Windows NT® Troubleshooting and Configuration

Windows NT® Troubleshooting and Configuration

Robert Reinstein, et al.

201 West 103rd Street
Indianapolis, Indiana 46290

This book is dedicated to my loving wife, Lisa, who has always given me the support that I needed during any of my endeavors.

I would also like to dedicate this book to the memory of my grandmother, Rosalie Epstein, who, at the age of 102, passed away during the editing of this book.

Copyright © 1997 by Sams Publishing

FIRST EDITION

All rights reserved. No part of this book shall be reproduced, stored in a retrieval system, or transmitted by any means, electronic, mechanical, photocopying, recording, or otherwise, without written permission from the publisher. No patent liability is assumed with respect to the use of the information contained herein. Although every precaution has been taken in the preparation of this book, the publisher and author assume no responsibility for errors or omissions. Neither is any liability assumed for damages resulting from the use of the information contained herein. For information, address Sams Publishing, 201 W. 103rd St., Indianapolis, IN 46290.

International Standard Book Number: 0-672-30941-6

Library of Congress Catalog Card Number: 96-68962

2000 99 98 97 4 3 2

Interpretation of the printing code: the rightmost double-digit number is the year of the book's printing; the rightmost single-digit, the number of the book's printing. For example, a printing code of 97-1 shows that the first printing of the book occurred in 1997.

Composed in AGaramond and MCPdigital by Macmillan Computer Publishing

Printed in the United States of America

Trademarks

All terms mentioned in this book that are known to be trademarks or service marks have been appropriately capitalized. Sams Publishing cannot attest to the accuracy of this information. Use of a term in this book should not be regarded as affecting the validity of any trademark or service mark. Windows NT is a registered trademark of Microsoft Corporation.

Publisher and President: *Richard K. Swadley*

Publishing Manager: *Dean Miller*

Director of Editorial Services: *Cindy Morrow*

Managing Editor: *Mary Inderstrodt*

Director of Marketing: *Kelli S. Spencer*

Product Marketing Manager: *Wendy Gilbride*

Assistant Marketing Manager: *Rachel Wolfe*

Acquisitions Editor
Kim Spilker

Development Editor
Robert L. Bogue

Software Development Specialist
Patricia J. Brooks

Production Editors
Heather E. Butler
Mary Inderstrodt

Copy Editors
Fran Blauw
Cheri Clark
Keith Davenport
Mitzi Foster
Kristin Ivanetich
Howard Jones
Carolyn Linn

Indexer
Benjamin Slen

Technical Reviewer
Chris Stone

Editorial Coordinator
Katie Wise

Technical Edit Coordinator
Lynette Quinn

Resource Coordinator
Deborah Frisby

Editorial Assistants
Carol Ackerman
Andi Richter
Rhonda Tinch-Mize

Cover Designer
Tim Amrhein

Book Designer
Alyssa Yesh

Copy Writer
David Reichwein

Production Team Supervisors
Brad Chinn
Charlotte Clapp

Production
Jenny Dierdorff
Chris Livengood
Tim Osborn
Andrew Stone

Overview

Contents

Part III Windows NT Configuration Essentials 159

Part VIII Keeping Windows NT Running—Troubleshooting Your Environment 693

Acknowledgments

A book of this size and nature requires the strength and dedication of many people.

Many people contributed to this book in their own way. First and foremost, I would like to thank the contributing authors, who each offered their expertise in areas of Windows NT. These authors deserve my thanks for helping complete this book while working under the tightest of deadlines. Their help in completing this book was invaluable, and as a reader, I'm sure that you'll agree with me that we have some very knowledgeable and talented people contributing to this book. I hope we get the chance to work together again on future projects.

I would also like to extend the greatest of thanks to the many people at Sams Publishing for their assistance and guidance. My lead editors, Kim Spilker and Robert Bogue, who were as patient as ever during a tumultuous time in my life, which just happened to coincide with the production of this book, are owed praise for their handling of this project. And let's not forget Mary Inderstrodt for her great help in reviewing these many chapters and making them appear as a cohesive unit. I would also like to thank Heather Butler for tying together all the loose ends down the homestretch. There were many other people at Sams who participated in the production of this book, and to you I offer my heartfelt gratitude for enabling this project to become a reality. Working with Sams has been a wonderful experience, and it is all because of the dedication and encouragement of these people.

I cannot help but thank Microsoft, for creating Windows NT and many other interesting products and technologies. A special thank you goes out to Elizabeth Fox, who, as part of the Microsoft Training and Certification team, took time out to review our appendix about Microsoft's excellent certification process.

I'd also like to thank the people at Manchester Equipment Company, especially Barry Steinberg, Joel Gilberts, Laura Fontana, Bill Scheibel, Morty Eisen, the entire Sales organization, and my comrades in the Sales Support department, for allowing me to continue my focus on Microsoft products and technologies.

Of course, I'd like to thank you, the reader, for sharing our interest in Windows NT. I hope this book enlightens you, or at the very least, helps you perform some troubleshooting with favorable results!

Last, but certainly not least, I thank my family (Lisa, Justin, Kevin, and Stephen) for the many nights and weekends that I spent in front of my keyboard banging out the bulk of this volume. Thank you for your understanding, thank you for your support, thank you for your patience, and thank you for being my family.

Oh, and I almost forgot. "Hi Mom!"

Robert Reinstein

About the Authors

Robert Reinstein has worked in the computer industry since 1984. He started beta testing for Microsoft in 1990, started Alpha testing Microsoft Windows NT in 1992, became a Microsoft Certified Professional in 1992, and is a sales support engineer at Manchester Equipment Company, Inc., a major systems integrator and Microsoft Solution Provider headquartered in Hauppauge, New York. He is a Microsoft Certified Systems Engineer for both the Windows NT 3.5x and 4.0 track. He is a major contributing author to the best-selling *Windows NT Server 4.0 Unleashed* also from Sams Publishing.

Although it seems like trying to stay on top of computer technology requires all of Robert's waking hour, he does find time to participate in non-computer–related activities. As a father of three, Robert spends whatever time he can find attending his kids' soccer, baseball, and roller hockey games, their karate activities, and their band concerts. Relaxation time is spent listening to Beatles music, and watching Beatles and other music-related videotapes. Visit Robert's Web site at `http://ourworld.compuserve.com/homepages/r_reinstein` to find out more about the Reinstein clan. You can send Robert e-mail at `robertr@mecnet.com`.

Robert L. Bogue owns Thor Projects, a consulting company located in Indianapolis, Indiana. Thor Projects specializes in solving the networking and integration needs of medium-sized organizations. Rob has been involved in more than 50 book projects on topics ranging from Visual Basic to Windows NT to Novell to Microsoft Office. He can be reached at `Rob.Bogue@Cyber-Wizard.Com` or (317) 844-5310.

Brett Bonenberger has been working with computer systems and networks for many years and is currently seeking his MCSE Certification. Brett holds a B.S. in Management Information Systems and a master's degree in Information and Communication Sciences, both from Ball State University. Currently he is Manager of Information Systems with the Indiana Chamber of Commerce in Indianapolis, Indiana. He also works with a small consulting team on many types of projects including Novell and NT network installations and Internet services. He can be reached via e-mail at `iccis@indy.net`. Brett would like to dedicate the work he has done for this book to his father-in-law, Chuck Anderson. We all miss you, Chuck.

Michael J. Carpenter is currently a consultant for Computer Sciences Corporation, in Falls Church, Virginia, the leader of the NT*Pro, Windows NT Server Users Group for the Washington, DC area. He is an avid mountain biker. He is a graduate of Methodist College, and a retired U.S. Army First Sergeant who now makes his home in Springfield, Virginia.

Les W. Harrison manages systems support at a real-time computing and control facility located in Raleigh, North Carolina. He has been directly involved in digital computing design and implementation since 1967. His primary interests are systems engineering, operating systems, networking and Internet technical writing, and golf. He has experience with systems covering the entire range of Intel platforms from i8008 (pre-i8088 vintage) to Pentium, including Multibus I. Les has worked with mainframe and mini-systems such as Xerox/SDS, Transdata, SEL, DEC PDP, VAX, and Alpha, and with operating systems including CPM, CCPM, DOS 3.0 to NT 4.0, RMX, UNIX, LINUX, RSX-11M, and VAX-VMS. He can be reached at `mrles@worldnet.att.net`.

Terry W. Ogletree is a consultant who divides his time between Atlanta, Georgia, and Raleigh, North Carolina. For more than 20 years he has worked with Digital's VAX/VMS systems and network products and has been involved with Windows NT since it was first released. He has been an active member of DECUS (Digital Equipment Computer Users Society) since 1985. Terry has consulted with Fortune 500 companies such as AT&T and Delta Airlines. He is a co-author of volume 2 of the *Windows NT 4 and Web Site Resource Library*, also from Sams Publishing. He can be reached at `ogletree@mindspring.com`, or you can visit his Web page at `http://www.biznesnet.com`.

Michael Tressler graduated from Ball State University in 1993 with a bachelor's degree in Computer Science. For the past four years he has been a Windows NT consultant, helping several of the largest companies in Indiana and the midwest with Windows NT support. He is now the co-owner of Intermix Systems, a company whose focus is the internetworking of Windows NT with legacy systems. He can be reached at `mtressle@iei.net`.

Since 1989, **John West** has been providing solutions for clients using the best in networking and application operating systems. As a Microsoft Certified Systems Engineer, Mr. West has installed client/server and mid-range integration solutions for companies such as Entergy, Lockheed Martin, and Siemens Corporation. He currently works as a technical analyst for Paranet, a premiere provider of installation, support, and management of distributed computer environments.

Tell Us What You Think!

As a reader, you are the most important critic and commentator of our books. We value your opinion and want to know what we're doing right, what we could do better, what areas you'd like to see us publish in, and any other words of wisdom you're willing to pass our way. You can help us make strong books that meet your needs and give you the computer guidance you require.

Do you have access to CompuServe or the World Wide Web? Then check out our CompuServe forum by typing `GO SAMS` at any prompt. If you prefer the World Wide Web, check out our site at `http://www.mcp.com`.

Note: If you have a technical question about this book, call the technical support line at 317-581-3833.

As the publishing manager of the group that created this book, I welcome your comments. You can fax, e-mail, or write me directly to let me know what you did or didn't like about this book—as well as what we can do to make our books stronger. Here's the information:

Fax: 317-581-4669

E-mail: `opsys_mgr@sams.mcp.com`

Mail: Dean Miller
Sams Publishing
201 W. 103rd Street
Indianapolis, IN 46290

Introduction

Welcome to the world of Microsoft Windows NT. Of course I'm presuming that you are new to Windows NT. If this book finds you early in your Windows NT experience, then hopefully this book will help you get up to speed a bit quicker than it took some of us, and if you are a seasoned Windows NT person, I hope that this book supplements your current knowledge. For all users, this book was designed not necessarily to be a "sit down and read" type of book, but as a reference that you can use whenever you're adjusting a configuration, or when you are first installing Windows NT.

My Windows NT experience dates back to the summer of 1992 when Microsoft made the alpha version of version 3.1 available to its corporate customers. As a Windows fanatic I had eagerly awaited this supposed "Windows-on-steroids" that I had read about in trade publications and Microsoft announcements.

Little did I expect an operating system that had very little to do with the MS-DOS that I was familiar with. I had been working with OS/2 around that time, which I found to be quite challenging, and felt that Windows NT was similar in the sense that I had to now relearn a lot of the configuration and troubleshooting techniques that I thought were PC standards.

I had been working in a Novell NetWare environment, and welcomed the administration of Microsoft Windows NT Advanced Server 3.1 with a sigh of relief. I knew Microsoft was doing something right.

Thank God the Windows Program Manager/File Manager/Control Panel interface was there, which eased my intimidation greatly.

However, the little nuances that were to become more of a norm to me, such as the BOOT.INI file, the Windows NT boot sequence (Ctrl+Alt+Del without rebooting the PC?), and NTFS permissions, soon became clearer and clearer, allowing me then to focus on this "new technology" and learn more and more about the fascinating operating system that has now developed into Windows NT 4.0.

Some of you may have already worked with Windows NT versions 3.x, and therefore are possibly in an adjustment period of becoming accustomed to the new interface. This is not a "Welcome to the new interface book," and I highly recommend Sams Publishing's *Windows NT Server 4.0 Unleashed* if you require an introduction to the interface. This book is geared toward the Windows NT user and administrator, whether for NT Server or NT Workstation, who needs that one more book to use as a reference when attempting a Windows NT 4.0 configuration task.

As we all know, you can never have too much information about Windows NT, because as one aspect of Windows NT becomes clearer, you come across another feature that you have to start researching. Hopefully this book will remain part of your Windows NT library.

Introduction

PART I

Understanding How Windows NT Works: Its Architecture and Design Structure

CHAPTER 1

The Windows NT Architecture

by Robert Reinstein

Discussed in this chapter are

- Microsoft networking
- The evolution of Windows NT
- The Windows NT kernel
- Windows NT's subsystems

In 1993 Microsoft introduced its new operating system, Microsoft Windows NT 3.1. This new operating system came in two flavors: a server-enhanced version that was packaged as Microsoft Windows NT Advanced Server and a desktop operating system simply titled Microsoft Windows NT.

Microsoft Windows NT has not always been the robust operating system with which you may be familiar. Originally Microsoft had a very hard time creating a widely accepted form of networking. Windows NT is truly a coming together of technologies that started in the late 1980s—back when Microsoft and IBM shared technologies (remember then?).

This chapter starts with some historical information (and maybe even some trivia) to help you understand how Microsoft Windows NT became such a popular network operating system. This history section also introduces the various components of the underlying architecture of Windows NT.

Then we introduce the subsystems that make Windows NT a unique operating system. The Windows NT Security model, which is a very large part of the Windows NT architecture, is covered in depth in Chapter 2, "Windows NT Security Architecture."

Microsoft Networking

Microsoft's first attempt at a network operating system, in 1985, was called MS-NET. 3Com Corporation has developed its OpenServer network operating system, which Microsoft licensed and renamed Microsoft LAN Manager. The most popular network operating system at the time of Microsoft's entry in the network operating system arena was Novell's NetWare.

NetWare offered server-based file and print services to client workstations, but Microsoft wanted to exploit a concept that had been used by others but had never been a commercial success. This concept is known as *peer-to-peer networking*.

Peer-to-peer networking offered client workstations the ability to act as both servers and workstations. With Microsoft Networking, client workstations could use resources offered by a stand-alone dedicated server and share their own local resources with other clients attached to the same network. Indeed, the appeal of peer-to-peer networking, especially for companies based on small networks, is that it does not even require the presence of a dedicated server.

Although the peer-to-peer networking concept was deemed very useful (and is still being used today by Microsoft's desktop operating systems and other non-Microsoft products, most notably Artisoft's LANtastic), the performance and administration for Microsoft LAN Manager had a lot to be desired.

However, LAN Manager did introduce concepts that are very familiar to users of Microsoft networking. LAN Manager introduced Microsoft domains, but the art of managing these domains was not fully realized until Windows NT. LAN Manager also included replication services, which allowed for directory synchronization across servers within the same domain. Remote Access Services, which should be very familiar to all Microsoft Windows NT Server administrators, was also originally implemented for LAN Manager.

LAN Manager's performance paled in comparison to NetWare and was used only by the most hard-core Microsoft enthusiasts, who apparently believed that Microsoft had the power to eventually create an upgrade that would offer file and print services on par with NetWare, or the other DOS- or UNIX-based counterparts. Or perhaps the loyalists just liked the way that LAN Manager implemented network services. Regardless, Microsoft LAN Manager was an MS-DOS program, or actually a set of MS-DOS device drivers and MS-DOS programs.

A version of LAN Manager was developed to run on the OS/2 operating system (then a joint effort from Microsoft and IBM), and this avenue was perhaps the way to offer a more powerful solution because OS/2 was, compared to DOS, a more stable and robust environment. LAN Manager also was ported for UNIX systems.

Perhaps the worst point about LAN Manager is the amount of resources required by the DOS clients in a LAN Manager domain.

LAN Manager allowed for two types of connections. One was an authenticated logon, which meant that the client would supply an account name, and permissions associated with that account would be granted to the client. The second type of connection was a non-authenticated attachment, which allowed the client to use a generic Guest account. Using the Guest account would not provide administrators with an audit trail for actions performed on a server.

To attain an authenticated logon to a LAN Manager server required a whopping 100KB of memory.

Note: Windows for Workgroups changed this situation, because it allowed an authenticated logon at a cost of only 40KB of memory, which could probably be loaded into high memory.

Incidentally, the IBM-developed NetBEUI protocol, which was originally introduced in 1985, was used as the network protocol for LAN Manager. This protocol, however, only contributed to the lack of support for LAN Manager because NetBEUI is a non-routable protocol, which means that it would be restricted to a single network segment, and, therefore, is not a good candidate for an enterprise solution. But NetBEUI is a very fast and efficient protocol.

Microsoft OS/2

In 1987 Microsoft and IBM released an operating system that they both deemed to be the successor to MS-DOS (which was being licensed to IBM who packaged it as PC-DOS). This new operating system would be designed from the ground up, allowing its developers freedom to ignore the limits that MS-DOS had made a standard.

This new freedom included not only the ability to eliminate the 640KB conventional memory barrier but also the ability to create a new file system that would be faster, allow for long filenames, utilize hard drive space more economically, and have a degree of fault tolerance built into it. MS-DOS developers had been using tricks to allow their programs to bypass the inherent limitations in MS-DOS. This new, advanced operating system would deliver a way for programmers to create their software without regard for the traditional limitations.

IBM and Microsoft would then both have rights and be able to develop applications for this new enhanced operating system, which they launched as OS/2.

Criticized by some as problematic because it was unable to run the more popular MS-DOS applications, OS/2 was launched to rave reviews. Because so many people had been growing tired of MS-DOS and its limitations, IBM hurried to get its productivity applications to run on OS/2 and Microsoft ported its most popular applications, such as Word and Excel, to run on this platform too.

The problem was that OS/2 had limited third-party support; many developers felt that it would not be profitable to spend the resources to write for this new operating system. They probably felt this way because OS/2 did not sell well. Only the business community, which were "true blue" shops seemed to jump on the OS/2 bandwagon, which accounted for lackluster sales. Programming for OS/2 also required expertise that would mean a severe learning curve for developers. And, since OS/2 was still a new and unproved platform, developers seemed to sit and wait for OS/2 to catch on.

Note that a few early third-party developers did port their software to OS/2, for example, Aldus with its PageMaker product. However, these programs, on the whole, were not commercially successful.

By the time OS/2 version 1.2 came out, support for a single DOS emulation session was included, thus allowing users to run legacy applications on the graphical OS/2 desktop, which was then called Presentation Manager.

Note that Microsoft had been developing Microsoft Windows in parallel with OS/2, had shipped Microsoft Windows 286 and Microsoft Windows 386 with the Presentation Manager GUI, and even went as far as advertising Windows as an introductory step to the operating system of the future, OS/2.

Again, limited support for legacy applications held back the commercial success of OS/2. IBM's stance on OS/2 was that it would like to make OS/2 backward compatible and allow more MS-DOS applications to run under it. Microsoft, on the other hand, saw OS/2 as a new beginning and did not want to compromise the integrity of the operating system by including code that could cause it to crash. Microsoft saw OS/2 as a full 32-bit operating system that would be fully protected from faulty applications and could be heralded as the optimum corporate desktop. Of course, Microsoft was also having great success with the release of the third version of Microsoft Windows and had the option of allowing OS/2 to be a step up, without looking back on MS-DOS. IBM did not have another GUI-based operating system and relied on OS/2 to be its "bread and butter."

At this point IBM and Microsoft decided to give up their cross-licensing of OS/2 so that Microsoft could pursue its dream of building a rock-solid operating system and IBM could work on OS/2 to achieve its own vision. By now IBM was working on what was to become OS/2 Version 2, and at the same time Microsoft was working on the next generation of OS/2.

IBM continued to create upgrades of OS/2, which included a licensed version of Microsoft Windows, and Microsoft continued development on a product that had been destined to become OS/2 Version 3.

Note: OS/2 is still in development by IBM. Version 2 introduced a new GUI named the Workplace Shell that had many advantages over Presentation Manager. OS/2 has a loyal group of users, but still does not have many commercially viable third-party developers supporting it. OS/2 is mostly used by the development community, as many robust programming environments run on OS/2. Many Lotus Notes servers have been running on

OS/2 because, prior to a Windows NT version, Notes required the multitasking ability of OS/2. Microsoft also marketed an OS/2 add-on for the Microsoft Mail package, but it has since gotten the product on Windows NT, although it does run on Windows NT's OS/2 subsystem. Version 2.1 of OS/2 included support for running Windows sessions in enhanced mode. Version 3 of OS/2, named Warp, sports a more mature interface, and since IBM has acquired Lotus, has a rich suite of applications available for it. Version 4 was released in 1996.

Microsoft Windows NT 3.1

In 1988 Microsoft hired David Cutler, now known as the father of Windows NT, who had been working at Digital Equipment Corporation (DEC). David had been involved in the design of operating systems at DEC, most notably with VMS.

David, along with some of his coworkers, joined Microsoft, and set out to create what is now known as Windows NT.

Microsoft finally released its new operating system in 1993 as Microsoft Windows NT Advanced Server and Microsoft Windows NT (the latter being the desktop operating system). NT stood for "New Technology," and indeed it was a whole new operating system based on the look and feel of Windows. But under the hood, NT was nothing like Windows, and for that matter, it was nothing like OS/2.

Microsoft Windows NT was a full 32-bit operating system that included various subsystems that could handle the tasks of running 16-bit DOS applications, 16-bit Windows applications, applications written to the Portable Operating System Interface for Computing Environments (POSIX) API, and character-based OS/2 applications. Interestingly enough, the native file system of OS/2, High Performance File System or HPFS, was originally supported on Windows NT, as was FAT and NTFS, which is Windows NT's native file system.

Note: Early beta copies of Windows NT 3.1 included a 3270 emulator, which was obviously targeted at the corporate market that had a heavy investment in mainframes.

Also note that any POSIX API calls that require file access will need an NTFS partition to handle these calls, because FAT does not have POSIX-compliant attributes.

These subsystems should not be confused with the so-called DOS Box emulation seen in Microsoft Windows. They are actually Windows NT processes that emulate the respective operating systems. By running as native Windows NT processes, each of these subsystems is fully protected. Windows NT does not contain MS-DOS!

Windows NT had built-in networking that was similar to LAN Manager but took the LAN Manager type feature set many steps further.

New features for Microsoft networking were GUI-based administration tools and a native file system (NTFS). Most notable was the inclusion of a single logon that would allow users to log on and gain access to multiple servers on multiple domains.

The implementation of NetBEUI was now called NBF, which stands for NetBEUI Frame. NBF surpasses NetBEUI as it breaks the 254-session limit on a computer and opens it up to 254 sessions per process. It is 100 percent backward compatible with NetBEUI and is still referred to as NetBEUI, as its packets are indistinguishable from NetBEUI. The implementation of NBF on Windows NT is what differentiates it from NetBEUI.

Built into the NT product was its Remote Access Services (RAS) that allowed dial-in clients to connect directly to the server and gain access to resources anywhere on the LAN. Microsoft included this remote-node software as part of the base Windows NT Advanced Server product and included its client piece as part of Windows for Workgroups.

Microsoft Windows NT was also designed for portability, which allowed Windows NT to run on both CISC and RISC processors. Windows NT was compiled to run on Intel, MIPS, and Alpha processors, which gave Windows NT users a very scalable path for implementing their Windows NT network.

Its portability was attributable to the modularity of Windows NT. This modularity is perhaps the strongest point to make about Windows NT, as it provided an operating system that was extendible, yet secure, and had a Windows facade, yet provided a bulletproof platform for deploying even the most mission-critical applications.

Windows NT's modularity was achieved by splitting the operating system into separate layers.

One layer, known as the Hardware Abstraction Layer (HAL) was unique for each type of processor. That layer allowed the other layers to operate transparently without concern for the server's or workstation's hardware. The HAL is the layer that device drivers are written to communicate with. The HAL also handles all the tasks related to symmetrical processing.

Windows NT was capable of running on a machine containing up to 32 processors. Its multithreaded processes took advantage of symmetric multiprocessing hardware.

Note: Symmetric processing allows individual threads, which make up a process, to run on an available processor in a multiple processor computer. Therefore, a single process, which includes the Windows NT operating system itself, can be executing on more than one processor at a time.

The kernel, which is the heart of the operating system, was identical, regardless of hardware platform. The kernel is the part of Windows NT that generates threads, or processes, and dispatches them. The kernel is part of the Windows NT Executive.

Various operating system services, including the HAL and kernel, comprise the Executive. These services are broken down into the following modules:

Object Manager assigns object handles that are required for processes to access system objects, such as directory objects, file objects, and port objects, to name a few. It also tracks the status of these objects and reports the status to the operating system.

Process Manager manages processes, which are actually address spaces and threads, which run within those processes. Starting an application creates a process. It is then responsible for creating one or more threads for this process.

The Virtual Memory Manager handles the task of mapping memory to a pagefile whenever virtual memory, which resides on a disk, is needed. The Virtual Memory Manager is also responsible for retrieving this paged memory from the disk when it is needed.

The Local Procedure Call (LPC) facility is the expediter of client/server calls, from one thread to another, that reside on the same machine.

The I/O Manager negotiates all I/O requests for the file system, device drivers, and network drivers.

The Security Reference Monitor along with the Logon and Security protected subsystems make up the Windows NT security model. Each time an object is accessed, the Security Reference Monitor intervenes and supplies the proper security information.

Windows NT is often referred to as a client/server operating system because of this modular approach. The interprocess communication (IPC) manager handles exchanging messages between these processes; hence, Windows NT is referred to as a message-based system.

The security that was implemented in the heart of the operating system allowed Windows NT to pass the strict security guidelines of the U.S. government. Finally, mission-critical, Windows-based applications could run on a strong and secure platform. Chapter 2 examines the security architecture of Windows NT in detail.

The flat memory model of Windows NT presented PC users with a fully protected environment in which to run their legacy applications, 16-bit Windows applications, and the forthcoming (at that time) 32-bit Windows applications. A scheme that allows each program to have its own address space creates this protection.

Preemptive multitasking sets Windows NT apart from Windows 3.1. Windows 3.1 used a form of multitasking called cooperative multitasking in which an application would take control of the CPU and then check for other waiting processes, such as printing or another application. Checking for waiting processes was in the hands of the programmer for the process that had control of the CPU, meaning that a selfish programmer could keep the CPU busy indefinitely without relinquishing control.

Preemptive multitasking in Windows NT gives control to the operating system, which hands out time slices of the CPU, thereby creating true multitasking.

The support for MS-DOS/Windows and OS/2 was enabled by subsystems that ran on Windows NT as separate processes. Each of these subsystems ran fully protected, meaning that it occupied its own memory address without the possibility of other processes being able to invade its memory space, which, if it happened, would cause the computer to crash. Even the sloppiest application could not bring down the operating system. These subsystems, along with the other subsystems in Windows NT, are discussed later in this chapter.

The problem with this version of Microsoft Windows NT was that it was very slow, noticeably slower than its 16-bit counterpart, Microsoft Windows, even with added memory. In addition, no support existed for integrating Windows NT with Novell NetWare, making the Windows NT desktop a poor choice when running on a non-Microsoft network.

Note: Novell eventually announced the development of a Windows NT–based client for NetWare, but this client seemed to remain in beta forever. Microsoft eventually created its own NetWare client, which apparently prompted Novell to move a little quicker to make its client available.

Another negative aspect of the workstation version was its poor support for 16-bit Windows applications, which could usually run, but at a snail's pace, rendering Windows NT 3.1 almost unusable.

The default network protocol for Windows NT was still LAN Manager's NetBEUI protocol (although Microsoft did supply an IPX/SPX-compatible protocol).

Inside this version of Windows NT was a core technology that is still being used by the product. This core is Windows NT's internal databases and includes the Registry and the Security Accounts Manager (SAM).

The Registry is a single database that contains all the information that Windows and LAN Manager had stored in INI and SYS files. Using the Registry allowed programmers to use this common database for storing program configuration settings and also gave administrators a single location to use in troubleshooting and configuration.

The SAM is the Windows NT security database; it holds information related to user accounts and security information. By replicating this database, multiple Windows NT servers in a domain can act in authenticating logons. Authenticating a logon is discussed in Chapter 2.

Microsoft Windows NT 3.5

Microsoft Windows NT 3.5 was a major upgrade. This time, Microsoft slimmed down the hardware requirements (mainly the RAM requirements) and produced a leaner, meaner operating system. Microsoft Windows NT 3.5 also introduced tools for integrating itself with Novell NetWare, which gave NetWare clients the ability to log in to NetWare servers. It also gave

NetWare administrators the ability to easily migrate their NetWare servers over to Microsoft Windows NT Server.

With this version Microsoft renamed the products to simply Microsoft Windows NT Server and Microsoft Windows NT Workstation.

> **Note:** When Windows NT 3.1 was released, I was evaluating software for an insurance company. Although I was thrilled with Microsoft's vision, I had to deem Windows NT 3.1 as unsuitable due to its lackluster performance and enormous hardware requirement, which, at that point in time, was cost prohibitive. This situation changed with the release of Version 3.5.

The NetBEUI protocol still shipped with Windows NT but was no longer the default protocol for Windows NT. A Microsoft-developed IPX/SPX-compatible protocol called NWLink became the default protocol for NT. TCP/IP was also integrated with the product, and Microsoft's implementation far exceeded other implementations of TCP/IP due to the addition of Microsoft's Dynamic Host Configuration Protocol (DHCP) which made the management of TCP/IP on a network almost child's play.

Support for 16-bit Windows applications was greatly enhanced, allowing these programs to run as fast, or faster, than they would within their native environment. Another support subsystem was the Win32 subsystem, which included the ability to run 16-bit Windows applications that used an extension of the Windows API known as Win32s.

Windows NT 3.5 also introduced the concept of server-based workstation management, allowing user profiles to be stored on the server that could control and manage the environment for client Windows NT workstations.

Microsoft Windows NT 3.51

Although only a point upgrade, major new features made this version of NT highly acceptable to the corporate world and is really the version of NT that allowed Microsoft Windows NT Server to become a contender as an enterprise network operating system.

Major improvements in this version include the ability to use long filenames on a FAT partition, real-time file compression and decompression, available add-ons for NetWare integration, and support for running Windows 95 applications.

Microsoft Windows NT 4.0

Another major upgrade, Version 4.0's features will be examined in detail throughout this book. This version of Windows NT features enhanced performance, sports the GUI used in Windows 95, and includes a system policy editor, much like the Windows 95 version, that allows for granular management of client workstation desktops. The Windows NT 4.0 Task Manager shows a graphical view of CPU utilization and a list of every active task running on the Windows NT machine. RAS Multilink Channel Aggregation allows multiple phone lines to be used to widen the RAS bandwidth.

NT 4.0 also integrates Internet services, with peer Web services on Windows NT Workstation and fully featured Web, Gopher, and FTP services in the server version. A new network protocol, Point-to-Point Tunneling Protocol (PPTP), supports secure RAS connectivity via the Internet.

Perhaps the only major change made to the underlying architecture of Windows NT since its inception has occurred in Version 4.0. The kernel has now taken on the task of Windows Manager (known as User) and of the Graphics Device Interface (GDI), the graphics output system. This change greatly improved performance. Whether or not the new design has an impact on the stability of Windows NT has yet to be seen.

Integration with NetWare is even stronger with client support for Novell's Network Directory Services (NDS).

Note: Missing from this release of Windows NT is support for HPFS, better known as the OS/2 High Performance File System. However, users of Version 3.51 can upgrade their servers and retain the device driver that supported HPFS.

Windows NT 4.0 gives hints of the upcoming object-oriented version of Windows NT, which Microsoft has referred to as Cairo. In the Cairo version of Windows NT we can expect to see a revised Directory Services, a device-driver model that is common to Windows 95, which will give Windows NT plug-and-play functionality, and Network OLE, which will allow for remote OLE objects. One can only imagine what else will find its way into the next major upgrade of Windows NT.

Note: As this book was being written, Microsoft had just released a beta version of its Distributed File System (DFS) that allows shares from multiple servers and workstations to appear as a single directory structure under a share on one computer. It's a very promising product.

The Windows NT Subsystems

As I mentioned earlier, Windows NT can emulate different operating systems through its environmental subsystems.

An environmental subsystem is a Windows NT process. Windows NT offers these subsystems:

MS-DOS
Win16
OS/2
POSIX
Win32

These processes, with the exception of the Win32 subsystem, are loaded only when an application calls for them.

After they are loaded, they remain active until the Windows NT session is terminated, even if the application that required the subsystem has already terminated.

MS-DOS Virtual DOS Machine

In the case of MS-DOS, a Virtual DOS Machine (VDM) is the actual process.

A VDM is an emulation of an *x86* computer running MS-DOS. Not only is the operating system a virtual system, but hardware is also "virtualized" to allow MS-DOS screen and keyboard emulation.

Note: This virtualized hardware allows MS-DOS–based applications to run on a RISC machine.

As each VDM is created, a memory space is given exclusively to the VDM, preventing any other applications from affecting the MS-DOS program. In addition, the MS-DOS VDM cannot affect any other subsystems.

A character-based application running in an MS-DOS VDM may be run in a window or in full-screen mode. Graphics-based applications must run in full-screen mode. On RISC computers, both character-based and graphical applications must run in a window.

WOW (Win16 on Win32)

Similar to the MS-DOS VDM, the Win16 subsystem is a multithreaded VDM that allows multiple 16-bit Windows programs to run seamlessly on the Windows NT desktop. This seamlessness gives 16-bit Windows programs the look and feel of the Windows NT 4.0 interface.

The WOW layer (Win16 on Win32) handles the translation of 16-bit API calls and messages. The subsystem allows the 16-bit application to think that it is running in a 16-bit environment. This translation process is known as "thunking."

Sixteen-bit Windows applications that require the use of virtual device drivers (VXDs) cannot run on the Win16 subsystem. These programs run in enhanced mode on *x*86 computers.

> **New to NT 4.0:** Sixteen-bit Windows applications also run in enhanced mode on RISC computers.

Because 16-bit Windows usually runs on top of MS-DOS, a 32-bit MS-DOS subsystem is also loaded when the Win16 subsystem is loaded. The MS-DOS subsystem uses two system files, `AUTOEXEC.NT` and `CONFIG.NT`, which are user modifiable and should be used to configure your emulated MS-DOS environment.

OLE and DDE services are available in the Win16 subsystem.

OS/2 Subsystem

The OS/2 subsystem enables character-based OS/2 executables to run on *x*86 computers. However, these executables are limited to programs that do not have API calls that go directly for hardware. Limited support is available for programs with direct video calls. Microsoft also has an add-on subsystem to support OS/2 applications that utilize the Presentation Manager interface.

> **Note:** The Microsoft Mail Multi-tasking Message Transfer Agent (MMTA) that ships with Microsoft Mail Server for PC Networks is an OS/2 application that has been designed to run on Windows NT. Microsoft's original MMTA was an OS/2 program but ran only on native OS/2. The OS/2 subsystem is utilized when running the MMTA.

POSIX

POSIX, which stands for Portable Operating System Interface for Computing Environments, is a set of standards that is maintained by the Institute of Electrical and Electronic Engineers (IEEE).

The POSIX API, which works with the programming language C, includes requirements that apply to file systems. NTFS partitions offer this compatibility. If a POSIX-compatible application does not require file access, then it may be run using any file system.

The Win32 Subsystem

Perhaps the single most important subsystem is the Win32 subsystem. As its name implies, this subsystem handles applications that have been written to the 32-bit Windows API. It also handles mouse, keyboard, and all screen output for all Windows NT subsystems.

Summary

Windows NT has been evolving for many, many years. Starting with the first version in 1993, this modular approach to an operating system has proven itself to be secure and stable.

The underlying architecture of Windows NT has proven that a strong, robust network operating system can be scalable, solid, and still easy to administer.

Its unique subsystems give Windows NT the ability to run the most popular programs. As time goes on, more and more incompatible software (that is, UNIX-based software) is being rewritten on a platform that is Windows NT compatible.

CHAPTER 2

Windows NT Security Architecture

by Robert Reinstein

The Windows NT security model is one of the main reasons why corporations and government agencies have been taking a close look at Windows NT.

The security services of Windows NT are built into its architecture. These system services track all access to Windows NT's object types, and of course, the design of the NT file system (NTFS) supports highly configurable security attributes.

This chapter introduces you to the following topics:

- The requirements for C2-level security
- Windows NT system level security
- The Windows NT logon process
- Assigning file permissions
- Sharing and securing resources
- Auditing Windows NT resources

C2-Level Security

The National Computer Security Center (NCSC) is the United States government agency responsible for performing software product security evaluations. They issue different levels of security, which are usually required for different organizations within the U.S. government. Windows NT was given the rating of adhering to the C2-level of security.

One of the most important aspects of the C2-level security specification involves ownership. Because it is very important for auditing files on a government server, ownership can decide who will actually be responsible for assigning permissions. Secure deletions is another important facet of C2-level security. So far, Windows NT does not include an undelete utility, which allows for a secure deletion process. Bear in mind that the Windows NT 4.0 Recycle Bin must be disabled for true C2-level compliance. Delivering a secure audit trail requires a secure logon process so that activities can be traced to the user. Recall that Windows NT auditing can be as granular as you want it to be, and the U.S. Department of Defense requires this type of auditing. Another requirement is that the audit logs themselves are secure and can be accessed only by administrators.

Note: Windows NT itself is C2-level compliant only when it is run on a non-networked computer, however, the NCSC has determined that Windows NT Server can be used as part of a C2-level certified system.

System Level Security

As I discussed in the first chapter, Windows NT modularity includes system services that are devoted to security. Intensive tracking allows Windows NT to monitor all access to Windows NT objects, such as user logons, files, and user accounts.

Security ID

These security attributes are assigned to individual users by their Security ID (SID). The SID is a randomly generated identifier and is always different for each user. Because this ID is always unique, a new user will never accidentally receive the SID once used by a deleted user. A SID is also assigned to user groups.

Security Access Token

When a user logs on to an NT domain, Windows NT creates a security access token. The security access token contains information about the user, such as the user's SID and name, and any SIDs and group names associated with groups of which the user is a member. This security access token is then passed to any program or process that the user starts or any object that the user attempts to gain access to. The program, process, or object then compares the security access token to its own list of access permissions, which is called an Access Control List (ACL).

Before examining the individual permissions, this section describes the entire process by which a user logs on to a Windows NT domain.

Even before the logon is performed, the first security check is the Ctrl+Alt+Del method of signaling Windows NT that a user wishes to log on. One of the simplest hacking programs to write is the type that presents a user with a phony logon screen. This type of program can then capture the user's name and password into a text file that the hacker can lift from the user's hard drive. Microsoft created this logon process to assure users that they are not entering their username and password into a bogus logon screen. Windows NT has the power to intercept the Ctrl+Alt+Del key combination, whereas under operating systems, a computer reboot would be forced.

After entering a username and password, the user clicks the OK button or presses Enter to process the logon. At this point the Local Security Authority kicks in. The Local Security Authority is the process that checks a user's right to log on to a Windows domain. It does so by generating access tokens. The Local Security Authority is also responsible for handling the domain's audit policies.

An authentication package checks the user accounts database to determine if the user belongs to the local domain and if so, determines whether the user has the right to log on to the domain.

If the authentication package determines that the user is not a local user, authentication packages from other domains that exist on the network attempt to grant the user a logon session.

After the username has been validated, the user's SID and the SIDs from any groups that the user is a member of are returned to the Local Security Authority by the Security Account Manager (SAM). The authentication package then creates a logon process.

If authentication fails, the logon process ends and an error is generated. Otherwise, the Security Access Token is now created. The logon process is shown in Flowchart 2.1.

Note: The SAM is limited to 15,000 entries.

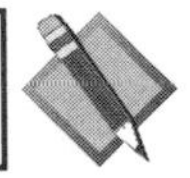

One of the main sources of problems for Windows NT domain clients having difficulty logging on to a Windows NT domain is using an invalid password. Because Windows NT uses a case-sensitive password, you need to stress to your users the importance of observing this case-sensitive rule. Otherwise, you can expect to get a lot of calls from users who are sure they entered the right password, only to discover that the Caps Lock key was engaged at the time.

Note: An administrator can revoke the right to log on to a domain through the User Manager for Domains application. A user account can also be disabled if the domain has been configured to create an account lockout based on previous unsuccessful logon attempts. This configuration is discussed in Chapter 14, "User Manager for Domains."

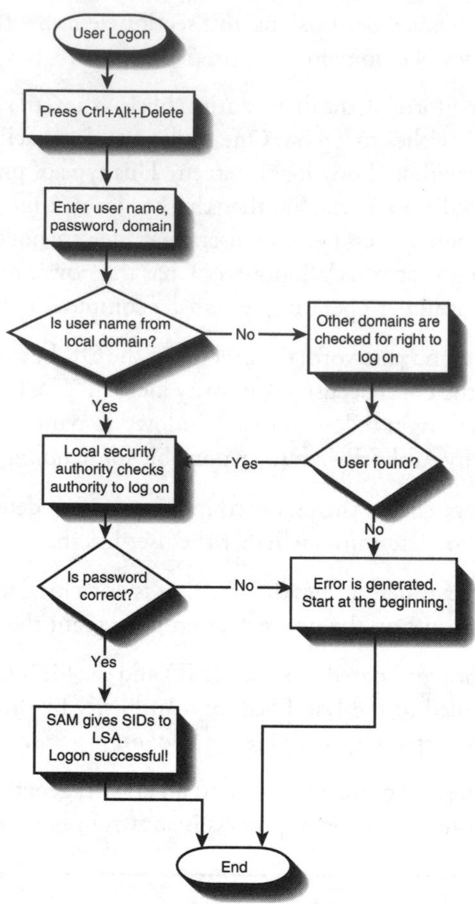

Flowchart 2.1. *The Windows NT logon process.*

Note: Microsoft has designed the Windows NT logon process to be extensible, which means that Microsoft published an application programming interface (API) for authentication packages so that the logon process can be modified by developers.

Windows NT Subjects

Once the Security Access Token has been created, the Win32 subsystem is called and a process is started. The user's Security Access Token is passed to the Win32-generated process, and then the process assumes the ACL, or the rights and permissions, of the user. This process is known as a *subject.*

A *subject* exists whenever a user starts a program. This type of subject is known as a *simple subject.* For example, if a user is allowed to read files in a particular directory, but not to modify any of those files, the program assumes those characteristics, and it is the program that cannot modify that directory. This status is known as running in the security context of a user.

A server process, such as one of the subsystems, is considered a *server subject.* A server subject can have other subjects as its clients. When a server subject has simple subjects as its clients, the server subject runs in the security context of its clients.

The server subject uses the Security Access Token of the client that is attempting to start a process. The server subject then extracts the client's SID and determines the permissions that the server subject is going to use for that process.

Windows NT Objects

All objects under Windows NT can have security. Files, directories, and printers are the main objects that come to mind. All of the objects in Windows NT contain a security descriptor, which contains all of the information required to allow the security system to perform its task of allowing users access, or restricting access, and to monitor for whether the action being performed requires auditing. The security descriptor also contains information about ownership of the object, and if running under the POSIX subsystem, group security information.

Windows NT supports two type of objects: container objects and noncontainer objects. A good description of a container object is a directory, which can contain files (which are noncontainer objects) and other directories. This arrangement is important, as objects within a container can have security attributes filter down from the container.

One of the items contained in the security descriptor is the Access Control List (ACL). This item contains information about the users and groups that are either allowed or denied access to a particular object. An ACL is a collection of Access Control Entries (ACE). Types of ACEs are the AccessAllowed ACE, the AccessDenied ACE, and the SystemAudit ACE, which is a system ACE that contains information about auditing.

An ACE contains an access mask. This mask is compared, by Windows NT, against the object's requirements for allowing an action, known as the desired access mask, or denying the action. The desired access mask is compared against the user's access token. This is the process where Windows NT security is defined.

The Security Reference Monitor is the process that monitors user requests and checks whether the user has the appropriate permissions to whatever object the user is interacting with. The Security Reference Monitor is also responsible for generating audit messages whenever an action that has been flagged for auditing has been executed. Auditing is explained later in this chapter, in the section titled "System Audit Policies."

File and Directory Permissions

The Windows NT security scheme is based on rights and permissions. *Permissions* apply to access to files, directories, or shares. File and directory permissions can be assigned to users through Windows NT Explorer by accessing the file or directory Properties page.

The extent of the permissions that can be assigned is based on the type of partition that the files reside on. If the partition is a FAT partition, then rights can be assigned only at the share level. Individual file permissions cannot be set on FAT partitions. The NTFS (NT file system) supports very granular user permissions on a file-by-file basis. A full explanation of these file systems appears in Chapter 5, "Windows NT File Systems."

These permissions can be assigned to usernames, to local groups, or to Everyone, which is a default Windows NT local group that includes every username within that domain.

In general, file and directory permissions are combinations of one or more individual permissions. Once you understand the individual permissions, the entire concept of the NTFS file and directory permissions will make more sense. The single letters shown in parentheses are often shown in security properties dialogs and summaries for permissions.

The individual permissions are shown in Table 2.1.

Table 2.1. File permissions.

Permission	*Definition*
Read (R)	The ability to browse the contents of a directory or file.
Write (W)	The ability to add files to a directory, or to change the contents of a file.
Execute (X)	Permission to execute an executable file.
Delete (D)	The user can delete a directory or a file.
Change Permissions (P)	Gives the user permission to make changes to the permissions settings without taking ownership.
Take Ownership (O)	The owner of a file can administer all permissions for that file. The creator of a file automatically becomes the owner of the file. The current owner of a file has the ability to grant the Take Ownership permission to others. If a user has the right to Take Ownership, then that user has the option to become the administrator for that file. Usually the Administrator will have ownership of most of the files on a server, because the Administrator is usually responsible for installing software. However, user files are usually owned by the individual users.

When accessing the security properties for files and directories, you will be able to pick from a list of standard permissions, which are a combination of two or more individual permissions. Of course, you also can create a custom permission by choosing a set of individual permissions.

Table 2.2 explains the NTFS standard permissions for directories.

Table 2.2. NTFS standard permissions for directories.

Permission	*Definition*
No Access	Includes no individual permissions. Users have no access to even view the contents of this directory.
List	Combines the Read and Execute individual permissions. The user can see the contents of a directory, but the user cannot access any new files created within that directory.
Read	Combines the Read and Execute individual permissions. The user can see the contents of a directory. Any new files created within this directory will also be flagged as Read.
Add	Combines the Write and Execute individual permissions. The user can add files to a directory, but cannot see the contents of the directory.
Add & Read	Combines the Read, Write, and Execute individual permissions. Users can add files to the directory, and read files, but do not have the ability to alter files. Files added to this directory assume the Read standard permission for files.
Change	Combines the Read, Write, Execute, and Delete individual permissions. Users can read files, modify files, add files to the directory, and remove files from the directory. All files added to this directory also assume the Change permission.
Full Control	Combines all of the individual permissions. New files in this directory also get marked with the Full Control permission.

Table 2.3 explains the NTFS standard permissions for files.

Table 2.3. NTFS standard permissions for files.

Permission	*Definition*
No Access	The user has no access to files with this permission.
Read	Combined Read and Execute individual permissions. User can access and execute these files.
Change	Combined Read, Write, Execute, and Delete permissions. User can read, modify, execute, and delete the file.
Full Control	Combines all individual permissions, so the user can read, write, execute, delete, set permissions, and take ownership of the file.

Also, three Special Access permissions allow you to specify any combination of individual permissions for files and directories:

Special Directory Access
Special File Access
Special Access

As I mentioned before, these permissions are available only to files and directories that are on an NTFS partition. Because this high level of security can be set only on NTFS partitions, I highly recommend that you use NTFS whenever possible.

Managing File and Directory Permissions

Setting permissions for files and directories is the only way that you will be able to protect your server's data. By default, users should not receive permissions to access any directories for which they do not require access. Although this explanation of permissions should give you a good understanding of the permissions that are available for you to implement, it is imperative that you understand how to apply these permissions in a manner that is easy to manage and provides your users with a safe server environment. Creating a security strategy is very important!

When assigning permissions for files and directories, you can usually plan which users will have particular permissions. Most of the time these permissions apply to a group of users. For instance, a financial application will probably be used by the accounting department, whereas the systems programmers will have absolutely no use for the application and should be protected from being able to access the application or the application's data.

The best way to handle permission assignments is to create logical groups of users, or local groups. For example, by defining only the people who are part of the accounting department, you can easily assign permissions to that group. This technique spares you the task of identifying each user and modifying their individual permissions for the financial application.

Of course, sometimes you are faced with an individual who does not logically fit into a particular group. Because of this type of user, you might have to assign permissions on an individual basis. However, grouping users should be the first consideration for you when deciding how to grant permissions for your applications.

Designing a disk volume should not be done by randomly installing programs into the root directory of the logical drive that has the most disk space available. Just as you should create groups for assigning permissions to users, you should consider grouping subdirectories under a main directory that is a logical parent for those subdirectories.

For example, by installing different financial applications into their own subdirectories that are under a financial directory, which is right off the root of the drive, you can then assign permissions to the main financial directory and force those permissions to filter down through the subdirectories. Then, when you assign permissions to users, you only need to assign permissions to the financial users group on that one directory.

The assignment of permissions is cumulative, so if a user has Read permissions based on membership in one group and also has Change permissions as a member of another group, then the user has both Read and Change permissions. If either of the user's groups has the permission No Access assigned to it, the No Access permission overrides any other permissions; that user will indeed have absolutely no access to that directory while the user is still a member of the group with No Access.

If that same user is part of a group that has Change permissions on a directory and is also a member of a group that has only Read permission on a particular data file within that directory, then the file permission overrides the directory permission.

Caution: A poorly designed directory structure can result in inadvertently changed directory and file permissions. You should always plan the directory structure on paper, possibly designed as a flowchart, during the design of your Windows NT server. See Flowchart 2.2.

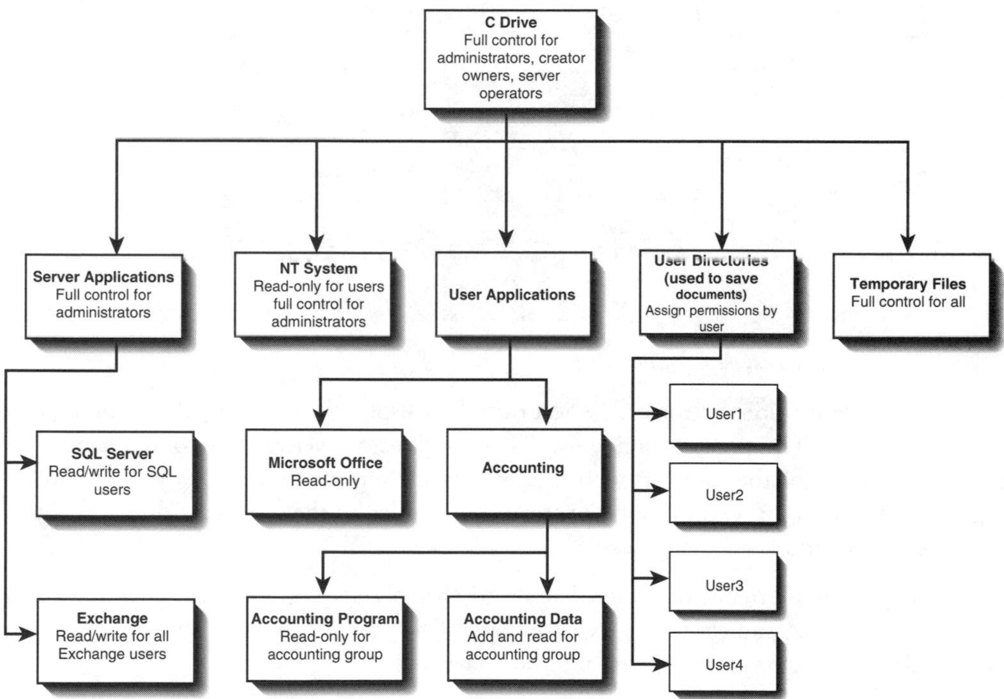

Flowchart 2.2. *Sample directory structure flowchart.*

Setting Permissions for a Directory

This example of setting permissions on a directory uses a sample directory, `C:\Justin`, in which the user account Justin saves certain documents. The folder method of accessing the Properties page will be used to demonstrate setting permissions.

Double-click the My Computer icon to display a list of logical drives. Open the C drive (or whatever drive is formatted for NTFS) by double-clicking the icon that represents that drive. Locate the proper directory (in this case, Justin) and click your right mouse button on that icon. Choose Properties from the pop-up menu (as shown in Figure 2.1). At this point, a summary of the `C:\Justin` directory is displayed. Next, click the Security tab. The Security page (see Figure 2.2) is where permissions can be set for that directory object, auditing can be enabled (which is discussed later in this chapter, in the "Auditing" section), or ownership of the directory object can be taken.

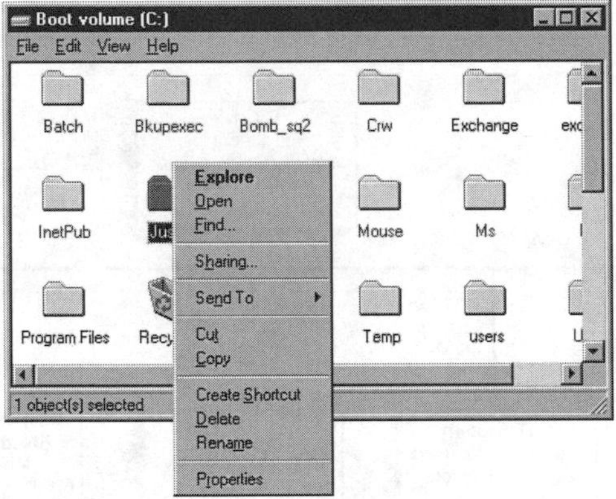

Figure 2.1. *Pop-up context menu for directories.*

Click the Permissions button on the Security tab to display the Directory Permissions page shown in Figure 2.3. This page contains a list of current directory permissions for `C:\Justin`, the name of the owner of the directory object, and various buttons that enable you to modify those permissions. In this example a new permission is added to the `C:\Justin` directory, but first I'll explain the modification process.

Highlight the username or group that already has permissions assigned, click the Permissions drop-down box, and choose a new permission. Click the OK button, and you have altered the existing permissions for that user or group. That's it!

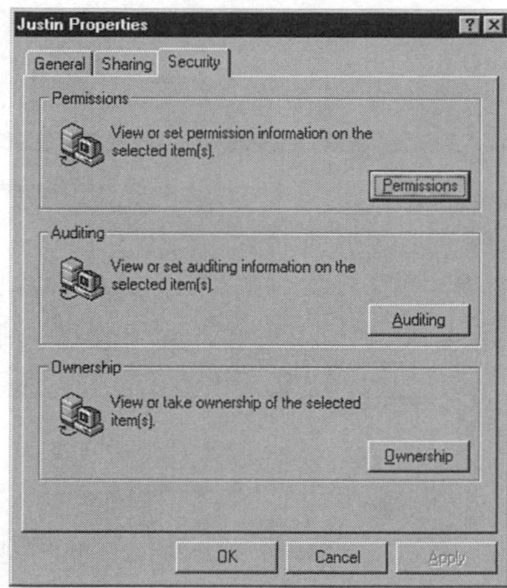

Figure 2.2. *Security page for directories.*

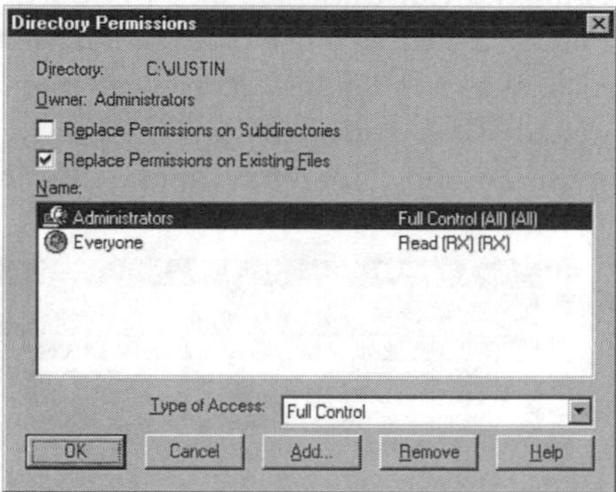

Figure 2.3. *Directory Permissions page.*

To add new permissions to `C:\Justin`, click once on the Add button. The Add Users and Groups dialog box (see Figure 2.4) displays a list that includes both global and local groups. Also on the list is the object `CREATOR OWNER`, which represents the user account that has ownership of the directory object, and the special groups, `INTERACTIVE` and `NETWORK`, which represent users that are accessing the computer locally or via the network, respectively. The operating system itself is represented by the special group SYSTEM.

By default, individual user accounts are not displayed on this list. Because the recommended way of assigning permissions is by group, Microsoft has decided not to show usernames in this list. However, if you click once on the button labeled Show Users, all usernames from that domain will be appended to the list, allowing you to modify rights on a user-by-user basis.

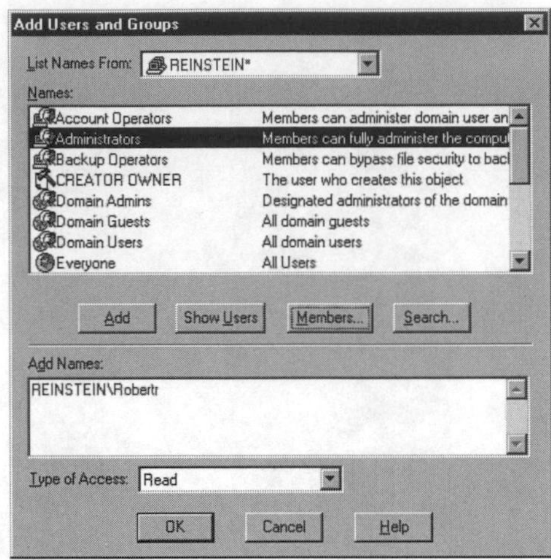

Figure 2.4. *Add Users and Groups dialog box.*

Another way of accessing individual usernames is by selecting a local group from the list and clicking once on the button labeled Members. This action will bring up a list of the members from the highlighted group, as shown in Figure 2.5. You can then choose from those members. This option is particularly handy when you are trying to locate only a subset of a group, such as only some of the Administrators group. This option applies only to local groups.

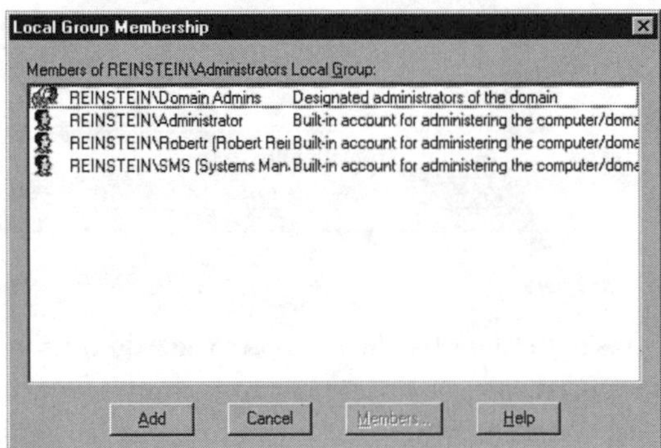

Figure 2.5. *Local group membership.*

Yet another way to select a username is by using the search function. In the Add Users and Groups dialog, click once on the button labeled Search to open the Find Account dialog box. (See Figure 2.6.) You can search in all of the domains on your network, or you can limit your search to one domain. Enter the username in the Find User or Group field and click the Search button. If that user is found, the user will be added to the Search Results list. When searching across multiple domains, the list might find multiple occurrences of the same username in different domains and display them all. However, these names will be fully qualified, showing the name of the domain in which the user account was found. For a full explanation of domains, see Chapter 3, "Domain Models."

Note: The search feature can also be used to search for local groups.

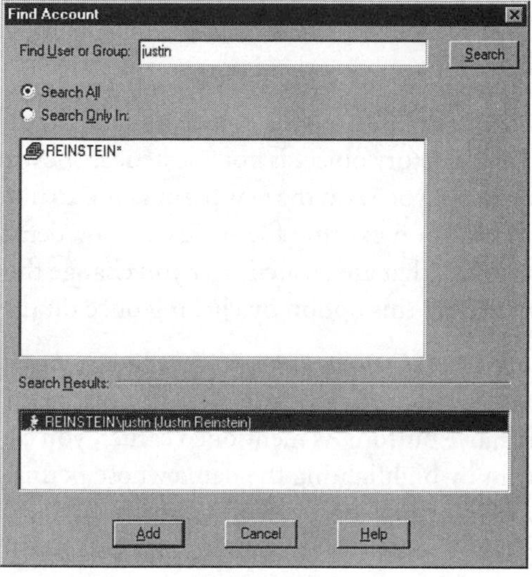

Figure 2.6. The Find Account dialog box.

Once you have completed adding usernames or group names to the Add Names list, choose the type of access that you want to assign to users and groups for the directory `C:\Justin`. Figure 2.7 shows the Type of Access drop-down list. Even if you want to assign different permissions to some of the newly added users or groups, click the OK button to add the names to the list of Names in the Directories Permissions dialog. Individual permissions for existing names and the newly added names can now be modified one at a time.

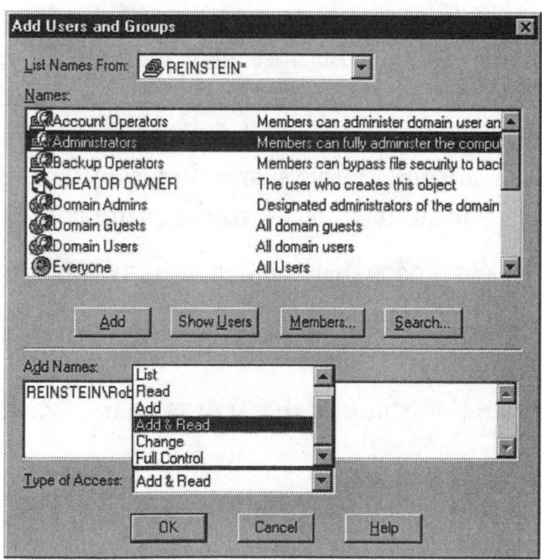

Figure 2.7. Use the Type of Access list to assign permission levels.

Note: Usernames can also be added manually by using the syntax `\domain\username`. Using this convention, you can add users from trusted domains as well.

To alter the permissions, you click the OK button, but before you do, consider the different methods that are available for applying these new permissions.

By default, when a Directory Permissions dialog is displayed, the option to replace permissions on subdirectories within this directory object is not selected, as shown in Figure 2.3. Check this box before changing permissions if you want the new permissions to filter down the directory tree. The option to replace permissions on existing files is selected by default. If you want to change the permissions only for new files that are created after you change the permissions for this directory object, then you must deselect this option by clicking once on the check box.

Changes to directory or file permissions sometimes include removing existing permissions, which is done by highlighting a username or group name in the Name list of the Permissions dialog and clicking once on the Remove button. As mentioned earlier, you can also alter permissions for the existing names on the list by highlighting the name whose permissions you want to change and selecting another permission from the Type of Access list.

Shared Disk Resources

The way to make resources available throughout Windows NT domains is to create a share. A *share* can be a hard drive, a directory, or a printer. Third-party utilities also allow you to create a modem share.

When you first install Windows NT Server, a number of default shares are automatically created for you. The administrative share is one type of default share. By default, each logical drive will have an administrative share. This type of share is a hidden share. A hidden share does not show up on any user's Browse list, but can be accessed manually. A share is hidden if the last character of the share name is a dollar sign (`$`). Because all Windows NT servers have a C drive, they will always have a share called `C$`, which is the entire C drive shared from the root directory and throughout the entire directory structure. By default, the user administrator is given full access to this share and to any other administrative shares. Logically, this permission makes a lot of sense because the administrator should have access to the entire contents of each logical drive.

Another default share is the `NETLOGON` share, which is the `SYSTEM32\REPL\IMPORT\SCRIPTS` directory under the Windows NT Server directory. This directory is used to keep logon scripts (which are explained in Chapter 14).

Another default administrative share is the `ADMIN$` share, which is the Windows NT Server directory.

Creating a Shared Disk Resource

One way to create a Windows NT share is by using Windows NT Explorer. By right-clicking a logical drive or on a directory, you will see Sharing on the pop-up menu. (See Figure 2.8.)

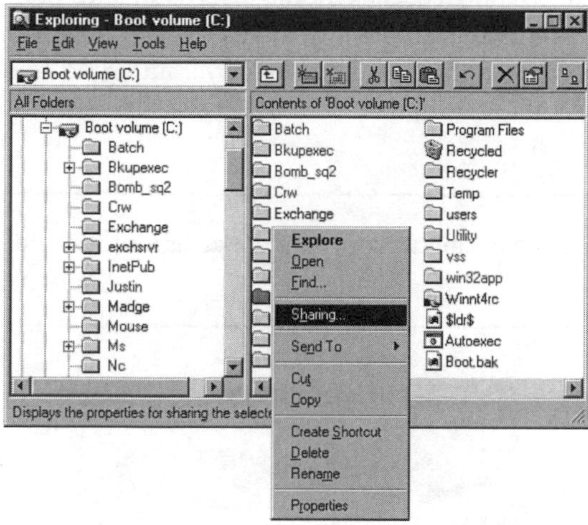

Figure 2.8. The Directory object pop-up menu.

Choose Sharing from the menu and click once to display the Sharing tab from the directory Properties page. (See Figure 2.9.) If this directory has never been shared, the option marked Not Shared will be chosen. If it is already being shared, the share name will appear. If the same directory has been shared multiple times (for reasons that will be discussed later in this chapter), then the drop-down Share Name box will show you the list of share names.

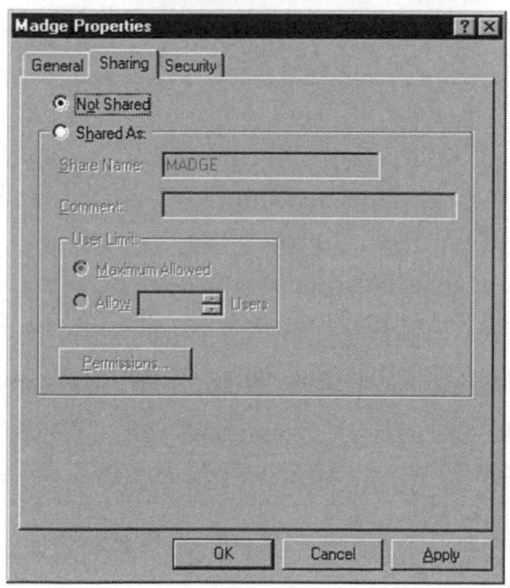

Figure 2.9. Directory Properties page.

Note: Windows gives you many ways to get to this Sharing tab from the Properties dialog; however, to avoid redundancy, I have included only one scenario.

If the directory has not been shared, click the Share As radio button. By default, as shown in Figure 2.10, the share name will be the same as the name of the directory. You have the option to change this name. You can define attributes for this share by limiting the number of users that can access the share concurrently, allowing the share to be accessed by any number of users, and assigning permissions for that share.

Tip: You also have the option to append a dollar sign to the end of the name if you want to hide the share.

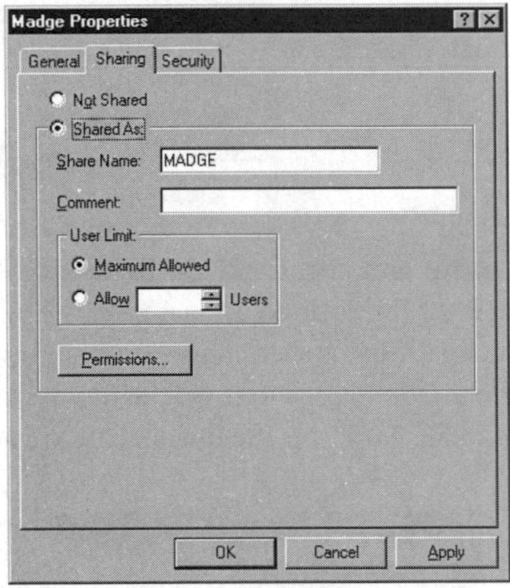

Figure 2.10. *The default share name is the same as the directory name.*

The next section in this chapter discusses how to assign permissions to the share. If the shared directory exists on an NTFS partition, then the Properties page also has a Security tab. This tab will give you more options on securing this directory, as I have already discussed. You might want to consider how you want to apply permissions.

The main purpose of creating more than one share for the same directory is to present a directory differently to different users or groups that require access to that directory. The differences can be as simple as the text description for the share or the permissions for the share.

Share-Level Permissions for Disk Resources

Permissions for shared drives and directories can be administered through Windows NT Explorer and Server Manager.

Table 2.4 shows the available permissions for a share.

Table 2.4. Share permissions.

Allowable Action	*No Access*	*Read*	*Change*	*Full Control*
View File and Directory Names		x	x	x
Change to the Subdirectories of the Shared Directory		x		x
View Data in Files and Run Executable Files		x	x	x
Change Data in Files			x	x
Delete Files and Subdirectories			x	x
Add Files and Subdirectories			x	x
Change Permissions (NTFS only)				x
Take Ownership (NTFS only)				x

Tip: When you are dealing with shares on an NTFS partition, the best way to assign permissions is through NTFS file and directory permissions. This method gives you greater control over the permissions for the files contained within the share.

Creating a share is the only way to make resources available across a Windows NT domain. Therefore, for files and directories, you must be careful to create the right balance of shares and file and directory permissions.

In some circumstances, an acceptable practice is to create a shared directory that uses only the simplistic permissions that are available for shares; for example, making the installation files for an application available to the domain. The directory that these installation files are copied into can be shared and its permissions can be set to Read for the Everyone group. This permission setting is acceptable because no one is required to write data to this directory. But whenever a user might add files to a share or modify a database within that share, it is in the best interest of the administrator to set individual file and directory permissions.

Note: If the share resides on a FAT partition, the only security that can be implemented on that share is share-level security.

To change permissions for a share, you can use Windows NT Explorer or Server Manager. Here is an example of assigning permissions for a shared disk resource through Windows NT Explorer.

Using Windows NT Explorer, locate the folder that you have set up as a share. Right mouse-click the folder to bring up the pop-up menu. Select Sharing from the menu. Click the Permissions button and the Access Through Share Permissions dialog box will appear (see Figure 2.11).

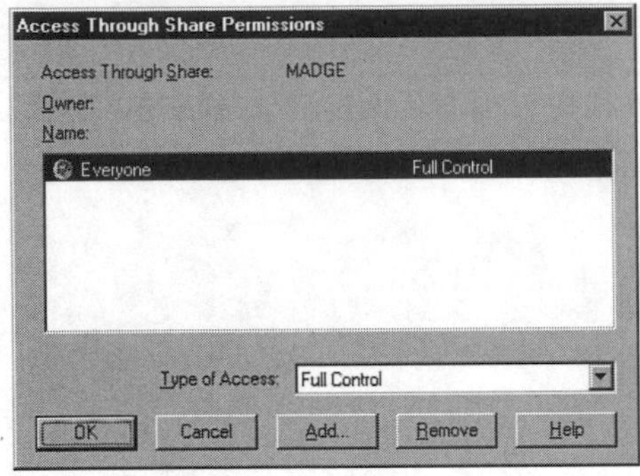

Figure 2.11. *Access Through Share Permissions dialog box.*

From this dialog box you can alter the existing permissions or click the Add button to select users or groups for whom you want to assign new permissions.

Administering Shares Using Server Manager

Another way to administer permissions for shares is through Server Manager in the Administrative Tools (Common) group. (See Figure 2.12.)

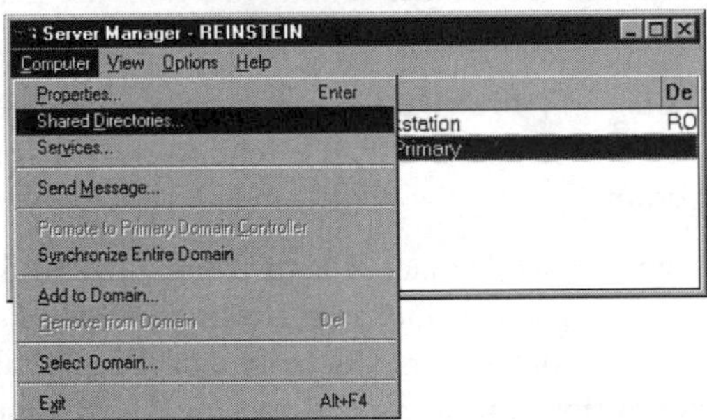

Figure 2.12. *Server Manager.*

In Server Manager select the domain controller that contains the shared directory for which you want to add, remove, or modify permissions. Then choose Shared Directories from the Computer menu to open the Shared Directories list, as shown in Figure 2.13. Highlight the share that you want to work on and click the Properties button. From the Share Properties dialog (see Figure 2.14), click the Permissions button. You will find yourself in the same Access Through Share dialog you opened earlier through Windows NT Explorer. (See Figure 2.14.)

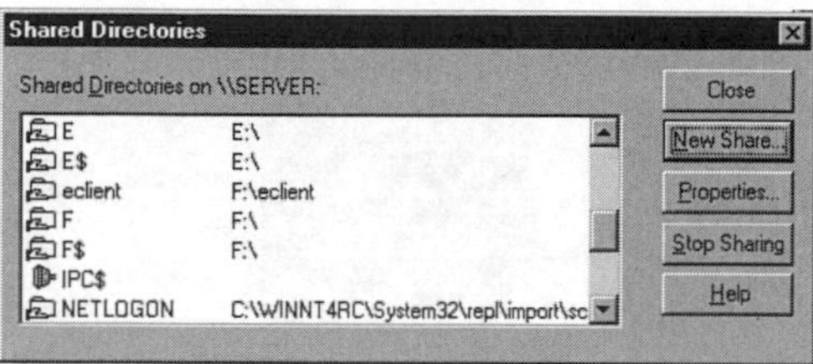

Figure 2.13. *Shared Directories list.*

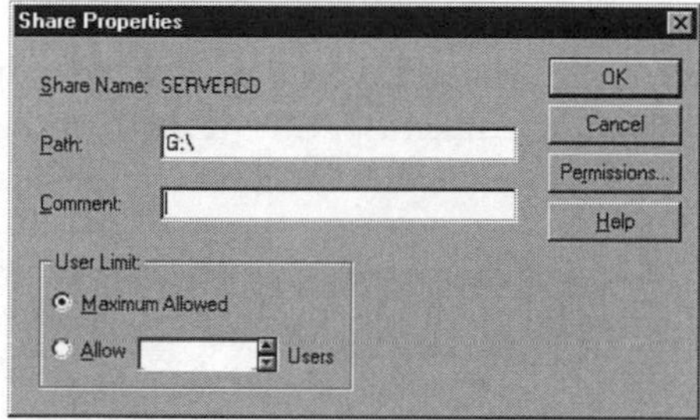

Figure 2.14. *The Share Properties dialog.*

Sharing Printers

Printers are another resource that users can share. Before you can share a printer, the printer needs to be installed on the Windows NT server.

Note: The printer does not need to physically reside on the Windows NT server, but must be installed into the server via the Add Printer process.

In order to create a shared printer, which will be using resources on the server, you must be a member of the Administrators, Server Operators, or Print Operators group.

Open the Printers display by using the Start button; then choose Settings | Printers. The installed printers will each be represented by an icon. To share a printer, right-click the icon that represents the printer you want to share and choose Sharing from the pop-up menu. (See Figure 2.15.)

This procedure is very similar to sharing disk resources. If the printer is not already shared, then the Not Shared radio button will be chosen. To start sharing the printer, click the Shared radio button. By default, the first eight characters of the printer's name appear in the Share Name box. (See Figure 2.16.) You can modify this name.

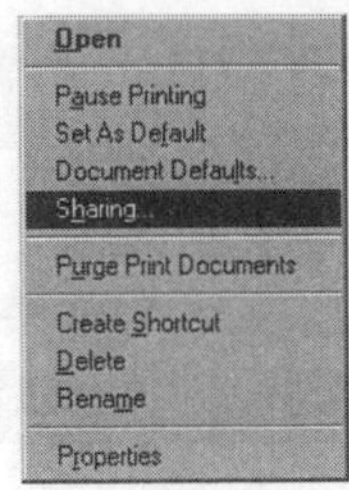

Figure 2.15. Printers pop-up menu.

You can also install drivers for the shared printer on the server; then clients can download the drivers when they attach to the printer. If you choose to store drivers on the server, you will be prompted to provide the drivers via diskette or CD-ROM to the installation program. As indicated on this page, to set permissions for the printer, you need to click the Security tab.

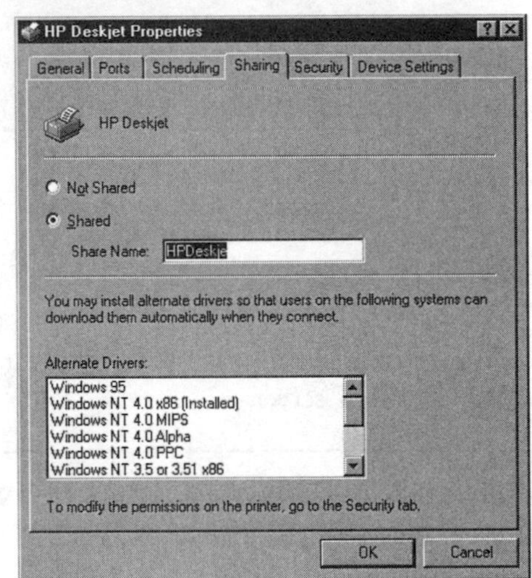

Figure 2.16. Enabling sharing for a printer.

The Securities page from the Printer Properties dialog is similar to the Security page you use to share directories or set NTFS-based permissions.

Choose Permissions to set the security for the printer that you have just shared. As shown in Figure 2.17, by default all users have access to a shared printer. Also, users have control over the print jobs that they submit to the shared printer.

You can set four permissions (Type of Access in Figure 2.17) for printers. By default, members of the Administrators, Server Operators, and Print Operators group have Full Control permission.

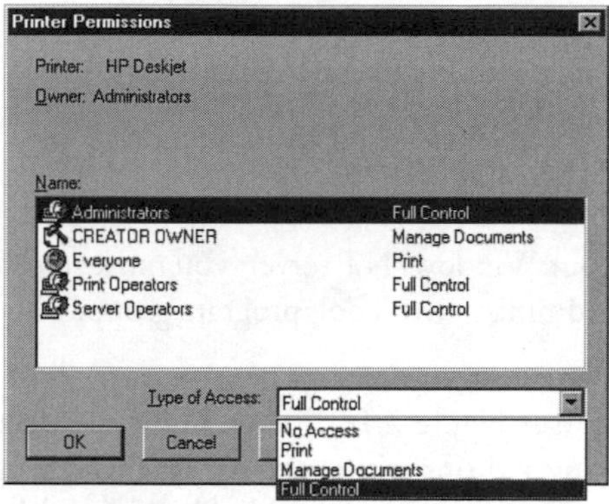

Figure 2.17. The Printer Permissions dialog box.

Table 2.5 explains the different printer permissions and the tasks these permissions allow them to perform.

Table 2.5. Printer permissions.

Permission	*No Access*	*Print*	*Manage Documents*	*Full Control*
Print		x		x
Alter Document Job Settings			x	x
Change the Order of Print Jobs				x
Delete, Pause, Resume, and Restart Print Jobs			x	x
Alter Printer Properties				x
Purge, Pause, and Resume Print Queues				x
Delete a Printer				x
Change Printer Permissions				x

Auditing

The auditing feature of Windows NT can allow you, as the Administrator, to create a log that can track almost every movement on your domain controllers. I say almost because certain events, which do not affect the integrity of your (network such as browsing a directory) are not tracked.

Everything that could have any type of impact on your network can be tracked and stored in the audit log, which is viewable with the Event Viewer utility.

System Audit Policies

To enable auditing on your Windows NT server, you must start the User Manager for Domains program, located in the Administrative Tools program group. This system utility will set the policy for auditing.

From the Policies menu (see Figure 2.18), select Audit. By default, Windows NT auditing is turned off because enabling auditing without properly considering the amount of disk space that the log will consume can result in a very quickly filled hard drive. However, you can limit the amount of disk space used for the audit log from within the Event Viewer application, which is an example of how granular the auditing feature of NT Server can be. Auditing also creates overhead for your server, so you should be selective about the items that you audit.

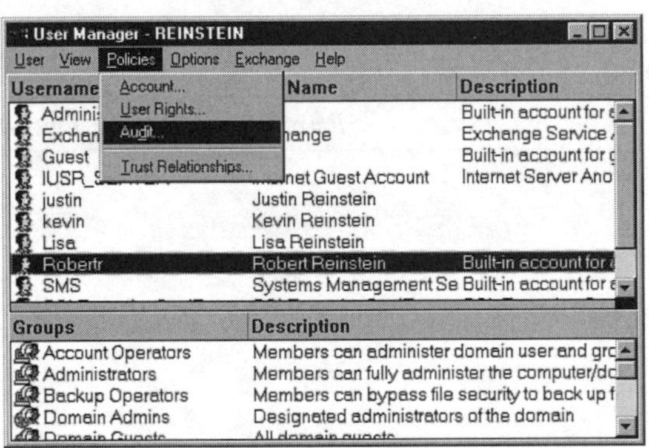

Figure 2.18. User Manager Policies menu.

Figure 2.19 shows the Audit Policy dialog box. Check the items that you want to have audited as a domain policy.

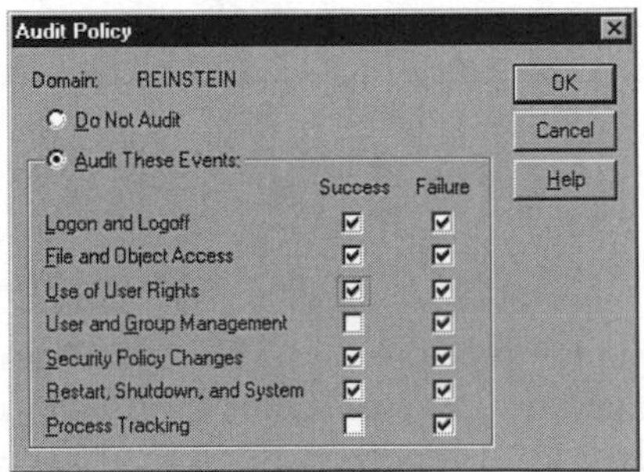

Figure 2.19. Audit Policy dialog box.

- Logon and Logoff auditing gives you a way to monitor network usage (indicated by successful logons and logoffs). A failure could mean an attempt to break into the network, or it could just be a forgotten password.
- File and Object Access can track all file and printer access. In the "File and Directory Auditing" and "Printer Auditing" sections later in this chapter, you will see how you are able to limit the number of audit messages for file and print access based on the type of action that has occurred.

Note: In order to audit file and print details, you must turn on File and Object Access auditing.

- Use of User Rights audits events that involve the rights that I discuss in the next section. But to give you an example now, a user can have the right to log on locally at the server console. Under normal circumstances, that logon is audited only as a logon; but when you enable the auditing for Use of User Rights, it is noted that the user has exercised the right to log on locally. This information is very useful because failures that are documented by Use of User Rights auditing could indicate a system problem.
- User and Group Management shows all events associated with the creation or modification of users or groups.
- Security Policy Changes tracks any changes to, or attempts to change, User Policies, Audit Policies, or Trust Relationships.
- Restart, Shutdown, and System will show if a restart or shutdown has been initiated, or if any attempt was made to stop the security log.
- Process Tracking gives a detailed account of the starting and stopping of system processes, including applications and threads.

File and Directory Auditing

To set up auditing for file access, you must go to the Properties/Security page for each disk resource that you want to audit. For this example I will set up auditing for the entire C drive.

Clicking the Auditing button on the Properties/Security page opens the Directory Auditing dialog shown in Figure 2.20. You can choose whether to apply these audit choices to subdirectories and to all the files within that directory. If an audit policy had already been set up for a particular file, not selecting Replace Auditing on Existing Files would retain the original auditing policy for that file. Selecting Replace Auditing on Existing Files will replace the original policy with the one you are now implementing.

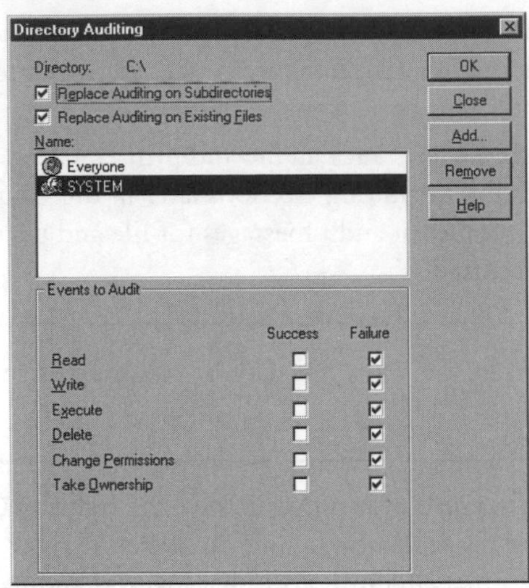

Figure 2.20. Directory Auditing dialog box.

Before you can choose the events to be audited, you must select the users or groups to audit. Click the Add button to view a list of groups. (See Figure 2.21.) Click the Show Users button in the Add Users and Groups dialog box to append all usernames to that list. For complete auditing, choose the Everyone group. Windows keyboard conventions apply for selecting multiple items from the list. Select the users or groups for whom you want to enable auditing and then click the OK button.

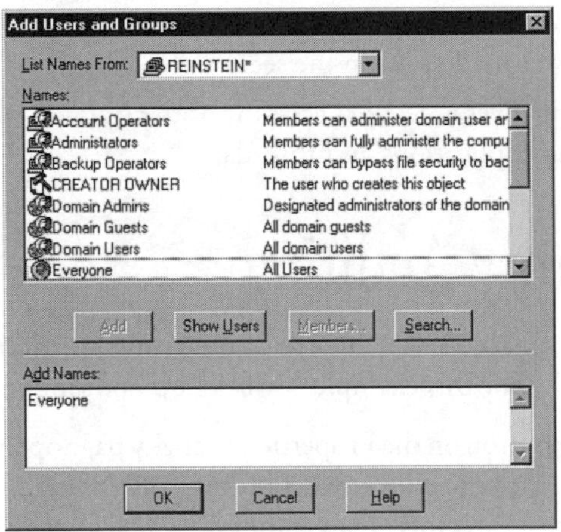

Figure 2.21. Adding users and groups for auditing.

Printer Auditing

To audit printer usage, click the Auditing button on the Properties/Security page for the printer you want to audit. As with file and directory auditing, you must specify the users that you want to audit. For complete auditing, select the Everyone group.

The options for printer auditing, shown in Figure 2.22, are explained by Table 2.6. The types of auditing are shown across Table 2.6, and the actions that are performed and audited are in the left column.

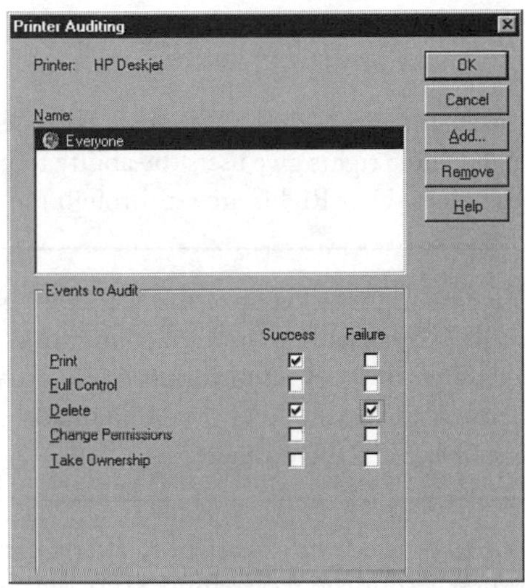

Figure 2.22. *Printer auditing.*

Table 2.6. Types and action for printer auditing.

Audit	*Print*	*Full Control*	*Delete*	*Change Permissions*	*Take Ownership*
Print Documents	x				
Alter Settings for Print Jobs		x			
Pause, Remove, Restart, and Move Documents		x			
Share a Printer		x			
Alter Printer Properties		x			
Remove a Printer			x		

continues

Table 2.6. continued

Audit	*Print*	*Full Control*	*Delete*	*Change Permissions*	*Take Ownership*
Change Permissions for a Printer				x	
Taking Ownership					x

User Rights

User Rights affect how users interact with the Windows NT operating system and the processes that run on Windows NT. These rights give users the ability to perform tasks above and beyond accessing file and print services. User Rights are set through the User Manager for Domains.

Note: A user must have the right to log on at the Windows NT server console. This right is called "Log on locally." By default, your average user does not have this right, but the Administrator and members of the Administrators group do have that right. This convention makes a lot of sense because you do not want an unauthorized user to walk up to the Windows NT server console and log on there!

Although the administrator, or users with the right to alter a user's rights, can modify the rights that are associated with a user account (and therefore a SID), the rights that are defined in Windows NT are not modifiable. Microsoft has mentioned that a future version of Windows NT will include the ability to create and define new rights.

Windows NT ships with predefined groups that already have some of these user rights assigned to them. For instance, the Administrators group has many of the user rights assigned to it, and the Print Operators group has only the rights that are required to administer print queues and printers. The Backup Operators group has the Back Up Files and Directories right.

The rights that can be assigned to users and groups are

Access this computer from network
Act as part of the operating system
Add workstations to domain
Back up files and directories
Bypass traverse checking
Change the system time
Create a pagefile
Create permanent shared objects
Create a token object

Debug programs
Force shutdown from a remote system
Generate security audits
Increase Quotas
Increase scheduling priority
Load and unload device drivers
Lock pages in memory
Log on as a batch job
Log on as a service
Log on locally
Manage auditing and security log
Modify firmware environment values
Profile single process
Profile system performance
Replace a process level token
Restore files and directories
Shut down the system
Take ownership of files or other objects

Most of these rights have already been assigned to the Administrators group.

To modify user rights, use the User Manager for Domains. Click the Policies menu and select User Rights.

As shown in Figure 2.23, the user right `Access this computer from network` is the current user right. The users or groups that have this right are shown in the Grant To list. From here you can add more users or groups to this list, or remove users or groups that already have the right. Click the down arrow to see the rest of the user rights that you can configure. The initial set of user rights that you'll see in this dialog is actually a subset of the complete list that I mentioned just above. To see the entire list of rights, you must click the Show Advanced User Rights check box. Then the drop-down list of Rights will expand to show all Windows NT user rights.

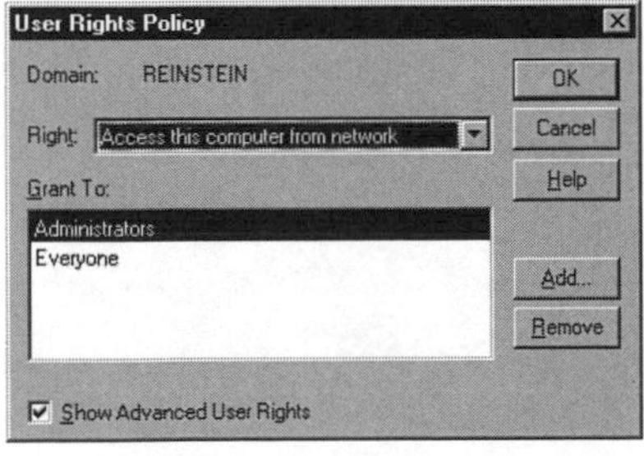

Figure 2.23. *User Rights policy.*

Summary

Security is one of the foremost features of Windows NT. Dedicated system processes are constantly checking authentication, making Windows NT possibly the most rock solid and secure operating system available.

Although it is reassuring to know that the operating system handles all aspects of security, it should be obvious that the creation of a Windows NT domain requires a great deal of planning, and setting security policies for your enterprise should be foremost on your list of tasks.

I strongly urge you to take advantage of all the security features that Windows NT has to offer. Take the time to decide how to implement your policies, rights, permissions, and auditing to make your network as secure as possible.

Domain Models

by Robert Reinstein

Ever since Microsoft released its Microsoft LAN Manager networking product, Microsoft Networking has worked with a server grouping method known as domains. By creating domains, Microsoft networking made administering a network much easier—no longer was it necessary to administer a network of user accounts and resources on a server-by-server basis.

This chapter explains the domain concept and the different types of domain models available for you to implement, as well as their pros and cons. From the information provided here, you should be able to decide which of these models best fits your organization.

What Is a Windows NT Domain?

Simply put, a Windows NT Domain is a logical grouping of computers. When a client logs on to Windows NT, he or she isn't actually logging on to a server, but a domain. The creation of a domain means that you, as the administrator, can configure and administer a logical grouping of servers. Whatever security you implement today on a single server will also apply to a new server running Windows NT Server that you have chosen to be part of the existing domain. A domain can actually include a Microsoft LAN Manager server and clients running Windows NT Workstation, Windows 95, Windows for Workgroups, Windows 3.*x*, MS-DOS, Apple, and OS/2.

When you install Windows NT Server on your first server, you're faced with naming that server. Later you have to specify the role that the server will play in your network, as either a Primary Domain Controller (PDC), a Backup Domain Controller (BDC), or a stand-alone server. A stand-alone server may or may not be part of a Windows NT domain, but is the only option that can be part of a workgroup.

Assuming that you want to take advantage of being able to centralize administration, you should have all servers and workstations join your domain.

Figure 3.1 shows a single domain with multiple servers.

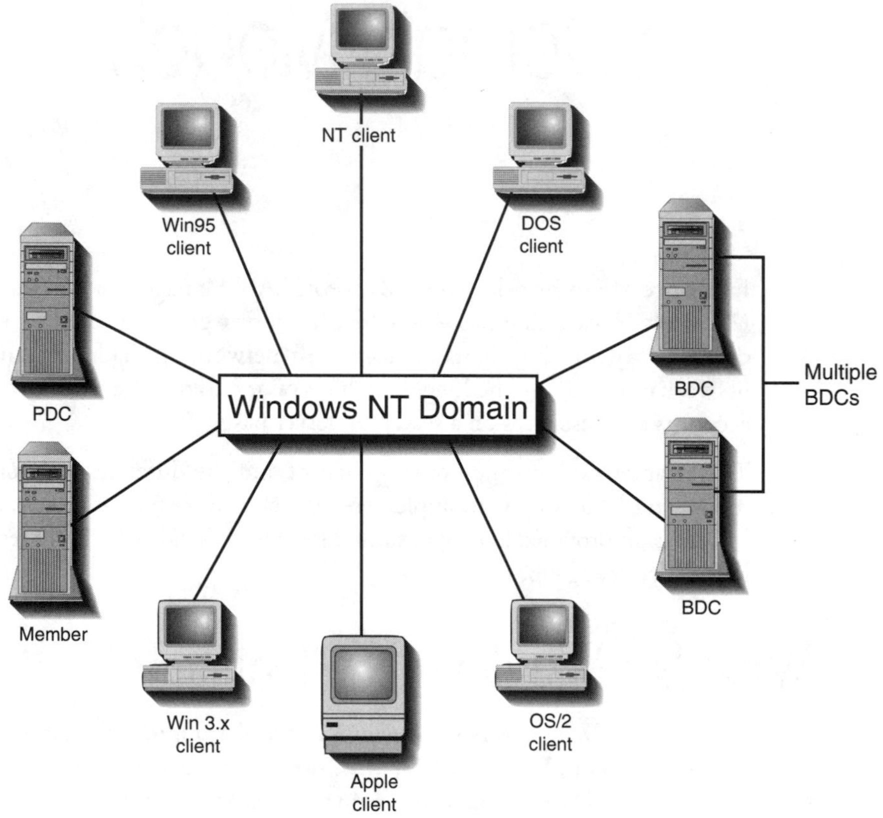

Figure 3.1. *Windows NT Domain.*

The average single domain might contain a Primary Domain Controller and one or more Backup Domain Controllers. The Primary Domain Controller is the host for the user account database and logon scripts. The Backup Domain Controllers replicate that data so that they can participate in the authentication of logon requests. A Backup Domain Controller also can be promoted to Primary Domain Controller if there's a problem with the actual Primary Domain Controller. The clients in a domain can be running Windows NT Workstation, Windows for Workgroups, Windows 3.*x*, MS-DOS, Windows 95, Apple, and OS/2.

Note: A Microsoft LAN Manager server can act as a Backup Domain Controller, but can't be promoted to a Primary Domain Controller.

Workgroups Versus Domains

An alternative to being part of a domain on a Windows NT network is to be part of a workgroup. Any PC running Windows NT Server, Windows NT Workstation, Windows 95, Windows for Workgroups, Windows 3.*x*, or MS-DOS can be part of a workgroup. This is another logical grouping of computers, but it doesn't have centralized security or administration. Each of the computers that participates in a workgroup handles its own administration.

Why would someone opt to run only in a workgroup?

Workgroup computing is really what is known as peer-to-peer networking. No one computer is the hub for all of the computers. Even though one or more of these computers may be running Windows NT Server, it doesn't make that computer any more important to the network, because it doesn't handle tasks like authenticating logon requests or storing user account information. All of the user account information for each of these computers is stored locally. This is fine for an organization that doesn't want to deal with administration or doesn't want to have the extra traffic on the network that is used for replication. Using workgroups is also the only way that a group of computers that doesn't include a server running Windows NT Server can use Microsoft networking. Any domain must have at least one Windows NT server that serves as the Primary Domain Controller.

Domains allow for the setting of standards on a network. For instance, after a security policy is set on a Primary Domain Controller, the other Windows NT servers in that same domain must follow those same policies. Using a domain also allows for the running of logon scripts.

There is also no problem having a domain and having workgroups with that domain. Microsoft Networking is very flexible and can be configured for whatever best suits your company.

Using multiple domains and trust relationships gives you flexibility that uses the best parts of both workgroups and domains. That is also part of the planning that must take place so that you can come up with the right domain model for you.

Multiple Domains

The single domain allows for central administration of user accounts and resources, such as disk drives and printers.

But what if your company has offices in different locations, or if different departments would prefer to administer their own users or resources?

These are only two scenarios in which you might need to evaluate the more complex Windows NT domain models.

There are ways for different domains to communicate. The next section is about trust relationships, which allow users from one domain to be given permission to utilize resources of another domain.

Trust Relationships

In a network that requires multiple domains, possibly due to geographical or departmental reasons, a single user might require a user account in each of these domains.

But Windows NT has an answer that allows for a user to be defined in only one domain, yet have access to resources to other domains. The answer is called a *trust.* A trust is an agreement between two domains.

Before you can examine some of the different domain models, you need to understand how trust relationships work. Trust relationships are very important to some of these domain models, so it's very important to understand what a trust is and why you should or shouldn't choose to implement trust relationships on your network.

The Trusting Domain and the Trusted Domain

One of the domains in a trust relationship is known as the *trusting domain.* The other domain involved in this trust relationship is known as the *trusted domain.*

Users and global groups from the trusted domain can be given permission to use resources (shared directories and printers) that belong to the trusting domain. This is accomplished by giving the trusting domain access to the trusted domain's user account database. This arrangement makes it possible to not have to set up the same user in more than one domain, which makes for easier administration of user accounts.

In Figure 3.2, the MANCHESTER domain is the trusting domain and the REINSTEIN domain is the trusted domain. This means that users that have been defined in the REINSTEIN domain can be assigned permission to access resources located in the MANCHESTER domain.

Trust relationships are one-way. Just because one domain trusts another, it doesn't mean that the reverse is true, unless it's explicitly set up that way. A two-way trust can be set up if the trusted domain also becomes a trusting domain and the trusting domain becomes trusted. In Figure 3.3, the MANCHESTER domain is both trusted and trusting, and the REINSTEIN domain is also trusted and trusting. This enables users in either domain to access resources in either domain (if the proper permissions are granted).

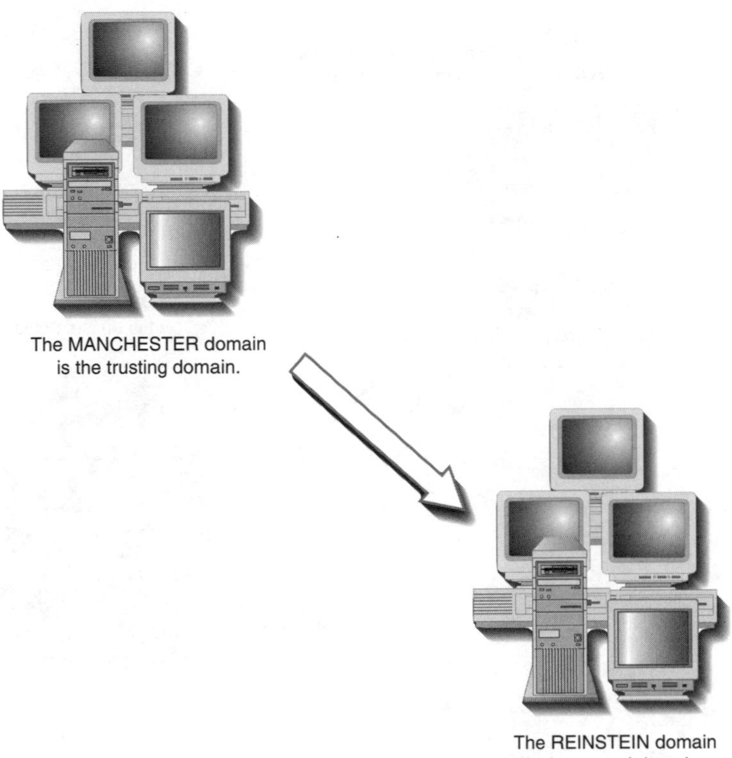
The MANCHESTER domain
is the trusting domain.
The REINSTEIN domain
is the trusted domain.

Figure 3.2. *A trust relationship*

If you have three domains, A, B, and C, and domain A trusts domain B, and domain B trusts domain C, domain A does not trust domain C automatically. All trusts must be set up explicitly.

Windows NT's security system handles trusts in the same manner that it handles user accounts. However, when a trust is defined, the trusted domain is set up as a global account on the trusting domain. This is handled internally and is really not something you need to concern yourself with.

The administrator of the trusting domain can assign permissions to users or global groups from the trusted domain. When a user from the trusted domain attempts to access a resource of the trusting domain, the trusting domain sends the request to a Domain Controller of the trusted domain to obtain authorization. This is known as pass-through authentication.

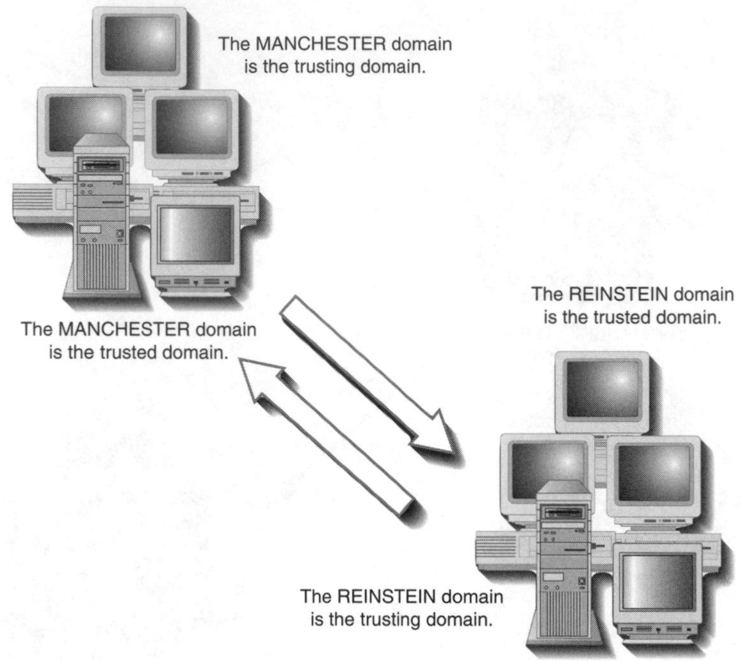
The MANCHESTER domain
is the trusting domain.
The REINSTEIN domain
is the trusted domain.
The MANCHESTER domain
is the trusted domain.
The REINSTEIN domain
is the trusting domain.

Figure 3.3. *Two-way trust relationship.*

How to Establish a Trust Relationship

Creating a trust relationship between domains requires cooperation from administrators in both domains. Before a domain can become a trusting domain, the domain that will become trusted should give the other domain permission to trust. These steps don't necessarily need to be performed in this order, but this order does ensure that the trust relationship can be tested immediately, as the password that is necessary to establish the trust relationship can then be verified.

NT4.0

In previous versions of Windows NT Server, the dialog to establish a trust explicitly called the first step to establishing a trust "permission to trust." Although version 4.0 doesn't explicitly call it that, it's the same process and is therefore used throughout this section.

Creating a trust relationship is accomplished by using the User Manager for Domains.

To establish the necessary permission to trust, an administrator for the domain that will be the trusted domain must run the User Manager for Domains program. Select Trust Relationships… from the Policies menu, as shown in Figure 3.4. The Trust Relationships dialog is broken into two parts, one to work with trusted domains and the other for trusting domains. To give the permission to trust, click the Add… button for Trusting Domains.

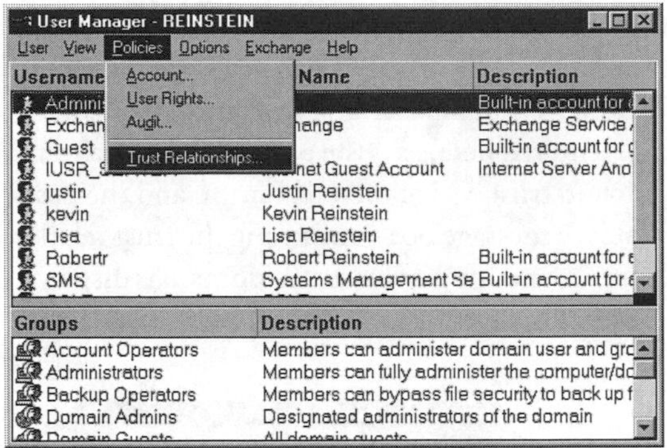

Figure 3.4. User Manager for Domains.

The Add Trusting Domain dialog (see Figure 3.5) prompts you to enter the name of the domain for which you will give permission to trust, and you must also enter a password that the administrator of the trusted domain will use when establishing the trust.

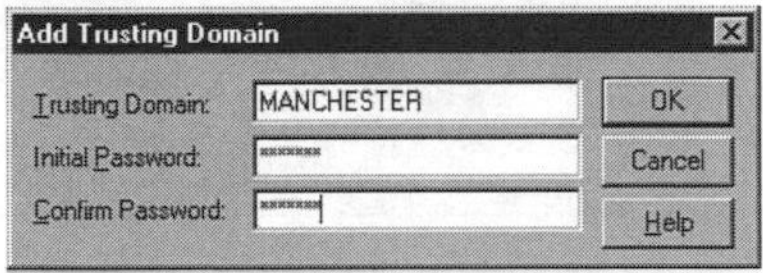

Figure 3.5. The Add Trusting Domain dialog box.

After this information is entered, click the OK button and the other domain will be listed as a trusting domain, as shown in Figure 3.6.

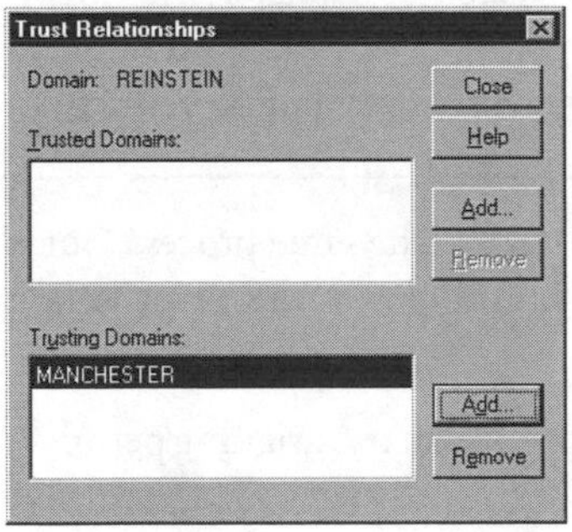

Figure 3.6. Completed permission to trust.

To complete the trust relationship, the other administrator also must run User Manager for Domains. To complete this part of the process, the administrator of the trusting domain must know the password that the administrator of the trusted domain established while giving permission to trust. Usually in a corporation, a password used to establish all trust relationships will be agreed upon.

From the Policies menu in User Manager for Domains, the administrator for the trusting domain selects Trust Relationships... . From the Trusted Domains part of the dialog, click the Add... button. The Add Trusted Domain dialog (see Figure 3.7) is now displayed. The name of the domain to be trusted is entered here, as is the password that was established by the trusted domain when giving permission to trust. Click the OK button and the password validation takes place. If the password is validated, a message box confirming the trust relationship is displayed. (See Figure 3.8.) Click the OK button, and the newly trusted domain is displayed in the list of trusted domains in the Trust Relationships dialog.

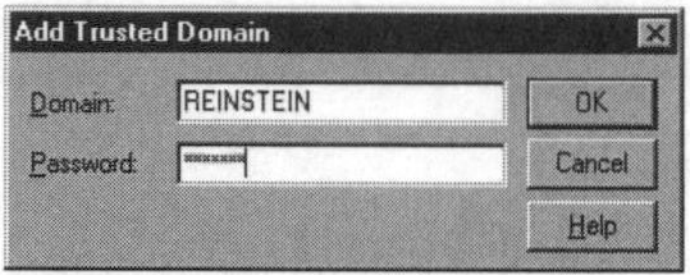

Figure 3.7. *The Add Trusted Domain dialog.*

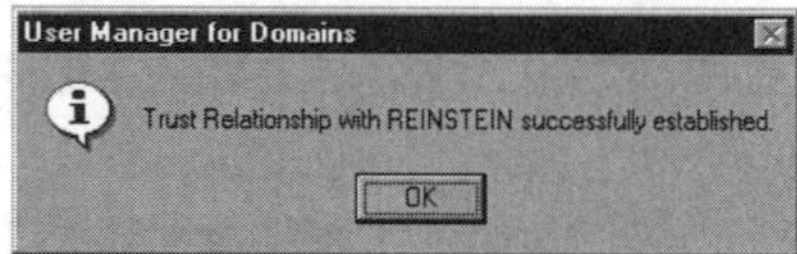

Figure 3.8. *A successful trust relationship.*

Caution: When setting up a trust, be sure to have the trusted domain give permission to trust first. Adding a trusted domain without getting this permission results in the other domain being added to the list of trusted domains, but the trust does not exist. An error message, displayed at the time the trusting domain adds a domain to its trusted list without permission to trust, mentions that the trust could not be verified.

To establish a two-way trust, repeat the same process, but with the trusted domain acting as the trusting domain. When this is completed, the Trust Relationships dialog will look as it does in Figure 3.9.

To test your trust relationship, you can try assigning permissions to a member of the other domain. Figure 3.10 shows the Add Users and Groups dialog, which now enables you to choose the domain you wish to list users and groups from, with the List Names From field as a drop-down box.

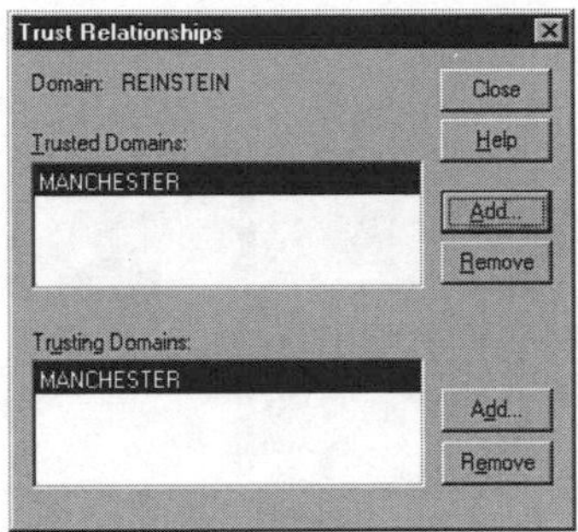

Figure 3.9. *Trust relationships with a two-way trust.*

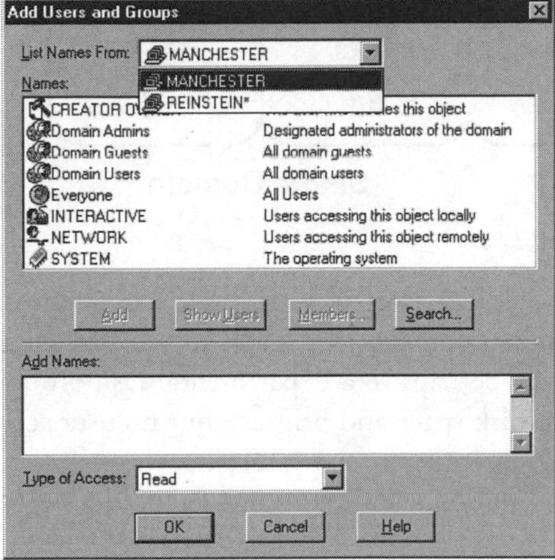

Figure 3.10. *Multiple domains for adding permissions.*

Popular Domain Models

The most popular Microsoft Networking Domain models are called the Single Domain model, the Multiple Domain model, the Multiple Master Domain model, and the Multiple Trust Domain model.

The Single Domain model is the most frequently used domain model because of its simplistic approach to networking. No trust relationships are necessary because there is only one domain. The Windows NT limit of 15,000 users per domain limits this model to organizations with no more than 15,000 users. Figure 3.11 illustrates a single domain, which can have one or more servers.

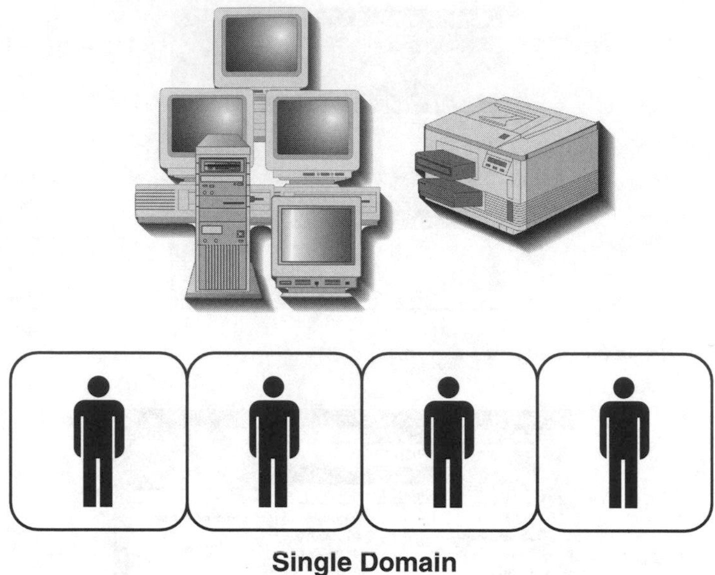

Figure 3.11. Single Domain model.

The Master Domain model, illustrated in Figure 3.12, takes one domain that administers all of the user accounts. The master domain defines and administers all user accounts for the network. Other domains are set up, perhaps in a departmental fashion or by geographical region, that contain resources such as disk space and printers, but no user accounts. These are the resource domains. Trust relationships are set up in which all of the resource domains are trusting and the master domain is the trusted domain.

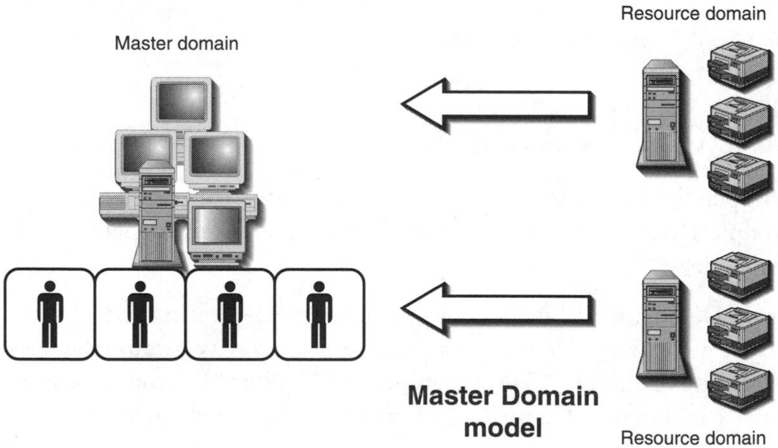

Figure 3.12. Master Domain model.

What makes this domain model work is that each of these departmental or regional domains can administer their own resources. User administration is still handled in one location, which limits the number of users to 15,000, but offers centralized user administration.

The Multiple Master Domain model, shown in Figure 3.13, is similar to the Master Domain model, but in this case there is more than one master domain. This is useful when resource domains are grouped in a logical fashion. The resource domains then set up a trust with a particular master domain. Once all of the resource domains are trusting and their respective master domains are trusted, the master domains set up a two-way trust with each other. This way, a user from any domain can gain access to resources in any other domain. This also enables breaking the 15,000 user limit of the models with only one master domain. At the same time, it creates a more difficult administrative task because the user accounts aren't centralized.

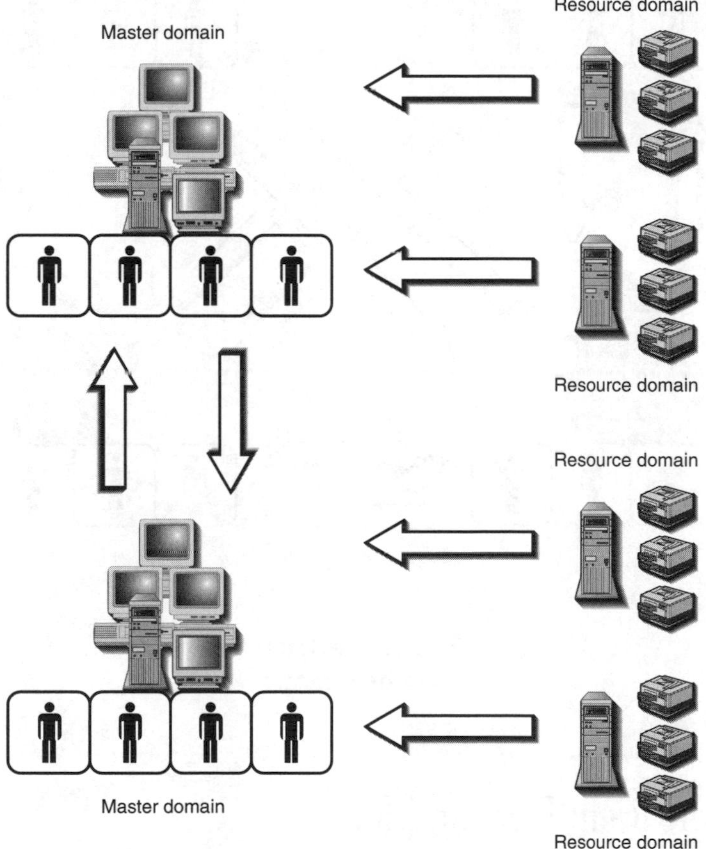

Figure 3.13. *Multiple Master Domain model.*

The Multiple Trust model (see Figure 3.14), also known as a Full Trust model, is basically a free-for-all. There are no master domains and no resource domains. The Multiple Trust model is for a company that has different departments or geographical regions that want to administer their own users and resources. Two-way trusts are set up to enable users from any domain to access resources on any other domain. This can be a headache to administer because there are so many trust relationships to implement and maintain; however, this may be the most suitable for your scenario.

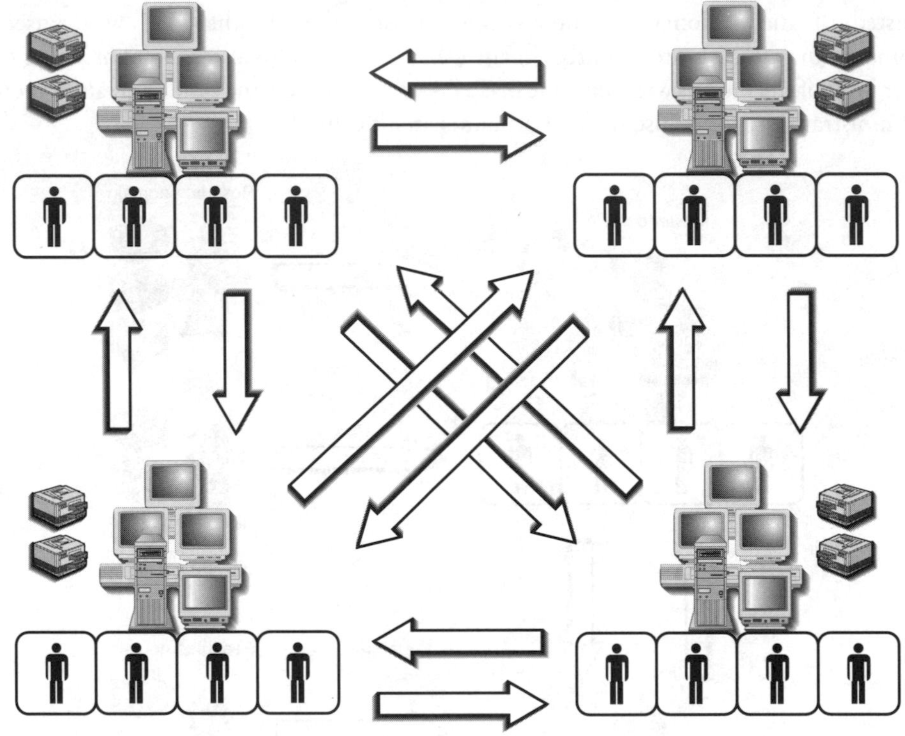

Figure 3.14. *Multiple Trust Domain model.*

Choosing the Right Domain Model

There are many decisions to make when planning your Windows NT domain model. The communications link between servers can help plan your domain model. Your company's requirements for administration are another concern. Do you have departments that don't want any "outsiders" administrating their user accounts or resources? Are there remote offices that don't have technical staff that can administer their servers? All of these items should be considered when defining your real needs. Flowchart 3.1 charts choosing a Domain model.

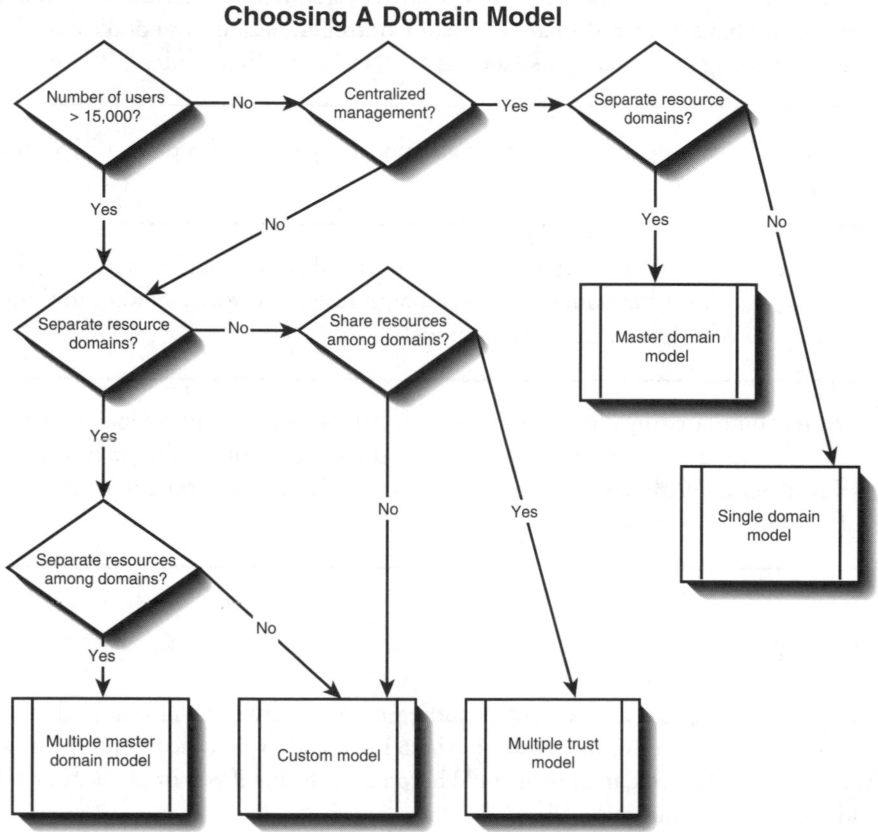

Flowchart 3.1. *Choosing a Domain model.*

The first thing you want to consider is central administration. If you have fewer than 15,000 user accounts, you can have central administration of the user accounts database. Now you have the choice to create either a Single Domain model or a Master Domain model. Do you also want to centrally administer all of the network resources? If so, the Single Domain model is the right one. Otherwise you should go for a Master Domain model.

If you want to break up administration of user accounts, either based on a large number of accounts or for corporate reasons, but still want to be able to share resource across domains, you need to decide whether you want to set up separate master domains and resource domains. If you want to break these up, then the Multiple Master Domain model makes sense. If your network will be a hodgepodge of domains with both resources and user accounts, the Multiple Trust model is probably the proper model.

If you work for a company that has two locations, and only one location has resources that need to be shared by both locations, you may want to set up a custom domain model.

For instance, if these two locations are separated by a slow link, each location should be in its own domain and have its own Primary Domain Controller, because you don't want logon authentication occurring over a slow link (such as ISDN or even 28.8 modem).

Note: You can use the Master Domain model if you can also place a BDC at the remote location.

In this scenario, you would set up the location with shared resources as trusting. If you also want the ability to administer both domains and both resources, you may want to think about a two-way trust, or Multiple Trust Domain model.

Note: Some large organizations, with thousands of users in multiple locations, use the Single Domain model. Other organizations with the same number of users run with a Multiple Trust model. With careful planning and communication, you can prepare the perfect model for your own purposes.

Summary

Careful planning and a good understanding of your network will ensure that you choose the domain model that fits your organization best. Be careful to plan and not jump into setting up your Windows NT network, because it could become confusing if you implement one domain model and then change your mind later.

Although some may criticize this way of managing a network, it is very simple to set up (once planned) and can be very easy to maintain—two strong points of a Windows NT network.

CHAPTER 4

Windows NT Registry Architecture

by Robert Reinstein

The Windows NT Registry is a database that holds all the Windows NT configuration settings. In order to administrate computers that are running Windows NT, it is important to have an understanding of how to manage the Registry.

This chapter covers these topics:

- An overview of the Windows NT Registry
- The structure of the Registry
- Registry data types

Overview of the Registry

The Windows NT Registry was designed as a way to store the different types of data that are necessary for the configuration of a computer running Windows NT.

In earlier versions of Windows, the main configuration files were `WIN.INI` and `SYSTEM.INI`. When Microsoft designed Windows NT, it had decided that having multiple files, plus possibly numerous configuration files created and maintained by application software, would be too cumbersome, and would actually not fit the needs of a multiuser system such as Windows NT.

As you may recall, the Windows INI files were designed in a very noncomplex way. A section within these files had a header that appeared in square brackets and values that were always defined as a text string. An example is shown in Listing 4.1.

Listing 4.1. A sample INI file section.

```
[ISVR.DRV]
IO Port=0x2E4
IRQ=15
Input Sync=0
keying=4
Algorithm=YVU9
Saturation=21
Tint=28
Contrast=63
Brightness=27
VCR=1
Connector=0
InputLoss=1
```

The example in Listing 4.1 is a section titled `ISVR.DRV`. Although three of the values, `IO Port`, `IRQ`, and `Algorithm`, contain different types of values (a hex value, a number, and a text string, respectively), they are all represented as a text string. The Windows NT Registry, on the other hand, allows for storage of values in their native format.

The INI files also did not contain a hierarchy. Each section was a separate entity without any way to imbed a section within a section. The Windows NT Registry allows for nested groups of values.

Allowing nested values is important because Windows NT will save settings based on a user's logon name.

Luckily, the days of searching for an individual application's INI files are over thanks to the strict guidelines for Windows NT software developers. In order to be qualified as Windows NT compliant, developers must write to the Windows NT Registry, keeping all configuration information in one place.

Keeping all configuration information in one place has many uses. One is, of course, not having to sweep across your hard drive(s) in order to find configuration settings that you may want to check or change. Another major enhancement of having configuration information in one place is the ability to back up a single Registry, knowing that all settings for a computer have been backed up, perhaps onto a single disk.

> **Note:** There still are INI files on your hard drive, as Windows NT supports usage of the `WIN.INI` and `SYSTEM.INI` for backwards compatibility with software that still utilizes those files. You may also be using software, usually 16-bit software, that has its own INI files.

Another major feature of the Windows NT Registry is the ability to assign security to any part of the Registry. The assignment of security in the Registry is discussed in Chapter 11, "Managing the Windows NT Registry."

Chapter 11 will discuss how to get into the Registry in order to browse or edit values contained within. The design of the Registry unfortunately has a side effect where any corruption to it can easily halt a Windows NT computer. Backing up the Registry is extremely important because of this, and luckily, the Emergency Repair Disk utility, `RDISK.EXE`, will handle backing up the Registry. In addition, the Windows NT Backup application and all third-party applications that are designed to back up Windows NT systems will work for backing up the Registry.

The Windows NT Registry should not be confused with the Windows 95 Registry. Although very similar in their basic structure, these are not compatible databases. Later in this chapter, the section "Structure of the Registry" will explain the exact structure of the Windows NT Registry.

Registry Terminology

When discussing the Registry, certain terminology is used:

> The *root key* is the name of an entire branch of the Registry. The Windows NT Registry is composed of five root keys.
>
> *Subkeys* are entries that exist under the root key. Each root key has one or more subkeys. You can think of a subkey as comparable to an INI file section name. However, a subkey can also have subkeys of its own, which is totally unlike an INI file section.
>
> Within a subkey are one or more value entries. These are three-part entries that contain a name, a data type, and a data value.
>
> A *hive* is a specific set of subkeys and value entries. The Windows NT Registry hives are stored within the `%SystemRoot%\system32\config` and `%SystemRoot%\Profiles\username` directories. Each of these hives also has an associated file with a file extension of LOG.

Registry Size

The actual size of the Windows NT Registry is determined by the amount of data that has been stored in the Registry. On a heavily used Windows NT computer, such as a PDC, the setting for the size of the Registry should be checked.

Figure 4.1 shows the dialog that enables you to view the current size of the Registry and set the maximum size allowed for the Registry. This value is also known as the Registry Size Limit, or RSL.

The RSL is set, by default, to 25 percent of the paged pool, which is an area in memory that is used to store system data. When the size of the paged pool changes, so does the RSL. The paged pool may be changed manually or dynamically by the system.

The dialog shown in Figure 4.1 is accessed through the Windows NT Control Panel by double-clicking the icon labeled System. Once into the System Properties dialog, click the tab labeled Performance. The dialog shown in Figure 4.1 is what you will see when you select the Performance tab.

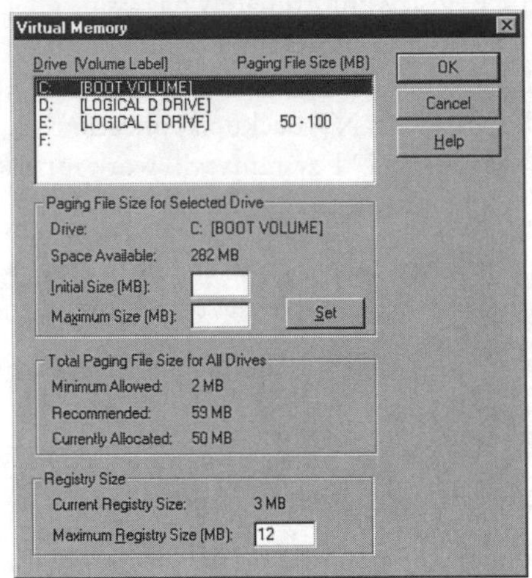

Figure 4.1. *Setting the maximum size of the Registry.*

The Registry Size section of the Performance tab does not actually affect performance, but is used as a gauge to see how much of the maximum allowable size for the Registry is being used.

The Maximum Registry Size (MB) setting does not reflect a space allocation, but rather a size that the system will allow the Registry to grow to, should it require expansion.

Having the maximum set too small may result in error messages during operations that modify data in the Registry. However, this setting does not guarantee available space for the Registry to grow.

Structure of the Registry

The Windows NT Registry is divided into five distinct branches, or root keys. These root keys are described in Table 4.1.

Table 4.1. Windows NT Registry root keys.

Root Key	*Description*
HKEY_LOCAL_MACHINE	Machine-specific information, including hardware, operating system, memory, and drivers
HKEY_CLASSES_ROOT	File associations and OLE information

Root Key	*Description*
HKEY_CURRENT_CONFIG	Information related to the currently active hardware profile
HKEY_CURRENT_USER	The current user's profile settings
HKEY_USERS	All user profiles, including the default user profile

This section first discusses what each of these root keys is and then discusses the structure that is used within all of these root keys.

HKEY_LOCAL_MACHINE

The HKEY_LOCAL_MACHINE root key contains information that is directly associated with the hardware on which the Registry is located. These subkeys are always present in a Windows NT Registry.

HARDWARE Subkey

The HARDWARE subkey includes a list of hardware devices, which is generated each time the computer is started. In Figure 4.2, the DEVICEMAP subkey is expanded, as well as many SCSI subkeys, eventually down to a subkey labeled Target Id 0, which is the SCSI boot device. Within that subkey a value entry Logical Unit Id 0 that has its two value entries, Identifier and Type, shown in the right panel.

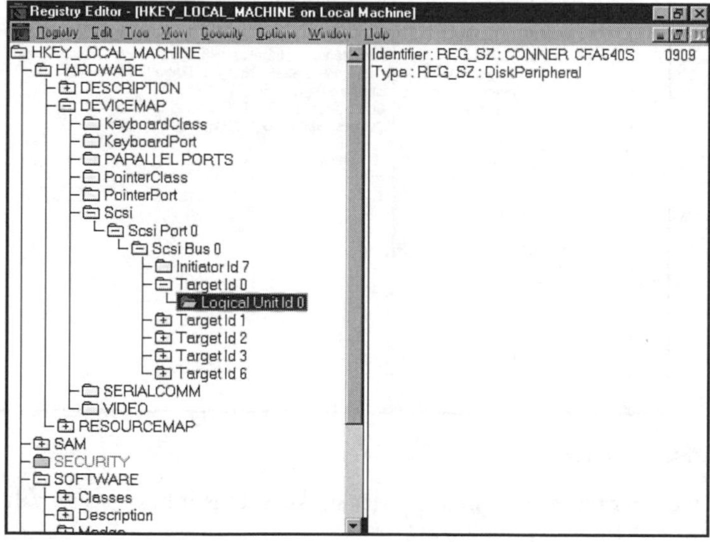

Figure 4.2. HARDWARE *subkey tree example.*

SAM Subkey

The Security Account Manager (SAM) is also contained here. On a PDC, this is the master account database for the domain and is replicated to any existing BDCs. For a Windows NT Workstation, or a member server, the SAM includes information that is local to the computer. This information may only be manipulated through the Windows NT tools, such as User Manager or Windows NT Explorer.

SECURITY Subkey

User rights are also stored in this root key. As with the SAM, this security is domain-wide if the computer is a PDC or BDC. On Windows NT Workstations, workgroup servers, or member servers, the information contained is local only.

SOFTWARE Subkey

Application-specific data, which is specific to the computer, is written and stored within this root key. For example, a subkey within this subkey is `Microsoft`. Within that subkey are subkeys for individual applications, such as Windows NT itself, as shown in Figure 4.3.

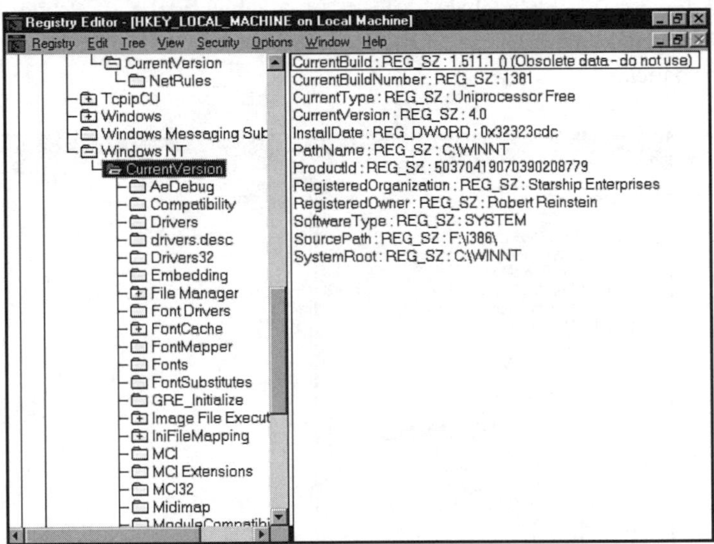

Figure 4.3. SOFTWARE *subkey tree example.*

The subkey `CurrentVersion` contains other subkeys, plus it has its own value entries, which are shown in the right panel in Figure 4.3.

Also within the SOFTWARE subkey is the CLASSES subkey. This contains information related to file associations, OLE, and DDE properties. Figure 4.4 shows the file extension AVI, and its value entries, which are for OLE and Web browser usage.

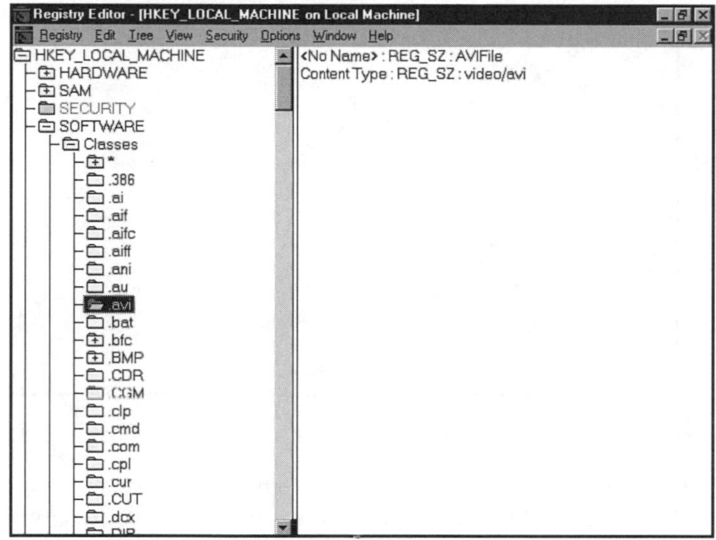

Figure 4.4. CLASSES *subkey example.*

HKEY_CLASSES_ROOT

The information contained in this subkey is identical to the information stored in the HKEY_LOCAL_MACHINE\Software\Classes subkey. This information is provided purely for Windows 3.1 registration database compatibility.

HKEY_CURRENT_CONFIG

This subkey is new to Windows NT and has been made compatible with the Windows 95 Registry. It has been added to Windows NT because of Windows NT 4.0's support for hardware profiles, which enable devices based on the current hardware profile. Previous versions of Windows NT did not support hardware profiles.

This root key is actually a pointer to the subkey HKEY_LOCAL_MACHINE\System\CurrentControlSet\Hardware Profiles\Current. Figure 4.5 shows the subkey Device0, which is under the subkey for a Western Digital video card.

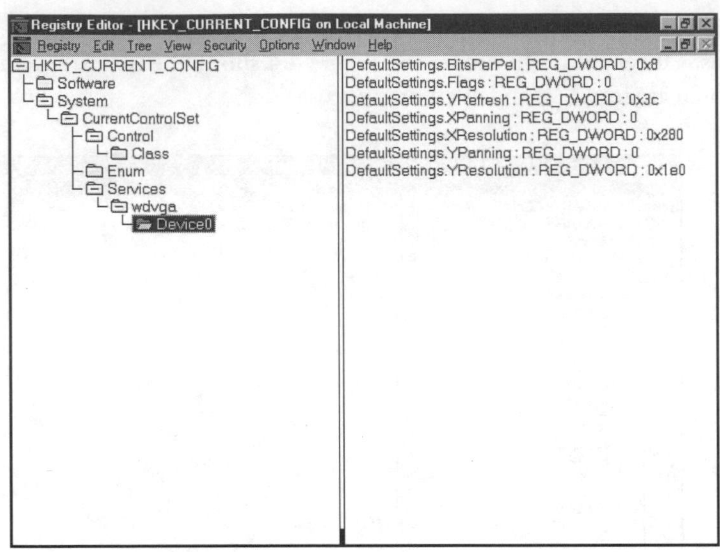

Figure 4.5. `HKEY_CURRENT_CONFIG` *sample subkey.*

The subkey `HKEY_LOCAL_MACHINE\System\CurrentControlSet\Hardware Profiles` contains all the hardware profiles that have been created using the Control Panel's System Properties' Hardware Profiles dialog, which is shown in Figure 4.6.

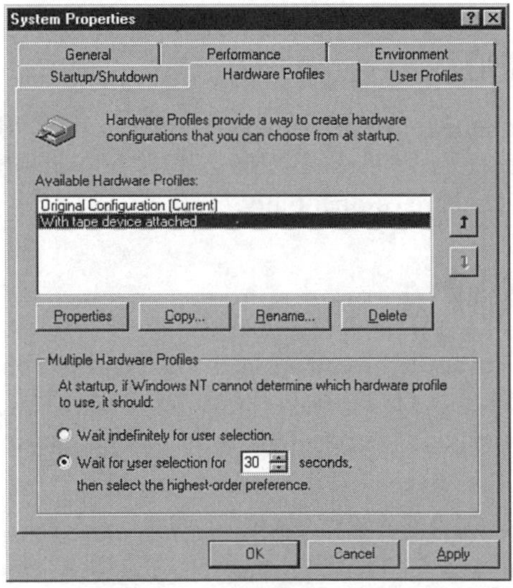

Figure 4.6. *Hardware Profiles properties dialog.*

When using hardware profiles, the currently selected hardware profile is copied into `HKEY_LOCAL_MACHINE\System\CurrentControlSet\Hardware Profiles\Current`.

HKEY_CURRENT_USER

This root key contains the subkey from HKEY_USERS that is associated with the currently logged on user account.

HKEY_USERS

As we already know, a user account is given a SID when the account is created.

The HKEY_USERS root key contains user profile information for the Windows NT default user, plus subkeys for each user account that uses a Windows NT user profile.

As shown in the example depicted in Figure 4.7, a subkey exists for .DEFAULT, and a subkey exists for a user account. The name of the subkey is actually the SID for that user account. The color choices stored for that user profile are shown on the right as value entries.

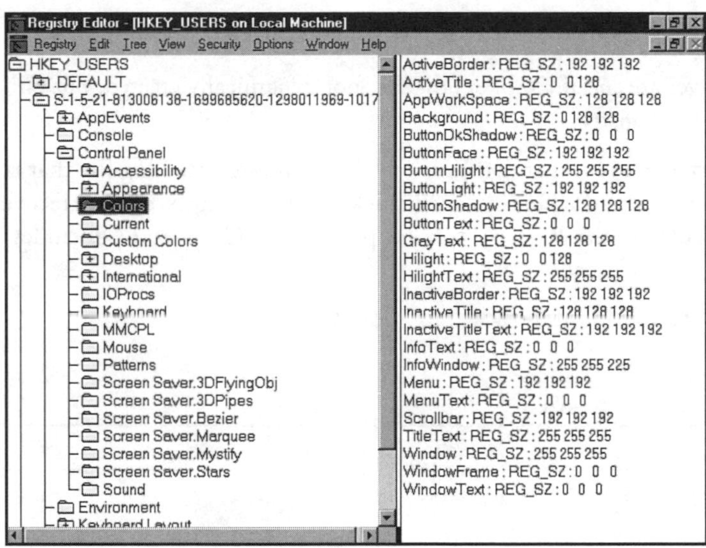

Figure 4.7. *A SID and user profile shown in the* HKEY_USERS *root key.*

Registry Data Types

Registry data is stored in a set number of data formats; these are what's known as the data type. The data types that are available in the Windows NT Registry are listed in Table 4.2.

Table 4.2. Windows NT Registry data types.

Data Type	*Description*
`REG_BINARY`	Binary data
`REG_DWORD`	Number that is four bytes long and displayed in hex format
`REG_SZ`	Readable text string
`REG_EXPAND_SZ`	Expandable data string and contains a variable
`REG_MULTI_SZ`	Multiple strings that can contain a list or multiple strings, and each value is separated by a null character

An example of the usage of the `REG_SZ` data type is shown in Figure 4.7. Figure 4.5 has value entries that use the data type `REG_DWORD`.

Registry Hives

Registry hives are specific subkeys that are not dynamically created, but rather they are required entries in the Registry.

The importance of hives is that they each have an associated log file that tracks changes to the associated subkey and value entries. By tracking these changes, disaster recovery or backing out of changes made to the Registry can be performed. Chapter 11 includes information about recovering the Registry.

The set of standard hives is shown in Table 4.3.

Table 4.3. Hives and their related files.

Hive Name	*Hive Filenames*
`HKEY_LOCAL_MACHINE\SAM`	`Sam.*`
`HKEY_LOCAL_MACHINE\Security`	`Security.*`
`HKEY_LOCAL_MACHINE\Software`	`Software.*`
`HKEY_LOCAL_MACHINE\System`	`System.*`
`HKEY_CURRENT_CONFIG`	`System.*`
`HKEY_USERS\.DEFAULT`	`Default.*`
`HKEY_CURRENT_USER`	`Ntuser.dat.*`

The file extensions used for these hive files have particular functions, which are listed in Table 4.4.

Table 4.4. Hive file extensions.

Types of Hive Files	*Description*
No filename extension	An exact replica of the hive.
`ALT`	A backup copy of the `HKEY_LOCAL_MACHINE\System` hive.
`LOG`	A log file that tracks changes made to each hive.
`SAV`	Default copies of hives that are generated during the text-mode installation of Windows NT.

These files can be used by the Registry Editor, which is discussed in Chapter 11.

Summary

As you've just learned, the Windows NT Registry is a versatile way of handling an enormous number of settings and parameters. Its intricate architecture is one that any serious Windows NT user or administrator must become familiar with. Chapter 11 will provide you with information on how to use the tools that come with Windows NT that will allow you to view, edit, and maintain a Windows NT Registry.

CHAPTER 5

Windows NT File Systems

by Robert Reinstein

When Windows NT was created, its security architecture was a high priority. Part of the security architecture depended on implementing a file system that would ignore the MS-DOS limitations and give the operating system a high performance file system with security that would surpass other available file systems.

This chapter covers the following topics:

- ◆ Different file systems: FAT, HPFS, and NTFS
- ◆ The Windows NT version of FAT
- ◆ Using compression on NTFS
- ◆ Converting FAT to NTFS

A History Lesson: The Three File Systems Originally Supported by Windows NT

One of the first questions you might ask when deciding to install Windows NT is whether to keep the existing file system or go to the more advanced native file system, NTFS.

Before deciding which file systems to keep, or whether NTFS should be implemented, you need to know the background on these file systems. This section introduces a brief history of the file systems, and discusses their pros and cons.

The FAT (File Allocation Table) File System

The FAT file system for personal computers was designed when floppy diskettes were the most common used media, and hard drives had an average capacity of ten megabytes. Because of this, FAT wasn't designed with larger capacities in mind, and has since required the use of new operating systems and system BIOSs to allow for the use of larger hard drives and directory trees of files that number in the thousands or millions.

Partitions formatted with FAT are broken into clusters. The FAT file system is also prone to fragmentation—the result of data being written to non-contiguous clusters. Using non-contiguous clusters to store one file slows down the read/write process. FAT writes files to the first available cluster it can find, and then skips ahead past used clusters to complete writing a file. These clusters are broken down into sectors. FAT also keeps track of a few attributes for each filc, such as the name of the file, the address of the starting sector, whether the file was deemed a system file, a read-only attribute, an archive bit (denoting if the file had been backed up or changed since the last time it was backed up), and a date for the file's creation or the last time the file was modified.

Tip: Because the overhead of using the FAT file system grows as partition size increases, you shouldn't use FAT on partitions that are greater than 200 megabytes.

The High Performance File System (HPFS)

HPFS was introduced in 1990 as part of OS/2 Version 1.2, when OS/2 was still co-developed by Microsoft and IBM.

HPFS allowed for greater hard drive capacity, and instituted technologies that would help prevent the occurrence of fragmentation, such as using physical sectors instead of clusters. It accomplished this by using a data structure called a B-Tree, which enables directory searches to occur in a manner more logical than that used by FAT's linear structure. HPFS also implemented physical separation between files, giving each file room for expansion, which resulted in less chance of fragmentation. HPFS also introduced long filenames of up to 255 characters, along with other attributes, such as the same attributes kept by FAT, and an access control list (ACL).

Of course, HPFS was designed with OS/2 in mind and is currently the file system of choice for that operating system. At one point, still during the time when Microsoft and IBM were co-developing OS/2, another file system, HPFS386, was introduced. It took advantage of the then new 386 processor, and was available for use on Microsoft's LAN Manager product. HPFS386 is back again in the most recent version of OS/2.

Note: Previous versions of the Microsoft Windows NT Server came with native support for HPFS. Microsoft Windows NT Server 4.0 doesn't come with a driver for HPFS, so the only way you can get Windows NT support for HPFS is if you are upgrading from a previous version of Windows NT (3.5 or 3.1).

Windows NT 3.51 only included support for booting from an HPFS partition.

If you have upgraded from a previous version of Windows NT and have support for HPFS installed, that support is retained.

Usually, HPFS partitions are kept on a non-dedicated Windows NT server to enable dual booting of both Windows NT and OS/2.

The access control lists associated with the data on the HPFS partitions aren't recognized by Windows NT's support for HPFS. If the server is a dedicated server, then the existing HPFS partitions can be converted to NTFS, using the `CONVERT.EXE` utility. The `CONVERT.EXE` utility is discussed later in this chapter in the section "Converting from FAT to NTFS."

NTFS: The Windows NT File System

Security: With the introduction of Windows NT in 1993, Microsoft took the advanced capabilities of HPFS and went many steps further. A major part of the security model that Windows NT offers is based on the NTFS file system. Although shared directories can be set up on a Windows NT server regardless of the file system used, it is only with NTFS that individual files can be assigned permissions. These rights, which also include rights to a directory, can be assigned permissions whether or not they're shared. Every attribute of the NTFS is kept as a file.

NTFS is the preferred file system for Windows NT because it enables the use of all of Windows NT's security features. A system can, however, use both of the natively available file systems at the same time. Of course, only the NTFS partitions will have the advantages of enhanced security.

Note: Incidentally, whenever Windows NT formats a diskette, it formats using FAT— the overhead of the NTFS file system would create too much extraneous, although important, information, making the actual capacity of the diskette too small. Therefore, NTFS is not a supported format on diskettes.

File descriptions on an NTFS volume are stored in a master file table (MFT), which is also a file. In addition to several records that contain data about the MFT itself, the MFT contains a record for each file and directory. The MFT also contains a log file. A mirror of the MFT is also kept elsewhere on the partition. Pointers to the MFT and its mirror are stored in the boot sector of the disk. A copy of the boot sector is stored in the logical center of the disk. With this many copies of the MFT, data recovery becomes even easier, which is why NTFS is known as a "recoverable file system."

Flowchart 5.1 shows the general format of the master file table. The master file table contains pointers that refer to external continuations, which are referred to in this diagram as extents.

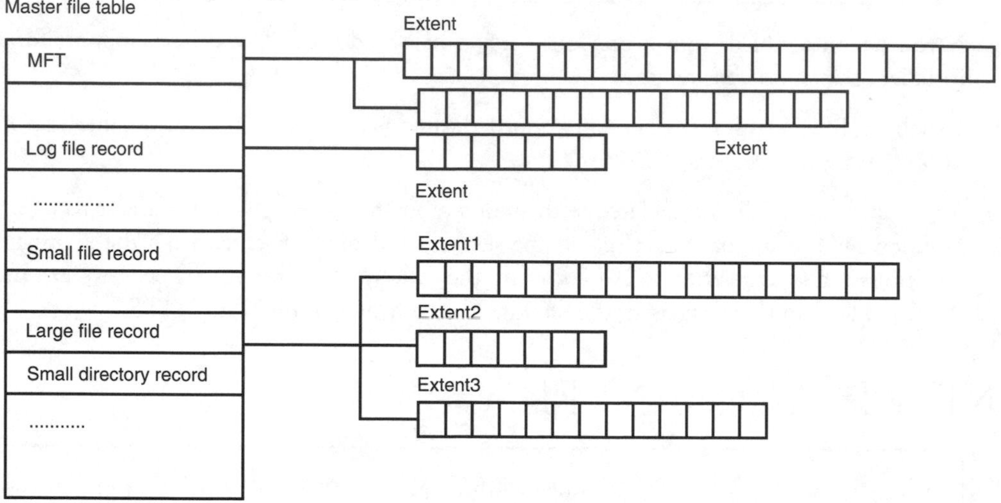

Flowchart 5.1. *NTFS master file table.*

When a file is called for on a FAT partition, a pointer to a list of sectors is read. NTFS cuts out one of these steps by having the sector map contained within the MFT. In cases of small files, it's possible for only a single record in the MFT to contain all of the information for that one file. Larger files require that extents are read, and directories require that the B-tree structure is read. All in all, this makes for a very speedy file system.

When a partition is formatted as NTFS, numerous system files that keep track of certain attributes of that partition are created. These system files are documented in Table 5.1.

Table 5.1. NTFS system files.

Filename	*System File*	*Description*
`$Mft`	Master File Table	The MFT
`$MftMirr`	Master File Table2	The mirror copy of the MFT
`$LogFile`	Log File	A file activity log that can be used to help rebuild information in case of a failure
`$Volume`	Volume	The name of a volume, along with other volume information

Filename	*System File*	*Description*
`$AttrDef`	Attribute Definitions	A table of attribute names, numbers, and descriptions
`$.`	Root Filename Index	The root directory
`$Bitmap`	Cluster Bitmap	A representation of the volume showing which allocation units are in use
`$Boot`	Boot File	If this partition is bootable, a bootstrap is included here
`$BadClus`	Bad Cluster File	Pointers to all of the bad clusters on this volume

The attributes of a file on an NTFS volume may contain all or some of the items listed in Table 5.2.

Table 5.2. NTFS file attributes.

Standard Information	*Includes time stamps, link count, and so on*
Attribute List	Lists all other attributes in large files only
Filename	The long filename (up to 255 characters) and the MS-DOS–compatible short filename
Security Descriptor	Contains permissions for the file, along with the owner's ID
Data	Various data attributes that may include unnamed attributes identified by keywords
Index Root	Required for directories
Index Allocation	Required for directories
Volume Information	The volume name and other information required by the volume system file
Bitmap	Pointers to records in use on the MFT or directory
Extended Attribute Information	Not used by Windows NT, but contains data that can be used by OS/2 systems
Extended Attributes	Not used by Windows NT, but contains data that can be used by OS/2 systems

Windows NT's Implementation of FAT

FAT is handled slightly differently under Windows NT. While Windows NT's FAT implementation is 100% backwards compatible, Windows NT also adds features to the FAT file system. Long filenames are allowed for FAT partitions, and are handled the same way as long filenames on a Windows 95 system. That is, the generated 8.3 filename is stored along with the long filename. As with HPFS, FAT partitions can be converted to NTFS. See the "Converting from FAT to NTFS" section, later in this chapter, for a discussion of the `CONVERT.EXE` utility.

Caution: Any FAT partitions that use DOS-based disk compression (such as Stacker or DriveSpace) won't have readable files when running Windows NT. Only the "host drive" will be visible.

Special partitioning software designed for DOS won't be recognized by Windows NT either, making the drive unreadable.

See the next section, "NTFS Disk Compression," to learn about the compression options available to you if you use NTFS partitions.

Keeping a FAT Partition on a Windows NT Server

One of the few reasons to keep FAT partitions on a Windows NT server is for certain DOS-based programs that might not be compatible with the NTFS file system.

An example of this is Computer Associates' AccPac Plus, which at the time of this writing has not been certified to run on a Windows NT server. The support staff at Computer Associates does recommend that if it must be run from a Windows NT server, their data should be kept on a FAT partition. Other software manufacturers may have similar concerns about running their software on NTFS, so if you're running any older 16-bit software from your Windows NT server, you should inquire whether the manufacturer supports running their software from NTFS.

There are reports that show DOS-based programs running slower from network partitions formatted as NTFS, as opposed to running from FAT partitions. If you plan to implement a DOS-based program from a Microsoft Windows NT server, you may want to run your own benchmarks.

Better yet, migrate to all 32-bit Windows-based programs.

Long Filenames on FAT

Another reason to keep a partition as FAT is if it is necessary to dual boot to DOS on the server.

When booting DOS on a Windows NT server, only the FAT partitions are recognized. Any long filenames that exist on the FAT partition are seen with a standard 8.3 filename. Windows NT creates an 8.3 filename (along with its long filenames) in the same way that Windows 95 creates 8.3 filenames along with long filenames.

The 8.3 version of a long filename of, for example "My Report," would be "MYREPO~1". Note that the imbedded space has been stripped out, and only the first six characters of the filename have been used. The following tilde character and the number one have been added in case there's another filename that started with the same first six characters. If another long filename existed named "My Report For September," then that file under DOS is seen as "MYREPO~2," and so on. Spaces aren't the only characters that are removed from a long filename. Any other special character that isn't supported in 8.3 filenames is replaced in the conversion by an underscore.

Because generating short filenames creates a certain amount of overhead on the server, you have the option to disable this feature and use only long filenames on your Windows NT computer.

To disable short filename support, use the registration database editor, `REGEDT32.EXE`, and then search the `HKEY_LOCAL_MACHINE` section for the entry `HKEY_LOCAL_MACHINE\System\CurrentControlSet\Control\FileSystem`. Change the value of the parameter `NtfsDisable8dot3NameCreation` to a value of `1` (one), and then short filename generation will be disabled.

NTFS uses the 16-bit Unicode character set, which contains many special characters, and supports most international special characters. Because many of these characters are deemed illegal by DOS file naming standards, these characters are also stripped.

NTFS File Naming Concerns

As mentioned in the preceding section, NTFS uses the 16-bit Unicode character set, which enables the use of some special characters, and includes both uppercase and lowercase letters of the alphabet. Therefore, a filename of `My Document` will retain the uppercase characters in its name, but NTFS won't differentiate between files that use the same characters with different cases. For instance, `my document` may co-exist in the same directory as `My Document`, but if you use Notepad to open the `My Document` file, the contents of `my document` are displayed in Notepad. This anomaly can create havoc for some users, and that is why it's important to standardize the way files are named.

> **Note:** Interestingly enough, although NTFS can handle filenames of up to 255 characters, files created from the command line can have filenames of only 253 characters in length.

There are special characters that can't appear in an NTFS filename:

```
? " / \ < > * ¦ :
```

When copying files from NTFS to either HPFS or FAT using command-line utilities, such as `XCOPY` and `COPY`, you may receive errors because those utilities can handle the long filename, but the receiving file system may "choke" on embedded spaces among other characters. To get around this, use the `/N` switch on those commands, and the short filename will be used. For example, to copy the contents of directory `C:\My Documents` from an NTFS partition to the directory `D:\DOCS` which is located on a FAT partition, use the following syntax:

```
XCOPY "C:\My Documents\*.*" D:\DOCS /N
```

Special attention must also be given when creating shortcuts to programs with file associations. If a type of file is associated with a 16-bit program, and the long filename is being used, the 16-bit program won't know how to interpret the filename and won't be able to load the file. This won't be a problem on a system running all Windows NT- or Windows 95-compliant programs.

Caution: Using any 16-bit program, such as the Windows 3.*x* File Manager, or a DOS utility like The Norton Commander, to manipulate files that have long filenames will wipe out the long filenames! If you use a 16-bit program to manipulate files on an NTFS volume, you run the risk of losing the security information too. Only use 32-bit programs that support long filenames to move or copy files on an NTFS volume!

NTFS: The Recoverable File System

Of course, the main purpose of file systems is to keep track of data stored on hard drives and to facilitate the reading and writing of this data. NTFS's recoverable file system is a great enhancement over FAT's careful-write file system and the lazy-write file system used by UNIX and FAT as implemented on Windows NT.

FAT's careful-write file system enables writes one at a time, and alters its volume information after each write. This is a very secure form of writing, but it is also a very slow process.

The lazy-write file system uses a cache. All writes are performed to this cache and the file system intelligently waits for the appropriate time to perform all of the writes to disk. This system gives the user faster access to the file system and prevents holdups due to slower disk access. It is also possible that if the same file is being modified more than once, the altered file may never actually be written to disk until the modifications are finished within the cache. Of course, this also can lead to lost data if the system crashes and unwritten modifications are still held in the cache.

Performance: NTFS's recoverable file system provides the speed of a lazy-write file system in addition to recovery features. The recovery features come from a transaction log that keeps track of which writes to disk have been completed and which ones have not. In the recovery process this log can ensure that only a few moments after a reboot the file system's integrity is back to 100 percent—without the need to run a utility such as `CHKDSK`, which requires the scanning of an entire volume. The overhead associated with this recoverable file system is less than the type used by the careful-write file system.

The recoverable file system also can ensure that an NTFS partition always remains accessible, even if the partition is bootable and the bootstrap has been damaged. In this instance, you can boot from another drive, or boot from diskettes and still have access to the formerly bootable volume.

NTFS supports hot-fixing as well. Instead of FAT's notorious "Abort, Retry, Fail?" message, NTFS attempts to move the data in a damaged cluster to a new location in a fashion that is transparent to the user. The damaged cluster is then marked as unusable. Unfortunately, it's possible that the moved data will be unusable anyhow, because the chance of corruption is very likely. However, if fault tolerance is enabled, the replicated data from the non-damaged cluster is used in its place. Chapter 17, "Disk Administrator," discusses the various ways of implementing fault tolerance on Windows NT.

The way that NTFS processes file actions as transactions is the key to its high degree of recoverability. Each write request to an NTFS partition generates redo and undo information. The redo information tells NTFS how to re-create the intended write. The undo information tells NTFS how to roll back the transaction, in case the transaction is incomplete or has an error. Once the write transaction is complete, NTFS generates a file update commit. Otherwise, NTFS uses the undo information to roll back the request.

The type of commit that NTFS performs is called a lazy commit which is similar to a lazy write in the sense that it will cache file commits and write them to the transaction log when system resources are high. This feature allows NTFS's high reliability features to have less overhead, overall, on the system.

In the case of a system crash, or unexpected shutdown of Windows NT (such as someone accidentally powering off the server before a clean shutdown is performed), NTFS performs a three-pass system check upon restarting.

As with most transactional-type logs, checkpoints are created once all log transactions since the last checkpoint have been confirmed. Checkpoint creation occurs every few seconds. The first pass that NTFS makes after a system restart is called the *analysis* pass. In this pass, NTFS compares items in the transaction log, since the last checkpoint, to the clusters those transactions dealt with. A second pass, called the *redo* pass, performs all of the transaction steps since the last checkpoint. The third pass, which is the *undo* pass, performs a rollback on any incomplete transactions.

Note: Whenever you start Windows NT, the NTFS volumes are checked to see whether they are "dirty." If it detects a potential problem, Windows NT automatically runs `CHKDSK /F`.

If the `CHKDSK` utility finds orphaned files or directories, they're moved to special directories that are named `FOUNDnnn` (if no other `FOUNDnnn` directories exist, the first one created is `FOUND000`, the next is `FOUND001`, and so on). Directories are named `DIRnnn.CHK`, and if they have files associated with them, those files are placed within that directory. Orphaned files are named `FILEnnn.CHK`.

If you want to run `CHKDSK /F` from the command line, run it from a drive other than the one you are checking. For example, to check the C: drive, from a D: prompt run `CHKDSK C: /F`. If `CHKDSK` can't get control of the drive because it's in use, it asks you whether it should run automatically the next time Windows NT is booted.

Flowchart 5.2 depicts a possible decision-making process for determining the best file systems for you to implement on your Windows NT server.

Converting from FAT to NTFS

The `CONVERT.EXE` utility is a command-line utility that can convert FAT partitions over to NTFS. It doesn't convert NTFS to FAT.

Deciding on a file system

RISC-based computer?

No

Require ability to boot Windows 95 or MS-DOS?

No

System partition should be NTFS

Yes

System partition must be FAT

Yes

System Partition must be FAT

Running any applications that require FAT?

No

Yes

Applications that must be run from a FAT partition must reside on FAT partition; otherwise, use NTFS

Non-system partitions require access when booting from MS-DOS or Windows 95?

No

Yes

Non-system partition must be FAT

Require granular file-by-file security?

Yes

No

Require C2-level security?

Yes

No

Require POSIX compliance?

Yes

No

Partitions under 100MB?

No

Yes

Format secondary partition(s) as FAT

Format secondary partition(s) as NTFS

End

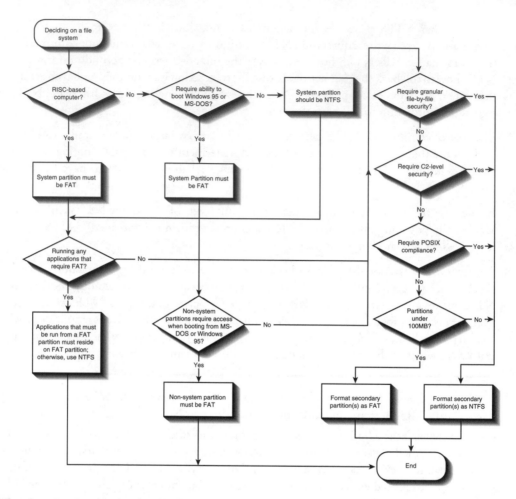

Flowchart 5.2. *Determining the right file system.*

The proper syntax for the `CONVERT.EXE` utility is `CONVERT d: /fs:ntfs` where `d` is the drive letter for the partition you're converting. You can't convert the boot partition while it's active, so if the `CONVERT` command is attempted on the boot partition, an entry is written to the Registry that initiates the conversion the next time the system is booted. Figure 5.1 depicts an actual conversion of a 300MB FAT volume into an NTFS volume. For this size partition, only 3KB was needed for the conversion.

Tip: Whenever possible, use NTFS as your file system. Its security and reliability is too good a thing to pass up. Also, the file compression for NTFS is another great advantage (see the following section for a discussion of Windows NT's unique file compression).

```
Command Prompt
Microsoft(R) Windows NT(TM)
(C) Copyright 1985-1996 Microsoft Corp.

C:\WINNT\profiles\Administrator\Desktop>convert m: /fs:ntfs
The type of the file system is FAT.
Determining disk space required for filesystem conversion
Total disk space:                  307184 kilobytes.
Free space on volume:              307016 kilobytes.
Space required for conversion:       3646 kilobytes.
Converting file system
Conversion complete

C:\WINNT\profiles\Administrator\Desktop>_
```

Figure 5.1. *Converting FAT to NTFS using* `CONVERT.EXE`.

If you're using a RISC-based system and want to use NTFS, create a one megabyte FAT partition for the system files. The remaining space can then be formatted as NTFS.

Caution: Because RISC processor-based machines require FAT on the boot partition, never run the `CONVERT.EXE` utility on these. If you do, the PC will no longer be bootable, and the program `ARCINST.EXE`, located on the Windows NT CD-ROM, will be needed to run and reformat the boot partition.

NTFS Disk Compression

NTFS includes a form of disk compression unlike the more familiar DOS-based programs, such as Stacker or DriveSpace.

Stacker and DriveSpace, which are DOS device driver-based programs, create one large file that contains all of the files contained in the drive that you compressed. This single file is a mountable volume that a DOS device driver mounts as its own drive. This drive is then viewed as a standard DOS FAT volume.

Windows NT uses Explorer and the `COMPACT.EXE` utility to individually compress files. These compressed files are then decompressed in real time when the files are opened.

Windows NT's type of compression is much safer than the DOS method, because it's possible for a corrupted compressed volume on DOS to result in the loss of the entire volume.

With Windows NT's compression scheme, each file is handled separately, therefore any corruption affects only that one file.

The algorithm used for NTFS Disk Compression is similar to the DoubleSpace one. In DoubleSpace, a file is searched for 2-byte pieces of data that are redundant throughout the file.

NTFS File Compression searches for 3 bytes of redundant data, making NTFS Disk Compression faster while sacrificing the amount of possible compression.

Tip: I personally use Windows NT's disk compression and have not had any bad experiences or noticeable lags due to compression. I would advise the following:

- Feel free to use the compression for seldom used files or archived data.
- Large documents compress very well.
- Don't use file compression for files that are already compressed, such as JPEG format graphics, or archive files like PKZIP or ARJ files.
- Don't use compression on files that are part of a highly critical application (you never know...).
- Back up. Back up. Back up. Whether there are compressed files or not, always keep a current backup.

Note: As with all file compression techniques, there's a certain amount of overhead for the decompression and recompression of these files.

Setting File and Directory Compression States

Each file and directory on an NTFS partition contains a compression state. This state can be modified either by using the `COMPACT.EXE` utility, or through the Windows NT Explorer.

Using Windows NT Explorer to Set Compression States

The properties dialog shown in Figure 5.2 is for a directory named `TEMP`. Note that the Attributes check boxes contain a Compress attribute. This check box is not checked, therefore this directory is uncompressed.

By placing a check mark in the check box and clicking on the Apply or OK button, Explorer prompts you to confirm your request to change the compression state for this folder, and also enables you to specify whether subfolders should also have their compression state changed. (See Figure 5.3.)

By clicking on the OK button, the files contained within the TEMP directory are compressed. (See Figure 5.4.)

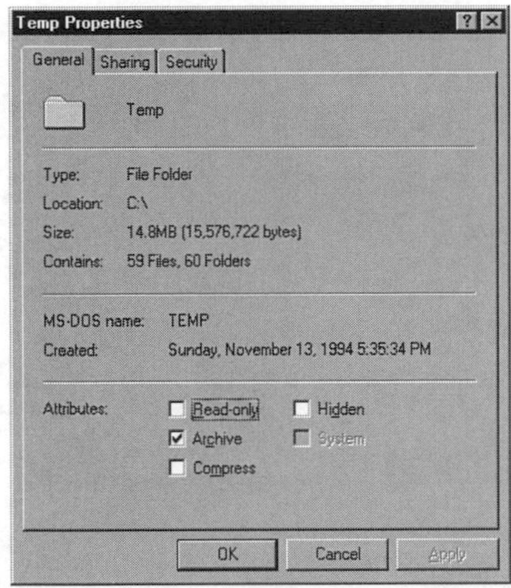

Figure 5.2. Folder properties.

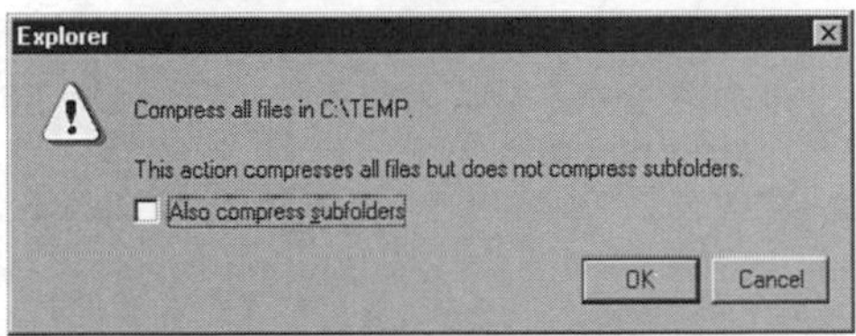

Figure 5.3. Compression confirmation.

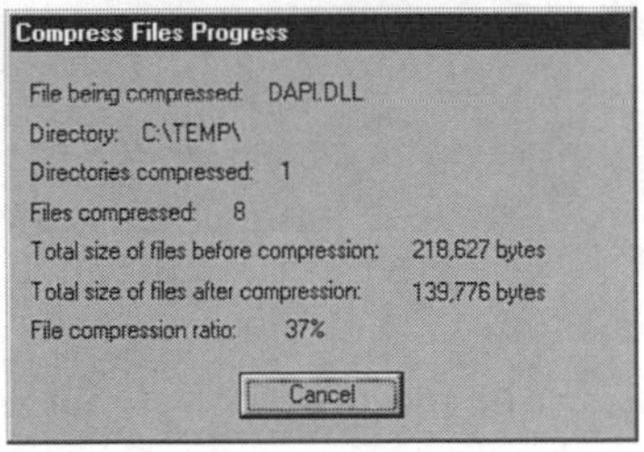

Figure 5.4. Folder compression in action.

As shown in Figure 5.5, the folder names in Windows NT Explorer are shown in blue if they have a compression state of compressed and remain black if the compression state is uncompressed.

Now, all the files within the TEMP directory have been compressed. Figure 5.6 shows the properties dialog of one of those files.

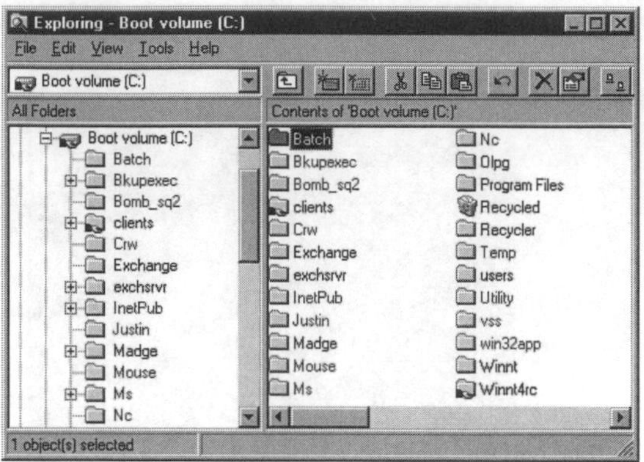

Figure 5.5. *Windows NT Explorer compression states.*

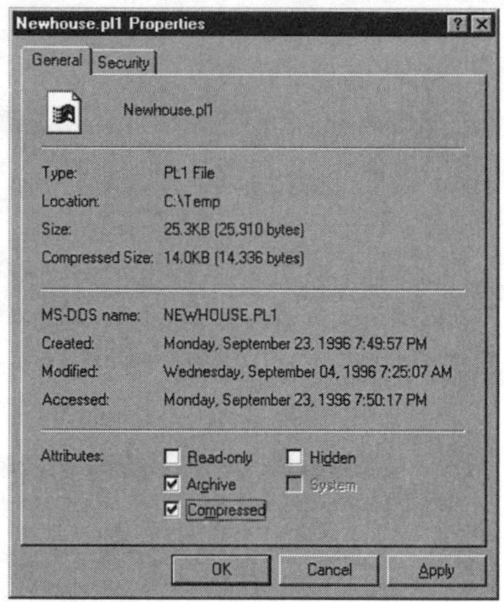

Figure 5.6. *File properties.*

If this were a file you wanted to be able to access without any of the lag time associated with real-time decompression, you could remove the check mark from the Compressed attribute and return that file to a compression state of uncompressed.

Even though you have changed the attribute for one file within a compressed folder, the compression state for the folder isn't altered. Any new files that are placed in that folder will automatically become compressed.

Using the COMPACT Utility

The `COMPACT.EXE` utility enables you to set compression states and check compression states through a command line.

There are two main reasons to use this method as opposed to using the Windows NT Explorer for configuring compression states.

First, you can use `COMPACT` to set compression states from a batch file. This can be handy, especially if you are using the `/I` switch, which allows for open files to be skipped. Otherwise, when you use Windows NT Explorer, the compression operation is halted if an open file is encountered.

Second, a compression state-setting operation that fails because of a system error or a power failure can result in a false compression state being reported through Windows NT Explorer. Using `COMPACT` is the only way to correct this.

The syntax for the `COMPACT` utility is as follows:

```
compact [/c] [/u] [/s[:dir]] [/a] [/i] [/f] [/q] [filename [...]]
```

- The `/c` switch compresses the specified folder or file.
- `/u` uncompresses the specified folder or file.
- `/s` tells `COMPACT` to apply the operation to all subfolders of the specified folder (dir), or to the current folder if no folder has been specified.
- `/a` displays files with the hidden or system attribute.
- `/f` forces compression or decompression of the specified folder or file.
- `/I` ignores any errors.
- `/q` reduces the amount of data that's reported.

Using no parameters with `COMPACT` simply displays the current compression state of the current folder. (See Figure 5.7.)

Filename enables you to specify a file, a folder, or multiple files using the wildcard character.

```
Command Prompt
 New files added to this directory will be compressed.

     9456 :      6144 = 1.5 to 1 C ABOUTTET.DLL
   145168 :     54272 = 2.7 to 1 C B&ARROW.EXE
       48 :        48 = 1.0 to 1 C B&ARROW.INI
    43680 :     23552 = 1.9 to 1 C LIGHT.EXE
    29306 :     15360 = 1.9 to 1 C LIGHT.HLP
    26467 :     14848 = 1.8 to 1 C RA.EXE
       33 :        33 = 1.0 to 1 C RUNAPP.INI
     2006 :       512 = 3.9 to 1 C STEPHEN.ELI
    61936 :     39936 = 1.6 to 1 C TETRIS.EXE
    25416 :     13312 = 1.9 to 1 C TETRIS.HLP
      660 :       512 = 1.3 to 1 C TETRIS.HST
      684 :       512 = 1.3 to 1 C TETRIS.INI
  1185849 :   1075200 = 1.1 to 1 C TSCONGME.EXE
    76480 :     48640 = 1.6 to 1 C WSLAM.EXE
    12377 :     10240 = 1.2 to 1 C WSLAM.HLP

Of 15 files within 1 directories
15 are compressed and 0 are not compressed.
1,619,566 total bytes of data are stored in 1,303,121 bytes.
The compression ratio is 1.2 to 1.

D:\WINAPPS>_
```

Figure 5.7. *The* `COMPACT` *utility.*

Moving and Copying Compressed File/Folders

When a file is moved to a folder on an NTFS partition, the compression state remains unaltered, regardless of the compression state of the destination folder.

This is an attribute of the NTFS file system.

If a file is copied to a folder on an NTFS partition, the file inherits the compression state of the destination folder.

Whenever files are moved or copied to a FAT partition, the compression state is lost, because the compression attribute doesn't exist on FAT.

Support for Removable Media

Windows NT supports formatting removable media, such as Bernoulli drives, as either FAT or NTFS. However, when working with removable media that has been formatted as NTFS, Windows NT requires that the system be shut down and rebooted in order to change media. It is recommended that the FAT file system is used to avoid this inconvenience. Of course, if the security of NTFS is required, then use the NTFS format.

A removable hard drive is restricted to having only one primary partition on Windows NT. Extended or logical partitions aren't recognized.

Drive letter assignments are handled automatically by Windows NT and can't be manually altered through Disk Administrator. Only SCSI devices are supported, not IDE.

Summary

Windows NT has a unique way of handling file systems.

Its NTFS file system is certainly leaps and bounds ahead of the FAT file system that you're probably accustomed to, and should be properly used to ensure the proper security you want for your Windows NT servers and domains.

See Chapter 17, for more information about the management of your hard drives and partitions.

Installing Windows NT

CHAPTER

The Windows NT Installation Process

by Robert Reinstein

The task of installing Windows NT Server can be a smooth, streamlined task if you are properly prepared. The previous chapter examined the hardware requirements, and Chapter 3, "Domain Models," discussed Windows NT domain models. If you are installing TCP/IP, you should research your options, such as whether or not to install Microsoft DHCP Server. Also, you'll need to know your company's addressing scheme. This information (and other information) can help make your Windows NT Server installation that much easier.

Since 1992, I've installed dozens of Windows NT servers and have found that the one most important task to prepare for in a smooth install is research.

In this chapter I will cover the following:

- Preparing your server
- Understanding what the Windows NT installation program will need to know
- Deciding on the role for your server
- Different methods for installing Windows NT
- The choices to make along the installation process
- Common Windows NT setup problems

Preparing For Your Installation

First, I'd like to discuss the type of research that can save you many painful hours of brooding over a failed Windows NT Server installation.

You've put together your server (installed the hard drives and network adapter; attached the UPS; installed the tape drive; installed and configured the RAID adapter; configured the CMOS and EISA configuration; installed the additional processor card(s); and slapped the case back together). The next task is installing the network operating system.

Now it's time to stop and prepare for the final task to get your Windows NT server up and running. If you've already worked with the same hardware configuration, you can proceed with the install program. If you haven't worked with this hardware configuration before, back up one moment and examine your choices for hardware.

The Microsoft Windows NT Hardware Compatibility List

As I've mentioned, Windows NT is particularly sensitive to hardware. That is why Microsoft publishes its Microsoft Windows NT Hardware Compatibility List, also known as the HCL. If you cannot find your hardware on the HCL that came with your copy of Windows NT Server, check Microsoft's Web site for an update of the HCL. Your hardware might be on the updated HCL. A new HCL is usually posted on Microsoft's Web site on a quarterly basis. You can also check with the hardware manufacturer to find out if their hardware has been submitted for testing by Microsoft and if the hardware has passed Microsoft's compatibility test.

If you want to ensure a clean install of Windows NT Server, you will get this list and abide by it, because even if you use hardware that is not on the list, if something fails down the road, you won't have any recourse with Microsoft, who might not offer you any technical support when you are running its operating system on unsupported hardware.

The hardware manufacturers represented in HCL have paid to have their hardware tested by Microsoft. You can rest assured that that manufacturer is also developing update drivers for their systems, because they realize that it is important for them to be 100 percent Windows NT-compatible.

The HCL covers the following hardware:

x86 architecture uniprocessor computers
x86 architecture multiprocessor computers
MIPS RISC architecture computers
MIPS RISC multiprocessor architecture computers
Digital Alpha AXP RISC architecture computers
Digital Alpha AXP RISC multiprocessor architecture computers

Processor upgrade products
PCMCIA-tested hardware
SCSI host adapters
SCSI CD-ROM drives
Non-SCSI CD-ROM drives
SCSI tape drives
Other tape drives
SCSI removable media
SCSI scanners
Disk controllers
Hard drives
Wide SCSI
Storage cabinets
RAID systems
Video capture adapters
Video display support
Network adapters
Uninterruptible power supplies
Multimedia audio adapters
Modems
Hardware security hosts
ISDN adapters
Multi-port serial adapters
X.25 adapters
Third-party remote access servers
Keyboards
Pointing devices
Printers
PowerPC hardware

Bear in mind that there are PCs on the HCL that are not necessarily "server grade" PCs. This is because the HCL is not restricted to Windows NT Server, but also applies to Windows NT Workstation.

I highly recommend using server hardware that has been designed to handle the task of acting as an enterprise server.

Caution: I've seen hardware manufacturers telling their customers that they only support Windows NT Workstation on their PC and not Windows NT Server. I recommend that you check with a manufacturer when there is a question of whether a PC is deemed suitable for running Windows NT Server or only Windows NT Workstation.

True servers have been designed to run 24 hours a day, 7 days a week. This is because they usually have been designed with fault tolerance (possibly redundant power supplies), have increased air flow, and have generally stronger parts that are able to withstand the rigors of being a production server.

Although there are all types of peripherals, communications adapters, hard drive controllers, tape drives, and so forth on the HCL, it is not necessarily a guarantee that all of the items on the HCL will work together. This is where your research starts.

When I've installed Windows NT Server on a piece of hardware that I've never had experience with, I check the online services, such as CompuServe, and see if there are any Windows NT issues posted in the manufacturer's forum. Sometimes you'll catch a reference to a reputable server, for instance a HP NetServer LS, but find that they are having a problem with a network card from, for example, SMC, who has numerous network adapters that are supported on Windows NT. If you can find any issues here that apply to your proposed configuration, you have the option to back out of using the troublesome piece and get something else that people have had success with.

Next go to the BBS or World Wide Web site from all of the manufacturers of the hardware components that make up your server and see if they have released any updated drivers. The Windows NT CD-ROM ships with numerous drivers; however, there have been drivers shipped on the CD-ROM in the past that just did not work!

An excellent source of information is on the Microsoft Network, where there are forums devoted to Windows NT and frequented by Microsoft engineers.

Once you have resolved your hardware and are sure that your configuration was born to run Windows NT, it's time to plan for the information that you will need to supply to the Windows NT Server installation program.

The most important decision you will have to make during the Windows NT Server install is whether the server will be part of a domain, and if it will be part of a domain, what role the server will play in a domain.

If you choose to have the server in a domain, and this is the first server in your domain, you're going to choose to make the server a primary domain controller (PDC). You also have to be prepared to name your server and name the domain that you will be creating. If there is an existing domain, you need to determine whether this server is going to be another domain controller (in this case a backup domain controller, or BDC) or a member server.

If the server will not be part of a domain, it will be a member server and will be assigned to a workgroup, not a domain. Flowchart 6.1 might help you make a decision on this.

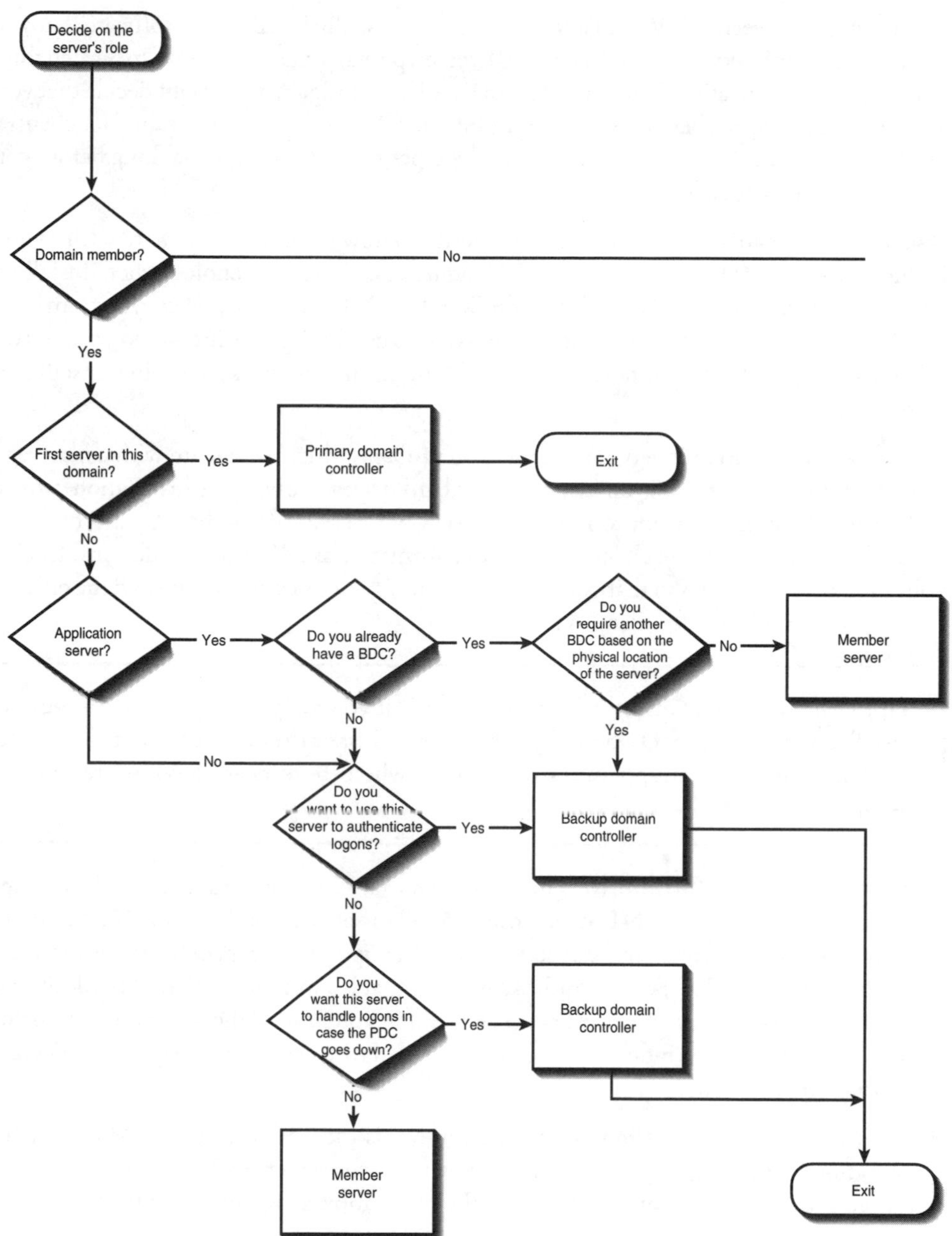

Flowchart 6.1. *Deciding on the server role.*

The decision between a BDC and a member server is usually based on the software that you plan on running on this server. If you'll have a SQL server, perhaps you do not want to burden this server with logon authentication, which a BDC can handle. Then again, you might decide that you need another domain controller in case of a failure on the PDC, and you would want your clients to still be able to log on to the network. These are the types of decisions to make long before you start piecing the server together.

If you are using cards that are not PCI, you need to know what their hardware settings are. This includes IRQs, DMA channels, and I/O addresses. A wrong choice when installing and configuring your network adapter during the Windows NT install can prevent you from being able to fully install Windows NT. Although it is possible to get through the installation process without fully installing network support, I'd suggest not having to backtrack after installation has completed.

Your disk configuration is very important. You probably already came up with a plan regarding implementing RAID before you installed your hard drives. Early in the installation process, you will be asked where you want to install Windows NT Server. If you have a hard drive that has already been formatted, and chances are it's been formatted as FAT, you should consider changing your file system to NTFS so that you can take advantage of its extra security and the efficient way it packs files into less space than FAT.

Tip: Usually the only reason not to use NTFS is if you are planning to leave a previously installed version of MS-DOS on the hard drive and want the option to boot to MS-DOS, or if you are installing an application on the server where the software developer recommends using FAT.

Also, on the subject of hard drives, make sure you have enough available hard drive space to accommodate the Windows NT Server install. A full installation of Windows NT Server requires around 100MB of hard drive space. Additionally, you might require space for applications and user directories. Windows NT Server requires a swapfile that is a minimum of 48MB. Ideally, you can allocate more space for virtual memory, so be sure that you have all the space you need before you start your install. Once Windows NT Server is installed, you can have multiple swapfiles on drives other than the boot drive.

Another decision, new to Windows NT Server 4.0, is the option to install Microsoft Internet Information Server (IIS). If you have planned on using the server as a World Wide Web server or just as an intranet server, you'll want to tell the installation program to install IIS.

Another consideration for installing Windows NT Server is the method of installation.

> **New to NT 4.0:** Windows NT Server 4.0 is a bootable CD-ROM, so if your server supports booting from the CD-ROM drive, use this method of installing Windows NT.

Another method is booting from the Windows NT Server boot floppy and then following the prompts to insert the second and third disks, until the installation is run from CD-ROM. In some cases, this method will not be available because you do not have a CD-ROM drive that is supported under Windows NT. If this is the case, you do have an option, which is an MS-DOS–based installation routine. The executable is `WINNT.EXE`, which will allow you to run a special installation routine that actually copies the installation files to a temporary directory on your hard drive and then proceeds to run the install directly from your hard drive. This method works only if you already have MS-DOS installed on your hard drive.

> **Note:** Sometimes you won't know if your CD-ROM drive is supported under Windows NT until you try using the standard installation method, which is using the Windows NT boot floppy, only to have the install program prompt you to insert disk four. Because disk four does not exist (Windows NT Server only comes with three disks and is not available as a disk-only version), this is a sign that there might be a problem with your CD-ROM drive or CD-ROM drive controller—or your CD-ROM is not supported and the WINNT method should be used.

See Flowchart 6.2 for the first phase of installation.

Another reason to run `WINNT.EXE` is if you are installing Windows NT Server from across a network. When you run install from the boot disk, you do not have access to any network resources; so if the Windows NT Server CD-ROM has been placed on a shared CD-ROM drive, you will be forced to run `WINNT.EXE`. Bear in mind that this install requires an additional 80MB of available hard drive space. See Flowchart 6.3 for other ways of installing NT Server.

The proper syntax for the `WINNT.EXE` command is

```
WINNT [/S: /T: /I:inifile]  [/B¦/C¦/F¦/OX¦/O¦/X]
```

where the `/S[:]` sourcepath specifies the source location of Windows NT files. This must be a full path of the form `x:\[path]` or `\\server\share[\path]`. The default is the current directory.

`/T[:]tempdrive` specifies a drive to contain temporary setup files. If a drive is not specified, Setup attempts to locate a drive for you. If you have developed a custom install script, you should use the `/I[:]inffile` parameter, which specifies the filename (no path) of the setup information file. The default is `DOSNET.INF`.

Other switches that you can use with `WINNT.EXE` are shown in Table 6.1.

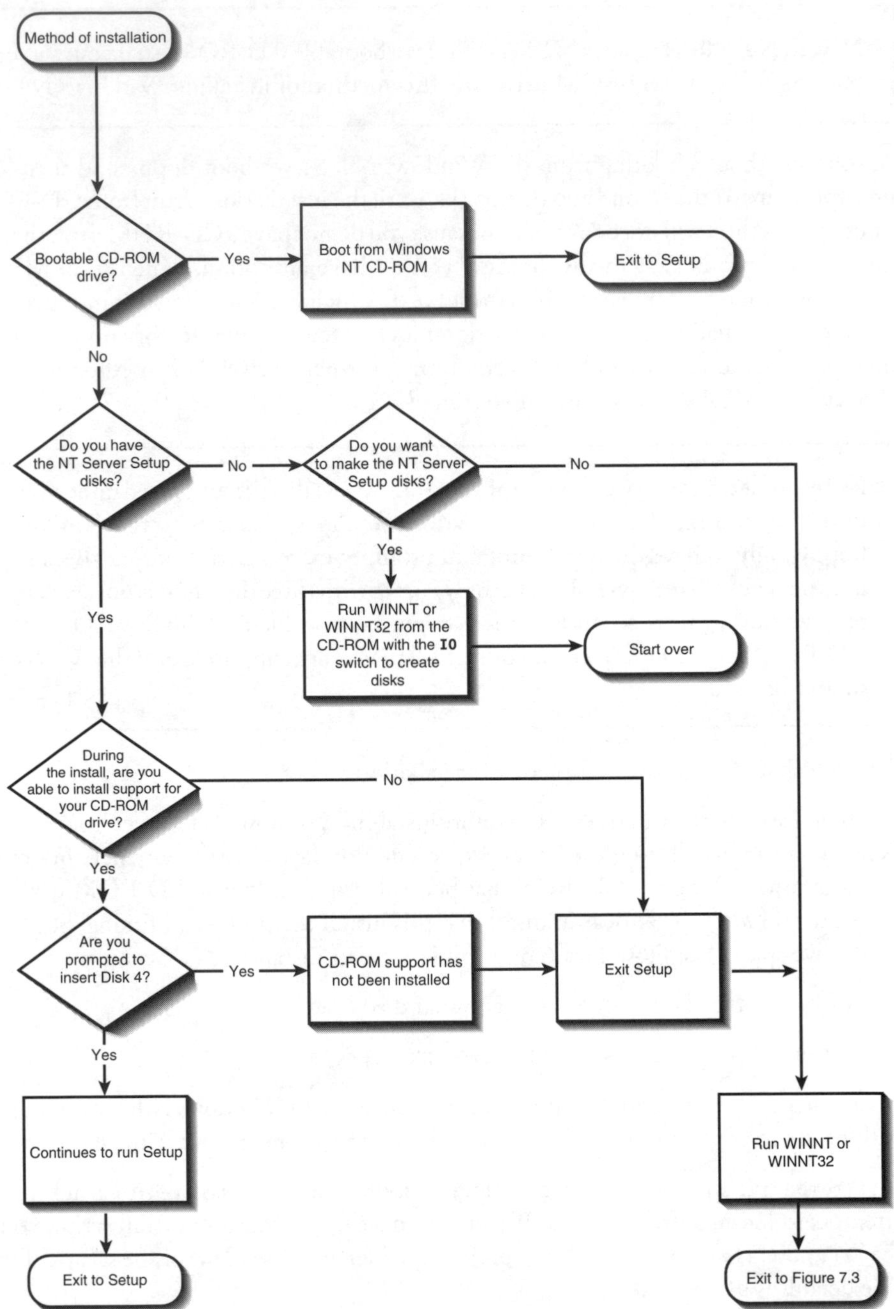

Flowchart 6.2. *Phase one of install.*

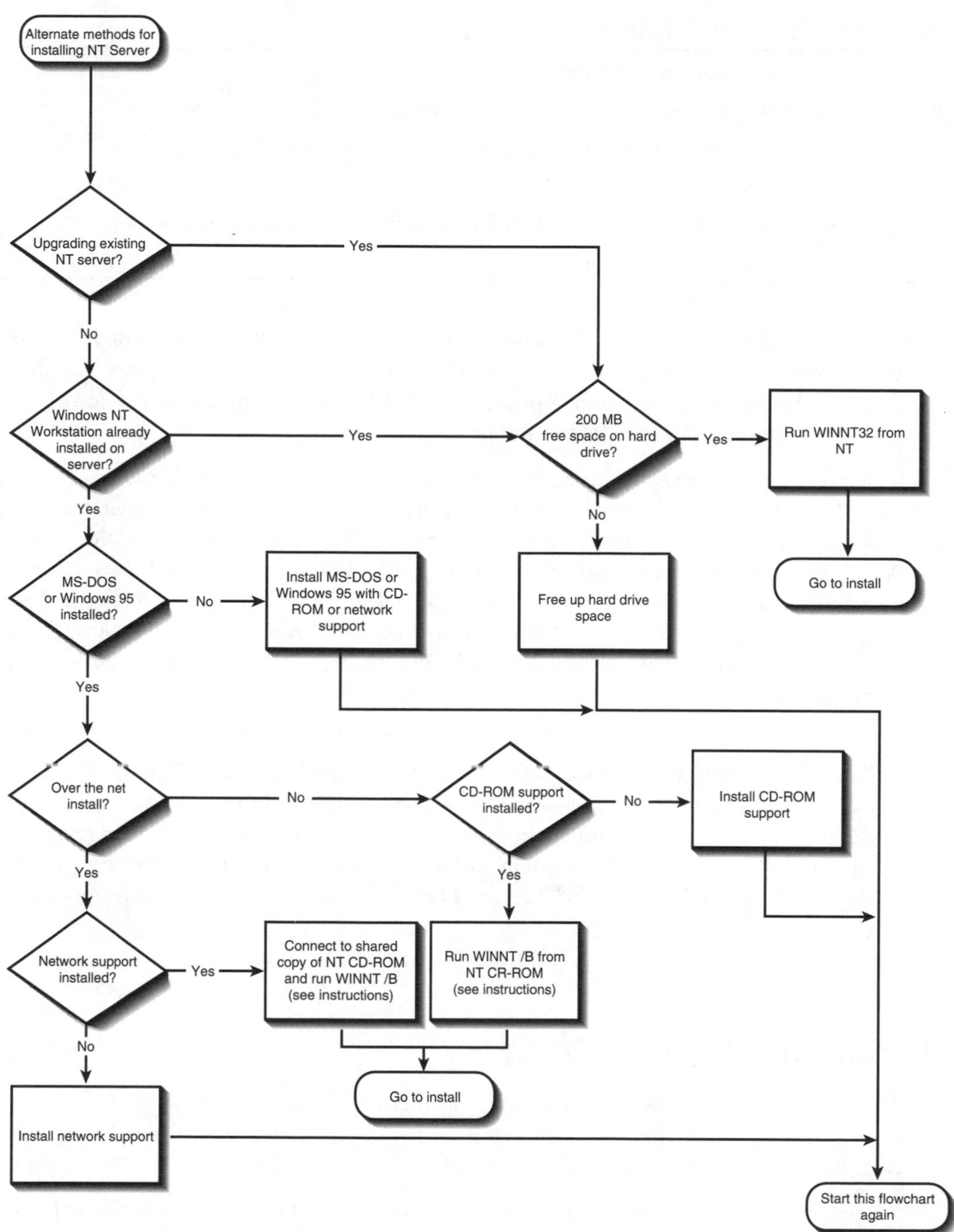

Flowchart 6.3. *Source of installation files.*

Table 6.1. `WINNT.EXE` command-line switches.

`/B`	Specifies floppyless operation
`/C`	Skips the free-space check on the Setup boot floppy disks you provide
`/F`	Does not verify files as they are copied to the Setup boot floppy disks
`/O`	Creates boot floppy disks only
`/OX`	Creates boot floppy disks for CD-ROM or floppy-disk–based installation
`/X`	Does not create the Setup boot floppy disks

The third method of installing Windows NT Server is using the `WINNT32.EXE` program, which is an NT-based setup routine similar to the `WINNT.EXE` method but run from a previously installed version of Windows NT Server or Workstation. See Chapter 7, "Upgrading Windows NT," for more information about the `WINNT32.EXE` program.

If Windows 95 is already running on your server and you insert the Windows NT Server CD-ROM, the Autorun feature of Windows 95 will kick off an introductory screen that gives you the option to install Windows NT Server or browse the contents of the CD-ROM. Currently, Windows NT Server will not migrate settings from a Windows 95 installation; however, Microsoft has committed to making this available in a future release of Windows NT. As I've said before, unless you require MS-DOS on the server, format the hard drives as NTFS. Of course, if you do this, it will not allow you to run MS-DOS, Windows 3.*x*, Windows For Workgroups, or Windows 95.

Tip: Some people just copy the `\I386` directory from the Microsoft Windows NT Server CD-ROM to an `\I386` directory on the server's hard drive and then run `WINNT /B` to avoid dealing with floppy disks. This method also enables you to make on-the-fly changes to your Microsoft Windows NT Server configuration after installation, without having to find the original Microsoft Windows NT Server CD-ROM. The space this `\I386` directory uses is minimal—only 80MB.

An Installation Overview

After you complete the installation process for Microsoft Windows NT Server 4.0, you should have a working server that you then can tailor by adding user accounts, setting permissions, creating shares, creating print queues, and performing many other tasks.

Keep in mind that your first task, the installation, should result in a bootable, working Microsoft Windows NT Server. Certain configuration should be saved until after the installation process, when the server is up and running. For example, there is no need to define any video mode beyond VGA, unless the installation program automatically detects it. An incorrect video driver could cause the computer to freeze during an installation process, which could force you to start the installation program over again. Sound support or any other peripheral device beyond the network adapter should also be saved for after the installation process has completed and the server has been restarted.

Make sure that you have read the section titled "Preparing For Your Installation," earlier in this chapter, and Chapter 9, "Capacity Planning." Have a disk handy to make your Emergency Repair disk and try to be sure that your hardware, including your network interface card, is functioning properly.

Note: If you have an existing network, sometimes it's easier to do a quick MS-DOS install and then load the appropriate drivers to connect to your network, just to check your network card, and if necessary, your network card and other cards' hardware settings. Don't expect a network card to function on Windows NT Server if it doesn't work with DOS!

The first portion of the installation, which is the character-mode portion, prepares your hard drive's master boot record by copying the necessary Microsoft Windows NT Server system files.

The second part of the installation, which is the graphical-mode part, enables you to configure basic networking and sets up the parameters for the server whenever someone is logging on locally at the system console.

Note: A properly planned Microsoft Windows NT Server installation should not take more than one hour.

In fact, with faster hardware, the installation process can take a much shorter amount of time. I've done an install on a DEC AlphaServer that took only 15 minutes.

The Installation Process

The first thing you need to determine before installing Microsoft Windows NT Server is whether you want to have another operating system on the server in addition to Windows NT.

If you are working with a system that already has an operating system on the hard drive, and you will be using the server as a dedicated Microsoft Windows NT Server, you should delete the existing partitions during the Windows NT install and have the installation program create one or more fresh partitions for you.

On the other hand, if you also need to be able to boot MS-DOS, Windows 95, or OS/2 on the server, you will be able to do that by using Windows NT's boot-loader. The boot-loader is a menu that is displayed each time a PC is started. This menu enables you to choose an operating system from which to boot. The full story on the boot-loader is explained in Chapter 10, "The Windows NT Boot Process."

As you learned earlier in the section titled "Preparing For Your Installation," you can use different methods for installing Microsoft Windows NT Server. This section assumes that you are using the preferred method, which is booting from the Microsoft Windows NT Server Setup Boot Disk and installing from the Microsoft Windows NT Server CD-ROM.

Before starting the installation process, I highly recommend that you physically attach the server to the network. The network setup of the installation process will expect to see a live network, and might not complete if you are not physically connected. It is also very important to be attached to the network if there already are live Windows NT servers on the network.

Booting the Server

Insert the Microsoft Windows NT Server Setup Boot Disk into your A: drive, which must be a 3 1/2-inch drive. After the system starts to boot from that disk, you'll see a message that says `Setup is inspecting your computer's hardware`. Next, the blue screen present throughout the character-based portion of Setup appears, and messages across the bottom of the screen inform you that the Windows NT Executive and the Hardware Abstraction Layer (HAL) are loading. You then see a prompt to insert Setup Disk 2 into your A: drive. Insert Disk 2 and press Enter to continue the installation.

The drivers and data necessary for the setup program to proceed are then loaded. These are fonts, locale-specific data, Windows NT Setup, PCMCIA support, SCSI Port driver, video driver, floppy disk driver, keyboard driver, and the FAT file system driver. After these drivers are loaded, you see the screen font change to a smaller font and the actual booting of Windows NT occurs. The first line identifies the operating system by name, version, and build number. The second line tells you the number of processors Windows NT can see and the amount of physical memory detected—and always shows that the multiprocessor kernel is loading. If you are running a single-processor server, the next time Windows NT boots, the single-processor kernel loads; but during installation, the multiprocessor kernel always loads.

The next screen gives you the following choices on how to proceed with your installation:

> You can get more information about the Microsoft Windows NT Server installation process by pressing the F1 key.
>
> You can proceed with the installation by pressing Enter.
>
> You can quit the installation process and restart the server.
>
> You can repair a previously installed copy of Microsoft Windows NT Server that may have been damaged.

The latter is the option you should choose if you are unable to boot Microsoft Windows NT Server or if you have made changes to your configuration and want to reinitialize the installation. You then can press R to be prompted to insert an Emergency Repair Disk.

The Emergency Repair Disk can be built during this installation process, or you can create it at any time from the command line. A formatted high-density 3.5-inch disk is required to create an Emergency Repair Disk.

Press Enter to continue with your installation. See Flowchart 6.4 for the character-based section of Setup.

Setting Up Your Hard Drive and CD-ROM Drivers

The next screen informs you about Windows NT's detection of SCSI and IDE controller chips. In order to have a bootable Microsoft Windows NT Server system, you must have NT install support for your boot device. You also need to have NT install support for the controller to which your CD-ROM drive is attached. (This might be the same as the controller for your boot device, but if they are different, you must ensure that support for both is installed.)

You have the option of letting the installation process try to identify which devices are in your system. (This process is known as *auto-detection.*) If your controllers are identified properly through this process, you can be assured that support for your boot drive and CD-ROM will exist the next time the Microsoft Windows NT Server installation routine reboots your server. If you have purchased a controller that came with its own set of Windows NT drivers or you know that the installation routine will not recognize your controller and you have a disk to use that contains the appropriate drivers, press the S key.

If you press the S key, the installation routine tells you that it did not detect any devices. Then press the S key again to choose from a list of drivers that come with Microsoft Windows NT Server. The last item on that list is Other, which enables you to point the installation program to a floppy drive.

Tip: You might want to try out auto-detection just to see whether Windows NT's native support includes support for your controllers. You should go straight to the S routine if your drivers are newer than the release date for Microsoft Windows NT Server 4.0.

If you use auto-detection and no devices are found, you can choose from the list of devices that ships with Microsoft Windows NT Server. Chances are that choosing from this list after trying auto-detection won't do you any good; however, if you had a compatible device, auto-detection would have picked up on it.

Tip: Another reason to choose the S option is if you attempt auto-detection and your server freezes up. It is possible for a server to seize during the auto-detection stage yet still be able to function properly through the entire installation process if auto-detection is skipped.

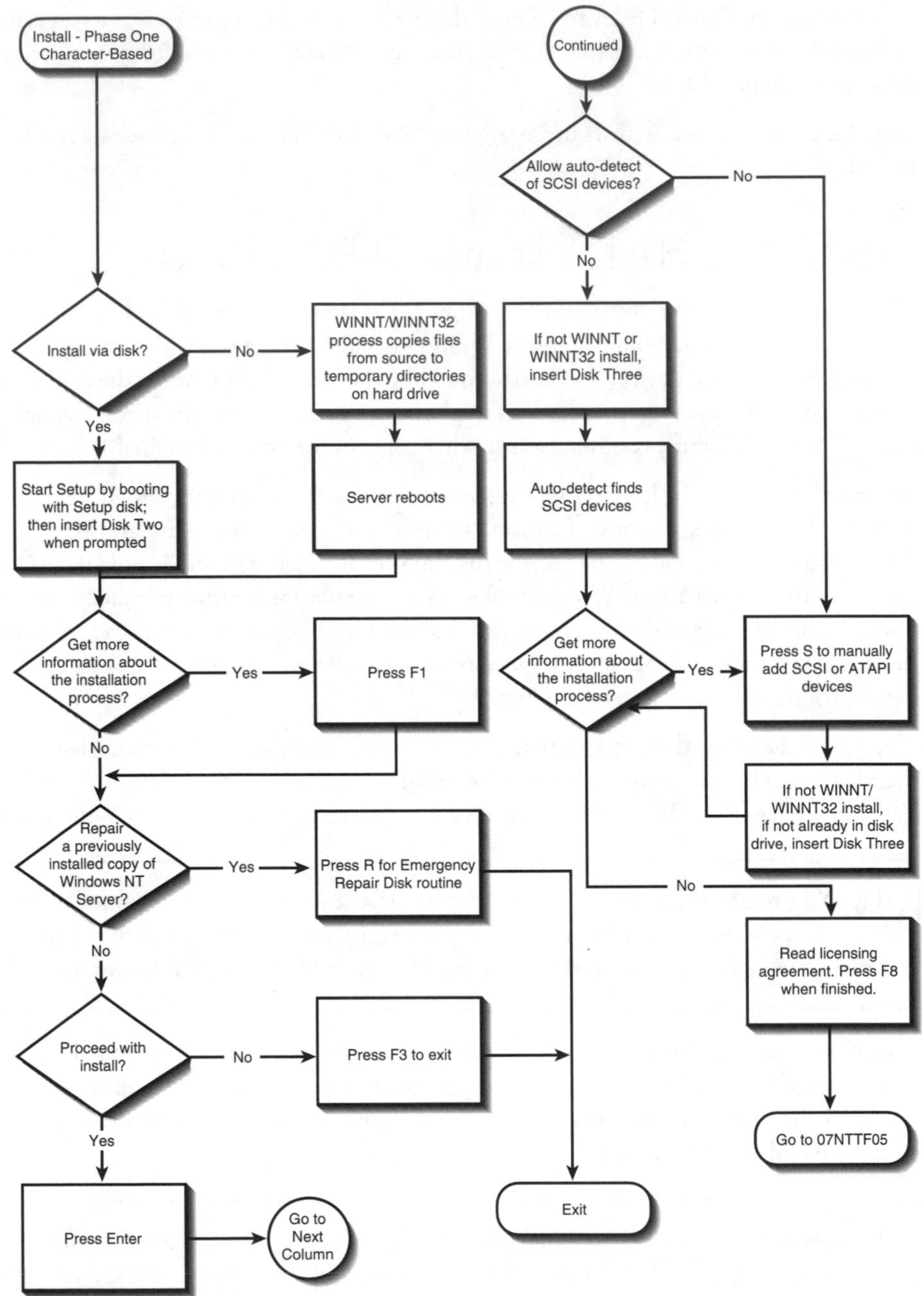

Flowchart 6.4. *Character-based section of setup.*

If you do choose to use auto-detection, the installation program prompts you to insert Setup Disk 3 into the floppy drive. After you press Enter, the installation program attempts to load each SCSI driver to see whether it can detect your SCSI controller(s). A list of found devices appears as they are detected. Not only are SCSI drivers loaded and tested, but some proprietary CD-ROM interfaces are also tested.

Assuming that auto-detection has found your controller or controllers, you now can press Enter to proceed with the rest of the installation—unless you want to install support for additional devices.

Note: I've seen many situations in which an IDE adapter for an IDE CD-ROM drive was not detected by auto-detection. This is something that you can choose from the list of SCSI controllers. Even though the list is presented as a list of SCSI controllers, there is a choice—ATAPI 1.2—that is the proper choice for an IDE interface. It is not necessary to specify IDE for an IDE hard drive, because this driver always is loaded during the installation routine, even if you do not have an IDE hard drive.

After you complete the process of identifying devices and you press Enter to continue the installation, additional drivers are loaded. This includes support for IDE and ESDI controllers, the NTFS file system, the CDFS file system, and, if appropriate, a SCSI CD-ROM, SCSI hard drives, and SCSI floppy drives.

Legalities

After the necessary SCSI or IDE drivers have loaded, you are presented with the Windows NT Server licensing agreement. You should take the time to read this, because it has some very interesting notes regarding licensing Microsoft BackOffice products and technologies. If you are using your Windows NT server to run BackOffice or any other parts of the BackOffice suite, you might want to examine this agreement more closely. The only way this could affect your install of Windows NT Server is if you choose not to honor the agreement and exit the installation process. I'll take it for granted that you understand the agreement; when you are at the final page, press the F8 key to continue with the installation.

Deciding Where to Install Windows NT Server

After your boot drive is examined, a search for a previous installation of Microsoft Windows NT Server is conducted. If a previously installed version of Microsoft Windows NT Server is found, you are asked whether you want to upgrade or install a fresh copy in its own directory.

If you do have another copy of Windows NT Server and want to preserve that copy, choose to install Windows NT Server in its own directory, separate from the previously installed version. I've seen installations where two copies of the same version of Windows NT Server have been installed.

The reason for this was that the administrator wanted one copy to remain that was a minimal installation, without any additional BackOffice components; that way, if there were a problem with some of those other applications, he could quickly boot up another copy of Windows NT Server to get his clients up and running with file and print services. If this is your case, both copies of Windows NT Server will be made available for you to choose from when the boot-loader menu appears each time you start the server.

Flowchart 6.5 shows the Installation destination.

If you do not have Microsoft Windows NT Server already installed on this server, you are asked to identify your type of computer, video display, mouse, keyboard, and keyboard layout.

These choices are very similar to the choices you have when running the old Windows 3.*x* setup routine. Because Microsoft Windows NT Server is so hardware-specific, it is very important that you do not make a wrong choice for any of these parameters.

Chances are that the appropriate choice for your server will be shown on-screen, although the video display usually defaults to VGA. You will have the option to change the video display during the latter part of the installation, where your specific video chip may be auto-detected, and after Microsoft Windows NT Server is installed.

If you are satisfied with the current choices shown, press Enter to proceed with the installation.

If a copy of Microsoft Windows 3.*x* is found on your boot drive, the installation routine asks you whether Microsoft Windows NT Server should be installed in the same directory.

It is possible to have Microsoft Windows NT Server and Microsoft Windows 3.*x* coexist in the same directory, sharing applications and settings. However, there is currently no way to have Microsoft Windows NT Server migrate Microsoft Windows 95 Registry settings, which can result in the inability to run the applications you had installed in Microsoft Windows 95 on Microsoft Windows NT Server—without the need to reinstall the applications again under Microsoft Windows NT Server.

It is strongly advised to install Microsoft Windows NT Server into its own directory if you want to continue running Microsoft Windows 95 on the same PC. You will then need to reinstall the software for use by Microsoft Windows NT Server, if you want to use the applications from there. Supposedly, the next version of Windows NT Server will include an upgrade path from Windows 95 to Windows NT Server.

Caution: If you decide to install to the same directory, keep in mind that it might be difficult to uninstall Microsoft Windows NT Server and leave your old Windows intact. I therefore recommend, in all cases, installing Microsoft Windows NT Server in its own directory.

Once again, I will remind you that if you need to run any of the other flavors of Windows on this server, you will not be able to convert your FAT partition to NTFS without losing the capability of running the other Windows.

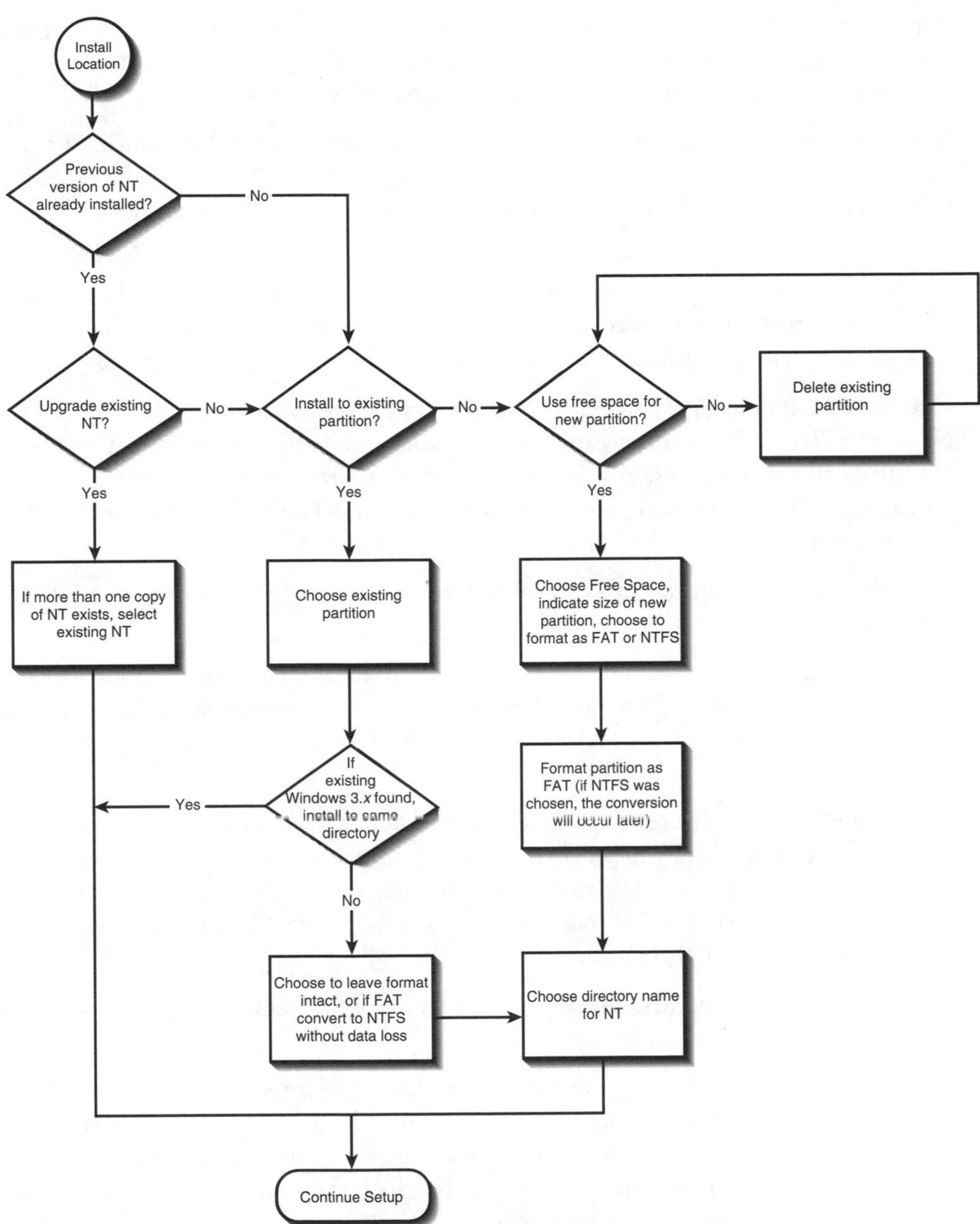

Flowchart 6.5. *Installation destination.*

If an old copy of Windows is found, you must press the N key to proceed without installing Microsoft Windows NT Server to the same directory. Press Enter if you do want to install Microsoft Windows NT Server to the same directory as Windows.

If you have not told the installation program where to install Microsoft Windows NT Server, you now will find a list of available partitions for installing Microsoft Windows NT Server. It is from here that you can choose to delete an existing partition—and you can create partitions from here as well.

The list shows the drive letter assigned to the partition, the current file system for that partition, and the total space and free space on the partition. Unpartitioned areas of your hard drive(s) also are shown. If you have decided to create or delete partitions, complete those tasks now.

Next, position the highlight bar over the partition to which you want to install Microsoft Windows NT Server. Remember that this partition must be large enough to accommodate approximately 100MB of files. Press Enter. You are asked whether you want to format the partition as FAT, format it as NTFS, convert an existing FAT partition to NTFS, or leave an existing FAT intact with no formatting.

Next, the installation program asks for a directory name. By default, the name is `\WINNT`, but you may change this.

After you select a directory name and press Enter, the installation program wants to check existing partitions for corruption. You can allow the program to perform an exhaustive secondary examination of those partitions. Press Enter to allow for both examinations or press Esc to perform only the first test.

If this is the first time you are using this server and you want to be assured that the hard drives are free from defects, let the Setup program run its exhaustive secondary examination. Although it takes up a lot more time for the install, which can be used as a coffee break, I highly recommend running it at least once. Then, if you need to reinstall Windows NT Server for some reason, you will not need to run the check again.

A Please Wait screen appears during the examination of the hard drive(s). After this process is completed, the file copy process begins.

The file copy process begins only if you successfully identified the device to which your CD-ROM drive is attached. If the installation program was unable to load the appropriate driver, the program prompts you for Setup Disk 4. Well, in case you were wondering, there is no Setup Disk 4. So, the next step is to abort the installation by pressing the F3 key and confirm the abort operation. Then you must find a drivers disk for your SCSI controller and start the installation process again.

If you specified SCSI drivers to be installed from a manufacturer's disk, you are prompted for that disk during this sequence.

After the copying process finishes, you are prompted to remove the disk from your floppy drive. You then can press Enter to proceed with the installation. You now have completed the character-based part of the Microsoft Windows NT Server installation program.

The Windows NT Server Setup Wizard

Now your server boots Microsoft Windows NT Server from the hard drive, and the graphical portion of the installation begins. You can file away those three disks until the next time you need to install Microsoft Windows NT Server or until you need to use your Emergency Repair Disk.

When your server reboots, you are presented with a menu of installed operating systems. The first item is your new installation of Microsoft Windows NT Server 4.0. If this is a dedicated server with no other operating systems, this is your only choice. If you originally had MS-DOS or another copy of Windows NT on the boot drive, those operating systems will also be listed as options on the menu. When installation has completed, you find yet another item on the menu. See Chapter 10.

The boot menu usually has a time-out of 30 seconds before a choice is made automatically, but for this installation, you immediately are launched into the next part of the installation.

You will again see the blue screen that identifies the operating system, version number, and build number. Again, under that information, you see the number of processors available to Windows NT and your physical memory, but this time the multiprocessor kernel is loaded only if your server has more than one processor.

> **Note:** Examine where Windows NT tells you which type of kernel is being loaded, because there have been instances in which a multiprocessor server has not had all of its processors recognized by Windows NT; thus, if the single-processor kernel is loaded, it's time to call tech support.

The graphical portion of the installation program now starts by initializing, and then some more files are copied from the CD-ROM to the hard drive. The Setup Wizard (see Figure 6.1) then starts its three-part process.

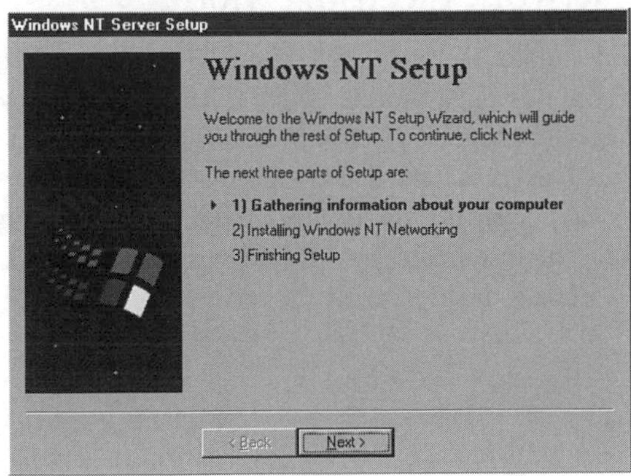

Figure 6.1. *The Windows NT Server Setup Wizard.*

The first part that the Setup Wizard will guide you through is defining information about the computer, including the computer name and licensing information, and determining which of the optional components of Microsoft Windows NT Server you want to install. The second part lets you define Microsoft Networking, which includes protocols and services. The final part is setting up your local workspace, which is used only when you log on locally to the server.

See Flowchart 6.6, which shows you the process that is handled by part one of the Setup Wizard.

The first part of the Setup Wizard routine is gathering information about your computer. Click the Next button. After some subdirectories are created within your Windows NT Server directory, you are prompted to enter your name and the name of your company (if any), as shown in Figure 6.2. This is standard procedure for all Microsoft installation programs. Enter these values and click the Next button.

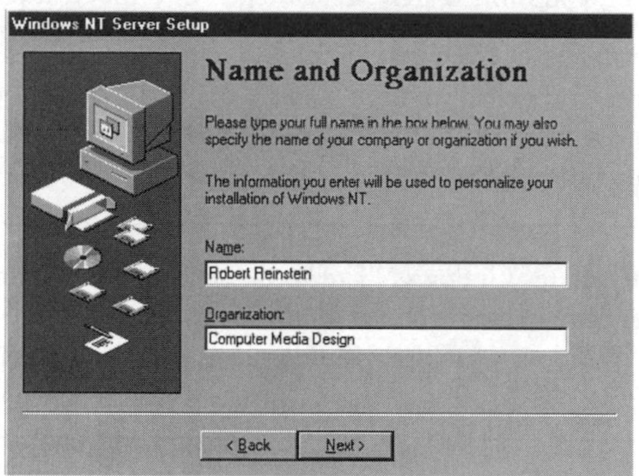

Figure 6.2. *Name and organization.*

Windows NT Network Licensing Modes

The Licensing Modes dialog appears. (See Figure 6.3.) You can license clients for Microsoft Windows NT Server in one of two modes. Per Server mode allows you to specify the number of concurrent users that will be accessing your physical server. A Per Seat mode allows you to purchase licenses for individual users to grant them access to all the servers contained within your corporation. After you specify this mode within the installation program, you have the option to change it from within the installed copy of Microsoft Windows NT Server, but you can change the mode only once during the lifetime of the server.

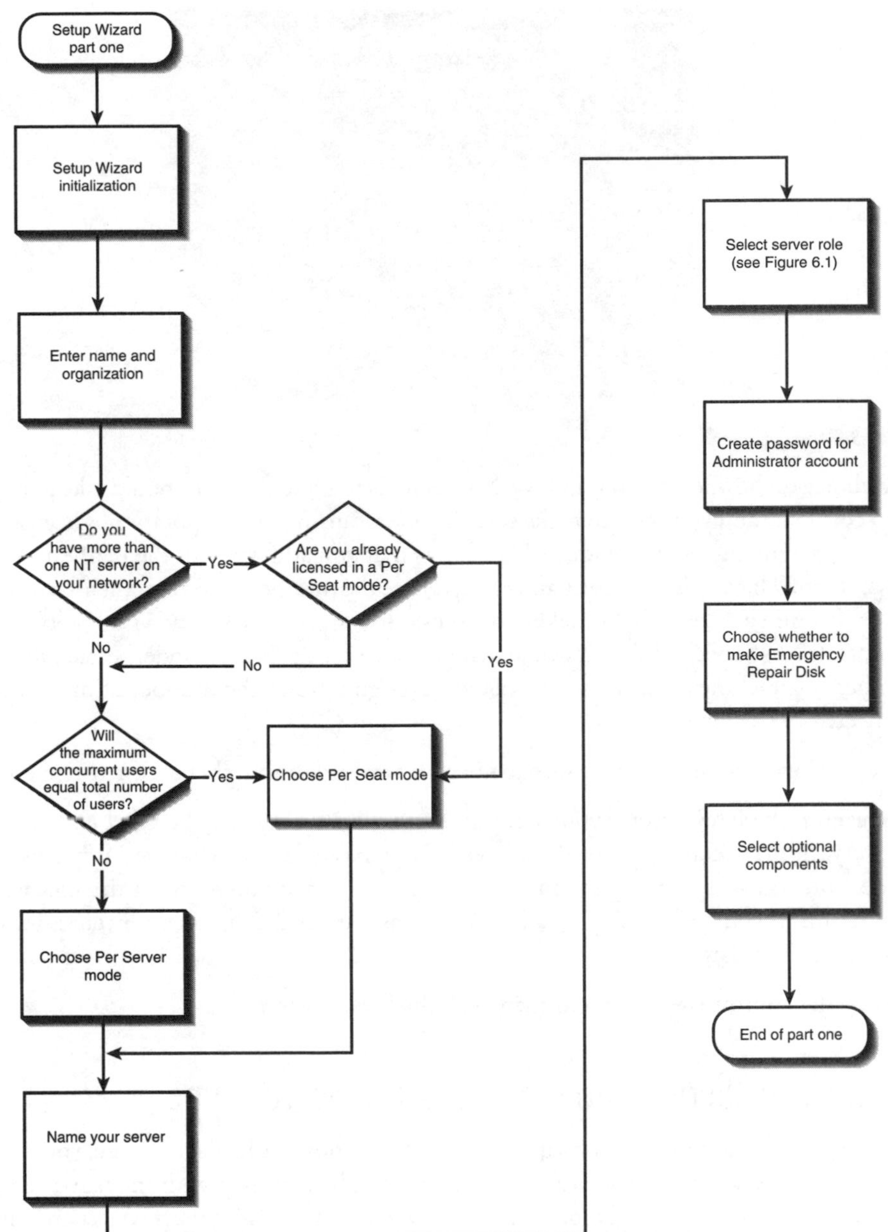

Flowchart 6.6. *Setup Wizard, part one.*

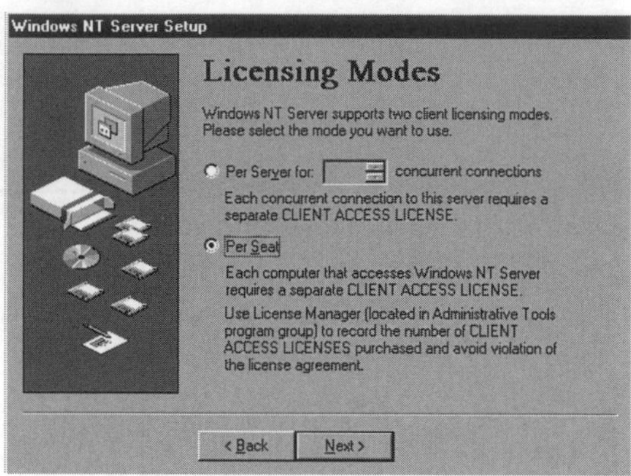

***Figure 6.3.** Licensing mode choice.*

The choice on how to license Windows NT Server is not one that you should take lightly. If there is no cost issue and you want to make sure that everyone in your corporation is licensed to access this server, plus any other Windows NT servers that you add, go with the Per Seat mode. If you expect to only have this one server and can estimate the number of concurrent attachments to the server, Per Server mode might make more sense. If you set up a Windows NT server strictly for Remote Access Services (RAS), it would make sense to use Per Server mode, because the maximum number of attachments to the server would never go beyond the number of modems you have connected to the server.

Note that logons at the server console do not count toward the number of concurrent connections.

However, if the RAS server is your second server and you're already licensed in a Per Seat mode for everyone in the company, you do not need to purchase additional licenses. When using Per Seat mode, you will be specifying the number of seats you have purchased in the License Manager application. If you are licensing on a Per Server basis, enter the number of licenses for this server during this installation routine.

Choose the appropriate mode and then click the Next button.

Naming Your Server and Choosing the Server Type

The Computer Name dialog, shown in Figure 6.4, will now be displayed. Here, you need to enter the name of the server. The server's name should not be confused with the name you give your domain. If you plan on having more than one server, you should give the server a name that enables you to easily identify the server when viewing a list of servers. The server's name must contain 15 characters or fewer, and it must be a name unique to your network.

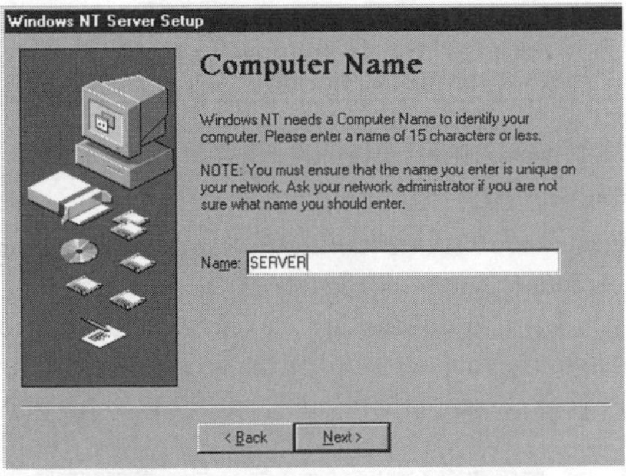

Figure 6.4. *Naming your server.*

Enter the name and then click the Next button.

The Server Type dialog (see Figure 6.5) is where you choose the role for this server. If this is your first server for this domain, choose Primary Domain Controller. If you have already established a domain and are adding this server as a BDC that will participate in administrative functions, choose that option. Otherwise, if this server will participate in an existing domain but you do not want it to participate in logon validation among other administrative tasks, or you do not want to implement a Windows NT domain model and just want this server to act as a peer-to-peer server, choose the Stand-Alone Server option.

Note: A stand-alone server is also known as a member server.

You must know the name of the domain you will create if you choose Primary Domain Controller, the name of the domain you are joining as a BDC, or the name of the workgroup or domain you will be part of as a member server. After you make your choice, click the Next button.

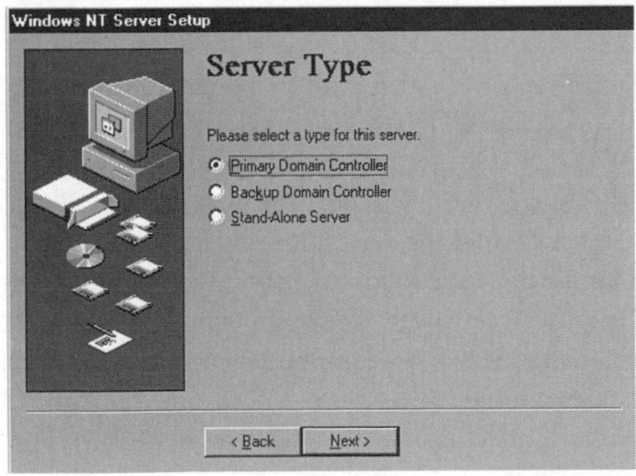

Figure 6.5. *Choosing the server type.*

> **Note:** Refer to Flowchart 6.1 to help you make a decision on your server's role.

Keep in mind that during the execution of the Setup Wizard, you can choose to go back to previous screens by clicking the Back button.

All PCs running Windows NT (both Workstation and Server) have an Administrator account. In the Administrator Account dialog (see Figure 6.6), you need to assign a password to that account for this server. If you want to do this later, assign a blank password for now by not entering anything. Remember to assign a password to the account before you allow other users to attach to this server. Make your entries, if applicable, and then click the Next button.

Figure 6.6. *Administrator Account.*

You are given the choice of creating an Emergency Repair Disk, as shown in Figure 6.7. Choose Yes, because you might need that disk to avoid having to reinstall Microsoft Windows NT Server from scratch. Important information regarding your partitions and administrative information is stored on this disk. If you do not make a disk now or if any information changes that you want to back up to a new Emergency Repair Disk, you can run the `RDISK.EXE` program from a command prompt.

Installing Windows NT's Optional Components

After you click the Next button, you have the option to install optional components for Microsoft Windows NT Server by making selections on the Select Components dialog. (See Figure 6.8.) These items are for use by a local logon and are not server tools. These optional components include Accessibility Options, Accessories, Communications, Games, Microsoft Exchange (which is not the Microsoft Exchange Server or client but a trimmed-down version of the Microsoft Exchange Server client that can be used to attach to a Microsoft Mail For PC Networks postoffice, or for mail from online services), and Multimedia. Check or uncheck the appropriate boxes and click the Next button.

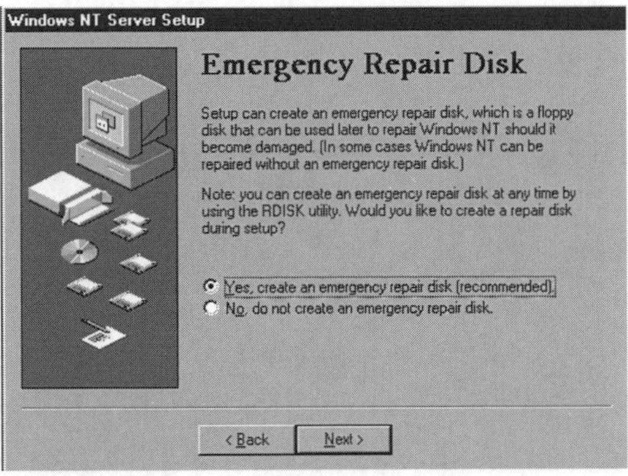

Figure 6.7. Emergency Repair Disk.

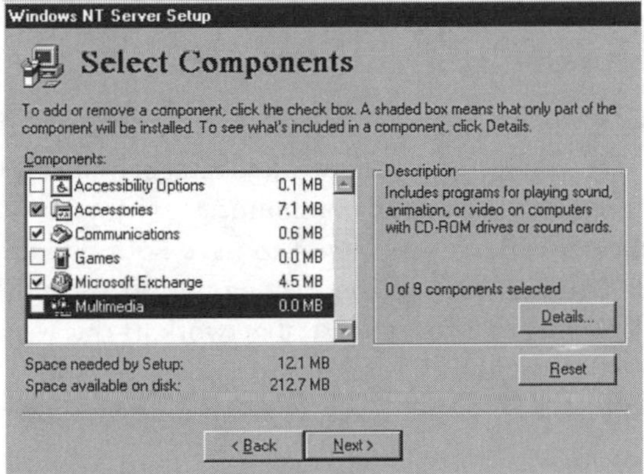

Figure 6.8. Select Components.

Note: Unless you plan to use your server as a workstation, it is not necessary to install all of the optional components—or for that matter, any of the optional components. For instance, Games and Multimedia are not usually used on a server, and the Communications group includes a phone dialer that you might not need to take up space on the hard drive. You have the option to add these items back into your server, but if you are trying to make the most out of your disk space, take the time to examine all of the optional components and decide whether they are necessary for this server.

That finishes up part one of the Setup Wizard. (See Figure 6.9.)

Part two of the Setup Wizard handles setting up the networking components of Microsoft Windows NT Server. Click the Next button to get started.

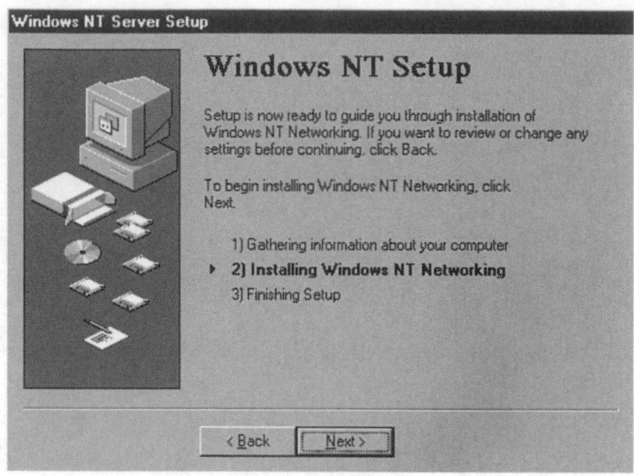

Figure 6.9. *Finishing part one of the Setup Wizard.*

Setting Up Microsoft Networking

The first question the Setup Wizard asks is how your server is connected to the network (as shown in Figure 6.10). If you are connected via a network adapter or by an ISDN connection, select Wired to the network. If this server is going to communicate with your network via a modem, select Remote access to the network. If you intend to have both connections available, select both choices. This section assumes that you are selecting the Wired to the network scenario because most of the servers are going to be on a physical network. If this were a server that had to dial in to join its domain, you would be prompted to answer questions about modems and other parameters, but in this step-by-step process, you will deal with a server that is on a hard-wired network.

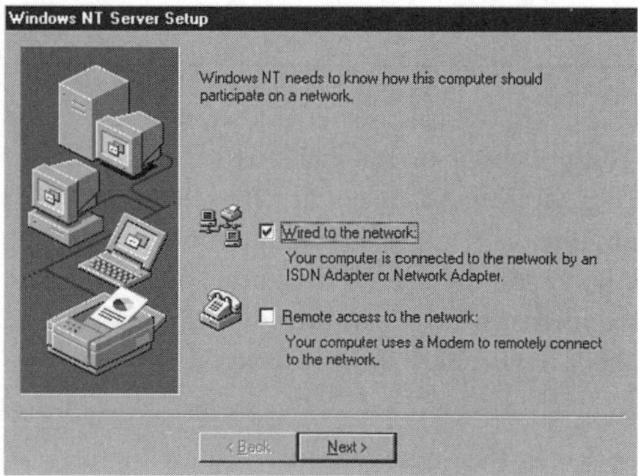

Figure 6.10. *Connecting to the network.*

Make your choice(s) and click the Next button.

The next dialog, Figure 6.11, lets you choose whether or not you will want to install Microsoft Internet Information Server. This is a fully functional World Wide Web (WWW), Gopher, and File Transfer Protocol (FTP) server that was available as an add-on for Microsoft Windows NT Server 3.51. The new version is fully integrated into the operating system and has gotten rave reviews about its speed and ease of administration.

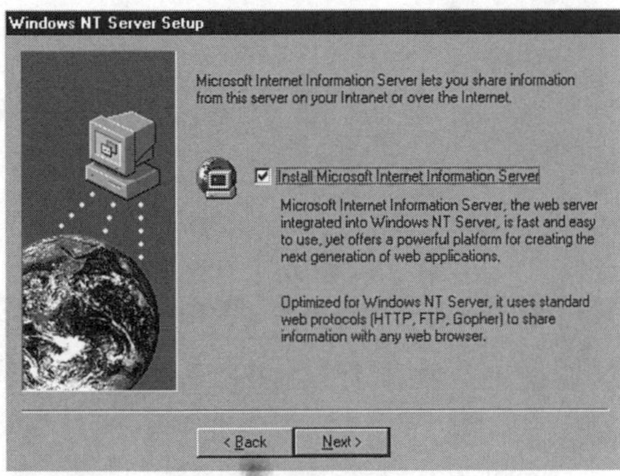

Figure 6.11. *Installing Microsoft Internet Information Server.*

Make your choice and click the Next button to resume installation.

The Network Adapter Card selection process is next. Again, an auto-detect feature can attempt to recognize your installed network interface card. As was the SCSI identification sequence, this can be a point of failure for the installation routine.

Caution: If you choose to allow for auto-detection and your server freezes up, you must start the installation process from the beginning.

You can choose to have a list displayed that you can choose from, or you can use a disk provided by the network interface card manufacturer. If you want to use auto-detect, click the Start Search button. Figure 6.12 shows the results of an auto-detect.

Click Select from list if you prefer to choose your card manually or if the auto-detect does not pick up on the card you have installed. If you are using a disk provided by a hardware manufacturer, choose Select from list. The resulting dialog includes a Have Disk button. Use this option. The Setup Wizard asks you for the location of the disk.

After you add one or more cards to the list, click the Next button to select the protocols you want to install on your server. (See Figure 6.13.)

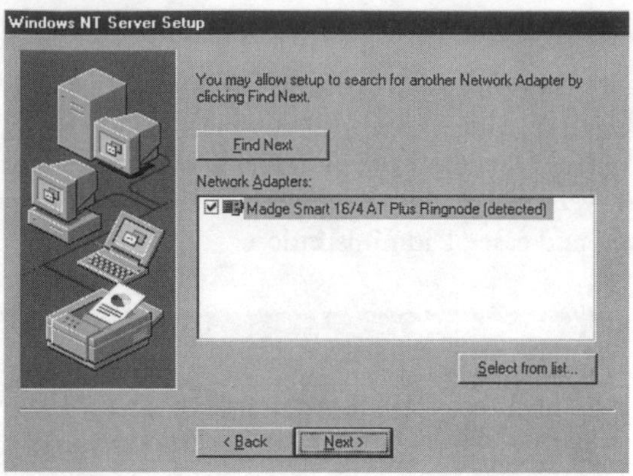

Figure 6.12. Choosing a network adapter.

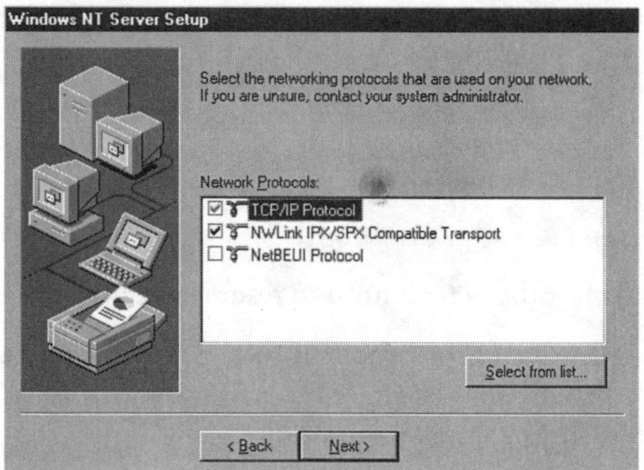

Figure 6.13. Select protocols.

NWLink, which is Microsoft's IPX/SPX-compatible protocol, and TCP/IP are chosen as the default protocols for your server. Choose whether you want these protocols installed and whether you want a fast nonroutable protocol; if you have an existing NetBEUI network, choose to install NetBEUI. You can install as many protocols as you want, but the more protocols you install, the more overhead there is on your server.

The Select from list button offers even more protocols, such as Microsoft's DLC protocol, which might be necessary if you plan on having 3270 connectivity that might require that protocol, or if you want to see a Hewlett-Packard Jet Direct card on your network. Microsoft's new Point To Point Tunneling Protocol (PPTP) is another option here. Install this if you plan on allowing clients to log on to the network through the Internet. A Have Disk button also is available on this dialog because you might want to install third-party implementations of TCP/IP or other protocols. Flowchart 6.7 shows select protocols.

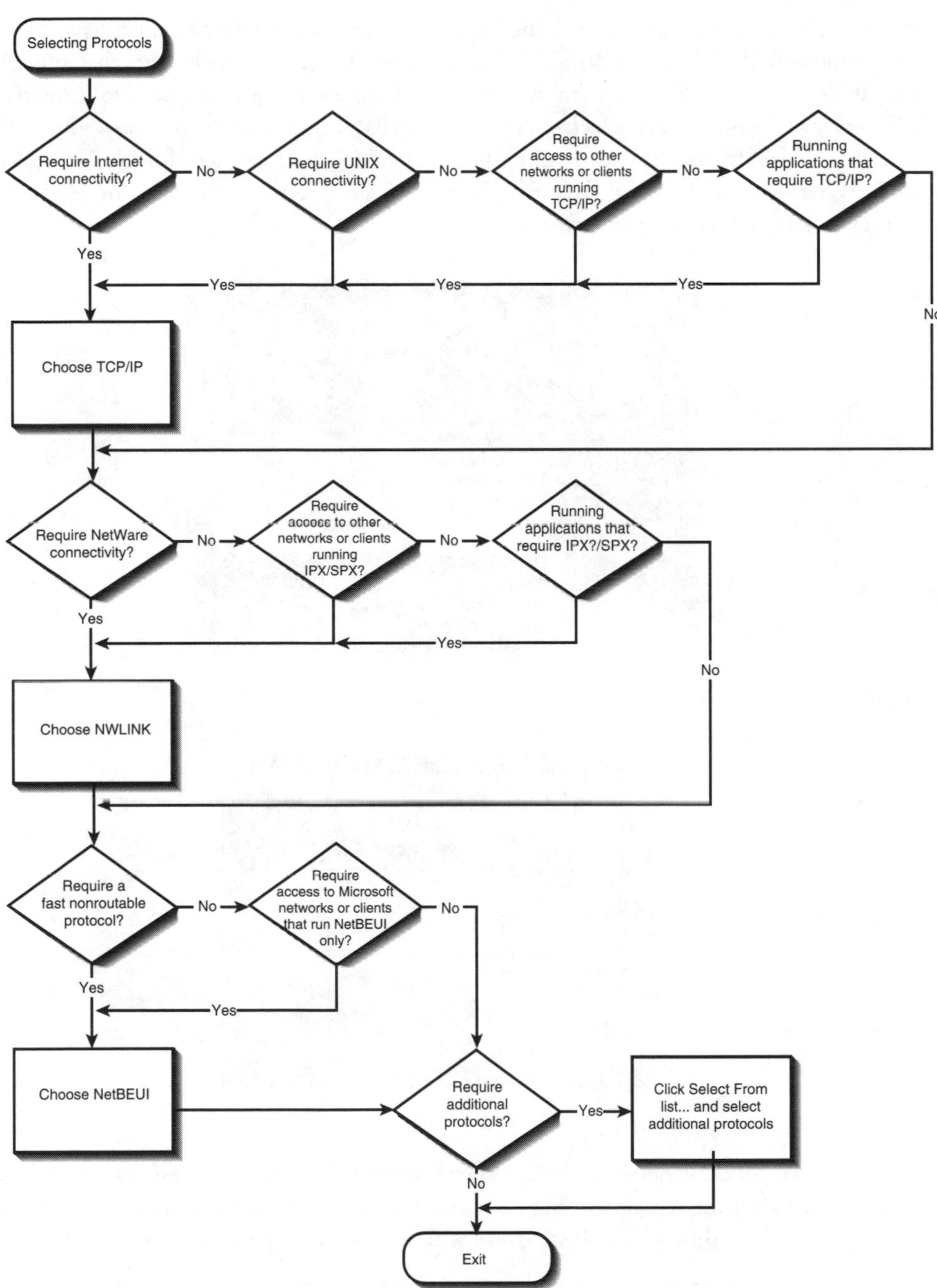

Flowchart 6.7. *Select protocols.*

After resolving your protocols, click the Next button to display a list of available network services that come with the Microsoft Windows NT Server package. The check boxes that appear grayed-out, shown in Figure 6.14, are that way because those services are necessary to properly run the NT server and cannot be deselected. A Select from list button again gives you additional choices (see Figure 6.15), such as for installing Gateway and Client Services for NetWare, Microsoft DHCP Server, Microsoft DNS Server, Remote Access Services, Services for Macintosh, and Windows Internet Name Service.

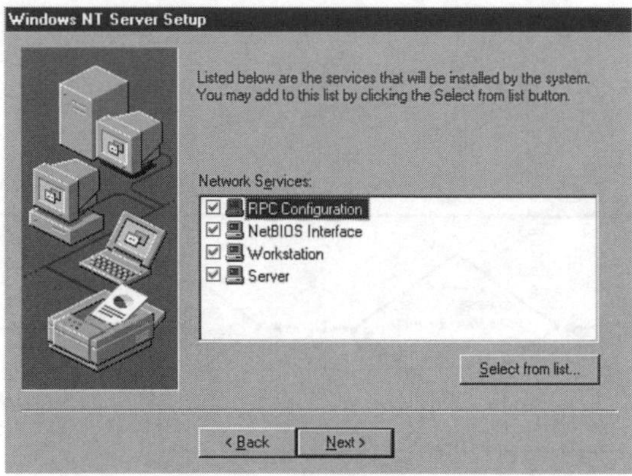

Figure 6.14. *Network Services.*

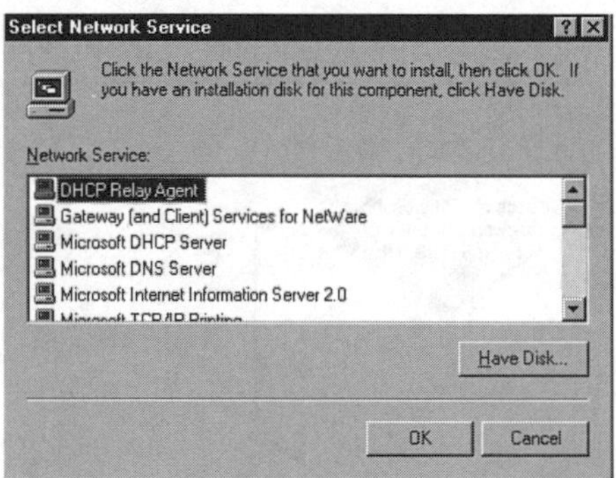

Figure 6.15. *Additional network services.*

You can make all these network choices after Microsoft Windows NT Server is installed. If you want to try to get the server running with minimum overhead, just accept the default network settings to get you through the installation with less possibility of something going wrong.

Caution: Selecting both Network Monitoring Agent and Network Monitoring Agent and Tools services can result in setup errors. Be sure to choose one or the other.

After the network services are resolved, you will be told that the network configuration is about to be installed. (See Figure 6.16.) This is the perfect time to click the Back button to review your choices. If you are sure you have made the right choices, click the Next button to start the file copy and network configuration process. If you are using a network adapter card that requires switch settings, you soon are prompted for the IRQ, DMA, and memory address for that card. Other configurable options also are presented to you, but be sure that you know the settings for your network adapter card because the network service attempts to start during this installation process.

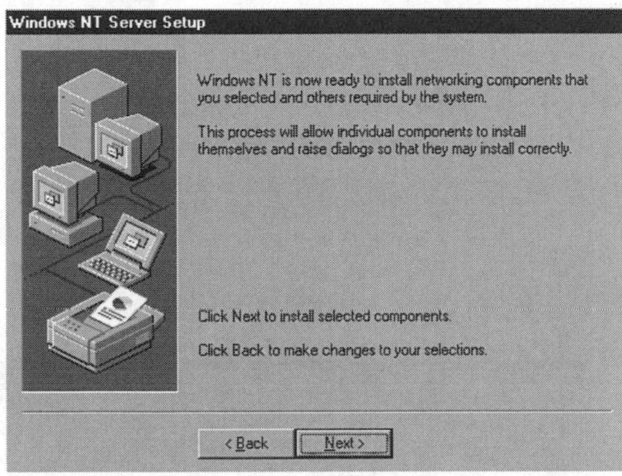

Figure 6.16. *Ready to install networking components.*

Any configuration dialogs can appear, so answer them accordingly. For instance, if you chose to install TCP/IP, you will be prompted to enter your IP address and subnet mask. If you are unsure what any of the right answers are, you can choose to proceed and clean up these network configurations after the installation of Microsoft Windows NT Server finishes. In the TCP/IP Properties screen, there is a button labeled Advanced. Click Advanced to get to the Advanced IP Addressing dialog (see Figure 6.17), which will allow you to configure security and PPTP Filtering. Additional information on these options is in Chapter 29, "Windows NT and TCP/IP." Click the OK button and then click Next to continue with your networking configuration.

The next dialog (see Figure 6.18) allows you to enable and disable bindings that have been created for you by default. You can deselect a binding by highlighting the binding and clicking on the Disable button. After you have completed verifying the bindings, click the Next button.

After the configuration and file copying process has completed, Windows NT will be ready to start the network. The dialog that tells you this (see Figure 6.19) is another good place to go back and check your settings. After you are certain that you have configured the networking services, your network adapter, your protocols, and the bindings correctly, click the Next button, and Microsoft Networking will attempt to start. Do not be concerned if you find that the server is taking a long time to respond. Besides initializing the network adapter, it is also resolving bindings.

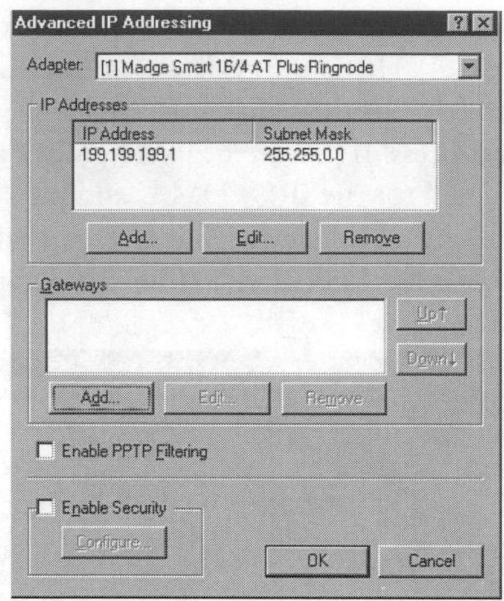

Figure 6.17. Advanced IP addressing.

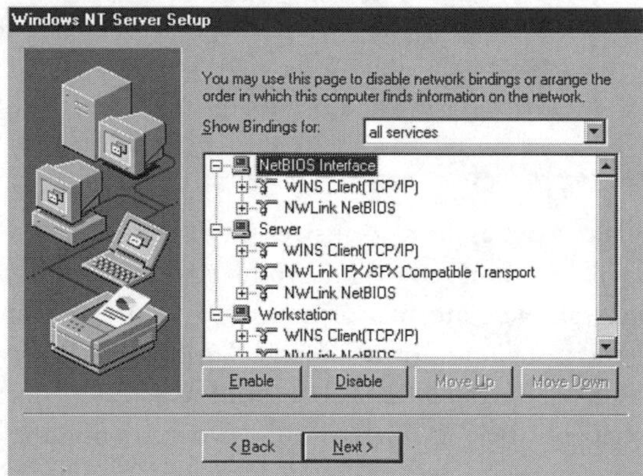

Figure 6.18. Bindings configuration.

If the network services start properly, you will proceed to the next dialog, but if they do not start properly, click the Back button a few times to go back to the network interface card dialog and check your settings again. Chances are that the network startup will fail if you gave NT the wrong settings or chose the wrong driver for your network adapter card.

Assuming that you have properly identified the card and its settings, you will be prompted for the name of the domain that you are starting or joining.

As shown in Figure 6.20, for a PDC you must enter the name of the domain you will be starting. There must not be another domain on your network with the same name. If the network services started properly and you do name a preexisting domain, you will get a warning about this, but it is possible to name an existing domain if you have not been able to connect to the network. So be sure that you have predetermined the name of the domain that you will be creating. If you chose to be a BDC, you must supply the name of the domain that you are going to join. You also must provide the administrator password, which verifies your authority to add this computer to the domain.

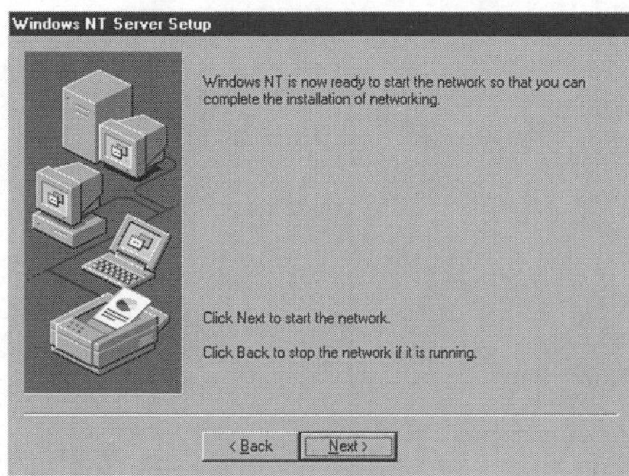

Figure 6.19. *Ready to start the network.*

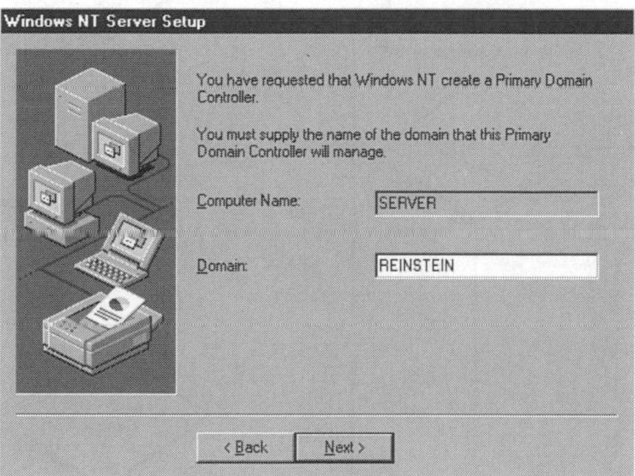

Figure 6.20. *Specifying a new domain.*

As a member server, it is not necessary for you to name a domain, but if you do want to join a preexisting domain, do it from here. The domain name, unless it is new, will be validated. If the domain cannot be found, you will not be able to proceed.

If you are joining an existing domain and get a message that the PDC cannot be found, be sure that the PDC is up and running. You also want to be sure that you typed in the correct name for the domain. Using naming conventions while you are planning your domain can help prevent this type of error. Try to avoid using names like SERVER1 and SERVER2. Domain names can be up to 15 characters long, so use that space effectively and you can avoid naming conflicts.

Clicking the Next button sends the Setup Wizard searching across the network for a preexisting domain or, when setting up a PDC, validates that the domain you are creating does not exist.

After adjusting many internal settings, which might make the server appear as if it has frozen, the network setup part of the Setup Wizard finishes, which brings you to the third and final stage of Microsoft Windows NT Server installation. (See Flowchart 6.8.) Figure 6.21 shows the final step for Setup Wizard.

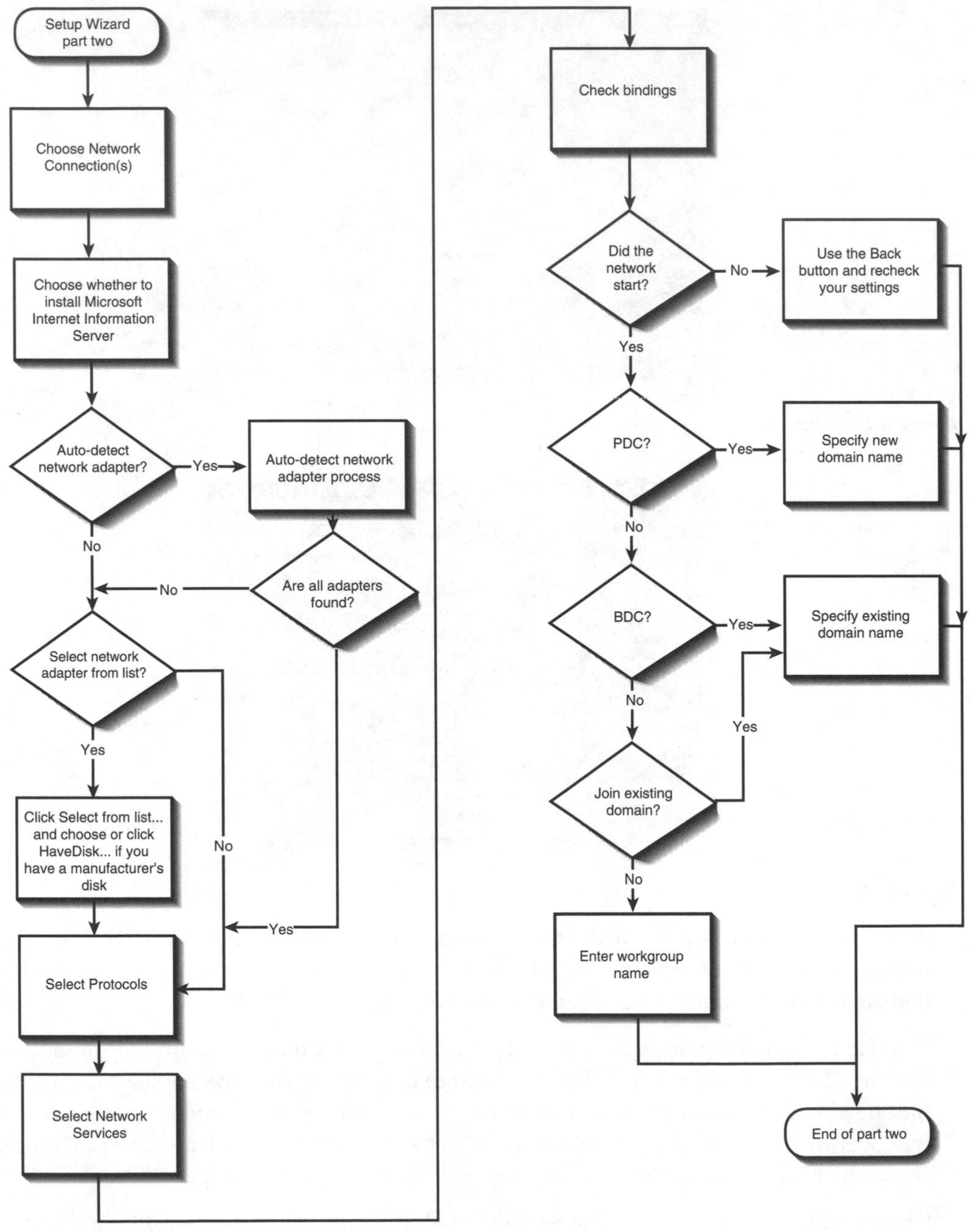

Flowchart 6.8. *Setup Wizard, part two.*

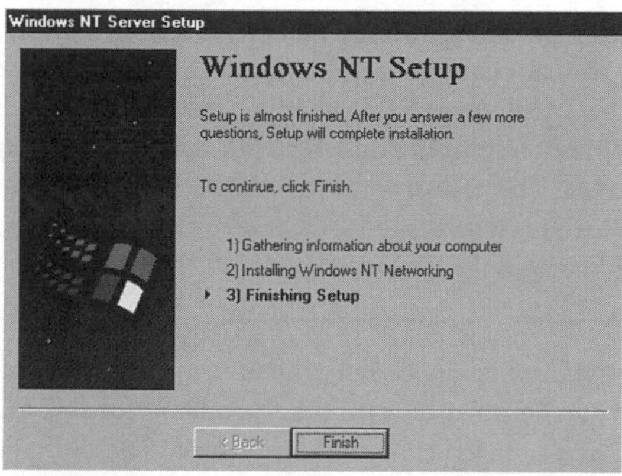

Figure 6.21. *The final step for Setup Wizard.*

IIS and Setting Up the Local Workspace

The Setup Wizard now sets up your menus and program groups. If you chose to install the Microsoft Internet Information Server (IIS), Microsoft Internet Information Server 2.0 Setup (see Figure 6.22) will begin.

Note: If you chose not to install Microsoft Internet Information Server, an icon will be placed on your desktop labeled Install Internet Information Server.

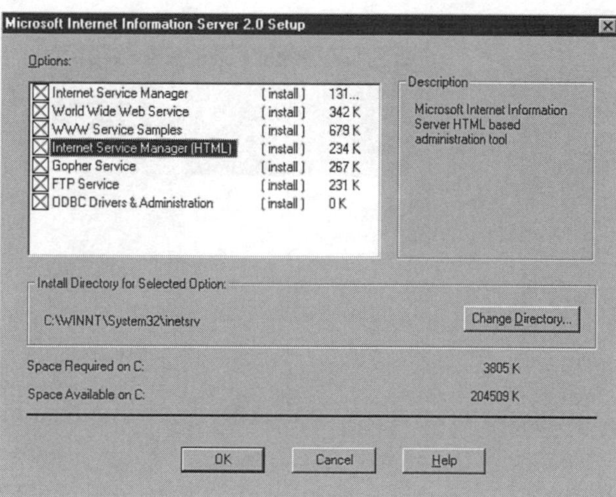

Figure 6.22. *Microsoft Internet Information Server 2.0 Setup.*

By default, IIS will be placed within an INETSVR directory within the Windows NT Server's SYSTEM32 directory. You can change this if you want. Choose the services that you want to run (such as World Wide Web, Gopher, and FTP) and click the Next button. Here you specify where you want the selected services' publishing directories to reside. By default, they will be placed with a directory called InetPub. The necessary files for the IIS services you selected are now copied to the server, and each service is started after those files are copied. See Chapter 49, "Internet Information Server," for more information.

Note: Installing the Gopher service will generate a message (shown in Figure 6.23) that says, "You do not have an Internet domain name declared for this machine. To insure proper gopher functionality, an Internet domain name should be configured through the Network Control Panel Applet." This can be configured after installation has completed and you restart the server.

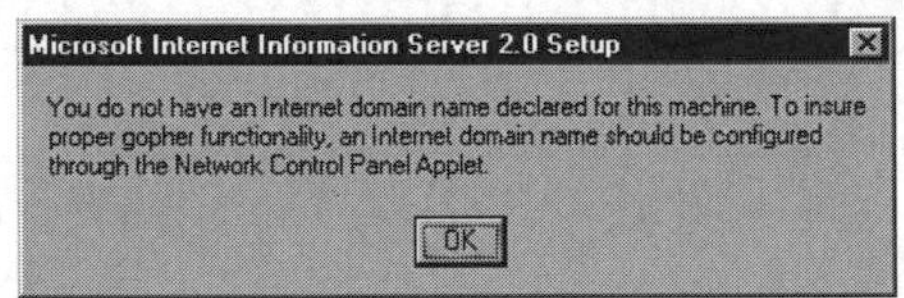

Figure 6.23. *Internet domain name error.*

Clicking the OK button allows the IIS setup to continue. If you had opted to install FTP services, those services would start and you would then be prompted to install ODBC drivers. (See Figure 6.24.) Microsoft Windows NT Server ships with drivers for Microsoft SQL Server, which you can choose to install at this time.

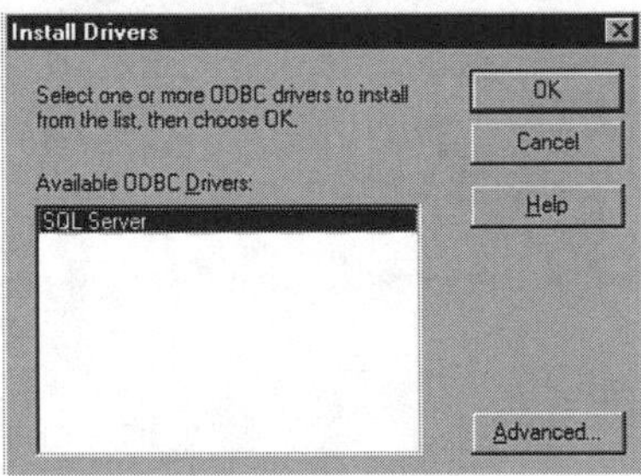

Figure 6.24. *Install ODBC drivers.*

Windows NT Setup continues to set up the default environment for Microsoft Windows NT Server.

The first item you are prompted for is your time zone. As shown in Figure 6.25, a graphical map of the world is shown, and all you need to do is choose from a list of time zones. If you are preparing this server for another location that has another time zone, choose the one that is applicable. Unlike the same option in Windows 95, you cannot just click the map for the proper time zone. You must make your selection from the list.

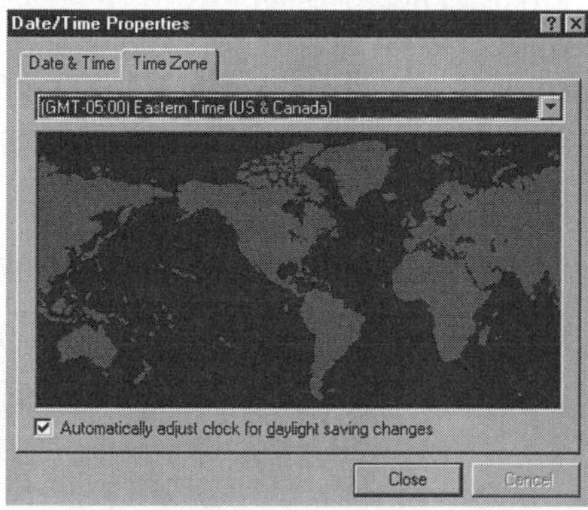

Figure 6.25. *Setting the time zone.*

Click the Date & Time tab to adjust the calendar and time settings for your server. Then click the Close button.

Next, the Setup Wizard tells you whether auto-detect has recognized your video display chip. If it has, it asks you to acknowledge this. If it has not detected it, stick with standard VGA, because you do not want to have to boot to an incomprehensible video display after installation has completed. You can click the Change Display Type button to see a list of video chips that are supported by Windows NT, and you always have the option to click the Have Disk button to use a hardware manufacturer-supplied video driver. As I've said before, however, you want to get through this installation process without incident. Changing the display type is something that you can do after Microsoft Windows NT Server is installed. In fact, when you reboot, you will see that another menu item has been added to the boot menu that enables you to boot NT Server in standard VGA mode, just in case you are having a video driver problem.

Click the OK button, set the horizontal and vertical resolutions by moving the slider, and adjust the color depth or click the List All Modes button to choose from a list of available resolutions and color-depth combinations. You also can set the refresh frequency and specify your preference for using large or small fonts in window titles and menu items.

Click the Test button to let Windows NT check the settings you have specified. After the test has completed, click OK to exit the video display configuration dialog.

After your video mode has been established, Windows NT starts its final file copying from the CD-ROM to your hard drive.

Windows NT then sets up Windows Messaging and, if you already have your hard drive formatted as NTFS, sets security on the system files.

Before you create the Emergency Repair Disk, Windows NT saves your configuration information.

To create the Emergency Repair Disk (see Figure 6.26), insert a 3 1/2-inch disk into your A: drive. The disk will always be formatted for you, so just make sure that it is not write protected. After the format, a number of files are copied to the disk. When it is finished, remove the disk, label it properly, and keep it in a location you will remember if you ever need to use it for recovery or when you need to update it.

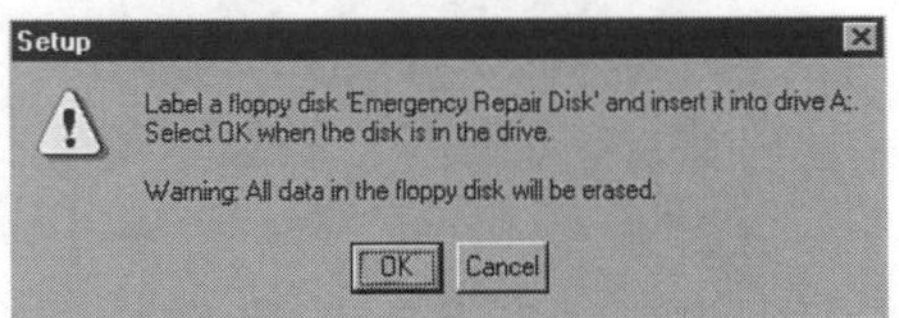

Figure 6.26. *Create the Emergency Repair Disk.*

As shown in Figure 6.27, you've finished installing Windows NT Server! Your server is ready to reboot and run as a Microsoft Windows NT server. Don't forget to make sure that the Emergency Repair Disk is removed from your drive A. Click the Restart Computer button, and your Microsoft Windows NT Server starts up ready for you to log in as Administrator, using the password you specified during setup.

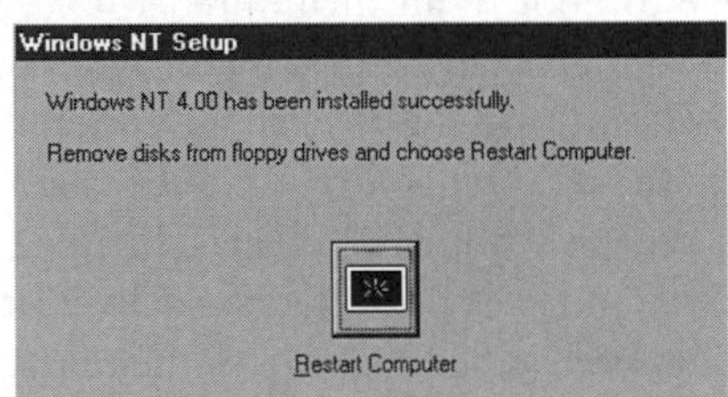

Figure 6.27. *Setup is finished.*

You then can create users, create groups, share drives or directories, create print queues, and do whatever it is that you wanted to do with Microsoft Windows NT Server in the first place.

If you had specified that a partition would be formatted as NTFS or converted to NTFS, it is during this first reboot that the NTFS is created. During the installation, you were still working with FAT. You'll see the conversion taking place, so keep your eye out for it.

Flowchart 6.9 shows the third step of the Setup Wizard.

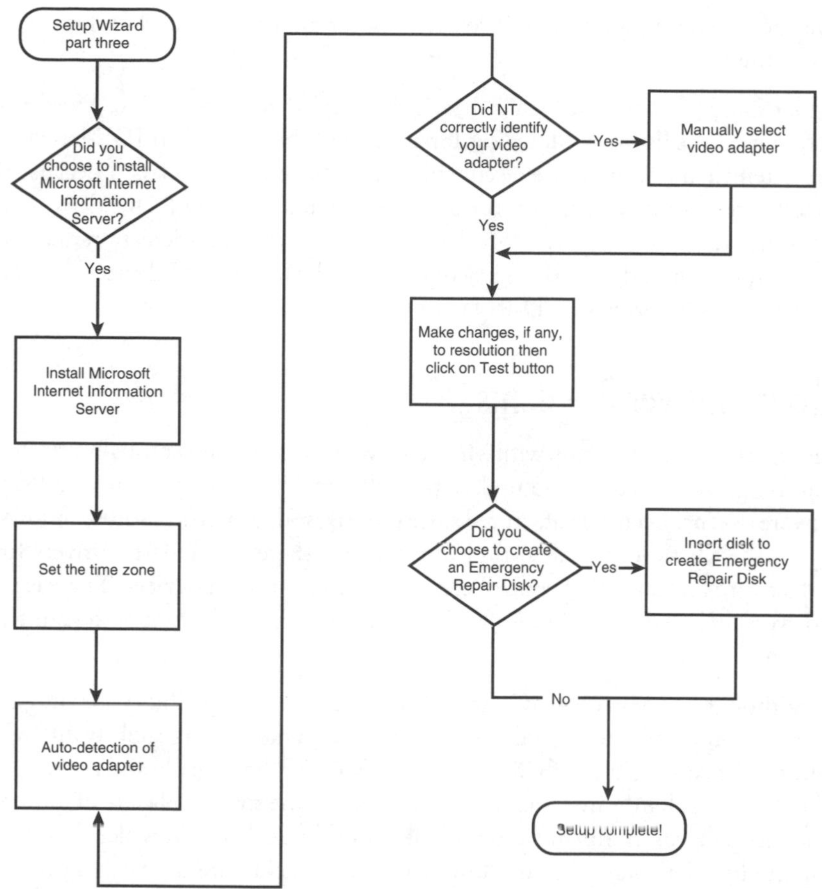

Flowchart 6.9. *Setup Wizard, part three.*

Examining Installation Problems

Sometimes a Microsoft Windows NT Server installation will go as smoothly as the one that I just showed you (and it really did go well the first time through). Then there are the times that things just get totally frustrating.

SCSI Problems

Other times I've had problems installing Microsoft Windows NT Server involved a SCSI controller. Under normal circumstances, a popular SCSI controller is identified properly. An improperly terminated SCSI chain, however, can create a condition that results in an Inaccessible Boot Device error during the first reboot after the character portion of the installation program. It is very important to make sure that both ends of the SCSI chain are terminated. Even if DOS or another operating system is able to overlook certain conditions, Windows NT can be affected by even the smallest error.

Another small problem I've seen is during the SCSI-detection routine. Most people don't think of looking on the list of SCSI devices for an ATAPI driver for their IDE-based CD-ROM drive. More often than not, users are faced with a message asking for Disk 4 because their CD-ROM controller was not detected. As more and more high-speed CD-ROM drives are produced with an IDE interface, it is important to remember that if the auto-detection does not see your IDE controller, you should press the S key to bring up the list of SCSI devices and choose the ATAPI 1.2 option to support your CD-ROM drive.

Hardware Driver Problems

Although the drivers that ship with Microsoft Windows NT Server usually are the latest at the time of shipping, manufacturers do update their drivers from time to time to reflect changes in the hardware that has been manufactured since the release date of Microsoft Windows NT Server. For this reason, whenever possible, find out whether there are updated drivers for your network interface card and any other controllers, sound cards, or other devices. There is no guarantee that the drivers included with Microsoft Windows NT Server will work with your particular piece of hardware.

Also, although the Microsoft Windows NT Hardware Compatibility List might list your server, it also is possible that the manufacturer has shipped a model with slightly different hardware that might not be compatible with Windows NT. Most of the larger brand names perform testing to ensure that their hardware remains compatible, but the smaller players might not be as efficient. Be sure to get a commitment from your dealer or Value Added Reseller regarding Windows NT compatibility. This way, if it turns out that Windows NT cannot install on your server, you have a recourse and can get your server replaced with one that will give you a smooth installation.

Setup Disk Errors

Another problem that can come up is setup floppy disks going bad. This can happen with any floppy disk, so as Murphy's Law would have it, why shouldn't a disk fail during Microsoft Windows NT Server installation?

Well, you do have the option to use the `WINNT.EXE` option and install from MS-DOS (that is, if MS-DOS is already installed on the boot device), but it's a good idea to have a good set of setup disks handy.

To create a new set of setup floppy disks, run the `WINNT.EXE` program from a DOS prompt. This program is located in the `\I386` directory of the CD-ROM, but add to that command line the `/OX` switch. This prompts you for three formatted 3 1/2-inch disks, one at a time. When finished, you will have a brand new set of setup disks from which to work.

General Troubleshooting

In order to troubleshoot a difficult installation, I suggest trying to install another operating system, such as MS-DOS, just to be able to perform simple troubleshooting techniques, such as IRQ or base memory conflicts. Although this method will not always show problems that Windows NT might see, it can help eliminate some of the most obvious problems and actually might clear the way for more easily identifying Windows NT-specific problems.

You also might want to create an MS-DOS bootable disk for quick troubleshooting.

Performing a RISC Installation

Installing Microsoft Windows NT Server on a RISC-based server is not much different from what I've described in the section of this chapter titled "The Installation Process." The major difference is in how to kick off the installation routine and the partitioning requirements.

Microsoft Windows NT Server is supported on servers using DEC's Alpha chip, a PowerPC chip, or a MIPS chip. These are Advanced RISC Computer (ARC)-compliant RISC systems, which are the only type on which Windows NT can run.

The Microsoft Windows NT Server CD-ROM has separate directories for each of these platforms. There is no need for a boot floppy disk because the installation program runs directly from the CD-ROM.

A minimum 2MB FAT partition is required on these systems for the boot partition; however, the rest of the hard drive space may be configured as NTFS.

If you are upgrading from a previous version of Microsoft Windows NT Server, you can use the `WINNT32.EXE` program from the directory that identifies the type of RISC chip that is in your server.

Incidentally, I'm convinced that a RISC-based Windows NT server is the ultimate Windows NT server. Using a DEC AlphaServer that was running on twin 233mHz Alpha chips took only 15 minutes to get up and running. I can only imagine what the 400 and 500mHz chips can do.

To install Microsoft Windows NT Server, insert the Microsoft Windows NT Server CD-ROM into your CD-ROM drive and restart your server. When the ARC screen appears, choose Run A Program from the menu. From the prompt, type whatever is appropriate to show that you are executing a program from the CD-ROM (`cd:`, for example) followed by a backslash (`\`), the type of system you are running on (MIPS, ALPHA, or PPC), another backslash, and then `SETUPLDR`.

On a DEC Alpha server, for example, enter the following:

```
cd:\alpha\setupldr
```

Then press Enter.

Note: Some of the recent DEC AlphaServers include a menu item, Install Microsoft Windows NT Server, on their ARC menu.

After you choose the option described in the preceding Note, the installation program will prompt you to specify where you want to install Microsoft Windows NT Server. If your system partition is large enough (more than 110MB), you can install Microsoft Windows NT Server onto it. Otherwise, only `OSLOADER.EXE` and `HAL.DLL` are copied into a subdirectory, `\OS\WINNT`.

Warning: Never delete the files that are in the `\OS\WINNT` directory. If you do, however, you can replace them, because they also are copied onto your Emergency Repair Disk.

Be sure that you use the video driver that has been supplied with the server, or contact Digital for an updated video driver. I have found that choosing VGA-compatible as your video driver just doesn't cut it on an AlphaServer.

Summary

Installing Microsoft Windows NT Server requires careful planning. The hardware must be carefully scrutinized to ensure that the installation process will run smoothly. If you are installing your first server, the design of your network should include creating naming standards and should take into consideration the amount of growth that your company may encounter.

Know how you want to set up your file system in advance. Be prepared to provide the installation program the necessary parameters, such as a computer name, domain name, server role, type of SCSI adapter, type of network adapter, and settings for the network adapter. Know what protocols and additional services you wish to install, such as Remote Access Services (RAS), Dynamic Host Configuration Protocol (DHCP), and the Microsoft Internet Information Server (IIS).

CHAPTER

Upgrading Windows NT

by Robert Reinstein

Upgrading from a previous version of Windows NT to version 4.0 is a very simple process. There are few decisions to make and there is limited interaction with the setup program during the installation.

This chapter covers the following subjects:

- Preparing for a Windows NT upgrade
- Different Windows NT upgrade methods
- Performing a Windows NT upgrade

Major Changes

Be aware that the major change from earlier versions of Windows NT is in the video portion, which will require an updated driver. Before you proceed on the upgrade process, be sure to check to see if Windows NT 4.0 comes with an updated video driver; otherwise, contact your video chip manufacturer.

The other major change is the Windows 95 interface that you will find after the upgrade process has completed and you reboot your computer. Although this interface is considered by most to be easier to use than the old Program Manager/ File Manager combination, it will create a learning curve for those of you who have not already been working with Windows 95.

Decisions to Make Before Upgrading

Prior to performing the installation process, there are questions you should ask yourself:

> Do I want to test this newer version of Windows NT before I actually upgrade?
>
> Are there newer versions of my applications that are required to run on Windows NT version 4.0?
>
> Are there updated drivers for my hardware included with Windows NT 4.0, or do I need to obtain them from the hardware manufacturer?
>
> Do I want the ability to back out of this upgrade and revert to my older version of Windows NT?

When you perform an upgrade of Windows NT, you are actually overwriting your older version of Windows NT, thus you cannot revert back to the older version. Therefore, a careful test of the newer version is important. Of course, you can install the new version to a different directory, but the settings from the older version will be ignored, forcing you to reconfigure (in order to add users, permissions, and so on).

Tip: It would have been nice if Microsoft provided a way to perform an upgrade to a different directory. This way system settings could be pulled in from the older version and placed into the new version without overwriting the older version of Windows NT. A roundabout way of doing this is to back up your current Windows NT directory to a new directory and then perform the upgrade. To return to the original version, delete the upgraded directory and rename the copy to the original directory. This will use a lot more disk space, but gives you a way to revert to the original version.

Newer software is being released that is "Windows NT 4.0 compatible." You need to find out from the manufacturers of your software if they have a newer version that is required to run on Windows NT 4.0. The HCL (Hardware Compatibility List) that ships in the Windows NT 4.0 box will let you know if a Windows NT 4.0 compatible driver is shipped for your hardware, most notably a SCSI and network adapter. If a new driver is not included, I suggest that you either call the manufacturer's bulletin board or go to its Web site to see if newer drivers are available.

Tip: To obtain a revised HCL, download it from Microsoft's Web site at `www.microsoft.com`.

A careful test of Windows NT 4.0 would be done by loading Windows NT 4.0 on a computer and simulating the types of work that would usually be done under production.

In the case of a server, a Windows NT 4.0 server could be added to the existing network as a member server or as a BDC without changing the production environment. However, there have been reports of incompatibilities when adding computers running Windows NT 4.0 to a Windows NT 3.51 or earlier domain.

Testing Windows NT 4.0 should be done outside of a production environment if you are able to simulate production conditions, such as user loads and print queues.

Load all the software that your users will be running on Windows NT 4.0 on a Windows NT 4.0 workstation and make sure that there are no incompatibilities that would prevent your clients from being able to carry on their usual day-to-day business.

Microsoft has documents and tools that can be helpful for evaluating the new version of Windows NT 4.0, such as white papers, that provide an excellent step-by-step evaluation plan. These are available at Microsoft's Web site.

After all these items have been considered, you should be able to make an informed decision on whether to perform the upgrade.

Note: The default installation directory for Windows NT 3.51 was WINNT35. Therefore, your Windows NT 4.0 upgrade may end up residing in a directory named WINNT35. You can only change the name of the target directory when performing a fresh install.

Upgrade Methods

The different methods that are available to you for performing the upgrade are the same as the different methods available for installing Windows NT. The recommended method of upgrading Windows NT is by using the `WINNT32.EXE` program. In Figure 7.1, I have started the WINNT32 program by issuing the command with the `/B` switch, which bypasses the creation of the setup floppies.

Note: An unattended upgrade can be performed by running either WINNT /U or WINNT32 /U. Unattended installations, including upgrades, are discussed in the next chapter, "Customizing the Installation Process."

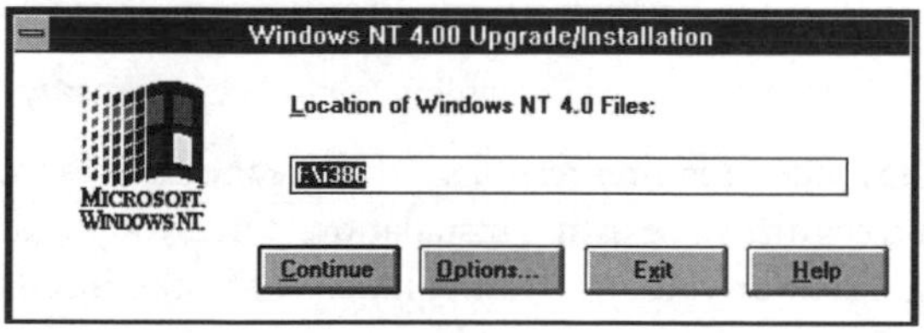

Figure 7.1. *The WINNT32 program.*

Performing the Upgrade

Caution: A full backup of your computer should be done prior to the upgrade procedure. An incomplete upgrade could render your operating system unusable, and your Emergency Repair Disk might not be helpful enough to bring back the system.

Running the WINNT32 program will create two temporary directories on the Windows NT computer. One is named `$WIN_NT$.~BT` and the other is named `$WIN_NT$.~LS`.

After these directories have been created, files are copied to both directories, as shown in Figure 7.2. After the copy routine has completed, you will be prompted to restart your computer. (See Figure 7.3.) When the computer reboots, the installation process will proceed as if you were using the setup boot disk.

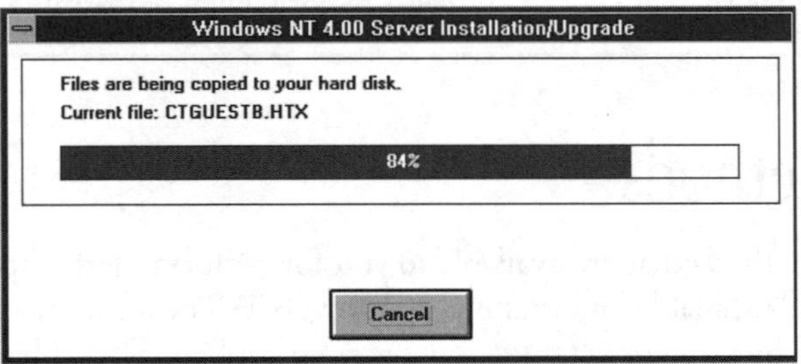

Figure 7.2. *WINNT32 copying files.*

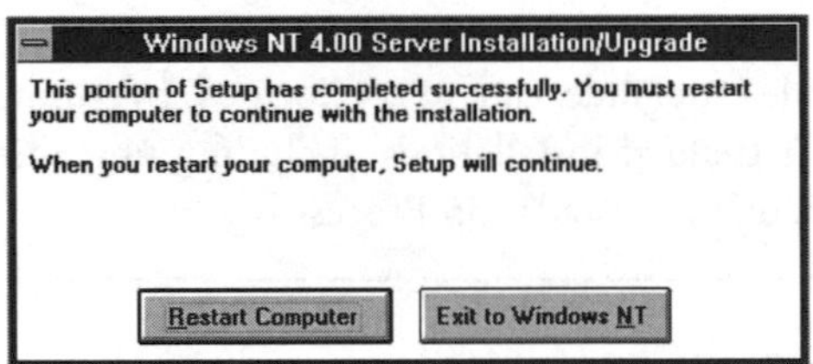

Figure 7.3. *The initial step of WINNT32, running on Windows NT 3.51, has completed.*

Starting the upgrade process requires responses that are the same as the full installation. However, at one point it will recognize the existing installation. Then you need to indicate whether you are performing a fresh install or you want to upgrade. When the installation program reaches that point, press Enter to perform the upgrade. Next, a list appears of previously installed versions of Windows NT, taken from the `BOOT.INI` file. Select the appropriate entry to proceed with the upgrade.

The upgrade routine will then delete some files that were used in the previous version, but are not used in the new version, and then copy files.

Because an upgrade is being performed, questions regarding the computer name and workgroup or domain settings will not be posed.

Note: During my upgrade, the installation program asked me if I wanted to overwrite my third-party network adapter drivers with Microsoft drivers. Because my drivers were designed for Windows NT version 3.51, and the Microsoft drivers were designed for Windows NT version 4.0, I opted to allow these files to be overwritten.

After the new files have been copied to the Windows NT directory and the new master boot sector has been created, the system will reboot again, just like a nonupgrade Windows NT installation process.

Upgrade Setup Wizard

The Setup Wizard used in the graphical part of the update process is almost the same as with the regular Windows NT installation process.

In this case though, as shown in Figure 7.4, the process is clearly identified as an upgrade, and many decisions that are required during the normal install are not needed for an upgrade. The Setup Wizard is still split into three sections, and any items that are new to Windows NT 4.0 will still require configuration.

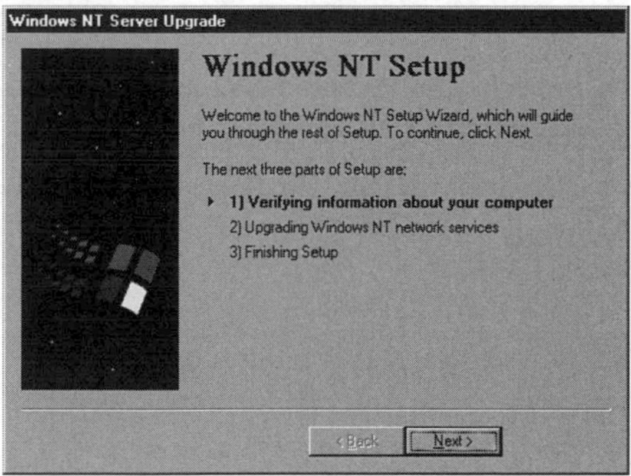

Figure 7.4. *The Upgrade Setup Wizard.*

New to NT 4.0: During the first step you will be asked if you want to install Microsoft Internet Information Server (IIS), which is Microsoft's Web, FTP, and Gopher server, or in the case of Windows NT Workstation, you'll be asked about installing peer Web services, which is Microsoft's new scaled-down version of IIS, which is to be used in a peer networking environment.

When you reach the second step (see Figure 7.5), which is when networking services are installed and configured, you will still be asked about installing additional services. You will also be required to verify the configuration for your network adapter(s) and protocols.

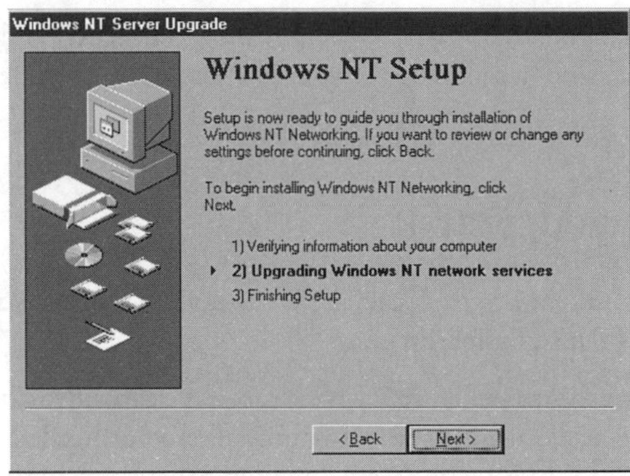

Figure 7.5. *Step two of Setup Wizard.*

After the networking issues have been resolved, the final copying of files will occur. Desktop settings will be retained, but these settings will now exist in Windows 95 style, which means that instead of Program Manager groups, your icons will appear in Start menu program folders. Your choice of wallpaper will remain, as will your system colors.

Once the completion dialog has been shown (see Figure 7.6), click the button and your computer will restart as a Windows NT 4.0 computer. The option of Windows NT in the OS Loader menu will also be updated.

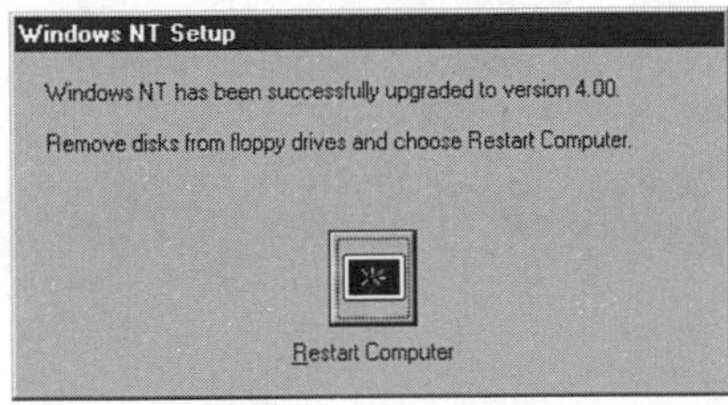

Figure 7.6. *Completed upgrade.*

Summary

The Windows NT upgrade process is a simple one, but you must be just as aware of your hardware and software settings as you had been when you first installed Windows NT on your computer.

Customizing the Installation Process

by Robert Reinstein

Installing Windows NT is fairly straightforward, if you know in advance the settings that are required during the installation process. But installing Windows NT onto multiple computers can get to be a tedious process, particularly if you have to roll out hundreds of workstations or set up dozens of servers. It's especially tedious if you have to make numerous configuration choices during each install. This is why Microsoft has furnished users with tools that allow for the creation of an unattended install and for customized installations.

This chapter discusses the following subjects:

- Rolling out Windows NT to multiple computers
- Using the Windows NT Setup Manager
- Modifying the Windows NT installation process using the SYSDIFF utility

Deploying Windows NT

Whether you're deploying computers running Windows NT Workstation or rolling out several servers running Windows NT Server, you have easier ways to carry out your task than having to perform the manual installation over and over again.

The key to a proper deployment of computers running Windows NT is being able to perform at least one successful manual installation for each type of hardware and software configuration you'll be using.

When you do perform a manual installation, you can identify the various hardware components you need to install drivers for, specify the proper video resolution, ensure connectivity to your LAN or WAN, and identify the needed software components included in Windows NT, or the unnecessary components of Windows NT.

It is also essential that any third-party software you want to run on Windows NT be thoroughly tested before you decide to start loading up multiple computers with Windows NT and that software. Because Windows NT is not 100 percent backward compatible, some tweaking might be necessary for the software to run properly or, in some instances, you might find that the software cannot run properly at all.

Types of Customized Windows NT Installations

After you have determined the proper Windows NT installation, you can decide which type of customized Windows NT installation technique would be suitable for you.

An unattended installation allows you to create a file, called an answer file, that will eliminate the need for you to be present during the entire installation process. This type of installation is great when all you need to do is set up computers running the Windows NT operating system, and nothing more.

If you want to pre-install one or more applications on each of these computers, you can use another tool that will make the necessary changes to the "plain vanilla" Windows NT installation and give you a computer that not only has a fully configured copy of Windows NT, but also has preinstalled application software. This task includes simply having additional bitmaps or other files added to the default Windows NT installation.

Performing either of these modified installation processes requires testing and patience, depending on how modified the installation becomes. It also depends on the complexity of the hardware you are using and whether third-party drivers support these methods of installations.

In most cases, you should be able to come up with a deployment scheme that is easier than having to perform a manual installation on every computer you want to install Windows NT on.

Unattended Installation

To summarize the ordinary Windows NT Workstation installation process, you must choose the target directory, the file system, the computer name, the name of a workgroup or domain, the type of network adapter, the type of video adapter, and other little options. A Windows NT Server installation includes the same choices as Windows NT Workstation but also requires determining a server's role, the licensing mode, and configuration of Microsoft Internet Information Server.

Microsoft has recognized that these decisions can be made during the installation of the first computer, and then those decisions can be utilized for any other computers getting the same installation. Of course, the computer name must always be unique, and in the case of servers, the role might be different; but on identical hardware within the same organization, many of the decisions are the same between computers.

The tool that Microsoft provides is what is called Setup Manager.

Setup Manager is not installed as part of the usual Windows NT installation, but it is located on the Windows NT CD-ROM in the `\SUPPORT\DEPTOOLS\I386` directory as `SETUPMGR.EXE`.

Setup Manager allows you to enter information you would usually provide during the installation routine and save that information as a text file. Then, whenever you want to install a fresh copy of Windows NT, all you need to do is open that text file in Setup Manager and change the appropriate items, such as Computer Name and perhaps Server Role. The Setup Manager on the Windows NT Server CD-ROM and the one on Windows NT Workstation are both the same program.

The output from Setup Manager can be used along with the `WINNT` or `WINNT32` command as an answer file.

As shown in Figure 8.1, Setup Manager has three buttons, each of which I refer to as a part of Setup Manager.

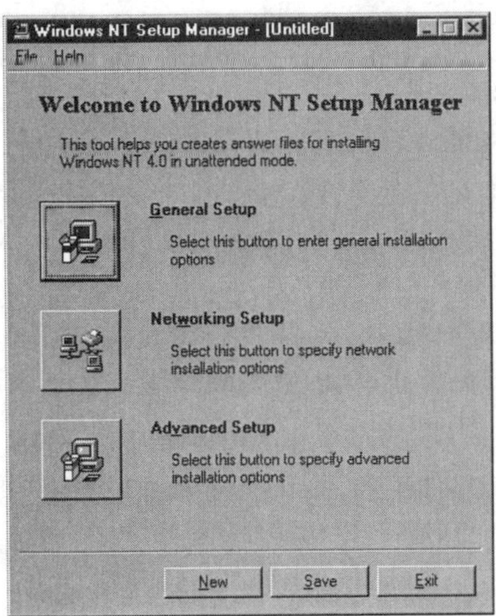

Figure 8.1. *Windows NT Setup Manager.*

Setup Manager, Part One: General Setup

The first part of Setup Manager is General Setup. The seven tabs in this dialog represent general information. The first tab, User Information, which is shown in Figure 8.2, contains the computer name, which must be different for each installation.

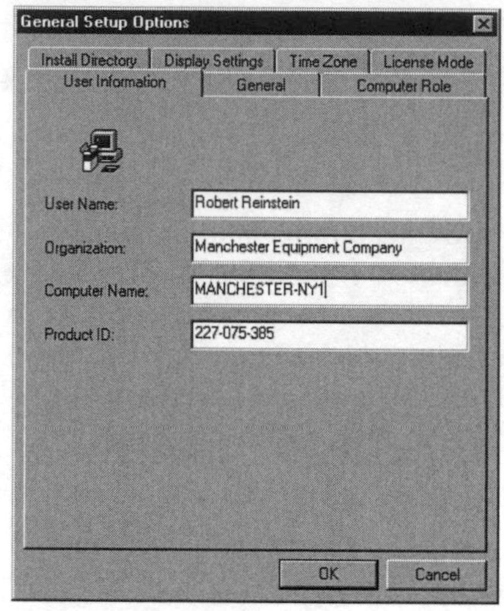

Figure 8.2. *The User Information tab of General Setup.*

The General tab, shown in Figure 8.3, allows you to specify whether to confirm hardware during the installation process. This can be important if you are installing onto computers that have different revisions of a BIOS on, for instance, a video card that might or might not work with the driver shipped with Windows NT.

The General tab also allows you to make a choice regarding upgrades. It lets you choose the installation to upgrade, upgrade the first installed version of Windows NT it finds, or upgrade Windows 3.1 or Windows for Workgroups.

The Overwrite OEM Files On Upgrade check box allows you to specify that older third-party drivers that were installed with an earlier version of Windows NT can be automatically overwritten by the new 4.0 version. By default, Microsoft does not overwrite third-party drivers.

The option to run a program along with setup is available from this tab, too.

The Computer Role tab, shown in Figure 8.4, lets you choose the type of computer you are installing Windows NT on. The choices include PDC, BDC, Server in a domain or Server in a workgroup for Windows NT Server, and Workstation in a domain or Workstation in a workgroup for Windows NT Workstation. You must also enter the domain name or workgroup name.

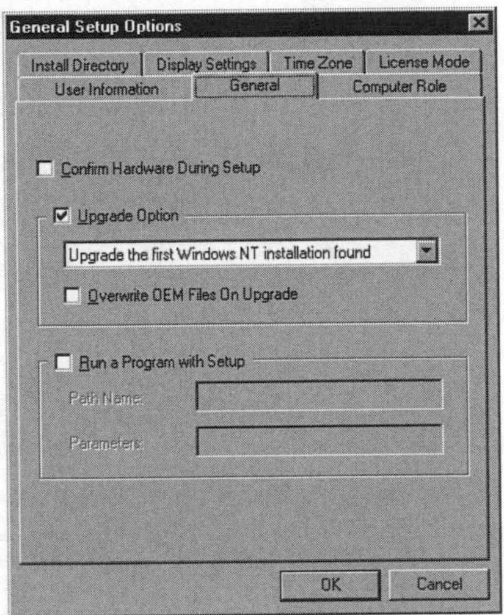

Figure 8.3. The General tab of General Setup.

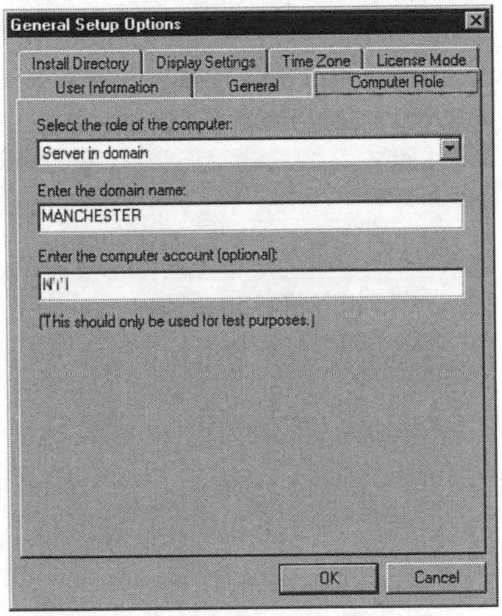

Figure 8.4. The Computer Role tab of General Setup.

If you're joining a domain, you should specify a computer account to allow the installation program to test access to the domain.

On the Install Directory tab, shown in Figure 8.5, you can choose the default `\WINNT` directory, specify a directory, or choose to be prompted for the directory during the installation process.

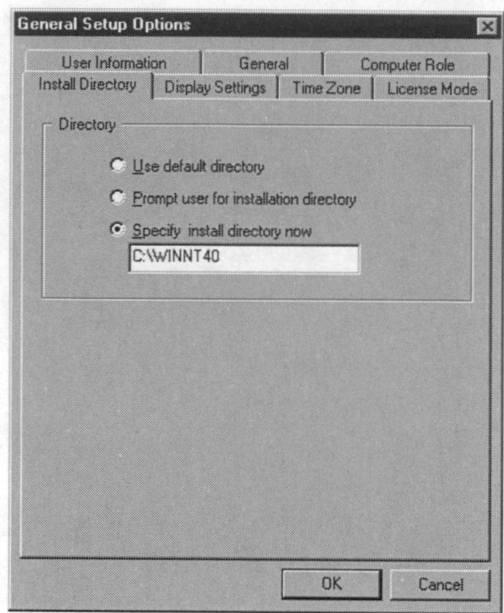

Figure 8.5. *The Install Directory tab of General Setup.*

As shown in Figure 8.6, the Display Settings tab allows you to enter values for the type of resolution you want automatically installed, or you can tell the installation program to wait to configure the video mode until the user actually logs on for the first time.

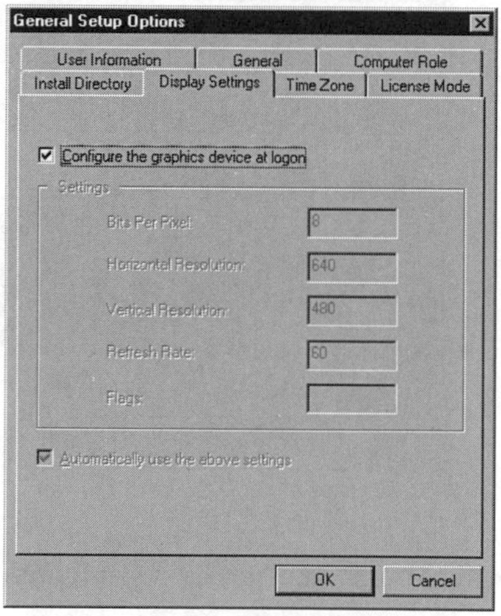

Figure 8.6. *The Display Settings tab of General Setup.*

The Time Zone tab lets you select the appropriate time zone for the computer.

If you are setting up this computer as a server, use the License Mode tab to specify whether to use Per Seat or Per Server licensing.

After you have completed these settings, click the OK button.

Setup Manager, Part Two: Networking Setup

The second part of Setup Manager is the Networking Setup, shown in Figure 8.7.

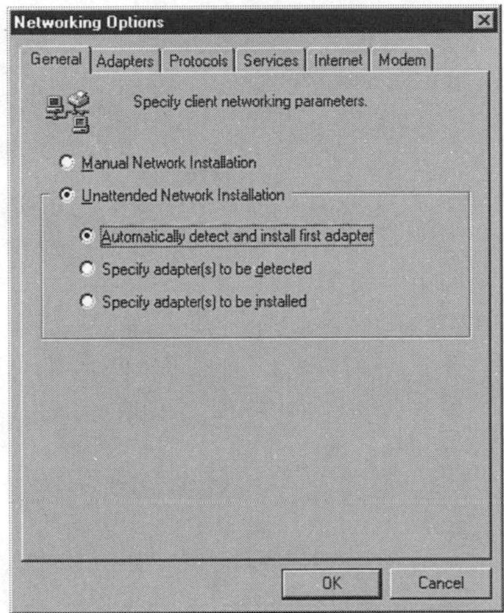

Figure 8.7. *The General tab of Networking Setup.*

From the General tab, you can opt to install networking manually, which is usually the route you would take if you had circumstances a totally unattended install could not handle, such as loading of third-party services or protocols.

You also have the option to manually select one or more network adapters from within the unattended installation.

If you have chosen to have Setup detect your adapter, you won't have access to the Adapters tab. If, however, you have specified that you want to select adapters or have a particular adapter detected, use the Adapters tab to select from a list of adapters. You can also choose to install a third-party adapter. Certain parameters are required, however, in order to install a third-party driver, and those parameters are not always readily available.

In one of the deployments I was part of, we wanted to load Windows NT Workstation on 200 laptops. For the most part, the creation of the answer file handled most of the tasks. However, the configuration for the driver for the PCMCIA Ethernet adapter did not support the unattended installation method, and we had to perform the configuration manually whenever the installation program got to the part where the network adapter is installed. After installing the driver, the unattended installation resumed without a hitch.

The Protocols tab, shown in Figure 8.8, allows you to choose NetBEUI, IPX, TCP/IP, or any combination of the three. In Figure 8.8, I've selected to install TCP/IP. By default, TCP/IP is configured to use DHCP. If this is not the case, click the Parameters button to configure the protocol. The TCP/IP Protocol Parameters dialog allows you to enter every possible parameter that is applicable to TCP/IP. Third-party or unlisted protocols can also be added here, but the parameters that are required to install the protocols properly require knowledge of what the required parameters are.

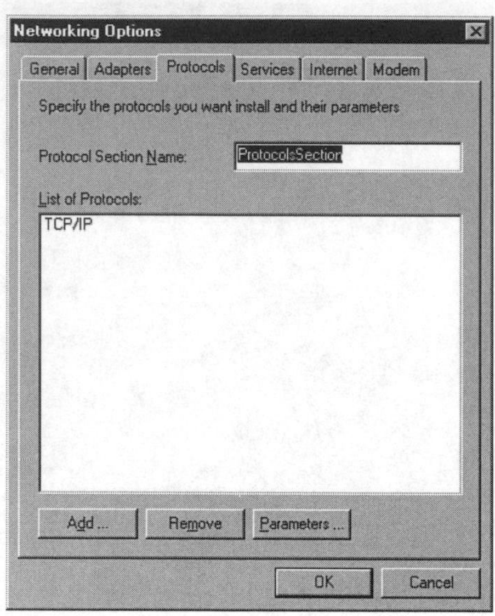

Figure 8.8. *The Protocols tab of Networking Options.*

> **Tip:** You can use a computer that already has the other protocol installed to derive the necessary parameters, but be sure to test the results before deploying the Setup Manager–generated answer file.

As shown in Figure 8.9, the Services tab allows you to easily choose the SNMP Server, Client Access for NetWare, and Remote Access Services (RAS). It, too, has a Parameters button for properly configuring these services. In the example shown in Figure 8.9, I had added the Client Access for NetWare service and clicked the Parameters button. The resulting dialog asks for a default server and gives a few login script options.

As with the Protocols dialog, you can add other services besides those listed, but you must be very familiar with the necessary parameters that are required to install these services properly.

If you choose to install RAS, many items require configuration, as shown in Figure 8.10. When you click the Parameters button for RAS, a multitabbed dialog is displayed. After this configuration is completed, you need to add modems to this Windows NT installation by choosing the Modems tab and adding a modem description.

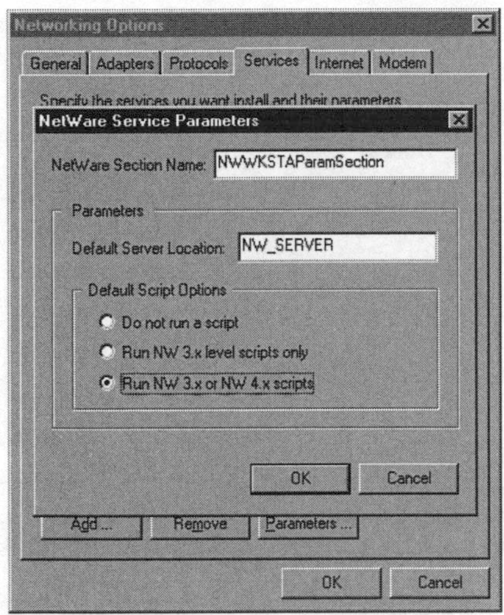

Figure 8.9. *NetWare Service Parameters.*

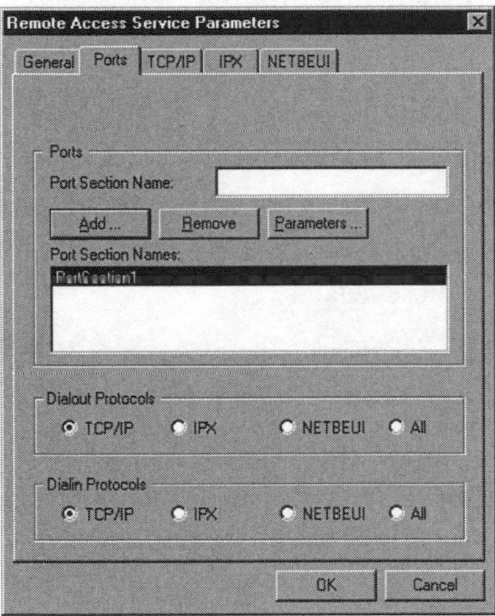

Figure 8.10. *Remote Access Service Parameters.*

The next tab is the Internet tab, which is used to configure the installation of Microsoft Internet Information Server (IIS). As shown in Figure 8.11, many configuration items need to be evaluated (shown here are the default settings). You also have the option of not installing IIS, by placing a check mark in the check box labeled Do not install Internet Server.

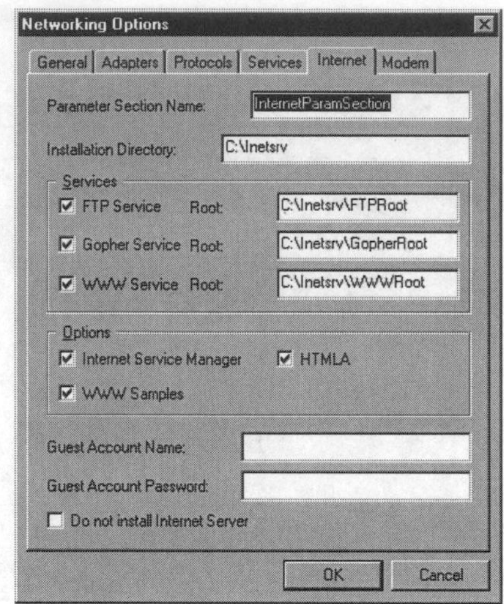

Figure 8.11. *The Internet tab of Networking Options.*

After you have completed your entries for the Networking Options, click OK to return to the Setup Manager main screen.

Setup Manager, Part Three: Advanced Setup

The third part of Setup Manager is the Advanced Setup. These options are, for the most part, items that would normally have a default behavior during the installation, but using these options gives you the ability to override those defaults.

The General tab for Advanced Setup, shown in Figure 8.12, allows you to specify a different HAL than the default Intel HAL. You can also specify a keyboard other than the default 101/102 U.S. layout.

The Reboot section comes in very handy when you want the unattended installation to run truly unattended. If you check the After Text Mode and After GUI Mode check boxes, the installation routine should run straight through without any user intervention.

The Skip Welcome wizard page check box removes another halt from an otherwise unattended installation. The Skip Administrator Password Wizard page sets the administrator's password default to null.

Tip: If you decide to use a null administrator's password for the sake of not having to enter it during the installation, be sure to create a password on the administrator's account after the installation is complete.

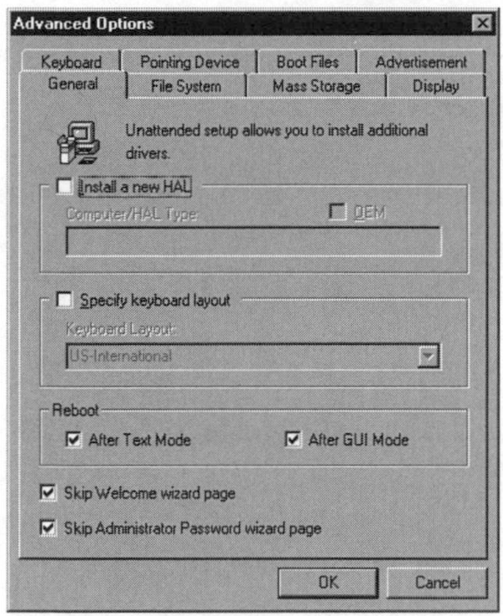

Figure 8.12. *The General tab of Advanced Setup.*

The File System tab allows you to have the installation program flag the system drive for conversion from FAT to NTFS.

The Advertisement tab lets you customize the background during the graphical portion of the installation routine. This is the one you can have fun with.

The other tabs in the Advanced Setup call for advanced knowledge in order to take advantage of them. I would highly recommend using them only if you test the use of these options before implementing them.

After entering the options you want to use, click OK to return to the Setup Manager main screen. When all three sections have been completed, click the Save button to create the text file.

The Setup Manager Answer File

The results of what I did with Setup Manager are shown in Listing 8.1.

Listing 8.1. The results from Setup Manager: The answer file.

```
[Unattended]
OemPreinstall = yes
NoWaitAfterTextMode = 1
NoWaitAfterGUIMode = 1
FileSystem = LeaveAlone
ExtendOEMPartition = 0
ConfirmHardware = no
NtUpgrade = no
Win31Upgrade = yes
```

continues

Listing 8.1. continued

```
TargetPath = C:\WINNT40
OverwriteOemFilesOnUpgrade = no

[UserData]
FullName = "Robert Reinstein"
OrgName = "Manchester Equipment Company"
ComputerName = MANCHESTER-NY1
ProductId = "227-075-385"

[GuiUnattended]
OemSkipWelcome = 1
OEMBlankAdminPassword = 1
TimeZone = "(GMT-05:00) Eastern Time (US & Canada)"
AdvServerType = SERVERNT

[LicenseFilePrintData]
AutoMode = PerSeat

[Display]
ConfigureAtLogon = 1

[Network]
DetectAdapters = ""
InstallProtocols = ProtocolsSection
InstallInternetServer = InternetParamSection
JoinDomain = MANCHESTER
CreateComputerAccount = NY1

[ProtocolsSection]
TC = TCParamSection

[TCParamSection]

[InternetParamSection]
InstallDir = C:\Inetsrv
InstallINETSTP = 1
InstallWWW = 1
WWWRoot = C:\Inetsrv\WWWRoot
InstallGOPHER = 1
GopherRoot = C:\Inetsrv\GopherRoot
InstallFTP = 1
FTPRoot = C:\Inetsrv\FTPRoot
InstallADMIN = 1
InstallW3SAMP = 1
InstallHTMLA = 1
```

To use the preceding answer file, which I had saved as `RR.TXT`, in an actual installation, you would use the command `WINNT/S:I:\I386/U:RR.TXT` or `WINNT32 /S:I:\I386/U:RR.TXT`, in which `I:\I386` is the source for the Windows NT installation files.

Tip: To perform an upgrade in unattended mode, you can simply run `WINNT/U` or `WINNT32 /U`, and the information from the current installation will be used in place of an answer file.

Automating Adding Programs to a Windows NT Installation

Windows NT 4.0 comes with a utility that allows you to modify the unattended installation that was just discussed in the section "Unattended Installation."

With the SYSDIFF utility, you can take a snapshot of a fresh Windows NT installation; then, after you make modifications to the installation, such as adding files to the Windows NT directories or installing programs, SYSDIFF creates a text file detailing the changes that were made. You can then use the resulting text file to perform an unattended installation that deploys not only Windows NT, but also additional files and applications.

Any files that have been added to the hard drive will be copied to a subdirectory within your Windows NT distribution share. SYSDIFF requires that you deploy Windows NT from a network distribution share.

Within the network distribution share, a directory named `$OEM$` is created. This is the directory that will hold the files that have been added to the base Windows NT installation.

Warning: The SYSDIFF utility does not make changes to the `HKEY_LOCAL_USER` tree in the Windows NT Registry; therefore, any programs that are user-specific and make changes to that part of the Registry may not be installed properly using SYSDIFF.

The SYSDIFF Files

The SYSDIFF utility is located on the Windows NT CD-ROM in the `\SUPPORT\DEPTOOLS\I386` directory. The two files used by SYSDIFF are `SYSDIFF.EXE` and `SYSDIFF.INF`.

`SYSDIFF.INF` is a text file that handles the configuration for the SYSDIFF program. The `SYSDIFF.INF` file is used to exclude drives, directories, or specific files from being profiled during the SYSDIFF routine. This is important if you are running SYSDIFF on a computer that already has data on it.

Tip: If you have installed Windows NT on a computer that has multiple hard drives that contain data, you might want to exclude from the SYSDIFF process the drives that are not part of the Windows NT installation, because the SYSDIFF process can take a long time to profile every directory.

Running SYSDIFF

Running the SYSDIFF program requires that the computer it is run on have a freshly installed copy of Windows NT on it. If the computer already had programs installed on its local hard drive, those files will be inventoried and counted as if they were part of the original Windows NT install. This brings up a problem: If you upgraded from an earlier version of Windows NT or Windows, whatever programs were already installed will not be carried over into the `$OEM$` directory.

The actual SYSDIFF process is a three-step process. The first step, shown in Figure 8.13, is known as the SNAP process. It runs through the local hard drives and creates a snapshot of all files and directories, paying closest attention to INI files, and also creates a snapshot of the Windows NT Registry.

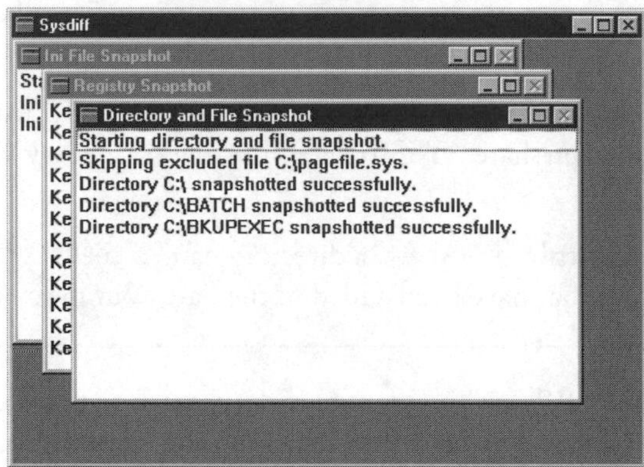

Figure 8.13. *The SYSDIFF SNAP process.*

The following is the proper syntax for the SNAP process:

```
sysdiff /snap c:\temp\snap.img
```

In this syntax, *`c:\temp\snap.img`* is the name of the output file for the SNAP process. The path can be any path, but a local path is preferred for performance.

During the SNAP process, you will see three windows open within the SYSDIFF program. One of the windows is scanning and tracking the Windows NT Registry. The second window is going through the directory trees and creating a snapshot of all the directories and files. The third window is creating a snapshot of the INI files that have been encountered by the directory scan.

> **Note:** This program is a great demonstration of Windows NT's preemptive multitasking.

Next, you install the programs or add the files you want to add to the Windows NT installation.

The second step is the DIFF process, shown in Figure 8.14, which identifies the changes that have been made to the system since the SNAP process took place.

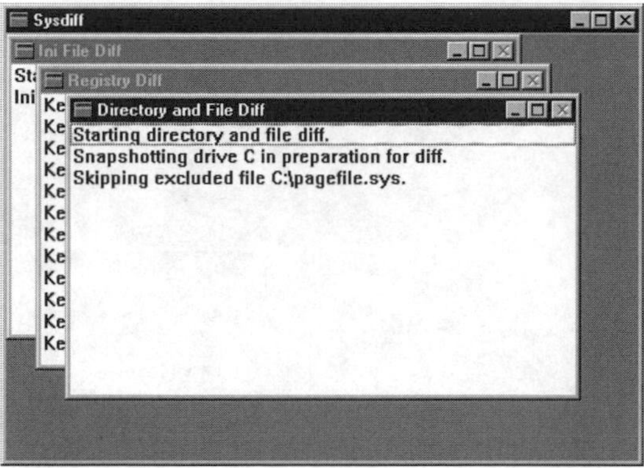

Figure 8.14. *The SYSDIFF DIFF process.*

The proper syntax for the DIFF process is this:

```
sysdiff /diff c:\temp\snap.img c:\temp\diff.img
```

Here, `c:\temp\snap.img` identifies the file created by the SNAP process, and `c:\temp\diff.img` is the output file for this step. Again, the path can be any path, but a local hard drive will increase the performance of this task.

The DIFF process appears similar to the SNAP process in that three windows open within the SYSDIFF program. This time, however, they are looking for the changes made to the directory structures, the INI files, and the Windows NT Registry.

The third step is the INF step, which builds the `$OEM$` directory within the Windows NT installation share.

Here is the proper syntax for the INF step:

```
sysdiff /inf /m c:\temp\diff.img z:\
```

The `/m` switch tells the SYSDIFF program to create shortcuts for the Windows NT Start menu, if any have been added. `c:\temp\diff.img` is the file that was created by the DIFF process. And `z:\` is the path for the Windows NT installation files share. If the Windows NT installation files have been placed within a directory, such as the `I386` directory, be sure to include that as part of this path, because this path is being used to indicate the path in which the `$OEM$` directory structure will be created.

When the INF process has completed, the message box shown in Figure 8.15 is displayed.

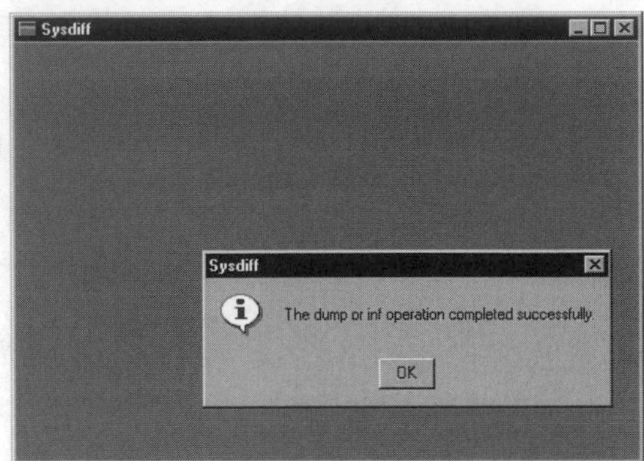

Figure 8.15. *The INF process has completed.*

OEM Installation

The SYSDIFF process takes advantage of a feature that is part of the Windows NT unattended installation process.

As shown in Listing 8.1, the first two lines in the output of Setup Manager were

```
[Unattended]
OemPreinstall = yes
```

It is the `OemPreinstall` line that identifies to the Windows NT installation process that a `$OEM$` directory might exist within the Windows NT installation files directory. The `$OEM$` directory structure is one that is known by the Windows NT installation program, and it is handled in a unique manner, which I will explain shortly.

The `OemPreinstall` option allows for the distribution of customized versions of Windows NT. The SYSDIFF utility then emulates the process that can be used by an OEM (Original Equipment Manufacturer) for creating its customized version of Windows NT.

The directory structure created for the `$OEM$` directory is very interesting.

When I ran SYSDIFF for these screen shots, I had installed the Microsoft Exchange client for Windows NT between the SNAP and DIFF processes. Within the `$OEM$` directory were two directories. One was the `$$` directory. This directory contained files to be copied or updated within the Windows NT installation directory.

Another directory was created within the `$OEM$` directory. Because I had installed the Microsoft Exchange client to my C: drive, a directory named `C` was created. Within this directory were the directory and files that needed to be copied to the C: drive.

Within both the `$$` and the `C` directory were files named `$$rename.txt`. Because the file copy part of the Windows NT installation process might occur under MS-DOS, files with long filenames do not copy with their long filenames left intact. The `$$rename.txt` file lists the files with their 8.3 filenames and their long filenames so that the files can be renamed to their appropriate filenames.

Listing 8.2 shows the contents of the `$$rename.txt` file that was created within the `$$` directory.

Listing 8.2. The `$$rename.txt` file.

```
[Profiles]
DEFAUL~1="Default User"
[Profiles\DEFAUL~1\SendTo]
MAILRE~1.LNK="Mail Recipient.lnk"
[Profiles\DEFAUL~1]
STARTM~1="Start Menu"
[Profiles\DEFAUL~1\STARTM~1\Programs]
MICROS~1.LNK="Microsoft Exchange.lnk"
MICROS~2.LNK="Microsoft Schedule+.lnk"
ACCESS~1="Accessories"
[Profiles\DEFAUL~1\STARTM~1\Programs\ACCESS~1]
SYSTEM~1="System Tools"
[Profiles\DEFAUL~1\STARTM~1\Programs\ACCESS~1\SYSTEM~1]
INBOXR~1.LNK="Inbox Repair Tool.lnk"
```

Within the root of the `$OEM$` directory, two text files were created. One is the `CMDLINES.TXT` file, which contains the appropriate commands that must be run to install the files and directories contained within the `$OEM$` directory. The contents of `CMDLINES.TXT` are given in Listing 8.3.

Listing 8.3. The `CMDLINES.TXT` file.

```
[Commands]
"rundll32 setupapi,InstallHinfSection DefaultInstall 128 .\diff.INF"
```

The other file is `DIFF.INF`, which is a configuration file used by the commands in `CMDLINES.TXT`. This is an interesting file that contains entries to identify the necessary changes that need to be made to the Windows NT Registry. The `DIFF.INF` file I created is shown in Listing 8.4.

Note: Some of the `AddReg` statements in Listing 8.4 have been truncated to 80-character lines so that they fit on the printed page.

Listing 8.4. The `DIFF.INF` file.

```
; Dump of sysdiff package c:\temp\diff.img
; File created with sysdiff version 40006
; Sysroot: C:\WINNT40
; Usrroot: C:\WINNT40\Profiles\Administrator
; Usrroot: C:\WINNT40\Profiles\ADMINI~1
; TotalDiffCount: 168

[Version]
Signature = "$Windows NT$"
```

continues

Listing 8.4. continued

```
[DefaultInstall]
AddReg = AddReg
DelReg = DelReg
UpdateInis = UpdateInis

[AddReg]
HKLM,"SOFTWARE\Microsoft\Exchange\Forms Registry","CacheSyncCount",65537,45
HKCU,"Software\Microsoft\Windows\CurrentVersion\Explorer\StreamMRU","MRUList",0,...
HKCU,"Software\Microsoft\Windows\CurrentVersion\Explorer\Streams\13","ViewView",...
HKCU,"Software\Microsoft\Windows\CurrentVersion\Explorer\Streams\18","ViewView",...
[DelReg]
[UpdateInis]
```

Testing the SYSDIFF Process

If you so desire, you can run the installation process manually to test SYSDIFF, using the APPLY process. Use the following syntax to test the results of SYSDIFF:

```
sysdiff /apply c:\temp\diff.inf
```

The `c:\temp\diff.inf` file is the file created from the DIFF process.

You can also use the APPLY process to create a patch that can be run against computers that already have Windows NT installed.

For instance, if you have a base Windows NT configuration and want to install the Microsoft Exchange client on an existing workstation running Windows NT, you can create the `DIFF.IMG` file and the `$OEM$` directory on a network share and then run the SYSDIFF APPLY process from the workstation using the same drive attachments that were used to create the `DIFF.IMG` file.

Note: In some cases, it's just as easy—or easier—to run the manufacturer's installation program.

Common SYSDIFF Problems

The SYSDIFF utility has specific requirements that enable it to work properly. Problems that frequently occur include failure due to open files or due to lack of hard drive space. Table 8.1 lists some of the error codes that can be returned during the SYSDIFF process, and some other symptoms of an unsuccessful SYSDIFF implementation.

Table 8.1. SYSDIFF error messages and symptoms.

Error Message or Symptom	*Possible Cause*
`System Error 5`	An attempt was made to access a reserved key in the Windows NT Registry. This is probably because SYSDIFF does not support installation of system services or drivers. Repeat the SYSDIFF process, but do not install the service or driver that caused this error; perform the installation of the service or driver manually.
`Diff Failed (error=2)`	A command-line parameter was incorrectly specified.
`Diff Failed (error=32)`	The SYSDIFF process tried to access an open file. Try to identify which file or files are causing this error; stop whatever process they are using, or exclude these files by editing the `SYSDIFF.INF` file.
Certain settings appear to be missing from an applied SYSDIFF installation	SYSDIFF does not modify the `HKEY_USERS` or `HKEY_CURRENT_USER` Registry sections and therefore might leave out some user-specific settings.
Additional drives appear in My Computer after a Windows NT installation	The computer on which SYSDIFF was run probably had network drives connected between the SNAP and DIFF processes. Either have the drives connected before the SNAP or do not attach to the drives before the DIFF.

Summary

Ideally, when you are rolling out multiple workstations running Windows NT or numerous servers, any shortcuts that enable you to shave off some installation time will be very helpful. If properly utilized, the Server Manager and SYSDIFF utilities can address these issues. We highly recommend that you thoroughly test these utilities before you perform an extensive implementation.

PART III

Windows NT Configuration Essentials

CHAPTER 9

Capacity Planning

by Robert Reinstein

Capacity planning for a Windows NT network requires a great deal of work in advance. Luckily, there are tools that can assist you in doing this, and this chapter can serve as your guide.

The first part of this chapter deals with the initial planning for a new network. Capacity planning can also be performed after you implement your network.

In this chapter you learn about the following aspects of capacity planning:

- Planning your hardware
- Identifying your goals
- Using tools to monitor performance after you've installed your network

Creating a Plan

When thinking about capacity planning, you have to first come up with a plan for undertaking this task. Right off the bat, you might be able to figure out the number of users on your network and the amount of disk space you require. In capacity planning, however, you also have to think about your growth, which could include multiple servers, and plan for your bandwidth. The bandwidth plan includes, depending on the scope of your network, multiple segments, routers, bridges, remote access, and other basic networking considerations.

Identifying Your Goals

Before you can come up with a plan, you should first identify your goals. You need to explore what exactly you are looking for in a Windows NT network and identify the overall purpose, or purposes, of this network. Your purposes could include file and print services, application servers, remote access, access to other networks (such as mainframe or mini-computers), communications, Internet access, database, intranet, client workstation management, groupware, and messaging.

Looking ahead, and not just identifying your plans for today, you need to know if you are thinking about just a LAN environment in a single location, or if you will be working with a WAN environment, possibly covering the globe.

Ideally, these are the goals for which you should be planning:

- High availability
- Sufficient resources (disk space, available print queues, and other services)
- Optimal user response time

Hardware Resources

When thinking about implementing a Windows NT network, there are some minimum requirements that need to be met before you think about the growth of your network.

Quantity of Servers

Throughout this discussion I will interject when I feel that more than one single server would best serve for a given situation. Obviously, a network that handles multiple offices in multiple locations is an excellent candidate for multiple servers. Applications that have such great overhead are also good examples of when multiple servers would best serve the network, even if the network exists within one physical location.

Domain Models

Another example of a consideration for multiple servers is domain planning.

Chapter 3 discussed domain models, and examining your network's need for a particular domain model might dictate the minimum number of servers necessary to get your network off the ground.

Load Balancing

Load balancing is another reason to have more than one server, even if you have chosen the single domain model. For instance, if your clients heavily utilize a word processing program that is installed on a server, you might find that having that application installed on two servers gives the clients faster access to some of the features of that application.

Certain software might recommend that it exist on its own server. Load balancing is thus performed by having one server exist solely for that application. A good example of this might be for Remote Access Services (RAS). While RAS can certainly exist on a single server network, it does create overhead that might affect other network services. Placing RAS on its own server will ensure that this overhead does not interfere with the processes on other servers.

Newer applications, such as Microsoft Exchange Server and Microsoft Systems Management Server, have been designed to allow the one application to run across multiple servers, which helps facilitate load balancing.

Clustering

Server clustering has only recently been introduced for the Windows NT platform. A proprietary system has been created by Digital Equipment Corporation (DEC). Digital Clusters for Windows NT allows multiple servers running Windows NT to share resources and appear as one virtual server to the network clients.

Microsoft has announced its own API for server clustering, which is named Wolfpack. As many manufacturers are either considering—or have already started planning—server clustering, Microsoft has asked that they write their clustering software to the Wolfpack API to allow a common clustering solution that is hardware independent. Currently, the Digital solution is proprietary, but it is available, and some people are going to be using it.

Fault Tolerance

Fault tolerance is yet another reason to extend your network beyond a single server. Usually the determining factor here is the amount of downtime you are willing to tolerate, or that your business can survive.

The average server might come with a 48-hour on-site warranty that can be upgraded to a 24-hour response, or even a 4-hour response.

In some cases even this is not enough protection, and that's when a second server is required.

Hardware components that are usually the cause for failures include CPUs, hard drives, power supplies, drive controllers, memory, and network interface cards.

Third-party solutions, such as Vinca Systems' Standby Server and Octopus Technologies' Octopus, provide real-time server mirroring that will have a server mirror kick in whenever the main server fails. The downtime here is minimized to only a few moments, and is transparent to the network clients.

Another approach that we recently used was having an extra server that is identical to two other servers we installed, but lacks hard drives, which stood in a closet. If one of the two live servers had a problem other than a hard drive problem—for which RAID solutions, such as those discussed in Chapter 17, "Disk Administrator," should handle the recovery—we would remove the hard drives from the failed server and put them into the spare server. This would provide a live server within minutes, but with a noticeable absence from the network that might affect network clients. This method also requires manual intervention that the real-time server mirroring solutions handle automatically.

Server Processors

The number of processors on a Windows NT computer can greatly improve performance, depending on the other software that is running on the computer.

A single processor computer running Windows NT might be capable of handling a great amount of network traffic and internal processes; however, the load that Windows NT running on a single processor can handle is limited. Windows NT has been built to be scalable, and can perform load balancing when running on multiple processors.

Out of the box, Windows NT Server can accommodate eight processors. If the hardware manufacturer provides the necessary drivers, Windows NT Server can take advantage of a computer with up to 32 processors.

Note: Windows NT Workstation is capable of handling only two processors.

Usually, simple file and print services will not justify the purchase of a multiple-processor computer.

If the computer running Windows NT Server is also running a processor intensive program, such as Microsoft SQL Server, Microsoft Systems Management Server, or Microsoft Exchange Server, and is handling a large number of requests, a second processor can boost the power of the computer 60 percent. A Web server is another example of a server that can get overburdened with requests. As you add each additional processor, the return is lessened. If you have the resources to test your production conditions in a lab and can set up a server with multiple processors, the results can be measured. Measuring might enable you to decide on whether the investment in a multiprocessor server would be cost-justified.

Tip: Microsoft Exchange Server includes a utility, LoadSim, which will simulate heavy usage, thereby enabling you to tune your system. This is a great utility to help you evaluate multiple processors.

Server Platforms

One of the main design elements for Windows NT is its portability. Currently Windows NT can run on the Intel x86, DEC Alpha, MIPS, and PowerPC platforms.

Note: Microsoft has announced that it has ceased development for the MIPS and PowerPC platform.

Deciding whether to implement a platform other than the Intel x86 has usually been based on cost and performance of RISC equipment.

Now, with the release of the Pentium Pro chip, the Intel versus RISC argument seems to be getting lessened, because a 200 MHz Pentium Pro is quite comparable to the 300 MHz RISC machines (according to Intel). However, there is no denying that RISC-based systems are impressive.

Alpha processors have been released with speeds of up to 400 and 500 MHz. At the time of this writing, the fastest Pentium Pro chip runs at 200 MHz. Of course, the actual architecture of the computer can offset the comparison of the speed of the chips.

New to NT 4.0: In previous versions of Windows NT, a 286 was emulated when running MS-DOS and 16-bit Windows applications on an Alpha chip. With version 4.0 of Windows NT, this emulation has been changed to that of a 486.

Memory Requirements

Out of the box, a single Windows NT server requires a server-grade computer that is on the Microsoft Hardware Compatibility List (HCL). The memory requirements are a minimum of 32MB. At my company, we prefer to see Windows NT servers running on 48MB of RAM.

Other applications that will reside on the server dictate additional memory requirements.

For instance, using Microsoft BackOffice and loading a copy of Microsoft SQL Server onto your Windows NT server can bring the minimum RAM requirement up to 64MB. Adding Microsoft Systems Management Server can drive that up to 96MB of RAM, depending on the number of users.

Ideally, using this scenario, there would be more than one server. One would be running the Microsoft Systems Management Server and another could have the Microsoft SQL Server installed on it. This type of load balancing was discussed earlier under the heading "Load Balancing."

Note: The license for Microsoft BackOffice is only for a single server, therefore the individual application might not be broken up between servers.

Computing Memory Requirements

The following equation might help you estimate the memory required for a Windows NT server:

- The base memory required for the system is 24MB. We will refer to this number as system memory.
- Estimate the total size of the average files that might be open on the server for each user.
- Multiply that number by the total number of users. We will refer to this as user memory.
- Estimate the average size of the applications being utilized on the server.
- Multiply the average size of applications running on the server by the total number of applications being run on the server. This will be referred to as the application memory.

To estimate the amount of memory necessary to run your server, add the server memory, user memory, and application memory. The result is the recommended memory for your server. Additional memory can be added to allow for caching.

Disk Requirements

Predicting the amount of disk space needed for a Windows NT server is difficult, because the size of applications and user information grow at an alarming rate. Luckily, the cost of adding disk space has been decreasing, which makes it easier to aim high and avoid running out of disk space.

The base Windows NT Server package can use 200MB of disk space. Each user directory can easily grow to hundreds of megabytes, depending on how you implement user directories. E-mail packages, such as Microsoft Exchange Server, can also occupy a large amount per user, plus a defined amount of disk space for public folders.

Expansion

Luckily, today's servers are built to accommodate a large number of hard drives. For example, the Hewlett-Packard LX Pro has 12 hot-swap drive bays. External expansion units can allow for terrabytes of data to be stored online.

Newer disk controller cards, such as the COMPAQ SmartArray II, allow for disk expansion without having to down the server.

In addition to using hard drives for storage, optical media, such as CD-ROM, can be used to hold unlimited amounts of data.

Note: If you are planning to use external units for storing data, be sure to check that these units are compatible with Windows NT, and more important, the disk controllers must be certified for Windows NT.

Fault Tolerance

In addition to the base requirements for hard drive capacity, you should be thinking about a fault-tolerant system.

Disk mirroring, which is also known as RAID Level 1, requires you to double the amount of usable drive capacity. Disk volumes that utilize disk striping with parity—also known as RAID Level 5—will use one drive in addition to the other drives that are part of the volume.

Hot swappable drives are hard drives that are enclosed in a shell that allow for quick removal from the server, or housing, and can be installed without the need to down the server. It is strongly advised that this type of media be used whenever possible.

Tip: The previously mentioned COMPAQ SmartArray II disk controller, and others like it, can enable you to switch your fault tolerance, or expand it, without having to down the server.

Network Topology

The size of your network, the need to integrate your network with other networks, and your budget will decide which is the favorable network topology for you to use.

Almost every year new ideas for increasing network bandwidth and speed are announced, but very few become standards.

Wireless networking exists, which is great for roving users or as a way to expand a network to areas that make wiring difficult, but we can't even consider that as a way to create a network that performs well.

Ethernet

Ethernet, which is by far the most popular network topology, is the most cost-effective form of networking. Network adapter cards sell for as low as $20, and an eight-port hub can cost as low as $90, which makes the cost per user as low as $33.

10-Megabit Ethernet

The longtime standard, 10-megabit Ethernet, is the most popular technology for setting up networks. The recent surge in implementing Ethernet Switching—which can allow a workstation to have full 10-megabit bandwidth—makes Ethernet a very smart, cost-effective, stable, and compatible choice. The most popular form of 10-megabit Ethernet is known as 10Base-T.

100-Megabit Ethernet

A recent standard is 100-megabit Ethernet. Most Ethernet network adapter manufacturers are selling cards that automatically adjust to 10 or 100 megabits. These are known as 10/100 cards.

The additional cost for 100-megabit Ethernet is usually the higher priced hubs, and the need for Category 5 wiring. Category 5 wiring is the standard nowadays for any installation, and it makes sense, as long as you're having a wiring job done, to use the best materials you can and avoid rewiring costs.

And gigabit Ethernet is just around the bend.

> **Note:** Hewlett-Packard was the first to bring out a 100-megabit Ethernet. Theirs is called 100VG and is not compatible with the newer, but more standard, 100Base-T. Actually, at the time of this writing, Hewlett-Packard was also producing 100Base-T.

Token Ring

Used initially by IBM environments, Token Ring, which can run at 4 megabits or at 16 megabits, depending on the wiring and the network adapter cards, lost in popularity to Ethernet a while ago.

There are still a lot of companies using Token Ring, and apparently enough cards are still being sold to justify the manufacture of new cards. Still, Token Ring is usually not used when implementing new networks.

ATM

ATM (Asynchronous Transfer Mode) is the only standards based technology that has been designed from the beginning to accommodate data, voice, and video. ATM can handle speeds in the gigabits, but its acceptance has been very slow, mainly due to its cost. The lowest cost per seat that I've seen is $500.

Identifying Bottlenecks

Let's say that you have set up your network using hardware and the network topology that you felt would be best for your needs.

Capacity planning does not stop there. In fact, capacity planning is an ongoing process. Identifying bottlenecks in your system as it stands or planning for expansion should be performed at regular intervals.

By definition, a bottleneck is a process in a chain of processes that prevents other processes from working as quickly as they could.

Once the network is in use, you can start to identify these bottlenecks and plan changes that need to be made to allow your network to perform as efficiently as possible.

Performance Monitor

The Windows NT Performance Monitor is a great place to start when looking for bottlenecks or when you need tips on fine-tuning.

Chapter 18, "Performance Monitor," gives you a more in-depth explanation of the Performance Monitor.

Performance Monitor is an application that can look at counters that exist on a Windows NT system in the form of DLLs and other programs.

These counters will keep track of items such as the number of reads from a disk or the number of CPU cycles to perform a transaction. Some of these counters are internal to Windows NT, and some might come with other software, such as Microsoft Exchange Server.

By keeping track of these counters and being able to graphically display the results of the counter, Performance Monitor can give you a real-time view of the performance of your server, other servers, and your network as a whole.

The activity that you choose to keep track of might be saved and then compared to the statistics that occur at another time, thus enabling you to spot times of the day that inhibit performance, or to compare the way a particular application acts over different links.

The amount of data that can be captured and analyzed is awesome, and can really give you great insight into your network's performance.

Task Manager

The Windows NT Task Manager is also a great resource for tracking performance and activity on a specific computer running Windows NT 4.0.

The Task Manager can be started by either pressing the Ctrl+Shift+Esc key combination, by right mouse-clicking the Task Bar, and then selecting Task Manager from the pop-up menu or, you can press the Ctrl+Alt+Del key combination and click the button labeled Task Manager. You can create a shortcut for the Task Manager by setting the command line to `TASKMGR.EXE`.

Working with Applications in Task Manager

Task Manager, shown in Figure 9.1, has three tabs. The first tab is Applications. This shows you the currently running programs. Figure 9.1 shows these applications in the Details view. You can also choose to show these as small icons or large icons.

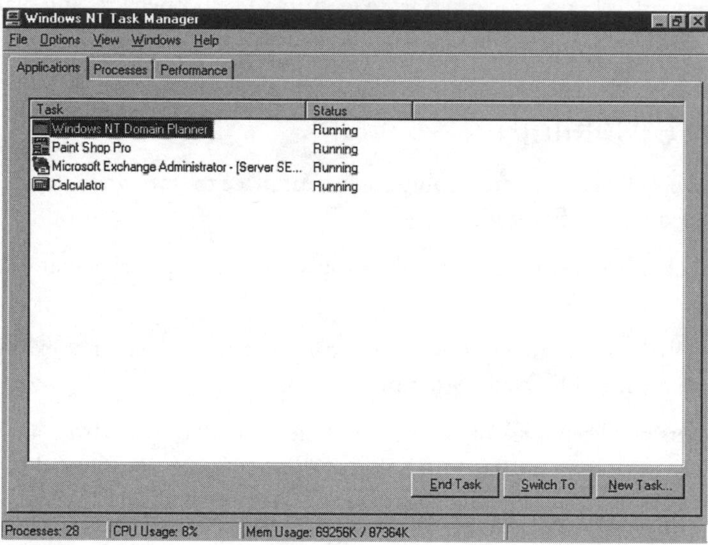

Figure 9.1. *Task Manager.*

At the bottom of the screen there are three buttons. The End Task button shuts down the currently highlighted program. The Switch To button brings the currently highlighted program to the forefront of your desktop and minimizes the Task Manager. The New Task button is the same as the Run... command found on the Start button.

The status bar at the bottom of the screen always displays the total number of currently running processes, the percent of CPU utilization, and the amount of virtual memory in use on the system.

If you right mouse-click an application, a pop-up menu gives you some options that are shown in Table 9.1.

Table 9.1. Task Manager application options.

Menu Item	*Performs This Task*
Switch To	Brings the highlighted application to the foreground and minimizes the Task Manager.
Bring To Front	Brings the highlighted application to the foreground. It does not affect Task Manager.
Minimize	Sets the highlighted application to a minimized state.
Maximize	Sets the highlighted application to a maximized state.
End Task	Ends the currently highlighted application.
Go To Process	Switches to the Processes view. The process that is the application is then highlighted.

Working with Processes in Task Manager

The second tab, Processes, which is shown in Figure 9.2, lists all of the individual processes running on the Windows NT computer.

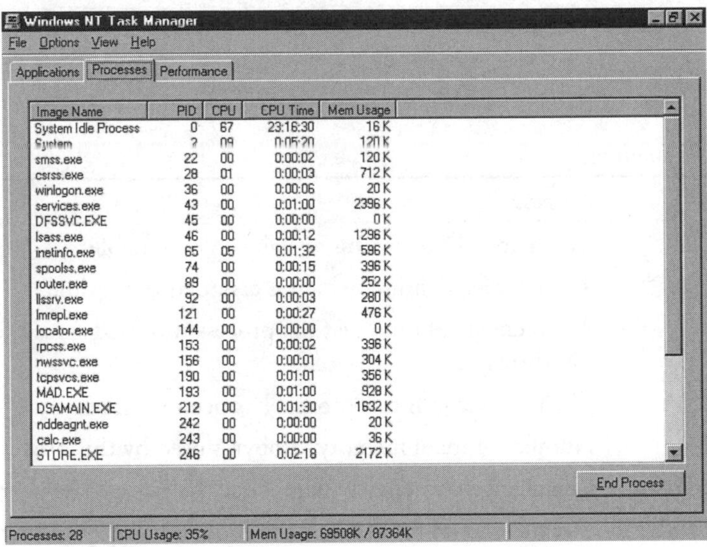

Figure 9.2. *The Task Manager Processes tab.*

Table 9.2 lists the columns that are shown for the running processes. By default, only the first five columns are shown. Additional columns can be selected to be shown by choosing Select Columns... from the View menu. Figure 9.3 shows the Select Columns dialog that allows you to choose which columns are shown. All these columns are resizable.

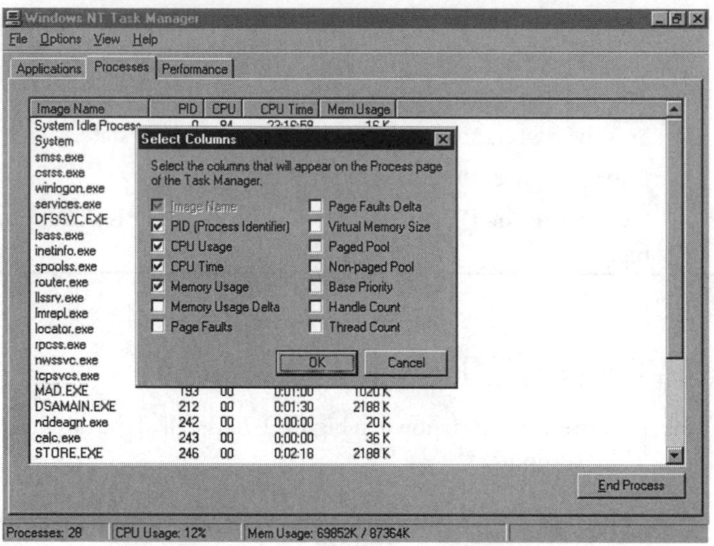

Figure 9.3. *The Processes Select Columns dialog.*

Table 9.2. Processes columns.

Column Name	*Purpose*
Image Name	The name of the process, usually an executable.
PID	The process identifier which is assigned at runtime.
CPU Usage	A percentage of time that the process was used since the last update of this display.
CPU Time	The total seconds this process has been running.
Memory Usage	Number of main memory kilobytes used by this process.
Memory Usage Delta	The change of memory usage since the last update of this display.
Page Faults	The number of times, since the process has been running, data had to be retrieved from disk because it was not found in memory.
Page Faults Delta	Reflects changes in page faults since the last update of this display.
Virtual Memory Size	Number of pagefile kilobytes used by this process.

Column Name	*Purpose*
Paged Pool	Number of kilobytes of user memory used by this process.
Non-paged Pool	Number of kilobytes of non-paged kernel memory used by this process.
Base Priority	The base priority of the process, which determines the order in which its threads are scheduled for the processor. Task Manager enables you to change the base priority. The choices are Realtime, High, Normal, and Low.
Handle Count	Total object handles used by this process.
Thread Count	Total number of threads in this process.

Viewing a Virtual DOS Machine

Figure 9.4 shows a process list with `ntvdm.exe` highlighted. This is a Windows NT virtual DOS machine, which is running a 16-bit Windows application. Note how the program, `olpg.exe`, and the 16-bit to 32-bit thunking mechanism, `wowexec.exe`, are indented beneath `ntvdm.exe`. This shows that only the one 16-bit program is running within this virtual DOS machine. You can use Task Manager to see if multiple 16-bit applications are sharing the same memory space, and then change it by restarting the program with the option to run in its own memory space.

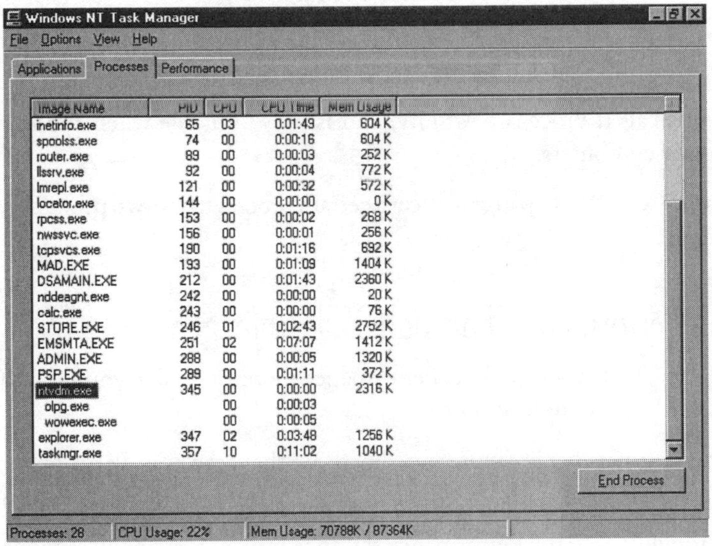

Figure 9.4. *A 16-bit Windows program in the Task Manager Processes list.*

Detecting Memory Hogs

Using the process list, you can identify the programs that are using or "hogging" memory, and then compare their memory usage with other similar programs.

Setting the Base Priority Class

The base priority class for a process determines the order in which threads are scheduled for the processor. This can be changed by right-clicking the process and then choosing Set Priority from the pop-up menu. Changing the base priority class only occurs for this instance of the process, because the base priority is set internally by the program. A program that is running as Normal can be changed to run as High, which boosts its performance. Or, programs running unnecessarily as Normal or High can be set to a Low base priority class, which allows other programs to be scheduled for processing more often.

> **Caution:** The primary drawback of changing the base priority class is that it might interfere with other processes and cause unstable behavior. It might be best to first set Task Manager to a high priority so that you always have access to Task Manager.

Choosing to Run a Process on Specific Processors

On a multiprocessor computer, Task Manager has the option of designating the processor, or processors, on which you want a process to run.

This option is called Processor Affinity, and is only available when running Windows NT on multiprocessor computers.

By using Processor Affinity you can direct a certain process to its own processor, which will increase its performance.

Monitoring Performance Through Task Manager

The third tab in Task Manager is its Performance monitor, which you shouldn't confuse with *the* Performance Monitor application.

Many of the statistics that are represented here are the same as in Performance Monitor, because they both get their statistics from the same place: Windows NT internal counters.

As shown in Figure 9.5, the Performance screen is broken into many sections. Table 9.3 lists the different sections of Performance and their uses.

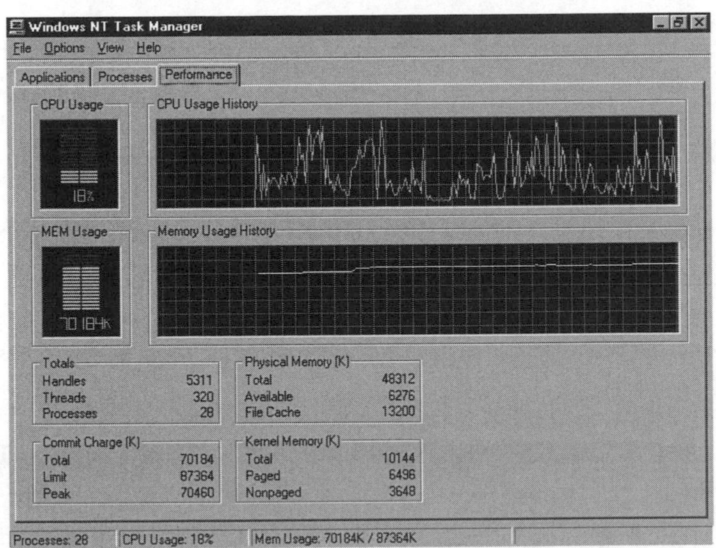

Figure 9.5. *Task Manager's Performance tab.*

Table 9.3. Task Manager Performance counters.

Counter	*Usage*
CPU Usage	The percentage of time the processor is running a thread other than the Idle thread.
MEM Usage	Number of kilobytes of virtual memory used
Total Handles	The number of object handles in the tables of all processes.
Total Threads	The number of running threads, including one Idle thread per processor.
Total Processes	The number of active processes, including the Idle process.
Total Physical Memory	Number of kilobytes of physical RAM installed in the computer.
Available Physical Memory	Number of kilobytes of physical memory available to processes.
File Cache Memory	Number of kilobytes of physical memory released to the file cache on demand.
Commit Change Total	Number of kilobytes of virtual memory in use by all processes.
Commit Change Limit	Number of kilobytes of virtual memory that can be committed to all processes without enlarging the paging file.
Commit Change Peak	The maximum amount of virtual memory used in the session, in kilobytes. The commit peak can exceed the commit limit if virtual memory is expanded.

continues

Table 9.3. continued

Counter	*Usage*
Total Kernel Memory	Total kilobytes of paged and nonpaged kernel memory.
Paged Kernel Memory	Total kilobytes of the paged pool allocated to the operating system.
Nonpaged Kernel Memory	Total kilobytes of the nonpaged pool allocated to the operating system.

Figure 9.6 shows the Performance page with the option to show kernel times, which is selected from the View menu.

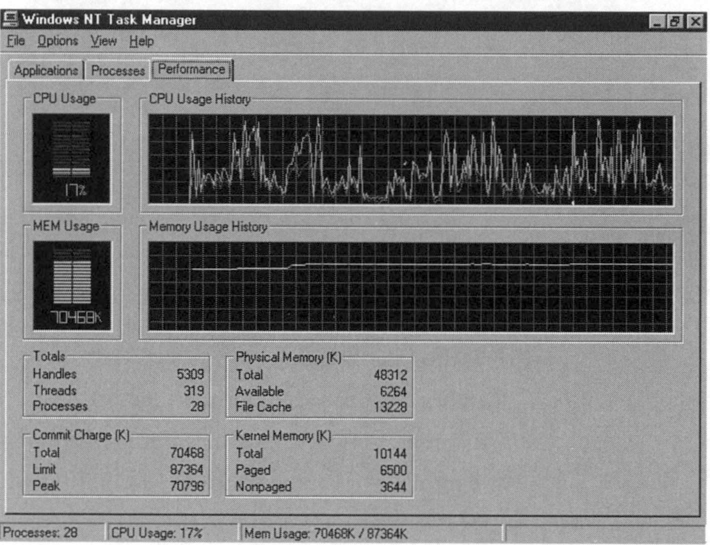

Figure 9.6. *Task Manager Performance page showing kernel times.*

The Show Kernel Times mode breaks up the CPU Usage into what the operating system is using, and what the applications are using.

When running Windows NT on a multiprocessor computer, the option CPU History on the View menu enables you to create separate graphs for each processor.

Note: Although Task Manager is highly accurate for monitoring performance, the program `TASKMGR.EXE` is also a process and runs a high base priority class. Therefore, the actual performance without Task Manager running should be better than the statistics read. You can minimize the impact of Task Manager on your system by changing its update speed to Low. This is done by choosing Update Speed from the View menu.

Other Tools and Third-Party Tools

There are many other performance monitoring programs, some of which were made by Microsoft, and others that come from third-party developers.

The Microsoft Windows NT 4.0 Resource Kit

The Microsoft Windows NT Resource Kit contains some very valuable performance monitoring tools.

Tools in the Windows NT Resource Kit include the following:

- The Performance Data Log Service, which enables you to export counters to a tab-delimited or comma-delimited text file that can then be used in a spreadsheet or imported into a database.
- Pperf, which monitors internal counters on Intel Pentium and Pentium Pro chips that monitor the activity of the chip.
- Process Monitor, which is a command-line character mode tool that provides a five second update of process statistics.
- Process Explode is the ultimate tool for viewing the internals of a single process. It will actually provide you with dozens of statistics about an individual process. This tool also gives you the functionality of Task Manager, because you can stop processes and change their base priority class.
- Process Viewer is a subset of Process Explode. It will, however, enable you to view processes running on other Windows NT 4.0 computers.
- Response Probe is a utility that enables you to simulate a load on a Windows NT computer.

Summary

Creating a successful Windows NT network takes careful planning. Determining your requirements will help ensure that the proper hardware is implemented. If after installing the network you find that there are noticeable lags (which will usually come to light by a number of users calling and complaining about their applications running slowly off of the network), there are a number of tools that can help you diagnose or fine-tune the existing network.

It might be beneficial to have an experienced network consultant help you get off the ground. If hiring a consultant isn't an option, however, using the methods and tools described in this chapter will enable you to get off to a good start.

The Windows NT Boot Process

by Robert Reinstein

When you compare the Windows NT boot process to the MS-DOS or Windows 95 boot process, you can see how Windows NT is unique. The process is really quite simple and is configurable, as you will see.

This chapter covers the following topics:

- How Windows NT alters the master boot record
- The `BOOT.INI` file
- ARC paths
- Dual-booting operating systems

The Boot Process—Step By Step

The Windows NT boot process is unique. Many checks are performed before the Windows NT operating system is allowed to start. Flowchart 10.1 shows the many steps in this process, which this section describes, starting with turning on (or restarting) the computer.

When you power on or restart a computer, the computer's built-in POST (Power On Self Test) is performed. Once this has completed, the master boot sector of the floppy disk and the first hard disk is searched.

When you install Windows NT, the installation process actually modifies the master boot sector of your boot hard drive. This is key to the way that the Windows NT boot process begins.

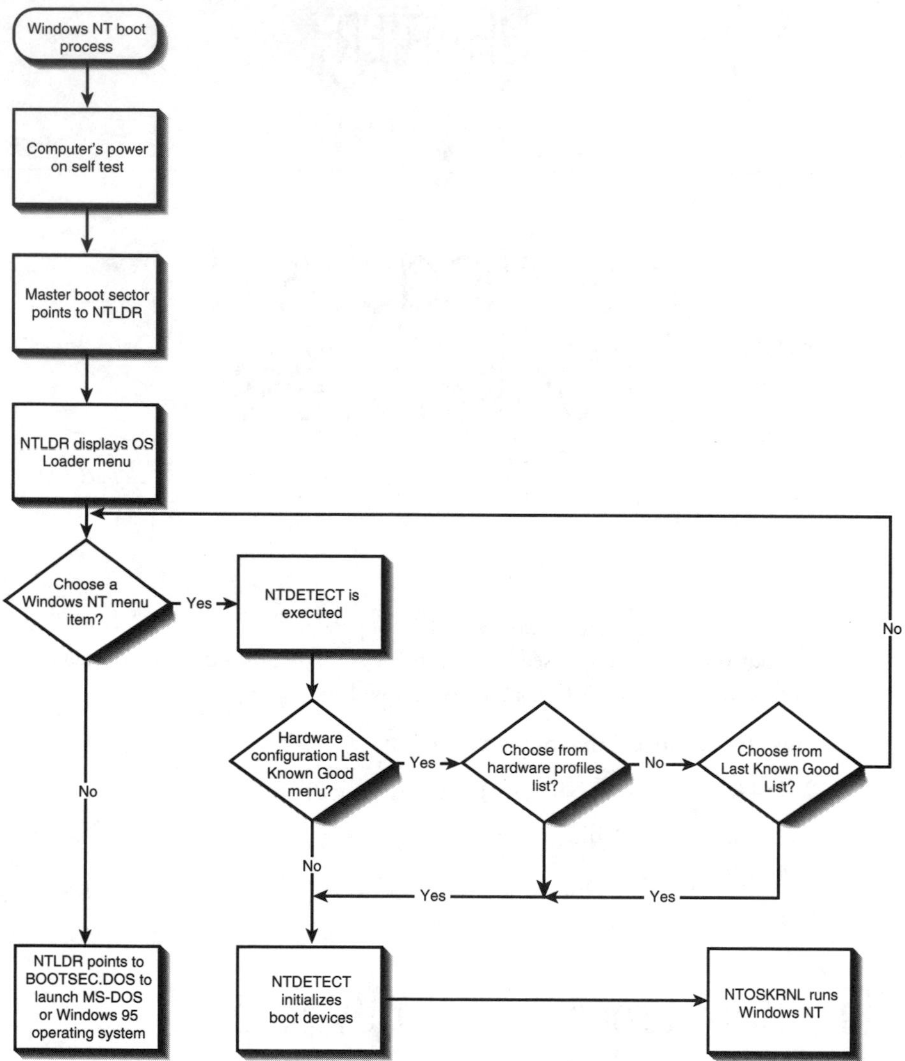

Flowchart 10.1. *The Windows NT boot process.*

Prior to MS-DOS 5.0, the master boot sector on a bootable PC hard drive contained the master boot record, the hard drive's partition table, and the file `IO.SYS`, which is the lowest-level MS-DOS system file.

Because MS-DOS 5.0 took IO.SYS out of the master boot sector and replaced it with a pointer to the actual IO.SYS file residing somewhere on the boot partition, Windows NT was able to make a modification to the master boot sector that would point instead to Windows NT's NTLDR file.

The NTLDR file processes a text file, which is named BOOT.INI. This is a read-only file that contains clear text that defines the Windows NT OS Loader Menu.

If Windows NT is chosen from the Windows NT OS Loader Menu, NTDETECT.COM is executed. NTDETECT is the program that detects the installed system devices and initializes those devices for the Windows NT environment.

First, NTDETECT will give you a chance to press the spacebar to enter the Hardware Profile/Configuration Recovery Menu, which is discussed later in this chapter in the section titled "Hardware Profiles/Configuration Recovery."

During this boot process, the blue screen shows the version of Windows NT, the build number, the installed memory for the computer, and if applicable, whether the Windows NT multiprocessor kernel is being loaded. If a Windows NT Service Pack has been applied, the service pack number will be shown also. The blue screen shows dots that indicate that the initialization of system devices is occurring. Anytime within this period, a defective device can show up as a screen full of debug information and an error message that may or may not be easily understood.

Several of the most common boot process error messages are covered in Chapter 39, "What to Do When NT Fails to Boot."

If the initialization process completes, NTOSKRNL.EXE is then executed, which completes the Windows NT boot process.

The BOOT.INI File

When NTLDR processes the BOOT.INI file, it is looking for a particular syntax (discussed here). This INI file is just like any standard INI file. Only two sections are necessary in BOOT.INI to fully define the Windows NT OS Loader Menu.

Listing 10.1 shows a typical BOOT.INI file.

Listing 10.1. A typical BOOT.INI file.

```
[boot loader]
timeout=30
default=multi(0)disk(0)rdisk(0)partition(1)\WINNT
[Operating Systems]
multi(0)disk(0)rdisk(0)partition(1)\WINNT="Windows NT Workstation Version 4.00"
multi(0)disk(0)rdisk(0)partition(1)\WINNT="Windows NT Workstation Version 4.00 [VGA
mode]" /basevideo /sos
C:\="MS-DOS"
```

boot loader

The `[boot loader]` section of `BOOT.INI` defines the default settings for the Windows NT OS Loader Menu, which are the default menu choice and the length of time before the default menu choice is automatically selected.

timeout=

The `timeout=` line sets the number of seconds that may pass before the default operating system (defined in the next line) is automatically chosen to boot.

By default, a time-out of 30 seconds is declared. You can lengthen this amount to as high as 999 seconds or as low as 1 second.

Another option for the time-out is the number zero, which will boot the default operating system without having a chance to select a choice other than the default operating system.

The final option is entering a value of `-1`, which will force the time-out period to be indefinite. Using `timeout=-1` will have the Windows NT OS Loader Menu stay onscreen until an operating system is chosen.

default=

The `default=` line of the `[boot loader]` section refers to the operating system that will be chosen as the default setting for the Windows NT OS Loader Menu. Depending on the value placed in the `timeout=` line, the operating system defined here will be launched either automatically or if the user presses the Enter key without using the arrow keys to move to another choice on the OS Loader Menu.

The operating system must be one that is defined in the second `BOOT.INI` section, `Operating Systems`. These definitions are presented in a format known as the ARC (Advanced RISC Computing) format, which is discussed in the next section about the second section of `BOOT.INI`, which is `[Operating Systems]`.

Operating Systems

The `[Operating Systems]` section defines the different boot paths from which the Windows NT OS Loader can launch an operating system.

As you can see in Listing 10.1, there are three default operating system choices if you have installed Windows NT over an existing MS-DOS or Windows 95 system. If this was a new install onto a system without MS-DOS or Windows 95, there will be only two choices for `[Operating Systems]`, which are both of the Windows NT entries.

The choice for MS-DOS does not use an ARC path, but a DOS path.

Advanced RISC Computing (ARC)

The Advanced RISC Computing path that is used in the `[Operating Systems]` section of `BOOT.INI`—and also used in the `default=` line of the `[boot loader]` section—is better known as an ARC path.

The proper syntax for creating an ARC path is presented in Table 10.1.

Table 10.1. ARC path keywords.

Keyword	*Description*
`scsi(x)` or `multi(x)`	`scsi` is used when a SCSI BIOS is going to be responsible for finding the Windows NT boot partition. `multi` can be used for SCSI, IDE, and ESDI hard drives, which rely on an INT 13 call to locate the bootable partition. The number `(x)` refers to the ordinal number of the drive adapter, which is usually zero, unless the boot partition is on a hard drive that is attached to another controller.
`disk(x)`	If `scsi` is used, this is the SCSI ID of the device that contains the bootable partition. If `multi` is used, this number must be zero.
`rdisk(x)`	Refers to the SCSI LUN (logical unit number) of the boot device. This is usually zero. This keyword is ignored by `multi`.
`partition(x)`	This is the partition number. All partitions receive a number except for type 5 (MS-DOS extended) and type 0 (unused) partitions, with primary partitions being numbered first and then logical drives. The numbering scheme here starts with the number one, whereas all of the other numbers start with the number zero.

The following line, taken from Listing 10.1, shows that this choice of operating system is using INT 13 of the system BIOS, resides on the first hard disk, is on the first partition of that hard disk, and is located in the `WINNT` directory.

```
multi(0)disk(0)rdisk(0)partition(1)\WINNT="Windows NT Workstation Version 4.00"
```

Multiple Windows NT Installations

It is possible to include multiple Windows NT installations on an OS Loader Menu.

This is accomplished by installing Windows NT into its own directory each time. For instance, a Windows NT Version 3.51 can co-exist with a Windows NT 4.0 just by having separate entries in the `[Operating Systems]` section of `BOOT.INI`.

Listing 10.2 provides an example of multiple Windows NT versions in the OS Loader Menu.

Listing 10.2. Multiple Windows NT installations.

```
multi(0)disk(0)rdisk(0)partition(1)\WINNT4WS="Windows NT Workstation Version 4.00"
multi(0)disk(0)rdisk(0)partition(1)\WINNT4WS="Windows NT Workstation Version 4.00
➥[VGA mode]" /basevideo /sos
multi(0)disk(0)rdisk(0)partition(1)\WINNT35="Windows NT Server 3.51"
multi(0)disk(0)rdisk(0)partition(1)\WINNT35="Windows NT Server 3.51 VGA" /basevideo
➥/sos
```

In Listing 10.2, a Windows NT 3.51 Server installation co-exists with a Windows NT 4.0 Workstation install.

The `[Operating Systems]` section is limited to 10 operating systems. If you list more than 10 in the list, the Boot Menu will simply ignore those entries past 10.

Note: If you do not specify a default operating system in the `[boot loader]` section, a new item is added to your `[Operating Systems]` list and is automatically made the default operating system. This item will be called "Windows NT (default)" and will point to the first copy of Windows NT that is found on your hard drives.

Booting Windows NT in Special Modes

For each of the operating systems in the previous example, there is a corresponding entry that is identified as VGA mode.

The `/sos` switch enables you to see the drivers that are being initialized during NTDETECT, instead of seeing the familiar progress dots.

The `/basevideo` switch is used to load minimal VGA support, which is handy in the event that you have a video driver problem and still need to boot into Windows NT in order to change the video driver you have installed.

Booting MS-DOS or Windows 95

When you make the choice to boot MS-DOS or Windows 95, which is choosing the menu choice associated with the DOS path C:\, you are actually telling NTLDR to look at the file `BOOTSECT.DOS` as the master boot sector. This then lets your system boot as a "normal" MS-DOS or Windows 95 computer.

Of course, if you have opted to format your boot drive as NTFS, there is no reason to have MS-DOS as one of your options, because MS-DOS cannot recognize partitions formatted as NTFS.

Modifying BOOT.INI

There are two ways to modify the contents of the BOOT.INI file without using a third-party utility.

- Modify BOOT.INI using the System applet, which is contained in the Windows NT Control Panel.
- In the System applet, choose the Startup/Shutdown tab.

As shown in Figure 10.1, the System Startup settings include a drop-down box that enables you to choose the default operating system for the OS Loader Menu. The time-out in seconds is determined by the Show list for *nn* seconds box. Making any changes within this dialog will alter the contents of the BOOT.INI file.

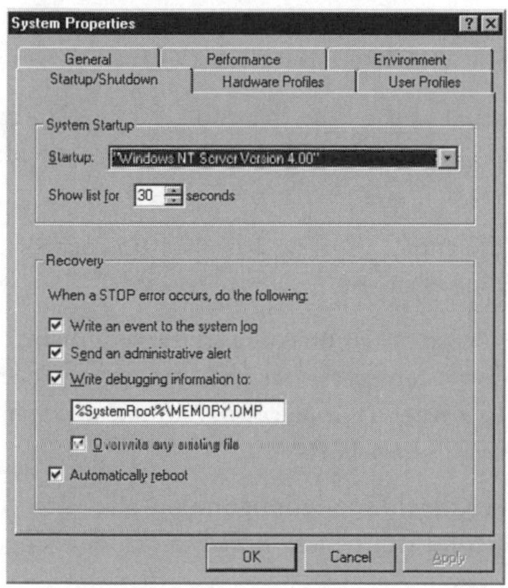

Figure 10.1. *The System Startup/Shutdown page.*

The System Startup settings option does not enable you to modify the choices for the OS Loader Menu, so it is up to you to edit the BOOT.INI file manually to make those changes.

The BOOT.INI file is a read-only file by default, so to edit it, you must first take off the read-only attribute. This can be done from within the Windows NT Explorer by clearing the check box associated with the read-only, hidden, and system attributes.

The read-only attribute can also be cleared from the command line. If you open a command prompt window, enter this command:

```
ATTRIB -S -H -R C:\BOOT.INI
```

This will take BOOT.INI and eliminate all of the attributes that designate it as a system, hidden, and read-only file. At this point, you are free to edit the file.

> **Caution:** Before you manually make changes to the `BOOT.INI` file, save a copy of the default version.

When editing the `BOOT.INI` file, be sure to follow the syntax shown in this chapter.

When you have finished editing the `BOOT.INI` file, I suggest that you place the attributes back on the file by issuing the following command:

```
ATTRIB +S +H +R C:\BOOT.INI
```

You can use Windows NT Explorer to add the read-only, hidden, and system attributes again, if that was the method you used to remove these attributes.

Hardware Profiles/Configuration Recovery

If you pressed the spacebar at the time that NTDETECT offered you the option to enter the Hardware Profile/Last Known Good Menu, you arrive at the Hardware Profiles/Configuration Recovery Menu.

This menu gives you the choice of using a backed up copy of the Registry or choosing to use optional configuration files that you may have created.

By default, a Windows NT installation contains the Original Configuration setting. If you have created additional hardware configurations, they can be selected from this menu or you can press the L key to select the Last Known Good configuration, which had been saved from the last time you successfully started Windows NT.

If you do choose the Last Known Good configuration, all changes that may have been made to your Windows NT configuration will be lost, which includes changes to the GUI configuration or added devices and services.

Master Boot Sector Recovery

Many, many times I have seen someone accidentally, or purposely, overwrite the Windows NT Master Boot Sector with a Master Boot Sector from MS-DOS.

Usually this happens when someone installs Windows NT onto a fresh hard drive and then decides afterwards that they also want to be able to boot MS-DOS, so they run the MS-DOS installation program and find out afterwards that their Windows NT OS Loader Menu has disappeared.

Another way this happens is if someone, for whatever reason, boots from a MS-DOS system disk and uses the `SYS` command on the hard drive.

The master boot record can also be affected by a computer virus.

There are a few methods that you can use to recover the Windows NT Master Boot Sector.

The first option is to run the Windows NT installation program again using the Windows NT boot disk. After you are prompted to insert disk 2, you will have the chance to choose to repair a damaged Windows NT installation. Choose to inspect the boot record, and your master boot record will be replaced.

Another method of recovering the Windows NT Master Boot Sector is by using a third-party utility that has been designed to do just that.

These utilities are not supported by Microsoft, so be sure to read whatever documentation comes with them and have a backup of your data before you proceed with either of them.

`MAKEBOOT` was the first freeware utility available for recovering the Windows NT Master Boot Sector. Written by Arthur Knowles, this little executable does nothing but rewrite the Master Boot Sector so that you once again have the OS Loader Menu.

A similar utility is Boot Partition 2.0 for WinNT written by G. Vollant. This utility not only can recover the Windows NT Master Boot Sector but can also modify the `BOOT.INI` file to include MS-DOS, Windows 95, OS/2, and Linux.

Summary

The Windows NT boot process is fairly simple to follow and allows Windows NT to check its resources before actually booting.

The NTDETECT sequence, in particular, will verify for you that your boot devices are functioning properly. It also performs a test on your RAM that is specific to Windows NT and may not be picked up by other diagnostic software.

With its configurable `BOOT.INI` file, you can let Windows NT front-end other operating systems as well, which makes it a very flexible operating system.

The next chapter introduces you to how Windows NT implements the FAT file system and Windows NT's own file system, NTFS.

CHAPTER 11

Managing the Windows NT Registry

by Robert Reinstein

In this chapter, you will learn about the following topics:

- Editing the Windows NT Registry
- Backing up and restoring the Windows NT Registry

As Chapter 4, "Windows NT Registry Architecture," noted, the Windows NT Registry is a series of root keys, subkeys, and value entries. Managing the Registry sometimes can be a daunting task. In fact, for the most part, you should never have to touch the Registry, and, as an end user as opposed to a "system administrator," you should never touch the Registry.

At times, however, an administrator might need to make manual adjustments to the Registry, including recovering a corrupted Registry. This chapter covers these types of manual adjustments.

Editing the Windows NT Registry

Every technical note put out by Microsoft that involves making a manual change to the Windows NT Registry has a disclaimer telling the user that modifying the Registry could result in an unusable system.

Microsoft is 100-percent right for doing this, because the Registry is like any other database—there is no room for errors. A corrupted Registry can prevent device drivers from loading, make the SAM unavailable, or cause hundreds of other problems.

Caution: I cannot emphasize how delicate the Registry is. All the material covered in this chapter discusses altering the Registry in a way that could create an unstable or unbootable system. You must use extreme caution when altering the Registry or using any of the tools described in this chapter. A backup of the Registry should be done before you attempt to make changes.

The Windows NT Registry Editor

The Windows NT Registry Editor is the program that enables you to view, edit, print sections of, and assign security to the Registry.

Warning: Most settings stored in the Windows NT Registry that are editable through the Windows NT Registry Editor can be changed more easily through utilities such as the Control Panel, User Manager (for Domains), and Server Manager; via configuration settings in applications; and by using other programs. The Windows NT Registry Editor should be used only by people who are sure of what they are doing and have no other way of changing a setting.

You can start the Windows NT Registry Editor by running the program `REGEDT32.EXE`.

When you start the Windows NT Registry Editor, it loads the Registry from the local computer. You also can load the Registry from another Windows NT computer by choosing Registry | Select Computer. Of course, you must have proper authority to edit the local Registry or a remote Registry. Security for the Registry is discussed later in this chapter in the section "Assigning Security to the Registry."

The Windows NT Registry Editor has many options that enable you to configure it. You can make the Windows NT Registry Editor run in read-only mode and have the Editor prompt you whenever you attempt to delete a subkey, for example. You choose these options from the Options menu.

Tip: Perhaps the easiest way to browse the system information contained in the Registry is by using the Windows NT Diagnostics program, which is located in the Administrative Tools program folder. This program provides a read-only environment and makes it easier to interpret the great amount of data in the Registry.

Figure 11.1 shows the Windows NT Registry Editor with the five root keys—each in its own window.

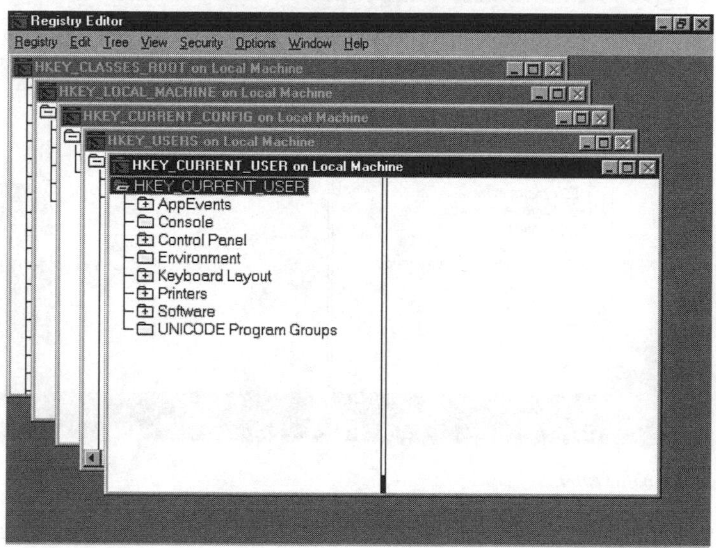

Figure 11.1. *The Windows NT Registry Editor.*

Using the Windows NT Registry Editor to view the Registry's contents is fascinating. The structure of the Registry in the Windows NT Registry Editor is simple and is presented in a File Manager–like fashion.

Each of the windows has two panels: one with subkeys and the other with value entries. After you click a subkey, the value entries associated with that subkey appear in the value entry panel. If no value entries are associated with the subkey, the value entry panel is blank.

Subkeys that contain more subkeys are indicated by a folder with a plus sign on it. You can expand this type of folder to reveal the next level of subkeys by double-clicking the folder. The plus sign then changes to a minus sign; you can close the current level of subkeys by double-clicking the folder again. Clicking any subkey displays any associated value entries in the value entry panel. Refer to Figure 11.1, which shows the root key highlighted. Because no value entries are associated with this root key, the value entry panel is blank.

Figure 11.2 shows the `AppEvents` subkey expanded. `AppEvents` includes the subkeys shown below it, as well as its own value entry, which is displayed in the value entry panel.

The `AppEvents` value entry, `Migrated Schemes`, has a data type of `REG_SZ`, and its value is `1`.

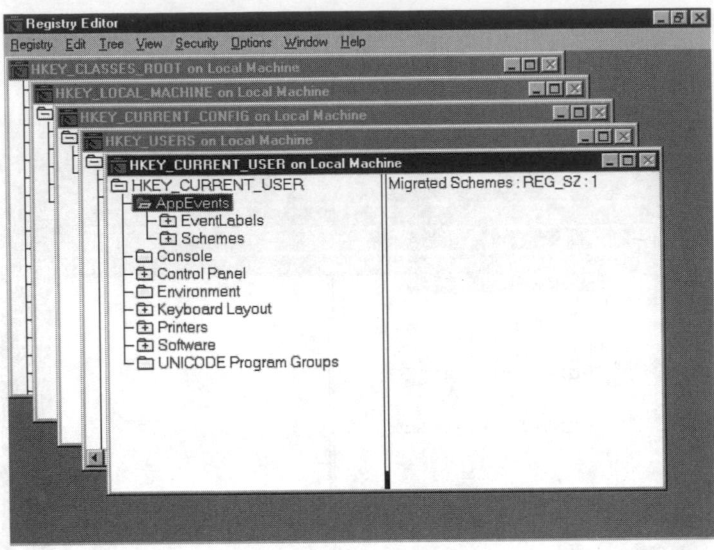

Figure 11.2. A subkey value entry.

Figure 11.3 shows a more descriptive and familiar group of settings that you might remember, not that you may still use them. The `[Restrictions]` settings in the Windows 3.*x* `PROGMAN.INI` still exist in Windows NT; however, for the Windows NT Program Manager, these settings appear in the Windows NT Registry as value entries for this subkey:

```
HKEY_CURRENT_USER\Software\Microsoft\Windows NT\CurrentVersion\Program Manager\
➥Restrictions
```

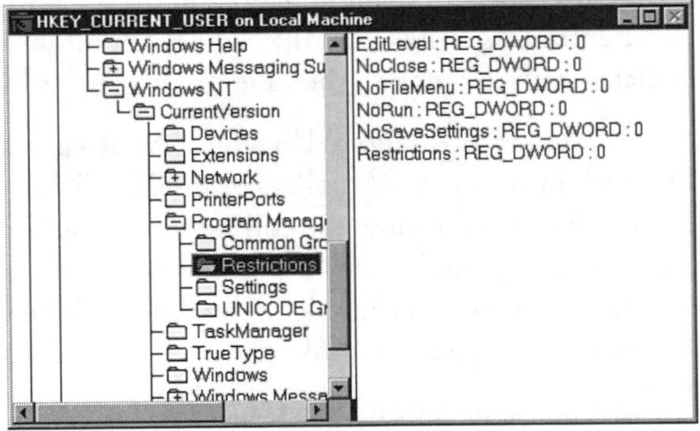

Figure 11.3. The Program Manager Restrictions settings in the Registry.

By default, these settings are a numeric zero, as they were in Windows 3.*x*. To edit these settings, however, you do not use the Windows Notepad; instead, you can double-click the value entry to access a value editor.

Value Editors

Each Registry entry is stored is a particular format. Some of these are numeric, and others are text strings. The Windows NT Registry Editor will automatically place you into the proper value editor when you choose to edit a value.

The DWORD Value Editor

The DWORD Editor shown in Figure 11.4 is only one of the four value editors in the Windows NT Registry Editor. The other editors are the String Editor, used for the data types `REG_SZ` and `REG_EXPAND_SZ`, the Multi-String Editor, which is for editing `REG_MULTI_SZ` values, and the Binary Editor, which stores editing values in the `REG_BINARY` data type format.

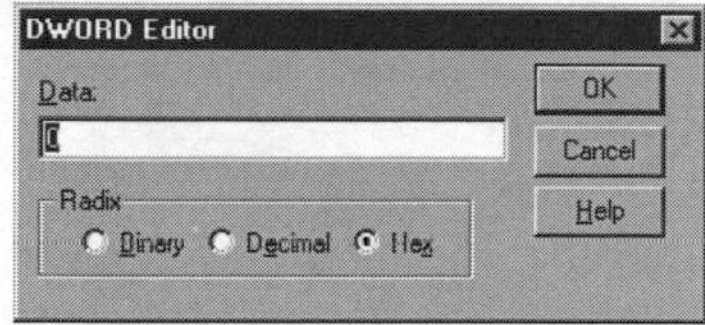

Figure 11.4. *The DWORD Editor.*

The DWORD Editor also enables you to change the way the data is displayed. The formats are a binary (base-2) number, decimal (base-10) number, or a hexadecimal (base-16) number.

The String Value Editor

The String Editor simply enables you to enter a data string.

The Binary Value Editor

You should use the Binary Editor very cautiously. As you can see in Figure 11.5, the data stored as a `REG_BINARY` data type is in hexadecimal format or true binary format. Both these formats are not easy to edit and actually are quite prone to typographical errors.

The Multi-String Value Editor

You can edit `REG_MULTI_SZ` data types by using the Multi-String Editor, which enables you to enter lists or multiple strings separated by a null character, which is not a space, but rather a "no value" character. You can press Enter to generate the null character in the Editor. Figure 11.6 shows two values contained in the same value entry.

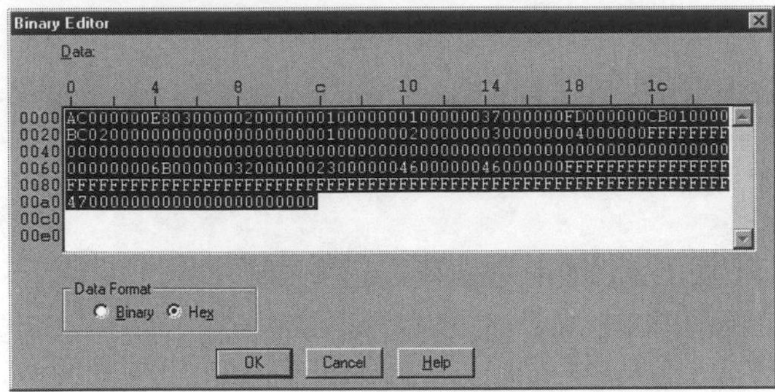

Figure 11.5. *The Binary Editor.*

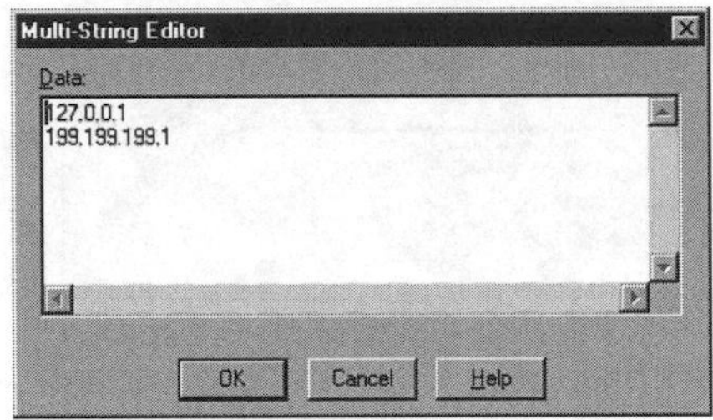

Figure 11.6. *The Multi-String Editor.*

The appropriate editor appears by default, based on the data type for the value entry. You can use a different value editor by highlighting the value entry you want to edit and then choosing the type of value editor you want to use from the Edit menu. It is best to use the default editor, though, because using the wrong value editor can result in corrupted data.

Searching the Registry

The search function in the Windows NT Registry Editor enables you to search by the name of a subkey. The REGEDIT Registry Editor, discussed in the next section, enables you to search under subkeys and value entries, which makes it easier to find items in the Registry.

To use the Windows NT Registry Editor to search Registry keys, choose View | Find Key. You can use the Find dialog to enter characters that might be all or part of a subkey name, as shown in Figure 11.7.

Note that only the subkeys, which are located in the left panel of the Registry, are searched; all value entries are ignored.

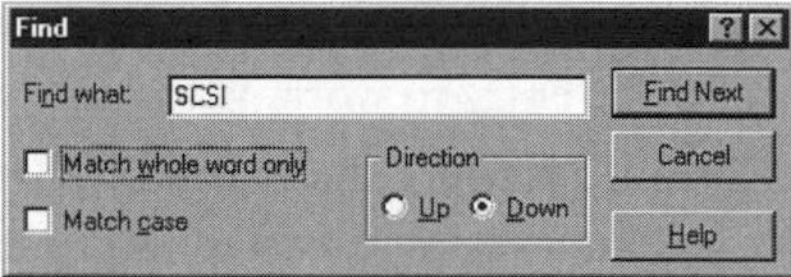

Figure 11.7. *Using the Find dialog to search the Registry.*

Adding Data to the Registry

Under normal circumstances, you should not need to add new subkeys or value entries to the Registry. However, you might have reasons to do this—either by fixes mentioned in Microsoft Windows NT Tech Notes and Microsoft Knowledge Base articles, or possibly at the advice of a software manufacturer.

The example used here creates a new subkey entry that is recommended to restrict access to a Windows NT Workstation computer's Registry from a remote computer. By default, Windows NT Server restricts remote access to its Registry only to members of the Administrators group. Windows NT Workstation has no provision for restricting access to its Registry, which is why this technique is being explained. In this case, the only way to restrict access to a Windows NT Workstation Registry is by adding a special subkey to the Registry.

The subkey that requires a value entry to enforce remote access on a Windows NT Workstation computer follows:

```
HKEY_LOCAL_MACHINE\System\CurrentControlSet\Control\SecurePipeServers
```

To add a value entry to the Registry, follow these steps:

1. Highlight the subkey to which you want to add the value entry. In this case, select `HKEY_LOCAL_MACHINE\System\CurrentControlSet\Control\SecurePipeServers`
2. Choose Edit | Add Key. The Add Value dialog appears.
3. Enter the name for the new value entry. In this case, the value name is `winreg`. The proper data type for this value entry is `REG_DWORD`, which you specify in the Data Type combo box. The Add Value dialog now should look similar to Figure 11.8.

Figure 11.8. *Specifying the value name and data type for a new value entry.*

4. Click OK. The appropriate editor—in this case, the DWORD Editor shown in Figure 11.9—appears. For this value entry to work, you must enter 1 as the value.
5. Click OK to exit the DWORD Editor dialog, and click OK to exit the Add Value dialog. The resulting entry appears, as shown in Figure 11.10.

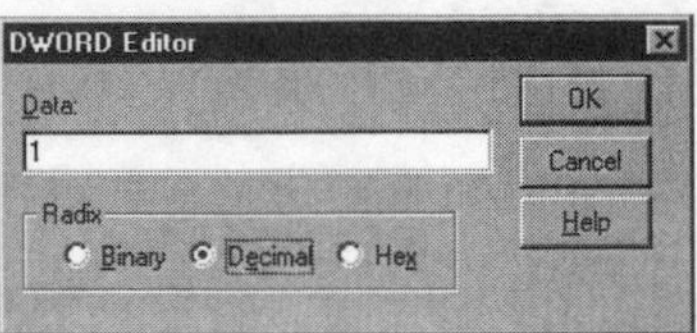

Figure 11.9. *Adding the value for the new value entry.*

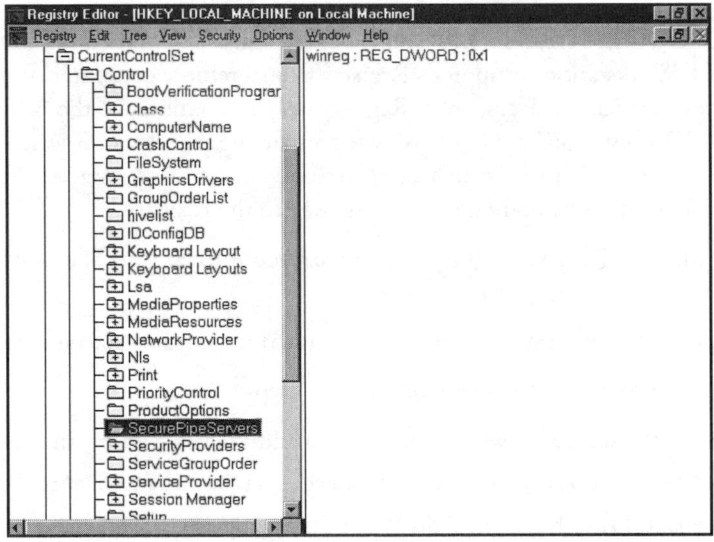

Figure 11.10. *A newly added value entry.*

You add a key to the Registry by using a similar procedure. You do not need to specify a value entry, however. Usually, you will not add a key unless a specific value entry needs to be added, but it is not mandatory.

Deleting Registry Objects

You can delete any object from the Registry if you have permission—whether it is a subkey or a value entry. The next section, "Assigning Security to the Registry," discusses Registry permissions.

You can delete a Registry object simply by highlighting the object and then pressing Delete or choosing Edit | Delete.

As with deleting objects from the Windows File Manager, if any subordinate subkeys (folders) exist, they are deleted as well.

Caution: Be extremely cautious before you delete any object from the Registry. One wrong move and you might be forced to use recovery techniques to avoid having an unstable system.

Assigning Security to the Registry

The example of adding a value entry showed you how to add a value entry to secure a Windows NT Workstation computer from having its Registry accessed across a network. Registry security is an issue of great concern. The Registry is fundamentally the heart of Windows NT, and it requires protection.

The Security menu in the Windows NT Registry Editor gives you choices of assigning permissions, configuring auditing, and assigning ownership, much like the NTFS file system. Under normal circumstances, the Registry is open to editing by anyone in the Administrators group. In addition to using the Windows NT Registry Editor to assign rights, setting User Rights from User Manager (for Domains) also can alter the permissions on certain keys. Members of the Backup Operators group, for example, have access to keys that a regular user does not.

Figure 11.11 shows the Registry Key Permissions dialog for the subkey you worked with in the "Adding Data to the Registry" section.

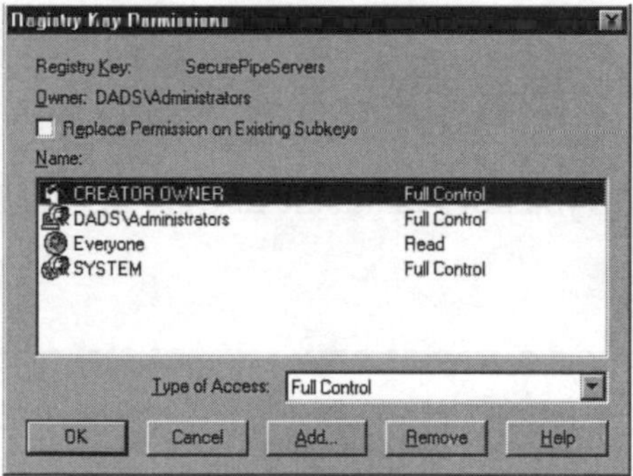

Figure 11.11. *Permissions for a Registry subkey.*

By default, the CREATOR OWNER, who is generally the user who added the subkey, has full control over the subkey. The Administrators group also has full control, as does the Windows NT System account. Also, by default, the Everyone account has read-only permission to the Registry subkey.

You can use the Auditing feature in the Registry to track all activity within the Registry, down to the subkey level. To enable auditing, first highlight the subkey you want to apply auditing to, and then choose Security | Auditing. The Registry Key Auditing dialog specifies the Registry key that has its auditing policies displayed, as shown in Figure 11.12.

You can enable the Audit Permission on Existing Subkeys check box in the Registry Key Auditing dialog to specify whether the auditing policies made in this dialog will apply to subkeys under this subkey. Next, you can flag specific user accounts and groups for auditing. You click the Add and Remove buttons to add and remove these accounts from the Name list in the Registry Key Permissions dialog.

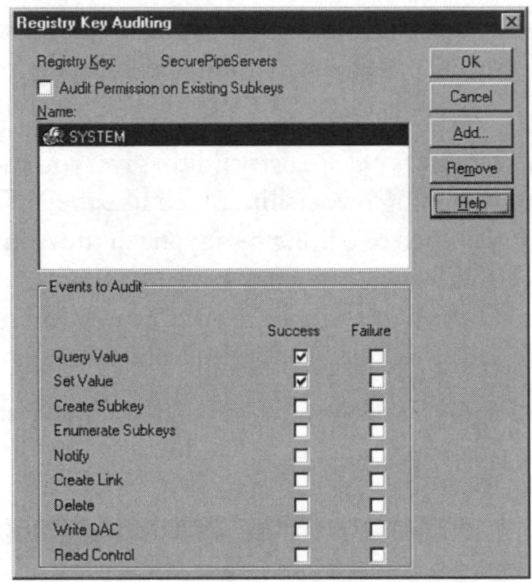

Figure 11.12. *The Registry Key Auditing dialog.*

Table 11.1 lists the events you can audit in the Registry Key Auditing dialog.

Table 11.1. Audited events.

Audit Property	*Audited Event*
Query Value	A value entry has been read
Set Value	A value entry has been written
Create Subkey	Creation of a subkey
Enumerate Subkeys	A read that scans through this subkey to find other subordinate subkeys
Notify	Subkey notification

Audit Property	*Audited Event*
Create Link	Creation of a pointer
Delete	Any deletion (subkey or value entry)
Write DAC	Write of a security permission
Read Control	Reading of a security permission

After you set the audit properties, click OK to enable these properties.

To take ownership of a Registry subkey and become the OWNER with or without being the CREATOR, you can choose Security | Owner. The Owner box appears, as shown in Figure 11.13; this is the same dialog you use to take ownership of NTFS objects.

Figure 11.13. *Taking ownership of a Registry subkey.*

The Other Registry Editor

The other Registry Editor available for Windows NT users is REGEDIT, which is modeled after the Windows 95 Registry Editor. I refer to this program as REGEDIT, even though its actual name is the same as the other Registry Editor, because the executable file for this program is `REGEDIT.EXE`.

Oddly enough, REGEDIT has a feature not available in the Windows NT Registry Editor: the capability to search through value entries. You can limit the level of searching to only subkeys or only value entries, which can come in handy if you are searching through a large Registry.

The Windows NT Registry Editor only enables you to search on a subkey, which sometimes is good enough, but not always.

The most noticeable difference between the two editors is that the Windows NT Registry Editor, REGEDT32, looks like a Windows 3.*x* program, whereas REGEDIT is designed with the Windows Explorer interface.

The Windows NT Registry Editor enables you to run the Editor in read-only mode, which is not available in REGEDIT. Users who just want to poke around to see what the Registry is about should use the Windows NT Registry Editor in read-only mode so that they do not accidentally modify any values.

REGEDIT does not enable you to set security for the Registry, so you probably will have reasons to use both these Registry Editors. REGEDIT is a great way to find data in the Registry, and the

Windows NT Registry Editor (REGEDT32) is the best way to edit the Registry—mainly because of its security-setting capability.

One other major difference between REGEDT32 and REGEDIT is that REGEDIT does not allow for the viewing or editing of the data types REG_EXPAND_SZ and REG_MULTI_SZ. In fact, if you try to view a REG_EXPAND_SZ with REGEDIT, it will be displayed as a binary value. Editing either of these values with REGEDIT will save the edited values as REG_SZ, which will render these values useless or possibly cause unpredictable behavior in the application or process that the Registry entry affects.

Figure 11.14 shows the same section of the Registry that is shown in Figure 11.3, but from within REGEDIT.

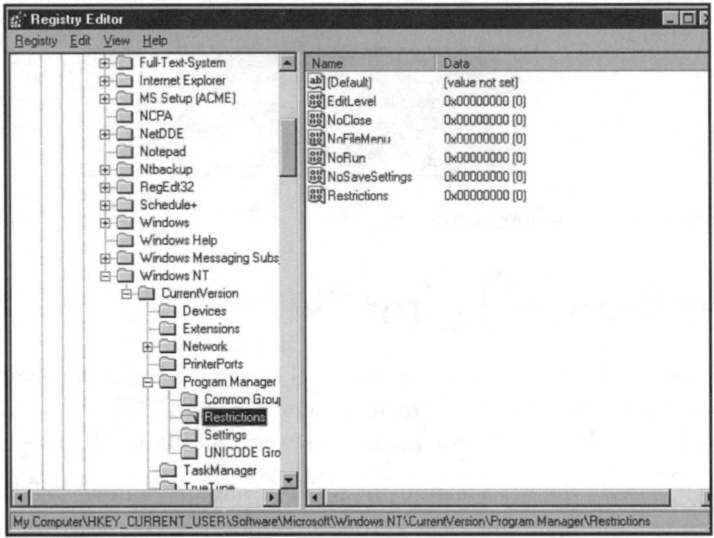

Figure 11.14. *The REGEDIT Registry Editor.*

Saving and Restoring the Registry

A corrupted Registry can prevent a Windows NT computer from booting. Several options are available for recovering from a corrupted or improperly edited Registry.

Backing Up the Registry

You can create a backup copy of the Registry in many ways. One way is by using the Windows NT Backup program or a third-party backup program. These programs offer an option to back up the Registry.

Restoring this backup requires a working Windows NT system and the proper permissions to restore the Registry. For more information on restoring the Registry in a nonbootable system, see Chapters 44, "Registry Recovery," and 45, "Disaster Recovery."

Another way to perform a Registry backup is to create an Emergency Repair Disk with the RDISK.EXE program, which creates a copy of the main Registry hives on the disk.

Saving Sections of the Registry

You can save subkeys and entire root keys by using commands on the Registry menu of the Windows NT Registry Editor. You can use the Save Key command to save subkeys as a hive, which is a non-readable format but can be restored to any Windows NT computer by choosing the Restore command from the same menu. You should use this method of saving a subkey as a precaution before modifying a subkey. The Save Subtree As command saves subkeys and their subordinate subkeys as readable text files. Listing 11.1 shows an example of a saved subkey structure.

Listing 11.1. A subkey saved as a text file.

```
Key Name:          SYSTEM\CurrentControlSet\Control\SecurePipeServers
Class Name:        <NO CLASS>
Last Write Time:   7/3/96 - 8:29 PM

Key Name:          SYSTEM\CurrentControlSet\Control\SecurePipeServers\winreg
Class Name:        <NO CLASS>
Last Write Time:   7/3/96 - 8:29 PM
Value 0
  Name:            Description
  Type:            REG_SZ
  Data:            Registry Server


Key Name:          SYSTEM\CurrentControlSet\Control\SecurePipeServers\
                   ➥winreg\AllowedPaths
Class Name:        <NO CLASS>
Last Write Time:   9/7/96 - 6:22 PM
Value 0
  Name:            Machine
  Type:            REG_MULTI_SZ
  Data:            System\CurrentControlSet\Control\ProductOptions
                   System\CurrentControlSet\Control\Print\Printers
                   System\CurrentControlSet\Services\Eventlog
                   Software\Microsoft\Windows NT\CurrentVersion
```

Summary

The importance of knowing how to properly handle the Registry and when to handle the Registry cannot be emphasized enough. After you become familiar with the Registry, you can use the various methods of viewing and editing the Registry as troubleshooting tools, and you will better understand how Windows NT works.

The next chapter, "Registry Values," introduces you to some of the most-used Registry objects, along with some obscure entries that might help you to understand Windows NT configuration.

Registry Values

by Robert Reinstein

This chapter is actually a tour of parts of the Windows NT Registry—with slight diversions—that will explain some of the more interesting sights along the way.

This chapter discusses the following:

- Where application settings are stored
- File associations and file type settings
- How to create an automatic logon
- Changing the default spool file path
- The location of the Last Known Good Configuration

Chapter 4, "Windows NT Registry Architecture," explained the general architecture of the Registry, which is a prerequisite for this chapter, as was Chapter 11, "Managing the Windows NT Registry," which showed how to use the editing and viewing tools for the Registry.

The Windows NT Registry can have hundreds of objects. Thus, not every single object is discussed in this chapter. There are certain objects, however, that you as an administrator should be able to seek out and verify, or possibly edit, when the need arises.

Caution: The Windows NT Registry is a delicate database that should be edited with extreme caution. An invalid value or any corruption to the Windows NT Registry can result in a non-startable Windows NT system.

HKEY_LOCAL_MACHINE

The HKEY_LOCAL_MACHINE root key holds the most important Registry information. This is the information that keeps the Windows NT computer running, and is the root key that you will most probably want to refer to in order to troubleshoot computer settings.

HKEY_LOCAL_MACHINE\HARDWARE

The HARDWARE subkey, shown in Figure 12.1, contains information about the hardware found on the Windows NT computer during the boot process. This is not data that can be edited, because it is always re-created at boot. This information is available in a readable format by running Windows NT Diagnostics, which is found in the Administrative Tools program folder. The value entry displayed in Figure 12.1 shows the SCSI driver that is in use on the Windows NT computer.

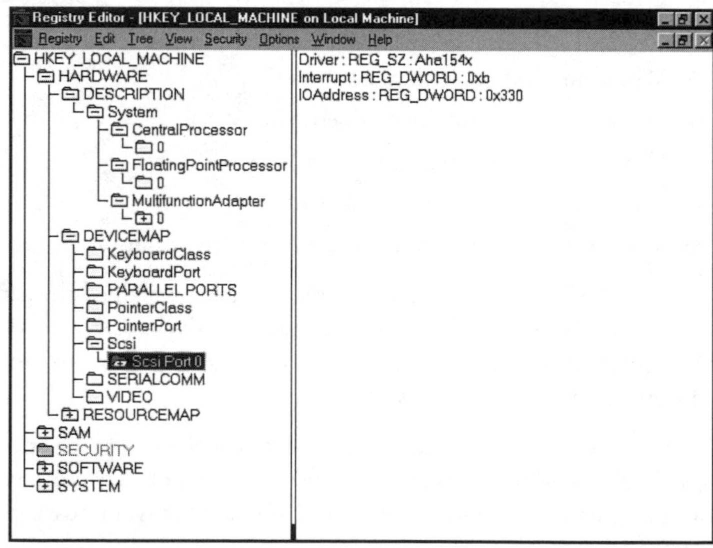

Figure 12.1. HKEY_LOCAL_MACHINE\HARDWARE.

The HARDWARE\DESCRIPTION contains low-level information about the computer. This includes information about CPUs, FPUs, serial ports, parallel ports, and input devices.

The HARDWARE\DEVICEMAP subkey duplicates some of the information from DESCRIPTION, but also has more detailed information about SCSI drives and the video configuration.

The HARDWARE\RESOURCEMAP subkey breaks down the hardware into subkeys that have value entries that identify the bus number and bus type for each. Within those values are detailed information regarding hardware interrupts, DMA channels, memory addresses, and other information that has been collected when NTDETECT.COM was run.

The SAM subkey is not viewable, and contains no editable value entries.

The SECURITY subkey is also not viewable, and contains no editable value entries.

HKEY_LOCAL_MACHINE\SOFTWARE

The SOFTWARE subkey contains configuration settings for software that has been installed under Windows NT, as well as settings for Windows NT itself.

The settings contained within SOFTWARE are limited to system-level software settings. All application software settings are kept in the HKEY_USERS root key.

Examples of the type of software settings kept in this subkey are network adapter drivers, protocols, ODBC software, Windows NT services, subsystems, and the Windows NT product itself.

Figure 12.2 shows the network adapter card drivers that have been installed. Many value entries have been created in order to document this driver.

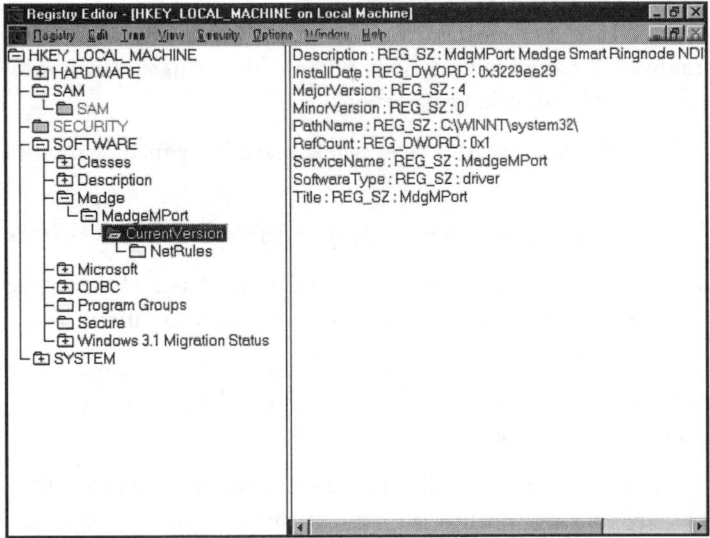

Figure 12.2. HKEY_LOCAL_MACHINE\SOFTWARE.

HKEY_LOCAL_MACHINE\SOFTWARE\Classes

The HKEY_CLASSES_ROOT root key is actually a pointer to the subkey HKEY_LOCAL_MACHINE\SOFTWARE\Classes, which is shown in Figure 12.3. This subkey contains subkeys and value entries that are all related to file extensions and OLE objects.

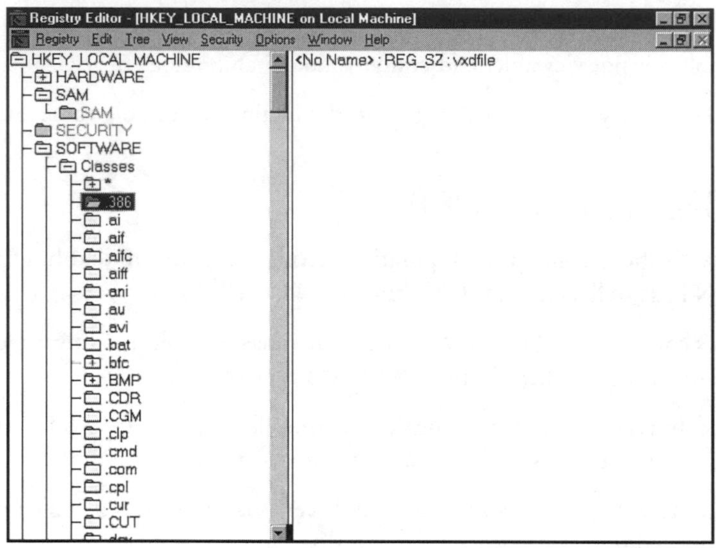

Figure 12.3. HKEY_LOCAL_MACHINE\SOFTWARE\Classes.

Although changing file extension associations is usually done by using the View/Options menu item in Windows NT Explorer or My Computer, editing this subkey is sometimes an easier way to make changes to file extension associations.

A subkey under HKEY_LOCAL_MACHINE\SOFTWARE\Classes may include multiple subkeys and value entries.

For example, a file extension may have a file type definition, such as curfile for extension .cur.

When this is the case, curfile also appears as a subkey that has a value entry defining it as a Cursor. It also has a subkey of DefaultIcon that specifies an icon association.

Other file types may have definitions that are used for the Microsoft Internet Explorer Web browser, such as .zip, which has a value entry titled Content Type, which has a value of application/x-zip-compressed.

Explorer shell extensions are also defined in HKEY_LOCAL_MACHINE\SOFTWARE\Classes. These add commands or redefine commands on context menus that are displayed when right-mouse clicking—or by double-clicking if it is set as the default action—on a file from within Explorer.

As shown in Figure 12.4, The file type `AVIFile` has many subkeys. The `shell` subkey defines the Open command from the context menu as the command shown on the right-hand panel, which is to execute the program Media Player (`mplay32.exe`) with switches that will play the file and then close Media Player.

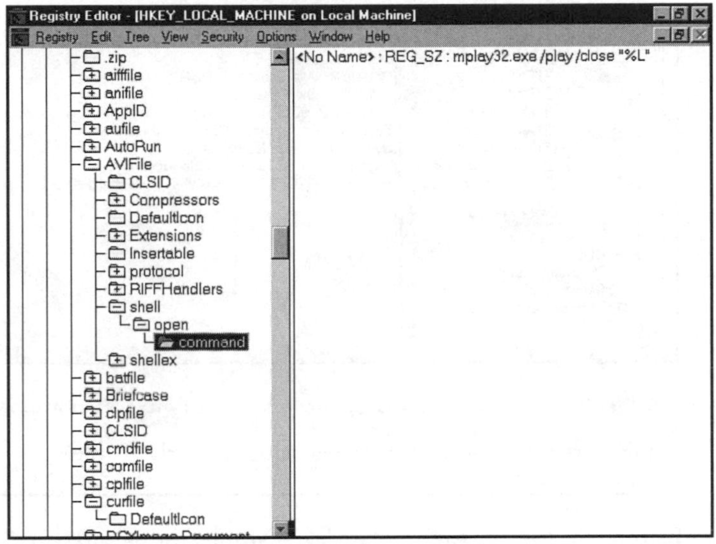

Figure 12.4. *Windows NT Explorer shell definition in* `HKEY_LOCAL_MACHINE\SOFTWARE\Classes`.

Creating an Automated Windows NT Logon

The subkey `HKEY_LOCAL_MACHINE\SOFTWARE\Microsoft\WindowsNT\CurrentVersion\Winlogon` defines the Windows NT logon process. It is here that an automated logon can be created. Although this may be a Windows NT security violation, it can be used when troubleshooting Windows NT and the need arises for booting Windows NT without requiring an interactive logon.

First, the value entry `AutoAdminLogon` needs to be enabled by changing the value to 1.

Next, the value entry `DefaultUserName` needs to be changed to the user account that will be used for an automatic logon.

And finally, a new value entry needs to be added. Add the value entry `DefaultPassword`, with a data type of `REG_SZ` and the password for `DefaultUser` as the value.

Figure 12.5 shows the `HKEY_LOCAL_MACHINE\SOFTWARE\Microsoft\WindowsNT\CurrentVersion\Winlogon` value entries.

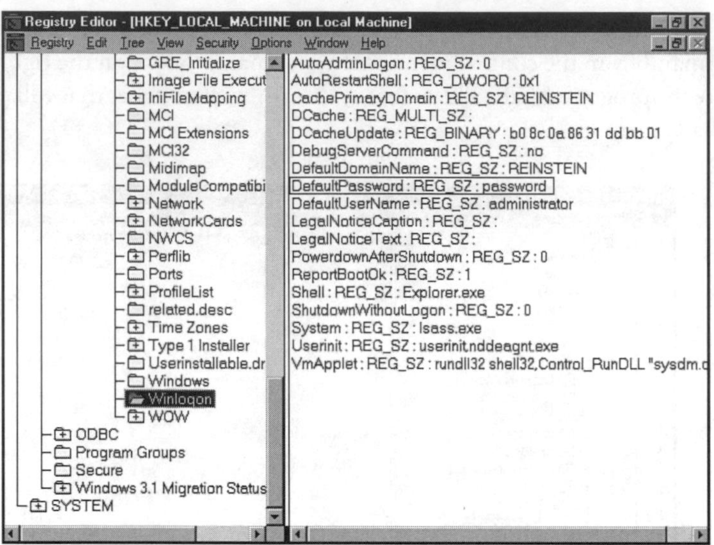

Figure 12.5. `HKEY_LOCAL_MACHINE\SOFTWARE\Microsoft\Windows NT\CurrentVersion\Winlogon` *value entries.*

In this list of value entries, the `DefaultPassword` value is clearly visible.

Caution: Because the `DefaultPassword` is clearly visible, the `DefaultUser` should only be a temporary account and not be a user account that carries a lot of permissions and rights.

Ideally, this method will be used using a `DefaultUser` that does not carry many permissions and rights.

HKEY_LOCAL_MACHINE\SYSTEM

The `HKEY_LOCAL_MACHINE\SYSTEM` subkey includes configuration settings that are essential for booting up a Windows NT computer.

The Last Known Good Configuration Location

Figure 12.6 shows the `Select` subkey, which contains value entries that have information regarding the `ControlSet` subkeys and the `CurrentControlSet` subkey.

The `ControlSet00x` subkeys contain devices, services, and configuration information that are used when Windows NT is booted. The value entries for the `Select` subkey refer to the `ControlSet00x` subkeys.

For instance, the value entry `Current` has a value of `1`, which refers to `ControlSet001`. The value entry `LastKnownGood` refers to the `ControlSet` that will be used when "Last Known Good Configuration" is chosen (by pressing the spacebar at boot time). In this case, `ControlSet002` would be used if "Last Known Good Configuration" is chosen. Actually, `CurrentControlSet` is always used, but in the event of a "Last Known Good Configuration" choice, the `ControlSet` designated as `LastKnownGood` would be copied to `CurrentControlSet` at boot time.

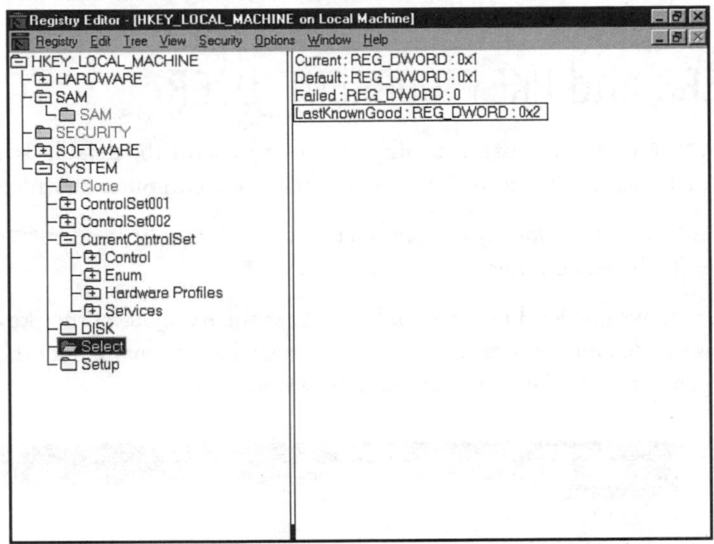

Figure 12.6. `HKEY_LOCAL_MACHINE\SYSTEM\Select`.

The `HKEY_LOCAL_MACHINE\SYSTEM\CurrentControlSet\Services` subkey contains the bulk of the settings for networking. The `HKEY_LOCAL_MACHINE\SYSTEM\Control\Hardware Profiles` subkey defines the different hardware profiles that are set up on the current computer.

Changing Spool File Paths

Almost all printer settings for Windows NT can be set from Control Panel or the Printer Properties dialogs. The only way to change where Windows NT puts spool files, however, is by directly changing the Registry.

Under the subkey `HKEY_LOCAL_MACHINE\SYSTEM\CurrentControlSet\Control\Print\Printers` is the value entry `DefaultSpoolDirectory`. This value can be changed to an alternate path for spool files.

Note: By default the directory is `SystemRoot\SYSTEM32\spool\PRINTERS`.

This value entry sets the spool file path for all printers. You can, however, assign separate spool file paths for each printer by changing the value entry that is under `HKEY_LOCAL_MACHINE\SYSTEM\CurrentControlSet\Control\Print\Printers\printername`, where *`printername`* is the assigned name for the printer. The value entry `SpoolDirectory` is, by default, blank, but can be changed.

HKEY_USERS and HKEY_CURRENT_USER

The `HKEY_USERS` root key contains configuration settings for the default user profile and a user profile for each user that has been identified for the current computer on which the Registry exists.

The `HKEY_CURRENT_USER` root key is actually a pointer to the subkey under `HKEY_USERS` that applies to the currently logged on user.

Figure 12.7 shows one level of three subkeys under the `HKEY_USERS` root key. The first subkey, `.DEFAULT`, is the default user profile. The other two subkeys are named for the SID that has been randomly generated for the user at the time they were created.

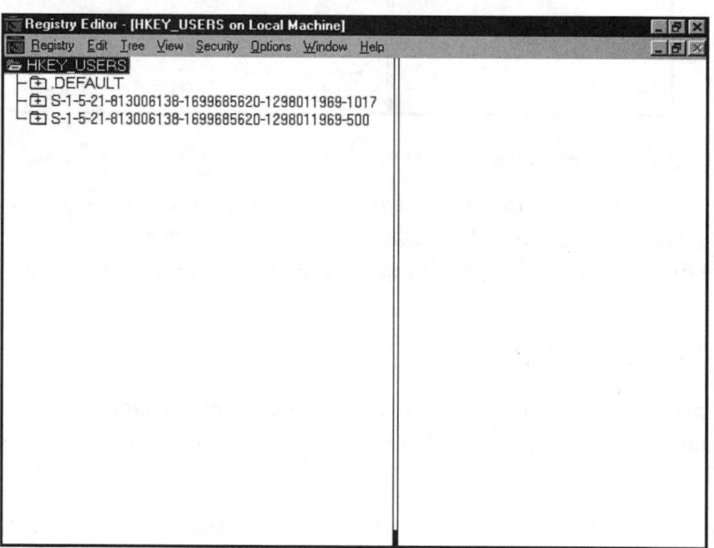

Figure 12.7. `HKEY_USERS` *subkeys.*

For each user profile, settings are kept in subkeys, including those listed in Table 12.1.

Table 12.1. User settings from `HKEY_USERS`.

Subkey	*Description*
`AppEvents\EventLabels`	Windows NT events create messages, such as `AppGPFault`. Event labels translate these events into readable English. For example, `AppGPFault` translates into `Program Error`.

Subkey	*Description*
`AppEvents\Schemes`	Associates system events and WAV (sound) files. Contains default and current settings for each of these events.
`Console`	Command prompt window settings. Multiple settings for `Console` can be created by creating a subkey under `Console` that has the name associated with the icon for the command prompt session. By default, the command prompt icon is labeled "Command Prompt." If no subkey is found with the name of the command prompt window, the `Console` default settings are used. If the name is found, those settings override the `Console` default settings.
`Control Panel`	Settings that are set from within the Control Panel, including screen savers, desktop, custom colors, mouse, keyboard, and patterns, among others.
`Environment`	Path settings for `TEMP` and `TMP` files.
`Keyboard Layout`	This is defined by the settings in Control Panel. A value in the `Substitutes` subkey would override the computer's default keyboard layout.
`Software`	Individual software settings. Software vendors will usually create a subkey for their company name and then add further subkeys for each of their applications. By default, all of the Windows NT applets and applications, such as Windows Help and Clock, have entries in here under the `Microsoft` subkey.
`UNICODE Program Groups`	Not used by Windows NT 4.0, but included for backwards compatibility.

Figure 12.8 shows one of the user profile subkeys expanded to show some of the other subkeys that are available. In this case, the Desktop subkey is expanded to show the 26 value entries that are kept for the desktop settings for each user profile.

Usually, the only subkey that should require manual modification (as opposed to using the Control Panel) is the `HKEY_USERS\.DEFAULT` subkey, which may be edited in order to set preferences for all new user profiles that are created on that computer.

The subkey `HKEY_CURRENT_USER\Software\Microsoft\Windows NT\CurrentVersion\Extensions` contains the file associations for the user currently logged on.

Settings that are comparable to the one that were handled in Windows 3.x from the `WIN.INI` file are located in the `HKEY_CURRENT_USER\Software\Microsoft\Windows NT\CurrentVersion\Windows` subkey.

Most notable here are the equivalents of the `RUN=` and `LOAD=` lines from `WIN.INI`.

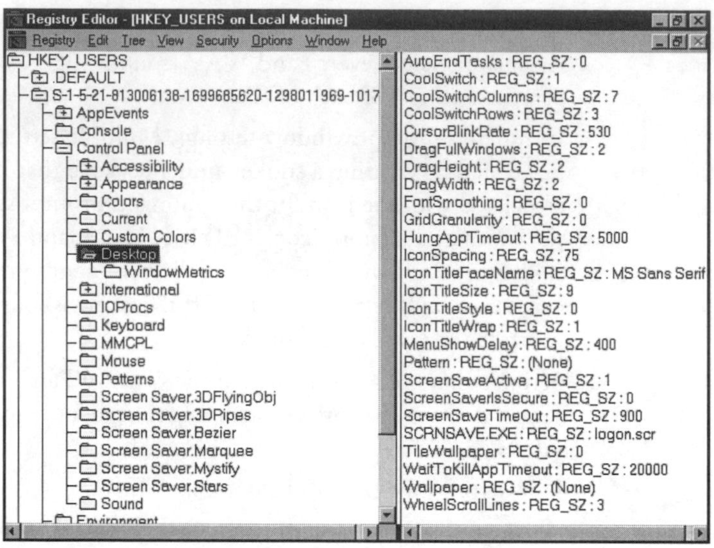

Figure 12.8. `HKEY_USERS\SID\Desktop` *subkey.*

Figure 12.9 shows the `HKEY_CURRENT_USER\Software\Microsoft\Windows NT\CurrentVersion\Windows` subkey. The equivalent of the old `WIN.INI LOAD=` line is the value entry `load`. The value entry `run` is the same as the old `WIN.INI RUN=` line.

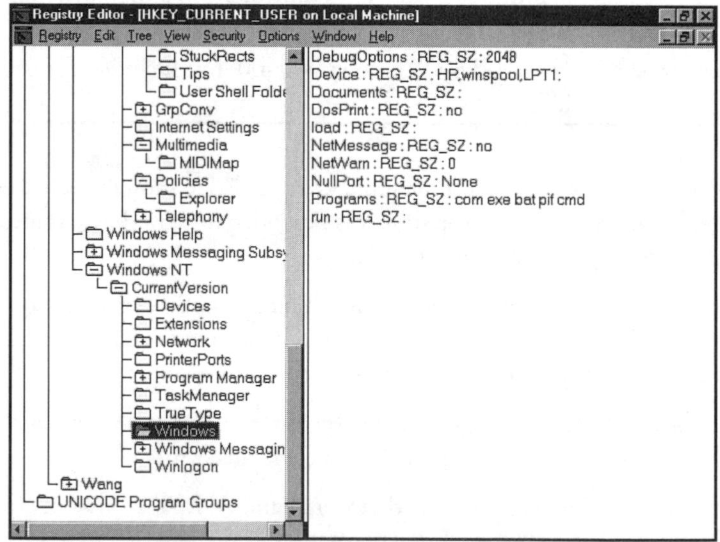

Figure 12.9. `HKEY_CURRENT_USER\Software\Microsoft\Windows NT\CurrentVersion\Windows.`

Summary

The Windows NT Registry may appear daunting at first, but once understood, it can easily be navigated and used as a troubleshooting tool. By having a single point to locate all of the computer and user settings, a great deal of understanding about the computer, user accounts, and Windows NT can be gained.

CHAPTER 13

Customizing the Windows NT Interface

by Robert Reinstein

With Windows NT 4.0, the Windows 95 interface came to Windows NT. The name of the interface is Explorer—not to be confused with the Explorer application or the Microsoft Internet Explorer.

Some diehard Windows 3.*x* users may be having a hard time getting used to the new interface, but there are ways to customize the new interface that will make the tasks of a Windows NT administrator easier.

Most of the administrative tasks could not be done with the previous interface.

This chapter introduces you to the following:

- The Windows NT Explorer shell
- System folders
- Tips for creating shortcuts

The Windows NT Desktop

Let me take you on a tour through the default Windows NT 4.0 desktop, which is shown in Figure 13.1.

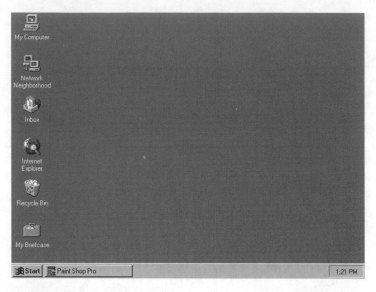

Figure 13.1. *The Windows NT 4.0 desktop.*

Running up and down the left side of the desktop are the default shortcuts.

Most of them are folders, which means that they contain other objects. There are system folders, which cannot be deleted, and there are regular folders, which are actually pointers to file directories. However, the vernacular for Windows NT 4.0 no longer uses directories as a proper term; what used to be called a directory is now called a folder.

The System Shortcuts

The first shortcut, My Computer, is a system folder. When it is opened by a double-click, as shown in Figure 13.2, it displays major system components such as logical drives, the Control Panel folder, the Printers folder, and the Dial-Up Networking folder.

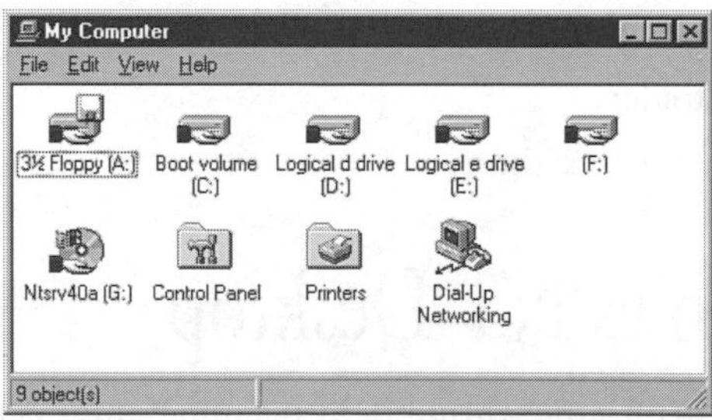

Figure 13.2. *The My Computer folder.*

The next shortcut, which is also a system folder, is the Network Neighborhood. As shown in Figure 13.3, the Network Neighborhood contains shortcuts for computers from the home domain. If other servers were on the network, these would be visible as well. The Entire Network shortcut, which is also a system folder, goes out to the entire network and provides shortcuts for domains and other networks that this computer has support to see. For instance, if a NetWare network were also on the network, the Entire Network folder would have a folder for NetWare and a folder for Microsoft.

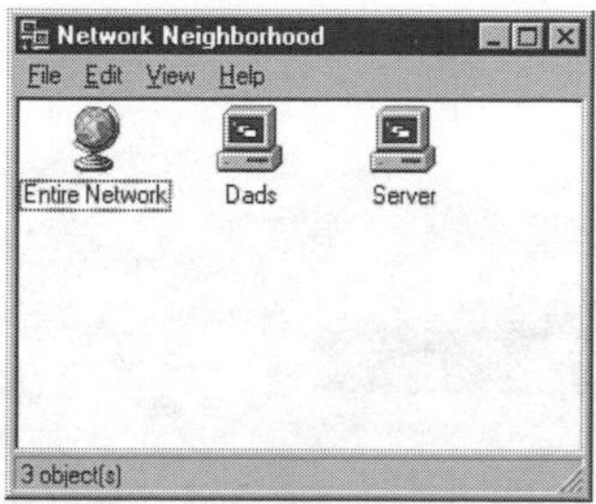

Figure 13.3. *The Network Neighborhood folder.*

The Inbox shortcut is actually a shortcut to Microsoft Windows Messaging. Double-clicking this will bring up the Windows Messaging client for Workgroups, which gives you access to a workgroup postoffice. Additional services may be added so that Windows Messaging can access Microsoft Mail postoffices and Internet mail.

If Microsoft Exchange Server and the Microsoft Exchange Server client software have been installed, the Inbox shortcut will point to the Microsoft Exchange Server Client instead.

The Internet Explorer shortcut is for Microsoft Internet Explorer. By default, version 2.0 of Microsoft Internet Explorer for Windows NT is installed with Windows NT 4.0. You can then upgrade to the latest version, which at the time of this writing was version 3.01. To download the latest version of Internet Explorer, go to the following Web page:

`http://www.microsoft.com/ie.`

The Recycle Bin is a system folder that contains deleted objects.

My Briefcase is a system folder that contains file objects that have been flagged for replication to another computer, usually a laptop.

The Windows NT Taskbar

At the bottom of the desktop is the Windows NT Taskbar. The Taskbar is similar to the Task Manager from Windows NT 3.51.

The difference here is that the Taskbar not only lists programs that are currently running, but it can always be visible without interfering with running programs. The Taskbar is also a container for other Windows NT objects such as the Start button and, by default, provides quick access to the Date/Time Properties dialog. The Taskbar is extendible, allowing third-party vendors to add items to it.

The Start Button

On the left side of the Taskbar is the Start button, which is really a shortcut that has many shortcuts within it.

Clicking the Start button once brings up a pop-up menu, shown in Figure 13.4, which shows the combined contents of the default Start folder and the user Start folder. Each user logging on to the computer can have unique Start folder items.

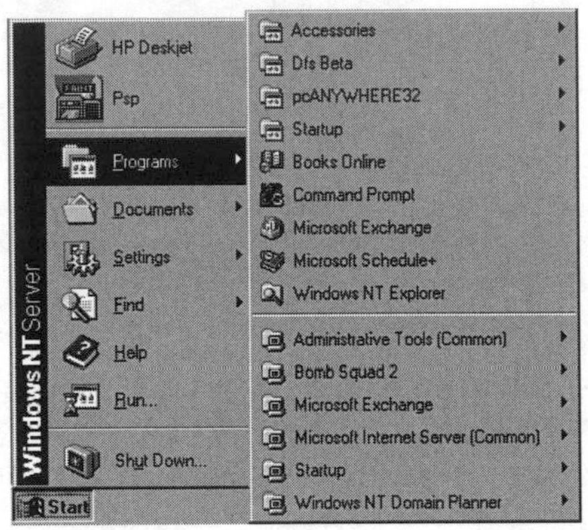

Figure 13.4. *The Start menu.*

Here's a list of the Start folder contents:

- The Programs folder, shown extended in Figure 13.4, contains common program folders and user program folders, which are delimited by a horizontal line.
- The Documents folder contains shortcuts to recently opened files.
- The Settings system folder contains shortcuts to the Windows NT Control Panel, the Printers folder, and the Taskbar Properties dialog.
- The Find, Help, Run, and Shut Down menu items are system commands that can be removed from the Start menu only by implementing User Profiles.

At the top of the Start menu are shortcuts that I placed there manually. These are added to the Start menu by dragging and dropping a shortcut onto the Start button. The user-definable Start button contents can be managed by using the Start Menu Programs tab in the Taskbar Properties dialog.

As shown in Figure 13.5, the top part of the Programs folder is pointing to the `%systemroot%\Profiles` folder. In this case, I'm logged on to the computer as Administrator. Thus, within the `%systemroot%\Profiles` folder is the Administrator folder. The list of folders within `%systemroot%\Profiles\Administrator` contains settings unique to the Administrator user account. One of these is the Start Menu folder.

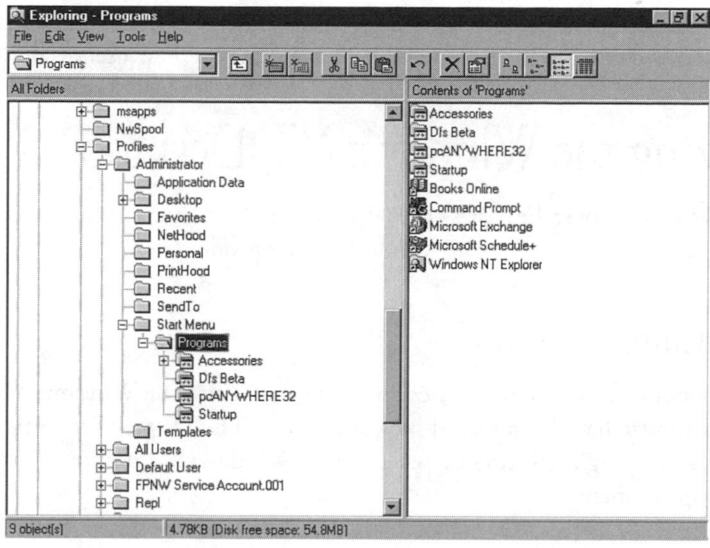

Figure 13.5. *The Administrator's Start Menu items.*

As you can see, on the right panel in this Explorer view are the contents of the Start Menu folder for Administrator. On the left panel, the contents of the Programs folders are exploded to show the subfolders. All these shortcuts make up part of the Start Menu.

The other part of the Start Menu comes from shortcuts within the `%systemroot%\Profiles\All Users\Start Menu` folder, shown in Figure 13.6.

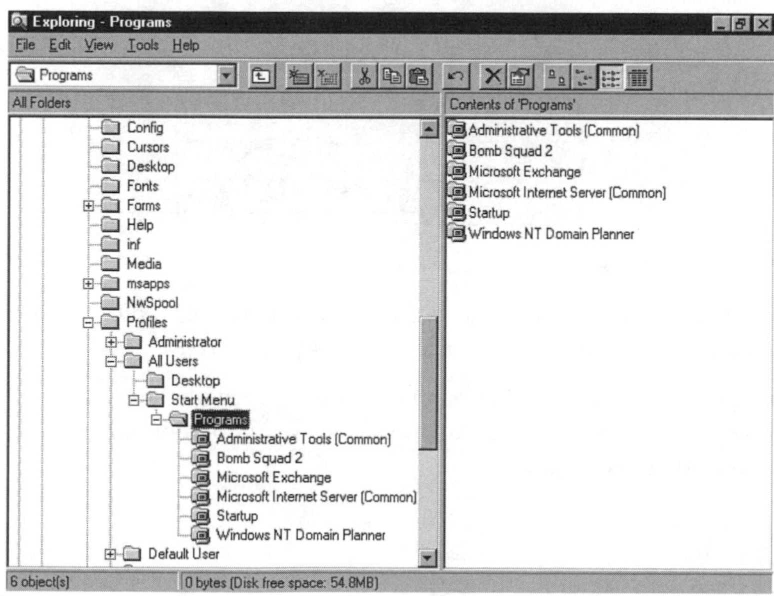

Figure 13.6. *All users' Start Menu items.*

When a user account is created on a Windows NT computer, the folder `%systemroot\Profiles\Default User` is copied to the unique folder created for the new user account.

Customizing the Windows NT Desktop

Now that we've gone over the basics of the Windows NT desktop, we can discuss how to customize the desktop in ways that will enable you to be more productive.

Basic Customization

Most of the items for which we're used to having to go into the Windows NT Control Panel in order to customize have been placed into one dialog. The Display Properties dialog (see Figure 13.7) is accessed by right-clicking anywhere on the Windows NT desktop and choosing Properties from the pop-up menu.

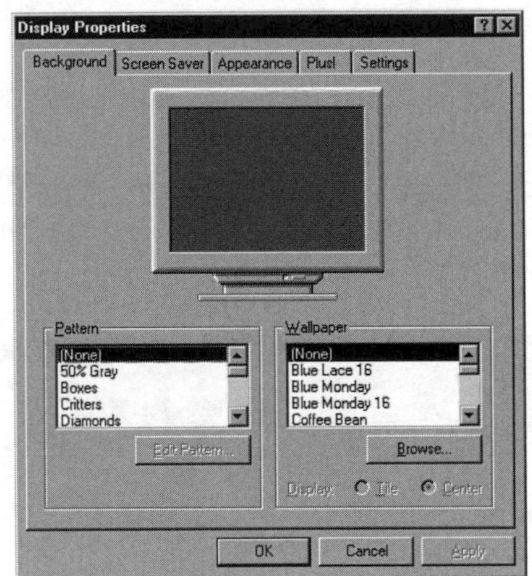

Figure 13.7. *Display Properties.*

The five tabs in the Display Properties dialog allow you to change your wallpaper, pattern, screen saver, color scheme, system fonts, icon size, and display driver.

These options are the same as those found in Windows 95, with the exception of the Settings tab, which forces you to test any changes to the video driver, resolution, color depth, or monitor type before committing to change these.

Folder Views

By default, when you open a folder, it opens in Folder view. Another type of view is the Explorer view. This default view can be changed by redefining the default double-click action on folder objects.

When you right-click an object, the pop-up menu that you see is a context menu, which means that, depending on the type of object you have clicked, the menu will show only options that pertain to that object.

For instance, Figure 13.8 shows a Context menu for a logical drive object that exists on a hard drive. The options include formatting, sharing, and opening the Properties dialog for this object.

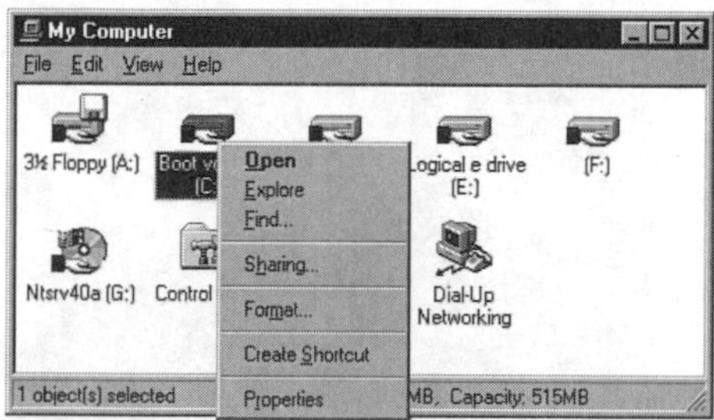

Figure 13.8. The Context menu.

You also can see that the menu item Open is in a bold font, which indicates that this is the menu item that will be chosen automatically if the object is double-clicked.

To change the default for this type of Context menu, which refers to any Context menu that has a choice of Open or Explore, choose Explore to get into Explorer view, as shown in Figure 13.9.

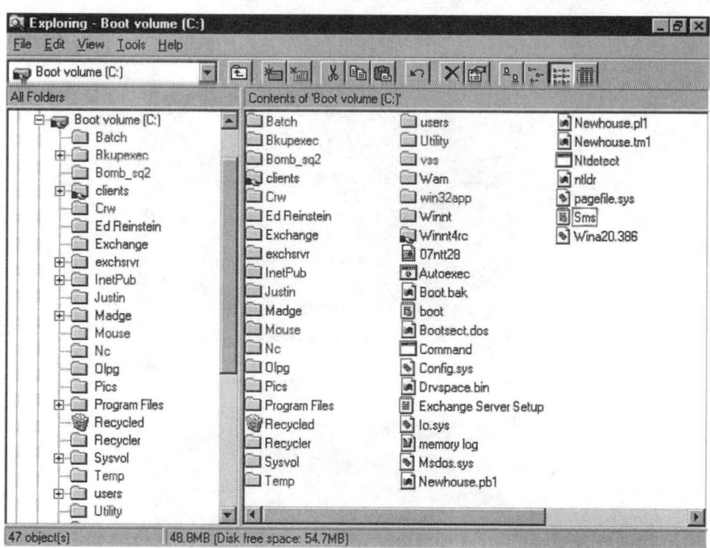

Figure 13.9. Explorer view.

Now select Options... from the View menu. Click the File Types tab in the Options dialog. Scroll down the list of Registered file types until you find the entry Folder (not File Folder), as shown in Figure 13.10.

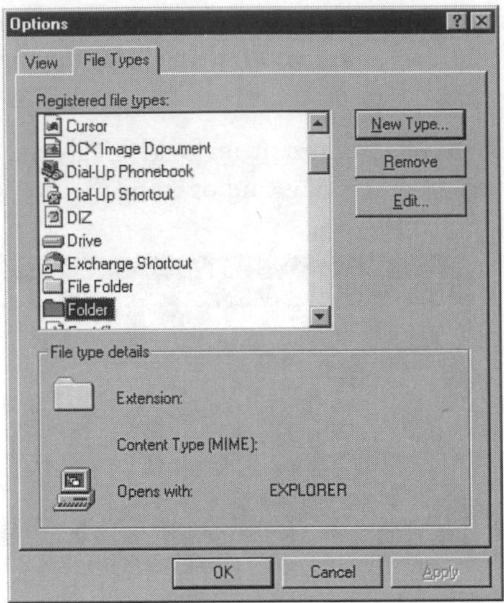

Figure 13.10. *The File Types options.*

Highlight the Folder entry and then click the button labeled Edit.... In the Edit File Type dialog, there are two Actions: open and explore. Highlight explore, and then click the button labeled Set Default. As shown in Figure 13.11, explore should now be boldface, which makes it the default action when double-clicking a folder. Try double-clicking a folder, such as My Computer or Network Neighborhood, and you'll see that explore is now the default view.

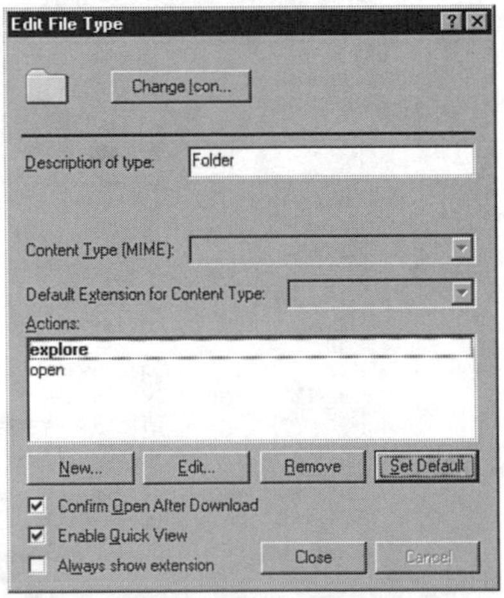

Figure 13.11. *The Edit File Type dialog.*

You can also modify the contents of the context menus, such as adding or deleting items on the menu. This is especially handy if you want to have a file extension associated with more than one program.

In Figure 13.12, I've gone into the Edit File Type for the file type Bitmap Image. Because I currently have a third-party image tool that is associated with the Open action, I'm going to click the New... button.

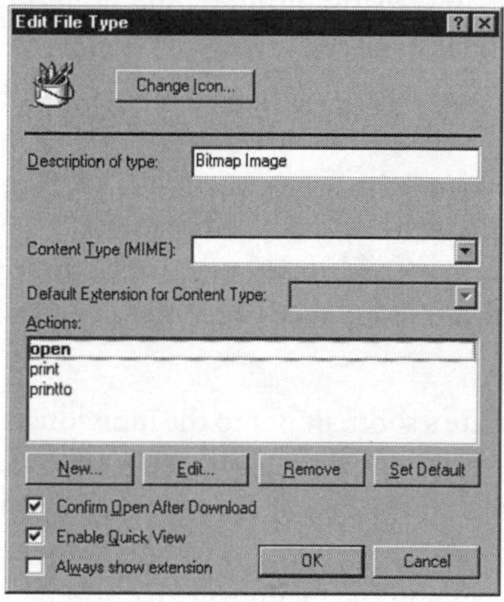

Figure 13.12. *Editing the Bitmap Image file type.*

Figure 13.13 shows the New Action dialog. The Action field is for the text that will appear on the context menu. The Application used to perform the action is entered as `pbrush.exe`, which is the Paint application included with Windows NT. Because `pbrush.exe` will automatically support this way of opening a file, I do not need to include any command-line parameters. As with a batch file, I could include a `%1` variable if the application requires a parameter.

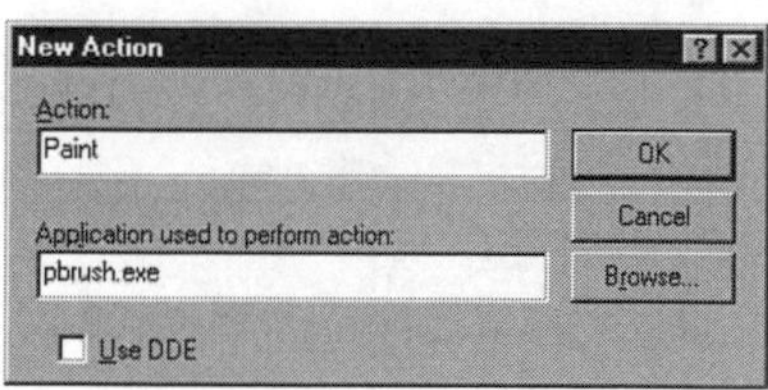

Figure 13.13. *Creating a new action for a context menu.*

Adding Useful Shortcuts

A shortcut is a small file that contains information about an object. This can include a file location, or in the case of a DOS executable, it will point to a PIF file.

Usually people will add shortcuts on their desktop for programs that they use on a regular basis. This is definitely one of the great uses for shortcuts. But because shortcuts can be a shortcut to not only a program, but for any type of object, there are some very useful shortcuts that people sometimes overlook.

The Explorer interface gives you the option to assign a shortcut not only to a program, but also to an object.

In the case of Windows NT 4.0, the list of objects includes files, directories, logical drives, computers, networks, domains, shares, printers, and even other shortcuts. Treating these many items simply as objects is one of the real strengths of shortcuts.

Folder Shortcuts

As the administrator of a network, chances are you use the Windows NT administrative tools often. In that case, you may have added the most-used administrative tools to your desktop. But after continual adding to the desktop, it can become very crowded, especially if you're running at a resolution of 640×480.

This is a good reason to create a shortcut not to the individual program, but to the Administrative Tools folder itself. This can be done by going to the path that I mentioned before, `%systemroot%\Profiles\All Users\Start Menu\Programs`. Once you have found your way there, click the Administrative Tools (Common) folder and drag the folder onto the desktop with your right mouse button. Drop it, and the menu will give you the option to Move Here, Copy Here, Create Shortcut(s) Here, or Cancel (shown in Figure 13.14). Choose Create Shortcut(s) Here, and you'll have a folder on your desktop with all the Administrative tools.

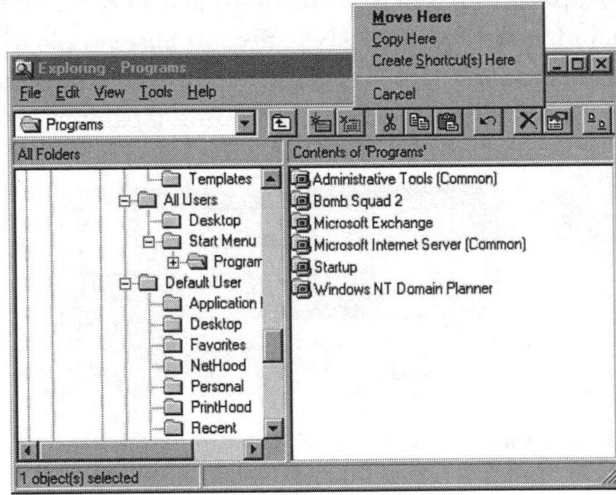

Figure 13.14. *Dragging a folder to the desktop.*

Tip: Do not choose Copy Here, or a folder that is a copy of an existing folder will be created on the desktop. A copy will not reflect any changes made to the original Administrative Tools (Common) folder, whereas a shortcut will.

After you have completed this, a folder will appear on your desktop, as shown in Figure 13.15. Now you can change the text under the icon or even change the icon if you want. This will not affect the original program folder.

Figure 13.15. *The Windows NT desktop with new shortcut folder.*

Computer Shortcuts

If you find yourself using the resources of another computer, such as a Windows NT server or workstation, a NetWare server, or another Windows computer that is sharing resources, you can create a shortcut to put right on your desktop.

Just as with creating the folder shortcut, drag a computer shortcut from Network Neighborhood with the right mouse button and choose Create Shortcut(s) Here.

Printer Shortcuts

To open a print queue directly, make a shortcut to a printer. You can also use this shortcut for drag-and-drop printing. Follow the directions for creating a folder shortcut, but do it from the Printers folder.

Drive Shortcuts

Making shortcuts for your most-used logical drives, or shares, can eliminate the need to drill down into the My Computer or Network Neighborhood system folders.

The Send To Folder

You might have noticed that when you right-click many objects, such as files or folders, there is a menu item called Send To. By default, the Send To menu lists 3 1/2 Floppy, My Briefcase, and Mail Recipient (if Windows Messaging is installed). The first two items come from the `%systemroot%\Profiles\Default User` folder and are copied to the default set of folders for each user account in the Profiles folder. My Briefcase is automatically added to the Send To folder for each user if the Briefcase application has been installed on Windows NT.

I find that many times I want to open a file in Notepad or WordPad, even if the chosen file does not have an associated file type or has another program as its destination in an Open action.

A quick way to make an application available to all files and folders is to add a shortcut to the program within the Send To folder.

To do this, open the Send To folder. (In Figure 13.16, I have the folder open in Explorer view.)

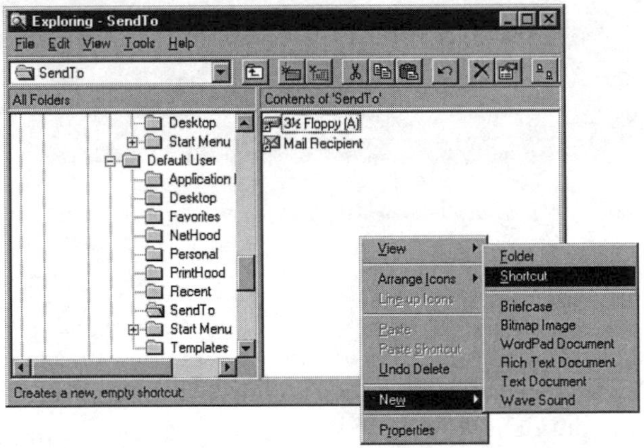

Figure 13.16. *Creating a new shortcut in the Send To folder.*

Right-click in the right panel and select New. Choose Shortcut from the list. The Create Shortcut Wizard (see Figure 13.17) will prompt you for the command line of the program for which you want to create a shortcut.

I've entered `notepad.exe` for the Notepad program. Finish the wizard, and the new shortcut will appear in the SendTo folder, as shown in Figure 13.18.

> **Note:** Because this is the Default User SendTo folder, it will not appear in the SendTo folder of existing users.

I've right-clicked the shortcut and chosen Copy. Then I went to the SendTo folder for the current user, Administrator, right-clicked, and chose Paste. Now the Send To menu for the Administrator has the Notepad shortcut.

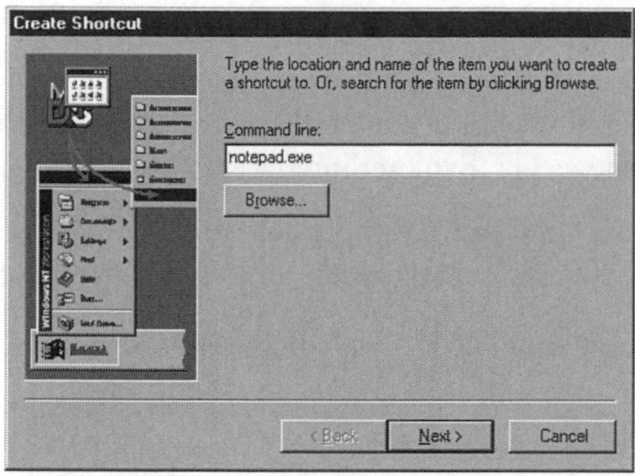

Figure 13.17. *The Create Shortcut Wizard.*

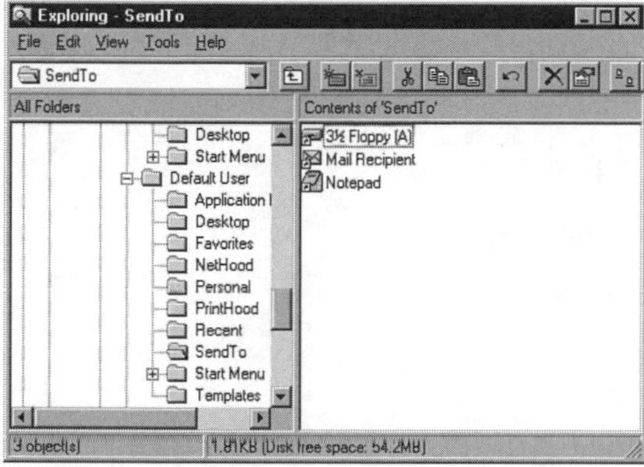

Figure 13.18. *Adding Notepad to the SendTo folder.*

Figure 13.19 shows that I've right-clicked on a file BOOT.BAK and chosen the Send To menu item. Notepad is now an option beside the regular items that usually appear on the Send To menu.

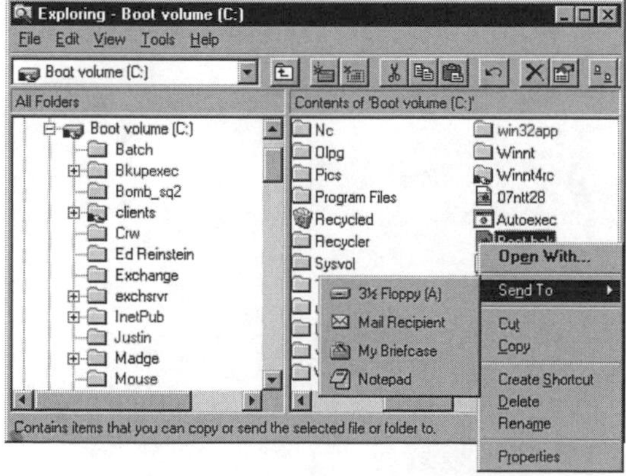

Figure 13.19. *Modified Send To menu.*

Summary

The items I've just mentioned only scratch the surface as far as what types of modifications you can make to the Windows NT Explorer interface.

What you have to think about is what you would prefer to have more easily available to you. Do you like the behavior of Explorer the way it is, or is there something about it you'd like to change?

If you want to change something, you just might be able to do it!

IV PART

Windows NT Administration

User Manager for Domains

by Robert Reinstein

User Manager for Domains is the primary tool for establishing user accounts and administering them. User Manager for Domains will serve as part of the Windows NT administrator's control center, along with Server Manager and Windows NT's other tools.

Note: Windows NT Workstation includes User Manager, which is used strictly to manage the local workstation, whereas User Manager for Domains can help administer an entire enterprise.

This chapter explains how to

- Add and modify user accounts
- Assign logon scripts to user accounts
- Assign user profiles
- Create local and global groups
- Manage trust relationships

The User Interface

User Manager for Domains is composed of three areas:

- The first area is the menu, which contains access to all the features and functions contained in User Manager for Domains.
- The second area is the User window, which shows a list of all the user accounts that exist within the current domain. User Manager for Domains can be used to administer multiple domains.
- The third window is the Groups window, where you'll see a listing of all the local and global groups that exist within the current domain.

Starting User Manager for Domains

The shortcut for User Manager for Domains can be found in the Administrative Tools program folder.

If you are executing User Manager for Domains from the command line, you also have the option to specify the domain you want to administer and the speed of the connection to that domain's PDC. The importance of the connection speed is explained later in this chapter, but to quickly fill you in, a low-speed connection will give you less functionality and fewer details, whereas a high-speed connection gives you complete functionality and all the details immediately.

In Figure 14.1 you see that—other than the user account that I set up for myself—these are the default accounts that are set up by the Windows NT installation process. In this case, I had also installed Microsoft Internet Information Server, so a Guest account for the Internet server part of my Windows NT server was also set up. But in any case, the Administrator user account and the Guest user account will always be found in a freshly installed copy of Windows NT Server.

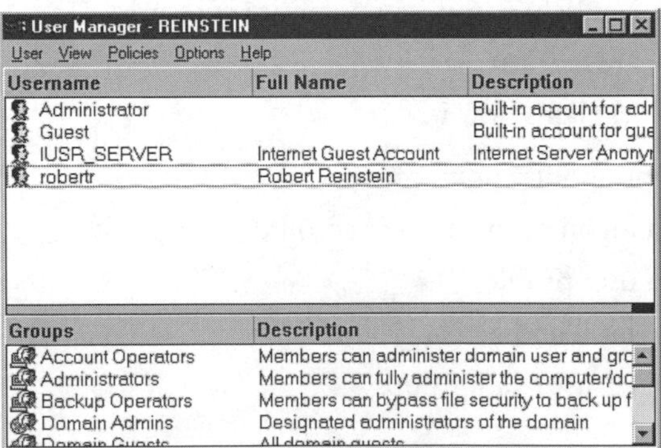

Figure 14.1. *User Manager for Domains.*

Also in Figure 14.1, you will see some of the groups that are installed by the Windows NT Server installation process.

Account Policies

Before you set up any user accounts, you should define the account policies that you want to enforce on your domain.

These policies are domain-wide rules that will be used for all user accounts. The main reason for setting account policies is to help avoid security violations on your network.

One of the greatest threats to a network is outsiders, usually hackers, who attempt to break into networks with the intent to damage the system. This damage usually results in data loss, or even the inability for users or administrators to log on to the domain, which can result in requiring a new installation of Windows NT.

To get to the configuration screen for your account policies, start User Manager for Domains.

Note: If you are working a multidomain environment, select the domain that you want to set account policies for by either starting User Manager for Domains from the command line with the name of the domain as a command-line parameter, as described in the section in this chapter titled "Running User Manager for Domains from a Command Line," or, after starting User Manager for Domains, make sure that your domain is named in the title bar. To change domains, choose User from the User Manager for Domains menu, and then click Select Domain.... Pick the appropriate domain, and again, verify that the proper domain is shown on the title bar.

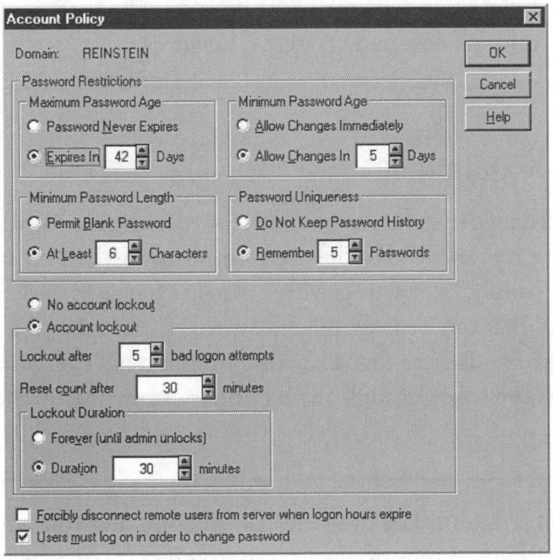

Figure 14.2. *Account Policy.*

From the User Manager for Domains menu, choose Policies and then select Account. As seen in Figure 14.2, you can set many policies related to passwords and user access.

Password Restrictions

Creating a policy for passwords is a very important part of setting up Windows NT security. The password is usually the only barrier keeping a hacker out of your network. Setting strict policies can enable you to keep your network private.

Forcing Password Expiration

The Password Restrictions section lets you choose the length of time that a user can continue to use the same password before he is forced to create a new password. In some cases, you might want to disable this by selecting Password Never Expires. Creating an expiration date for passwords, however, makes the network more secure because sometimes user passwords are discovered by other users. A user may also have other passwords for other networks or perhaps online services, and people assume that a person may be using the same password for different protected systems. Changing a password on a regular basis can make a potential hacker's job more difficult.

Tip: Suggest to your users that it is a *bad* idea to use the same password for external systems as they do for your network systems because of the potential risks. These risks involve someone who is familiar with one of your outside passwords using one of those passwords to break security on your internal network, possibly using your user account to delete data or perform other types of destruction. You should make sure they know that they can use the same password for all company systems, however.

Password Length Requirement

Minimum Password Length can force your users to create passwords that are more difficult to hack than, say, a one-character password or the users simply using their initials. There are programs that generate passwords simply by starting with a single character and trying every possible letter, number, and symbol that can be used in a password. By lengthening the password, it makes the number of possible combinations that a hacking program has to try that much more. Other types of hacking programs can scan through the dictionary from a spell-checker in an attempt to find a password.

Note: The section "Account Lockout" describes action that you can take to prevent a hacker from having the ability to repeatedly attempt to crack a password.

Minimum Password Age

The Minimum Password Age prevents a user from making changes to his password too often. The Minimum Password Age setting can prevent users from purposely changing their passwords numerous times in a row, just to flush out passwords that are kept in the password history list.

Password Uniqueness

Password Uniqueness stores previously used passwords. If a user changes his password more than once in a day, the Password Uniqueness History will not retain passwords that have been changed the same day that they were created. Password Uniqueness enables you to control how often users can reuse passwords that they have used before. Configurable from 0 to 24, this is usually used to prevent users from flipping between two passwords over and over again.

Account Logon Restrictions

Other account policies determine when a user is allowed to log on to a domain. The first, Account Lockout, can help prevent a hacker from gaining access to your network. The second option can forcibly remove users from the network, again, helping to prevent hackers from gaining entrance to the network "after hours."

Account Lockout

Next is the capability to create an Account Lockout.

If enabled, an Account Lockout will prevent a user from gaining access to the domain if a wrong password has been used. You can configure this to kick in after the user makes only one logon attempt with a wrong password, or you can keep a counter and only start the lockout period after up to 999 attempts.

This is usually used for two reasons:

- One reason is that if a hacker is trying to find out the user's password, chances are he will be making numerous attempts at logging on. Using this feature will bring these logon attempts to the attention of the administrator because the "real" user will be unable to log on to the domain and will most probably call for technical support in this matter.
- Another reason to enable the lockout feature is if you do want users to contact you. Sometimes users will keep trying to log on to the domain with a bad password and start blaming the system for not accepting what they believe is the correct password. By telling them that they are locked out and should contact the administrator, you can quickly clarify to them that they have not been using the proper password, and you can then have them choose a new password.

Of course, in some cases, you do not want people locked out if they only make a mistake every so often. That is why you can also configure the duration of time between logons that will increment the "bad logon attempt" counter. For instance, if a user makes one mistake each month, and the Lockout After count is set to 6, in six months you will receive a phone call from that user. But if you set the Reset Count After to 43,200 minutes, which is 30 days, each month the counter will be reset to zero.

Account Lockout Duration

You can also configure the Lockout Duration. This comes in handy if you do not want to penalize users because of a hacker's attempts to use their accounts. By setting the Lockout Duration to, for instance, one hour, the users may not even get to see a lockout if the hacker was trying to break their passwords in the middle of the night. But this will prevent the hacker from repeatedly trying different passwords with a single user account, in order to break into the network.

On the other hand, you do have the option to make the Lockout Duration *forever*, which always requires manual intervention on the part of the administrator. This option would allow an administrator to talk to the user to determine the reason why the wrong password had been used. One company I worked for had this requirement as a means to help educate users on the importance of remembering their passwords.

Automatically Disconnecting Users

As you will see, the hours of the day in which a user is permitted to access the network may be defined. Here, by placing a check mark in the check box next to where it says "Forcibly disconnect remote users from server when logon hours expire" you can "kick off" a user from the network if he remains on the network past the time that he is allowed to log on. By not checking the box, an already-connected user may remain on the network, as long as he has logged on during the hours that he is allowed to log on.

By setting the appropriate logon hours for a user and then using this option to forcibly disconnect the user, you help prevent unauthorized users from accessing the network during off hours.

The Makeup of User Accounts

Before we dive into creating a user account, let's examine what it is that makes up a user account.

A user account usually represents a person or client on your network. It can also represent a function, such as the Guest account, which is a one-size-fits-all user account giving anyone who logs on as Guest limited access to the server. Other user accounts can be put in place because of a requirement for a piece of software, such as the Microsoft Systems Management Server user account that is required when you install that software. This type of account is known as a *service account.*

Tip: While on the subject of software that relies on its own user account or service account: There are programs that install their own service account that is uniquely named and includes an explicit description, such as Cheyenne's InocuLAN. Also, there is software that will ask you to name the account to use, such as Microsoft Systems Management Server.

In some cases, the installation routine for that program will default to using the Windows NT domain's Administrator account. Do not allow software to use the Administrator account for its own purposes! In fact, you should probably copy the Administrator account and then delete it.

The Administrator account is the most-often hacked account, because most hackers expect to find that user account in all Windows NT domains or workstations. By creating another account, which is uniquely named but carries all of the rights and permissions of the default Administrator account, you will be able to prevent break-ins through this account and also be assured that software installations will not have the Administrator account to use for its own purposes.

You might decide to change the rights on the Administrator's account without remembering that the changes you made also affect that software's rights to your system. Sometimes the installation program will make its own changes to the Administrator account by granting it the rights it needs to function properly.

It is because of this that a user account should be created solely for use by any software that requires a service account. This account can be created before the installation of the software if you know that it will be required by the installation program, or you can create a service account during the software's installation process.

In all cases, a user account represents an entity. Along with that entity being described to the server, rights and permissions are also part of the user account.

These rights, which are mostly listed in Chapter 2, "Windows NT Security Architecture," are supplemented by attributes that directly relate to the user's right to log on to the domain.

These logon attributes include the user account's right to log on, which may be dependent on the time of the day, the number of concurrent connections to the domain, the computer or computers that the user can log on from, and whether the user can log on through Windows NT's Remote Access Services (RAS).

In order to achieve this logon, the user enters a username and a password. The user must also specify the domain the user wants to log on to. A number of security checks are performed, which are described in detail in Chapter 2. The user's right to log on may be affected by certain parameters, or policies, that you as the administrator have set up, as discussed earlier in this chapter.

Note: In this discussion I am referring to true user accounts, and not the aforementioned service accounts that usually have the Windows NT right to "Log on as a service," which creates a logon session at the time of the booting of Windows NT and occurs without interaction from a physical client.

User Environment Profile

After a user logs on successfully, the account is checked for setting up a User Environment Profile. The User Environment Profile, which is defined on an account-by-account basis, includes the following:

- User Profile
- Logon Script
- Home Directory

These three items should be carefully considered when you are planning your network and may be difficult to implement after you add all of your users.

A User Profile applies only to clients running Windows NT (Workstation or Server). User Profiles contain workstation environment settings, such as program items, screen colors, and resource connections, among other settings. User Profiles can be specific to a user, or more than one user can share a profile (although profiles can be shared only by users running the same version of Windows NT).

Note: Windows 95 also offers User Profiles; however, these are not compatible with the type created on Windows NT.

Under normal circumstances, a User Profile will be updated when a user logs off the workstation. You can make a mandatory profile, which means that the settings are not saved each time the user logs off the workstation, that gives the user the same desktop each time he logs on. Roving profiles enable users to get the same workstation environment no matter where they log on (as long as they are running the same version of Windows NT at the time).

You might decide that there are certain program groups that you would like to make available to certain people in your organization. By creating a User Profile on the server that has this particular group and assigning that profile to the users who need those programs, you can be assured that those users will get that program group on their desktops.

There are numerous reasons to use User Profiles, and by being creative you can probably come up with some unique ways of using this feature.

To take matters even further, the System Policy Editor, available in Windows NT 4.0, can make granular restrictions to a User Profile, such as restricting any changes on the desktop or preventing access to the Control Panel or a command prompt.

Note: There is also a Policy Editor for Windows 95 workstations that can be administered by the Windows NT administrator.

A logon script is essentially a batch file that can be forced to execute whenever a user logs on to a domain. Examples of using Logon Scripts include making connections to printers and disk shares, executing virus scanners, and basically executing any command.

A user's home directory is a directory that can be either local or on the server. The home directory is used by programs that do not automatically assign a working directory or if a working directory has not been defined for the application. This way, if you want to create individual directories for users to store their documents on the server, you can just assign a home directory of (assuming that you have already created a share called `USERS` on the server) `\\USERS\%USERNAME%`. The `%USERNAME%` is a Windows NT variable that will be changed to the user's logon ID after this value has been assigned.

By default, a home directory will be assigned to Windows NT users on their local hard drive in a directory named `\USERS\DEFAULT`.

Account Naming Conventions

Another matter to think about before you spend a lot of time entering user account information is a naming convention for user accounts.

Identify the type of naming convention that will give you flexibility to add more users, because just using first names may cause conflicts.

For security reasons you might want to assign alphanumeric account names.

Here are some examples of using naming conventions. Using my name, Robert Reinstein, you can use the following:

- `RREINSTE`
- `ROBERTR`
- `RRNSTN`
- `RR7218`

The first example uses my first initial followed by the first seven characters of my last name. The second example uses my first name followed by my last initial. The third example uses my first initial followed by my last name, but eliminating any vowels. The final example uses my first and last initials, followed by my extension number.

Other types of user account names can be generated by using a person's Social Security number, employee ID number, or any other unique combination that may not be easily guessed by hackers.

As I just mentioned, if you are going to assign home directories, you might want to keep the length of account names to a maximum of eight characters to allow for MS-DOS compatibility.

Adding a User Account

After you have worked out your plan on how to implement users, start User Manager for Domains.

To add a user, you have two options. You can create a user from scratch, or you can choose to copy an existing user. For this scenario, a new user will be created from scratch.

Select New User from User Manager for Domains' User menu.

The New User dialog, shown in Figure 14.3, requires that you enter a username, or logon ID, for the account you are adding. Enter a full name that will be used purely for descriptive purposes. An optional description enables you to enter even more descriptive text.

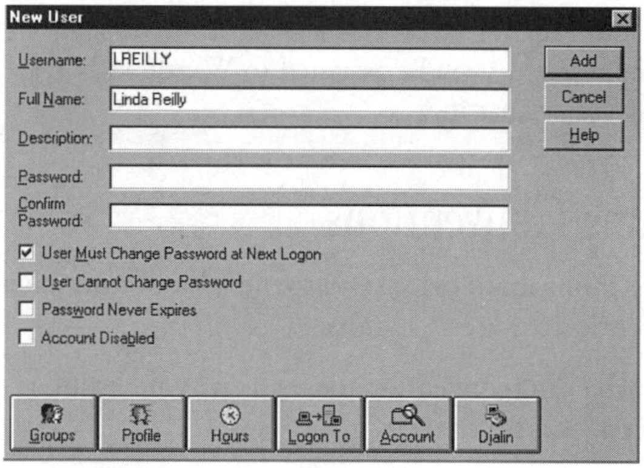

Figure 14.3. *New User dialog showing the most common fields.*

Creating a Password

For the Password field, you can set the user's password or leave the Password field blank. If you predefine the user's password, reenter the same password in the Confirm Password field.

Chances are that unless you have already been informed by the user what he would like his password to be set to (which would be a breach of security, because even the administrator shouldn't know the client's password), you will want to check the check box that says User Must Change Password at Next Logon.

This option will force the user to change his password, therefore setting his initial password the next time he logs on to the domain.

Enabling User Cannot Change Password would require that only administrators have the power to create and change passwords. This could be used in a situation in which an account is created with rights to perform a specific task. If one of the users using this special account changed the password, the other users would not have access to this special account. By enabling this option, the users using this account would not be able to change the password.

Setting Password Never Expires overrides the Account Policies that you may have set up that requires the changing of passwords. This option should only be used for service accounts.

The Account Disabled check box does just that. This is a quick way to disable someone's account, for instance, if he goes on vacation or leaves the company. By simply disabling the account, you can keep all of the attributes attached to the account. By deleting the account, you also delete the SID that had been created for the account, thus eliminating all permissions and rights for that account. So, in most cases, it pays to disable the account.

Group Memberships

The next item to configure for a user is the Group Memberships dialog (see Figure 14.4), which is accessed by clicking on the button labeled Groups.

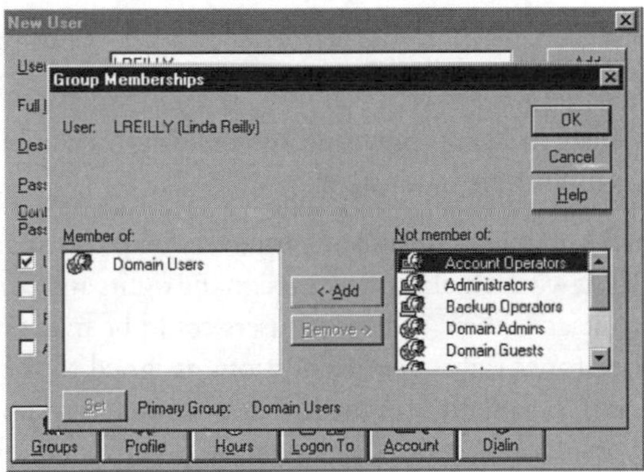

***Figure 14.4.** Group memberships.*

Groups are a way of logically grouping two or more accounts, in order to make administering the system much easier. By having a group that will share rights and permissions, those attributes only have to be set for the group. The individual users within the group then get those rights and permissions.

Windows NT Server comes with many preconfigured groups. As seen in Figure 14.4, this user is shown as a member of the group Domain Users. Not shown is that the user is also a member of a system group named Everyone. On the right of the dialog is a list of the other predefined groups that this user is not a member of. Each of these groups has certain rights assigned to them.

For instance, if you wanted this user to have the right to be able to back up servers, you could simply add the user to the Backup Operators group, which has the right to back up files and directories.

Local Groups and Global Groups

There are two different types of groups for Windows NT: local and global groups.

Local groups belong to the domain and can be assigned permissions and rights. Local groups can contain global groups.

Global groups do not have permissions or rights assigned to them, but they can become members of local groups. A global group can contain user accounts only from the domain in which the global group is created.

Users can become members of both local groups and global groups.

The primary reason for creating global groups is that global groups can be assigned to local groups that are outside of their domain. The same cannot be said about local groups. Therefore, the global group Domain Admins, which by default includes the Administrator account from the local domain, can join the local Administrators group from another domain, thus giving the local Administrators permissions and rights for administering an outside domain.

This cross-domain assignment of rights involves trust relationships, which are thoroughly discussed in Chapter 3, "Domain Models."

Perhaps the best example of local groups within an organization would be using two departments, the Financial department and the MIS department.

Because the Financial department consists of employees who require access to the same files and utilize the same printers, it would make sense to assign the rights and permissions to those resources to a group called "Financial." Then, individual users could be made members of that group and automatically have the proper rights and permissions assigned to them. The same would occur with the MIS department. If a member of the MIS department is responsible for working with the Financial department or is currently working on a project with them, that user could also be made a temporary member of the Financial group. This avoids having to assign rights and permissions to the MIS person for the duration of the project and then having to remove the same rights and permissions after the project is completed. The MIS person just needs to be removed from the Financial group.

The creation of groups is shown later in this chapter.

When you have completed specifying the groups that you want the new user to be a member of, click OK to save the configuration and return to the New User dialog.

By default, Windows NT contains the following local groups:

Administrators
Account operators (Windows NT Server domain controllers only)
Backup operators

Guests
Power Users (Windows NT Workstation and Windows NT Server member servers only)
Print operators (Windows NT Server domain controllers only)
Replicator
Server operators (Windows NT Server domain controllers only)
Users

By default, Windows NT Server contains the following global groups:

Domain admins
Domain users

User Environment Profile

As previously discussed in this chapter, a User Environment Profile may be set up for individual user accounts. To access this dialog, click the button that is labeled Profile.

In some cases, the profiles will be the same for all users, or the profiles may be the same for members of the same department. Of course, these profiles can also be set up for each individual.

In Figure 14.5, this user's profile was assigned to a share setup on the server than has been named Profiles. This is actually a directory named `Profiles` that is in the Windows NT (`\%SystemRoot%`) directory. The `Profiles` directory keeps all the profiles for all the users in this domain. Implementing profiles this way results in a roving profile, because users can log on from any workstation, and as long as that workstation is running the same version of Windows NT, the user's individual settings will be downloaded to that computer.

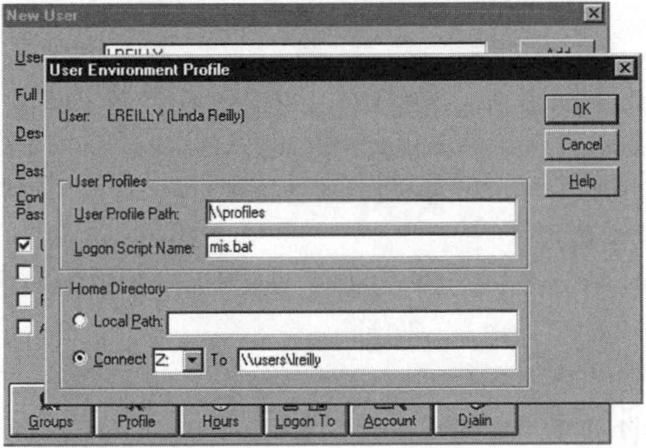

Figure 14.5. *User Environment Profile.*

By setting the Profile Path, a directory is created within that share, titled the same as the username. In this case, the directory is `C:\WINNT\PROFILES\LREILLY`. Because I have used a UNC (Universal Naming Convention) path (`\\SERVER\PROFILES`), that directory will be found from any computer in the domain.

The logon script assigned to this user account, `MIS.BAT`, is kept by default in the server's `NETLOGON` share. For this instance, a logon script was created for the MIS department that performs connections to shared resources that all members of the MIS department require.

For the user's home directories, a share was created on the server that shares the `\USERS` directory as `USERS`. Each user account has been given his or her own directory within this share.

Click the OK button to save this configuration and return to the New User dialog.

Logon Hours

Each user can be assigned hours in each day of the week where they can, or cannot, log on to the network. This is done by clicking the button labeled Hours.

In my example, shown in Figure 14.6, the user cannot log on to the network any day before 6:00 a.m. or after 6:00 p.m. I have also blocked out all day Sunday.

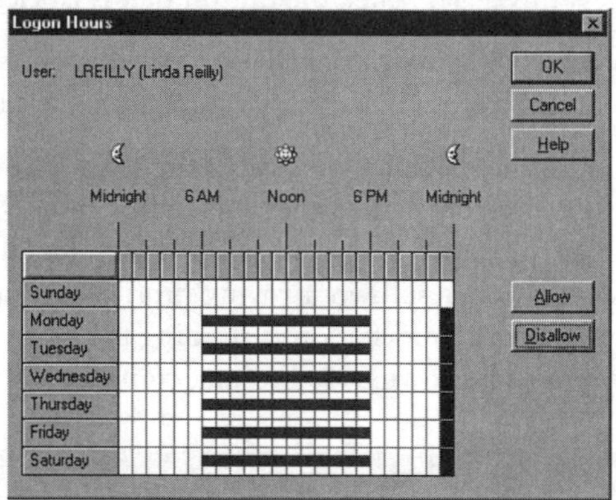

Figure 14.6. *Logon hours.*

If you had set the Account Policies to force a logoff when the user's hours have expired, this user would be kicked off the domain at 6:00 p.m. and not allowed to log back on until 6:00 a.m. the next day (with the exception of Sunday).

After the hours have been chosen, click the OK button to save this configuration and return to the New User dialog.

Logon Workstations

You can restrict a user to only being able to log on to the domain from particular workstations.

For my scenario, shown in Figure 14.7, I have chosen to let this user truly "float" and have the ability to log on from any Windows NT computer, with the exception of the server itself. Logging on from the actual server's console requires the right Logon Locally, which is given only to the

Administrator group, the Backup Operators group, Print Operators, and Server Operators by default. For security reasons, this is not a right that you want to hand out to all users.

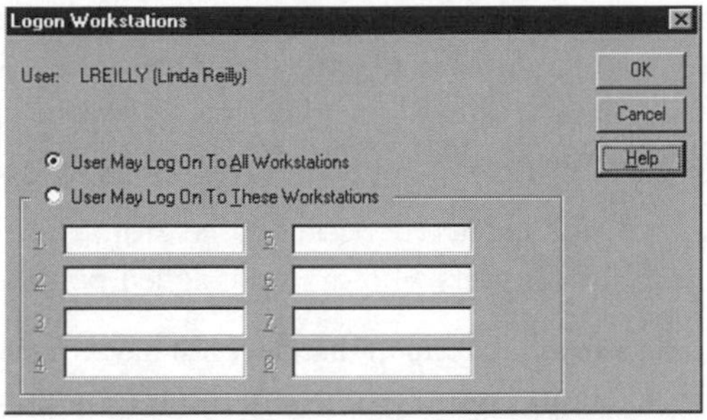

Figure 14.7. *Logon Workstations.*

If you did want to restrict the user and specify workstations that the user can log on from, you would click the radio button next to User May Log On To These Workstations and specify the computer names of workstations that are members of the domain. Adding a workstation to the domain is a process that would have been done during the installation of Windows NT Workstation, or it can be done using the Server Manager administrative tool.

When you have completed this dialog, click the OK button to save the configuration and return to the New User dialog.

Account Information

Additional information about the user account can be found by clicking the Account button.

An expiration date for the account can be set here, as shown in Figure 14.8. This is usually used when there is a temporary employee or a consultant working within this domain and you want to set the account to expire on a specific date. This way, the account still exists, which will come in handy if the person comes back. This also relieves the administrator from having to remember when someone is going to be leaving the company.

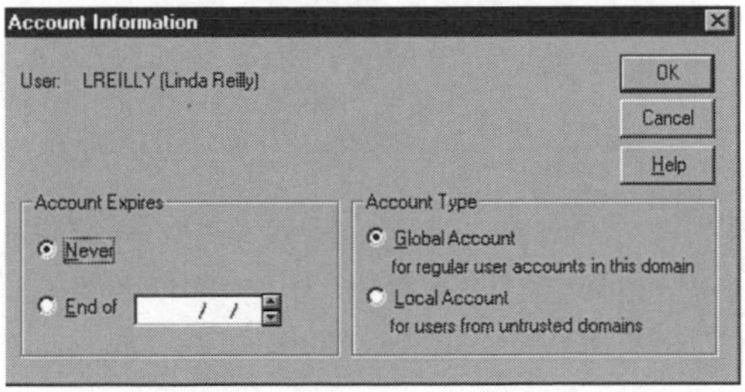

Figure 14.8. *Account Information.*

The choices for Account Type enable you to specify if the user belongs to this domain or if the user is actually a member of another domain that is untrusted. By specifying that a user is a member of an untrusted domain, a local account is created. This user account cannot be used to log on directly to this domain and can only be assigned permissions for accessing resources. That user will still have to log on to his own domain to gain access to the network. To receive pass-through authentication, the user account should use the same password in its own domain and in the definition for the local account.

For trusted domains this is not a concern, because users from trusted domains already have their names listed locally in the list of users who can be assigned permissions.

For instance, if a user is in a another domain that does not have a trust relationship with the current domain and the user requires access to a resource in the current domain, the options are either to create a user account that is maintained by the current domain, as if that user did not exist elsewhere on the network, or to create a local account, which simply allows a user to be defined as an outside user. Being flagged as a local account means that this user account will not be made available to other domains for which a trust relationship exists with the current domain.

When you are done with this dialog, click the OK button to save the configuration and return to the New User dialog.

Dialin Information

If Remote Access Services (RAS) has been enabled on this domain, use the Dialin Information dialog to configure users for using RAS. As shown in Figure 14.9, the Dialin Information dialog, which is accessed by clicking the button labeled Dialin, enables you to grant permission to the user to log on to the server via RAS.

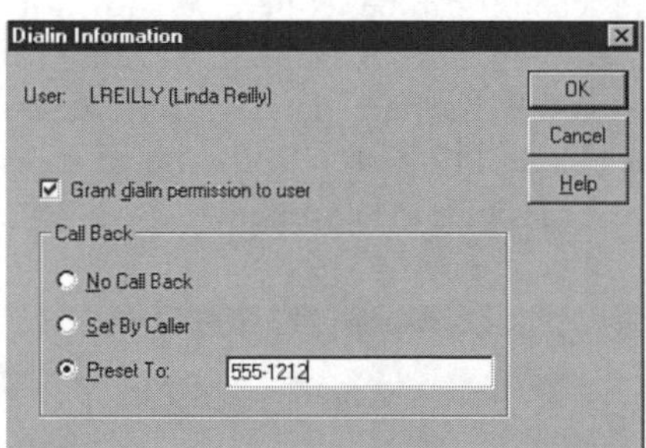

Figure 14.9. *Dialin Information.*

If the user is granted permission to use RAS, security can be set up for callback, which forces the server to call the user back at a specific phone number.

Other options here enable the user to specify a callback number at the time of logging on.

The last option is the ability for a user to log on without a callback.

See Chapter 20, "Installing Windows NT Workstation," for a more detailed discussion on how to implement and maintain Windows NT's very powerful Remote Access Services.

Completing the Addition of the User

When you have entered the information you want for this user account, click the Add button and the account will then be established. Notice that User Manager for Domains does not close the New User dialog, and you can continue to add users until you choose the Close button.

Copying a User Account

Another way to create users is to copy an existing user account. When you copy an account, which is done by highlighting the account you want to copy and selecting Copy from the User menu, all the settings, from Groups to Dialin, are copied from the original user.

As you can see in Figure 14.10, this copy of the LREILLY account has the same User Environment Profile as LREILLY, with the exception of the paths that used the username as part of their path. Here the username has been substituted with the variable %USERNAME%.

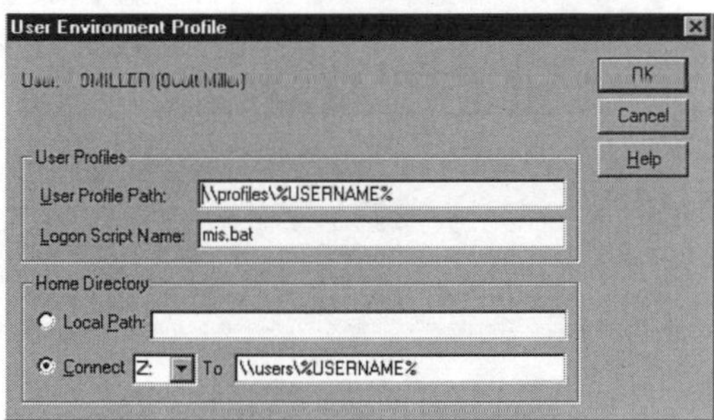

Figure 14.10. *Copying a user account.*

When this copy is saved, the %USERNAME% variable will automatically translate into the username of the new account. This is demonstrated in Figure 14.11, where I saved that new "cloned" account and reopened it for editing. As you can see, what had been %USERNAME% is now SMILLER.

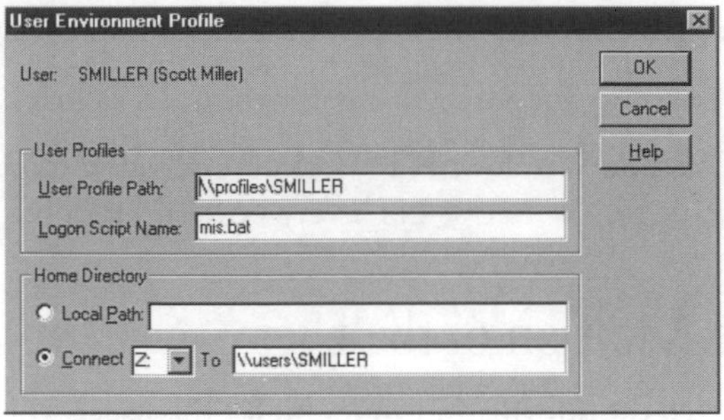

Figure 14.11. %USERNAME% *substitution.*

Renaming an Account

It is possible to rename an account. Just go to the User menu and select Rename.... The Rename dialog (see Figure 14.12) will appear and prompt you to enter the new name for this user. Once you have entered the new name, click OK and the account will be renamed. By renaming an account rather than deleting and creating a new account, the user will retain his or her SID, which then allows the user to keep existing permissions and rights.

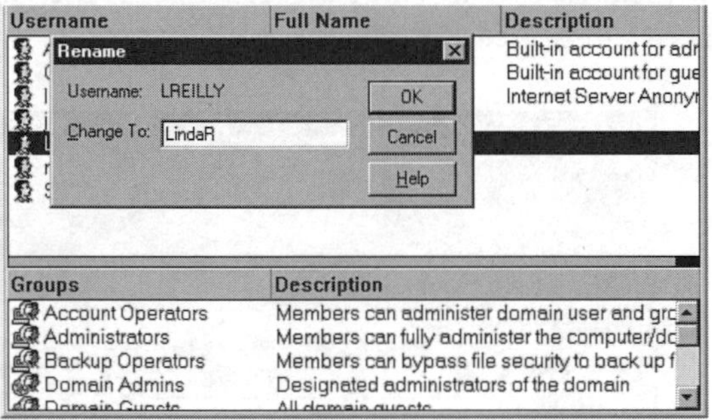

Figure 14.12. Rename dialog.

Editing User Properties

After a user account has been configured, you always have the option to make changes to it. Changes can be made to individual accounts, or you can select multiple user accounts that can be modified all at once.

To edit one user account, you can either double-click the user's name or highlight the user's name and choose Properties... from the User menu.

Multiple user accounts can be selected by using the standard Windows conventions of selecting multiple items from a list. This is by using the method of holding down the Ctrl key while making selections. You can also select a range of user accounts by highlighting the first user account and then holding down the Shift key and selecting the user account at the end of the range. Now all the items within that range will be highlighted.

At this point, you can make modifications to all the selected accounts by choosing Properties from the User menu.

As shown in Figure 14.13, the selected usernames are shown toward the top of the User Properties dialog. Any settings that are changed here will be made to all the usernames specified in the Users list.

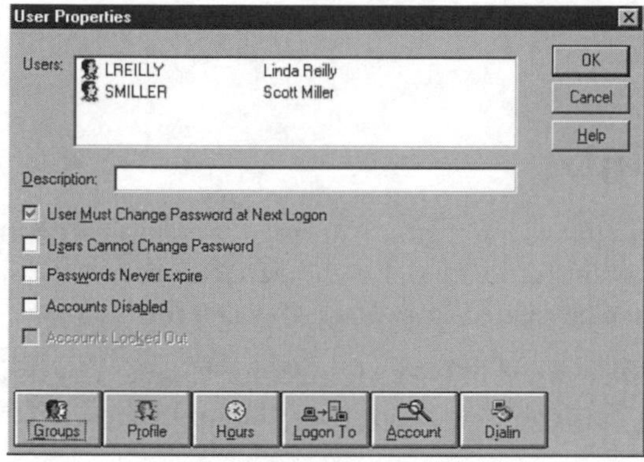

Figure 14.13. User Properties.

One other way to select multiple usernames is by selecting all the users who are members of a particular group.

By selecting Select Users from the User menu, a listing of the groups that are defined for the domain will appear. As shown in Figure 14.14, I have selected the Domain Admins group and clicked the Select button.

Note that the three users who are selected in User Manager for Domains are the members of the Domain Admins group.

At this point you can continue to select groups and add to the selected user accounts. You can also deselect user accounts from those that are already selected.

If you wanted to assign a policy to all user accounts except the Domain Admins members, you could first select all the user accounts while in the main User Manager for Domains screen (using the range selection method) and then use Select Users to deselect the members of the Domain Admins group.

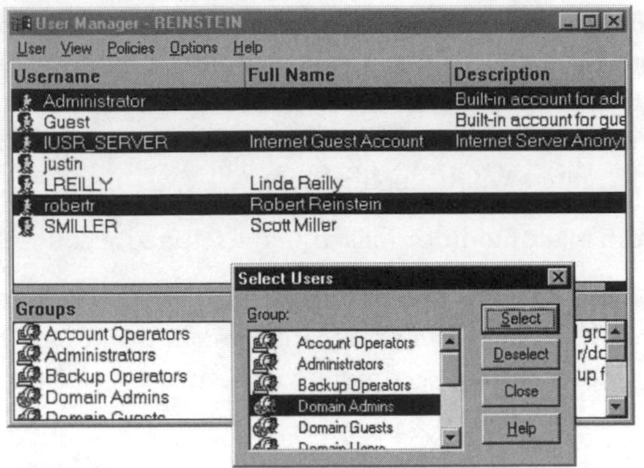

Figure 14.14. Select Users.

Creating Groups

As explained earlier in this chapter, groups are used to easily give permissions and rights to a group of users and make administration of rights and permissions much easier. The two types of groups, Local and Global, can be created from User Manager for Domains.

The type of group is identified in User Manager for Domains by its icon, which shows two users in front of an object. If that object is a computer, the group is local. If the object is a globe, the group is global.

Creating a Local Group

To create a group, first highlight one or more members of the proposed group in the User Manager for Domains window. Then, from the User menu, choose New Local Group.

As shown in Figure 14.15, you need to give the group a name, and you have the option to enter descriptive text for this group.

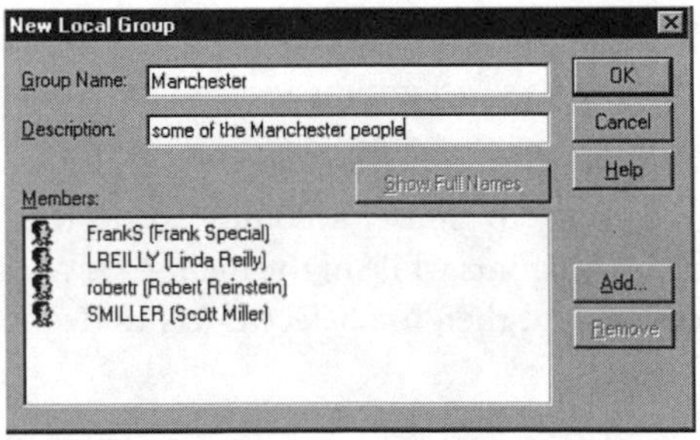

Figure 14.15. New Local Group.

The user account or accounts that you highlighted are automatically placed in the Members list. You can add more members or global groups to this new group by clicking the Add... button.

The Add Users and Groups dialog (see Figure 14.16) is one that you will see often in Windows NT. This same dialog is used when assigning permissions to NTFS files and directories, among other security configuration dialogs.

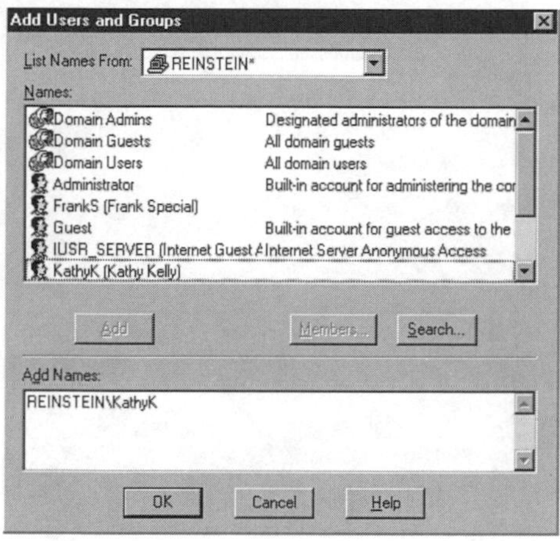

Figure 14.16. *Add Users and Groups.*

You have the option to display your proposed group members by just their usernames or by both their usernames and their full names. Toggling to the full name is done by clicking the Show Full Names button.

At the top of the dialog is the Domains list, which will contain more than one domain if your current domain is involved in a trust relationship. If this is the case, choose the domain that contains the user accounts or global groups that you want to add to your new group. Double-click the name to add that name to the Add Names list at the bottom of the dialog. To remove names from the Add Names list, you must actually delete the name from the list, by either backspacing or highlighting and deleting the name. You can also perform a search across multiple domains by clicking the Search button.

By clicking the Search button, you are presented with the Find Account dialog. (See Figure 14.17.)

The Find Account dialog enables you to enter the name of a user or group and either search across the current domain and all domains that you have a trust relationship with or select a subset of those domains for your search. After entering your search text, click the Search button to initiate the search.

When you locate the user or groups that you want to add to the new group, click the Add button.

Once you have identified the group of users and global groups that you want to include in your new local group, click the OK button and the group will be created and added to the Groups list in User Manager for Domains.

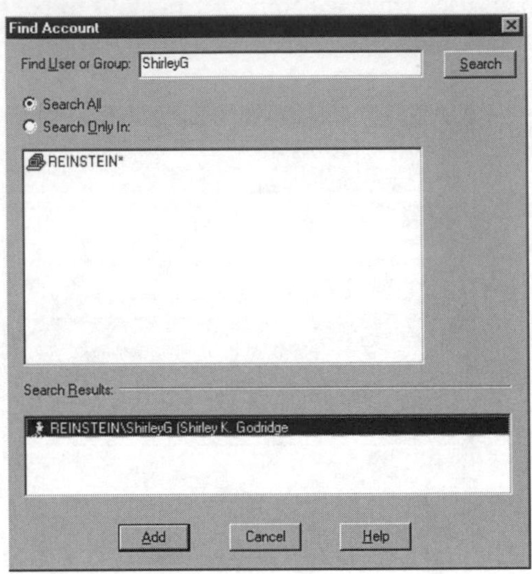

Figure 14.17. *The Find Account dialog.*

Creating a Global Group

Creating a global group is similar to creating a local group. You are restricted, however, to only adding members who are local users. This makes sense, because global groups are only for use by other domains in which you have a trust relationship.

To create a global group, you may first highlight any users whom you would like to initially add to the group as members (this is optional).

Select New Global Group from the User Manager for Domains Users menu.

The New Global Group dialog (see Figure 14.18) enables you to type in a name for the group and an optional description. The list on the left side of the dialog is for members whom you want to add to the group. In the list on the right side are user accounts from your domain that are currently not members of the new group. Double-click or highlight and click <-Add the user accounts that you want to add to the group.

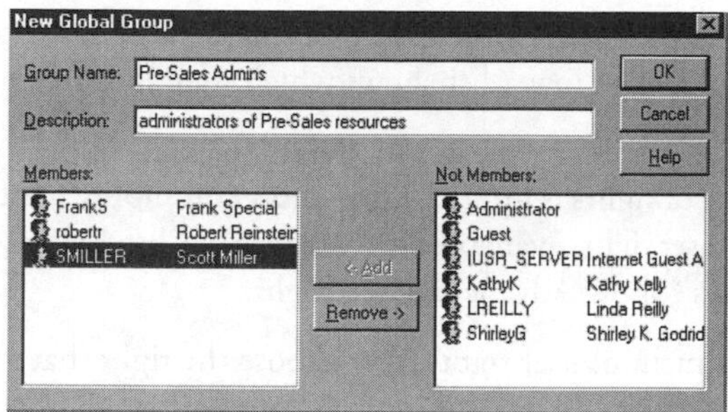

Figure 14.18. *New Global Group.*

Assigning User Rights

User rights are permissions that can be assigned to users or groups. Windows NT comes with predetermined user rights. There is currently no way of creating your own user rights, but for administrative purposes, the built-in user rights are sufficient to handle most of the security issues you may face.

> **Note:** There are plans to allow for the creation of custom user rights in a future version of Windows NT.

Certain user rights have already been assigned to the default user accounts and local groups. When you access the User Rights Policy dialog, you will see which rights have already been assigned.

To access the User Rights Policy dialog (see Figure 14.19), select User Rights from the User Manager for Domains Policies menu.

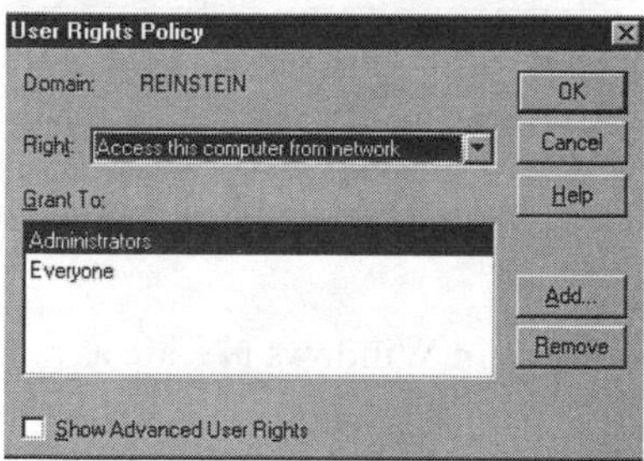

Figure 14.19. *User Rights Policy.*

This dialog shows you the name of the current domain and has a drop-down list of the available rights in Windows NT. The lower list shows which user accounts or groups have the currently visible right assigned to them.

By default, the listing of rights is limited to the most commonly used rights. You can change this list to include all the user rights available on Windows NT by clicking the check box at the bottom of the dialog that says "Show Advanced User Rights."

To change the assignment of user rights, first choose the right that you want to deal with. Based on the list of user accounts and groups that have that right, use the Add or Remove button to make your changes.

When you click the Add button, the Add Users and Groups dialog (see Figure 14.20) appears. This is a similar dialog to the one that is used to add users to groups, but this dialog will only show a list of local and global groups at first. If you also want user accounts to appear on the list, you must first click the button that says Show Users.

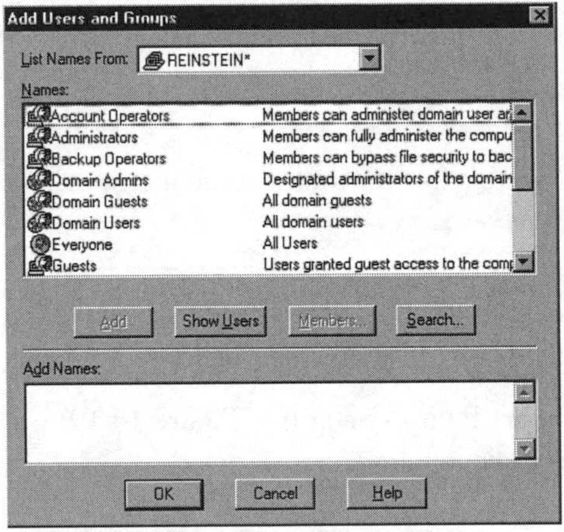

Figure 14.20. *Add Users and Groups.*

Once you have selected the names that you want to assign to the current right, click the OK button, and that right will be assigned to the users you have chosen and the members of the groups you identified.

The user rights that are available in Windows NT are as follows:

Access this computer from network
Act as part of the operating system
Add workstations to domain
Back up files and directories
Bypass traverse checking
Change the system time
Create a pagefile
Create a token object

Create permanent shared objects
Debug programs
Force shutdown from a remote system
Generate security audits
Increase quotas
Increase scheduling priority
Load and unload device drivers
Lock pages in memory
Log on as a batch job
Log on as a service
Log on locally
Manage auditing and security log
Modify Firmware environment variables
Profile single process
Profile system performance
Replace a process level token
Restore files and directories
Shut down the system
Take ownership of files and other objects

Auditing

Windows NT includes auditing features that can allow administrators to trace almost every move a user makes on the network. This can be especially useful for environments that have sensitive data, are required to keep detailed usage history, or utilize charge backs, to name but a few reasons to use the auditing features.

By choosing the Audit... item on the User Manager for Domains Policies menu, the Audit Policy dialog (see Figure 14.21) will be displayed.

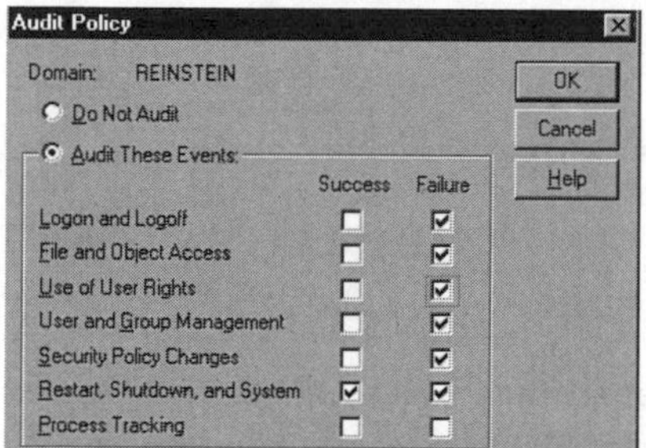

Figure 14.21. *Audit Policy.*

You have the choice to run off auditing or to turn on success and failures for the following categories:

1. Logon and Logoff
2. File and Object Access
3. Use of User Rights
4. User and Group Management
5. Security Policy Changes
6. Restart, Shutdown, and System
7. Process Tracking

The beautiful thing about Windows NT's auditing is how very granular you can get. The reporting can show you every single logon and logoff, each and every access for files on an NTFS volume, who's trying to shut down the server (unsuccessfully, hopefully), and basically every move that an administrator or non-administrator could make while attempting to make changes to your Windows NT domain.

You have to be careful not to overdo it though, because the audit logs can grow very large in an environment that has hundreds of users and tracks every logon and logoff.

For more information about Windows NT auditing, see Chapter 2.

Trust Relationships

Trust relationships allow domains to gain access to each other's user account database for the purpose of being able to assign permissions to resources across domains.

User Manager for Domains is the tool that is used to create these relationships.

This final item on the Policies menu that handles trust relationships is covered thoroughly in Chapter 3.

Low Speed Connections

As I mentioned earlier in the chapter, User Manager for Domains gives you the option to use a low-speed connection. This option, which is available on the Options menu, hides the username and group listings. This way, you can connect to a remote domain and not have to download the entire username and group listing, which, in a large environment, could be hundreds of entries, possibly thousands. This will enable you to manage a large domain from a dial-up connection.

Figure 14.22 shows User Manager with a low-speed connection.

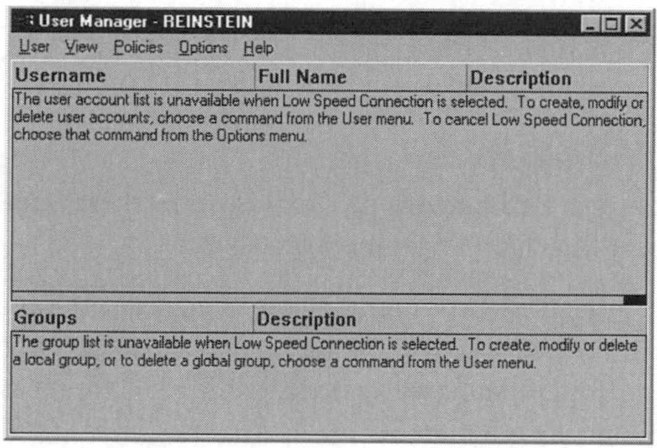

Figure 14.22. *Low-speed connection.*

When you are using User Manager for Domains with a low-speed connection, you rely solely on using the User Manager for Domains menus. The option to create a global group is not available with a low-speed connection, and neither is the Select Users option. You have to know the exact name of the user account that you are going to copy, delete, or modify.

When selecting Copy, Delete, Rename, or Properties from the User menu, you will be prompted to enter the user or group with which you want to work. Figure 14.23 shows the Manage User or Group Properties dialog that you would see if you chose Properties from the User menu. As with the other options I mentioned, you must directly enter the proper name of the user or group with which you want to work. When selecting New User or New Local Group you will see the same dialog that would be displayed if this was not a low-speed connection.

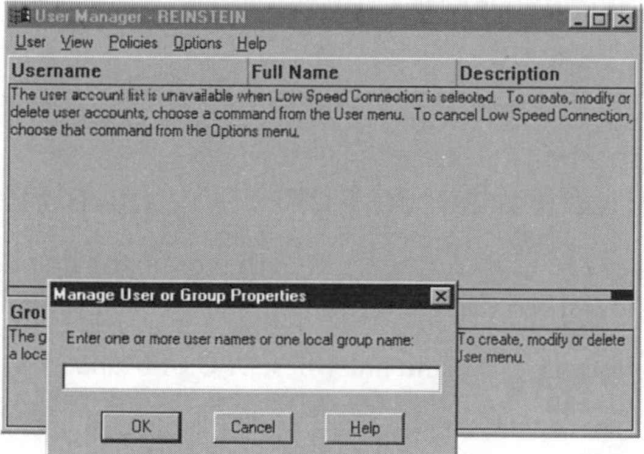

Figure 14.23. *Manage User or Group Properties.*

Running User Manager for Domains from a Command Line

The actual User Manager for Domains program exists in the %systemroot%\SYSTEM32 directory. The filename for User Manager for Domains is USRMGR.EXE.

The options that are available when running User Manager for Domains from the command line are to specify a domain and to specify the speed of the connection to the PDC for the domain. By default, User Manager for Domains will connect to the PDC for the domain that the user running User Manager for Domains is a member of.

Specifying the Domain to Manage

Under normal circumstances, User Manager for Domains will be used to manage accounts, policies, and trust relationships for the current domain. The current domain is the domain that the user running User Manager for Domains is a member of.

However, in an enterprise setup, where multiple domains can be administered from another domain, it might be necessary to override the default domain and specify the actual domain that you want to administer through User Manager for Domains.

This can be done by adding the name of the domain to the command line for User Manager for Domains.

For instance, if you want to manage the MANCHESTER domain, you could use the following command line:

```
USRMGR MANCHESTER
```

Specifying Connection Speed from the Command Line

The connection speed to a PDC can be set from the command line. Use the /l switch if you want to connect using a low-speed connection. The /h switch will force a high-speed connection.

For example, the following command line will start User Manager for Domains with a low-speed connection:

```
USRMGR /l
```

The low-speed connection is usually used when connecting through a slow link to a PDC. If you want to connect to a PDC from a domain that is different from your own, you can combine command-line switches.

For instance, to administer the MANCHESTER domain and specify a low-speed connection, use the following command line:

```
USRMGR MANCHESTER /l
```

Summary

The User Manager for Domains is a very powerful tool for handling most of your security requirements.

Before you dive into creating groups and user accounts, plan carefully how you would like to implement your network. Planning in advance will enable you to have a much easier time at administering your users and setting up your security policies.

The next chapter tells you about User Manager for Domains' counterpart in Windows NT domain administration, the Server Manager.

Server Manager

by Robert Reinstein

The Windows NT Server Manager application is the administrative tool with which you can monitor all the servers in your Windows NT domains.

The functions of Server Manager discussed in this chapter include

- Monitoring resources in use
- Seeing which users are logged on to the domain
- Configuring replication

The Server Manager application icon is located in the Administrative Tools program folder.

A version for Windows 3.*x*, Windows 95, and Windows NT workstations is located on the Windows NT Server CD-ROM in the `Clients\Srvtools` directory.

The Server Manager Main Window

When you first start Server Manager, the computers running Microsoft Networking in the current domain are listed and identified. In Figure 15.1 the Server Manager shows that the computer SERVER is a primary domain controller. The computer named DADS is a Windows NT Workstation client. KEVIN is a Windows 95 client workstation. Any other computers that are participating in the domain would also be shown in this list.

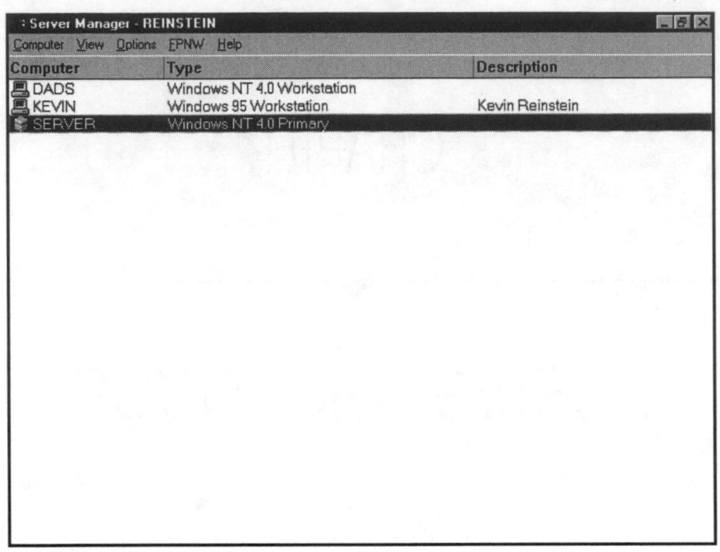

Figure 15.1. *Server Manager dialog.*

Icons to the left of the computer's name indicate its role on the network.

You can filter this list by clicking the View menu item. By default, all computers are shown, but by selecting from the View menu item, you can limit the list to servers or workstations. You can also limit the list to show only members of the domain, which will limit the list to Windows NT computers that have joined the current domain.

The Low Speed Connection option located on the Options menu will prevent Server Manager from refreshing its list automatically. This is especially useful for domains that you are managing over a WAN or slow link, such as a modem. If this option is turned on, which is shown as a check mark next to the menu item, you can refresh the display by choosing Refresh from the View menu.

If you have multiple domains in your network, choose to view and administer another domain by choosing Select Domain from the Computer menu item.

Administration

Windows NT servers and workstations can be administered from Server Manager. By double-clicking the computer you want to administer, the resulting dialog enables you to view and configure some aspects of that computer.

A summary in the top half of the Properties dialog shows the number of users currently connected to the selected computer, the total number of open files on the computer, the total number of files that are locked by connected users, and the total number of open named pipes, which are interprocess communication mechanisms that can be either local or to a process occurring on another computer.

In the description field, you can enter descriptive text that will show up on the Server Manager list of computers. If this has already been filled in, that description will always appear here when the properties for that computer are displayed.

Viewing Connected Users

Click the button labeled Users to display the User Sessions dialog.

As shown in Figure 15.2, User Sessions lists users who are connected to the selected computer, the name of the computer the user is using, the number of files opened, status information, and whether that user is connected to the Windows NT computer via the Guest account.

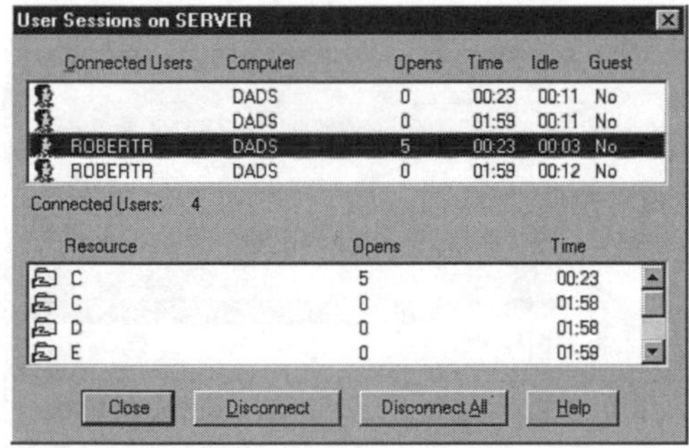

Figure 15.2. *User Sessions dialog.*

Note: You may notice that the first user shown in Figure 15.2 is blank. This is known as a null connection. A *null* connection is a connection that is being used by an interprocess communication, also known as an IPC.

The lower half of the User Sessions dialog lists the shares that the highlighted user is accessing and shows the number of open files for each of these shares.

Using the buttons at the bottom of the dialog, you can disconnect the highlighted user or all of the connected users from the selected computer.

Caution: Disconnecting users while they have files open is not recommended, because doing so may corrupt those files or the file may remain open and unavailable to other users until the computer is shut down.

Viewing Shared Resources

By clicking the Shares button located on the Properties dialog, you will see a list of all the shares, including shared printers and administrative shares, that are located on the current computer.

This list displays the number of users currently using the share and the physical path to the share.

When you highlight one share name in the list, the lower part of the Shared Resources dialog displays the connected usernames, the length of time the user has been attached to the share, and whether the user is actively accessing the share.

In the example shown in Figure 15.3, the C share is being accessed by the same user in two instances. One instance is active and the other is not. If this was a live network where dozens, hundreds, or thousands of users were contending for access of a single share, you would want to limit the number of people who can access the share at the same time to eliminate poor performance.

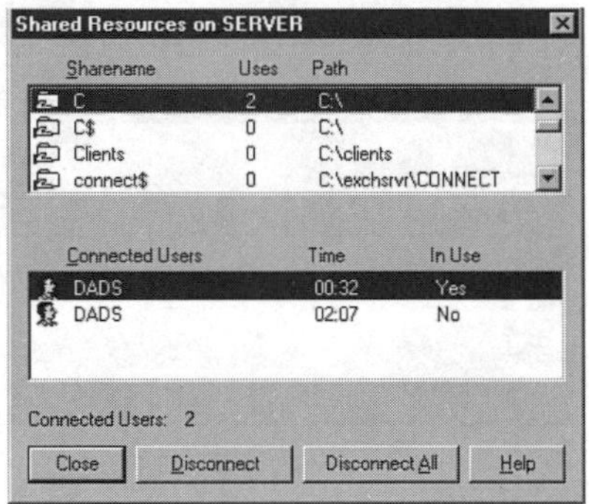

Figure 15.3. *Shared Resources dialog.*

When you originally set up the share, you were able to specify the maximum number of concurrent connections to the new share.

In this case, if that number had been two, the C share would have hit its maximum number of users. To make another slot available, use the Shared Resources dialog to disconnect a user from a share. You could also use the disconnect feature to disconnect all users from a share if, for instance, you needed to update a file and needed exclusive access to the file to do that.

Viewing Open Resources

To view a list of the actual files that are open and in use on the selected computer, click the In Use button from the Properties dialog. The resulting dialog will look like the one shown in Figure 15.4.

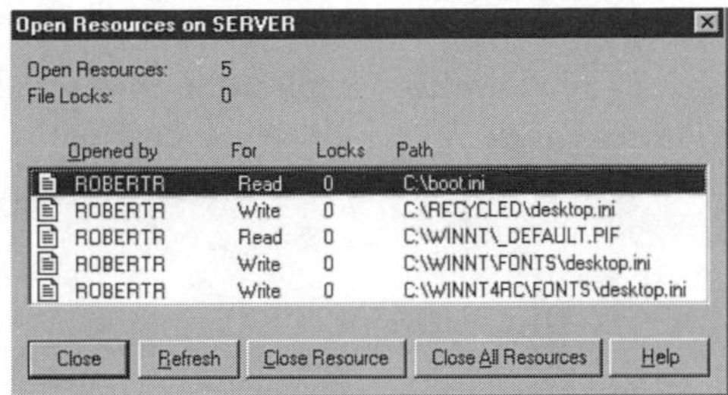

Figure 15.4. *Open Resources dialog.*

The Open Resources dialog displays a list of the files that are currently in use on the selected computer. The status of each of these files is shown as either open in a read-only mode or open in write mode, which means the user can read and write in the file.

This dialog is especially useful in case you need to disconnect users. There is no harm in disconnecting a user from a resource as long as the user is in read-only mode. Take the individual file from the user by highlighting it in the list and then clicking the Close Resource button. All of the users attached to that particular file will be disconnected from the file.

To close all of the files, click the Close All Resources button.

Setting Up Directory Replication

With Windows NT, you can replicate directories, which is particularly useful if you need to distribute data between PCs in an automated manner.

NT Workstation: Windows NT workstations can only import data; they cannot export directories.

Note: OS/2 LAN Manager 2.*x* servers can also import directories.

Usually, replication is used in a Windows NT domain to make sure that logon scripts are kept synchronized between domain controllers.

The directories that are exported must be within the same structure. As a default, the path `%systemroot%\System32\Repl\Export`, and any directories placed under this directory, are used for exporting. The default import path is `%systemroot%\System32\Repl\Import`.

Setting up replication requires configuring on both export computers and import computers. If the two do not have a synchronized configuration, replication will fail. In other words, setting up replication requires the closest attention to every detail.

Note: You can also configure Directory Replication through the Server applet located in the Windows NT Control Panel.

Enabling the Directory Replication Service

By default, the Directory Replication service is installed on all Windows NT computers. You must take necessary steps so that this service can start automatically whenever the computer is started, however.

The first step to enabling Directory Replication is to create an account that the Directory Replication service will use. This is necessary because Directory Replication must be assigned.

Using User Manager for Domains, add an account with the attributes shown in Figure 15.5. You can name the account any name you want. Pay attention to the check boxes because this account will be unable to change its own password; it must never be required to change its password.

Tip: When enabling some features of Windows NT and installing many other products on Windows NT, you might find that special accounts, known as service accounts, must be created. Sometimes the software will volunteer to create the account, and other times the service account must be created manually. In all cases, it's wise to use a prefix for service account names so that they are more easily distinguishable.

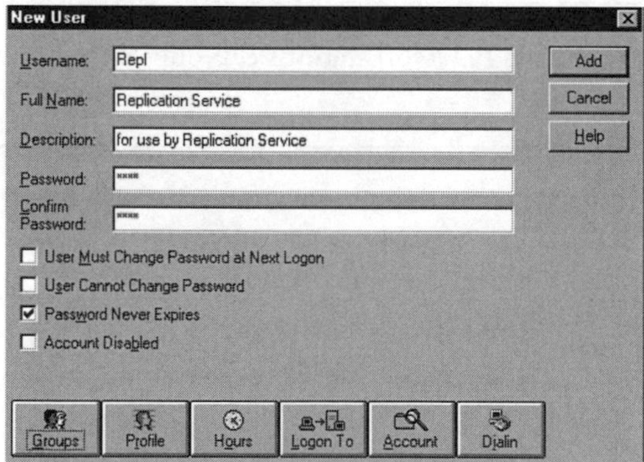

***Figure 15.5.** Adding a user account for Directory Replication.*

You must also make this account a member of the Backup Operators group. If you have set up your Windows NT default user account template with any logon hour restrictions, you must remove them for this account.

After you have created the account, go into the Control Panel and open the Services dialog.

> **Note:** The Services dialog is also accessible directly from Server Manager by highlighting the computer and choosing Services from the Computer menu item. To have access to both the Directory Replication dialog and the Services dialog, however, you must use the Control Panel applet.

Locate and double-click the Directory Replication service to open the Service configuration dialog. As shown in Figure 15.6, change the Startup Type to Automatic and under Log On As, select This Account and enter the name of the account that you had created for this service to use.

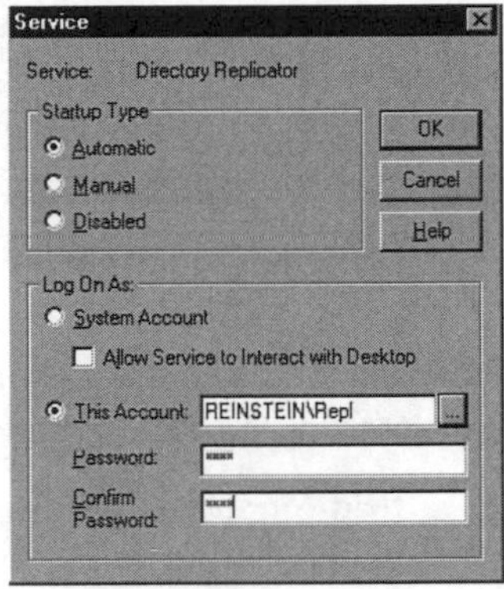

Figure 15.6. Service configuration.

Enter the password for the account and click the OK button. The resulting dialog (see Figure 15.7) will inform you that the specified account has been given the right to Log On As A Service and has been added to the Replicator local group.

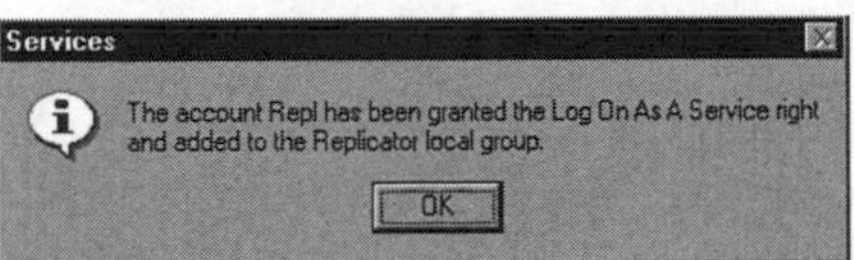

Figure 15.7. Successful configuration of the Directory Replication service.

Click the OK button to return to the Services dialog.

Now the Directory Replication service has been configured, and you may continue to configure the directory replication from Server Manager.

Setting Up the Export Server

From the list of computers in Server Manager, double-click the computer that will serve as the export server. When you click the Replication button on the server's Properties dialog, the Directory Replication dialog is displayed, as shown in Figure 15.8.

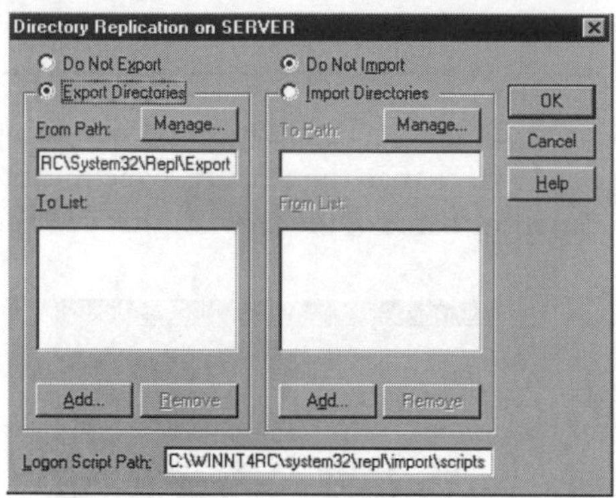

Figure 15.8. *Directory replication.*

The left side of the Directory Replication dialog works with the export directory. The right side of the dialog handles the task of receiving a directory exported from another computer.

At the bottom of the dialog is a field for specifying the server's path for Logon Scripts. As I mentioned, distribution of logon scripts is usually the reason to set up replication. This field defaults to `%systemroot\System32\Repl\Import\Scripts`, which is the default `NETLOGON` share, but you can change it to wherever you want to keep the logon scripts.

To enable directory replication, you must choose the Export Directories radio button and place the appropriate path that you want to export in the From Path.

By default, members of the export server's domain will automatically receive the exported directories if those computers have enabled the import mechanism for directory replication.

If computers are outside the domain of the export server, you must add them to the To List. When you add computers to this list, you override the automatic replication to the export server's domain members and must specify them manually if you still want to enable local domain replication.

Tip: If you set up directory replication across a WAN, you should explicitly name the individual computers that you want to export to, even if you want to include an entire domain. If you only name the domain, directory replication might not be successful.

To add computers to the To List, click the Add... button. A list of domains will appear. Choose to add entire domains or double-click a domain name to see a list of the computers within that domain beneath the domain name. Select an individual computer by double-clicking its name.

Continue to add domains and computers until you have added all the computers or domains that you want to import to the exported directory.

The directory that you choose to export can then be configured. Click the button labeled Manage... in the Directory Replication dialog to find a list of the subdirectories that appear under the directory you chose as the export directory. In the example in Figure 15.9, the only subdirectory is `Scripts`.

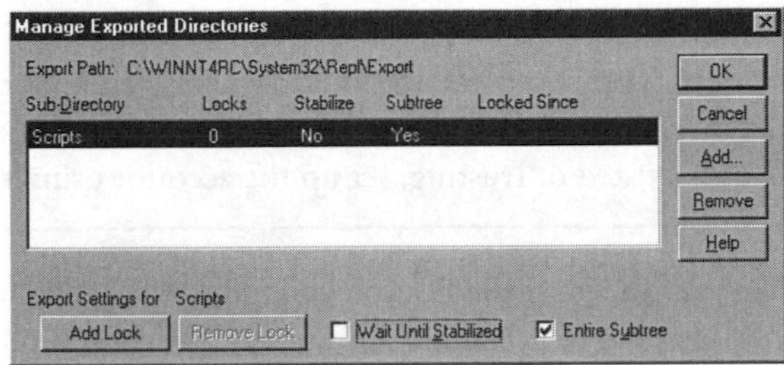

Figure 15.9. Managing exported directories.

Your options for configuring this subdirectory are shown in Table 15.1.

Table 15.1. Export directory configuration.

Locks	Prevents the subdirectory from being exported
Stabilize	Requires no changes to the subdirectory for two minutes before an export can occur
Subtree	Indicates whether any subdirectories within the selected subdirectory will also be exported
Locked Since	Shows the date and time a lock was placed on this subdirectory

You can place a lock on a subdirectory by highlighting the chosen subdirectory and clicking the button labeled Add Lock. You can add multiple locks, and no exporting will be performed unless the number of locks is zero.

To set Stabilize, check the check box labeled Wait Until Stabilized. By default, this box is unchecked.

The Subtree setting is controlled by the check box labeled Entire Subtree. By default, this box is checked so that all subdirectories beneath the highlighted subdirectory can be exported. If this box is unchecked, only the root of the selected subdirectory will be exported.

Setting Up the Importing Computer

For any export operation to be successful, a properly configured import computer must be ready to receive the transferred data.

To properly configure a computer to receive exported directories, you must make the same changes to the Directory Replication service as for the Export Server, which is to make the service start automatically and use the This Account setting.

Note: If the importing computer is on the same domain as the export server, use the account that the export server had set up. Otherwise, create an account for your domain to use. If the other domain is trusted or trusting, set up the account using the same account name.

Figure 15.10 shows the Directory Replication configuration dialog for Windows NT Workstation. As I mentioned earlier in this chapter, Windows NT Workstation cannot export but can only import directories. In this example, I have chosen to import data from SERVER, the computer that I configured in the previous section, "Setting Up the Export Server."

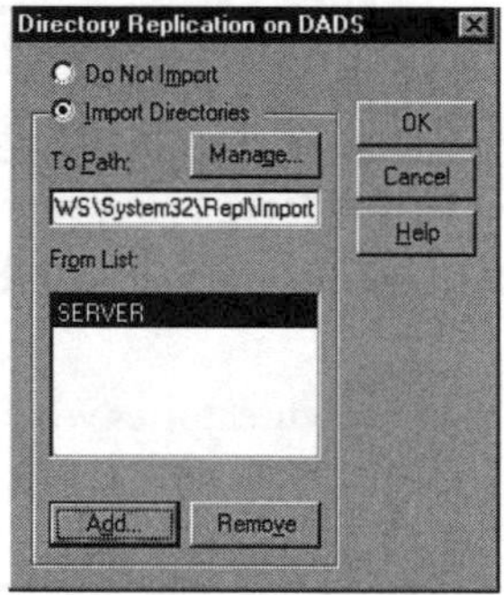

Figure 15.10. *Directory Replication on Windows NT Workstation.*

After the settings have been made to allow importing, the Directory Replication service will automatically start. To ensure that the service starts every time the computer is booted, however, the settings in Services (located in the Control Panel) for Directory Replication must be set to Automatic. The Event Viewer application can be checked for information regarding successful, or unsuccessful, replication.

To configure the import directory, click the Manage button from the Directory Replication dialog in the Import Directories area. Figure 15.11 shows the Manage Imported Directories dialog.

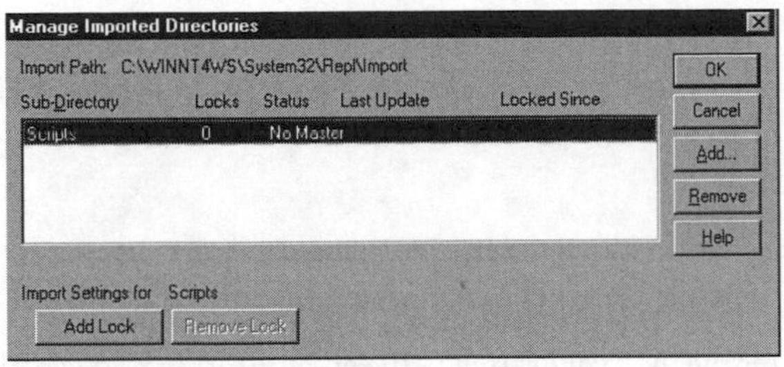

Figure 15.11. *Manage Imported Directories.*

Table 15.2. shows the settings in the Manage Imported Directories dialog.

Table 15.2. Imported Directories settings.

Locks	Gives a count of the number of locks placed on the selected import directory. When a lock is placed on an import directory, no data can be imported into the directory. To add a lock, click Add Lock in the Manage Imported Directories dialog. To remove locks, click the button labeled Remove Lock.
Status	The status of an import directory can be OK, which means that successful importing has occurred and the import directory is currently synchronized with the import directory; No Master, which means that the subdirectory is not receiving data; No Sync, which means that replication is occurring but the directories are not in synch; and a blank status, which means that replication has not occurred, possibly meaning that there is a configuration problem.
Last Update	Shows the date and time that the last import occurred.
Locked Since	Shows the time and date that a lock was placed on this subdirectory.

Optimizing Directory Replication Settings

Directory replication occurs whenever a change is made to the data contained within directories that are flagged for exporting. It is possible to change the interval at which replication occurs, using the Registry Editor, `REGEDT32`, but you should only use this if you are sure you can be extremely careful.

> **Caution:** An improperly edited Registry may result in an inoperable Windows NT system.

The following settings apply only to Windows NT servers that are configured as Export servers.

In the HKEY_LOCAL_MACHINE section of the Registry, the subtree named System\CurrentControlSet\Services\Replicator handles the settings for the Directory Replication service.

Most of the settings within this subtree are configurable by using Server Manager, though two values are not configurable unless they are edited directly using REGEDT32.

These items can alter the interval of time between replication and can also change the amount of time required for stabilization.

The Interval setting defaults to five minutes, hence the initial setting of 5. Valid values for Interval are from 1 to 60. By changing the setting to 1, the directories that have been flagged for replication will be checked once a minute. If you are experiencing trouble due to replication occurring too often, you can have the Directory Replication service check the export directories up to only once an hour.

The GuardTime setting shows the number of minutes assigned to stabilization, which I discussed earlier in this chapter. The valid setting for GuardTime ranges from 0 to one-half of the setting for Interval. Giving GuardTime a value of 0 will disable stabilization.

Directory Replication Errors

When you are configuring Directory Replication, be sure to enter a valid pathname for the import and export paths; otherwise, you will find an error in the Event Viewer that says The System Cannot Find the File Specified or The System Cannot Find the Path Specified. This error will occur when the Directory Replication service attempts to start.

Another cause for errors in starting the Directory Replication service is when the information entered via Server Manager for directory replication does not match the entries for directory replication kept in the Registry. This could be due to corruption to the Registry, the inadvertent deletion of entries in the Registry, or an unusual shutdown of Server Manager.

To reset the Directory Replication service, go to the Services applet in the Control Panel and set Directory Replication to Manual. Then stop the service.

Once the service has stopped, start REGEDT32, the Registry Editor, and look for the HKEY_LOCAL_MACHINE subtree System\CurrentControlSet\Services\Replicator.

Now make the following changes, shown in Table 15.3, to the following entries under System\CurrentControlSet\Services\Replicator.

Caution: Do not delete the entire System\CurrentControlSet\Services\Replicator subtree in an attempt to reset the Directory Replicator service or you will generate additional errors.

Table 15.3. Resetting Registry entries for Directory Replication.

`Exports`	Deletes all values
`Imports`	Deletes all values
`Parameters\ExportPath`	Sets the string to `C:\`
`Parameters\ImportPath`	Sets the string to `C:\`
`Parameters\ImportList`	Deletes the string value

From the Directory Replication dialog in Server Manager, manually enter the Export path and Import path (if applicable) as `%systemroot%\System32\Repl\Export` or `%systemroot%\System32\Repl\Import`. Also, you will need to reenter the Logon Script path, which is usually `%systemroot%\System32\Repl\Import\Scripts`.

When you close the Directory Replication dialog, the Directory Replication service should start.

After these settings have been saved, you should synchronize the domain. Instructions on this are located later in this chapter.

Administrative Alerts

The final button available on the Server Manager Properties dialog is labeled Alerts. Clicking this button will bring up the Alerts dialog. (See Figure 15.12.)

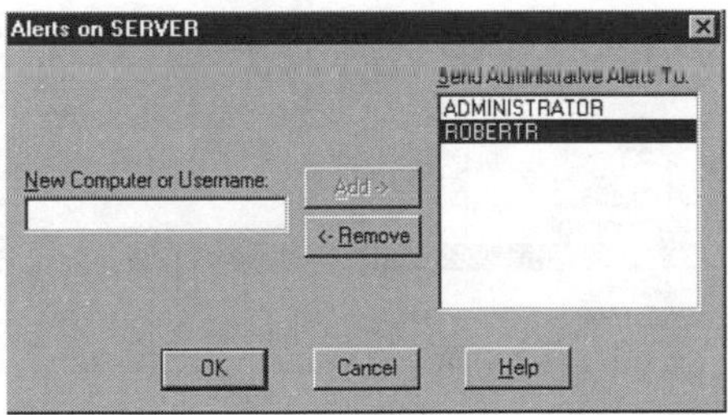

***Figure 15.12.** Alerts dialog.*

Windows NT generates Administrative alerts when there is a resource security, or server problem, such as a shutdown due to power loss.

The mechanisms driving the alert process are the Alerter service and the Messenger service. To receive these alerts, the Messenger service is required. By default, Windows NT computers run both the Alerter and Messenger services.

Of course, all the messages that the Alerter service would send are logged to the Event log, though sometimes you want to notify certain personnel of an event immediately.

In the dialog shown in Figure 15.12, the account names ADMINISTRATOR and ROBERTR have been added to the Send Administrative Alerts To list. These users will receive a pop-up notification of any activity on the selected computer, in this case, SERVER.

Troubleshooting Alerts

Troubleshooting: If you find that the designated recipients are not getting these alerts, verify that the Alerter and Messenger services are running on the source computer. Also make sure that the Messenger service is running on the recipient's computer.

Administering Shares Through Server Manager

The first section of this chapter dealt with the properties for Windows NT computers on your network. Server Manager is also used to administer the shared directories on your Windows NT computers.

Located on the Computer menu item of Server Manager, the Shared Directories... option will show you a list of all the shared directories for the selected computer. (See Figure 15.13.) These shares include user-created system and administrative shares. From this list, you can see the share name and the actual path for the share.

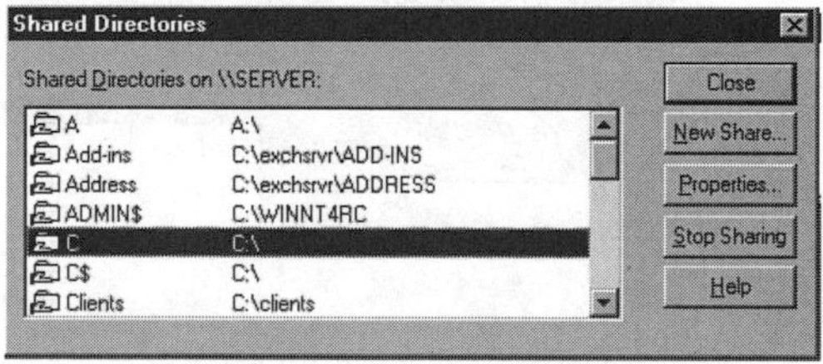

Figure 15.13. *Shared Directories dialog.*

From this dialog, you can choose to stop sharing the share, display the properties for the share (with which you can then make any changes to the configuration for the share), or create a new share.

Unique to using Server Manager to manage your shared directories is the ability to create and maintain shares that exist on other computers. Of course, you must have the proper rights and permissions to perform these actions.

For complete details on creating and setting permissions on shared directories, refer to Chapter 2, "Windows NT Security Architecture."

Administering Services Through Server Manager

The Services dialog that is displayed when you choose Services from the Computer menu in Server Manager is the same dialog that you would see by running the Services applet, located in the Windows NT Control Panel.

Using Server Manager, however, you can also administer the services that are running on remote computers. Of course, this is achieved only if you have sufficient rights to administer the other computer.

The Services dialog, shown in Figure 15.14, lists all the services that are installed on the selected computer. The Status column identifies whether the service is currently active ("Started"), has been paused ("Paused"), or is inactive, which would be shown as a blank status. The Startup column shows how the service will start, whether it will start automatically at boot time or whether it must be started manually (either by a user or by a service). The other option for Startup is Disabled, which makes the service unable to start at any time.

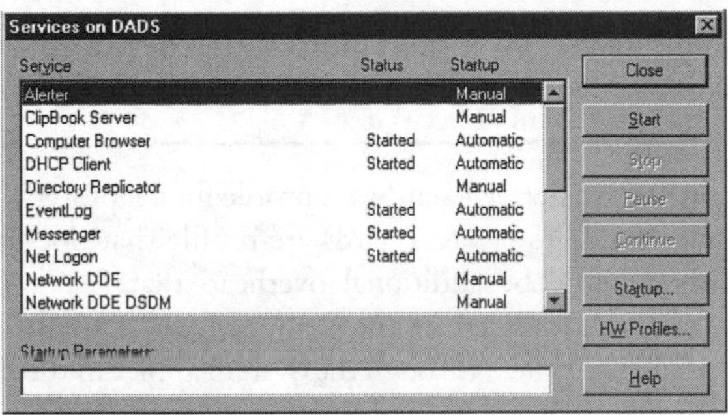

Figure 15.14. *The services installed on the selected computer.*

When a service that has not already started is highlighted, the Start button will be available to manually start the service. Clicking the button makes the system attempt to start the service. Once started, the Stop button will be available to stop the service. Sometimes, but not always, the Pause button is also available to pause a service. Paused services will show the Continue button, which when pressed will change the status from Paused to Started again.

Clicking the Startup button will bring you into the configuration dialog for the highlighted service, where you can choose the startup mode for the service. As I described previously in the section about starting the Directory Replication service, sometimes it is necessary to have the service use permissions that are granted to a user account. In most cases, though, a system account will be used as the default, shown in Figure 15.15, which shows the default settings for the Net Logon service.

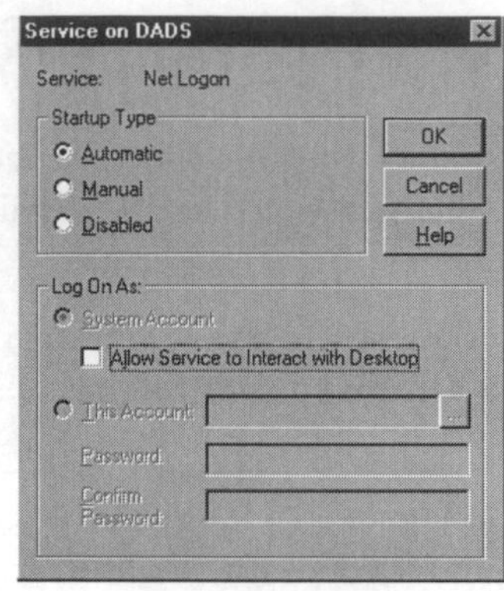

Figure 15.15. Net Logon Service settings.

With the Allow Service to Interact with Desktop check box, you can specify whether a specific service requires the capability to run a front end on the desktop.

New to NT 4.0: With the HW Profiles button on the Services dialog, you can configure the different optional hardware profiles that can be set up on Windows NT 4.0 computers.

For example, if you were to define a hardware profile for a laptop that is not always connected to a network, you may decide to create a hardware profile that does not include any networking services because they would be additional overhead that is not necessary for a stand-alone computer. In this case, you could create another profile (all copies of Windows NT 4.0 default to a profile called "Original Profile") through the System applet in the Windows NT Control Panel and use the HW Profiles... dialog to disable the services that are not necessary while acting as a stand-alone computer.

In Figure 15.16, I have done just that for the Server service running on the computer DADS.

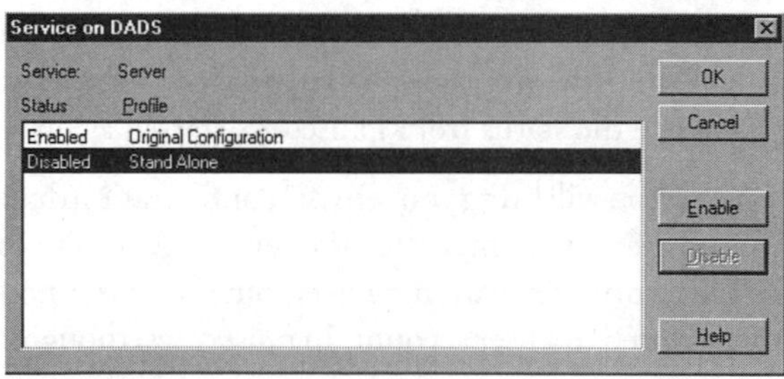

Figure 15.16. Service settings for hardware profiles.

Sending Messages

Server Manager gives you the ability to send messages to all users connected to a computer, as long as the computer is listed in Server Manager and is running Windows NT. Figure 15.17 illustrates the Send Message dialog.

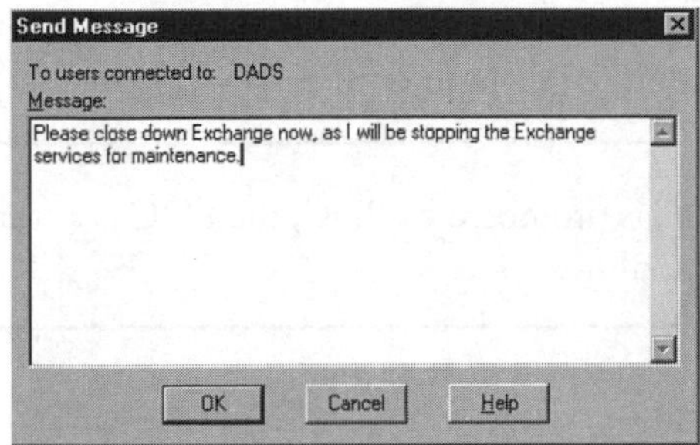

Figure 15.17. *Sending a message.*

In Server Manager, highlight the computer to which the users to whom you want to get the message are connected and select Send Message... from the Computer menu item.

Type the message you want to send in the Send Message dialog and then click the OK button.

Promoting a Backup Domain Controller to a Primary Domain Controller

If a Primary Domain Controller (PDC) is taken offline because of a server crash or maintenance or because the server is being retired, you will need to promote a Backup Domain Controller (BDC) to be the new PDC.

By highlighting a BDC in Server Manager, you can use a menu item on the Computer menu to promote the BDC to a PDC.

Note: If a BDC is promoted to a PDC while the PDC is still online, it might force the PDC to be demoted to a BDC.

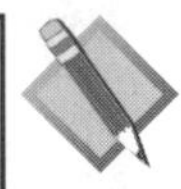

After you select the menu item Promote to Primary Domain Controller, the request will go out to let the other BDCs in the domain know that a PDC now exists.

Demoting a Primary Domain Controller to a Backup Domain Controller

When a BDC is promoted to a PDC, it is usually because the PDC was taken offline, perhaps for a repair. When the PDC is put back online, the former BDC must be demoted back to a BDC by highlighting the former BDC on the Server Manager list and then choosing Demote To Backup Domain Controller from the Computer menu.

Note: When a BDC is promoted to PDC, the PDC is automatically demoted to BDC, if the former PDC is online.

Forcing Domain Controller Synchronization

Under normal circumstances, the administrative database of a PDC is replicated to all of the BDCs that are part of the domain. Sometimes, connection problems will result in non-synchronized domain controllers. The Server Manager contains two options that can force this synchronization.

Usually using these options to "kickstart" synchronization will help rectify any synchronization problems that your domain may be experiencing.

Synchronizing the Domain

When a PDC is highlighted in Server Manager, the menu item Synchronize Entire Domain will appear on the Computer menu. This option forces replication of the administrative databases between the PDC and any BDCs that are currently available in the domain. Once the request has been made to the system, a confirmation dialog will let you know that the synchronization process has started.

Tip: Use this option whenever you are planning to shut down the PDC. This way, any revised account information on the PDC will be forced to the BDCs.

Forcing a BDC to Synchronize with a PDC

Another menu item that is visible when a BDC is highlighted in Server Manager enables you to force the synchronization of the BDC with its domain's PDC. This menu item, Synchronize with Primary Domain Controller, is located on the Computer menu.

This option is used when a BDC unexplainably is rejecting valid user logons. Although you can force synchronization from the server, if you have many BDCs but are only concerned about one BDC, the synchronization process will complete faster using this method.

Managing Domain Membership

Windows NT domains require that computers are added to the domain to obtain a fully authenticated logon. That computer can also assign permissions to accounts and global groups that belong to that domain.

Usually, it is during the installation of Windows NT that a computer opts to join a domain. To join a domain, the user must have rights to add a computer to a domain. As you saw during the installation of Windows NT Workstation, the option to join a domain required the name of the domain, an authorized account name, and the password for that account.

The Server Manager list of computers will indicate whether a computer is a member of a domain. With one option on the View menu of Server Manager, you can filter out computers that are not domain members.

Because each computer in a domain must have a unique computer name, it is essential that Server Manager is used to verify the existence, or lack thereof, of a particular computer name before an attempt is made to use it again.

The Computer menu in Server Manager offers two choices that involve the management of computers membership in a domain.

Adding a Computer to a Domain

One choice in Server Manager is for adding computers to a domain. Select Add To Domain from the Computer menu and the Add Computer To Domain dialog (see Figure 15.18) will be displayed.

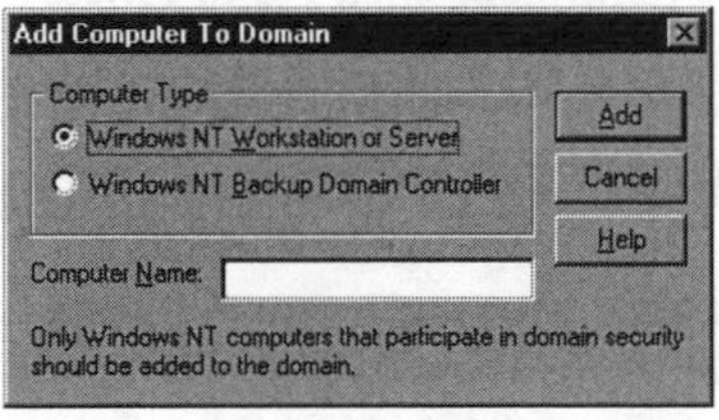

Figure 15.18. *Adding a computer to a domain.*

Within this dialog, you must indicate whether the computer you are adding to the domain is a Windows NT Workstation, a Windows NT Server that is not acting as a domain controller, or a Windows NT Server BDC.

Next, enter the unique name that you assign to this computer. This name may be up to 15 characters long and cannot be the same as any other computer or domain name in the entire network. This name is not case-sensitive.

Click the OK button and that computer will be allowed to participate in the Windows NT domain security.

Security: Be careful using this utility, because once a computer is added to the domain, any computer may log onto the domain using that name. If a computer logs onto the domain using a new computer name assigned to a BDC, the security database will be replicated to that computer.

Removing a Computer from a Domain

The other option in Server Manager for controlling domain members is to remove a computer from a domain.

To do so, highlight the computer in Server Manager and then choose Remove From Domain, which is on the Computer menu.

When you choose to remove a computer from a domain, you will first see a message box (see Figure 15.19) with which you can confirm your choice of removing the computer from the domain.

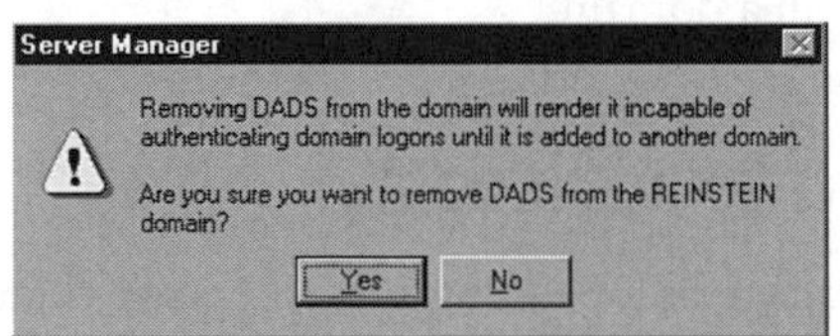

Figure 15.19. *Removing a computer from a domain.*

Click Yes to continue the removal or click No to cancel the process.

Starting Server Manager from a Command Line

You can start Server Manager from the command line using the command `SRVMGR`. The proper syntax for Server Manager is

```
srvmgr [domain [/l¦/h]]
```

You can use two optional parameters with this command:

The first is the name of the domain that you want to administer through Server Manager.

The second parameter is a switch that can set Server Manager to a low-speed or high-speed connection. Use `/l` for low speed and `/h` for high speed.

Summary

The Windows NT Server Manager is a very powerful tool that you can use to manage your entire network of Windows NT domains.

Along with User Manager for Domains, these two applications make up most of the management functions available to you under Windows NT.

The Network Client Administrator, which is discussed in Chapter 19, "Network Client Administrator," is another very powerful tool for Windows NT administrators.

Print Manager

by Robert Reinstein

The printer-sharing capabilities in Windows NT Server have many features. This chapter introduces you to printer support in Windows NT:

- Adding printer support
- Creating a local shared printer
- Attaching to network-interface printers
- Creating print queues for remote printers
- Managing print queues
- TCP/IP printer support

New to NT 4.0: In previous versions of Windows NT, Print Manager was the tool used to define and manage printers. This application no longer exists with version 4.0.

Defining Printers

Before you can do any network-specific work with printers, you must define the printers to the operating system.

Access the Printers folder (see Figure 16.1) via the Start button. Click the Start button and select Settings. From the resulting submenu, choose Printers.

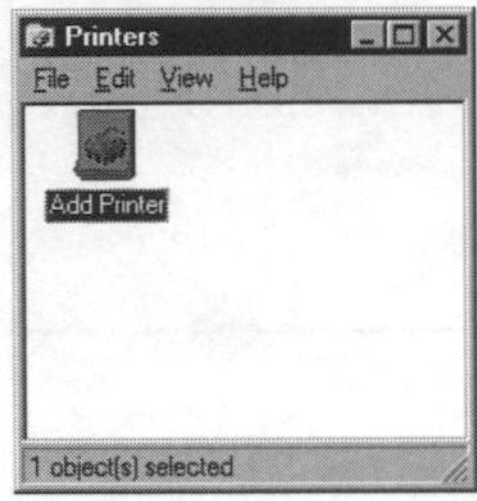

Figure 16.1. The Printers folder.

By default, the Add Printer icon is the only icon that appears in the Printers folder. This icon is a system shortcut and cannot be removed.

Double-click this icon to start the Add Printer Wizard.

The Add Printer Wizard

The purpose of the Add Printer Wizard is to step you through creating a printer.

The first question the Add Printer Wizard asks, as shown in Figure 16.2, is whether the printer that you are creating is a local or a network printer.

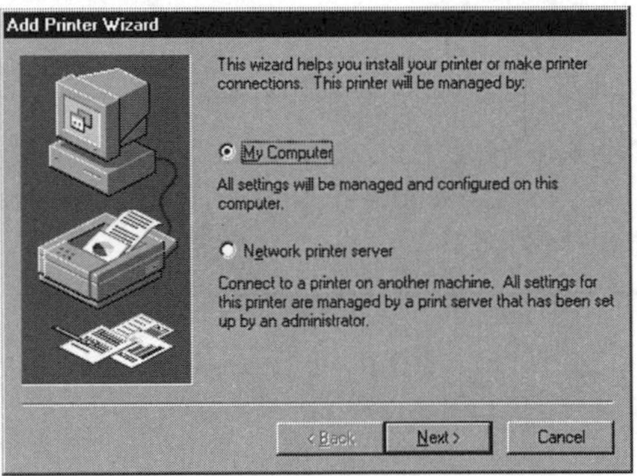

Figure 16.2. The Add Printer Wizard.

Creating a Locally Connected Printer Definition

If you are defining a printer that is attached to a local port, such as LPT1, the radio button labeled My Computer would be the appropriate choice. To attach to a printer that is available on the network via Microsoft networking, choose Network printer server instead.

For this first example, I will define a printer that is attached to the LPT1 port on the Windows NT server.

After selecting the My Computer radio button, continue by clicking the Next button.

Selecting a Printer Port

Next, the Ports dialog displays a list of local ports. This includes LPT and COM ports—plus FILE, which prompts users for a filename, and then directs printed output to that file. NetWareCompatiblePServer ports are also listed if File and Print Services for NetWare is installed.

In Figure 16.3, the LPT1 port has been chosen for this printer.

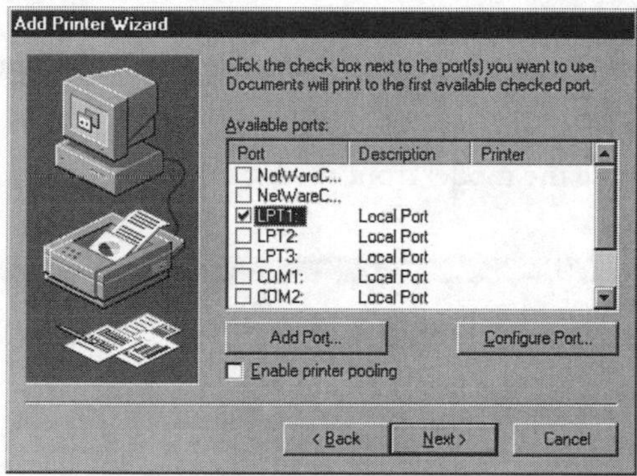

Figure 16.3. *Printer port selection.*

In the Enable printer pooling check box, you can select more than one port for one printer. This way, if two or more identical printers are attached to the computer, you can choose multiple ports for the same printer definition, and load balancing will be performed when print jobs are sent to this one printer definition. Although pooling printers can allow a user to get print jobs to a printer quicker, the user will not actually know which physical printer the output will appear from.

Figure 16.4 shows printer pooling enabled with both LPT1 and LPT2 chosen as the port for this one printer.

Connecting to Printers with Network Adapters

On this same dialog, you have the option to create a port. Creating a port is usually used when you want to attach to a printer that uses a network interface card, such as a Hewlett-Packard JetDirect card.

I discuss this later in this chapter in the section titled "Creating Printer Ports."

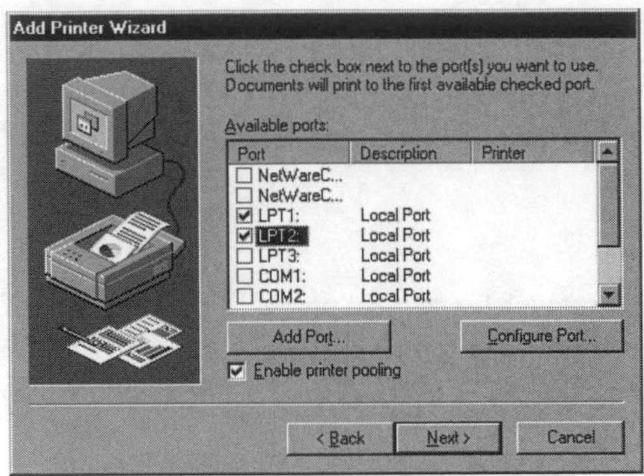

Figure 16.4. *Printer pooling enabled.*

After you have chosen the proper port or ports, click the Next button to continue.

Next, choose the type of printer, as shown in Figure 16.5. Select the brand name from the list on the left, and then choose the model from the list on the right.

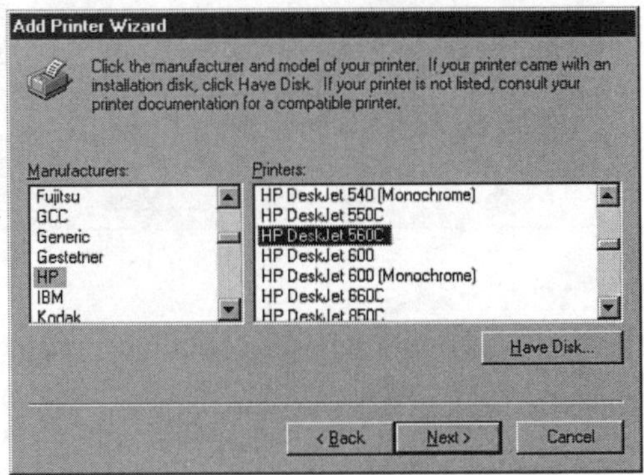

Figure 16.5. *Printer brand and model selection.*

After you have chosen the proper printer, you are asked to name the printer. By default, as shown in Figure 16.6, the actual printer name and model will be used, though you can choose a name up to 31 characters long for this printer definition. This name will not be used when the printer is shared but rather will be used when the printer folder is viewed locally.

After you have chosen the name for the printer definition, click the Next button.

Sharing the Printer and Enabling Point and Print

In the next dialog, choose whether the printer you are defining will be shared on the Microsoft network.

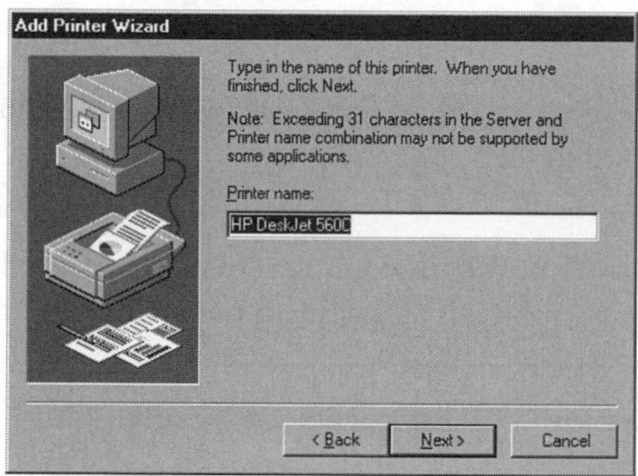

Figure 16.6. *Naming the printer definition.*

If it is shared, you have the option to install drivers that clients of the Windows NT computer or Windows NT domain may use. This enables a feature known as Point and Print. Point and Print is available for Windows NT and Windows 95 computers. All other platforms must install a print driver locally.

Figure 16.7 shows a list of the platforms from which you can choose to install drivers. Of course, if you want to install drivers other than for Windows NT, the drivers will need to be available from an alternate source.

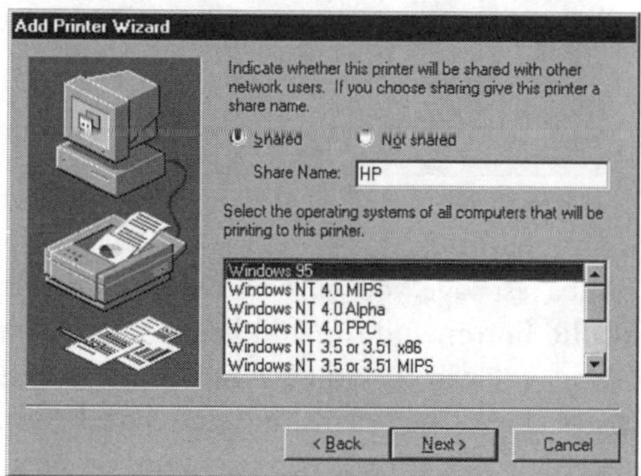

Figure 16.7. *Shared printer drivers.*

In this case, printer sharing is chosen, and the shared printer's name is HP. Installing drivers for Windows 95 clients is also chosen.

Note: Note that both Windows NT 4.0 and Windows NT 3.51 are listed here. This is because Windows NT 4.0 printer drivers, as with most of the Windows NT 4.0 drivers, have been updated.

When installing drivers for another platform, you make it very easy for those users to install the shared printer. When they attach to the printer on the network and the printer drivers have already been installed onto the server (as I have chosen to do for Windows 95), the necessary printer drivers are automatically copied to their computer.

Note: If a Windows NT or Windows 95 client wishes to have full control of the print queue, they should define the printer by installing it into their own Printers folder.

When you are finished with this dialog, click the Next button.

The next step in the Add Printer Wizard is to choose whether to print a test page. (See Figure 16.8.) You should print a test page to ensure that the proper driver has been installed. This will also let you know whether the other options that you chose are correct.

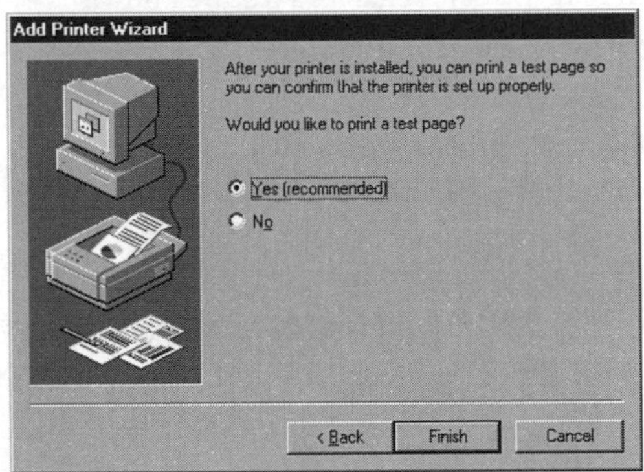

Figure 16.8. *Print a test page.*

If you have chosen to print a test page, you will be asked whether the test page has printed properly. If it has, click the Yes radio button and the Add Printer Wizard will be completed. If there is a problem with the test page, you can click the No radio button and Windows NT Help will give you some tips on things to check, such as making sure that the printer is turned on and that the cable is properly connected. You can then step backward by using the Back button in the Add Printer Wizard to see whether you selected a wrong port or whether you were given any incorrect information for this printer definition.

Once the Add Printer Wizard has completed, the Printers folder will show the newly created printer definition, as shown in Figure 16.9.

Creating a Printer Definition for a Network Printer

Besides creating a printer definition for a printer that is directly connected to a Windows NT computer, you can also create a printer definition for a printer that is on the network.

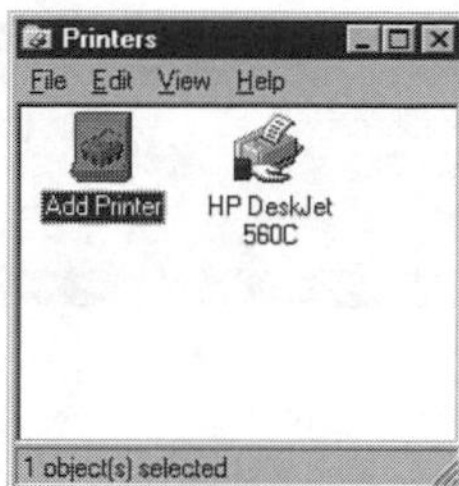

Figure 16.9. *The Printers folder with a newly created printer definition.*

This type of printer may be connected to another computer running Windows NT, Windows 95, or Windows for Workgroups.

When you choose this type of printer, control still exists on the other computer that has defined the network printer, but you can still create a queue on your Windows NT computer and share the printer under another name, creating your own security for this printer.

Using Add Printer Wizard for Defining a Network Printer

To start the Add Printer Wizard, double-click the Add New Printer icon in the Printers folder. This time, you want to select the radio button labeled Network printer server, as shown in Figure 16.10.

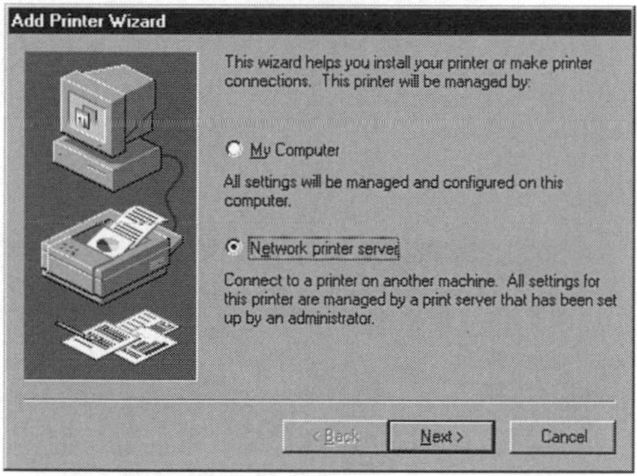

Figure 16.10. *Defining a network printer server.*

Click the Next button, and you will be prompted for the name of the printer that you want to define on this computer. A list of available printers will appear from which you can choose, or you can enter the printer name directly into the field labeled Printer. In Figure 16.11, I have entered the printer name `\\DADS\LASERJET` directly.

If the printer to which you are connecting is attached to a Windows NT computer, then the drivers you need to print to this printer are already installed. If the print server is a Windows 95 or Windows for Workgroups computer, however, you need to install Windows NT drivers.

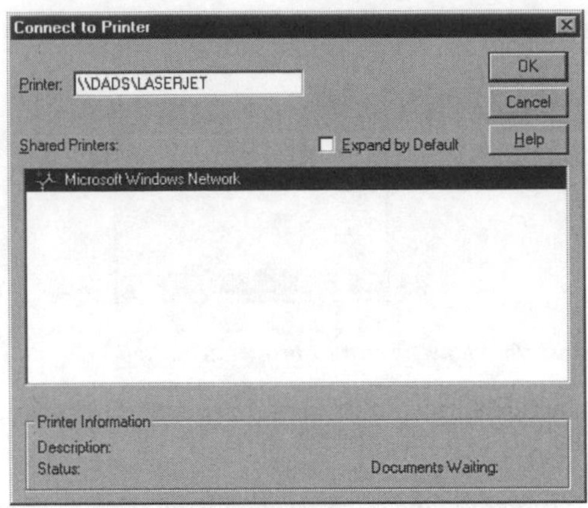

Figure 16.11. Network printer server name.

The computer acting as the print server for the printer I'm attaching to is running Windows 95, so the dialog shown in Figure 16.12 pops up to let me know that Point and Print is not available for this printer. If this is unacceptable, click the Cancel button. Click the OK button for the prompt to select the manufacturer and model of the printer, as shown in Figure 16.13.

Figure 16.12. Printer drivers not installed.

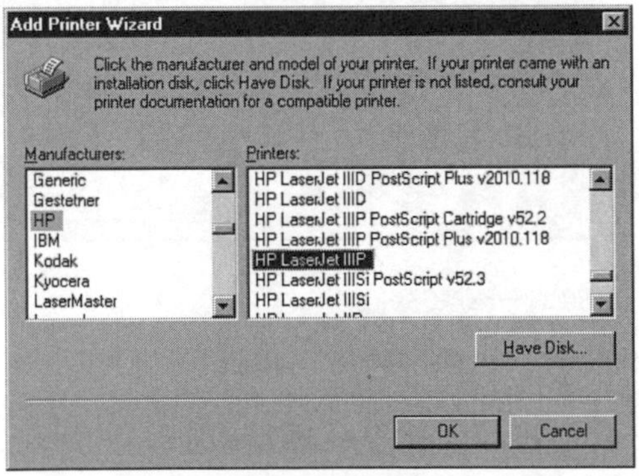

Figure 16.13. Select printer manufacturer and model.

After selecting the manufacturer and model, click the Next button. If more than one printer is defined, the Add Printer Wizard will ask whether this printer should be set to be the default printer for the local computer. If this dialog is shown, make your selection and then click the Next button.

Next, select whether this printer will be shared on the network by the Windows NT computer. If so, enter a name for the shared printer and choose the optional printer drivers for other platforms that can be installed to allow for Point and Print. In Figure 16.14, I have chosen to install Windows 95 drivers as well, as the clients on this network are all Windows NT or Windows 95.

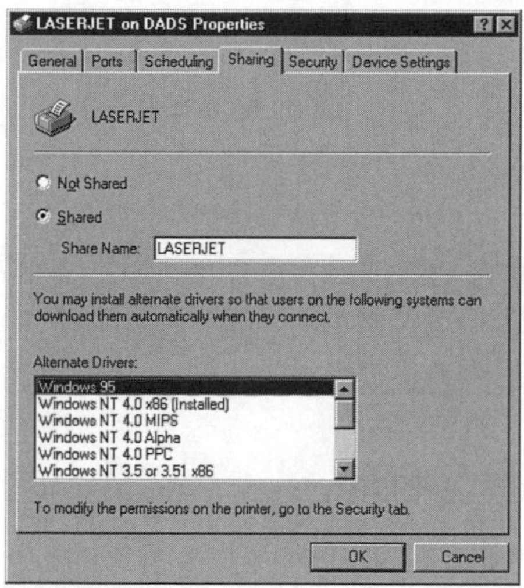

Figure 16.14. *Sharing and Point and Print settings.*

Because I have chosen Windows 95, the Add Printer Wizard prompts for the location of the Windows 95 drivers for this printer. Figure 16.15 shows the dialog where the path for the printer will be found. In this case, the Windows 95 CD-ROM includes these printer drivers, so that is the path to which the dialog is pointed.

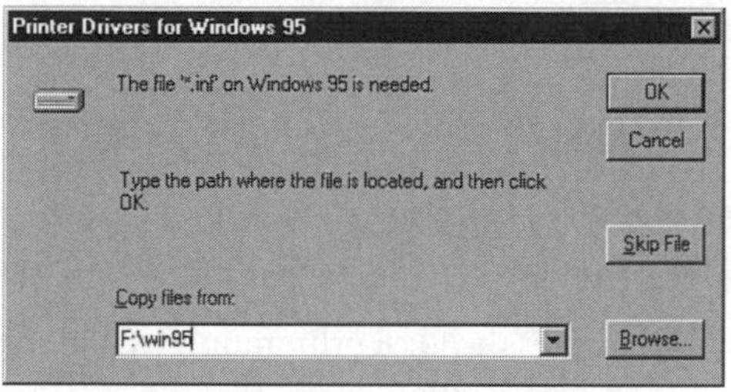

Figure 16.15. *Source path for alternate printer drivers.*

Once the file copy has completed, the last option for the Add Printer Wizard is the option to print a test page. After this, the printer definition is added to the Printers folder, as shown in Figure 16.16.

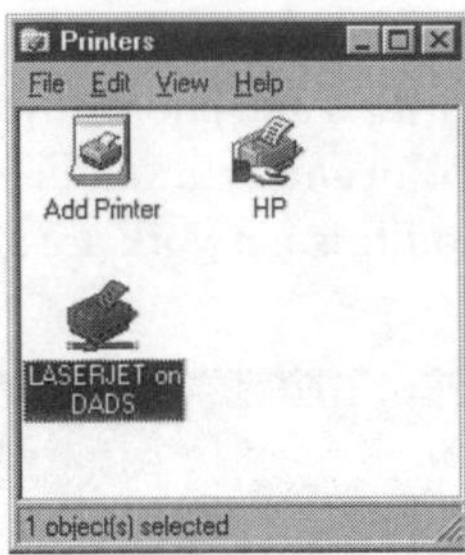

Figure 16.16. Printers folder with network printer.

Note: The hand shown under the icon for the printer named HP denotes a locally attached, shared printer, whereas the other printer icon, for LASERJET on DADS, refers to a network printer.

Assigning Security to Printers

Chapter 2, "Windows NT Security Architecture," discussed the security attributes that you can assign to a shared printer resource. The items discussed there are assigned through the Printers folder by selecting a printer icon, clicking it with the right mouse button, and selecting Properties from the resulting pop-up menu.

The Security tab has buttons with which you can assign permissions, configure auditing, and take ownership of these printers.

Even if a printer is not directly connected to the Windows NT computer, you can create permissions for a printer definition created on the computer here.

Creating Printer Ports

Windows NT has the capability to create many different types of printer ports based on the services that you have installed. These ports are dependent on the drivers, called printer monitors.

By default, Windows NT installs the local print monitor, making available the standard LPT and COM ports and the option of printing directly to a file.

The following optional print monitors are also available:

- Hewlett-Packard Network Port print monitor
- Line Printer (LPR) Port print monitor (listed as Microsoft TCP/IP Printing in the Network Services dialog)
- Macintosh print monitor

- Digital Network Port print monitor
- LexMark Mark Vision print monitor
- PJL Language Monitor

You can install each of these print monitors by adding the appropriate service.

For instance, the most widely used of these optional ports is the Hewlett-Packard Network Port print monitor. This gives you the option of connecting to a Hewlett-Packard JetDirect device or to a Hewlett-Packard printer that includes a built-in network adapter. In all cases, connectivity to these devices requires the DLC protocol, which is how the print devices communicate.

Installing protocols is discussed in Chapter 20, "Installing Windows NT Workstation," and in Chapter 6, "The Windows NT Installation Process." To summarize the process, protocols are installed through the Network applet, which is in the Control Panel. Select the Protocols tab, then choose to add a protocol, and DLC will be on the list for you to add easily. After the DLC protocol is installed, you will be able to see the network address for any JetDirect devices on your network.

The DLC protocol itself is not a routable protocol, so the printer must be on the same segment as the Windows NT computer or the segment must be bridged onto the same segment as the Windows NT computer.

After the DLC protocol is installed, you must use the Add Printer Wizard to connect to a network printer and choose to manage the settings locally. When the ports dialog appears, click the Add Port button. The list of print monitors will appear, as shown in Figure 16.17. Select Hewlett-Packard Network Port, and a list of available printer addresses will appear. Select the appropriate printer and the new port will be created. Continue with the installation of the printer as detailed earlier in this chapter.

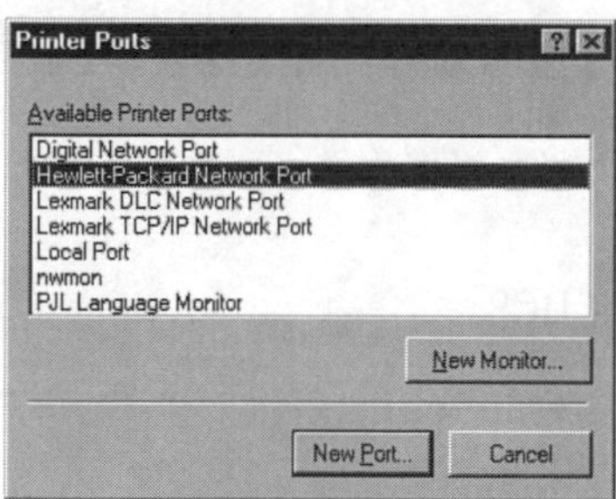

Figure 16.17. *Printer Ports list after installing DLC.*

Another popular print monitor requires that you install the TCP/IP Printing Service, which is added through the Networks applet in Control Panel. Click the Services tab and choose the Add Service option. Microsoft TCP/IP Printing will appear on the list for you to add. The resulting service will allow for a connection to UNIX computers or any other type of computer running an LPD service that requires TCP/IP.

You can also attach to printers that natively run TCP/IP.

After you restart the computer, the Printer Ports dialog will have renamed the Printer Port to LPR Port, which stands for Line Printer Port.

The print monitors that you can add to Windows NT are unlimited because the Add Printer Wizard allows for the addition of third-party print monitors.

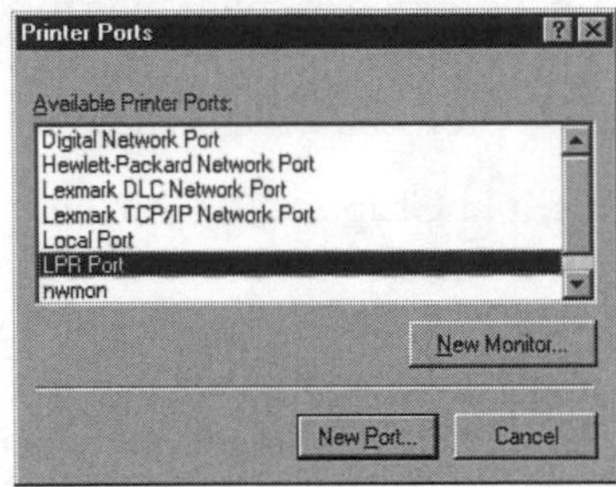

Figure 16.18. Printer Ports list after installing TCP/IP Printing service.

Double-click the LPR Port entry to display the Add LPR compatible printer dialog. (See Figure 16.19.) This dialog is looking for two entries: the name or address of a computer running the LPD service or a printer running TCP/IP, and the name or address of the printer or print queue running on that server.

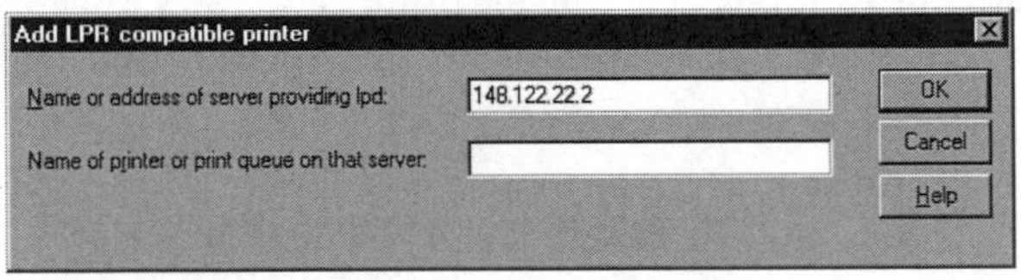

Figure 16.19. The Add LPR-compatible printer dialog.

Managing Print Queues

To manage print queues on Windows NT, open the Printers folder and double-click the icon that represents the printer definition.

The print queue for the printer I defined as HP DeskJet 560C is shown in Figure 16.20.

Two print entries are waiting on that queue. The first print job is paused because the printer is offline, as indicated in the status field. The second print job is in the process of being spooled to this print queue.

You can manipulate and configure both the print queue and the individual print jobs by using the menu or by right-mouse-clicking on the print jobs themselves.

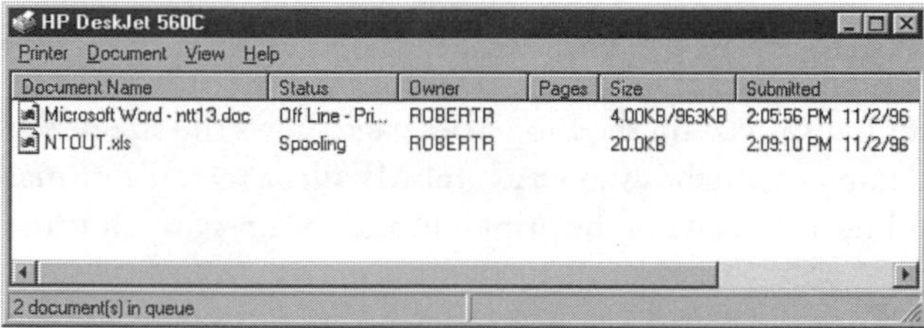

Figure 16.20. HP DeskJet 560C print queue.

Figure 16.21 shows the Printer menu. Within this menu, you can pause the print queue, set this queue as the default local printer, configure page setup defaults, configure sharing for the printer, choose to purge all print jobs currently on the print queue, or access the properties page for this printer definition.

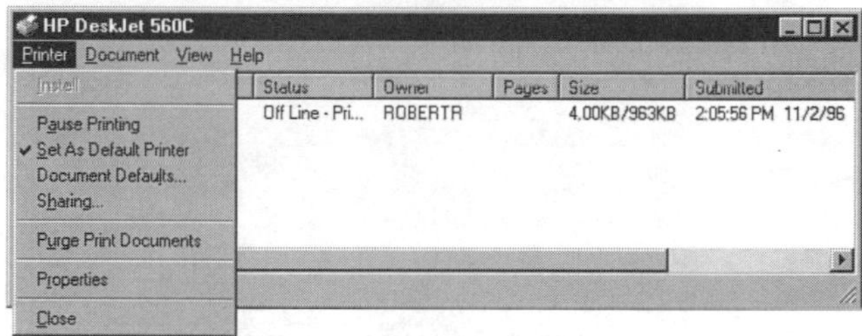

Figure 16.21. The Printer menu.

The Document menu is active only if a print job is highlighted. This menu will also appear when you right-click a print job, as shown in Figure 16.22. The options available here are to pause that particular print job (not the whole queue), resume a paused print job, restart a print job from the beginning, remove a job from the print queue, or show the properties page for that specific print job.

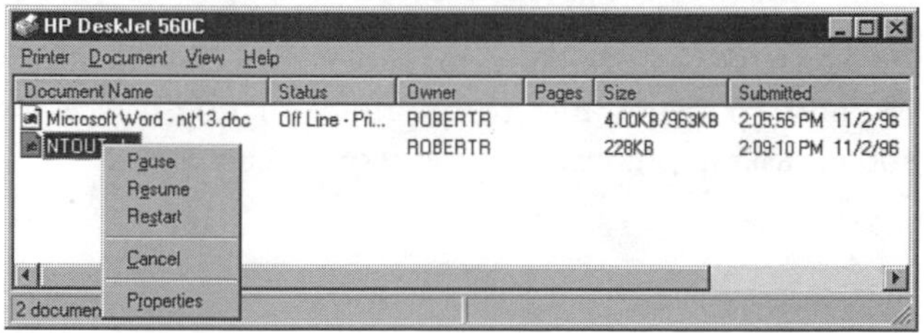

Figure 16.22. The Document menu.

The Properties page for a print job, shown in Figure 16.23, offers general information about the document itself. It also enables you to alter the priority of the print job, making it print sooner or later than other print jobs in the same queue. Other than the priority setting, the Notify field, and the Schedule settings, you may change no other settings for this document, and the other settings that you can view from the Properties page are for reference only.

The information displayed on the Properties page shows the size of the print job, the number of pages, the dDatatype (which is shown as an EMF file, a metafile format), the Processor (which is usually Winprint), the owner of the print job, and the date and time the print job was submitted.

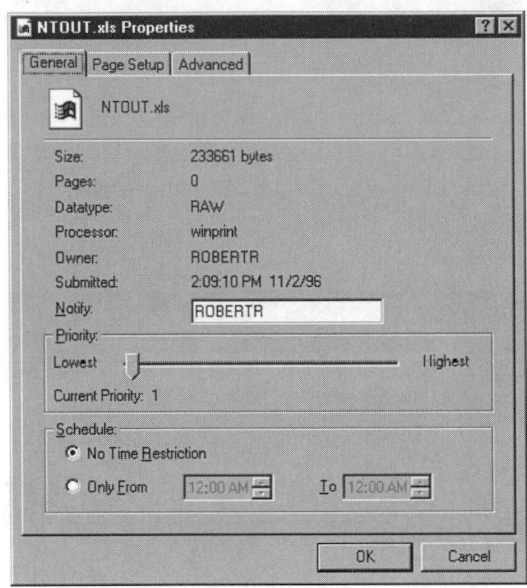

Figure 16.23. *A document Properties page.*

Summary

Windows NT is an excellent print server that offers connectivity across platforms and is a clear example of one of Windows NT's main attributes: cross-platform compatibility.

Its capability to assign server-based security to printers shared by client computers, TCP/IP printer support, and support for many third-party printer sharing devices makes Windows NT an excellent method of making printers available across an enterprise.

CHAPTER 17

Disk Administrator

by Robert Reinstein

FDISK has always been sort of a challenge to me when I'm dealing with a multitude of physical hard drives and partitions.

In many instances, I've found myself cycling through the hard drives display in FDISK, hoping that the partition I just deleted was the one I really wanted to delete.

And too many times I've found out that I just purged the wrong partition (or the right partition, but from the wrong hard drive).

The Windows NT Disk Administrator provides a way to manage all your hard drives and partitions in one window, making disk management a less intimidating procedure.

This chapter discusses the following topics:

- Creating and deleting drive partitions
- Formatting drive partitions
- Managing volume sets
- Managing stripe sets
- Disk mirroring

Using Disk Administrator, Windows NT Server, and Windows NT Workstation, users can view all their physical hard drives and CD-ROM drives at the same time.

Major changes to your hard drives, such as the deletion of partitions or the creation of partitions, will not occur until you have committed the changes!

New to NT 4.0: New to Disk Administrator for Windows NT 4.0 is that CD-ROM drives are now viewed in the graphical display. Previous versions had CD-ROM drives only as a menu item.

Basic Facts About Disk Administrator

During the installation of Windows NT, the option of creating, deleting, and formatting partitions is your first exposure to Windows NT's file systems configuration. The Windows NT Disk Administrator utility is the primary utility for handling your physical and logical hard drives after you have installed Windows NT.

Disk Administrator is available only to members of the Administrators group in the Windows NT domain or on a Windows NT Workstation.

Usually you will use Disk Administrator to add a new physical drive to the server, although you can use it also to modify existing drives and to implement fault tolerance.

As you can see in Figure 17.1, Disk Administrator shows a graphical representation of your physical hard drives and CD-ROM drives. At a glance you can see the different partitions and their size, the volume names, the file systems in use, the drive letter assignments, and the amount of free space that is available for creating new partitions.

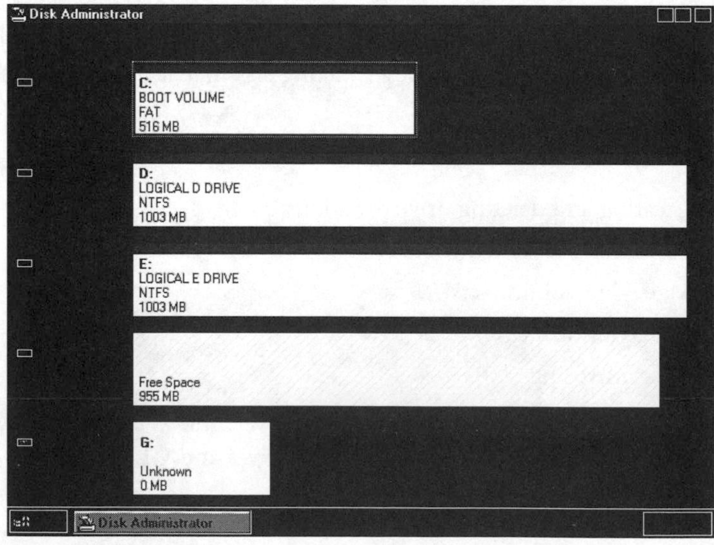

Figure 17.1. Disk Administrator.

Disk Administrator's menu choices give you the following options:

- Create a partition
- Create an extended partition
- Format a partition
- Label a partition
- Delete a partition
- Mark a partition as active
- Assign a drive letter
- Create a volume set
- Extend a volume set
- Establish a mirror set *
- Break a mirror set *
- Create a stripe set
- Create a stripe set with parity *
- Regenerate a member from a missing or damaged stripe set with parity *
- Save or restore a Disk Configuration file
- View a partition's properties
- Choose a physical or logical view for Disk Administrator
- Customize Disk Administrator's toolbar

NT Workstation: The items marked with * are not available on Windows NT Workstation. These menu items deal with RAID options that are supported only on Windows NT Server.

Note: After you use Disk Administrator to alter information about your disks, you should run the `RDISK.EXE` utility, which is the program that creates your Emergency Repair Disk. This will create a new Emergency Repair Disk with the updated disk information.

Starting Disk Administrator

To start the Disk Administrator, choose Disk Administrator, located in the Administrative Tools program folder. You can also start Disk Administrator by running the program `WINDISK.EXE`.

The first time you start Disk Administrator, you will be prompted to allow Disk Administrator to write a non-destructive signature to each of your hard drives. (See Figure 17.2.) This signature is written to an otherwise inaccessible part of the hard drive and is used by Windows NT to identify whether a change of hardware has occurred. You should choose OK on this dialog box unless you are using only a temporary drive. This prompt will appear each time you add a new hard drive to your system.

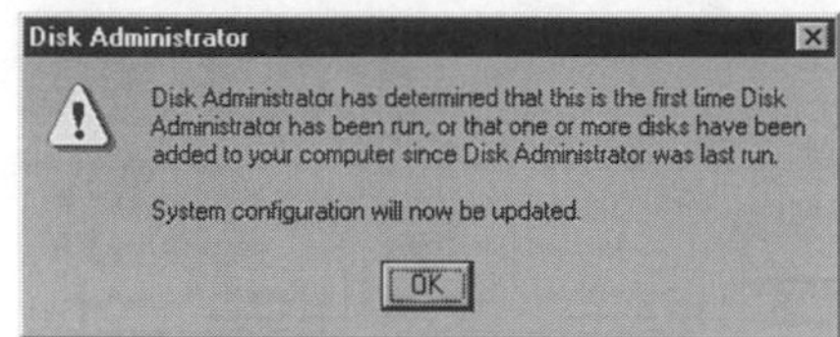

Figure 17.2. *Prompt to write a signature to the hard drives.*

Configuring the Disk Administrator Display

Disk Administrator uses visual cues so that you can easily identify the size and type of partitions on your hard drives.

Disk Administrator Color Options

Different colors and patterns are used as a legend to identify a primary partition, a logical drive, a stripe set, a mirror set, and a volume set. Free space does not have a color bar associated with it; instead, it uses diagonal lines as a background. You can customize this legend by choosing Colors and Patterns from the Options menu. These options are shown in Figures 17.3 and 17.4.

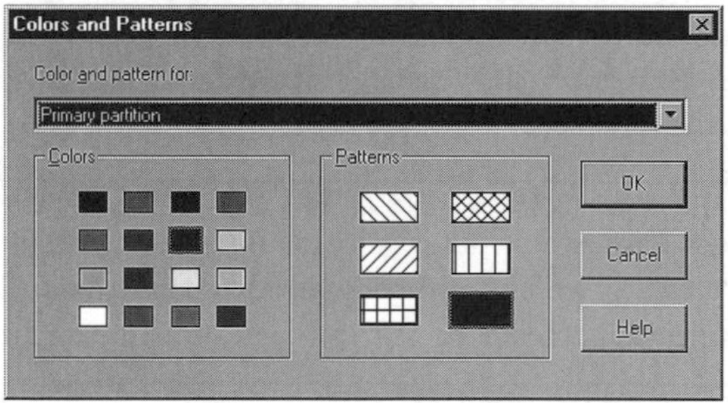

Figure 17.3. *Color options.*

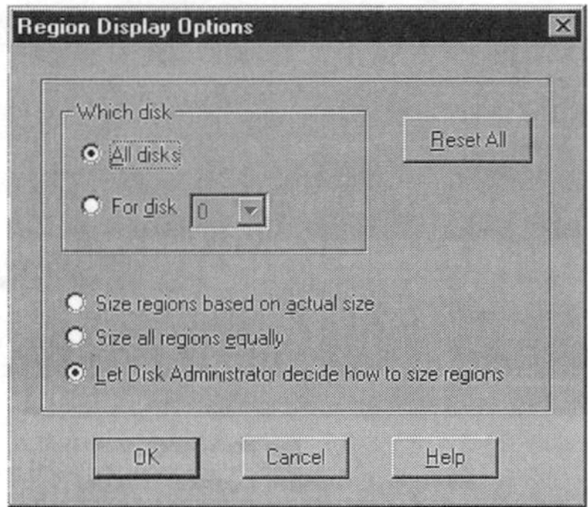

Figure 17.4. *Region Display Options.*

Disk Administrator Region Sizing

The Options menu also has choices for whether to show the status bar at the bottom of the Disk Administrator and how to size the disk regions. Disk Administrator will size these regions so that they are easier to read and identify, but you have the option to make the length of the individual bars, which represent the individual hard drives and the partitions or free spaces contained within, in a more proportional manner. (See Figure 17.5.)

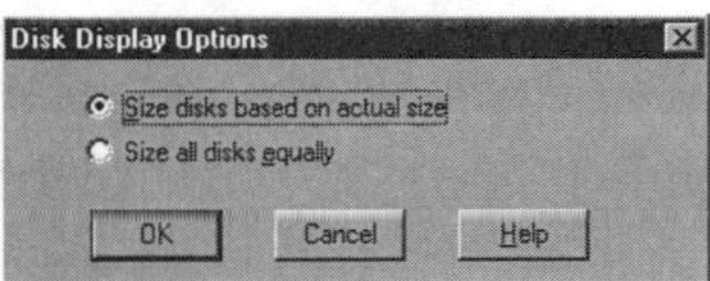

Figure 17.5. *Disk Display Options.*

> **Tip:** To ensure that you can see all of your drives' partitions, use the option "Size all disks equally." Hard drives that vary in size may result in displaying a hard drive too small, making details difficult to read, or running a large hard drive's display off the side of the window, making it impossible to view!

No matter how you choose to display your drives, an asterisk in the upper-left corner of the color bar of the disk region identifies an active partition.

Customizing the Disk Administrator Toolbar

Another configurable option for Disk Administrator's display is the capability to customize the Disk Administrator toolbar. The Customize Toolbar dialog (see Figure 17.6) is shown when you choose Customize Toolbar from the Options menu.

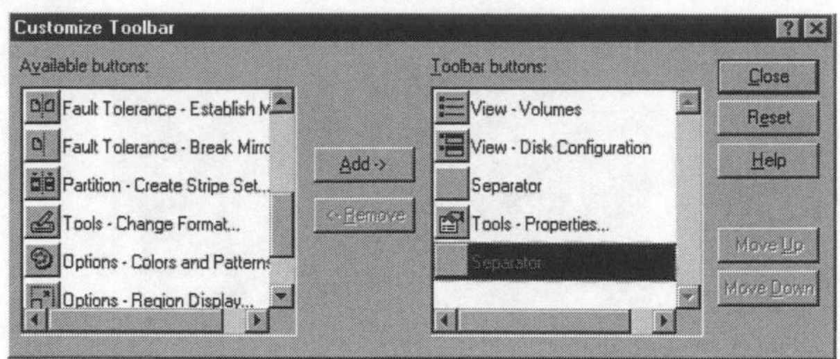

Figure 17.6. Customize Toolbar dialog.

You can add every menu item from Disk Administrator as a button on the toolbar, which can make configuring your storage media even easier than hunting through the many menu items that Disk Administrator offers.

Changing the View

Besides the "bar chart" representation of hard drives, removable media, and CD-ROM drives, the View menu item enables you to switch to a grid-like listing of the different volumes that exist on the server. (See Figure 17.7.) This is done by choosing Volumes from the View menu. This listing ignores unpartitioned space and shows a logical view of the server's storage devices. You can switch back to a physical view of the storage media by choosing Disk Configuration from the View menu.

Disk Administrator

Partition Fault Tolerance Tools View Options Help

Volume	Name	Capacity	Free Space	% Free	Format	Fault Tolerant?	Volume Type	Fault
C:	BOOT VOLUME	516 MB	125 MB	24 %	FAT	yes	Mirror set	516 M
D:	LOGICAL D D...	1003 MB	67 MB	6 %	NTFS	no		
E:	LOGICAL E D...	1003 MB	253 MB	25 %	NTFS	no		
F:		300 MB	0 MB	0 %	Unknown	no		
G:		0 MB	0 MB	0 %	Unknown	no		

Mirror set #1 [INITIALIZING] 516 MB FAT C: BOOT VOLUME

Figure 17.7. Volume view.

Working with Partitions

As with any operating system, there must be a way to manage your hard drive or hard drives. The Disk Administrator gives you a graphical way to look at the partitioning schemes that you have implemented on these drives. It is much easier to work with these partitions, or unpartitioned space, when you are able to view the entire drive or set of drives.

Working with Existing Partitions

In the case of a new server, where no partitions existed on the hard drives prior to the installation of Windows NT, Disk Administrator should have no problem recognizing all of your server's partitions. If you are installing Windows NT on top of a hard drive that already has MS-DOS or another operating system previously installed, however, there are cases in which Windows NT will not be able to understand a disk's existing partitioning. This happens when a partition table does not comply with the strict requirements that Windows NT enforces. When this occurs you must first boot from the operating system that created the disk partitions. Then, back up any information that you would like to retain from those partitions. Once completed, delete the partitions by using FDISK for MS-DOS or the appropriate utility for that particular operating system.

To re-create the partitions, use either a recent version of MS-DOS or the Windows NT installation program if you have deleted the partition that contained Windows NT. Otherwise, you can boot Windows NT and use Disk Administrator to re-create the partitions.

Note: Using an older PC as a server with today's large IDE hard drives usually causes problems with Windows NT because not all the cylinders of an IDE hard drive greater than 540 megabytes will be recognized by the setup program for the PC.

Working with large hard drives will be much easier if you use either SCSI hard drives with a supported SCSI controller or a server that has built-in support for large IDE hard drives.

The latest version of On Track's Disk Manager does come with Windows NT drivers, although you should probably not use this software implementation of cylinder translation on mission critical servers, due to its overhead. But in some cases, it is absolutely necessary, and I have used it and can attest to the fact that it works well.

Creating a Partition

When creating a partition, you need to first decide on the method that you want to use. MS-DOS allows for only two types of partitions: a primary partition that is usually used for the operating system, and an extended partition. Windows NT will allow for up to four partitions on a hard drive, one of which may be an extended partition. An extended partition can contain one or more logical partitions. If you create a primary partition that is formatted as FAT, MS-DOS will be able to recognize this as an MS-DOS drive. Any extended partition containing logical drives that are also formatted as FAT will also be recognized by MS-DOS as valid drives.

Non-extended partitions beyond the first FAT drive will not be recognized as valid drives, nor will any partitions that are formatted as NTFS or HPFS. Be sure to keep this in mind if you are planning to dual-boot the server as both Windows NT and MS-DOS. Even FAT partitions may not be recognized by MS-DOS if the partitioning scheme is not one that is MS-DOS compliant. (See Figure 17.8.)

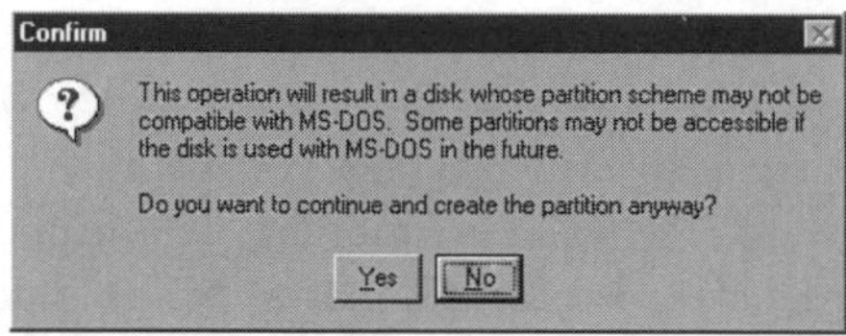

Figure 17.8. *Message regarding the creation of a non–DOS-compatible primary partition.*

Usually drives will contain more than one non-DOS partition if you are planning to dual-boot Windows NT and UNIX or OS/2.

To create a primary partition, select the hard drive by clicking the representation of the drive that is noted as free space, as shown in Figure 17.9. Then choose Create from the Partition menu. A dialog will appear that will display both a minimum and a maximum number of megabytes that can be used for this partition. You will be prompted to enter the number of megabytes that you would like to use. (See Figure 17.10.) If this is the only partition that you would like on this drive, you may use the maximum. If you plan on also creating additional partitions, which may or may not include an extended partition, be sure to leave enough space for the other partitions you might create. After you finalize your decision, the new partition will appear on the graph. These changes will not take effect until the changes are committed, either by choosing the Partition menu item Commit Changes Now or by exiting Disk Administrator and then confirming the changes. Once completed, you may create more partitions, if space allows. As soon as you create a non-extended partition, a drive letter is assigned to that partition.

Formatting a Partition

After creating a partition, the new partition may now be formatted, which is accomplished by selecting the new partition and then choosing Format from the Tools menu.

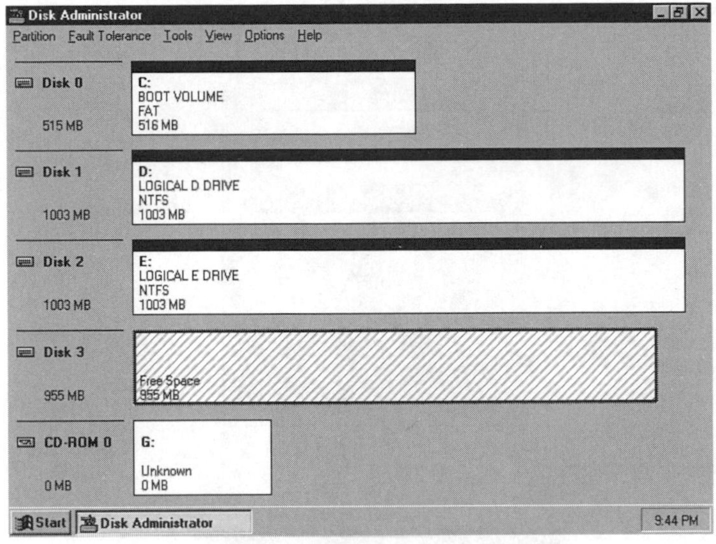

Figure 17.9. *Free space.*

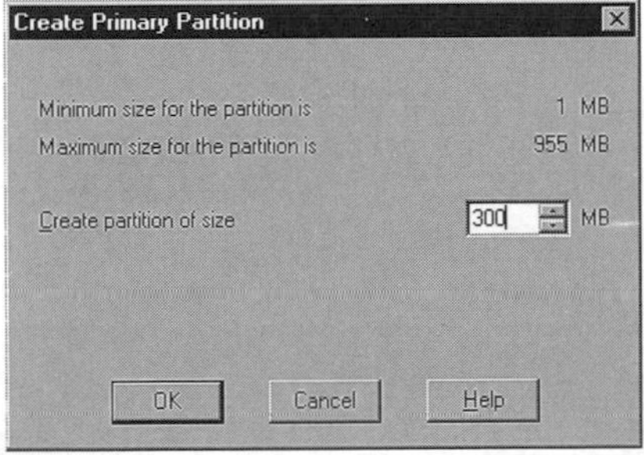

Figure 17.10. *Creating a primary partition.*

Note: You can format an existing partition using Windows NT Explorer. And you can still use the FORMAT and LABEL command from the command prompt for formatting and labeling a volume.

Choose the appropriate type of file system (note that the choices are NTFS and FAT in Figure 17.11) and click the OK button to start the format process. In the checkbox, choose whether to perform a quick format. This type of format will bypass checking the physical drive during the format process. It is recommended that you do not use this option unless you have recently formatted the same partition without incident. Before proceeding, a confirmation dialog box, shown in Figure 17.12, will appear for you to confirm that you want to format the selected partition.

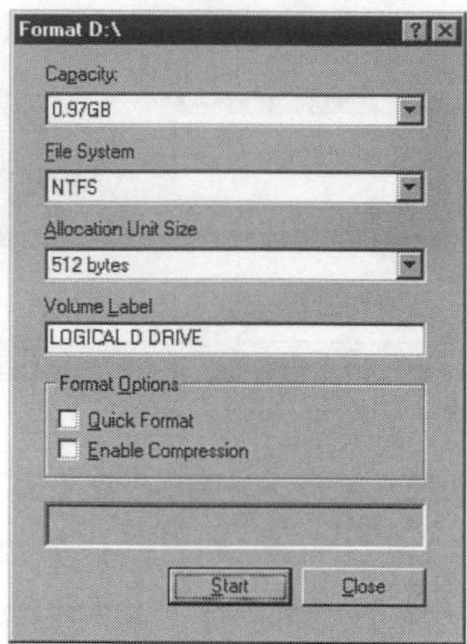

Figure 17.11. *Formatting a partition.*

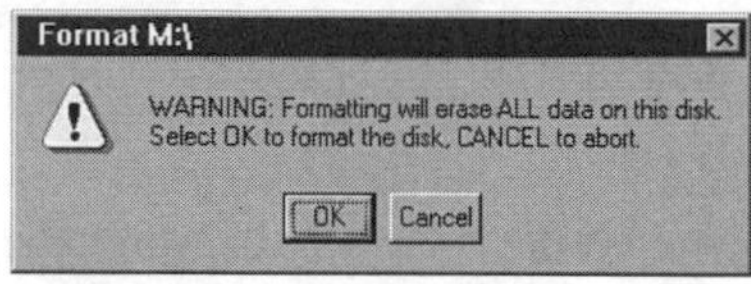

Figure 17.12. *Format confirmation dialog.*

While formatting proceeds, a status box, shown in Figure 17.13, will appear to let you know how far along the formatting process is.

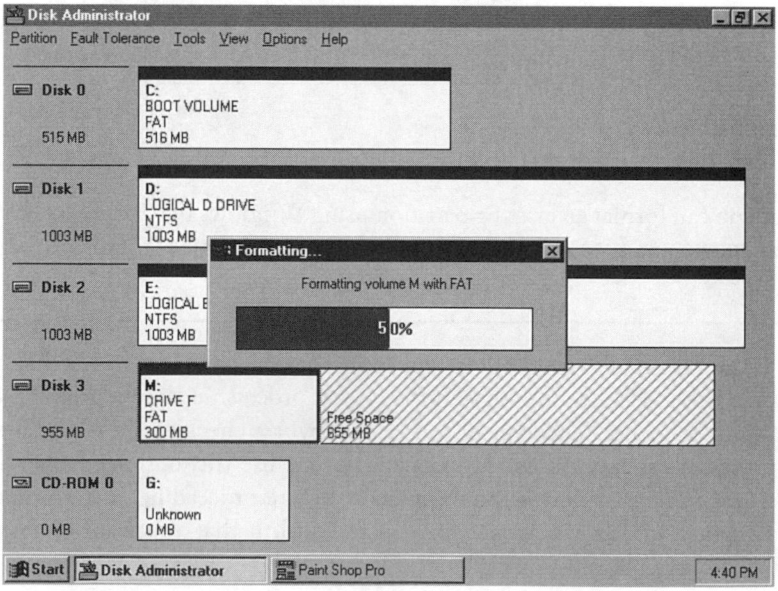

Figure 17.13. *The format status dialog.*

Caution: You may cancel the format from within this status box, but be aware that if the partition was formerly formatted, canceling this format will not restore the partition to its former state.

Windows NT gives you the option of changing logical drive letters. This can be very useful if, for instance, the computer has an IDE drive and a SCSI drive, so the IDE hard drive is logical drive C: and the SCSI drive is automatically assigned as logical drive D:. Take into account that if another IDE drive might be added in the future, this will bump up the SCSI drive to logical E:. This could force you to move data from the SCSI drive to the IDE drive, just to keep some programs settings synchronized, such as shortcuts and INI settings. Using Disk Administrator, you could make the SCSI drive logical drive E: now, before you install software, which would then make room for a second IDE drive, which will automatically be given the logical D: drive letter when it is installed.

If you would like to change the drive letter that was automatically assigned by the operating system for the new partition or for any other existing partition, select the partition and then choose Drive Letter from the Tools menu. A drop-down box, shown in Figure 17.14, with a choice of unused drive letters will appear. Choose the drive letter you would like to use and click the OK button. That drive letter will be assigned to the selected partition instantly.

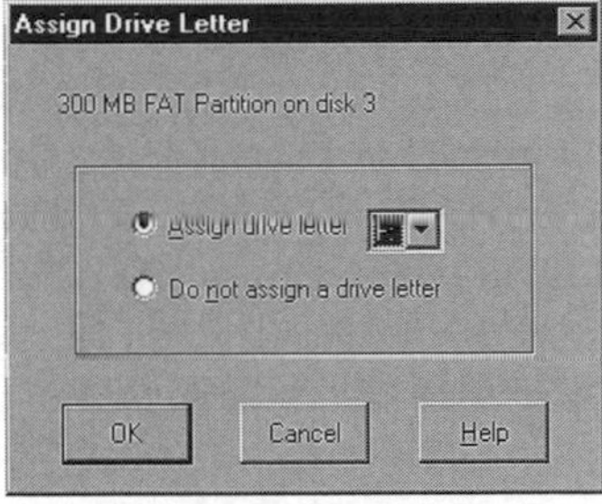

Figure 17.14. *Changing a drive letter.*

You can also use this option to change the drive letter that is assigned to CD-ROM drives, as shown in Figure 17.15.

Figure 17.15. *Changing a CD-ROM drive letter.*

With primary partitions, you can choose which of the primary partitions should be the active partition, which is the partition used at the boot volume. Usually the first partition on the first hard drive will be used as the active partition, although in certain scenarios you might want to change this.

For instance, if you want to set up a second C drive as a small partition contained on your first hard drive (drive 0) that is formatted as bootable MS-DOS, you can then have the option to reboot your PC to that partition instead of the current Windows NT-bootable partition. This can be useful if you want to keep your Windows NT partition formatted as NTFS but still want the option to boot MS-DOS.

After changing the active partition through Disk Administrator and restarting the server, you can use MS-DOS, but you will not have access to your Windows NT boot partition. When you want to go back to booting from the Windows NT-bootable partition, use MS-DOS's FDISK to make the non-DOS partition the active partition again.

Marking an Active Partition

An active partition is the primary partition that can be used to boot from. In most cases, the active partition will be the first partition on the first hard drive. It is possible to have different operating systems installed on the same computer and allow the computer to boot from different partitions.

A good example of why you would alter the active partition on your first hard drive is when you install Microsoft Windows NT Server onto a computer that already has the OS/2 Boot Manager installed. By default, Microsoft Windows NT Server marks the partition that contains the Windows NT system files as active. Before the installation, the OS/2 Boot Manager partition had been marked as active. The only way to re-enable Boot Manager would be to use Disk Administrator. You would do this by highlighting the Boot Manager partition, then click the Partition menu. Choose Mark Active from that menu and you will get the confirmation message shown in Figure 17.16. The next time the system restarts, the Boot Manager will appear.

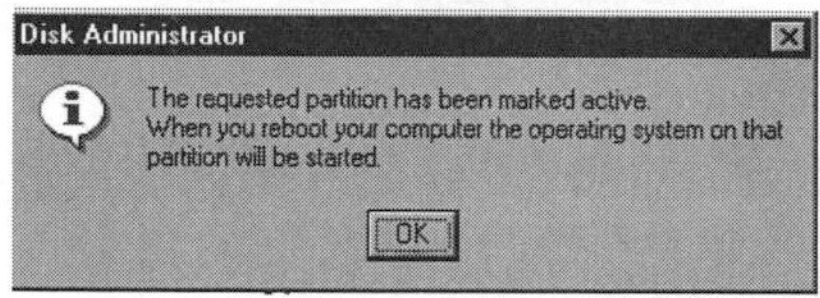

Figure 17.16. *The Mark Active confirmation message.*

Creating an Extended Partition

Creating an extended partition is similar to creating a primary partition except that afterwards you have the option to create logical partitions within the extended partition. To create an extended partition, select a free space on a hard drive that already has an existing primary partition. Then choose Create Extended from the Partition menu. You will be prompted for the size of this partition, as shown in Figure 17.17. Once the size is entered, click the OK button to create the partition. When completed, the extended partition will appear as free space, but the status bar at the bottom of the screen will indicate that it is an extended partition. You may now create logical partitions within the extended partition.

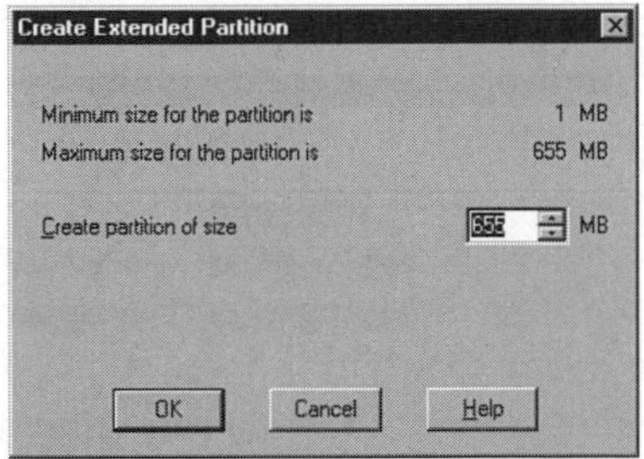

Figure 17.17. *Creating an extended partition.*

Creating Logical Partitions

To create logical partitions within the extended partition, choose the extended partition, then choose Create from the Partition menu. A dialog box similar to Figure 17.17 will enable you to choose the size of the logical partition. (See Figure 17.18.) The maximum size displayed is the amount of free space within the extended partition. After entering the size, click the OK button and the logical partition will be created. As with primary partitions, a drive letter is instantly assigned.

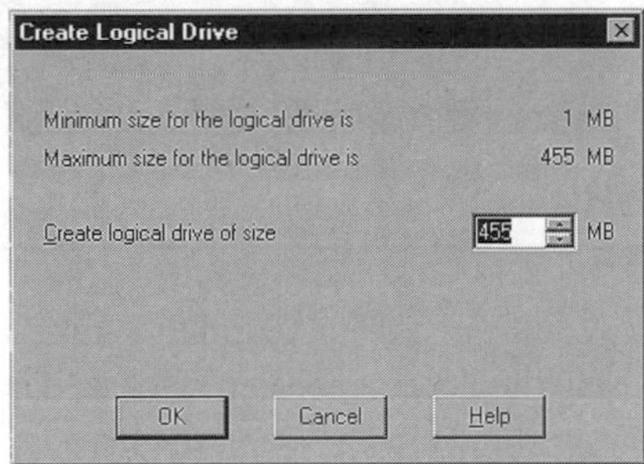

Figure 17.18. *Creating a logical partition.*

Deleting Partitions

To delete a partition, select the partition you want to delete, then choose Delete from the Partition menu.

Caution: Be sure to back up all the information on the partition before you proceed with the deletion.

As seen in Figure 17.19, when you attempt to delete a partition, a confirmation dialog will appear to warn you about losing data. If you are sure that you want to continue, click the OK button and the partition will then be shown as free space. As with all the options within Disk Administrator that permanently alter a hard drive's partition map, the final changes to the affected partition will not occur until you choose to commit these changes. You can manually commit the changes by choosing the Commit Changes Now menu item or by committing the changes when exiting Disk Administrator. After committing the changes, Disk Administrator will warn you that the changes will be permanent. Choose the OK button to continue or click the No button to cancel the changes. If you have committed the changes, you are reminded to update your Emergency Repair Disk using the `RDISK` utility, as shown in Figure 17.20.

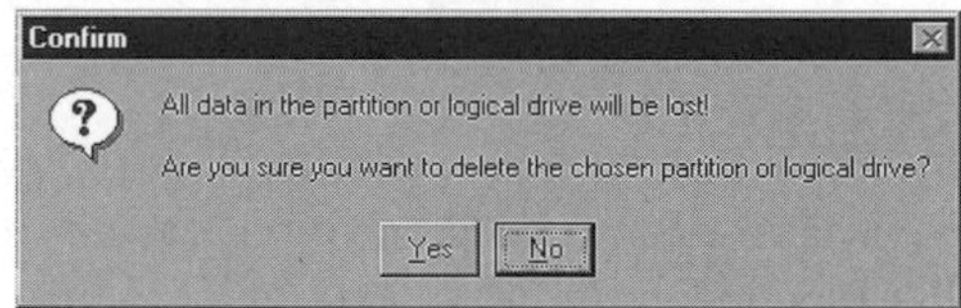

Figure 17.19. *Deleting a partition.*

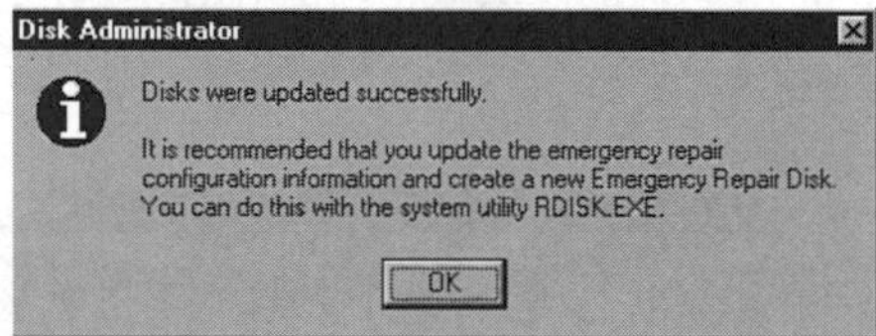

Figure 17.20. *Committing changes.*

Tip: I've accidentally committed changes to Disk Administrator, and then have been able to reverse them by using the Emergency Repair Disk. That disk contains all your partition information that was captured either during the installation of Windows NT or from the last time that you ran the `RDISK` utility.

Partition Properties

With Disk Administrator, you can check your partitions for errors, which is the equivalent of MS-DOS's CHKDSK. This option is available from within the Properties option.

When selecting Properties from the Tools menu, you will be presented with a pie chart view of the partition. As shown in Figure 17.21, the amount of free space and used space are shown, as is the Volume Name, which can be changed directly from within the Properties box.

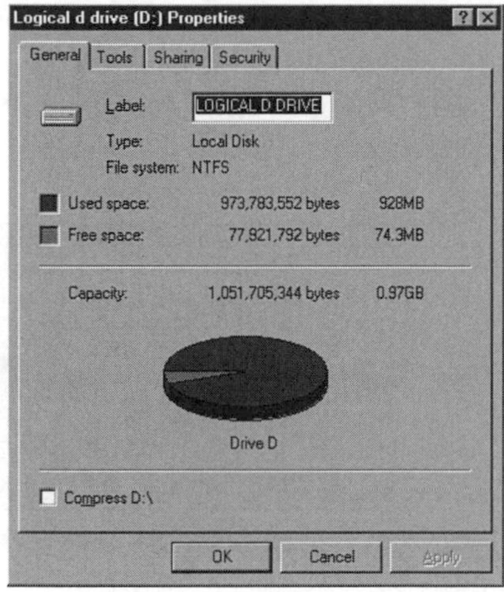

Figure 17.21. *Volume properties.*

The Tools tab (see Figure 17.22) contains the option to inspect the partition for any damage, such as cross-linked files, by clicking the Check Now button. The Backup Now button launches Microsoft Windows NT Backup. If a third-party defragmentation utility has been installed, the Defragment Now button will not be grayed out and will be available to defragment the current volume.

Figure 17.22. *Volume tools.*

> **Note:** Because the volume in Figure 17.21 is formatted as NTFS, the Compress check box is shown. Also, the Security tab is available. Neither of these features appears in the Properties for FAT volumes.

When selecting the Check Now option, you will be presented with a dialog box (see Figure 17.23) that gives you the choice to fix file system errors automatically, or perform a complete disk scan which will search for physical damage.

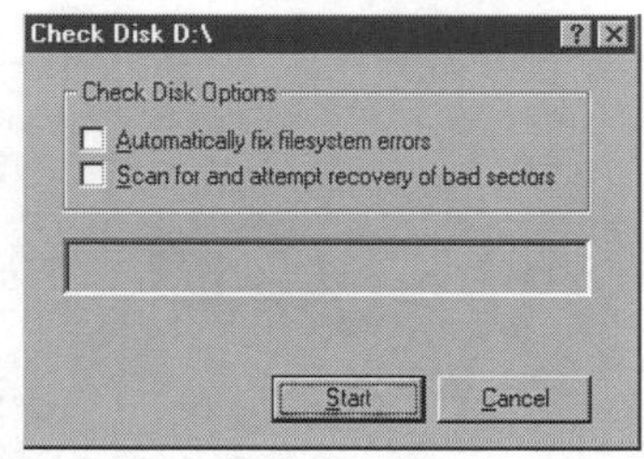

***Figure 17.23.** Choosing Check for Errors from the Volume tools.*

If you select a volume that is busy with a process and cannot be locked for inspection, you will receive a message that will ask you whether you want to check the volume the next time the system is started (see Figure 17.24). You can choose to allow this or to cancel the Check Now option. If this is not the case, the disk check will proceed. Once the disk check is completed, you will be presented with a summary of events that occurred during the disk check. (See Figure 17.25.)

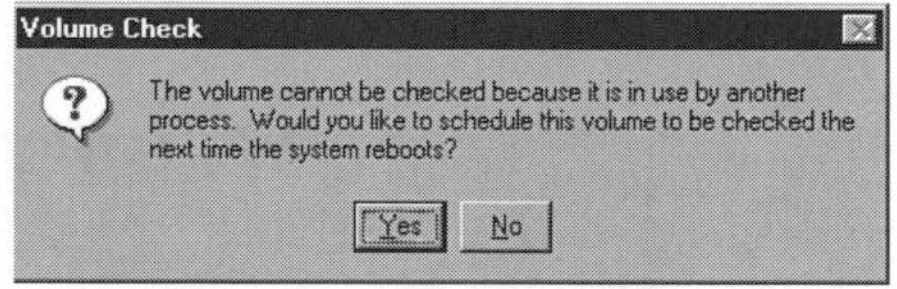

***Figure 17.24.** Disk Locked message.*

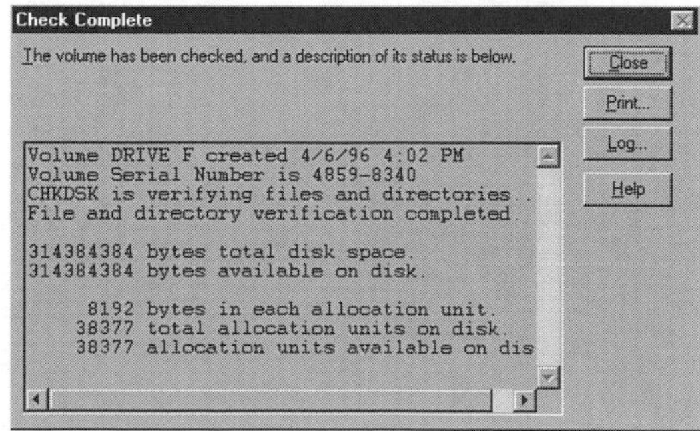

***Figure 17.25.** Results from checking a disk for errors.*

Disk Volumes

A Windows NT Server disk volume is comprised of one or more partitions on one or more hard drives that are formatted with a file system and can be assigned a drive letter. With MS-DOS, a volume was simply a partition on one hard drive, but with Windows NT Server, you can create different types of volumes that offer greater flexibility and fault tolerance.

Fault Tolerance

A few of the options that Windows NT gives you for handling your drives involve RAID, which stands for Redundant Array of Inexpensive Disks. RAID levels above level 0 offer fault tolerance, which is very important when data loss is a concern. Although a tape backup can offer the restoration of data that is as recent as the last time a tape backup was made, fault tolerant disks provide restoration of data that is as recent as the data that was last written before a drive failure occurred.

Working with Volume Sets

A volume set is created by combining free space from 1 to 32 hard drives and creating a logical volume that is seen by the operating system as one partition. In reality, once the first segment of a volume set is used, the file system continues on the next segment of the volume set. One advantage of using a volume set is that you can save drive letters by combining areas on different hard drives, as opposed to assigning a drive letter to each individual area (partition). Disk I/O can also improve because it is possible that data from the same program is being read from multiple physical drives at the same time, instead of queuing instructions for one physical drive. You may also run across a partitioning scheme that ends up with small empty areas at the end of multiple hard drives. These can easily be combined to form one volume.

To create a volume set, select all of the free areas you want to include in the volume set by clicking the first area you want to include. Then hold down the Ctrl key and select the next area for inclusion. Continue this until all the free space areas that will comprise the volume set are selected. Then choose Create Volume Set from the Partition menu. Just as it is shown in Figure 17.26, you will be prompted to enter the amount of disk space you would like to allocate to this volume. Clicking the OK button then creates the volume set.

You can also extend a single NTFS partition by selecting an NTFS partition and selecting free space. Choose Extend Volume Set from the Partition menu and then enter the number of megabytes from the free space that you would like to append onto the current NTFS partition, as seen in Figure 17.27. Click the OK button and the chosen free space will now appear as part of the NTFS volume. Note that the color bar on all the included partitions will now share the color that has been designated as signifying a volume set.

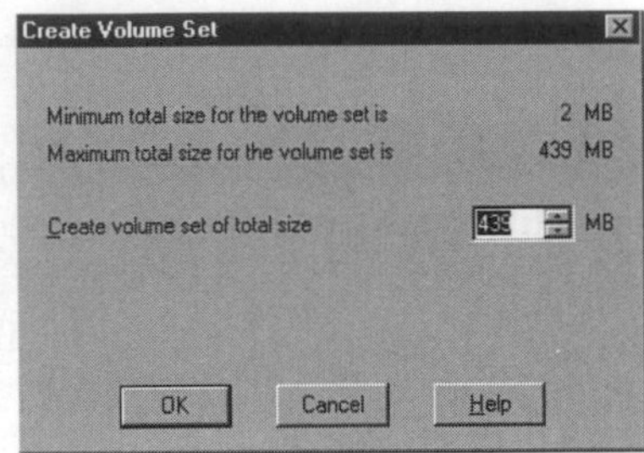

Figure 17.26. *Creating a volume set.*

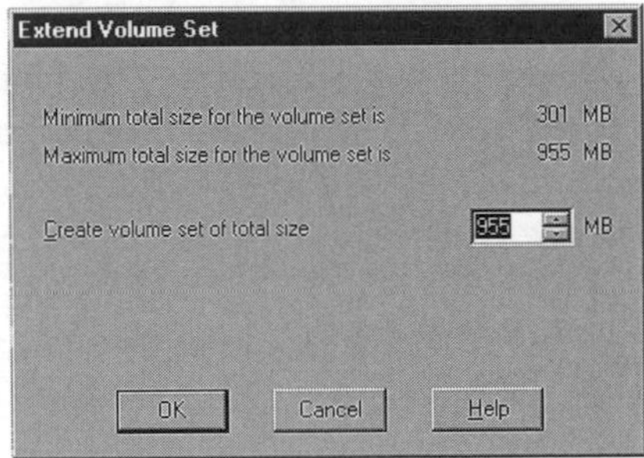

Figure 17.27. *Extending a volume set.*

Also, you cannot extend the volume where Windows NT's system files reside. Attempting to do so will result in the error message shown in Figure 17.28.

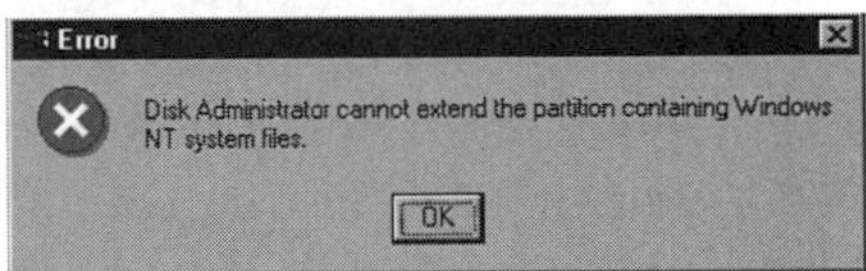

Figure 17.28. *Attempting to extend a volume with Windows NT system files.*

You may delete a volume set by selecting any of the regions that are part of the volume set and then choosing Delete from the Partition menu.

Caution: Be sure to back up all the information on the volume set before you proceed with the deletion.

A confirmation dialog (see Figure 17.29) will then enable you to proceed or cancel the deletion.

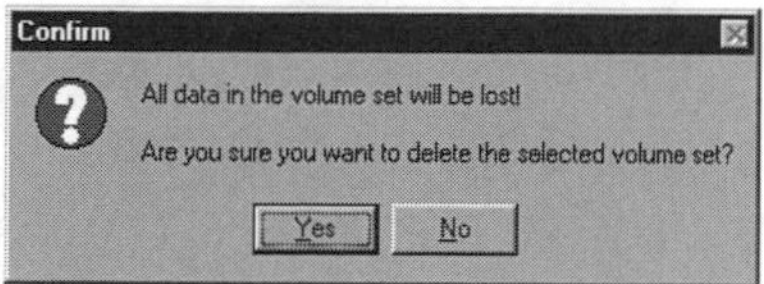

Figure 17.29. *Deleting a volume set.*

Working with Mirrored Partitions

NT Workstation: This section applies only to Windows NT Server because Windows NT Workstation does not support mirroring of hard drives through Disk Administrator.

With mirroring, you can create a mirror image of a partition on another drive. This form of fault tolerance is also known as RAID level 1. Usually you will want to mirror all of the partitions on a server so that in case of a drive failure you will be able to easily install a working drive that contains all the data that was on the faulty drive.

Note: If the drive that contains your system partition fails, you need to use your Emergency Repair Disk to re-enable the operating system. Recovering from this situation is covered in Chapter 39, "What to Do When Windows NT Fails to Boot."

To mirror a partition, select the partition that you would like to mirror. Then hold down the Ctrl key and click the free space in which you would like to contain the mirror.

Note: The free space that you select for the mirror must be as large as or larger than the partition you want to mirror.

Choose the Establish Mirror option from the Fault Tolerance menu, and a partition the same size as the original partition will be created. Both of these partitions will share the same drive letter.

As shown in Figure 17.30, when mirroring the boot partition, you will be instructed to create a boot floppy that will be needed in case of a drive failure. This is discussed further in Chapter 45, "Disaster Recovery."

After the mirror has been established, Disk Administrator will indicate that the mirror is in progress by a message on the status bar. (See Figure 17.31.) In addition, the color of the mirror partition's statistics will appear in red until the partition has finished initializing. Once initialized, the mirror partition will protect your data in case of a drive failure.

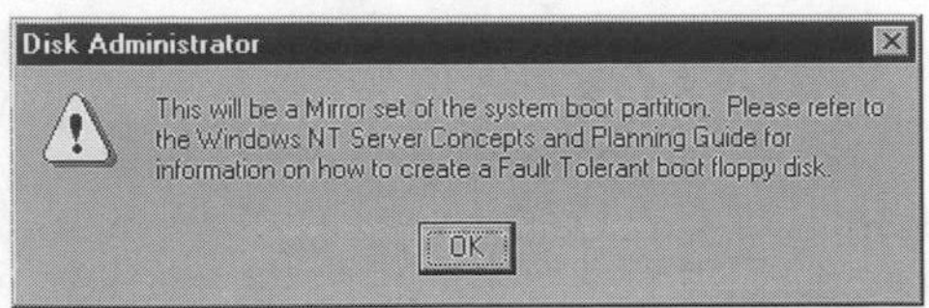

Figure 17.30. *Mirroring a boot partition.*

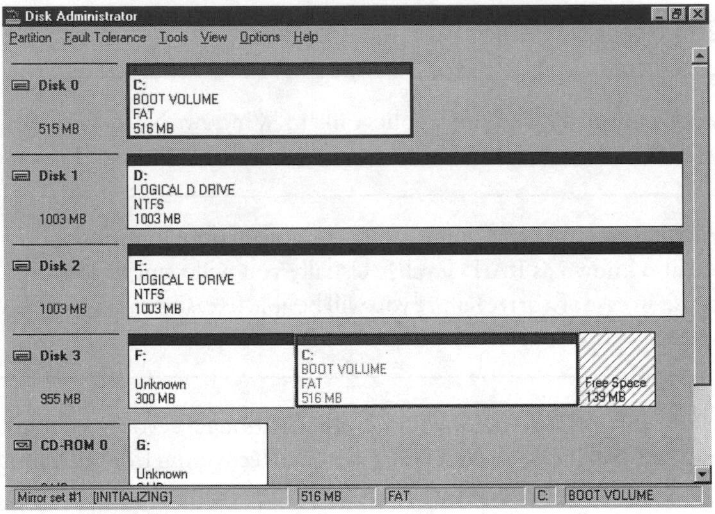

Figure 17.31. *Mirror initialization.*

Figure 17.32 shows the entry that is written to the System Event log once the mirror starts to initialize. Once the mirror has completed, the entry shown in Figure 17.33 will also be written to the System Event log.

Whether to reclaim disk space, remove a hard drive, or simply to rearrange your partitions, you may find yourself in the position of needing to break a mirror. To break a mirror, select the partition you would no longer like to be mirrored and choose Break Mirror from the Fault Tolerance menu. As in Figure 17.34, you will first be warned that breaking the mirror will result in two separate partitions. Once confirmed, the break will be established, and the former mirror partition will now have a new drive letter assigned to it, retaining the same data it had while it was part of the mirror set. To reclaim the space, you must now delete the partition or reformat the partition.

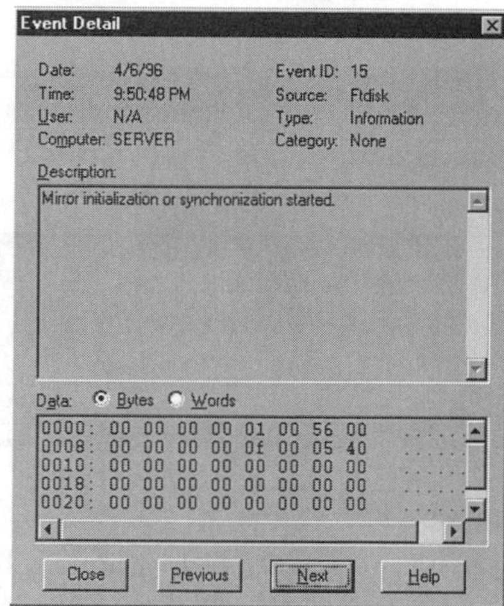

Figure 17.32. *The System Event log entry for the start of a mirror initialization.*

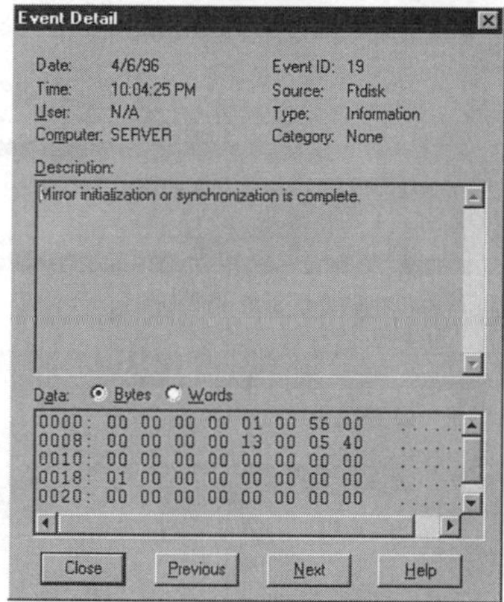

Figure 17.33. *The System Event log entry for a completed mirror initialization.*

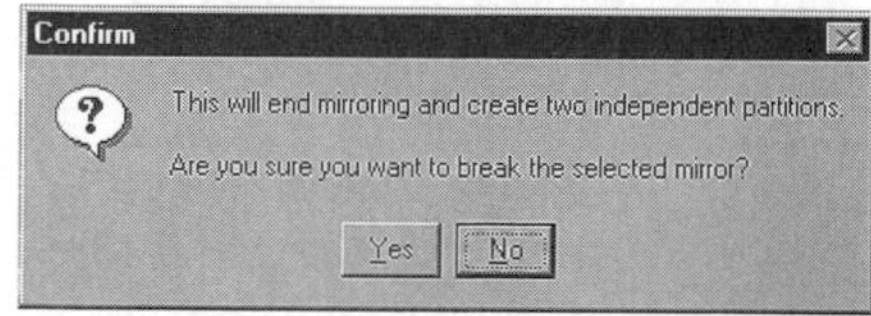

Figure 17.34. *Breaking a mirror.*

In some cases, you will not be able to break the mirrored volume while the system service that resides on that volume is active because Windows NT cannot lock the mirrored set while it is active. A message, shown in Figure 17.35, will let you choose whether to break the mirror the next time the system starts or to cancel the breaking of the mirrored set.

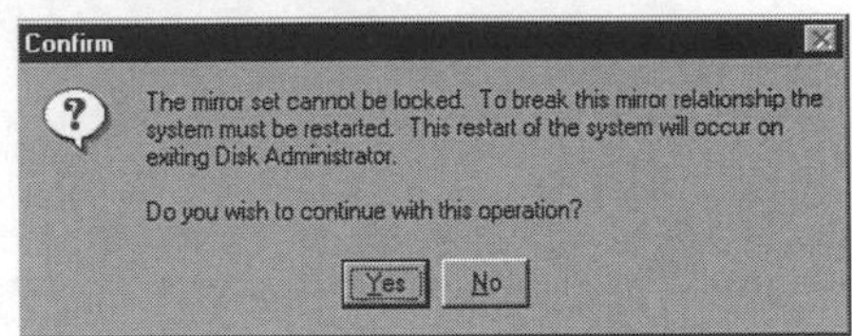

Figure 17.35. A mirror set cannot be locked.

Once the mirror is broken, the next available drive letter will be given to the mirror partition. (See Figure 17.36.)

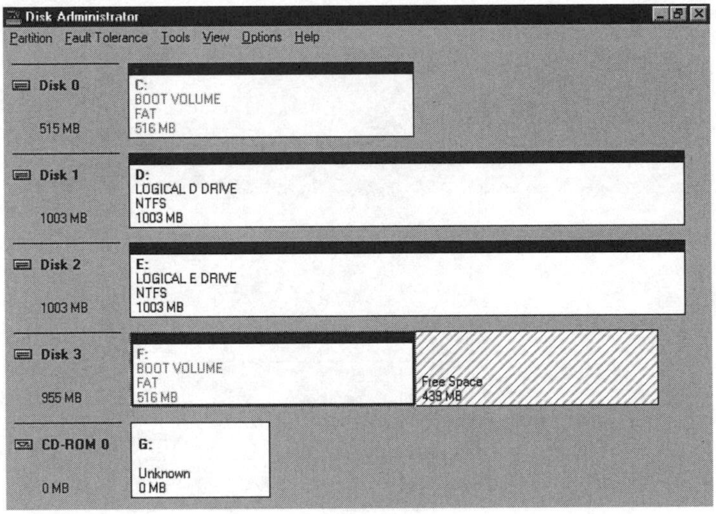

Figure 17.36. The result of a broken mirror.

Working with Stripe Sets

Disk striping is a way to evenly distribute data across two or more hard drives, thus increasing performance. There are two types of disk striping. One is simply disk striping, also referred to as RAID level 0. The other is disk striping with parity, also known as RAID level 5. In both cases, data is written across multiple drives, which can allow data to be written faster.

Stripe Sets Without Parity

While offering no fault tolerance, disk striping offers increased performance. Disk striping will evenly distribute a volume across multiple physical hard drives so that a read or write to a single volume can be broken into separate instructions that can be executed at the same time.

Caution: While a stripe set without parity is a cost-efficient way to increase disk performance, the entire volume can be lost if any of the hard drives that contain part of the stripe set has a failure.

Creating a Stripe Set

Using free space on each drive (from 2 to 32 hard drives), select the free space areas by clicking the first free space region, holding down the Ctrl key, and selecting the remaining free space regions you would like to include in the stripe set. Then select Create Stripe Set from the Partition menu. You will be shown the minimum and the maximum size of the stripe set that can be created. If you want to use the maximum size, just click the OK button; otherwise, first alter the size and then click the OK button. Windows NT will then allocate the appropriate slices from the free space regions to build the stripe set. Once the stripe set is built, these members of the stripe set will be identified by a color bar and background that symbolizes stripe sets (which is green for both by default). Exit Disk Administrator, and you will be prompted to shut down and restart the server. After rebooting, your stripe set will be available for use.

Note: Because all the regions used for the stripe set must be the same size, the smallest free space region will determine the size of the stripe set volume.

Removing a Stripe Set

To remove a stripe set, select one of the members of the stripe set and then select Delete from the Partition menu. After you confirm that you want to remove the entire stripe set, those regions are then marked as available. Commit your changes to allow these disk areas to be reused.

Caution: Be sure to back up all the information on the stripe set before you proceed with the deletion.

Disk Striping with Parity

NT Workstation: Disk striping with parity is not supported on Windows NT Workstation through Disk Administrator.

Of Windows NT Server's choices for a software RAID solution, disk striping with parity at RAID level 5 is the most secure and robust form of disk fault tolerance available.

RAID-5 disk striping is very similar to disk striping without parity, but it also involves one more hard drive. Data is written across two or more hard drives, while another hard drive holds the parity information. This way, if one of the hard drives fails, the two remaining drives can recalculate the lost information and place this information back onto a newly installed working hard drive. This then brings the minimum number of hard drives involved in disk striping with parity to three, with a maximum number of 32 hard drives.

Parity Bits

A parity bit is derived by multiplying the data bits from all but one drive. For instance, in a three-drive scenario, if the first bit on the first drive was equal to 1 and the first bit on the second drive was also 1, then the parity bit would be calculated to a value of 1.

Table 17.1 demonstrates the first four bits on a three-drive stripe set with parity.

Table 17.1. Parity bits in a RAID-5 configuration.

	Disk 1	*Disk 2*	*Disk 3*
Bit 1	Data=1	Data=0	Parity=0
Bit 2	Data=0	Parity=0	Data=1
Bit 3	Parity=1	Data=1	Data=1
Bit 4	Data=1	Data=0	Parity=0

If Disk 3 were to fail, a new drive would be substituted in its place. For Bit 1, no data had been lost because Disk 3 contained only parity information. On Bit 2, the data from Disk 3 was lost, so the data on Disk 1 is compared to the parity bit on Disk 2. Using multiplication, the lost bit from Disk 3 is reconstructed as a value of 1.

Creating a Stripe Set with Parity

To create a stripe set, first select one free area on three or more disks, then select Create Stripe Set with Parity from the Fault Tolerance menu. You will be shown the minimum and maximum size of the stripe set that you can create. If you want to use the maximum size, just click the OK button;

otherwise, first alter the size and then click the OK button. Windows NT will then allocate the appropriate slices from the free space regions to build the stripe set with parity. After the stripe set is built, these members of the stripe set will be identified by a color bar and background that symbolizes stripe sets (which is green for both by default).

Note: If there is not sufficient disk space or not enough drives with sufficient free space, the Create Stripe Set with Parity option will be grayed out.

Exit Disk Administrator, and you will be prompted to shut down and restart the server. After rebooting, your stripe set will be available for use.

Note: As with stripe set without parity, all of the regions used for the stripe set must be the same size; therefore, the smallest free space region determines the size of stripe set volume.

To remove a stripe set, select one of the members of the stripe set and then select Delete from the Partition menu. After you confirm that you want to remove the entire stripe set, those regions are then marked as available. Commit your changes to allow these sections to be reused.

Caution: Be sure to back up all the information on the stripe set before you proceed with the deletion.

Regenerating a Stripe Set

With a stripe set with parity, you have protection against a single hard drive failure. When this occurs and you replace the hard drive, the first task you should perform is to regenerate the stripe set.

After installing your new hard drive and restarting Windows NT Server, the autocheck phase will determine that the stripe set has been broken and the stripe set will be locked. To re-enable the stripe set, you must start the Disk Administrator program and select one of the regions that belongs to the stripe set with parity. Once selected, hold down the Ctrl key and select the new empty region that you would like to replace with the missing stripe set partition. Next, select Regenerate from the Fault Tolerance menu, and the system will acknowledge the new member of the set. Exit Disk Administrator and restart the system to enable the stripe set again.

Tip: While Microsoft Windows NT Server's Fault Tolerance options are very useful, a hardware implementation of fault tolerance will be a more efficient way to run your server. This is because the specialized RAID disk controller will take over and provide the necessary processes, leaving the CPU(s) to handle other tasks. Of course, this solution is more costly.

> Another reason to go with hardware fault tolerance is the newest breed of controllers with which you can increase storage on a RAID system without requiring reinitialization of the hard drives, thus enabling you to leave the server active while upgrading the disk space.
>
> Another feature of some new external disk subsystems is the capability to share a disk subsystem between two or more servers.

Saving Disk Configuration Information

With Disk Administrator, you can save and restore disk configuration information, such as drive letter assignments, stripe set, mirror, and volume set information.

You can save this information to a floppy diskette by selecting Configuration from the Partition menu, and then selecting Save from the submenu. You will be prompted to insert a floppy diskette into the A drive on the server. This information is important to keep on hand, should you accidentally make changes in Disk Administrator from which you would like to revert. You can also use it if you have to reinstall Windows NT Server because reinstalling will reset your disk configuration information to its default state. If you ever decide to perform a fresh installation of Windows NT Server, this information could save you a lot of time in reconfiguring disk information.

To restore the information from diskette, select Configuration from the Partition menu and then select Restore from the submenu. You are prompted to insert the disk configuration information diskette into the A drive on the server. After a confirmation, the information is restored. You then should restart the system to allow all the disk configuration changes to take effect.

Although saving the partition information is very important, it is even more important to keep a current Emergency Repair Disk. This disk is created by running the `RDISK.EXE` program. Information on using an Emergency Repair Disk can be found in Chapter 39.

Summary

After you have determined the most appropriate file system configuration, you are ready to configure and implement the rest of your Microsoft Windows NT Server network.

Using the NTFS file system on your server will give you the most flexibility in implementing security and fault tolerance.

Be careful when using Disk Administrator. One wrong move and you'll wipe out a partition. Remember that it is practically the same as using MS-DOS's FDISK, so be sure to plan carefully before you make any changes to your partitioning scheme.

Do use the `RDISK.EXE` utility. If you make a mistake and accidentally remove a partition, you can restore a saved configuration. While you may have made your Emergency Repair Diskette during installation, any changes made to your disk configuration since you made the original disk will be lost. The Emergency Repair Disk should be updated whenever any changes are made to your partitioning scheme, and using `RDISK.EXE` will keep the Emergency Repair Disk up-to-date.

Performance Monitor

by Robert Reinstein

Chapter 9, "Capacity Planning," discusses the overhead on Windows NT and ways to ensure that your hardware is capable of running on a Windows NT network. It also discusses ways to monitor the performance of your Windows NT server and mentions the Windows NT Performance Monitor.

This chapter discusses the following:

- How to successfully utilize Performance Monitor
- Common types of bottlenecks
- Analyzing Performance Monitor data

Why Monitor Performance on Your Server?

When you are setting up a Windows NT server, you are creating a computer that will be capable of handling tasks such as print serving, file serving, e-mail, anti-virus, and communications (data, faxing, gateways). These types of servers used to be file servers, but now they are usually much more than that.

When a network client is sitting at his computer, and he attempts to run software that requires assistance from the server, he is going to expect a response comparable to running the software directly from his hard drive.

Sometimes a user will notice a time lag or get disconnected from an application due to a time-out of sorts. And you, as the network administrator, will receive an irate phone call, or many phone calls, as users call to let you know that "the network isn't working."

This is when performance monitoring is the most important.

Server Bottlenecks

Perhaps the greatest cause of performance problems on computers are bottlenecks. These bottlenecks are usually caused by hardware or software that is running slowly, which impacts the performance of other software or hardware.

Being able to diagnose and find bottlenecks is one of the most important ways to maintain a server, because with detection and the proper diagnosis you can address the bottlenecks and do something about them.

The most common bottlenecks are memory (or lack of), hard drives, network adapter cards, the network in general (which means either the topology, protocol, insufficient wiring, or two or more of these), poorly written network applications, and the computer's CPU.

Being able to pick apart these entities and examine them on an individual basis is the way to identify a bottleneck.

The Windows NT Performance Monitor

The Windows NT Performance Monitor is a tool that enables you to do just that—pick apart individual components on a computer (including hardware and software), record statistics, graph those statistics, and view real-time statistics. Right out of the box, Performance Monitor offers over 350 statistics for your Windows NT system.

Figure 18.1 shows you the Performance Monitor application. This application is started by choosing it from the Administrative Tools program folder from the Start menu, or by running the command `PERFMON`.

When you start Performance Monitor, the application opens up by default into what is known as Graph View. This is the view that is used the most, and will enable you to view statistics in real time.

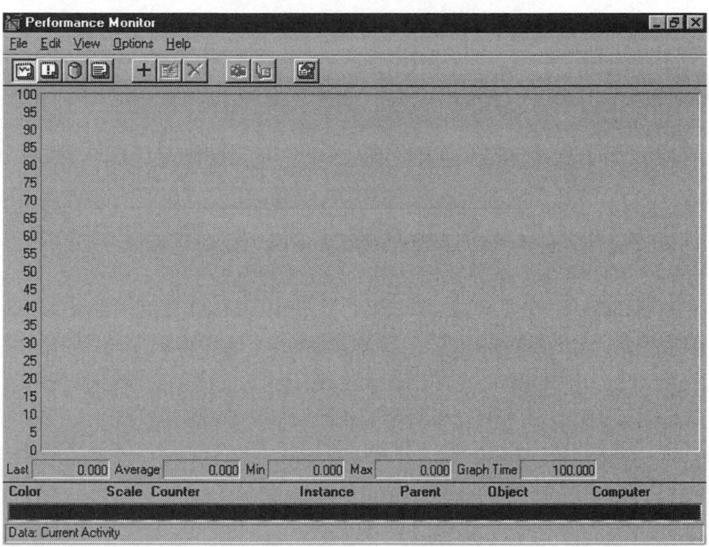

Figure 18.1. *The Windows NT Performance Monitor.*

Objects and Counters

The statistics that Performance Monitor can monitor are many. Table 18.1 lists some of the items that can have a great impact on how well your Windows NT computer and your network is running. Performance Monitor refers to the entity that is being monitored as an object and the statistic that it captures as a counter.

In Chapter 6, "The Windows NT Installation Process," I mentioned that Windows NT has internal counters that monitor activity on the computer, and showed you how Task Manager can display these counters.

Performance Monitor uses the same counters, but can access a greater depth of these counters.

Table 18.1. Performance Monitor objects and counters.

Object	*Counter*
Processor (CPU)	Percent of Processor Time Used
	Interrupts per second
Hard Drive (physical)	Average Disk Queue Length
	Disk Reads per second
	Disk Writes per second

continues

Table 18.1. continued

Object	*Counter*
Paging File	Percent of Usage
System	System Uptime
	File write operations per second
	File Read operations per second
Server	Bytes Received per second
	Bytes Transmitted per second
	File Open
	Files Opened Total
	Logons per second
	Total Logons
Cache	Copy Reads per second
	Copy Read Hits Percentage
Network Segment	Network Utilization percentage
	Broadcast frames received per second
	Total Bytes Received per second
Process	Processor Time percentage
	Working Set

This is only a small subset of the objects that can be monitored by Performance Monitor. And the objects that can be monitored by Performance Monitor is extensible. All of the Microsoft BackOffice products will add objects to Performance Monitor. Microsoft has provided an API (application programming interface) to enable developers to add objects to Performance Monitor that relate to their applications.

This chapter introduces you to the different methods of capturing and viewing data that are available to you by using the Performance Monitor tool.

Before we look at navigating Performance Monitor, let's examine what kind of data you should be looking for within Performance Monitor.

Analyzing Captured Data

What you really need to know is what data is necessary to capture when trying to detect bottlenecks or other adverse conditions.

Performance Monitor is a great tool just to get a good idea of how your Windows NT computers are running and to analyze network segment traffic. But the primary reason to implement the Performance Monitor tool lies in the objects and counter that are shown in Table 18.1 and the other available objects and counters.

Methods of Analyzing Memory

To monitor the memory usage of a particular program, you can have Performance Monitor look at the Process object. The counter Working Set can tell you the amount of memory that the program has reserved for its use. This can be very handy for spotting memory hogs or for evaluating software.

When there is not enough physical memory installed, the paging file (`PAGEFILE.SYS`) is used as virtual memory. To determine the usage of the paging file, look at the Physical Disk object for the disk or disks that contain a paging file. When added together, the Avg. Disk sec/Transfer and Pages/sec counter values should not exceed 0.1. If they do, it means that at least 10 percent of disk access time is being used for writing to a paging file, which is not acceptable. This means you should really consider adding memory to the computer.

Tip: If the maximum paging file size, as defined in the System applet in Control Panel, is close to the actual size of the paging file, you should increase the size of the paging file.

Analyzing Processor Activity

The Processor object can enable you to monitor activity on a CPU. And in the case of multiprocessor computers, there will be multiple Instances for the Processor object, along with an instance that shows overall processor activity.

The % Processor Time counter enables you to view a percentage of elapsed time that a processor is executing a process. When this number is up towards the 100 percent limit, you know that a faster processor may help the computer handle these processes more efficiently. Even more important, however, is to check the Processor Queue Length counter for the System object. This queue will tell you how many processes are sitting idle waiting for the processor to be freed. If this queue is low, your processor(s) may be sufficient.

General I/O Monitoring

A hardware problem can be diagnosed by looking at the Processor object's Interrupts/sec counter. This counter tells you the number of I/O requests that are waiting for processing. If this number rises without processor utilization rising, it may mean that there is another bottleneck in an I/O device or, for that matter, a malfunctioning I/O device.

Disk Drive Monitoring

Performance Monitor gives you counters that can help you look at each drive in your Windows NT computer and see if they are operating properly and efficiently.

Note: In order to turn on physical disk monitoring, you must run the command `DISKPERF -Y`.

The Physical Disk object has counters that enable you to observe each hard drive in your system. The % Disk Time counter can let you identify the usage of each of your hard drives. The Current Disk Queue Length counter will report the number of waiting I/O requests for a hard drive.

If the % Disk Time is over 90 percent, which is high, the Current Disk Queue Length will tell you if the drive is handling requests efficiently. Disk Queue Lengths that are over two times the number of spindles making up the hard drive (which is usually one spindle, although RAID drives can have more) can be a symptom of a faulty controller, indicate the need for faster disks, or even indicate a bad drive cable. Resolving these performance problems may involve buying new drives, adding drives, adding or replacing controllers, and possibly moving data to another computer.

These statistics can be looked at for each individual drive, but there is also an instance called `_Total` that will give you an overview of all your disks.

Network Monitoring

While Performance Monitor is not a replacement for advanced network monitoring tools such as Hewlett-Packard Open View, or network packet analyzers such as Data General's Sniffer, you can get statistics that will help you evaluate and analyze how specific computers and network segments are handling network traffic.

The Redirector object monitors transmissions from the computer, and the Server object monitors requests to the computer. Using the counters associated with these objects can tell you how well the computer is handling the task of operating as a server. Monitor the Processor object at the same time, and you will be able to tell if problems stem from an overutilized CPU. The same holds true for monitoring the Physical Disk object in conjunction with the Redirector and Server objects.

Note: The Network Monitor application, which ships with Windows NT Server 4.0, is a subset of the Network Monitor that ships with Microsoft Systems Management Server. Used in conjunction with Performance Monitor, the Network Monitor can help you evaluate your computer's overall performance and help identify bottlenecks on your network, which includes identifying network adapter cards out on the network that may be malfunctioning.

Types of Views for Performance Monitor

The Performance Monitor can be displayed four ways. The first four buttons on the toolbar represent these four different views.

The first button represents Graph View. The second button is Alert View. The third is the Log File view, and the fourth button changes the display to a Report View.

These views are explained in the following sections.

Charting in Performance Monitor

To create a chart in Performance Monitor, click the plus sign toolbar button.

The Add To Chart dialog, shown in Figure 18.2, will present many options for adding monitored objects to the Performance Monitor display.

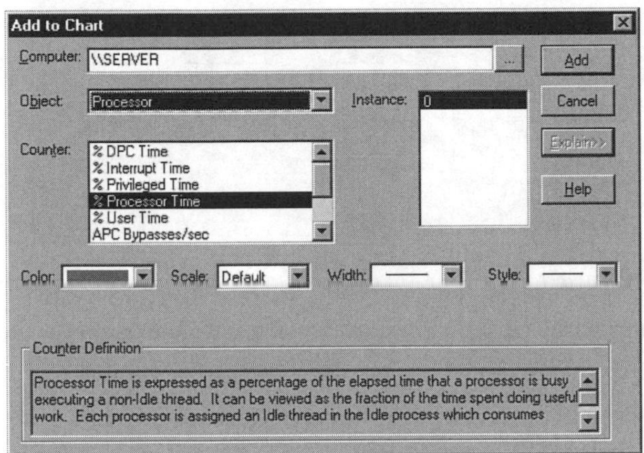

Figure 18.2. *Add To Chart dialog.*

The first item that can be chosen is the computer that will be monitored. By default, the local computer is the chosen computer. By clicking the browse button, a list of available computers on the network will be displayed. You can choose any computer that is running Windows NT for remote monitoring.

> **Note:** Although other computers will be displayed, only Windows NT computers can be monitored using Performance Monitor. Choosing another type of computer will give you an error message.

Next, the Object list is a drop-down list. Choose the appropriate object you want to monitor. By default, Processor is already chosen.

Under the object list is the Counter list. The counter definition, shown near the bottom of Figure 18.2, explains the counter's purpose. This definition is only shown if you click the button on the right side of the Add to Chart dialog labeled Explain>>.

The Instance list will show values only for the selected object. For instance, in Figure 18.2 the Instance list shows the value zero. This is because there could be multiple processors in a computer, and in this case, only processor zero exists.

Figure 18.3 shows Physical Disk as the chosen object, and the Instance list has five values. The first is a total of all physical drives, and the other values represent the four hard drives installed in the computer.

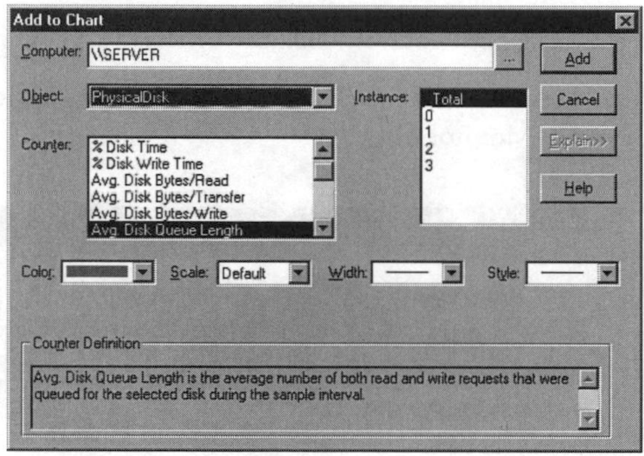

Figure 18.3. *The Object Instance list.*

Because the Performance Monitor chart can track multiple counters at the same time, in order to tell them apart you need to specify the attributes for each line that will occupy the graph.

The Color, Scale, Width, and Style drop-down boxes enable you to select these attributes so that you can make each counter appear unique.

Click the Add button to add the currently selected counter to the graph. Next, you can choose to add another counter. Click the Done button when you have finished adding counters to the graph.

You may want to limit the number of counters in a graph to a minimum so that the display does not get too crowded. You can run multiple instances of Performance Monitor and have a few counters represented in each instance of Performance Monitor.

Viewing a Chart

After you have selected the counters for the graph, a real-time display of these counters are displayed, as shown in Figure 18.4. At the bottom of the screen is a legend that shows the different counters and the type of line that is being drawn to represent the counter.

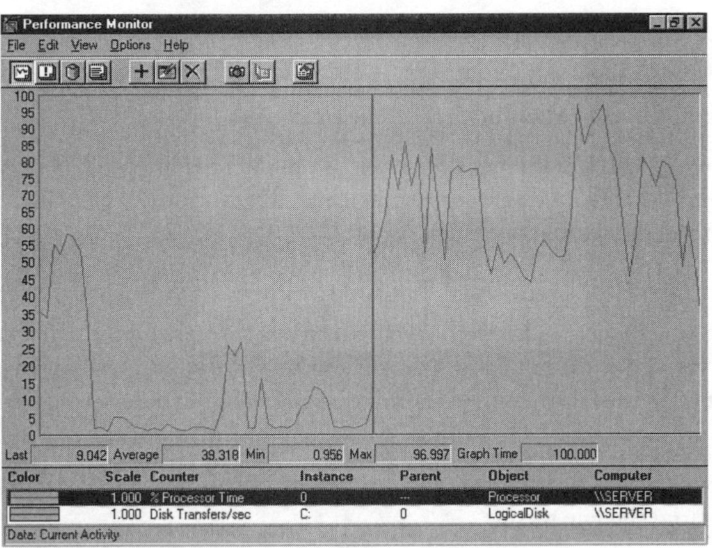

Figure 18.4. *A Performance Monitor chart.*

By highlighting one of these counters in the legend, you can display statistics in a status line that is directly below the graph.

Properties for the chart can be changed by choosing Chart from the Options menu. Figure 18.5 shows these options.

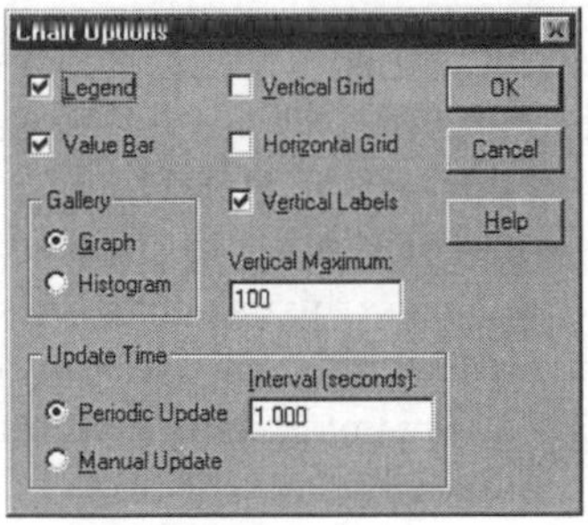

Figure 18.5. *Chart options.*

These options enable you to configure the way the chart is displayed. As you can see, a choice is there to display either a graph or a histogram. The labels, shown here as 0 to 100, can be changed from horizontal to vertical. The maximum value for the labels can be changed as well. A horizontal or vertical grid can also be displayed behind the lines, which makes the chart values easier to read.

The Update Time settings enable you to choose between an automatic or a manual update, which requires clicking the toolbar button that shows a camera to chart the counters.

Additional Chart Options

After counters have been selected for the chart, and you are in Chart View, you have the option to remove individual counters or clear all the counters.

Removing a counter is accomplished by selecting a counter in the legend. Next, you press the delete key or choose Delete From Chart on the Edit menu. The button on the toolbar with the X graphic will also remove the currently selected counter.

You can clear all the counters by choosing Clear Display from the Edit menu.

Because selecting the counters to be monitored can be a tedious task that you may not want to have to re-create each time you run Performance Monitor, you can save your settings by choosing Save Chart Settings on the File menu. An unlimited number of different settings can be saved because the settings are saved into a file (with a PMC extension) that you can name descriptively.

The settings for all views (chart, alert, log, and report) can be saved in a PMW file by choosing Save Workspace from the File menu.

> **Note:** A log file can provide historical data to be shown in Chart View. The option to use a log file for display is picked by choosing the menu item Data From on the Options menu. See the Performance Monitor Log View section for information on creating a log file.

Using Performance Monitor Data for Reporting

You can also export the data that is currently in the Performance Monitor windows into a tab-delimited file or to a comma-delimited file. When displaying real-time information that is updated on a one-second interval, this is not very helpful. However, if you manually take snapshots of system performance or set Performance Monitor to update on a larger interval (for instance, every 60 seconds, or 3600 seconds), you can use this data for comparison with previously captured data. The types of files that Performance Monitor can save can be imported into Microsoft Excel or almost any other data analysis tool. A sample comma-delimited file is shown in Listing 18.1.

Listing 18.1. Performance Monitor data in comma-delimited format.

```
Reported on \\SERVER
Date: 11/7/96
Time: 7:42:10 PM
Data: Current Activity
Interval:   1.000 seconds

,,% Processor Time,
,,0,
,,,
,,Processor,
Date,Time,\\SERVER,
```

```
11/7/96,7:37:32 PM ,      2.055,
11/7/96,7:37:33 PM ,      7.108,
11/7/96,7:37:34 PM ,     30.490,
11/7/96,7:37:35 PM ,     21.816,
11/7/96,7:37:36 PM ,      9.051,
11/7/96,7:37:37 PM ,      9.969,
11/7/96,7:37:38 PM ,      1.996,
11/7/96,7:37:39 PM ,      7.061,
11/7/96,7:37:40 PM ,     12.962,
11/7/96,7:37:41 PM ,     18.128,
11/7/96,7:37:42 PM ,      7.849,
11/7/96,7:37:43 PM ,      8.978,
11/7/96,7:37:44 PM ,     33.091,
11/7/96,7:37:45 PM ,     23.944,
11/7/96,7:37:46 PM ,      2.957,
11/7/96,7:37:47 PM ,      1.986,
11/7/96,7:37:48 PM ,      3.996,
11/7/96,7:37:49 PM ,      7.015,
11/7/96,7:37:50 PM ,      5.949,
11/7/96,7:37:51 PM ,      9.060,
11/7/96,7:37:52 PM ,      1.947,
11/7/96,7:37:53 PM ,      3.015,
11/7/96,7:37:54 PM ,      1.977,
11/7/96,7:37:55 PM ,      5.053,
11/7/96,7:37:56 PM ,      4.987,
11/7/96,7:37:57 PM ,     12.005,
11/7/96,7:40:44 PM ,      1.322,
11/7/96,7:40:58 PM ,      8.558,
11/7/96,7:40:59 PM ,      7.766,
11/7/96,7:41:00 PM ,      5.959,
11/7/96,7:41:01 PM ,      2.006,
11/7/96,7:41:02 PM ,      1.967,
11/7/96,7:41:03 PM ,      3.025,
11/7/96,7:41:04 PM ,      2.010,
11/7/96,7:41:05 PM ,      2.006,
11/7/96,7:41:06 PM ,      1.947,
11/7/96,7:41:07 PM ,      3.054,
11/7/96,7:41:08 PM ,      1.996,
11/7/96,7:41:09 PM ,      1.947,
11/7/96,7:41:10 PM ,      2.006,
11/7/96,7:41:11 PM ,      1.996,
11/7/96,7:41:12 PM ,      6.024,
11/7/96,7:41:13 PM ,      3.015,
11/7/96,7:41:14 PM ,      3.025,
11/7/96,7:41:15 PM ,      1.937,
11/7/96,7:41:16 PM ,      2.055,
11/7/96,7:41:17 PM ,      1.996,
11/7/96,7:41:18 PM ,      2.986,
11/7/96,7:41:19 PM ,      2.967,
11/7/96,7:41:20 PM ,      1.996,
11/7/96,7:41:21 PM ,      2.006,
11/7/96,7:41:22 PM ,      2.035,
11/7/96,7:41:23 PM ,      2.006,
11/7/96,7:41:24 PM ,      1.967,
11/7/96,7:41:25 PM ,      2.045,
11/7/96,7:41:26 PM ,      1.986,
11/7/96,7:41:27 PM ,      1.957,
11/7/96,7:41:28 PM ,      1.986,
11/7/96,7:41:29 PM ,      1.996,
```

continues

Listing 18.1. continued

```
11/7/96,7:41:30 PM ,      2.025,
11/7/96,7:41:31 PM ,      2.055,
11/7/96,7:41:32 PM ,      1.986,
11/7/96,7:41:33 PM ,      3.977,
11/7/96,7:41:34 PM ,      2.016,
11/7/96,7:41:35 PM ,      2.016,
11/7/96,7:41:36 PM ,      2.977,
11/7/96,7:41:37 PM ,      1.967,
11/7/96,7:41:38 PM ,      1.986,
11/7/96,7:41:39 PM ,      2.006,
11/7/96,7:41:40 PM ,      2.065,
11/7/96,7:41:41 PM ,      1.986,
11/7/96,7:41:42 PM ,      5.987,
11/7/96,7:41:43 PM ,      3.025,
11/7/96,7:41:44 PM ,      2.025,
11/7/96,7:41:45 PM ,     17.038,
11/7/96,7:41:46 PM ,      1.859,
11/7/96,7:41:47 PM ,      2.016,
11/7/96,7:41:48 PM ,      4.025,
11/7/96,7:41:49 PM ,      2.025,
11/7/96,7:41:50 PM ,      2.996,
11/7/96,7:41:51 PM ,      1.977,
11/7/96,7:41:52 PM ,      2.016,
11/7/96,7:41:53 PM ,      1.996,
11/7/96,7:41:54 PM ,      1.967,
11/7/96,7:41:55 PM ,      2.006,
11/7/96,7:41:56 PM ,      4.006,
11/7/96,7:41:57 PM ,      6.015,
11/7/96,7:41:58 PM ,     12.023,
11/7/96,7:41:59 PM ,      8.024,
11/7/96,7:42:00 PM ,      7.108,
11/7/96,7:42:01 PM ,     11.944,
11/7/96,7:42:02 PM ,     14.971,
11/7/96,7:42:03 PM ,     64.042,
11/7/96,7:42:04 PM ,     18.891,
11/7/96,7:42:05 PM ,     27.019,
11/7/96,7:42:06 PM ,      8.680,
11/7/96,7:42:07 PM ,      4.289,
11/7/96,7:42:08 PM ,      1.967,
11/7/96,7:42:09 PM ,      3.967,
11/7/96,7:42:10 PM ,     12.076,
```

Capturing Alerts in Performance Monitor

The second view in Performance Monitor is the Alert View. This is a fantastic tool that enables you to create thresholds for performance and capture an alert if that threshold is exceeded.

Choose Alert View from the View menu or click the second toolbar button.

When Alert View is chosen, you still have the same toolbar that Chart View gives you, so to add an alert, click the toolbar button that has a plus sign.

The Add to Alert dialog (see Figure 18.6) enables you to choose from the same counters that were available for Chart View. In this case you also need to specify the threshold.

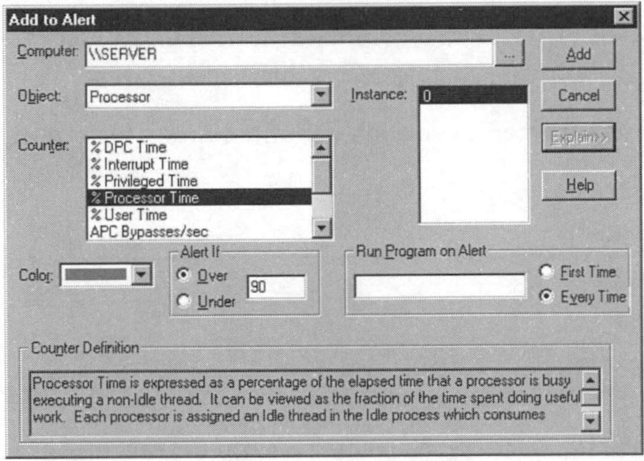

Figure 18.6. The Add to Alert dialog.

In Figure 18.7, the Alerts that I have chosen include checking for the percentage of free space on each of the logical volumes. I've configured these to add an alert when the free space is lower than 25 percent.

Within the Add to Alert dialog you can also specify a program to run when an alert is generated.

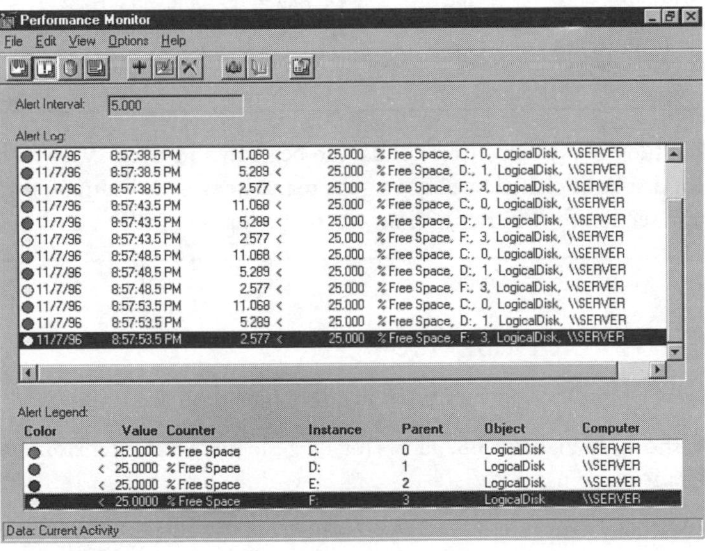

Figure 18.7. Alert View.

It is from within the Alert View that you can specify the interval at which Alert View will check the thresholds.

As with Chart View, you can save the settings for Alert View by choosing Save Alert Settings from the File menu, or you can save all four views into one file by choosing Save Workspace from the File menu.

These alerts can also be exported to a comma-delimited or tab-delimited file that can be used to import into a data analysis tool such as Microsoft Excel.

A sample list of Alerts exported to comma-delimited files is shown in Listing 18.2.

Listing 18.2. Alert output.

```
Reported on \\SERVER
Date: 11/7/96
Time: 9:05:11 PM
Data: Current Activity
Interval:    5.000 seconds

Date,Time,Value,Trigger Condition,Counter,Instance,Parent,Object,Computer
11/7/96,8:57:33 PM ,      11.068,<      25.000,% Free Space,C:,0,LogicalDisk,\\SERVER
11/7/96,8:57:33 PM ,       5.289,<      25.000,% Free Space,D:,1,LogicalDisk,\\SERVER
11/7/96,8:57:33 PM ,       2.577,<      25.000,% Free Space,F:,3,LogicalDisk,\\SERVER
11/7/96,8:57:38 PM ,      11.068,<      25.000,% Free Space,C:,0,LogicalDisk,\\SERVER
11/7/96,8:57:38 PM ,       5.289,<      25.000,% Free Space,D:,1,LogicalDisk,\\SERVER
11/7/96,8:57:38 PM ,       2.577,<      25.000,% Free Space,F:,3,LogicalDisk,\\SERVER
11/7/96,8:57:43 PM ,      11.068,<      25.000,% Free Space,C:,0,LogicalDisk,\\SERVER
11/7/96,8:57:43 PM ,       5.289,<      25.000,% Free Space,D:,1,LogicalDisk,\\SERVER
11/7/96,8:57:43 PM ,       2.577,<      25.000,% Free Space,F:,3,LogicalDisk,\\SERVER
11/7/96,8:57:48 PM ,      11.068,<      25.000,% Free Space,C:,0,LogicalDisk,\\SERVER
11/7/96,8:57:48 PM ,       5.289,<      25.000,% Free Space,D:,1,LogicalDisk,\\SERVER
11/7/96,8:57:48 PM ,       2.577,<      25.000,% Free Space,F:,3,LogicalDisk,\\SERVER
```

Note: A log file can provide historical data to be shown in Event View. The option to use a log file for display is picked by choosing the menu item Data From on the Options menu. See the next section for information on creating a log file.

Performance Monitor Log View

Select Log View from the View menu or click the third toolbar button.

The log view, shown in Figure 18.8, allows for a log file (with the extension .LOG), which is used to capture data for later use.

A log file is essentially a capture of data that is only readable by Performance Monitor and can be displayed in any of its views as if it were incoming real-time data. It's sort of a "playback" mechanism for historical data.

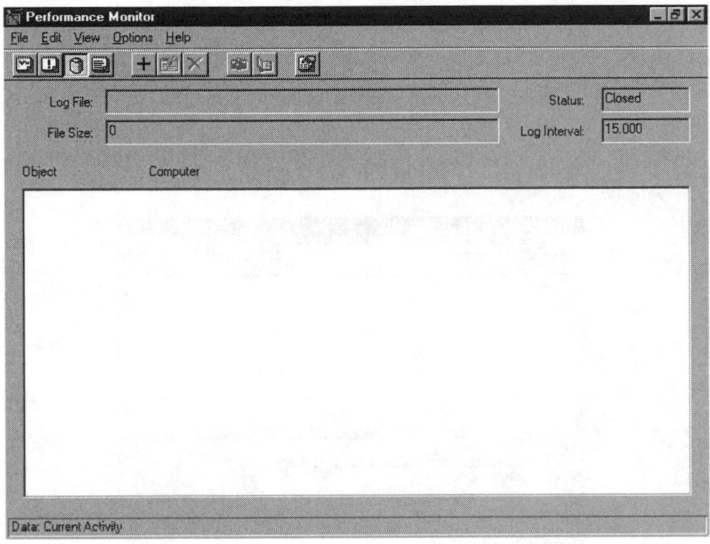

Figure 18.8. Performance Monitor Log View.

> **Tip:** A perfect time to create a log file, perhaps at 5 or 15 minute intervals for a full day, is right after you've installed Windows NT. This log file can be kept as historical data that should show your system running optimally. As you add on software or devices you can then compare to see the type of effect the hardware or software is actually having on the computer.

To start a log file you must first choose the statistics that you want to log. In Figure 18.9 I had clicked the plus sign button and the Add To Log dialog popped up. The object Memory is being chosen for logging.

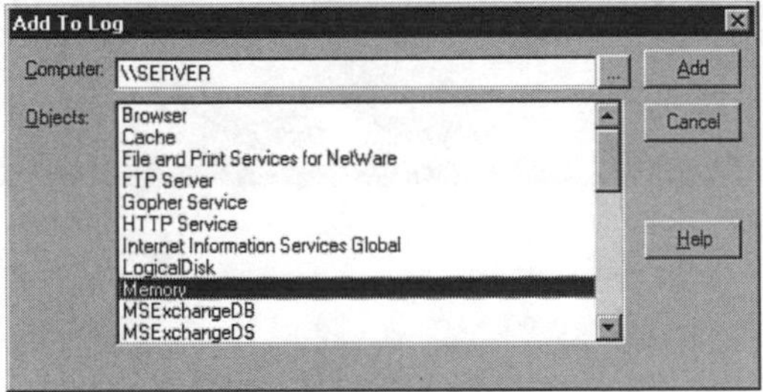

Figure 18.9. The Add To Log dialog.

Additional items can be added, but in order to save space in my log, I've chosen memory only.

Next, a log file needs to be chosen. You can choose to append to an existing log file or create a new log file. Figure 18.10 shows that a filename MEMORY.LOG is being created. The option for this log file is to log statistics every 15 seconds. This can be changed to a different value or it can be set to accept statistics on a manual basis, which is done by choosing the Update Now command from the Options menu.

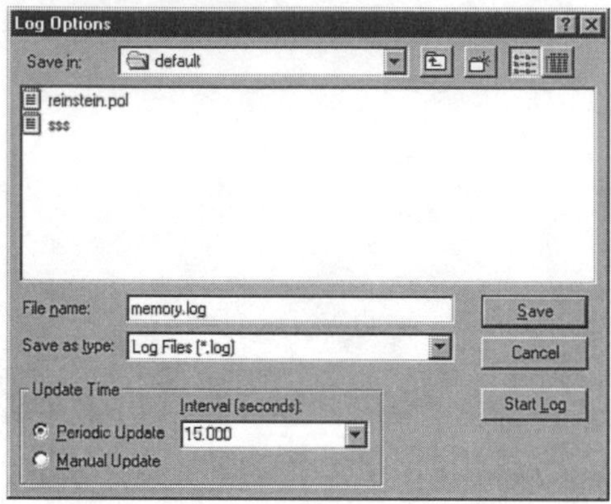

Figure 18.10. The Log Options dialog.

Once the proper entries have been made, the file can be saved, or the logging can be started by clicking the Start Log button.

Figure 18.11 shows logging in progress. It is not necessary to leave the Performance Monitor window open, because logging will occur in the background. You can, however, use the Performance Monitor window to monitor the size of the log.

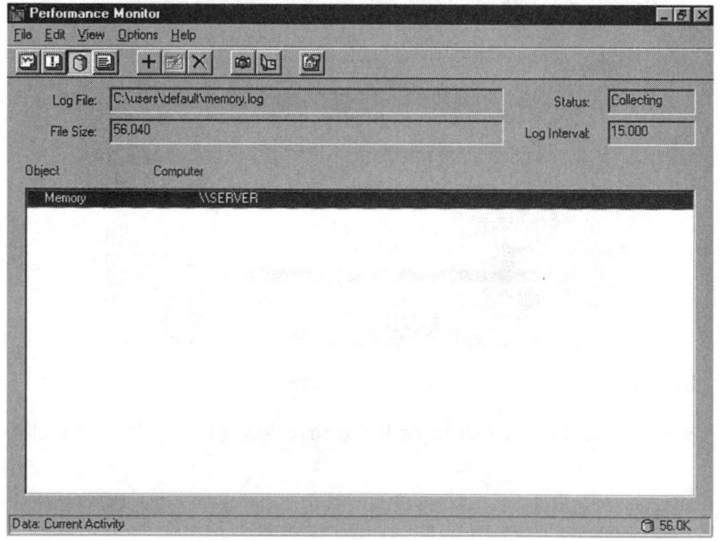

Figure 18.11. Logging in progress.

You may also decide to add a bookmark to the log, which is adding descriptive text to the log at any point. A bookmark can help you add text that will remind you of what you were trying to accomplish, or perhaps for you to make a note of a particular application that is running. Adding a bookmark is accomplished by choosing Bookmark... from the Options menu. The Add Bookmark dialog (Figure 18.12) allows you to enter the text.

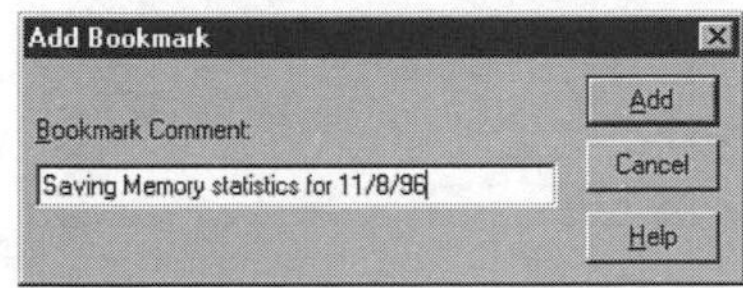

Figure 18.12. *The Add Bookmark dialog.*

Note that the log filename is displayed along with the current size of the file and the status (which may be Collecting as shown in Figure 18.11, or Closed, which means that the log file is not collecting data). The log interval is displayed, as is the size of the log file, which is displayed at the bottom-right corner of the screen.

When you want to stop logging, choose Log from the Options menu and click the Stop Log button, as shown in Figure 18.13.

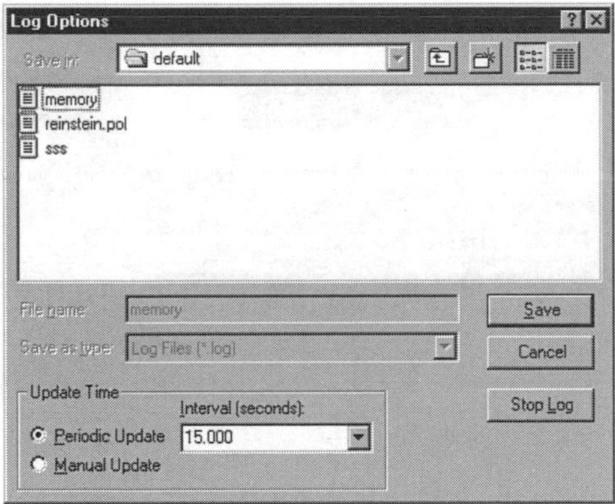

Figure 18.13. *The Stop Log button.*

Settings can be saved for logging the same way that settings can be saved for all the Performance Monitor views, which is done through the File menu.

Performance Monitor Report View

So far, you've seen Chart View, which can display data as a graph or a histogram, Event View, which looks for thresholds and reports on events of interest based on those thresholds, and Log View, which can capture data directly to a log file.

Report View provides a simple text display of statistics, either in real-time or from a log file.

The choice between live data or using data from a log file is done by choosing Data From on the Options menu. This is shown in Figure 18.14.

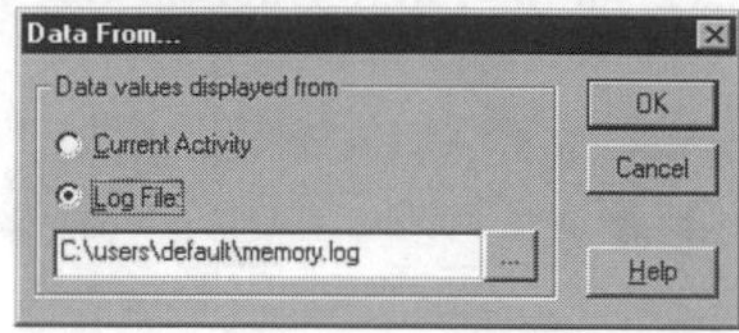

Figure 18.14. *Choosing live data or using a log file.*

In Figure 18.14 I have chosen to use data that I captured into a log file named `MEMORY.LOG`, which is the file I created in the Log View example.

Once a log file has been chosen, a time slice needs to be selected. This is done by picking Time Windows from the Edit menu. Figure 18.15 shows the entire time range that is contained within the chosen log file. The bookmark list enables you to pick a starting time for the time slice that will be shown in the current Performance Monitor view, and you must also choose the end time for this time slice.

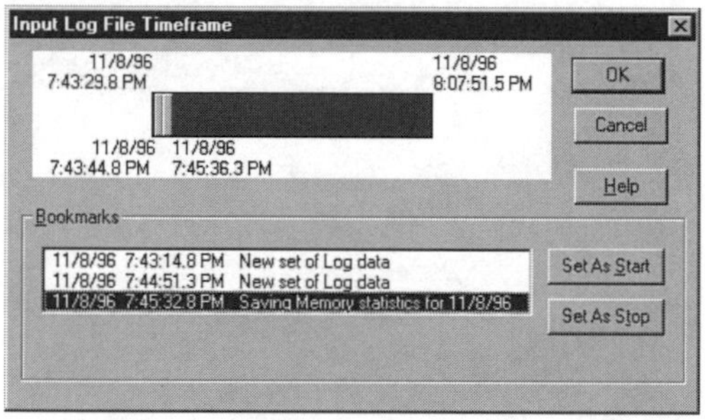

Figure 18.15. *Creating a time slice from a log file.*

Once this has been selected, click the OK button.

Now, as with all views, whether coming from current data or from a log file, you must select the objects and counters that you wish to display. Because this log file only contained information about the Memory object, the only available object for display will be Memory.

Choose the object by clicking the plus sign button. As shown in Figure 18.16, the Add to Report dialog shows the only object available in the selected log file, Memory, and its counters. Add the counters you want to view, and when finished choosing, click the Done button.

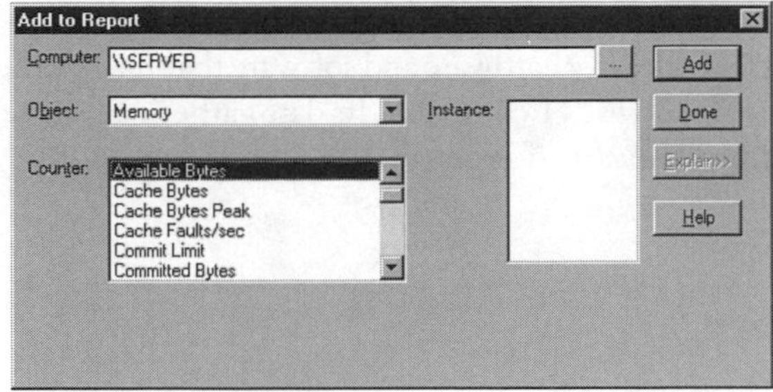

Figure 18.16. *The Add to Report dialog.*

Figure 18.17 shows Report View and the two counters that were selected for viewing. This report can then be exported to a comma-delimited file or a text-delimited file.

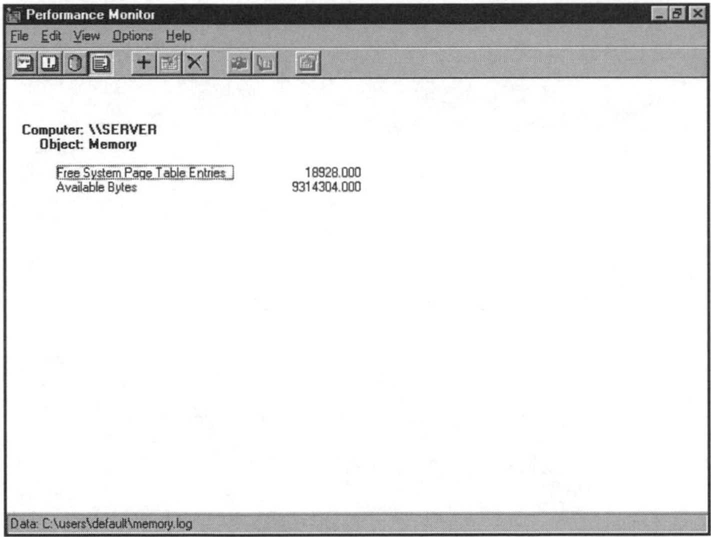

Figure 18.17. *Performance Monitor Report View.*

Thus, Report View can be used to view historical data and then prepare the data to be exported into a data analysis tool.

Summary

Even though Microsoft touts Windows NT as "self-tuning," there is a considerable amount of ways that a Windows NT computer can require manual tuning. It was for this reason that Microsoft included Performance Monitor as a part of Windows NT.

While viewed by some as a nuisance to use, Performance Monitor can really help you pinpoint bottlenecks and help you identify hardware and software that may be the cause of occasional poor performance on your Windows NT computer. Its data gathering features can also help you justify the need for upgrading hardware, if necessary.

Network Client Administrator

by Robert Reinstein

One of the greatest headaches in setting up a network—any network—is getting your clients connected to the network. If your clients are running Windows NT Workstation, Windows 95, or Windows for Workgroups, getting them onto a Microsoft Network is not too difficult and usually requires just a little tweaking; however, the workstations that are still running DOS, DOS/Windows 3.*x*, or OS/2 require a lot of time and configuration. A lot of that time is spent installing the client software that is necessary to make that network connection.

This chapter will show you how to use the Network Client Administrator to

- Copy network client software to a server share
- Make a set of disks that contain Microsoft Networking components
- Create a network startup disk that will attach any workstation to a Windows NT network
- Modify the Network Client Administrator to allow it to create any type of custom disk

Note: Microsoft Windows 95 and Microsoft Windows NT Workstation are the preferred clients for a Microsoft Windows NT network because of their ease of installation and seamless networking.

The Windows NT Server Network Client Administrator is a tool that can help the administrator ease the installation of Windows- and DOS-based clients onto the Windows NT Server domain.

You can use the Network Client Administrator to help with client software installation and also to distribute additional software, from the 32-bit implementation of Microsoft TCP/IP for Windows for Workgroups to almost any type of software.

These tools include the means to copy all the client software contained on the Windows NT Server CD-ROM to a network share, to create disks that can be used to have a client attach to the network and access that share, and to copy administrative tools that can be used on PCs that are not running the Windows NT operating system.

The Network Client Administrator also has features that you can modify to provide even more functionality than is explained in the documentation. In the section titled "Customizing the Network Client Administrator" later in this chapter, I will explain these modifications.

Starting the Network Client Administrator

The shortcut for the Network Client Administrator is located in the Administrative Tools Common folder on the Windows NT Server Start Programs menu.

This simple yet very effective application, shown in Figure 19.1, gives you four choices of functionality (although one of them is nothing more than an instruction to refer to a section of the Windows NT Resource Kit).

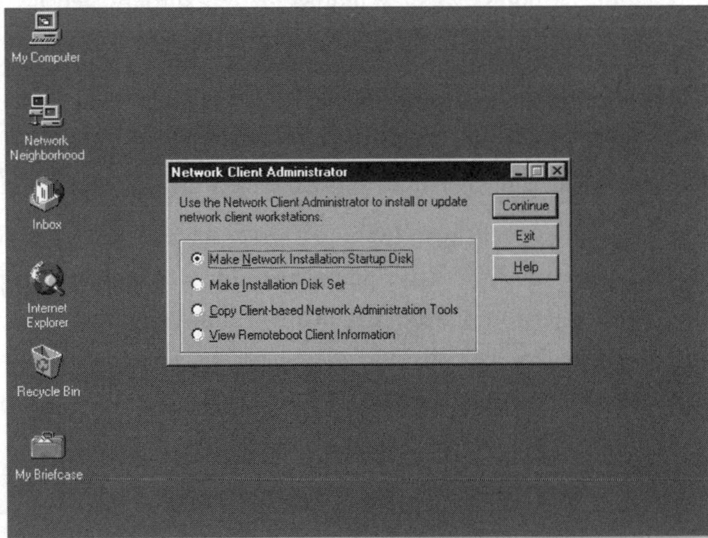

Figure 19.1. *The Network Client Administrator.*

The Network Client Administrator Tools

The choices Make Network Installation Startup Disk and Make Installation Disk Set depend on the existence of copies of the Microsoft Network client installation software. The Windows NT Server CD-ROM contains a directory structure, located under the `\CLIENTS` directory, that contains Microsoft Network client software for MS-DOS, Windows 3.*x*, and OS/2. The CD-ROM also contains fully installable copies of Microsoft Windows 95, Microsoft's 32-bit TCP/IP for Windows for Workgroups, Microsoft's Remoteboot, and Remote Access Services (RAS) for MS-DOS.

The full copy of Microsoft Windows 95 on the Microsoft Windows NT Server CD-ROM contains updated files that are not found in the shrink-wrapped version of Microsoft Windows 95. If you are configuring workstations that are already running Microsoft Windows 95, you need to copy the files located in the `\CLIENTS\UPDATE.W95` directory. Updated files for already installed copies of Microsoft Windows for Workgroups are contained in the `\CLIENTS\UPDATE.WFW` directory.

Sharing the Network Client Installation Files

When starting either Make Network Installation Startup Disk or Make Installation Disk Set, you will be prompted to configure the network share from which the client software can be copied.

If you have not run either of these options before, you can choose to create a new share on your server or specify another server that already has the client software share established. In Figure 19.2, the `Path` field refers either to the location of the Microsoft Windows NT Server CD-ROM and the path where the client software can be copied from or to another location that you specify, such as a share on another server that has that same directory structure. Copying the client installation files to your server is optional. However, having a copy of these files on the server can be very convenient, because you won't have to dig out the Microsoft Windows NT Server CD-ROM whenever you need client software.

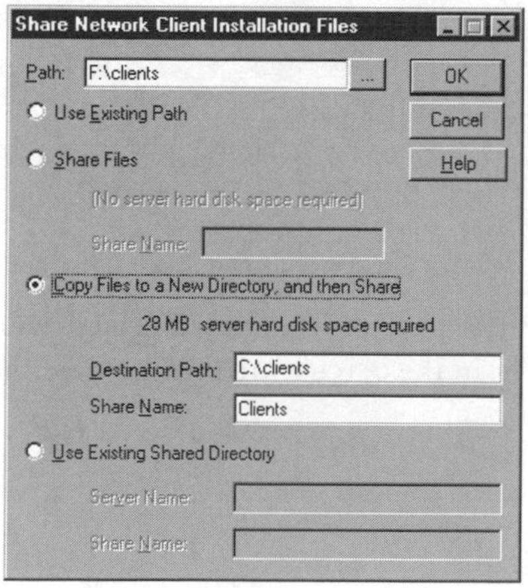

Figure 19.2. *The Share Network Client Installation Files dialog.*

Note: Note that the Share Network Client Installation Files option says `64 MB server hard disk space required`. In reality, if you should decide to perform some customization, as I will explain later, that number can grow to well over 200 megabytes!

Note: Unless you have another server on your LAN containing the Microsoft Network Client Software that you will access for the purpose of making client installation disks, you need to specify the `Path`.

After filling in the `Path` field, you need to specify whether you want create a share that points directly to the source for the files or create a new share. Figure 19.2 shows the default setting of creating a new share called `Clients` in the `C:\CLIENTS` directory.

After the new directory is created, 64MB of files are copied to the new directory (see Figure 19.3) to create the `Clients` share.

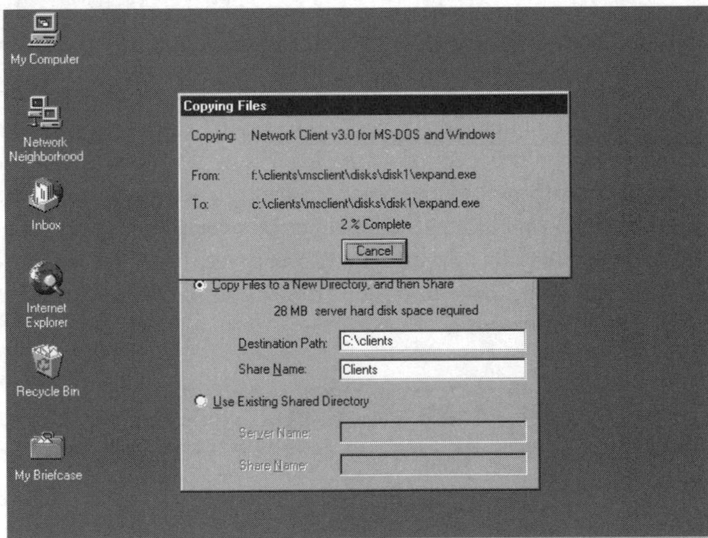

Figure 19.3. *Copying files from the NT Server CD-ROM to a network share.*

When the copying is complete (see Figure 19.4), you can delete unneeded parts of the directory structure. The subdirectories in the `C:\CLIENTS` directory are shown in Table 19.1.

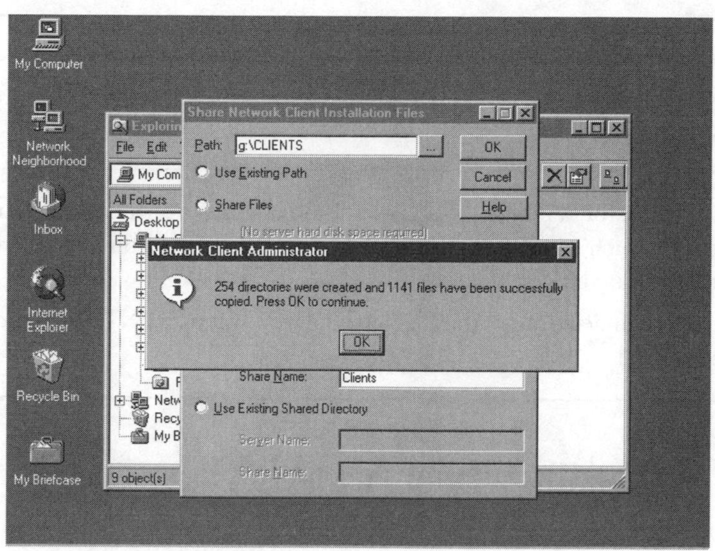

Figure 19.4. `C:\CLIENTS` *directory creation completed.*

Table 19.1. Network client software directory structure.

Directory	*Description*
`\CLIENTS\LANMAN`	Microsoft LAN Manager for MS-DOS
`\CLIENTS\LANMAN.OS2`	Microsoft LAN Manager for MS OS/2
`\CLIENTS\MSCLIENT`	Microsoft Network Client for MS-DOS
`\CLIENTS\RAS`	Microsoft RAS for MS-DOS
`\CLIENTS\RPL`	Remoteboot Service for Microsoft Windows NT Server
`\CLIENTS\SRVTOOLS\WINNT`	Client-based network administration tools for Windows NT Workstation
`\CLIENTS\SRVTOOLS\WIN95`	Client-based network administration tools for Windows 95
`\CLIENTS\SUPPORT`	Network Client Administrator `readme` file
`\CLIENTS\TCP32WFW`	Microsoft TCP/IP-32 for Windows for Workgroups
`\CLIENTS\UPDATE.W95`	Updated files for Windows 95
`\CLIENTS\UPDATE.WFW`	Updated files for Windows for Workgroups
`\WIN95`	Microsoft Windows 95

Tip: The LAN Manager client is available because LAN Manager servers can be incorporated into a Windows NT Server domain.

Tip: Server Tools for Windows NT Workstation includes utilities for the various flavors of Windows NT, such as I386, MIPS, Alpha, and PowerPC. You can delete any of these subdirectories that you don't need.

Similarly, you can delete any other Server Tools for Windows NT Workstation for which you have no need.

Making a Network Installation Start-Up Disk

Installing Microsoft Network client software to a workstation that is running MS-DOS or Windows 3.*x* can bc accomplished either by creating a network installation start-up disk or using disks created by the Network Client Administrator.

In fact, you can use Network Client Administrator to install a fresh copy of Windows 95, or another operating system, on a newly formatted hard drive.

New to NT 4.0: The previous version of Windows NT Server, version 3.51, shipped with a complete copy of Windows for Workgroups, but did not include Windows 95.

At times you may prefer to create installation disks in advance and keep them handy for future installations. However, the `Make Network Installation Startup Disk` option is geared toward a specific workstation and cannot be reused.

This option will copy the necessary software to a single floppy disk that will load the appropriate network interface card driver, attach to the network, connect to the share that has the Microsoft Network client software, and execute the setup program for the type of client that was specified when creating the disk.

Note: The disk that you use for making a network installation start-up disk must be formatted and bootable.

The Target Workstation Configuration dialog (see Figure 19.5) lets you choose which type of network client software you want to install on the workstation. The two choices you will see here, by default, are MS-DOS/Windows 3.*x* and Windows 95.

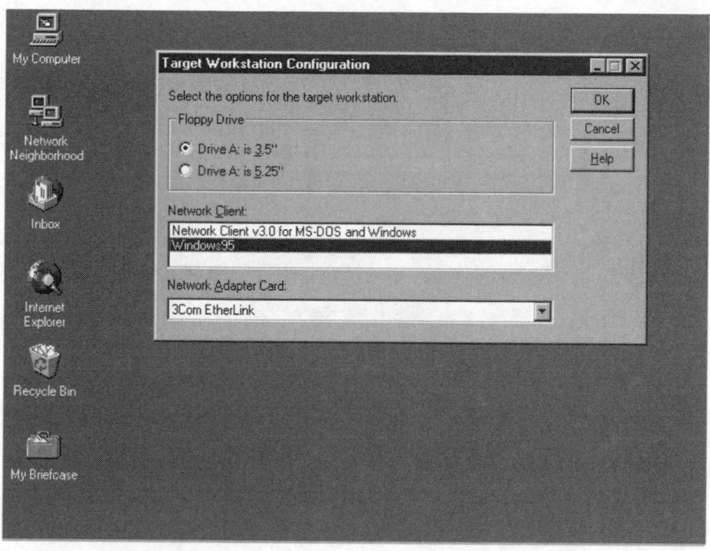

Figure 19.5. Target Workstation Configuration dialog.

Note: The client software for DOS and Windows 3.*x* does not need to be licensed and is included for part of the cost of the Windows NT Server Client Access License that you or your company should have already purchased.

The other option, Windows 95, is not included as part of the Windows NT Client Access License and requires separate licensing. If the workstation is currently running Windows 3.*x*, you will qualify for upgrade pricing. If the workstation is running DOS only, you must purchase a full copy of Windows 95 to properly license the Windows 95 installation. (See Figure 19.6.)

Tip: Whenever possible, install Windows 95. The built-in networking components of Windows 95 more than justify its price. A Windows 95 workstation does not require the Microsoft Network full redirector, which is a 100KB hog. The navigation tools, for connecting to a network printer or network share, are worth the price by themselves.

Usually, only a computer running on less than 8MB of memory and/or a 386 or under CPU should be excluded from being a Windows 95 workstation.

From a pick list of available network interface card drivers, choose the workstation's network adapter card. This setting must be accurate, as the start-up disk will attempt to load this driver.

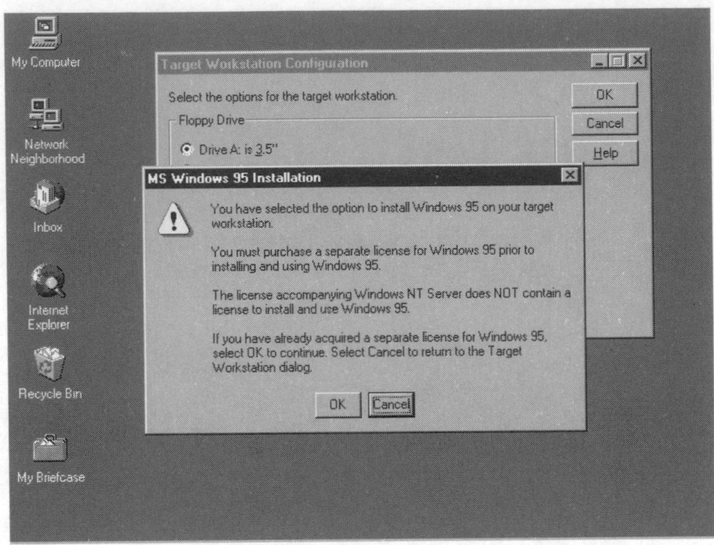

Figure 19.6. MS Windows 95 installation.

The Network Startup Disk Configuration dialog (see Figure 19.7) asks for a unique computer name for the client workstation. Any user account can be used to access this share, so a preexisting account must be entered into the `User Name` field. Enter the name of the domain that this workstation will join and the initial protocol that will be used for the network client software installation.

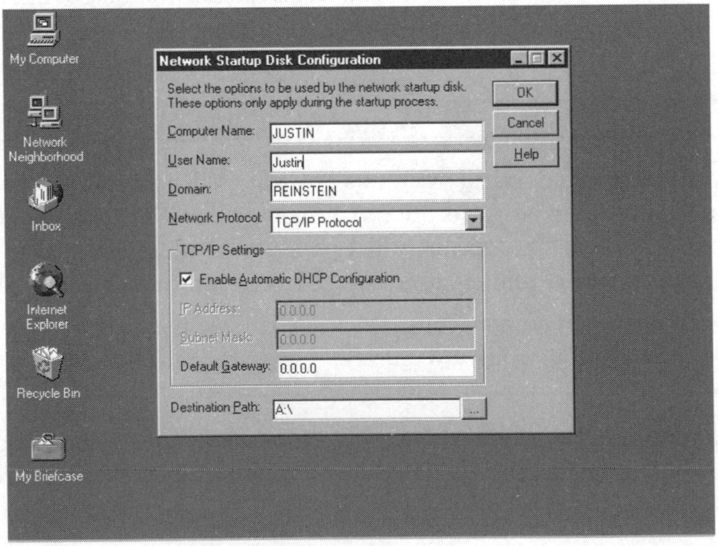

Figure 19.7. The Network Startup Disk Configuration dialog.

> **Note:** If a Windows NT Server in the entered domain is running DHCP services, you can opt to install TCP/IP and check the box that says Enable Automatic DHCP Configuration. If you use this option, then you do not have to enter the IP address and subnet mask for the DHCP server.

The last field (`Destination Path`) is where you specify a target for the files that will be copied. This field should be a drive letter associated with a floppy drive; however, you may wish to copy these files to a local hard drive or a network share for future use.

> **Note:** The floppy disk that you use as a network installation start-up disk must be formatted and bootable.

On this disk, a `CONFIG.SYS` file and an `AUTOEXEC.BAT` file are created, along with a directory called `NET`.

As shown in Listings 19.1 and 19.2, the necessary drivers are loaded in `CONFIG.SYS`, the appropriate bindings are created in `AUTOEXEC.BAT`, a connection to the network share is made, and the `SETUP.EXE` program from the Windows 95 directory is run.

Listing 19.1. A sample startup disk `CONFIG.SYS`.

```
files=30
device=a:\net\ifshlp.sys
lastdrive=z
DEVICE=A:\NET\HIMEM.SYS
DEVICE=A:\NET\EMM386.EXE NOEMS
DOS=HIGH,UMB
```

Listing 19.2. A sample startup disk `AUTOEXEC.BAT`.

```
path=a:\net
a:\net\net initialize
a:\net\nwlink
a:\net\net start
net use z: \\SERVER\Clients
echo Running Setup...
z:\win95\setup.exe /#
```

> **Tip:** Although only a limited number of network interface card drivers are available in the Target Workstation Configuration dialog (refer to Figure 19.5), you can edit some of the files on the start-up disk to reflect a driver that comes from a third-party driver disk. This task is accomplished by editing files from the `NET` directory that have the extensions `.INI` and `.INF`. These files refer to the specific network interface card driver that was chosen during

the Target Workstation Configuration dialog. To determine the appropriate changes, perform a manual installation from disks of the client software and indicate that you want to use another driver, rather than an included driver. Use the hardware manufacturer's driver disk, and when the installation is complete, note the `netcard=` entries in `SYSTEM.INI` and `PROTOCOL.INI`. You will also have to install the manufacturer's version of `PROTMAN.DOS` to the `NET` directory on the start-up disk.

After the necessary entries have been made, the Network Client Administrator will confirm your settings with a dialog (see Figure 19.8) that explicitly states the type of disk that will be created.

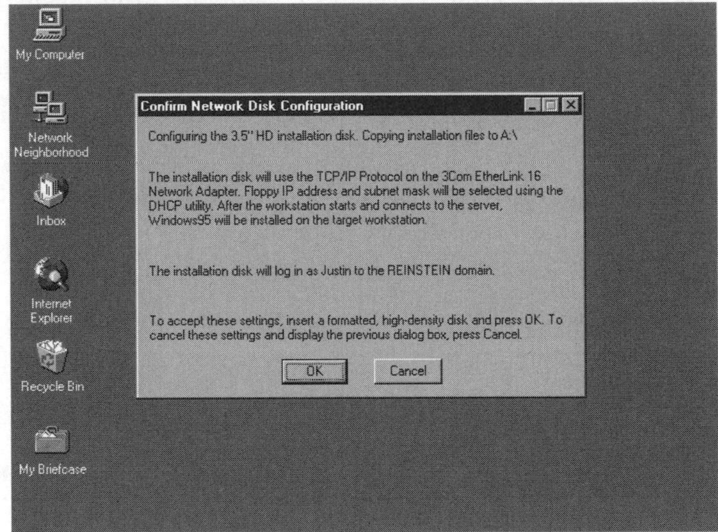

Figure 19.8. *Confirm Network Disk Configuration dialog.*

Making Network Installation Disks

When you choose Make Installation Disk Set from the Network Client Administrator dialog, you will first be prompted for the location of the client setup installation files. If you have already performed this setup, those settings will be retained and shown for confirmation.

The available disk sets that can be made through this process are

Microsoft TCP/IP 32 for Windows for Workgroups 3.11
Microsoft Network Client v3.0 for MS-DOS and Windows
Microsoft LAN Manager v2.2c for MS-DOS
Microsoft LAN Manager v2.2c for MS OS/2
Microsoft Remote Access v1.1a for MS-DOS

The Make Installation Disk Set dialog (see Figure 19.9) lists these items and allows you to choose the letter of the floppy drive on which you want to create the disks. The number of disks required is also displayed (one disk each, except for the LAN Manager options, which take four disks each), as is a choice for the Network Client Administrator to format the disks before copying the chosen files to them.

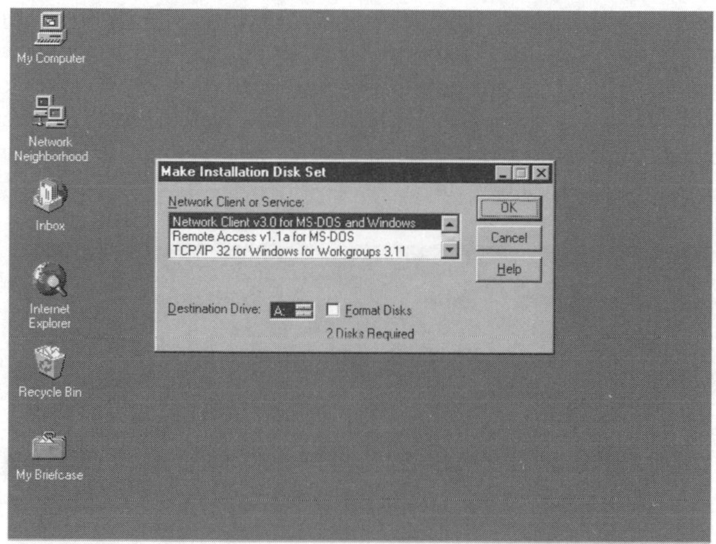

Figure 19.9. *The Make Installation Disk Set dialog.*

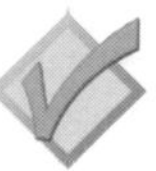

Tip: Although you might want to have a copy of Remote Access Services For DOS or TCP/IP for Windows for Workgroups, once you have connectivity to the server, it is just as easy to install these items directly from the `Clients` share.

After choosing the drive and product for which you want to make disks, click OK and you will be prompted to insert the necessary disks.

Copy Client-Based Network Administration Tools

The third utility available in the Network Client Administrator copies Windows NT Server administration tools that can run on Windows NT Workstation and Windows 95, including versions of User Manager for Domains, Server Manager, and Event Viewer.

These tools enable a client to administer certain functions on the server. In addition, for Windows NT Workstation you also get copies of System Policy Editor, DHCP Administrator, RPL Manager, RAS Administrator, and WINS Administrator.

The missing administration tool, Disk Manager, is rightly kept as a local tool that should be used only by an administrator at the server's console.

The minimum requirement on the workstation that runs these tools is 8MB of RAM and 3MB to 5MB of hard drive space.

The Share Client-based Administration Tools dialog (see Figure 19.10) is similar to the Share Network Client Installation Files dialog. First you need to identify a source path for the tools. On the Windows NT Server CD-ROM, this file is in the `C:\CLIENTS\SRVTOOLS` directory. If the tools have already been copied to another directory on a network share, click on the Use Existing Shared Directory radio button and type in the server name and share name. You can use this utility to create a share that points directly to the CD-ROM, to create a share for a preexisting directory on a network drive, or to create a new directory on a network drive.

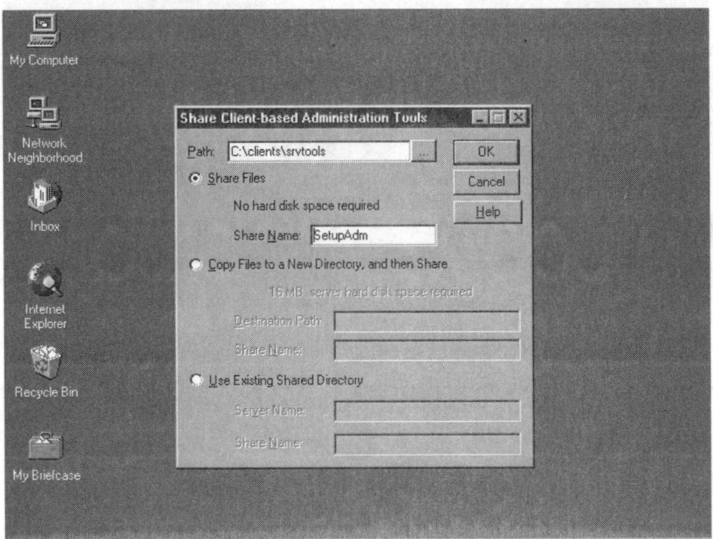

Figure 19.10. *The Share Client-based Administration Tools dialog.*

If one of the latter two methods is chosen, the files are also copied to the new share.

Note: For this example, the Windows NT Server CD-ROM `\CLIENTS` directory was copied while making the network installation start-up disk, so the client-based administration tools already exist within the share called `CLIENTS`. Therefore, this step creates a share for the `C:\CLIENTS\SRVTOOLS` directory that will be called `SETUPADM` by default.

View Remoteboot Client Information

The final function of the Network Client Administrator is actually not much of an option. As Figure 19.11 shows, choosing this option merely tells the user to refer to the Windows NT Resource Kit.

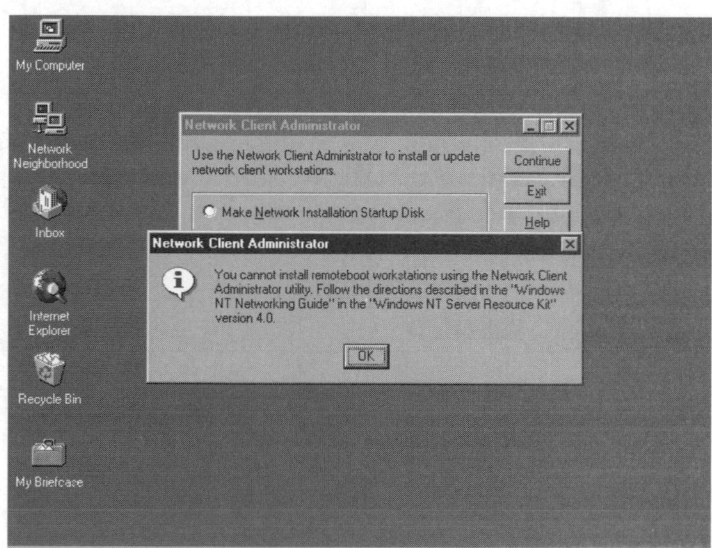

Figure 19.11. *View Remoteboot Client option.*

I'm still wondering why Microsoft opted to include this option in the Network Client Administrator.

Customizing the Network Client Administrator

One of the great features of the Network Client Administrator is that it can be modified to extend its functionality.

Because it can create a disk that will enable an over-the-network installation of Windows 95 or the MS-DOS Client for Microsoft Networks, why not make it a way to implement an over-the-network installation of Windows NT Workstation, Windows NT Server, Windows for Workgroups, or any other application?

Actually, Microsoft planned to allow users to modify this file; in fact, entries in some of the sections of file `NCADMIN.INF` show that an over-the-network install of Windows NT Workstation was under consideration.

The driving force behind the Network Client Administrator is a file that is placed on the shared directory. The NCADMIN.INF file looks like a standard Windows INI file, using bracketed sections with values within each section. The only noticeable difference is that Microsoft uses the pound sign (#) for commented lines instead of semicolons (;).

Customizing the Make a Network Installation Startup Disk Option

In Listing 19.3, the section called OTN (for over-the-net) lists the subdirectories that could be included in the share that contains the client software. The first two entries in the OTN section name directories created by the Network Client Administrator when you originally create the network share. The last three entries in the OTN section name directories that are not created by the Network Client Administrator, but can be manually created by you; then the contents of the respective products can be copied to those directories.

Listing 19.3. The OTN section of NCADMIN.INF.

```
[OTN]
#
#       list of sub dirs of the client tree that should be presented
#       for creating an Over-The-Net install disk
#
# SubDirName=DisplayName
wfw=Windows for Workgroups v3.11
msclient=Network Client v3.0 for MS-DOS and Windows
win95=Windows95
winnt=Windows NT Workstation
winnt.srv=Windows NT Server
```

When you use the Network Client Administrator to create a network installation start-up disk, it reads the OTN section of the NCADMIN.INF file, but then it checks to see which of these directories are available in the share. If it doesn't find a directory, it does not list the item in the list of possible client software installations to run.

For instance, if your network share is in the C:\CLIENTS directory on the NT server and you manually create a directory called WINNT and copy the contents of the \I386 directory from the Windows NT Workstation CD-ROM into the C:\CLIENTS\WINNT directory, Windows NT Workstation will be a choice in the Network Client Administrator Target Workstation Configuration dialog. (See Figure 19.12.)

Tip: I previously mentioned that the best choice for DOS workstations is to upgrade to Windows 95. Using this method, however, you can give your clients the option of using the best Microsoft networking client software, Microsoft Windows NT Workstation.

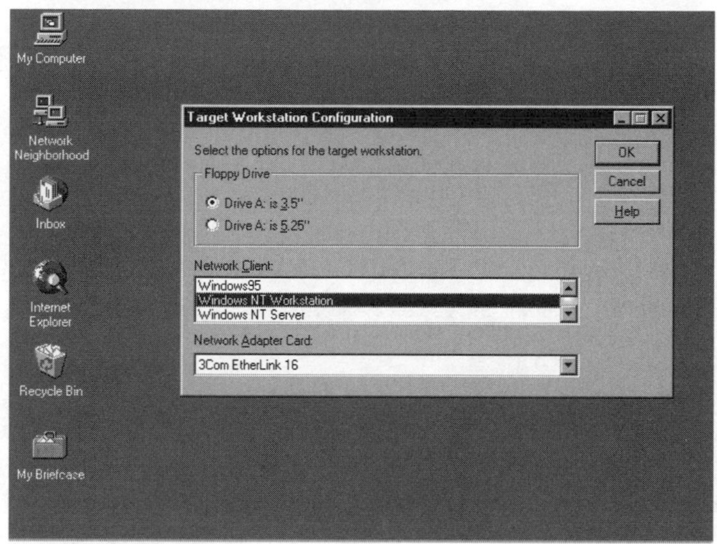

Figure 19.12. *A customized Target Workstation Configuration dialog.*

The next section that pertains to the over-the-net installation is the Warning Clients section (see Listing 19.4). This section contains the text that will be displayed whenever network client software is chosen for the network installation start-up disk. This text can be modified by adding instructions. I have highlighted the text that I modified in Listing 19.4.

See Figure 19.13 for an example of the resulting dialog created by a modification to the Warning Clients section. If any of the OTN values are not represented in this section, then no dialog is shown.

Listing 19.4. The Warning Clients section of `NCADMIN.INF`.

```
[WarningClients]
# ClientDir_n = text string
#  where n is a decimal number
#  more than one string can be displayed in the warning popup by
#  adding more lines, each with an incremented decimal digit. The
#  strings will be concatenated before display.
#
wfw_caption="MS Windows for Workgroups Installation"
wfw_1="You have selected the option to install Windows For Workgroups
➥ on your target workstation.\r\n\r\n"
wfw_2="You must purchase a separate license for Windows for Workgroups
➥ prior to installing and "
wfw_3="using Windows for Workgroups.\r\n\r\nThe license accompanying
➥ Windows NT Server does NOT contain a "
wfw_4="license to install and use Windows for Workgroups.\r\n\r\n\If
➥ you have already acquired a separate "
wfw_5="license for Windows for Workgroups, select OK to continue.
➥ Select Cancel to return to the Target "
wfw_6="Workstation dialog."
```

continues

Listing 19.4. continued

```
#
win95_caption="MS Windows 95 Installation"
win95_1="You have selected the option to install Windows 95 on your
➥ target workstation.\r\n\r\n"
win95_2="You must purchase a separate license for Windows 95 prior to
➥ installing and "
win95_3="using Windows 95.\r\n\r\nThe license accompanying Windows NT
➥ Server does NOT contain a "
win95_4="license to install and use Windows 95.\r\n\r\nIf you have already
➥ acquired a separate "
win95_5="license for Windows 95, select OK to continue. Select Cancel to
➥ return to the Target "
win95_6="Workstation dialog."
#
winnt_caption="MS Windows NT Workstation Installation"
winnt_1="You have selected the option to install Windows NT on your
➥ target workstation.\r\n\r\n"
winnt_2="Contact your network administrator for a license, and get the proper "
winnt_3="parameters that you will require to properly install Windows NT
➥ Workstation \r\n\r\n"
winnt_4="Select OK to continue. Select Cancel to return to the Target
➥ Workstation dialog."
#
winnt.srv_caption="MS Windows NT Server Installation"
winnt.srv_1="You have selected the option to install Windows NT Server
➥ on your target system.\r\n\r\n"
winnt.srv_2="You must purchase a separate license for each Windows NT
➥ Server system prior to "
winnt.srv_3="installing and using Windows NT Server on that system.\r\n\r\nThe
➥ license accompanying Windows NT Server does "
winnt.srv_4="NOT contain a license to install and use additional Windows
➥ NT Servers.\r\n\r\n"
winnt.srv_5="If you have already acquired an additional license for Windows
➥ NT Server, "
winnt.srv_6="select OK to continue. Select Cancel to return to the Target
➥ Workstation dialog."
```

The next relevant section in NCADMIN.INF for the over-the-net installation is the SetupCmd section. (See Listing 19.5.) This section provides the generated AUTOEXEC.BAT for the floppy disk, its final command, to kick off the setup program for the installed network client software. You should examine the command-line switches in the listing to determine whether they apply to what you want to accomplish. The switches for the WINNT program can be found in Chapter 6, "The Windows NT Installation Process."

Listing 19.5. The SetupCmd section of NCADMIN.INF.

```
[SetupCmd]
msclient=setup.exe /$
wfw=setup.exe /#
win95=setup.exe
winnt=winnt.exe /B /S:Z:\WINNT\NETSETUP
winnt.srv=winnt.exe /B /S:Z:\WINNT.srv\NETSETUP
```

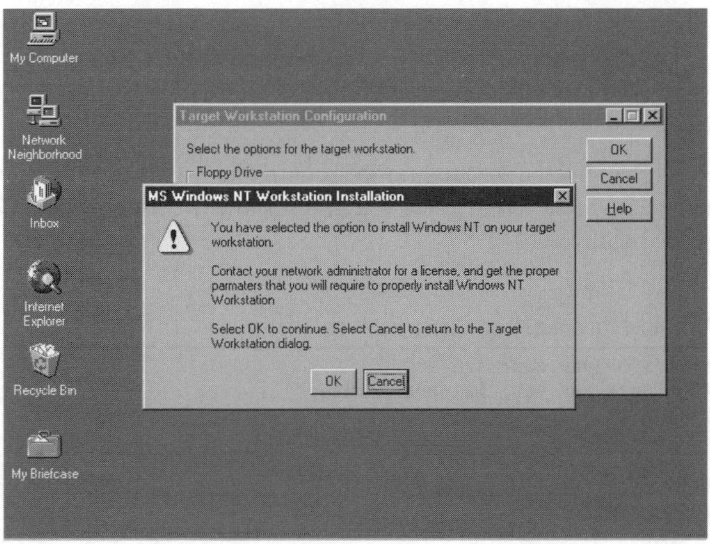

Figure 19.13. *The result of a modified Warning Clients section.*

You should examine the other sections in `NCADMIN.INF` as well. You will see that, depending on the protocol stack selected for use on the over-the-net installation, different commands are added to the `AUTOEXEC.BAT` on the floppy disk. You might want to add commands to this `AUTOEXEC.BAT` based on the topology of your network or to adhere to certain standards.

Tip: For instance, you might want to have an anti-virus program scan the client's hard drive at the time of installation. By adding an anti-virus program to the list of files copied to the floppy disk and adding the command to kick off the anti-virus scan, you can make a customized version of the network installation start-up disk.

Customizing the Make Installation Disk Set Option

As shown in Listing 19.6, the `NCADMIN.INF` file contains entries that pertain to disk images within the `Clients` share. The first entry shown in Listing 19.6 is for making disks for the Microsoft client.

To customize Network Client Administrator for making other types of disks, perform the following steps.

First, after deciding on what disks to make available, create a directory within the `Clients` share.

In this example the disk includes the latest network card drivers for a particular card and the directory is within the `Clients` share called `NIC`.

Within that directory is another directory called DISKS, and within that directory is a new directory called DISK1. If this software was packaged as a multiple disk set, create a DISK2 directory, then DISK3, and so on. A copy of the contents of the disk also appears in the \CLIENTS\NIC\DISKS\DISK1 directory.

The next step is to modify the NCADMIN.INF to accommodate this new disk creation scenario. The first modification is to add a section to NCADMIN.INF, as shown in Listing 19.6. The modified section is highlighted by bold type.

Listing 19.6. Disk label for a new installation disk set.

```
[Updated Network Driver names]
disk1=""New Drivers For Your Network Adapter""
disk1_label=NEWNICK

[msclient_names]
disk1_label=MSCLNTDISK1
disk2_label=MSCLNTDISK2

[ras_names]
disk1_label=DOSRASDISK1
```

The second modification occurs in the DiskSet section. The change is highlighted in Listing 19.7.

Listing 19.7. Modified DiskSet section.

```
[DiskSet]
#
#       list of the clients that have installation floppy "images" for
#       copying to a floppy disk(s) for floppy installation
#
# SubDirName=DisplayName
msclient=Network Client v3.0 for MS-DOS and Windows
ras=Remote Access v1.1a for MS-DOS
tcp32wfw=TCP/IP 32 for Windows for Workgroups 3.11
lanman=LAN Manager v2.2c for MS-DOS
lanman.os2=LAN Manager v2.2c for OS/2
nic=Updated Network Drivers
```

Now, with these modifications in place, you can choose the Network Client Administrator's Make Installation Disk option, and after identifying what share to use, the Make Installation Disk Set dialog (see Figure 19.14) will have the new disk definition.

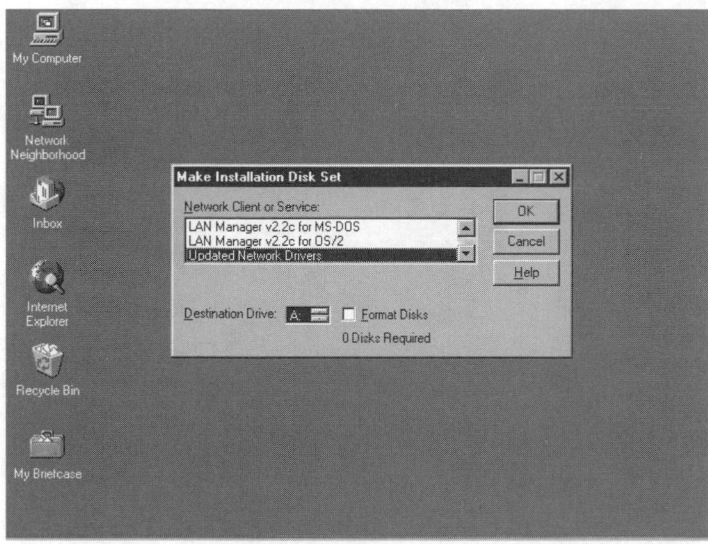

Figure 19.14. *The modified Make Installation Disk Set dialog.*

You can format the disks you are going to use for this process by selecting the Format Disk check box.

After choosing the option to creating a new disk, you will be prompted to insert a blank disk (see Figure 19.15). If you choose to format the disk, you will be warned about files being erased on the target disk, and then a quick format will occur.

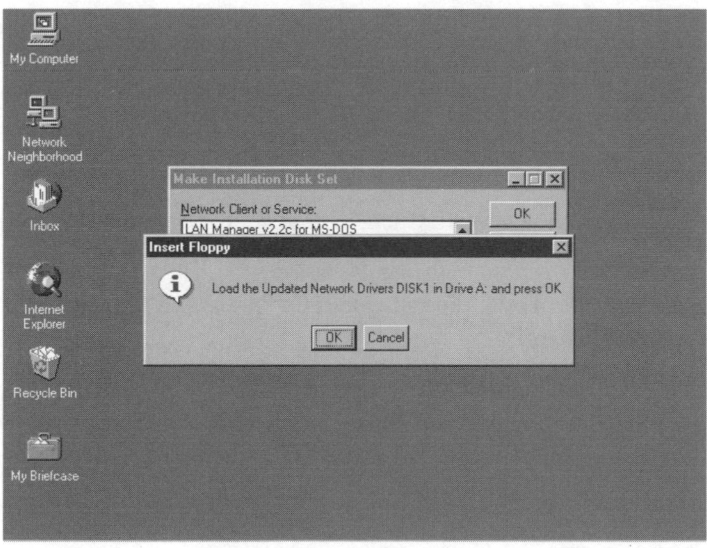

Figure 19.15. *Prompt for a disk.*

The files from within the DISK1 subdirectory will be copied to the disk, as shown in Figure 19.16.

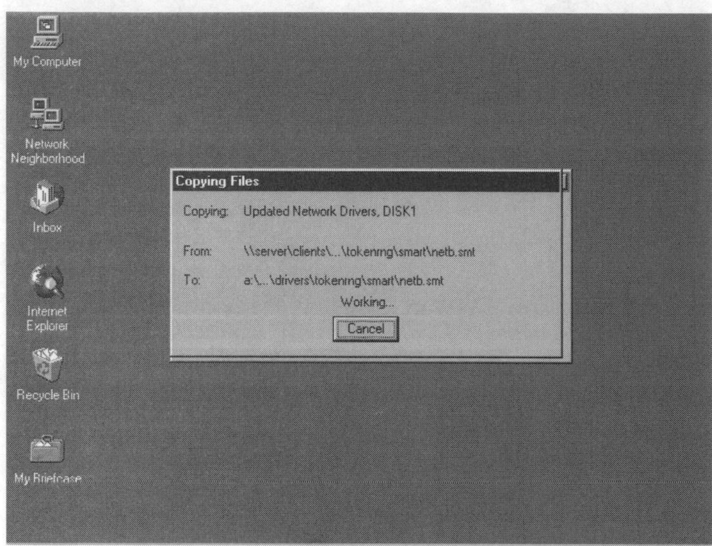

Figure 19.16. *File copy operation.*

Note: You can copy any files within the DISK1, DISK2, and so on directories to disk. Just be sure that the size of these directories does not exceed the capacity of your disk.

After the files have been copied, you will be notified to insert another disk, if necessary. If the process is successful, you will receive a confirmation, and you will be told how many files have been copied.

Summary

When properly utilized, the Network Client Administrator program can be one of the best tools a Microsoft Windows NT network administrator can have.

For example, you can use network installation start-up disks to control a roll-out of a Microsoft Windows NT–based network.

You can use the Make Installation Disk Set option for all types of tasks in addition to the ones that are directly related to creating disks for Microsoft clients. Just think of the possibilities!

PART V

Windows NT Domain Clients

Installing Windows NT Workstation

by Robert Reinstein

The task of installing Windows NT Workstation is very similar to that of installing Windows NT Server, so most of what was in Chapter 6, "The Windows NT Installation Process," will be repeated here. I'm including the installation process in its entirety so that you don't have to flip back and forth between chapters to get a full picture of the install.

In Chapter 9, "Capacity Planning," I examined the hardware requirements for Windows NT Server. Very little is different for Windows NT Workstation; however, Windows NT Workstation is limited to using only up to two processors. The overall memory requirement is also less than for Windows NT Server, but Windows NT Workstation still can use all the memory you can throw at it.

This chapter discusses these installation tasks:

- Preparing for the installation
- Installation methods
- Decisions to make during a Windows NT installation
- Joining a Windows NT domain
- Installing TCP/IP
- How to install network adapters, protocols, and services

This chapter also discusses how to configure a Windows NT Workstation as a network client, after you install the operating system.

As with Windows NT Server, the one most important task to prepare for a smooth install is research, which I discuss next.

Preparing for Your Installation

The success of your Windows NT Workstation install will depend on certain choices you make during the installation routine. But even before you think about that, you must be sure that you have chosen the proper hardware for your workstation.

The Microsoft Windows NT Hardware Compatibility List

The Windows NT operating system is particularly sensitive to hardware. That is why Microsoft publishes its Microsoft Windows NT Hardware Compatibility List (HCL). If you cannot find your hardware on the HCL that came with your copy of Windows NT Workstation, check Microsoft's Web site for an update of the HCL. Your hardware might be on the updated HCL. A new HCL is usually posted on Microsoft's Web site on a quarterly basis. You can also check with the hardware manufacturer to find out if its hardware has been submitted for testing by Microsoft and whether the hardware has passed Microsoft's compatibility test.

If you want to ensure a clean install of Windows NT Workstation, you will get this list and abide by it, because if you use hardware that is not on the list, if something fails down the road, you won't have any recourse with Microsoft, who might not offer you any technical support when you are running its operating system on unsupported hardware.

The hardware manufacturers that are represented in HCL have paid to have their hardware tested by Microsoft. You can rest assured that those manufacturers are also developing updated drivers for their systems, because they realize the importance of being 100 percent Windows NT-compatible.

The HCL covers the following hardware:

x86 architecture uniprocessor computers
x86 architecture multiprocessor computers
MIPS RISC architecture computers
MIPS RISC multiprocessor architecture computers
Digital Alpha AXP RISC architecture computers
Digital Alpha AXP RISC multiprocessor architecture computers

Processor upgrade products
PCMCIA-tested hardware
SCSI host adapters
SCSI CD-ROM drives
Non-SCSI CD-ROM drives
SCSI tape drives
Other tape drives
SCSI removable media
SCSI scanners
Disk controllers
Hard drives
Wide SCSI
Storage cabinets
RAID systems
Video capture adapters
Video display support
Network adapters
Uninterruptible power supplies
Multimedia audio adapters
Modems
Hardware security hosts
ISDN adapters
Multiport serial adapters
X.25 adapters
Third-party remote access servers
Keyboards
Pointing devices
Printers
PowerPC hardware

Although all types of peripherals, communications adapters, hard drive controllers, tape drives, and so forth are on the HCL, this is not necessarily a guarantee that all the items on the HCL will work together. This is where your research starts.

When I've installed Windows NT Workstation on a piece of hardware that I've never had experience with, I check the online services, such as CompuServe, and see whether any Windows NT issues are posted in the manufacturer's forum. Sometimes you'll catch a reference to a reputable computer, for instance, an HP Vectra VL3, and find that it is having a problem with a network card from, for example, SMC, which has numerous network adapters that are supported on Windows NT. If you can find any problems here that apply to your proposed configuration, you have the option of backing out of the troublesome piece and getting something else that people have had success with.

The next step is to go to the BBS or World Wide Web sites of all the manufacturers of the hardware components that make up your workstation and see whether they have released any updated drivers. Yes, the Windows NT CD-ROM ships with numerous drivers, but some drivers shipped on the CD-ROM in the past just did not work!

An excellent source of information is Microsoft's own Microsoft Network, where you can find forums devoted to Windows NT that are frequented by Microsoft engineers.

If you are using any cards that are not PCI or EISA, you need to know what their hardware settings are. This includes IRQs, DMA channels, and I/O addresses. Making a wrong choice when installing and configuring your network adapter during the Windows NT install can prevent you from being able to fully install Windows NT. Although it is possible to get through the installation process without fully installing network support, I'd suggest not having to backtrack after installation has completed.

Your disk configuration is very important. Early in the installation process you are asked where you want to install Windows NT Workstation. If you have a hard drive that has already been formatted (and chances are it has been formatted as FAT), you should consider changing your file system to NTFS. This way, you can take advantage of its extra security and the efficient way it packs files into less space than FAT.

Tip: Usually the only reason not to use NTFS is if you are planning to leave a previously installed version of MS-DOS or Windows 95 on the hard drive and want the option to boot to MS-DOS/Windows 95, or if you are installing an application on the server where the software developer recommends using FAT (I've seen it happen).

Also on the subject of hard drives, make sure that you have enough available hard drive space to accommodate the Windows NT Workstation install. A full installation of Windows NT Workstation requires around 100 megabytes of hard drive space. Additionally, you might require space for applications and for user directories. Windows NT Workstation requires a swapfile that is a minimum of 48 megabytes. Ideally, you can allocate more space for virtual memory, so make sure that you have all the space you need before you start your install. After Windows NT Workstation is installed, you can have multiple swapfiles on drives other than the boot drive.

Another consideration for installing Windows NT Workstation is the method of installation. The preferred method is booting from the Windows NT Workstation boot floppy and then following the prompts to insert the second and third diskette, until the installation is run from the CD-ROM disc. In some cases, this method will not be available because you don't have a CD-ROM drive that is supported under Windows NT. If this is the case, you do have an option, which is an MS-DOS–based installation routine. The executable is `WINNT.EXE`. It allows you to run a special installation routine that actually copies the installation files to a temporary directory on your hard drive and then proceeds to run the install directly from your hard drive. This method works only if you already have an operating system installed on your hard drive. If you do, however, have problems accessing your CD-ROM from Windows NT, you won't discover the trouble until you attempt to install using the floppy disks, only to find that after disk 3 the install program prompts you to insert disk 4, which does not exist.

You also should run `WINNT.EXE` if you are installing Windows NT Workstation from across a network. When you install from the boot disk, you don't have access to any network resources, so if the Windows NT Workstation CD-ROM has been placed on a shared CD-ROM drive, you will be forced to run `WINNT.EXE`. Bear in mind that this install requires an additional 80 megabytes of available hard drive space.

See Chapter 6 for a couple of flowcharts that can help you determine which method of installation to use.

This is the proper syntax for the `WINNT.EXE` command:

```
WINNT [/S:sourcepath /T:tempdrive /I:inifile]  [/B¦/C¦/F¦/OX¦/O¦/X]
```

`/S:`*`sourcepath`* specifies the source location of Windows NT files. This must be a full path of the form `x:\[path]` or `\\server\share[\path]`. The default is the current directory.

`/T:`*`tempdrive`* specifies a drive to contain temporary setup files. If a drive is not specified, Setup attempts to locate a drive for you. If you have developed a custom install script, you should use the `/I:`*`inifile`* parameter, which specifies the filename (no path) of the Setup information file. The default is `DOSNET.INF`.

Other switches you can use with `WINNT.EXE` are shown in Table 20.1.

Table 20.1. The `WINNT.EXE` command-line switches.

Switch	*Description*
`/B`	Specifies floppyless operation
`/C`	Skips the free-space check on the Setup boot floppy disks you provide
`/F`	Does not verify files as they are copied to the Setup boot floppy disks
`/O`	Creates boot floppy disks only
`/OX`	Creates boot floppy disks for CD-ROM or floppy-disk-based installation
`/X`	Does not create the Setup boot floppy disks

The third method of installing Windows NT Workstation is by using the `WINNT32.EXE` program, which is an NT-based setup routine that is very similar to the `WINNT.EXE` method but is run from a previously installed version of Windows NT Server or Workstation. See Chapter 7, "Upgrading Windows NT," for more information about the `WINNT32.EXE` program.

If Windows 95 is already running on your workstation and you insert the Windows NT Workstation CD-ROM, the Autorun feature of Windows 95 kicks off an introductory screen that gives you the option to install Windows NT Workstation or browse the contents of the CD-ROM. Windows NT Workstation does not upgrade a Windows 95 installation, so don't think you can do that. As I've said before, unless you require MS-DOS on the server, go with formatting the hard drives as NTFS. Of course, if you do this, you will be unable to run MS-DOS, Windows 3.*x*, Windows for Workgroups, or Windows 95.

Note: A Windows 95 to Windows NT Workstation upgrade path should be available with the next release of Windows NT Workstation.

Tip: Some people just copy the `\I386` directory from the Windows NT Workstation CD-ROM to an `\I386` directory on the local hard drive and then run `WINNT /B` just to avoid dealing with floppy disks. This method also enables you to make on-the-fly changes to your Microsoft Windows NT Workstation configuration after installation without having to find the original Windows NT Workstation CD-ROM. The space this `\I386` directory uses is minimal—only 80MB.

A Windows NT Workstation Installation Overview

Keep in mind that your first task, the installation, should result in a bootable, working Windows NT Workstation computer. Certain configuring should be saved until after the installation process, after the workstation is up and running. For example, there is no need to define any video mode beyond VGA, unless the installation program automatically detects it. An incorrect video driver could cause the computer to freeze during an installation process, which could force you to start the installation program all over again. Sound support, or any other peripheral device beyond the network adapter, should also be saved until after the installation process has completed and the computer has been restarted.

Make sure that you have read the section "Preparing for Your Installation," earlier in this chapter, and Chapter 9. Have a disk handy to make your Emergency Repair Disk, and try to be sure that your hardware, including your network interface card, if applicable, is functioning properly.

Note: If you have an existing network, sometimes it's easier to do a quick DOS install and then load the appropriate drivers to connect to your network, just to check your network card and, if necessary, your network card's and other cards' hardware settings. Don't expect a network card to function on Windows NT Workstation if it doesn't work with DOS!

The first portion of the installation, which is the character-mode portion, prepares your hard drive's master boot record by copying the necessary Windows NT Workstation system files.

The second part of the installation, which is the graphical-mode part, enables you to configure basic networking and sets up the parameters for the user's desktop and applications.

Note: A properly planned Windows NT Workstation installation should not take more than half an hour.

The Windows NT Workstation Installation Process

The first thing you need to determine before installing Windows NT Workstation is whether you want to have another operating system on the computer in addition to Windows NT.

If you are working with a system that already has an operating system on the hard drive, you might want to use the `FDISK` and `FORMAT` commands to start with a clean hard drive formatted as FAT. If you also need to be able to boot MS-DOS, Windows 95, or OS/2, you will be able to do that by using NT's boot loader. The boot loader is a menu, displayed each time a PC is started, that enables you to choose an operating system from which to boot. The full story on the boot loader is explained in Chapter 10, "The Windows NT Boot Process."

As you learned earlier, in the section "Preparing for Your Installation," you can use different methods for installing Windows NT Workstation. This section assumes that you are using the preferred method, which is to boot from the Windows NT Workstation Setup Boot Disk and install from the Windows NT Workstation CD-ROM.

Before you start the installation process, I highly recommend that you physically attach the computer to the network, if applicable. The network setup of the installation process will expect to see a live network, and it might not complete if you are not physically connected. It is also very important to be attached to the network if you want to join an existing Windows NT domain during the installation process.

Booting the Workstation

Insert the Windows NT Workstation Setup Boot Disk into your A: drive, which must be a 3 1/2-inch drive. After the system starts to boot from that disk, you'll see a message stating that Setup is inspecting your computer's hardware. Next, the blue screen present throughout the character-based portion of Setup appears, and messages across the bottom of the screen inform you that the Windows NT Executive and the Hardware Abstraction Layer (HAL) are loading. You then see a prompt to insert Setup Disk 2 into your A: drive. Press Enter to continue the installation.

The drivers and data that are necessary for the Setup program to proceed are then loaded. These are the fonts, locale-specific data, Windows NT Setup, PCMCIA support, SCSI port driver, video driver, floppy disk driver, keyboard driver, and FAT file system driver. After these drivers are loaded, you see the screen font change to a smaller font, and the actual booting of Windows NT occurs. The first line identifies the operating system by name, version, and build number. The second line tells you the number of processors Windows NT can see and the amount of physical memory detected and always shows that the multiprocessor kernel is loading. If you are running a single-processor computer, the next time Windows NT boots, the single-processor kernel loads; during installation, however, the multiprocessor kernel always loads.

The next screen gives you the following choices on how to proceed with your installation:

You can get more information about the Windows NT Workstation installation process by pressing the F1 key.

You can proceed with the installation by pressing Enter.

You can quit the installation process and restart the computer.

By pressing the R key, you can repair a previously installed copy of Windows NT Workstation that might have been damaged.

The last of these options is the one you should choose if you are unable to boot Windows NT Workstation or if you have made changes to your configuration and want to reinitialize the installation. You then can press R to be prompted to insert an Emergency Repair Disk. You can build the Emergency Repair Disk during this installation process or you can create it at any time from the command line.

Press Enter to continue with your installation.

Setting Up Your Hard Drive and CD-ROM Drivers

The next screen informs you about Windows NT's detection of SCSI and IDE controller chips. To have a bootable Windows NT Workstation system, you must have Windows NT install support for your boot device. You also need to have NT install support for the controller to which your CD-ROM drive is attached (of course, this might be the same as the controller for your boot device, but if they are different, you must ensure that support for both is installed).

You have the option of letting the installation process try to identify which devices are in your system (this process is known as auto-detection). If your controllers are identified properly through this process, you can be assured that support for your boot drive and CD-ROM will exist the next time the Windows NT Workstation installation routine reboots your workstation. If you have purchased a controller that came with its own set of Windows NT drivers or you know that the installation routine will not recognize your controller and you have a disk to use that contains the appropriate drivers, press the S key.

If you press S, the installation routine tells you that it did not detect any devices, and you then can press S again to choose from a list of drivers that come with Windows NT Workstation. The last item on that list is Other, which enables you to point the installation program to a floppy drive.

Tip: You might want to try auto-detection just to see whether Windows NT's native support includes support for your controllers. You should go straight to the S routine if your drivers are newer than the production date for Windows NT Workstation 4.0, which was July 29, 1996.

Tip: Another reason to choose the S option is if you attempt auto-detection and your workstation freezes up. It is possible for a workstation to seize during the auto-detection stage yet still be able to function properly through the entire installation process if auto-detection is skipped.

If you use auto-detection and no devices are found, you can choose from the list of devices that ships with Windows NT Workstation. Chances are that choosing from this list after trying auto-detection won't do you any good, however, because if you had a compatible device, auto-detection would have picked up on it.

If you do choose to use auto-detection, the installation program prompts you to insert Setup Disk 3 into the floppy drive. After you press Enter, the installation program attempts to load each SCSI driver to see whether it can detect your SCSI controllers. A list of devices found appears as they are detected. Not only are SCSI drivers loaded and tested, but some proprietary CD-ROM interfaces are also tested.

Assuming that auto-detection has found your controller or controllers, you now can press Enter to proceed with the rest of the installation, unless you want to install support for additional devices.

Note: I've seen many situations in which an IDE adapter for an IDE CD-ROM drive was not detected by auto-detection. This is something you can choose from the list of SCSI controllers. Even though the list is presented as a list of SCSI controllers, there is a choice, ATAPI 1.2, that is the proper choice for an IDE interface. It is not necessary to specify IDE for an IDE hard drive because this driver always is loaded during the installation routine, even if you don't have an IDE hard drive.

After you complete the process of identifying devices and you press Enter to continue the installation, additional drivers are loaded. This includes support for IDE and ESDI controllers, the NTFS file system, and the CDFS file system, and, if appropriate, support for a SCSI CD-ROM, SCSI hard drives, and SCSI floppy drives.

Windows NT Workstation Legalities

After the necessary SCSI or IDE drivers have been loaded, you are presented with the Windows NT Workstation licensing agreement. You might want to take the time to read this agreement, because it has some very interesting notes regarding Java and the notorious TCP/IP connections issue regarding Windows NT Workstation.

I'll take it for granted that you understand the agreement and that at the final page you pressed the F8 key to continue with the installation.

Deciding Where to Install Windows NT Workstation

After your boot drive is examined, a search for a previous installation of Windows NT Workstation is conducted. If a previously installed version of Windows NT Workstation is found, you are asked whether you want to upgrade or install a fresh copy in its own directory.

If you do have another copy of Windows NT Workstation and want to preserve that copy, you can choose to install Windows NT Workstation in its own directory, separate from the previously installed version. It is no problem to have multiple copies of Windows NT Workstation coexist on a computer. Each installation will still have an entry on the OS Loader Menu. See Chapter 6 for a flowchart to help determine where to install Windows NT Workstation.

Assuming that you don't have Windows NT Workstation already installed on this computer, you are asked to identify your type of computer, video display, mouse, keyboard, and keyboard layout. These choices are very similar to the choices you have when running the old Windows 3.*x* setup routine. Because Windows NT Workstation is so hardware-specific, however, it is critical that you don't make a wrong choice for any of these parameters.

Chances are that the appropriate choices for your computer will be shown on-screen, although the video display usually defaults to VGA. You will have the option to change the video display during the latter part of the installation, where your specific video chip can be auto-detected, and after Windows NT Workstation is installed.

If you are satisfied with the current choices shown, press Enter to proceed with the installation.

If a copy of Windows 3.*x* is found on your boot drive, the installation routine asks you whether Windows NT Workstation should be installed in the same directory. It is possible to have Windows NT Workstation and Windows 3.*x* coexist in the same directory, sharing applications and settings. Currently, however, Windows NT Workstation cannot migrate Windows 95 Registry settings, which might result in the inability to run the applications you had installed in Windows 95 on Windows NT Workstation without the need to reinstall the applications under Windows NT Workstation.

If an earlier version of Windows NT Workstation is found, you will be asked whether you want to upgrade that installation or perform a clean install to another directory.

You're strongly advised to install Windows NT Workstation into its own directory if you want to continue to run Windows 95 on the same PC. You will then need to reinstall the software for use by Windows NT Workstation if you want to use the applications from there. As previously mentioned, the next version of Windows NT Workstation is supposed to include an upgrade path from Windows 95 to Windows NT Workstation.

Caution: If you do decide to install to the same directory, keep in mind that it might be difficult to uninstall Windows NT Workstation and leave your old Windows intact. I therefore recommend, in all cases, installing Windows NT Workstation in its own directory.

Once again, I will remind you that if you need to run any of the other flavors of Windows on this computer, you cannot convert your FAT partition to NTFS without losing the ability of running the other Windows.

If an old copy of Windows is found, you must press the N key to proceed without installing Windows NT Workstation to the same directory. Press Enter if you do want to install Windows NT Workstation to the same directory as Windows.

If you have not yet told the installation program where to install Windows NT Workstation, you now will find a list of available partitions for installing Windows NT Workstation. Here is where you can choose to delete an existing partition or create partitions.

The list shows the drive letter assigned to the partition, the current file system for that partition, and the total space and free space on the partition. Unpartitioned areas of your hard drive also are shown. If you have decided to create or delete partitions, complete those tasks now.

Next, position the highlight bar over the partition to which you want to install Windows NT Workstation. Remember that this partition must be large enough to accommodate approximately 100MB of files. Press Enter. You are asked whether you want to format the partition as FAT, format it as NTFS, convert an existing FAT partition to NTFS, or leave an existing FAT intact with no formatting.

Next, the installation program asks for a directory name. By default, the name is `\WINNT`, but you can change this name if you want to.

Note: The previous version of Windows NT Workstation used the default directory `\WINNT35`.

After you select a directory name and press Enter, the installation program wants to check existing partitions for corruption. You can allow the program to perform an exhaustive secondary examination of those partitions. Press Enter to allow for both examinations, or press Esc to perform only the first test.

If this is the first time you are using this computer and you want to assure yourself that the hard drives are free from defects, let the setup program run its "exhaustive secondary examination." Although it takes up a lot more time for the install, which can be used as a coffee break, I highly recommend running this examination at least once. Then, if you need to reinstall Windows NT Workstation for some reason, you will not need to run the check again.

A "please wait" screen appears during the examination of the hard drive. After this process is completed, the file copy process begins.

The file copy process begins only if you successfully identified the device to which your CD-ROM drive is attached. If the installation program was unable to load the appropriate driver, the program prompts you for Setup Disk 4. In case you were wondering, there is no Setup Disk 4. So the next step is to abort the installation by pressing the F3 key and confirm the abort operation. Then you must find a drivers disk for your SCSI controller and start the installation process all over again. If you also specified SCSI drivers to be installed from a manufacturer's disk, you are prompted for that disk during this sequence.

After the copying process finishes, you are prompted to remove the disk from your floppy drive. You then can press Enter to proceed with the installation. You now have completed the character-based part of the Windows NT Workstation installation program.

The Windows NT Workstation Setup Wizard

Now your computer will boot Windows NT Workstation from the hard drive, and the graphical portion of the installation begins. You can file away those three disks until the next time you need to install Windows NT Workstation or until you need to use your Emergency Repair Disk.

When your computer reboots, you are presented with a menu of installed operating systems, which is the OS Loader Menu. The first item is your new installation of Windows NT Workstation 4.0. If you originally had MS-DOS or another copy of Windows NT on the boot drive, those operating systems are also listed as options on the menu. The OS Loader Menu is discussed further in Chapter 10.

The OS Loader Menu usually has a time-out of 30 seconds before a choice is made automatically, but for this installation, you immediately are launched into the next part of the installation.

You will again see the blue screen that identifies the operating system, version number, and build number. Again, under that information, you see the number of processors available to Windows NT and your physical memory, but this time the multiprocessor kernel is loaded only if your computer has more than one processor.

Note: Examine where Windows NT tells you which type of kernel is being loaded, because there have been instances in which a multiprocessor computer has not had all of its processors recognized by Windows NT. Therefore, if the single processor kernel is loaded, it's time to get some technical support.

The graphical portion of the installation program now starts by initializing, and then some more files are copied from the CD-ROM to the hard drive. The Setup Wizard then starts its three-part process.

In the first part, the Setup Wizard guides you through defining information about the computer, including the computer name, licensing information, and your choice of which of the optional components of Windows NT Workstation to install. The second part lets you define Microsoft Networking, which includes protocols, and services. The final part is setting up your local workspace.

The first part of the Setup Wizard routine is "Gathering information about your computer." Click the Next button. After some subdirectories are created within your Windows NT Workstation directory, your first choice in this graphical portion of the installation routine appears.

Windows NT Setup Options

Four setup options are then presented. The first is a typical installation, which automatically installs most of the Windows NT Workstation components that Microsoft has deemed the "typical" items for a Windows NT Workstation installation.

The second option is to perform a "portable" installation, which installs optional components that are useful for running on a Notebook.

The third option is the compact installation, which eliminates all the unnecessary components from the Windows NT Workstation installation. This choice results in a working operating system that is without any optional components.

Fourth is the custom installation, which allows you to pick and choose each option individually.

Next, you are prompted to enter your name and the name of your company, if applicable. This is standard procedure for all Microsoft installation programs. Enter these values and click the Next button.

The Windows NT Workstation registration process involves entering the CD Key. This is a number that appears on a sticker affixed to the back of the Windows NT Workstation CD cover. Enter this number and then click the Next button.

Naming Your Computer

The Computer Name dialog is now displayed. Here, you need to enter the name of the workstation. The workstation's name should not be confused with your account name. The computer's name must contain 15 characters or fewer, and it must be a unique name for your network.

Enter the name and then click the Next button.

> **Note:** Keep in mind that during the execution of the Setup Wizard, you can choose to go back to previous screens by clicking the Back button.

All PCs running Windows NT (both Workstation and Server) have an Administrator account. In the Administrator Account dialog you need to assign a password to that account for this computer. If you want to do this later, just assign a blank password for now by not entering anything—but do remember to assign a password to the Administrator account later. Make your entries, if applicable, and then click the Next button.

You are given the choice of creating an Emergency Repair Disk. Choose Yes, because you might need that disk to avoid having to reinstall Windows NT Workstation from scratch. Important information regarding your partitions and administrative information is stored on this disk. If you don't make a disk now or if any information changes that you want to back up to a new Emergency Repair Disk, you always can run the `RDISK.EXE` program from a command prompt.

Installing Windows NT's Optional Components

After clicking the Next button, you can install optional components for Windows NT Workstation by making selections on the Select Components dialog.

These optional components include Accessibility Options, Accessories, Communications, Games, Microsoft Exchange (which is not the Microsoft Exchange Server or client, but a trimmed-down version of the Microsoft Exchange Server client that can be used to attach to a Microsoft Mail For PC Networks postoffice, or for mail from online services), and Multimedia. Check or uncheck the appropriate boxes and click the Next button.

That finishes part one of the Setup Wizard. Part two handles setting up the networking components of Windows NT Workstation. Click the Next button to get started.

Setting Up Microsoft Networking

The first question the Setup Wizard asks is how your computer is connected to the network. If you are connected via a network adapter or by an ISDN connection, select Wired to the network. If this computer is going to communicate with your network via a modem, select Remote access to the network. If you intend to have both connections available, select both choices. This section assumes that you are selecting the Wired to the network scenario because most of the computers will be on a physical network. If this were a computer that had to dial in to log on to a domain, you would be prompted to answer questions about modems and other parameters, but in this step-by-step process, you will deal with a computer that is on a hard-wired network. Make your choices and click the Next button.

The Network Adapter Card selection process is next. Again, an auto-detect feature can attempt to recognize your installed network interface card. As was the SCSI identification sequence, this can be a point of failure for the installation routine.

> **Caution:** If you choose to allow for auto-detection and your computer freezes up, you must start the installation process from the beginning.

You also can elect to have a list displayed that you can choose from, or you can use a disk provided by the network interface card manufacturer. If you want to use auto-detect, click the Start Search button. Click Select from List if you prefer to choose your card manually or if auto-detect does not pick up on the card you have installed.

If you are using a disk provided by a hardware manufacturer, choose Select from List. The resulting dialog includes a Have Disk button. Use this option and the Setup Wizard asks you for the location of the disk.

After you add one or more cards to the list, click the Next button to select the protocols you want to install on your computer.

TCP/IP is chosen as the default protocol for your computer. Choose whether you want this protocol installed. If you want a fast, nonroutable protocol or you have an existing NetBEUI network, choose to install NetBEUI. NWLink, which is Microsoft's IPX/SPX-compatible protocol, is also available here. You can install as many protocols as you want, but the more protocols you install, the more overhead you have on your computer.

The Select from List button offers even more protocols, such as Microsoft's DLC protocol, which might be necessary if you plan on having 3270 connectivity that might require that protocol, or if you want to see a Hewlett-Packard Jet Direct card on your network. Microsoft's new Point-to-Point Tunneling Protocol (PPTP) and AppleTalk are other options here. Install PPTP if you plan on logging to a Microsoft network through the Internet. A Have Disk button also is available on this dialog because you might want to install third-party implementations of TCP/IP or other protocols.

After resolving your protocols, click the Next button to display a list of available network services that come with the Windows NT Workstation package. Some check boxes appear grayed out because those services are necessary to properly run Windows NT and cannot be deselected. A Select from List button again gives you additional choices, such as installing Client Services for NetWare, Microsoft Peer Web Services, and Remote Access Services.

All these network choices can be made after the installation of Windows NT Workstation, so if you want to try to get the computer running with minimum overhead, just accept the default settings to get you through the installation with less possibility of something going wrong.

After the network services are resolved, you are told that the network configuration is about to be installed. This is the perfect time to click the Back button to review your choices. If you are sure you have made the right choices, click the Next button to start the file copy and network configuration process. If you are using a network adapter card that requires switch settings, you soon are prompted for the IRQ, DMA, and memory address for that card. Other configurable options also are presented to you, but be sure that you know the settings for your network adapter card, because the network service attempts to start during this installation process.

Any configuration dialogs can appear, so answer them accordingly. For instance, if you choose to install TCP/IP, you are first asked whether a DHCP (Dynamic Host Configuration Protocol) server is available to provide you with a TCP/IP address. If you respond No, you are prompted to enter your IP address and subnet mask. If you are unsure what any of the right answers are, you can choose to proceed and clean up these network configurations after the installation of Windows NT Workstation finishes. The TCP/IP Properties screen includes a button labeled Advanced. Click this button to get to the Advanced IP Addressing dialog, which allows you to configure security and PPTP Filtering. Additional information on these options is in Part VI, "Networking with Windows NT." Click OK and then click Next to continue with your networking configuration.

The next dialog allows you to select and deselect bindings that have been created for you by default. After you have completed verifying the bindings, click Next.

After the configuration and file copying process has completed, Windows NT is ready to start the network. This is another good time to go back and check your settings. When you are certain you have configured the networking services, your network adapter, your protocols, and the bindings correctly, click Next, and Microsoft Networking attempts to start. Don't be concerned if you find that the computer is taking a long time to respond. Besides initializing the network adapter, it is also resolving bindings.

If the network services start properly, you proceed to the next dialog, but if they don't start properly, click the Back button a few times to go back to the network interface card dialog and check your settings again. Chances are that the network startup will fail if you gave Windows NT the wrong settings for your network adapter card or if you chose the wrong driver for your network adapter card.

Assuming that you have properly identified the card and its settings, you are now prompted for the name of the workgroup or domain you are joining. As a domain member, you need to name a domain. This domain name must be validated. If the domain cannot be found, you will not be able to proceed and will be forced to join or create a workgroup.

If you are joining a domain and have not already been set up as a member of the domain via the Windows NT Server Manager utility, you must place a check mark in the box labeled Create a Computer Account in the Domain.

To create a computer account in the chosen domain, you must supply the Setup program with an account that has the permission to add a workstation to the domain and that account's associated password. After you do this, the computer's account is added to the domain, and the second step of the installation program is complete.

Setting Up the Local Workspace

The Setup Wizard now sets up your menus and program groups.

The first item you are prompted for is your time zone. A graphical map of the world is shown, and all you need to do is choose from a list of time zones. If you are preparing this computer for another location that has another time zone, choose the one that is applicable. Unlike the same option in Windows 95, you cannot just click the map for the proper time zone. You must make your selection from the list.

Click the Date & Time tab to adjust the calendar and time settings for your computer. Then click the Close button.

Next, the Setup Wizard tells you whether auto-detect has recognized your video display chip. If it has, it asks you to acknowledge this information. If it has not detected your video display chip, stick with standard VGA, because you don't want to have to boot to an incomprehensible video display after installation has completed. You can click the Change Display Type button to see a list of video chips supported on Windows NT, and you always have the option to click the Have Disk button to use a hardware-manufacturer-supplied video driver. As I've said before, however, you want to get through this installation process without incident. Changing the display type is something that you can do after Windows NT Workstation is installed. In fact, as you might have already seen, a menu item has been added to the OS Loader Menu that enables you to boot Windows NT Workstation in standard VGA mode, just in case you are having a video driver problem.

Click the OK button, set the horizontal and vertical resolutions by moving the sliders, adjust the color depth, or click the List All Modes button to choose from a list of available resolutions and color-depth combinations. You also can set the refresh frequency here, and you can specify your preference for using large or small fonts in window titles and menu items.

Click the Test button to let Windows NT check the settings you have specified. After the test has completed, you can click OK to exit the video display configuration dialog.

After your video mode has been established, Windows NT starts its final file copying from the CD-ROM to your hard drive. Windows NT then sets up Windows Messaging and, if you already have your hard drive formatted as NTFS, sets security on the system files.

Before you create the Emergency Repair Disk, save your configuration information.

To create the Emergency Repair Disk, insert a 3 1/2-inch disk into your A: drive. The diskette will always be formatted for you, so just make sure that it is not write-protected. After the format, some files are copied to the disk. When the copying is finished, remove the disk, label it properly, and keep it in a location you will remember if you ever need to use it for recovery or when you need to update it.

Now you've finished installing Windows NT Workstation!

Your computer is now ready to reboot and run. Don't forget to make sure that the Emergency Repair Disk is removed from your A: drive. Click the Restart Computer button and your computer starts, ready for you to log in as Administrator, using the password you specified during Setup. You then can create users, create groups, share drives or directories, add printers, and do whatever it is you wanted to do with your Windows NT Workstation in the first place.

If you had specified that a partition would be formatted as NTFS or converted to NTFS, it is during this first reboot that the NTFS is created. During the installation, you were still working with FAT. You'll see the conversion taking place, so watch for it.

Check out the section "Examining Installation Problems," in Chapter 6, because a lot of common problems associated with installing Windows NT Server are the same as for Windows NT Workstation.

The Windows NT Workstation v4.0 Client

Of all the clients you can have in a Windows NT domain, the Windows NT Workstation client is the ideal client.

Why? Because not only is the configuration of networking on this client almost identical to the Windows NT Server settings, but Windows NT Workstation is totally manageable because it can join a domain and be administered remotely through the Windows NT Server Manager application.

This section highlights the client setup for a computer already running Windows NT Workstation 4.0.

Configuring the Client

During the installation of Windows NT Workstation 4.0, the client has the choice of identifying itself to the domain and handling all aspects of adding protocols, network adapters, and certain services.

Windows NT Workstation was designed to be a network client. If configured properly during the installation, there should be no need to enter the configuration dialog for networking unless you need to add or update drivers, protocols, or services.

Installing support to connect to a server requires knowledge of certain parameters, such as the appropriate protocol or protocols necessary to be part of the network.

The details of joining a domain and configuring Windows NT Workstation during the installation process were discussed in detail earlier in this chapter.

Although the Windows NT installation process steps you through network configuration, you must manually configure the Windows NT Workstation domain client if you have already installed the operating system without network support.

Adding your workstation to the domain requires the help of an administrator for the Windows NT domain. As discussed in Chapter 15, "Server Manager," the computer running Windows NT Workstation has to be added to the domain before the client can actually log on to the domain. Adding the computer to the domain can be handled either through the Windows NT Workstation Control Panel or by using the Windows NT Server administration tool, Server Manager. See Chapter 15 for instructions on using Server Manager. This chapter includes instructions on how to add the computer to the domain directly from the Windows NT Workstation computer. The Server Manager also can be used to remotely administer a computer running Windows NT Workstation.

Adding Networking Components Through Control Panel

From the Windows NT Workstation Control Panel, double-click the Network icon. The resulting tabbed dialog, shown in Figure 20.1, lets you enter all the information needed to enable a Windows NT Workstation to log on to a Windows NT domain, which includes your network adapter, protocols, and the name of the domain that you are a member of.

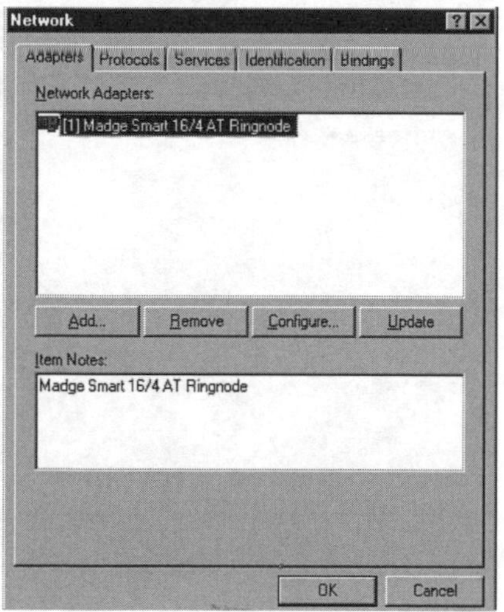

Figure 20.1. *The Network settings in Control Panel.*

Selecting Network Adapters

The first tab in the network dialog is Adapters, which enables you to specify one or more network adapter cards. Click the Add button for a list of drivers that ship with Windows NT Workstation.

Note: If a network adapter was installed prior to the installation of Windows NT Workstation, the network adapter may have been automatically detected and installed.

In most cases, you can simply scroll down the list and choose the appropriate card. However, you may be better off using updated drivers obtained directly from the hardware manufacturer.

If you are using drivers that are not supplied on the Windows NT Workstation CD-ROM, choose the Have Disk button and point to the path that has these newer drivers. If applicable, a configuration dialog will follow. Once you have configured the card, you can proceed to the next tab.

Installing Protocols

Click the Protocols tab to view the Protocols dialog. (See Figure 20.2.) The Protocols dialog enables you to specify one or more protocols that you will use to communicate with servers and, if necessary, other workstations.

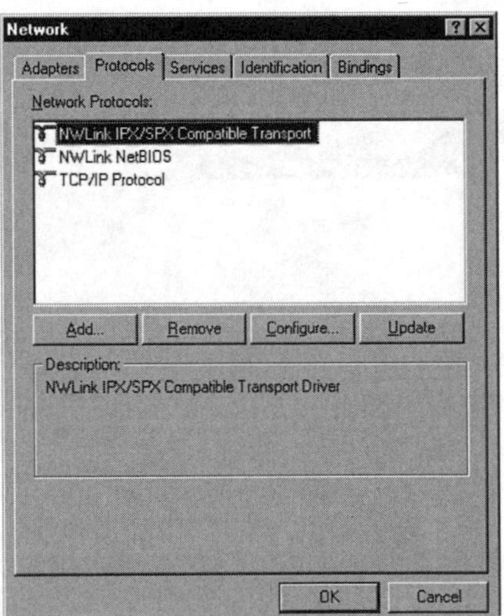

Figure 20.2. *Network Protocols dialog.*

In my example, I have added both NWLink, which is the IPX/SPX-compatible protocol, and Microsoft's TCP/IP. The configuration dialogs for these protocols are accessed by highlighting the protocol and then clicking the button labeled Configure.

Configuring Network Services

Clicking the next tab, Services, reveals the Services dialog, which will have some options already chosen for you. These are shown in Figure 20.3. These services will be sufficient to give the client Microsoft networking connectivity.

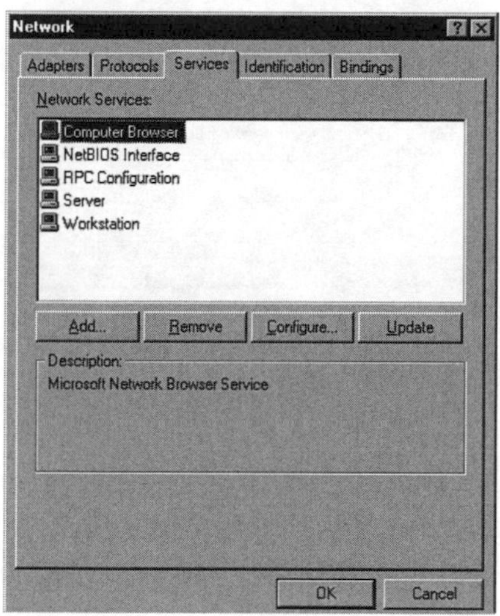

Figure 20.3. *The Network Services dialog.*

An example of the additional services that are included with Windows NT Workstation is Remote Access Services (RAS), which is explained in full in Chapter 27, "Troubleshooting the Remote Access Service (RAS) and Dial-Up Networking (DUN)."

Identify the Computer

In order to identify your computer to the Windows NT Server domain, you must have a unique name for the computer and specify whether you are going to log on to a workgroup or a domain. The Identification dialog, shown in Figure 20.4, allows those specifications to be made. When first entering this dialog, the original choices made during installation are displayed.

Click the Change button to modify the current entries. Here, you again will get a choice of which type of logon should be made when logging in to the workstation and the option to change the computer name. This computer name should already be defined as part of the domain. If this is not already done, however, a user with permission to add workstations to the domain—usually an administrator—may click the check box that will add the computer to the domain. When adding the computer to a domain, the user account and password for a user with the required permissions must be entered.

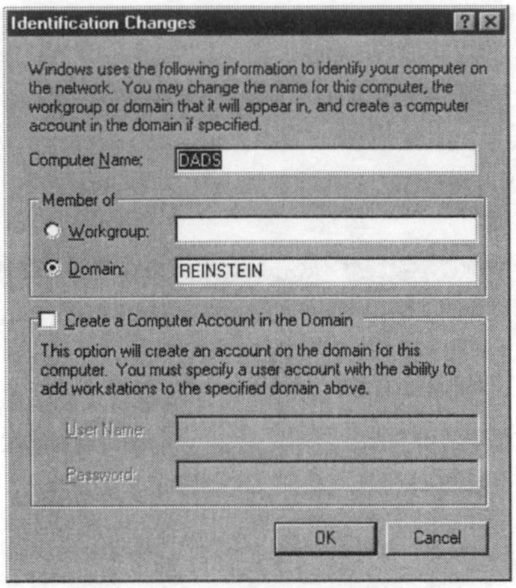

Figure 20.4. *The Network Identification Changes dialog.*

Review Bindings

The final tab in the Control Panel Network settings is Bindings. Clicking this tab brings up the Bindings dialog, which is shown in Figure 20.5.

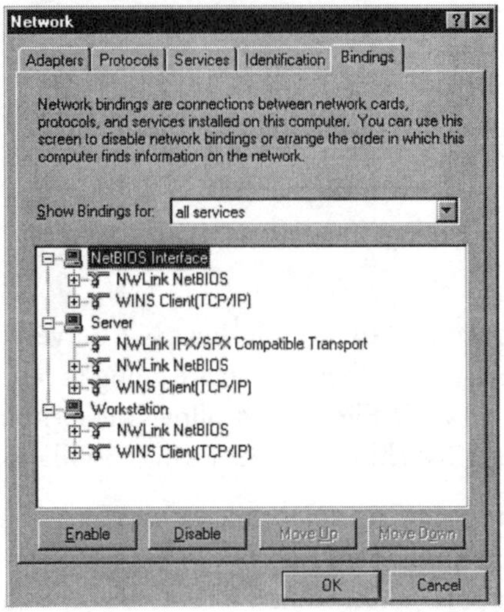

Figure 20.5. *The Network Bindings dialog.*

By default, all protocols are bound to all network services. You can disable or change the order of the bindings through the Network Bindings dialog.

It is important to review these bindings before finalizing your network settings, because any unnecessary bindings will create unnecessary overhead.

> **Note:** If NWLink is not needed for a RAS connection, you can disable the NWLink protocol from the bindings for the dial-up adapter that is installed for RAS.

Applying the Changes

Once these settings have been finalized, click the OK button, and, if necessary, you will be prompted for additional configuration information. You will then be prompted to restart the system with the new settings.

Updating Network Components

Using the networking configuration dialogs that I just discussed, you can update drivers, protocols, and services.

As new versions of a protocol or updated drivers for a network adapter are made available, you will want to implement them. There is no need to remove the existing driver, protocol, or service to implement these updates, because there is a built-in facility for such updates.

The method for applying updates for drivers, services, and protocols is the same in each case.

For example, if you want to apply an update to Microsoft's TCP/IP protocol, from the Protocols dialog, highlight TCP/IP. Then click the button that is labeled Update. You will be prompted for the path of the TCP/IP update. The original protocol will be overwritten with the newer version, and any obsolete files will be removed.

Summary

As with Windows NT Server, installing Windows NT Workstation requires careful planning. The hardware must be carefully scrutinized to ensure that the installation process will run smoothly.

Know how you want to set up your file system in advance. Be prepared to provide the installation program the necessary parameters, such as a computer name, domain or workgroup name, type of SCSI adapter, type of network adapter, and settings for the network adapter. Know what protocols and additional services you need to install.

21 CHAPTER

Windows NT Workstation 3.51

by Robert Reinstein

Adding Microsoft Networking support on Windows NT Workstation 3.51 is not much different from Windows NT Workstation 4.0. In both cases, Microsoft Networking is an integrated part of the operating system, Windows NT.

Detailed instructions for installing Windows NT Workstation 4.0 are provided in Chapter 6, "The Windows NT Installation Process," and the steps for installing Windows NT Workstation 3.51 are very similar. This chapter does not cover the process in as much detail.

When installing Windows NT Workstation 3.51, the user is prompted for all the information that is necessary to load the appropriate drivers for network connectivity. Attaching the computer to a Windows NT domain is also handled automatically during the installation process. Installing support to connect to a server requires knowledge of certain parameters, such as the appropriate protocol(s) necessary to be part of the network.

This chapter explains how to

- Add network support to a previously installed Windows NT Workstation 3.51
- Enable a computer running Windows NT Workstation 3.51 to obtain an authenticated logon from a Windows NT domain

> **Note:** Currently, Windows NT Workstation 3.51 has been discontinued by Microsoft, but there are many copies still in use.

Configuring Network Settings

The configuration of Windows NT Workstation 3.51 is handled by the Network applet located in the Windows NT Workstation Control Panel, shown in Figure 21.1.

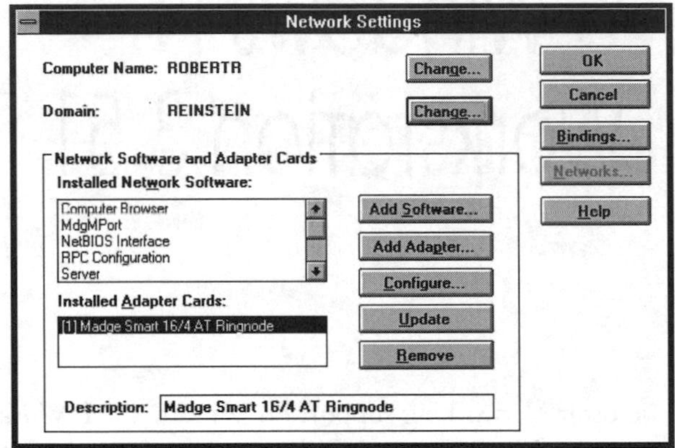

Figure 21.1. *Network Settings.*

Double-click the Network icon in Control Panel to open the Network Settings dialog that enables you to add, remove, or configure all the networking protocols, services, and adapters.

At the top of this dialog is the Windows NT Workstation computer name that was defined during installation. As with all computers on a Microsoft network, the computer name must be unique to the network.

Defining a Domain or Workgroup

Under the computer name is either a workgroup name or a domain name, depending on which of the two were chosen during installation.

Click the Change button next to the Workgroup or Domain name to bring up the Domain/Workgroup Settings dialog, shown in Figure 21.2. In this dialog, specify the name of the Windows NT domain that you are a member of or will be joining.

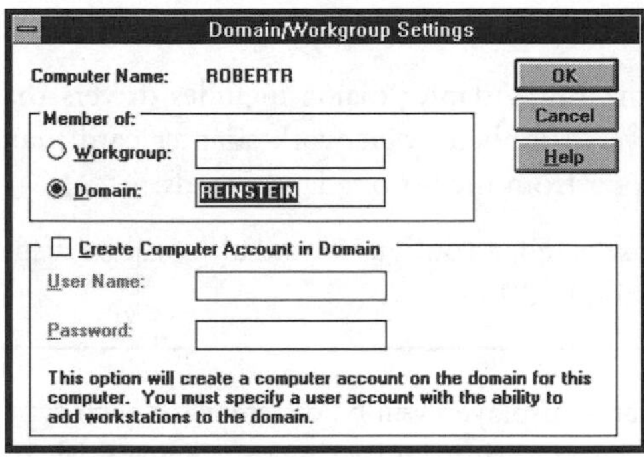

Figure 21.2. *Domain/Workgroup Settings.*

To change from a workgroup to a domain name, or change the name of a workgroup or domain, click within the Member of: area on the radio button that reads Domain. Then enter the name of the domain in the associated text box.

Before you can join a domain and get an authenticated logon, the computer must be added to the Windows NT domain.

This can be done from the Domain/Workgroup Settings dialog or by using Windows NT Server Manager. (See Chapter 15, "Server Manager.") Only a user that has the right to add a computer to a domain can accomplish this task.

To add the computer to a domain from the Domain/Workgroup Settings dialog, place a checkmark in the check box labeled Create Computer Account in Domain. Next, fill in the user account and password for a user who has the right to add a computer to a domain, usually an administrator.

Adding Network Client Support

In Windows NT Workstation 3.51, the installable network components are broken down into software and hardware. The software includes protocols, network clients, and services. The network adapters are hardware.

Click the Add Software button to display a list of software including TCP/IP, Remote Access Services, and Client Service for NetWare. Items can be added to the list by selecting the list item Unlisted Software.

After you have chosen the appropriate software, click OK. Now it's time to choose the network adapter card(s).

If Remote Access Services has been chosen as an Installed Network Software, then a dial-up networking adapter would already be listed as an Installed Adapter Card.

To add a network adapter, click the Add Adapter button.

The list displayed on the Add Adapter dialog includes drivers that come with Windows NT Workstation 3.51. Drivers supplied by network adapter card manufacturers can be added by choosing Unlisted Adapter from the list of adapter cards.

After an adapter card is selected, a configuration dialog will be displayed if it is necessary for the card to be manually configured.

Note: The dialog that is displayed will be different for each type of adapter. Settings may include IRQ, DMA, card location, and various settings specific to Ethernet or Token Ring.

Reviewing Bindings

By default, all protocols are bound to all network services. You can disable or change the order of the bindings through the Network applet in Control Panel, as shown in Figure 21.3, by clicking the button labeled Bindings.

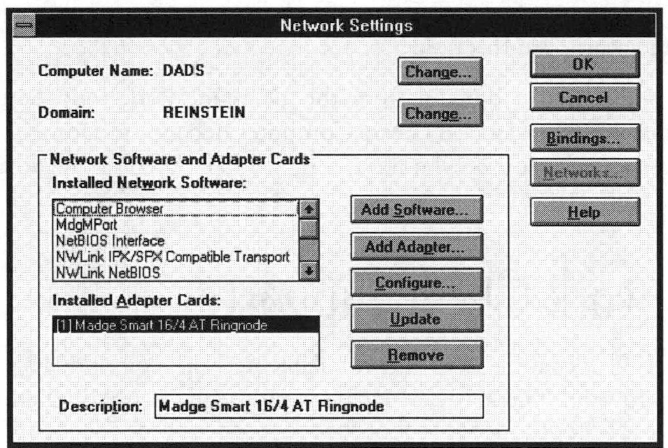

Figure 21.3. *The Network Settings dialog.*

It is important to review these bindings before finalizing your network settings, because any unnecessary bindings will create overhead that can be avoided. You can enable or disable bindings by double-clicking them. A lighted bulb indicates an enabled binding. Placing the most used bindings toward the top of the list also improves performance.

In Figure 21.4, a binding for the NetBEUI protocol is highlighted. This particular binding is for Remote Access Services. After double-clicking on this binding, the lightbulb icon goes dim, as shown in Figure 21.5.

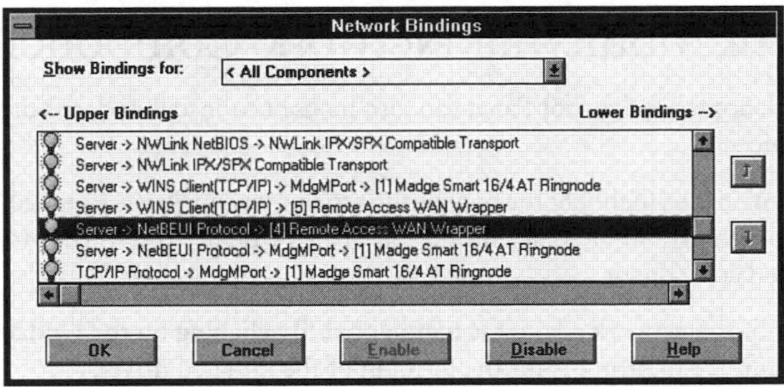

Figure 21.4. *An enabled binding.*

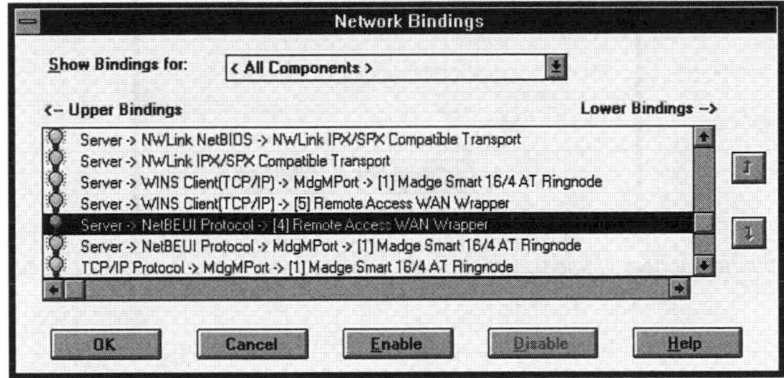

Figure 21.5. *A disabled binding.*

Applying the Settings

After all protocols, services, and adapters have been installed and added to the lists of installed components, click OK.

If any additional configuration is necessary, such as for the TCP/IP protocol, the configuration dialog will appear.

After the settings have been saved, you will be prompted to restart Windows NT. After the computer has been restarted, the network support will be installed.

When the system logs on to Windows NT, the From: field in the Logon dialog will become a drop-down box where you can select either the local computer name or the domain/workgroup name. Logging in to the domain name will give the Windows NT Workstation an authenticated logon to the Windows NT Server domain.

Updating or Modifying Network Components

The Network applet in Control Panel can also be used to install updated drivers, protocols, or network services.

To perform an update, highlight the previously installed version in the Installed Network Software or Install Adapters list and then click the button labeled Update. You will be prompted for the path of the updated component.

In Figure 21.3, the network adapter is highlighted. By clicking on the Update button, a dialog, shown in Figure 21.6, prompts for the location of the updated driver.

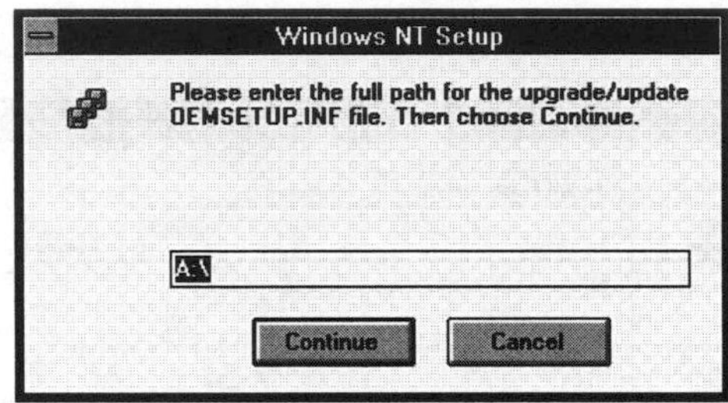

Figure 21.6. *Prompt for location of updated drivers.*

Summary

Configuring Windows NT Workstation 3.51 is essentially the same as configuring Windows NT Workstation 4.0 because the network settings have remained the same between versions; only the user interface has changed.

The easiest way to install Microsoft networking support on Windows NT Workstation 3.51 is during the original installation of the operating system; however, adding the support afterward is a very simple process.

The Windows 95 Client

by Robert Reinstein

With Windows 95, Microsoft has integrated its Windows NT domain client in such a way that makes it truly part of the operating system. One great thing about Windows 95 is its capability to be configured easily as a Windows NT domain client, along with a client for other types of networks.

The networking protocols that come with Windows 95 include Microsoft TCP/IP, which makes configuring Windows 95 as a DHCP client that much easier.

This chapter will discuss

- The necessary steps of installing support for a Windows 95 workstation that will act as a client on a Windows NT domain
- Automating Windows 95 installation by using the Batch Setup utility

Installing Windows 95

You can install Windows 95 manually, by either disks or the Windows 95 CD-ROM. You can also install Windows 95 by running the setup routine from a network share; that will be quicker, easier, and more standardized.

Regardless of how you install it, Windows 95 will install the client for Microsoft Networking by default. If you did not need the client on a previous installation, the network client support may have been removed, meaning that you will have to install Microsoft Networking after the fact. Adding Microsoft Networking to an existing installation of Windows 95 is discussed later in this chapter.

Windows NT Server's Network Client Administrator can create a share point on a Windows NT Server for the installation of Windows 95. A startup disk also can be created to get the client onto the server and point to the Windows 95 installation files directory. If the client is already a Microsoft Networking client running an earlier version of Windows, the upgrade to Windows 95 can also be performed using this directory as the source of the Windows 95 files.

An automated installation is also available, which you should use if you are going to be rolling out many Windows 95 workstations that will be connecting to a Windows NT domain.

Windows 95 Batch Setup

> **Note:** This section is not intended as a thorough explanation of this Windows 95 installation method, but is briefly discussed because it is a highly recommended method of installing Windows 95 clients on a Windows NT network. For more information, please check your local bookstore.

Windows 95 Batch Setup is very similar to the Windows NT Setup Manager in that it will create a script that can be used to answer almost all the responses that are needed during a Windows 95 installation.

If any information is not entered through Windows 95 Batch Setup when you run the installation program using the script that Batch Setup generates, the installation program will halt and wait for you to enter the information.

It is highly recommended that all possible information be entered through Batch Setup and that the resulting script be thoroughly tested.

Running Windows 95 Batch Setup

On the Windows 95 CD-ROM in the `\ADMIN\NETTOOLS\NETSETUP` directory is a program called the Windows 95 Batch Setup. Start this program by running the file `BATCH.EXE`.

When you run Batch Setup, the main screen (see Figure 22.1) will display numerous entry fields along with buttons that you will use to navigate through all aspects of Windows 95 setup.

Once you have identified the user and computer, click the Network Options button.

Network Options

With the Windows 95 Network Options dialog, shown in Figure 22.2, you can specify all aspects of the network setup that are essential to establish Windows 95 computers on the network.

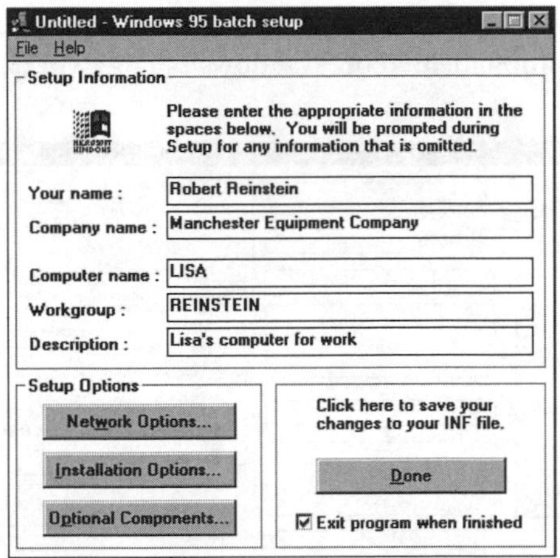

Figure 22.1. Batch Setup Manager.

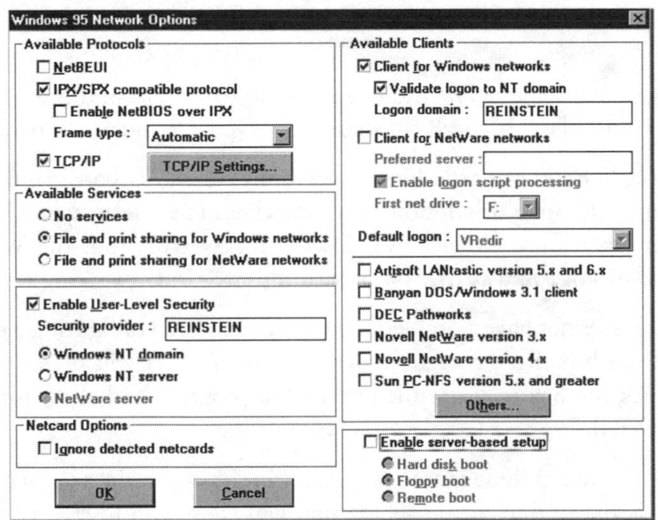

Figure 22.2. Windows 95 Network Options.

In the Available Protocols area, choose the protocols you want to install. When selecting TCP/IP, you must also click on the TCP/IP Settings button to specify whether DHCP will be used, or to specify addresses for the client computer, WINS, and DNS servers.

The TCP/IP Options dialog (see Figure 22.3) contains all aspects of TCP/IP settings. In this example I have opted to use DHCP because a DHCP server is located on the network, and chose to have the WINS settings inherited from DHCP. I have not chosen to point to a gateway or to use DNS.

Chapter 29, "Windows NT and TCP/IP," provides you with detailed information about the protocol and how it is implemented on Windows NT networks.

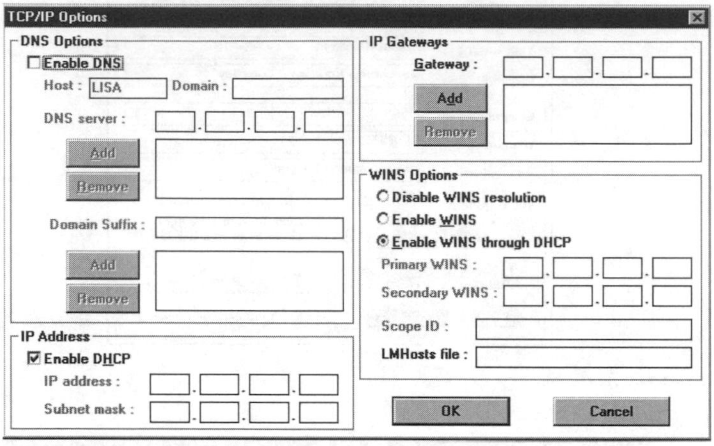

Figure 22.3. *TCP/IP settings.*

You may choose to install the File and Print sharing services from this dialog. It is recommended that you do not use the File and Print sharing for NetWare networks on a Microsoft network.

If you do enable File and Print sharing for Microsoft Networks, consider the Enabling User-level Security option. Choosing this option allows the client to set security levels on local shares based on usernames taken from either a Windows NT server or from the Windows NT domain. Otherwise, security is based strictly on password protection.

If Windows 95 does not have a problem auto-detecting and configuring a network adapter, then do not check the box that says Ignore detected netcards. If you prefer to make these settings manually, check the box to pause the installation program and allow for manual setup of the network adapter(s).

Of special importance in these settings is the area in the upper-right corner that is titled Available Clients. This is the section of this dialog that will allow you to specify that the Windows 95 workstation will connect to a Windows NT domain.

The box labeled Client for Microsoft Networks must be checked, as well as the box labeled Validate Logon to NT Domain. Be sure to specify the proper Logon Domain to ensure that this client will obtain a logon.

The last area in the Network Options is Enable Server-based Setup. Use this only if you want the client to use a shared copy of Windows 95 located on a server.

When you have finished selecting the Network Options, click the OK button and then click the Installation Options button.

Installation Options and Optional Components

The Windows 95 Installation Options dialog (see Figure 22.4) offers settings for most of the other aspects of the Windows 95 installation. One option, the Type of installation, will determine whether you will have access to the Optional Components screen. Only if Custom is selected from the list of installation types will you have access to the Optional Components screen, as shown in Figure 22.5.

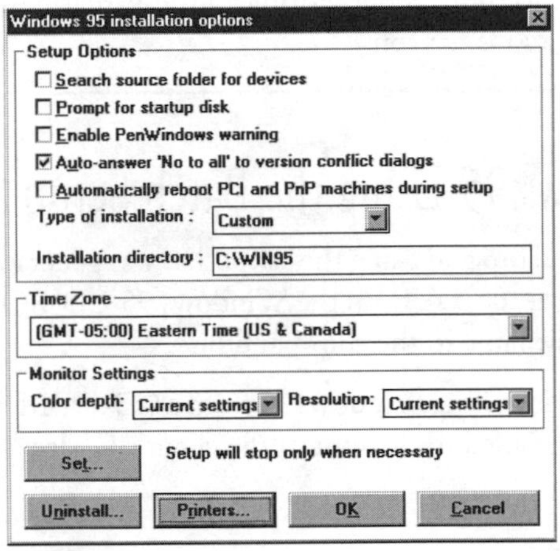

Figure 22.4. *Windows 95 Installation Options dialog.*

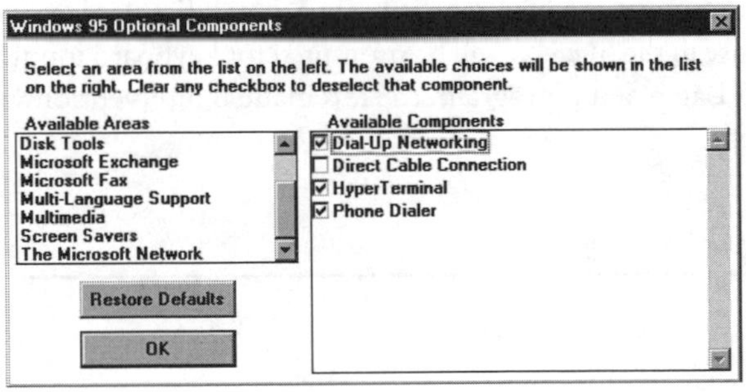

Figure 22.5. *Windows 95 Optional Components dialog.*

After you have made your choices on the Windows 95 Installation Options screen, click the OK button to return to the Windows 95 Batch Setup main screen.

If you chose an installation type of Custom, you can click on the Optional Components button and choose the individual applications, accessories, and files that are available for Windows 95. Once you complete this, click the OK button.

To save your file, click the Done button. You will be prompted for a filename and path to save the file.

Listing 22.1 is the file that I created using Windows 95 Batch Setup. Note the [Network] section of the file, where you will have to manually change the Computer Name and Description for each computer for which you will use this script.

Tip: You may want to think about writing a little Visual Basic application that will make these small modifications for you.

Installing Windows 95 Using the Batch Setup Script

Running Windows 95 setup and using the script that was generated by Windows 95 Batch Setup is as simple as running `SETUP.EXE` from the Windows 95 CD-ROM, disks, or network share and adding the path and filename to the command line.

For instance, if you are installing Windows 95 from a CD-ROM, which is your F: drive, and have the Batch Setup script copied to the root of the client's C: drive, you can run

```
F:\WIN95\SETUP C:\BSETUP.INF
```

If the Batch Setup script is not found, the installation program will not run.

If the Batch Setup script is found, the Windows 95 setup program will appear to run normally, but instead of prompting you for keyboard input, it will first look at the `BSETUP.INF` file. If there is no valid response in the file, you will be prompted for keyboard input. So the more you put into the Windows 95 Batch Setup program, the less manual intervention will be required during the actual installation.

Listing 22.1. Windows 95 Batch Setup.

```
[BatchSetup]
Version=1.0a
SaveDate=10/21/96

[Setup]
Express=1
InstallDir="C:\WIN95"
EBD=0
ChangeDir=0
OptionalComponents=1
Network=1
System=0
CCP=0
CleanBoot=0
Display=0
PenWinWarning=0
InstallType=3
```

```
DevicePath=0
TimeZone="Eastern"
Uninstall=0
VRC=0
NoPrompt2Boot=0

[NameAndOrg]
Name="Robert Reinstein"
Org="Manchester Equipment Company"
Display=0

[Network]
ComputerName="LISA"
Workgroup="REINSTEIN"
Description="Lisa's computer for work"
Display=0
Clients=VREDIR
Protocols=NWLINK, MSTCP
Services=VSERVER
IgnoreDetectedNetCards=0
Security=domain
PassThroughAgent="REINSTEIN"

[NWLINK]
FrameType=4
NetBIOS=0

[MSTCP]
DHCP=1
DNS=0
WINS=DHCP
Hostname=LISA

[NWREDIR]
FirstNetDrive=F:
ProcessLoginScript=1

[VREDIR]
LogonDomain="REINSTEIN"
ValidatedLogon=1

[OptionalComponents]
"Accessibility Options"=0
"Briefcase"=0
"Calculator"=1
"Character Map"=0
"Clipboard Viewer"=0
"Desktop Wallpaper"=0
"Document Templates"=1
"Games"=0
"Mouse Pointers"=0
"Net Watcher"=0
"Object Packager"=1
"Online User's Guide"=0
"Paint"=1
"Quick View"=0
"System Monitor"=0
"System Resource Meter"=0
```

continues

Listing 22.1. continued

```
"Windows 95 Tour"=0
"WordPad"=1
"Dial-Up Networking"=1
"Direct Cable Connection"=0
"HyperTerminal"=1
"Phone Dialer"=1
"Backup"=0
"Defrag"=1
"Disk compression tools"=1
"Microsoft Exchange"=0
"Microsoft Mail Services"=0
"Microsoft Fax Services"=0
"Microsoft Fax Viewer"=0
"Central European language support"=0
"Cyrillic language support"=0
"Greek Language support"=0
"Audio Compression"=1
"CD Player"=1
"Jungle Sound Scheme"=0
"Media Player"=1
"Musica Sound Scheme"=0
"Robotz Sound Scheme"=0
"Sample Sounds"=0
"Sound Recorder"=1
"Utopia Sound Scheme"=0
"Video Compression"=1
"Volume Control"=1
"Additional Screen Savers"=0
"Flying Windows"=1
"The Microsoft Network"=0
```

Note: At two points during the Windows 95 installation program, the user is told to remove the disk if one is in drive A:. Using a Batch Setup script, you will not get those prompts, so be sure to remove any disks before you install or, if you are installing from disks, remove the disk each time the PC reboots.

Installing Microsoft Networks Support

By default, when you install Windows 95, it will automatically set up support for Microsoft Networks.

If you are upgrading an existing Windows for Workgroups installation that has support for Microsoft Networks, those settings will be carried over.

But on a new install, sometimes people will deselect the support for Microsoft Networks so that they can run Windows 95 without that overhead. If this is the case, then Microsoft Networks support must be added to the Windows 95 configuration.

Installing Microsoft Networks Support on an Existing Windows 95 Installation

The Windows 95 Control Panel has a Network icon that contains all the settings that are pertinent to setting up the user for access to a Windows NT domain, among other networks. It is also the place to install and configure networking protocols, peer-to-peer networking, and other networking services that Windows 95 and third-party developers offer.

The following description of the Network configuration dialog includes tasks that can be performed during the initial installation of Windows 95 or after Windows 95 has been installed.

During a Windows 95 installation, you will be prompted for each component to be installed. The process that I describe here is for manually adding Microsoft Networks support using the Network applet in the Windows 95 Control Panel.

The installation process of the client software is very similar to the Windows for Workgroups client support installation. Windows 95 was designed to better fit into heterogeneous networks, however, and Microsoft Networks is only one of many types of network support that can be installed through the network setup portion of the Windows 95 installation or the Networks applet in Control Panel.

Windows 95 introduces the "Network Component." These components include Network Clients, Network Adapters, protocol stacks, and network services.

Windows 95 uses the protected-mode virtual device driver `VREDIR.VXD` so that the Windows 95 workstation can communicate with any Microsoft Networks-compatible computer, including other Windows 95 workstations, Windows NT servers and workstations, Windows for Workgroups workstations, and MS-DOS computers running the Workgroup Add-on for MS-DOS.

The Network dialog, shown in Figure 22.6, has three tabs. The first tab, Configuration, must be selected to add Microsoft Networks support.

As I mentioned during a Windows 95 installation, you will be asked if you want to participate in Microsoft Networking. If you choose Yes, the Client for Microsoft Networks will automatically install.

From a previously installed version of Windows 95, click the Add button in the Network dialog. This displays the Select Network Component Type dialog. (See Figure 22.7.)

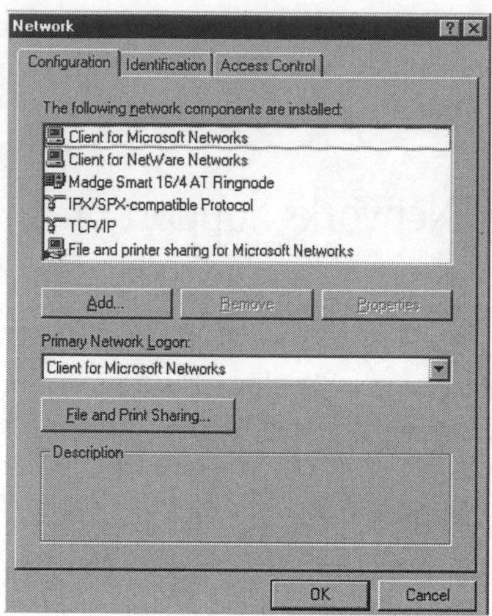

Figure 22.6. *Windows 95 Network dialog.*

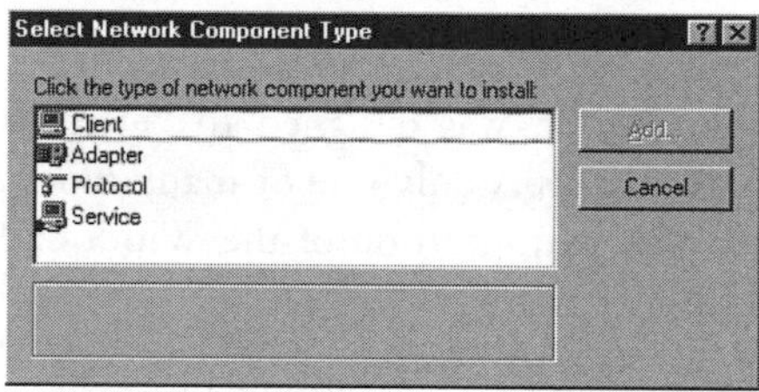

Figure 22.7. *The Select Network Component Type dialog.*

Select Client from the list and click on Add. Windows 95 has many choices for network clients, including Novell, Banyan, and SunSoft clients. Choose Microsoft from the Manufacturers list, and highlight Client for Microsoft Networks in the Network Clients list. (See Figure 22.8.) Click the OK button and the Client for Microsoft Networks will now appear on the list of installed Network Components. By default, the IPX and NetBEUI protocols will be installed.

If you want to remove the default protocols from the Network dialog, highlight the protocol you want to remove and click the Remove button.

To add a protocol, click the Add button and choose Protocol from the Select Network Component Type dialog. (See Figure 22.7.)

The Select Network Protocol dialog (see Figure 22.9) lists protocol manufacturers on the left, and the available protocols on the right. For clients of a Windows NT domain, when you are adding a protocol, be sure to select Microsoft as the manufacturer. The protocols listed as manufactured by Microsoft are all included with Windows 95 and are compatible with Windows NT Server.

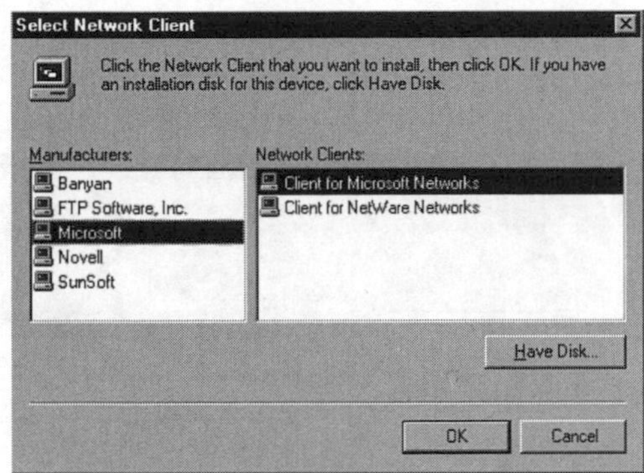

Figure 22.8. *The Select Network Client dialog.*

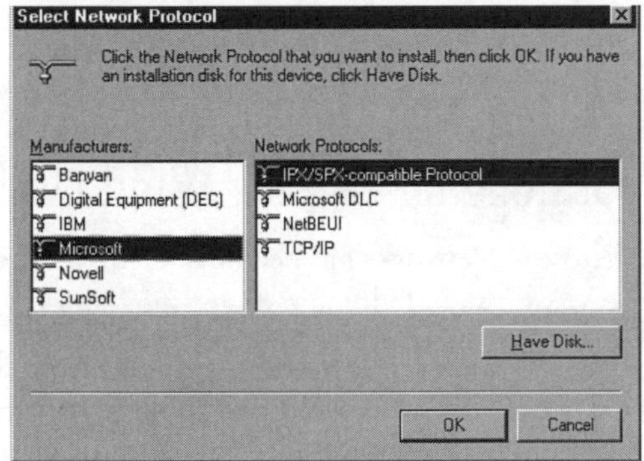

Figure 22.9. *The Select Network Protocol dialog.*

Usually a network adapter will be sensed automatically when you start Windows 95 with the adapter already installed, though you can use the Select Network Adapter dialog to add drivers from network adapters before you actually install the card or to add support for an adapter that Windows 95 did not sense.

The steps that I have described will enable your computer for Microsoft Networks the next time you restart Windows 95.

In addition to enabling the basics, you can also add services, such as File and Print Sharing for Microsoft Networks, which enables the client computer to make its locally attached hard drive(s), CD-ROM (if applicable), and printers available to other Microsoft Networks-enabled clients.

To add a service, click Add from the Network dialog, then select Services from the Select Network Component list. File and Printer Sharing for Microsoft Networks will appear to the right of the Select Network Service dialog (see Figure 22.10) if Microsoft is selected on the left. Other services include File and Printer Sharing for NetWare Networks, with which you can emulate a NetWare server and support attaching directly to a printer attached to a Hewlett-Packard JetDirect device, among other services.

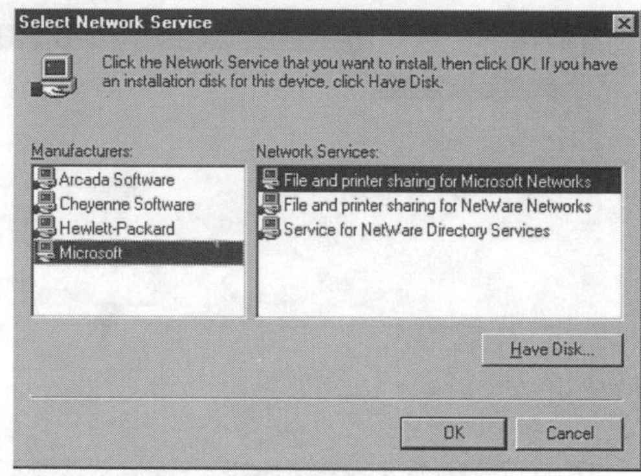

Figure 22.10. *The Select Network Service dialog.*

Adding Support for Logging On to a Windows NT Domain

After the Client for Microsoft Networks has been installed, you need to configure it so that the client can log on to the Windows NT domain each time Windows 95 is started.

To configure the Client for Microsoft Networks, highlight Client for Microsoft Networks in the list of installed Network Components. Click the Properties button to bring up the Client for Microsoft Network Properties dialog. (See Figure 22.11.) With this dialog, you can tell Windows 95 to log you on to the named Windows NT domain and how to restore persistent connections each time Windows 95 is started.

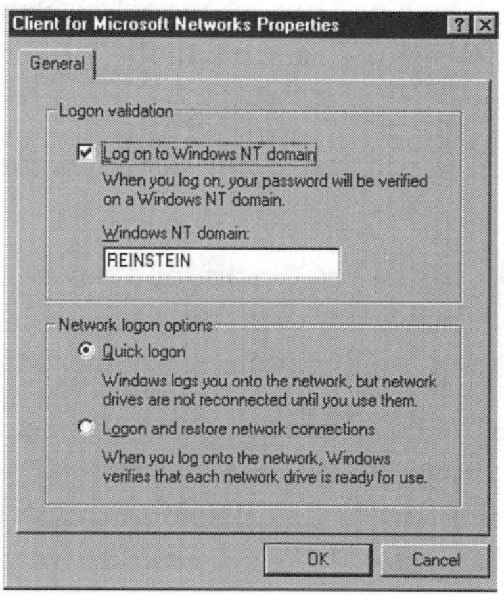

Figure 22.11. *Client for Microsoft Network Properties dialog.*

When you choose a Quick Logon, the Network Client will not verify attached drives until you actually try to use the network shares. This will slow down the first time you go to access a network share, but speeds up the logon process. Click the OK button to save these settings, and you're well on your way to establishing yourself as a network client.

> **Note:** Password caching must not be disabled as a system policy for Quick Logon to work.

Next, click the Identification tab to identify the computer to the network.

The Identification dialog (see Figure 22.12) is where you name your computer or rename this computer. You can use the Workgroup field for peer-to-peer networking, though in this case, you would name the Windows NT domain in which the client is going to be participating. The last field, `Description`, is strictly a comment field and will help the Windows NT administrators to further identify this computer.

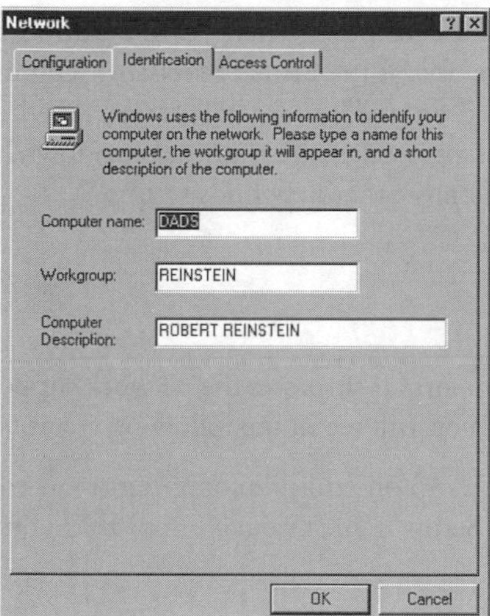

Figure 22.12. *Network identification.*

The third and final tab, Access Control, is only used when you have installed the File and Print Sharing for Microsoft Networks. With this tab, you can specify whether you want to use the user list and group list from your Windows NT domain to identify security on the shared resources on your computer.

If you do want to share a locally attached printer for only a select group of people, you must enable user-level security so that you can specify the user accounts that can access the printer.

By only granting use of the printer to the Administrator, the Administrator can set up a print queue on a Windows NT server and grant permissions for the server's queue.

Synchronizing User Account Names

When installing Windows 95, the user is asked for a logon name and password for Windows 95. This is the first item that you need to consider when readying a client for access to a Windows NT domain. To use Microsoft's single logon feature, the Windows 95 username should be the same as the username set up on the Windows NT domain user account. This way, when the client logs on to the network, the same username will be used for logging on to the actual workstation. Additionally, if support for other networks is going to be installed, using the same username for all networks and for the Windows 95 workstation will enable the single logon feature.

If these usernames are not synchronized between the Windows 95 logon, the Windows NT domain logon, and any other network logons, the user will be prompted for the username for each attachment where that username does not exist. This is not necessarily the case for clients who have different usernames for Windows 95 and Windows NT Server, but this will be discussed in the following discussion of the Primary Network Logon. If necessary, you can synchronize passwords via the Password applet in the Windows 95 Control Panel.

If you are installing support for other networks in addition to Microsoft Networks, you must designate Microsoft Networks as the Primary Network Logon to take advantage of user profiles and system policies stored on a Windows NT Server. Having the Primary Network Logon as Microsoft Networks will also make sure that the Windows NT Server domain logon script, if available, will be run after any other network's scripts.

Summary

Windows 95 network support far surpasses the network support that is offered for Microsoft 16-bit operating systems, as you will see in the following chapters.

When you install Windows 95 on multiple computers that require Windows NT domain access, the Windows 95 Batch Setup is an invaluable tool that you should seriously evaluate for this deployment.

The Windows for Workgroups Client

by Robert Reinstein

Microsoft released Windows for Workgroups as a network-ready version of Windows 3.1.

Enabling a Windows for Workgroups computer as a client for Windows NT domain is a fairly simple process, especially if Windows for Workgroups has already been configured for its built-in, peer-to-peer networking.

Whether it's a first-time installation of Windows for Workgroups or an existing installation, enabling the Microsoft Networking client is achieved in the same manner.

This chapter will explain

- How to enable Windows for Workgroups as a Windows NT domain client
- Adding the TCP/IP protocol to Windows for Workgroups

Installing Support for Microsoft Networks

From an already installed Windows for Workgroups, locate the Network Setup program icon in the Networks program group.

During the Windows for Workgroups installation program, you will be presented with the Network Setup dialog, which is the same as the Network Setup program. Within this dialog, tell Windows for Workgroups that you want to install support for Microsoft Networking.

Note: Figure 23.1 depicts a completed Network Setup. When first run, Network Setup will show that no network support is installed or, in the case of the initial installation of Windows for Workgroups, it will default to installing support for Microsoft Networks.

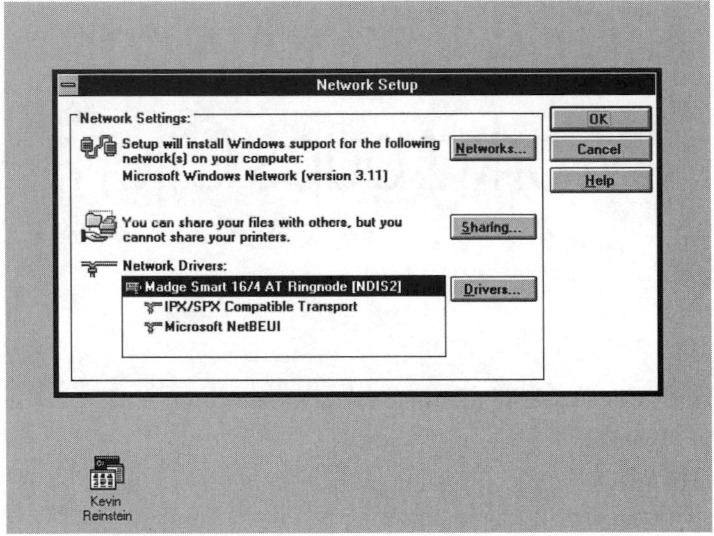

Figure 23.1. *The Network Setup program.*

Click the Networks button to open the Networks dialog (see Figure 23.2), where you can install support for a Windows NT domain by choosing the option Install Microsoft Windows Network. Once you have completed this, click the OK button to return to Network Setup.

Because Windows for Workgroups includes support for peer-to-peer networking, you can choose to create shares on the client computer and make printers attached to the computer available to the network.

You can choose to share files and printers by clicking the Sharing button that displays the Sharing dialog. (See Figure 23.3.) From here, click the checkbox for each option that you want to enable, then click the OK button to return to Network Setup.

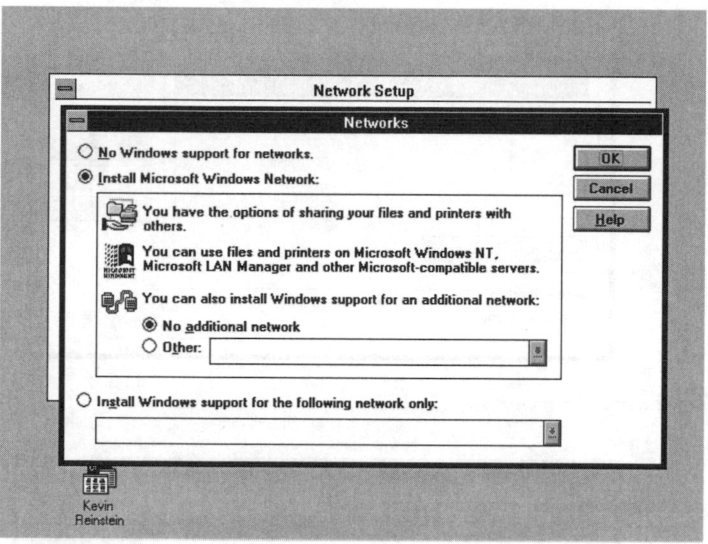

Figure 23.2. *Install Microsoft Windows Network.*

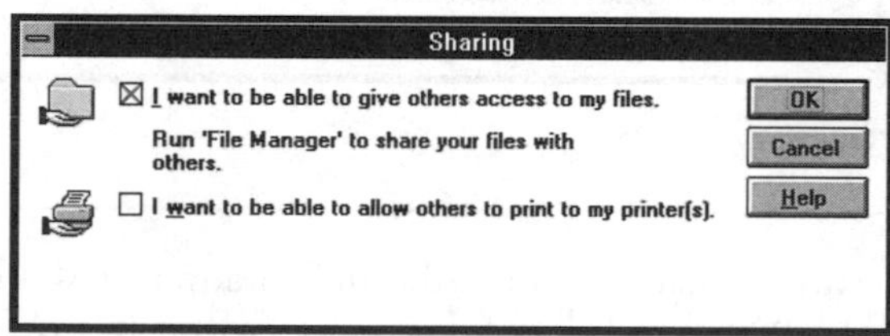

Figure 23.3. *The file and printer Sharing dialog.*

Installing Network Adapters and Protocols

Next, you need to add support for your network adapter. By clicking the Drivers button, the Network Drivers dialog (see Figure 23.4) is displayed, and from here you can install drivers for network adapters and install networking protocols.

First, click the Add Adapter button to choose the network adapter that you have installed. You can choose from the list of included network adapter drivers or you can use the driver that came with the network adapter by choosing Unlisted or Updated Network Adapter from the list of adapters, as shown in Figure 23.5.

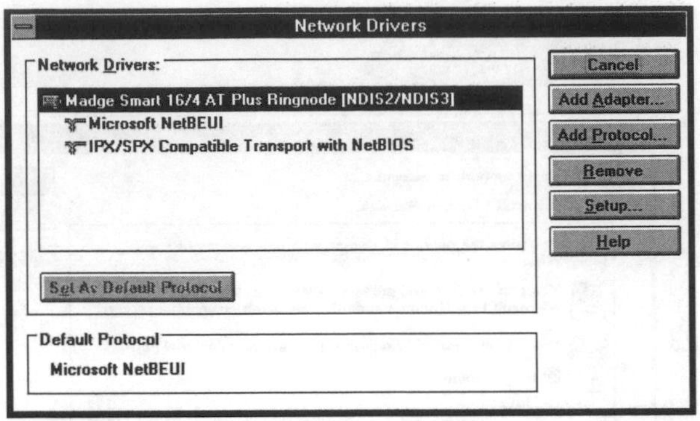

Figure 23.4. The Network Drivers dialog.

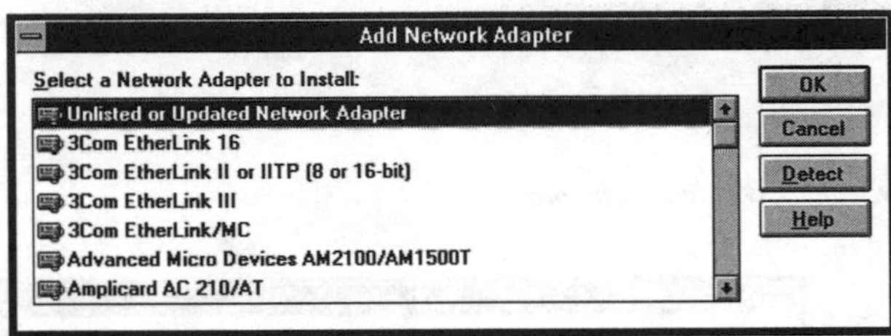

Figure 23.5. The Add Network Adapter dialog.

Tip: Because the drivers that were shipped with Windows for Workgroups can be dated as far back as the early 1990s, I highly recommend contacting the manufacturer of the network adapter to obtain an updated driver. Although the drivers that come with Windows for Workgroups might still work, an updated driver can give you increased capabilities or may be more compatible or stable.

Next, choose the protocols that you require to communicate on your network. The protocols that ship with the Windows for Workgroups product are NetBEUI, which is the default for Microsoft Networking on the client side, and NWLink, which is Microsoft's IPX-compatible protocol.

To add protocols, click the Add Protocol button to display the Add Network Protocol dialog. (See Figure 23.6.) Choose a protocol from the displayed list to install and click the OK button.

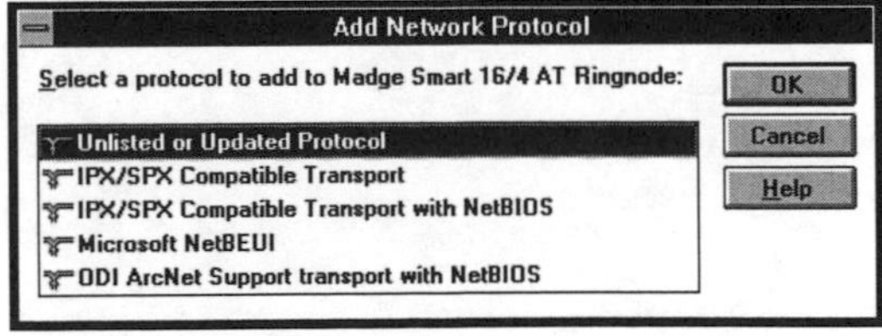

Figure 23.6. The Add Network Protocol dialog.

Installing TCP/IP-32

At the time of the original release of Windows for Workgroups, TCP/IP was not used as much on PC networks as it is now. Because most networks are now running TCP/IP, it may be important for you to install Microsoft's 32-bit implementation of TCP/IP for Windows for Workgroups.

The Windows NT CD-ROM comes with this installable protocol. If you set up a client software share on the server, the installation files for the TCP/IP protocol may be located in the `\\servername\clients\tcp32wfw\netsetup` directory.

Note: If this is a new Windows for Workgroups installation and you do not have access to the network while installing Windows for Workgroups, use the Network Client Administrator program to create a disk that contains Microsoft's TCP/IP for Windows for Workgroups. Refer to Chapter 19, "Network Client Administrator," for instructions on how to create the TCP/IP disk.

To install Microsoft TCP/IP from the Network Drivers dialog, click the Add Protocol button. The Add Network Protocol dialog's list of protocols, shown in Figure 23.6, starts with Unlisted or Updated Protocol, which is the item that you want to select.

The Install Protocol dialog will then prompt you for the source of the protocol installation files. If you have made a disk with Microsoft TCP/IP-32, enter the drive letter for the disk; otherwise, if you are attached to your network and have Microsoft TCP/IP-32 on a network drive, use the Browse button to locate the network drive, or just enter a previously assigned path for the Microsoft TCP/IP-32 files.

If the proper files are found, the Unlisted or Updated Protocol dialog (see Figure 23.7) will then list Microsoft TCP/IP-32. Click the OK button to install the protocol and then files will be copied to the client computer.

Note: When installing TCP/IP-32, a new program group that provides icons for Microsoft's TCP/IP utilities is created. The Microsoft TCP/IP-32 program group, shown in Figure 23.8, will give you an FTP program, a Telnet program, a Help file that explains the configuration of Microsoft TCP/IP-32, and a text file with more information about Microsoft TCP/IP. Not shown are other MS-DOS-based utility programs, including ARP, TRACERT, and IPCONFIG. TRACERT and IPCONFIG are very important programs because they may be used to troubleshoot TCP/IP.

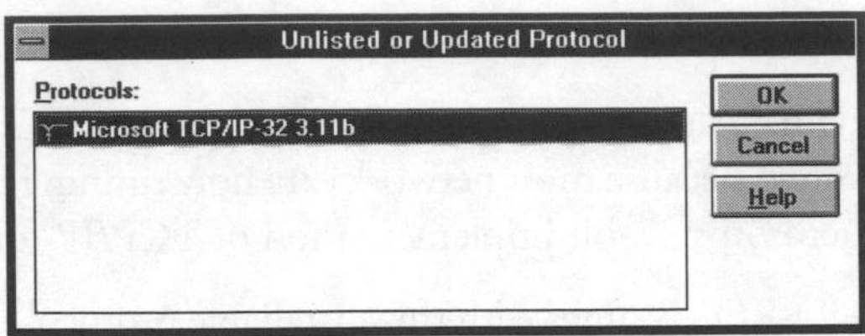

Figure 23.7. Unlisted or Updated Protocol dialog.

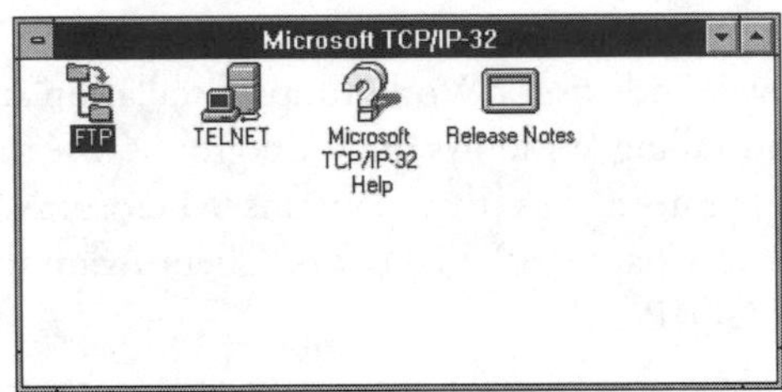

Figure 23.8. Microsoft TCP/IP-32 program group.

When you have completed adding TCP/IP, the Network Drivers dialog will show Microsoft TCP/IP-32 installed. (See Figure 23.9.)

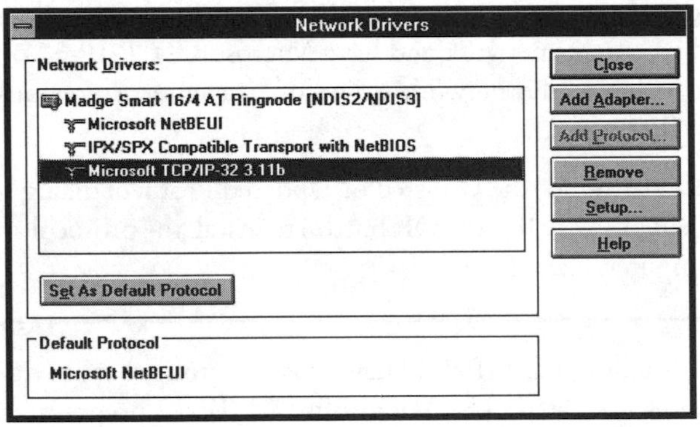

Figure 23.9. Network Drivers dialog with TCP/IP installed.

Next, configure Microsoft TCP/IP-32 by highlighting Microsoft TCP/IP-32, and click the Setup button.

In the Microsoft TCP/IP Configuration dialog (see Figure 23.10), you can specify that you will be either using Microsoft's DHCP Server services (which is discussed at length in Chapter 30, "Windows NT and Dynamic Host Configuration Protocol (DHCP)") or manually configuring the TCP/IP address and the location of WINS servers and gateways.

After you have completed installing Microsoft TCP/IP-32 and any other protocols that you want to run on the client, return to Network Setup by clicking the OK button. At Network Setup, click the OK button to exit and you will be prompted to restart your computer.

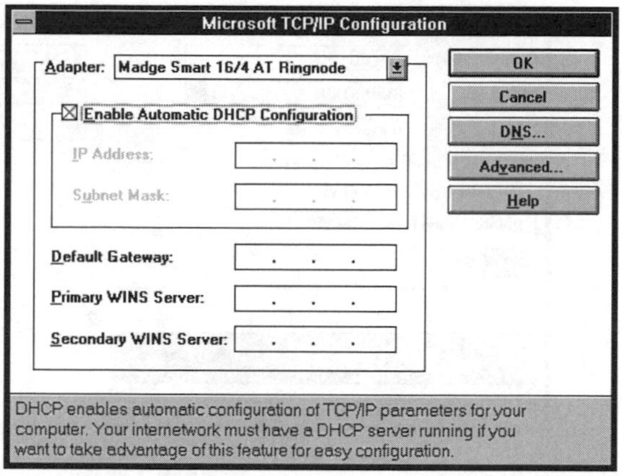

Figure 23.10. Microsoft TCP/IP Configuration dialog.

Changes Made to the Client Computer

Besides adding network support to the client computer, the following modifications were made to the MS-DOS startup files:

- `IFSHLP.SYS` is added to `CONFIG.SYS`
- `NET START` is added to `AUTOEXEC.BAT`

Additionally, changes are made to the `SYSTEM.INI` file in the `WINDOWS` directory, and a `PROTOCOL.INI` file is created in the `WINDOWS` directory.

Configuring a Logon to the Windows NT Domain

After the network drivers have been configured and the computer has been restarted, you must configure Windows for Workgroups to log on to the Windows NT Domain.

To do so, double-click the Networks icon in the Windows for Workgroups Control Panel. In this dialog, shown in Figure 23.11, the user can change his or her computer name, add a text description for his or her computer, and change his or her workgroup.

The computer name should be something that is meaningful to you as an administrator. All computers in a workgroup must have a unique computer name. When browsing through the computers on your domain, you will see all these computer names listed. A descriptive name will enable you to identify the computer more easily. You should also use the description field to identify the client properly; I would suggest using the client's full name for this description. Or, in the case of clients using different computers, use the description and name to indicate the physical location or purpose for the computer.

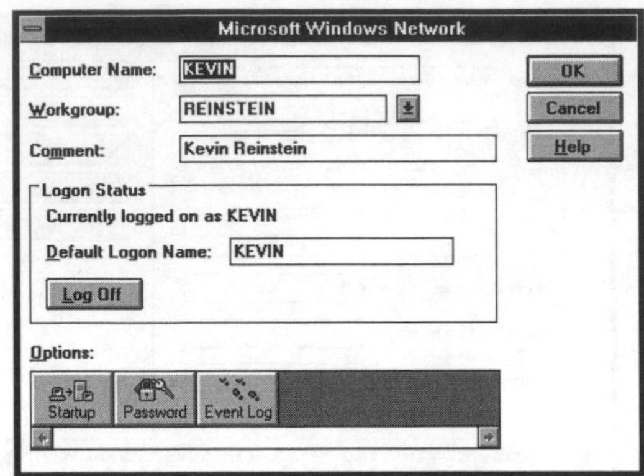

Figure 23.11. *Network Control Panel.*

The workgroup is a virtual network that clients running the Microsoft Network Client can use, regardless of the operating system running on their computer. By naming a common workgroup, clients can have access to disk drives, CD-ROM drives, and printers that have been made available by enabling sharing.

Note: When you install Microsoft Networking on a Windows for Workgroups client, the default value for the workgroup name will be WORKGROUP. Remember this when you browse the network for computers and find a few of them in their own little workgroup named WORKGROUP. This will probably mean that they have not been configured correctly for a Windows NT domain.

The default value for a computer name is the first eight characters in the name that was used during the installation of Windows for Workgroups. For example, my default computer name is ROBERTRE. You should also review and change this if necessary.

You can also use the Network Control Panel to log on or log off from Microsoft Networking. Use the row of buttons at the bottom of the Network Control Panel to configure various other options for Microsoft Networking.

The most important button from the standpoint of configuring for a Windows NT domain is the Startup button. Click this button to bring up the Startup Settings dialog, shown in Figure 23.12.

Configure these items in the Startup Settings dialog:

- Logging on to Microsoft Networking when Windows for Workgroups first starts
- Enabling Network DDE services
- Ghosted, or non-established, network drive connections
- Starting the WinPopup dialog service
- Logging on to either a Windows NT domain or a Microsoft LAN Manager domain

- The Microsoft NT or LAN Manager domain name
- Displaying a confirmation dialog for logging on to a server
- Changing a password
- The CPU time slice given up for sharing resources on the client's computer

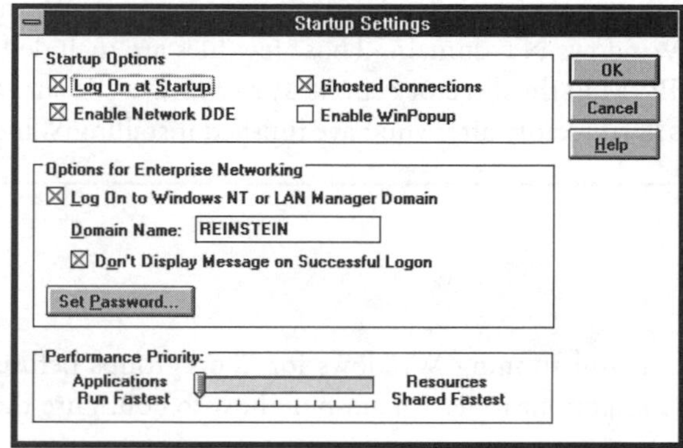

Figure 23.12. *The Startup Settings dialog.*

Specific to configuring the computer for a Windows NT domain is checking the checkbox that states Log On to Windows NT or LAN Manager Domain. Checking this box will force an authenticate logon attempt whenever Windows for Workgroups is started.

Tip: Be aware that Windows for Workgroups clients cannot see long filenames that may be stored on the Windows NT domain. They will instead see the eight-dot-three MS-DOS filenames that are generated for MS-DOS clients. If you have used long filenames via a Windows NT server, Windows NT Workstation, or Windows 95 PCs, consider upgrading all your Microsoft Network-enabled PCs to operating systems that can view long filenames.

If an authenticated logon takes place and the box that states Don't Display Message on Successful Logon is left unchecked, a confirmation dialog indicating the username and level of authentication will appear each time Windows for Workgroups is started.

When logon occurs, if it is a logon script for the client, it will run from within a DOS window.

Accessing Microsoft Networking Resources

The Windows for Workgroups client can access resources within the Windows NT domain and on other Microsoft Networking computers by using File Manager to access shared disk resources, and from within Print Manager to connect to shared printers.

The `NET` command, among other functions, is another way to access network resources. A discussion of the `NET` command and its many uses is in Chapter 24, "MS-DOS/Windows 3.*x*."

Note: Windows NT Server 3.51 contained an updated version of Windows for Workgroups 3.11. This updated version of Windows for Workgroups contained only a few updated files that contained fixes to problems related to connecting a Windows for Workgroups computer to a Windows NT domain. Those few files are included on the Windows NT Server 4.0 CD-ROM in the directory `CLIENTS\UPDATE.WFW`. Be sure to copy these files into the `WINDOWS\SYSTEM` directory after you have finished installing Windows for Workgroups.

Summary

Corporate America is still running Windows for Workgroups before going to Windows NT Workstation, so it's important to have a grasp on how to configure these computers.

Integrating a Windows for Workgroups computer on a Windows NT domain is very simple, but be sure to have the latest drivers and settings for your network adapter.

Because TCP/IP is not included with the base Windows for Workgroups package, be sure to create a disk with Microsoft TCP/IP-32 before enabling Windows for Workgroups computers for a Windows NT domain.

Also be sure to consider the many reasons to upgrade to a better Microsoft Network client, Windows 95, or Windows NT Workstation. Windows 95 offers the Explorer shell, support for plug-and-play, the capability to run the new breed of Windows 95 applications, and lower overhead when attaching to networks. Windows NT Workstation is the ultimate Windows NT network client, offering a high level of security and a rock-solid (stable) operating system.

MS-DOS/ Windows 3.x

by Robert Reinstein

This chapter will show you

- ◆ How to install support for Microsoft Networking on MS-DOS
- ◆ How to install support for Microsoft Networking on Windows 3.x
- ◆ How to access network resources from within Windows 3.x

Microsoft Networking

Before there was Windows NT Server, there was Microsoft LAN Manager. This form of networking, which required using a NetBIOS layer on top of a networking protocol, used networking concepts that are still being used in Windows NT networks.

Curiously enough, the MS-DOS/Windows 3.x Client software for Windows NT Server is the same client software that would be used to attach to a Microsoft LAN Manager 2.1 server and is clearly identified as such in the `README.TXT` file that accompanies it.

Note: Current clients of Microsoft LAN Manager can keep their current client software and log on to a Windows NT server. The latest revision of the client software is version 3.0, at the time of this writing.

For an MS-DOS or Windows 3.x client to log on to a Windows NT server, the client must run the Microsoft Networking Client Full Redirector to load MS-DOS drivers that occupy around 100KB of memory.

Note: Because of this overhead, the MS-DOS Redirector is the least preferred method of attaching into a Windows NT server.

It is understood that many companies still use MS-DOS and Windows 3.x as their standard operating environment, which is why Microsoft still includes the software required to log on to a Windows NT server.

Installing the Microsoft Networking Client for MS-DOS/Windows 3.x

The software required for the Microsoft Networking Client Redirector is located on the Windows NT Server CD-ROM. You can install the software to a share on the server created by the Network Client Administrator, from the installation disks the Network Client Administrator created, or directly from the CD-ROM.

To install the client software, run `SETUP.EXE` from either the disk, the network share, or the CD-ROM. The setup program, shown in Figure 24.1, will ask for the name of the computer and the name of the domain to which the client will log on.

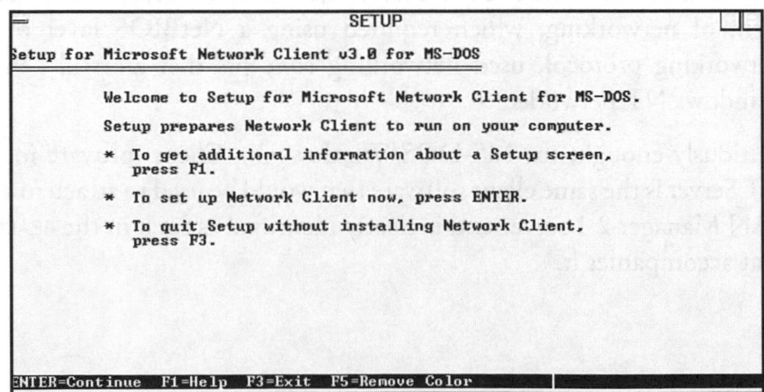

Figure 24.1. *The Microsoft LAN Manager Client Installation program.*

You must specify the type of network card you are using to load drivers that come either with Windows NT Server or from a disk you received with your network adapter. These settings are saved in the directory containing the client software in files named `SYSTEM.INI` and `PROTOCOL.INI`.

The network adapter drivers that ship with the Microsoft LAN Manager Client are very limited, so be sure to set drivers from the hardware manufacturer to ensure a clean installation.

The modifications made to the MS-DOS startup files are

- `IFSHLP.SYS` is added to `CONFIG.SYS`
- `NET START` is added to `AUTOEXEC.BAT`

With these modifications, you can then log on to the server. To be authenticated by the server, you must load the Network Client Full Redirector. The Network Client Basic Redirector, which uses only half the memory of the Network Client Full Redirector, is sufficient to allow clients to attach to shares and print queues on the server but gives them limited capabilities.

Start the Microsoft Networking Client Basic Redirector by using the `NET` command.

The `NET` command is the main command for Microsoft Networking. Besides starting Microsoft Networking for MS-DOS/Windows 3.x and Windows for Workgroups, the `NET` command is also very useful for troubleshooting.

Used alone, the `NET` command starts the basic redirector, which is also known as the Workstation Service. The Workstation Client pop-up utility (see Figure 24.2) will then appear. With this utility, you can point and click to attach to shares and print queues. The pop-up utility toggles between drive attachments and printer attachments. (See Figure 24.3.)

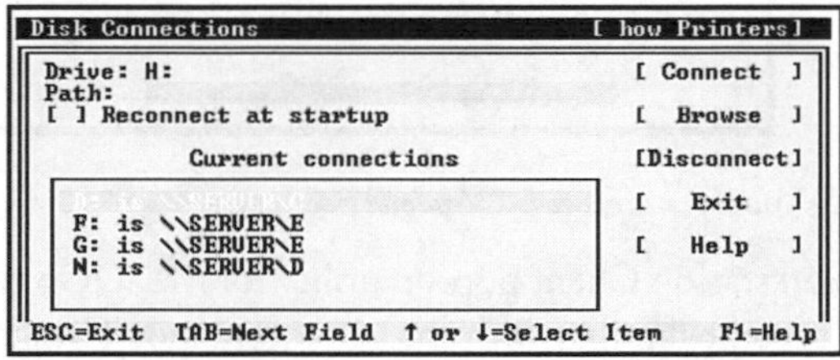

Figure 24.2. Workstation Client pop-up utility.

```
Printer Connections                          [ how Disks ]
Port: LPT                                    [ Connect ]
Path:
[ ] Reconnect at startup                     [ Browse ]
            Current connections              [Disconnect]
                                             [ Exit ]
  LPT2: is \\SERVER\LASERJET
                                             [ Help ]
                                             [Show Queue]
ESC=Exit TAB=Next Field ↑ or ↓=Select Item   F1=Help
```

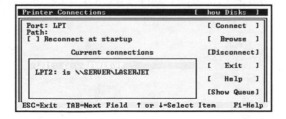

Figure 24.3. Workstation Client printer attachments.

Using the NET START WORKSTATION command will make the non-authenticated attachment to the server without bringing up the Workstation Client pop-up utility.

With the Microsoft Networking Client Basic Redirector, you can create attachments to drives and printers before starting Windows 3.x so that those connections can remain in effect during the Windows 3.x session. No other attaching can be done from within Windows 3.x, however.

To start the Microsoft Networking Client Full Redirector, which is necessary for full functionality under Windows 3.x and allows for an authenticated domain logon, use the NET START FULL command. If the Windows NT Server has been configured with a logon script, that script will be executed as part of the logon sequence.

The protocols available for the Microsoft Networking MS-DOS/Windows 3.x client are NetBEUI, NWLink (IPX-compatible), Microsoft DLC, and TCP/IP. An MS-DOS–based Remote Access Services (RAS) client is also included.

To make attachments from within Windows 3.x, you must install support for Microsoft Networking by using the Windows Setup (either through the MS-DOS-based setup or the icon in the Main program group) and specifying that you are using Microsoft LAN Manager (see Figure 24.4). This will give you full functionality of attaching to shares (see Figure 24.5) and print queues (see Figure 24.6) through the Windows-based client software that will be added to Windows 3.x after you make this selection.

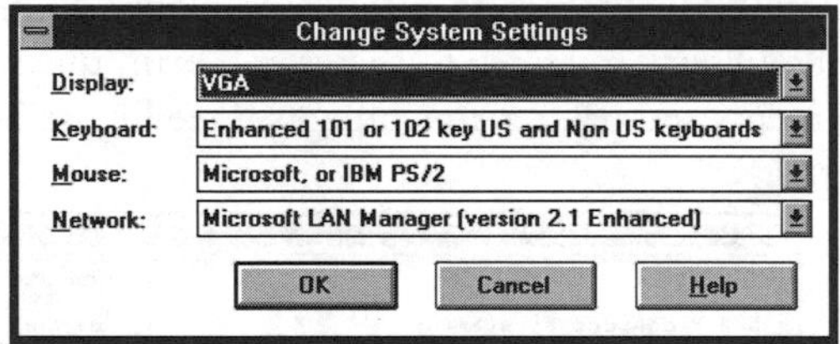

Figure 24.4. *Installing LAN Manager support in Windows 3.x.*

Besides using the Workstation Client pop-up utility for MS-DOS to connect to shares and print queues, you should become familiar with the NET command. The NET command gives you all the functionality in the Workstation Client pop-up utility plus more, but it is totally command-line-driven with which you can create batch files to run various network utilities. Table 24.1 contains the NET command with its parameters and the result of using those parameters.

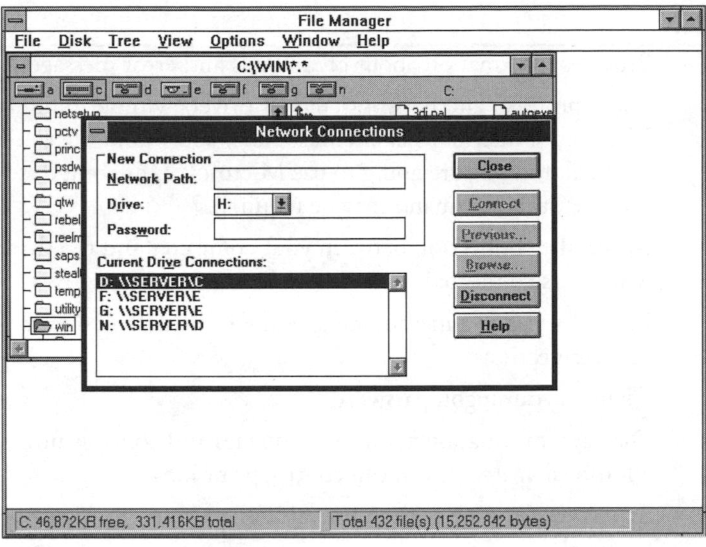

Figure 24.5. *Network drive attachments in Windows 3.x.*

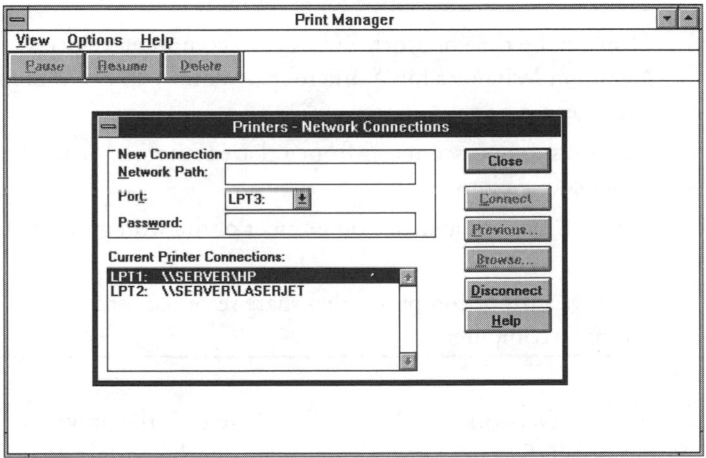

Figure 24.6. *Printer attachments in Windows 3.x.*

Table 24.1. The `NET` command.

`NET CONFIG`	Displays your current workgroup settings including your computer name, username, redirector version, and workgroup name.
`NET DIAG`	Runs the Microsoft Network Diagnostics program to display diagnostic information about your network. Usually you would run this on two computers to test the connection between computers.

continues

Table 24.1. continued

`NET HELP`	Provides information about commands and error messages.
`NET INIT`	Loads protocol and network-adapter drivers without binding them to Protocol Manager. Under normal circumstances, you would not need to use this command; if you are going to use Microsoft DLC or a third-party protocol, however, this command may be required.
`NET LOGOFF`	Breaks the connection between your computer and the shared resources to which it is connected.
`NET LOGON`	Identifies you as a member of a workgroup and reconnects you to any persistent connections.
`NET PASSWORD`	Changes your logon password.
`NET PRINT`	Displays information about print queues and controls print jobs. With additional switches, you can control print jobs.
`NET START`	Starts services such as the basic and full redirector or loads the NetBEUI protocol.
`NET START POPUP`	Loads the pop-up utility as a TSR.
`NET STOP`	Stops services as mentioned for `NET START`.
`NET TIME`	Displays the time or synchronizes your computer's clock with the clock on a Microsoft Windows for Workgroups, Windows NT, Windows 95, or LAN Manager time server.
`NET USE`	Connects to or disconnects from a shared resource or displays information about connections.
`NET VER`	Displays the type and version number of the workgroup redirector you are using.
`NET VIEW`	Displays a list of computers that share resources or a list of shared resources on a specific computer.

Although the Microsoft Networking Client Full Redirector is the only way to be fully authenticated by a Windows NT Server Domain Controller, the Microsoft Networking Client Basic Redirector uses MS-DOS conventional memory sparingly, which may be a requirement for some workstations, yet still allows for basic functionality.

Resources on the server that are available to Windows NT Server's guest account will also be available to clients running the Microsoft Networking Basic Redirector. If the client running the Microsoft Networking Client Basic Redirector has permission for access to shared resources that are not available to the Guest account, then those resources will not be available. Non-secure environments can use the Microsoft Networking Client Basic Redirector for their clients, though more secure environments will want to load the Microsoft Networking Client Full Redirector for full authentication.

Loading the Microsoft Networking Client Full Redirector is wise mainly because the Guest account may be removed in a more secure environment. It is also necessary to use the Microsoft Networking Client Full Redirector to allow for network functionality under Windows 3.x. Without the Microsoft Networking Client Full Redirector, Windows 3.x will not recognize that the client is connected to a network, therefore disabling all network functions.

The Windows 3.x client for Microsoft Networks, even with the Microsoft Networking Client Full Redirector, is limited in its features compared to the client software for Windows for Workgroups, Windows 95, or Windows NT Workstation. Figure 24.7 shows the limited configuration options available for the Windows 3.x client for Microsoft Networks.

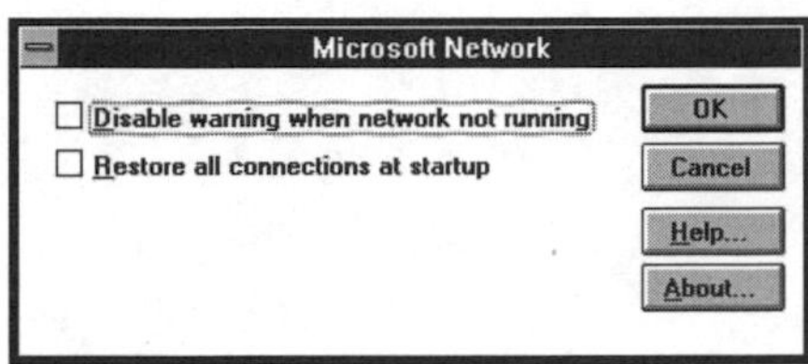

Figure 24.7. *Control Panel options for Microsoft Networks in Windows 3.x.*

When a client wants to attach to a share on the server, the client is required to enter the full Universal Naming Convention (UNC) name for the target share. This lack of point-and-click ease of use makes this client software a poor example of what usually makes the Windows environment shine.

Tip: I highly recommend that any MS-DOS or Windows 3.x client be upgraded to Windows for Workgroups, Windows 95, or Windows NT Workstation. These operating systems have client software that truly exploits the Windows environment and makes accessing the Windows NT Server much easier. Besides that, the 100KB overhead that the MS-DOS/Windows 3.x client has is one big chunk that cannot be loaded high, so you don't have a chance of running your client workstation on more that 540KB. In my experience, this makes Windows 3.x much less stable, and the chance of opening multiple applications, regardless of the amount of extended memory on the PC, is almost nonexistent.

Caution: Be aware that MS-DOS and Windows 3.x clients cannot see the long filenames that may be stored on the Windows NT Server. Instead, they will see the eight-dot-three MS-DOS filenames that are generated for MS-DOS clients.

Summary

Windows for Workgroups offers a 32-bit networking client and enhanced performance. Windows 95 offers those things as well, plus the ability to run the new breed of Windows 95 applications. It also offers lower overhead when attaching to networks. Windows NT Workstation is the ultimate Windows NT network client and offers a high level of security.

Because there are still many Windows 3.x clients running on networks, Microsoft will continue to support them; however, based on the many reasons to upgrade to Windows for Workgroups, Windows 95, or Windows NT Workstation, an upgrade should be highly considered.

PART VI

Networking with Windows NT

Securing Your Windows NT Environment

by Mike Carpenter

What Are the Security Issues for the Windows NT Environment?

Security in the Windows NT 4.0 environment is a complex mix of physical security, network security, security policy, and the built-in security features of the Windows NT operating system. I will try to explain each of these issues separately and as they relate to each other.

Whenever I am asked about Windows NT security, it seems the issue of C2 security comes up. In a nutshell, C2 security is the National Computer Security Center's (NCSC) designation for a level of security called Controlled Access Protection. It requires that users be held accountable for their actions and that the system has a way of keeping track of processes as well as identifying in the records which user initiated the process. When a user is done with an object, it must not be available for reuse by another user who does not have proper authority. Users may individually grant others access to their data but not to a level higher than delegated to them by the administrator. I will cover C2 security a bit more in this chapter as it pertains to the section.

Physical Security

No area of security will work without the proper physical security of your server. You must lock up your server when there is no administrator sitting at it. If someone can get to your server, someone can get to your network—simple as that. An intruder wanting to take down your network can do so by simply turning off the power or unplugging a cable. Even someone being near enough to the server with coffee or any other fluid can bring down the system if an accident occurs.

Keep all nonessential people away from the server if you can. Have a good lock installed on the door, make sure any windows cannot be opened from the outside, and don't forget to look to the ceiling and floors for paths to get in. Many office environments have crawl spaces in the floor and ceilings for cabling and for utilities such as heat and water. These need to be secured also, to the best possible degree.

If the server has reset buttons, power switches, floppy drives, or a case that can be easily opened, you should invest in housing of some sort to protect the server. Don't forget to put the uninterruptible power supply inside that case, too. If that is not practical for you, use CMOS settings to disable booting from the floppy drive and set user passwords or an administrator password on the server itself. Failing to protect the floppy drive can mean that an intruder could simply reload Windows NT, take ownership of the objects on the system, and compromise your data and security at will. C2 certification would require the server to be locked in a secure room when unattended. This would include over-the-wall access and crawl spaces under the floor.

An organization should have a well-planned physical security policy that ensures keys are tracked and secured, or even the strongest of doors and locks will not keep out an intruder. When the server's operation or security of the data becomes more critical, the security policy must be reviewed to bring it to the level necessary to ensure those needs are met.

Network Security

If the Windows NT server is going to be a member of a network, you need to take certain precautions to ensure that assaults on the server cannot be made through that network. These threats to security can come in many forms, such as unauthorized access via a modem in a client machine and the monitoring of data between machines on the same segment; if a network is connected via the Internet to a WAN, you will have even more security issues to deal with.

Modem Access

If computers must access the network remotely by modem, use a server to connect to the modem and make sure all physical security and security policy issues are addressed. Never give out the modem access number to anyone but authorized users. Having a password policy that requires regular periodic changes of the password is essential. There is a feature in Remote Access Server

(RAS) that forces a callback to a specific phone number for the user. If the remote computer has a fixed phone number, that is an excellent way to increase the level of security.

If your network's users can install a modem on their computers, they should be able to install a number of programs that allow access to that computer, and therefore to the network. If possible, do not allow any modems to be connected to computers that are part of your network. If you must, it is essential that no program that would allow remote access to the network is installed on it.

If a program such as PC Anywhere or Windows NT Remote Access Server is loaded and configured on the computer, it is simple to connect to the network and have the same permissions as any registered user. If there is a breach of security policy, such as someone finding the modem's phone number, the username, and password, the entire network's security is compromised to the degree of the users' access and permissions.

Monitoring Data

Data being sent over a network is subject to monitoring by many different methods. It can be done from any computer that is a member of that segment, by plugging a device into an active network jack or by tapping into the cables that make up the network. Good physical security can go a long way to prevent this, as can a good security policy.

Within a segment of a LAN, all information is broadcast to all devices. Modern software filters the data so that you see only what is intended for you, but all data from all devices on that segment is there for all to see. Keeping the segment itself as small as possible can greatly increase security. Connecting segments with a router of some kind also helps to keep the monitor more controlled. Ethernet switches don't operate in that same manner; they localize the traffic to the address that it is intended for. You might even consider using different segments for different security groupings, rather than just by location, which further ensures that all data is kept secure within devices used only by others of the same level.

Any 10BaseT or Ethernet port can be a potential source of compromise to network security. Disable any unused ports or wall jacks. Make sure unused offices with hot jacks are secured too—or, if your need for security is high and general access to your offices is not restricted, enforce a policy that all offices be locked when there is nobody in them, further denying access to hot jacks.

Cables that comprise the LAN are susceptible to compromise if they are not properly protected with good physical security. Make sure that all are well protected from any intruder who could attach a monitoring device, and protect them from being spliced and having a jack added. Regular inspections of the cables are required to make sure security breaches have not occurred. This should be part of the security policy. Using fiber-optic cables is a good way to increase the level of security and, generally speaking, can improve performance of your system, too. If you cannot ensure the physical security of the cabling or of jacks, consider using encryption to secure the data sent between machines on the network. There are several encryption techniques and software solutions, as well as some hardware-encryption devices that can be used to accomplish this.

Internet Security Issues

Connecting your network to the Internet can increase the ways your network can be expanded to include remote offices or connections and provide your network with the WWW, FTP, e-mail, and other services available. The downside is that the entire world has potential access to your network via the same connection. Physical barriers such as firewalls can help prevent unauthorized access, but cheaper software solutions, including the security features built into Windows NT, can provide a high degree of security.

Hardware firewalls are computer devices that stand between the server and the Internet itself. Each has its own unique features but the end result is that firewalls can filter out unauthorized intrusion and facilitate the connection of authorized users. Another benefit to some firewall products is that they can help enforce policies such as limiting the duration of Internet access time for users, and opening and closing ports at scheduled times. Other features include restricting the sites that are visited and the types of files transferred. Software-based firewalls are available, too. They provide much the same protection features but take up resources on the servers they are installed on, and do not fully isolate the server as a hardware firewall can.

Windows NT 4.0 includes a feature called Point-to-Point Tunneling Protocol (PPTP), which is an extension of RAS. It enables users and administrators to set up what Microsoft calls *virtual private networks* (VPNs) that can help increase the security of any remote access. Using a 40-bit key and an RC4 algorithm, the VPN utilizes RAS's bulk data encryption to create a secure channel to transmit data on the Internet.

The security provided by properly setting up a security policy on your Windows NT server is your very best defense from unauthorized Internet access. Ensure that the guest account is disabled. Rename the administrator account. Make sure that you understand completely the security implications of installing software such as FTP servers, WWW servers, or e-mail servers. Log all traffic passing through the servers and check regularly for behaviors that might indicate a breach of security.

The Built-In Security Features of the Windows NT Operating System

The Windows NT operating system provides many security features. The primary means of applying these features are through access control and the New Technology File System (NTFS). Windows NT was designed to provide security as a central concept in its design, with the objective of meeting C2 security requirements, as described earlier in this chapter.

Access Control

Access control in Windows NT is enforced by mandatory logon, wherein each user must log on and is assigned an access token that is used by the operating system to determine whether or not access to an object is permitted. When your access token matches the permission level required for that object, you are given access; if not, you are denied access. You cannot run user-mode applications until a valid logon has occurred.

The Windows NT logon process, called WinLogon, happens like this:

1. The user is prompted to press Ctrl+Alt+Del to invoke the WinLogon dialog box. This is a hardware interrupt sequence that would be extremely difficult to duplicate through software virus or hacking, because that sequence cannot be remapped.
2. The user enters a username and password.
3. The username and password are compared in the Security Accounts Manager of the Security Subsystem. If there is a match, the Security Subsystem assigns an access token to the user.
4. The access token is then used by the Win32 subsystem whenever access to a new process is required.

The access token is made up of a security ID representing the user, the group IDs representing the groups the user is a member of, and individual permissions assigned to the user, as explained here:

- Security ID: Windows NT assigns a unique security ID for each user and group as it is entered into the user accounts database through the User Manager. If a user or group is deleted and reentered, it is given a new security ID and will not be the owner of files or groups previously owned, even if the username and password are identical.
- Group ID: Although similar to the security ID because it allows access by permissions, a group ID does not represent a certain user. When a user becomes a member of a group, that group ID becomes a part of the user's access token when he next logs on. If a user is logged on while an administrator removes that user from a group, the user will still have access to objects that allow that group's access until he logs off.
- Permissions: Permissions are the specific access control entries that are a part of an object's access control list. In that access control list is a list of security and group IDs and the associated rights each has to the object.

Note: Because the user access token is assigned the group IDs and permissions when the user logs on, changes to group membership or permissions will not take effect until the user logs off.

Another method to increase the security of your Windows NT environment is to disable the default username. By default, Windows NT will keep the last username in the WinLogon dialog box. All that needs to be done then is for the user to enter a password. To make it harder for an intruder to use the logon, especially for someone not familiar with the usernames, you can add a Registry entry, `DontDisplayLastUserName`, and set it to `1`. To do this follow these steps:

1. Click the Start Button and select Run.
2. Type `regedit` in the Open input box and click OK.
3. Double-click the HKEY_LOCAL_MACHINE key.
4. Double-click the SOFTWARE key.
5. Double-click the Microsoft key.
6. Double-click the Windows NT key.
7. Double-click the Current Version key.
8. Double-click the WinLogon key.
9. Select New from the Registry menu.
10. Select String value from the pop-up menu.
11. Type `DontDisplayLastUserName` in the field of the entry and press Enter.
12. Double-click the `DontDisplayLastUserName` field and type `1` in the entry field of the Edit String dialog box.
13. Click OK.
14. Close the Registry Editor, log out, and log back in to check the results. You should see no username in the Logon dialog box. (See Figure 25.1.)

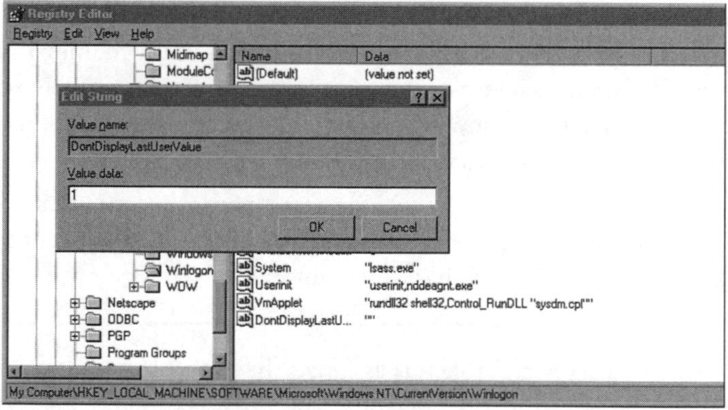

Figure 25.1. *The Edit String dialog box in the Registry Editor.*

Note: Carefully check any entries you make to the Registry. If you corrupt the Registry, you might have to run Windows NT Setup and use your Emergency Repair Disk to restore a broken Registry. Now is a good time to update that disk, *before* you edit the Registry.

Automatic Account Lockout

By default, Windows NT allows an unlimited number of logon attempts. You can set your Windows NT environment to lock out a user if a certain number of unsuccessful attempts are made. Then, only an administrator can unlock the account. You can select any number, but 3–5 is the normal range; more than that would give an intruder a great advantage at guessing the password. To set the Automatic Account Lockout, do the following:

1. Log on as the administrator.
2. Select User Manager from Start | Administrative Tools.
3. Select Policies and then Accounts Policies from the Administrative Tools menu.
4. Click the Account Lockout radio button.
5. Select the number of attempts you want to set in the Lockout after _ bad logon attempts box.
6. Select the number of minutes you want the account to be locked out in the Reset count after _ minutes box.
7. Close the User Manager and log off the system.
8. Attempt to log on as someone other than the administrator, using the wrong password to test the setup. (See Figure 25.2.)

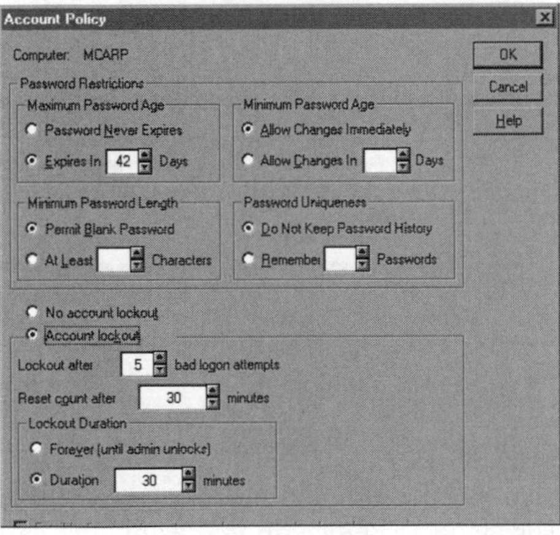

Figure 25.2. *The Account Policy dialog box.*

> **Note:** The Default Administrator account cannot be locked out with the Automatic Account Lockout feature. To further prevent intrusion, rename the administrator account.

Renaming the Administrator Account

By default, Windows NT installs with an account named administrator that has full control over your operating system. If you do not rename this account, any intruder already has the username for the account, and would only need to find a password that works, because the Automatic Account Lockout feature does not apply to this account.

To change the name of the default administrator account, do the following:

1. From the Start menu, select Administrative Tools | User Manager.
2. Select the administrator account in the User Manager.
3. Select the User menu and Rename from the pop-up list.
4. Enter the name you want to have for the account in the dialog box and click OK.
5. Close the User Manager and log off the computer.
6. Attempt to log on using the new administrator account name. (See Figure 25.3.)

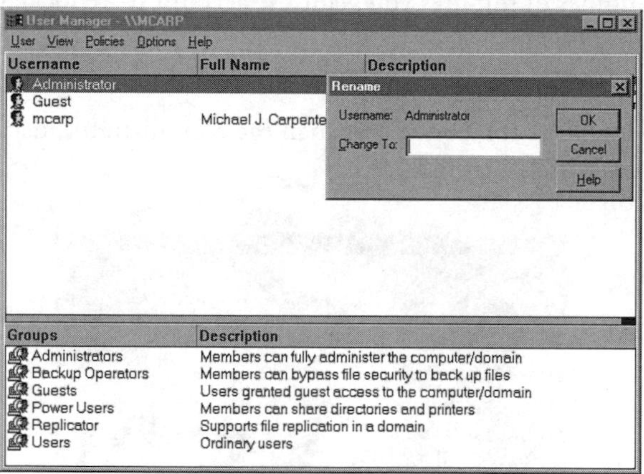

Figure 25.3. *The Rename dialog box in the User Manager.*

NTFS

Windows NT was designed to be operated using the New Technology File System (NTFS). Aside from providing a degree of fault tolerance, more flexible file and partition sizes, long filename support, POSIX compliance, and an increase in performance, it works hand in hand with the

Windows NT file system to provide a high degree of security to files and directories. The primary NTFS security features are

- Permissions: NTFS provides different levels of access to groups or users either to individual files or directories.
- Auditing: Windows NT can be set to log all security-related events.
- Transaction logging: NTFS is a log-based file system that records information to allow later undo or redo of changes made to a file.
- Ownership: NTFS assigns ownership of a file to the user who creates it and then tracks changes to ownership.

Permissions

Every file or directory is an object in the NTFS that can have permissions set either at the time of sharing, or by user or group. User or group permissions are additional to any directory sharing permission, with the most restrictive permission setting being used if user or group permissions are different from the directory sharing permissions. (See Table 25.1.)

Table 25.1. A list of operations that a user is allowed with the settings shown.

Permission	*R*	*X*	*W*	*D*	*P*	*O*
No Access						
Read	X	X				
List (Directory Only)	X	X				
Add (Directory Only)		X	X			
Add & Read (Directory Only)	X	X	X			
Change	X	X	X	X		
Full Control	X	X	X	X	X	X
Special Access	*	*	*	*	*	*

X = Operation that can be performed
*= Operation that may be available as determined by the Special Access setting
R = Read or display data, attributes, owner, and permissions
X = Run or execute files in the directory
W = Write to the files or directory, or change the attributes
D = Delete the file or directory
P = Change permissions
O = Take ownership

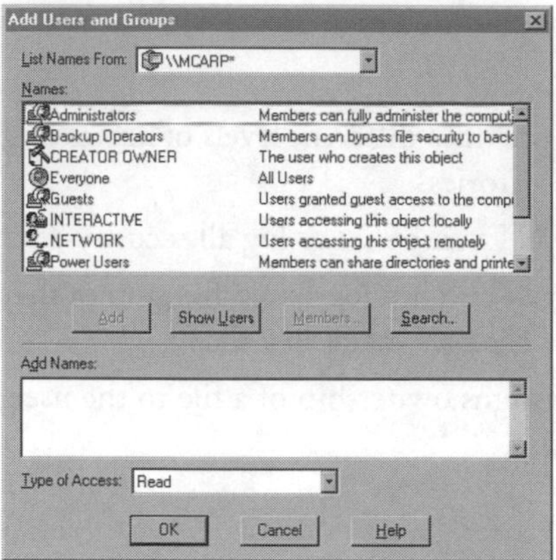

Figure 25.4. *Setting user and group permissions.*

Note: Remember, the user who creates a file or directory has full control of it; administrators can take ownership and also have full control of all files and directories.

To change the permissions of a file or directory, you must have full control assess to it, have change permissions access to it, or be the owner of it. You can make permission changes by selecting the file or directory in Windows Explorer, right-clicking it with the mouse, choosing Properties from the pop-up list, selecting the Security tab, and clicking the Permissions button. A File or Directory Permissions dialog box will come up; when you click the appropriate button, new users or groups can be added or removed from the permissions.

The key to security through file and directory permission is to have a good security policy in place and then ensure that all files to be protected have permissions properly set. You should make careful decisions about group permissions, not only to allow for security but to protect from inadvertent removal and changing of files or attributes.

Auditing

You can use NTFS auditing to track the successful and unsuccessful attempts to access or change a file or directory. These attempts are logged to the Security Log of the Event Viewer. You can customize this log to record only the attempts to perform the operations selected by the administrator, and for only the groups or users specified.

Auditing is first enabled in the User Manager. After auditing is enabled, the file or directory is selected in the Windows Explorer; Security is selected under Properties, and Auditing selected. From the File or Directory Auditing dialog box, groups or users can be specified as well as which operations are to be logged and whether successful or unsuccessful attempts at those operations can be selected by checking the boxes, as shown in Figure 25.5.

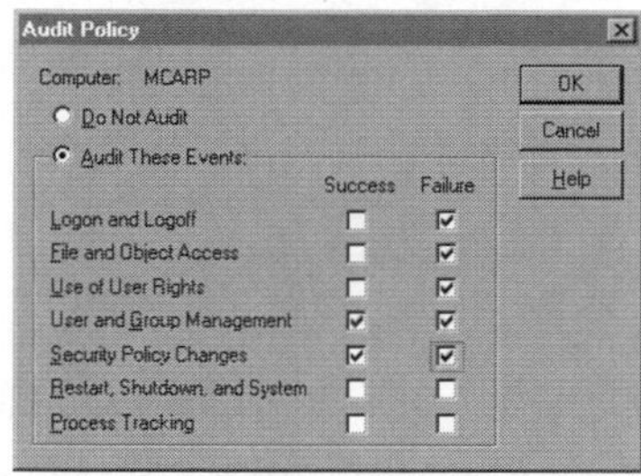

Figure 25.5. *The Audit Policy dialog box.*

Remember, these audits are useful only for preventing security problems if they are reviewed frequently for patterns that indicate a breach of security. They can also be used after the security problem is found through other means, but will only show what happened, by whom, and when.

Windows NT Browser Service

by Robert Reinstein

This chapter discusses the Windows NT browser service. The NT browser service builds a list of all computers on the local network. Here's what you'll learn today:

- What network browsing is
- Browser process
- Browser configuration
- Support of different environments

What Is Network Browsing?

Network browsing is similar to browsing a book. When you browse a book, you look at the table of contents or the index to find out what information is available and where to find it. Browsing on the network is similar in that you're trying to find out what servers and resources are available and where to find them.

A special service in NT, called the computer browser, is responsible for maintaining an up-to-date list of available resources. The computer browser is much like a continuously updated table of contents. As new servers come online, the service is registered with the browser. As servers go offline, they are eventually removed.

Browsing works so that all computers announce themselves on the network at the time they are started and at certain intervals thereafter. These announcements are gathered on the browser computer and added to the browser list. This computer list can then be requested by other computers when a user wants to view a list of the currently available computers on the network. The fact that computers constantly announce themselves to the computer maintaining the browser list means that if a computer does not announce itself within a certain period, it will be taken off the list. This ensures that the list will contain an almost up-to-date list of computers in the network.

Browser Categories

There are several different roles for a browser computer:

- Master browsers
- Domain master browsers
- Backup browsers
- Potential browsers
- Nonbrowsers (clients)

A master browser is a computer that gathers all the announcements sent by the other computers and creates and maintains the browser list from these announcements. The master browser then can serve clients by sending them the browser list when they request it. There is at least one master browser computer for each domain or workgroup. If the domain spans several subnetworks, there can be several master browsers within that domain, one for each subnetwork, depending on the protocol used.

In a domain network there is also a special type of a master browser called the domain master browser. The domain master browser receives the announcements for the whole domain and is responsible for distributing the list of a domain's resources to the master browsers within that domain. The domain master browser is always the primary domain controller.

Note: A workgroup cannot span multiple subnetworks. If you are running a workgroup environment, there won't be a domain master browser. Instead, there will be a master browser for each combination of subnetwork and workgroup.

Backup browsers receive the list of available domains and computers from the master browser and are responsible for serving client browser list queries. The backup browsers query the master browser every 15 minutes to get the latest list of computers, which they will then pass on to the client computers upon request. The master browser is responsible for designating a computer as a backup browser according to certain rules.

Potential browsers are computers that are capable of maintaining a list of available computers and can be elected as a master or backup browser. Most computers are capable of becoming a master browser, and are thus potential browsers.

Nonbrowsers are computers that have been specially configured so that they cannot perform any of the previously mentioned browser roles.

Browser Election

The `browse` function relies on the fact that there is always a master browser for the network. If a browser computer cannot be found or if two computers believe themselves to be the master browser, a new master browser is elected. This is called a browser election.

A browser election will occur in the following cases:

- A computer cannot locate the master browser
- A preferred master browser or an NT server comes online

Note: A computer can be defined as a preferred master browser by setting a specific value in the computer's Registry. (See the section "Browser Configuration" later in this chapter.) A preferred master browser will force a browser election when it comes online in the same way a domain controller will force an election when it comes up. A Preferred Master Browser has an advantage in the election of a new browser.

Browser election is based on election criteria. The criteria affecting browser election are operating system type, whether the computer is a Primary Domain Controller or is running a WINS server, whether the computer is running a master or backup browser, whether the computer is a Preferred Master Browser, how long the computer has been up, and the name of the computer.

A computer initiates a browser election by sending out an election datagram. When a browser receives an election datagram, it will examine the election criteria contained in the datagram to see whether the computer sending the datagram has greater criteria than the browser. Based on this criteria, the browsers will then elect a new master browser among themselves.

The election process is conducted by each system capable of serving as a master browser advertising its configuration via a single number. The potential browser with the highest number wins the election. That number has the following format:

Operating system type	`0xFF000000`
Election version	`0x00FFFF00`
Settings	`0x000000FF`

The operating system that the potential master browser is running is the most important. The election process gives the highest priority to NT Server, then NT Workstation, then other Windows systems. The operating system and the value it uses for operating system type are listed here:

Operating System	*Value*
Windows NT Server	`0x02`
Windows NT Workstation	`0x01`
Windows for Workgroups, Windows 95	`0x00`

The next most important criteria is the election version. This is set each time an election starts and should be the same for all servers in the election.

The final components are computer settings that can control how willing the server is to become a master browser. The following are the values used for each option:

Option	*Value*
Primary Domain Controller	`0x80`
Preferred Master Browser	`0x08`
Current Master Browser	`0x04`
Maintains Server List	`0x02`
Current Backup Browser	`0x01`

Unlike previous sections of the election number, this section can have more than one value. Thus, both a Primary Domain Controller that is a Preferred Master Browser and the Current Master Browser will have a value of `0x8B`, which is `0x80` for being a Primary Domain Controller plus the `0x08` for being a Preferred Master Browser and the `0x04` for being the Current Master Browser.

For more information on the browser election process, search the Microsoft Knowledge base for article Q102878.

Browsing Process

If you are running a Windows NT domain environment, it's safe to assume that the first computer that is up in the domain is the domain controller. The domain controller will become the domain master browser for its domain and also the master browser for that particular subnetwork. If you are running a workgroup environment, the first computer that comes up will become the master browser for that particular workgroup and subnetwork.

Whenever a Primary Domain Controller comes online, it will automatically become the domain master browser, as well as the local subnet browser. Due to the election criteria of the browser service, a Primary Domain Controller will always be a browser, as will any backup domain controller that isn't on the same subnet with the Primary Domain Controller.

A master browser receives announcements from computers running any of the following software:

- Windows NT 3.1
- Windows NT 3.1 Advanced Server
- Windows for Workgroups
- Windows 95
- Windows NT Workstation 3.5, or later
- Windows NT Server 3.5, or later
- LAN Manager systems

When a computer running any of the above mentioned operating systems starts, it will make an announcement to the master browser indicating that it is an available resource. Or, the computer might decide to force a browser election if it doesn't find the master browser in time.

If a master browser is found and accepted, the master browser will determine the computer's role. In other words the master browser will decide whether the computer that just started will become a backup browser or stay a potential browser. The configuration of the computer can also prevent it from becoming a backup browser. (See the section "Browser Configuration" later in this chapter.) If the computer is not a LAN Manager system, the master browser will also return to the computer a list of available backup browsers.

When browsing has been initialized and the computer has not been elected as a master browser, it will start announcing itself to the master browser at specified intervals. The first announcement will occur 1 minute after the initial startup, the next one 2 minutes after that, the next one 4 minutes after that, the next one 8 minutes after that and then every 12 minutes. If computer power is turned off, the master browser will wait for 3 announcement cycles (36 minutes by default), and if it has not received an announcement from the computer, it will remove the computer from the browse list.

Browser Shutdown or Failure

The browser election process should make sure that there is always a master browser for a given network. If a master browser is shut down properly, it will force an election to elect a new master browser. If the master browser fails, a backup browser requesting an update to its browse list or a client performing a browse request will notice this and force an election.

If a backup browser is shut down properly, it will announce to the master browser that it will not be available anymore, and the master browser removes it from the list of available backup browsers. The same happens when a nonbrowser is shut down. The master browser will automatically remove any computer from the browse list if it has not received an announcement from the computer in three announcement cycles (3 times 12 minutes). Because of this delay a computer may still be visible in the browse list, even though it is not available on the network. This delay may be even longer for backup browsers, because they get their updated list from the master browser only every 15 minutes. Thus, it may take a full 36 minutes before the master browser removes a computer from the browse list, and an additional 15 minutes for the removal to be visible to the backup browsers.

Browse Requests

A computer requesting the browse list will initially send the request to the master browser. The master browser will then send the computer a list of backup browsers, and the requesting computer will select three backup browsers it will use for the actual browse requests. The number of available backup browsers is dependent on how many computers there are on the network:

- All Backup Domain Controllers will become backup browsers.
- If the `MaintainServerList` value in the `CurrentControlSet\Services\Browser\Parameters` key is set to Yes, the computer will become a backup browser.
- If no backup browsers are selected based on the above mentioned criteria, the master browser will designate a computer to become a backup browser. There must be at least 1 backup browser for every 32 computers in the subnetwork.

Browser Configuration

The browser process relies mostly on default values. There are, however, some values and parameters an administrator can change to affect the way browsing works. All of the browser configuration is done in the Windows NT Registry. All the Registry entries for the Browser service are located under the following Registry subkey:

```
\HKEY_LOCAL_MACHINE\System\CurrentControlSet\Services\Browser\Parameters
```

The `MaintainServerList` parameter defines whether the computer can become a browser or not:

Value	*Description*
`Yes`	This computer will become a browser. Upon startup the computer will either be elected a master browser or will become a backup browser. This value is the default for a computer running Windows NT Server.
`No`	This computer is a non-browser, and cannot become a backup or a master browser.
`Auto`	This computer is a potential browser, and will become a backup browser depending on the decision by the master browser. This is the default value for a computer running Windows NT Workstation.

> **Note:** This chapter covers the parameters and their settings for a Windows NT environment. Similar parameters exist for both Windows 95 and Windows for Workgroups environments as well, and their values are set in a way characteristic for these environments.

The parameter `IsDomainMasterBrowser` defines whether this computer is a Preferred Master Browser. A Preferred Master Browser is given a priority during a browser election. The value of this parameter is `False` by default. If you want to define the computer as a Preferred Master Browser, set the value to `True`.

You can also increase or decrease the time that a computer waits between announcements. By default the time between announcements is 12 minutes, or 720 seconds. If you want to decrease the number of announcements on the network, you can increase the time. The negative effect of increasing the time between announcements is that in the event of a failure or shutdown it takes longer for this computer to disappear from the browser list.

The announcement time can be changed by adding a parameter called `Announce` (type `REG_DWORD`) under the Registry key `HKEY_LOCAL_MACHINE\System\CurrentControlSet\Services\LanmanServer\Parameters` and set the value for this parameter to the number of seconds you want to pass between announcements.

Browsing in a Multiple Domain Environment

When a computer becomes a master browser within a domain or a workgroup, it will announce itself to the master browsers within other domains or workgroups using datagrams called domain announcements. This will allow the master browsers to create and maintain a list not only of available computers within their own domain, but also of available domains and workgroups in the network. The master browsers will then announce their domain or workgroup at certain intervals, and if a domain or workgroup is not announced for a certain period of time, the other master browsers will remove this domain or workgroup from their browse list.

If a domain spans several subnetworks, the domain master browser (the domain's Primary Domain Controller) is responsible for maintaining a list of all available resources in that particular domain. The master browsers in each of the subnetworks announce themselves to the domain master browser at certain intervals, so that the domain master browser will know to obtain the browse list from that particular master browser. The domain master browser then merges the browse lists from the various master browsers to form a complete list for the domain, and will propagate this list back down to the master browsers. This will enable the clients to view the complete browse list for a domain.

In order for the master browsers in each subnetwork to announce themselves to the domain master browser, they must know how to locate the domain master browser. There are two ways of providing this information:

- Using the WINS service
- Using LMHOSTS files

For more information on WINS and LMHOSTS, see Chapter 31, "The Windows Internet Naming Service (WINS)."

These two methods will provide the master browsers with the IP address of the domain master browsers, which will enable the master browser to send a directed datagram to the domain master browser and announce its presence.

All the NetBIOS over TCP/IP broadcasts are sent using UDP port 137. It is possible to enable some routers to automatically forward these broadcasts, which will enable browsing to occur over subnetworks without configuring WINS or LMHOSTS files. This will, however, create some unnecessary broadcast traffic on the network, which is generally inadvisable.

Troubleshooting the Browser Service

If you are running the browser service in a single LAN environment, the process should be more or less automatic. As has been discussed earlier in this chapter, the browsers will themselves take care of always having one master browser and a suitable number of backup browsers on the network.

If you are, however, running the browser service in an internetwork consisting of many subnetworks, you need to do some configuring to let the master browsers in each of the subnetworks know where they can find the domain master browsers for each domain. This can be done using an LMHOSTS file or a WINS server as discussed earlier in the section "Browsing in a Multiple Domain Environment."

When troubleshooting the browser service, always remember that deleting a machine or a domain from the browser list will take some time. An administrator's greatest gift is a bit of patience!

Summary

The NT browsing services allow browsing to work across multiple networks. They also bring strength and reliability to the browsing process.

Browsing is the cornerstone of networking. Even a quick glance at the browsing election process shows how much of a priority Microsoft gave NT when browsing.

CHAPTER 27

Troubleshooting the Remote Access Service (RAS) and Dial-Up Networking (DUN)

by Terry W. Ogletree

The remote access capabilities of Windows NT enable the user to dial in to an NT Server through a telephone connection and establish a basic connection to the network. You can also use other telephone network services such as ISDN and X.25 interfaces to communicate remotely. Windows NT Server can run the Remote Access Service (RAS) to provide dial-in capabilities for your users. Both NT Server and Workstation can use the Dial-Up Networking component of RAS to dial out to other RAS servers.

The RAS that was supplied with versions of Windows NT prior to version 4.0 had a single GUI application that you could use to administer both the dial-in and dial-out services. In Windows NT 4.0, an attempt was made to provide the user with an interface that is similar to the one that comes with Windows 95. Thus, you can still use the Remote Access Admin program (found under the Administrative Tools menu) to configure and monitor dial-in users, and you can use the Dial-Up Network icon (found in the My Computer desktop folder) to establish outgoing RAS communication sessions. Although the Dial-Up Network program appears at first glance to be the same as the one you find in Windows 95, the similarities are on the surface only.

Troubleshooting RAS problems from the client or server side can become difficult when you consider the many different parts of the operating system that become involved in RAS communications. You have to be sure the hardware, such as the modem and telephone line, is functioning properly. You need to be sure the dial-in users are correctly set up in the security directory database and have the rights needed to access resources on the network. Manufacturers are updating software drivers for modems all the time. Even Microsoft can cause problems by releasing a service pack (known to laymen as a *bugfix*) that breaks as much code as it fixes.

Tip: Unless you have a specific problem that is fixed by Service Pack 2, don't install it! Although many of the bugs reported by users have been repaired in this service pack, it has a bad track record of introducing a whole new host of problems. Skip Service Pack 2 and install Service Pack 3 instead!

This chapter gives you a brief overview of RAS, along with information on configuring the service. Additional topics include the following:

- Troubleshooting modem and X.25 PAD problems
- Computer name resolution for RAS connections
- RAS configuration files
- Using the `DEVICE.LOG` file for troubleshooting computer-modem communications
- Windows NT Resource Kit utilities that can help you with RAS problems
- Problems with browsing and other common RAS errors

Overview of the Remote Access Service

The RAS found in Windows NT 4.0 is a powerful network communications program. Using RAS, you can connect to your workplace computer and use the same procedures to connect to network drives, printers, and other resources, as if you had an actual network card installed and hooked up to the network.

Of course, if you're using a modem you will notice one difference right away: RAS can be slower than a direct connection. If you have an ISDN line, you will notice a significant increase in speed. Some user management utilities of Windows NT, such as User Manager for Domains, include an option called "Slow speed connection," which means a slow network connection or a RAS connection.

However, as new technologies mature (such as Asynchronous Digital Subscriber Line [ADSL]), remote users can expect an ever-increasing bandwidth from public communications networks.

When you install Windows NT, you are given the option of installing RAS during the initial setup. If you choose to do this after installing the operating system, you can do so simply by using the Network applet in the Control Panel to install the service.

Installing RAS

To install RAS, double-click the Network icon in the Control Panel. Select the Services tab (see Figure 27.1) and look to be sure you do not already have the service installed. If it is not visible in the Network Services box, click the Add button. You can then select the service from the list of available services in the Select Network Service dialog box.

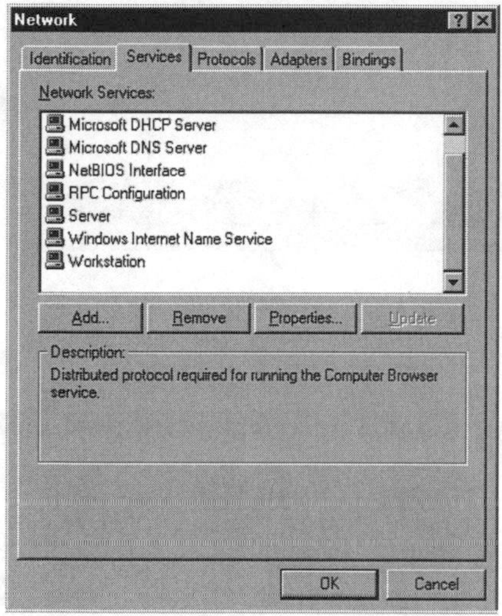

Figure 27.1. *The Services tab in the Network dialog box shows the network services currently installed. Use the Add button to install the Remote Access Service.*

> **Note:** Install the network protocol you want to use with RAS before installing RAS. Usually, this is TCP/IP (if, for example, you are connecting to the Internet for World Wide Web access). However, RAS also supports the NetBEUI (for NetBIOS applications) and NWLink (for Novell network connections) protocols using PPP (Point-to-Point Protocol). If you do not install the protocol first, it will not be available under RAS.

The installation procedure will then prompt you for the location of the installation files and copy the appropriate programs to your local drive.

If you have not already installed a modem or other communications port (ISDN terminal adapter, X.25 PAD, and so on) the Setup program will prompt you to set up a modem or other RAS-compatible device by invoking the modem installation dialog. (See Figure 27.2.)

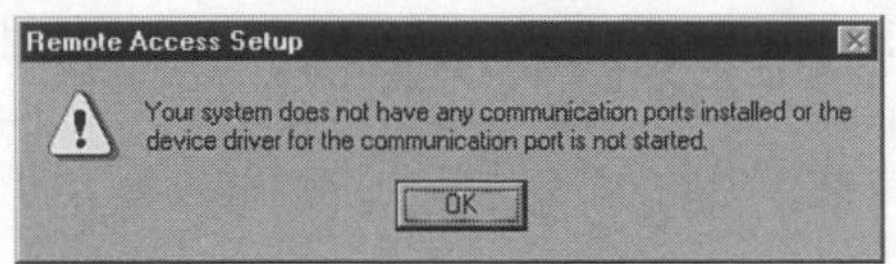

Figure 27.2. Setup will prompt you if you have not already installed a modem or other communications hardware.

After you click the OK button, you see another dialog box that shows any communication devices already on the system (see Figure 27.3). If you have none, click the Add button and you will get the Add RAS Device dialog box (see Figure 27.4).

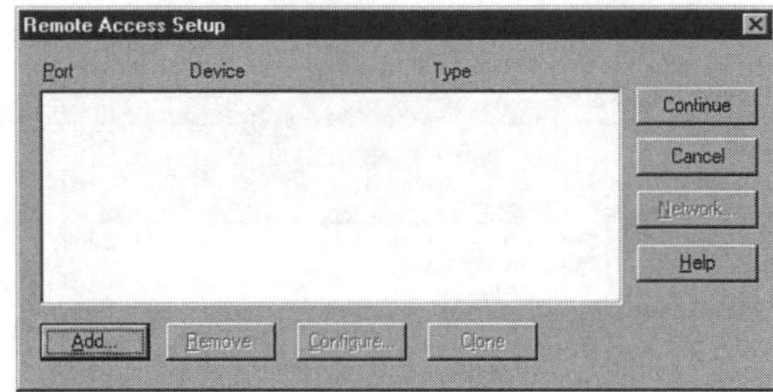

Figure 27.3. The Remote Access Setup dialog box shows whether you have any modems installed. The Add button enables you to install a new device.

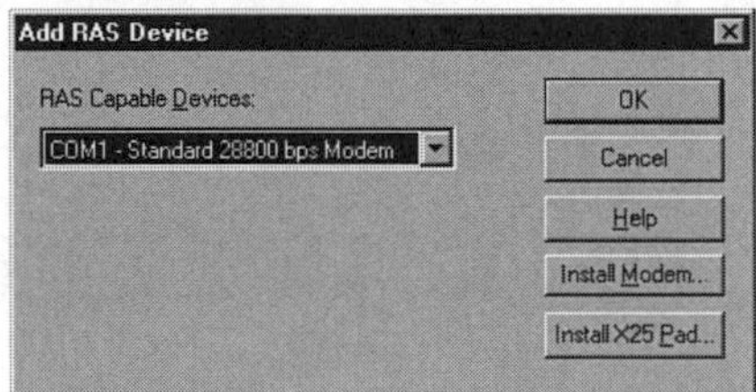

Figure 27.4. The Add RAS Device dialog box enables you to add modems and other communication devices.

To add a modem from the Add RAS Device dialog box, do the following:

1. Click the Install Modem button.
2. From the list of available ports that is presented, select the port that your modem is attached to.
3. Click on the Install Modem button.
4. Windows NT will attempt to detect what type of modem is connected to your system. If it does not recognize the modem, it will display a list of modems from which you can select your modem.
5. If you can find your modem in the list, select it. Otherwise, use the Have Disk button and, when prompted, insert a floppy disk that has the appropriate files from your modem manufacturer. Click Next.

6. The Configure Port Usage dialog box will appear. You can use this dialog box to configure the modem port for one of three types of access: Dial out only, Receive calls only, or Dial out and Receive calls.

After you add the modem, the Remote Access Setup dialog box displays the modem (see Figure 27.5).

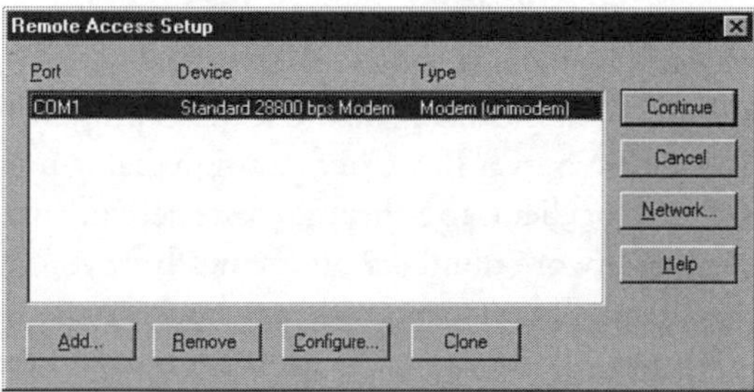

Figure 27.5. *The newly added modem now shows up in the Remote Access Setup dialog box.*

Finally, the Setup program enables you to select whether you want NetBEUI RAS clients to access just the RAS server or the entire network the server is attached to (see Figure 27.6). It then enables you to configure the TCP/IP protocol if you have it installed (see Figure 27.7).

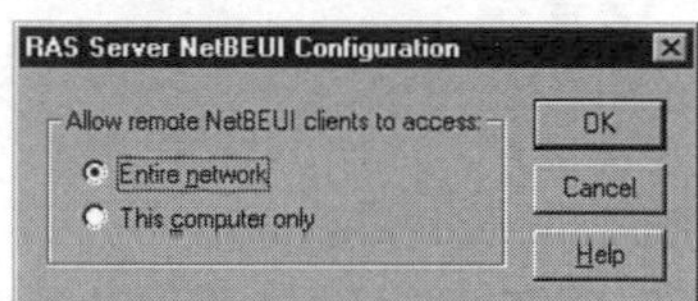

Figure 27.6. *You can restrict NetBEUI RAS clients to just the RAS server or allow them to access the entire network.*

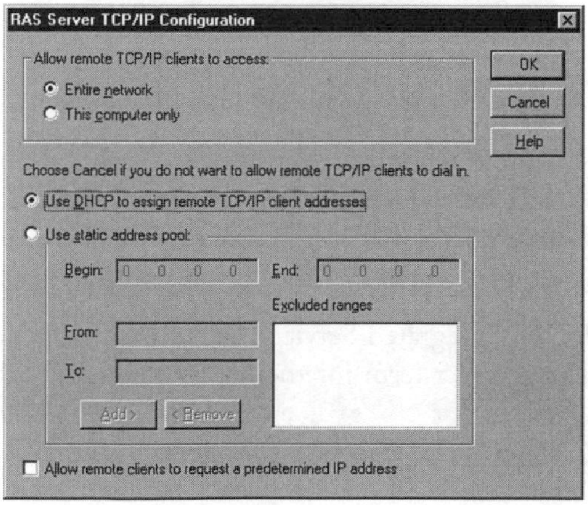

Figure 27.7. *If you have installed the TCP/IP protocol, the Setup program enables you to configure it for RAS clients.*

One of the most common mistakes when installing RAS is forgetting to select an address configuration mechanism. Using the RAS Server TCP/IP Configuration dialog box, you can select to use a DHCP server or a static pool of addresses you specify for RAS clients. If you choose to enter a range of addresses in the static pool section of the dialog box, make sure that you use a range of addresses that is not being used by any other computer or DHCP server. Remember that all IP addresses on the network must be unique.

If you have the IPX protocol installed on your system, you can configure it also for use with RAS. In the Remote Access Setup dialog box, select the Network button and then check the IPX check box in the Server Settings part of the dialog box. Use the Configure button found next to the IPX check box to bring up the RAS Server IPX Configuration dialog box. Here you can configure the IPX protocol to allow access for clients to either the entire network or just the RAS server computer. You can choose to allocate network numbers automatically or you can specify a range of numbers that RAS can assign to clients. If you want, you can choose to use the same network number for all clients using the IPX protocol, and you can permit clients to request a specific IPX node number.

When you have finished configuring the protocols to be used for the RAS server, the Setup program reminds you that you have to first grant permission to users before they can dial in to your server (see Figure 27.8).

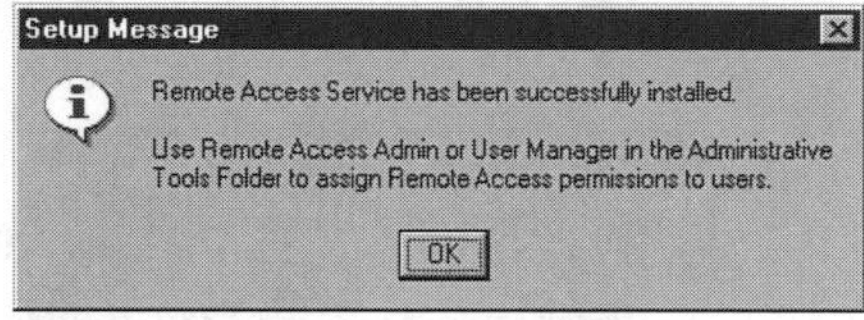

Figure 27.8. *Setup reminds you to grant permission to your users. If you forget, the users will not be able to dial in!*

As with most network modifications, you will have to reboot the machine before the new services can be used.

Troubleshooting Modems and PADs

The modem is the usual piece of hardware you associate with dial-up connectivity. Modem stands for modulation-demodulation, which describes what the device does: It modulates digital signals into analog signals for transport across the telephone network and, on the other end, demodulates the signal to produce a digital signal that the remote computer can understand.

When you use an ISDN (Integrated Services Digital Network) connection, you don't need a modem. For ISDN the correct term for the hardware you attach to the line with is TA (for Terminal Adapter).

Note: Routers are also available that can terminate the ISDN connection at your site. Using a router instead of a TA gives you the ability to allow more than one computer to share access to the ISDN connection.

Modems are pretty standard devices in most respects. The Hayes compatible command set, which is named for the manufacturer that originated it, Hayes Microcomputers, is the basic command set that dominates the modem market. It is easy to find out the exact commands you need to control your modem (hey, read the handbook).

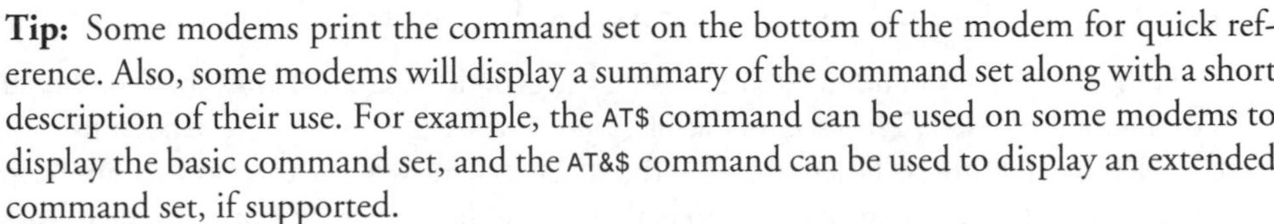

Tip: Some modems print the command set on the bottom of the modem for quick reference. Also, some modems will display a summary of the command set along with a short description of their use. For example, the `AT$` command can be used on some modems to display the basic command set, and the `AT&$` command can be used to display an extended command set, if supported.

Both modems and X.25 interface devices use serial communications ports. Both devices can be configured using information files (`MODEM.INF` and `PAD.INF`), and you can diagnose many problems with either type of device using a file called `DEVICE.LOG`.

The `MODEM.INF` and `PAD.INF` Files

Windows NT 4.0, like Windows 95, provides support for TAPI (the telephone application programming interface) and the Universal Modem Driver (Unimodem). However, if you are using an older modem for which you cannot obtain a TAPI driver, you can configure the modem for use with RAS by using the `MODEM.INF` file.

This file is found in the `%systemroot%\System32\RAS` directory. It is a large file that contains configuration information for a large number of different modems. If your modem is not supported by Windows NT (check the Hardware Compatibility List), you may be able to edit this file and create the entries needed to make your modem work with NT. A similar file called `PAD.INF` can be found in the same directory and is used to configure X.25 PADs.

Tip: Always check Microsoft's Web site for the newest copy of the Hardware Compatibility List (HCL). There is also a white paper you can read that discusses hardware compatibility issues and Windows NT. The white paper is available at the following URL:

`http://www.microsoft.com/syspro/technet/boes/bo/winntas/technote/mscompt.htm`

To find the most recent copy of the HCL, point your Web browser to `www.microsoft.com`, select the Support option and then the product Windows NT Server.

Also, manufacturers are constantly updating drivers for hardware devices used with NT. If your modem is not on the HCL, you might try searching the Internet to find the manufacturer's home page. There's a good chance they have developed a driver that is compatible with Windows NT.

If your modem is listed on the HCL, it has been certified according to standards set by Microsoft to work with Windows NT. If you obtain a newer driver from the manufacturer, it may or may not be certified.

If you cannot find your modem in the `MODEM.INF` file and the manufacturer does not supply a revised version of the file, you can experiment with the current file to try to make it work.

The first thing you should do is to try using the generic modem entries that are included in the file. These are titled "Hayes Compatible *baud rate*" modems, where *baud rate* can be from 1,200KB to 28,800KB. These entries in the `MODEM.INF` file will use the most common commands implemented by different manufacturers that claim Hayes compatibility. If one of these generic modem types does not work, you might try a different modem model by the same manufacturer. While you may not find an entry that is completely compatible, you might find one that is partially compatible and use it to clone your own entry.

Tip: This solution won't work in all cases, but you can try using the `MODEM.INF` file from Windows 95 to install a modem under Windows NT. Some of the definitions found in the Windows 95 file are valid for use under Windows NT.

When you add the modem, do not instruct the wizard to detect the modem. Instead choose the "I will select it from a list" selection. Use the Have Disk button and insert a disk containing the Windows 95 `MODEM.INF` file into the A drive.

Editing the file and creating your own entry appears to be a simple matter. The first section of the file that contains *global responses,* which are the most common responses used by a large number of different manufacturers, is listed here. Following this section, you will see entries for individual modems. Each new modem section begins with the name of the modem in square brackets ([ ]). The text you place here is also the text that is displayed when you are presented with choices while using the Modem Wizard to install a modem.

To create a new entry, simply supply a name for your modem and define the command strings that you think will be necessary. You will note that the `ALIAS=` keyword can be used to include the definitions from another entry. Many entries in this file have an `ALIAS=` keyword followed by the name of a Hayes modem, followed by command definitions that differ from the included definitions. Using the `ALIAS=` keyword can prevent a lot of typing and cut down on the size of the file.

Note: The `ALIAS=` keyword must reference another modem entry that is completely self-contained. That is, you cannot alias an alias. If you use the `ALIAS=` keyword to include command-string definitions from another modem entry, the referenced entry cannot also contain an `ALIAS=` keyword.

Corrupted or Missing .INF and .INI Files (ERRORS 657 and 659)

The information files described in the preceding section are required for the Remote Access Service to work. Other initialization files may also be needed. The following errors indicate that a file is missing or has been corrupted:

Error 657: The `device.inf` file could not be opened.

Error 659: The `media.ini` file refers to an unknown device name.

When you make modifications to any of the information or initialization files, you should always first create a backup copy. The easiest way to do this is to use the `COPY` command:

```
> COPY MODEM.INF MODEM.ORIGINAL
```

This will create a file called `MODEM.ORIGINAL`, which you can always go back to should you screw things up in the `MODEM.INF` file.

When you get error 657 or error 659, replace the file named in the error message with a backup copy. If you do not have a backup copy, the only alternative you have is to try to back out any errors made in the file or reinstall the Remote Access Service so that it will replace the files with original files from the distribution source. The disadvantage of using reinstall to fix the problem is that you will lose any other edits you have successfully made to the file before you corrupted it.

Caution: Rule of thumb: *Always* create backup copies of any configuration files you edit!

The DEVICE.LOG File

To make things easier, you can create a log file that shows the interaction between the modem and the RAS software. If you have problems getting your modem to connect to an Internet provider and you are using a script file, the `DEVICE.LOG` log file can be a lifesaver.

You need to edit the Registry to instruct RAS to create the `DEVICE.LOG` file:

1. Start the Registry Editor (use `REGEDIT.EXE` or `REGEDT32.EXE`) at the command prompt.
2. Locate the following key:

   `HKEY_LOCAL_MACHINE\System\CurrentControlSet\Services\rasman\parameters`

   (If the key does not exist, use the Add Value option on the Edit menu to create it.)

3. Whether you edit or create the key, the following values must be used:

   Value Name: `logging`

   Data Type: `REG_DWORD`

   String: `1`

4. Exit the Registry Editor.
5. Stop and restart the Remote Access Service. To do this, use the Services applet in the Control Panel, highlight the service, and click Stop. Wait a few seconds and then click Start. See Figure 27.9 for an example of the Services dialog box.

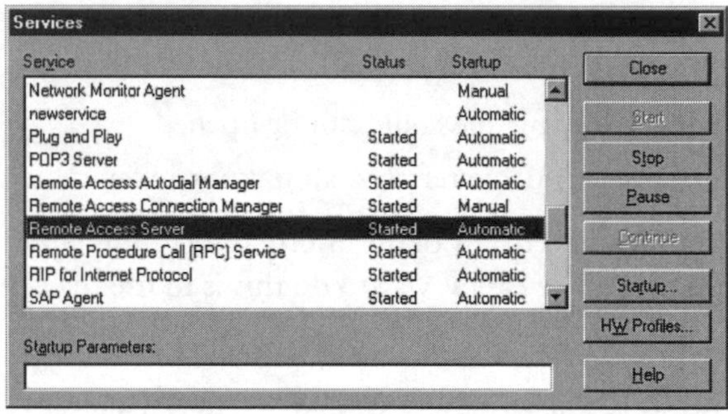

Figure 27.9. *The Services applet enables you to stop and restart the Remote Access Service.*

Note that you can also use the Server Manager to select the server on which RAS is running and then use the Server menu selection Services to stop and start the service.

After restarting the service, you can try using the modem with RAS again. After you fail to connect, exit the Remote Access program and examine the contents of the `DEVICE.LOG` file. You will find the log file in the `%systemroot%\system32\RAS` directory. Use the `EDIT` command to examine this simple ASCII file.

The `DEVICE.LOG` file should contain all text sent to the modem (or X.25 interface device) by the RAS program and all echoes and responses from the device.

The `DEVICE.LOG` file can be a helpful tool when debugging problems with your `MODEM.INF` file. You see the actual command strings that RAS sends to the modem and the responses. Specifically, the `MODEM.INF` symbol `COMMAND_INIT` is used to define the string RAS sends to the modem for initialization and setup. If you are trying to tweak an entry in `MODEM.INF` to make it work for an unsupported model, the information logged to `DEVICE.LOG` can be of great value.

ISDN Problems

Integrated Services Digital Network (ISDN) service can give you a large boost in bandwidth for a RAS connection. Although you can achieve a maximum of around 33KB using a modem, an ISDN connection gives you two 64KB 'B' channels (which can be combined into one 128KB link).

Another channel in an ISDN connection is used for signaling and call setup procedures. Two B channels and one D signaling channel is called BRI (Basic Rate Interface). Another version of ISDN offered by most telephone companies is PRI (Primary Rate Interface). The main difference is that PRI gives you more B channels.

If you need more than the BRI setup, you should consider the economics of using fractional T1 or full T1 lines for your connection. Of course, when dialing into work from a home computer, a T1 can be considered expensive overkill. Who can afford several thousand dollars a month for a telephone line?

Remote Access Server Failing to Answer Incoming Calls

When using ISDN for your RAS server, you may encounter a problem where RAS doesn't answer incoming calls. This is usually due to the inclusion of non-numeric characters (such as the dash character) in a phone number.

When using ISDN, do not use non-numeric characters in the phone number.

Connectivity and Name Resolution

After you have confirmed that your modem is communicating with your ISP's modem and that RAS has successfully logged you onto the remote server and has started PPP, you may encounter problems accessing Internet resources due to name resolution problems.

When you configured the RAS Phonebook entry, you had the option of entering the addresses of DNS servers that would be used on the remote network or having the ISP's server provide the information. Either way, you can confirm that the addresses have been correctly assigned and can be located on the network using a few simple steps.

First, use the `IPCONFIG/ALL` command to show current TCP/IP configuration information. Listing 27.1 is a sample output from this command. As you can see, it gives you much more than just the addresses of the name servers.

Listing 27.1. Output from the `IPCONFIG/ALL` command.

```
Windows NT IP Configuration

    Host Name . . . . . . . . . . : bcatlanta1.ono
    DNS Servers . . . . . . . . . : 207.69.188.185
                                    207.69.188.186
    Node Type . . . . . . . . . . : Broadcast
    NetBIOS Scope ID. . . . . . . :
    IP Routing Enabled. . . . . . : Yes
    WINS Proxy Enabled. . . . . . : No
```

continues

Listing 27.1. continued

```
    NetBIOS Resolution Uses DNS : No

Ethernet adapter NDISLoop4:

    Description . . . . . . . . : MS LoopBack Driver
    Physical Address. . . . . . : 20-4C-4F-4F-50-20
    DHCP Enabled. . . . . . . . : No
    IP Address. . . . . . . . . : 10.10.10.10
    Subnet Mask . . . . . . . . : 255.255.0.0
    Default Gateway . . . . . . :

Ethernet adapter NdisWan6:

    Description . . . . . . . . : NdisWan Adapter
    Physical Address. . . . . . : 00-01-B0-10-67-80
    DHCP Enabled. . . . . . . . : No
    IP Address. . . . . . . . . : 207.69.217.99
    Subnet Mask . . . . . . . . : 255.255.255.0
    Default Gateway . . . . . . : 207.69.217.99

Ethernet adapter NdisWan5:

    Description . . . . . . . . : NdisWan Adapter
    Physical Address. . . . . . : 00-00-00-00-00-00
    DHCP Enabled. . . . . . . . : No
    IP Address. . . . . . . . . : 0.0.0.0
    Subnet Mask . . . . . . . . : 0.0.0.0
    Default Gateway . . . . . . :
```

If the addresses listed for your DNS servers are correct, try using the `PING` command to see if you can actually send and receive packets from the addresses.

```
> PING <address>
```

> **Tip:** If you are not sure about the IP addresses for the DNS servers, you can contact your ISP or the administrator of the network you are dialing in to in order to get the correct addresses. Because the DNS servers on a TCP/IP network (such as the Internet) are the computers that translate network names to network addresses, your computer must have the address of one or more DNS servers in order to establish a session with a remote computer using network names.

If you have assigned the correct addresses (check with your ISP) and you can communicate with them, you should have no problems resolving TCP/IP names using the servers. If a problem persists, you should have your ISP check to make sure that the DNS servers are functioning correctly.

Note: When you try to use an Internet domain name to access a resource, keep in mind that if the name has just recently been registered with InterNIC it might take them a few days, or possibly a week, to get the information into the domain name servers.

Another possible problem you can encounter when connecting to an ISP is an address conflict. You cannot use the same IP address for your network adapter card and your RAS connection. Even if you have installed the Microsoft Loopback Adapter (a software driver that simulates a network adapter), you still must use a unique address for it.

Again, you can see the addresses assigned to your various network connections by using the `IPCONFIG/ALL` command. If you see that an adapter and your RAS adapter share the same address, you should change one of them. If you are using the loopback adapter, you can remove it if you have no need for remote clients to browse your computer.

Finally, if you are still having communication problems, try disabling software compression. To do this perform the following steps:

1. Bring up the Dial-Up Networking application (found under My Computer).
2. Click the More button.
3. Select Edit Entry and Modem Properties from the More menu.
4. Select the Server tab and then clear the Enable Software Compression check box.

After you have cleared the check box, try to connect to your ISP once more.

Problems Using AutoDial

The AutoDial feature of Windows NT 4.0 can be used to automatically dial out to a remote connection when you try to access a network service that requires it.

Using RASAUTOU

If you are experiencing problems with AutoDial, you can use the command-line (character-based) interface to view and modify information stored by AutoDial.

`> RASAUTOU -S` will give you a list of names and addresses that AutoDial has a record of. If you run this command and see addresses or names that you no longer need, you can use the Registry Editor to remove them. To do so, follow these steps:

1. Start the Registry Editor. (Use either `REGEDIT.EXE` or `REGEDT32.EXE`.)
2. Locate the following key:

   `HKEY_CURRENT_USER\Software\Microsoft\RASAutodial\Addresses`

3. Delete the addresses or names you no longer need by highlighting the value and using the Delete selection on the Edit menu (see Figure 27.10).

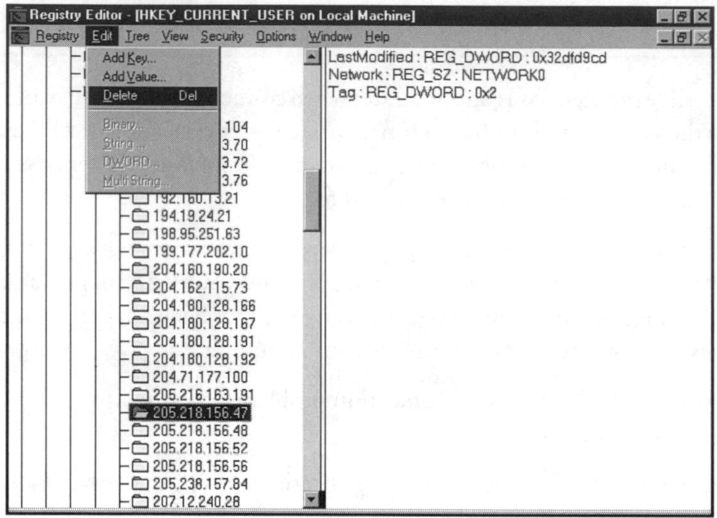

Figure 27.10. *Use the Delete selection from the Edit menu to remove unnecessary addresses from AutoDial.*

Tracing AutoDial Events

The `DEVICE.LOG` file discussed in this chapter can be used to create a log file of the interaction between the RAS software and the serial hardware device. By requesting an additional utility file from Microsoft Technical Support, you can do something similar for AutoDial.

The file you need is `RTUTILS.DLL`. When calling technical support, mention the Knowledge Base article number Q152220. The file should be available at no charge.

To use `RTUTILS.DLL`, perform the following steps:

1. Copy the file to the `%systemroot%\System32` directory on your hard disk.
2. Start the Registry Editor (use either `REGEDIT.EXE` or `REGEDT32.EXE`).
3. Locate the following subkey:

   `HKEY_LOCAL_MACHINE\SYSTEM\CurrentControlSet\Services\Tracing\RASAUTO\EnableFileTracing`
4. Change the value for this subkey from `0` to `1`. You can do this by double-clicking the key to bring up the editing dialog box.
5. Exit the Registry Editor.
6. Stop all Remote Access Service processes. You can use the Services applet in the Control Panel to do this.
7. After waiting about a minute, restart the Remote Access Service(s). Be sure that the RASAUTO service is restarted.

From this point forward, you will find log entries for the actions taken by AutoDial in a file called `RASAUTO.LOG`. To find out what directory the log file will be written in, examine the `FileDirectory` value under the same Registry key that you found `EnableFileTracing`.

The log file is an ASCII text file that you can read using any regular text-file editor.

User Authentication and RAS

When RAS clients are not able to connect to your RAS server, most of the time you will find it to be a problem in user authentication. This can be something simple, such as a user entering the wrong password or a user not having been granted the permission to dial in. Or, it can be something much more complicated, such as a duplicate name on the network or a hardware failure.

The Default Domain for RAS Clients

When a RAS client dials in to a Windows NT Server running RAS (and does not specify a domain name), the server will attempt to authenticate the username and password in the domain security directory database that the RAS server belongs to, or the local security directory database if the server is not a domain member.

If the RAS server is not a member of a domain and you use third-party RAS client software, you will not be able to pass the name of a logon domain to the NT RAS server. Therefore, if you use a standalone server for your RAS server, you will need to create an account in the local security directory database for third-party clients. For Windows NT (and Windows 95) clients you can use a domain account, and the RAS server will forward the logon information to the appropriate domain controller for validation.

If you have a need to force the authentication to use a different domain for NT clients (which the server must have access to), you can do so by editing the Registry.

To use a Registry key to specify the default domain, perform the following steps:

1. Run the Registry Editor (`REGEDIT.EXE` or `REGEDT32.EXE`) at the command prompt.
2. Find the following key:

   `HKEY_LOCAL_MACHINE\System\CurrentControlSet\Services\RASMAN\PPP`
3. From the Edit menu, select Edit Value. The name of the value to edit is `DefaultDomain`.

The data type for this value should be `REG_SZ`, and you can specify a domain name (up to 15 characters) for the value.

Granting Dial-In Permissions to RAS Clients

To grant dial-in access to users in a domain, you simply use the Remote Access Admin utility (found under the Administrative Tools menu), select Permissions from the Users menu, and select the users (or all users) that you want to grant the right to. After a domain user account has been granted the right to dial in, that account can be used on any RAS server in the domain.

Tip: As of version 4.0, you can also use the User Manager administrative tool to grant dial-in permission to your users. In the User Properties dialog box for any user you can click on the Dialin button to get to the Dialin Information dialog box. In that dialog box you can select the check box Grant Dialin Permission to User and you can also configure callback options for this user if you use that feature.

If you want to allow certain users to dial in only to selected servers, you will not be able to do this on a server-by-server basis in a domain. You can, however, simulate the same thing by denying another right on servers that you do not want the user to dial in to.

In addition to the dial-in permission, a user also needs to be granted the "Access this computer from network" right on each server for which dial-in access is desired. Therefore, if you want to limit users to certain RAS servers, simply use the User Manager on each server to revoke the "Access this computer from network" right for those users.

If the RAS server offers other services to the network, such as file or print shares, this solution will not work. Removing the "Access this computer from network" right will deny not only RAS access, but also local area network access, to the shares offered by the RAS server.

RASDIAL Fails to Connect Using the Scheduler Service

You can use the Scheduler Service (the `AT` command) to run commands at a predefined time on Windows NT. However, you should remember that unless you change it (using the Services applet on the Control Panel), the Scheduler Service runs under the System account. This account, you will remember, does not have granted to it the right "Access this computer from network."

This can cause a peculiar situation to happen when dialing in to a RAS server. If you specify (on the command line) the username and password for the RAS client to pass to the RAS server, that name and password are used to authenticate you for the RAS session.

If you do not specify the name and password, the RASDIAL program will use the name and password for the account under which it is being run. Therefore, if you run the `RASDIAL` command through the Scheduler Service, which uses the System account, you will not be able to log on to a remote RAS server. The remote server will use the default username (System), which does not have the right to log on through the network!

To rectify the situation, you can create a command file that runs and contains the `RASDIAL` command, along with the username and password. However, this can present a security risk that is unacceptable at many sites. Also, you can set up a different user account under which to run the Scheduler service and create the same account on the RAS server, granting the account the right to log on through the network and granting the account dial-in permission.

RAS Routing Naming and Addressing Issues

When you use RAS to provide remote access to resources on your LAN, you must be sure that you configure RAS and your network protocols correctly. Simple problems, such as using the same address for your RAS adapter as you use for your network card adapter, can be easy to fix. Problems with browsing for resources can be a little more difficult.

Browsing Across Router on LAN Fails

When you connect to a remote Windows NT network using RAS, you have the option "Use default gateway on remote network," available in the TCP/IP configuration dialog box under the Phonebook. Enabling this feature is necessary if you want to use an Internet utility, such as FTP or a Web browser, to access resources on the remote network.

However, this can cause problems when the RAS client tries to access resources on the network it is connected to by its physical network card. Although all resources on the local subnet should be available, those on the other side of a router cannot be seen.

This is because when you check "Use default gateway on remote network," a new route is added to the routing table to reflect this. If you use the `ROUTE PRINT` command, you will see that the first two entries have the network address of `0.0.0.0` (the default address for packets that don't match any other routing table entry). The first will be the default gateway on the LAN to which the computer is physically attached. The second entry will be the default gateway on the remote server connected through RAS.

The main difference is to be found in the column labeled `Metric`. This is the number of hops the packet must take to reach its destination when using this route. The metric for the first entry is `2`, and the metric for the RAS gateway is `1`.

You might think that the easiest way to remedy this would be to use the `ROUTE` command to delete the second entry. However, if you do this, RAS will replace the first entry with its own and you will effectively end up deleting the first entry!

To solve this problem, you need to use the `ROUTE` command to add a static route for the network on the other side of the router. The gateway address you specify should be the same one you see in the first routing table entry for the LAN default gateway. If you have more than one router on the LAN, create a route table entry for each network.

Unable to Acquire an IP Address (Event ID 20091)

This error occurs when you are using DHCP to administer client addresses for your RAS server. The following error message is recorded in the system log on the RAS server (use the Event Viewer administrative tool to view event records):

```
Event ID: 20091
Source: RemoteAccess
```

```
Type: Error
Description: The Remote Access Server was unable to acquire an IP address from the
DHCP Server to be used on the Server Adapter. Incoming users will be unable to
connect using IP.
```

The preceding error is caused by one of the following problems:

1. There is no DHCP server available on the network (you forgot to install one or the DHCP server you rely on is down).
2. A DHCP server is available on the network but you forgot to activate a scope that includes addresses for the same subnet as the RAS server's subnet address.

To solve the problem, you can assign a static pool of IP addresses using the Remote Access Server utility, or you can configure and activate a compatible scope of addresses on a DHCP server. Of course, if you already have a DHCP server and you get this error, your server is either down or unavailable to the RAS server. In that case, investigate the DHCP server and connectivity problems.

The Name Already Exists on the Network (Error 642)

Error 642 can occur when you attempt to dial in to a RAS server that is on the local area network to which your RAS client is connected.

This error usually occurs when a user is experimenting with RAS and chooses to use a server on the local network for practice. Because computers—the client and the RAS server—are connected physically to the LAN, each has already registered several NetBIOS names on that network. When the client tries to register names through RAS, the RAS server notices that the names already exist on the network.

To avoid this error, either disconnect the RAS client from the physical LAN, or, if appropriate, change the configuration of the RAS server so that access is granted to "This computer only." To change the RAS server's access mode, use the Network applet in the Control Panel.

Multihomed RAS Servers—Binding RAS to One Network Card

If you have a RAS server with two network interface cards (NICs) you may get the following error message in the System Event Log:

```
Event ID 20026
Source: RemoteAccess
Type: Error
Description: Remote Access Server Security Failure. A network error has occurred when
trying to establish a session with the security agent on LANA x. The error code is
the data.
```

where `LANA x` is a number for a network card on the system.

When assigning TCP/IP addresses, a RAS server can use a static pool of addresses or make use of a DHCP server to provide addresses to clients. This error occurs when RAS is bound to more than one network card, only one of which is valid for the subnet of addresses used by RAS. To prevent this error from occurring, you need to remove the incorrect binding.

1. Use the Network applet in the Control Panel.
2. Choose the Bindings tab.
3. Select Remote Access Server Service in the Show Bindings box.
4. Select the TCP/IP binding for the NIC that is not being used by the same addresses as the RAS clients, and then click the Disable button.
5. Exit the Network applet and reboot the computer for the binding change to take effect.

After you unbind the second NIC, the problem should no longer occur.

Using DHCP to Assign RAS Client Addresses

The Remote Access Service enables you to assign client addresses in three ways: a static address pool, a DHCP server, or configuring the server to allow the client to request a specific address. If you do not have a DHCP server on your network, the easiest method to use is to assign a range of available network addresses to RAS and use the static address pool option.

If you use DHCP, however, the addresses used by the Remote Access Service for clients are stored in the Registry. This will cause no problems—that is, until you reconfigure the DHCP server with a new range of addresses and delete the old range. Because the RAS server stores these values in the Registry until the lease expires, it will continue to use these addresses with RAS clients. If you have changed the address subnet on your LAN, you can end up with lots of addressing problems.

The solution is to remove the range of addresses from RAS by editing the Registry:

1. Start the Registry Editor (`REGEDIT.EXE` or `REGEDT32.EXE`).
2. Locate the following key:

   `HKEY_LOCAL_MACHINE\System\CurrentControlSet\Services\RemoteAccess\Parameteres\IP`
3. Under this key, locate the `DhcpAddresses` subkey and delete it.
4. Exit the Registry Editor and reboot Windows NT.

After the reboot, your RAS server will request new addresses from the DHCP server when a client dials in to the system.

SPX/IPX Network Issues

The capability to closely integrate Windows NT networks with Novell-based networks is one of the main reasons NT is making such huge inroads into previously all-NetWare shops. NetWare, which uses the SPX/IPX protocols for network communications, is the most widespread network operating system for personal computers in the world today.

RAS supports remote access for not only TCP/IP- and NetBIOS-based networks, but also for NetWare networks. In general, if you configure everything according to the help files that are included with Windows NT and with associated products such as the NetWare Gateway, you will have no problems. However, this section looks at a few things that can go wrong.

Multiple RAS Servers (IPX) Cannot Dial In to Another IPX Network

If all your IPX clients are configured as dial-out clients, you will probably not experience this problem. However, if you get the following error message when attempting to dial out from a RAS IPX-configured server to another IPX network

```
IPX CP reported error 744: Cannot use the IPX network number assigned by remote
server. Check the eventlog.
```

you may have more than one RAS IPX-configured server trying to dial into the remote IPX network.

The Event Log shows the following error:

```
The IPX network number <number> configured for the WAN interface is already in use on
the LAN. Possible solutions: 1) Disconnect this computer from the LAN and wait 3
minutes before dialing again; 2) Configure this computer for dialout only.
```

Although at first this might seem confusing, there is a good reason why you can have more than one RAS IPX-configured server dial in to the same remote IPX network.

When the first server dials in to the remote network, it is assigned a network number by the remote IPX network server. On its local area network, the RAS client—because it is configured also as a RAS server using the IPX protocol—will automatically be seen on the network as an IPX router. Thus, *it will advertise the network number it receives as a client* from the remote network on the local network. When a second IPX server—also configured as a RAS server for the IPX protocol—tries to dial in to the remote network, it also receives a network number from the remote IPX server, but cannot use it because *it already has that number in its routing tables* for the first IPX server.

Figure 27.11 is a diagram that shows the relationship between the two networks.

If the RAS server on Network B is set up to assign the same network number to each dial-in client, only RAS Server 1 on Network A will be able to use that number. RAS Server 2, which is also a RAS server (IPX) and thus an IPX router, cannot use the same number. However, RAS Client 3 can use the same number because it is not a RAS server for IPX and therefore is not an IPX router by default.

The only way around this type of situation is to make all but one of your IPX RAS servers dial-out RAS clients only. Doing this will prevent them from advertising the number on the network. Alternatively, you could temporarily disconnect a server from the local area network, wait a few minutes, and then use it as a dial-out client. The network number will be dropped from the routing table after about three minutes, and no conflict will then exist on the local machine.

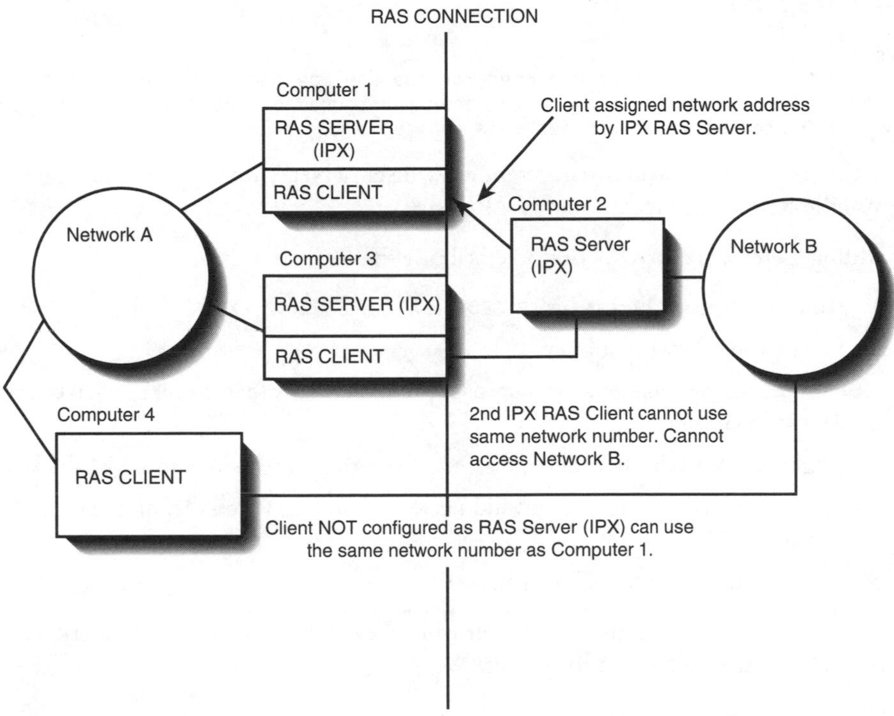

Figure 27.11. *Only one client on Network A can use the same network number assigned by the IPX RAS server on Network B.*

Also, if the remote network you are dialing in to is a Windows NT RAS server, you can configure it to assign different network numbers to IPX clients that dial in:

1. Use the Network applet in the Control Panel.
2. Select the Services tab and highlight Remote Access Service.
3. Select the Network option and then Server Settings.
4. Select IPX and then Configure.
5. Make sure the check box Assign same network number to all IPX clients is unchecked.

Error Using NWLink to Dial in to Windows NT RAS (Event ID 20087)

When you use NWLink on a RAS client to dial in to an NT RAS server that does not have a valid IPX network number, you will get an error:

```
Event ID: 20087
Source: RemoteAccess
Type: Error
Description: The IPX network number for the LAN adapter with the MAC address <ad-
dress> on the local machine has not been configured or could not be auto-detected.
The IPX Router will not work on this LAN segment.
```

You can solve this problem two different ways: install a NetWare server on the local LAN segment or use the Registry Editor to modify a Registry value.

If adding a NetWare server is not practical, use the Registry Editor:

1. Run the Registry Editor (use `REGEDIT.EXE` or `REGEDT32.EXE`).
2. Locate the following subkey:

   ```
   HKEY_LOCAL_MACHINE\System\CurrentControlSet\Services\NwLnkipx\NetConfig\<network
   or RAS adapter>
   ```
3. Highlight the value `NetworkNumber` and from the Edit menu choose Multi String.
4. Change the value from `0` to a valid network number. Click OK and exit the Registry Editor.
5. Reboot the Windows NT server.

When the system reboots, the RAS server will believe it has a valid IPX network number, which should enable the RAS client to connect.

Browsing Through RAS

Browsers and master browsers in a Windows NT network provide a list of services available to clients on the network. Browsing enables you to use the Explorer to see a list of services and then click the ones to which you want to connect.

Computers on RAS Server's Network Cannot Browse a RAS Client's Resources

If you are using RAS on a stand-alone computer (that is, one not connected to a network, such as your home PC), you will have problems browsing.

This is because the expected behavior of a RAS client in a non-networked situation is that it will be dialing in to a network and will therefore browse the services on that network. For the reverse to be true—to allow clients from the network on which the RAS server resides to browse shares on the RAS client—you must make it appear to be networked.

To do this, you can do one of two things: install a network card (expensive solution if you don't need it) or install the Microsoft Loopback Adapter to simulate a network.

The Microsoft Loopback Adapter can be installed like any other adapter, by using the Network applet in the Control Panel. It is used to test network functions when no physical network is attached to the PC. To install the Loopback Adapter, perform the following steps:

1. Bring up the Network applet in the Control Panel.
2. Select the Adapters tab.
3. Click on the Add button.
4. From the dialog box presented (see Figure 27.12) select MS Loopback Adapter and then click OK.

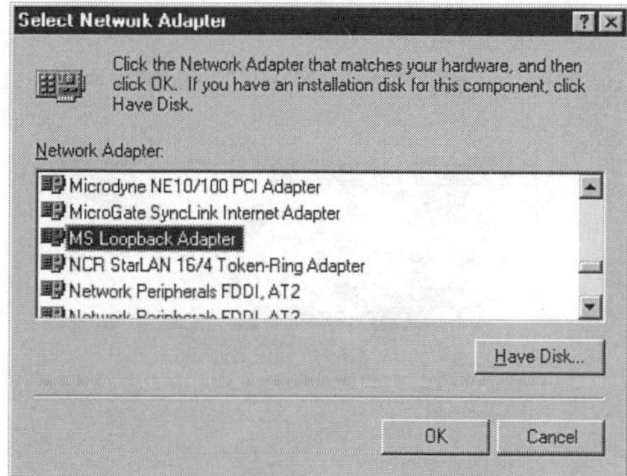

Figure 27.12. *Select the MS Loopback Adapter from the choices shown in the Select Network Adapter dialog box.*

5. The installation process will prompt for the path to the source files and then copy the appropriate files to your local hard drive.
6. Reboot the PC so that the Loopback Adapter will be installed on boot.

Note that if you have not previously installed and configured a network protocol (such as TCP/IP), the installation process will prompt you to do so before you reboot. The network card (or Loopback Adapter) needs to have an address assigned to it, just like the RAS client software adapter is assigned a network address when it dials in to a RAS server.

Note that under a previous version of Windows NT (version 3.5), you could use the same address for the network card (or Loopback Adapter) and the RAS client software. This was due to a problem in the file `RASIPHLP.DLL`, not by design. As of version 3.51, this has been corrected. To route traffic through your RAS connection, each adapter needs to have a unique TCP/IP address.

RAS Client Cannot Browse RAS Server's Network Using Just TCP/IP

If your RAS client uses only TCP/IP (and does not use NWLink or NetBIOS), you may have a problem browsing the network to which the RAS server is connected. If the RAS client belongs to the domain on the RAS server's network (or a workgroup with the same name), you should have no problems.

If the RAS client does not belong to a workgroup or domain that is the same as the RAS Server, you need to be sure the WINS service is installed somewhere on the network. In addition, you need to be sure the RAS server (and any other computers on the network that you want to browse from the RAS client) has WINS name resolution enabled. To enable WINS name resolution, add the name of a primary and possibly a secondary WINS server to these computers' TCP/IP configuration. To change this, perform the following steps:

1. Use the Network applet in the Control Panel.
2. Select the Protocols tab and then double-click the TCP/IP protocol. This will bring up the TCP/IP Properties page. Click the WINS Address tab (see Figure 27.13).

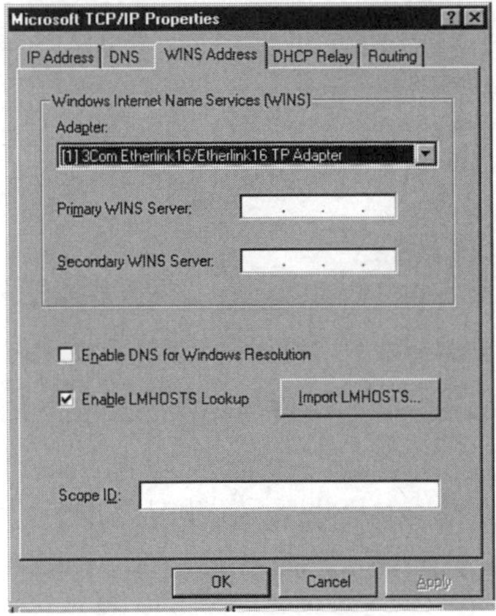

Figure 27.13. *The TCP/IP Properties page, with the WINS Addresses tab selected, is where you add WINS servers to be used for name resolution on the network.*

3. Enter the address of a primary WINS server and, if applicable, a secondary WINS server.
4. Click OK. Reboot the computer for the new TCP/IP configuration to take effect.

Finally, to enable WINS name resolution on the RAS client, you can either instruct the client to use server-assigned name server addresses (this is the default) or you can configure the RAS client to use specific name servers and enter the addresses yourself. Figure 27.14 shows the PPP TCP/IP Settings dialog box, in which you can configure the name servers.

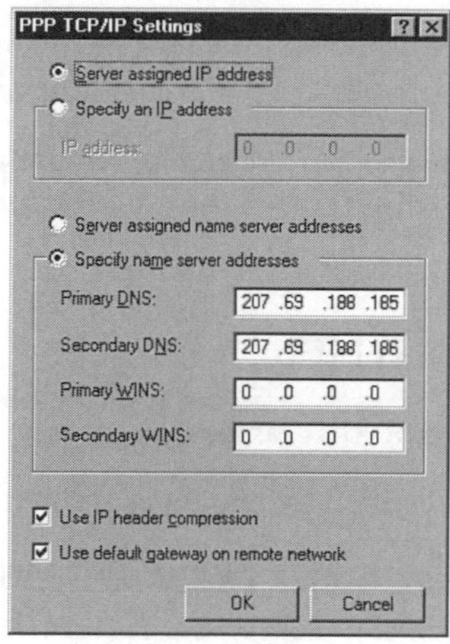

Figure 27.14. *The PPP TCP/IP Settings dialog box under the Phonebook enables you to add name servers or to instruct the client to use server-assigned addresses.*

To configure TCP/IP for the RAS client, perform the following:

1. Edit the Phonebook entry on the RAS client for the RAS server you are calling.
2. Click the Network button.
3. Select TCP/IP Settings.
4. Either add the appropriate WINS server addresses (for the WINS servers on the remote network you will be dialing in to) or check the "use server-assigned addresses" check box.

Remote Administration Through RAS

You can administer a RAS server from a RAS client. However, in order to do so you must have an account on the RAS server's domain and grant yourself the appropriate rights (by group membership) or use an account on the RAS server's local security database with the appropriate rights.

To administer a RAS server, you can be a member of the Domain Administrators group (or the Local Administrators group on a local directory database). Alternatively, you can administer portions of the service by being a member of the Account Operators group or the Server Operators group.

The Account Operators group gives the account the capability to grant or revoke the dial-in permission. That is, you can control who is allowed to dial in to the RAS server.

The Server Operators group gives the account the capability to start and stop the RAS server service, disconnect clients, and send messages to RAS clients. The Server Operators group does not grant you the ability to grant or revoke dial-in permissions.

By having membership in both groups or by having membership in the Administrators or Domain Admins group, you can perform all of the previous functions.

Thus, when trying to diagnose problems related to remotely administering the RAS server, check the users' group memberships first.

Other Event Log Entries

This section lists a variety of errors that can be viewed using the Event Viewer administrative tool.

The following errors can be rectified by removing and reinstalling the RAS service:

- `20001`—`Cannot load the NetBIOS gateway DLL components.`
- `20002`—`Cannot open the RAS Server parameters Registry key.`
- `20003`—`Can't access Registry key values.`
- `20005`—`Cannot enumerate Registry key values.`
- `20006`—`Parameter %1 has an invalid type.`
- `20029`—`Remote Access Connection Manager failed to start because RASHUB could not be opened.`
- `20040`—`Remote Access Server failure. Cannot find the LANA numbers for the network adapters.`
- `20043`—`RASMXS.DLL cannot load RASSER.DLL.`

Other miscellaneous error codes:

- `20004`—`Memory allocation failure.`

  Add more memory, close applications not being used, or stop unnecessary services.
- `20007`—`Cannot enumerate the RAS Connection Manager ports.`

  This error message indicates that a multiport adapter may have been installed incorrectly.
- `20008`—`The Remote Access Server is not configured to receive calls.`

  Either some other program is using the port or Remote Access Server has been set up for dial-out only.
- `20009`—`Cannot receive initial frame on port %1. The user has been disconnected.`

  This indicates that RAS may not be installed on the client trying to dial in. Check the client and if the problem persists, reinstall the software on the client.

- `20010—The user connected to port %1 has been disconnected due to inactivity.`

  You can change the timeout value if it is too short for your users. Otherwise, advise the client to dial in again.

- `20011—The user connected to port %1 has been disconnected because there is not enough memory available in the system.`

  Again, install additional memory or free up memory by stopping programs or services that are unnecessary.

- `20012—The user connected to port %1 has been disconnected due to a system error.`

  This error is usually accompanied by other error messages that may be more specific to the problem.

- `20013—The user connected to port %1 has been disconnected due to a fatal network error on the local network.`

  This usually indicates a problem with the physical connection to the network. Check the network adapter card and cabling to be sure all are functioning properly.

- `20014—The user connected to port %1 has been disconnected due to a fatal network error on the async network.`

  This indicates possible problems with the serial port. Check the hardware to be sure it is functioning correctly.

- `20015—The communications device attached to port %1 is not functioning.`

  Verify the modem and cabling are functioning.

- `20016—The user <user> has connected and failed to authenticate on port <port>. The line has been disconnected.`

  This can be either a permissions problem or a bad password. Check to see that the user has been granted the dial-in permission and verify the user's password.

- `20017—The user <user> has connected and has been successfully authenticated on port <port>.`

  This is an informational success event message. Nothing is in error. You can use these events to track when users log in to your system. See event number `20019` for the logoff message.

- `20018—The user connected to port <port> has been disconnected because there was a transports-level error during the authentication conversation.`

  Ask the user to dial in again.

- `20019—The user has disconnected from port <port>.`

  This is another informational message. No action is necessary. Use this type of event record to track users logging off your system.

- `20020—Cannot reset the network adapter for LANAx. The error code is the data.`

  Check the RAS configuration. If the problem persists, reinstall RAS.

- `20021—Remote Access Server Security Failure. Cannot locate the computer name.`

  This message indicates that RAS cannot get the computer name of the RAS client. Check the RAS client configuration.

- `20022—Remote Access Server Security Failure. Cannot add the name for communication with the security agent on LANAx.`

  Check to be sure that another server on `LANAx` does not have the same name.

- `20023—Remote Access Server Security Failure. Cannot access the network adapter address on LANAx.`

  Check the RAS configuration.

- `20024—Remote Access Server Security Failure. The security agent has rejected the Remote Access server's call to establish a session on LANAx.`

  This indicates that a remote access security agent is running on your network.

- `20025—Remote Access Server Security Failure. The security agent has rejected the Remote Access server's request to start the service on this computer on LANAx.`

  This indicates that a remote access security agent is running on your network.

- `20026—Remote Access Server Security Failure. A network error has occurred when trying to establish a session with the security agent on LANAx. The error code is the data.`

  See "Multihomed RAS Servers—Binding RAS to One Network Card," earlier in this chapter, for a discussion of this message.

- `20027—The user connected to port <port> has been disconnected because there are no operating system resources available.`

  This is indicative of a memory shortage. Again, free up memory by closing unnecessary applications or stopping unneeded services, or buy more memory.

- `20028—The user connected to port <port> has been disconnected because of a failure to lock user memory.`

  Try the connection again.

- `20030—Remote Access Connection Manager failed to start because it could not initialize the security attributes.`

  If the problem continues to occur, reboot the computer. If that does not help, reinstall RAS.

- `20031—Remote Access Connection Manager failed to start because no endpoints were available.`

  If the problem continues to occur, reboot the computer. If that does not help, reinstall RAS.

- `20032—Remote Access Connection Manager failed to start because it could not load one or more communication DLLs.`

  This may indicate a hardware problem. Check your modem, cables, and ports. If the problem continues to occur, reboot the computer. If that does not help, reinstall RAS.

- `20033—Remote Access Connection Manager failed to start because it could not locate port information from Media DLLs.`

  This may indicate a hardware problem. Check your modem, cables, and ports. If the problem continues to occur, reboot the computer. If that does not help, reinstall RAS.

- `20034—Remote Access Connection Manager failed to start because it could not access protocol information from the Registry.`

  Reboot the computer. If that does not help, reinstall RAS.

- `20035—Remote Access Connection Manager failed to start because it could not register with the Local Security Authority.`

  This is a problem accessing the Registry. Reboot the computer. If that does not help, reinstall RAS.

- `20036—Remote Access Connection Manager failed to start because it could not create shared file mapping.`

  Reboot the computer. If that does not help, reinstall RAS.

- `20037—Remote Access Connection Manager failed to start because it could not create buffers.`

  Reboot the computer. If that does not help, reinstall RAS.

- `20038—Remote Access Connection Manager failed to start because it could not access resources.`

  Reboot the computer. If that does not help, reinstall RAS.

- `20039—Remote Access Connection Manager failed to start because it could not start worker threads.`

  Reboot the computer. If that does not help, reinstall RAS.

- `20041—RASSER.DLL cannot open the SERIAL.INI file.`

  Check the RAS configuration (use the Network applet in the Control Panel).

- `20042—An attempt by RASSER.DLL to get a async media access control handle failed.`

  Check the RAS configuration (use the Network applet in the Control Panel). If you find nothing wrong, reinstall RAS.

- `20044—The Remote Access Server cannot allocate a route for the user connected on port <port>. The user has been disconnected.`

  Check the configuration of your Remote Access Service. Check the RAS configuration (use the Network applet in the Control Panel). If you find nothing wrong, reinstall RAS.

- `20045—Cannot allocate memory in the admin support thread for the Remote Access Service.`

  Check the RAS configuration (use the Network applet in the Control Panel). If you find nothing wrong, reinstall RAS.

- `20046—Cannot create an instance thread in the admin support thread for the Remote Access Service.`

  Reboot the computer. If this does not help, reinstall RAS.

- `20047—Cannot create a named pipe instance in the admin support thread for Remote Access Service.`

  Reboot the computer. If this does not help, reinstall RAS.

- `20048—General named pipe failure occurred in the admin support thread for Remote Access Service.`

  Reboot the computer. If this does not help, reinstall RAS.

- `20049—An invalid request was sent to the admin support thread for Remote Access Service, possibly from a down level admin tool. The request was not processed.`

  Reboot the computer. If this does not help, reinstall RAS.

- `20050—The user <user> was active on port <port> for <minutes> minutes.`

  This is an informational message. You can use this type of message to track the time a user spends on your system.

- `20051—Using the default value for Registry parameter <parameter> because the value given is not in the legal range for the parameter.`

  Review Registry entries for RAS. Check the parameter specified in the error message.

- `20052—The user connected to port <port> has been disconnected due to an authentication time-out.`

  The user is taking too long for the authentication sequence. Ask the user to type faster!

- `20053—The user <user> connected to port <port> has been disconnected because the computer could not be projected onto the network.`

  Check to be sure the user's computer name is unique on the network. Ask the user to try again.

- `20054—The user <user> connected to port <port> has been disconnected because an internal authentication error occurred.`

  Ask the user to try again. If the problem persists, reboot the computer. If that does not help, reinstall RAS.

- `20055—The Remote Access Server could not be started because it has been configured to access the network and there are no network adapters available.`

  The RAS configuration does not match the computer configuration. If you have changed hardware (network adapter card), reconfigure RAS. Alternatively, if there is no adapter, install one or install the Microsoft Loopback Adapter.

- `20056—The user <user> established a NetBIOS session between the remote workstation and the network server.`

  This is an informational message. No action is necessary.

- `20057—Remote Access Service failed to start because the Remote Access Connection Manager failed to initialize.`

  This message indicates that RAS is not correctly configured. Usually there will be additional messages that are more specific to the problem.

- `20058—Cannot add the remote computer name <computername> on LANAx. The error code is the data.`

  This indicates a name duplication problem. A computer on the local network has the same name as the RAS client trying to dial in. Change the RAS client's computer name or the name of the computer on the local network.

- `20059—Cannot delete the remote computer name <computername> from LANAx. The error code is the data.`

  This indicates that an internal has occurred in RAS. Print out the data (using the Event Viewer) and contact Microsoft Technical Support for further diagnosis.

- `20060—Cannot add remote computer group name <name> on LANAx. The error code is the data.`

  The remote group name conflicts with a computer name. Change either the computer's name or the group name the remote RAS client is trying to register.

- `20061—Cannot delete the remote computer group name <group name> from LANAx. The error code is the data.`

  This indicates that an internal has occurred in RAS. Print out the data (using the Event Viewer) and contact Microsoft Technical Support for further diagnosis.

- `20062—The modem on <port> moved to an unsupported BPS rate.`

  The modem has tried to switch to a baud rate that the serial port does not support. Try a different COM port or use the Ports applet in the Control Panel to change the communication rate for the port.

- `20063—The serial driver could not allocate adequate I/O queues. This may result in an unreliable connection.`

  This indicates an out-of-memory error, or, if you are using a multiport adapter, it might be configured to use too many ports. The solution is to free up or buy more memory or check the number of ports being used by the multiport adapter.

- `20064—Remote Access connection Manager could not re-open bi-plex port <port>. The port will not be available to calling in or calling out. Restart all Remote Access Service components.`

  This may indicate a hardware configuration problem. First try stopping and restarting all components associated with RAS. If this does not help and the hardware is correctly configured, reinstall RAS.

- `20065—Internal Error: Disconnect operation on <port> completed with an error.`

  RAS has disconnected from the remote user and has encountered an error. Have the remote RAS client try again to connect. If the problem persists, reboot the computer.

- `20066—General named pipe failure occurred in the Point to Point Protocol engine.`

  Try rebooting the computer. If this does not help, reinstall RAS.

- `20067—Remote Access Connection Manager failed to start because the Point to Point Protocol failed to initialize.`

  Try rebooting the computer. If this does not help, reinstall RAS.

- `20068—The user <user> on port <port> was called back at the number <number>.`

  This is an informational message. No action is required.

- `20069—The Remote Access Gateway Proxy could not create a process.`

  Check the configuration of the RAS gateway.

- `20070—The Remote Access Gateway Proxy could not create a process.`

  Check the configuration of the RAS gateway.

- `20073—Cannot open or obtain information about the PPP key or one of its subkeys.`

  This indicates a possible Registry problem. Check the entries for PPP in the Registry.

- `20074—Point to Point Protocol engine was unable to load the <module> module.`

  Reinstall the Point-to-Point Protocol.

- `20075—The Point to Point Protocol module <module> returned an error while initializing.`

  Reinstall the Point-to-Point Protocol.

- `20076—The Point-to-Point Protocol failed to load the required PAP and/or CHAP authentication modules.`

  Reinstall the Point-to-Point Protocol.

- `20077—An error occurred in the Point-to-Point Protocol module. The error code is the data.`

  Print out the data (using the Event Viewer) and contact Microsoft Technical Support for further diagnosis.

- `20078—The IPX network number <number> configured for the WAN interface is already in use on the LAN.`

  Reconfigure the IPX network number.

- `20079—The IPX network number <number> requested by the remote client for the WAN interface cannot be used on the local IPX router because the router is not configured to change its local WAN network numbers.`

  You should configure the IPX Remote Access Service to allocate addresses automatically and use different addresses for remote IPX clients.

- `20080—The password for user <username> connected on port <port> has expired. The line has been disconnected.`

  Change the RAS client user's password.

- `20081—The account for user <username> connected on port <port> has expired.`

  Check the user account using User Manager for Domains.

- `20082—The account for user <username> connected on port <port> does not have Remote Access privilege. The line has been disconnected.`

  Use the RAS Manager administrative tool or the User Manager tool to grant the user the privilege.

- `20083—The software version of the user <username> connected on port <port> is unsupported. The line has been disconnected.`

  Upgrade the RAS client's software.

- `20084—The server machine is configured to require data encryption. The machine for user <username> connected on port <port> does not support encryption. The line has been disconnected.`

  Use the Phonebook on the RAS client to configure the RAS client to use encryption.

- `20088—The Remote Access Server was unable to renew the lease for IP Address <address> from the DHCP Server. All connected users using IP will be unable to access network resources. Users can reconnect to the server to restore IP connectivity.`

  This is indicative of a possible DHCP server problem. Check the DHCP server.

- `20089—The Remote Access Server was unable to renew the lease for IP Address <address> from the DHCP server. The user assigned with this IP address will be unable to access network resources using IP. Reconnecting to the server will restore IP connectivity.`

  This is indicative of a possible DHCP server problem. Check the DHCP server.

- `20090—The Remote Access Server was unable to acquire an IP Address from the DHCP Server to assign to the incoming user.`

  This is indicative of a possible DHCP server problem. Check the DHCP server.

- `20091—The Remote Access Server was unable to acquire an IP Address from the DHCP Server to be used on the Server Adapter. Incoming users will be unable to connect using IP.`

  See "Unable to Acquire an IP Address (Event ID 20091)," earlier in this chapter, for a fuller discussion of this message.

- `20092—The Remote Access Server acquired IP Address <address> from the DHCP Server to be used on the Server Adapter.`

  This is an informational message. No action is required.

- `20093—The Remote Access Server's attempt to callback user <username> on port <port> failed with RAS error code <code>.`

  Check the RAS configuration on the RAS server and on the RAS client.

- `20094—A general error occurred writing to the named pipe in the Remote Access Proxy.`

  Try rebooting the computer. If this does not help, reinstall RAS.

- `20095—Cannot open the RAS security host Registry key.`

  This indicates a possible problem with the Registry. Try rebooting the computer. If this does not help, reinstall RAS.

- `20096—Cannot load the Security host module component.`

  This indicates a possible problem with the Registry. Try rebooting the computer. If this does not help, reinstall RAS.

- `20097—The user <username> has connected and failed to authenticate with a third party security on port <port>. The line has been disconnected.`

  Check the configuration of the third-party security module.

- `20098—The user connected to port <port> has been disconnected because an internal authentication error occurred in the third party security module. The error code is the data.`

  The third-party security module has not authenticated the user. Check the user's configuration and the third-party security module's configuration.

- `20099—Cannot receive initial data on port <port>. The user has been disconnected.`

  This indicates a possible hardware problem with the modem or maybe a bad (noisy) phone line.

- `20101—A user was unable to connect on port <port>. No more connections can be made to this remote computer because the computer has exceeded its client license limit.`

  Purchase additional client licenses.

Summary

Windows NT comes with many tools you can use to troubleshoot Remote Access problems. The Event Viewer enables you to view error log entries created by the system or application. Using TCP/IP diagnostic utilities (such as the `ROUTE` command or the `PING` utility), you can examine and modify network configuration information.

The most important troubleshooting tool a network administrator has, however, is his knowledge of the system. You need to know such things as the topology of the network, how user accounts have been set up, and protocols running on the network, in order to solve problems in a timely manner.

This chapter covered many common problems that are encountered when administering a RAS server. Because RAS clients are really just like other network clients (except for the communications media), normal network problems can cause them grief. When you troubleshoot RAS, don't stick to just the Remote Access Manager or RAS client and associated software. A truly knowledgeable system administrator will look at the whole picture and use the symptoms to track down where the problem actually exists.

Network Protocols Available with Windows NT

by Robert Reinstein

This chapter covers the different network protocols that are available with Windows NT and discusses properties and uses of the protocols. Some of the protocols are introduced fairly thoroughly in this chapter, whereas some of the protocols are discussed in detail elsewhere in this book. The topics covered are as follows:

- Supported protocols and their properties
- Selecting a protocol
- Installing a protocol
- Protocol bindings

Supported Protocols

Protocols make up the language that computers use to communicate with each other. Protocols allow computers to share files, printers, e-mail, and client/server databases.

NT supports a variety of protocols that can be used for file and print sharing, as well as protocols that have special uses such as encrypting and tunneling data or printing to a network printer.

All protocols must communicate to the network card, as well as to the operating system. In the old days, protocols were network-card specific. Each network card came with a combined driver and protocol package. This was very inefficient and unreliable.

Microsoft developed an NDIS standard, which separated the protocol driver from the network card driver. Novell developed a competing standard ODI around the same time. Both standards allowed one protocol driver to be used on every card.

On the other side of the protocol driver is sometimes the TDI (Transport Driver Interface); when the protocol provides this interface, it can be used for file and print sharing.

The following protocols are supplied with Windows NT:

- Transmission Control Protocol/Internet Protocol, or TCP/IP
- NetBEUI
- NWLink IPX/SPX Compatible Transport
- Data Link Control (DLC)
- AppleTalk
- Streams Environment
- Point-to-Point Tunneling Protocol (PPTP)

These protocols can be divided into two categories depending on their use:

- Network server protocols

  These are protocols that enable you to connect a client computer to your NT server machine and use the server's file and print resources. These protocols include TCP/IP, NetBEUI, NWLink, and AppleTalk.
- Special protocols

  These are protocols that can't be used to connect a client computer to your NT server to use file and print resources. These protocols are used for special purposes, such as connecting the NT computer to a mainframe or a networked printer. DLC is a special protocol.

The following sections discuss the properties and use of each of these protocols.

TCP/IP

Transmission Control Protocol/Internet Protocol (TCP/IP) is a routeable protocol that will allow your network to span a wide area. TCP/IP is the standard protocol for the Internet, and because of the popularity of the Internet network, TCP/IP has gained a lot of popularity during the past few years. In addition, NT introduced new management tools such as DHCP, WINS, and TCP/IP, making it easier to manage large networks.

TCP/IP is now the default protocol for Windows NT. For Windows NT 4.0 much of the TCP/IP protocol has been rewritten, and the protocol has gained significant improvements in performance.

Benefits of the Windows NT TCP/IP implementation follow:

- Supports building routeable Internetworks networks that can span several networks.
- Provides access to the Internet.
- Includes a set of its own server services, such as the WINS and DHCP services, plus a brand new DNS server service.

Implementing TCP/IP is a complicated process. There are several chapters of this book dedicated to the correct implementation of TCP/IP. See Chapter 29, "Windows NT and TCP/IP," for more information on setting up TCP/IP. You can learn more about DHCP in Chapter 30, "Windows NT and Dynamic Host Configuration Protocol (DHCP)," and WINS in Chapter 31, "The Windows Internet Naming Service (WINS)."

NetBEUI

NetBEUI (NetBIOS Enhanced User Interface) is a protocol specifically developed by IBM in 1985 for local area networks. As the name states, NetBEUI is an extension of the NetBIOS interface. These two are often confused; however, NetBIOS is a user interface familiar from commands such as the NET USE command, and NetBEUI is a protocol that is sometimes used to transport these commands and their data over the network. Other protocols such as TCP/IP may also be used to transport NetBIOS commands over the network.

In Windows NT, the separation of NetBIOS the interface and NetBEUI the protocol is much more clear than in previous implementations of NetBEUI. Previously, it was customary to combine the upper-layer NetBIOS interface with the default transport NetBEUI. In Windows NT, however, the NetBEUI upper layer conforms to the Transport Driver Interface boundary layer and the NetBIOS interface has been implemented completely separately. Although the implementation differs quite significantly from other NetBEUI implementations, NetBEUI 3.0 still supports the NetBEUI Frame Format protocol (NBF) and is completely compatible with earlier versions of NetBEUI.

NetBEUI is designed to be used in single LAN environments and cannot be used in a WAN environment. That can be an advantage because there is no overhead for a WAN, and the protocol is one of the quickest available. If you want to join two networks running NetBEUI together—in other words, use resources of one network from the other using NetBEUI—the networks have to be connected using a bridge.

Bridges are special pieces of communication hardware that make two physical networks look like one big network. Bridges are generally more expensive than routers and less efficient because bridges have to hold physical addresses of each node on each side of the communication line to determine whether a packet on the local network must be forwarded to the remote network. The increased number of addresses that must be held and the amount of processing makes them poor choices.

NetBEUI has some significant benefits over other protocols:

- NetBEUI requires no configuration. The only addresses used by NetBEUI are the NetBIOS character-based computer name and the hardware or MAC address of the network adapter, which are both defined elsewhere. Address resolution is done using broadcast datagrams.
- It requires only a small amount of system resources. It requires the least amount of memory when implemented, and is a good fit for environments with DOS-based PCs.
- The performance of NetBEUI is excellent in small LAN environments.

Windows NT 4.0 includes NetBEUI Version 3.0. The performance of this version has been somewhat improved over the previous versions. Version 3.0 also breaks the 254 session limit of previous NetBEUI implementations. This limitation in the amount of sessions has previously limited the number of computers sharing data in a single LAN using NetBEUI.

Even though there are no parameters for NetBEUI that you could configure through the Network application in Control Panel, NetBEUI has parameters that are defined in the Registry. The NetBEUI parameters are located in the Registry under the following key:

```
HKEY_LOCAL_MACHINE\System\CurrentControlSet\Services\NBF
```

As always, changing values in the Registry is not recommended unless you know what you're doing. A single incorrect value in the Registry can cause NT not to boot. There are currently no knowledge-based articles recommending changing the NetBEUI settings in the Registry.

NWLink IPX/SPX Compatible Transport

NWLink is the Microsoft implementation of the IPX/SPX protocol for Windows NT. NWLink can be used to establish connections between computers running Windows NT and any other Microsoft network-compatible network operating system, such as Windows 95 and Windows for Workgroups.

NWLink is just an IPX/SPX-compatible protocol. It does not, by itself, allow computers running Windows NT to establish connections to computers running the Novell NetWare network operating system, or share files and printers to client computers running a Novell client. In order to access files or printers on a NetWare server, Novell-compatible client software must be installed on the Windows NT computer. Microsoft ships Gateway (and Client) Services for NetWare with NT Server and Client Services for NetWare with NT Workstation. It is also possible for a Windows NT Server computer to share files and printers with NetWare clients using the File and Print Services for the NetWare software component. File and Print Services for NetWare is sold separately. For more information on Windows NT services for NetWare, see Chapter 33, "Integrating with NetWare."

Selecting a Transport Protocol

Selecting protocols on an NT server and deciding which to use on the network can be complex but normally isn't a big decision once you realize what protocols have what strengths.

Although it is possible to configure NT with all of the protocols it has available, it's not normally the best approach. However, even if you decide that TCP/IP is going to be the protocol for your network you might consider loading up a few other protocols as well.

In the past, this wasn't a good idea. Each protocol chews up network and computing resources from the server; however, if the protocol is not actually in use on your network, the resource demands are minimal.

If there are network protocols on your network that the NT server does not yet need to utilize, you can still load them. NT requires a reboot every time a protocol is added to the system. This can be a real hassle because it almost ensures that you have to add the protocol at night or on a weekend. Adding the protocols allows you to install software that uses the protocol during the day. Some packages will still require a reboot, but not very many of them require this anymore.

The first thing to decide is which transport protocol you will be using. Table 28.1 outlines when to use each of the three included transport protocols. AppleTalk is not included because it cannot be used to provide native Microsoft file and print services.

Table 28.1. Transport protocol choices.

Type of Network	*TCP/IP*	*IPX/SPX (NwLink)*	*NetBEUI*
Small network	No	Yes	Yes
Medium network, Low administration	No	Yes	No
Medium network, Growing	Yes	No	No

continues

Table 28.1. continued

Type of Network	*TCP/IP*	*IPX/SPX (NwLink)*	*NetBEUI*
Large network	Yes	No	No
Any size network with Novell currently installed	Yes	Yes	No
Any size network where Internet access is required	Yes	No	No

Generally speaking, NT works best in small environments (fewer than 20 users) with NetBEUI or IPX/SPX, because both are relatively easy to configure and get running.

In a medium-sized environment (20–75 users), NetBEUI is no longer an option. If growth is a substantial factor in your network, you will want to choose TCP/IP. However, if a lower administration alternative is needed, IPX/SPX will work.

In a large network (more than 75 users), TCP/IP is the best solution because Microsoft has developed the tools to make TCP/IP easier to administer in a large environment. TCP/IP was designed to handle large environments, and much of the administrative burden that makes it a poor choice for small networks helps when larger networks are involved.

Some special considerations can affect the decision to go with one protocol over another. For instance, if you are already running a Novell environment, it's probably best to choose IPX/SPX—at least initially—for your network protocol. It's already being run by Novell, and everything is preconfigured.

When the network will be connected to the Internet, it almost always makes sense to run TCP/IP. The easiest step in using TCP/IP is setting it up. Because you already need to set it up in order to facilitate Internet access, it makes sense to just run TCP/IP internally as well.

Caution: The Internet can be a significant security risk. Make sure that you investigate the necessary security precautions before connecting any network to the Internet.

An advantage of IPX/SPX is that it can be used internally, and users from the Internet will be unable to access any internal machine because they won't have the same protocol installed. This also means, however, that you must have a nonstandard configuration in order for your users to access the Internet.

After you've decided on your standard protocol, you might want to load all of the protocols anyway so that visitors to your company can easily get access to your network with their system. It might seem like a silly thing, but a fair amount of time can be devoured by a CEO and the banker he brought in because the banker wants to use one of your printers.

After you decide which transport protocols to use, you need to review the nontransport protocols. Special protocols such as DLC or Streams Environment should be loaded.

Data Link Control (DLC)

The Data Link Control (DLC) protocol is a special-purpose protocol that provides applications with access to the OSI data-link layer of the NT networking model. The Windows NT DLC protocol does not support the TDI interface and cannot be used for communication between Windows NT- or Microsoft Network-based computers.

The DLC protocol has three functions in Windows NT:

- To connect the NT computer to IBM's mainframes using the SNA protocol suite
- To support the Windows NT remoteboot service
- To connect the Windows NT computer to a printer supporting DLC connections, such as the Hewlett-Packard LaserJet family of printers

The DLC does not contain any settings that could be configured through the Control Panel Network application. You can, however, configure some of the DLC parameters located in the Registry under the following key:

```
HKEY_LOCAL_MACHINE\System\CurrentControlSet\Services\DLC
```

AppleTalk

AppleTalk is a collection of protocols used almost exclusively by Apple's Macintosh computers. AppleTalk support has been added to NT to enable Macintosh computers to use NT's file and printer resources. This protocol is part of the Services for Macintosh service. This service enables you to configure your NT server to act as a Macintosh server for your Macintosh client computers and share both files and printers.

The AppleTalk protocol is usually not installed by itself; it is part of the Services for Macintosh network service. When you install this service, the AppleTalk protocol will also be installed. The AppleTalk protocol settings are not configured through the Control Panel Network applications Protocols tab, but instead by opening the Services tab, selecting Services for Macintosh, and then clicking Properties. The Microsoft AppleTalk Protocol Properties window will appear.

The Properties window contains two tabs—General and Routing. The General page is used to select the adapter used for the Macintosh services and to define the default zone name. The Macintosh zone is a bit like an NT domain; it groups computers and services together, and can be seen in the Macintosh computer when selecting the file share or printer in the Chooser program. By default the Macintosh services are only visible to the network connected to the default adapter, which is selected from the General page. If you want to have the services available to multiple networks and network adapters, you have to have at least one AppleTalk router configured in the network.

The Routing tab is used to configure AppleTalk routing. When you configure NT to be an AppleTalk router, not only will the files and printers from the NT server be visible to all of the connected networks, but services from one network will be available to the other.

The AppleTalk parameters can be set through the Registry as well. The Registry location for the AppleTalk parameters is as follows:

```
HKEY_LOCAL_MACHINE\System\CurrentControlSet\Services\AppleTalk
```

Point-to-Point Tunneling Protocol

New to NT 4.0 is the Point-to-Point Tunneling Protocol (PPTP). This protocol was developed by a Microsoft-lead consortium of vendors, including U.S. Robotics and 3Com (when they were separate companies).

The protocol works in conjunction with PPP to encapsulate and encrypt data for transmission across the Internet. Not just IP can be encapsulated, but NetBEUI and IPX can be tunneled across the Internet. *Tunneling* is the process of wrapping a protocol in another protocol and unwrapping at the other end. This utilizes the network infrastructure for the outer protocol. This allows non-routed protocols to be used at a remote location.

When encryption is included with tunneling to transport private data over a public network, it is generally referred to as a virtual private network (VPN). A VPN is desirable because the costs associated with it are generally much less than the costs of running a dedicated private network.

PPTP is designed to allow remote users to gain access to the corporate network over the Internet. Each user would form his own virtual private network when dialing into the Internet, and this would allow each user to use all the company resources.

PPTP can be used in one of two ways:

- The terminal server that the client dials into can have PPTP installed on it as a PPP extension and would take over the overhead burden of encapsulating and encrypting the data.
- The only method currently available is to use a PPTP-enabled client to establish the VPN itself. In this scenario, the client's CPU is responsible for the encapsulation and encryption. The only operating system that is PPTP-enabled at this time is Windows NT.

If you have a distributed company with small remote offices, PPTP might be a cost-effective way to connect the offices to the corporate network. PPTP is controlled by NT's Remote Access Service (RAS). More information on PPTP can be found in Chapter 27, "Troubleshooting the Remote Access Service (RAS) and Dial-Up Networking (DUN)."

Windows NT and TCP/IP

by Michael Tressler

Windows NT has excellent support for the TCP/IP protocol. TCP/IP is the most widely supported protocol in use today and is the language of the Internet. This chapter consists of three sections. The first section examines TCP/IP setup options, and the second section explains the tools and utilities Windows NT provides to help troubleshoot TCP/IP problems. The third section discusses the troubleshooting steps you should take to solve TCP/IP problems, and also includes some answers to common TCP/IP questions. This chapter assumes that you are familiar with the basic addressing scheme of TCP/IP.

In this chapter, we will focus on the following topics:

- TCP/IP setup on Windows NT
- TCP/IP configuration
- TCP/IP utilities for use in Windows NT
- Troubleshooting Windows NT

TCP/IP Setup

Knowing how to properly configure TCP/IP is one of the most important aspects to a successful TCP/IP implementation. Most of the options within Microsoft's TCP/IP setup are straightforward. However, due to the legacy of older Microsoft TCP/IP products, some of the options can be confusing. It is often these obscure settings that can help debug many problems you may run into.

The first step to successfully set up TCP/IP is to make sure it is properly configured. To access the TCP/IP settings, follow these steps:

1. Click the Start button and choose Settings | Control Panel.
2. In the Control Panel, double-click the Network icon. The Network dialog appears.
3. Select the Protocols tab and double-click the TCP/IP entry. You must be logged in as a member of the Administrators group in order to change these settings.

Setting the IP Address and Default Gateway

After you have accessed the TCP/IP settings, you are always presented with the information as shown in Figure 29.1. In this section of the TCP/IP settings, you will be entering the most important TCP/IP parameters. These are the parameters that give your machine a distinct number on your TCP/IP networks. This distinct number is known as an IP address. An *IP address* is a grouping of four numbers; each of the four numbers ranges from 0 to 255. If you are unsure of what your IP address should be, check with your network administrator. He or she should have a list of all used and unused IP addresses for your network.

You also need to provide a subnet mask value. Windows NT automatically configures this value based on the class of the IP address you entered. If your network uses a nonstandard subnet mask, you must enter this value manually. If you need to hard code your IP address, instead of allowing it to be automatically assigned, you must fill in the IP Address and Subnet Mask boxes with valid numbers for your network.

You can choose whether to obtain an IP address from a *Dynamic Host Configuration Protocol* (DHCP) server or by specifying an IP address by selecting the corresponding radio button. A DHCP server is a machine on the network that automatically assigns TCP/IP settings to systems. If you want your system to become a DHCP client, select the Obtain an IP address from a DHCP server option. You must have a DHCP server available on your network. If you enable DHCP without there being a DHCP server on your network, you will not be able to communicate on your network over the TCP/IP protocol. If you choose to enable DHCP support on your client, a warning message appears, as shown in Figure 29.2.

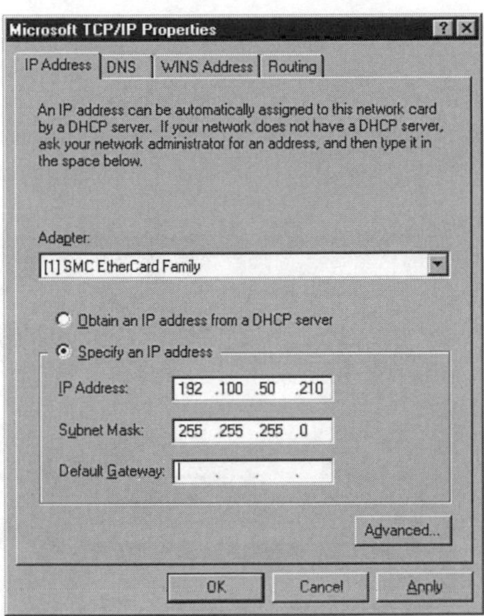

Figure 29.1. *The Microsoft TCP/IP Properties dialog.*

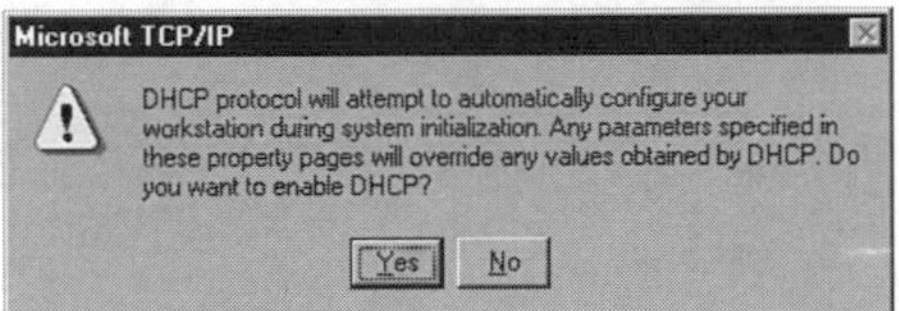

Figure 29.2. *A DHCP client warning message.*

This warning tells you that any TCP/IP properties that contain values will not be overridden by information provided by the DHCP server. In general, it is best if you make sure that all the TCP/IP properties are empty. This helps avoid any conflicts between what properties the client should have and what properties the client receives from the DHCP server. For a complete discussion of DHCP, see Chapter 30, "Windows NT and Dynamic Host Configuration Protocol (DHCP)."

Tip: As a general rule, if you are setting up Windows NT Server, do not enable the DHCP client option. Your network will be much more stable if your servers have solid, consistent IP addresses. Windows NT will not allow you to have a DHCP client enabled on a DHCP server.

The Default Gateway entry is optional. If you are on a network with routers, enter the IP address of your primary router, or default gateway. A *default gateway* is a device, usually a router, that can forward TCP/IP packets to another network. If you leave this entry blank, you will not be able to send packets outside your local TCP/IP network.

Advanced IP Addressing

Windows NT enables you to establish multiple IP addresses for the same network card and to define multiple gateways or routers. You can do this by clicking the Advanced button on the TCP/IP Properties page. This displays the Advanced IP Addressing dialog shown in Figure 29.3.

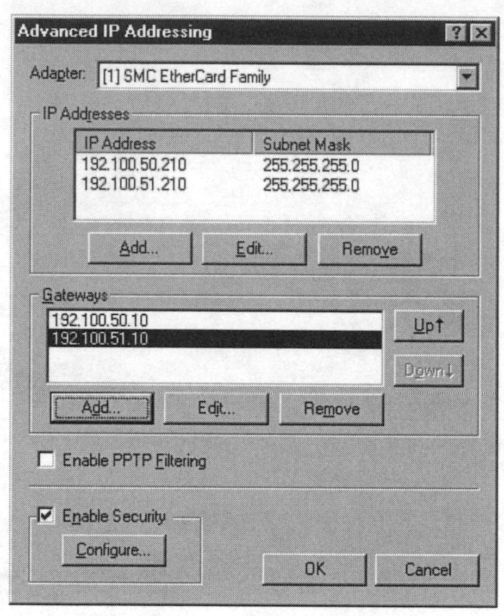

Figure 29.3. *The Advanced IP Addressing dialog.*

You use the Adapter option to select which adapter you want to work with. After you select the appropriate adapter, you see a window with a list of currently assigned IP addresses for that network adapter. By default, only the IP address you assigned in the Advanced IP Addressing dialog box appears. If you want to add more IP addresses to this adapter, click Add. The TCP/IP Address dialog box appears; you can define up to five IP addresses per adapter here. After you enter the IP address and its related subnet mask value, click OK to close the TCP/IP Address dialog box. On the Advanced IP Addressing dialog box you also have the option to Edit an IP address or its related subnet mask. You can also click Remove to delete an IP address for your network adapter.

Tip: To add more than 5 IP addresses, you need to edit the Registry. The Registry key for adding additional IP addresses is

```
HKEY_Local_Machine\System\CurrentControlSet\Services\TCPIP\Parameters\
➥IPEnableRouter
```

The Gateways section on the Advanced IP Addressing dialog box is for the addition of gateways. Your default gateway is automatically added to the list. To add another gateway, click the Add button underneath the Gateways list and enter the IP address of the additional gateway. You might want to add more gateways for several reasons. Perhaps you want to have a backup router in case the primary router fails. Or, if you are using multiple IP addresses in different subnets, each subnet might have its own gateway. To set the priority of the gateways, click the up and down buttons next to the Gateways list.

You should enable the Enable PPTP Filtering checkbox only if you will be connecting to a server that also is running the *Point-to-Point Tunneling Protocol* (PPTP). Enabling this checkbox effectively disables all other protocols bound to the selected adapter and allows only PPTP packets into the system through that adapter.

You use the Enable Security checkbox if you want to enable packet filtering. *Packet filtering* is a way to specify which types of traffic you want to allow to reach your server. Applications written to support sending and receiving of TCP/IP data use ports of communications. The FTP utility, for example, uses TCP port 21 to establish communications between the client and the server. So when you enter a command such as `ftp 1.1.1.1`, you actually are issuing the command `ftp 1.1.1.1:21`, where `:21` specifies that communications between the FTP client and the FTP server should use *port 21*. You can view a list of assigned ports by opening the `\winnt\system32\drivers\etc\services` file with Notepad. If your particular application is not listed, contact the software vendor, who should be able to tell you which port it is using. When the Enable Security check box is marked, the Configure button becomes available. Figure 29.4 shows the TCP/IP Security Properties window.

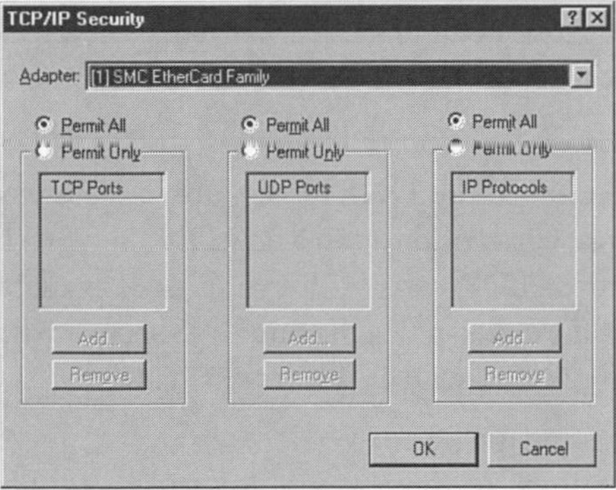

Figure 29.4. *The TCP/IP Security Properties dialog.*

Once again, make sure that you select the appropriate adapter with which you want to work. After you select the appropriate adapter, you can proceed to limit the type of traffic allowed into this system. The only time you should have to change these values is if this system is going to be on the Internet or on any other unsecured public network.

To limit packets, click the Permit Only radio button for the protocol type you want to limit. You then can disable or enable certain ports. Suppose that you only want to allow FTP access to this machine. You would select Permit Only in all three boxes, click Add under the TCP Ports window, and enter the number `21`.

Domain Name Service

The second tab on the Microsoft TCP/IP Properties dialog is the DNS tab, as shown in Figure 29.5. You can select this tab and set the system's DNS name, DNS service search order, and domain suffix search order. DNS is a naming service that enables you to map names to IP addresses to help users find things on a TCP/IP network. It is easier to remember `www.microsoft.com`, for example, than it is to remember `207.168.156.58`. Note that any settings entered here have no effect on Microsoft's Windows Internet Naming Service (WINS). WINS is a NetBIOS naming resolution system used almost exclusively on Microsoft Networks. DNS is an open, cross-platform name resolution system found prominently on the Internet and UNIX-based networks. Until the release of Windows NT 4.0, Microsoft had no support for a Windows NT-based DNS server. Using NT as a DNS server is covered in Chapter 32, "The Domain Name System." WINS is discussed in Chapter 31, "The Windows Internet Naming Service (WINS)."

Every client in a DNS naming scheme must have a hostname. By default, Windows NT uses your machine name as your hostname. In almost every case, you should not change this hostname. If you know your domain name, you should enter this into the domain name property field. If you are on the Internet, your organization has a domain name. Enter this value here. If you are not on the Internet and want to use DNS as your naming system, I recommend that you register your domain name with InterNIC anyway. You can contact InterNIC via the Internet at `http://www.internic.org`. That way, if your company joins the Internet at a later date, your name will be available for you to use. In Figure 29.5, the domain name is `domain.com`. Other examples of domain names are `microsoft.com`, `iei.net` and `atl.carpediem.com`. Windows NT joins the hostname with the domain name to create your machine's unique DNS name. In Figure 29.5, the DNS name is `tfs.domain.com`.

You specify the IP addresses of the DNS servers on your network or internetwork in the DNS Service Search Order area. Click Add to add a new DNS server, click Edit to change an IP address, or click Remove to remove a DNS server from your list of available DNS servers. You click the up and down buttons to set the order in which your DNS servers will be searched to map DNS names to IP addresses. In Figure 29.5, the DNS server `10.1.1.14` always will be searched before the server `206.216.124.1`.

In the DNS Suffix Search Order area, you specify the order in which suffixes are appended to hostnames during name resolution. You can add up to five domain suffixes.

When attempting to resolve a *fully qualified domain name* (FQDN) from a short name, Windows NT first appends the local domain name. If this is not successful, Windows NT uses the Domain Suffix list to create additional FQDNs and query DNS servers in the order listed.

Click Add to add a domain suffix. A domain suffix is usually the same as a domain name. In Figure 29.5, the domain suffixes are `domain.com` and `indy.domain.com`. You can click Edit to correct an entry, and you can click Remove to remove an entry. You click the up and down arrows to set the search order, with the top entry being searched first.

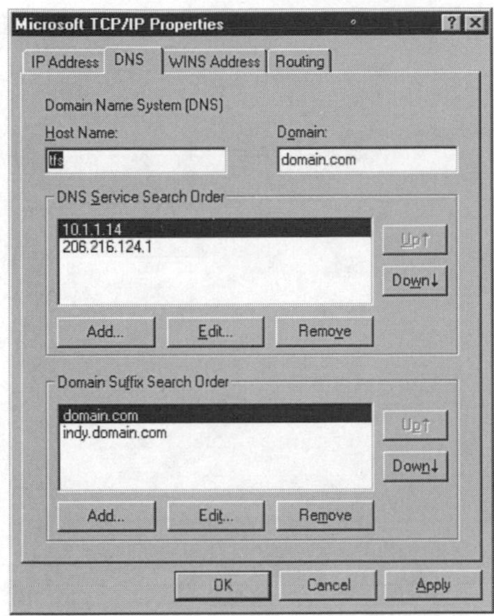

Figure 29.5. *The DNS tab of the TCP/IP Properties dialog.*

WINS Address

You use the WINS Address tab to set *Windows Internet Name Services* (WINS) properties, as shown in Figure 29.6. WINS provides a similar function to DNS. WINS name resolution is based on NetBIOS names and DNS is based on IP names. *NetBIOS* is a protocol that Microsoft network clients use to broadcast their presence on the network. However, NetBIOS is a nonroutable protocol, which means that names will not make it across routers that do not forward broadcasts. The NetBIOS names on one network, therefore, are invisible to the machines on other networks connected via routers. To overcome this limitation, Microsoft developed WINS. WINS allows for the dynamic addition of client machines to the NetBIOS name list. WINS is incompatible with most implementations of DNS. One notable exception is Microsoft's DNS server that ships with Windows NT 4.0. For more information on WINS and DNS, see Chapters 31 and 32.

As does the IP Address tab, the WINS tab enables you to set properties for each network adapter installed on your system. Whenever you make changes, verify that you are working with the appropriate network adapter selected. Your *primary WINS server* is the server your system queries for name-to-IP mapping. If that system is not available, your system uses the address found in the Secondary WINS Server entry.

The Enable DNS for Windows Name Resolution checkbox enables you to resolve NetBIOS names using DNS. By default, this box is not checked. By checking this box, Windows NT will attempt to resolve NetBIOS names by mapping them to DNS.

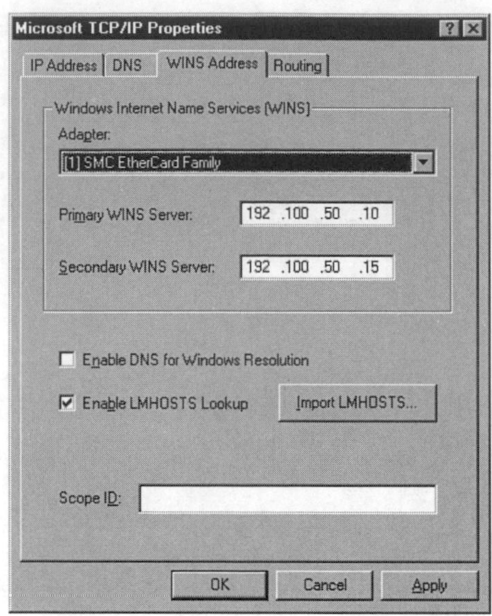

Figure 29.6. *The WINS Address Properties tab.*

The Enable LMHOSTS Lookup checkbox enables name resolution using the `LMHOSTS` file. The `LMHOSTS` file is a static text file that contains static network names and IP addresses. Because of the growth and use of WINS and DNS, `LMHOSTS` and the related hosts files are used mostly for troubleshooting.

The Import LMHOSTS button is most useful when installing Windows NT. Importing an `LMHOSTS` table enables you to join a domain across a router when WINS is not available to facilitate name resolution. More information on `LMHOSTS` and hosts files is available later in this chapter, in the "Troubleshooting TCP/IP" section.

The Scope ID property in the TCP/IP configuration provides a way to isolate a group of computers that communicate only with each other. By default, this field is left blank, and under only the rarest of circumstances should you enter a value here. At best, it is a way to secure NetBIOS communications. By adding a character string value in this field, that value is appended to all NetBIOS names. When two machines attempt to communicate with one another and the scope ID is the same, NetBIOS communications continue unhindered. If the scope ID is different, however, the machines simply disregard NetBIOS packets from any other scope ID. Regular, non-NetBIOS communications can continue. You will be able to ping a machine, for example, but a `net view` command to the same machine will fail.

Routing

If your system has more than one network adapter, you can enable Windows NT to act like a router. Packets from one network adapter then can be forwarded to another network adapter.

To enable IP routing, enable the Enable IP Forwarding checkbox, as shown in Figure 29.7. After you enable this box, you need to establish static routes by using the `route.exe` utility or installing the Router Information Protocol (RIP) service. More information on routing is available later in the "TCP/IP Utilities" section of this chapter.

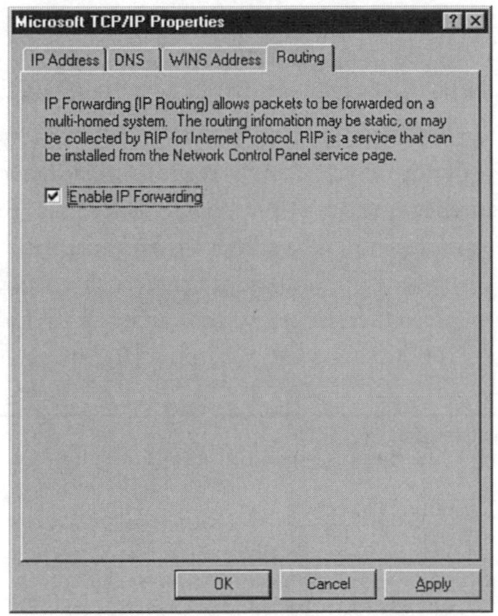

Figure 29.7. *The Routing Properties tab.*

Enabling the IP Forwarding setting sets the Registry value

```
HKEY_Local_Machine\System\CurrentControlSet\Services\TCPIP\Parameters\
➥IPEnableRouter
```

to `1` for enabled or `0` for disabled. In versions prior to Windows NT 4.0, this value must be added manually to the Registry.

Note: Windows NT Server offers an additional configuration tab called DHCP Relay, which has no direct bearing on this chapter and is discussed in Chapter 32.

TCP/IP Utilities and Related Protocols

In this section, you'll examine the tools Microsoft provides to help you troubleshoot TCP/IP problems. TCP/IP offers a wealth of tools that easily can help pinpoint problems. You also will look at protocols such as RIP and *Point-to-Point Tunneling Protocol* (PPTP) in this section.

The TCP/IP utilities Microsoft ships with Windows NT are command-line utilities that must be run from a command shell. Anyone can run these utilities, which makes it easy to talk a user through remote troubleshooting. All these utilities are located in the `\winnt\system32` subdirectory.

PING

`PING.exe` is probably the most widely used TCP/IP troubleshooting utility. *Packet Internet Groper* (PING) is used to test the reachability of other hosts. When you issue a PING, you simply are issuing an *Internet Control Message Protocol* (ICMP) echo request that waits for a reply. ICMP is part of the TCP/IP suite of protocols. ICMP is responsible for error handling when datagrams are discarded or when systems become congested. By using the Echo Request and Echo Reply Message portion of ICMP, a system can send out a request to a remote machine to reply to its message. This is what happens when a system PINGs an address. To use PING, simply open a command shell and type `PING` *`<Destination>`*, where *`destination`* can be an IP address or a machine name. Figure 29.8 shows a successful PING using a DNS name.

```
Microsoft(R) Windows NT(TM)
(C) Copyright 1985-1996 Microsoft Corp.

C:\>ping www.microsoft.com

Pinging www.microsoft.com [207.68.137.53] with 32 bytes of data:

Reply from 207.68.137.53: bytes=32 time=230ms TTL=55
Reply from 207.68.137.53: bytes=32 time=270ms TTL=55
Reply from 207.68.137.53: bytes=32 time=251ms TTL=55
Reply from 207.68.137.53: bytes=32 time=240ms TTL=55

C:\>
```

Figure 29.8. *A successful PING.*

You can glean very valuable information by looking at the data PING returns. Because I used a fully qualified DNS name, my system needed to resolve the name to an IP address. PING displays this IP address. Next, PING makes four attempts to reach the remote system. Each attempt displays a summary. In the summary, you can see which IP address replied, how many bytes replied, how many milliseconds the round-trip took to respond to your request, and the *Time to Live* (TTL) that was set for this PING. TTL simply means the length of time PING should wait before it determines that the ICMP packet failed. PING has numerous command-line options, as shown in Table 29.1, but for the most part, the default settings will work correctly.

Table 29.1. PING command-line options.

Option	*Function*
`-a`	Resolves addresses to hostnames
`-f`	Sets the Don't Fragment flag in the packet

Option	*Function*
`-i TTL`	Specifies the time to live
`-j` *`host-list`*	Specifies the loose source route along the *`host-list`*
`-k` *`host-list`*	Specifies the strict source route along the *`host-list`*
`-l` *`size`*	Sends the buffer *`size`*
`-n` *`count`*	Specifies the number of echo requests to send
`-r` *`count`*	Provides the record route for *`count`* hops
`-s` *`count`*	Provides the timestamp for *`count`* hops
`-t`	Pings the specified host until interrupted
`-v TOS`	Specifies the type of service
`-w` *`timeout`*	Specifies the *`timeout`* in milliseconds to wait for each reply

PING does not tell you the path it took to find the destination machine. I did a PING once using an IP address. PING responded successfully, yet I was still unable to address or connect to this machine using anything else. Finally, I determined that a router was not configured properly, and it was redirecting my PING to the Internet instead of the internal network. PING also does not usually work through a firewall or proxy server. Most of these devices do not forward the ICMP protocol.

TRACERT

`Tracert.exe`, which stands for *Trace Route*, is the second most useful utility that ships with Windows NT. And if it weren't for its lack of speed, I'd probably use it more often than PING. TRACERT does basically the same thing as PING; however, it also tells you the route it takes to get to the remote machine.

The TRACERT utility helped me detect an improperly configured router that PING couldn't help me with. PING responded with a successful connection to the machine, but I couldn't access this machine using other tools. By running a TRACERT to the remote machine, I was able to see the path that was being taken to reach the machine. By viewing the path, I was able to determine that a router was misconfigured.

To use TRACERT, open a command window and type `tracert` *`<destination>`*, where *`destination`* is an IP address or a hostname. Table 29.2 lists the TRACERT command-line options.

Table 29.2. The TRACERT command-line options.

Option	*Specifies*
`-d`	Do not resolve addresses to hostnames
`-h` *`maximum_hops`*	Maximum number of hops to search for target

continues

Table 29.2. continued

Option	*Specifies*
`-j` *`host-list`*	Loose source route along *`host-list`*
`-w` *`timeout`*	Wait *`timeout`* milliseconds for each reply

TRACERT also gives you a wealth of information. It gives you the IP address it is attempting to reach, as well as up to 30 hops to find its location. A *hop* can be thought of as a network that had to be crossed. By default, TRACERT crosses up to 30 networks. TRACERT also shows how long it takes to get to each hop, and, most important, TRACERT tells you where it went.

Figure 29.9 shows a sample output of a TRACERT from a PC dialed in to the Internet to `www.microsoft.com`. The first line where the request timed out was because TRACERT tried to first find its way to `www.microsoft.com` via my network card instead of the modem. The first successful hit was to the router at Internet Exchange, my ISP (`rtr1.iei.net`). From there, it hit a nationwide MCI backbone until it showed up at Uncle Bill's house. This utility is exceptionally beneficial inside a closed internetwork.

```
Microsoft(R) Windows NT(TM)
(C) Copyright 1985-1996 Microsoft Corp.

C:\>tracert www.microsoft.com

Tracing route to www.microsoft.com [207.68.137.59]
over a maximum of 30 hops:

  1     *        *        *     Request timed out.
  2   140 ms   150 ms   140 ms  rtr1.iei.net [206.154.216.221]
  3   240 ms   481 ms   220 ms  border7-serial2-2.NorthRoyalton.mci.net [204.
211.45]
  4   140 ms   140 ms   140 ms  core2-fddi-0.NorthRoyalton.mci.net [204.70.98
]
  5   561 ms   170 ms   160 ms  bordercore1-loopback.Atlanta.mci.net [166.48.
1]
  6  1112 ms   600 ms   641 ms  microsoft.Seattle.mci.net [166.48.209.250]
  7   280 ms   661 ms   251 ms  microsoft.Seattle.mci.net [166.48.209.250]
  8   240 ms   231 ms   230 ms  microsoft.Seattle.mci.net [166.48.209.250]
  9   251 ms   240 ms   240 ms  207.68.145.46
 10   281 ms   250 ms   251 ms  www.microsoft.com [207.68.137.59]

Trace complete.

C:\>
```

Figure 29.9. *A TRACERT to* `www.microsoft.com`.

TRACERT also uses ICMP and therefore is unable to pass through most firewalls and routers. TRACERT begins by setting the ICMP TTL to 1 and increments the TTL by 1 after each transmission until the target responds or the maximum TTL expires. The route is determined by examining the `ICMP Time Exceeded` messages sent back by intermediate routers. TRACERT can use this information to reconstruct the path taken by the ICMP echo request.

NBTSTAT

NBTSTAT.exe, which stands for *NetBIOS transport over TCP/IP Status*, checks NetBIOS name-resolution values. NBTSTAT can tell you what names were registered for your machine, as well as under what names or IP addresses other machines were registered. NBTSTAT works by querying your local name cache or a WINS server. To run NBTSTAT, open a command window and type NBTSTAT with one of the options listed in Table 29.3.

Table 29.3. NBTSTAT options.

Option	*Stands For*	*Function*
-a	Adapter status	Lists the remote machine's name table, given its name
-A	Adapter status	Lists the remote machine's name table, given its IP address
-c	Cache	Lists the remote name cache, including the IP addresses
Interval		Redisplays selected statistics, pausing *interval* seconds between each display; press Ctrl+C to stop redisplaying statistics
IP address		Provides a dotted decimal representation of the IP address
n	Names	Lists local NetBIOS names
-r	Resolved	Lists names resolved by broadcast and via WINS
-R	Reload	Purges and reloads the remote cache name table
RemoteName		Specifies the remote host machine name
-s	Sessions	Lists the sessions table, converting destination IP addresses to hostnames via the hosts file
-S	Sessions	Lists the sessions table with the destination IP addresses

To determine what names you were registered as, type NBTSTAT -N. To see what another system was registered as, you can type

```
NBTSTAT -a <hostname>
```

or

```
NBTSTAT -A <IP Address of host>
```

Suppose that you've been receiving some error logs on network-monitoring software that points to a potential problem with a system at IP address 192.100.50.210. A simple way to find out what this machine does is by issuing the command

```
NBTSTAT -A 192.100.50.210
```

as shown in Figure 29.10.

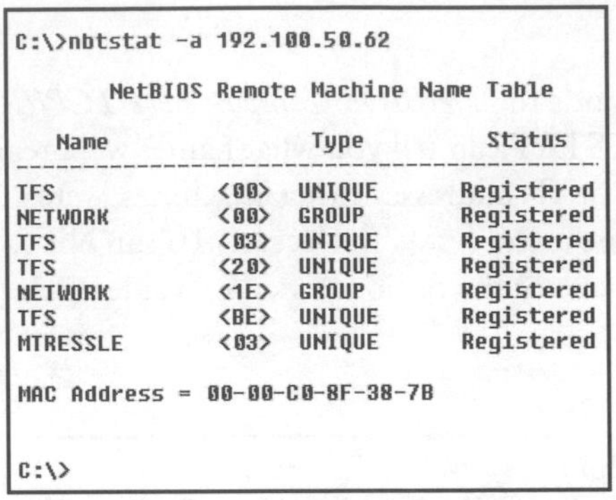

```
C:\>nbtstat -a 192.100.50.62

        NetBIOS Remote Machine Name Table

    Name               Type         Status
---------------------------------------------
TFS            <00>  UNIQUE      Registered
NETWORK        <00>  GROUP       Registered
TFS            <03>  UNIQUE      Registered
TFS            <20>  UNIQUE      Registered
NETWORK        <1E>  GROUP       Registered
TFS            <BE>  UNIQUE      Registered
MTRESSLE       <03>  UNIQUE      Registered

MAC Address = 00-00-C0-8F-38-7B


C:\>
```

Figure 29.10. *An NBTSTAT resolution via IP address.*

Fortunately, this system is a WINS client, so this utility returns a wealth of information. Line 1, `NetBIOS ID <00>`, tells you the hostname: `TFS`. Line 2, `NetBIOS ID <00>`, tells you the domain to which this machine belongs: `NETWORK`. And Line 4, `NetBIOS ID <03>`, tells you who is logged in: `Administrator`. Finally, it also gives you the MAC address of the remote machine.

IPCONFIG

`IPCONFIG.exe` is a utility that displays a system's current IP configuration. It is extremely useful in DHCP environments. To use IPCONFIG, open a command window and type `IPCONFIG`.

By default, IPCONFIG gives you an overview of your IP settings—your IP address, subnet mask, and default gateway for each network adapter. By adding the `/all` switch, IPCONFIG displays most TCP/IP settings for your system. Figure 29.11 shows the results of an `IPCONFIG /All` command.

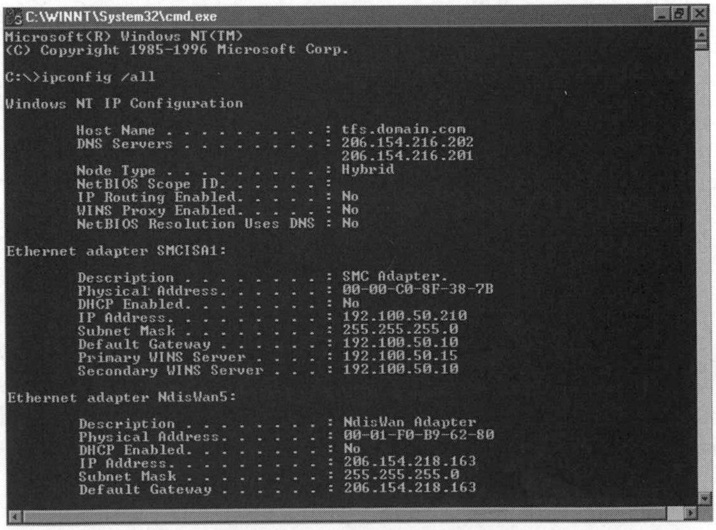

```
C:\WINNT\System32\cmd.exe
Microsoft(R) Windows NT(TM)
(C) Copyright 1985-1996 Microsoft Corp.

C:\>ipconfig /all

Windows NT IP Configuration

        Host Name . . . . . . . . . : tfs.domain.com
        DNS Servers . . . . . . . . : 206.154.216.202
                                      206.154.216.201
        Node Type . . . . . . . . . : Hybrid
        NetBIOS Scope ID. . . . . . :
        IP Routing Enabled. . . . . : No
        WINS Proxy Enabled. . . . . : No
        NetBIOS Resolution Uses DNS : No

Ethernet adapter SMCISA1:

        Description . . . . . . . . : SMC Adapter.
        Physical Address. . . . . . : 00-00-C0-8F-38-7B
        DHCP Enabled. . . . . . . . : No
        IP Address. . . . . . . . . : 192.100.50.210
        Subnet Mask . . . . . . . . : 255.255.255.0
        Default Gateway . . . . . . : 192.100.50.10
        Primary WINS Server . . . . : 192.100.50.15
        Secondary WINS Server . . . : 192.100.50.10

Ethernet adapter NdisWan5:

        Description . . . . . . . . : NdisWan Adapter
        Physical Address. . . . . . : 00-01-F0-B9-62-80
        DHCP Enabled. . . . . . . . : No
        IP Address. . . . . . . . . : 206.154.218.163
        Subnet Mask . . . . . . . . : 255.255.255.0
        Default Gateway . . . . . . : 206.154.218.163
```

Figure 29.11. *The* `IPCONFIG /All` *command.*

The first section in Figure 29.11 shows system-wide TCP/IP settings. You can see the fully resolved hostname: `tfs.domain.com`. You also can see which DNS servers are defined for this system and the individual settings for the network adapters in the system: `SMCISA1`, an SMC Ethernet adapter, and `NdisWan5`, a *Point-to-Point Protocol* (PPP) connected modem. All this information can help you verify that the settings you entered in the TCP/IP dialogs are correct. This also is the only place you can see DHCP values sent to you via a DHCP server.

IPCONFIG has two other command-line parameters: `/release` and `/renew`. These values, with a DHCP server, enable you to dynamically reacquire DHCP values. Typing `IPCONFIG /release` sends a release packet to the DHCP server telling it that you no longer are using the IP address. It also disables the local IP protocol, because you do not have a valid IP address. Typing `IPCONFIG /renew` begins the DHCP discovery sequence, which should provide you with a new IP address. For more on this process, see Chapter 32.

NETSTAT

`NETSTAT.exe` is a utility that displays the status of all activity on TCP and *User Datagram Protocol* (UDP) ports on the local system, as well as current TCP/IP connections. The most beneficial use of NETSTAT is with the `-e` or the `-s` switch. `NETSTAT -e` displays interface statistics, such as bytes sent and received, errors sent and received, and discarded packets. You also can use NETSTAT simply to see whether an interface is alive and sending or receiving data. Figure 29.12 shows an example of statistics produced by the `NETSTAT -e` command.

```
C:\>netstat -e
Interface Statistics

                           Received            Sent

Bytes                      24805868        10278838
Unicast packets               35103           40343
Non-unicast packets           29106           26395
Discards                          0               0
Errors                            0               0
Unknown protocols             12092

C:\>
```

Figure 29.12. *Interface statistics provided by the* `NETSTAT -e` *command.*

You use the `NETSTAT -s` command to view per-protocol statistics. Statistics for TCP, UDP, ICMP, and IP are shown by default. A nice feature of this command is its capability to show all statistics of the major protocols. You can use these statistics to look for abnormally high error counts. These numbers, along with statistics from a program such as Network Monitor or HP OpenView, can help you pinpoint problems on individual systems. Figure 29.13 shows an example of statistics produced by the `NETSTAT -s` command.

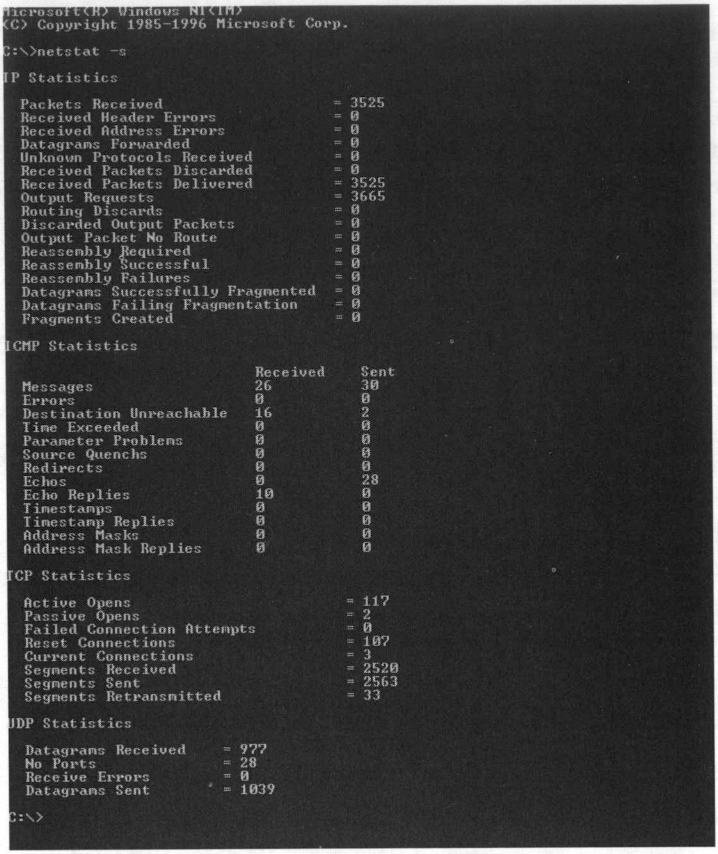

```
Microsoft(R) Windows NT(TM)
(C) Copyright 1985-1996 Microsoft Corp.

C:\>netstat -s

IP Statistics

  Packets Received                    = 3525
  Received Header Errors              = 0
  Received Address Errors             = 0
  Datagrams Forwarded                 = 0
  Unknown Protocols Received          = 0
  Received Packets Discarded          = 0
  Received Packets Delivered          = 3525
  Output Requests                     = 3665
  Routing Discards                    = 0
  Discarded Output Packets            = 0
  Output Packet No Route              = 0
  Reassembly Required                 = 0
  Reassembly Successful               = 0
  Reassembly Failures                 = 0
  Datagrams Successfully Fragmented   = 0
  Datagrams Failing Fragmentation     = 0
  Fragments Created                   = 0

ICMP Statistics

                          Received    Sent
  Messages                26          30
  Errors                  0           0
  Destination Unreachable 16          2
  Time Exceeded           0           0
  Parameter Problems      0           0
  Source Quenchs          0           0
  Redirects               0           0
  Echos                   0           28
  Echo Replies            10          0
  Timestamps              0           0
  Timestamp Replies       0           0
  Address Masks           0           0
  Address Mask Replies    0           0

TCP Statistics

  Active Opens                        = 117
  Passive Opens                       = 2
  Failed Connection Attempts          = 0
  Reset Connections                   = 107
  Current Connections                 = 3
  Segments Received                   = 2520
  Segments Sent                       = 2563
  Segments Retransmitted              = 33

UDP Statistics

  Datagrams Received    = 977
  No Ports              = 28
  Receive Errors        = 0
  Datagrams Sent        = 1039

C:\>
```

Figure 29.13. *Protocol statistics produced by the* `NETSTAT -s` *command.*

ROUTE

`ROUTE.exe` is a very important utility in a *multihomed* machine (a machine with more than one network card). By using the `route` command, you can add static routes to Windows NT's route table. With the correct static routes in place, your machine will be able to forward packets from one network adapter to another, and vice versa. In effect, you can set up Windows NT to act like a network router.

To see which routes are already established on your system, open a command prompt and type `route print` to print your system's current route table. Figure 29.14 shows the output from a `route print` command.

```
C:\>route print

Active Routes:

  Network Address          Netmask  Gateway Address        Interface  Metric
          1.0.0.0        255.0.0.0          1.0.0.1          1.0.0.1       1
          1.0.0.1  255.255.255.255        127.0.0.1        127.0.0.1       1
    1.255.255.255  255.255.255.255          1.0.0.1          1.0.0.1       1
        127.0.0.0        255.0.0.0        127.0.0.1        127.0.0.1       1
        224.0.0.0        224.0.0.0          1.0.0.1          1.0.0.1       1
  255.255.255.255  255.255.255.255          1.0.0.1          1.0.0.1       1

C:\>
```

Figure 29.14. *The output of a* `route print` *command.*

Now look at all that the `route print` command tells you. Even if you have only one network card in your system, at first glance it looks as if your machine is overloaded with routes. The reason for this is that every path to the network needs to be defined. Realize that if you ever need to connect back to your system, there needs to be a path defined for that communication. These paths are known as routes. Think of it as the highway system. There are tons of highways throughout America, but you have only one or two local on-ramps to the highway system. Because you know your local neighborhood and street layout, you almost always make the correct choice as to which on-ramp to take to reach your destination most quickly. Your network computer also needs to know which on-ramps it has, and which ramp will best get it to its remote destination.

On the system in Figure 29.14, the IP address is `1.0.0.1`, and the subnet mask is `255.0.0.0`. Line 1 tells you that anytime you need to communicate with subnet `1.0.0.0`, which has the subnet mask `255.0.0.0`, you should use gateway address `1.0.0.1`, which is your local network adapter—your primary on-ramp. Line 2 tells you that for the specific address `1.0.0.1` with subnet mask `255.255.255.255`, you should use gateway `127.0.0.1`. Subnet mask `255.255.255.255` is the local broadcast address (a special, reserved IP address), and routers do not forward broadcasts. `127.0.0.1` is the local loopback adapter. Basically, this line means that any data destined for `1.0.0.1` should be forwarded to the local loopback adapter or back to the system itself. Using our highway example, this means that you're already at your destination, so don't waste time using the highway. Line 3 tells you that broadcasts to address `1.255.255.255` should be forwarded to `1.0.0.1`. Line 4 tells you that data destined for the `127.0.0.0` subnet should be forwarded to `127.0.0.1`, the local loopback adapter. Line 5 is a special line, much like line 4. Line 5 declares the use of `224.0.0.0` as a multicast address that is used internally by Windows NT. Finally, all local broadcasts should be forwarded to `1.0.0.1`.

To add a route, you use the following command syntax:

```
route add [destination] [MASK netmask] [gateway] [METRIC metric]
```

The `route add` command is used to tell your system about new or better ways to get to its destination. Calling back to the highway example, `route add` lets us tell the computer about new highways or preferred highways to use. *`destination`* represents the IP subnet you want to add, `MASK` is the subnet mask for the IP subnet you want to add, *`gateway`* represents the IP address you want to send the destination through, and *metric* is the expense of this route. Suppose you have a machine with two network cards. Network card 1 has the IP address `1.0.0.1` with the subnet mask `255.0.0.0`, and network card 2 has the IP address `2.0.0.2` with the subnet mask `255.0.0.0`. For Windows NT to route data from subnet `2.0.0.0` to subnet `1.0.0.0`, you need to enter the following static route:

```
route add 2.0.0.0 MASK 255.0.0.0 1.0.0.1 METRIC 1
```

If you want to make this a persistent route, meaning that Windows NT should remember this route the next time you reboot the machine, you can add a `-p` switch to the command line. The command then looks like this:

```
route -p add 2.0.0.0 MASK 255.0.0.0 1.0.0.1 METRIC 1
```

> **Note:** The `MASK` and `METRIC` values are optional. If you omit `MASK`, NT uses the default subnet mask for the IP class range into which your destination address falls. If you omit `Metric`, it defaults to 1.

To delete a route, open a command prompt and execute this command:

```
route delete [destination]
```

In this example, this command would look like this:

```
route delete 2.0.0.0
```

ARP

`ARP.exe` is a utility you can use to maintain your local ARP cache. *Address Resolution Protocol* (ARP) performs IP-address-to-MAC-address resolution for outgoing packets. A MAC address is the actual, physical hardware address found on all your network equipment. IP addresses are logical, friendly addresses but it is the MAC address that truly represents your machine as a distinct entity on the network. As outgoing IP packets are created, source and destination MAC addresses must be inside the packet. It is the job of ARP to obtain the destination MAC address. It is possible that ARP can obtain the wrong MAC address, which will cause you no end of problems in attempting to communicate with another system. In almost all cases, ARP returns the wrong MAC address if two machines on the same network have the same IP address.

To save time and bandwidth, ARP maintains a cache of recently discovered IP-address-to-MAC-address mappings, called the *ARP cache.* ARP checks every outbound packet against its cache of addresses. If it finds a match, ARP uses its cached information; otherwise, ARP broadcasts an ARP request packet asking the owner of the IP address to respond with its MAC address. After it receives a reply to its broadcast, ARP updates its cache.

You can view the ARP cache by opening a command window and typing ARP -a. Figure 29.15 shows an example of the output of an ARP -a command.

```
C:\>arp -a

Interface: 192.100.50.210 on Interface 2
  Internet Address      Physical Address      Type
  192.100.50.10         00-20-af-34-05-4d     dynamic

C:\>
```

Figure 29.15. The output of an ARP -a print *command.*

In Figure 29.15, you can see that for interface 192.100.50.210, ARP has cached the mapping of IP address 192.100.50.10 to MAC address 00-20-af-34-05-4d, and that this is a *dynamic mapping*. A dynamic mapping means that ARP has discovered this automatically and that it is subject to being aged out of the cache. Entries are aged out of the ARP cache if they are not used by any outgoing datagrams for two minutes. Entries that are being used are aged out of the ARP cache after 10 minutes.

You can add a static mapping to the ARP cache. You might want to do this if two machines on the network have the same IP address, and you want to be sure that you are talking to the correct one. Ultimately, it is the MAC address that matters, not the IP address. To add a static mapping, use the following syntax:

ARP -s [*IP Address*] [*MAC Address*] [*Interface Address*]

Figure 29.16 shows a static mapping for IP address 192.100.50.31, for which the MAC address is 00-a0-24-74-d3-4e on system interface 192.100.50.210.

```
C:\>arp -s 192.100.50.31 00-a0-24-74-d3-4e 192.100.50.210

C:\>arp -a

Interface: 192.100.50.210 on Interface 2
  Internet Address      Physical Address      Type
  192.100.50.10         00-20-af-34-05-4d     dynamic
  192.100.50.31         00-a0-24-74-d3-4e     static

C:\>ping 192.100.50.31

Pinging 192.100.50.31 with 32 bytes of data:

Reply from 192.100.50.31: bytes=32 time<10ms TTL=255
Reply from 192.100.50.31: bytes=32 time<10ms TTL=255
Reply from 192.100.50.31: bytes=32 time<10ms TTL=255
Reply from 192.100.50.31: bytes=32 time<10ms TTL=255

C:\>
```

Figure 29.16. The output of an ARP -s *command.*

Executing ARP -a shows that the addition to the cache was added as a static mapping. Finally, a successful PING shows that you are able to successfully reach the machine with the new ARP mapping.

To delete an ARP mapping, use the following syntax:

```
ARP -d [IP Address] [Interface Address]
```

If you want to delete your static mapping, you can enter

```
ARP -d 192.100.50.31 192.100.50.210.
```

Troubleshooting TCP/IP

Earlier in this chapter, we looked at the settings and tools available in Windows NT's implementation of TCP/IP. In this section, we'll look at how to analyze and solve TCP/IP problems.

Steps for Troubleshooting TCP/IP

You can use the following procedure to find the source of errors in almost all possible TCP/IP configurations:

1. *PING your local host.* By issuing the `PING 127.0.0.1` command, you safely can determine that TCP/IP is installed correctly on your machine. If this fails, you should reinstall TCP/IP.
2. *Use the `IPCONFIG /ALL` command.* This tells you what your system says its IP configuration is. Verify this information closely, looking for typing errors. If you find an error, make the appropriate change by choosing Settings | Control Panel | Network. If all your addresses are blank, it's possible that you did not receive an address via DHCP. Verify that there is a DHCP server configured for your subnet. If this is the case, and an `IPCONFIG /renew` command still fails to get you an IP address, check your network cabling. Also, verify that your network adapter initialized properly. Look in Event Viewer for any error messages for the network card, and also look in Control Panel | Devices to make sure that the device driver for your network card has started. If your network card didn't start, verify that you installed the correct device driver for your network card and that you entered the correct configuration information for your card. If your network card driver asks you for the transceiver type (UTP, AUI, and so on), make sure you selected the correct type.
3. *Ping your adapters.* If your adapter's IP address is `192.100.50.10`, ping this address to ensure that what the computer says it has and what it responds to are the same. If steps 1 and 2 are correct, step 3 should never fail. If there is an error, however, return to steps 1 and 2. Repeat step 3 for any additional adapters.
4. *Ping any other IP address on your subnet.* This step tests numerous things. It verifies that your network adapter can physically communicate with the network and that your IP address and subnet mask are correct. If your ping fails, there are several things to check. Verify that your network adapter is plugged in to a live network port using good cables. In my experience, bad cables are the main cause of a failed ping.

5. *Verify that the IP address you pinged is on a live, networked machine.* Make sure that this machine is turned on and plugged in to the network. Check Event Viewer for any errors reported by the network adapter on bootup. It is possible that you might have an incorrect adapter driver, IRQ, I/O address, or other conflict keeping your adapter from communicating with the network. Make sure that you are using only IP addresses at this stage, because you could be having name-resolution errors. Also, try to ping an IP address that is on your subnet and not on another network via a router. Disable the PPTP checkbox if it is enabled and any NetBIOS scope ID settings in the Network dialog (by choosing Settings | Control Panel and double-clicking the Network icon).
6. *Ping across a router.* Ping another system that is separated from your subnet by a router. This step verifies that your default gateway is defined properly on your system. If this step fails, return to the Network dialog and verify your default gateway setting. Make sure that other, known good clients can ping across the router to verify that the router is working correctly. Try pinging the IP address of your default gateway. If this fails, you have a problem in your network cabling configuration or your router might be down. If everything checks out, use TRACERT against the remote system and observe the path that is echoed back. Check your local system's route table by using the `ROUTE` command, and make any necessary changes. If you add or change a route that you want to keep, remember to use the `-p` switch to make that route a permanent route.
7. *Issue a ping by name on your subnet.* Execute a `PING` command using a machine name—for example, `PING CLIENT1`. This tests your name resolution.

   If this test fails, check whether your system is configured properly to use your name servers. You can use the `IPCONFIG /all` command to list your DNS servers, if any, as well as your primary and secondary WINS servers, if any. If you have name servers and these values are blank, return to the Network dialog and enter correct values for WINS and/or DNS servers. If these values are present and pinging by name fails, verify that the addresses for your name servers are correct.

   Next, verify that your name servers are running and available to your subnet. You can do this by pinging from a known good client on your subnet. If you obtain your IP address via DHCP, check with the DHCP administrator that DHCP is providing values for WINS and/or DNS servers. If you are using DHCP and the name servers are not being pushed to the client, you can manually enter these values in the Network dialog. Check that you spelled the remote system's name correctly and that it is alive and connected to the subnet.

   Check your hosts and `LMHOSTS` files in the `\winnt\system32\drivers\etc` directory. By default, these are empty. If you are on a network that uses hosts or `LMHOSTS` files, verify that they are set up correctly and that there are no misspellings or incorrect IP address mappings.

You also can see what the remote machine thinks its name really is by executing the `NBTSTAT -A [machine name]` command. This command returns a list of the remote machine's NetBIOS registered names.

8. *Ping by name across a router.* This should work in most instances. Possible reasons for failure are incorrect secondary DNS and/or WINS server settings in the Network dialog or incorrect default gateway settings. Verify that the remote machine is enabled. Verify steps 6 and 7.
9. *Use a TCP/IP application.* You can use FTP, Telnet, Web browsers, or `NET USE` statements to see whether the machine can connect to the remote server. If any of these tests fail, check that the remote machines are alive and connected to the network. Also, use the `PING` or `TRACERT` command with these machines to verify that there is not some other error now appearing, such as a problem with security permissions. Check to see whether you have security enabled inside the advanced IP addressing options in the Network dialog.
10. If you've made it to this step, any errors most likely are not TCP/IP-related, and instead are related to individual applications or other system settings. For advanced troubleshooting at this stage, check the local ARP cache and look at the statistics generated by the `NETSTAT` command. Using a network analyzer, such as Microsoft's Network Monitor, is a good way to verify that the proper packets are being passed from the client.

Solutions to Common TCP/IP Problems and Questions

This section presents some common problems and asks some common questions about TCP/IP networks and potential solutions to these problems.

Q I receive error 53 when trying to connect to other machines. What is this error, and how should I correct it?

A Error 53 occurs when the remote computer's name cannot be resolved. Confirm that the name is spelled correctly and that the remote computer has TCP/IP correctly installed. Next, make sure that the remote machine is visible to your name servers. You can test this by pinging or browsing for that machine on a WINS-based network or pinging it on a DNS-based network. Edit your `LMHOSTS` file and add the remote machine.

Q What are hosts and LMHOSTS files?

A *Hosts* and `LMHOSTS` files are simply text files that contain name-to-IP-address mappings. These files reside in the `/winnt/system32/drivers/etc` directory and can be edited with any text editor, such as Notepad. Before the development of DNS and WINS, no easy, centralized network name servers were available. On these networks, all clients had to have an updated copy of the hosts files to be able to address remote machines on the network by name. Hosts files are static text files, which means that anytime a change occurs on the network, all hosts files on the network must be updated to reflect these changes. This is a considerable administrative task on large networks. Some hosts files implementations, notably `LMHOSTS`, support references to a centralized hosts file, but this did not provide nearly the ease and power of a good name service. Also, because hosts files are static text files, it can take a client a very long time to search through a list on a large network line by line to find the IP address for a name.

On install, a usable `LMHOSTS` file does not exist, and the installed hosts file contains the following uncommented line:

```
127.0.0.1       localhost
```

This line enables you to refer to your local machine by the name `localhost` as well as by IP address `127.0.0.1`. Instead of executing `PING 127.0.0.1`, for example, you can execute `PING localhost`. Because `localhost` is referenced in the hosts file, this executes a ping to `127.0.0.1`.

Both hosts and `LMHOSTS` files have the same syntax for adding an entry: an IP address followed by at least one space and then the name you want to map (with no spaces). You can add comments to the files by using the pound (`#`) sign. Suppose that you want to add a mapping to your `LMHOSTS` file so that you don't have to ping `192.100.50.15`. Instead, you want to ping that machine by its name, which is `banana`. To do this, you edit the `LMHOSTS` file and add the following line to the bottom of the file:

```
192.100.50.15    banana    #Banana is the accounting server
```

`# comment` is optional, but it is a good idea to use it. Now, you can execute `PING banana`, and if machine `192.100.50.15` is awake and on the network, you should receive a successful ping response.

Tip: Microsoft ships a sample `LMHOSTS` file named `LMHOSTS.SAM`. It is a good idea to copy this file to `LMHOSTS` (no file extension) before editing it. That way, you always can restore the original `LMHOSTS.SAM` file. The `LMHOSTS.SAM` file also contains instructions and samples for the use of the `LMHOSTS` file.

Q What is the difference between the hosts file and the LMHOSTS file? When should I use them?

A In general, the hosts file is for TCP/IP utilities, and the LMHOSTS file is for Windows NT NET utilities. If you want to ping a computer by name, edit the hosts file. If you want to use a NET VIEW command by name, edit the LMHOSTS file. For more information on the LMHOSTS file, see the LMHOSTS.SAM file located on any Windows NT station with TCP/IP installed in the \winnt\system32\drivers\etc directory.

In general, avoid using hosts and LMHOSTS files in place of a good network name server. If your network name server does not have a particular name on it, using the LMHOSTS file is preferred. A good use of the LMHOSTS file is to enable access to a machine across the Internet. Suppose that you want to administer a machine across the Internet. You would edit the LMHOSTS file and add a reference to the Internet-connected machine. Suppose that the machine is named Server1 with an IP address of 1.2.3.4. Add the following line to the LMHOSTS file:

```
1.2.3.4     Server1     #Pre
```

The #Pre directive simply tells Windows NT to preload the name into its name cache. After this file is edited, open a command prompt and execute the following command:

```
NBTSTAT -R
```

This purges and reloads the cache name table. Now, assuming that you have permissions, you should be able to use User Manager, Server Manager, or most other Windows NT administrative tools to access the machine Server1. These same steps hold true for file and print access to this machine. To verify that the LMHOSTS mapping worked, escape to a command prompt and type

```
NET VIEW \\Server1
```

You now should see a list of available file and print shares.

One final use of the LMHOSTS file is to enable the installation of a *Backup Domain Controller* (BDC) in a routed environment. When installing a BDC, the BDC *must* be able to communicate with the *Primary Domain Controller* (PDC). By default, NT broadcasts to find the PDC. In a routed environment, this broadcast fails. Your installation of the BDC therefore fails. To work around this, enter the name of a primary WINS server in the IP configuration screen during installation, or use an LMHOSTS file that has at least an entry for the PDC and the #DOM:*<domainname>* extension.

During installation, you can import the LMHOSTS file from a diskette. Suppose that you need to add the current BDC to a domain named Company. The PDC is named PDCServer and has an IP address of 1.2.3.4. The LMHOSTS file should look like this:

```
1.2.3.4     PDCServer #DOM:Company
```

Q I received a `Bad IP Address <name>` error, and I'm using an `LMHOSTS` file. I know my values are correct. How can this be?

A Check your settings in the Network dialog to make sure the Enable LMHOSTS lookup check box is enabled. Also, make sure that the file was not accidentally saved as a Unicode file. Opening the file in Notepad and saving it back should fix this.

Q I'm attempting to reinstall TCP/IP, but I receive the error message `The Registry Subkey Already Exists`. How do I correct this?

A Using the Registry Editor, verify that the following keys have been removed. If they exist, remove them manually.

- Connectivity Utilities

  If you have removed the TCP/IP service components, you must also remove the following Registry subkeys:

  ```
  HKEY_LOCAL_MACHINE\Software\Microsoft\NetBT
  HKEY_LOCAL_MACHINE\Software\Microsoft\Tcpip
  HKEY_LOCAL_MACHINE\Software\Microsoft\TcpipCU
  HKEY_LOCAL_MACHINE\SYSTEM\CCS\Services\DHCP
  HKEY_LOCAL_MACHINE\SYSTEM\CCS\Services\LMHosts
  HKEY_LOCAL_MACHINE\SYSTEM\CCS\Services\'NetDriver'\Parameters\Tcpip
  HKEY_LOCAL_MACHINE\SYSTEM\CCS\Services\NetBT
  ```

- Simple Network Management Protocol (SNMP) Service

  If you have removed the SNMP service components, you also must remove the following Registry subkeys:

  ```
  HKEY_LOCAL_MACHINE\Software\Microsoft\RFC1156Agent
  HKEY_LOCAL_MACHINE\Software\Microsoft\Snmp
  HKEY_LOCAL_MACHINE\System\CCS\Services\Snmp
  ```

- TCP/IP Network Printing Support

  If you have removed the Microsoft TCP/IP Printing (LPDSVC) service components, you also must remove the following Registry subkeys:

  ```
  HKEY_LOCAL_MACHINE\Software\Microsoft\Lpdsvc
  HKEY_LOCAL_MACHINE\Software\Microsoft\TcpPrint
  HKEY_LOCAL_MACHINE\SYSTEM\CCS\Services\LpdsvcSimple TCP\IP Services
  ```

  If you have removed the simple TCP/IP services components, you also must remove the following Registry subkeys:

  ```
  HKEY_LOCAL_MACHINE\Software\Microsoft\SimpTcp
  HKEY_LOCAL_MACHINE\SYSTEM\CCS\Services\SimpTcp
  ```

- DHCP Server Service

  If you have removed the DHCP server service components, you also must remove the following Registry subkeys:

  ```
  HKEY_LOCAL_MACHINE\Software\Microsoft\DhcpMibAgent
  HKEY_LOCAL_MACHINE\Software\Microsoft\DhcpServer
  HKEY_LOCAL_MACHINE\SYSTEM\CCS\Services\DhcpServer
  ```

- WINS Server Service

  If you have removed the WINS server service components, you also must remove the following Registry subkeys:

```
HKEY_LOCAL_MACHINE\Software\Microsoft\Wins
HKEY_LOCAL_MACHINE\Software\Microsoft\WinsMibAgent
HKEY_LOCAL_MACHINE\SYSTEM\CCS\Services\Wins
```

Q I've just added a second network card to my system to connect to a different network. Now I can't ping my original adapter! I can ping the gateway associated with the second *Network Interface Card* (NIC). What should I check?

A Try switching the order of the bindings of the two adapters in the Network dialog and restarting your computer.

Q I'm trying to use Performance Monitor to measure my TCP/IP network traffic. But I don't see the counters within Performance Monitor. I have TCP/IP successfully installed. Where did the counters go?

A These counters are installed with the SNMP service. Install the SNMP service, and Performance Monitor adds the counters for TCP, UDP, IP, and ICMP.

Q How do I add more than five IP addresses to my system?

A Open the Registry Editor and look under

```
HKEY_LOCAL_MACHINE\SYSTEM\CurrentControlSet\Services\<AdapterName>\Parameters\
➥Tcpip
```

Locate the `IPAddress` value. This value will be of type `REG_MULTI_SZ`. Each of the lines represents one of the IP addresses that the NIC has. If you have entered three IP addresses using the Network dialog, those three IP addresses are listed. Double-click the `IPAddress` value, and the Multi-String Editor dialog appears. You should see all the IP addresses you have assigned there. Add more IP addresses by appending them to the list—one on each line.

You also need to add associated subnet masks for each IP address you add. In the Registry key, under `IPAddress`, you should see a key named `SubnetMask` of type `REG_MULTI_SZ`. By double-clicking this value, you will see an edit box. Add matching subnet masks for each IP address you entered.

When you finish adding IP addresses, reboot your machine. To verify that all your IP addresses were added correctly, type `IPCONFIG` at a command prompt. Also, check the Event Viewer for any TCP/IP-related errors.

Summary

TCP/IP is the most complex protocol shipped with Windows NT. It also is the protocol with the best utilities for troubleshooting. After you master these utilities, TCP/IP will become easier to install and troubleshoot.

A good understanding of this chapter will help you in the next chapter, "Windows NT and Dynamic Host Configuration Protocol (DHCP)."

Windows NT and Dynamic Host Configuration Protocol (DHCP)

by Mike Tressler

There are times when things come along in the computer industry that are so simple, elegant, and brilliant that you can't help but wonder why it took so long for it to happen. DHCP is such a thing. Dynamic Host Configuration Protocol (DHCP) is so simple and elegant, it's worthy of the label *genius.* However, many people are hesitant to use DHCP, mostly because of ignorance about its workings. This chapter looks in detail at the implementation of DHCP. You will learn what is happening at the lowest packet level of this protocol. You will also look at the communications that occur between the client that is requesting an IP address and the server that is providing an IP address.

This chapter shows how to configure a DHCP server, including what the requirements are for a DHCP server, where best to place DHCP servers in a network topology, and how to configure the values and parameters of the DHCP server. You will see many new features of DHCP, including support for the BOOTP protocol and new collision-detection mechanisms in DHCP.

Finally, this chapter goes through the steps needed to troubleshoot properly a DHCP installation. You can follow a list of steps to ease the troubleshooting process and see how to detect errors at the packet level using Microsoft's Network Monitor utility.

After reading this chapter, you will be able to understand how a DHCP client and server communicate, how to configure a DHCP server, and how to properly troubleshoot the Dynamic Host Configuration Protocol.

DHCP Implementation Details

DHCP is a protocol that enables clients to dynamically acquire IP addresses from a DHCP server. A DHCP server can be any machine that is running Windows NT 3.51 or later.

DHCP is actually pretty easy to troubleshoot and debug. However, most people I've met have not had a formal introduction to DHCP's inner workings, and thus they are confused and irritated at what appear to be some magical, mystical, uncontrollable reactions that DHCP appears to be giving. I urge everyone who is unfamiliar with DHCP to read this section of the chapter and not skip ahead to the troubleshooting section at the end. It is in the understanding of DHCP that most problems will become obvious.

DHCP in a Nutshell

DHCP is simply a four-line conversation between the client requesting an IP address and the server providing the IP address. Let's think through what steps should be required for a client to obtain an IP address. Obviously, the client does not have an IP address preconfigured; otherwise there would be little need for DHCP in the first place. Because there is no IP address, the client needs to get one. Thus, at boot time the client broadcasts to the network, asking if someone is configured as a DHCP server. Barring any network communications errors, one or more DHCP servers respond by offering an IP address to the client. The client will then request the use of one of those addresses. Finally, the server agrees that the client can have the address, and the client begins using the IP address. That's about all there is to DHCP. A client asks for an address, a server offers one, and the client accepts the address and begins using it.

The History of DHCP

Obviously, DHCP clients and servers are a bit more formal than in the previous paragraph. So let's look a little more closely at the technical implementation of DHCP. As stated in the opening, DHCP is genius, and part of that genius lies in the use of existing protocols and RFCs. Using existing protocols and RFCs dictates that most existing network equipment will work just great with DHCP. DHCP was developed by the Internet Engineering Task Force (IETF) to reduce the amount of configuration required on a TCP/IP network. DHCP is defined in Request for Comments (RFCs) 1533, 1534, 1541, and 1542. A quick look at these RFCs reveals RFC titles such as "DHCP Options and BOOTP Vendor Extensions," "Interoperation Between DHCP and BOOTP," and "Clarifications and Extensions for the Bootstrap Protocol." So what is BOOTP, and why does it show up in the RFCs that define DHCP?

BOOTP, which stands for Bootstrap Protocol, is the precursor to DHCP. BOOTP is a protocol that allows devices to receive IP addresses from a network BOOTP server. However, unlike DHCP, BOOTP provides static addresses for BOOTP devices. What happens in a BOOTP conversation is similar to what happens in a DHCP conversation. According to RFC 951, the BOOTP server should "Attempt to lookup the client hardware address in our [the server's] database," meaning that the servers must already know the hardware or MAC address of the requesting client. Then, based on this hardware address, the server sends back the same IP address every time. Thus, BOOTP is static. That's not all bad, though. Think of a network printer that supports lpd printing. How could you print to this printer if its IP address changed all the time?

DHCP is a superset of BOOTP. The latest BOOTP RFC is RFC 1542, which includes support for DHCP. Because BOOTP was so close to the desires of DHCP, it was very easy to use the existing BOOTP messages to support DHCP because BOOTP already provided a variety of configuration parameters to configure a workstation. The DHCP message format is nearly identical to BOOTP, but DHCP includes some new fields and uses some existing BOOTP fields differently. Another major advantage of basing DHCP off of BOOTP is that most existing routers can act as RFC 1542 relay agents that can be used to relay DHCP messages between subnets. Therefore, with a router acting as an RFC 1542 relay agent, you can provide IP addresses to machines on remote subnets.

How a DHCP Client Leases an IP Address

In DHCP, clients don't own IP addresses; they lease them. By default, a successfully leased IP address is the client's to use for three days. Over the course of these three days, the client will attempt to renew his lease. In many cases, once a client receives an IP address lease, that client keeps the IP address for a very long time—if he can successfully renew that lease. The concept of leasing might seem like an odd way to control IP addresses, but consider a network that has used nearly all of its IP addresses. If there were no lease concept, when new clients were added to the network, they would keep an address forever. In a class-C addressing scheme, what would happen after the 254th client was added to the network? There would be no more addresses to hand out. But what if some of the machines that have received an IP address are broken, or if laptops with IP addresses are off the network? Why shouldn't the server be able to give an IP address to the new (255th) client? The only way the server can determine if one of the previous 255 machines is broken or off the network is by seeing how recently that client asked to have its address renewed. And by default, if the client hasn't asked to use that address for the past three days, the server will then give out this address again. A lease arrangement is the only way to be assured that the server can reuse IP addresses.

For the client to obtain an IP address lease, a DHCP conversation occurs. Figure 30.1 shows the steps involved in an IP address conversation.

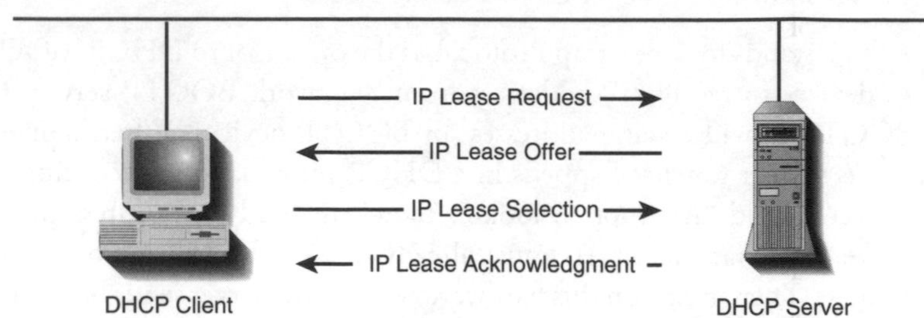

Figure 30.1. *The four steps in a DHCP conversation.*

The Initializing State and DHCPDISCOVER

When a DHCP client boots and begins its search for a DHCP server, the client is in what is called the *initializing* state. At this point, the client's TCP/IP stack initially loads and initializes with a null IP address. The null IP address is used so that the client knows it must obtain a legal IP address. Also, if a legal IP address were assigned in this state, there would be the possibility of an IP address conflict on the network. The DHCP client broadcasts a `DHCPDISCOVER` message to its local subnet using BOOTP UDP server port 67. The `DHCPDISCOVER` message contains the client's name and its MAC address. In the event that this client has previously received an IP address, it also sends its last known IP address in the `DHCPDISCOVER` message. This is done so that the client can try to lease the same IP address again.

Because the client cannot use its last known IP address, the source IP address for the `DHCPDISCOVER` broadcast is `0.0.0.0`, and the destination is `255.255.255.255`. In this step, the DHCP client basically broadcasts to the network that it needs to find a DHCP server.

A graphical view of the `DHCPDISCOVER` phase is shown in Figure 30.2.

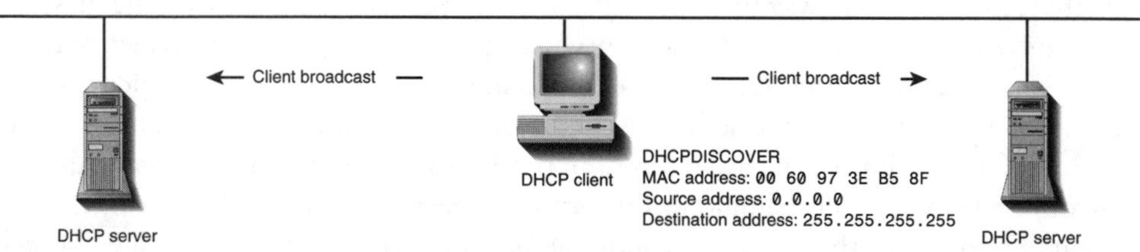

Figure 30.2. *The* `DHCPDISCOVER` *phase of a DHCP conversation.*

The Selecting State and DHCPOFFER

DHCP servers on your network sit around listening for DHCPDISCOVER messages. If the DHCP servers hear one of these requests, they will respond to the client with a DHCPOFFER message using BOOTP UDP port 68. The DHCP servers look into their administrator-configured address databases and see if they have a valid address to offer to this client. If they do, the DHCP server selects an available IP address from its database, marks it as used, and embeds it into the DHCPOFFER message. When the server sends the DHCPOFFER message, it sends it as a broadcast because the DHCP client does not yet have an IP address. This broadcasted DHCPOFFER message carries the following information: the DHCP client's MAC address used to properly identify the client, an offered IP address, an appropriate Subnet Mask, a server identifier (which is the IP address of the offering DHCP server), and the length of the lease.

If a client does not receive a DHCPOFFER message from a DHCP server, the client will retry its DHCPDISCOVER broadcast four times every 5 minutes. The four retries are sent at 2-, 4-, 8-, and 16-second intervals, plus a random interval between 0 and 1,000 milliseconds. If a DHCP client does not receive an offer after its four attempts, it will sleep for 5 minutes and try again.

A DHCP server will use the following criteria to determine which IP address to offer:

- The server has an unexpired lease for that client and therefore already has a reserved IP address for that client.
- The client sent an IP address as part of its DHCPDISCOVER message, and this address is available on the DHCP server.
- If neither of the above is available, the server will offer an available address from its pool.

A key point to observe is that a DHCP client will always try to re-lease the last IP address it received. This offers some stability to the network. Also, the client assumes it's a known good IP address that worked the last time and did not cause any IP addressing conflicts. Figure 30.3 shows a graphical representation of the DHCP offer phase.

Note: Under Windows NT 4.0, you now have the option to send unicast responses to DHCP clients, as opposed to broadcast responses. Previous versions of DHCP Server ignored the client broadcast flag. If you would like to enable the unicast support in Windows NT 4.0, edit the following Registry location:

`HKEY_LOCAL_MACHINE\SYSTEM\CurrentControlSet\Services\DHCPServer\Parameters\IgnoreBroadcastFlag`. Set this value to `reg_dword type 0`. Setting it to `1`, the default, forces DHCP server to broadcast all its responses.

Setting this value does decrease network traffic. However, it should only be used when clients are on the same homogenous Ethernet or token ring network, not when there is a router or bridge that performs MAC address translation, such as an Ethernet-to-token ring gateway.

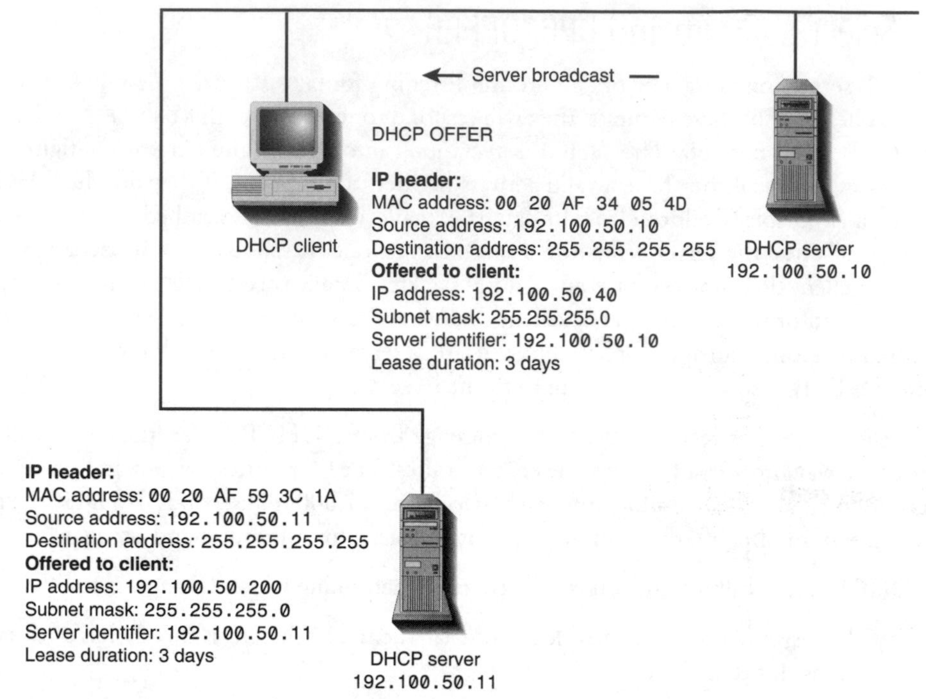

Figure 30.3. *The DHCP offer phase of a DHCP conversation.*

The Requesting State and DHCPREQUEST

The DHCP client collects all the valid DHCPOFFER messages and selects an offer. The selection of a valid offer is usually the first offer received. The client then sends a DHCPREQUEST message to the DHCP server, accepting the offered IP address. It is a request message, because the client still does not have an IP address and is requesting to use the one offered by the server.

The DHCPREQUEST message contains at least the server-identifier field from the DHCPOFFER message, which is the IP address of the chosen DHCP server. On most DHCP clients, the DHCPREQUEST message also includes a request from the client for any more configuration information that the DHCP server can provide. This additional configuration information could include information such as a default gateway or primary DNS server.

Because the client is still not fully bound to TCP/IP, the client again must broadcast to the network the DHCPOFFER it is accepting. Because the DHCPREQUEST message includes the IP address of the DHCP server the client selected (located in the server identifier field), and because it's a broadcast, all DHCP servers that offered an IP address will hear the DHCPREQUEST. The DHCP servers look at the server-identifier field and determine if they were selected to provide the IP address for that particular client. Those whose DHCPOFFERs were rejected mark the offered DHCP address as available in their pool of available IP addresses. Figure 30.4 shows the DHCP request phase.

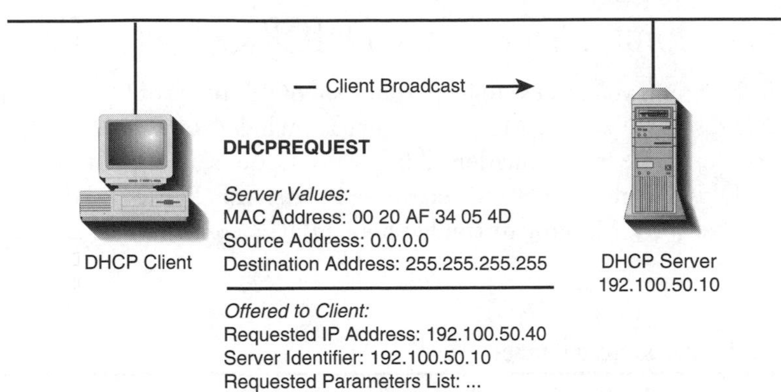

Figure 30.4. *The DHCP request phase of a DHCP conversation.*

The Bound State and DHCPACK

One last step! Upon receipt of the DHCPREQUEST message by the DHCP client, the DHCP server responds to the client with a DHCPACK message as an acknowledgment that the client may go ahead and use this address. The DHCPACK message contains a valid lease for the negotiated IP address and any additional configuration parameters that the client requested and that the server can provide. When the client receives the DHCPACK message, it completes initialization of TCP/IP and is now considered a bound TCP/IP client that can communicate over the network using TCP/IP. The client will also save this IP address in the Registry (Windows 95 and NT systems) or in a file called DHCP.DAT (Windows 3.*x* stations). It then requests this IP address in future DHCPDISCOVER messages. Refer to Figure 30.5 for a graphical view of this state.

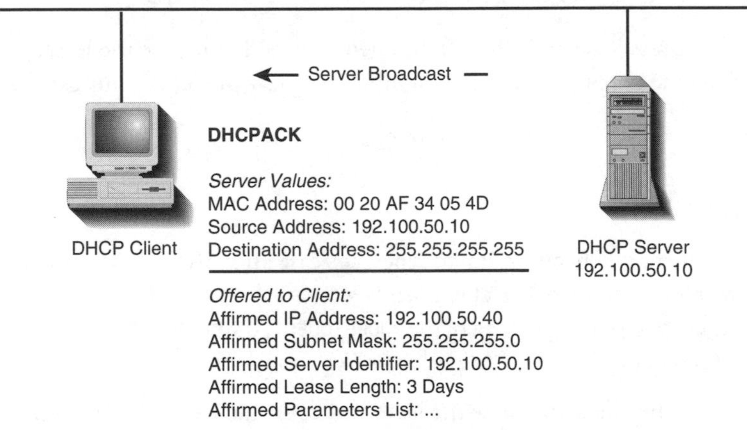

Figure 30.5. *The DHCP acknowledgment phase of a DHCP conversation.*

A Network Monitor View of the DHCP Conversation

One of the best tools you can use to help troubleshoot this phase of DHCP is a protocol analyzer such as Microsoft's Network Monitor, which is included in Windows NT 4.0. Table 30.1 summarizes the source and destination address conversations. Using this table, you should be able to dissect a DHCP conversation and determine where it is failing. More detailed information on how to use Network Monitor to troubleshoot DHCP conversations is available later in this chapter.

Table 30.1. DHCP conversation addresses.

State	*Source MAC Address*	*Destination MAC Address*	*Source IP Address*	*Destination IP Address*	*Description*
`DHCPDISCOVER`	DHCP client	Broadcast	`0.0.0.0`	`255.255.255.255`	DHCP discover
`DHCPOFFER`	DHCP server	Broadcast	DHCP server	`255.255.255.255`	DHCP offer
`DHCPREQUEST`	DHCP client	Broadcast	`0.0.0.0`	`255.255.255.255`	DHCP request
`DHCPACK`	DHCP server	Broadcast	DHCP server	`255.255.255.255`	DHCP acknowledgment

How a DHCP Client Renews a Lease

After an IP address lease has expired, the client can no longer use the leased IP address. In order to avoid this, the client periodically attempts to renew the lease, thus extending the use of that address.

The Renew State

The DHCP client will begin trying to renew its lease after 50% of the lease duration has expired. In order to renew its lease, the client sends a `DHCPREQUEST` to the DHCP server from which it obtained its lease. Upon the receipt of the `DHCPREQUEST`, the `DHCPSERVER` will respond with a `DHCPACK` to the DHCP client. The `DHCPACK` performs two functions:

- It allows the client to renew the lease and continue using the IP address.
- The `DHCPACK` contains all configuration information for the client. In the event that the administrator updated the TCP/IP configuration information, the client receives these changes and begins using them.

After the DHCP client receives the DHCPACK, the client once again becomes a bound TCP/IP client that can communicate over the network using TCP/IP.

The Rebinding State

If the DHCP client is unable to reach the DHCP server that provides its IP address, the DHCP client will attempt to contact *any* DHCP server when 87.5% of the client's lease has expired. The client attempts to contact the DHCP servers by using DHCPREQUEST broadcasts in an attempt to locate any server that can renew its lease. Any other DHCP servers on the network can respond with either a DHCPACK or a DHCPNACK message. If a DHCPACK message is received, the client resets its lease duration and continues using its IP address. If the client receives a DHCPNACK message, the client must reinitialize and obtain a new IP address. A DHCPNACK message is sent by DHCP servers to inform DHCP clients that they have incorrect configuration information.

If the lease expires or a DHCPNACK is received, the client must immediately cease using the leased IP address. The client will then enter the initialization stage and attempt to negotiate a new DHCP lease.

Additional DHCP Messages

There are two more DHCP messages that have not yet been discussed. Microsoft clients have just recently supported the DHCPDECLINE message, which is used to communicate IP address conflicts. The DHCPRELEASE message is an optional housekeeping message.

DHCPDECLINE

A DHCP server can send additional configuration information along with its DHCPACK message. Upon receipt of this information, the client reviews the IP configuration information received. If there is an invalid configuration parameter, the client will broadcast a DHCPDECLINE message to the DHCP server. After issuing the DHCPDECLINE message, the DHCP client will return to the initializing state and try again to lease an IP address.

On Windows NT 4.0 Service Pack 2 and subsequent releases, DHCP clients now support this message. After the client receives the lease from the server, it issues an ARP to see if the IP address is in use. If it is, it will issue a DHCPDECLINE to the DHCP server. If the server is also running Windows NT 4.0 Service Pack 2 or later versions of DHCP Server, it will flag the IP address as a BAD_ADDRESS in its DHCP database. After the client issues the DHCPDECLINE, the client returns to the initializing state.

DHCPRELEASE

A `DHCPRELEASE` message is sent by a DHCP client to notify the DHCP server that the client is canceling its lease and relinquishing its IP address. A `DHCPRELEASE` message includes the client's IP address that it is relinquishing, as well as the client's MAC address. Upon receipt of this message, the DHCP server marks the address as available.

Although it seems that this is a sensible thing for clients to do, most clients do not send this message when shutting down. There are several reasons for this. If a client does not send a `DHCPRELEASE` message, the DHCP server will still think that the client is online using this address. Therefore, the DHCP server will not mark this address as available and there will be a higher likelihood that when the DHCP client boots again, its previous IP address will be available. Another reason for not sending a `DHCPRELEASE` message is that it lowers the amount of network traffic, as well as the amount of work that the DHCP server must do. If all machines on a network are constantly sending `DHCPRELEASE` messages and then booting up again throughout the day, the original leases have most likely not expired. Therefore, the DHCP server doesn't have to go through the routine of unnecessarily marking and unmarking available IP addresses.

An end user can force the release of a DHCP address by using either the `ipconfig.exe` or the `winipcfg.exe` utility. On Windows and Windows 3.*x* clients, executing the `ipconfig /release` command from a command-prompt window will send a `DHCPRELEASE` message to the DHCP server. On Windows 95 stations, running the graphical `winipcfg.exe` utility and clicking either the Release or Release All button sends the `DHCPRELEASE` message. After executing either of these commands, the client station will not be able to communicate over the network via TCP/IP until the client's IP addresses have been renewed. This is done by executing `ipconfig /renew` (Windows NT or Windows 3.*x* clients) or by clicking the Renew button (Windows 95). Performing the renew action begins the entire DHCP cycle anew.

Summarizing How a DHCP Client Leases and Renews an IP Address

The last few sections technically detailed the steps involved in a client leasing and renewing an IP address. An understanding of this process is one of the most powerful tools you can use to troubleshoot DHCP.

For reference, here are the steps a client uses to lease an IP address:

1. Upon boot, initialize TCP/IP using IP address `0.0.0.0`.
2. Broadcast a `DHCPDISCOVER` message, looking for a DHCP server.
3. A DHCP server receives the `DHCPDISCOVER` message, checks to see if it can respond—and if it can, broadcasts a `DHCPOFFER` message back to the client and marks the offered IP address as leased.

4. The client selects which DHCPOFFER to accept and sends a DHCPREQUEST to the DHCP server whose offer the client accepts.
5. The DHCP server accepts the DHCPREQUEST message and sends a DHCPACK message back to the client. Inside the DHCPACK message are additional configuration parameters.
6. Finally, the client binds TCP/IP using the DHCP address provided by the DHCP server.

In order to renew a DHCP lease, the following steps occur:

1. After 50% of the lease has expired, the client sends a DHCPREQUEST message to the server.
2. If the server is found, it returns a DHCPACK to the client; the client waits until 50% of the lease has expired and repeats step 1.
3. If 85% of the lease has expired, the DHCP client broadcasts a DHCPREQUEST message on the network. At this point, the DHCP client is saying that it will accept *any* valid IP address, not just confirmation and renewal of its current IP address.
4. Upon expiration of its lease or receipt of a DHCPNACK message, the client forfeits its use of its IP address and enters the initializing state.

DHCP Servers and Scopes

For a DHCP client to obtain an IP address using DHCP, that client must successfully contact a DHCP server. A DHCP server can be any machine running at least Windows NT Server 3.5 that has a static IP configured and has the DHCP service successfully configured and running. The focus of the next few sections is to help you understand what is involved in successfully configuring and installing a DHCP server.

DHCP servers distribute ranges of IP addresses to DHCP clients. These ranges of IP addresses are called *scopes*. A scope is a definition of IP ranges and related attributes. When determining what scopes to define and how many scopes to use, there are a few rules you should keep in mind.

You should always have more than one DHCP server per scope. This means that you should split a scope across two servers. If you have only one DHCP server, and if it were to go offline for an extended period of time, DHCP client leases could expire. If this were to happen over a weekend, you could have a big problem on your hands Monday morning. Therefore, if you have a second server that also distributes IP addresses for the same subnet, you have protected yourself from a potential problem during extended server downtime. You also receive the side benefit of a load-balanced DHCP server. Because both servers can validate DHCP requests, one server won't be flooded with DHCP broadcasts. An individual DHCP server can support about 10,000 clients.

If you do exercise the option to utilize two DHCP servers for the same IP subnet, you must be certain to segregate your scopes so that they do not overlap. There is currently no mechanism to synchronize assignment of IP addresses from multiple servers' IP address pools. This means that each DHCP server must be responsible for its own independent address pool. For example, you want to offer 100 IP addresses for DHCP clients. You decide that you want to use two servers and assign 50 addresses to each server's DHCP address pool. Your best option is to assign addresses 1–50 to DHCP server A and addresses 51–100 to DHCP server B. Note that there is no overlap in this scenario. Server A cannot give out an address in server B's pool, and vice versa. If you have an overlap in your defined address pools, it is possible that server B might provide an address that server A has already assigned to one of its DHCP clients.

> **Note:** DHCP server does not know what IP addresses are already used on your network, and in versions prior to Windows NT 4.0 Service Pack 2, it does not attempt to determine whether the IP address it is leasing is an available address on your network. It is up to you, the DHCP Administrator, to tell DHCP server which IP addresses it should distribute. If you make an error, it is very likely that there could be duplicate IP addresses assigned on your network, causing unpredictable results and problems on your network. Before you begin configuring DHCP server, make sure that you have a detailed listing of all available and unavailable IP addresses in your subnet.

Windows NT Server 4.0 Service Pack 2 and later versions have a crude method for determining if an IP address is available for lease on the network. There is an option labeled Conflict Detection Attempts. To enable this feature, select the Server Menu option within the DHCP server administration program, and then select Properties. By setting a value in the pull-down list, you are effectively telling DHCP Server to send this many pings before offering this address as a valid lease. For example, setting this value to `3` will force DHCP Server to issue three pings before leasing the address in question. After each ping, DHCP Server waits 2 seconds. Therefore, setting the Conflict Detection Attempts to `3` will cause a 6-second delay (3 pings × 2 seconds) in the DHCP lease cycle.

If the DHCP server receives a reply to the ping, it will mark the address as a `BAD_ADDRESS` and will try again by leasing the next address in the scope. After the offending IP address has been dealt with, you can then return the `BAD_ADDRESS` to the address pool by deleting it from the scope Active Leases window.

If a client is leasing an IP address it already had, or if the client is renewing its address, the DHCP server will not attempt a ping operation. It will only ping when leasing addresses that have not yet been successfully leased.

Remember that no amount of DHCP server ping testing can help you in your administration of an IP network. It is important that you keep a close eye on which IP addresses you have used on your network.

What happens if you are on a network with multiple subnets? Your best bet is to place a DHCP server on each subnet and connect the subnets with routers that can act as RFC 1542 relay agents. Routers that support RFC 1542 have the capability to modify DHCP packets to signify from which subnet the broadcast came. The reason you would want routers capable of forwarding DHCP requests is for fault tolerance. For example, if one of your DHCP servers went down for a period of time, clients could receive DHCP addresses from DHCP servers on other subnets. The DHCP servers on the router-separated subnets need to have a properly configured scope for each subnet for which you want to provide backup. Realize that these routers will forward all DHCP communication across their connected subnets.

When a DHCP server receives a DHCP broadcast, the server must determine where the broadcast came from so that it can provide a valid IP address to the client. In order to help the DHCP server determine where this broadcast came from, RFC 1542–enabled routers edit a field in the `DHCPDISCOVER` broadcast. The router examines the field `giaddr` (also known as the `Relay IP address` field) before the broadcast is forwarded to the remote subnet. If the `giaddr` field in the broadcast packet has an IP address of `0.0.0.0`, the RFC 1542 relay agent on the router edits this field and enters its own IP address. If the field has already been changed, the RFC 1542 relay agent will not modify this field.

When Client 1 issues its `DHCPDISCOVER` broadcast, nothing needs to be done to the broadcast packet. The DHCP server will detect that it is on its local subnet because the `giaddr` field is still `0.0.0.0`. It will therefore dole out an IP address from its scope range, `192.100.50.30` to `192.100.50.149`.

For Client 2, things are a bit more involved. When Client 2 issues its `DHCPDISCOVER` request, the RFC 1542 relay agent on the router will change the `giaddr` field in the broadcast packet to `192.100.51.254`. It will then forward this packet to all subnets to which the router is connected. This is done because the router does not know which subnet has a valid DHCP server. Therefore, the `192.100.50.0` subnet and the other subnets will all receive this broadcast. When the DHCP server sees that the `giaddr` field is set to `192.100.51.254`, it will respond with a `DHCPOFFER` for the scope `192.100.51.40` to `192.100.51.149`.

If the router does not support the RFC 1542 Relay Agent, only Client 1 will be able to obtain a lease. If you are on a network with subnets separated by a router, verify with your router vendor that support for RFC 1542 is installed and enabled.

There are some points to keep in mind when setting up a network with DHCP servers separated by routers. Suppose you have two DHCP servers. The first DHCP server is on subnet `192.100.50.0`, and the second is on subnet `192.100.51.0`. DHCP Server 1 has 120 defined IP addresses for dissemination on its local subnet, and DHCP Server 2 has 110 addresses available for its local subnet. In order to provide a level of fault tolerance, you should set up scopes on each DHCP server to service the other's subnet in case of failure. In our example, on DHCP Server 1 we will establish a 50-address scope for the `192.100.51.0` subnet. On DHCP Server 2, we will establish a 51-address scope to cover for the `192.100.50.0` subnet. There are scopes on both servers for both subnets. Should one of the servers fail, the other server would be able to provide leases for the failed server. Notice also that the servers do not cover as many addresses for the remote subnet as they do for the local subnet. This is because, due to network latency, the local DHCP server will provide most of the DHCP leases for the local clients. Also, in case of router failure, there is an optimal number of local IP addresses in the range so that if the router fails, it can still support a large number of clients. Figure 30.6 shows a graphical view of this example.

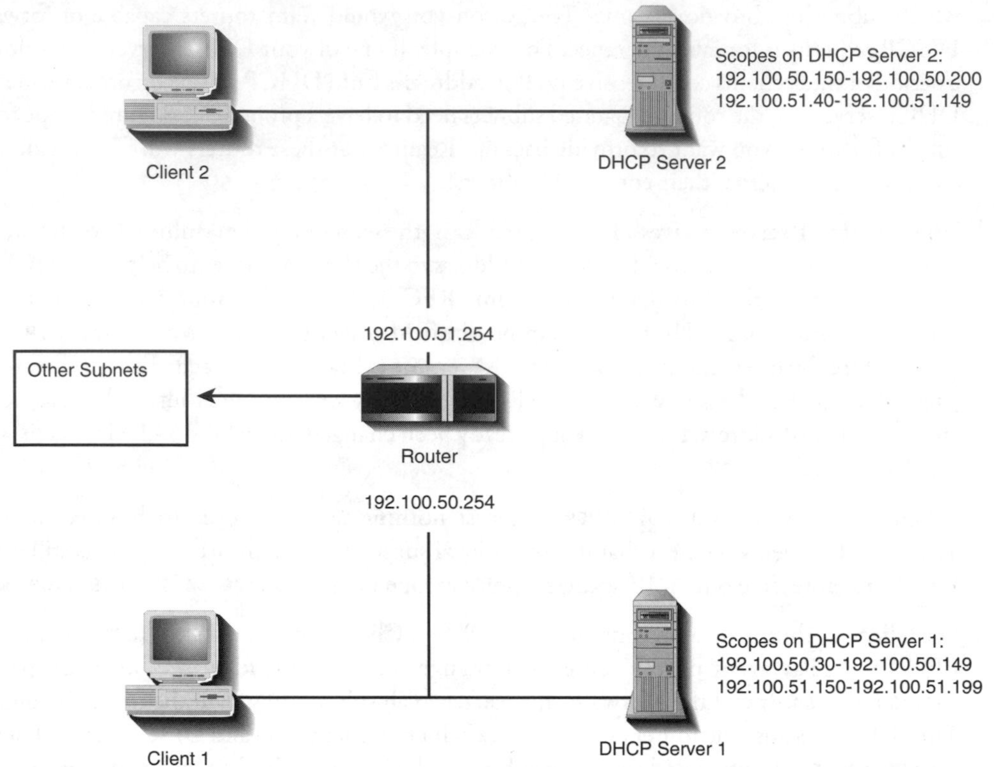

Figure 30.6. *A network with multiple subnets and multiple DHCP servers.*

When a local client broadcasts a `DHCPDISCOVER` packet, the local servers will usually provide the client with the DHCP lease. Be aware, however, that the `DHCPDISCOVER` packet is still forwarded to all subnets by the RFC 1542 agent on the router, and that the remote DHCP server could initiate the lease with the local client.

You can also set up a multihomed Windows NT server and assign a different subnet to each of the network cards in the server. This way, the DHCP server would be able to provide addresses for multiple subnets without the need for a router.

You can also use one server to provide multiple subnets on the same network by using superscopes. Superscopes are discussed in more detail later in this chapter.

Installing DHCP Server

Microsoft DHCP Server is a network service. To install this service, go to Control Panel | Network | Services and click the Add button. (See Figure 30.7.)

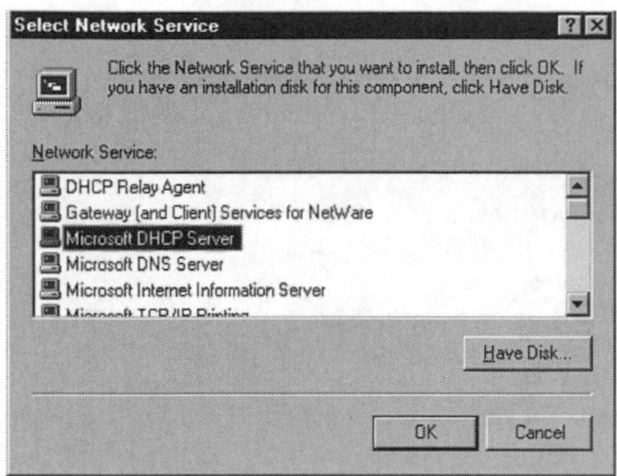

Figure 30.7. *Installing a DHCP server.*

After a DHCP server has been installed, you will be asked to restart your server. After your server has restarted and you have logged in successfully, you are ready to begin configuring your DHCP server.

The DHCP Manager program is found in the Administrative Tools program group. DHCP Manager shows only one server, the local machine, and a blank Option Configuration pane, as shown in Figure 30.8.

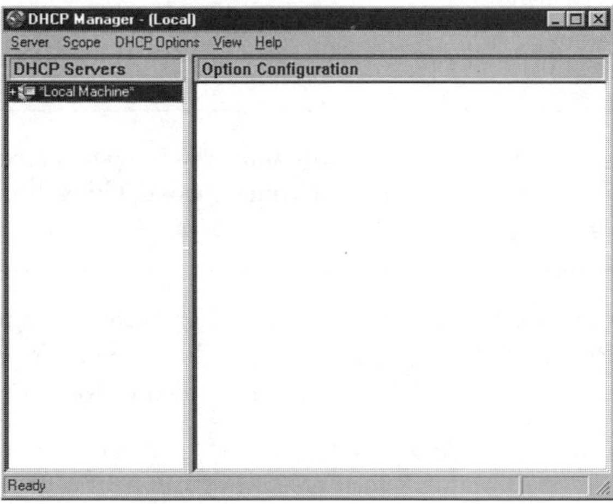

Figure 30.8. *DHCP Manager shows both the known servers and the options on the opening screen.*

The first step in setting up a DHCP server is to create a scope of IP addresses. In DHCP Manager, you'll notice that the left window pane has an entry labeled Local Machine. This entry will hold all the DHCP scopes defined for the server on which you are currently working.

To create a scope for this server, double-click the Local Machine icon. This will change the plus sign preceding the Local Machine icon to a minus sign. Once this is done, select Scope from the pull-down menu. If you are running DHCP Manager on Windows NT 4 with Service Pack 2 or later, you will notice that you have two options: Create and Superscopes. On earlier versions of Windows NT, you will see only Create. In either case, select Create. I will discuss superscopes later in this chapter.

A new window appears, titled Create Scope – (Local). It is in this form that your most important scope settings will be created. The first two fields ask for the start and end addresses of your IP address pool. This range determines the minimum and maximum IP values that DHCP will distribute. For example, if your server is on IP subnet `1.1.1.0` and you would like to distribute IP addresses from `1.1.1.80` to `1.1.1.200`, you would enter `1.1.1.80` in the first field and `1.1.1.200` in the second field. The third field asks for the subnet mask. Enter the subnet mask of your server at this time. For example, `255.0.0.0` could be entered in the third field.

The Exclusion Range is a device to allow you to exclude an individual address or a range of addresses from the pool of IP addresses you defined previously. For example, suppose you have four network printers with IP addresses `1.1.1.100`, `1.1.1.156`, `1.1.1.157`, and `1.1.1.158`. You could exclude these addresses from the IP address pool by adding them to the exclusion range. In order to remove IP address `1.1.1.100` from the IP address pool, enter `1.1.1.100` as the start address and click the Add button. In order to remove the three consecutively addressed printers in the previous list, enter `1.1.1.156` as the start address and `1.1.1.158` as the end address. Click the Add button after entering these values.

Tip: A useful option is to define an entire subnet as the pool of available IP addresses and then exclude addresses already defined on your network. This will give you greater flexibility in redefining your scope in the future.

Next, you are asked to determine the lease duration. Earlier in the chapter, you learned that clients lease their DHCP addresses and that after 50% of the lease has expired, the DHCP client will attempt to renew its lease. Lease duration is asking you how long you want the lease to last.

There are several factors in this decision. If you are on a static network where nothing changes very often and you have very few DHCP clients and a large number of IP addresses available, it might be a good idea to increase the lease duration. This will also provide for less network traffic because clients will renew their IP addresses less often. However, if there are few available IP addresses and a great number of DHCP clients, you might want to decrease the length of the lease duration. This will increase the turnover of leased addresses, thus improving the odds that there will be an available address for a client.

Setting the scope duration to Unlimited is not advised. Rather, set a very long lease range. This will provide you some flexibility that the Unlimited option does not provide.

Note: The maximum lease duration is 999 days, 23 hours, and 59 minutes.

Finally, you are asked to provide a name and a comment for this scope. You may enter any useful information here. This information is for your benefit only and has no effect on the performance of DHCP. When you have finished filling out this screen, click OK. An example of a properly filled-out DHCP scope is shown in Figure 30.9.

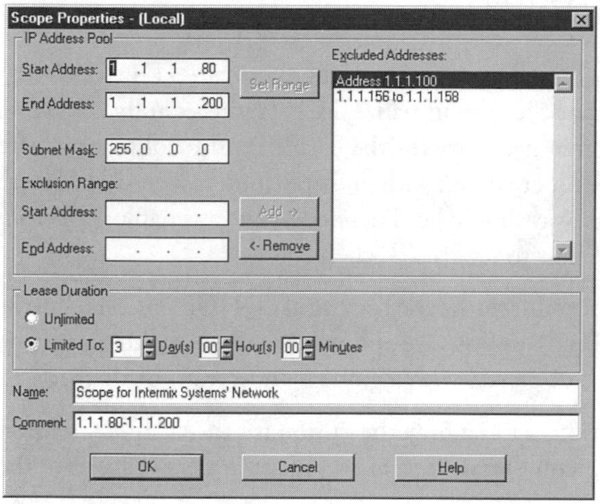

Figure 30.9. *A properly created DHCP local scope.*

After you click the OK button, a dialog pops up, informing you that the scope has been successfully created. It also asks you if you would like to activate this scope now. The default option is No. If you do not need to add any additional scope parameters, such as WINS Server or Router (Default Gateway) values, you may go ahead and pick OK.

Your scope will then be active and respond to `DHCPDISCOVER` broadcasts. If, however, you want to add some more parameters for your DHCP clients to receive, select No. This will ensure that no clients will issue a `DHCPDISCOVER` before your server is configured to supply complete information to the client.

To activate or deactivate a scope after it has been created, select the Scope menu option, and select either the Activate or the Deactivate option. If the light bulb icon preceding the scope is yellow, the scope is active. If the light bulb is gray, the scope is deactivated. (See Figure 30.10.)

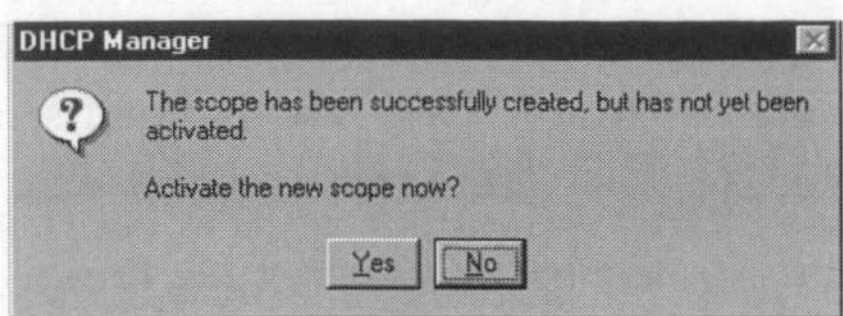

Figure 30.10. The DHCP Manager dialog box after a scope has been created.

DHCP Options

As you saw earlier, DHCP server only needs to provide a DHCP client with a valid IP address and subnet mask for that client to initialize TCP/IP successfully. However, there are many TCP/IP settings that are often necessary for the TCP/IP protocol to work effectively on a network. For example, if you are on a network with multiple routers, you should be able to tell the DHCP client what its default gateway should be. Therefore, you can enable numerous DHCP options that your DHCP server can pass to its DHCP clients.

There are four methods that can be used to set DHCP options. First, you can set Global DHCP options. Global DHCP options are options that are set for all scopes on the selected DHCP server. Global options are displayed with a globe icon in front of them.

Scope DHCP options will set only the option for the currently selected scope. Scope options are displayed with an icon that depicts a row of computers in front of them.

You can also set DHCP server options on a client-by-client basis. However, this only applies to clients that have a client reservation for them. This enables you to not only provide a predefined IP address for a client, but also to provide this client with specific or custom DHCP options.

Finally, setting default DHCP options modifies the setting for one specific DHCP option. By setting up a default value, you save yourself trouble in the future when trying to remember what the exact values should be for a particular global or scope option. After setting a default DHCP option, the next time you add a global or local DHCP option, the default value will automatically appear.

If you enable multiple levels of DHCP options, there must be a way to determine which option gains precedence over another. The following list shows the hierarchy of DHCP options:

Client DHCP options override both global and scope DHCP options.

Scope DHCP options override global DHCP options.

If there is no client or scope DHCP option, global DHCP options will take effect.

Common DHCP Options

There is a core group of DHCP options that administrators should consider setting. There are numerous other options that an administrator can set, but many of these have no effect on Microsoft DHCP clients. However, other vendor- and platform-specific implementations of DHCP clients can utilize various DHCP options beyond those of Microsoft's DHCP client implementation. Check the documentation for your DHCP client to see which DHCP options it supports.

The DHCP option `003 Router` should be set on any network that has a router or default gateway. Simply enter the IP address of this router.

If your network has a DNS server, or if your network is connected to the Internet, you will most likely want to define a DNS server by using DHCP option `006 DNS Servers`. By entering a list of DNS server IP addresses here, your clients will be prepared to access DNS servers for name resolution.

If you are on a DNS network, including the Internet, you should set DHCP option `15 Domain Name`. This will set your client's domain name. For example, `microsoft.com` is a domain name.

To define WINS servers on your network, use option `044 WINS/NBNS Servers`. Entering a value here will allow your DHCP clients to find a WINS server for name resolution.

When setting option `044 WINS/NBNS Servers`, you will be prompted to also set a value for `046 WINS/NBT node type`. You have four options with this setting: `0x1` (b-node), `0x2` (p-node), `0x4` (m-node), and `0x8` (h-node).

In most cases, you'll want to select `0x8` (h-node) for your `046 WINS/NBT node type`. When telling your clients to use h-node as their node type, you are effectively decreasing your network traffic.

Clients can perform name resolution in several ways, one of which is by using broadcasts (b-node) to resolve names. This is undesirable. Instead, to optimize network traffic, your client should make a direct request to a name server to fulfill the requested address resolution. This is done using the p-node type. M-node is a mixture of both the b-node and the p-node types. Using m-node, a client will attempt a broadcast name resolution and, if that fails, it will then use a p-node name resolution. This is an improvement over either b-node or p-node, because if one resolution fails, the other is used. However, in m-node, broadcast resolution (b-node) is used before p-node is attempted.

h-node name resolution is the inverse of m-node name resolution. In h-node, a client will always attempt p-node–directed sends and will use b-node only as a last resort. Therefore, the broadcasts on your network should diminish greatly.

In order to set your network clients to use a particular node type, enter the numeric value in the entry box, preceded by `0x`. For example, to set h-node as your `046 WINS/NBT node type`, enter `0x8` in the entry field.

Advanced DHCP Server Options

There are many interesting and useful features and parameters for you to consider when establishing DHCP services on your network. The following sections detail these options.

Client Reservations

Over the course of supporting a network, it might become necessary that a certain client always receive the same IP address. With this in mind, you can create a client reservation. A client reservation is the capability of DHCP to always provide the same IP address to a given client. The client that is to receive the IP address is identified by its network card's unique Media Access Control (MAC) address. Because the MAC address is always sent during the DHCP process, the DHCP server simply checks its Client Reservations table to see if there is a reservation for that MAC address. If there is, the server returns that IP address in its `DHCPOFFER` broadcast. If there is no match in the Client Reservations table, the DHCP server continues with its normal scope lookup for an available IP address.

To enable client reservations, select Scope from the menu and then Add Reservations. After making these selections, you will see a screen similar to that in Figure 30.11.

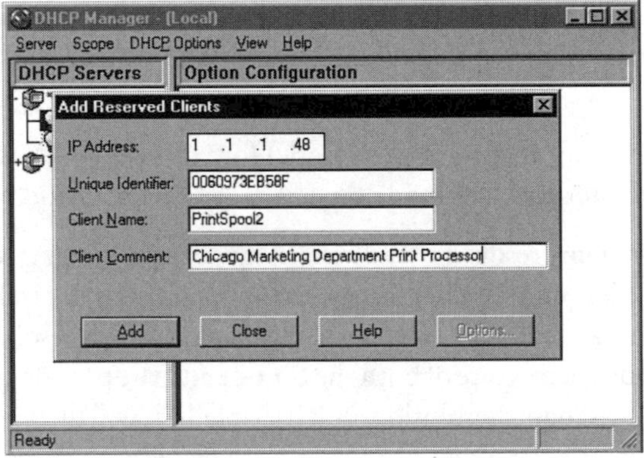

Figure 30.11. *Adding a client reservation.*

The first entry you need to add is the IP address that you would like to reserve. Next, you must enter the Unique Identifier, which is the client's MAC address. To determine a client's MAC address, you can enter the following command on most Microsoft DHCP clients: `IPCONFIG /all`. On Windows 95 systems, run the `WINIPCFG.EXE` utility to see a listing of the client's MAC address. Verify that you correctly entered the MAC address in the Unique Identifier field.

You are then asked to provide a client name and a client comment. These are optional; however, you are advised to fill them out with pertinent information that will enable you to remember why exactly you reserved these addresses.

BOOTP Services

At the beginning of this chapter, you learned that BOOTP is a predecessor to DHCP. The primary differences between DHCP and BOOTP are that BOOTP clients assume that their address is infinite in its duration, the BOOTP address received by the client is static, and in BOOTP you can pass a bootfile to the client. With versions of Windows NT 4.0 after Service Pack 2, you can now enable a DHCP server to also act as a BOOTP server. Future versions will support assigning dynamic IP leases to BOOTP devices.

Adding BOOTP reservations is similar in every way to adding DHCP client reservations. However, there are some additional client options that you might want to apply to a client reservation that is relevant only to BOOTP.

BOOTP clients that do not specify the parameter request list option (55) can still retrieve the following options, which are sent to the BOOTP client in the following order:

1	Subnet Mask
3	Router
5	Name Server
12	Host Name
15	Domain Name
44	NetBIOS over TCP/IP Name Server
45	NetBIOS over TCP/IP Datagram Distribution Server
46	NetBIOS over TCP/IP Node Type
47	NetBIOS over TCP/IP Scope
48	X Window System Font Server
49	X Window System Display Manager
69	SMTP Server
70	POP3 Server
9	LPR Server
17	Root Path
42	NTP Server
4	Time Server

The DHCP server will return as many of the preceding options as will fit into the response packet. If the BOOTP client needs additional options, that BOOTP client must specify the parameter request option (55).

You can set additional BOOTP values in the server's BOOTP table. This table is found by selecting your server in DHCP Administrator, picking properties, and then picking the BOOTP table tab. Check your BOOTP client's documentation on what information you should enter into this table for your client to work properly.

For more information concerning BOOTP, check the BOOTP RFCs on the Internet at `http://www.pasteur.fr/other/computer/RFC/`.

Superscopes

Some networks have more than one subnet running across the same physical cabling. I've worked on a network that had a backbone similar to the one in Figure 30.12.

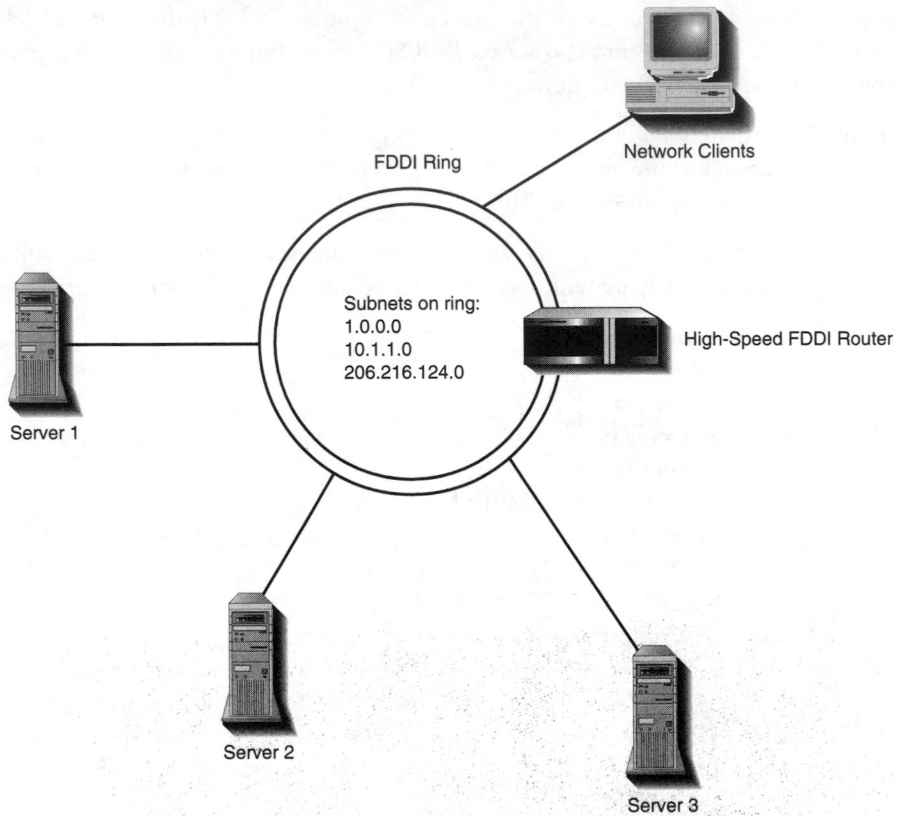

Figure 30.12. *A network backbone with multiple subnets.*

On this network, there is an FDDI ring providing a high-speed backbone that supports several IP address subnets and hundreds of clients. On the FDDI ring is a high-speed router that allows the various subnets to communicate with one another on the ring. Servers 1, 2, and 3 are all on the same subnet. When DHCP was rolled out on this network, the problem that was run into was that all the clients received IP addresses only from the subnet that the servers were on. This is because the `giaddr` field in the `DHCPDISCOVER` broadcast was still set to `0.0.0.0`. Because the clients could directly broadcast to the servers without needing the router, none of the other scope addresses were ever used. These servers were running Windows NT 3.51, so the only way the servers could provide addresses to the other subnets on the network was by changing the IP addresses of two of the servers so that they were on the other subnets.

This is an undesirable solution. There was no redundancy or load balancing of the DHCP servers. If one were to have failed, it is likely that there would have been problems with clients not receiving IP addresses. To avoid situations like this, Microsoft has introduced the concept of *superscopes*. A superscope is a scope that allows a DHCP server to support multiple logical IP subnets on the same network wire. Superscopes can be created only on Windows NT 4.0 with Service Pack 2 or later.

To create a superscope, you must already have scopes created for all the subnets that you would like this server to support. Once these individual (or child) scopes are created, you can package them together into a superscope. Make sure that these scopes are active and have global and local scope values defined, as appropriate.

Once your individual scopes are defined, select the Scopes menu option and then the Superscopes option. Pick Create Superscope, enter a name for this superscope, and select OK.

You must now add the child scopes you created earlier into this new superscope. According to Microsoft, the order in which the scopes are added is the order that this server will use to assign IP addresses. Using the sample network in Figure 30.10, if we set up a superscope on Server 1 that listed the scopes in the order of `1.0.0.0`, `206.216.124.0`, and `10.1.1.0`, the DHCP server would first dole out addresses from the `1.0.0.0` subnet. Next, it would hand out addresses from the `206.216.124.0` subnet, and finally it would give out addresses for the `10.1.1.0` subnet.

If you want to load-balance the distribution of these subnets (that is, you want all of your subnets equally distributed), you would need to create a superscope on a second server that had a different child scope ordering. However, when actually trying to do this, there is no indication that the scope order has any effect on the way superscope works today.

Active Leases

DHCP enables administrators to see which addresses are currently leased, how much time is left on the lease, and to whom the addresses are leased. In order to see this information, select the Scope menu item and then pick Active Leases. This will bring up a dialog box similar to the one shown in Figure 30.13.

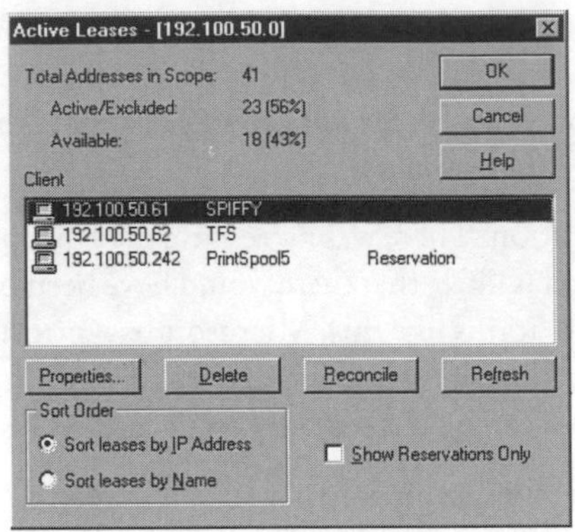

Figure 30.13. *Viewing active leases.*

In the client window is a list of all active leases, sorted by IP address. Following the IP address is the client name that has the reservation. Optionally, there can be a reservation comment to show whether the active lease is a reservation. You can also sort this client name by checking the radio box at the bottom of this dialog box labeled Sort leases by Name.

Clicking the Properties button enables you to get more detailed information concerning a given lease.

Reconciling the DHCP Database

Within the Active Leases window that we discussed in the previous section is a button labeled Reconcile. This button triggers a consistency check between what DHCP server has in the Registry and what DHCP server has stored in its database. If you suspect that there are some inconsistencies between what you see in the Active Leases window and what you think is actually leased, reconciling the database can bring things back together. This is a safe button to click and can be a very valuable tool when you're experiencing DHCP problems.

Maintaining and Backing up the DHCP Database

DHCP uses a database to help keep track of leased IP addresses. This database is stored in `\%windir%\system32\dhcp`. Under Windows NT 3.5*x*, the database and related files require a bit more maintenance than under Windows NT 4.0.

Windows NT 3.5*x* DHCP Database Maintenance

By looking in the `\%windir%\system32\dhcp` directory on a Windows NT 3.5*x* machine, you should see the following files:

- DHCP.MDB, which is the actual DHCP database. Although the extension is .mdb, you cannot view this file by using Microsoft Access. The database does utilize the Microsoft Jet engine, but it is modified from the standard Microsoft Access database format.
- SYSTEM.MDB, which the DHCP server uses to track the structure of the DHCP database.
- JET.LOG and JET*.log files are the transaction logs for the DHCP database. This log file is used to recover the database in case of failure. For a mild improvement in system performance, you can disable this logging by setting the Registry value HKEY_LOCAL_MACHINE\SYSTEM\CurrentControlSet\Services\DHCPServer\Parameters\DatabaseLogging to 0.
- DHCP.TMP is a temporary file used by the DHCP server to store database information. If DHCP is properly stopped or shut down, this file will be removed and re-created the next time DHCP starts up successfully.

By default, the DHCP database is backed up after 15 minutes of inactivity. The files DHCP.MDB, SYSTEM.MDB, and JET.LOG are backed up into the \%windir%\system32\dhcp\backup\jet directory. In addition, the Registry HKEY_LOCAL_MACHINE\SYSTEM\CurrentControlSet\DHCPServer subkey is stored in the file DHCPCFG.

If you would like to control the backup process, you must edit the Registry entry BackupInterval or BackupDatabasePath. These entries are found in HKEY_LOCAL_MACHINE\SYSTEM\CurrentControlSet\DHCPServer. BackupInterval tells the DHCP server how much inactivity can occur before it should back up the database. This value can be between 5 and 60 minutes.

The BackupDatabasePath entry is used to tell the DHCP server where it should place the backed-up files. It is a good idea to edit this value to point to another drive on your machine. That way, if there is a drive failure on your DHCP server, you can recover the information after the server is repaired. Do not point to a network drive for this backup path, because the network might not be available.

In order to restore a DHCP database, stop the DHCP Server Service. Delete any files in the \%winroot%\system32\dhcp subdirectory, and copy the backed-up files to this directory. Run Registry editor and restore the contents of the HKEY_LOCAL_MACHINE\SYSTEM\CurrentControlSet\DHCPServer\Configuration key by choosing Restore from the Registry menu and then selecting the DHCPCFG file. Finally, restart the DHCP Server Service.

You can use the preceding steps to move a DHCP server from one machine to the other. However, you should be aware that the installation of Windows NT Server on the new machine must be on the same drive letter and in the same path as the original DHCP server. Also, TCP/IP and the DHCP server must already be installed on the new server.

Over the course of time, the DHCP.MDB database will continue to get larger and larger, eating up drive space unnecessarily. In order to compact the DHCP.MDB file, you can run the jetpack.exe utility. This utility is located in the \%windir%\system32 directory.

In order to run jetpack.exe, you must shell out to a command prompt and change the directory to \%windir%\system32\dhcp. Next, stop the DHCP Server Service by executing the following command: net stop "Microsoft DHCP server". Execute the jetpack command to compress the DHCP.MDB file. This is done by using the following command-line syntax: jetpack *<database name>* *<temporary database name>*. In our case, the database name is DHCP.MDB. The temporary database can be anything but temp. I like to use x as the name of the temporary database. For example: jetpack.exe DHCP.MDB X. Finally, restart the DHCP Server Service by executing the following: net start "Microsoft DHCP Server".

Windows NT 4.0 DHCP Database Backup and Maintenance

Unlike the Jet database engine Microsoft used for the DHCP database in Windows NT 3.51, Microsoft has a new database engine for DHCP in 4.0. Microsoft is now using the performance-enhanced Exchange Server version 4.0 database engine.

The same directory path is used, \%windir%\system32\dhcp, but the file structure has changed:

- DHCP.MDB still stores the core DHCP database, but it is now in the Exchange Server form rather than the Jet form of 3.51.
- DHCP.TMP is still the temporary file used during database index operations.
- J50.LOG and J50#####.LOG are the database transaction logs. These files are used in case DHCP needs to recover any data.
- J50.CHK is a checkpoint file.

These files are backed up on a 15-minute interval; this interval can be set through the Registry by editing the following key:

```
SYSTEM\current\currentcontrolset\services\DHCPServer\Parameters\BackupInterval.
```

Under Windows NT 4.0, you do not need to compact the DHCP database using the jetpack.exe utility. This is now done automatically.

When converting a Windows NT 3.5*x* DHCP server to a Windows NT 4.0 DHCP server, most of the work is done automatically. Because the 3.5*x* and 4.0 use different database engines, the DHCP.MDB file must be converted from the Jet engine to the Exchange Server engine. Using the jetconv.exe conversion process does this. When the DHCP Server Service starts for the first time after upgrading to 4.0, it detects that the DHCP.MDB file is still in the 3.5*x* version. The administrator receives a warning message explaining that the database is about to be converted to the 4.0 version of DHCP.MDB. When the administrator clicks OK, the DHCP Server Service is stopped and the conversion begins.

Note: This conversion also converts WINS and RPL databases if they are installed.

Before you upgrade to Windows NT Server version 4.0, verify that the old database is in a consistent state. Simply stopping and starting the DHCP service while still in NT 3.51 does this. An inconsistent database can cause the conversion to fail.

The conversion requires approximately 5MB of disk space for each database that it converts. The old databases are backed up into a subdirectory named `\351db`. For DHCP, you can find your original 3.51 databases in the `\%windir%\system32\dhcp\351db` directory.

This conversion can take several minutes to an hour, depending on the size of the database being converted. You should not stop or restart the DHCP service during this conversion.

In case the conversion fails, you can manually start the conversion by using the `upg351db.exe` utility. This utility is found in the `\%windir%\system32` directory. For help on using this utility, shell to a command prompt and execute `upg351db -?`. Once a database is converted to 4.0 format, it cannot be converted back to a 3.51 database. Also, a converted database will not work with Windows NT 3.51 services.

To restore a DHCP database under NT 4.0, stop the Microsoft DHCP Server Service. Delete all files in the `\%windir%\system32\dhcp` directory. Copy a backed-up version of the `DHCP.MDB` file to this directory, and restart the service.

To move a DHCP server to another machine, follow the previous steps in restoring a DHCP server. Make sure that the drive letter you're moving to is the same as the one where it resided. If the directory name has changed, move only the `DHCP.MDB` files and not the `*.log` or `*.chk` files.

Using DHCP Manager to Manage Multiple DHCP Servers

Like most of Microsoft's administrative tools, DHCP Manager can be used to administer remote DHCP servers. To add a remote DHCP server to DHCP Manager, select the Server menu item and then the Add option. At this point you will be asked to enter the address of the server you would like to administer. You can enter either the server name or its IP address.

After DHCP Manager has successfully contacted the remote DHCP server, you will see another entry on the DHCP server's window pane. Double-clicking this server will enable you to administer it as if it were your local DHCP server.

When working with multiple DHCP servers in DHCP Manager, make sure that you always select the correct server before doing administrative work.

Deleting Scopes

To delete a scope, highlight the scope you want to remove. Next, select the Scope menu option and then the Delete option. You will then be asked to verify this deletion.

Troubleshooting DHCP

If you've read this chapter, you should realize that DHCP is actually a very simple protocol. However, there is no simple tool to debug when things are going wrong. My favorite tool to break out when things go wrong is Microsoft's Network Monitor. I've used this tool to debug errors ranging from servers not listening for DHCP broadcasts, to routers not forwarding DHCP messages, to unexpected broadcast paths to DHCP servers.

Tip: If you have the Windows NT Resource Kit, there is a utility named `DHCPLOC.EXE` that is ultimately a DHCP-specific packet sniffer. For those of you uncomfortable with the complexity of Microsoft's Network Monitor, I recommend that you use this tool. Full documentation and examples are provided in the Resource Kit.

Microsoft Network Monitor

For those of you not familiar with Microsoft Network Monitor, I recommend that you spend an hour or two playing around with it, especially because it is shipped with Windows NT 4.0. Microsoft Network Monitor can help you track down plenty of other problems in your network besides DHCP problems, and can be a very valuable tool in your administrative toolbox. If you don't have Windows NT 4.0, use the version of Network Monitor that ships with Microsoft's Systems Management Server product.

The best strategy to use with Network Monitor is to set a filter between your DHCP servers and one particular test client. This will help filter out any extraneous network traffic. In the first half of this chapter, I discussed the four transactions that occur in a DHCP conversation: `DHCPDISCOVER`, `DCHPOFFER`, `DHCPREQUEST`, and `DHCPACK`. A successful DHCP dialog is shown in the network capture in Figure 30.14.

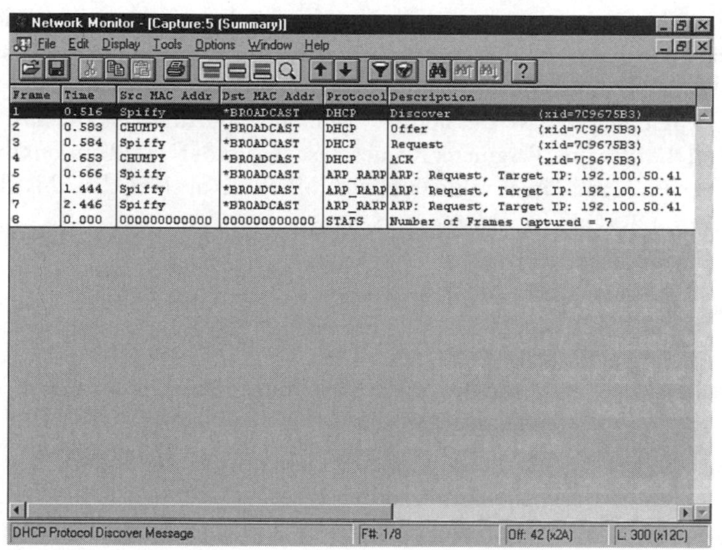

Figure 30.14. A successful DHCP Network Monitor capture.

A Packet-Level View of `DHCPDISCOVER`

Frame 1 shows the client Spiffy broadcasting a `DHCPDISCOVER` request. By expanding this broadcast, as shown in Figure 30.15, we can see just what this `DHCPDISCOVER` request broadcasted. In the bottom window we see the `giaddr` field. Because this value is set to `0.0.0.0`, we know that this packet did not go through a router. Otherwise, this field would hold the value of the first router that forwarded the broadcast.

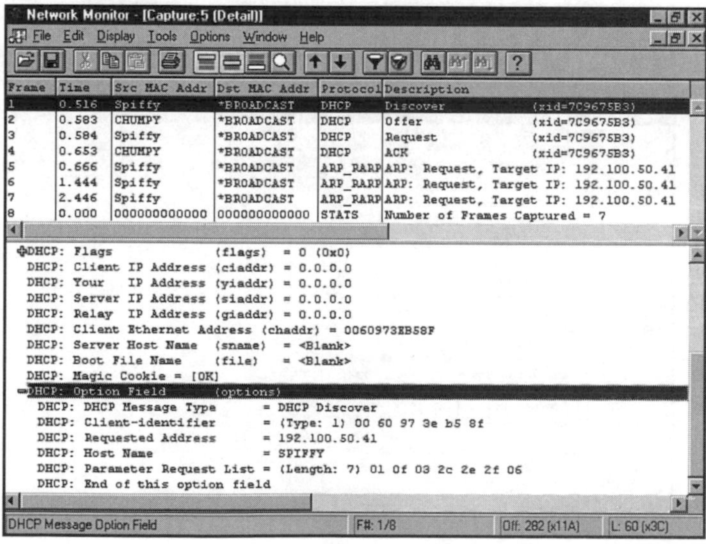

Figure 30.15. A detailed view of a `DHCPDISCOVER` *broadcast.*

By expanding the Option field, we can see an exact snapshot of what this broadcast contained. We see in the first line that it was a `DHCPDISCOVER` broadcast. The next line is Spiffy's MAC address (`00-60-97-3e-b5-8f`). In line 3 we see that Spiffy previously had the IP address of `192.100.50.41` and that Spiffy would like to have this address again. The fourth line is the hostname of this client (Spiffy). And the fifth line, Parameter Request List, is a list of DHCP options that the client would like filled. These hexadecimal values are a list of all the options that this client supports. For example, option 2C correlates to `044 WINS\NBNS Server`.

A `DHCPDISCOVER` broadcast frame is either 342 or 590 bytes total. Microsoft Windows for Workgroups TCP/IP 3.11a and Windows NT 3.5 used 590-byte frames. Here is a breakdown of a `DHCPDISCOVER` broadcast:

First 14 bytes	Ethernet header, which includes the destination address of `255.255.255.255`
Next 20 bytes	IP header, which includes the source address (`0.0.0.0`) and the destination address (`255.255.255.255`)
Next 8 bytes	UDP header, which contains the source and destination ports (BOOTP ports 68 and 67)
Bytes 43–300	`DHCPDISCOVER` Packet component, which contains the Option Field and is shown in Figure 30.15

A Packet-Level View of `DHCPOFFER`

The second line in Figure 30.15 is the server's `DHCPOFFER` response. By expanding the view of the `DHCPOFFER` response, as shown in Figure 30.16, we can analyze what Chumpy, our server, sent back to the client.

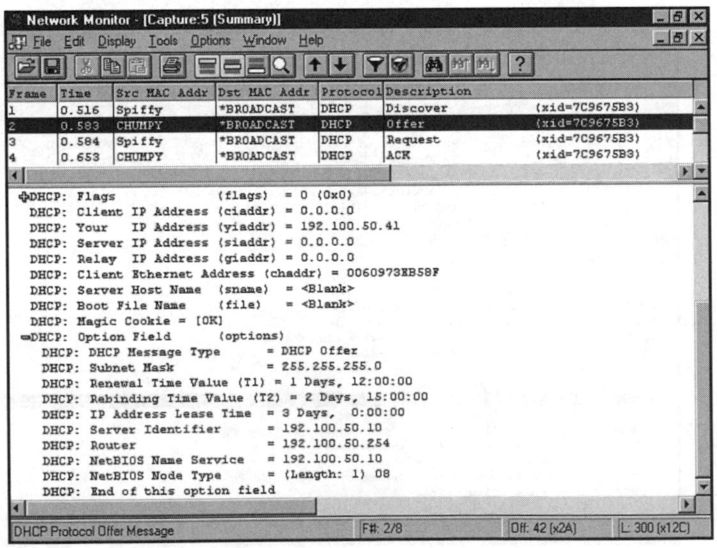

Figure 30.16. *A detailed view of a* `DHCPOFFER` *broadcast.*

The third line we see in the packet-analysis portion of Figure 30.16 is the `yiaddr` field. This is the IP address that Chumpy is offering to Spiffy, our client: `192.100.50.41`. If we look at Figure 30.16, we see that this is the address that Spiffy requested. Therefore, Spiffy will get the address requested.

By looking at the Option field in Figure 30.16, we see that this message is indeed a `DHCPOFFER`. Chumpy is also offering values for Spiffy to use, such as Subnet Mask, Renewal, Rebinding, and Lease duration values. Chumpy is also sending its IP address so that when Spiffy replies to this `OFFER` with a request, Chumpy will know that it was selected to be the DHCP server. Chumpy also passes along the router, NetBIOS name server (WINS Server), and node type to Spiffy. These last values come from the DHCP Options scope values that I defined for this scope.

A `DHCPOFFER` frame is 342 bytes in size. A breakdown of a `DHCPOFFER` packet follows:

First 14 bytes	Ethernet header, which has a destination address of `255.255.255.255`
Next 20 bytes	IP header, which includes a source address of the DHCP server and a destination address of `255.255.255.255`
Next 8 bytes	UDP header, which contains the source and destination ports (BOOTP ports 68 and 67)
Final 300 bytes	`DHCPOFFER` packet component

A Packet-Level View of `DHCPREQUEST`

The third line in Figure 30.14 is Spiffy's `DHCPREQUEST` response to Chumpy's `DHCPOFFER` broadcast. Figure 30.17 shows a detailed packet analysis of Spiffy's `DHCPREQUEST`.

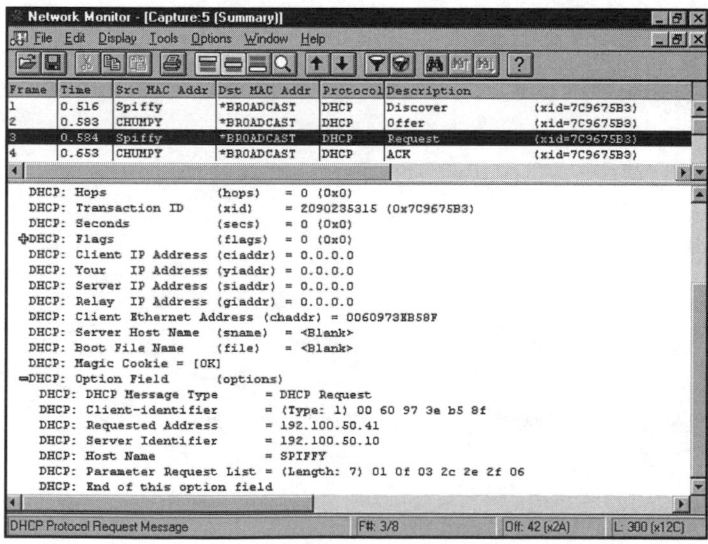

Figure 30.17. *A detailed view of a* `DHCPREQUEST` *broadcast.*

Midway down the Flags section, we see a chaddr entry, which is Spiffy's Ethernet address. Spiffy sends this so Chumpy knows which client he is dealing with. Note that this is the only identifier that Spiffy can use, because at this point Spiffy cannot yet use the IP address that Chumpy DHCPOFFERed previously.

By looking into the DHCP option field, we can see that indeed, this is a DHCPREQUEST. The second option field shows Spiffy's MAC address. The third line shows that Spiffy is willing to accept IP address 192.100.50.41, and that server 192.100.50.10 is who should validate the lease. We again see that Spiffy is the hostname requesting this IP address. Spiffy is also asking once more for a list of DHCP options.

Had Chumpy offered a different address in his DHCPOFFER broadcast shown previously, Spiffy would have turned around and performed up to two more DHCPDISCOVER broadcasts before finally settling on Chumpy. This is because Spiffy is trying ardently to reuse a previous IP address. If no server is willing to let Spiffy use that address, Spiffy will then accept any DHCPOFFERED address.

A DHCPREQUEST frame is either 342 or 590 bytes total, depending on the size of the DHCPDISCOVER frame. A breakdown of a DHCPREQUEST packet follows:

First 14 bytes	Ethernet header, with a destination address of 255.255.255.255
Next 20 bytes	IP header, with source address of 0.0.0.0 and destination address of 255.255.255.255
Next 8 bytes	UDP header, which contains the source and destination ports (BOOTP ports 68 and 67)
Final 300 bytes	DHCPOFFER packet component, as shown in Figure 30.16

A Packet-Level View of DHCPACK

The final phase in this conversation is the DHCPACK, as shown in Figure 30.14. At this point, Chumpy acknowledges that client Spiffy can have that IP address. Figure 30.18 shows a detailed look at the DHCPACK packet.

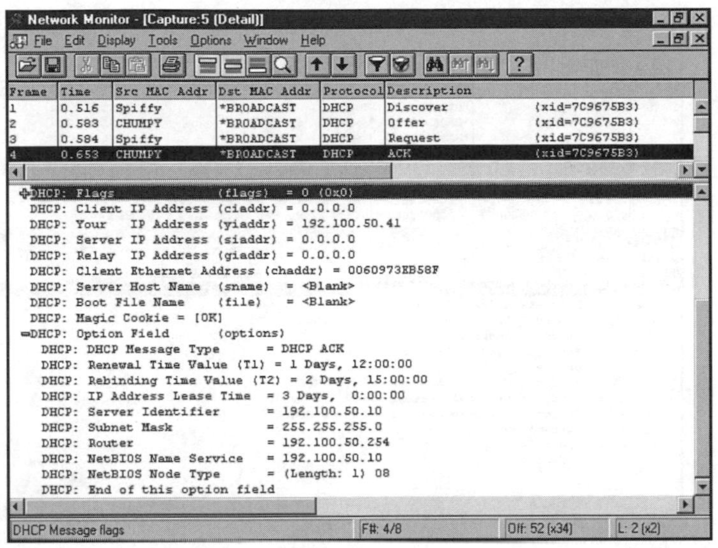

Figure 30.18. *A detailed view of a* `DHCPACK` *broadcast.*

In the packet-analysis portion, we see that Chumpy definitively tells Spiffy that its client IP address (the `yiaddr` field) is `192.100.50.41`. We also see Spiffy's Ethernet address in the `chaddr` field. Remember, Spiffy has not yet fully initialized its IP stack, and must therefore still rely on broadcast messages for communications.

In the Option Field portion of the packet, we see that Chumpy is resubmitting the DHCP scope option information to Spiffy.

The `DHCPACK` frame is 342 bytes. Following is a breakdown of a `DHCPACK` packet:

First 14 bytes — Ethernet header, with destination address of `255.255.255.255`

Next 20 bytes — IP header, with source address of `192.100.50.10` (Chumpy) and destination address of `255.255.255.255`

Next 8 bytes — UDP header, which contains the source and destination ports (BOOTP ports 68 and 67)

Final 300 bytes — `DHCPACK` packet component

ARP Verification of This IP Address

Because Spiffy is a Windows NT 4.0 client with Service Pack 2 installed, Spiffy now attempts to verify the validity of its new IP address. The three `ARP_RARP` broadcasts shown in Figure 30.15 are broadcast to see whether there is another device on the network with the IP address of `192.100.50.41`.

By looking at the packet breakdown of the ARP broadcast in Figure 30.19, we can determine that there was no such conflicting device.

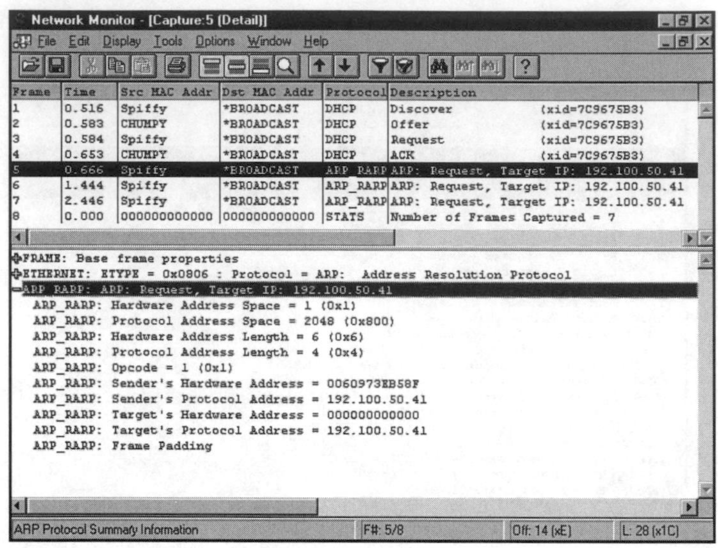

Figure 30.19. *A successful ARP_RARP broadcast.*

The important information in the `ARP_RARP` packet is the final four entries in the ARP packet. We see Spiffy's MAC address as the sender's hardware address, and Spiffy's newly acquired IP address (`192.100.50.41`) as the Sender's Protocol address. Spiffy is trying to determine if this IP address exists on the network, and as such, there is no Target Hardware address. For the Target's protocol address, we see `192.100.50.41`.

Had Spiffy found another machine with IP address `192.100.50.41` on the network, it would have immediately sent a `DHCPDECLINE` to the DHCP server. Upon receipt of the `DHCPDECLINE`, the Windows NT 4.0 Service Pack 2 or later server would have marked the address as a `BAD_ADDRESS`.

Also, if you were using a Windows NT 4.0 Service Pack 2 or later server that was leasing an address for the first time and had conflict detection enabled, you should see pings in your network capture. These are marked in Network Monitor as `ARP_RARP` broadcasts. Figure 30.20 shows an example of a network capture with server-side conflict detection enabled.

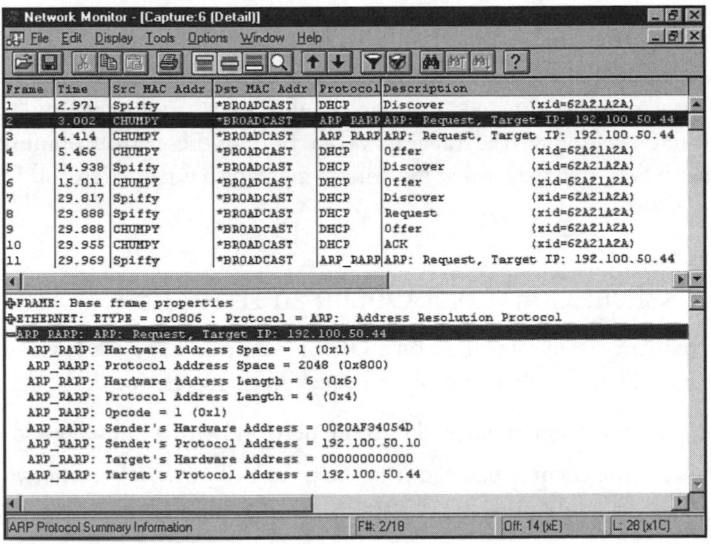

Figure 30.20. *DHCP conflict detection.*

We see in frame 1 that client Spiffy is attempting to discover a DHCP server. Server Chumpy receives this `DHCPDISCOVER` broadcast and, realizing that it has no previously used DHCP leases available, instantly pings for address `192.100.50.44`. I set the conflict detection level to 2, so we see 2 `ARP_RARP` broadcasts on our capture. You'll also notice a string of `DHCPOFFER`s and `DHCPDISCOVER`s in frames 4 through 7. This is because Spiffy is attempting to reuse its last known IP address, and Chumpy is offering it a different one. Spiffy will try three times to find a server that will allow it to use its old address. If it can't, it then accepts the first `DHCPOFFER` request it received, as shown in frame 8. Frames 9 and 10 finalize the transaction. Then, we see in Frame 11 that Spiffy is now verifying that the address it received is valid on the subnet.

Network Monitor Summary

I hope that through the preceding examples and discussion you've been able to learn what you need to look for when analyzing a DHCP discussion with Network Monitor. It is well worth your time to spend a few hours working with Network Monitor so that if the time comes when inexplicable things are happening with DHCP, you'll be able to see exactly what is happening.

General DHCP Troubleshooting Tips

The next few sections should help answer some commonly seen DHCP errors.

Errors in Connecting to Remote Servers with DHCP Manager

If you try to connect to a remote DHCP server through DHCP Manager, you might receive the following error messages: `The RPC Server is Unavailable` or `Error 1753: The DHCP Server service is not running on the target system`. Both of these errors point to the same problem. Verify through Server Manager that the remote machine has the Microsoft DHCP Server Service running.

The DHCP Client Could Not Obtain an IP Address

The most frequent error you will see on a DHCP network is `The DHCP client could not obtain an IP address`. There are several things to check in this scenario:

- Make sure the client is plugged into the network with a known good cable.
- Make sure the client is patched into the hubs and other related network devices.
- Verify that the DHCP Server Service is running on your DHCP servers.
- If your client is trying to connect from across a router, make sure that the router supports RFC 1542.
- Verify that you received no errors when installing TCP/IP to the client.
- Hard-code your client's IP address and see if you can communicate with the server, directly or across a router.
- Make sure your DHCP server has an available lease for this client.
- Use Network Monitor to determine where the broadcast packet is going, and what, if anything, the DHCP server is replying.

If you are using a client reservation, make sure that the client identifier (the client's Media Access Control value) is entered correctly.

The DHCP Client Could Not Renew the IP Address Lease

The `The DHCP client could not renew the IP address lease` error would occur if the client tried to renew its lease and was unable to contact a DHCP server. The troubleshooting steps are the same as in the previous section. However, pay particular attention to hardware problems and DHCP server problems. Because this client at one time was able to correctly receive an IP address, the software on the client is correctly installed and configured.

Verifying Client Configuration with `IPCONFIG`

To see just exactly what TCP/IP values your DHCP client has received, run the `IPCONFIG /ALL` command from a command-prompt window. In Windows 95, the `IPCONFIG` command has been replaced with the less robust yet prettier `WINIPCFG` command. If you see values that are not what you expected, verify that the local client machine does not have a predefined setting in its TCP/IP configuration. If this looks correct, verify your scope information on your DHCP servers.

In some situations, it might be desirable to have your clients release and renew their IP addresses every time they log on to the network. Using the IPCONFIG command in the logon script can do this. If you have Windows 95 clients, you must use the IPCONFIG utility from Windows for Workgroups 3.11 to achieve this functionality because the WINIPCFG utility does not support command-line parameters. The following is a code fragment that you could use in your network logon scripts to force clients to reinitialize their IP addresses. This script assumes that the Windows for Workgroups IPCONFIG utility is in the netlogon share.

```
IF EXIST C:\WINDOWS\IPCONFIG.EXE IPCONFIG.EXE /RENEW ;WFW
IF EXIST C:\WINNT\SYSTEM32\IPCONFIG.EXE IPCONFIG.EXE /RENEW ;WINNT
IF EXIST C:\WINDOWS\WINIPCFG.EXE %0\..\IPCONFIG.EXE /RENEW ;WIN95
```

Tip: The %0\..\ syntax used in the last line of the script means "use the current drive letter." Because there is no way of knowing ahead of time which drive letter a client can use to connect to the netlogon share, the %0\..\ syntax acts like a variable. At runtime, it is replaced with the drive letter that is connected to the netlogon share.

Location of DHCP Information

Windows NT clients store their DHCP configuration information in the following Registry key:

```
HKEY_LOCAL_MACHINE\SYSTEM\CurrentControlSet\<Your Network Adapter Device>\Paramters\TCPIP
```

Windows NT Server DHCP configuration is stored in the following location:

```
HKEY_LOCAL_MACHINE\SYSTEM\CurrentControlSet\Services\DHCPSERVER
```

Windows 95 client DHCP information can be found in the following Windows 95 Registry location:

```
\HKEY_LOCAL_MACHINE\SYSTEM\CurrentControlSet\Services\VxD\DHCP\DhcpInfo00
```

LAN Manager 3.0 and MS-DOS LAN Manager 2.2c client information is stored in a file named dhcp.prm, found in the *network_root* directory.

Windows for Workgroups with TCP/IP-32 stores the DHCP-related information in the Dhcp.bin file under the <WINDOWS_SYSTEM_ROOT> subdirectory. If you really want to force your client to discover a new IP address, exit Windows, delete this file, and enter Windows again.

DHCP Options Supported by Windows Clients

Here is a list of the DHCP options that Microsoft Windows clients currently support:

1	Subnet Mask	Defined in the Create Scope/Scope Properties dialog box.
3	Router	Used to define the client's default gateway.
6	DNS servers	Lists the DNS servers that the client computer has available to it.
15	Domain Name	Specifies the DNS domain name for the client.
44	WINS/NBNS Servers	Lists the NetBIOS Name resolution servers the client should use.
46	WINS/NBT Node types	Specifies the node type the client should use for NetBIOS over TCP/IP name resolution.
51	Lease Time	Specified in seconds, this value tells the client how long its lease is. This value is set in the Create Scope/Scope Properties dialog box.
58	Renewal (T1) Time	Specifies the time in seconds until the client enters the renewal state. This value cannot be set directly through DHCP Manager.
59	Rebinding (T2) Time	Specifies the time in seconds until the client enters the rebinding state. This value cannot be set directly via DHCP Manager.

DHCP Server Logging

Windows NT 4.0 DHCP server supports DHCP logging. To enable this option, select your DHCP server in DHCP Manager, select Server, and then select Properties. On the General tab is a checkbox to Enable DHCP Logging. DHCP will then generate a log file named `DHCPSRV.LOG` that tracks all its activity. Using this checkbox can slow down the system's overall performance.

The `DHCPSRV.LOG` file can be found in the `%WINDIR%\system32\dhcp` directory. Figure 30.21 shows an example of this file.

```
dhcpsrv.log - Notepad
File Edit Search Help
                    Microsoft DHCP Server Activity Log

Event ID  Meaning
00        The log was started.
01        The log was stopped.
02        The log was temporarily paused due to low disk space.
10        A new IP address was leased to a client.
11        A lease was renewed by a client.
12        A lease was released by a client.
13        An IP address was found to be in use on the network.
14        A lease request could not be satisfied because the scope's
          address pool was exhausted.
15        A lease was denied.
20        A BOOTP address was leased to a client.


ID Date,Time,Description,IP Address,Host Name,MAC Address
12,02/25/97,01:47:35,Release,192.100.50.44,SPIFFY,0060973EB58F
10,02/25/97,01:47:39,Assign,192.100.50.44,SPIFFY,0060973EB58F
10,02/25/97,01:49:25,Assign,192.100.50.61,SPIFFY,0060973EB58F
```

Figure 30.21. *The* DHCPSRV.LOG *file.*

No More Data Is Available

When creating a new scope in DHCP Manager, you might get the error message that `No more data is available`. This is a bug in the Windows NT 4.0 DHCP Manager. To work around this bug, add the server `127.0.0.1` to your list of DHCP servers. This bug has no adverse effects on your scopes or DHCP services, other than being annoying.

Summary

DHCP is a simple little protocol. Ultimately, only four broadcasts happen on your network. Client configuration is as simple as checking one box, and you only need to provide three values to the DHCP server to start enjoying the benefits of DHCP. It is my experience that most people's simple ignorance of what DHCP is and what it does scares them away from this most valuable of services.

By understanding how DHCP works, you can troubleshoot most errors without using any tools or utilities. And with the use of Network Monitor, you can see exactly what DHCP traffic is happening on your network.

CHAPTER 31

The Windows Internet Naming Service (WINS)

by Terry W. Ogletree

From the user's point of view, locating another computer or resource on a modern network is done using familiar "friendly names." These names are designated by administrators to specify hosts or resources so that the user need not be bothered with remembering complicated physical or logical addresses that a particular protocol may employ.

Two key components that can be used in Microsoft networks have been discussed in previous chapters: Dynamic Host Configuration Protocol (DHCP) for assigning IP addresses and Domain Name Services (DNS) for providing IP address to host name resolution. This chapter briefly reviews these two components and shows how they can operate with the Windows Internet Naming Service (WINS), which is used to resolve IP addresses to NetBIOS names.

Topics that are covered in this chapter include

- Integrating NetBIOS with TCP/IP (NetBT)
- Dynamic name registration using WINS
- Important databases used by WINS
- Enabling WINS lookup by DNS

- Monitoring WINS
- Replication between WINS servers
- Static mappings in the WINS database
- Backing up and restoring the WINS database
- Useful utilities found in the Resource Kits

Network Address Assignment and Name Resolution

Computers connect to local area networks (LANs) via a network interface card (NIC), sometimes called simply the network adapter. Each NIC manufactured has hardcoded into its firmware a hardware, or physical, address that it uses to identify itself when it places data onto a network.

Network cards are not protocol specific, but are actually signaling devices that can be programmed to send out different formats of organized data. Network protocols are the specifications that determine how programs interact with the network card and the format and rules used in transmitting data from one networked computer to another.

Each computer uses the NIC's physical address to identify itself on the network; therefore, network protocols must have some method of determining how to address packets of data to make sure they get to the correct destinations. In other words, a computer must somehow find out the address of another computer's NIC before it can send data directly to it.

The physical address is most often referred to as the Media Access Control (or MAC) address. When it gets down to the bits and bytes of networking, the transport protocol must use the MAC address. Most protocols shield the programmer and user from this by mapping a logical address or name to the MAC address and use this name or logical address in organizing and routing traffic throughout a network.

NetBIOS and NetBEUI

NetBIOS (Network Basic Input/Output Operating System) is a network-interface specification that specifies a name-based interface to the network. NetBIOS was developed in the early 1980s by IBM as a session-layer protocol that allowed programs to connect to resources on a network based on names rather than MAC addresses. The NetBEUI (NetBIOS Extended User Interface) protocol was developed as a transport protocol for the NetBIOS interface. NetBEUI mainly uses broadcasts to resolve a name to the correct MAC address.

Simply put, when a computer needs to locate a resource such as another computer, it sends out a broadcast packet that all computer hosts on the local LAN segment examine. The broadcast packet contains the name of the resource it is looking for. When a computer intercepts a packet that contains its name, it responds to the computer that originated the packet by sending a packet to it that contains the MAC address needed to communicate directly with it. The originating computer can then use the MAC address to send packets of data directly to that computer so that other hosts on the network can ignore the packets and communication will take place directly between the two computers.

Of course there are other mechanisms (such as name caching) that allow a computer using NetBEUI to store a list of addresses of computers it has recently had connections to, but the first basis of discovery is always done with broadcasts. This can consume a lot of network bandwidth and thus limits the number of computers you can effectively put on a LAN before data-throughput performance begins to suffer.

Transmission Control Protocol/Internet Protocol (TCP/IP): A Routable Protocol

Transmission Control Protocol/Internet Protocol (TCP/IP) is a set of protocols and standards that use a 32-bit (4-byte) IP address to identify computer hosts on a network. The IP address, as discussed in Chapter 29, "Windows NT and TCP/IP," is a logical address. Depending on the class of network you are using, different portions of the 32 bits are used to designate a network while the remaining bits are used to identify hosts on the network. Because TCP/IP can identify different networks as well as hosts on a LAN (in other words, in is routable), it is much more suited to larger networks that scale beyond the LAN to worldwide WANs, such as the Internet.

TCP/IP also associates "friendly names" with the logical IP addresses to make it easier for users to identify and remember how to access resources on the network. TCP/IP uses a variety of methods to provide name resolution. Perhaps the simplest method is the `HOSTS` file, which is a text file that a computer can use to look up the IP address of a host by using the host's name.

Whereas NetBEUI is limited to communicating with hosts on the local subnet that can hear the broadcast messages, TCP/IP can enable hosts on different subnets to communicate with each other. TCP/IP is indeed two protocols. The Internet Protocol (IP) is a connectionless-oriented protocol that provides an unreliable method of transporting data packets, whereas the Transmission Control Protocol (TCP) uses IP and builds on it to reliably route packets destined for other subnets or networks to the correct gateway that either connects to the destination network or knows how to get the data packet to the destination.

IP uses a method similar to NetBEUI—Address Resolution Protocol (ARP)—to locate hosts on the local subnet. TCP is logically abstracted from the MAC address because the IP protocol resolves details at that level.

The Domain Name Service (DNS) is a common method used by TCP/IP networks to resolve names to IP addresses. Maintaining `HOSTS` files on a large number of computers can be difficult and consume a lot of administrative time. DNS allows for a distributed database of names to IP addresses to be managed in an efficient way.

If NetBIOS applications could use TCP/IP as a transport method, and a method of translating NetBIOS names to IP addresses could be devised, the two could easily be joined together.

Windows NT provides this functionality using NetBT (NetBIOS over TCP/IP). NT services, such as the Browser and Netlogon services, use the Transport Driver Interface (TDI) in order to use NetBT. A NetBIOS emulator is also available to assist NetBIOS programs by translating their requests to TDI functions.

Integrating NetBIOS and TCP/IP

Microsoft versions of TCP/IP include Application Programming Interfaces (APIs), which enable an application program to make a network request using a NetBIOS name and have that name translated to an IP address. Thus, NetBIOS applications can be written to use the TCP/IP protocol for communications and therefore extend the scope of NetBIOS applications beyond the local network segment.

One of the first methods used by TCP/IP to resolve IP address to host names was the `HOSTS` file. It consisted of a text file in which each line had an IP address and its associated name.

The `LMHOSTS` file was developed to provide a similar function, but instead resolves NetBIOS names to IP addresses. The `LMHOSTS` file can work well when a network is quite small. However, maintaining synchronized `LMHOSTS` files on larger networks can become as cumbersome as maintaining individual `HOSTS` files on TCP/IP networks.

The Microsoft Domain Name Server that is available with Windows NT 4.0 can be used to resolve NetBIOS names to IP addresses. It accomplishes this by passing unknown names to WINS for resolution.

The Dynamic Host Configuration Protocol (DHCP)

Although DNS solves the name resolution problem for large networks by providing the name resolution process and essentially eliminates the need for a `HOSTS` file, a network administrator must still configure each host computer on the network and assign it an IP address, along with other configuration information such as a subnet mask, a default gateway, and so on. This can also be a time-consuming task, especially in a networking environment where the network changes frequently. Adding and removing computers from the network requires that the pool of available network addresses be tracked to ensure that an address is always unique on the network.

DHCP is an automated client/server mechanism that was developed to eliminate the manual labor involved in tracking network addresses and in configuring clients. (See Chapter 30, "Windows NT and Dynamic Host Configuration Protocol (DHCP).") It was developed from BOOTP, a protocol originally used by network nodes such as diskless workstations, to allow a client to request an operating system download and network configuration from a central server.

DHCP manages IP addresses by leasing them to host computers for a set period of time. Host computers request a network address from the central server when they boot and are required to renew the leases before they expire and thus, when computers are removed from a network, the address used is eventually released for use by another client. Administrators do not need to keep track of IP addresses in a spreadsheet and consult it every time they want to find an address to use for a new host computer. Adding and removing computers from a network is automated by the DHCP server.

A problem quickly becomes apparent. Because the DNS architecture is based on statically assigning an address to a host client, and DHCP is based on dynamically assigning and reassigning addresses, the two seem at first to be incompatible. If you want to combine a NetBIOS-based network that takes advantage of a dynamic service like DHCP with a static name resolution service like DNS, then some method must be found to mediate between the two.

WINS Provides Dynamic Name Resolution Service

The Windows Internet Naming Service (WINS) was developed to allow for dynamic registration and resolution of network names-to-address translations. After a WINS client determines its network address, whether it be statically assigned or dynamically leased from a DHCP server, it then contacts a WINS server to register itself. The WINS server and the DHCP server are complementary services. DHCP dispenses network configuration information to clients as needed and WINS tracks client addresses and names. You can also add static records to a WINS database, so it can provide name resolution for both static and dynamic address assignment mechanisms.

If you are having problems getting a client to resolve names using WINS, check the client's TCP/IP configuration:

1. Using the Network applet in the Control Panel, select the Protocols tab. (See Figure 31.1.)
2. Click the TCP/IP protocol and then click the Properties button.

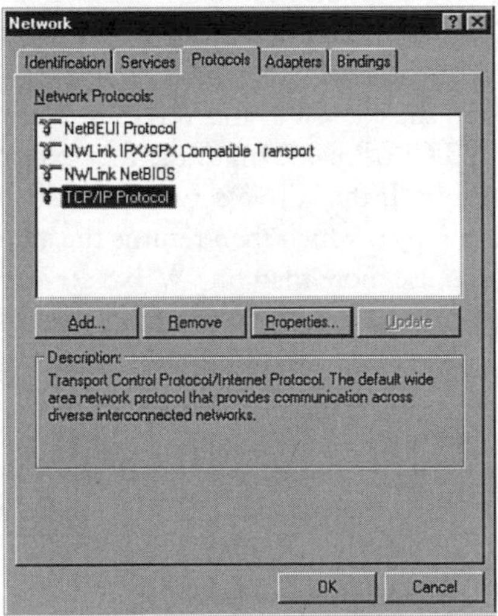

Figure 31.1. *The Protocols tab.*

3. In the Microsoft TCP/IP Properties dialog, select the WINS Address tab. (See Figure 31.2.)

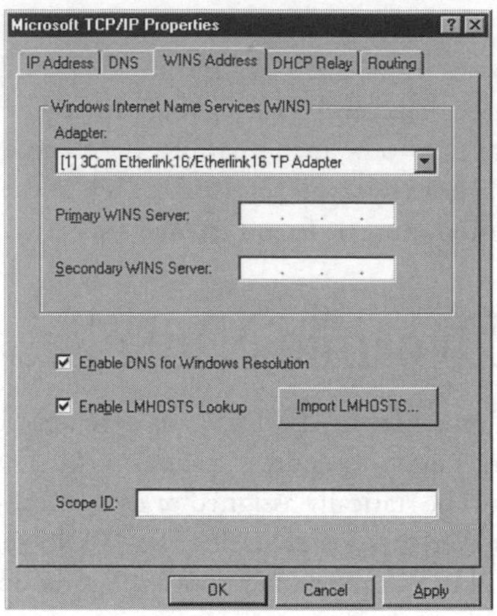

Figure 31.2. *You can enter WINS server addresses that the client computer will use on the WINS Address page.*

4. Check the addresses for your primary and secondary WINS servers. (A secondary WINS server is recommended for fault-tolerance purposes, but not required.) If the WINS server's address is correct and your computer still cannot resolve addresses using WINS, you should then check to be sure that your computer is not having problems communicating with each WINS server. You can do this by using the PING utility.
5. If you want the client to also query DNS servers when a WINS query fails, be sure the Enable DNS for Windows Resolution check box is selected. If you have this option enabled on your computer and DNS cannot resolve the name using an A record (address record), it will forward the request to the WINS server. It does this by using the host-name (the text of the TCP/IP name up to the first period) to request that the WINS server resolve the address. If the WINS server can locate the hostname in its database, it returns it to the DNS server, which then returns the address to the client. If the client has been configured to use more than one WINS server, the DNS server will query each one until it gets the address, or until there are no more WINS servers to query.
6. If you want the client to use an `LMHOSTS` file when a WINS query fails, the Enable `LMHOSTS` Lookup check box should be selected.

By configuring the client computer to use not only WINS but also DNS, you increase the chances that the client will be able to resolve resource names. If you need an `LMHOSTS` file, you should enable it also.

Reinstalling the WINS Server

If you have incorrectly installed the WINS, or if your database has become corrupted and the backup copies do not work (or, worse yet, you have no backup copies and the service will not start and create new data files), then you may need to reinstall the WINS server.

1. Bring up the Network applet in the Control Panel. Select the Services tab.
2. Click the Windows Internet Name Service and click the Remove button.
3. Click OK.

When you remove the WINS Server service and then attempt to reinstall it, you may get this error:

```
The Registry Subkey Already Exists.
```

If this happens, you must use the Registry Editor (use `REGEDIT.EXE` or `REGEDIT32.EXE`) to remove keys that were left behind by the previous installation. Remove the following keys:

```
HKEY_LOCAL_MACHINE\Software\Microsoft\Wins
HKEY_LOCAL_MACHINE\Software\Microsoft\WinsMibAgent
HKEY_LOCAL_MACHINE\SYSTEM\CurrentControlSet\Services\Wins
```

As always, use extreme caution when using the Registry Editor to modify your system configuration. It is possible to render the system unusable by deleting or modifying the wrong keys.

To reinstall the WINS server do the following:

1. Bring up the Networks applet in the Control Panel. Select the Services tab (see Figure 31.3) and click the Add button.

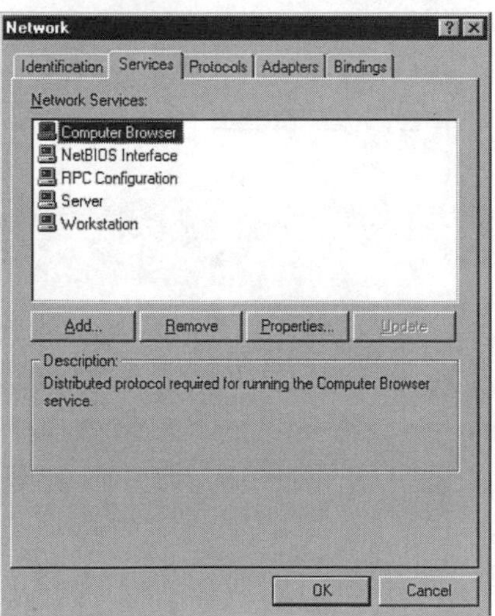

Figure 31.3. *You can add the WINS at the Services tab in the Network dialog.*

2. The Select Network Service dialog will appear. (See Figure 31.4.) Use the scrollbar on the right to scroll through the services until you find Windows Internet Name Service. Click it and then the OK button.

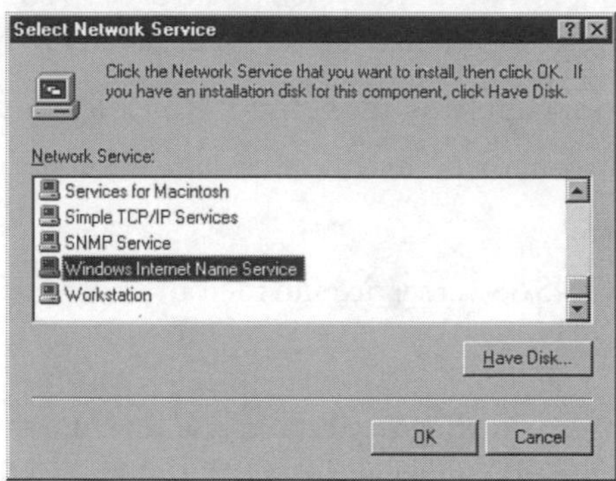

Figure 31.4. Use the Select Network Service dialog to install the WINS network service.

3. You will be prompted to supply the path for the Windows NT distribution source. This can be your CD or a network drive on which the distribution has been placed.
4. After you enter the path, the setup program will copy the needed files from the source to your local computer and when finished, the Network dialog (see Figure 31.5) will show the Windows Internet Name Service on the list of installed network services. Click the Close button and when prompted, reboot your computer.

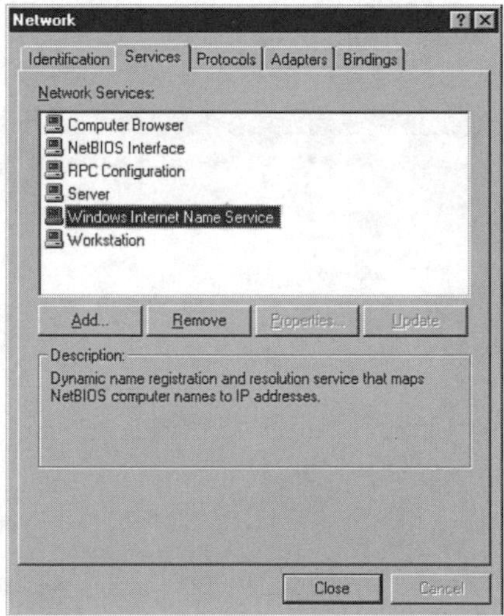

Figure 31.5. When properly installed, the Windows Internet Name Service shows up on the Network dialog.

Problems with WINS Server Database Files

The WINS server uses several files found in the `%systemroot%\SYSTEM32\WINS` directory. The following files are used by the WINS server:

- `J50.log` and `J50#####.log`

  All transactions done by the server are logged in these files. WINS uses these files to recover the database when necessary.

- `J50.chk`

  This is a checkpoint file used with the log files.

- `WINS.MDB`

  This is the actual WINS name/address database. It contains two tables: an IP address-Owner ID mapping table and a Name-to-IP-address table.

- `WINSTMP.MDB`

  This file is a temporary file that the service uses to store data when performing maintenance on the index. After a system crash, this file may remain in the directory.

Compacting the `WINS.MDB` Database File

In versions of Windows NT prior to 4.0, the database file `WINS.MDB` used by the WINS server would not recover unused space left over when obsolete records were deleted. Because of this the `JETPACK` program was used at the command prompt to compact the database when it became larger than 30MB. Compacting the database improves server performance.

This should no longer be necessary. Under Windows NT 4.0 the compaction process takes place automatically in the background during idle time.

However, occasionally you may find performance suffering and if the database is approaching the 30MB mark, you might want to try compacting the database. Before running the `JETPACK` program, however, be sure to switch to the `%systemroot%\SYSTEM32\WINS` directory. The program expects to find the file `SYSTEM.MDB` in the current directory. If you get the error message

```
Jetpack failed with error = -1811
```

then you are probably in the wrong directory. Check your default.

Use this syntax for `JETPACK` to compact the WINS database:

```
JETPACK WINS.MDB temporaryfile
```

where `WINS.MDB` is the WINS database file and *`temporaryfile`* is a temporary filename you create. Note that you cannot use the filename `TEMP.MDB` for the *`temporaryfile`* filename. This is because the `JETPACK` program will create a file called `TEMP.MDB` before it creates your temporary file and you will get an error indicating that the file already exists (`"Jetpack failed with error = 80"`).

Also note that you must stop the service before you attempt to compact the database. Failure to do so may corrupt the database and you will have to use a backup copy. Following is an example of the commands you need to execute to compact the WINS database:

```
> CD %SYSTEMROOT%\SYSTEM32\WINS
> NET STOP WINS
> JETPACK WINS.MDB TMP.MDB
> NET START WINS
```

This stops the service, compacts the database, and then restarts the WINS. When you are finished, your temporary file should be gone if you were successful. The `JETPACK` program deletes the original `WINS.MDB` and renames the temporary file to that name.

DNS and WINS Cooperation

If the entire network were composed of only Microsoft networking clients, then it would be okay to stop at this point. However, one of the main goals in the design of Windows NT networking is to allow for interoperability with other networks that do not use the WINS service to resolve network resource names; therefore, it is important that Windows NT find a way to allow non-WINS clients to resolve the dynamic addresses leased by DHCP to NetBIOS clients. In other words, DNS and WINS, like DNS and DHCP, must work together.

In Version 4.0 of Windows NT this has been implemented by modifying the behavior of the Microsoft DNS so that it will query a WINS server if it is unable to resolve a name query using its own static database.

NetBIOS names are 16 characters long, with the last byte reserved to indicate the type of name. Names that are stored in a DNS database consist of a host computer name and a domain name. This two-part name is referred to as a fully qualified domain name (FQDN). To provide compatibility with the DNS naming convention, Windows NT uses the NetBIOS computer name with the DNS domain name (not to be confused with the Windows NT domain name) to create an FQDN.

When you enable WINS lookup on the Microsoft DNS server, and the DNS is unable to locate the name in its database, it will remove the domain name and use the computer hostname to query the WINS server.

However, you must enable WINS lookup on the DNS server. To do so, follow these steps:

1. Bring up the Domain Name Service Manager, found under the Administrative Tools menu.
2. Click the zone for which you want to enable DNS lookup. (See Figure 31.6.)

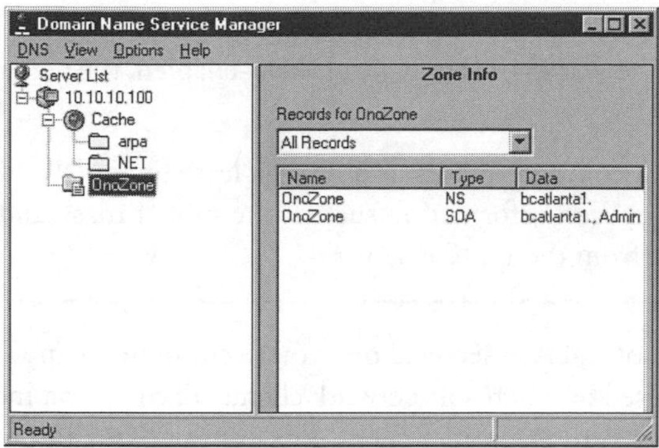

Figure 31.6. Click the zone in the Domain Name Service Manager that you want to enable WINS lookup for.

3. From the DNS pull-down menu, select Properties. The Zone Properties dialog will appear. Select the WINS Lookup tab.
4. Enable lookup by selecting the Use WINS Resolution check box. (See Figure 31.7.)
5. In the WINS Servers box, enter the address of a WINS server that can resolve names for hosts in this zone. Click the Add button. You can add one or more WINS servers to be queried.

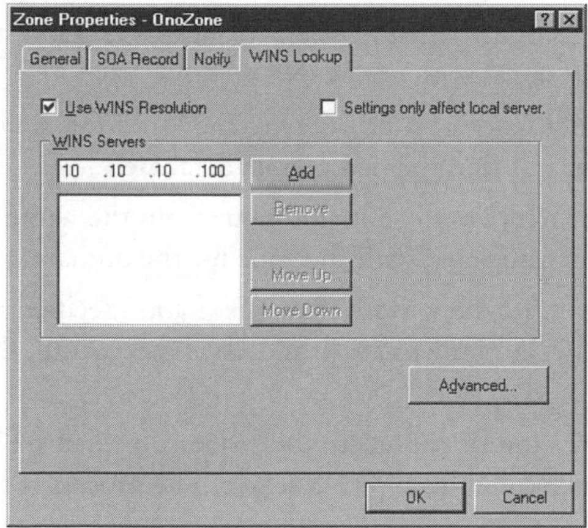

Figure 31.7. The Zone Properties dialog with the WINS Lookup tab selected.

That's all there is to it. Now when NetBIOS computers, such as Windows NT–based network clients, are set up to be WINS-, DHCP-, and DNS-enabled, the name resolution process proceeds as follows:

1. When the NT computer boots, it obtains a lease on an IP address from a DHCP server. Other configuration information such as the subnet mask and a list of WINS servers, is also obtained from the DHCP server.

Tip: The Microsoft DHCP server allows you to configure many DHCP options, although only a subset is used by Microsoft network clients. Each option indicates a type of data that the DHCP server can return to a client. For example, in addition to an IP address and a subnet address, a DHCP server can be configured to return to the client the addresses of one or more WINS servers (option 44) and one or more DNS servers (option 6). Other advanced TCP/IP options are supported so that the Microsoft DNS server can be used by non-Microsoft clients. However, the DHCP packet that the Microsoft DNS server uses can use only up to 312 bytes for DHCP options.

Some third-party DNS servers and client software allow for using other unused space to provide additional options, called *option overlays.* This is not supported by the Microsoft DNS server.

2. The NT client computer then registers its NetBIOS name and the IP address it obtained from the DHCP server with the WINS server.
3. When a computer sends a name query to the DNS for the DHCP-configured host, the DNS server does not find the name in its database.
4. The DNS server removes the domain name from the name and sends a name query to the WINS server associated with the zone for the domain.
5. The WINS server (possibly more than one if you specified more than one) attempts to resolve the NetBIOS name to an IP address. If successful, the results are returned to the DNS server.
6. The DNS returns the IP address to the requesting client. The client is not aware that the information was located by a WINS server. The process is transparent to the DNS client.

Managing WINS Servers

The WINS Manager, found under the Administrative Tools menu, is used to configure and manage the WINS server. Figure 31.8 shows the main window of the WINS Manager.

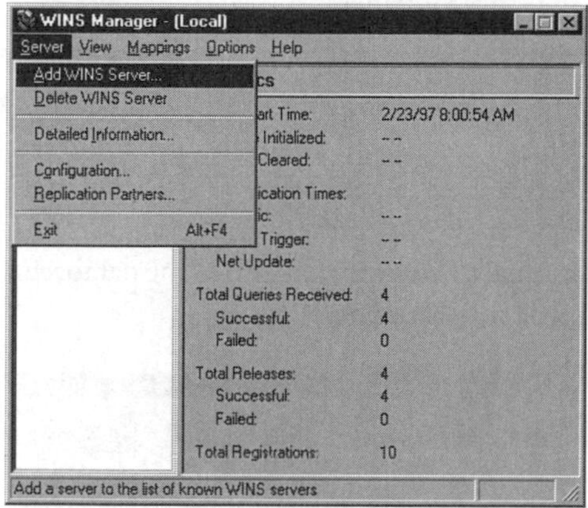

Figure 31.8. *The main window of the WINS Manager.*

Before you can administer a WINS server using the WINS Manager, you must add the WINS server using the Server pull-down menu. If you do not see the WINS server that you want to administer, click the Server menu, then select the Add WINS Server choice. (Refer to Figure 31.8.)

A dialog will prompt you for the name of the WINS server to add (see Figure 31.9).

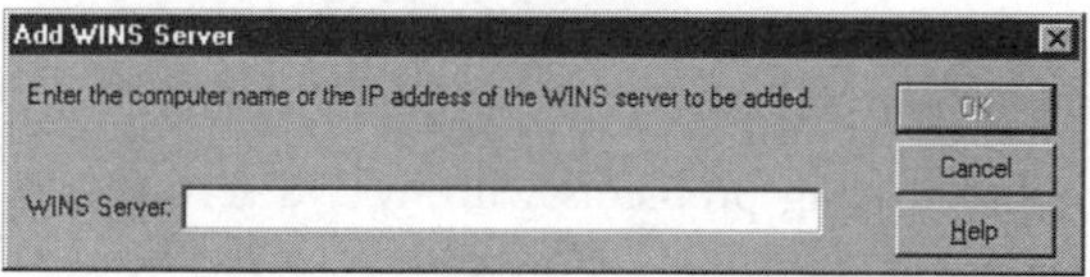

Figure 31.9. *Enter the name of the WINS server you want to add in this dialog.*

After you add a server, it will show up in the WINS Manager under the WINS Servers column. In order to perform management functions on a server, you first select it by clicking the server address to highlight it. To delete a WINS server, select it and use the Delete WINS Server selection from the Server pull-down menu.

> **Note:** When you delete a server using the Server menu, you do not remove the service from the computer that is running the WINS server. You only remove the capability to manage it from the WINS Manager. You can add or delete WINS servers using the WINS Manager as often as you want. To actually remove the WINS from a computer, you must use the Network applet in the Control Panel.

The Statistics pane in the WINS Manager will show standard statistics for the server you have highlighted in the WINS Servers pane. If you want to see more detailed statistics, select Detailed Information from the Server menu. (See Figure 31.10.) The statistics that you can examine will help you determine whether name registrations and resolution are taking place as you would expect them to. You can check to see whether replication of the database with push/pull partners is being performed, and the time it was last done.

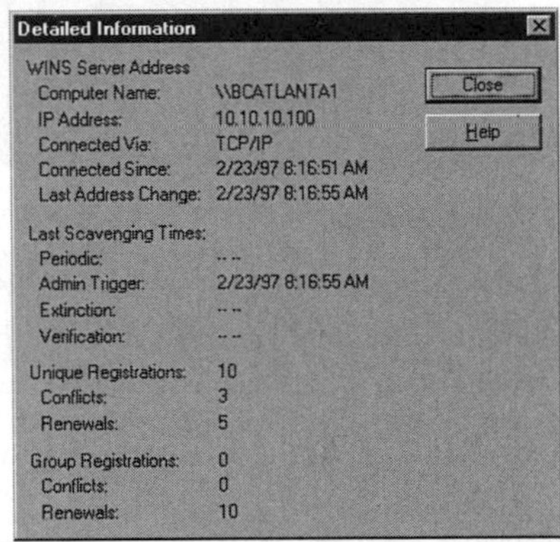

Figure 31.10. *You can view detailed statistics about the selected WINS server in the Detailed Information dialog.*

When you are troubleshooting problems with WINS servers, the statistics can be useful in determining where a problem lies. For example, the Last Replication Times statistic tells you the last time the database was replicated. If this time does not change, then a problem exists communicating with the pull partner. If the Total Queries Received statistic remains zero, then perhaps you have used the wrong address for the WINS server when you configured client computers.

These are the basic statistics you see:

- **Database Initialized.** This is the last time that static mappings were imported into the database.
- **Statistics Cleared.** The last time the Clear Statistics command from the View menu was used.
- **Last Replication Times.** The last time the database was replicated. The following three methods show the times that can cause a database replication:

  Periodic—Replication performed at an interval specified in the Preferences menu.

Admin Trigger—The Replicate Now button was selected in the Replication Partners dialog.

Net Update—The server received a push request message from another WINS server wishing to receive updates.

- **Total Queries Received.** There are two categories:

  Successful—The number of queries the WINS server was able to resolve.

  Failed—The number of queries the WINS server could not resolve from its database.

- **Total Releases.** There are two categories:

  Successful—The number of name releases as a result of notification from a NetBIOS program that shut down normally.

  Failed—The number of name releases the WINS server was unable to release.

- **Total Registrations.** The number of name registrations from WINS-enabled clients that were registered on the WINS server.

When you use the Detailed Information selection from the Server menu, the following statistics are displayed:

- **Last Address Change.** The last time that a database change was replicated.
- **Last Scavenging Times.** The last time database entries were removed (scavenged) from the database. Statistics are shown for the following types of events that can initiate scavenging:

  Periodic—The renewal interval found in the WINS Server Configuration (local) dialog expired.

  Admin Trigger—Initiate Scavenging was selected from the Mappings menu.

  Extinction—The extinction interval found in the WINS Server Configuration dialog.

  Verification—The verify interval found in the WINS Server Configuration dialog.

- **Unique Registrations.** The number of name registration requests the server has accepted.
- **Unique Conflicts.** The number of conflicts when name registrations were received for existing unique names that are owned by this server.
- **Unique Renewals.** The number of unique name renewals.
- **Group Registrations.** The number of group name registrations accepted by this server.
- **Group Conflicts.** The number of conflicts when group name registrations were received for existing group names already owned by this server.
- **Group Renewals**. The number of group name renewals received.

Replication Among WINS Servers

Although you can get by with just one WINS server in your network, it is best to have more than one. Having more than one WINS server comes in handy when you are troubleshooting problems with a primary WINS server. You can stop and start it without worrying about clients not being able to resolve names during the down time.

You can configure WINS servers to replicate data to each other (by establishing push and pull partners) so that the entire database is stored in more than one place on the network. Should one WINS server fail, clients can use secondary WINS servers to continue name resolution until the primary WINS server is restored to service.

A pull partner is a WINS server that you have configured to pull database entries from another WINS server. A push partner is a WINS server that is configured to send its database entries to other WINS servers.

The simplest scenario is to have two WINS servers that replicate to each other. Each server becomes a push and a pull partner of the other. In Figure 31.11, WINS Server A pushes database records to WINS Server B and pulls database records from WINS Server B. It is important to realize that you must configure the relationship on both sides. If you simply configure WINS Server A to be a push partner to Server B and to be a pull partner from Server B, you will have accomplished only half of the process. You must also configure WINS Server B to be a push partner to Server A and to be a pull partner from Server A.

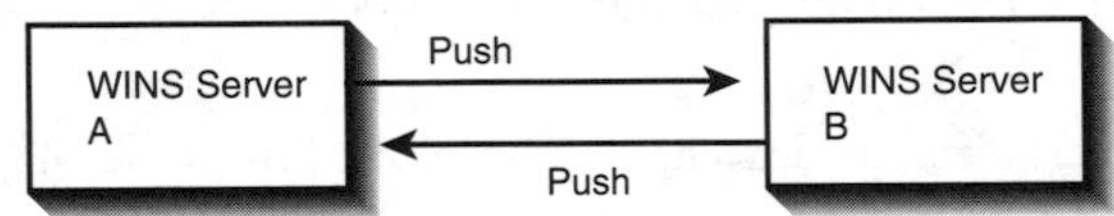

Figure 31.11. *Two WINS servers can fully replicate the WINS database on a small network by being push and pull partners of each other.*

To go one step further, if you have more than two WINS servers, you can designate all WINS servers on your network to be pull and push partners of each other. In a large network, you may want to use a circular chained set of push and pull partners as shown in Figure 31.12.

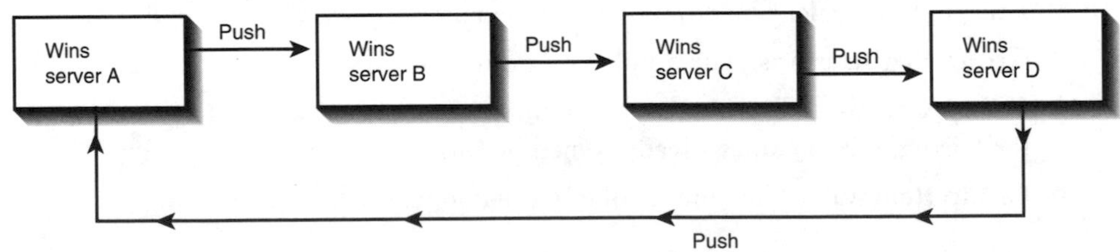

Figure 31.12. *A chain of push and pull partners can reduce the network traffic involved in keeping a fully replicated WINS database on the network.*

In Figure 31.12, WINS Server A is configured to be a push partner of WINS Server B. WINS Server B is configured to be a pull partner of Server A. The other servers are configured in a similar manner so that changes move from A, to B, to C, and to Server D. Server D, however, is configured to be a push partner to Server A. WINS Server A is configured to be a pull partner from Server D.

Using this scheme, all WINS database registrations and releases will eventually be propagated to all other WINS servers without having to configure each server to be a push and pull partner of all other WINS servers.

The downside to this is that it will take longer for the changes to be fully replicated throughout the network. You can use the WINS Manager to establish push and pull partner relationships and to adjust the parameters that affect the timing of the updates.

Configuring Push and Pull Partners

If you see the following event in the system log using the Event Viewer, you probably have incorrectly configured your push and pull partners for this WINS server:

```
Event ID: 4102
Source: WINS
Description: The connection was aborted by the remote client.
```

If this occurs, you should check to be sure that each partner to which this server is a pull partner has this server set up as a push partner, and vice versa. A push/pull relationship is two-sided. Both sides must be defined.

Push and pull partners are configured using the Server menu in the WINS Manager program. If you suspect, looking at the Last Replication Times statistics, that the WINS server is not replicating its database (pushing) to its pull partners, you should check to be sure that the push/pull relationships are properly configured.

Click Replication Partners on the Server menu to view the current push/pull partnerships. You should get a list of WINS servers (see Figure 31.13). The highlighted computer is a partner of the local computer if the Replication Options (Push Partner and Pull Partner) are not grayed-out when you highlight a server and the check boxes for push or pull partner are selected.

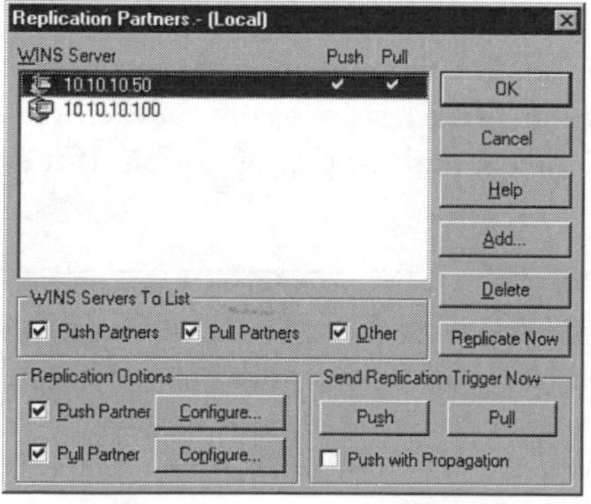

Figure 31.13. *The Replication Partners dialog.*

You can also use the Add and Delete buttons here to add or remove a WINS partner from the list. To remove one, simply highlight the server address and click the Delete button. To add a new partner, click the Add button. You will get the Add WINS Server dialog (see Figure 31.14), where you enter the new partner's addresses.

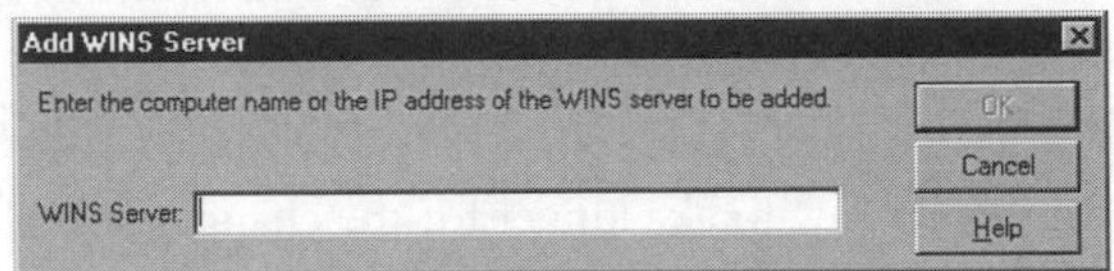

Figure 31.14. *In the Add WINS Server dialog, you enter the address of the new push or pull partner.*

If a pull partner is missing, for example, you should use Add to reestablish the relationship. If the partner already exists, but isn't functioning properly, go back to the opening window of the WINS Manager, highlight the partner server, and select the Configuration option from the Server menu to examine the configuration for that partner. Figure 31.15 shows the WINS Server Configuration dialog with the Advanced button selected.

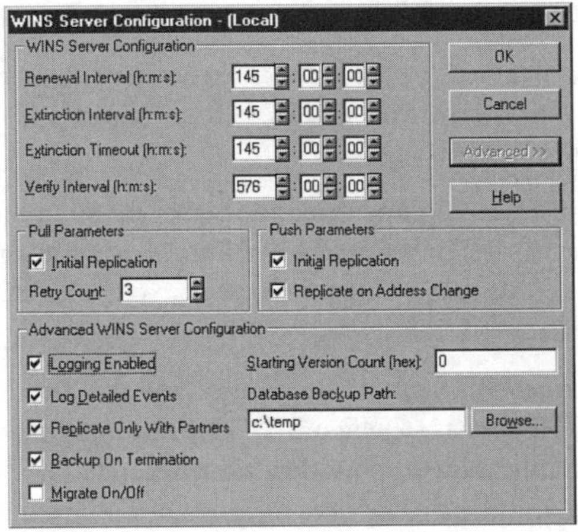

Figure 31.15. *The WINS Server Configuration dialog can be used to show the configuration of a push or pull partner.*

If you suspect that replication is not occurring at the correct interval, use the Push or Pull buttons under the Send Replication Trigger Now section of the Replication Partners dialog, shown in Figure 31.13. This will force a push or pull operation. If it succeeds, the periodic replications should also work.

> **Tip:** The Push with Propagation check box can be used to send a copy of the database to a pull partner. The "with propagation" part means that the pull partner will then turn around and push the data to all of its pull partners, and so on, down the line. If you have configured your partners in a chain as shown in Figure 31.16, then this will cause a full replication to take place after a short period of time.

Timers Used by the WINS Service

The WINS service uses four timers to determine when name records are to be purged from the database and when a database replication should occur. Microsoft does not recommend you change the values of these timers. However, they are configurable, so you can change them if you think you have a good reason.

You can view these timers (or change them) from the WINS Server Configuration - (Local) dialog. To bring up this dialog, select Configuration from the Server menu in the WINS Manager dialog. The four timers are shown in Figure 31.16.

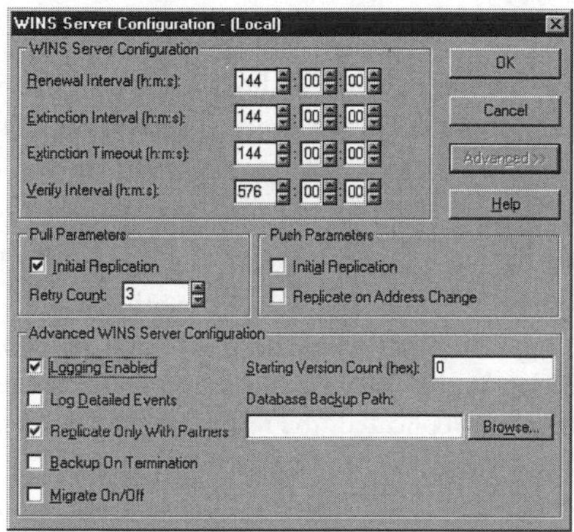

Figure 31.16. The WINS Server Configuration - (Local) dialog with the Advanced button selected.

The timers used by the WINS service to determine whether or not a registration is still valid are the following:

- **Renewal Interval**

  This is a Time to Live (TTL) value. When a name is registered with a WINS server, it will remain in the database for only a set period of time. After that time, the client must contact the WINS server and renew the name registration. Upon an initial name registration, the current time plus this Renewal Interval time is used to determine when the name will be marked as released by the WINS server.

  When a record is marked as released, the change is not replicated to other WINS servers. When a new name registration is received for this name, it can be accepted by the WINS server immediately. The WINS server assumes that because the previous client did not renew the name, it must no longer be using it.

  The default value for this timer under Windows NT 4.0 is six days (144 hours).

- **Extinction Interval**

  When a name is marked as released, it is time-stamped with the current time plus the Extinction Interval. After this time has passed, the name is marked as extinct. The version ID of the record is incremented so that this information will propagate to other WINS servers at the next replication time. The WINS servers that pull in this record during replication will mark it with the current time plus the value of the next timer, the Extinction Time-Out.

  The default value for the Extinction Interval is also six days (144 hours) for Windows NT 4.0.

- **Extinction Time-Out**

  When a record becomes older than this value, it is removed from the database. The default, generally, is also six days (144 hours) under Windows NT 4.0. However, it can vary depending on the value set for Renewal Interval and on the maximum replication time interval.

- **Verify Interval**

  There is always a chance that a record that has been marked as extinct will be scavenged from the database before it is replicated to the other WINS servers. For example, the system administrator may manually remove the record by using the Mappings/Initiate Scavenging selection in the WINS Manager program. If the change from active record to extinct record is not replicated, the record will never be removed from the other WINS servers.

  For that reason, when an active record is replicated to a pull partner, it is time-stamped with the current time plus the Verify Interval. When scavenging occurs (manual or periodic) and a record is found that is older than this timestamp, the WINS server will query the WINS server that owns this record (the WINS server that originated the record) to see if the name is still valid. If it receives a negative response, the record can be removed from the database. Otherwise, it is not removed. This is true even when the owner-WINS server cannot be contacted. Active records are never removed unless the owner-WINS server can be contacted to verify it.

  The default value for this timer under Windows NT 4.0 is 24 days (576 hours).

Note: The preceding values for the timers are not specific. The algorithms used by NT are not definitely documented by Microsoft because they are subject to change.

Missing Name Registrations

If clients that use the WINS server are having problems resolving names of hosts that you know are on the network, you can look into the WINS database to check whether or not the correct database records exist.

When a WINS-enabled client boots, it will try to register at least three names with the WINS server: the computer name, the username, and the domain name. If you do not see these in the database for each client, you may have a problem.

NetBIOS names that are registered in a WINS database can be of many types. The 16th byte of the name is used to indicate what type of name it is. NetBIOS names can be unique (only one can exist in the network) or group names (more than one address can be associated with the name). The following types of NetBIOS names can be found in the WINS database:

- `computer_name[00h]` (unique name)

  This type of name is registered by a workstation service on the WINS client.
- `computer_name[03h]` (unique name)

  The messenger service on the WINS client registers this name.
- `computer_name[06h]` (unique name)

  This name is registered by the remote access service (RAS) when it starts.
- `computer_name[1Fh]` (unique name)

  The Network Dynamic Data Exchange (NetDDE) Services will register this type of name when it starts.
- `computer_name[20h]` (unique name)

  The server service running on the WINS client will register this type of name.
- `computer_name[21h]` (unique name)

  The RAS client service on the WINS client will register this type of name when the service starts.
- `computer_name[BEh]` (unique name)

  The network monitoring agent service will register this type of name when it starts. This name will be padded with plus symbols (+) if the name (minus the 16th character) is not 15 characters long.
- `computer_name[BFh]` (unique name)

  The network monitoring utility (from the systems management server, or SMS) will register this type of name. Again, the name is padded with plus symbols to make it 15 characters long before the 16th character is added.

- `username[03h]` (unique name)

  When a user logs on to an NT computer, the username is registered with the WINS database using this type of name. If a user is logged on at more than one computer, the name is registered only once. This type of name is used by net send commands to locate a user.

- `domain_name[1Bh]` (unique name)

  The Windows NT Primary Domain Controller (PDC) that is running as a domain master browser registers this name type. When WINS is queried for this name, it returns the IP address of the computer that registered the name.

- `domain_name[1Dh]` (unique name)

  This name type indicates a master browser. Although there can be only one domain master browser, there can be multiple master browsers—but only one per subnet. The backup browsers use this name to locate master browsers.

  Note that when a computer attempts to register this name with WINS, it returns a positive registration response to the computer, but does not actually register the name in the WINS database. When a WINS client queries for this name, it receives a negative response, and then uses broadcasts on the local subnet to find the browser.

- `domain_name[00h]` (group name)

  The workstation service registers this type of name. It is used to receive browser broadcasts from LAN Manager computers.

- `domain_name[1Ch]` (group name)

  Domain controllers register this type of name. It can have up to 25 addresses associated with it, the first being the Primary Domain Controller (PDC) and the others being Backup Domain Controllers (BDCs).

- `domain_name[1Eh]` (group name)

  Browsers use this name during the election of a master browser. The WINS server returns the network broadcast address (for the requesting client's local network) when queried for this type of name.

- `_MSBROWSE_,[01h]` (group name)

  The master browser on each subnet registers this type of name. The WINS server returns the network broadcast address (for the requesting client's local network) when queried for this type of name. This type of name is different from the rest; instead of postfixing a single byte as the sixteenth byte, it adds on the entire 11 character string `_MSBROWSE_,`.

Dynamic Mappings

There are two types of records you can view: static and dynamic. Static entries are those that you enter using the Static Mappings selection from the Mappings menu. Dynamic registrations, in which a client registers its name(s) when it starts up, can be viewed by using the Show Database selection under the Mappings menu. Figure 31.17 shows the Show Database window.

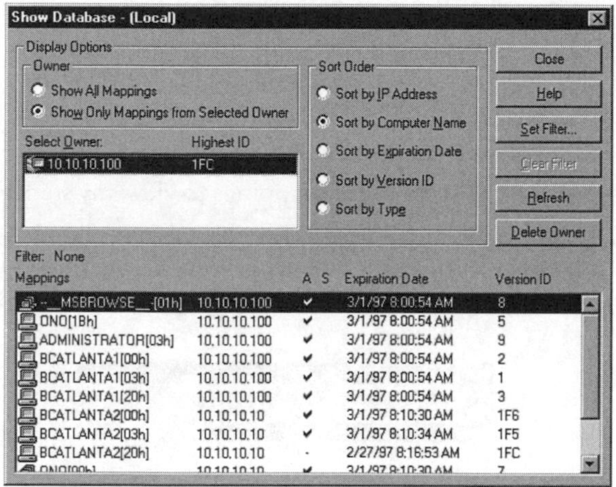

Figure 31.17. *The Show Database window can be used to show all address-to-name mappings in the database, both those that are and those that are not owned by the server.*

In Figure 31.17 you see that you can narrow your search by rearranging the records' sort order. You can set a filter using the Set Filter button. (See Figure 31.18.)

Figure 31.18. *Enter a computer name or an IP address in the Set Filter dialog to narrow your search of the WINS database.*

By examining records in the database, you can determine whether WINS clients are registering the correct NetBIOS names when they reboot. If a client's NetBIOS names are not showing up, then you should again use `ping` to check the communications path between the WINS server and the client. Be sure to check from both directions.

Tip: Another possible problem you may encounter when using static mappings involves the interoperation with DHCP. If you have a multihomed computer that uses a DHCP-reserved address for a unique name (a computer hostname), this reserved name/address combination will override any static mapping in the WINS database if you have selected the Migration On/Off option in the WINS server's advanced configuration dialog. When you encounter static address mappings that don't seem to be working, be sure to check the DHCP server for reserved IP addresses that may conflict.

Checking Static Mappings

Use the Mappings menu and select Static Mappings to view any static records you have added to the database. Figure 31.19 shows the Static Mappings - (Local) dialog with three names listed. You can use the Add Mappings button to bring up another dialog to add more static mappings (see Figure 31.20), or you can import them from an `LMHOSTS` file, using the Import Mappings button.

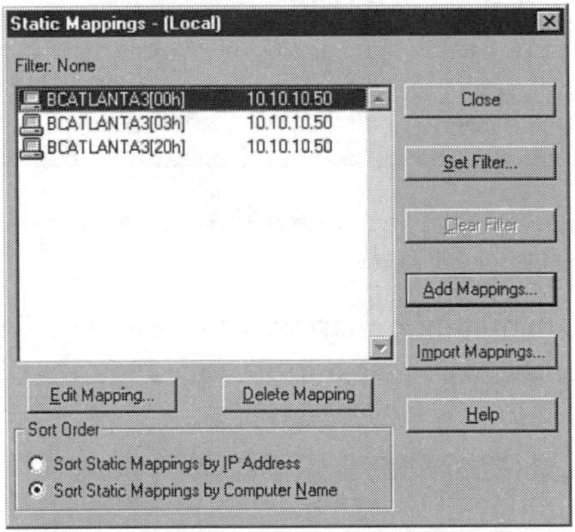

Figure 31.19. *The Static Mappings dialog shows current static mappings and can be used to add or remove static mappings.*

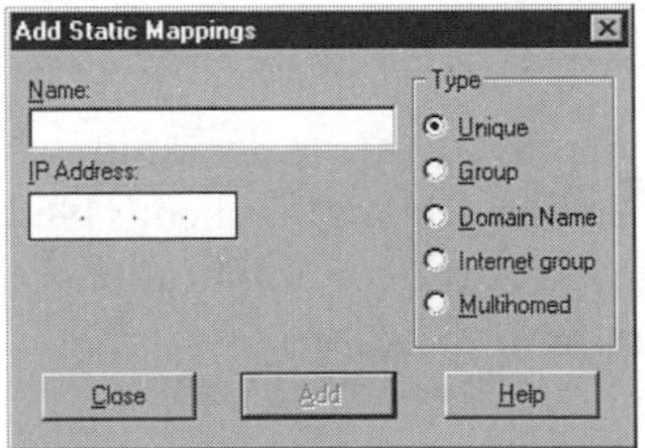

Figure 31.20. *When you add a static mapping in the Add Static Mappings dialog, you enter the NetBIOS name and IP address, and then select the type of NetBIOS name.*

Note: If you choose the Edit Mapping button in the Static Mappings dialog, you can edit only the NetBIOS name and IP address. You can't change the type of NetBIOS name. If you entered a record with an incorrect type, delete it and re-add the record with the correct NetBIOS name type.

Note: Static mappings are replicated to partners. However, they do not show up under Mappings|Static Mappings on the partner. They will show up as a regular dynamic database entry. You can, if you want to, add static mappings on each partner for a name/address pair, but the default is to replicate all entries, both static and dynamic, to partners.

Backup and Restore of the WINS Database

If you use push and pull partners to distribute the WINS database throughout your network, you are essentially maintaining a complete copy of the database even if a particular WINS server should fail. A few records might be lost in such a case, but only those that were awaiting a periodic pull or push. To keep a complete backup copy, you should add a backup path using the WINS Manager so that the server will create a backup copy of itself every three hours. This is automatic if you create the directory.

Note: You cannot use a network drive for the backup path for WINS database backups. The path must be on a local drive.

To add a backup path for your WINS database files, select the Mappings menu and then the Backup Database selection. The Select Backup Directory dialog (see Figure 31.21) appears and you can then enter the pathname for the backup copy of the WINS files.

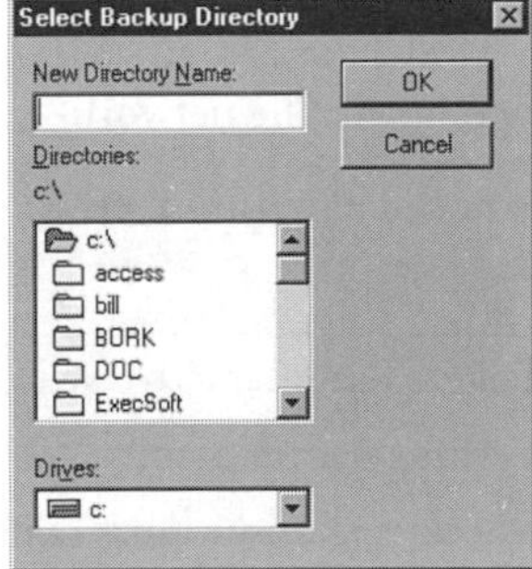

Figure 31.21. *Enter a path where you want to store copies of the WINS database in the Select Backup Directory dialog.*

If you find that the WINS database files have become corrupted, you can use the backup copy to restore them. If you find that you cannot connect to the WINS server with the WINS Manager, and you verify that the WINS service is actually running on the computer, you probably have corrupted files.

Here's how to manually restore the database from the backup files:

1. Make a backup of the suspected corrupted files. You never know, they might not be corrupted.
2. Set default to the `%SYSTEMROOT%\SYSTEM32\WINS` directory and delete the following files:

   `J50.LOG`

   `J50#####.LOG`

   `WINS.TMP`

   `WINS.MDB`
3. Copy the `WINS.MDB` file from the backup directory to the `%SYSTEMROOT%\SYSTEM32\WINS` directory.
4. At the command prompt enter this line:

   `NET START WINS to start the service.`

If the service does not start, shut down the computer and power it off for about 15 seconds, then reboot. If the service still does not start, your backup files may also be corrupted. If that seems to be the case, you need to reinstall the WINS server service.

Resource Kit Utilities

The Windows NT Resource Kit (Version 4.0) contains two utilities you can use to assist in troubleshooting the WINS database: `winschk` and `winsdmp.exe`.

`winschk` is a command-line utility that

- ◆ Checks for version number inconsistencies.
- ◆ Monitors replication activity.
- ◆ Verifies the replication topology in the network.

In the menu for the program, you can enter numbers to select functions as follows:

Number	*Function*
0	Toggle the interactive switch
1	Test for names against WINS servers
2	Check version number consistencies
3	Monitor WINS servers and detect communication failures
4	Verify replication configuration setup

Use the value 99 to exit the program. The default mode of operation is interactive. If you toggle this off, the record of activity is logged to a file called `WINSTST.LOG` in your local directory. If you select function 3 and run it non-interactively, the process runs in the background and dumps its results to a file called `MONITOR.LOG`.

If you select function 1, you must create two text files:

- `SERVERS.TXT`, which should contain the IP address of a WINS server from which a list of all replications WINS servers is built up for the query.
- `NAMES.TXT`, which should contain a list of NetBIOS names (one per line) that will be checked. Names in this file must be in all uppercase letters and the sixteenth byte should be postfixed to the name, separated from it by the asterisk (*) character. For example, `FOOBAR*20` is a valid name to put into this file.

When you use function 1, the names contained in the `NAMES.TXT` file will be checked against all servers on the list created from the `SERVERS.TXT` file. It will report `"name not found"` errors and mismatched IP addresses for each name. WINS servers that do not respond will also be listed.

Function 2 checks for version numbers that get out of sync. Version numbers are associated with each name in the WINS database and are incremented when the record for the name changes. Version numbers tell the replication process which records need to be propagated to the other servers, thus reducing network traffic, as all records will not be sent.

This function also checks to be sure that the server that owns a name (where it was first registered) always has the highest version number.

Function 3 monitors communication failures between WINS servers. You can run this interactively as a one-time execution, or set it up to run as a background process that checks WINS servers every three hours.

Function 4 checks to be sure each push partner has a pull partner, and vice versa, and also makes sure the time interval is defined.

The second tool, `winsdmp.exe`, dumps the contents of the WINS database to a comma-separated list. The output goes to `stdout`, so you will need to pipe this to a file if you want to save it.

The fields, in order, are as follows:

1. Owner IP address
2. Name
3. Sixteenth character (hexadecimal)
4. Name length
5. Type of record
6. State of record
7. Version ID (high-order word)
8. Version ID (low-order word)

9. Static/dynamic flag
10. Timestamp
11. Number of IP addresses
12. IP addresses

Dumping the database to a file and then importing it into a spreadsheet will enable you to quickly locate records and detect missing names.

WINS Proxy Agents

You can also configure Windows NT servers to be WINS proxy agents if you have non-WINS client computers on your network that rely on broadcasts to resolve names. A WINS proxy agent will listen on the subnet for these broadcasts and then, if it has the name already in its cache, it will send the information to the client. If the name is not found in its cache, it will forward a name resolution query to a WINS server for resolution. The agent will then return the information to the non-WINS client so that it can resolve the address.

Because WINS proxy agents can query WINS servers on the other side of a router, and broadcasts are not usually forwarded by routers, you should consider placing a WINS proxy agent on each subnet that has several non-WINS enabled clients.

However, WINS proxy agents *will not* register or deregister names with the WINS server for these non-WINS–enabled clients. The function of the proxy agent is only to answer name queries. When a proxy agent receives a name release request, it only removes the name from its own cache.

Warning: Although you can have more than one WINS server on a subnet, Microsoft does not recommend that you have more than one proxy agent on a subnet (or at the most, two). Having multiple proxy agents on the same subnet can overload a WINS server on that subnet with requests.

Summary

The Windows Internet Naming Service (WINS) is a name registration/resolution service for network clients to use in locating other computers and services. The main difference between WINS and the Domain Name Server (DNS) name resolution service is that computers using WINS can dynamically register their names and addresses. Using DNS, an administrator must keep track of client addresses and names and statically add the information to the database that DNS clients access. WINS adds the capability to provide an accurate naming service for dynamic clients that obtain their network address and other configuration information from a DHCP (Dynamic Host Configuration Protocol) server.

To troubleshoot the WINS service, you need to understand that it registers and resolves NetBIOS names, which are not the same thing as a computer hostname on a TCP/IP network. Actually, if you limit the name to 15 characters, you can use the same name for both a NetBIOS name and an IP name. Doing so makes system administration in a large network much easier because there is only one name associated with each computer host.

Another feature of WINS that improves upon the DNS concept is that it is a distributed database. Whereas the DNS system on the Internet is a hierarchical system with name servers pointing to other name servers in the tree that can either resolve a name or point to another name server in the path, WINS replication partners completely replicate the entire network database. Changes made by clients coming on and going off the network are propagated in a timely manner to replication partners. The use of multiple WINS servers also provides for a load-balancing effect.

The files used by WINS are all found in the same directory. You can set up the WINS server to automatically produce a backup of these files (even when they're open) by copying them to another directory on the local system. The NT Backup program may not produce a viable copy if the files are opened and in use during the backup. If you keep a current backup of the files, you can restore the database under almost any circumstances and have your network back in order without having to resort to restoring from backup tapes or other offline storage media.

The Windows NT Resource Kit (server version) comes with a host of utilities that can aid in troubleshooting computer and network problems. Two utilities are included that are specific to solving WINS problems. Trying to manage a large Windows NT network without the utilities and information contained in the Resource Kit is a foolish endeavor.

The most basic tool for resolving WINS problems, however, is the WINS Manager program. Using this tool, you can detect when replication partners are not pushing or pulling database records. You can find out the number of name registrations and resolutions carried out by each WINS server. By regularly reviewing the statistics available under the WINS Manager, you can keep a good eye on your WINS server performance.

The Domain Name System

by Les Harrison

In the 1970s, the Internet was primarily the communication and research medium of educators, the military, and government agencies. Even then, the numeric addresses of hosts (computers) were related to human-friendly names by a simple table lookup structure. Host name to address mappings were maintained by the SRI-NIC (Stanford Research Institute—Network Information Center) in a single ASCII file called `HOSTS.TXT`. This one file contained the name and address and all other administrative information for all the host machines on the Internet. Every host machine address change (new or modified) required a corresponding change to the SRI-NIC `HOSTS.TXT` file. System administrators had to routinely FTP a current version of the `HOSTS.TXT` file from the SRI-NIC machine to bring their own machines up to the current database version.

The rapid growth of the Internet created the need to develop the domain name system. The number of hosts increased rapidly and projections of the future growth showed that the existing `HOSTS.TXT` file transfer would be not only unwieldy but virtually impossible to maintain accurately or within any reasonable period of time. Delegating the FTP load to more machines would not provide a solution in the near future.

Another and perhaps more critical problem was the lack of control for domain name collisions. No two hosts in the `HOSTS` file could have the same name. Although SRI-NIC could assure that each numeric address was unique, it did not have authority over names. When duplicate names were entered in the file, the scheme had a flaw. A name conflict for a mail hub could result in disrupting mail exchange for a large part of the ARPAnet. As the user database grew larger, it took longer to get updates across the Internet to all machines, so at any point in time, many machines were not up-to-date.

Advances in technology brought on smaller, more powerful and more diverse classes of machines. Local administrators could support their own organizations but had to wait for the SRI-NIC to change `HOSTS.TXT` to make changes visible to the remainder of the Internet users. Organizations also wanted some local structure and a general-purpose name service.

The struggle to control the explosive name service problems brought about ideas for name spaces and their management. The idea of a hierarchical name space, with the hierarchy roughly corresponding to organizational structure and names using "." as the character to mark the boundary between hierarchy levels, was the winner.

Note: You can find the original Domain Name System description in the Request for Comments (RFC) documents RFC-882 and RFC-883 and the current versions of these documents RFC-1034 and RFC-1035 by searching for the document numbers at

`http://ds.internic.net/ds/dspg1intdoc.html`

From the original concepts, the Domain Name System (DNS) has grown to be the set of protocols and services in use today on the Internet. You have used the DNS if you have used a Web browser with similar TCP/IP utilities on the Internet.

The DNS protocol's best-known function is mapping user-friendly names to IP addresses. For example, suppose the FTP site at `biznesnet.com` had an IP address of `207.2.225.190`. You would reach this computer by specifying `ftp.biznesnet.com` and not the more difficult-to-remember IP address. Using a name is more reliable because the numeric address can change. For instance, the domain `biznesnet.com` could move to another Internet service provider and be given a new IP address.

Microsoft has included a robust DNS application with Microsoft Windows NT Server 4.0. Also included is a user-friendly DNS administration program called DNS Manager. These place MS Windows NT in the running with the BIND applications. The original and still the most popular implementation of the DNS protocol, BIND was developed at Berkeley for the 4.3 BSD UNIX operating system. BIND stands for Berkeley Internet Name Domain. The DNS server in Windows NT 4.0 is a completely new rendition of code, and because it is written to the requirements of the RFCs, it is fully compatible with BIND.

This chapter discusses the technology behind DNS. It does not discuss the use of the Microsoft DNS Manager or implementation steps for establishing a domain. The critical points of DNS files and records are described and some of the more common errors involving DNS are included.

DNS—The Technology

The Domain Name System is a complex distributed database of domain records. The DNS database names establish a logical structure called the *domain name space* that can be compared to a root directory structure having many subdirectories extending downward through many levels. Another analogy for the DNS is to describe it as an upside-down tree that has the roots as the highest level of authority, the limbs next in the levels of authority, and the leaves as the lowest level of authority (the end users). Each node or domain in the domain name space is named and can contain subdomains. Domains and subdomains are grouped into *zones* to allow for distributed administration of the name space. (Zones are discussed later in this chapter.) The domain name identifies the domain's position in the logical DNS hierarchy in relation to its parent domain by separating each branch of the tree with a period (.). Figure 32.1 shows a few of the top-level domains, where the biznesnet domain fits, and a host called `biznesnetcom1` within the biznesnet domain. Someone who wanted to contact that host would use what is called the *fully qualified domain name* (FQDN), which is `biznesnetcom1.biznesnet.com`.

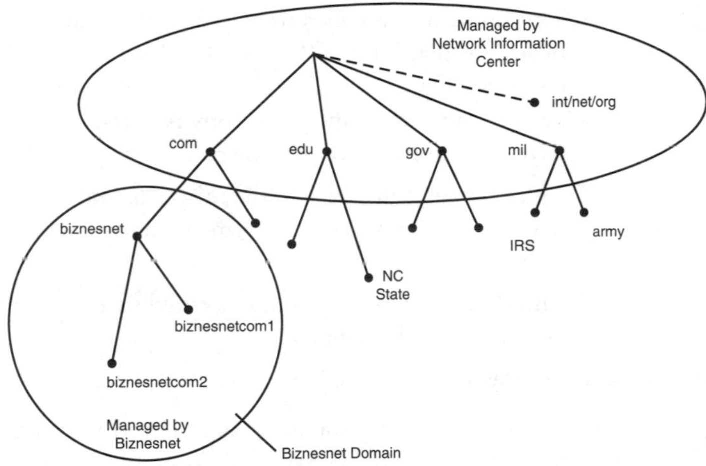

Figure 32.1. *Where the biznesnet domain fits in the DNS hierarchy.*

Top-Level DNS Domains and the Internet

The root of the DNS database on the Internet is managed by the Internet Network Information Center (InterNIC).

> **Note:** You can find more information about InterNIC at
> `Http://rs.internic.net`

The top-level domains (TLD) were originally assigned organizationally and by country. Of these generic domains, five are international, and two are restricted to use by entities in the United States.

The five international domains are

`COM` Intended for commercial entities, this domain has grown very large and many are concerned about the administrative load and system performance if the current growth pattern is continued. It may become necessary to subdivide the COM domain and allow only future commercial registrations in the subdomains.

`EDU` This domain was originally intended for all educational institutions. Many universities, colleges, schools, educational service organizations, and educational consortia are registered under EDU. Currently, new registrations are limited to four-year colleges and universities. Schools and two-year colleges are to be registered in the country domains. (See explanation of U.S. domain, especially K12 and CC, following this list.)

`NET` This domain is intended to hold only the computers of network providers, that is the NIC (Network Information Center) and NOC (Network Operations Center), the administrative computers, and the network node computers. Customers of the network provider would have domain names of their own.

`ORG` This domain is intended as the miscellaneous TLD for organizations that don't fit anywhere else. Some nongovernment organizations may fit here.

`INT` This domain is for organizations established by international treaties or international databases.

The two domains that may be used only in the United States are

`GOV` Originally intended for any kind of government office or agency, only agencies of the U.S. federal government may currently use this domain. State and local agencies are registered in the country domains.

`MIL` This domain is used by the U.S. military.

An example of a country domain is `US`, which provides for the registration of all kinds of entities in the United States. Addresses within this domain follow this syntax: *`entity name.locality.state code`*`.US`. For example, the address for NEC in Raleigh, North Carolina would be `NEC.Raleigh.NC.US`. Branches of the US domain include K12 for elementary and secondary schools; CC for community colleges, TEC for technical schools, STATE for state government agencies, COG for government councils, LIB for libraries, MUS for Museums. For instance, the Riverdale-Hs K12 entity located in Tennessee, USA would have a domain like: `Riverdale-Hs.Rcsd.K12.TN.US`.

Note: You can find details on the `US` domain at `http://www.isi.edu/in-notes/usdnr/`.

DNS Domains

Each node in the tree of a DNS database, along with all the nodes that it services, is called a domain. Domains can include hosts (computers) and other domains or subdomains. For example, the domain biznesnet could contain both computers such as `ftp.biznesnet.com` and subdomains such as `dev.biznesnet` that, in turn, could contain hosts such as `ntserver.dev.biznesnet`.

Note: In general, domain names and hostnames have restrictions in their naming that allow only the use of characters *a z*, *A Z*, *0 9*, and the dash or minus sign (-). Characters such as the slash (/), period (.), and underscore (_) may not be used.

DNS Zones

A *zone* represents the portions of the DNS name space for which a particular DNS server is the authority. In other words, a zone is some portion of the DNS name space whose database records are maintained in a zone file. A single DNS server might be configured to manage one or multiple zone files, and each zone file is referenced to a domain node known as the zone's *root domain.*

Zone files do not have to include all subdomains under the zone's root domain. For a comparison of domains and zones, take a look at Figure 32.2. In this example, `biznesnet.com` is a domain, but the entire domain is not controlled by one zone file. Part of the domain is actually broken off into a separate zone file for `dev.biznesnet.com`.

Note: A zone is a physical file composed of resource records that defines a group of domains. A domain is a node in the DNS name space and all subdomains below it.

DNS Name Servers

DNS name servers provide the repository for information about the domain name space. Name servers usually are responsible for one or more zones. A key point is that name servers have *authority* over the zones for which they are responsible. When name servers are defined by their administrators, they are informed of the zones for which they have responsibility. This is important for the transfer of zone files to other name servers as changes are made to the database.

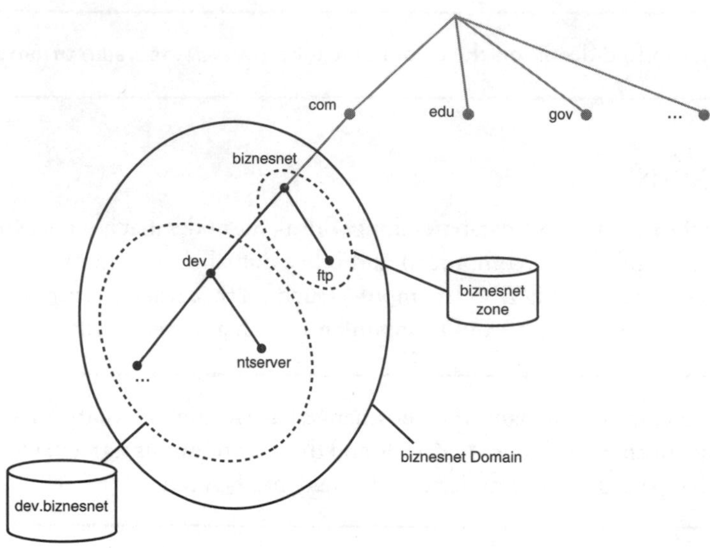

Figure 32.2. *Comparison of domains and zones in the DNS.*

DNS Primary, Secondary, and Master Name Servers

Name servers come in three flavors: primary, secondary, and master. A *primary name server* gets the data for its zones from local files stored on its own disks or on the local network. Changes to a zone, such as adding domains or hosts, are performed on the primary name server.

A *secondary name server* gets the data for its zones from another name server across the network that is authoritative for that zone. The primary name server makes a *zone transfer* to the secondary name server when the database is modified on the primary name server.

Here are three good reasons to have *secondary* servers:

- To provide redundancy. Two DNS name servers serving each zone, a primary and at least one secondary for redundancy, provide a fault-tolerant system.
- To better serve remote locations. Secondary servers should be provided in remote locations to ensure name resolution continues when the network connection to the primary name server fails.
- To reduce the load on the primary server.

Separate files are used to store information for each zone so the primary or secondary designation is defined at the zone level. This way, a particular name server can be a primary name server for certain zones and a secondary name server for other zones.

Secondary name servers must be identified in the primary name server that is to provide the zone transfers when database changes are made. This is also true in the opposite direction. In this case, the primary name server is called the master name server because it is the source of zone information for its authoritative name space. When changes are made in the master name server, it will notify the secondary and cache a zone transfer. If the secondary name server is booted, it will contact the master name server and request that a zone transfer be cached. Caching the zone transfers means that the server will put the transfer in the queue for processing.

DNS Forwarders and Slaves

Determining the IP address for the given domain name is called *name resolution.* Resolving a name request starts in the local DNS server's own zone files. If that server is not authoritative for the requested domain, it will have to contact other name servers to obtain a resolution for the request.

DNS includes a concept called *forwarders.* You can select a specific DNS name server to be a forwarder to limit the number of machines you have accessing the Internet directly for name service. When you select a machine to be a forwarder, you configure all other DNS name servers in your area of administration to use forwarders and provide them with the IP address of the selected forwarder machine. Figure 32.3 illustrates the use of a forwarder.

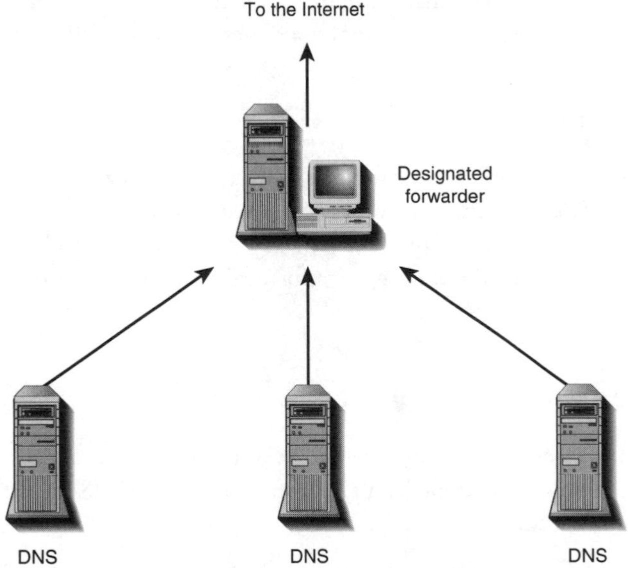

Figure 32.3. *Forwarders limit Internet exposure for your network.*

Servers that are to use forwarders pass any DNS request that they cannot resolve with their own zone files to the designated forwarder. The forwarder proceeds to resolve the request and return the results to the requester. If the forwarder cannot resolve the request, the requesting machine attempts to resolve the request as if it were not configured to use a forwarder. If the requesting machine has also been configured to be a *slave*, it will return a failure message to the user that it cannot resolve the name.

Cache-Only DNS Servers

All DNS name servers cache queries that they have resolved. *Cache-only servers* are DNS name servers that only make queries, cache the answers, and return the results. They are not authoritative for any domains.

Cache-only servers are mindless when they are booted. They will have no cached name resolution information until they have been in service over time and users have made name service requests. They have no zone information; therefore, they do not make zone transfers with other servers.

Name Resolution Types

There are three types of queries that a client can make to a DNS server: *recursive*, *iterative*, and *inverse*. DNS servers can be both a client and a server to another DNS server.

Recursive Queries

In a recursive query, the queried name server is asked to respond with the requested data or return an error. The error must state that data of the requested type does not exist or the specified domain name does not exist. This type of query is typically done by a DNS client (a *resolver*) to a DNS server. If a DNS server is configured to use a forwarder, the request from this DNS server to its forwarder will be a recursive query.

Iterative Queries

In an iterative query, the queried name server gives its best current answer back to the requester. This type of query is typically done by a DNS server to other DNS servers after it has received a recursive query from a resolver.

Figure 32.4 shows examples of both types of queries. Query 1/8 is a recursive query from a client resolver to its DNS server, and 2/3, 4/5, and 6/7 are iterative queries from the DNS server to other DNS servers.

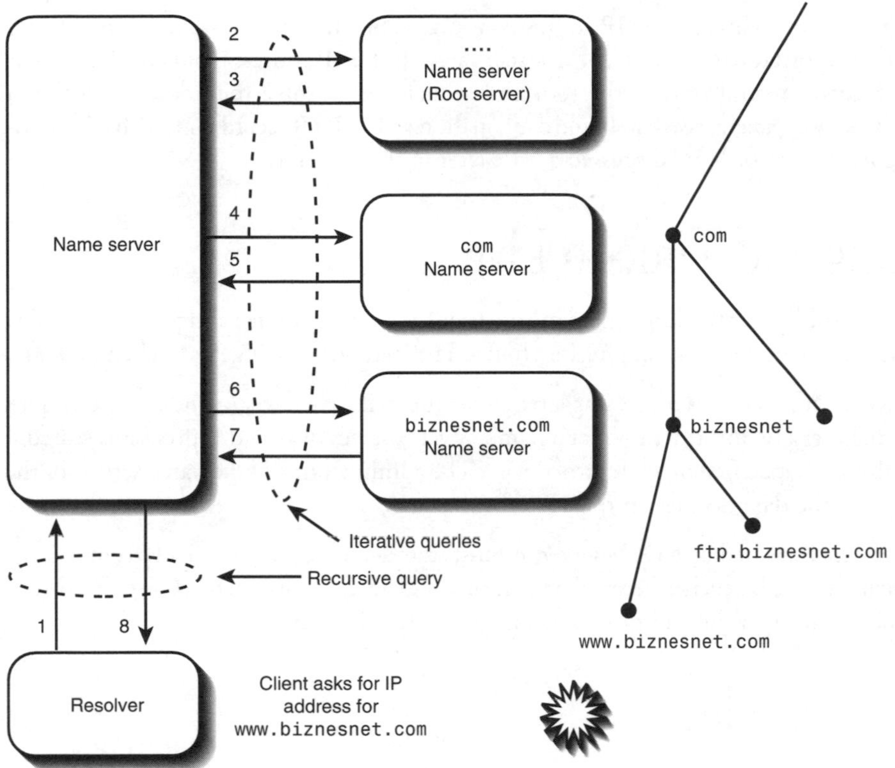

Figure 32.4. Query types in a name lookup transaction.

The Inverse Situation: `in-addr.arpa`

Perhaps you have a hot Internet tip from an officemate but it has been handed to you as dotted decimal notation like `207.2.225.190`. No problem, you just type it into your browser and press Return and there you are, `biznesnet.com`. There is no correlation in the DNS name space between the domain names and the associated IP addresses they contain. Finding the domain "owned" by this IP address would require an extensive search of IP addresses. This is why the domain `in-addr.arpa` in the DNS name space was created.

Node names in the `in-addr.arpa` domain are based on the numbers in the dotted-octet representation of IP addresses (dotted-octet is usually used instead of byte in networking because some machines have bytes longer than eight bits). IP addresses are more specific from left to right and domain names are less specific from left to right. Therefore, the order of IP address octets must be reversed when building the `in-addr.arpa` tree.

To find a host name for the IP address `207.2.225.190`, the resolver queries the DNS server for a pointer record for `190.225.2.207.in-addr.arpa`. If this IP address is outside the local domain, the DNS server would start at the root and sequentially resolve the domain nodes until finding `225.2.207.in-addr.arpa` that should contain the resource PTR record for `190` (that is, `207.2.225.190`). The pointer records are discussed a little later in this chapter.

Caching and Time to Live

In the world of networking, there must be a way to cause packets and processes to die or cease to float around the networks looking for a home. The method for doing this is called *Time to Live* (TTL).

When a name server is processing a recursive query, it may have to send out many queries to find the answer. The information that a name server receives during this process is stored in its cache for the TTL specified in the returned data. The administrator of the name server for the zone that contains the data decides on the TTL for the data.

After data is cached by a DNS server, it must start decrementing the TTL from its original value. When the TTL reaches zero, it will flush the data from its cache. Client resolvers also have mechanisms to cache and flush data based on the TTL value.

The DNS Files

DNS servers are configured by editing text files. Microsoft DNS in Microsoft Windows NT Server 4.0 includes the usual text files and a user-friendly interface to generate and edit these text files. The new administration interface called DNS Manager makes it much easier to configure both local and remote Microsoft DNS servers. The DNS administrative tool configures the RFC-compatible text files for you as you enter the records in the DNS Manager GUI.

The use of the DNS Manager is not discussed here because the primary goal of this chapter is to familiarize you with the concepts of DNS and the details of the DNS zone files themselves. In RFC-compliant DNS systems such as Microsoft NT 4.0 DNS, there are several files that define the DNS system configuration and database. These files are explained in detail in the following sections.

The Database File

The *zone file* contains the resource records for that part of the domain for which the zone is responsible. Windows NT 4.0 includes a file as a template to work with called `place.dns`. This file must be edited and renamed before you use it on your DNS server. You should name this file the same as the zone it represents because it will be replicated between your master and secondary name servers.

Note: You can find the DNS files in this directory:

```
\%systemroot%\System32\Dns
```

The Start of Authority (SOA)

The first record in any database file is the SOA record. This is the syntax for the SOA record:

```
IN SOA <source host> <contact e-mail> <ser. no.> <refresh time> <retry time>
➥<expiration time> <TTL>
```

The elements of the SOA record are

Source host	The host on which this file is maintained.
Contact e-mail	The Internet e-mail address for the person responsible for this domain's database file.

Note: Instead of writing the @ symbol in the e-mail name as would normally be done, the @ must be replaced with a period when placed in the zone files. In other words, the e-mail address `lesh@biznesnet.com` would be represented as `lesh.biznesnet.com` in the zone file.

Serial number	The version number of this database file. This number should increase each time the database file is changed.
Refresh time	The elapsed time (in seconds) that a secondary server will wait between checks to its master server to see if the database file has changed and a zone transfer should be requested.
Retry time	The elapsed time (in seconds) that a secondary server will wait before retrying a failed zone transfer.
Expiration time	The elapsed time (in seconds) that a secondary server will keep trying to download a zone. After this time limit expires, the old zone information will be discarded.
Time to Live	The elapsed time (in seconds) that a DNS server is allowed to cache any resource records from this database file. This is the value that is sent out with all query responses from this zone file when the individual resource record does not contain an overriding value.

To span a line in a database file, enclose the line breaks with ().

Note: In a zone file, the @ symbol represents the root domain of the zone. In the following records, `IN` represents Internet, the class of the data. Other classes exist, but none of them is currently in widespread use. Another critical point is that any domain name in the database file that is not terminated with a period (.) will have the root domain appended to the end.

The following example further illustrates the format of the preceding record elements.

```
@  IN SOA  nameserver1.biznesnet.com. lesh.biznesnet.com. (
1          ; serial number
10800      ; refresh [3 hours]
3600       ; retry [1 hour]
604800     ; expire [7 days]
86400      ; time to live [1 day]
```

The Name Server Record

The *name server* record lists the name servers for this domain. This record provides name server information to other name servers that are looking up names in your domain. This is the syntax of a name server record:

```
<domain> IN NS <nameserver host >
```

Here are some sample name server records:

```
@ IN NS  nameserver2.biznesnet.com.

@ IN NS  nameserver3.biznesnet.com.
```

The Mail Exchange Record

The *mail exchange* record points to the host machine that operates the mail service for this domain. If multiple mail exchange records exist in the file, the resolver will attempt to contact the lowest ASCII value mail server name. In the following sample records, mail addressed to `lesh@biznesnet.com` is delivered to `lesh@mailserver0.biznesnet.com` first or to `lesh@mailserver1.biznesnet.com` if `mailserver0` is unavailable.

This is the syntax for mail server records:

```
<domain> IN MX <preference> <mailserver host >
```

Here are some sample mail exchange records:

```
@    IN MX  1  mailserver0

@    IN MX  2  mailserver1
```

The Host Record

The *host* record associates hostnames with IP addresses within a zone. You should include in it entries for all hosts that require static address to name mappings. These records will be the majority record type when static records are used in a database file.

This is the syntax for a host record:

```
<host name> IN A <ip address of host>
```

Here are some sample host records:

```
biznesnetcom1  IN A  207.2.225.190

nameserver2    IN A  207.2.225.189

mailserver1    IN A  207.2.225.188
```

The Local Host Record

A *local host* record allows lookups for `localhost` to return `127.0.0.1`. This address is reserved for the `localhost` address in all networked machines. The following is an example of the local host record in the database:

```
localhost  IN A  127.0.0.1
```

Canonical Name Records (CNAME)

CNAME records are aliases pointing to the host's official domain name; these records enable you to use more than one name to point to a single host. Using a CNAME record, you can search for a domain with WWW as part of its name.

Using canonical names makes it easy to do such things as host both an FTP server and a Web server on the same machine. The syntax of the CNAME record is as follows:

```
<host alias name> IN CNAME <host name>
```

Assume that `www.biznesnet.com` and `FTP.biznesnet.com` are on the same machine. If this is the case, you might have the following entries in your zone file:

```
FileServer1 IN A 207.2.225.190

ftp CNAME FileServer1

www CNAME FileServer1
```

Suppose you need to move the FTP server to another machine. To do this, you just change the CNAME in the DNS server for FTP and add an address record for the new server. For example,

```
FTP - CNAME FileServer2

FileServer2 IN A 207.2.225.189
```

The Cache File

The cache file is made up of host information needed to resolve names outside the authoritative domain. It contains names and addresses of root name servers. Microsoft DNS Server 4.0 includes a file that lists the root name servers at the time the product was manufactured; it should work for your initial setup. You will need to establish your own cache file if you are using the DNS server on an internal system or intranet. Following is an example of the DNS cache file contents:

```
; DNS CACHE FILE
;
; Initial cache data for root domain servers.
;
; YOU SHOULD CHANGE:
; —Nothing if connected to the Internet. Edit this file only when
;   update root name server list is released.
;   OR
; —If NOT connected to the Internet, remove these records and replace
;   with NS and A records for the DNS server authoritative for the
;   root domain at your site.
; Internet root name server records:
;  last update: Sep 1, 1995
;  related version of root zone: 1995090100
;
; formerly NS.INTERNIC.NET
.      3600000 IN NS A.ROOT-SERVERS.NET.
A.ROOT-SERVERS.NET.  3600000  A  198.41.0.4
; formerly NS1.ISI.EDU
.      3600000  NS B.ROOT-SERVERS.NET.
B.ROOT-SERVERS.NET.  3600000  A  128.9.0.107
; formerly C.PSI.NET
.      3600000  NS C.ROOT-SERVERS.NET.
C.ROOT-SERVERS.NET.  3600000  A  192.33.4.12
; formerly TERP.UMD.EDU
.      3600000  NS D.ROOT-SERVERS.NET.
D.ROOT-SERVERS.NET.  3600000  A  128.8.10.90
; formerly NS.NASA.GOV
.      3600000  NS E.ROOT-SERVERS.NET.
E.ROOT-SERVERS.NET.  3600000  A  192.203.230.10
; formerly NS.ISC.ORG
.      3600000  NS F.ROOT-SERVERS.NET.
F.ROOT-SERVERS.NET.  3600000  A  39.13.229.241
; formerly NS.NIC.DDN.MIL
.      3600000  NS G.ROOT-SERVERS.NET.
G.ROOT-SERVERS.NET.  3600000  A  192.112.36.4
; formerly AOS.ARL.ARMY.MIL
.      3600000  NS H.ROOT-SERVERS.NET.
; End of File
```

Note: For a current Internet cache file, see `FTP://rs.internic.net/domain/named.cache`.

The Reverse Lookup File

The in-addr.arpa record, mentioned earlier in this chapter, is maintained in a database file that is used for reverse lookups. Reverse lookups are for particular IP DNS zones of host names that belong to given IP numbers. A resolver can use this record type by providing an IP address and requesting a matching host name. This file contains SOA and name server records similar to other DNS database zone files. It also contains pointer records.

Reverse lookup is needed by applications that provide the capabilities to implement security based on the connecting host names. For example, if a client tries to link to a Network File System (NFS) volume with this security arrangement, the NFS server would contact the DNS server and do a reverse-name lookup on the client's IP address. If the host name returned by the DNS server is not in the access list for the NFS volume, or if the host name was not found by DNS, then the NFS mount request would be denied.

Here are a couple of sample zones for different IP class networks.

Sample class C zone:

```
100.200.192.in-addr.arpa
```

Sample class B zone:

```
55.157.in-addr.arpa
```

The Pointer Record

Pointer records (PTR) are a mapping of IP addresses to host names within a reverse-lookup zone. IP numbers are written in reverse order and in-addr.arpa. is appended to the end to create this pointer record. As an example, looking up the name for 207.2.225.190 requires a PTR query for the name 190.115.2.207.in-addr.arpa. Following is the syntax of the PTR:

```
<ip reverse domain name> IN PTR <host name>
```

This is a sample pointer record:

```
190.2.225.207.in-addr.arpa.  IN PTR  mailserver1.biznesnet.com.
```

The arpa-127.rev File

The 127 address always belongs to the localhost machine. The arpa-127.rev file is a database file for the 127.in-addr.arpa. domain, providing a pointer to the local machine. Only the SOA and NS records change in this file.

The BIND Boot File and Microsoft DNS

Microsoft DNS server does not use a boot file; it is configured at boot time from data contained in the Registry. The boot file is a BIND requirement and is not part of the official requirements spelled out in the RFCs. The Microsoft DNS will allow use of a boot file if you make a manual edit to the Registry to force use of the boot file method. If you attempt to start Microsoft DNS server and you receive this error message

```
The DNS server could not start because the requested file was not found
```

it usually means that the Registry is configured to use a boot file and none exists. Look in `\%systemroot%\Winnt\System32\Dns\backup` or `\%systemroot%\Winnt\System32\Dns\samples` to find a boot file you can move into `\%systemroot%\Winnt\System32\Dns`. The DNS server should boot after this file is in place.

This file controls the startup behavior of the DNS server. Commands must start at the beginning of a line and no spaces may precede commands. Recognized commands are `directory`, `cache`, `primary`, and `secondary`. The syntax for the file records is described in the following sections.

`directory` Command

The `directory` command specifies a directory where other files referred to in the boot file can be found. The `directory` command syntax is as follows:

```
directory <directory>
```

Sample `directory` command:

```
directory c:\winnts\system32\dns
```

`cache` Command

The `cache` command specifies a file used to help the DNS service contact name servers for the root domain. This command and the file it refers to must be present. A cache file for use on the Internet is provided with Windows NT 4.0. The `cache` command syntax is as follows:

```
cache  . <filename>
```

Sample cache command:

```
cache . cache
```

primary Command

The `primary` command specifies a domain for which this name server is authoritative and a database file that contains the resource records for that domain (zone file). The `primary` command syntax is the following:

```
primary <domain> <filename>
```

Sample `primary` commands:

```
primary biznesnet.com microsoft.dns
```

```
primary dev.biznesnet.com dev.dns
```

secondary Command

The `secondary` command specifies a domain for which this name server is authoritative, and a list of master server IP addresses from which to attempt to download the zone information rather than read it from a file. It also defines the name of the local file for caching this zone. The following is the `secondary` command syntax:

```
secondary <domain> <hostlist> <local filename>
```

Example:

```
secondary test.biznesnet.com 157.55.200.100 test.dns
```

forwarders Command

The `forwarders` command specifies another server willing to try resolving recursive queries on behalf of the system. The following is the `forwarders` command syntax:

```
forwarders <hostlist>
```

Sample `forwarders` command:

```
forwarders 157.55.200.100 157.55.200.101
```

slave Command

The `slave` command specifies that the use of `forwarders` is the only way possible to resolve queries. This command can follow only a `forwarders` command. Here is the `slave` command in use:

```
forwarders 163.53.212.109 163.53.212.110
slave
```

Introduction to Microsoft NT 4.0 DNS

The Microsoft DNS server is not a port of the Berkeley BIND code. Microsoft decided to write a new DNS server that is fully RFC-compliant and compatible with BIND. It is also not an extension of the standalone DNS server previously provided in the Resource Kits. The DNS server in Windows NT 4.0 is an RFC-compliant implementation of DNS.

Because Microsoft DNS is an RFC-compliant DNS server, it creates and uses standard DNS zone files and supports all standard resource record types. This makes it interoperable with other DNS servers.

Note: Microsoft DNS supports RFCs 1033, 1034, 1035, 1101, 1123, 1183, and 1536.

A plus feature of Microsoft DNS is that DNS Manager allows for easy administration of any other Microsoft DNS server on the network and over the Internet via a Remote Procedure Call (RPC). The administrative UI also contains a Zone Wizard that enables someone less familiar to DNS to be successful in creating zones and zone database files. However, you cannot administer non-Microsoft DNS servers with DNS Manager.

The Microsoft DNS server can use the database, boot, cache, rev, and other files from any other DNS server implementation (that is, UNIX or other Windows NT DNS implementation) as long as that DNS server is RFC-compliant. All that needs to be done to port the files over to Microsoft DNS is to change the filenames and locations in the boot file.

Note: Although Microsoft DNS will support a boot file on initial installation, the boot file is a BIND-specific implementation and not a requirement of the RFCs. This is provided for migration from BIND-based DNS servers. If the Microsoft DNS Manager UI tool is used to create and administer zone files, this Boot From BootFile option will be set to Boot From Registry and Microsoft DNS will store and use data in the Windows NT Registry for locating and loading the zone file databases. A message will be written to the boot file that states that the information is now in the Registry. To go back to booting from the boot file, the value of the `EnableRegistryBoot` key in the Windows NT Registry will have to be modified manually.

The Microsoft DNS server can also be a primary or secondary to any other operating system (or other vendors Windows NT implementations).

The DNS Manager Program in Windows NT 4.0

DNS Manager displays statistics about the traffic received on the computer running Microsoft DNS server. These statistics are automatically started and displayed in the right pane of DNS Manager after you add a server and create at least one zone on that server. By default, these statistics are cumulative and are normally not cleared until the computer running Microsoft DNS server is stopped.

You can use the `dnsstat.exe` utility provided in the Windows NT Server 4.0 Resource Kit to clear the statistics without stopping the Microsoft DNS server.

This command-line utility provides a dump of statistics about traffic received on a computer running Microsoft DNS server. You also can use `dnsstat` to clear these statistics without stopping the DNS server. By default, these statistics are cumulative and are normally not cleared until the computer running Microsoft DNS server is stopped.

`dnsstat` syntax is as follows:

```
dnsstat {servername ¦ IP address} [{-c ¦ /c ¦ -clear ¦ /clear}]
```

Where `servername` returns all DNS server statistics on the server named `servername`. IP address returns all DNS server statistics on the server with the IP address indicated. The options `-c` or `/c` or `-clear` or `/clear` reset DNS statistics on the server indicated.

To clear the Microsoft DNS server statistics by using the `dnsstat` command, click Start, and select Run | Open from the menu and type

```
dnsstat <servername> -c or dnstat <servername> /c
```

Click OK.

This resets the value of the DNS statistics to zero. Open DNS Manager to verify that the statistics have been cleared and restarted.

DNS Tools

BIND has been around longer than Microsoft DNS, so there are a lot more BIND-related tools available to assist in the sometimes laborious task of cleaning up a nonfunctioning DNS. In the Microsoft Windows NT 4.0 world, there are only the usual TCP/IP tools such as `ping`, `nslookup`, `nbtstat`, `arp` and the other handy utilities supplied with Windows NT 4.0. The primary tool for DNS troubleshooting is the `nslookup` utility.

Lookup tools display the data returned by a name server when it receives a query. These tools, such as the `nslookup` function, assist the system administrator in validating DNS changes made to his or her domain name servers.

Lookup tools can be used to obtain delegation information from servers in nonlocal domains. This allows the system administrator to determine whether the parent domain is correctly parsing and returning the address of the local DNS server. `Nslookup` includes an interactive mode and a debug mode.

An overlooked source of information about name server behavior is the system event log. The server log and applications log in Windows NT 4.0 enable the system administrator to monitor zone loading, reloading, and zone transfers. Using the Event Viewer, you can obtain a quick feel for the health of your server.

DNS and WINS

It is difficult to discuss Microsoft DNS server without including a discussion of WINS. You can find plenty of details on Windows Internet Name Service (WINS) in this book's chapter on WINS. The fact remains, however, that DNS is not WINS. DNS is a mostly static database whereas WINS is highly dynamic. DNS performs IP name resolution and is a universally accepted Internet standard. WINS, on the other hand, is a Microsoft standard that resolves NetBIOS names and is not a universally accepted Internet standard.

Many of the topics discussed in this chapter apply equally to Microsoft DNS and BIND and any other RFC-compliant DNS product. Because WINS is not currently an Internet standard, name translation on the global Internet today is performed by DNS. When the Microsoft DNS is employed wholly within the intranet environment, the use of WINS in conjunction with DNS effectively provides a dynamic DNS. The discussion in this chapter is limited to the global Internet use of DNS via the Internet Protocol (IP).

Common DNS Problems

DNS problems usually are caused by one or more of a discrete set of mistakes or omissions in DNS management. The following sections summarize the common administrative errors that occur in setting up DNS, regardless of which DNS server you are using.

Failure to Increment SOA Record's Serial Number

Failure to increment the start of authority (SOA) record's serial number is the primary cause of DNS errors. Without the serial number increment, the secondary name server will not recognize when a change has been made. The secondary server does not automatically test for changes in the SOA record. Any changes in the SOA must be accompanied by a change in the SOA record serial number, and this change must be broadcast to the secondary name server. Whenever you are making changes to the SOA record, always test the secondary name server to ensure that it recognizes the change. Be sure to check this important detail if you are having zone transfer problems.

No Period at End of FQDN

Failure to end domain names in the database with a period can have adverse consequences. Microsoft DNS server assumes that the domain names in the database are relative to the domain currently being defined. For instance, in the database file defining `biznesnet.com`, an entry such as

```
biznesnet.com. IN NS.biznesnet.com
```

really means

```
biznesnet.com. IN NS ns.biznesnet.com.biznesnet.com.
```

You can see this was not what was intended in this record.

Absence of Reverse Lookup Records

Forgetting reverse DNS or pointer (PTR) records can result in slow startup of client applications that reverse DNS lookup to translate IP numbers to names (for example, Telnet). This can also be observed when running `traceroute`. The delay is caused by `traceroute` trying repeated reverse DNS lookups for IP addresses on each hop in the route. Missing reverse DNS records can also result in denial of connection when the user is attempting to access another host.

Glue Records That Are Missing or Incorrect

You, as administrator of a domain, must inform your parent domains to change their glue records (glue records are the A name resource records) to match any change you make in the IP address or alias of your primary or secondary name servers. If you neglect to do this, the glue records maintained by the parent domain will become invalid. The common symptom of invalid glue records is the inability of a host to access a host in a different domain via its domain name while being able to access the other host via its IP address.

Administrators Who Do Not Communicate

The DNS parent and child zone administrators must inform each other of changes in a zone. Their most common errors are lame delegations and missing delegations. A lame delegation occurs when a parent domain zone file includes a name server for a subdomain that knows nothing about its zone of authority. A missing delegation means the parent domain name server's listing does not include the name of one or more primary name servers within the parent's domain. Changing the IP address of an organization's primary server without ensuring that the parent domain reflects the change is a common error. This is indicated by the inability of nonlocal hosts to find the primary domain server.

Outdated Root Cache Files

The root cache contains the domain name and IP address of the root server for each domain. System administrators must proactively keep the root cache files up-to-date because there is no automatic refresh mechanism from the root domain level. A system with an out-of-date root cache file will be unable to access the root server for one or more domains, thus blocking access to the entire domain. The current copy of root cache files is available via FTP from

```
rs.internic.net/domain/named.root
```

Using NetBIOS Scope with DNS

In DNS Manager you can elect to submit the domain as a NetBIOS scope. You should use this option *only* if you already are using NetBIOS Scope in your Windows NT network.

When this option is selected, DNS server will submit the host (computer) name and the domain name from a DNS request to WINS for resolution. The host name is submitted as the NetBIOS computer name, and the domain name is submitted as the NetBIOS Scope. For this option to work, you will need to make sure that you have implemented NetBIOS Scope names in a consistent manner on your network. The main potential problem lies in the case of the names. With DNS, names are case insensitive. With NetBIOS Scope, they are case sensitive.

Troubleshooting TCP/IP-Related Name Resolution Problems

If you are unable to connect to a server on the Internet using a fully qualified domain name such as `www.biznesnet.com`, try connecting to a server on the Internet using that server's IP address.

In the address field of your Web browser, connect by typing the following address

```
http://<###.###.###.###>
```

where `<###.###.###.###>` is the IP address of the server.

You also can test connectivity to the site's IP address by using the `ping` command. From a command prompt in Windows NT, type the following line:

```
ping <###.###.###.###>
```

where `<###.###.###.###>` is the IP address of the server.

If you are communicating properly with the site, you should receive a reply from it.

The inability to communicate with a server on the Internet using the IP address may indicate only a problem with your ISP's Domain Name Service (DNS). To determine whether the problem is with DNS, make sure you are connected to your ISP, and at the command prompt type the following line:

```
ipconfig /all
```

This command displays Windows NT IP configuration information, including the IP address of the DNS server.

The `IPCONFIG.EXE` utility has been included with Windows NT since Version 3.5. The purpose of this utility is to provide the user with diagnostic information related to TCP/IP network configuration. `IPCONFIG` also accepts various Dynamic Host Configuration Protocol (DHCP) commands, enabling a system to update or release its TCP/IP network configuration. Following is the syntax for the IPCONFIG utility:

```
IPCONFIG [/? ¦ /all ¦ /release [adapter] ¦ /renew [adapter]]
```

The switches in the preceding line of code perform the following functions:

Switch	*Function*
`/?`	Displays this help message
`/all`	Displays full configuration information
`/release`	Releases the IP address for the specified adapter
`/renew`	Renews the IP address for the specified adapter

With no parameters, `IPCONFIG` will display only the IP address, subnet mask, and default gateway for each adapter bound to TCP/IP.

With the `/all` switch, `IPCONFIG` will display all the current TCP/IP configuration values including the IP address, subnet mask, default gateway, and WINS and DNS configuration.

If the adapter name is not specified with either the `/Release` or `/Renew` switch, the IP address leases for all adapters bound to TCP/IP will be released or renewed.

The `/Release` and `/Renew` switches can be used only on a system configured with DHCP.

The `IPCONFIG` command displays Windows NT TCP/IP settings for all network adapters and modem connections. The address for the modem connection is displayed as the NDISWAN(x) adapter. The default gateway for the NDISWAN(x) adapter is the same as the IP address; this is normal and by design. More than one NDISWAN(x) adapter may be displayed. Any NDISWAN(x) adapters not currently in use display zeros for the IP address.

If you have difficulty connecting to a particular server, even when specifying the same name, use the `nbtstat -n` command to determine (authoritatively) what name the server registered on the network. The output of this command lists several names that the system has registered using NetBIOS over TCP/IP. One resembling the system's computer name should be present. If not, try one of the other unique names displayed. The `nbtstat -n` command can also display the cached entries for remote systems—either `#PRE` loaded from `LMHOSTS` or recently resolved names—due to current network activity. If the name the remote users are using is the same, and the other systems are on a remote subnet, make sure that they have the system's mapping in their `LMHOSTS` file.

When you cannot connect to foreign systems with host names using Telnet, FTP, and so on, but can connect using only IP addresses, check the host name resolution configuration (found under the TCP/IP Connectivity option in Control Panel) to be sure that the appropriate HOSTS and DNS setup has been configured for the system. If you are using the HOSTS file, make sure the remote system is spelled the same way in the file as it is being used by the application. If you are using DNS, make sure the IP addresses of the DNS servers are correct and in the proper order. To determine whether the host name is being resolved properly, try using ping with the remote system by typing both the host name and IP address.

When a TCP/IP connection to a remote system appears to be hung, the NETSTAT -a command can be used to show the status of all activity on TCP and UDP ports on the local system. The state of a good TCP connection is usually established with 0 bytes in the send and receive queues. If data is blocked in either queue or if the state is irregular, there is probably a problem with the connection. If not, you are probably experiencing network or application delay.

Conflict with Other Network Adapters

Verify that the IP address assigned to you by your ISP for this connection is not the same as the IP address for your network card or loopback driver (if installed). Also, the IP address of your network card or loopback driver should not be on the same network as the IP address assigned to you by your ISP for this connection.

To view and edit the IP addresses of your network adapter or loopback driver, open the Network tool in Control Panel. The Network tool is only for your network adapters. When you are configuring the IP address for your Dial-Up adapter, all configuration should be done in the Dial-Up Networking tool.

H-Node and B-Node Computers

Windows NT 4.0 allows you to resolve NetBIOS names using the HOSTS file or domain name service (DNS) server. To do this, you must select the Enable DNS for Windows Name Resolution check box in the Advanced Microsoft TCP/IP Configuration dialog box that you reach when you make the menu choices Control Panel | Network.

In addition, Windows NT uses WINS, b-node broadcasts, and the LMHOSTS file for NetBIOS name resolution. If all of these name resolution methods are used, an h-node host computer implements them in the following order:

1. NetBIOS name cache
2. WINS server
3. B-node broadcast
4. LMHOSTS file
5. HOSTS file
6. DNS server

The HOSTS file is used by some TCP/IP utilities, such as ping and ftp, even though the Enable DNS for Windows Name Resolution check box is cleared.

Using NetBIOS Names to Troubleshoot DNS

Windows NT 4.0 allows you to use a domain name server (DNS) to resolve a computer name to an IP address for Windows networking functions, or to connect directly to an IP address without knowing the NetBIOS name. Some examples are

```
net use * \\ftp.biznesnet.com\data
```

and

```
net view \\10.57.8.191
```

When this new functionality is used, it still is necessary for the calling computer to know one of the NetBIOS names registered on the remote computer. There are currently two ways of finding a valid NetBIOS name to connect to on the target computer:

- Trying a NetBIOS session setup to the new `*SMBSERVER` name that recent implementations support.
- Issuing a NetBIOS adapter status request to the destination IP address, and then parsing the returned name table for the name registered by the server service (`<computername>[0x20]`).

NetBIOS sessions are established between two NetBIOS names. A session setup involves the following phases:

1. NetBIOS name resolution (via a name server, broadcast, or static file)
2. NetBIOS name query request
3. NetBIOS name query response

   A TCP connection is established:
4. SYN
5. SYN-ACK
6. ACK

   A NetBIOS session is set up over that connection:
7. NetBIOS session setup request
8. NetBIOS session setup response

When using a DNS to resolve names, or when connecting directly to an IP address, there is no assurance that the NetBIOS name for the called system is known.

The DNS (host) name is not necessarily the same as the NetBIOS name, and in many cases the DNS name is actually an alias for any number of different computers. This means that the NetBIOS name must be verified before a session can be set up.

Windows NT 4.0 computers verify or obtain the NetBIOS name by one of two methods if a DNS was used to resolve an address for a NetBIOS resource:

- Attempting to set up a session to the newly supported `*SMBSERVER` NetBIOS name or, if that fails:
- Sending a NetBIOS adapter status request to the called IP address, and obtaining the list of NetBIOS names registered for that adapter.

The NetBIOS adapter status response contains the name table for the computer queried. It is parsed for the name registered by the server service, and then a TCP connection and NetBIOS session can be established.

RFC 1002 states the following:

"NBNS can (optionally) ensure that the node is down by sending a NODE STATUS REQUEST. If such a request is sent, and no response is received, it can be assumed that the node is down."

In order to establish a connection from a Windows NT 4.0 computer to another computer using DNS name resolution, the remote computer must either support NetBIOS sessions to the special case `*SMBSERVER` name, or respond properly to an adapter status request. You can use the Windows NT `nbtstat -A <ipaddr>` command to test this. A sample is shown here:

```
D:\>nbtstat -A 207.2.225.190
NetBIOS Remote Machine Name Table
Name      Type   Status
BIZNESNET   <1F> UNIQUE Registered
BIZNESNET   <00> UNIQUE Registered
PSS-BP      <00> GROUP  Registered
BIZNESNET   <03> UNIQUE Registered
BIZNESNET   <20> UNIQUE Registered   <-The server service name
PSS-BP      <1E> GROUP  Registered
MAC Address = 00-80-5F-50-E3-CC
```

Summary

The Domain Name System is a set of rules applied to the network as Robert's Rules of Order are applied to a meeting. In the expanded context of the Internet, there must be rules of order or chaos will result. The DNS is the implementation of the rules that are clearly defined in the RFCs. If you are having DNS difficulties, you may not be in a position to carefully sit down and read through the rules of the game you are trying to play. It may be necessary to obtain help first, then become the self-proclaimed expert later. Of course, you can call the Microsoft help desk at any time. These Usenet newsgroups also offer collective advice on DNS:

`comp.protocols.dns.bind`

`microsoft.public.windowsnt.dns`

`microsoft.public.windowsnt.domain`

`microsoft.public.windowsnt.protocol.tcpip`

Querying for DNS on any major Internet search site will find hundreds or thousands of documents, so narrow your query with other terms, such as *setup* or *troubleshooting*.

Reference lists on the World Wide Web include the following:

`http://www.dns.net/dnsrd`

`http://rs.internic.net/help/domain/dns.html`

An excellent source of information on DNS concepts is the book *DNS and BIND* by Paul Albitz and Cricket Liu, published by O'Reilly & Associates, Inc. The revised edition is now available. This book is primarily for the UNIX world, but DNS concepts are platform independent and the principles apply to Microsoft DNS server in Windows NT 4.0.

PART VII

Integrating with Other Networks

CHAPTER 33

Integrating with NetWare

by Robert Reinstein

Of course, Microsoft Windows NT Server is a great server and can handle all the file, print, and application server requirements for a small company or a large corporation. But other network operating systems still exist in the marketplace.

When Microsoft released the first version of Windows NT Server, Novell NetWare held the greatest market share for network operating systems. At the time of this writing, NetWare still does, with Microsoft Windows NT Server catching up quickly.

Note: There are indications that this will change by the year 2000, and Windows NT Server will have the leading market share.

Because of the huge base of installed NetWare servers, Microsoft decided, beginning with Microsoft Windows NT Server 3.5, to incorporate some features that would enable Microsoft Windows NT Server to coexist with NetWare. Microsoft also offered tools that enable an easy migration from NetWare to Microsoft Windows NT Server.

This chapter discusses the following:

- Migrating a NetWare server to a Windows NT server
- Integrating NetWare into a Windows NT network
- Having a Windows NT server emulate a NetWare server
- Managing NetWare through Windows NT administrative tools

A Little History: Microsoft and Novell

When Microsoft Windows NT Server was first released in 1993, it seemed as though there would never be connectivity between Windows NT and NetWare. Microsoft didn't care to include its version of a NetWare client, and Novell seemed to have even less of an interest in allowing Windows NT PCs to see NetWare servers.

Perhaps this was because of the differences that Novell and Microsoft encountered with the release of Windows for Workgroups.

In case you're unfamiliar with this issue, Microsoft had been given permission to include a NetWare client in Microsoft Windows 3.0. When Microsoft Windows 3.1 was released, it too had a NetWare client.

Microsoft also took the liberty of including Novell's NetWare Client for Windows in the first release of Windows for Workgroups. According to Novell, Microsoft had not asked permission to include this client software, and Novell demanded that Microsoft remove its software from the product. This was the start of a feud that would be short-lived but would result in no production of a NetWare client for Windows NT in time for the release of Windows NT.

Note: The Microsoft versus Novell feud over the inclusion of the Novell NetWare client in Windows for Workgroups 3.1 resulted in a lack of support for NetWare in Windows for Workgroups 3.11, which prompts the user for a Novell-supplied client disk when attempting to install support for a NetWare network.

As a user in a NetWare environment at the time, I found it very frustrating to have to live without network connectivity when running Windows NT as my desktop operating system.

Due to customer demand, Microsoft decided to create its own NetWare client for Windows NT. Apparently not wanting to be outdone by Microsoft, Novell released its own NetWare client for Windows NT, albeit in beta form. Both clients offered nothing more than basic connectivity and, in my opinion, the Microsoft client was a little more feature-rich than the Novell client, which appeared to be a rush job. Both products really only performed minimal connectivity.

Both companies then started to play leap-frog, releasing their respective beta versions of the NetWare client for Windows NT, each time adding a little more functionality.

Not until Microsoft released Windows NT Server 3.5 was a client for NetWare built into the Windows NT product.

Microsoft's client depended on a NetWare bindery to gain access to a NetWare server. With the release of NetWare 4.*x* with its new NDS tree, Microsoft's NetWare Client for Windows NT required NetWare 4.*x* servers to run in a Bindery Emulation mode. Novell soon released its NDS client for Windows NT, but this was supported for use only on a Windows NT Workstation.

New to NT 4.0: Not until Microsoft Windows NT Server 4.0 has Microsoft finally included the capability for a Windows NT server to log into a NetWare NDS tree (although this functionality has been available for Windows NT Workstation from both Microsoft and Novell). The NDS login is only usable for logging in as a client, however. This chapter discusses functionality within Windows NT Server, which still requires Bindery Emulation mode.

The next section of this chapter discusses the feature built into Windows NT Server, called Gateway (and Client) Services for NetWare, which enables a Windows NT server access to a NetWare server.

Gateway (and Client) Services for NetWare

Gateway (and Client) Services for NetWare is an installable service that enables access to a NetWare server through the Windows NT Server. With this service, a client can run only the client software for a Windows NT network and still have access to NetWare resources.

NT Workstation: Windows NT Workstation includes Client Services for NetWare. This is similar to the service that is included with Windows NT Server; however, it allows for the Windows NT Workstation to attach only to the NetWare resources. The Windows NT Workstation cannot make the NetWare resources available as shares.

There are a few guidelines for using this service. First, *this is not a way to bypass NetWare security.* A client who uses the gateway must have an account on the NetWare server and must have permission to access whatever resources to which he or she tries to attach.

Second, Gateway (and Client) Services for NetWare is not a replacement for making a direct connection to a NetWare server. Gateway (and Client) Services for NetWare uses only one connection to NetWare and cannot achieve the same performance as a direct connection. In fact, if more than one user is using the resources that have been created by the Gateway (and Client) Services for NetWare, the performance degrades even more. That is why you are strongly advised to use Gateway (and Client) Services for NetWare only if the resources on the NetWare server are seldom used. See Flowchart 33.1 to help you make a decision as to whether to use the Gateway (and Client) Services for NetWare.

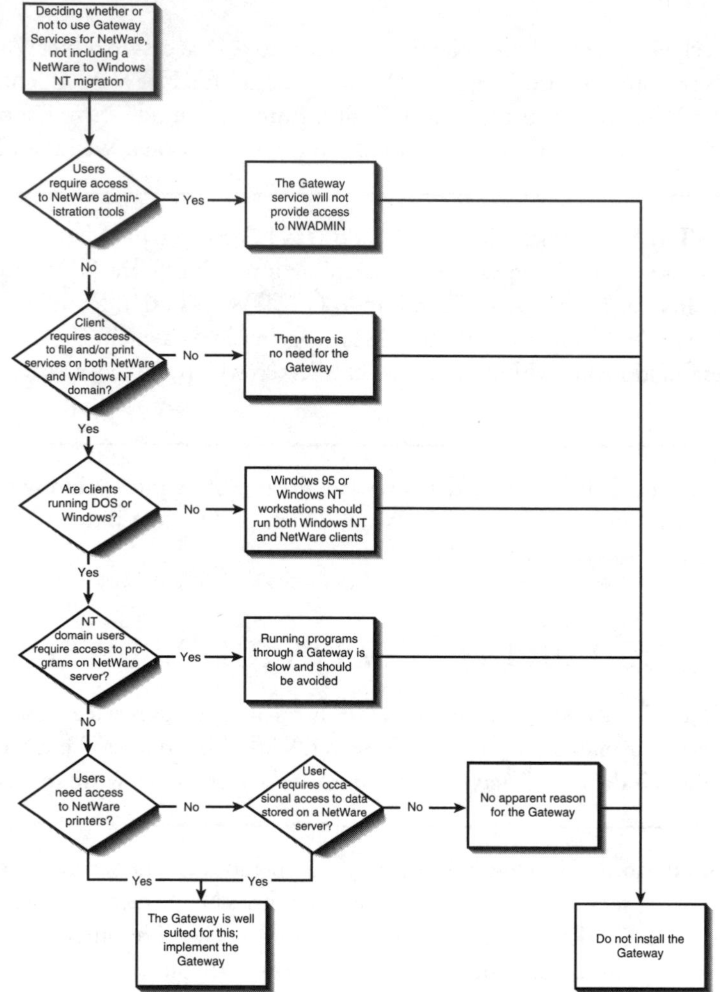

Flowchart 33.1. *Choosing whether to install Gateway (and Client) Services for NetWare.*

For instance, if a NetWare client decides to migrate to a Windows NT domain and run only the client software for Windows NT, possibly to avoid unnecessary overhead, there is still a chance that there is a shared directory on the NetWare server to which the user requires access. To retrieve an occasional document, or to print to a NetWare print queue, Gateway (and Client) Services for NetWare is the perfect tool. It should not be used for running applications. Yes, you can run an application, but again, there is a good chance that there will be a performance issue.

> **Performance:** Users who do want access to applications residing on a NetWare server should run native NetWare client software and make a direct connection.

Installing Gateway (and Client) Services for NetWare

Before you install Gateway (and Client) Services for NetWare, you need to do some preliminary work on the NetWare side to enable the Gateway (and Client) Services for NetWare to function properly. Therefore, you will require Supervisor equivalency for NetWare and have administrative rights for the Windows NT domain.

Configuring NetWare

In this example I'm using a NetWare 4.1 server. I have logged into the NetWare NDS tree, which enables me to run the `NWADMIN.EXE` administration program from Windows 95. I am using Microsoft's Client for NDS to get access to the NetWare server.

For a NetWare 3.*x* server, you would use SYSCON to perform the same activities I describe here. If you are using NetWare 3.*x*, you'll need to repeat these steps for each NetWare 3.*x* server to which you want to give your Windows NT clients access. NDS enables you to go through this routine only once.

One account used on the NetWare server functions as the service account for Gateway (and Client) Services for NetWare. This is the NetWare account that will be used by the Gateway (and Client) Services for NetWare, and it determines the greatest level of access that any client accessing NetWare resources through this gateway will have, based on the security permissions granted to the service account.

Using NWADMIN, choose to create a new user object. The name of the user can be anything, but the same ID must exist on both the NetWare server(s) and in the Windows NT domain. For this example, I will use the name NTSERVER (see Figure 33.1).

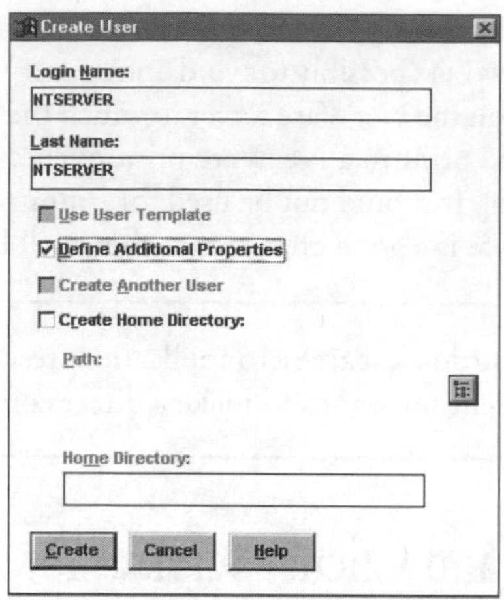

Figure 33.1. Adding the Gateway (and Client) Services for NetWare service account to NetWare.

Click the Define Additional Properties checkbox because you will want to continue configuring this account.

The next dialog, shown in Figure 33.2, has several configuration tabs from which to choose. In this case, I've added a description to the account so that someone else doesn't accidentally delete the account.

> **Tip:** Documenting your actions regarding setting up this gateway will help you in troubleshooting and will also help you remember the groups and user IDs you've set up for the future.

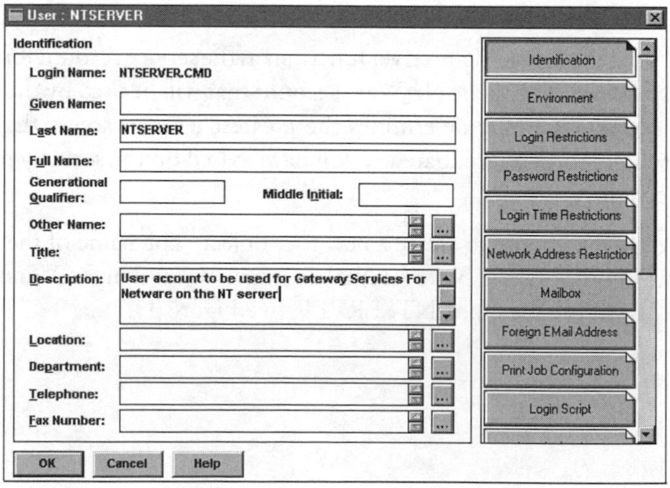

Figure 33.2. User identification in NWADMIN.

Click the Password Restrictions tab to set the password for the Gateway (and Client) Services for NetWare service account (see Figure 33.3).

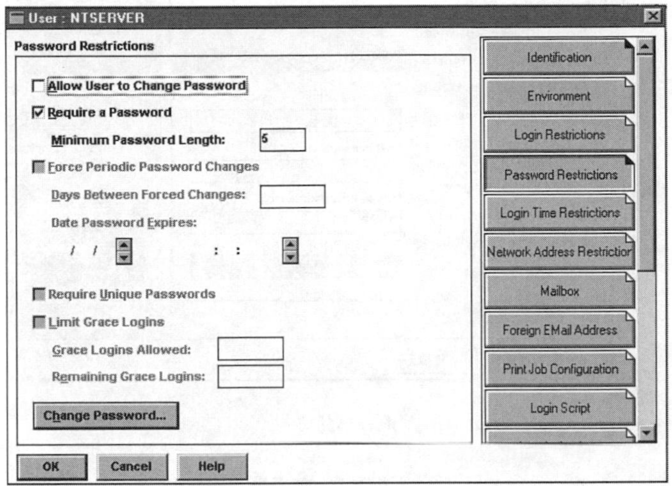

Figure 33.3. *Password restrictions in NWADMIN.*

Tip: As with all networks, defining a password is strongly advised. Chances are that you already have a default user profile set up to dictate the password standards for your organization. In the case of this service account, however, you don't want the user to be able to change the password, and you don't want the account or the password to expire.

Click the Change Password button to set the password (see Figure 33.4).

Click the OK button and you have finished configuring the Gateway (and Client) Services for NetWare service account in NetWare. You still need to create this account in the Windows NT domain.

Next on the NetWare side, you need to create a new group (see Figure 33.5). Call the group NTGATEWAY and click the Define Additional Properties checkbox for this group (see Figure 33.6).

In the Identification page shown in Figure 33.7, type in a description for this group so that no one accidentally deletes the group. Without this group, Gateway (and Client) Services for NetWare does not function at all.

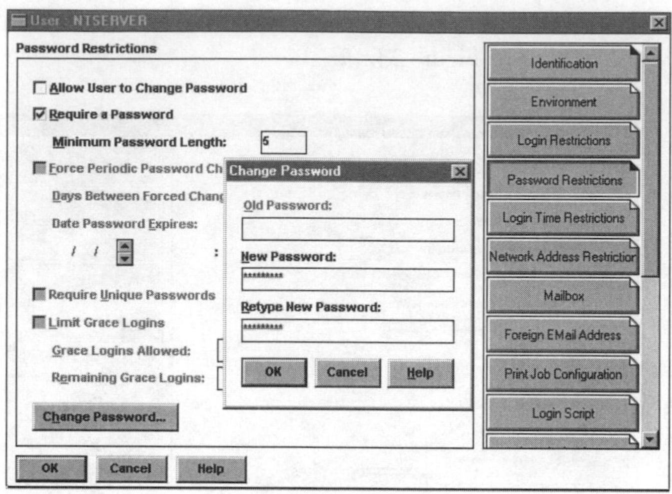

Figure 33.4. *The Change Password dialog in NWADMIN.*

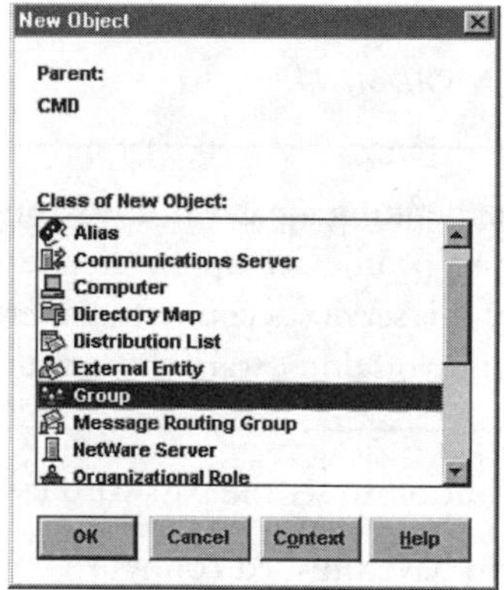

Figure 33.5. *Creating a new object in NWADMIN.*

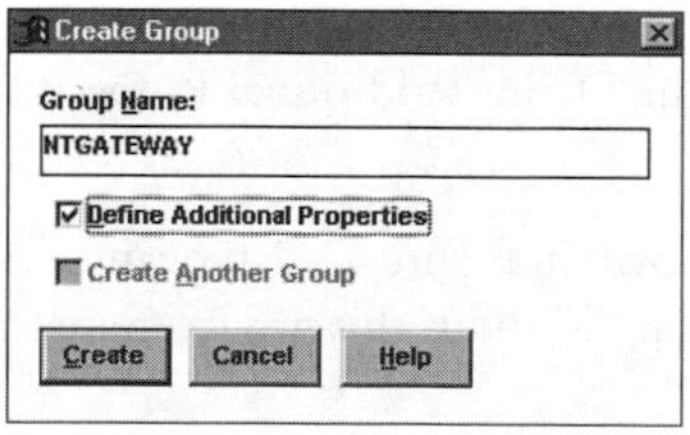

Figure 33.6. *Naming the new group.*

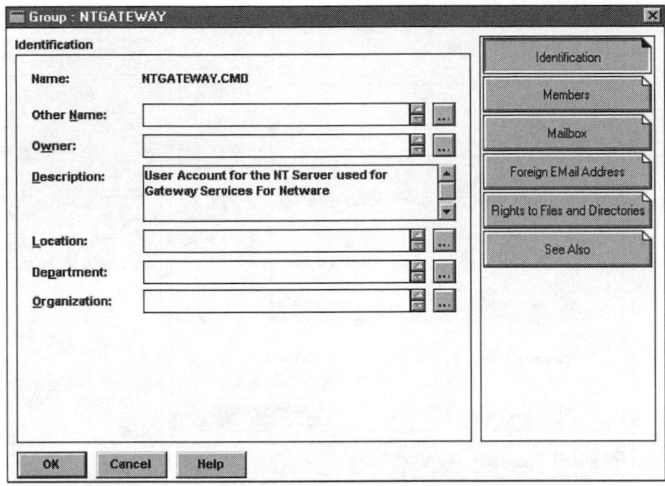

Figure 33.7. Describing the NTGATEWAY group in NWADMIN.

Next, click the Members tab. Here is where you add the Gateway (and Client) Services for NetWare service account to this group (see Figure 33.8).

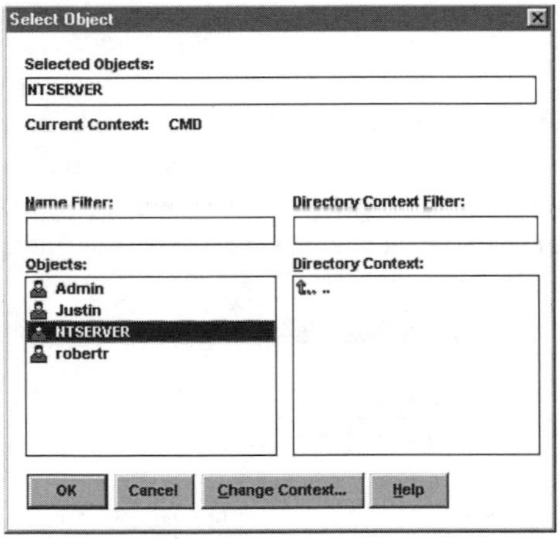

Select Object
Selected Objects:
NTSERVER
Current Context: CMD
Name Filter:
Directory Context Filter:
Objects:
Admin
Justin
NTSERVER
robertr
Directory Context:
OK
Cancel
Change Context...
Help

Figure 33.8. Selecting the Gateway (and Client) Services for NetWare service account for the NTGATEWAY group.

Click the Add button and go through the tree to find the Gateway (and Client) Services for NetWare service account NTSERVER.

Once the Gateway (and Client) Services for NetWare service account has been added to the NTGATEWAY group, scroll down the tabs and click the Rights to Files and Directories tab (see Figure 33.9).

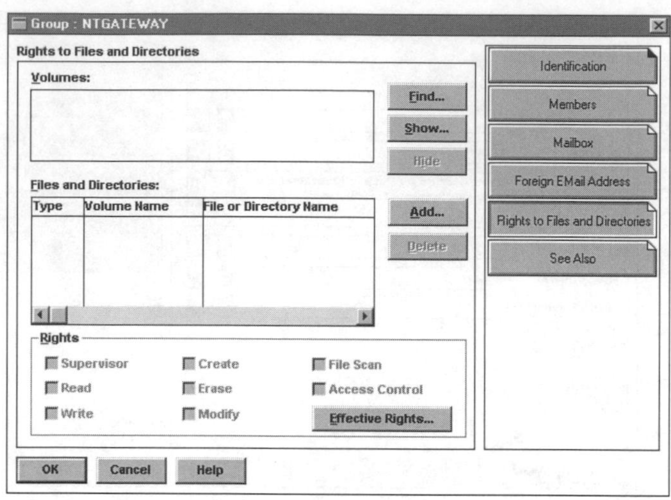

Figure 33.9. *The Rights to Files and Directories page in NWADMIN.*

You can configure the NTGATEWAY group to have as much or as little access to NetWare as you like. Because the users still have access to only the files and directories that their own NetWare accounts have access to, you might want to give Supervisor rights to all the NetWare volumes. You also have the option to assign lesser rights to limit the usage of the Gateway (and Client) Services for NetWare service account.

Click the Add button to find the volumes that are available in the NDS tree. Navigate through the tree, and when you see a volume you want to enable the Gateway (and Client) Services for NetWare service account to access, highlight it, as shown in Figure 33.10, and click the OK button. Continue doing this until you have identified all these volumes.

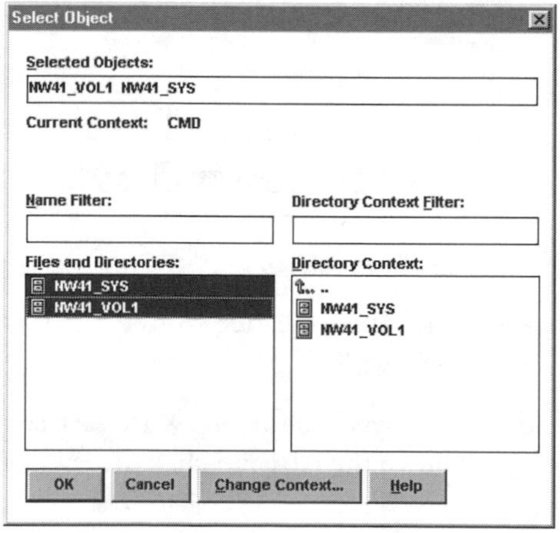

Figure 33.10. *Selecting volumes for the gateway.*

After you have added the last volume you want to make available, highlight each volume and assign the appropriate rights for that volume. To assign Supervisor rights for all the volumes, select all the volumes and click the Supervisor check box (see Figure 33.11).

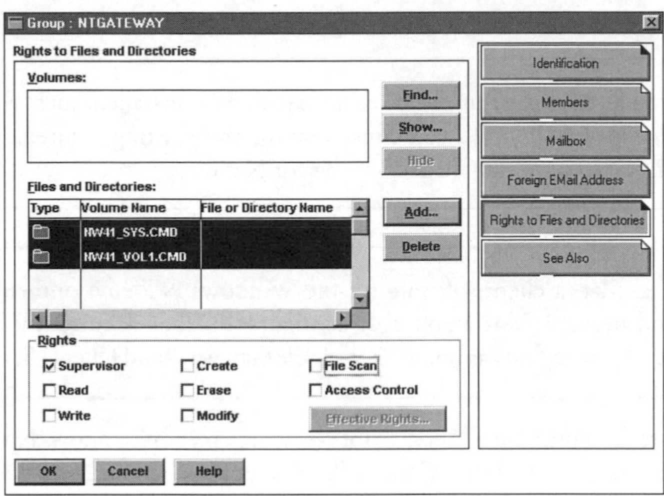

Figure 33.11. *Assigning Supervisor privileges for volumes.*

Once these rights have been set, click the OK button, and your work configuring NetWare is complete (see Figure 33.12).

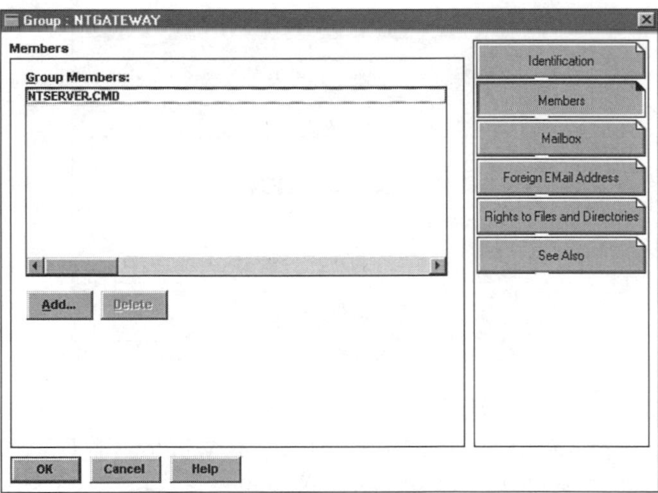

Figure 33.12. *Completing the creation of the NTGATEWAY group.*

Configuring the Windows NT Server

On the Windows NT Server, you need to create a user account that will act as the service account for the Gateway (and Client) Services for NetWare service account. This account must have permission to create shares and a password. The password must be set to never expire.

Note: If you already have another NetWare redirector installed, such as Novell's NetWare Services for Windows NT, you must remove the existing redirector before installing Microsoft's Gateway (and Client) Services for NetWare.

Tip: Novell's latest client software for the Windows NT environment has become very mature and offers a great amount of configuration that is currently not available from Microsoft, although you cannot use it with the Gateway (and Client) Services for NetWare.

To install Gateway (and Client) Services for NetWare on your Windows NT Server, click the Start button, choose Settings, and click Control Panel. Double-click the Network icon. In the Network dialog, click the Services tab. A list of services that have already been installed appears. Click the Add button, and a list of installable services is displayed. This is the Select Network Services dialog.

From the Select Network Service listing, highlight Gateway (and Client) Service for NetWare (see Figure 33.13) and click the OK button.

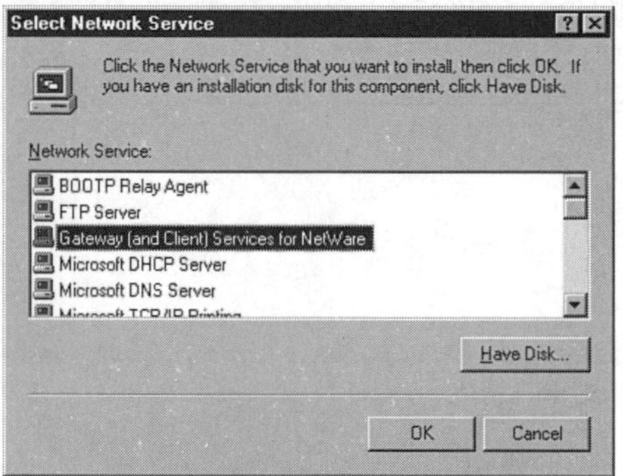

Figure 33.13. *The Select Network Service dialog.*

You are prompted for the location of the Microsoft Windows NT Server CD-ROM, and the appropriate files are copied to the Microsoft Windows NT Server directory. When the copy has completed, Gateway (and Client) Services for NetWare appears on the installed services list. Click the Close button, and you are prompted to restart the server.

If you did not already have the NWLink IPX/SPX–compatible protocol installed, Gateway (and Client) Services for NetWare will automatically install this protocol. If the NWLink IPX/SPX–compatible protocol is installed for you during this process, the NWLink IPX/SPX Properties dialog, shown in Figure 33.14, will prompt you for a network number and a frame type before you are prompted to restart the server.

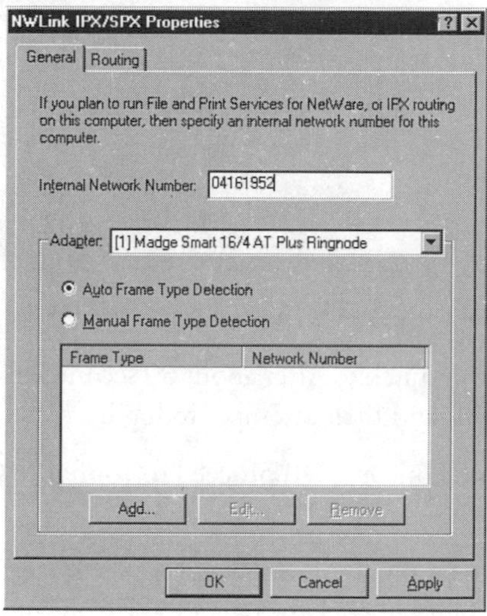

Figure 33.14. *The NWLink IPX/SPX configuration dialog.*

After the server has restarted, the user name used in the local logon must be a valid user on both the Windows NT Server and the NetWare server where Gateway (and Client) Services for NetWare is used. The user name must also have permission to create shares on the Windows NT Server.

After logging on, the Select Preferred Server for NetWare dialog, shown in Figure 33.15, prompts for a server name, if you are connecting to a NetWare 3.*x* server; a NetWare 4.1 server in bindery emulation mode; or a Tree and Context for attaching to an NDS tree on a NetWare 4.*x* server. In this example, I have chosen to use the NDS tree for the login.

Tip: You have the option of choosing to execute a login script when logging on locally, although there really shouldn't be any reason to do that if your only intent is to create a gateway.

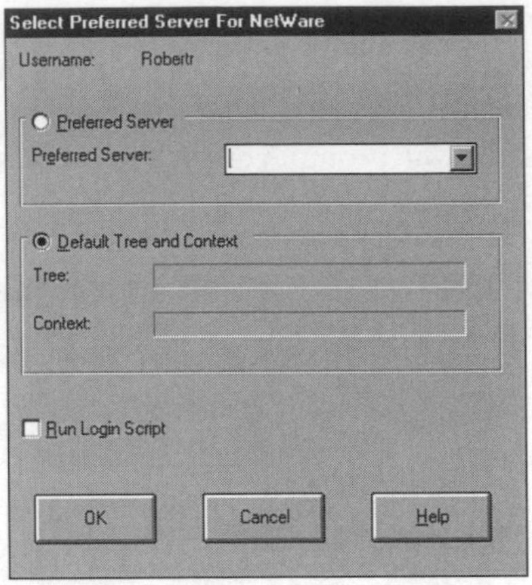

Figure 33.15. The Select Preferred Server For NetWare dialog.

Select your Preferred Server quickly. After about 60 seconds, this dialog times out, logs you on to the Windows NT domain, and then attempts to log in to the first NetWare server found.

Once you have been logged on, you can proceed to configure Gateway (and Client) Services for NetWare.

After you install Gateway (and Client) Services for NetWare, a new icon appears in the Control Panel (see Figure 33.16). Double-click the red GSNW icon, and the Gateway (and Client) Services for NetWare applet appears (see Figure 33.17). You can change your preferred server choice and make printing configuration choices for NetWare here. This configuration information applies only to the username that appears at the top of the dialog.

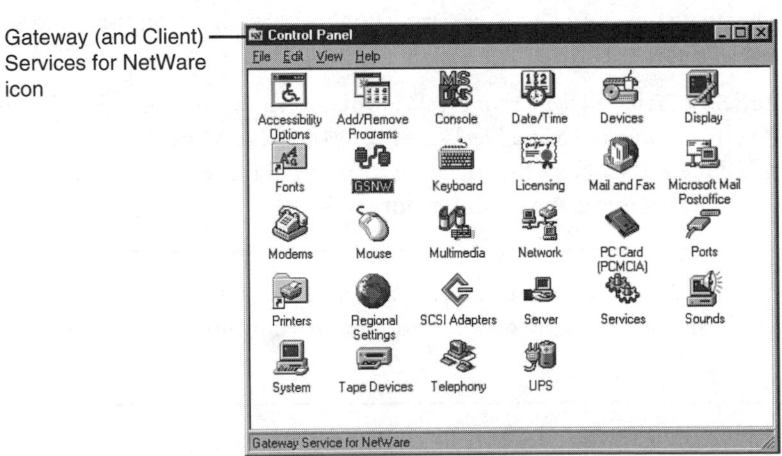

Figure 33.16. The Control Panel with the Gateway (and Client) Services for NetWare icon.

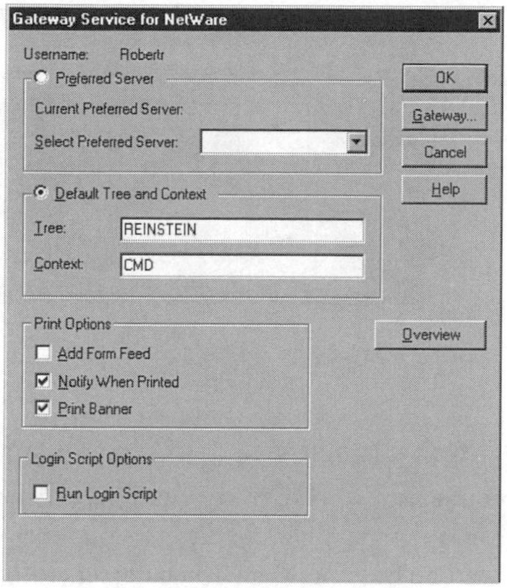

Figure 33.17. The Gateway (and Client) Services for NetWare applet.

By clicking the Gateway button, you enter the Configure Gateway dialog (see Figure 33.18).

The first thing to do in this dialog is check the box that says Enable Gateway, which will enable you to specify the Gateway (and Client) Services for NetWare service account and password defined in NetWare. In Figure 33.18 you see that no shares are defined. These shares are the same type you might already be used to as a Windows NT Server administrator. The main difference is that the shares defined here point to volumes located on a NetWare server.

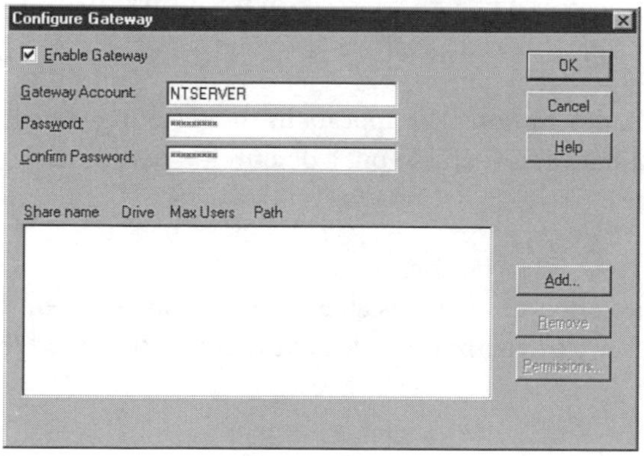

Figure 33.18. The Configure Gateway dialog.

To create shares, click the Add button. The New Share dialog, shown in Figure 33.19, prompts you to enter the following:

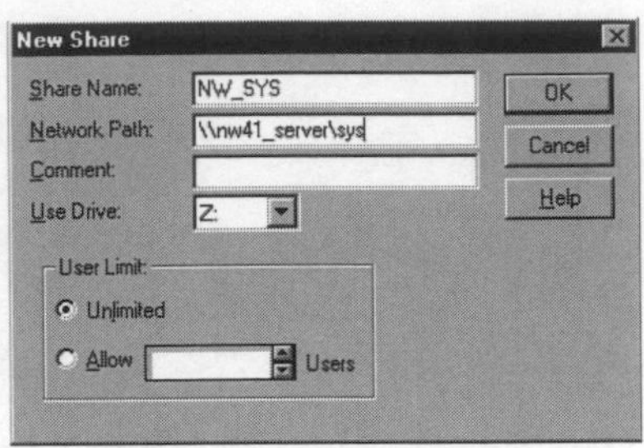

Figure 33.19. *Creating a new share for the Gateway.*

◆ Share Name

As with the usual type of Windows NT Server share, you should enter a name that you want to display to clients in a browse list. MS-DOS workstations cannot access names longer than eight characters. If names are longer than eight characters, you receive a warning, as shown in Figure 33.20. The share name can be no more than 15 characters long.

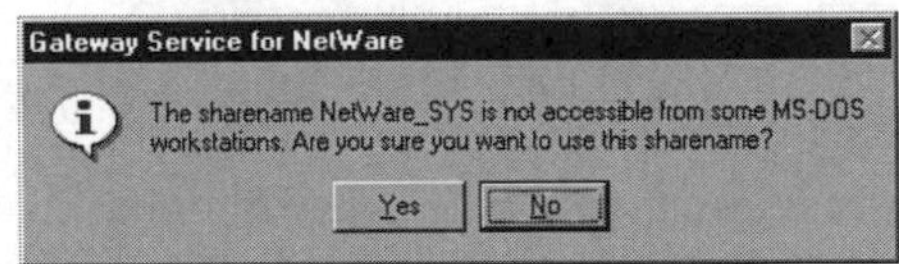

Figure 33.20. *Warning for non-DOS-compatible share names.*

◆ Network Path

Specify the volume to be used for this share using Universal Naming Convention (UNC). In this example, I am pointing to the server named NW41_SERVER and the volume SYS.

◆ Comment

This comment is a description that appears in the resulting list of gateway shares and will be available to your clients. It is useful to put a description here to identify the share to your users as a NetWare volume.

◆ Use Drive

An unused drive letter on the server is chosen for this share. Even though the gateway is active without a local logon, a currently available drive letter must be used to establish the gateway share originally.

◆ User Limit

Enter the maximum number of concurrent connections allowed to access this share. Choose Unlimited to allow unlimited connections.

Click the OK button, and the share will be established.

Tip: You might receive an error message like that shown in Figure 33.21. This is an interesting error message because it does not always mean what it says. You can get this error message if you have incorrectly specified a service account that was not set up properly under NetWare or if you made a typo while entering an account name. In this case, I invoked this error message by attempting to exceed the number of licensed connections available on the NetWare server. Incidentally, an incorrect or mistyped password results in an Incorrect Password message, and an incorrect or mistyped network path gets a Server Not Found or Network Path Not Found message.

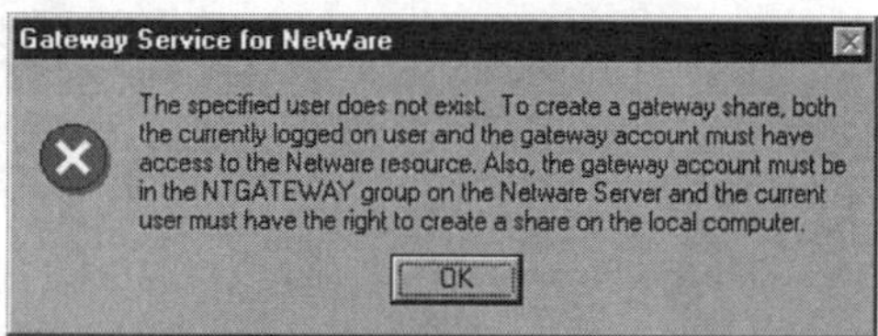

Figure 33.21. *The User Does Not Exist error message.*

If the share was created successfully, the Configure Gateway dialog should now list your newly created share (see Figure 33.22).

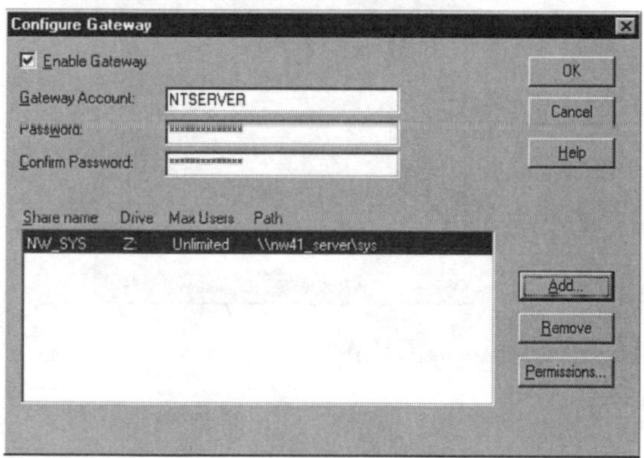

Figure 33.22. *The newly created share.*

Now you can work on setting the permissions for this share. This is an interesting piece of configuring the gateway, because even if a user has full permissions on a NetWare volume, the permissions set on this share can lessen the user's actual permissions. For instance, if I have read and write permission on the `\\NW41_SERVER\SYS` volume and the permission for the `NW_SYS` share gives Full Control to the Everyone group, I am still limited to read and write permissions, as set in NetWare. But if I alter the Gateway Configuration permissions to give the Everyone group only read permission (see Figure 33.23), my access to that volume is now limited to read only.

Furthermore, if I have limited permissions set on the NetWare NTGATEWAY group, the user's permissions cannot exceed the permissions set for that group.

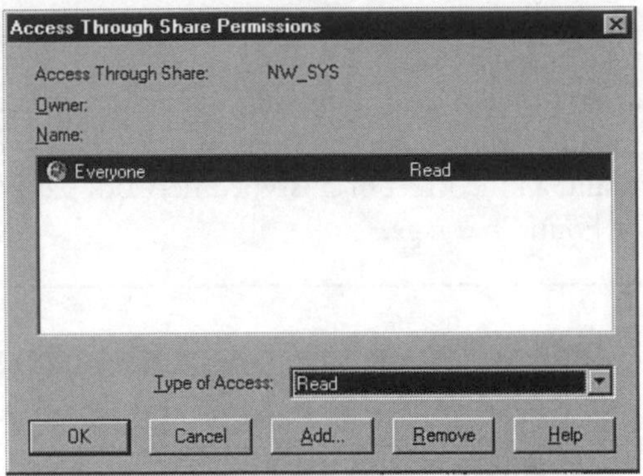

Figure 33.23. *Setting permissions for the new share.*

Click the OK button in the Configure Gateway dialog to make the share available to the network. As shown in Figure 33.24, the share list for SERVER shows `NW_SYS` as one of the shares on that Windows NT Server. Opening up the `NW_SYS` folder shows your standard NetWare SYS volume.

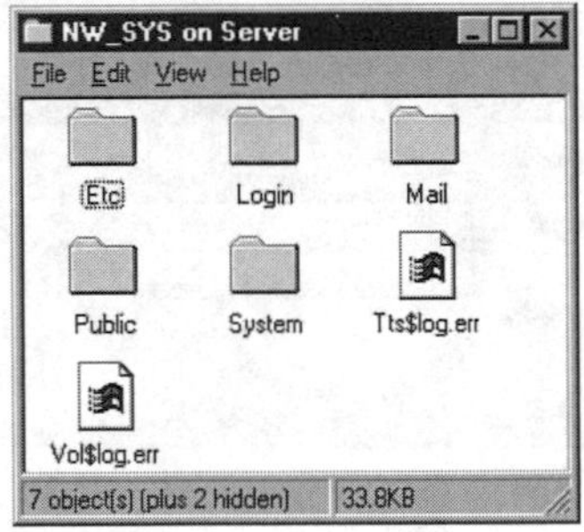

Figure 33.24. *The Gateway share, as seen by a client.*

The Migration Tool for NetWare

Although with Gateway (and Client) Services for NetWare you can integrate Microsoft Windows NT Server and Novell NetWare, with the Migration Tool for NetWare you can upgrade from NetWare to Windows NT. This is done by having both servers on the same network and performing an over-the-wire transfer of administrative information and data.

The Migration Tool for NetWare relies on the existence of a NetWare bindery. The bindery is the database of administrative information used in NetWare 3.*x*.

NetWare 4.*x* uses NDS to hold its data, but there is a Bindery Emulation mode for NetWare 4.*x*. This emulation mode is required if you want to migrate from NetWare 4.*x* to Windows NT using the Migration Tool for NetWare.

Caution: Any branches in the NDS tree that are not in Bindery Emulation mode will not be copied or even recognized by the Migration Tool for NetWare.

Another requirement is that your destination directory on the Windows NT Server must be formatted as NTFS so that Windows NT can take in the security information contained on the NetWare server. If you are migrating files to a FAT volume, all the files and directories will lose their security information.

Of course, you must match hard-drive capacity on the Windows NT Server or have more available so you have enough space to bring over the information you want to migrate.

Caution: Usually, a NetWare server will not be running only the NetWare network operating system but may also be running some utilities such as backup software, anti-virus tools, or communications software. In most cases, the executable program for this software is a NetWare Loadable Module (NLM). NLMs are useless for a Windows NT server and cannot be migrated. Before you fully migrate from NetWare to Windows NT, be sure to purchase Windows NT–compatible replacements for these programs.

In the case of backup software, the backup tapes created from an NLM backup program may not be compatible with a Windows NT backup program. You might want to keep your original NetWare server and backup software available until you are sure that you no longer require it. Once you have migrated to Windows NT, be sure to create a full backup.

Two parts of the NetWare environment cannot translate to a Windows NT domain: login scripts and user account passwords. There is a way to configure the Migration Tool for NetWare to set passwords, but the only way to migrate login scripts is to translate them manually into Windows NT Logon scripts.

See the section, "File and Print Services for NetWare," to learn about an alternate strategy for migrating from a NetWare environment to a Windows NT domain.

Note: Actually, by using the add-on File and Print Services for NetWare, you can bring over and use login scripts on a Windows NT domain. If you plan to use this facility, be sure to also migrate the NetWare Mail directories.

Preparing for the Migration

When you migrate NetWare servers to a Windows NT domain, you can make many choices. If you are migrating a single NetWare server to a Windows NT domain, you will have a relatively easy time. If you are migrating multiple NetWare servers to a single Windows NT domain, you run the risk of duplicate user accounts, groups, and data.

Flowchart 33.2 can help you identify the steps you will require in your migration process.

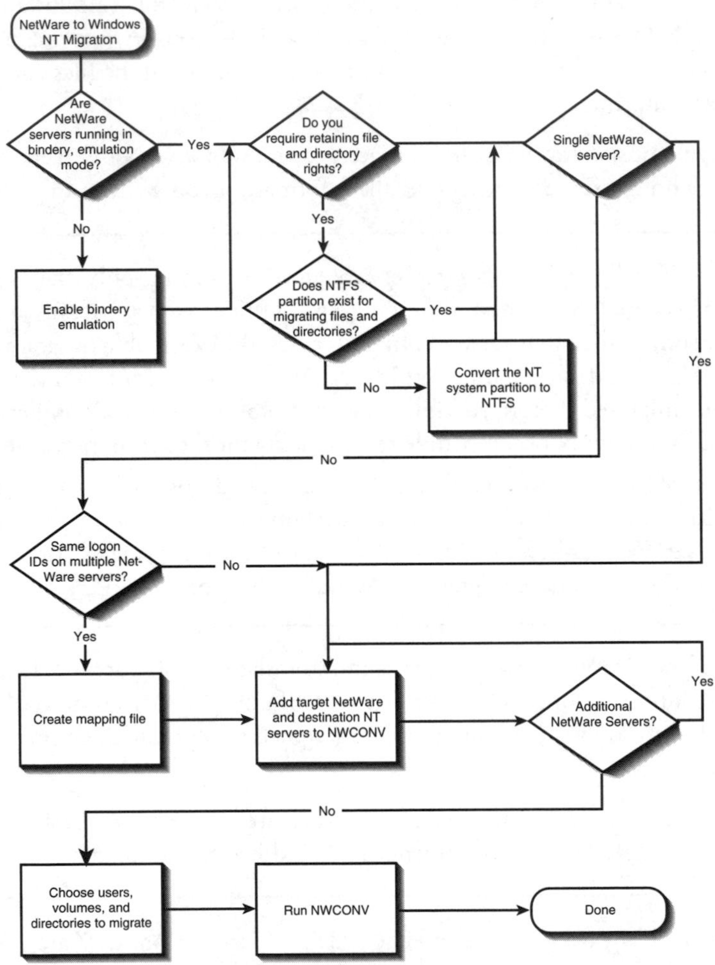

Flowchart 33.2. *NetWare to Windows NT migration flowchart.*

Along the path of setting up the migration, you are given options on how to handle potential problems.

> **Tip:** This is a great time to go through your NetWare servers and weed out unused groups, user accounts, and files. Why deal with these during the migration if you don't need them?

Before you can run the migration utility, you must be logged on to your Windows NT Server as a member of the Administrators group. You also must use a NetWare user account that has supervisory equivalency.

Let's start preparing for the migration by starting the `NWCONV.EXE` program found in the `SYSTEM32` subdirectory in your Windows NT directory.

The Migration Tool for NetWare starts out by displaying the Select Servers For Migration dialog (see Figure 33.25). Click the button next to the From NetWare Server entry field, and the Select NetWare Server dialog is displayed (see Figure 33.26). Highlight the first NetWare server you want to migrate and click the OK button.

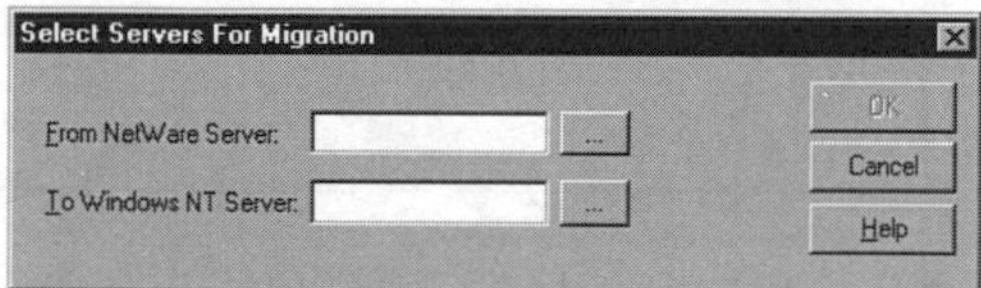

Figure 33.25. The Select Servers For Migration dialog.

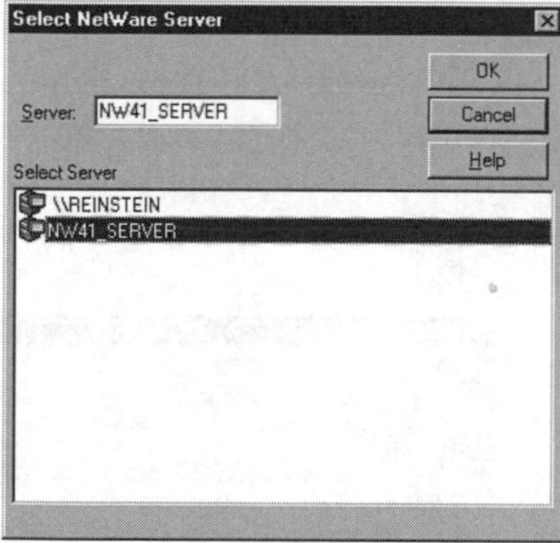

Figure 33.26. The Select NetWare Server dialog.

Next, click the button to the right of the To Windows NT Server entry field to bring up the Select Windows NT Server dialog (see Figure 33.27). After you have selected the destination server, click the OK button to return to the Select Servers For Migration dialog (see Figure 33.28).

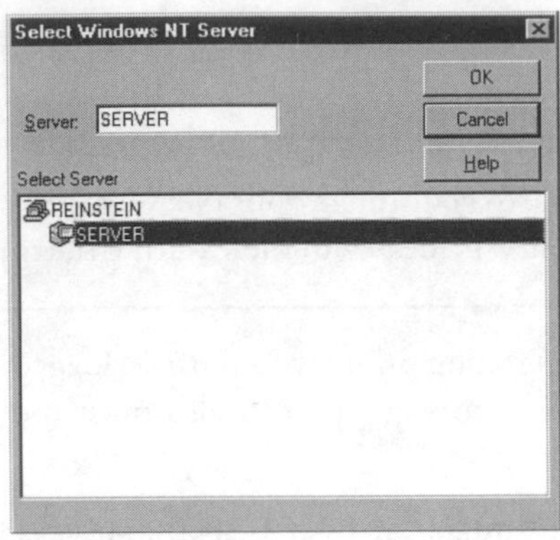

Figure 33.27. The Select Windows NT Server dialog.

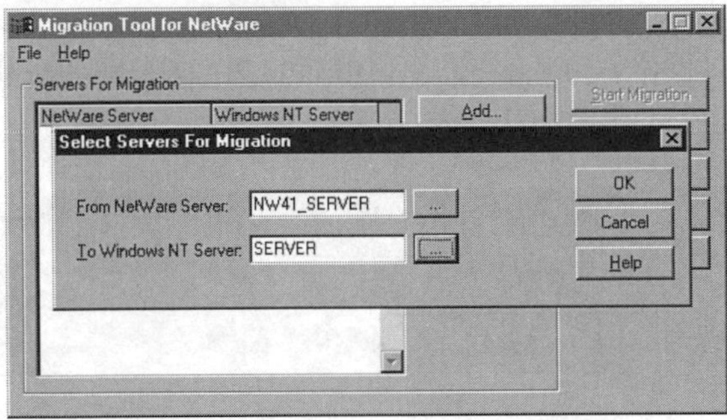

Figure 33.28. The Select Servers For Migration dialog with selection results.

Click the OK button to add the selected set of servers to the main Migration Tool window. If NetWare cannot use your current Windows NT logon name and password, you are prompted for the user account on the NetWare server that gives you full access to the bindery and the volumes (see Figure 33.29). Once you have entered the appropriate information, click the OK button and the pair of servers will appear on the Servers For Migration list (see Figure 33.30).

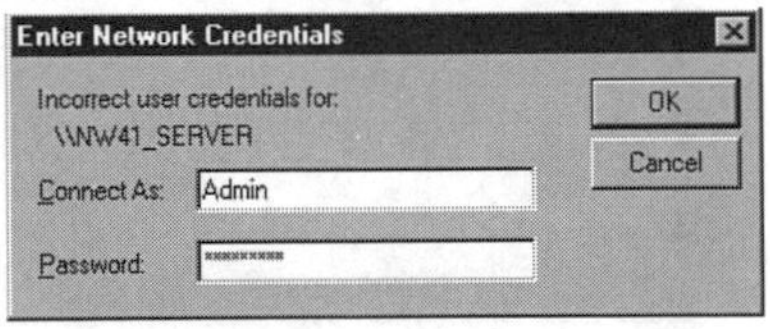

Figure 33.29. The Enter Network Credentials dialog.

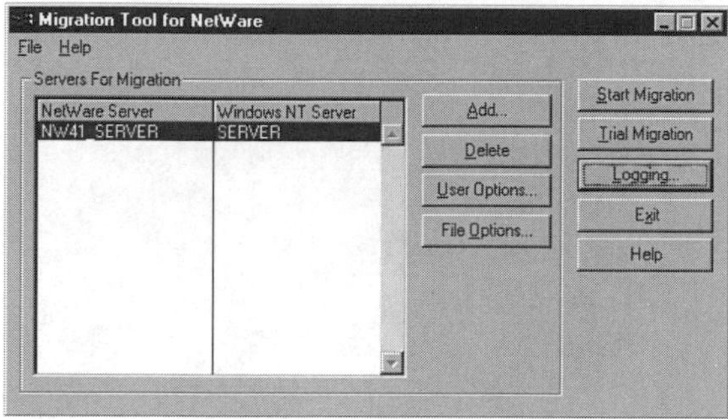

Figure 33.30. *The Servers For Migration list.*

If you want to migrate more NetWare servers, repeat this process until you have identified all the servers you want to migrate to Windows NT.

Tip: Even if you want to migrate more than one server from NetWare, you might want to handle them one at a time so that you don't have to handle several possible conflicts in one shot. A slow migration is sometimes best, although some people opt to perform the entire migration at one fell swoop, just to get it done quickly. Luckily, there is a trial migration mode that can identify these conflicts in advance.

After you have selected all the servers for migration, you can start to configure the different options.

Before you proceed with configuring your migration, you should be aware of some options that are available to you during the configuration process.

With the File menu in the Migration Tool for NetWare main dialog, you can save the currently configured migration. By default, when you exit the Migration Tool for NetWare dialog, all the configuration options you set during the last time you ran the program are saved and brought into the current session. You can also click the File menu and choose Save Configuration to save all the current options to a file with the file extension `.CNF`. You can also restore previously saved settings by choosing Restore Configuration from the File menu. To start the Migration Tool for NetWare with a clean slate, just choose Restore Default Config from the File menu.

Now, back to configuring your migration.

To configure the user and group options, click the User Options button.

With the User and Group Options dialog, shown in Figure 33.31, you can specify whether user accounts and groups will be transferred to the Windows NT domain. If they will be transferred, you can configure how this transfer will be handled.

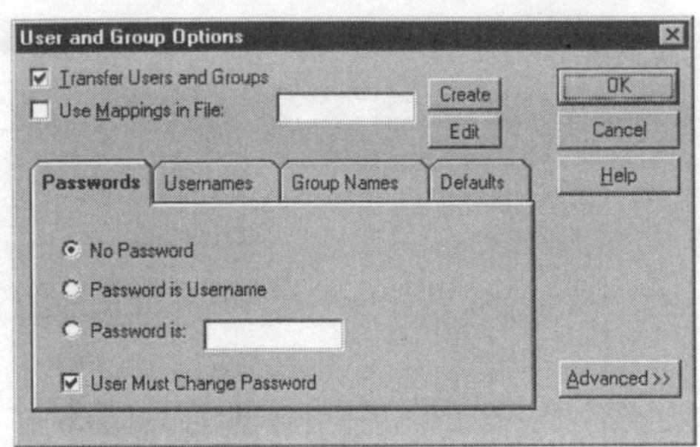

Figure 33.31. *The User and Group Options dialog.*

You can specify whether the passwords for all the migrated users should be blank, set to be the same as their username, or set to a password you specify to be used for all user accounts. You can also specify whether the user is forced to change his or her password the first time he or she logs on to the Windows NT domain.

You can also specify how to handle duplicate usernames during the migration. A duplicate username can occur if a Windows NT account has the same name as a NetWare account or if you are migrating more than one NetWare server to the same Windows NT domain.

Your options are to skip the duplicate username and log an error, skip the duplicate username and ignore the error, add information from the duplicate user to the existing user account, or add a prefix to the duplicate username.

The same options are available for groups, although you cannot add information from the duplicate group to the existing group.

You can also choose to add NetWare users who have Supervisor equivalency to the Windows NT domain's Administrators group.

You also have the choice of overriding all the preceding settings by creating a mapping file. A *mapping file* is a text file with the file extension `.MAP` that tells the Migration Tool exactly how to handle each username and group.

To create a mapping file, click the checkbox in the User and Group Options dialog labeled Use Mappings in File. Then enter the name of the file you would like to create. Do not type in the file extension. In my example, shown in Figure 33.32, I used the name NW2NT for the mapping file. Click the Create button, and the Create Mapping File dialog appears (see Figure 33.33).

In this dialog, choose whether usernames and group names appear in the mapping file. If usernames appear in the mapping file, you can specify whether you want to put a default password into the mapping file. In this example, I opted to include both usernames and groups. I chose to leave the password blank because I want to fill in my own passwords for the users I want to migrate.

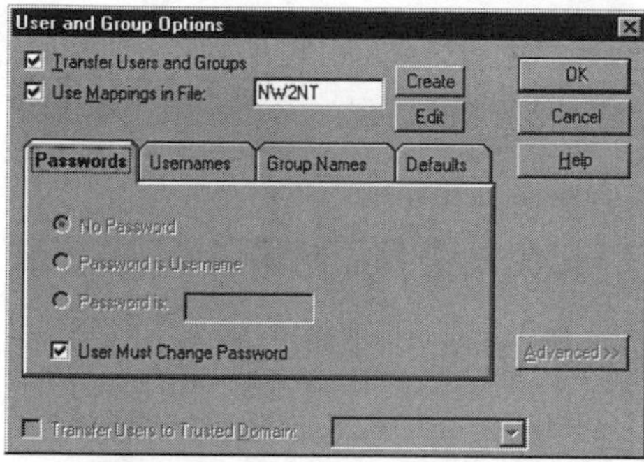

Figure 33.32. Using the User and Group Options dialog to create a mapping file.

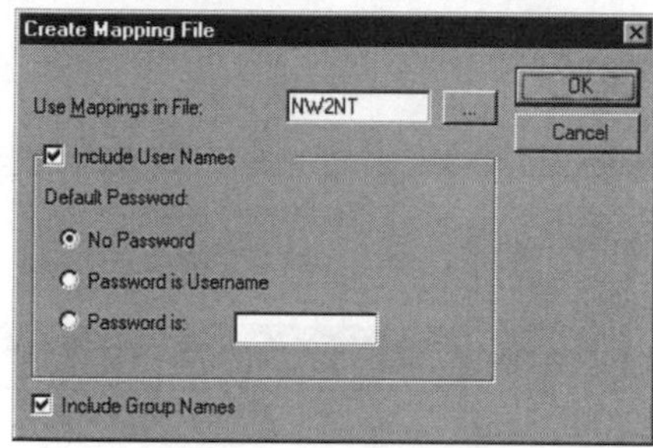

Figure 33.33. The Create Mapping File dialog.

When you have completed these options, click the OK button. A file-creation confirmation box asks whether you want to edit the mapping file (see Figure 33.34). Click Yes to bring your newly created mapping file into Notepad for editing.

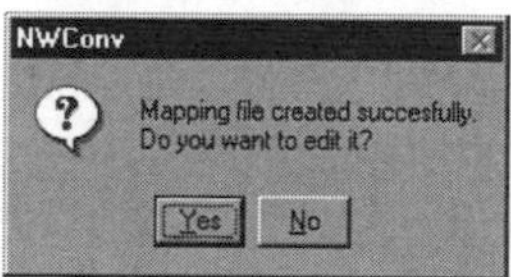

Figure 33.34. Confirming that the mapping file has been created.

In Figure 33.35, you see that the options you chose (in this case, both users and groups) have been brought into this file along with whatever password you have chosen (none in this case). The syntax for the mappings is OldName, NewName, Password.

In Figure 33.36, I changed the NetWare username JUSTIN to JUSTINR for the Windows NT domain account. I also set that account's password to HOME and altered the NetWare KEVIN account and set a password for it. I left the other accounts alone because those accounts already exist in the Windows NT domain and are flagged as duplicated. I decided to leave the group name alone as well. I then saved the mapping by exiting Notepad as I normally would.

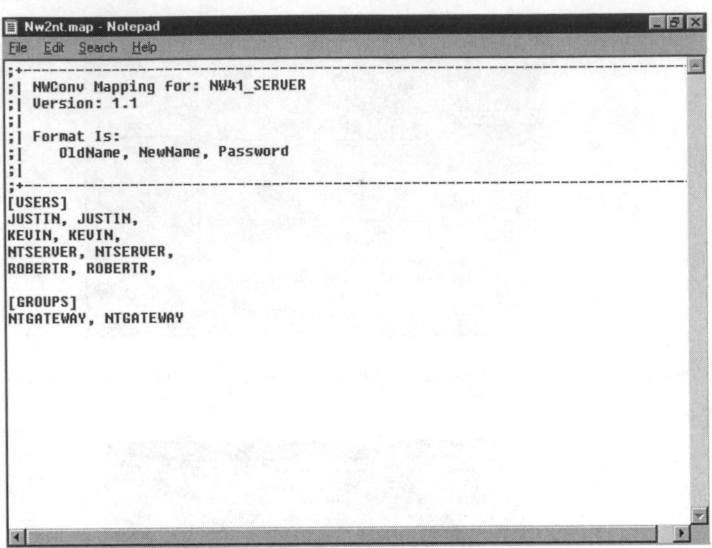

Figure 33.35. *The default mapping file.*

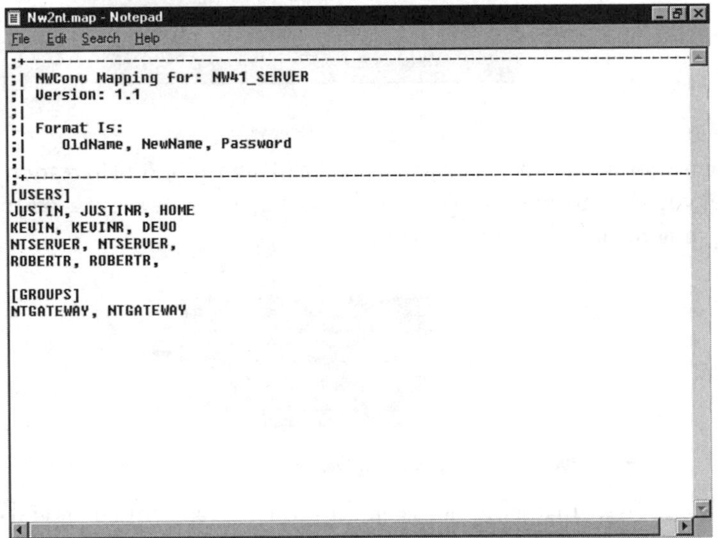

Figure 33.36. *The mapping file after editing.*

The Migration Tool reads the mapping file when either the trial migration or the actual migration is run. It can be altered at any time, even outside the User and Group Options dialog.

Now you are back to the User and Group Options dialog. If your settings here are completed, click the OK button to return to the Migration Tool for NetWare main dialog.

The next area of configuration is the File Options. By clicking the File Options button, you can specify what volumes and files are migrated and what their destinations are.

By default, if you choose to migrate the NetWare volumes, they are copied to the first NTFS partition found in drive letter order. A directory is created with the same name as the volume name, and the share name, by default, is also the volume name. In the example, two volumes are on the NetWare server: SYS and VOL1. You can override this and specify where the files and directories will be copied, but copying them to a FAT partition will cause you to lose all security information for those files and directories.

Also by default, the `\SYSTEM`, `\MAIL`, `\LOGIN`, and `\ETC` directories from the NetWare SYS volume will not be migrated unless you choose them for copying.

In the User and Group Options dialog, click the File Options button to display the File Options dialog (see Figure 33.37), listing the volumes from the selected NetWare server. Your first choice is whether to copy these volumes to the Windows NT Server. Because the default action, which is to migrate the volume, has been left unchanged, the NetWare volumes are listed, and now the specific configuration options can be specified.

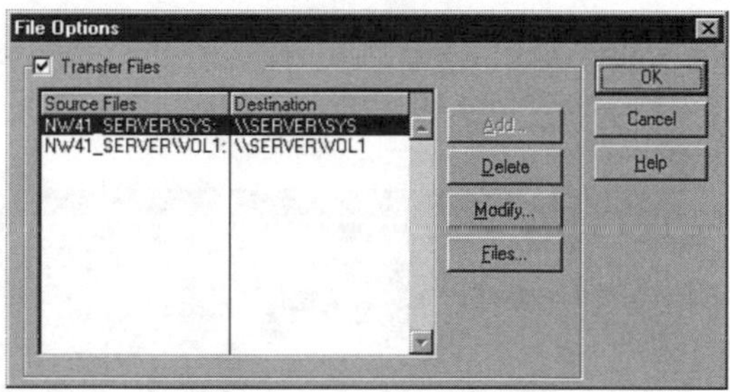

Figure 33.37. *The File Options dialog.*

As shown in the Destination column, the shares that are created are the same names as the volumes. This is the default option, which you can override. You can also choose to remove one or both volumes from the list by highlighting the volume and clicking the Delete button. I wanted to change the destination of the SYS volume, so I highlighted the SYS volume and clicked the Modify button.

The Modify Destination dialog, shown in Figure 33.38, gives you the option to change the share name and/or the destination directory for the selected volume. I wanted to change both of these, so I clicked the New Share button.

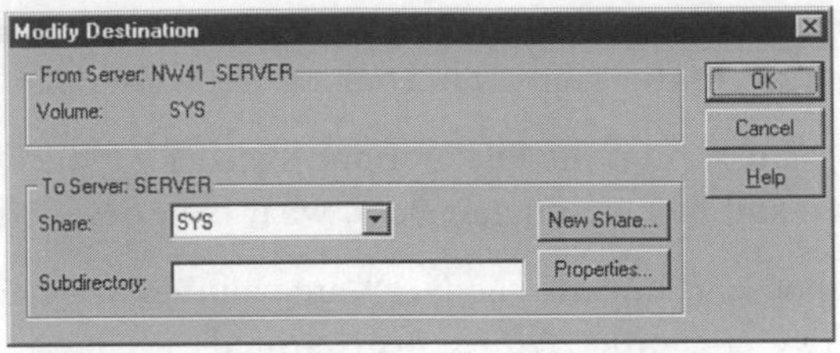

Figure 33.38. The Modify Destination dialog.

The resulting dialog, shown in Figure 33.39, enabled me to type in the share name I want to use, which is NW_SYS. I also changed the default migration directory, which was `D:\SYS`, because my C drive is formatted as FAT, to a directory of my choosing on the E drive, named Old NetWare SYS Volume.

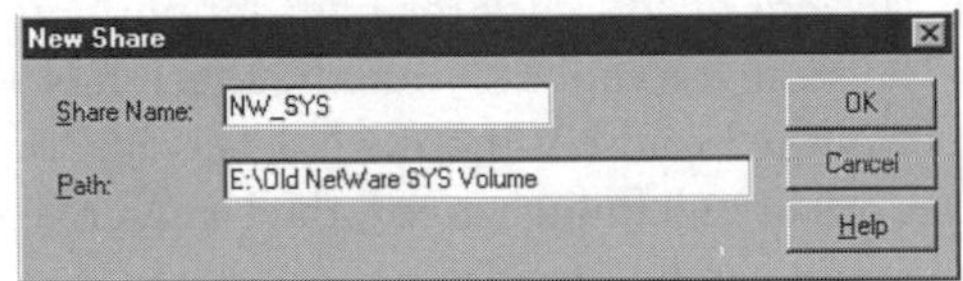

Figure 33.39. The New Share dialog.

After you click the OK button, the File Options dialog is displayed, with the new information reflected in the Destination column (see Figure 33.40).

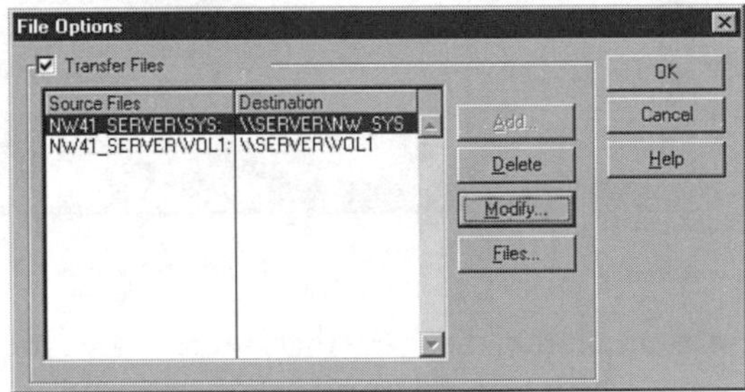

Figure 33.40. File Options after changing the destination share.

By clicking the Files button, you can choose individual files and directories contained on the volume that you want to migrate. As shown in Figure 33.41, by default the Files to Transfer dialog selects most of the non-NetWare-specific files and directories to be migrated. It is up to you to check the unchecked boxes next to the items the Migration Tool has automatically chosen to omit or to uncheck the boxes of the files or directories you don't want to migrate. If the migrated files are going to be copied to an NTFS partition, most of the file attributes will travel along with them.

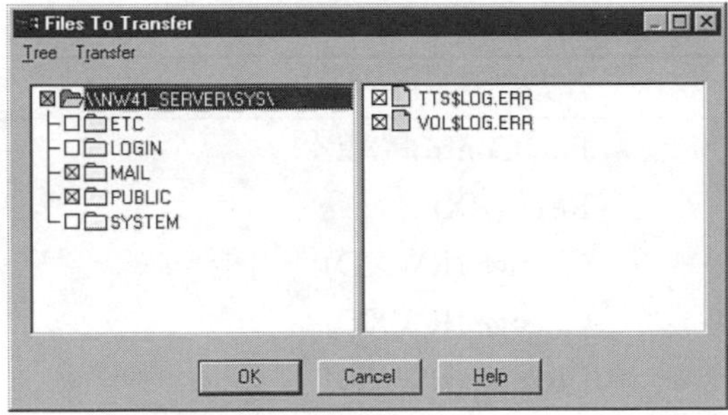

Figure 33.41. *The Files To Transfer dialog.*

Note: Hidden and system files are not migrated by default. In the Files to Transfer dialog (see Figure 33.41), click the Transfer menu and choose Hidden Files to transfer all hidden files in the directories selected for transfer. To migrate system files, click the Transfer menu and choose System Files to transfer all system files in the directories selected for transfer.

The actual translation methods of file and directory attributes are shown in Tables 33.1, 33.2, and 33.3.

The effective rights for a directory are translated to the NTFS permissions shown in Table 33.1.

Table 33.1. Directory rights translation.

NetWare Directory Rights	*NTFS Directory Permissions*
Supervisory (S)	Full Control (All) (All)
Read (R)	Read (RX) (RX)
Write (W)	Change (RWXD) (RWXD)
Create (C)	Add (WX) (not specified)
Erase (E)	Change (RWXD) (RWXD)
Modify (M)	Change (RWXD) (RWXD)
File Scan (F)	List (RX) (not specified)
Access Control (A)	Change Permissions (P)

The effective rights for a file are translated to the NTFS permissions shown in Table 33.2.

Table 33.2. File access rights translation.

NetWare File Rights	*NTFS File Permissions*
Supervisory (S)	Full Control (All)
Read (R)	Read (RX)
Write (W)	Change (RWXD)
Erase (E)	Change (RWXD)
Modify (M)	Change (RWXD)
Access Control (A)	Change Permissions (P)

Note: The Create (C) and File Scan (F) rights are ignored when files are transferred.

NetWare file attributes are translated to the NTFS file attributes shown in Table 33.3.

Table 33.3. File attributes translation.

NetWare File Attributes	*NTFS File Attributes*
Read Only (Ro)	Read Only (R)
Delete Inhibit (D)	Read Only (R)
Rename Inhibit (R)	Read Only (R)
Archive Needed (A)	Archive (A)
System (SY)	System (S)
Hidden (H)	Hidden (H)
Read Write (Rw)	None, because files without the R attribute can be read and written to

The following NetWare file attributes are not supported by NTFS and are therefore ignored: Copy Inhibit (C), Execute Only (X), Indexed (I), Purge (P), Read Audit (Ra), Shareable (SH), Transactional (T), and Write Audit (Wa).

After you have set the options for the first volume, repeat the procedure for all the other volumes from the NetWare server you are migrating.

When you have completed all the file and directory options, click the OK button to return to the Migration Tool for NetWare main dialog.

You now can choose the logging options for your migration. Click the Logging button to display the Logging dialog (see Figure 33.42), with which you can turn on or off three options.

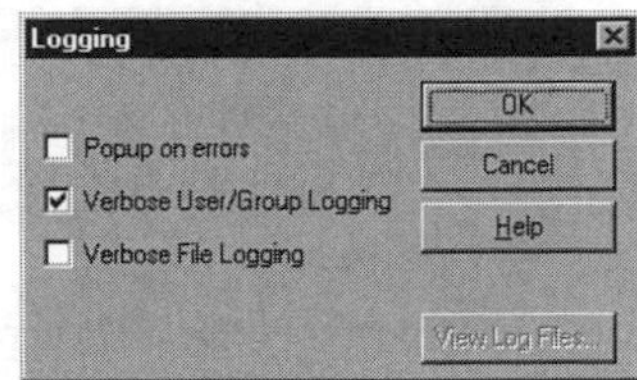

Figure 33.42. *The Logging dialog.*

With the first option, Popup on Errors, choose whether you want to display a message whenever an error situation has been encountered. If you are running a trial migration, which simply creates a log and does not actually perform the migration, you might want to turn off this option. The intent is to run a trial migration and then make changes based on the error log.

The second option, Verbose User/Group Logging, gives you the option to explicitly log every translation performed on users and groups. If you require a complete record of the migration, turn on this option by checking the box.

The third option, Verbose File Logging, gives you a list of each file and directory that has been transferred from the NetWare volume to the Windows NT Server. Again, if you require a complete log of your migration, turn this on by checking the box.

Regardless of which options you choose, all errors are placed in an error log.

Starting the Migration

You are now ready to perform your migration, but you have the option of performing a trial migration first. This trial puts the Migration Tool for NetWare through the motions of an actual migration using the options you have specified without actually migrating users, groups, or volumes.

Kick off the trial migration by clicking the Trial Migration button. As shown in Figure 33.43, the migration is performed just as if it were the real migration. Users, files, and directories are examined. If any contentions are found, the Migration Tool reacts according to however the options have been configured. Figure 33.44 shows one such error, where a duplicate username has been encountered. Here you are given the choice to manually give that user a new name (and then click the OK button to continue), abort the entire procedure, or cancel the migration of this particular user.

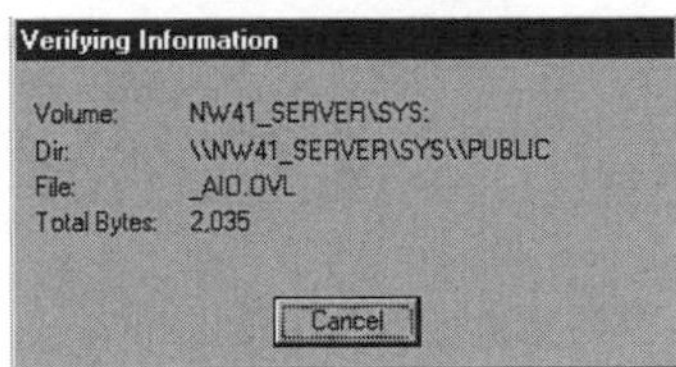

Figure 33.43. *A trial migration in the works.*

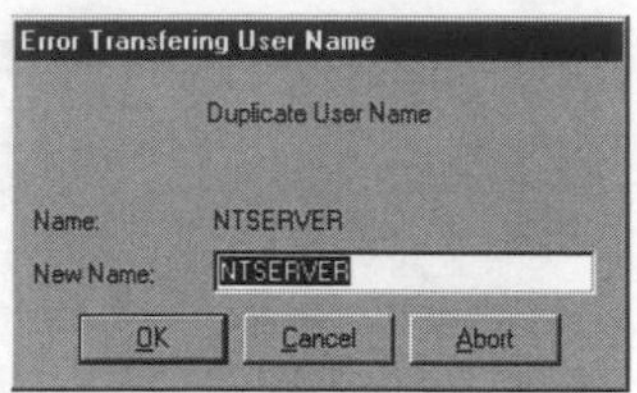

Figure 33.44. *An error with transferring a username.*

When the trial migration is complete, you are notified in exactly the same way you would be if this were the real migration. A summary of the migration gives you the vital statistics (see Figure 33.45). You can also choose to view the three log files in an application called LogView (see Figure 33.46).

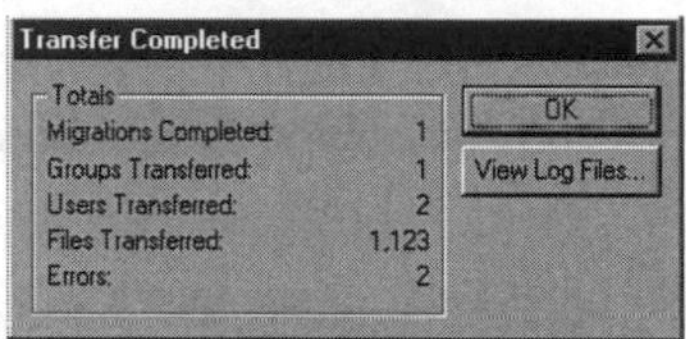

Figure 33.45. *Trial migration has completed.*

```
LogFile.LOG
[Servers]
   From: NW41_SERVER     To: SERVER

;+-------------------------------------------
;| Server Information
;+-------------------------------------------

[SERVER]
   Windows NT(R) Server
   Version: 4.0
```

Figure 33.46. *The LogView application.*

The `LogFile.LOG` (see Figure 33.47) is where you find detailed information about the actual conversions that have occurred. If you have chosen Verbose File Logging, this is where you will find it.

The `Summary.LOG` (see Figure 33.48) gives you a brief account of what translations have been completed.

The `Error.LOG` (see Figure 33.49) shows you what went wrong in the translation process.

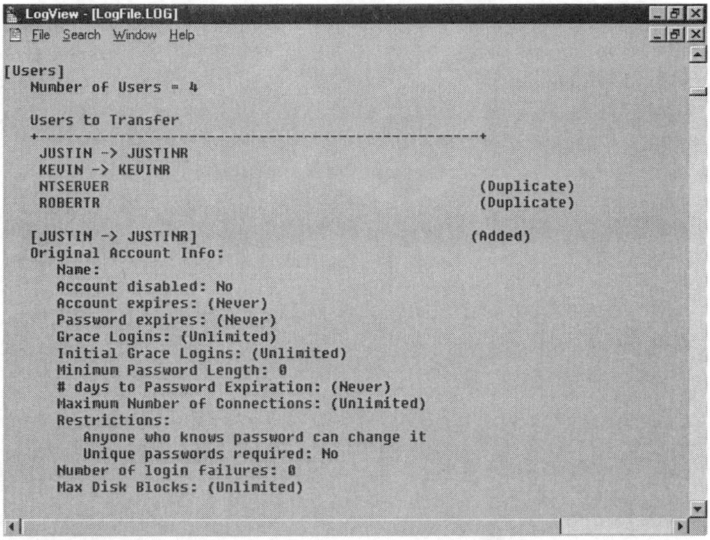

```
LogView - [LogFile.LOG]
File  Search  Window  Help

[Users]
   Number of Users = 4

   Users to Transfer
   +---------------------------------------------------+
    JUSTIN -> JUSTINR
    KEVIN -> KEVINR
    NTSERVER                                           (Duplicate)
    ROBERTR                                            (Duplicate)

   [JUSTIN -> JUSTINR]                                (Added)
   Original Account Info:
      Name:
      Account disabled: No
      Account expires: (Never)
      Password expires: (Never)
      Grace Logins: (Unlimited)
      Initial Grace Logins: (Unlimited)
      Minimum Password Length: 0
      # days to Password Expiration: (Never)
      Maximum Number of Connections: (Unlimited)
      Restrictions:
         Anyone who knows password can change it
         Unique passwords required: No
      Number of login failures: 0
      Max Disk Blocks: (Unlimited)
```

Figure 33.47. *The* `LogFile.LOG` *file.*

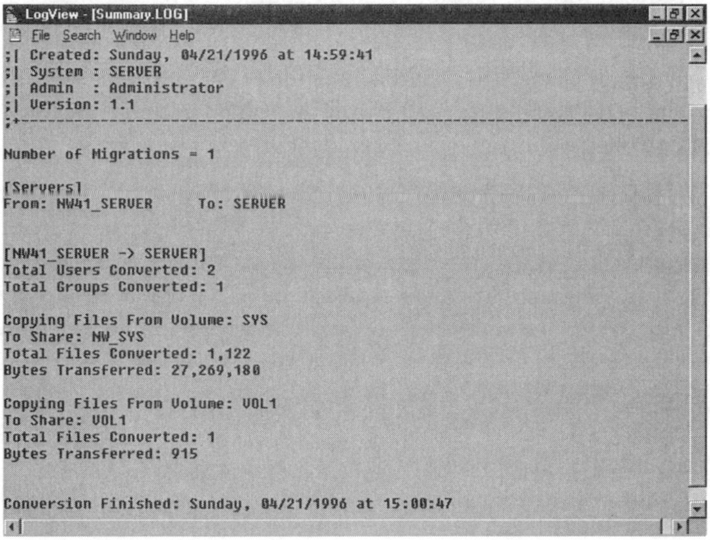

```
LogView - [Summary.LOG]
File  Search  Window  Help
;| Created: Sunday, 04/21/1996 at 14:59:41
;| System : SERVER
;| Admin  : Administrator
;| Version: 1.1
;+---------------------------------------------------------------------

Number of Migrations = 1

[Servers]
From: NW41_SERVER     To: SERVER


[NW41_SERVER -> SERVER]
Total Users Converted: 2
Total Groups Converted: 1

Copying Files From Volume: SYS
To Share: NW_SYS
Total Files Converted: 1,122
Bytes Transferred: 27,269,180

Copying Files From Volume: VOL1
To Share: VOL1
Total Files Converted: 1
Bytes Transferred: 915


Conversion Finished: Sunday, 04/21/1996 at 15:00:47
```

Figure 33.48. *The* `Summary.LOG` *file.*

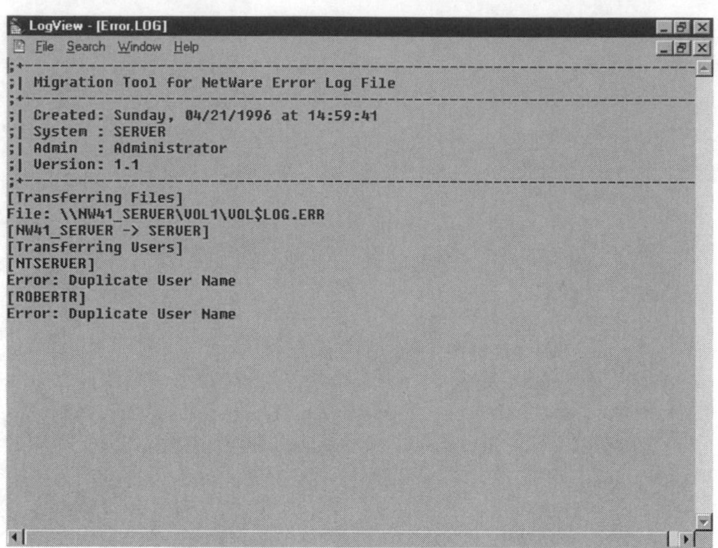

Figure 33.49. *The* `Error.LOG` *file.*

Before you proceed with the actual migration, you should review these logs and make sure that what you are about to do is the right thing. The migration cannot be reversed.

After you have made changes to your mapping file or changed some of the logging options, you might feel comfortable with proceeding with the real migration. When you are ready, click the Start Migration button and you will see exactly what you saw when you tried the trial migration. This time, though, it's for real.

As you can see in Figure 33.50, the NetWare user JUSTIN has been transferred to the Windows NT domain as JUSTINR. As you might recall, this transformation was dictated by the mapping file `NW2NT.MAP`. In the group listing, you can see the NTGATEWAY group that had been set up on the NetWare server to enable Gateway (and Client) Services for NetWare to function. Figure 33.51 shows the NetWare to Windows NT translated NTGATEWAY group, which has retained its only member: NTSERVER.

In Figure 33.52, you can see the new directory from the Windows NT Server's E: drive called Old NetWare SYS Volume. This translation was also configured through the use of the `NW2NT.MAP` mapping file.

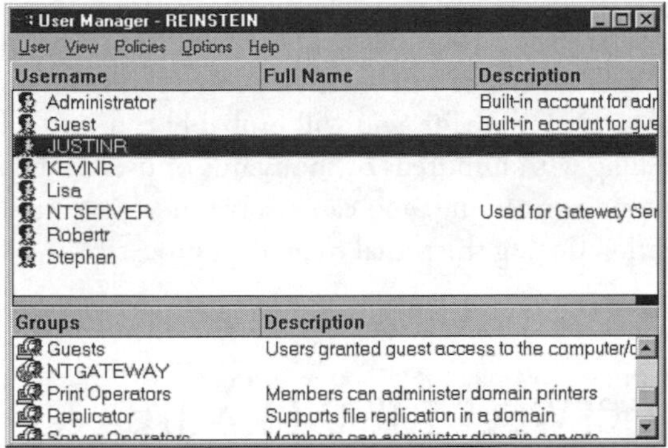

Figure 33.50. *User administrator for domains with a newly migrated NetWare user.*

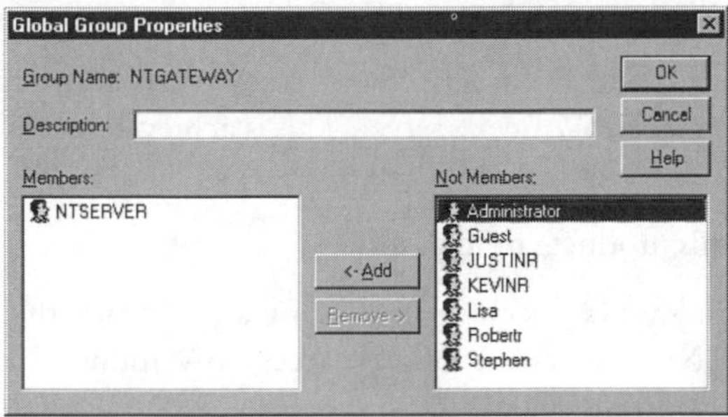

Figure 33.51. *A NetWare group after migration to Windows NT.*

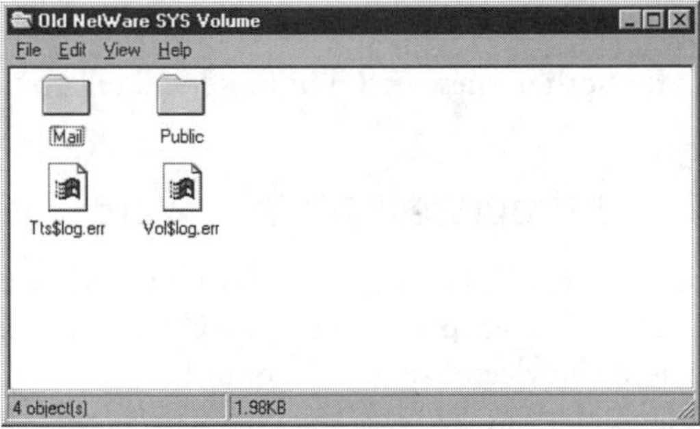

Figure 33.52. *A NetWare SYS volume after migration to Windows NT.*

Tip: A mapping file is a very powerful way to run a NetWare migration without errors and with the result looking exactly as you want. When you migrate multiple NetWare servers over to one Windows NT domain, you will probably run into a lot of naming conflicts. Unless you are dealing with hundreds or thousands of users, which might make editing a mapping file too time-consuming, you can resolve most conflicts without having to deal with user intervention during the actual migration process.

File and Print Services for NetWare

Microsoft produces a tool that can be very helpful for easing NetWare–to–Windows NT migrations: File and Print Services for NetWare. This exceptional product is available separately from the Microsoft Windows NT Server 4.0 product.

The basic premise of File and Print Services for NetWare is allowing a Windows NT server to appear to the network as a NetWare 3.*x* server. This is achieved by adding a service to a Windows NT server that emulates a NetWare bindery.

Two major uses for this product come to mind.

One is allowing a Windows NT server to coexist on a predominantly NetWare network, giving workstations running NetWare client software access to Windows NT resources without having to run a Microsoft networking client.

Another use for File and Print Services for NetWare would be to ease a migration from NetWare to Windows NT by making the Windows NT server emulate an existing NetWare server, making a switch from NetWare to Windows NT transparent to the end user.

I will discuss scenarios for both of these uses, but first I will tell you about installing the service.

Installing File and Print Services for NetWare

Installing File and Print Services for NetWare is the same as adding any other network service to Windows NT Server. Open the network applet in the Control Panel, and click the Services tab. Click the Add button in the Services dialog. A list of installable services is shown in the resulting dialog, but because File and Print Services for NetWare is not supplied with the Microsoft Windows NT Server product, click the Have Disk... button. As shown in Figure 33.53, you will be prompted for the location of File and Print Services for NetWare installation files. Enter the proper path and click the OK button.

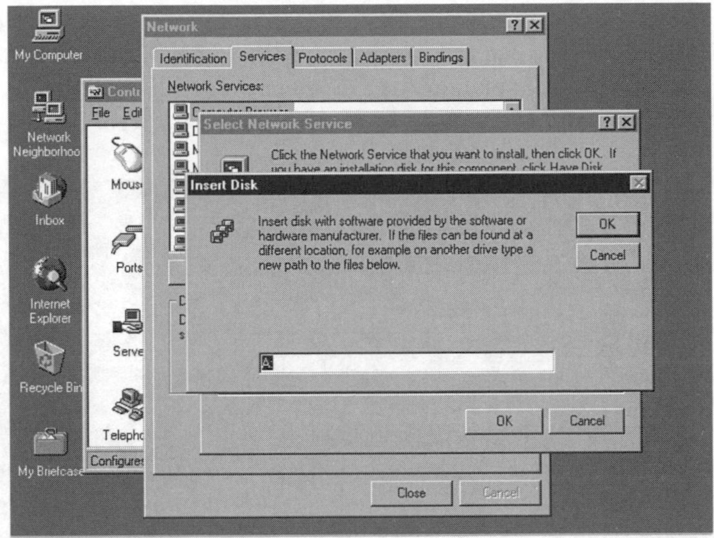

Figure 33.53. *Selecting a Source Path.*

You now have the option to install the File and Print Services for NetWare service and administrative tools or only the administrative tools. In Figure 33.54, I have chosen to install the File and Print Services for NetWare service and administrative tools. You would install only the administrative tools if you already have this service running on another server in the same domain and want to add the File and Print Services for NetWare extensions to User Manager for Domains and Server Manager.

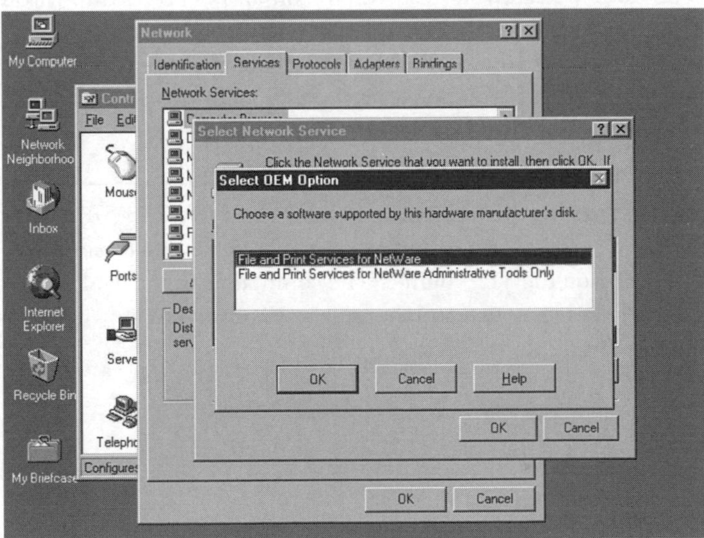

Figure 33.54. *File and Print Services for NetWare install options.*

After you copy the files, the installation dialog for File and Print Services for NetWare (see Figure 33.55) is displayed. It is here that you can give your pseudo-NetWare server a name, and you need to define a path for your SYS volume. The SYS volume on a File and Print Services for NetWare server will resemble the SYS volume on an actual NetWare 3.*x* server.

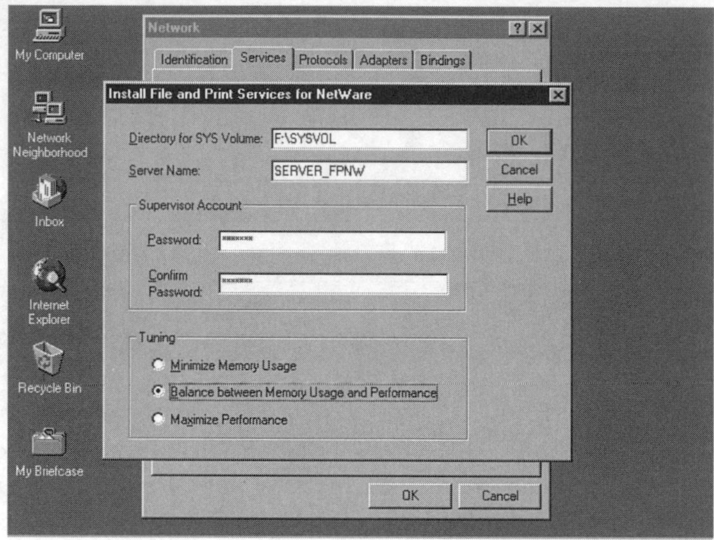

Figure 33.55. *Install for File and Print Services for NetWare.*

Note: If you do not create your SYS volume on an NTFS partition, you will receive the message shown in Figure 33.56. For you to be able to place permissions on the SYS volume in the same manner that you would on an actual NetWare server, the NTFS file attributes are absolutely necessary. If you do create the SYS volume on a FAT partition, you will be limited to assigning only Read or Read/Write permissions.

The directory structure for the SYS volume, shown in Figure 33.57 as the directory SYSVOL, contains the `login`, `system`, `mail`, and `public` directories that NetWare administrators are accustomed to seeing on the SYS volume. The commands in the `public` directory are Microsoft versions of the familiar NetWare commands. These commands are 100% compatible with their NetWare counterparts.

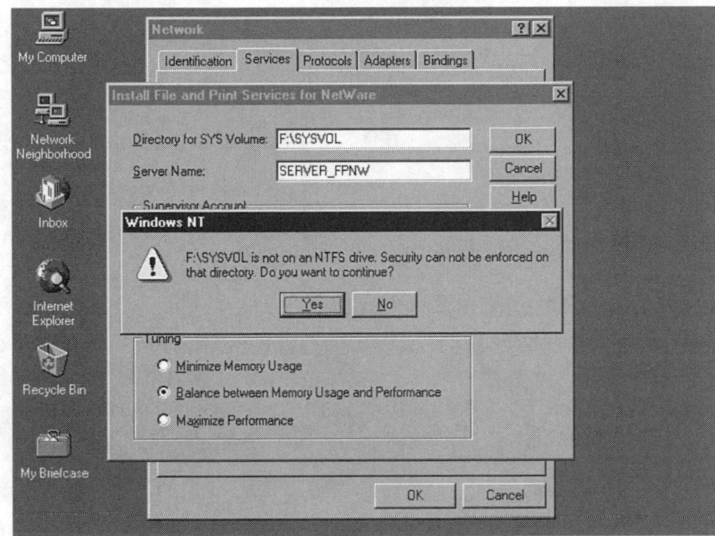

Figure 33.56. *The NetWare SYS volume should be placed on an NTFS drive.*

When the File and Print Services for NetWare service was installed, a Supervisor account was created for the Windows NT domain. This account is automatically added to the Administrators group. In this configuration dialog, you define the password for the Supervisor user account. You can also fine-tune the service by choosing the amount of resources to be used to handle this service.

After you have finished installing File and Print Services for NetWare, you are prompted to enter a password for the service account that will be created and used for File and Print Services for NetWare (see Figure 33.58). Enter the password twice and click the OK button to finalize the installation of File and Print Services for NetWare. The newly installed service will now appear in the list of installed services along with the SAP service that has also been automatically installed. Click the Close button and you will be prompted to restart the Windows NT server. Click the Yes button and your server will shut down and restart. When the server reboots, the File and Print Services for NetWare service will be active.

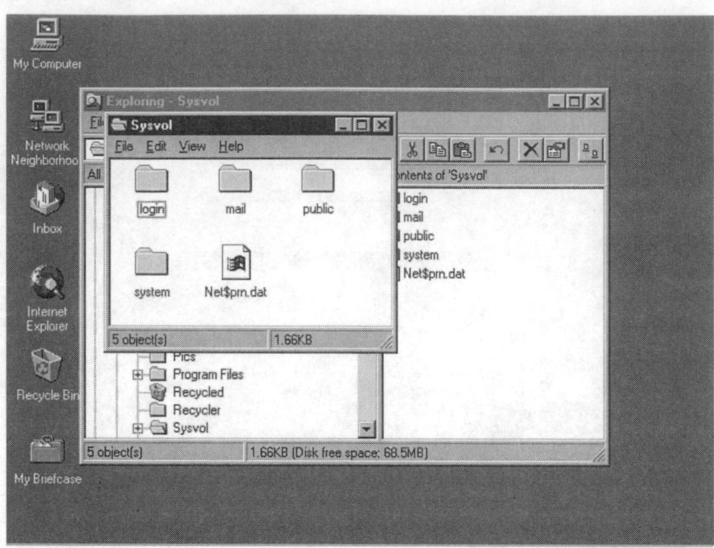

Figure 33.57. The File and Print Services for NetWare SYS volume structure.

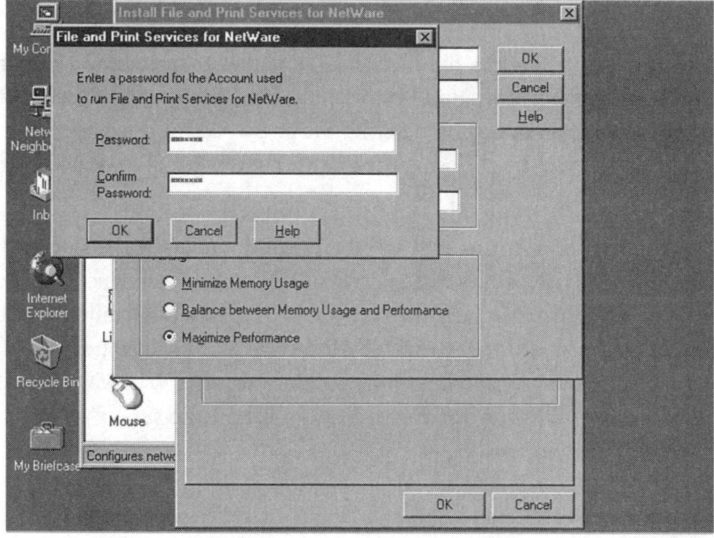

Figure 33.58. Setting the password for the File and Print Services for NetWare Service account.

You can test the service by running the NetWare `SLIST` command from any NetWare client workstation. The Windows NT server will appear on the list of NetWare servers, using the server name that you specified in the installation dialog.

File and Print Services for NetWare Extensions

Both User Manager and Server Manager will have new menu items that can help you administer the NetWare-compatible facilities that File and Print Services for NetWare has given your Windows NT server. With these extensions, you can perform tasks that are available through User Manager and Server Manager, although with these extensions, you can treat NetWare-compatible users as if they are logging into a separate NetWare server. We will explore this in the next section, "Configuring File and Print Services for NetWare."

Configuring File and Print Services for NetWare

A new icon will appear in the Windows NT Control Panel (see Figure 33.59). Double-click the File and Print Services for NetWare icon to bring up the File and Print Services for NetWare applet. In this applet (Figure 33.60), you can change the server name, define the server as an "open system," and define whether you want clients who have not specified a preferred server in their `NET.CFG` file to be allowed to log in to the pseudo-NetWare server. You can also gain access to the User Manager and Server Manager extensions that are also available through those administrative tools.

Figure 33.59. *The FPNW icon in Control Panel.*

The User Manager for Domains extensions, shown in Figure 33.61, add a check box with which you can specify whether a user account will maintain a NetWare-compatible login. If this box is checked, you have access to the NW Compat button. Click the NW Compat button to bring up the NetWare Compatible Properties dialog (see Figure 33.62). Here you can set attributes for a user account that are not available for native Windows NT clients but are found on genuine NetWare administration tools. This includes limiting the number of concurrent connections for a user and editing a login script. The login script for a NetWare-compatible user uses the same syntax that is used on NetWare servers for login scripts.

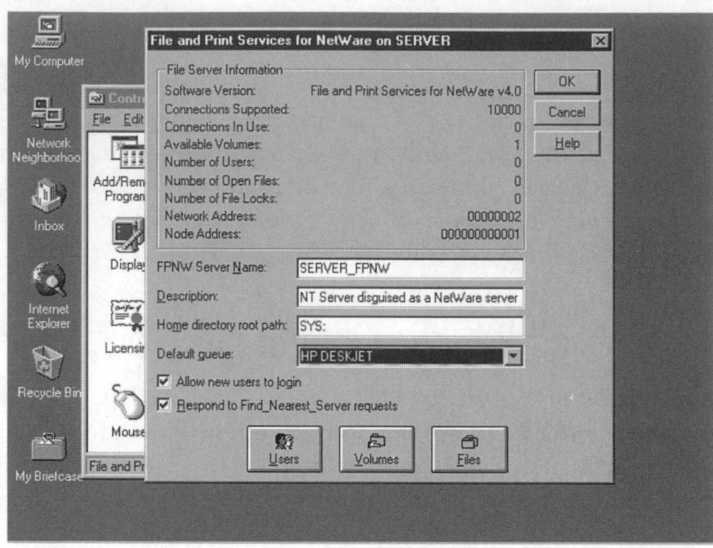

Figure 33.60. *The File and Print Services for NetWare applet.*

Note: For users running Windows NT Workstation who want to administer File and Print Services for NetWare running on a Windows NT server, you must copy the version of Server Manager that File and Print Services for NetWare installed from the Windows NT server to the Windows NT workstation.

New to NT 4.0: The Client-based Server Tools, which include a version of User Manager for Domains for Windows 95, will not automatically be updated with the User Manager for Domains extensions for File and Print Services for NetWare. The File and Print Services for NetWare package does include a revised version of User Manager for Domains that will give you remote administration of NetWare-enabled users, however.

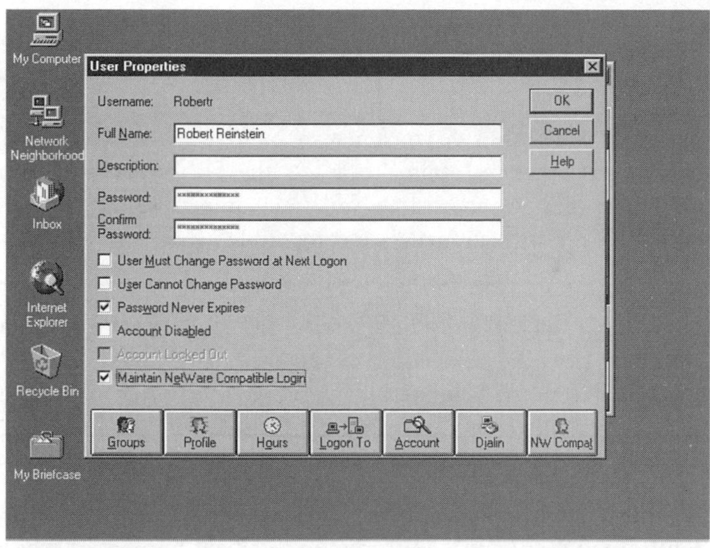

Figure 33.61. *User Manager with FPNW extensions.*

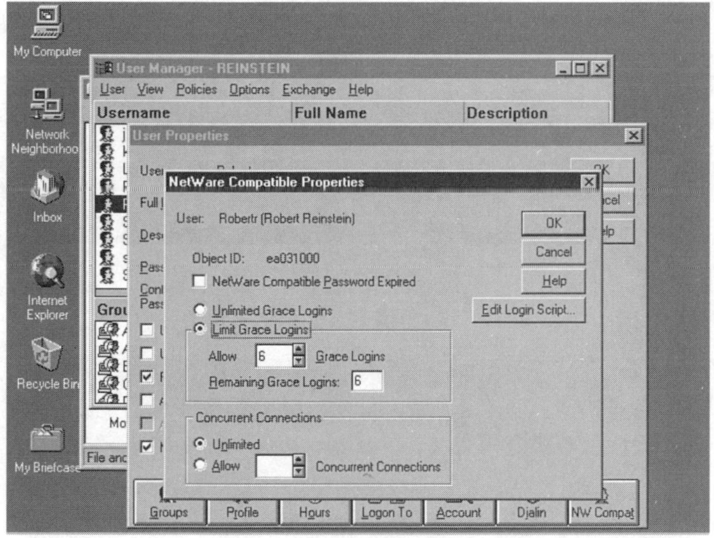

Figure 33.62. *The NetWare Compatible Properties dialog.*

Using Server Manager to Administer File and Print Services for NetWare

The Server Manager extensions give you a new menu item. As shown in Figure 33.63, a FPNW drop-down menu gives you the ability to access the FPNW Control Panel applet, manage NetWare-compatible volumes, and define NetWare-compatible print servers. You can also send NetWare-compatible messages to NetWare-compatible users.

Note: For Windows NT Workstation users who want to administer a Windows NT domain, you must copy the new version of Server Manager that File and Print Services for NetWare installed from the Windows NT server to the Windows NT workstation.

New to NT 4.0: The Client-based Server Tools, which include a version of Server Manager for Windows 95 and Windows NT Workstation, will not automatically be updated with the Server Manager extensions for File and Print Services for NetWare. The File and Print Services for NetWare package does include a revised version of the Windows 95 client tool that will give you remote administration of FPNW-enabled domains, however.

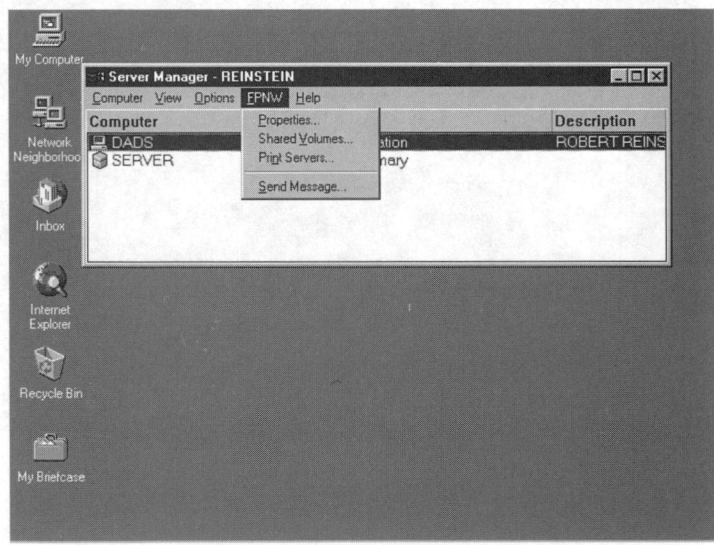

Figure 33.63. *The menu for the Server Manager FPNW extensions.*

When I mention NetWare-compatible, I mean that these are resources for which you can use the NetWare-compatible commands, such as CAPTURE and MAP. These are also the commands that you can use to create NetWare-compatible login scripts.

Creating and Maintaining NetWare-Compatible Volumes

Using the FPNW menu in Server Manager, you can create, delete, or alter NetWare-compatible volumes that you create using File and Print Services for NetWare. Figure 33.64 shows the Volumes dialog that appears after selecting Shared Volumes... from the FPNW menu. The volume listed is the SYS volume that was created when you installed File and Print Services for NetWare. To create an additional volume, click the Add... button. The Create Volume dialog (see Figure 33.65) prompts you for a volume name and an existing directory to use for the new volume. You can also configure permissions and user connection limits here. An upcoming section in this chapter, "Migrating from NetWare to Windows NT Using File and Print Services for NetWare," will show you how to use this dialog for a smooth NetWare–to–Windows NT migration.

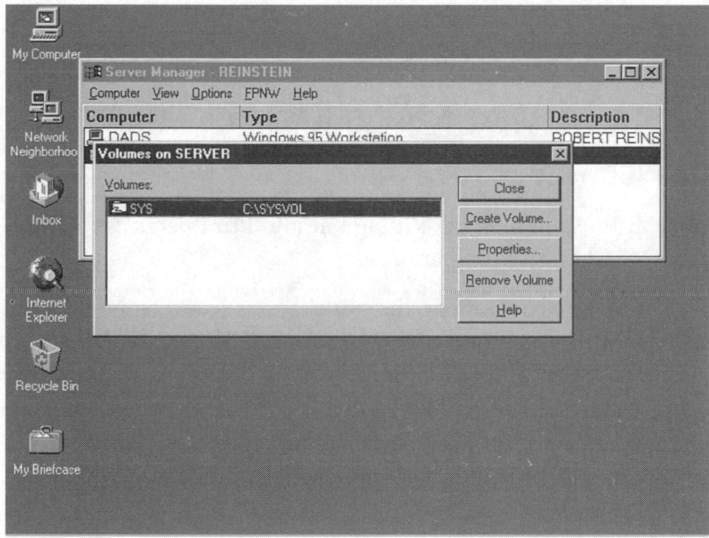

Figure 33.64. *The NetWare-compatible Volumes dialog.*

Click the OK button to complete the creation of the new volume, and the resulting list of volumes will show both the original and the new volume.

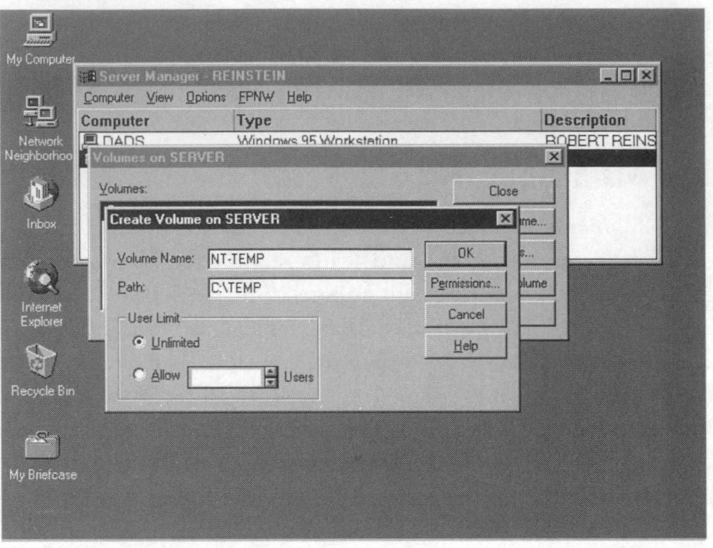

Figure 33.65. The Create Volume on SERVER dialog.

Migrating from NetWare to Windows NT Using File and Print Services for NetWare

You can realize the greatest benefit of using File and Print Services for NetWare when you plan a NetWare–to–Windows NT migration.

If you are in a NetWare environment, the workstations accessing NetWare are probably running different versions of the NetWare client, such as NETX and VLM, and running on different platforms, such as DOS, DOS/Windows, OS/2, Windows 95, and Windows NT. These workstations probably are running login scripts that handle their connections to printers and volumes. Changing from a NetWare environment to a native Windows NT client workstation involves a lot of work and planning, especially when you are dealing with dozens, hundreds, or even thousands of client workstations.

The Migration Tool for NetWare does a beautiful job in assisting with this process, but it is possible to perform a phased migration, and that is where File and Print Services for NetWare comes in very handy.

Let's use a simple example. A NetWare server named NW_SERVER has two volumes, SYS and VOL1. VOL1 has a directory called APPS that contains numerous applications, each in its own subdirectory. A system login script maps drives for users based on their group memberships.

Under normal circumstances, a NetWare–to–Windows NT migration would entail using the Migration Tools for NetWare to copy user accounts, groups, and volumes. Then you could create

Windows NT logon scripts that emulated the commands used in the NetWare system login script. And finally, each workstation would require changing over its NetWare client software to a Microsoft networking client. Depending on the number of users, this could take hours, days, or months. It probably would also require leaving the NetWare server online while users are slowly migrated over to the Windows NT environment.

Now picture this: Use the Migration Tool for NetWare to copy the user accounts, group, and volume. Install File and Print Services for NetWare, giving the pseudo-NetWare server the name NW_SERVER. Now a login specifying NW_SERVER as the preferred server would give the user the same login, but this time, after the NetWare server was taken offline, it would be to the Windows NT server. Next, create a directory on the Windows NT server and place the APPS directory from the NetWare server into this directory on the Windows NT server. Then create a volume named VOL1 using this directory as the path. The users would then still find their applications within the APPS directory on VOL1, only this time it's not on the NetWare server but on the Windows NT server. All you have to do now is flag all the users as NetWare compatible and assign them their old system login script (after copying it over, of course). Follow the same logic for creating print queues with the same name as the original NetWare queues. Now you are free to bring down the NetWare server and have all your users function the same as they had, without them even knowing that any type of change has occurred.

This then would give you time to slowly bring workstations over to Microsoft networking by installing their new client software, creating a Windows NT logon script or creating persistent connections to the network shares they require, and removing their User Manager attribute of being NetWare compatible.

Using File and Print Services for NetWare to Integrate Windows NT into a NetWare Environment

Sometimes a NetWare shop will require the use of a Windows NT server because of one application that runs only on Windows NT Server. Most of the Windows NT servers my company sells into NetWare environments are due to programs that need Microsoft SQL Server as their database, so I see this a lot.

Because a Windows NT server has a lot of power to offer and a company may not want to upgrade the hardware it is using for its NetWare servers, the ideal is to add new services to the Windows NT server.

For instance, we have had customers who decided to attach CD-ROM drives to a Windows NT server because they didn't want to invest in a dedicated CD server or didn't want to attach any peripherals directly to their NetWare servers. File and Print Services for NetWare is the perfect solution for allowing current NetWare users to access resources on a Windows NT server without having to change their client software. By adding users to the Windows NT server and flagging them as NetWare compatible, they can map a drive, using their NetWare tools, to one of the CD-ROMs attached to the Windows NT server.

File and Print Services for NetWare creates resources that are so NetWare compatible that they can even be seen as part of a Novell NetWare NDS tree. Figures 33.66 through 33.68 show the NWADMIN program that is used to administer a NetWare 4.*x* environment. In Figure 33.66, I am adding a Windows NT server that is running File and Print Services for NetWare to the NDS tree. In Figure 33.67, I'm adding a NetWare-compatible volume to this same NDS tree. Figure 33.68 shows the new NDS tree with the new server and volume defined.

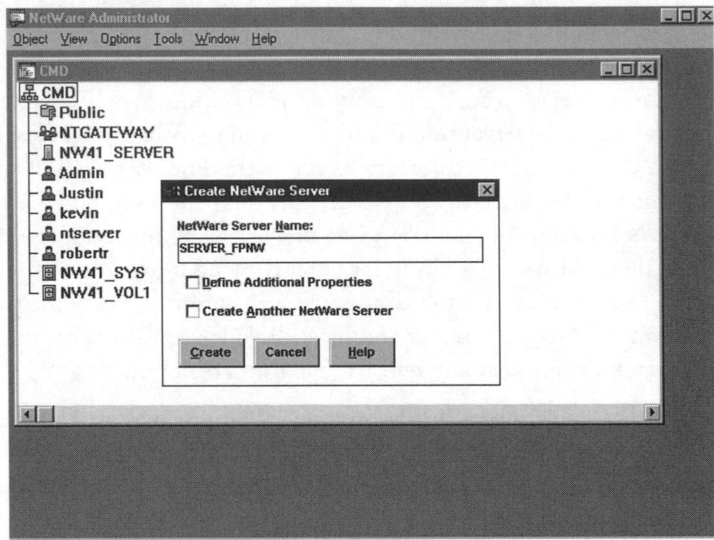

Figure 33.66. *Adding a Windows NT Server with File and Print Services for NetWare to a NetWare NDS tree.*

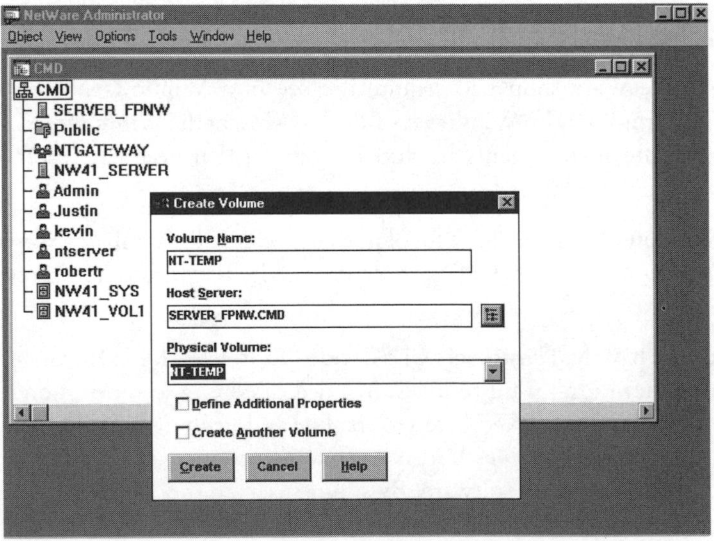

Figure 33.67. *Adding a Windows NT Server File and Print Services for NetWare volume to a NetWare NDS tree.*

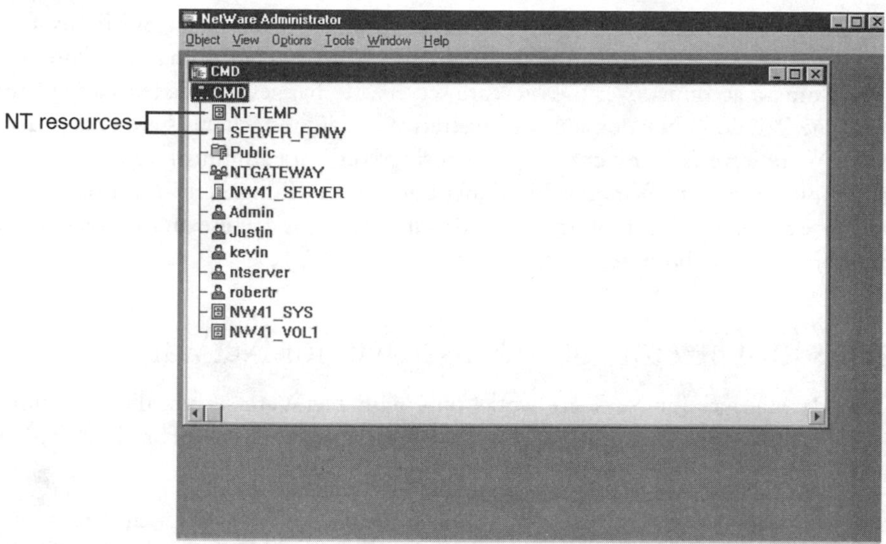

Figure 33.68. *A NetWare NDS tree showing Windows NT resources.*

You also can define any Windows NT–supported printer as a NetWare-compatible print queue, which will make the print queue accessible by any NetWare client workstation.

Of course, anyone using these services on the Windows NT server must be licensed as a Windows NT client, but the cost for this is minimal, and the benefits are great.

Should File and Print Services for NetWare Be Used?

I highly recommend using File and Print Services for NetWare, but would prefer to see its use limited to acting as a "bandage" for a migration or enabling a NetWare client access to a Windows NT domain until that user is prepared to run the native Microsoft Networking client.

At this point, with most PCs running with 8MB of memory and a 486 or Pentium processor, most users should be migrating to Windows 95 and Windows NT Workstation, allowing users to run both the Microsoft Networking client and the NetWare client without creating much overhead.

The administrative headaches of having both native Microsoft clients and NetWare-compatible clients definitely results in more administrative responsibility and a greater margin for error when changing user configurations.

Directory Service Manager for NetWare

Another add-on that Microsoft sells is its Directory Service Manager for NetWare.

With this interesting utility, user accounts and groups from both NetWare and Windows NT domains can be managed and have synchronized passwords.

The way Directory Service Manager for NetWare works is that it will copy—or, as Microsoft calls it, *propagate*—user and group accounts from NetWare to a Windows NT domain, and propagate Windows NT domain accounts over to NetWare servers. If changes are made to any of these accounts from the Windows NT domain administrative tools, those changes are then reflected over to the NetWare server(s). Any changes made using NetWare administrative tools are not automatically copied over to the Windows NT domain accounts. Microsoft has furnished versions of many NetWare command-line tools that users or administrators can use on the NetWare side to force synchronization on both networks.

Requirements for Directory Service Manager for NetWare

Directory Service Manager for NetWare works only with NetWare servers that are running NetWare versions 2.*x* and 3.*x*. It cannot work with NetWare 4.*x* servers, even if bindery emulation is enabled.

The Windows NT domain's PDC must be running the Gateway (and Client) Services for NetWare to use Directory Service Manager for NetWare. Running this ensures that the Windows NT domain's PDC is running the NWLink IPX/SPX–compatible protocol and gives the Windows NT domain access to the bindery on NetWare servers.

Up to 32 NetWare servers can share users with one Windows NT domain. Directory Service Manager for NetWare enables you, the Windows NT administrator, also to flag Windows NT domain users to join a NetWare server. NetWare has a limit of 2,000 users per server, so you should be selective about the Windows NT domain clients that you copy over to NetWare.

Installing Directory Service Manager for NetWare

The installation procedure for Directory Service Manager for NetWare is practically the same as for File and Print Services for NetWare, which is simply a matter of adding network services. Simply follow the directions I had included in the previous section about File and Print Services for NetWare to add the Directory Service Manager for NetWare and Directory Service Manager for NetWare Administrator Tools services to your Windows NT PDC.

Account Information

Table 33.4 lists NetWare user account information values, whether they are copied from a NetWare server to a Windows NT domain, and how and whether they can be administered from Windows NT's User Manager for Domains.

Table 33.4. User account attributes.

NetWare Account Restriction	*Windows NT Server Equivalent*	*User Manager for Domains Setting*
Account Expiration Date	Account Expiration Date	Carried over from NetWare.
Intruder Lockout	Account Lockout	Taken from Windows NT Account Policy.
User Disk Volume Restrictions	None	Not handled by Directory Service Manager for NetWare.
Account Disabled	Account Disabled	Carried over from NetWare.
Allow User to Change Password	User Cannot Change Password	Carried over from NetWare.
Days Between Forced Changes and Password Expiration Date	Maximum Password Age	Taken from Windows NT Account Policy.
Force Periodic Password Changes	Password Never Expires	Carried over from NetWare.
Grace Logins	Grace Logins	Carried over from NetWare.
Intruder Detection/Lockout	Account Lockout	Taken from Windows NT Account Policy.
Limit Concurrent Connections	Limit Concurrent Connections	Carried over from NetWare.
Minimum Password Length	Minimum Password Length	Taken from Windows NT Account Policy.
Require Password	Permit Blank Password	Taken from Windows NT Account Policy.
Require Unique Passwords	Password Uniqueness	Taken from Windows NT Account Policy.
Station Restrictions	Logon Workstations	Carried over from NetWare.
Time Restrictions	Logon Hours	Carried over from NetWare; Windows NT specifies logon hours at the whole hour, however, whereas NetWare uses half-hours. In the translation, the user is given more time.

Directory Service Manager for NetWare Client Tools

With the utilities that come with Directory Service Manager for NetWare, users can keep their passwords synchronized across networks and perform basic NetWare functions.

The client tools are copied automatically to the NetWare server's `system` directory. To ensure that NetWare clients have access to these tools, you will probably want to copy them manually to the NetWare server's `public` and `login` directories.

The `CHGPASS` program works just as the NetWare version does, except that it changes not only the NetWare password but also the Windows NT domain password for that user. The proper syntax for `CHGPASS` is

```
CHGPASS [-s] [server] [/username]
```

- The `-s` switch restricts the command to a Windows NT domain. Because CHGPASS will automatically detect the type of client that is running the command, there is no reason to use this switch.
- The term `server` denotes the server that should accept the password change. By default, the current server will receive the change request.
- Use `/username` if you are changing the password for a user other than the person currently logged on.

With `MSLOGIN`, a client can log onto a specific server and run the appropriate login script for that server. You are logged out from all other servers when using this command. The syntax for the `MSLOGIN` command is:

```
MSLOGIN [server[/name]] [clearscreen] [/noattach] [/script path]
```

- The `server` is the name of the server you want to log in to.
- The `name` is the account ID you want to use for the login.
- Use `/clearscreen` to clear the screen before you are prompted to enter your password.
- The term `/noattach` forces the `MSLOGIN` command to not log you in to a server nor out from a server, but rather just run the login script you specify with the `/script` parameter.
- With the `/script` parameter, you can specify a specific login script without being forced to run a system login script or a personal login script.
- The `path` parameter names the fully qualified path for the selected script.

`MSMAP` is the Directory Service Manager for NetWare equivalent to NetWare's `MAP` command, but it includes not only NetWare drive mappings but also Microsoft networking drive connections. It uses the same syntax as the native NetWare `MAP` command.

`MSATTACH` is the functional equivalent to NetWare's `ATTACH` command and uses the same syntax as the `ATTACH` command.

Synchronization Manager

When you have installed Directory Service Manager for NetWare, a new program will be added to your Administrative Tools program folder: Synchronization Manager. With Synchronization Manager, you can select the NetWare server or servers that you want to manage through Directory Service Manager for NetWare.

From here, pick and choose the users and groups that you want to pull over into the Windows NT domain for administrative purposes.

Remember, Directory Service Manager for NetWare is not the same as the Migration Tools for NetWare, even though it is very similar.

The users who you bring into the Windows NT domain for administration are not converted to Windows NT domain user account. The accounts are created as NetWare-enabled and are viewed as NetWare accounts.

In fact, if you are going to be managing accounts from more than one NetWare server or there are NetWare accounts that share the same name as an account from the Windows NT domain, although these accounts are not the same user, you will create a mapping file that is very similar to the mapping file that may be used during a NetWare–to–Windows NT domain migration.

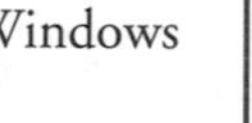

New to NT 4.0: New to the version of Directory Service Manager for NetWare for Windows NT Server 4.0 is the `DSMCHK` command.

This command is used to test for password synchronization. You can run it directly from the command line or include it as part of a login script.

The syntax for the `DSMCHK` command is:

```
DSMCHK -d domain -u username [-n Nwserver] [-r retriesinterval]
```

- `-d domain` specifies the Windows NT domain that contains the user account.
- `-u username` is the user account to check.
- `-n Nwserver` is the NetWare server that contains this user account. The default is to try all the NetWare servers on the domain.
- `-r retriesinterval` enables you to specify a number of retries and the number of seconds between each retry.

Using the `DCMCHK` command will return an error code. These codes are

`0`: Successful synchronization

`1`: Unsuccessful synchronization

`2`: NetWare server not found or not administered by Directory Service Manager for NetWare

`3`: Domain name not found

4: User account not found or not administered by Directory Service Manager for NetWare
5: User account not found on PDC

Note: At the time of this writing, the new version of Directory Service Manager for NetWare for Windows NT Server 4.0 was still in beta test. That is why some of these instructions are vague.

This section was included here as an introduction to the Directory Service Manager for NetWare services, and should you decide to implement those services, I fully recommend using the documentation that is included with the released package of Directory Service Manager for NetWare.

Summary

As you have just seen, Microsoft Windows NT Server makes it easy to integrate or even to migrate from NetWare.

The tools that are available both with Windows NT Server and as separate products can make your NetWare and Windows NT integration easier than you probably thought.

Both Microsoft and Novell have been working to enable these two network operating systems to interact, and it seems that the ties are getting closer and closer.

Don't forget that migrating from one environment to the other requires a lot of planning. But if you become familiar with the tools I've just told you about, you should be able to create a plan that will run very smoothly.

CHAPTER 34

Integrating Windows NT and UNIX

by Michael Tressler

Any discussion of computer networks ultimately must mention UNIX, the granddaddy of network operating systems. UNIX and its derivatives are found in nearly every decent-sized network, running on everything from data-entry terminals to high-end graphics workstations to Internet hosts and to mainframe-powered database servers supporting billions of daily transactions.

UNIX has been around since the 1960s, making Windows NT a mere child in terms of age. Microsoft knew that for Windows NT to succeed in corporate networks, it had to be able to interact and work well with the more mature UNIX-based systems. This chapter will explain the several methods that Windows NT and UNIX interoperate, as well as highlight ways to ensure a successful intermixing of UNIX with Windows NT.

In this chapter, we will look at the following connectivity options:

- FTP, the File Transfer Protocol
- LPR/LPD printing support
- Telnet terminal emulation
- NFS, the Network File System
- SAMBA, which allows for near-native connectivity

Connectivity Native to Windows NT

If it were not for UNIX, TCP/IP would not have grown to become the de facto standard protocol of networks. All UNIX platforms ship a version of TCP/IP as well as all versions of Windows NT. Therefore, there's no need to decide which protocol to use when connecting UNIX and Windows NT: Use TCP/IP. For more information on the configuration and troubleshooting of TCP/IP on Windows NT, see Chapter 29, "Windows NT and TCP/IP."

Just because UNIX and Windows NT both support TCP/IP does not mean they can interoperate easily. For example, there is no native way to share files between UNIX and Windows NT.

The File Transfer Protocol

The simplest way to move files between UNIX and Windows NT is with the *File Transfer Protocol* (FTP). Just as every version of UNIX ships TCP/IP, every version of UNIX also ships FTP client and server software. Because Windows NT also contains native FTP client and server support, FTP becomes the only native way to move files between UNIX and Windows NT systems. Unfortunately, FTP can be used only to move files between systems, and its command-line interface can be intimidating to people who only know how to operate in graphical user interfaces. Even the point-and-click implementations of the FTP client can cause grief to users.

By default, FTP listens on TCP port 21 for incoming client connections. After receiving a client request to connect, the FTP server responds with a login prompt. The user then must enter a valid username and password to gain access to the server. Because Windows NT and UNIX do not share user lists and passwords, the administrator must set up an account for every UNIX user who wants to access a Windows NT system, and vice versa.

Warning: FTP logins are not encrypted, which means that anyone running a packet sniffer on your network can intercept plain text passwords. Therefore, FTP is an inherently insecure protocol because passwords can be captured easily.

Anonymous FTP is another potential security risk with FTP server software. Anonymous FTP enables any user to connect to the FTP server using the username `anonymous` and a password of the user's choice, but the standard is the client's e-mail address. If you've ever transferred files from public FTP sites on the Internet via your Web browser, you've used anonymous FTP. If you enable support for the anonymous user on your FTP site, be sure to set your security policy to allow access only to the directories and files you want the world to see.

The FTP client that ships with Windows NT is a command-line application. To run it, type `ftp` at a run prompt or in a command-prompt window. You then see the `ftp>` prompt. You now are inside the FTP utility. To see a list of valid commands, type a question mark (`?`) and press Enter.

To connect to a host, use this syntax:

```
OPEN <FTPHOST>
```

To connect to Microsoft's public FTP server, for example, type this command:

```
OPEN ftp.microsoft.com
```

If you successfully connect to an FTP server, you see a login prompt. If you see the message `Connection refused`, the FTP server software is not running on the remote host.

After you are logged in successfully, you can transfer files to or from your system, or navigate the directory structure. To navigate the remote system's directory structure, use the `cd` keyword, which stands for *change directory*. The `cd` keyword is similar to the `cd` command in DOS or the Windows NT command prompt. To see a directory listing of the remote server, use the `ls` or `dir` keyword. To change the working directory of your local system, use the `lcd` keyword, which stands for *local change directory*. Any file you get will then be placed into the directory you specify.

To download files from the remote server, use the `get` keyword. To upload files to the remote server, use the `put` keyword. The only caveat is that, by default, FTP uses an ASCII transfer mode to move files between the systems. ASCII mode does offer the benefit of converting UNIX line-feed characters in text files to MS-DOS standard carriage-return and line-feed characters. If you try to move a binary file using ASCII mode, for example, your binary file will become corrupted. To make sure that the FTP client is using the correct transfer modes, you can use the `asc` and `bin` keywords to set ASCII or binary modes.

On Windows NT, the FTP server software runs as a service. If the FTP server service is installed, it starts automatically whenever the machine is booted. On Windows NT 4.0, the FTP server service is installed as part of the *Internet Information Server* (IIS). For more information on Microsoft's FTP server, see Chapter 49, "Internet Information Server."

Printing Support

Printing support is the only other native client and server support Windows NT provides for interoperability with UNIX. Windows NT supports the *Line Printer Remote* (LPR) and *Line Printer Daemon* (LPD) services. LPR supports printing to UNIX hosts (as well as other Windows NT print servers), and LPD supports client print requests. LPR and LPD are defined in RFC 1179.

Line Printer Remote (LPR)

The LPR service enables Windows NT and UNIX clients to print to servers running the LPD service. To set up a Windows NT client to use the LPR service, you first need to install the service. On Windows NT 4.0 machines, choose Start | Settings | Control Panel. In the Control Panel, double-click the Network icon. Select the Services tab. You should see an entry for Microsoft TCP/IP Printing.

Connecting to an LPD-serviced printer is not much more difficult than connecting to a typical Windows NT-based print share. To create a connection to the LPD serviced printer on a UNIX server, you need to know the IP address or DNS name of the remote print server, the name of the printer on the remote print server, and the make and model of that printer.

On Windows NT 4.0, start the Add Printer Wizard by choosing Start | Settings | Printers. Double-click the Add Printer icon. In the Add Printer dialog, select the My Computer option and click Next. Click Add Port and then choose LPR Port from the Add Port dialog. Press the New Port button, and enter the IP address or DNS name of the remote print server in the first field, titled `Name or address of server providing lpd:`. Next, enter the name of the printer on that host in the `Name of printer or print queue on that server:` field.

Note: If you are setting up a connection to a single-port Hewlett-Packard JetDirect card, you do not need to enter a value in the `Name of printer or print queue on that server:` field of the Add Port dialog.

Note: After pressing the OK button in the "Add LPR compatible printer" dialog box, Windows NT performs a simple test to verify that the remote LPD server and printer are available. If the test fails, an "LPR Port Configuration Warning" appears, offering several reasons why the test may have failed.

After closing the Add LPD Port dialog box and continuing with the Add Printer Wizard, you are prompted to enter the make and model of the remote printer. You also are asked for a name for the printer, and whether you want to share the printer. By sharing the printer, you are enabling the LPD service that will let LPR clients connect to this printer. Sharing this printer will allow your Microsoft client machines to print to a UNIX printer. In essence, Windows NT is acting as a gateway between your clients and the UNIX print server. After you finish with the wizard, your test print should come out successfully.

Troubleshooting LPR

Setting up a connection to a UNIX-served printer is a straightforward operation, and Microsoft has done an excellent job with its Add Port Wizard. The first step to troubleshooting LPR is to verify that the UNIX LPD server is able to print to the printer. If that proves successful, there are several other reasons why LPR may fail.

- You entered an incorrect IP address or DNS name.
- You mistyped the printer name on the remote host.
- You selected the wrong make and model of printer.
- The remote server is not available, or the LPD service has stopped on that machine.
- The remote printer has a security policy preventing connectivity.

If you are receiving output, but it is not formatted correctly, verify that you selected the correct make and model of printer. Also, check to see what port monitor software is running on the remote print server. When a Windows NT LPR client ships a print job to an LPD server, the print job contains the LPR `l` command. This command tells the LPD server to ship the job through unaltered. Your LPD server may require a different value for this field, however. You can set this value by editing the Windows NT Registry in the following location:

```
HKEY_LOCAL_MACHINE\System\CurrentControlSet\Control\Print\Monitors\LPR Port\
Ports\<portname>\Timeouts
```

By adding the value `PrintSwitch` of data type `REG_SZ`, you can enter a string that your LPD server software may require.

The LPR Utility

You also can use the command-line LPR utility that ships with Windows NT 4.0. This utility may be useful in a batch file that needs to send printed output to a remote print server. The syntax of the command follows:

```
LPR -S <servername> -P <printername> <filename>
```

Suppose that you want to print the text file `c:\winnt\setuplog.txt` to the printer `HP3` on server `LINUX1`. You can use the following command:

```
LPR -S LINUX1 -P HP3 c:\winnt\setuplog.txt
```

If you want to print a binary file, such as a binary PostScript file, you need to add the `-ol` switch to the LPR command. If you want to print the binary PostScript file `c:\winnt\results.ps` to the same printer, your command should look like this:

```
LPR -S LINUX1 -P HP3 -ol c:\winnt\results.ps
```

If a UNIX client wants to print to a Windows NT LPD server, the UNIX client can use the LPR client software, using the same parameters as in this example for the Windows NT LPR command. There is one slight difference: To print binary files, the switch is simply `-l` on UNIX clients instead of `-ol`.

The LPQ Utility

You can use the command-line LPQ utility to see what is in the queue on a remote LPD print server. LPQ is also a command-line utility. The parameters are very similar to that of the LPR utility:

```
LPQ -S <servername> -P <printername> -l
```

The `-l` switch is optional, and it simply means that you want to receive a detailed status of the remote queue.

The Line Printer Daemon (LPD) Service

Simply put, the LPD service receives print jobs from LPR clients. The LPD service then spools this print job to an output device. The LPR and LPD standards were published as *Request for Comment* (RFC) 1179. Establishing an LPD printer in Windows NT 4.0 is very easy. You first must create a printer on the local machine.

Adding a printer to Windows NT is briefly discussed in the previous section, "Line Printer Remote (LPR)." However, if you intend to make this printer available to LPR clients, you must enable sharing of this printer.

For more information on troubleshooting and configuring a printer on Windows NT, see Chapter 46, "Troubleshooting: Microsoft Exchange and Microsoft Mail."

The LPD service does not pass extended error messages back to the LPR client, and the LPD service does not use the print data type defined in the Print Processor dialog on the Printer Properties tab. Instead, LPD is told by the client which print processor data type to use. Windows NT will respond to two LPR data types: Text, and all other data types are treated as a RAW data type.

Telnet

Telnet is a terminal-emulation application that enables clients to access command-line sessions on remote computers running the TelnetD service. Windows NT ships with only a Telnet client and not a TelnetD server. Microsoft is working on a TelnetD service, and a beta version of this service is located in the Windows NT 4.0 Server Resource Kit. For more information on the TelnetD server, you can send e-mail to `telnetd@microsoft.com`.

Telnet is used primarily to run applications on a remote host. In most cases, a user starts a Telnet session, successfully logs in, and then runs applications on the remote host. Almost all the processing takes place on the remote host, and the Telnet client only sends and receives characters and screen updates.

Thousands and thousands of UNIX applications can be run from Telnet clients. Generally, these applications must all be command-line character-cell driven applications. Many of these applications are slowly being replaced by client/server applications with graphical front ends. All the processing is done on the Telnet server, which requires a very powerful server to host all the clients who will be processing on that machine.

You also can use Telnet to gain access to UNIX shell accounts. A great example of this capability is completely administering a UNIX server from a remote location, including over the Internet.

Caution: Telnet poses the same security risk that FTP poses: Passwords transmitted across the network are not encrypted and therefore can be "sniffed" by unscrupulous users.

Microsoft's Telnet Client

Microsoft's Telnet client that ships with Windows NT is a very limited Telnet client. It *is* free, however, and you can use it to connect to servers running TelnetD, which provides some functionality that will get you by in most instances. If you find yourself confined by the minimal functionality of Microsoft's Telnet client, a large third-party and shareware market provides WinSock-compliant Telnet applications.

On Windows NT 4.0, you can find the Telnet client by choosing Start | Programs | Accessories. After Telnet starts, you can connect to a remote host by choosing the Remote System option from the Connect menu. A dialog appears that enables you to specify the remote host by IP address or DNS name. This dialog box also allows you to specify a port other than Telnet, as well as the terminal emulation type for your client to use during TermType subnegotiation. TermType subnegotiation is usually not used, but on some TelnetD servers it is used to define the client type that is connecting. Note that setting the TermType is not the terminal emulation you will be using during this session; it is only a value used to tell TelnetD what kind of client you are. You still control terminal-emulation settings from the Terminal/Preferences dialog. Figure 34.1 shows the Microsoft Telnet client connecting to a Telnet server.

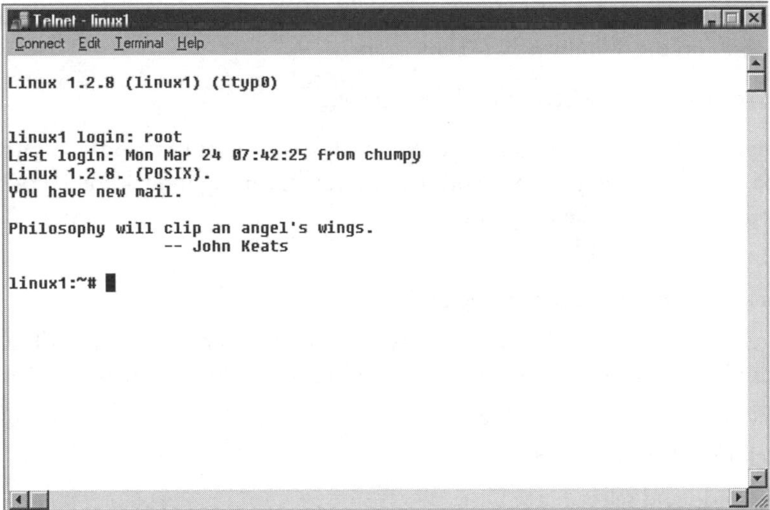

Figure 34.1. *Using Microsoft's Telnet client.*

Microsoft's Telnet Server

In Microsoft's words, the

> Telnet Server Beta (TELNETD.EXE) provides a solution for running command-line utilities, scripts, and batch files from OS-independent clients. It is not intended to be a full commercial-grade Telnet solution. Telnet Server Beta supports remote, character-based sessions, while Windows NT 4.0 is designed primarily to support graphics-based applications.

Microsoft's last sentence points to some of the problems with running applications via Telnet on Windows NT servers. There is no set way to determine whether an application will run correctly on a Windows NT Telnet server except by testing it.

Most graphically driven applications will not even start using Microsoft's TelnetD server, and those graphically driven applications that will start will be seen only on the desktop of the host computer.

Applications that do run properly as text-mode applications but reflect error messages in graphical dialog boxes can cause some interesting moments. The Telnet client will not see these dialog boxes. Some applications can adjust for this limitation by redirecting their dialog boxes to the command-line interface.

The Microsoft Telnet server service consists of two parts: the TelnetD service itself, and an underlying component called the *Remote Session Manager* (RSM). The Telnet server accepts incoming connections and routes them to the RSM.

The RSM is responsible for initiating, terminating, and managing the character-oriented remote Telnet session on the Windows NT Telnet server.

Use these steps to install Microsoft's Telnet server:

1. Open the Network configuration tool by choosing Start | Settings | Control Panel and then double-clicking the Network icon. Or, you can right-click the Network Neighborhood icon and choose Properties.
2. Select the Services tab.
3. Click Add and then select Have Disk.
4. Enter the path to the Telnet server distribution files. The Windows NT Resource Kit Setup installs these files to the Telnet subdirectory below the Resource Kit directory.
5. Select the Remote Session Manager.
6. Click OK. Don't reboot.
7. Click Add and select Have Disk.
8. Select the Telnet Service Beta (Inbound Telnet).
9. Click OK and reboot your system.

Caution: The `OEMSETUP.INF` file that ships with the Windows NT Server 4.0 Resource Kit is out-of-date. It does not provide the option to install the Remote Session Manager. An updated version of the `OEMSETUP.INF` file, which fixes this bug, is available at

`ftp.microsoft.com/bussys/winnt/winnt-public/reskit/nt40/telnetd`

After successfully rebooting your machine, the Telnet service should be running. To test it, use the Microsoft Telnet client and Telnet to your local Telnet server. Figure 34.2 shows what you see if you connect successfully.

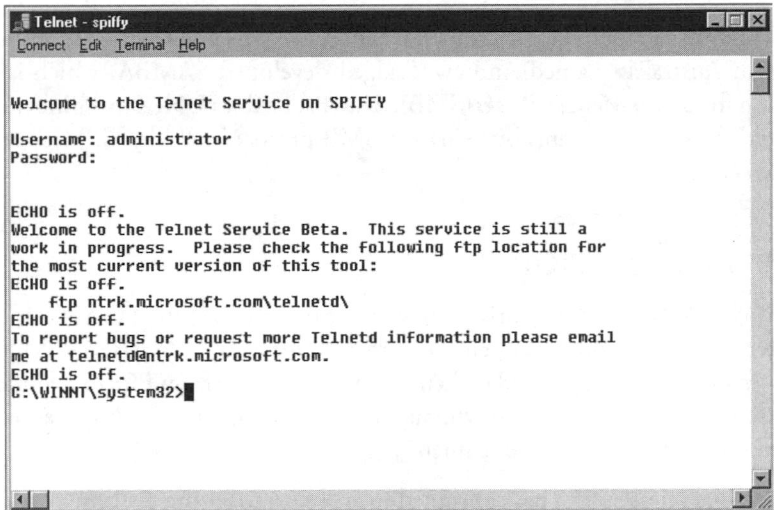

Figure 34.2. *Successfully Telneting to a Windows NT Telnet server.*

The login and password are determined by the local Windows NT accounts database. Several of the user account options are invalid. The Guest user and a member who is only a member of the Guest group will not be able to log in. Setting the User Must Change Password at Next Logon option also causes logins to fail.

If a user executes a `net use` drive redirection command, that `net use` drive redirection becomes active on the Telnet server desktop. Also, any drive letters already redirected on the desktop will not be available for Telnet clients to redirect. Finally, if a client makes a network redirection and exits, that drive redirection remains active on the server's desktop, but the client loses that redirection on the next logon, meaning that it then must redirect another drive letter to get back to where it was. On a busy server, you could quickly run out of drive letters to redirect.

Warning: The only security you have is file-level security, so be sure to lock down your file system appropriately with the proper security settings.

Third-Party Integration Utilities

Earlier in this chapter, we looked at the native interoperability that Windows NT provides with UNIX. In many cases, that may be all you need to use. In most UNIX environments, however, you want to be able to use file sharing beyond the simple file moving provided by FTP.

In this section, we will look at two popular methods used to share files between UNIX and Windows NT. The first is the *Network File System* (NFS). NFS is a protocol developed in the mid-'80s by Sun Microsystems to facilitate file sharing between UNIX systems. The popularity of this protocol quickly grew, and now NFS client and NFS server software is offered for every major operating system available, including Windows NT.

Another widely used method for sharing files between UNIX and Microsoft operating systems is SAMBA. An Australian named Andrew Tridgell developed SAMBA, which is a play on the abbreviation for *Server Message Blocks* (SMB). SAMBA enables UNIX machines to communicate natively with Microsoft systems by using the SMB protocol used by all Microsoft networking clients and servers.

The Network File System

The *Network File System* (NFS) originally was released in 1985 by SunSoft, a division of Sun Microsystems. It has become an open standard for distributed file systems. NFS implements a client/server architecture supported on heterogeneous systems from PCs to mainframes. NFS has been licensed to hundreds of vendors who supply NFS-based solutions. NFS has been defined and updated in several Internet RFC documents.

Since its original release, NFS has continued to evolve to meet the distributed file system needs. For example, a version of NFS for the Internet named WebNFS is now available. WebNFS is intended to simplify FTP activities and to provide a Web interface to mounting remote file systems. As new versions are introduced, performance and scalability are improved. NFS is capable of easily scaling from small- to enterprise-size environments. NFS also has flexible and extensible security architectures.

Benefits and Architecture of NFS

NFS was designed with several goals in mind:

- *Transparent access:* Users can access remote files as if they were local. Users do not need to know where the file physically exists.
- *Portability:* NFS is a machine- and operating-system–independent standard, as is proven by its availability on just about every major and minor operating system in existence today.

- *Fast recovery from failure:* NFS is designed to handle network outages gracefully and to reconnect quickly and easily to lost network resources.
- *Network protocol independence:* NFS is transport-protocol–independent. In most cases, though, it runs on top of TCP/IP.
- *Security:* NFS was designed to use multiple security mechanisms. NFS will be able to use future security mechanisms as they become available. NFS also enables administrators to decide what type of security they want to implement, instead of forcing them to use one method.

The architecture of NFS has been successful in meeting these goals. NFS clients communicate with an NFS server using *Remote Procedure Calls* (RPCs), which operate over the *User Datagram Protocol* (UDP) transport on a TCP/IP network. Using RPCs, the NFS client contacts the *Port Mapper*, a program that translates RPC service requests to a specific TCP/IP socket on the NFS server. After the client is connected to the NFS server, it can perform a number of functions—primarily, listing the available mount points or connecting to a mount point. NFS is a *connectionless* protocol, which means that a connection to an NFS server is established and disconnected for every transaction.

A *mount point* is the NFS equivalent of a Windows NT share. It is a directory on the NFS server to which a client can connect. An NFS share is created in many ways, depending primarily on the operating system. On Sun systems, for example, the `share` command is used to create NFS mount points, whereas on many other UNIX systems, an `exports` file is created.

Clients connect at boot time or through an interactive mount command. When the NFS server receives the mount request from the Port Mapper program, the server checks whether that directory is available for export and whether the client has proper permissions to access that mount point. After the client mounts the remote drive, he can use it as if it were a local drive. This should sound similar to mounting drives on a pure Microsoft network using shares. Both methods are very similar as far as an end user is concerned, although much more is going on in the background.

When PC support was introduced to NFS, some inherent problems needed to be solved. Because most PCs ran DOS, there were two major issues: DOS did not support long filenames like UNIX does, and DOS has no user validation.

The first problem was solved on the PC side by providing filename mapping similar to that used when a DOS client connects to a Windows NT server. A filename might become mangled (for example, `thislongfile.name` might be converted to the much less descriptive `thislo~1.nam`), but it is at least accessible by the client.

The bigger problem was user validation. To solve this problem, SunSoft introduced the *PC-NFS daemon* (PCNFSD). PCNFSD is a program that, when used with a client-side piece, verifies usernames and passwords before allowing NFS connectivity. The client-side piece is responsible for asking for the username and password, and the server-side piece is responsible for validating that information. All user information is on the NFS server. PCNFSD also allows for printer redirection from the PC to the NFS server.

PCNFSD is still around with Windows NT. When a Windows NT client wants to mount an NFS drive, the client passes the username and password of the logged-in user. If the NFS server has a matching username and password, the client is authenticated. One of the administrative hassles between Windows NT and an NFS server is that usernames and passwords are not automatically synchronized.

NFS Clients on Windows NT

Currently, several vendors provide NFS solutions for Windows NT. Most of these solutions enable Windows NT to be an NFS client or an NFS server. A recent product from Intergraph, AccessNFS Gateway for Windows NT, enables Windows NT to act as an NFS gateway for non-NFS clients. This method is similar to that of the Windows NT NetWare gateway, where Windows NT provides *Server Message Blocks* (SMB) to *NetWare Core Protocol* (NCP) translation. With this product, Windows NT performs SMB-to-NFS protocol translation.

Figure 34.3 is an example from Intergraph's Disk Access for Windows NT. You should notice the clean integration with the Explorer shell. The newer versions enable you to browse through the directory structure without having to mount a drive.

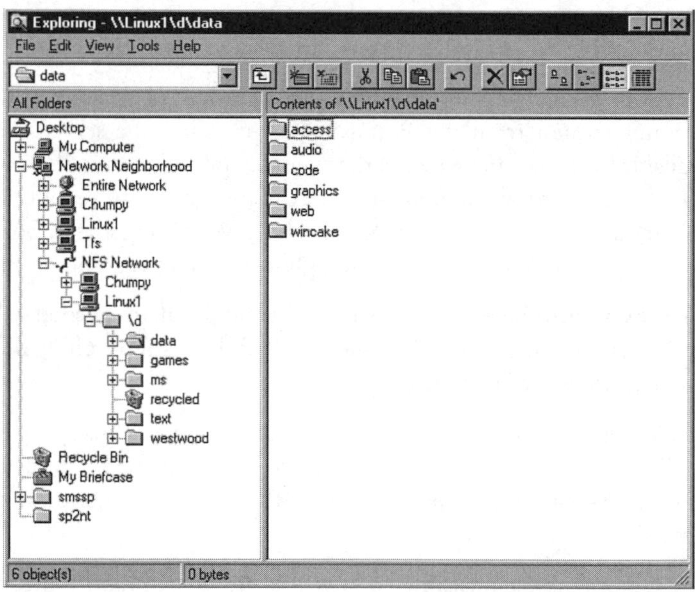

Figure 34.3. *Browsing an NFS share from Windows Explorer.*

You can mount an NFS share on Windows NT and have it appear as a drive letter on your desktop. This sort of native integration makes it easy to set up and install NFS client support for users.

NFS Servers on Windows NT

Just as products are available to enable Windows NT to access NFS servers, other products are available that enable Windows NT itself to be an NFS server. In most cases, creating a mount point is the same as creating a regular Windows NT share. After the share is created, you need to run the NFS Server Administration program and mark your newly created share as an NFS share. Some NFS server programs enable you to create NFS shares separate from standard Windows NT shares. In either case, after an NFS share is created, it is available to NFS clients. In Figure 34.4, you can see how simple it is to create an NFS share when using Intergraph's DiskShare NFS server.

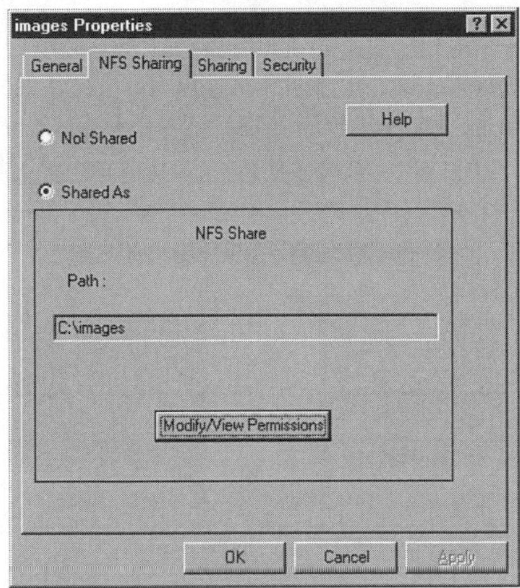

Figure 34.4. *Creating an NFS share for the directory* `c:\images`.

The main point of concern is the mapping of NFS client usernames to Windows NT usernames. In general, you run a utility on the Windows NT NFS server that lets you enter the username and password of the remote NFS client and associate that client with a Windows NT username. When an NFS client passes its username and password, Windows NT maps this information to the local or domain username you defined. If a mapping is found, the client can mount any mount points for which he has permission. Some programs automatically map similar names, which means that you don't have to explicitly map usernames if usernames and passwords match up on the NFS client and the NFS server.

SAMBA

As you learned earlier in this chapter, SAMBA is a play on the abbreviation for *Server Message Blocks* (SMB). SMB is a protocol developed jointly by Microsoft, Intel, and IBM. SMB defines a series of commands used to pass information between networked computers. It is the standard protocol

Microsoft uses in file and print sharing among its various operating systems. Various PC operating systems also have varied support for SMB; most notably, OS/2 Warp supports networking via SMBs. Unfortunately, no native support is available on UNIX for Microsoft clients. Administrators are forced to use FTP or NFS to share files between Microsoft clients and UNIX servers. This limitation of SMB causes great expense, because NFS client software must be procured and installed on every client's desktop. Also, NFS software doesn't support the browse list concept very well, so users need to know the server and mount point to which they want to connect.

With the release of SAMBA, the expense and complication of connecting SMB clients to UNIX servers disappeared. End users now can use their network browsers and see UNIX servers as if they were any other Microsoft server. There is no need to install additional software on Microsoft clients, no additional software expense, and—perhaps best of all—SAMBA is available freely over the Internet. So, aside from installation and configuration on the UNIX server, there is no expense. The trade-off is that there is no support for SAMBA besides the various Internet newsgroups and mailing lists. Plenty of documentation and support exists for SAMBA, but many times it's much easier and less expensive to pick up the phone and call for support instead of wading through piles of documentation that never seem to answer your specific question.

SAMBA Installation

> **Warning:** If you are not an experienced UNIX administrator, it is a good idea to have a UNIX support person handy when installing SAMBA. It is a pretty straightforward installation, but some of the obscurities of UNIX can quickly bite you if you aren't sure of what you are doing.

This section doesn't go through a detailed set of instructions for installing SAMBA. Not only are there better instructions available on the Internet than what I could provide, but differences exist in all UNIX systems that make a detailed set of instructions impractical. Regardless of the UNIX system you are using, you need to follow similar steps.

You first must obtain a copy of SAMBA for your version of UNIX. SAMBA is located on the Internet at `http://lake.canberra.edu.au/pub/samba/samba.html`. This site has plenty of documentation, as well as the source code, so that you can compile it to your specific UNIX variant. Some precompiled versions of SAMBA also are available for a few specific versions of UNIX. SAMBA support is available for most of the major UNIX systems, including LINUX, Solaris, SunOS, IRIX, HP-UX, OSF1, and AIX.

After you pull down SAMBA to your UNIX system, you must expand the archive by using the UNIX `tar` command. After you expand the installation set, you need to edit the makefile for your specific version of UNIX. You can find the makefile in the `/samba/samba-`*`<version number>`*`/source` directory. At the top half of the file are some settings you might want to look at closely. For example, this is where you can set the workgroup to which this UNIX server will belong. SAMBA supports only the workgroup model—not the Windows NT domain model. Also, no method exists to replicate user accounts to and from a SAMBA server. In essence, a SAMBA server cannot be a domain controller. SAMBA can be told to authenticate login requests by forwarding them to a Windows NT host, though.

Note: There is a utility available at `ftp://samba.edu.au/pub/samba/pwdump` that allows you to schedule an export of Windows NT passwords to a SAMBA machine. Using this, the Windows NT accounts become "native" to the SAMBA machine. Though some misinformed people call this a security hole in Windows NT, all passwords stay encrypted. The security hole comes in by being able to run password cracking/guessing software against the file. But by having a competent password policy in place, even the best password cracking/guessing software won't be of much value, and your accounts and passwords will still be secure.

About one-third of the way down the makefile is a listing of all the operating systems SAMBA supports, along with the appropriate compilation switches. Simply find your version of UNIX and remove the pound (`#`) signs to uncomment the switches. Then save the makefile and exit.

Next, execute the UNIX `make` command to compile SAMBA. After a few minutes, you should have a compiled version of SAMBA. Any errors most likely are caused by an incorrect edit of the makefile. Finally, you need to install the executables that you just compiled by executing the `make install` command. This puts the executables and man pages into their appropriate locations.

To verify successful creation of the man pages, type `man smbd` or `man nmbd` at a UNIX command prompt. You should now see the man pages for these two programs.

To run SAMBA, you can execute the `smbd -D` command and then the `nmbd -D` command at the command prompt. `smbd` is the SAMBA daemon responsible for handling SMB communications, and `nmbd` is used to handle NetBIOS name resolution similar to the functionality of the WINS service on Windows NT Server. You can use a SAMBA server as a WINS server by pointing your clients to the SAMBA server as their WINS server. SAMBA's `nmbd` does not support options such as push/pull partners and static mappings, however.

You can also edit the `inetd.conf` file to start SAMBA on demand, or you can edit the `rc.local` file to start SAMBA every time the system boots. It is up to you which method to use, and full documentation is available to help you set this up as it pertains to your version of UNIX.

SAMBA Configuration

Now that SAMBA is running, you need to make shares available to your clients; you do this by editing the `smb.conf` file. This file is located in the `/usr/local/samba/lib` directory, and it controls almost every aspect of SAMBA operation. In this file, you specify shares and permissions.

Toward the top of the `smb.conf` file, you'll see a section called `global`, which you can comment out. If you want to enable user validation by forwarding requests to an NT Server, edit this section and add the following two entries:

```
security = server
password server = <name of domain controller>
```

After adding these entries, you don't need to worry about creating user accounts or password synchronization between UNIX and Windows NT. You also will need to edit your `/etc/hosts` file and add the IP address mapping for the server name you entered in the Password Server field.

> **Note:** In my experience with SAMBA on a LINUX server, things ran very smoothly. I did run into a bug when using the Guest account with browsing, however. SAMBA does not like LINUX Guest accounts with a large amount of *user IDs* (UIDs). In my case, the UID was set into the upper 60,000s. I was unable to browse the SAMBA server until I set the UID down to 400. Bugs and errors like this can cause you to easily spend hours with SAMBA trying to find answers. It took me about four hours to find this fix.

The bottom half of the `smb.conf` file enables you to define your shares and printers. There are plenty of options for you to define, and the comments in this file provide some help.

You can get plenty of help on configuring printers and shares for SAMBA by viewing the man page for the `smb.conf` file by typing `man smb.conf` at your SAMBA server's command prompt. Also, any changes you make to the `smb.conf` file do not take effect until `smbd` and `nmbd` are stopped and restarted.

After SAMBA is up and running, users won't know the difference between the SAMBA server and a typical Windows NT server. As Figure 34.5 shows, SAMBA servers appear in the user's browse list just as any other Microsoft server does.

Notes About SAMBA

Although SAMBA appears to be the answer to all your Windows NT-to-UNIX needs, SAMBA does have some downsides. The lack of dedicated support for the product could be reason enough to make you hesitant to roll out SAMBA as your main desktop link to the UNIX world. You must support SAMBA yourself. Plenty of newsgroups and mailing lists are available to help you get answers to your questions, though.

SAMBA also makes your UNIX server vulnerable to SMB-based security attacks, especially when connected to the Internet. To help prevent this, close UDP ports 137 and 138, and TCP port 139 on your routers and firewalls. Closing these ports prevents SMB clients from mounting your server's shares. You can also use the Hosts Allow option in the `smb.conf` file to explicitly list the clients who can access the shares on your SAMBA server.

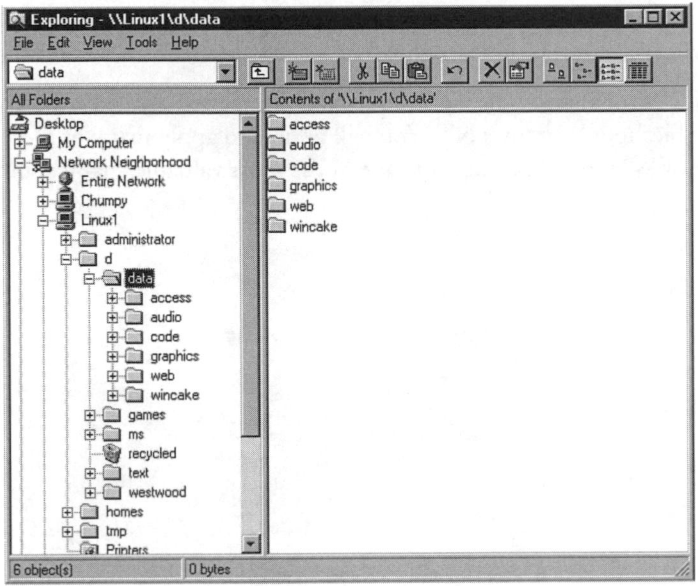

Figure 34.5. *Browsing a SAMBA share on server* `Linux1`.

When working with files on a SAMBA host, remember that UNIX filenames are case sensitive. Also, filenames might not show up in the directory at times because they are not DOS- compliant. To view these files from a client, set the `mangled names = yes` entry in the `smb.conf` file.

SAMBA also is available for VMS, Novell, and OS/2, which provides some level of cross-platform support.

Summary

In almost every diverse network, there will surely be UNIX systems offering valuable and irreplaceable benefits to the organization. Simply throwing out UNIX for Windows NT often is an unwise and unacceptable solution. Fortunately, making UNIX and Windows NT work together isn't as daunting as it seems. By using the out-of-box connectivity that Windows NT provides, along with third-party solutions, connecting these two systems can be surprisingly simple and painless.

To see what other products are available for connecting Windows NT with UNIX, such as X Window clients and servers, you can look at Microsoft's Windows NT Resources page at

`http://www.microsoft.com/ntserver/tools/`

This page lists both client and server applications to help you find the products you need to solve your connectivity problems.

You also might want to consider a Web-based solution for connecting Windows NT and UNIX. For information on this solution, see the discussion of Microsoft's IIS in Chapter 49.

In Chapter 35, "Troubleshooting Techniques and Strategies," we take a look at steps you should follow to troubleshoot Windows NT. You will be able to apply many of these methodologies to your support of Windows NT, and it is one of the most valuable chapters in this book.

PART VIII

Keeping Windows NT Running—Troubleshooting Your Environment

Troubleshooting Techniques and Strategies

by Terry W. Ogletree

Perhaps the most frustrating part of trying to diagnose problems on a computer attached to a network is the overwhelming number of factors that can be involved in isolating a problem. Is it hardware or software? Is it the local computer, or is there a resource problem on the network? When a user attempts to vocalize a problem, it is human nature to frame the words in the context of the impact the problem has on the user.

Suppose that a user complains that the word processor software is broken. What he really means is that he cannot open a document. The problem might lie in resource permissions, users' rights, or network communications. The user might even be using the wrong set of commands to open the document. But, to the user, it's the word processor that is malfunctioning, because he cannot do the same job he usually does every day using the program.

The first thing you should keep in mind when you enter troubleshooting mode is that you must listen and gather evidence that relates to the symptoms the user reports. To gather evidence and evaluate the data in a systematic, scientific way, you should record your observations to help determine what is relevant and what has been tried before.

This chapter briefly examines some of the techniques you can use to make your problem-solving tasks more productive. Three important topics will be discussed:

- Recording your observations, actions, and results
- Examining the problem thoroughly and localizing the symptoms before deciding on a plan of action
- Testing the assumptions from your plan and, if the results do not direct you to a solution, reexamining the remaining facts and modifying your plan

Write It Down

Record keeping is an important tool in problem solving. If you are working in a fast-paced environment and are dealing constantly with myriad problems, keeping a written record of your observations, actions, and results can result in a significant time savings. When problems are passed to a subordinate, does that person have to start all over in the information-gathering process? If you require that all problems begin with a succinct statement of the problem (instead of a vague "it's broke" type of problem statement), and if each person who works on the problem is required to record his actions, it can be easier to logically step closer and closer to a solution.

Another reason to write down your observations and actions is that when you read over a problem statement, you sometimes will find that a seemingly insignificant bit of information now stands out; this enables you to detect patterns. Although the symptoms that cause the user the most distress might get the most attention in the written record, the little details that recur sometimes can point the way to a whole new understanding of the situation—and thus a solution to the problem.

So, when you are in the process of solving computer problems, keep a running problem statement that contains these three elements:

- An initial problem statement that describes the problem in objective terms
- A list of further observations and actions taken during the problem-solving effort
- Conclusions reached during the problem-solving process

The last item might not help you during the first round of problem solving, but it might be of great value in the future. Instead of reinventing the wheel each time a problem arises, you can draw on your experience by keeping a database of problems and their effective resolutions. Many help desks are built around this concept. A user calls in with a problem. The first thing the help-desk person does is search the `Problems` database to see whether a similar situation has occurred. If so, he usually can use the written problem reports to help quickly resolve problems that recur.

Examine the Problem and Gather Information

After you receive a problem complaint and compose the initial problem statement, you need to gather further data that relates to the problem.

Using the scientific method, you divide and conquer. You take your observations and act on them. First, evaluate the symptoms you have. Formulate a possible scenario that explains the data you have. Test the scenario by selectively isolating factors that you know are related to the scenario. Did the test succeed or fail? As you isolate selected factors and the problem still arises, you can eliminate factors that are not relevant to the problem.

Use Windows NT Diagnostic Utilities and Log Files

Gathering information means more than just getting a problem description from a user. Windows NT comes with many utilities you can use to obtain diagnostic information. The Event logs (System, Application, and Security) can provide a wealth of information—as long as you have configured the system to audit the events. Deciding which events to audit is something you will develop a feel for over time. A good way to start is to audit all events, become familiar with the messages that are logged, and then begin to filter the events you consider important on your system.

You always can turn auditing on and off. If your system resources are limited, and you cannot always audit a lot of events, you can choose to audit selected events when you are troubleshooting. You can use the Performance Monitor to examine your system in the same manner. If you decide to turn on statistics for disk events, you might notice a slight degradation in performance. For that reason, logical and physical disk counters are not enabled by default when you use the Performance Monitor. You use the `DISKPERF` command to enable or disable counters for disk-related activity.

Log files also can be a great source of information. If you are running the *Internet Information Server* (IIS), for example, you can use the log files it generates for each of the services (WWW, Gopher, and FTP) to locate information specific to the time frame in which a problem occurs.

Many protocol-specific utilities, such as the PING utility, come with Windows NT to provide standard troubleshooting tools. The next chapter discusses in more detail the tools and utilities provided with NT that you can use to track down problems.

Localize the Symptoms

When you begin to formulate tests that can be used to eliminate symptoms systematically, you should not just blindly strike out and hope you will hit something. Plan your actions using reasonable hunches as to where the problem lies.

Find the First Point of Failure

You should try to localize the symptoms you observe. In other words, you should try to pin down the actual point of failure. More than one point of failure might exist in any particular problem. There might even be a cascading set of problems—each set off by the problem preceding it. Windows NT is a complex operating system. Services do not necessarily run in a vacuum. By examining entries in the Registry, you can see that some services depend on the successful startup of other services. These dependencies can complicate your troubleshooting efforts if you do not take the time to understand which symptoms to examine first and to find out exactly where these symptoms are occurring.

Examine the following Registry key, for example:

```
HKEY_LOCAL_MACHINE\SYSTEM\CurrentControlSet\Control\Services
```

In this example, you can see each service that is configured to run on your NT computer and the parameter values the operating system uses to start and run the service. The value `DependOnGroup` is present for some services (as well as the `DependOnService` parameter) which, when present, shows the service group or service that needs to be started successfully before the selected service can run.

If you use the Event Viewer to examine messages, you often will see a message that indicates that the service failed to start due to a dependency such as this. The point is that you should not start your investigation with the service that produces the last event message. You should trace down through the messages, correlating them with the values in the Registry that show you the dependencies, and try to determine which was the first error to occur.

Is It the Network or the Computer? (Or Both?)

The preceding section was an example of localizing the symptoms to a particular service on a computer. You should begin the process of tracking down exactly where a problem actually occurred, however, by looking at the entire situation. A good system administrator is aware of the network topology and the devices connected to the network. If you do not keep up with the elements that make up your network, you will spend a lot of time trying to track down network problems, because you won't even know which devices to consider when trying to form an idea of the problem.

Use your common sense and the various tools provided by Windows NT (and the Resource Kit) to determine whether you have a network problem or whether the problem exists on a particular computer or other device on the network. It should seem quite sensible that if a user cannot read a file from a floppy disk that the problem is highly unlikely to be a network problem. If a user cannot log on to a domain, but the workstation works just fine otherwise, you might have a problem with the domain controller or with the user entering invalid information. Again, common sense helps you arrive at valid conclusions most of the time if you have a good understanding of the layout of your network and the patterns of use associated with it.

If you determine that the problem is most likely occurring on a particular computer, you should try to vary the circumstances under which the error occurs to eliminate possible causes of the error.

You should ask questions such as these of the user who reported the problem:

1. Has the computer, the application, or some other device or software component ever worked before, or is this the first time the problem has occurred?
2. If this has worked before, what is different now?
3. If the user was able to perform this task in the past, was it on a computer different from the one he currently is using?
4. Has anything at all changed on the network or the computer (such as a password)?
5. Has the hardware been modified in any way?

If a user is trying to perform an action for the first time, you should start with a simple procedure: Follow the directions the user is given to perform the task and see whether it works for you. If the user has performed the task before, go over the instructions with him to be sure that the user is entering the correct information.

Is the user performing the task on a different computer than he normally uses? Workstations and servers can be set up to optimally perform certain tasks and can be configured to run some services and not others. A user might install a software package on a computer and not realize that it doesn't work because the package depends on the installation of some other piece of software.

Has the user's password expired? Has someone changed the permissions on a resource? Is a network server down? Is the network protocol functioning?

If the hardware has been changed, was the *Hardware Compatibility List* (HCL) checked to see whether the device is supported under Windows NT?

The questions you can come up with can be endless. The secret is to use common sense. Narrow down the problem to find the cause instead of blindly trying to examine every possible reason why something could go wrong.

Be Proactive

As stated earlier, a good administrator is aware of the devices connected to the network and has some idea of the usage on the network. If you have a small office LAN that rarely changes, it can be simple to keep in your head an idea of how the network functions.

That will not help on the day you're out of the office and someone else is saddled with a problem, though. What seems so simple to you might involve a whole day of troubleshooting and frustration for another person. One of the most needless mistakes an administrator can make is to patch a problem when it is discovered instead of correcting the problem. Often, it can be simple to perform a quick fix just before the office closes and tell yourself that you surely will fix it in the morning.

But then a meeting comes up, and then something else comes up, and before you know it, you've forgotten all about the problem—and the fix, because you never wrote it down and you don't keep good records of your system.

To see a perfect example of this situation, suppose that you use an `LMHOSTS` file to map a network name to an address when a computer is having problems using a DNS or WINS server to resolve names and addresses. When another user has the same problem, you might remember that you fixed a similar problem just last week, but you cannot remember how you did it. Not only do you have to research the problem all over again, but you also leave behind a trail of other problems that are really only half-fixed.

Document the Network Layout

Many software packages are available on the market to help you map the devices on your network and their configurations. If your network is large enough, you can perform a lot of this task by using the *Systems Management Server* (SMS) BackOffice product. If you want graphical representations of your network, third-party tools are available that will draw these for you.

Using something as simple as a spreadsheet to keep information on each computer or other device on the network and to record important configuration parameters (such as IP address and computer name) can be a big help. Not only can you use such a database to assist in problem solving, but also to perform other network administrative chores, such as alerting you when computers that are leased are about to go offlease.

Prepare for the Unexpected

It's easy to prepare for things if you know they are going to happen. If you have pagers at your workplace, you know in advance that the battery used in each pager has a time limit on how long it will continue to power the pager. You plan ahead by purchasing replacement batteries and keeping them at the office. If you produce a lot of hard-copy output, you know in advance that you will need more paper, and you schedule the purchases accordingly.

Preparing for what you cannot predict is a little harder. You can use the backup procedures that come with some system services and utilities, such as the automatic database backup in the WINS server software. You can keep distribution disks and CD-ROMs offsite for the software you use on your computers. Because the last resort you have when you encounter a problem that has no solution is to use your backup resource, you should give a high priority to maintaining adequate backup procedures. When you add computers and interconnections to your network, you should continually reevaluate the plan you use for your backup to be sure that it will meet your needs if disaster strikes.

Plan Your Backup Procedures for Recoverability

There are many standard plans for creating backup tapes and ensuring secure storage of the backup media. One of the most common plans consists of these steps:

1. Create a full backup of each computer system once a week—usually, during non-peak office hours. An automated backup on a weekend day is a good time for this.
2. Run an incremental backup each day during the week to capture just the data that was created or modified during that day.
3. Each week, send the most current full backup to an offsite storage site and bring back the older backup media.
4. Keep the incremental backups for two weeks to ensure recoverability if the most recent full backup is compromised.

Using this simple plan, you always can recover data from the full backup set and the intervening incremental backups to restore files up to the time of the most recent incremental backup. By storing the most recent full backup offsite, keeping two weeks of incremental backups, and keeping the next most recent full backup, you will have two paths of restoration if one of the full backups becomes unusable.

Warning: The backup utility included with Windows NT makes a complete backup of your Registry files only if you perform the backup locally, and only if you are making a backup of the drive on which the Registry files are stored. If you use the utility to back up other computers on the network, the Registry files from those computers will not be backed up. You can only back up Registry files by making a backup locally on the computer that these files reside on.

For this reason, if you back up computers via the network, you should use one of the other tools provided by NT, such as the `REGBACK.EXE` and `REGREST.EXE` programs, to keep copies of important files offline.

Note that this plan does not take any precaution to recover from the destruction of one of the incremental backups. You can elaborate on this simple plan to develop a backup schedule that gives you the amount of recoverability required by your business needs.

Back Up Important System Files

In addition to keeping a full backup of your System disk and any additional data disks, you should keep the necessary floppy disks to boot the system if a catastrophic problem arises. If necessary, you can just reinstall the operating system and then spend a lot of time reinstalling software and recovering data. If the point of failure is a corrupted System file, however, you can recover more quickly by keeping a set of Setup boot disks used when you install the operating system and an *Emergency Repair Disk* (ERD).

Create Setup Floppy Disks

The three Setup boot disks come with the CD-ROM software distribution and are used during the initial installation of NT on a computer. If you do not have the disks, you can create a set by using the Setup program with the following syntax:

```
> WINNT.EXE /O
```

or

```
> WINNT32.EXE /O
```

Create an Emergency Repair Disk

You can create the Emergency Repair Disk by using the `RDISK` command at the command prompt. You then have to insert a formatted diskette, so it's best to create that disk first and then execute the command. Figure 35.1 shows the Repair Disk Utility dialog box that appears when you run RDISK.

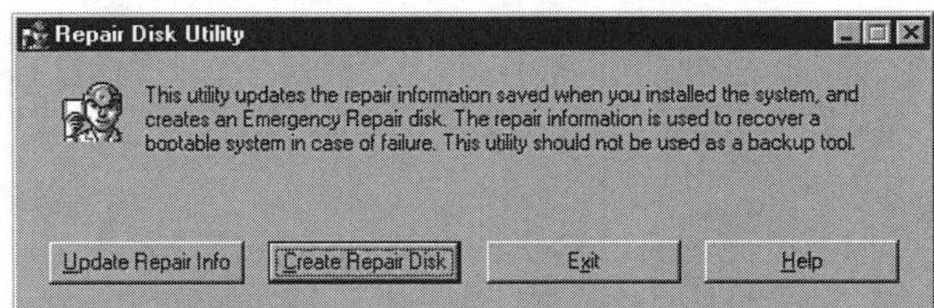

Figure 35.1. *The Repair Disk Utility (RDISK.EXE) allows you to update configuration information and to create an Emergency Repair Disk.*

When you install Windows NT, the Setup program creates the directory `%SYSTEMROOT%\Repair` and copies the files from `%SYSTEMROOT%\System32\Config` to that directory as a backup. The RDISK utility places these files onto a diskette, and also can be used to update the information in the Repair directory (Update Repair Info button in Figure 35.1). Table 35.1 lists the files saved by the RDISK utility.

Table 35.1. Files saved by the RDISK utility.

File	*Description*
`Autoexec.nt`	Used by `Default.pif` file (when user runs an MS-DOS application without specifying a PIF file). Many, but not all commands available for use in the `Autoexec.bat` file can be used.
`Config.NT`	Used by `Default.pif` file (when a user runs an MS-DOS application without specifying a PIF file). Many, but not all commands available for use in the `Config.bat` file can be used.
`Default._`	A compressed file copy of the `HKEY_USERS\DEFAULT` Registry key.
`Ntuser.da_`	A compressed file copy of `%SYSTEMROOT%\Profiles\Default\user\Ntuser.dat.`
`Sam._`	A compressed file copy of the `HKEY_LOCAL_MACHINE\SAM` Registry key.
`Security._`	A compressed file copy of the `HKEY_LOCAL_MACHINE\SECURITY` Registry key.
`Setup.log`	Contains setup information used by the repair process (this log file is created by the Setup program).
`Software._`	A compressed file copy of the `HKEY_LOCAL_MACHINE\SOFTWARE` Registry key.
`System._`	A compressed file copy of the `HKEY_LOCAL_MACHINE\SYSTEM` Registry key.

When you use the RDISK utility to repair the information in the Repair directory the only files that are copied, by default, to the Repair directory are the System and Software Registry hive files. If you invoke the utility using the command-line switch `/s` (`RDISK /S`), then the Sam and Security files are copied to the Repair directory also.

After RDISK finishes updating files in the Repair directory it will prompt you to create or update your Emergency Repair Disk (see Figure 35.2). You can also select to do this from the opening dialog box (refer to Figure 35.1).

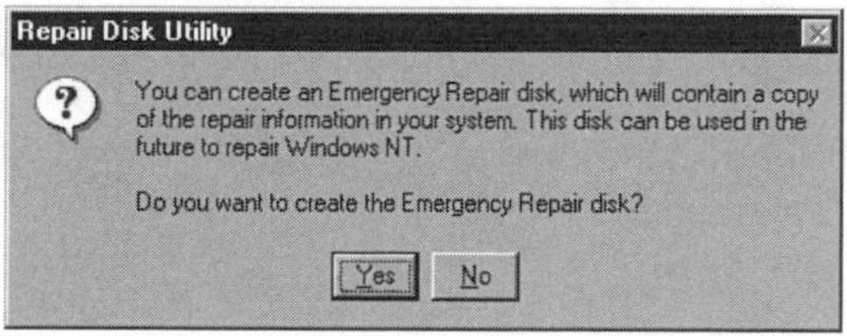

Figure 35.2. *After the information in the Repair directory is updated, you are prompted to create the ERD.*

When you choose to create an ERD, the utility will ask you to insert a diskette into the floppy drive and will also warn you that the diskette will be formatted before the ERD is created. If you choose to proceed, the utility will format the disk and copy the appropriate configuration files to the floppy.

It is important to note that an ERD is not a replacement for a backup of the System disk. It is a tool that can be used with a corrupted disk or with a disk restored from a backup when the System disk is too badly damaged to be repaired. The ERD stores a minimum of information needed to attempt a repair. You will notice from looking at Table 35.1 that the user accounts are not stored on the ERD. This is because the size of the security directory database can become quite large—in excess of 30MB. You cannot possibly fit this much information on a convenient number of diskettes!

If you keep a regular backup of the System disk, however, you can use the ERD with that backup to fully restore the system in most instances.

Use Other Backup Utilities

In addition to using the RDISK utility and keeping a good backup of the System disk, you can use a few other utilities to prepare for problems with the System disk.

The Windows NT Server 4.0 Resource Kit contains the utilities `Regback.exe` and `Regrest.exe`, which can be used to save and restore copies of the Registry files. You can use these utilities to save and restore all the Registry files or just portions of them. If your troubleshooting skills are keen enough that you are confident manipulating the Registry, then using these two tools may enable you to more quickly fix problems as long as you are sure that you know what you are doing.

You can save the Registry key `HKEY_LOCAL_MACHINE\SYSTEM` by choosing Registry | Save Key from the `Regedt32.exe` Registry Editor program. You also can use the Disk Administrator to do the same thing (choose Configuration | Save), but it will only enable you to save the information to a diskette, whereas the Registry Editor enables you to specify the path.

Before installing new hardware drivers or making other major changes to your system, you always should be sure to have as many backup resources to fall back on as you might need to restore the system. Using more than one resource practically ensures that you will be able to recover from most problems.

Summary

To effectively troubleshoot problems on your computer or network, it is important to attack the problems in an orderly, defined manner. Keep a written record of the problem and the steps you take when trying to find a solution. Use your history of written solutions to make problem resolution easier in the future.

Take the time to investigate a problem thoroughly. Don't get bogged down with irrelevant details; formulate an action plan you can use to create test situations that point to the relevant factors.

When gathering information for problem resolution, do not forget the many tools and utilities that come with Windows NT, or with the Resource Kits that you can purchase separately. The next chapter will go into more detail about tools that can be helpful for troubleshooting.

If you prepare for the worst by having a good backup policy in place, you can recover from almost any problem. You cannot always predict what is going to happen, but if you prepare for a complete disaster, you usually will have enough resources to recover from even the largest problem.

Windows NT Troubleshooting Utilities

by John West

Having things go wrong is never any fun, and though it may not happen often, it's important to know what utilities are available to help get your NT system up and running as quickly as possible. This chapter is designed to introduce you to some of the utilities available to help troubleshoot the NT operating system. Using these utilities can help you to resolve the problems you are experiencing.

In this chapter we are going to look at the following:

- The troubleshooting utilities included with Windows NT
- The troubleshooting utilities included with the Windows NT Resource Kit
- The utilities that Microsoft offers through electronic services such as the Internet or CompuServe

Utilities Provided in the NT Package

Windows NT provides useful tools to assist in troubleshooting problems with NT. Utilities included in the NT operating system are the Windows NT Hardware Detection tool, Windows NT Diagnostics, Performance Monitor, and Event Logs. This section examines each of these utilities.

General Utilities

The utilities under this section can help troubleshoot the system and software applications, and can help maintain accurate records on your system configuration.

Windows NT Hardware Detection Tool

The Windows NT Hardware Detection Tool (NTHQ) is provided on the Windows NT CD-ROM in the `\support\hqtool` directory. This utility provides information on the configuration of your hardware. The information provided by NTHQ includes the following:

- PCI, EISA, and ISA bus information
- A report on whether items like your video and network card are compatible with NT
- Information and capabilities on installed mass storage devices

NTHQ requires you to reboot your system and boot off the disk that is created by the `makedisk.bat` file located in the `\support\hqtool` directory. Once it has started, it will query the system for its configuration information. When NTHQ finishes querying your system, you can save a copy of the report to your local hard drive only if it is partitioned as FAT, or save it to the NTHQ disk.

Generally, this utility is used to send data to support personnel when working on a technical problem with your system. Support engineers can use the data provided from this utility to get an accurate picture of what is running on the system. It is also helpful to use this utility for maintaining configuration data sheets on your system.

Windows NT Diagnostics

Windows NT diagnostics is a terrific utility included as part of every NT installation. This utility has seen some major modifications in release 4.0 of Windows NT, which includes information on the configuration and status of your workstation. You can start Windows NT diagnostics by going to the Administrative Tools folder and clicking the NT diagnostics icon. The following tabs are available:

- Version—The Version tab provides information on the version level of Windows NT and any service packs that have been installed. In addition, you will see the CD Key, product code, and platform version of the installed operating system.

- Display—The Display tab shows the version and creator of the currently installed video driver, current refresh setting, amount of installed RAM, and other details related to the video driver.
- Drives—The Drives tab enables you to view information on physical and networked drives available to the machine. Drives can be grouped by type or by connection. Information about the drive's geometry and file system can also be viewed.
- Services—The Services tab gives the name and state of all installed services. This tab also gives you the ability to view installed devices and the status of the devices.
- Resources—The Resources tab shows the resources the system is using. Resources like IRQ, I/O, DMA, and memory can be viewed here.
- Environment—The Environment tab shows information on path parameters, commspec configuration, library paths, and installed OS.
- Network—The Network tab enables you to view information on network-related information such as number of users logged on, received SMB blocks, maximum locks, and other related items.
- Memory—The Memory tab allows you to view information concerning memory use and allocation in the NT Operating System.
- System—The System tab provides system hardware information. This includes the systems BIOS, HAL, and installed processors.

Windows NT diagnostics gives you the ability to view any of these items on local or remote systems. This enables you to check on what driver versions are installed on separate machines or print reports to compare the differences between the two. In addition, you may print any of the items or a summary report to help you keep track of the resources used by your system over a period of time.

Performance Monitor

Windows NT provides a flexible and solid tool to monitor the performance of applications and the system's hardware. The Performance Monitor in Windows NT gives numerous data collection counters and flexible views.

Counters

Counters are specific items in NT on which data can be collected. An example of a counter would be the average throughput of data of a hard disk. The Windows NT Performance Monitor groups counters based on object type. Object types usually represent a physical item like a hard drive or a processor. Here is a list of the common object types you will find on most NT machines:

Cache	Paging File	Redirector
LogicalDisk	PhysicalDisk	Server
Memory	Process	System
Objects	Processor	Thread

Performance Monitor has a ton of counters available for monitoring. If that's not enough, additional counters can be added to it by other applications that are installed to the NT operating system.

Views

The Performance Monitor in Windows NT enables you to view data collected in either chart, alert, log, or report view. Each of these views enables you to examine collected data in ways that the other views may not offer.

- Chart—This view provides a chart view of information, as shown in Figure 36.1. This view is good for looking at peaks and doing comparisons against multiple counters.

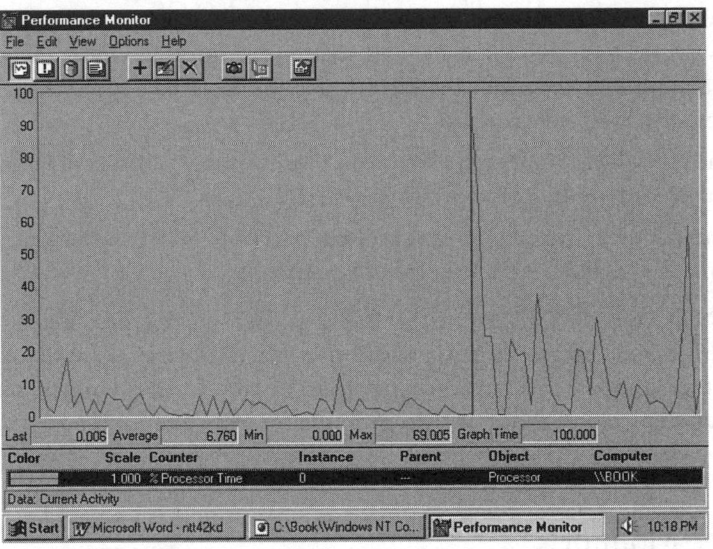

Figure 36.1. *Chart view in the Windows NT Performance Monitor.*

- Alert—Alert view enables you to take counters and establish thresholds that will send out system alerts if the counter threshold is reached.
- Log—The log view enables you to view the values of counters that have been or are being saved to disk. Using the log view is necessary if you plan to archive information over a long period of time.
- Report—Working in this view is particularly useful for doing long-term comparisons in troubleshooting studies. This view enables you to view summaries of the data stored by counters during your test.

The Performance Monitor included with Windows NT is a powerful and flexible tool. It provides the ability to collect and view data in many different ways. By using its strengths and flexibility, the Performance Monitor can be a powerful tool in determining and even preventing problems from happening on your operating system.

Server Manager

Server Manager for Domains, which comes with Windows NT Server, is a utility that can be useful when trying to troubleshoot problems with NT. One important thing that the Server Manager will enable you to do is to shut down a service from a remote workstation. This comes in handy if you have an NT server that will not let you log on locally but is still available to the network. Using Server Manager, you can shut down applications such as SQL Server safely before shutting the server down.

Event Logs

NT's event logs are capable of storing just about anything that goes on in the operating system. NT was designed from the ground up to include support for C2 security. In meeting this goal, the NT operating system had to provide auditing capabilities on all actions performed by the operating system, applications, and users. This data is collected and stored in one of three event logs: the application, system, or security log.

Application

The application log records all messages concerning applications running on the NT operating system. You should always check this log if you are having a problem with an application on your NT system. A properly written application will leave a message in this area that explains the problem that it is having.

System

The system log provides information on systems events, such as network card failures, or when the event log is started. If you are having hardware problems with your NT system, this is a good place to look.

Security

The security log, as you probably have already guessed, contains information on the security events that happen inside NT. Security logging must be turned on before data is written to this log.

Network Utilities

Figuring out why your machine cannot communicate with the rest of the network can be a tedious and time-consuming task. NT provides utilities that are helpful in making this task a little easier on you. The utilities listed in this section are useful in troubleshooting problems with your network.

Network Monitor

Network Monitor gives you the ability to view network data as it passes across the network. Windows NT version 4.0 now ships with a version of Network Monitor. Those of you familiar with the Network Monitor that ships with SMS should note that the version that ships with NT 4.0 is trimmed down so that it only shows traffic destined to and leaving from the server on which the Network Monitor program is running. Figure 36.2 gives you an idea what the Network Monitor looks like. As you can see, the Network Monitor enables you to view all packets coming into the local system. Details such as packet type, destination, and source are available. This is a great tool for working out bandwidth and other network-related problems.

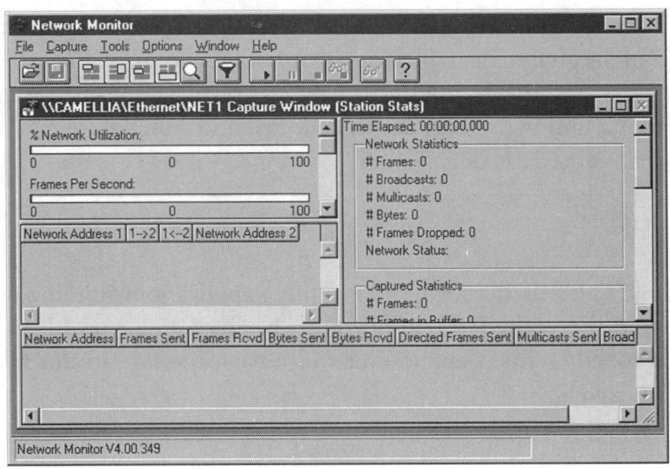

Figure 36.2. *The Network Monitor.*

ipconfig

`ipconfig` is a terrific utility used to determine current IP configuration data to all devices in the system. For example, if you are trying to figure out the IP address of a Windows NT system that receives configuration information through the dynamic host configuration protocol (DHCP), you could run `ipconfig` from the command prompt to view the system's TCP/IP address. Figure 36.3 shows what the results of running `ipconfig` look like.

```
Command Prompt
Microsoft(R) Windows NT(TM)
(C) Copyright 1985-1996 Microsoft Corp.

D:\>ipconfig

Windows NT IP Configuration

Ethernet adapter NdisWan7:

        IP Address. . . . . . . . . : 199.5.54.101
        Subnet Mask . . . . . . . . : 255.255.255.0
        Default Gateway . . . . . . : 199.5.54.101

Ethernet adapter NdisWan6:

        IP Address. . . . . . . . . : 0.0.0.0
        Subnet Mask . . . . . . . . : 0.0.0.0
        Default Gateway . . . . . . :

D:\>_
```

Figure 36.3. *The* `ipconfig` *utility.*

ping

`ping` is provided as part of most TCP/IP capable systems. You use `ping` to send a message to a specified computer and await its return. This is a terrific way to see if you are capable of contacting anyone else on the network. Figure 36.4 lists the results of using `ping`. Another great thing about `ping` is that you can use either the IP address or the fully qualified domain name of the system you are trying to contact. This enables you to determine whether you are having Domain Name Server (DNS) or IP configuration problems with your system.

```
Command Prompt
D:\>NBTSTAT -R

Successful purge and preload of the NBT Remote Cache Name Table.

D:\>tracert 199.5.54.1

Tracing route to CAMELLIA [199.5.54.1]
over a maximum of 30 hops:

  1   3095 ms   2894 ms   2964 ms   CAMELLIA [199.5.54.1]

Trace complete.

D:\>
```

Figure 36.4. *Results from using the* `ping` *utility.*

NBTSTAT

`NBTSTAT` provides important information about NetBIOS name resolution and table configurations. One very important thing to know about `NBTSTAT` is that if you use LMHOSTS files in your network configuration and you make a change to this file, it will be necessary to run `NBTSTAT -R` to flush the cache and reload the file. This will give you access to the systems that you added to the LMHOSTS file.

Tracert

Tracert is a utility used to show the path your data takes when communicating with a remote node. If you are having network problems, this utility can help you determine where a breakdown in communications is occurring.

Utilities Provided in the Resource Kit

The Windows NT Resource Kit from Microsoft can be found on the Technet CD-ROM, or it can be purchased in full text form from most bookstores or directly from Microsoft. The utilities included on the CD-ROM in either the Technet or book version are a terrific resource for troubleshooting. The bottom line is that if you do not have these utilities already, get them. Outlined in the next few sections are some of the more useful utilities for troubleshooting.

Crystal Reports Event Viewer

The Crystal Reports Event Viewer is useful for collecting and parsing through the data stored to the event logs. Using this utility, you can create customized reports to let you know of any errors that have occurred over a specified period of time. This is really useful for sights that have a lot of traffic on their systems and are looking for a quick and easy way to collect the data necessary for an accurate analysis of the network.

Blue Screen Utilities

If you have ever had the opportunity to witness a blue screen firsthand, you already know blue screens are bad. Blue screens occur when something in the operating system has gone so bad that the only thing NT can do is stop functioning, dump its memory contents to a file on the hard drive, and start over. If you do get one of these, you are sure as heck going to want to find out what caused it as quickly as possible. The utilities discussed in the following two sections are designed to assist you in determining what exactly is killing your system so that you can then figure out how to fix it.

Dumpchk

Dumpchk is a command-line utility used to verify that a dump file is in good condition. To use the Dumpchk utility, jump out to the command prompt and type in the command along with the path to the dump file. The program will then go out and report back any errors with the file.

Dumpexam

The `Dumpexam` utility is used to convert data in the memory dump file into a more legible text file. The text created by this utility can usually provide a support engineer with the information needed to determine the cause of the problem.

Disk Utilities

Disk utilities provided in the resource kit give users advanced functions for troubleshooting problems with the disk subsystem. You will find utilities used for troubleshooting disk problems outlined in the following two sections.

FTEDIT

`FTEDIT` is used to help re-create and edit the Registry parameters that apply to the fault-tolerant partitions. This utility is very useful if you had to re-install NT and you do not have a fault-tolerant boot disk. `FTEDIT` enables you to go in and re-create the Registry parameters necessary to access your fault-tolerant drives.

Dumpflop

The `Dumpflop` utility is used to dump the memory dump file created by a Windows NT blue screen to a floppy disk instead of the hard drive. I do not recommend using this utility unless you really have no other choice. You see, the memory dump will be the size of whatever the physical and virtual memory space size happened to be—minus what the disk compression can take off—at the time of the blue screen. Most NT systems have a minimum of 32MB of RAM, so you are already at a potential 10-15 floppy disk minimum download. Not a whole lot of fun.

Utilities Available Online

Most technology companies make utilities and resources available through online services such as the Internet. In addition to utilities, lots of companies also provide discussion areas and white papers online to assist users in using their products. Microsoft provides some of the best online resources for their products of the companies around. The resources Microsoft uses to provide access to electronic data are discussed in the following sections.

World Wide Web on the Internet

The popularity of the Internet and the World Wide Web has made this area one of the most popular places to post updated materials on products and issues. The following are just some of the Web sites that Microsoft provides.

Microsoft Windows NT Server Home Page

This page provides access to the latest information and utilities available from Microsoft. You can also get access to the Windows NT Knowledge Base that Microsoft makes available online. This is a terrific resource that you can query for information on problems you are experiencing:

`http://www.microsoft.com/NTServer`

Microsoft Windows NT Workstation Home Page

Similar to the Windows NT Server Home Page, the Windows NT Workstation home page gives you access to resources that allow you to keep your NT Workstation working at peak efficiency:

`http://www.microsoft.com/NTWorkstation`

Microsoft Windows NT Server Support Options

This area provides NT Server support options. Here you will find technical white papers and will be able to access and query online databases for solutions to your problems:

`http://www.microsoft.com/ntserver/support`

Microsoft Windows NT Workstation Support Options

This area supports data for Windows NT Workstation and provides access to troubleshooting databases and white papers:

`http://www.microsoft.com/NTWksSupport`

Windows NT Troubleshooting Guides

The Windows NT Troubleshooting Guides walk you through a series of questions concerning the problem you are experiencing. After you have gone through the series of questions, you are presented with a solution to your problem:

`http://www.microsoft.com/NTWksSupport/content/nttroubleshoot`

Microsoft Technet

The Microsoft Technet CD-ROM is available as a subscription service from Microsoft. This CD-ROM contains more than 1,500 technical documents related to Microsoft products. These technical documents contain information on troubleshooting, network planning, installation, and maintenance of NT products. A directory list of all NT-related areas of the Technet CD-ROM follows:

MS BackOffice
- MS Windows NT Server
  - Technical Notes
    - Windows NT Hardware and Licensing Planning Guide
    - Capacity Planning for Your Windows NT Server Network
    - Implementing Directory Services Using MS Windows NT Server
    - MS Windows NT Server Domain Strategy
    - Windows Desktop Family Integration into Business Environments
    - Windows NT and the Internet
    - Coexistence and Migration in Windows NT
- MS Windows NT Workstation
  - Product Facts
    - The Best Way to a 32-bit Desktop: Windows NT Workstation 4.0 and Windows 95
    - Microsoft Windows NT Operating System
    - Rescue for the HelpDesk—The Impact of Windows NT Workstation
    - Windows 95 and Windows NT Workstation Product Comparison
    - What's New in Windows NT Workstation Shell Update Release
  - Tools and Utilities
    - MS Windows 32-bit Financial Impact Analysis Tool

FTP on the Internet

The Microsoft FTP site provides access to patches, updates, documents, and software trials. This is a terrific area for getting the latest service pack for NT. Some of the software available for download includes the following:

- ◆ Microsoft Proxy Server
- ◆ Exchange 5.0
- ◆ SQL 6.5
- ◆ Microsoft Project

The following paths have information available through ftp from Microsoft:

```
ftp://ftp.microsoft.com/bussys/winnt-Root of the winnt ftp area. Service Pack,
➥White Papers and utilities are just some of the items that can be found here.
```

CompuServe

CompuServe provides a forum to post questions and receive answers to problems you are having with your Windows NT operating system. You can also get patches for the NT operating system from here.

```
Go to the Windows NT forum
```

America Online

Similar to CompuServe, America Online is a service provider that provides areas for discussing NT and receiving patches on the NT operating system.

Use the Windows NT Workstation folders under `software/operating systems/Windows/Windows NT`.

Summary

The Windows NT operating system provides a variety of utilities to assist in troubleshooting the NT operating system. These utilities can help reduce network downtime, increase user productivity, and even help detect potential problem areas. For more information on NT and its utilities, check out the Microsoft Windows NT home page at `www.microsoft.com/ntserver`.

CHAPTER 37

Third-Party Utilities

by Brett Bonenberger

Windows NT has several good utilities built into it, but there are many utilities that are not included. There was a time when NT was not supported by software vendors. With earlier versions of NT, it was difficult to find software utilities to use. Utilities such as virus scanning and backup software were just about non-existent. As NT began to gain popularity with versions 3.51 and 4.0, utilities began to come out of the walls. At Fall Comdex last November, most of the vendors there were touting new utilities for NT 4.0. It is amazing how quickly a product can gain popularity and show tremendous growth.

There has been an even greater growth in popularity for NT in the past few months. Most of this popularity stems from the release of NT 4.0. Many more vendors have begun to develop products. Products for Network Management, Disk Control, and Internet applications have all been coming out of the woodwork. I will explore some of the third-party utilities that are applicable to NT and give you a good understanding of the types of products that are available. Some of those types of products include the following:

- Virus scanning
- Network management
- Fax software
- Modem sharing software
- Backup software

I will cover these products by vendor so that you have an idea of the wide assortment of utilities that each vendor can provide for Windows NT.

The Applications

The following sections present brief descriptions of applications that are available for NT from Symantec and McAfee. Symantec and McAfee have both been in the software market for many years. The high quality of their older products has extended into NT. These utilities will help you maintain a reliable and stable system. The utilities include virus scanning, faxing, and desktop management applications.

Symantec

Symantec was one of the first companies to develop NT applications, and its list of NT software continues to grow. Additional information on the software packages discussed in this section can be found on Symantec's Web site at `http://www.symantec.com`.

Norton AntiVirus

Norton AntiVirus has been around for a while and just recently became available for Windows NT. Like most antivirus software, it searches and destroys any virus that exists on the network. A virus is a small software program written to purposely do harm to your computer systems. Viruses can affect boot sectors, rendering a hard drive useless. Viruses can also affect files, creating a large problem in a network situation where infected files can be shared to other users. You can receive a virus through files attached to e-mail or from diskettes brought in from another company or employee. Virus scanning and removal is a practice that should be a part of your network planning. I've always had a belief that the people who write viruses should be using their time to develop their programming skills and do something useful.

Norton AntiVirus offers auto-protection that automatically scans all local and remote files as they are downloaded, opened, saved, or created. Norton AntiVirus will run on an NT 3.51 or 4.0 server or workstation. You can buy a licensed pack version that will give you the ability to distribute all Norton AntiVirus configurations and virus definitions to your workstations for complete protection of your network.

Some of the other key features that Norton AntiVirus has include

- A patented polymorphic virus detection system called Striker
- LiveUpdate for automatically updating your virus signature files over the Internet or through a modem
- Protection for Windows NT-based FTP and Web Servers
- Detection of application macro viruses

Figure 37.1 shows the Norton AntiVirus application.

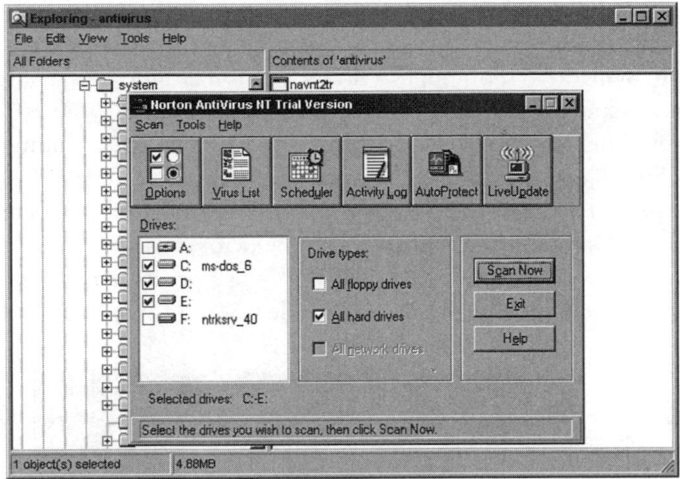

Figure 37.1. *Norton AntiVirus application.*

Norton NT Tools

Norton NT Tools is a combination of several programs that can help you with your administration of NT. NT Tools offers antivirus software, file management, and monitoring of system information.

The Norton AntiVirus software protects network resources and eliminates any virus that is found. It is also able to automatically update virus signature files so that you are assured of protection from viruses.

The file management supports compression and encryption and is also able to recognize UNC paths. With the Norton File Manager, you can drag and drop from FTP sites on the Internet.

System monitoring is accomplished through the System Doctor, which monitors all vital resources on the network and also provides you with statistics about hardware, memory, and peripherals.

Norton Secret Stuff

Lately, several articles have been published about e-mail and privacy, and ask the question: Who is reading your e-mail? This is causing a lot of controversy and people are looking for a way to prevent others from reading their e-mail. Norton Secret Stuff is a solution for this.

Norton Secret Stuff can be used to encrypt files that are attached to your e-mails so that no one except the intended receiver can read the files. The receiver does not need to have Secret Stuff to even read their e-mail. All attachments are sent in an executable form that prompts the receiver for a password when he clicks to open the executable. Attention multinational corporations: This product has been approved to be used in sending files overseas.

Norton Utilities

This is perhaps Symantec's most popular utility. Norton Utilities was first released in 1982—the early DOS days—and was a valuable tool then as it is now. Norton Utilities 2.0 for NT 4.0 enables you to do everything that the Windows 95 version is able to do, including defragmenting hard drives with Speed Disk, recovering deleted files with the Norton Protected Recycle Bin, monitoring system resources, and obtaining system information. System resource monitoring is done through the Norton System Doctor. System Doctor runs in the background, monitoring all vital system resources, and can auto alert you if there is a potential problem. Figure 37.2 shows a trial version of Speed Disk which is downloadable from the Symantec Web site.

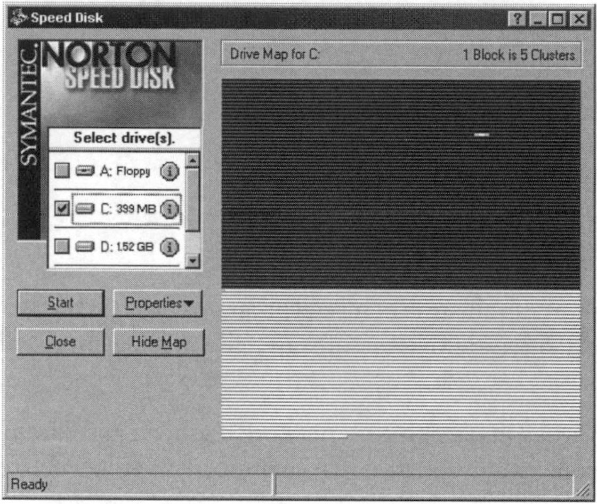

Figure 37.2. *Norton Speed Disk trial version.*

WinFax Pro 8.0

WinFax Pro is the best-selling personal fax software on the market. A network edition is now available that enables users on your network to fax from their desktop through network modems. The only limitation is that you can only use up to four modems simultaneously. WinFax Pro can integrate into an existing NET SatisFAXtion fax server. This installation will enable you to use up to eight fax ports simultaneously.

WinFax Pro offers many other benefits for those who have great needs for easy communication. TalkWorks allows for constant communication through WinFax Pro from remote locations. You can use TalkWorks to retrieve faxes, listen to voice mail messages, and if waiting for that critical fax, it will notify you of the fax and offer to forward it to a number where you are! The voice messaging features of TalkWorks allow you to maintain a log of every received message and will interact with Caller ID if you subscribe to the service. Another nice feature for those who have only one phone line is TalkWorks' capability to automatically detect the type of incoming call and answer it appropriately. You can also develop your own Fax On Demand solution!

WinFax Pro offers so many features, it is hard to find a more robust product. This product is perfect for the home office or small business owner.

Open Agent

There hasn't been a really good network management system for Windows NT. Most are not built to work fully with NT. Symantec has helped bridge the gap with Open Agent. Open Agent uses an existing SNMP monitoring console such as HP OpenView or IBM NetView and provides NT-specific monitoring capabilities within the SNMP console. Open Agent enables viewing all statistics from all NT workstations and servers and provides key information on server utilization, trends, and events.

Norton Administrator Suite

Norton Administrator Suite is an integrated package of different Symantec utilities to assist in network administration. The utilities included are

- Norton Administrator for Networks
- Norton Desktop Administrator
- Norton AntiVirus
- PcANYWHERE/32
- Symantec Exposé

As you can see, the Norton Administrator Suite gives you most of the tools that you need to effectively administer your network. You can manage all network and end-user resources from a single console, inventory desktop resources, plan and implement operating system and application upgrades, meter software licensing, and protect your network from viruses.

McAfee

McAfee also established itself in the early DOS days and has since become a leader in the software industry. McAfee began, of course, as a supplier of virus protection software. It now supplies a variety of software applications that can be used on a network or desktop. McAfee's support for Windows NT has not been as great as Symantec's, but they are moving toward that end. More information on the following McAfee products can be found at `http://www.mcafee.com`.

VirusScan for Windows NT

VirusScan made McAfee famous, and the company has extended its excellent virus protection software into the NT environments. VirusScan for NT is a native 32-bit application. It can scan all system areas including local and network drives, CD-ROMs, floppies, boot areas, and compressed files. It is also able to detect recursive infections of the same file and automatically work to stop reinfections. Figure 37.3 shows the VirusScan application for Windows NT Server.

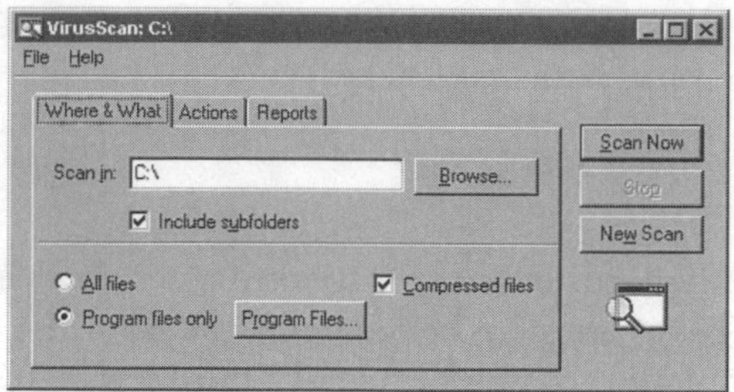

Figure 37.3. *McAfee VirusScan application for Windows NT.*

Netshield for Windows NT

Netshield is an extension of McAfee's VirusScan for networks. It scans and detects viruses in real time; in other words, as a file is written, created, or stored on the network, Netshield detects viruses and either isolates the file, deletes it, or cleans it. Netshield also runs scheduled scans on all local and networked drives. When a virus is found, Netshield will immediately send out notification.

Groupshield for Windows NT

Groupshield is McAfee's first virus protection system for groupware environments. Currently, it only supports Lotus Notes implementation. Groupshield detects and cleans macro viruses and bombs that are imbedded into e-mail messages and attached files. It will capture any virus that is routed through the enterprise.

SaberLAN Workstation

SaberLAN is a network management tool that includes several excellent utilities. With SaberLAN, you can monitor software licensing, software and hardware inventory, and software distribution, and restrict access to features and resources on the desktop. This is a standalone product that does not need any other third-party SNMP console software. SaberLAN will work in mixed Novell and NT environments.

Specialized Companies

Several companies operate within a specific product line. Most of the products developed for NT were first developed to work under Novell or UNIX.

Castelle

Castelle is known as the number one fax solution provider for Novell and is now moving into NT environments. Castelle uses a dedicated box called a FaxPress with a number of fax ports. You can use as many FaxPresses as you need. When you use multiple FaxPress boxes, one is configured as the master and the others as slaves. Each box acts as a network node. Like a desktop, the FaxPress can use TCP/IP for its communication protocol. Users are able to send faxes from within applications and receive faxes directly to their desktops. Outgoing faxes can be monitored from any workstation that has the FaxPress software installed. Each user can see the number of faxes that are going out but can only see details concerning his or her faxes.

FaxPress is an excellent solution for anyone who needs to do small broadcasts or receive personal faxes on the desktop. A very simple installation process and an intuitive interface make Castelle an excellent product for administrators and users alike. Figure 37.4 shows the Castelle FaxPress application. To get more information on Castelle, visit `http://www.Castelle.com`.

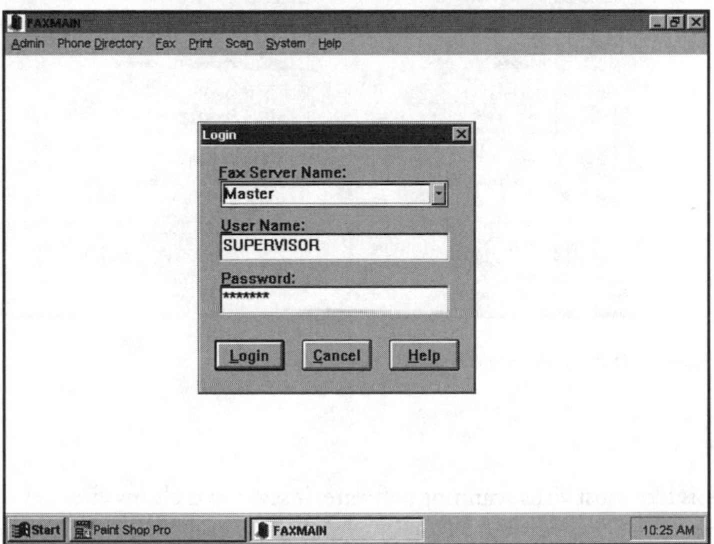

Figure 37.4. *The Castelle FaxPress application.*

Cheyenne

Cheyenne has several packages for use on NT, including its storage management software, ArcServe, and its virus scanning software, InocuLAN. To get more information about Cheyenne products, visit the company's Web site at `http://www.cheyenne.com`.

ArcServe

Cheyenne ArcServe is probably one of the best backup software packages on the market. With Version 6, Cheyenne has added some unique features. ArcServe supports tape RAID levels 0, 1, and 5. If you are using the RAID levels, and a tape fails, you will be able to complete a restoration.

ArcServe has included another very helpful feature: the Disaster Recovery Option. Tape restoration has always been the most scrutinized aspect of backup software. You could always back up data, but without an operating system installed, you cannot restore. The Disaster Recovery option uses a boot disk that will load drivers for the tape drive and begin restoration off a tape. It will restore all information, including the fully functioning operating system. Figure 37.5 shows the Cheyenne ArcServe Version 6 for NT.

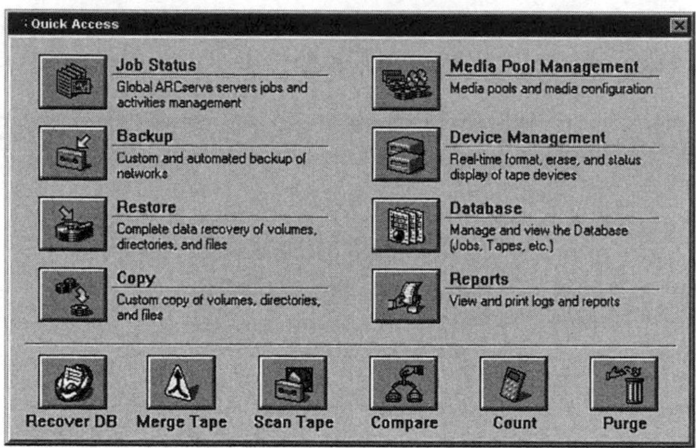

***Figure** 37.5. Cheyenne ArcServe Version 6.*

InocuLAN

InocuLAN is like most virus scanning software; it scans and cleans viruses from files. InocuLAN takes the cleaning a step further. Before InocuLAN cleans a file, it creates a backup of the file. If the clean fails and the file is damaged, the user will not lose the file. True, the virus is still present, but the way that virus scanning software develops, a cure will probably be found quickly. Most companies will gladly take the file to examine the virus structure for future signature updates.

Another unique feature: if a workstation on the network attempts to upload a file that is infected, the client workstation will be automatically logged off. When this happens, InocuLAN will log which workstation the file came from so that the administrator can focus on destroying the virus.

You can also control how much processor time is used for scanning and monitoring—no more lag of network performance.

SpartaCom

SpartaCom offers several products for use with Windows NT, including ZetaFAX and SAPS. SAPS is produced by SpartaCom, but they are the reseller for ZetaFAX in the United States. To find out more information about these and other SpartaCom products, visit `www.spartacom.com`.

SpartaCom Asynchronous Port Sharing Software (SAPS)

SAPS is modem-sharing software. All the clients can share modems that are connected to an NT server. This is a perfect solution for allowing your users to use dial-up solutions. A user can easily accomplish connections to the Internet, BBSs, D&B, or any other service. SAPS solutions are both economical and easy to install and use. You can even use the same modems that you would use for your RAS dial-in solution. Troubleshooting is very simple and most of the time a problem lies somewhere other than in the software configuration. I highly recommend this type of solution for anyone who needs to provide dial-out solutions for their users. Figure 37.6 shows the SAPS application for NT.

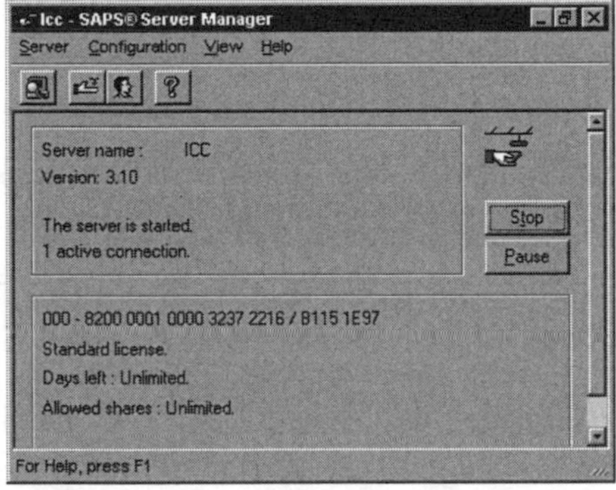

Figure 37.6. *SAPS application for NT.*

ZetaFAX

ZetaFAX Version 5 is a scalable and efficient fax solution for Windows NT. You can easily add more fax ports or users to the system without a lot of configuration overhead. ZetaFAX maintains a single queue for messages that are sent to all users and fax modems. Messages can be set with a higher priority to rush them through the queue.

ZetaFAX was designed with Microsoft BackOffice integration. ZetaFAX runs as a 32-bit service under NT 3.51 or NT 4.0. An e-mail gateway allows Microsoft Exchange users to integrate their e-mail with faxing.

One of the nicest features that ZetaFAX has over other solutions is the capability to automatically resend only the remaining pages of a fax that has been cut off. Other solutions start the entire fax over and the recipient can sometimes receive the same pages over and over.

If your organization or company uses billback codes to bill departments for their usage, ZetaFAX offers an easy-to-use export utility to export the billing log to a spreadsheet or database application.

ZetaFAX also uses DID or Direct Inward Dialing to automatically distribute inbound faxes to the proper person or department. With the e-mail integration, the fax can even appear in a person's in-box!

Seagate

Remember back in the early days when Seagate was nothing more than a hard drive manufacturer? Now the company is producing software, and within the past two years has acquired Arcada and the Arcada product line. Seagate has created some very good software applications. Among those are Backup Exec and NerveCenter NT. For more information about Seagate and its application solutions, visit its Web site at `http://www.seagate.com`.

Backup Exec

Backup Exec is Seagate's NT backup solution. Several characteristics are important to note. The first is that all copies of Backup Exec within the enterprise can be centrally administrated. Imagine being able to monitor and view the status of a backup happening in a remote office 1,000 miles away.

The second is its support of the native NT Backup. This is a big plus. Many people give NT Backup a chance before they go out and spend money on a third-party solution. After they realize the limitations of NT Backup, they buy the third-party solution. Unfortunately, tapes created by NT Backup will most likely not be recognized under the new backup application. Backup Exec eliminates that problem. Any tape created by NT Backup can be read through Backup Exec.

The third is Backup Exec's capability to back up all clients, including DOS, Windows, WFW, NT, 95, OS/2, NetWare 3.*x* and 4.*x* servers, Macintosh, and UNIX. So this product is a complete, enterprise-wide backup solution.

NerveCenter NT

NerveCenter NT is a network management and diagnostic tool for NT. NerveCenter NT can monitor your network to find potential problems and can alert you by paging, by e-mail, or by generating a trouble ticket. NerveCenter NT works with you to solve your problems rather than just notifying you of the problem. If a traffic spike occurs on the network, NerveCenter NT will see that, but instead of notifying you that there is a problem, it will begin to monitor the segment in which the spike occurred. If the spikes are frequent and begin to turn into more than spikes,

NerveCenter NT will let you know. As a problem is reported, a traffic and alarm summary window is updated. Every time there is a potential problem, the problem is logged and assigned a level of severity so that you can quickly determine what problem is the most critical. Is there going to be a time when the world does not need network administrators?

Intel

Intel has always been known for its processors—its primary business—but not everyone knows about Intel's LANDesk Management Suite. LANDesk makes it possible to manage many different network operating systems. Some of the features of LANDesk include software distribution and metering, asset inventory, remote control, event handling, server monitoring, and printer management. You can view all of these reports through an integrated reporting system. LANDesk is also able to dynamically discover and manage Microsoft networking products, including Windows 95 and Windows 3.*x* clients.

A companion product to the LANDesk Management Suite is the LANDesk Virus Protect. Virus Protect offers real-time, on-demand, and scheduled scanning for viruses, scheduled downloads of virus signature files, and an integrated event log that provides the user detailed information about the origin of any virus. Take a look at Intel's Web site at `http://www.intel.com`. There you will see numerous awards that Intel LANDesk Management Suite has won.

Summary

There are many more applications for Windows NT than could be covered in this chapter. This chapter has introduced you to the type of products that are out there and discussed modem sharing, faxing, virus protection, and network management solutions. Companies such as Intel, Castelle, SpartaCom, and McAfee have met the demand for application software for NT and will continue to help strengthen the NT market.

Troubleshooting Windows NT Installation

by Mike Carpenter

Failures can occur during the installation of Windows NT. Complex modern systems can be made up of many hardware combinations—some with new plug-and-play attributes—that may present unique problems. The key to solving installation problems is in the strategy you use.

Strategy

The following steps have to occur to properly load Windows NT:

- Kernel Load—This phase is where the actual kernel is loaded, the core of the Windows NT operating system. This includes the loading of the Hardware Abstraction Layer. The Hardware Abstraction Layer then determines which drivers should be loaded, but they are not yet initialized during this phase.
- Kernel Initialization—This phase initializes the kernel and drivers that were loaded during the Kernel Load Phase. Windows NT then creates a list of hardware in the Registry based on the information passed to it by NTLDR and OSLOADER.

- Services Load—During this phase, the Session Manager is loaded. The Session Manager uses the key `HKEY_LOCAL_MACHINE\SYSTEM\CurrentControlSet\Control\SessionManager\bootExecutive`. The default program contained at that pointer is Autocheck. This program will detect damaged files on the system and attempt to repair them. The repair process may not be able to repair files broken by defective hardware or power outages and those types of failures. The Session Manager also sets up the paging files for memory management and loads the subsystems specified by the Registry. Normally, the subsystem loaded is the Win32 subsystem.
- Windows System Start—During this phase, the Windows NT logon screen is displayed and the Service Controller looks to the Registry for services that are to be started automatically, and starts them, as well as any services required by those services.
- Windows Logon—When the user logs on, the boot process is completed and the Clone control set is written to the LastKnownGood control set.

Failure can occur in any one of these steps, so you should pay attention to the process as the system initializes the first time through during installation to get a feel for in which of those phases the error occurred.

Note: If you are not sure why your installation is hanging, remove all unnecessary devices, install Windows NT 4.0, and then reinstall the devices one by one. This will ensure that your strategy is uncomplicated by the incompatibilities of individual devices.

Keeping things simple is usually the best way to approach the problem. If the system is fully loaded with devices such as sound cards, video capture adapters, modems, network interface cards, or other such devices, try removing all but the most essential.

Usually you need only a video adapter and the drive controllers. Try the installation again, and if you are successful, add the devices one-by-one, configuring each device fully before adding the next.

If this strategy is not successful, you will wind up with the infamous BSOD, or Blue Screen of Death, signaling a failure to the kernel mode. While the BSOD is frustrating to the installer when it appears, it does have a wealth of knowledge with it in the form of codes to help determine what caused the failure. These can be indications of problems with drive controllers or SCSI adapters, improper drivers for installed devices, or even hardware failure.

Inaccessible Hard Drive

A BSOD warning of inaccessible hard drive can indicate several different types of problems. The solutions are different if you have SCSI or IDE boot drives.

During installation, Windows NT offers automatic detection of your drives and controllers. If you choose to use automatic detection, make sure that the correct devices have been identified. If not, be prepared to set the selection manually. You may also be required to provide software drivers if they are not on the installation CD-ROM.

Multiple drives, especially mixing SCSI and IDE, may also present problems. Try installing only the necessary boot drive first, and then add additional drives and adapters later if you don't need them during your installation. It will be a lot easier to identify and fix problems if you have eliminated as many of the possibilities of conflict as possible.

SCSI

If you have a SCSI drive, first check to see if the adapter is fully seated. Check the cable connections, both at the adapter and on the drive, and ensure the terminations are accomplished in accordance with manufacturer's instructions. Ensure that the adapter is on the Hardware Compatibility Listing, and that during the installation, the adapter was properly recognized and the correct driver was loaded.

Some new 7200 RPM drives can overheat if they are not installed in a way that allows heat to dissipate properly. Likewise, if the ventilation is blocked, overheating can cause intermittent failures or failure after a short period of time.

IDE

If your IDE drive is larger than 540MB, make sure your system BIOS is set to LBA. If your BIOS does not accept drives with LBA settings, first check to see if there is a BIOS upgrade. If not, check with the drive manufacturer to see if there is a utility you can use to install an overlay that will enable your system to work with larger drives. A boot-sector virus may also be the culprit. Scanning the disk with a good virus checking and cleaning program is good practice before any installation.

Network Problems

If you select the option to connect to a network during installation, and you have a failure during booting, your problem may be related to the network interface card or the software drivers for it.

Windows NT will attempt to automatically identify your network interface card during the installation. This can cause a kernel mode failure and the infamous BSOD. If this occurs, you will need to restart the installation from the beginning. When you get to the part that prompts you to decide whether you want to automatically detect the network interface card, select no and configure it manually.

If automatic detection has properly identified your network interface card, you might have either a defective card or software driver. If you have another network interface card, try removing the original card and replacing it with the new one. Always check to make sure interrupt settings are not in conflict with other devices. If you still have the same problem, try another type or brand of network interface card.

You also should contact the manufacturer to determine whether there is a newer or better version of the software driver available for that device. Follow their instructions for the installation of that driver.

If these methods fail, try to install NT without the network installation, complete the process, and then install the network interface card again when all other devices are configured.

Video Adapters

First, check to see whether your adapter is on the Hardware Compatibility List. If it is not, you might have to try one that is on the list in order to continue the installation. Some video adapters fail to properly install during Windows NT installation. You will get either no video, a scrambled screen, or your screen will appear off-center or misaligned.

You can attempt to correct this by restarting the computer and selecting to boot into VGA mode. If you can boot this way, try setting the video to another resolution or frequency, being sure to test it before continuing.

If this does not work, try first to see if there is a newer software driver available. If there is, load it following the manufacturer's instructions. You may also try a different video adapter. It is always good to keep a simple VGA adapter available to troubleshoot video problems during installation. You can then attempt to correct the problems after you successfully install Windows NT.

Sound Cards

Sound cards can present many problems with Windows NT installations. Some are plug-and-play, some have game ports or other I/O devices, and many simply do not have drivers written for use with Windows NT 4.0.

Note: Creative Labs Sound Blaster 16 sound cards seem to work well in Windows NT 4.0. Be careful of sound cards that are "Sound Blaster 16 compatible" or ones that can emulate the SB 16 characteristics. Check the Hardware Compatibility List before you buy.

First, check the Hardware Compatibility List to verify that your exact make and model sound card is listed. If it is not, check with the manufacturer to see whether it has developed a driver for the card. If it has not, it probably will not work with Windows NT 4.0 and quite possibly will cause problems during your installation.

Some plug-and-play type sound cards are compatible with Windows NT 4.0, but are not able to use plug-and-play configuration. To solve this problem, boot the computer with a bootable DOS diskette and use the manufacturer's instructions to set the plug-and-play variables such as IRQ or Base Memory settings. Record the settings before you turn off the machine, because you might need those settings to properly set up the card when you install Windows NT 4.0.

Tape Backup Drives

Tape Backup Drives normally are SCSI devices, but not always. These devices may cause problems during installation if they are not properly detected or if the wrong driver is used.

Again, first check the Hardware Compatibility List to ensure your exact make and model drive is listed. If it is not, check with the manufacturer for drivers compatible with Windows NT 4.0.

If it is a SCSI device, check to make sure the device number is set to a unique setting so that it does not interfere with other SCSI devices on that adapter. Check the manufacturer's instructions to ensure that it is properly installed.

If it is not a SCSI device and uses an adapter card, either PCI or EISA, check the card's jumper settings to ensure the IRQ or other settings don't conflict with other devices in the computer.

Summary

Keeping your Windows NT 4.0 installation as simple as possible will help you eliminate installation headaches. If your computer and all additional devices and peripherals are listed in the Hardware Compatibility List, you still might run into problems due to conflicts between the devices.

Check all IRQ settings, SCSI device number settings, and for port conflicts before you attempt the installation. Have all the settings for each device handy because you might need to manually set them as you install Windows NT 4.0.

What to Do When NT Fails to Boot

by John West

The Windows NT boot process follows a series of defined steps; during this process, any one of many types of failures can, and sometimes does, occur. Never fear—most of the failures that can occur are documented here. This chapter breaks down the boot process into six specific areas. Under each of these areas, potential problems and their resolutions are listed. This chapter is designed so that you first can identify which step of the boot process is failing and then drill down so that you can find the resolution to your problem. Good luck.

Boot Fails During Power-On Self Test

The power-on self test is the first step that occurs during Windows NT bootup. This test occurs when the server first is powered on. During this test, the following actions occur:

- The system performs hardware checks on the memory, video, and hard drive controllers.
- SCSI cards with their BIOS enabled are started and perform a self test.

System Beeps or Produces Error Messages

This indicates that you have some sort of hardware failure. Check the manual from your motherboard manufacturer for the error code's specific meaning.

System Hangs at the SCSI BIOS After Adding Another Controller

This generally means that you have some sort of conflict in your I/O, DMA, or IRQ settings between the new and old SCSI cards. Check your settings and make sure that they are not in conflict with each other.

Boot Fails During Hard Drive Initialization

After checking the controllers, video, and memory, the system checks the status of the hard drives. If the hard drive query fails, you see an error message similar to this:

```
Hard Drive Controller Failure
```

As the message suggests, you have a failure in your controller card or on the hard drive. Try swapping out the controller and see whether it fixes your problem.

Common SCSI Controller Problems

The SCSI bus has its own set of unique problems that can creep up on you. Although the SCSI bus provides greater device flexibility and higher data throughput, these advantages come at a price. The price includes additional configuration options that must be correctly set for SCSI bus to work correctly in your system. Configuration options that must be set include BIOS settings, SCSI IDS, and termination. This section is designed to assist you in troubleshooting problems with your SCSI bus.

BIOS setup has changed

A SCSI card can operate under NT with the SCSI BIOS enabled or disabled, as long as you have it configured the way you want it to run when NT is installed. When the BIOS is enabled on a SCSI card, NT mounts the drive and takes care of managing all communication with the operating system. This includes the capability to apply sector translation so that a drive's geometry can have the highest compatibility with operating systems. Changing any settings in the BIOS after NT is installed on your system can cause NT to fail.

BIOS has been disabled

If you turn off the BIOS on the SCSI card on a system that had NT installed on it while the BIOS was active, NT fails to boot. Turning back on the BIOS should restore operations.

BIOS has had sector translation changed

Changing the sector translation in the BIOS makes NT look in the wrong place for the boot partition, which causes NT to fail. Changing the sector translation back to its original setting generally fixes the problem.

Conflicting SCSI IDs

If you add a new SCSI device and no longer are able to see your hard drive, you probably have conflicting SCSI IDs. Make sure that each device in the SCSI chain has a unique SCSI address.

SCSI Termination

In order for a SCSI bus to work properly, the system must have terminators at each end of the cable. Improper termination can lead to unreliable operation of your SCSI devices. For example, if you have two internal drives and one external drive hooked to the same SCSI controller, it would be necessary to have a termination enabled on the internal hard drive that is farthest from the controller, and have termination enabled on the external drive. You would not have termination enabled on the SCSI card. You should only have SCSI card termination enabled if there are no external devices present.

Drive Not Ready

A `Drive Not Ready` error might indicate problems with the hard drive. Sometimes it can be as simple as having the drive's jumpers set for drive spin up on detection instead of power up. Drives that do not spin up fast enough end up timing out and reporting the `Drive Not Ready` error you are getting. Check your hard drive manual for the proper jumper setting on your particular hard drive.

Problem with a Bus Master SCSI VESA Local Bus Adapter

The VESA Local Bus specification uses slots that play a role as master or slave. When using a bus-mastering VL-BUS SCSI adapter, it is important that it is plugged in to the master VL-BUS slot.

PCI SCSI Adapter Stops Responding and BIOS Has Installed Successfully

This condition usually is caused by a hard drive that has failed or is not spinning up fast enough. Check the jumper settings on the hard drive and see whether they are set up to spin the drive up on power up. This error can also be caused by improper termination.

Boot Fails After Hard Drive Initialization But Before the Boot Menu Appears

After the hard drive has been initialized, the operating system proceeds to the master boot record, which is located on Head 0, Cylinder 0, Sector 1. The master boot record is non-operating system dependent—no matter what operating system you have installed, you always will have a master boot record that the hardware CMOS uses to turn control over to the operating system. This section lists some of the problems you might experience during this stage of the Windows NT boot.

`Error Loading Operating System`

This message could indicate that you have a damaged boot block or that you might have a damaged hard drive. Use the NT Recovery disk to see whether you can rebuild the boot sector. If you do not have the NT Recovery disk, you can try running the NT installation and perform an upgrade on your existing version of NT.

`Bad or Missing Operating System`

This error usually signifies that your boot sector is good, but there is a problem locating the partition with the operating system on it. Some of the reasons why this error might happen follow.

You Changed Your SCSI Controller

Not all SCSI controllers handle hard drives in the same way. If you have to swap out your SCSI controller, you should be prepared to perform a complete reinstallation of Windows NT.

You Added an IDE or EIDE Drive to a SCSI System

If you have been working in an all-SCSI environment and add an IDE or EIDE drive, the EIDE or IDE drive takes the SCSI drive's old drive letter and pushes the SCSI drive down to a new drive letter. This process causes the NT operating system to lose the boot partition. You can copy the `winnt` directory to your new IDE drive and run the NT upgrade process to re-create the boot partition.

Primary Drive of a Mirror Set Has Failed

If the primary drive of a mirror set fails, you must update the `Boot.ini` file to point to the right drive for boot or to reconfigure the mirror to be the same SCSI ID or to be the master drive in an EIDE/IDE drive environment.

A Hardware RAID Change Has Occurred

Changing your hardware RAID level or controller can make your system partition inaccessible. If you need to change the RAID settings, be prepared to reinstall the operating system. You'll need to make sure that you have a good backup available.

`Couldn't find NTLDR`

This error message can occur under the following circumstances:

- The file has become corrupted.
- You have changed SCSI controllers.
- You have some type of data corruption on your hard drive.

To correct this problem, try using the Emergency Repair disk. If you do not have an Emergency Repair disk handy, you can try running an NT install and performing an upgrade on your currently installed version of NT.

Boot Fails After Selecting Windows NT from the Boot Menu

After accessing the master boot record, the CMOS is directed to the area that contains the active partition and current operating system. In an NT installation, this area contains a boot menu application. This application enables you to choose which operating system you want to start up. If you left a hard drive with the DOS operating system, you would have the opportunity to boot into it now. The options you generally see here follow:

- Windows NT 4.0
- Windows NT 4.0 (VGA mode)
- Windows or MS-DOS

If you take a look at the `boot.ini` file, which is where these options are stored, you also will find that there are mappings that tell the boot operating system where to find the operating system you selected from the menu. The values are *absolute*—they will not update their paths if the partitions are moved or drives are exchanged. This section describes some common problems that can occur after selecting an operating system from the boot menu.

Windows NT could not load because the following file is missing or corrupt

Common causes for this error follow:

- The file has become corrupted.
- You have changed SCSI controllers.
- You have some type of data corruption on your hard drive.

To correct this problem, try using the Emergency Repair disk. If you do not have an Emergency Repair disk handy, you can try running an NT install and performing an upgrade on your currently installed version of NT.

Missing or Invalid Control\ServiceGroupOrder\List Registry Setting

This error generally is caused by an improper sequence in the kernel load sequence. This error can be caused by the following:

- You set the startup for a device to boot in the Control Panel of Windows NT.
- A device driver has become corrupted.

To fix this problem, try using the Last Known Good option during startup. If this does not help, you will need to use your NT Recovery disk.

NTLDR I/O Error Reading Disk

This error can be caused by advanced IDE controllers or problems with the timers and wait states on the bus. To correct this problem, refer to your hardware manual for your hard drive controller card. For additional information, look up the knowledge base article Q102776. This can be found on the Microsoft Web site or on a Technet CD.

Error Opening NTDETECT

This error is caused by a missing or corrupted `NTDETECT.com` file.

To replace the `NTDETECT.com` file on a system with the FAT file system, copy the file from an NT boot disk or from the NT Install CD-ROM to the root directory of the boot drive.

On a system that uses the NTFS file system on its boot partition, you can use the Windows NT Emergency Repair disk or run the NT Install program and upgrade current operating system.

`Windows NT could not start because the following file is missing or corrupt:Winnt\system32\config\(hive file)`

This error usually is caused by corrupted or deleted files in the `winnt\sytem32\config` directory. To correct this problem, use the NT Emergency Repair disk and replace all system files.

If you do not have an Emergency Repair disk, you can start an NT installation and select the Upgrade option for your current version of NT to produce the same effect.

`Couldn't open boot sector file mult(0)Disk(0)Rdisk(0)Partition(1):Bootsect.dos`

The boot file for your MS-DOS operating system has been deleted. To correct this problem, boot from an MS-DOS floppy disk and run the `sys.com` command against the hard drive to transfer the system files of MS-DOS. You then have to use the Emergency Repair disk to replace your NT boot files.

If you do not have the NT Recovery disk, you can start an NT install and upgrade your existing NT operating system. This method updates all files without altering your system's Registry.

Boot Fails After Control Is Turned Over to NTDETECT and Returns to NTLDR

During this phase of the NT boot, control is turned over to `NTDETECT`, which detects currently installed hardware and passes this information back to `NTLDR`. `NTLDR` continues booting the Windows NT operating system by starting the `NTOSKRNL`. Actions that occur during this phase follow:

- A blue background appears on-screen.
- System memory is checked.
- The number of processors is checked.
- HAL is initialized.
- `CHKDSK` may be run on the hard drives.

This section explains some error messages that might occur during this phase.

CHKDSK Errors

If your system reports CHKDSK errors and fails to boot, this indicates that you have corrupted files on your hard drive. To recover, use the NT Emergency Repair disk.

If you do not have the NT Recovery disk, you can start an NT install and upgrade your existing NT operating system. This action updates all files without altering your system's Registry.

HAL Errors

The *Hardware Abstraction Layer* (HAL) is used by Windows NT to provide a programmable layer that enables NT to work on multiple hardware platforms. This means that different HALs are used by NT, depending on the hardware platform on which they are running.

```
HAL: Bad APIC version. HAL: This HAL.DLL requires an MPS version
1.1 system. Replace HAL.DLL with the correct HAL for this system.
The system is halting.
```

This message appears when NT detects a motherboard with multiple processors, but the motherboard has only one processor installed. To fix this problem, choose a custom installation during Windows NT setup and make sure that AT-compatible is selected—not a multiprocessor board.

If you are performing an upgrade, you can press the F5 key during the NT startup phase and choose the correct kernel to use.

Boot Fails After Graphical Operating System Is Loaded

The final step of the boot up of NT is the graphical phase of startup. During this phase, the following actions occur:

- The system switches to a graphical backdrop.
- NT services listed in the Registry are started.
- A logon prompt is displayed.

The System Freezes

If your system freezes while you are in the graphical mode of Windows NT (you can see the `Ctrl+Alt+Del to Logon` sequence), you probably have a misbehaving service.

To correct this problem, first select the Last Known Good option from the boot-up sequence if you recently have installed a new device driver or software package.

If your system is still frozen, try using the Windows NT Recovery disk to recover your system.

If you do not have the NT Recovery disk, you can start an NT install and upgrade your existing NT operating system. This choice updates all files without altering your system's Registry.

Summary

The problems presented in this chapter are common experiences people have faced when booting the Windows NT operating system. Of course, in the tradition of computers and the software that accompanies them, new problems always are waiting to be discovered. For the latest information on this type of troubleshooting and other NT topics, visit the NT Workstation and NT Server Web pages at

```
www.microsoft.com/ntworkstation
www.microsoft.com/ntserver
```

Troubleshooting the System Logon Failures

by Terry W. Ogletree

When you use Windows NT Servers and Workstations in your network, there are several ways that you can log on to a computer or to the network. The most basic method is to use a domain-based security directory database and have users log on only once to access resources on any computer in the domain. If you use only Windows NT Workstation, you cannot form a domain, because you would need a domain controller to do so, which must be a Windows NT Server computer.

However, with an NT Workstation network you can use the local computer's security directory database to store usernames and passwords. Under this scheme when you access a resource on another computer in the network you must enter a name and password for each computer you access. Since it's not necessary for you to use the same username and password on each workstation, and since password expiration times may expire after different intervals, maintaining multiple accounts can become quite a chore.

In this chapter we will discuss the different methods you can use to authenticate users on your Windows NT network and give you some background information on the logon process so that you will be better equipped to troubleshoot failures. Other topics that will be discussed include the following:

- Logging on locally versus logging on remotely
- Pass-through authentication
- Trust relationships between domains

- Logging on using remote access
- The NetLogon service
- Controlling user logins using policies
- Helpful utilities you can find in the Windows NT Resource Kit

Domain Versus Workgroup Logons

The domain method is the preferred method for managing user accounts if you want to have centralized, tight control over your network security. Although the directory database is stored in a central location, by using Backup Domain Controllers (BDCs) you can ensure fault tolerance—the database is backed up in a timely manner to the BDCs by the Primary Domain Controller (PDC) so that if the PDC were to fail, the BDCs could continue processing user logons. Additionally, if you choose to have one or more BDCs, they can help with processing user logons, especially when the PDC is on a different network segment.

The workgroup method gives you the same security you had when you were using Windows for Workgroups. Using this method you protect file and print shares. You cannot assign individual permissions to each file on the system. Each person who accesses a share must use a single password that protects that share. The result is that you must depend on the goodwill of many users who access the same resource using the same password. This setup doesn't do much for accountability.

Under the domain system each username has a password associated with it. You grant rights to the user account and you can protect resources, down to the file level, with a set of permissions. You can give different users different rights and you can use different permissions for each user when protecting resources.

Note: Logging on to the network or computer does not necessarily give a user the right to access any resources protected by permissions. It simply gives the user the *ability* to access resources provided that the computer or domain administrator has granted permission to do so. For more information about granting permissions to resources, see Chapter 41, "Introduction to Access Problems."

To sum it up, using a domain-based security directory database gives you more control over your network security and gives your users the ability to log on to the network one time and not have to enter any more passwords to access resources for which you have granted them permission.

This chapter describes briefly the logon process used for different types of logons and hints for tracking down the reasons for failed logons. Common mistakes will be pointed out and suggested policies and procedures will be addressed. Solving user logon problems will also be discussed throughout the chapter.

Check the Event Log First

When troubleshooting logon problems, the first thing you should check is the Security log using the Event Viewer. If the problem is a simple, common one such as the user has forgotten a password, you will see it here, provided that you have enabled auditing for this event. The Event Viewer can be found on the Administrative Tools menu. To use the Event Viewer to troubleshoot logon failures, select the Security log from the Log menu. To see the details for any event listed in the Security log, double-click the event.

Figure 40.1 shows a detailed example of a logon failure. As you can see from the message, the user entered either an unknown username or a bad password. You can see that the username that was used was Administrator. Since you know the account exists, the problem must be a bad password.

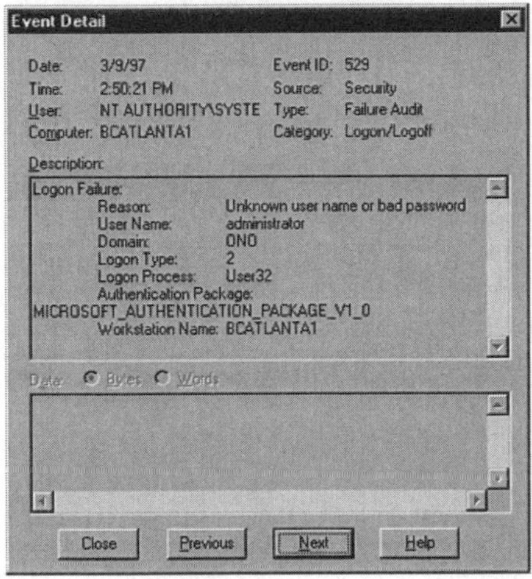

Figure 40.1. *An example of a logon failure as recorded in the Security log.*

Figure 40.2 shows an event log message caused by a *successful* logon. Remember again that these messages will not appear in the log file unless you set your system auditing policy to include these types of messages. Figure 40.3 shows the dialog box you use to set the auditing policy. To get to this dialog box, bring up the User Manager and select Audit under the Policies menu.

In addition to event records that show password failures, you will also find other helpful messages in this file. For example, if a user tries to log on outside the hours permitted to the account, an event log record will be recorded.

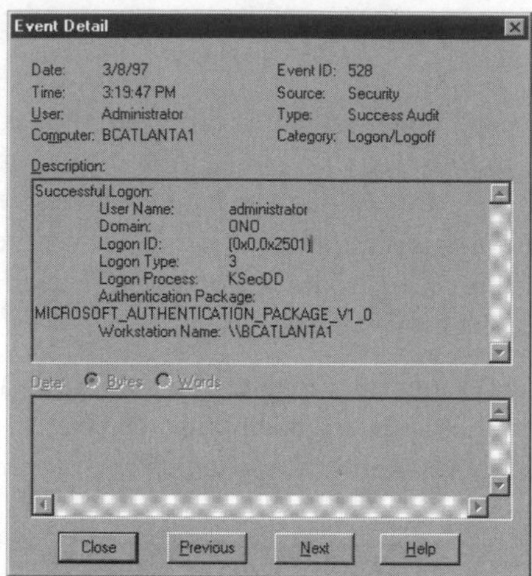

Figure 40.2. An example of a successful logon as recorded in the Security log.

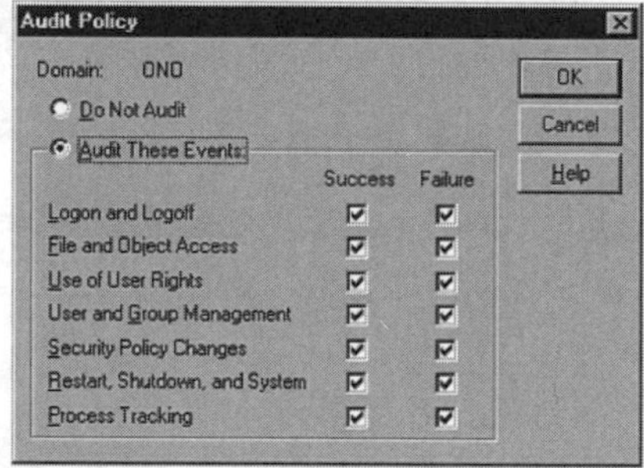

Figure 40.3. Setting the Audit Policy to record Logon and Logoff events, both successful and failed attempts, can make troubleshooting much easier.

Overview of the Logon Process

Windows NT allows for two types of logons: interactive (or local) logon and remote logon. An interactive logon occurs when a user logs on to a Windows NT computer at the keyboard. An example of a remote logon is when a user accesses a resource on a Windows NT computer via the network.

Another type of logon is used to extend the single logon concept throughout the network. When a user accesses a resource on a Windows NT computer that resides in a trusted domain, without having to enter a new password, pass-through authentication occurs. Although pass-through authentication is really another type of remote logon, it is significant in NT networking, and it deserves a detailed discussion by itself.

Note: Pass-through authentication will not work for Macintosh clients, even if you set up Services for Macintosh to use the Microsoft User Authentication Module. A Macintosh client *must* re-enter a username and password when trying to connect to servers in trusting domains.

When you log on to an NT computer your logon will be verified against one of the following:

- The local security directory database that resides on the computer you are logging on to.
- A domain directory database that resides on a PDC or a domain directory database that resides on a BDC.
- A domain directory database that resides on a PDC or BDC in another domain that trusts your domain, using pass-through authentication.

When you are trying to determine why a logon attempt fails, you should first understand where the logon is being validated. This will be difficult to do unless you know the structure of your network and are aware of where user accounts are stored. For example, if you change a password for a user on the PDC and that user tries to log on with a computer attached to a different subnet, the user will be validated by a BDC on that subnet, if there is one. Because changes are propagated to BDCs at regular intervals, the logon will fail if the information has not yet reached the logon BDC.

The logon box allows you to select the computer database or domain database that you want to log on to. Depending on the domain model used in your network (see Chapter 3, "Domain Models," for more information), your user account can reside on a workstation or almost any server in the network that acts as a domain controller. Even if you have a domain account, *you can still have an account* on a workstation's local database (or the local database of an NT Server not acting as a domain controller).

Figure 40.4 shows a network where four users have logged on, each using a different method. Computer A has logged on to the local computer interactively. This user can access files and other resources on the local computer. Computer B has logged on to Domain X using a domain account. This user was validated against the domain directory database for Domain X and can access files and resources throughout the domain. Computer C has logged on to Domain X, but was validated against the directory database stored on a PDC in Domain Y. In this case Domain X has a one-way trust relationship with Domain Y and the administrator of Domain X has granted rights to access resources to selected users from Domain Y.

This is a quick overview of the types of logons that you can use to access a Windows NT network. One other method which is now becoming more popular is RAS, or Remote Access Service via a modem or other communications media (see Chapter 27, "Troubleshooting the Remote Access Service (RAS) and Dial-Up Networking (DUN)"). Users logging in to your network using RAS can have almost the same access that you can provide to your LAN users. You can even administer your network using a RAS connection, although you will be limited to the speed your communication media provides. Whereas an Ethernet network can run from 10MB/sec to 100MB/sec, RAS connections are much slower. Modems are just now getting up to speed with a new 34.4KB standard and, in the next few months, up to a 56KB standard that comes close to ISDN speeds. You should be aware, however, that even though modems are getting faster, the throughput you will achieve will come nowhere near the performance you get when the computer is directly wired to the network.

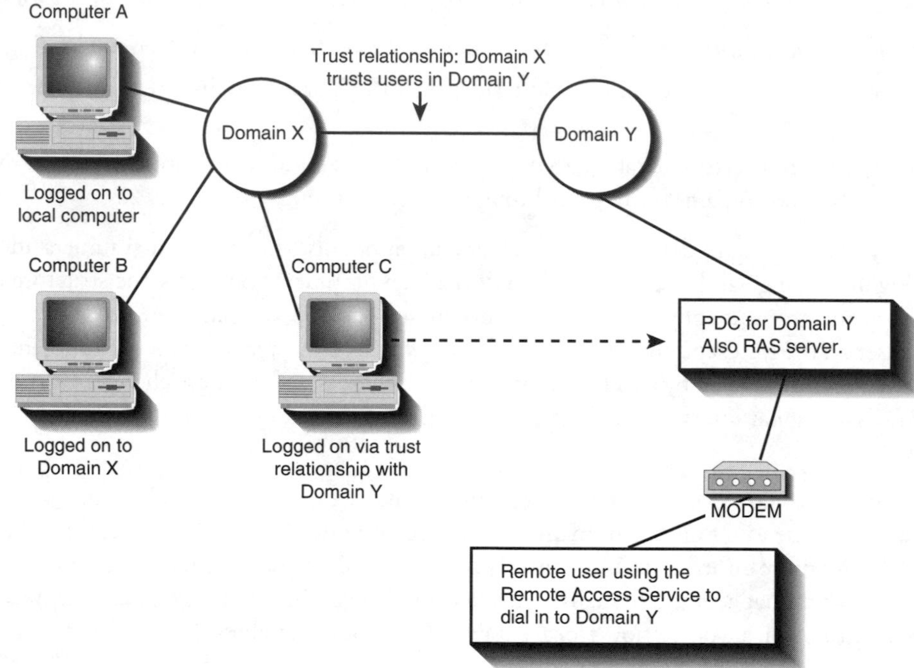

Figure 40.4. *Users can be validated against different security directory databases under NT networking.*

In addition to the standard logon/logoff event log messages, you can use the Event Viewer to examine the Application log (select Application from the Log menu in the Event Viewer). The Remote Access Server logs messages to this file, which may be helpful when users are having problems logging in.

Logging On Locally

Logging on to an NT computer from the keyboard is the oldest type of logon used for personal computers. Before networking had evolved to a sophisticated level, users traded files with floppy disks, and password/menu systems were popular as a method of locking out unwanted users. Hardware password implementations soon followed so that you couldn't even boot the computer if you didn't know the hardware password.

In order to log on locally at a computer in a Windows NT network, your user account must have the "Log on locally" right granted to it.

By default, only the following user groups are allowed to log on locally to an NT Server operating as a domain controller:

- Administrators
- Server operators
- Print operators
- Backup operators
- Account operators

On Windows NT Workstation computers (and NT Servers not acting in a domain controller mode), the groups are a little different. In that case the following groups are granted the "Log on locally" right by default:

- Administrators
- Backup operators
- Power users
- Users
- Guests

Although the group Domain Users is not granted the right to "Log on locally" on NT Servers, you will note that the group Users can log on interactively (locally) at an NT Workstation computer. This is by design, because logging in at a workstation to do a day's work is the normal pattern of usage in an NT network. The group Users also, by default, does not possess the right to log on interactively at an NT Server. Servers are designed to provide services to client computers. Although you can grant any user the right to log on to an NT Server, only administrative users have the right by default.

This doesn't mean you cannot grant individual users or groups the right. Indeed, that is how you allow a user to log on locally without having to put him in one of the more privileged groups. If a user complains that he can no longer log on to a workstation, you should first determine whether he is authorized to do so. In a large network this might mean contacting a user's supervisor or checking with a person who is in charge of computer security. After you have determined that the user is authorized to log on locally to the computer, you can grant the user the right to log on locally by using the User Manager:

1. Select User Manager for Domains from the Administrative Tools menu.
2. Select User Rights from the Policy menu.
3. Select the right "Log on locally" from the Right pull-down menu (see Figure 40.5).
4. The Grant To box shows the users who already have the right granted to them. If the user's name does not appear here, click the Add button to add the name.

5. Select the user or groups from the Names box in the Add Users and Groups dialog box and click Add to move the name to the Add Names box (see Figure 40.6).
6. When you have finished selecting the users or groups, click the OK button at the bottom left of the dialog box. If you have changed your mind, you can use the Cancel button. You can also select users in the Add Names box and click on the Remove button to cancel the addition of that particular user, while leaving intact the others you have selected.
7. Click the OK button on the User Rights Policy dialog box and you are finished.

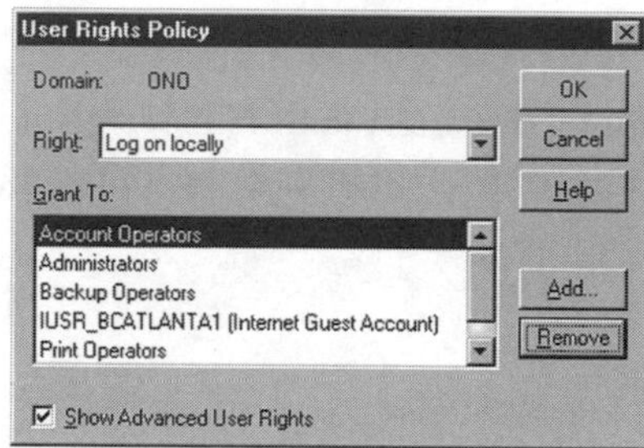

Figure 40.5. *Select the "Log on locally" right and then click the Add button to select the users to whom you want to grant this right.*

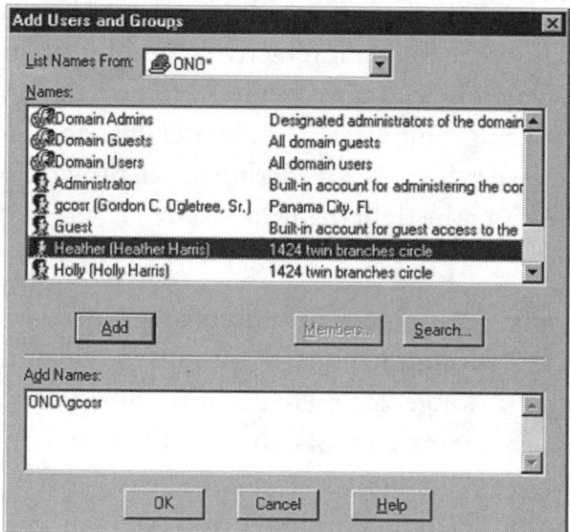

Figure 40.6. *The Add Users and Groups dialog box allows you to select the user/group that you want to grant rights to.*

Remote Logons

Remote logons occur when you access a resource via the network. In the preceding section you saw that a user must be granted the right to log on locally or must be in a group that holds that right. The same goes for remote (network) logons. If you determine that a user needs network access to a computer and you want to grant him the right, use the same procedure described in the preceding section, but choose the right "Access this computer from network" instead (see Figure 40.7).

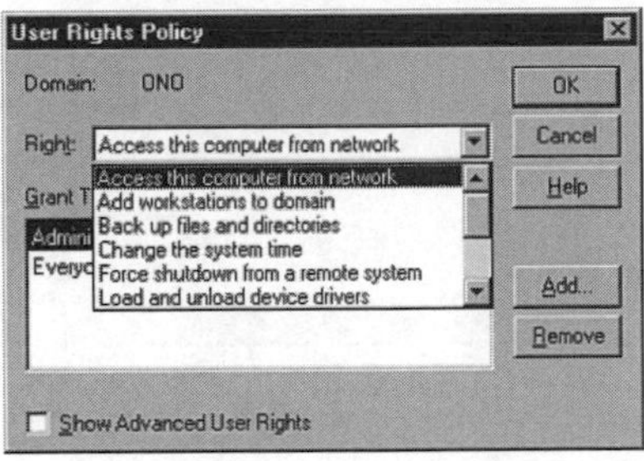

Figure 40.7. *You can also grant a user the right to make remote (network) logons by using the User Manager.*

Pass-Through Authentication

As discussed at the start of this chapter, one of the best features of using Windows NT for your network is the concept of a single logon that can be used to grant access to resources to a user throughout the network. By having a domain account instead of an account on a local directory database, the user can be granted access to resources throughout the domain. The concept of pass-through authentication can be used to extend this to all domains in the network.

Pass-through authentication occurs when a user accesses a resource via the network that is on a computer in a trusting domain. To understand pass-through authentication, you must first understand the concept of a trust relationship.

Workstations (or servers not acting as a domain controller) can be a member of only one domain. Administrators in the domain can grant access to resources in the domain on a user-by-user basis. To allow users to interact with computers in other domains, the administrator must establish a trust relationship with the other domain. This is a simple thing to do using the User Manager for Domains tool.

Select Trust Relationships from the Policies menu in the User Manager for Domains. Figure 40.8 shows the Trust Relationships dialog box that appears.

The first box in the dialog box shows domains that are already trusted by your domain. If a domain is trusted by your domain, it means that users from that domain will show up in the dialog boxes you use for granting permissions to files or printers, along with other resources. When a user from a trusted domain tries to access a resource on your domain, he will not have to give a username and password. Of course, since the user doesn't have an account in your domain, it would do him no good to even try!

The trust relationship says that your domain trusts the other domain. You trust that that domain has authenticated the user's logon credentials and you accept this on a trust basis.

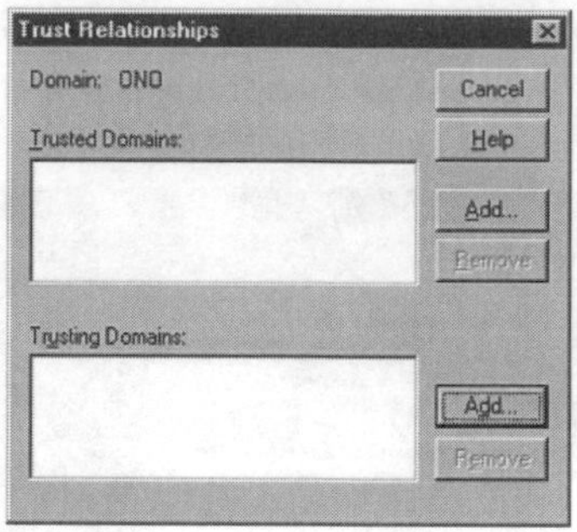

Figure 40.8. *You establish trust relationships using this dialog box from the User Manager for Domains.*

It is important to point out again that a trust relationship by itself does not guarantee access. The administrator in the trusting domain has to use resource permissions to grant or deny access for the trusted domain's users, just like the administrator grants or denies access to users in the domain.

If a user from a domain that you trust is having problems accessing resources in your domain, check this dialog box to be sure that the trust relationship still exists.

To add a domain to your trusted domain list, click the Add button in the Trust Relationships box. Figure 40.9 shows the Add Trusted Domain dialog box that you use to add a domain to your trusted domain list.

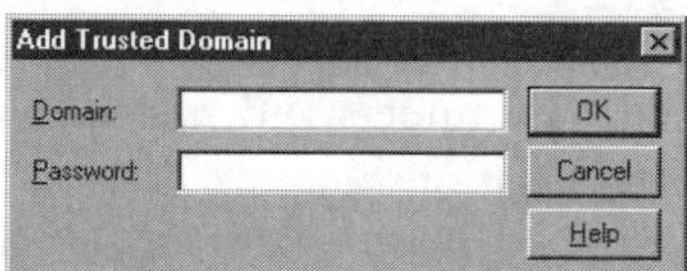

Figure 40.9. *You use the Add Trusted Domain dialog box to add domains to your trusted domain list.*

Note: Microsoft suggests that you first establish the trusting domain relationship, and then establish the trusted domain relationship. When you establish a trust relationship in this order, the interdomain trust password is immediately verified by the trusted/trusting domains. Also, when you decide that a trust relationship is no longer needed, you should be sure that it is removed from both sides of the relationship—in other words, from both domains.

After you have established a trust relationship with another domain, pass-through authentication can occur. If, for example, the administrator of Domain A wants to grant access to resources in the domain to users in Domain B, he first establishes a one-way trust with Domain B. Then the administrator grants access permissions to selected users (usually by using local groups) for certain resources in Domain A. When a user attempts to access one of these resources, Domain A does not prompt for a username/password. Instead it allows the user to access the resources based on the trust relationship. It is assumed that the trusted domain has already authenticated the user's logon.

This is pass-through authentication.

By using this method, administrators throughout the network can establish trust relationships, thereby allowing users the ability to log on to not just the domain, but also the network, using one logon.

Remote Access Logons

Chapter 27 covers a lot of problems you may encounter when using RAS and Dial-Up Networking. For the sake of clarity and to put logon information in one place, a quick review of how to set up users for remote access needs to be discussed.

You can grant a user or a group the ability to use RAS from either the User Manager for Domains or by using the Remote Access Admin utility. Both are found under the Administrative Tools menu.

If you want to use the Remote Access Admin utility, select Permissions from the Users menu.

This brings up the Remote Access Permissions dialog box (see Figure 40.10), which lists the users you can grant the permission to. To grant a user the permission, select the username by highlighting it with a single click and then select the "Grant dialin permission to user" check box. Click the OK button and you are done.

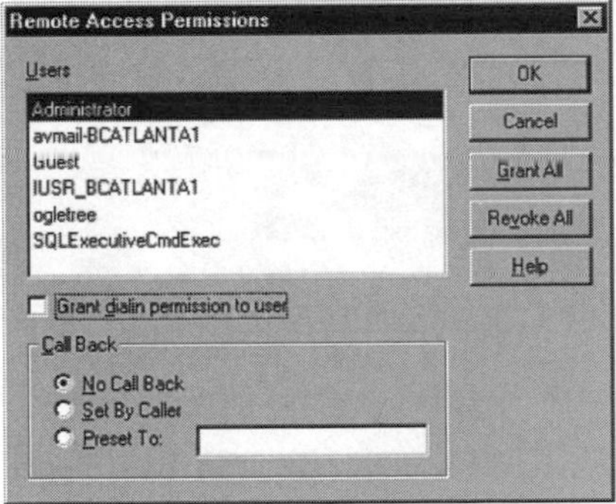

Figure 40.10. *From this dialog box you select the users to whom the remote access permission is given.*

You can use the Grant All and the Revoke All buttons in the Remote Access Permissions dialog box if you want to grant or remove the permission to all the listed users.

You can also use the User Manager for Domains to grant a user the remote access permission. Bring up the User Manager for Domains and double-click on the user you want to grant permission to. Alternatively, you can highlight the username with a single click and select Properties from the User menu. You will then get the User Properties dialog box, as shown in Figure 40.11.

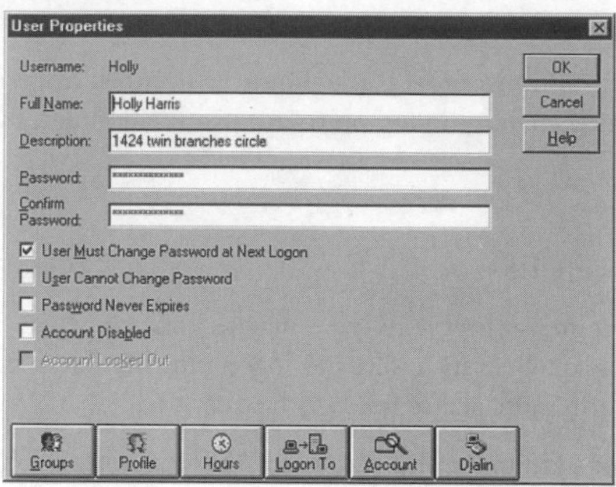

Figure 40.11. The User Properties dialog box allows you to configure many aspects of a user account, including the dial-in permission.

Unlike the Remote Access Admin utility, you can only use the Dialin Information dialog box (see Figure 40.12) to grant dial-in permissions to the user you have selected. There are no Grant All or Revoke All buttons in this dialog box.

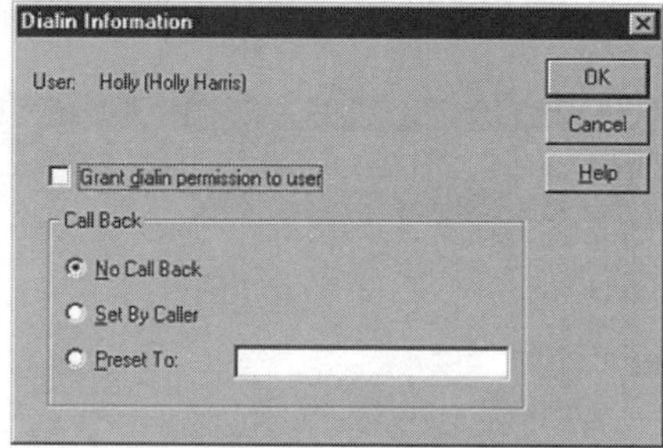

Figure 40.12. The Dialin Information dialog box from the User Manager administrative tool.

If you have determined that a user correctly holds the dial-in permission, be sure (using either tool described) that the Call Back options are correct. For example, if you use the Preset To option to specify a number that will be dialed for the call-back attempt, the logon will fail if the user tries to use RAS from another telephone number. If you have users who travel, then setting the call back to a preset number will not always work. Once again, if your user has problems logging in via RAS, be sure to use the Event Viewer to check the Security log.

Passwords

Another thing you should consider when users are having problems logging on to your system is the password. Under most circumstances in an NT network, passwords are case sensitive. If the machine you log in to and the machine that offers the resource you want to connect to are both

Windows NT computers, the password will be stored, and you must enter it, in a case-sensitive mode.

If you log on to a non–Windows NT computer (such as a Windows for Workgroups computer) and try to access resources on another non–Windows NT computer, the password is not case sensitive. However, if you change your password from a non–Windows NT computer, and your account is stored on an NT computer, the password is stored in the same format that the non–Windows NT computer uses: case-insensitive. Even if you log on next at a Windows NT computer, the password is still case insensitive because you have changed it from a non-NT computer (using NET PASSWORD from a Windows 95 or Windows for Workgroups client, for example).

If you have any LAN Manager 2.x clients on your network, you will have to use a LAN Manager–compatible password. If you used the PORTUAS utility to move users from your LAN Manager database to an NT database, the LAN Manager password will be stored in the directory database. If you add users to the database using the User Manager for Domains utility, the user will have an NT-compatible password. The important differences between the two are the following:

1. A LAN Manager password cannot be longer than 14 characters.
2. A Windows NT password can be up to 128 characters long.
3. LAN Manager passwords use the Original Equipment Manufacturer (OEM) character set and it is case insensitive.
4. Windows NT passwords are case sensitive and are stored using the Unicode character set.

Tip: Frequently you can resolve user logon problems by investigating the user's password. Because NT passwords must be entered in the exact case as the stored password, many users coming from other environments will have to learn this. When you add users to your network, be sure to point out to them how their passwords are stored.

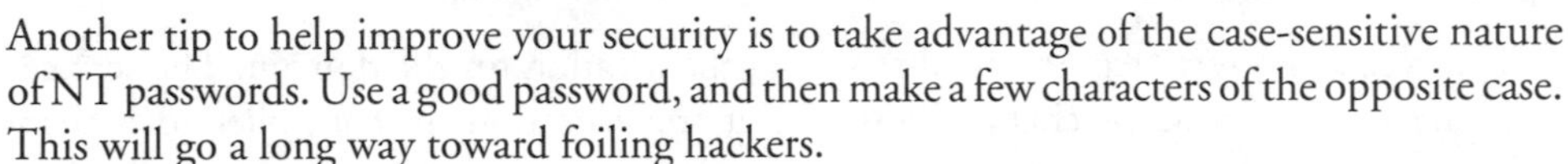

Another tip to help improve your security is to take advantage of the case-sensitive nature of NT passwords. Use a good password, and then make a few characters of the opposite case. This will go a long way toward foiling hackers.

If you change your password, and you enter a new password that is consistent with the LAN Manager type and the Windows NT type, then both passwords will be updated in the database.

The NetLogon Service

When you add a new user account to a PDC, it is the responsibility of the NetLogon service to propagate this information to any BDCs that may be configured in the domain. By default, the NetLogon service sends modifications to the security directory database to BDCs every five minutes. For this reason, it might take a few minutes after you create or modify a user account before the user can use it throughout the network. If, for example, a new user wants to log on to a server or workstation that is on a different subnet from the PDC, you should wait a few minutes after adding the account for the PDC to copy that information to the remote BDC.

As you make changes to the security directory database, the changes are recorded in a *change log*. The change log can hold approximately 2,000 entries before the oldest changes are removed to make room for newer changes. It is easy to see that if a BDC is out of service for an extended period of time when changes were made to the domain security database, the BDC might not have all the updated information when it boots again. If it has been down for a time long enough for modifications to be dropped from the change log (because they were replicated while the BDC was down or because the change log became full), then the BDC will have to undergo a *full synchronization* with the PDC. This means that the entire contents of the security directory database will be copied to the BDC, instead of just the changes recorded in the change log.

Partial synchronization is the name given to the incremental updates that are performed periodically by the NetLogon service.

You can force a complete update of a BDC by using the Server Manager administrative tool:

1. Bring up the Server Manager by double-clicking it in the Administrative Tools menu.
2. Select the Synchronize Entire Domain entry from the Computer menu.
3. An informational message will appear to let you know that the action might take some time. Click on Yes to continue (see Figure 40.13).

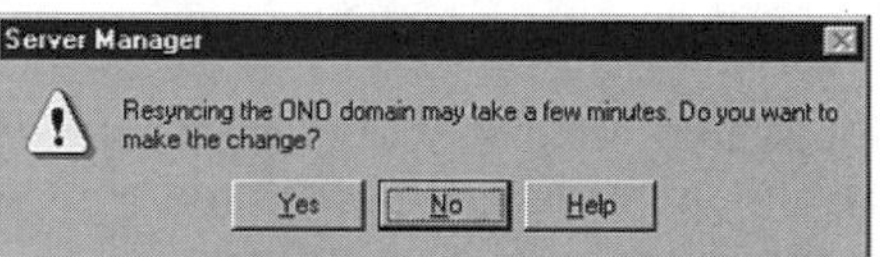

Figure 40.13. *You can continue or abort the full synchronization at this point.*

The NetLogon service is also used in user authentication for the domain. The service sets up a secure communications channel with the appropriate domain controller to exchange logon information. The domain controller downloads to the computer information that is needed to process the logon. One important thing to note is that if you are using NT clients, the logon information for the past 10 successful logons is stored locally. This means that if all your domain controllers are down, you can still log on, provided that you use one of the past 10 usernames that was logged on at the computer. This cached-logon feature will work on both Windows NT Server and Workstation. It will not, unfortunately, work for other NT network clients such as those using Windows 95 or Windows for Workgroups.

What Is MSV1_0?

When you log on to an NT computer, the logon request is validated by a security package called MSV1_0. This is the default security authentication package for Windows NT. If you want, you can write your own (no small feat for nonprogrammers) and edit the Registry to replace MSV1_0 with your own package.

The MSV1_0 authentication package is divided into two parts. The top half of the package prompts the user for a password and passes it, along with a domain name and username, to the lower half of the package. The lower half proceeds to authenticate the logon information against the computer's local security directory database. If you are logging in locally to a domain controller, or logging in to a workstation's local directory database, both halves of the process complete on the computer you are logging in to. If you are logging in to a domain and the computer you are using is not a domain controller, the MSV1_0 package passes the request to the NetLogon service instead. The NetLogon service on the domain controller passes the information to the bottom half of its MSV1_0 package, which then queries the domain directory database.

Two illustrations show the logic used to validate user logons depending on the information supplied by the user. Figure 40.14 shows the process when you specify a domain name along with your username and password. Figure 40.15 shows the process when you do not specify a domain name.

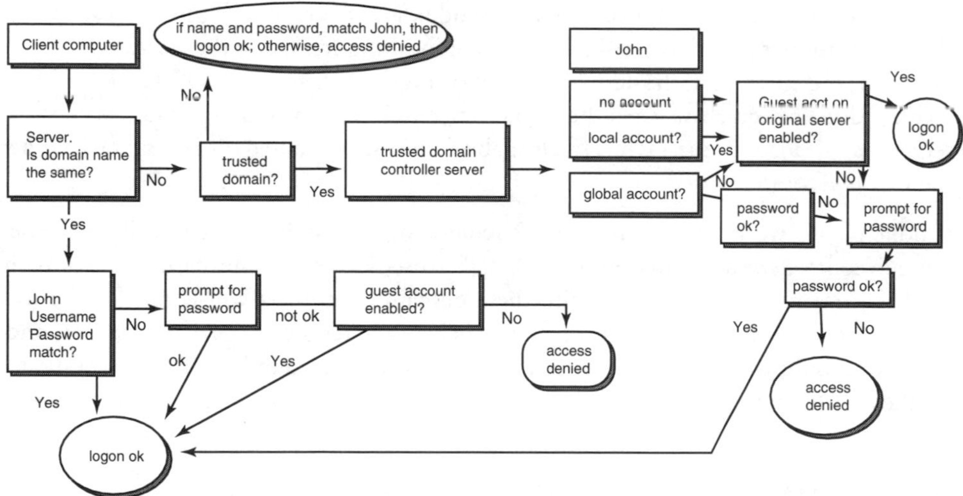

Figure 40.14. The steps involved in authenticating a user when a domain name is included in the logon information.

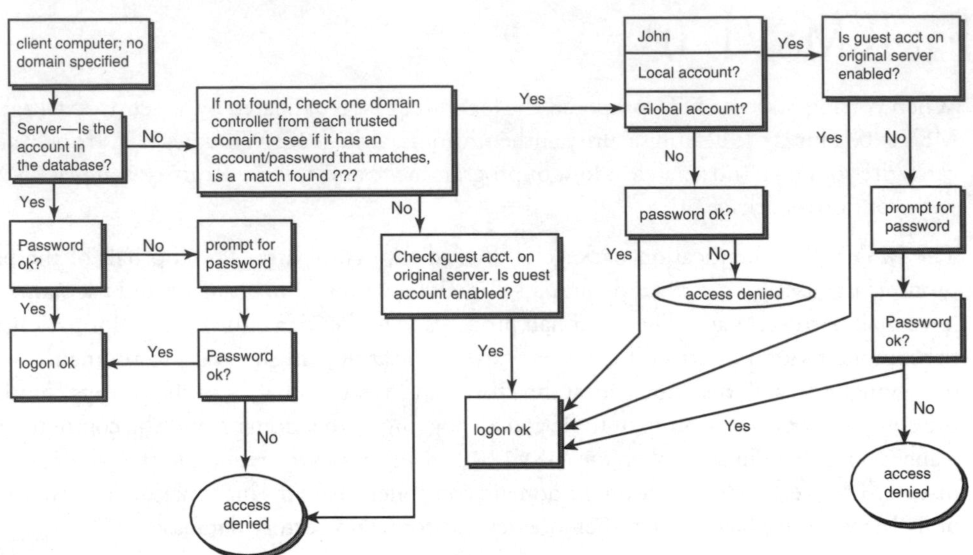

Figure 40.15. The steps involved in authenticating a user when a domain name is not included in the logon information.

LAN Manager 2.x clients do not understand the domain concept. Those clients are the ones that will be attempting to log on remotely to NT computers without using a domain name. When trying to access an NT Workstation, the first attempt to validate the logon is via the workstation's local directory database. If a matching name and password are found, the logon succeeds. If not, the information is passed to a domain controller for the domain that the workstation is a member of, for another attempt. If the domain controller finds a username/password match in the domain security directory database, then the logon succeeds. If not, the Guest account is checked on the server that the logon request is for. If it is enabled, the user is granted the access you have permitted the Guest account.

If none of this works to authenticate the remote logon, the domain controller will check with domain controllers in each of the domains that it trusts. Hopefully one of those domain controllers will return a successful logon. Again, these domain controllers will check for the username/password in their domain security directory database and report success if a match is found. If not, and the account used is a local account, the logon will succeed only by using the Guest account on the originating computer.

The Account Policy

When user logons fail and the password and username appear to be valid, you should check your Account Policy (as set up under the User Manager for Domains) to be sure that nothing there is restricting the user from logging in.

To get to the Account Policy dialog box (see Figure 40.16), bring up the User Manager for Domains and select Accounts from the Policy menu.

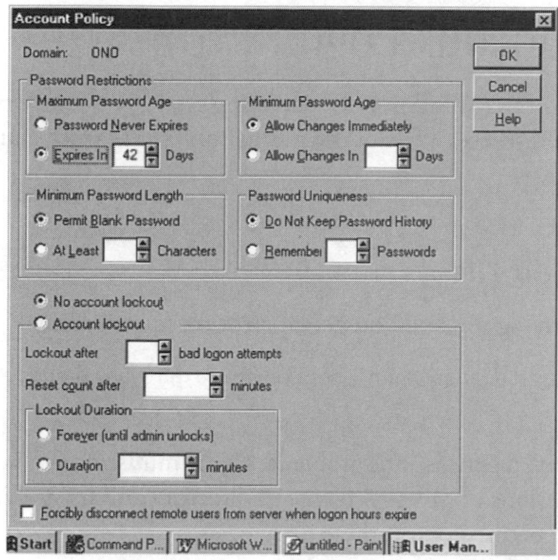

Figure 40.16. *The Account Policy dialog box sets policies for all accounts in the directory database.*

Several fields in this dialog box could be preventing a user from logging in:

- Maximum Password Age: Have you set an expiration date for the password?
- Account lockout: Have you enabled the lockout feature for failed logon attempts? If so, the user will not succeed in logging in with the correct username/password until the lockout time expires, if the user has exceeded the number of bad logon attempts.

Did the user log on and then become disconnected and not able to log on again? Check to see whether the "Forcibly disconnect remote users from server when logon hours expire" check box is checked in the Account Policy dialog box.

> **Note:** You use the Hours button on the User Properties dialog box (in the User Manager for Domains) to set the hours that the user is allowed to log on. It is important to note that if the logon server and the user's computer are in different time zones, the time used for determining access is the time on the logon server.
>
> When adding users and setting restrictive hours for network access, be sure to use the correct time!
>
> Be aware that unless you check the "Forcibly disconnect ..." check box on the Account Policy dialog box, a user who stays logged on past the time allowed can keep working. Only new logons are blocked!

Other Miscellaneous Logon Errors

Many different parts of the Windows NT operating system can cause problems during the logon process. This section discusses a few of the more prominent errors that can occur and how to fix them.

Unable to Load Profile

When you attempt to log on, and you get an error message stating

```
Unable to log you on because your profile could not be loaded, please contact your
administrator.
```

then you probably have a permissions problem. The administrator should log on to the computer and check the permissions on the `%systemroot%` directory and its subdirectories. The user should have at least Change permission on these directories.

A common mistake is to try to protect the system files by restricting access to Read-only for the group Everyone. When you encounter this problem, the easiest method to correct it is to reapply the Change permission to these directories for the group Everyone.

Environment Variables and Windows 95 Clients

Windows NT provides a few environment variables that you can use for logon scripts for most clients. Those variables are

- %HOMEDRIVE%
- %HOMEPATH%
- %HOMESHARE%
- %OS%
- %PROCESSOR_ARCHITECTURE%
- %PROCESSOR_LEVEL%
- %USERDOMAIN%
- %USERNAME%

If you are logging in from any Windows NT computer, all the preceding variables will work in your logon script. However, because many networks at this time have Windows 95 clients (and Windows 3.x clients), you should be aware that the following variables will not work when logging on to an NT network from these clients:

- %USERNAME%
- %USERDOMAIN%

- %OS%
- %PROCESSOR%

If you want to use these environment variables in a logon script for a non-NT client, you must define the variables first. You can find several scripting utilities on the Internet to help you perform this function.

Helpful Resource Kit Utilities

If you haven't already acquired the Windows NT Server 4.0 Resource Kit, you probably should. The kit comes with three books that extensively cover a lot of topics that are only hinted at in the standard NT documentation. The kit also includes many utilities and tools that can be used to accomplish many tasks on the network.

> **Tip:** The Windows NT 4.0 Resource Kit, Supplement One, was recently released. It provides updates to utilities that were included in the first Resource Kit release and a few new utilities, in addition to another book that covers new territory and corrects mistakes in the original documentation. A must-have for any good administrator.

Two of those utilities might come in handy when you try to diagnose problems with users accessing your network.

Setting Up a Computer for Automatic Login

If you have a low-security need for a particular NT Workstation or Server and want to bypass the logon box, you can accomplish this in two ways. The first is to edit the Registry. That process is as follows:

1. Log on to the computer using the Administrator account (or an account that is a member of the Administrators or Domain Admins group, whichever is appropriate for the computer).
2. Start up the Registry Editor (`REGEDT32.EXE` at the command prompt).
3. Locate the following key:

   `HKEY_LOCAL_MACHINE\SOFTWARE\Microsoft\Windows\NT\CurrentVersion\Winlogon`
4. From the Edit menu, select Add Value.
5. In the dialog box titled Add Value, enter the text `AutoAdminLogon` into the Value Name field.
6. In the field named Data Type, select `REG_SZ`.

7. Click on OK. This brings up the String Editor dialog box, where you should enter the value of `1`.
8. On the right-hand side of the Registry dialog box, you will see the value named `DefaultUserName`. Double-click it.
9. After you double-click on the value, the String Editor will reappear. This time enter the user account name that you want to be used for the automatic logon.
10. Now you need to add another value. From the Edit menu, select Add Value. The Add Value dialog box appears.
11. Select the REG_SZ datatype.
12. For the Value Name field, enter `DefaultPassword`.
13. For the value of this entry, enter the password for the user account you entered in step 9.
14. On the right-hand side of the Registry Editor dialog box, select the value `DefaultDomainName` by double-clicking it.
15. In the String Editor dialog box, you can enter either a domain name or a computer name that will be used in authenticating the logon. Of course, this should be the workstation (or nondomain controller server) or domain where the user account resides.
16. Exit the Registry Editor and log out. You should immediately be logged in again, using the account you specified above. If this does not happen, log in and check your entries. If all is okay, reboot the computer and you should be logged in automatically.

Sounds easy, doesn't it? Well, in the Resource Kit you will find a graphical tool that does all the Registry entries for you. You simply enter the password for the account you are logged in to and click the OK button. In Figure 40.17 you can see that the current user is Administrator. Set Auto Logon has been selected (note that you can remove the automatic logon in this dialog box also). The password can be entered into the Password field and, after the OK button is clicked, you can log off to test the automatic logon.

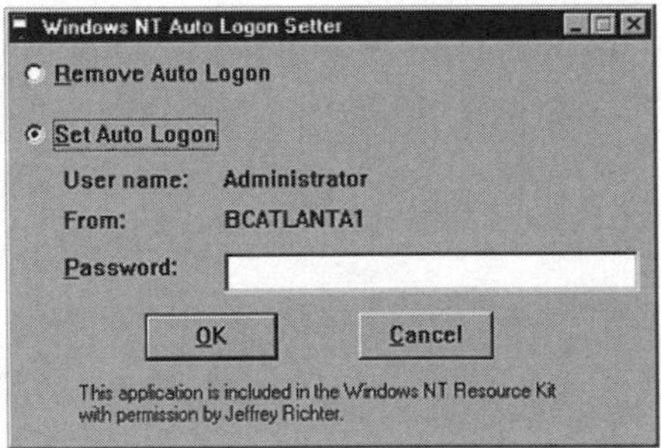

Figure 40.17. *The Windows NT Auto Logon Setter is a tool you will find in the Windows NT 4.0 Resource Kit.*

Whether you intend to use this feature often or only occasionally, you should use the tool that comes with the Resource Kit. Why? Because when you edit the Registry, you must be very careful not to make any mistakes. Editing the Registry can render the system unbootable. As always, if you find you need to edit the Registry, make sure you have a complete backup of the system and an Emergency Repair Disk on hand in case of emergency.

Tip: If you have a computer set up for automatic logon, which uses the username you specified, there might come a need to log on to the computer interactively as a different user. To do this you simply reboot the computer and, during the initial logon phase (after the blue screen), hold down the Shift key. The Logon dialog box will appear and you can log on as another user.

However, when you bypass automatic logon, the username that you use to log on to the computer will replace the name that you specified when you used the Registry Editor or the Resource Kit tool. You will need to re-enable automatic logon when you are finished. Rebooting the computer will not produce an automatic logon until you do.

Warning: You should use the automatic logon feature only when you are absolutely sure that no security problems exist for the particular computer or username you select. The username is stored in the Registry as text and anyone who has access to the key can read it! Locking a computer in an office and using automatic logon is not enough to secure it. Any user who has access to the Registry key can use the Registry Editor remotely to look at the username and password, and can use it to log on at other computers in the network.

Using thc Domain Monitor

Another Resource Kit tool that is useful in tracking down logon problems is the Domain Monitor. This tool enables you to continually monitor servers in your domain or trusted domains. Figure 40.18 shows the opening window for the Domain Monitor. Double-clicking on the ONO domain brings up the Domain Controller Status window (see Figure 40.19) where you can see the domain controllers for this domain.

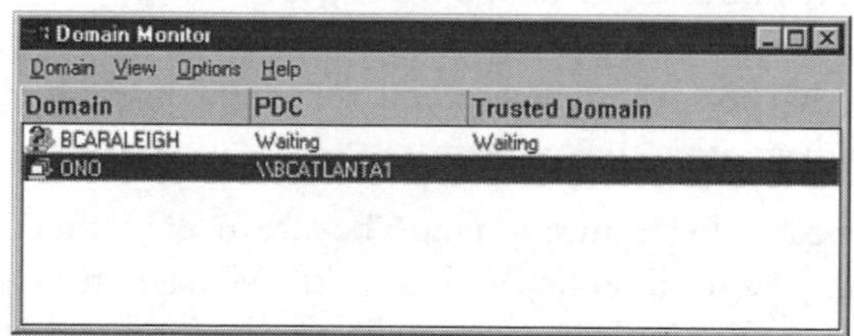

Figure 40.18. *The Resource Kit tool Domain Monitor can be used to obtain a frequently updated status of the domains on your network.*

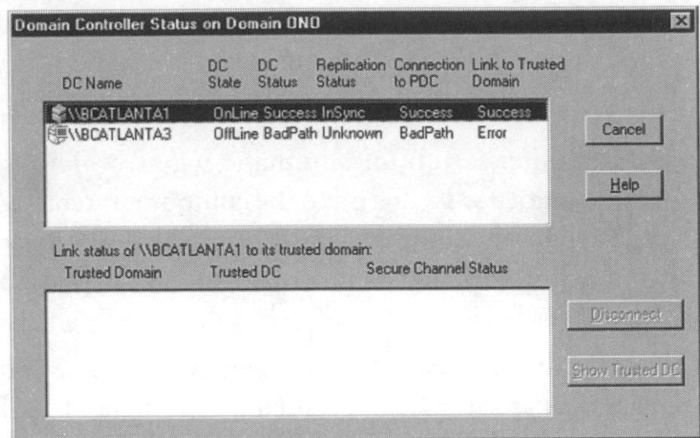

Figure 40.19. *The Domain Controller Status window shows you the status of domain controllers in the domain you select.*

If a user is trying to log on to the network and is supposed to use the Backup Domain Controller BCATLANTA3, you will be able immediately to see that the server is down. The user cannot log on because the domain controller is out of service.

When you first start the Domain Monitor, you must add the names of domains you want to monitor. To do this, select Add Domain from the Domain menu in the main window of the monitor. A small dialog box allows you to enter the name of the domain to be added. You can also use the Remove Domain option under the same menu to remove a domain when you no longer want to monitor it.

The Domain Monitor can show you a lot of other information also, and is a great tool for quickly diagnosing simple network or logon problems. You can adjust the time interval at which the display is refreshed, thereby giving yourself a frequently updated information display you can monitor.

Summary

Troubleshooting logon problems in a Windows NT network need not be difficult. If you first can determine what security directory database is being used to validate a user's logon (a PDC, BDC, or local computer database), then you have already narrowed your search tremendously. After you locate the computer that hosts the database, you can use the Event Viewer to examine the Security log as a first step in diagnosing the problem.

In order to use the Security log feature you must be sure to set up the events that you want to audit. You do this by setting the Audit Policy with the User Manager for Domains. If you do not want to audit these events continuously, you can still turn them on and off during troubleshooting.

Windows NT supports logging on interactively (locally) at a computer, logging in remotely (a network connection, for example), pass-through authentication (user verified by a domain controller on a trusted domain), and logging in using the Remote Access Service. If a user is having problems logging in, be sure you understand exactly what the user is trying to do before you start trying to solve the problem. If the user is logging in at an NT computer, for example, you should remember that passwords are case sensitive, whereas they are not when logging in to an NT computer remotely from a LAN Manager 2.x computer.

Although selected built-in user groups are granted the right to "Log on Locally" or to "Access this computer from the network," you can also grant these individual rights to a user or to a group. Thus, you do not have to give a user more rights than needed just to make a logon possible.

The Windows NT administrative tools, such as the User Manager for Domains, the Server Manager, and the Remote Access Admin utility, provide a wealth of information you can use to track down problems. You should become familiar with these tools.

Introduction to Access Problems

by Brett Bonenberger

Almost everyone has had resource access problems. With the integration of network operating systems and the growth of LANs, a resource problem can be complex to solve. For most of us, the types of problems that arise include access to printers, shares, and server applications. It's amazing that one day everything is working fine and the next day you lose the ability to print or retrieve that important file from the server. Your users begin to panic and the phone begins ringing. We have all been in this situation. Sometimes, the solution is simple; other times, it is not. This chapter explores what you need to know to solve your own network resource problems including shared resources, user authentication, printers, and trust relationships.

Troubleshooting Shared Folders and Files

One of the frequent changes made on a system involves security access on a folder or on individual files. The following are two examples that I find to be common on networks.

When a user creates a new folder, he or she has the option to grant and restrict other users from the folder. This is a great feature in Windows NT. It allows the users to manage themselves in workgroup situations without an administrator forming groups for them. It takes a lot of overhead off the administrator. But, there have been times when users make mistakes with security settings. A common problem is when users remove themselves from a group that they just formed. It is a frustrating experience.

Another example of change in security is when you are working with groups. Similar to the previous example, it is common to create user groups for access to databases, files, and folders. When granting or denying access to these groups, it is easy to make a mistake and leave a group off the access list. A good hierarchy of groups should help to eliminate this problem.

Tip: If you manage a large number of users and groups, it is wise to maintain a manual documentation of the users, the groups they belong to, and their access rights. It is a nice list to have available when planning your security rights.

If documentation is not your thing, Windows NT has some built-in utilities that will help you create your own documentation. One of these utilities is CACLS. CACLS is a command-line utility that you can use to list, change, or overwrite the Access Controls for a file or directory structure. Using this list you can save the output to a file and print the file or keep it online.

If you notice, a change on the system had been made in each of the examples. Lost access to a resource rarely occurs on its own. In fact, I have never known something like that to occur. It might appear that way, but if you investigate deep enough you will probably discover a human hand somewhere. This is especially true in a large network. If you are a member of a large network administration team, changes could be made to the system without everyone's knowledge. Each action or change taken by an administrator should be documented for everyone. This is a good practice. Have fun with it. If you enjoy working with databases, create a small system database in any desktop database application. In the database, you should include who made the change, why the change was made, users affected by the change, and the date and time. There are many other items you could include, but those are the basics. If you have an intranet, create an intranet solution to keep track of changed information. If you are the only person who would be making changes to the system, a good simple way to keep track of what changes you have made is to maintain a log. A small notebook or desktop calendar would be sufficient. Write down every change you make, when you made it, and the result of the change. A log could also help you when you are troubleshooting performance problems.

User Authentication and Identification

Windows NT has a very complex security structure built in. I always see things as the more complex, the more things can go wrong. Windows NT security architecture was explained in Chapter 2, "Windows NT Security Architecture." Included in the security architecture is user authentication.

User Authentication

User authentication is dependent on a unique security ID called, appropriately, a SID. A SID is automatically created whenever you add a new user. Statistically speaking, there are no two SIDs alike anywhere, meaning no two users anywhere in the world will have the same SID!

Every security authentication that a user might have during an NT session is reliant on the SID. If you delete a user, all security settings for that user are lost. There is no way to get the settings back. If you re-create the user with the same username, it will have a different SID. Windows NT does not recognize the previous and current accounts as being the same, so it will issue a new SID each time.

Therefore, your security context covers the range of permissions and privileges that are associated with your SID. Because the security context is lost when a user is deleted, your security context is focused on your SID.

It is general practice that if a user is taking a leave of absence for whatever reason, the account should be disabled rather than deleted. If you are working with fairly deep security rights, re-creating a user can take some time.

When a user logs on, Windows NT creates a security token for the user that contains the SIDs for the user. Whenever a user attempts to access an object, the SIDs are compared with the access permissions of the object.

All SIDs for all users on the network are contained in the Registry, so it is possible to track a user by using his unique SID. The Registry key that contains all the SIDs is `HKEY_LOCAL_MACHINE\SOFTWARE\Microsoft\Windows NT\CurrentVersion\ProfileList`. The SID is composed of user information, date, time, and domain information, and a SID is represented by the following:

S-1-X-Y^1-Y^2-......-Y^n

- The prefix S-1 indicates that this is a revision 1 security ID. There is no revision 2 security ID, so there may be plans on enhancing the SID.
- The X is the value that represents the identifier authority. The identifier authority value identifies who issued the security ID.
- The Y^n values represent subagencies that were involved in issuing the SID.

The following example illustrates how a problem with a SID can cause problems with accessing resources.

Users on your network are having problems accessing shared resources across the network. Whenever certain users would attempt to access a resource sitting on your Backup Domain Controller (BDC), they would receive an error stating that the specified object could not be found. The same was true for your application servers. Still, some users were able to access the resources on all servers. Being in a multiple server environment you have a Primary Domain Controller (PDC) and a Backup Domain Controller.

Isolating a problem like this would not be easy. One of the first things you would check would probably be the security settings for each resource. What many people do not know is that if the SIDs for the administrator user for the domain had different SIDs on each domain controller, access attempts would be futile. To solve this you would require the use of a tool that could look up the SID for an account on the PDC and compare it to the SID on the BDC. Such a tool exists in the Windows NT Resource Kit. The tool is a command-line utility called `getsid`.

Unfortunately, to correct a problem with different SIDs would require you to rebuild the BDC so that when the server rejoins the domain, all information in the SAM database will be replicated properly to the BDC.

Note: There are many shareware utilities available on the Internet that will do the same thing. A great site for Windows NT related files is `http:\\www.bhs.com`.

Problems with Trust Relationships

If you are managing a multiple domain environment, you are likely using trust relationships so that users from each domain can access resources on the other domain. Remember, there are two roles in a trust relationship: the trusted domain and the trusting domain. The trusted domain is the domain that hosts the SAM database for user authentication. The trusting domain is the domain that relies on another domain to authenticate users and privilege levels.

There are many benefits to having a trust relationship:

- It provides a secure communication channel between two or more domains.
- It allows administrators to see the network as a single administrative system.
- It places centralized administration at the enterprise level rather than the domain level.

Although a trust relationship can make administration easier, there are many problems that can prevent a user from accessing shared resources across a trust. Each problem is defined as configuration, security, or connectivity.

Configuration Problems

A configuration problem will occur when you first establish the trust relationship. The problem could be that the trust was established in the wrong direction. The problem here would be that the trusting domain was set up as the trusted domain and the trusted domain was set up as the trusting domain. This is a common mistake. In fact, this is covered in great depth in the NT Server Certification exam. You must add the trusting domain before you add a trusted domain.

Not using identical passwords when first establishing the trust relationship is another configuration problem. Each administrator must have clear and accurate documentation about the trust outlining the trusted and trusting domains.

Security Problems

I have already discussed security problems with file and folder access, but security problems with trusts are a little more involved. When a trust relationship is first established, the operating system immediately changes the password used and it constantly changes for the life of the trust.

Therefore, if a trust relationship is broken, the trust cannot be reestablished on the broken end because the administrator will not know the password. Each administrator must delete and re-create the trust.

Connectivity Problems

Connectivity problems in a trust relationship depend on the physical layer of the network. A problem could arise because of a misconfigured protocol or a bad connection between domains. Chapter 43, "Identifying, Isolating, and Repairing Network Problems," provides some troubleshooting steps that you can use to help determine where a connectivity problem lies.

Troubleshooting Printing Problems

Another important resource users might lose access to is printers. There are many types of printers out there: UNIX-based, Novell, and NT printers, all of which need to be shared across a multiplatform network. Here are some basic steps to try when working with a printer problem.

- Check all your cable connections at the hub, network jack, and printer. Verify that the printer is turned on. Check the printer port assignment under the Printer settings on the server and under NT Workstation clients.
- Verify that you have the correct printer selected in your application. You could be printing to a different printer and not realize it! This is done in most Windows applications through the printer setup.
- Make sure you have enough disk space available for the spooler. The spooler is configured by default to use the system partition. This directory is `%SystemRoot%\system32\SPOOL\PRINTERS`.
- Verify that you have the correct and most recent drivers installed. Also, check the configuration of the drivers and make sure you are using the correct print monitor.
- Determine whether you are able to print from a simpler application, such as Notepad or Write. Verify that there is not a problem with your spooler. An easy way to check this is to copy either your `autoexec`, `.ini`, or other text file to the printer port.

Some Common Printing Problems

Now that I have given you some simple troubleshooting steps, I would like to talk about some of the more common printing problems. This is not meant to be all-inclusive but rather cover some of the problems that I and others have had. I have talked with several of my professional peers to put this list together.

Just as with file and folder access, users can be assigned the right to access or use a printer to prevent unauthorized use of a printer. For example, on one of our networks, we have restricted access to a printer that is used by the accounting and finance department. This printer is in a fairly public area; so, by restricting the access to the printer we can shield confidential documents from the rest of the staff. If possible, you should try to keep departmental printers in a non-public area to protect confidential documents.

To track the types of attempted or successful access to a printer, you can set up *auditing*. Auditing lets you monitor attempted or actual misuse of printer access privileges. Setting up auditing is an easy process. Under the Security tab on the Printer Properties dialog box is the Auditing button. There you can set up the audit log to track who does what and to track conditions of the printer, such as failed print jobs. By default, auditing is turned off. To activate, use the Add button and select the users or groups you want to audit. Print audit logs can become very large and care should be taken not to fill up your Event Logs. Normally, you would only want to audit unsuccessful attempts or print jobs to a special printer that is expensive to print on.

Again like ownership of folders or files, ownership of the printer can be by an individual or a group of people. Ownership provides the ability to control the printer object. In the example with the finance department, printing rights are granted to the finance group. Within that group, one person is the print operator, so the ultimate control of the printer is given to the finance department.

What Does This Mean to Me?

By now, you must be wondering whether permissions cause problems with printing? In a dynamic environment where permissions are granted and revoked often, mistakes can be made easily. In an environment in which you would have many print operators, mistakes can be made. Most of the time, these mistakes can be avoided if changes to the printing system are done in an orderly and controlled fashion. Figure 41.1 shows the Property dialog box for a LaserJet 5SI. Controlling permissions, auditing, and ownership is done under the Security tab. Administrative privileges are required to make any changes.

Permissions

Setting permissions for a printer is very simple and is similar to setting file and folder permissions. There are four levels of print permissions: No Access, Print, Manage Documents, and Full Control. Figure 41.2 shows the Finance group with Full Control and the four permission levels available. Each permission level of course has a different level of access. Table 41.1 shows each level of permission and a brief explanation of the type of access.

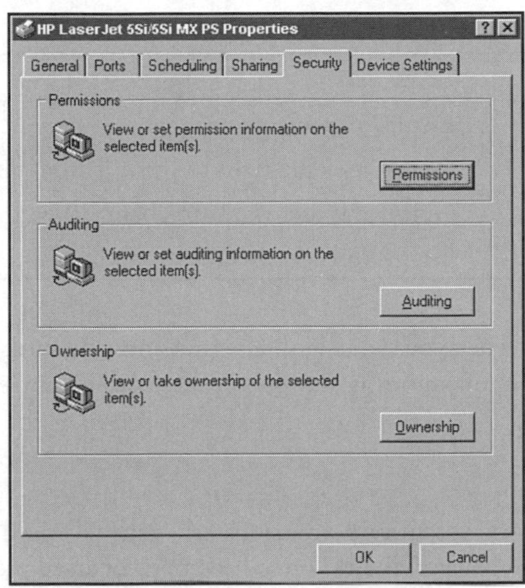

Figure 41.1. The Security tab allows for control of the permissions, auditing, and ownership.

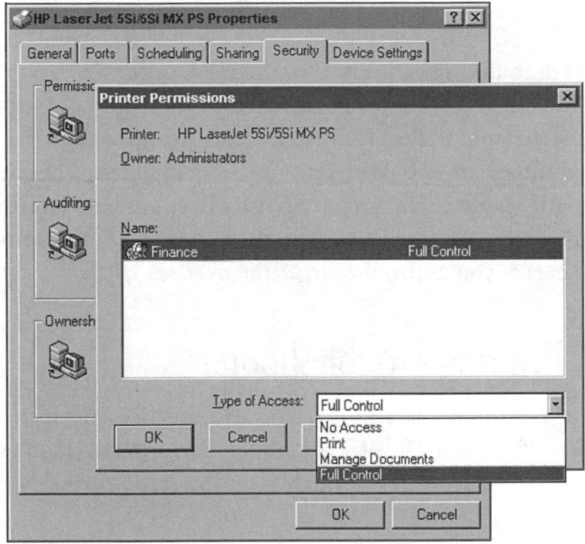

Figure 41.2. Finance group with Full Control.

Table 41.1. Permissions and explanations.

Permission Level	*Access Level*
No Access	Denies all access to printer.
Print	Grants user the right to print, pause, resume, or delete jobs.
Manage Documents	Grants the user rights to change the status of any print job.
Full Control	Grants full administrative access and control.

Care should be taken when you are assigning permissions. Be sure you track this information on paper and that all print operators have copies of these permission settings.

Auditing

Now that you have your security permissions set, you will need to audit the printer object. Auditing, as mentioned earlier, allows you to keep track of attempted misuse of the printer; or, if a user is presenting you with a printing problem, you can audit the user's attempts to give you a starting point for troubleshooting. Before you can audit any individual, you must set the individual to be audited. This is done through User Manager for Domains, which was covered in Chapter 14, "User Manager for Domains."

Figure 41.3 shows the auditing dialog box for the HP LaserJet 5SI. In that box, the Finance group is being audited for failed print jobs. If I wanted to monitor another user or group because of suspected misuse of the printer, I could add the user or group to the list of names and track all failed events. All audited information is written to the Security Event Log. Because of this, you should keep a close eye on the audited events. Your Security Event Log can get full very quickly if you audit a large number of events. Auditing an event also requires a small amount of overhead on your server. The more events you audit, the larger the overhead.

Windows NT Printing Troubleshooter

In an attempt to make using operating systems easier, Microsoft includes troubleshooters in its software. Windows 95, Microsoft Office, and NT Server have troubleshooters. This software is designed to help you solve problems through a step-by-step process. NT Server 4.0 has a printing troubleshooter.

Accessing the troubleshooter is done through the online help. If you search for troubleshooting in the help index and select printing problems, the troubleshooter will load.

Figure 41.4 shows the first screen of the troubleshooter. Notice its first question: "What's wrong?" From here until the problem is or is not solved, you will need to select an answer for each question the troubleshooter asks. Eventually, you will reach a solution, as shown in Figure 41.5, or you will exhaust the troubleshooter of ideas and end up with the screen in Figure 41.6.

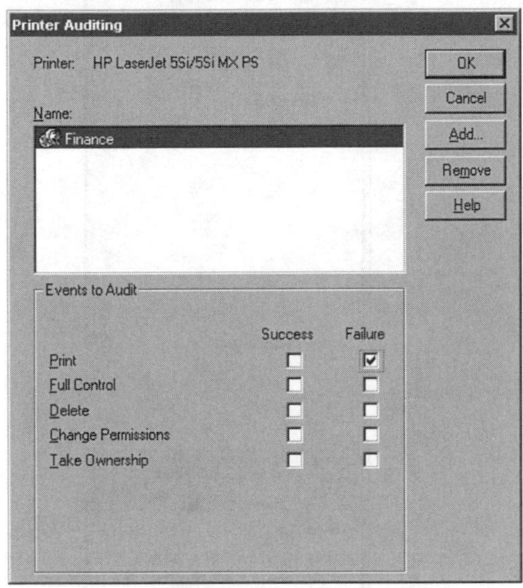

Figure 41.3. *Auditing dialog for the HP LaserJet 5SI.*

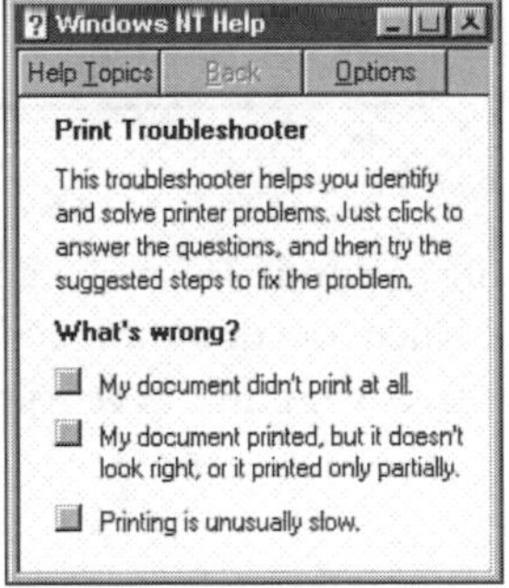

Figure 41.4. *The troubleshooter asks, "What's wrong?".*

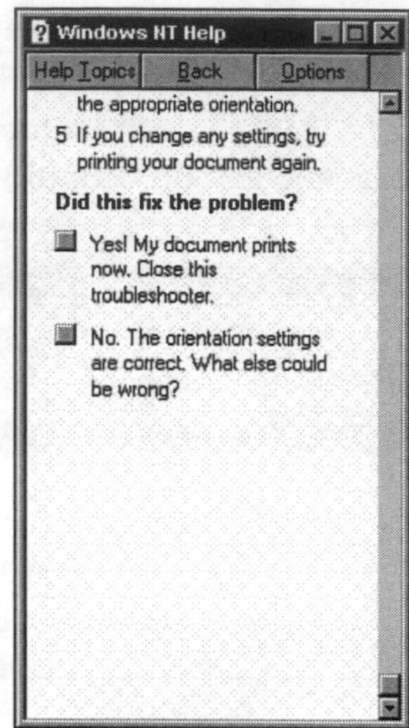

Figure 41.5. *The troubleshooter's solution.*

Figure 41.6. *The troubleshooter has no more ideas.*

Whatever your result, Microsoft continues to make advances in its troubleshooting software. There might someday be a time when you don't touch the keyboard and the system autocorrects the problem for you. But most of us wouldn't have a job anymore, would we?

Summary

Solving resource access problems can take a lot of valuable time. The problems are not always easy to solve and there never seems to be enough time to solve them. In this chapter we looked at several resource access problems including shared folders and files, user authentication, problems with trust relationships, and printing. This chapter is designed to help you get started in resource troubleshooting and to learn how your resource access problems can be solved.

Solving Printer Problems

by Terry W. Ogletree

Windows NT offers a variety of solutions to printer problems. In a large network of personal computers, it could be quite expensive to purchase a printer for each user's workstation. You can, if you need to, connect a single printer to a single workstation and restrict its use to that workstation. However, if you decide to set up print servers, much like file servers, you can use a much smaller number of printers and offer them to some or all clients on your network.

This chapter will cover some of the basic concepts about printing under Windows NT and the procedures involved in setting up printers, as well as a few other troubleshooting topics:

- Print devices versus printers
- Printer pools and multiple printers for a print device
- Creating printers versus connecting to printers
- Overview of the NT internal mechanisms involved in printing
- Ports and print processors
- Auditing printing events and using the Event viewer

Basic Printer Concepts

Before you try to understand the concepts involved in printing under Windows NT and how to troubleshoot problems as they arise, you should first be aware of these technical terms used in the NT documentation that may not mean exactly what you think they do:

- Printer

  Under most computer operating systems, a printer is a physical device that produces hardcopy output. Under Windows NT, a printer is a logical construct that is the software interface to that physical print device. This is an important distinction. When you see the word "printer" in the documentation or in this chapter, it does not refer to an actual printer, such as a laser printer.

- Print Device

  This is the term used in Windows NT to designate the physical device that produces the hardcopy output. In NT, a printer (sometimes referred to as a logical printer) sends output to the print device.

Another important concept to remember in relation to Windows NT printing, especially when you are trying to figure out why a user cannot access a printer, is that, like file shares, you can assign permissions to printers. You can allow everyone on the network to print to a printer, or delete documents from the printer, and so on. Rights and permissions are central to the security model that is deeply embedded into Windows NT.

The Relationship of Printers to Print Devices

When personal computers were first introduced, there was a one-to-one relationship between the computer and the print device. With the advent of networking, it became possible to associate many computers with one print device.

Under the Windows NT networking model, you can allow many computers to share print devices, and you can do it in several interesting ways.

Figure 42.1 illustrates three different relationships that can be set up between printers and print devices.

In the one-to-one relationship between a printer and a print device, Printer A sends output to Print device 1. It is a very simple relationship. Keep in mind that the printer in Figure 42.1 is not a computer. It is a logical construct that can reside on more than one computer. The point is that, no matter which computer the output comes from, the actual formatting and spooling of the job are done on a one-to-one basis between the printer and the print device.

Printer B and Printer C have a different type of relationship. Here, two different logical printers send different kinds of output to a single print device. Printer B prints one-sided (simplex) output and Printer C prints two-sided (duplex) output on the same print device. You could buy two different printers to do the same thing. Or, you could have users specify the simplex/duplex option in their applications' Printer Setup dialogs. However, this is a simple illustration. You can set up many different printers for the same print device with each one having a different combination of printer properties. For simplicity's sake, it is much easier to set up several different print devices and allow the user to choose the printer based on the characteristics needed for the output.

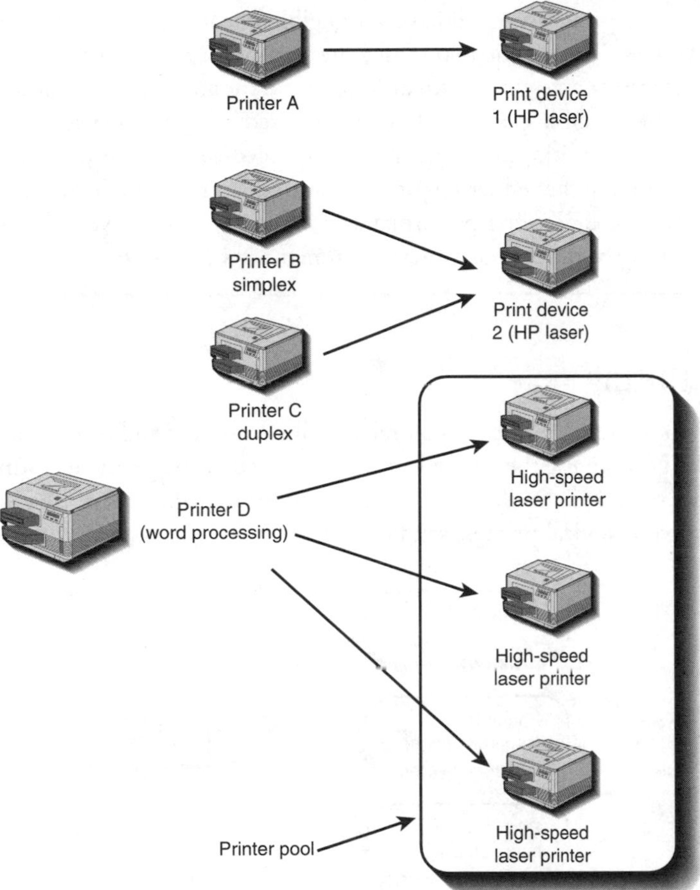

Figure 42.1. *You can associate printers with the actual print devices in several ways under Windows NT.*

Printer D in Figure 42.1 is set up in what is called, under Windows NT, a *printer pool*. This is the opposite of how Printers B and C are set up. In this situation, a single printer can send output to more than one print device that resides in a printer pool. Of course, you would want each print device in the pool to be of the same make and model or at least have the capability to emulate the same type of print device. In high-volume situations such as a company's word processing department, this solution can greatly improve productivity. When a user prints to Printer D, and one of the print devices in the pool is already printing, the output is directed to a printer that is currently idle. Although all users print to the same logical printer, the output is spread out among several print devices to improve throughput—much like an office telephone system is set up to "hunt" the next available free telephone before it routes the call.

Tip: There is no limit to the number of print devices you can use in a printer pool. However, you will be constrained by the resources on the print server you are using. You can use a dedicated Windows NT computer to be a print server, or you can use an NT computer that is already acting as a file server. Because NT places a higher priority on file services, using a file server as a print server will have a negligible impact on users who access the computer for file services. Perhaps the two most important resources to consider when setting up a print server are the amount of hard disk space and the amount of physical memory installed on the computer. Disk space is only a limiting factor when you expect to have a number of large documents waiting to print; they are spooled to a file on the disk while they wait. Memory is used in the rendering process and in queuing operations and, as always in NT, more memory means better performance. Of course, if you have only a few print devices attached and they all stay busy, increasing memory will not speed up the printer.

Delayed Printing

If you have an office where a large volume of printing occurs and all of it does not need to print immediately, you can use the delayed-print feature. You can specify in a printer's Property sheet the times that the printer is allowed to send output to the print device. Figure 42.2 shows another example of several logical printers sending output to a single print device.

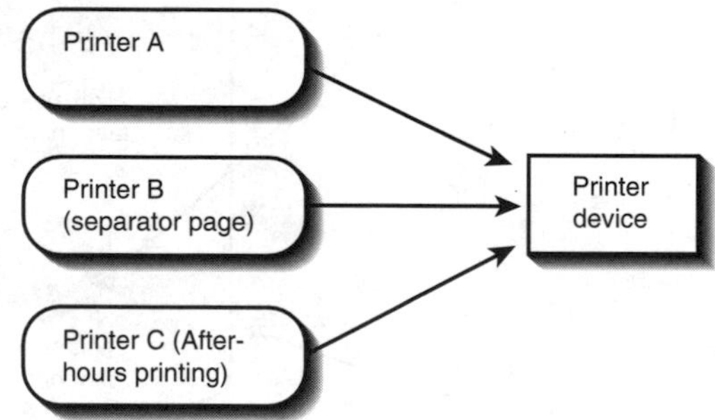

Figure 42.2. *Two printers can print 24 hours. Printer C prints only after office hours.*

Using this setup, you can send jobs that can wait until tomorrow to Printer C and let users use Printer A and Printer B during normal office hours. Note again that the first two printers have different characteristics. You could set up more than one printer to print after hours, with different characteristics, and they could compete for the print device after hours.

What Is Printer Priority?

When you have more than one printer sharing a print device, you can use the delayed print feature described in the previous section to delay less important jobs until a time when most other printing is not likely to happen.

If you want to be sure that all documents print during your regular office hours, though, and you want to make sure that certain users (your boss?) get their print jobs done first, you can use the Priority selection in the printer's Property sheet to designate the relative priority that is assigned to a printer's documents. If you set up Printer A to have a higher priority than Printer B and both share the same print device, and even if Printer B has many documents waiting to print, when Printer A sends a document, it will move to the top of the list of documents to print. When the printer device becomes available again, Printer A's document will be the next document to print.

Creating and Connecting to Printers

As explained, you can attach a physical print device to a computer, or you can connect to a printer offered as a print share by a print server. Additionally, Windows NT supports printing to networked printers using TCP/IP or Data Link Control (DLC), along with AppleTalk and NetWare printers. The TCP/IP function is enabled using the LPR/LPD protocols, which were first developed on UNIX systems. LPR stands for line printer remote and LPD stands for line printer daemon. In UNIX, a daemon is a background process that is available to service requests as they come in, without requiring the intervention of another user.

Windows NT supports both protocols. You can set up a Windows NT server to be a print server using the LPD protocol, or you can set up NT clients to use the LPR protocol to send print jobs to other LPD servers, even those that are not running Windows NT. (See Figure 42.3.) For example, many HP LaserJet printers now come with a JetDirect network card that enables them to receive print jobs using either LPR or DLC.

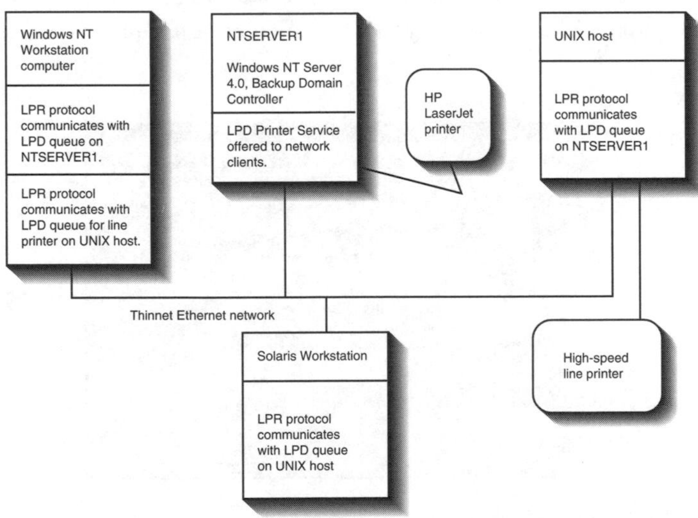

Figure 42.3. *The LPR/LPD protocols from the TCP/IP protocol suite are used to offer print services on the network.*

Creating a Printer

You use the Printer Wizard to create a printer for a print device attached to your computer. You also use the Printer Wizard to connect to a printer that resides on the network or is offered as a service by another computer.

You activate the Printer Wizard by double-clicking on the Add Printer icon in the Printers folder. (See Figure 42.4.) The Printers folder can be found under the Network Neighborhood icon, in the Control Panel, and by selecting Settings from the Start menu.

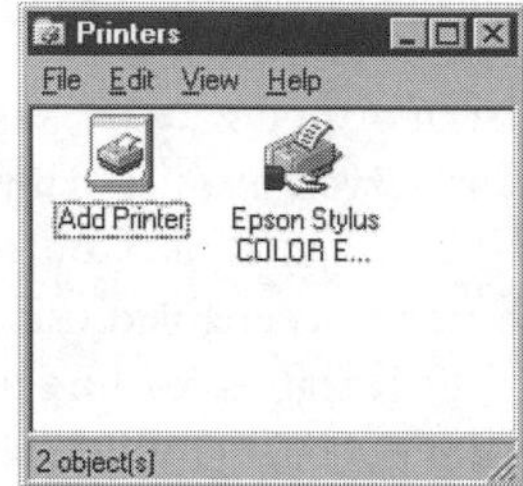

Figure 42.4. *The Add Printer icon is found in the Printers folder. Use it to add a new printer to your computer.*

Tip: You also can select the Add a Printer selection under the Administrative Tools/ Administrative Wizards menu.

The Printer Wizard will ask you a few questions and walk you through the process painlessly. The first dialog that appears asks whether you want to create a printer or connect to a printer. (See Figure 42.5.)

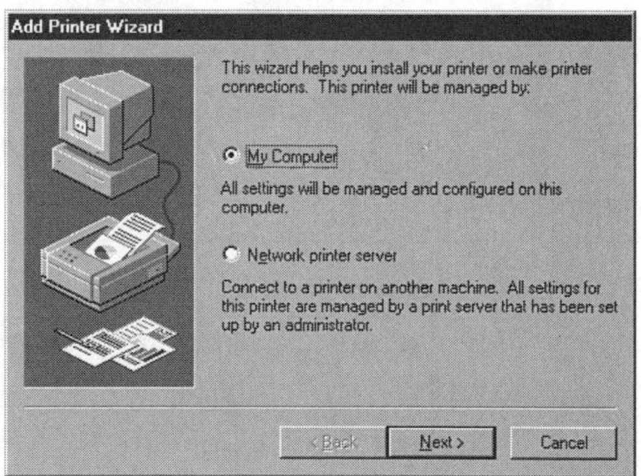

Figure 42.5. *Select My Computer if you are creating a printer on your workstation or server.*

Click the Next button and the Printer Wizard asks you to select a port that will be used to access the printer. If the printer is attached to your computer, this is probably an LPT port or perhaps a parallel port. If you are creating a printer to send output to another kind of port, such as an LPR/LPD printer, you should use the Add Port button if the port does not appear in the Available ports box. (See Figure 42.6.)

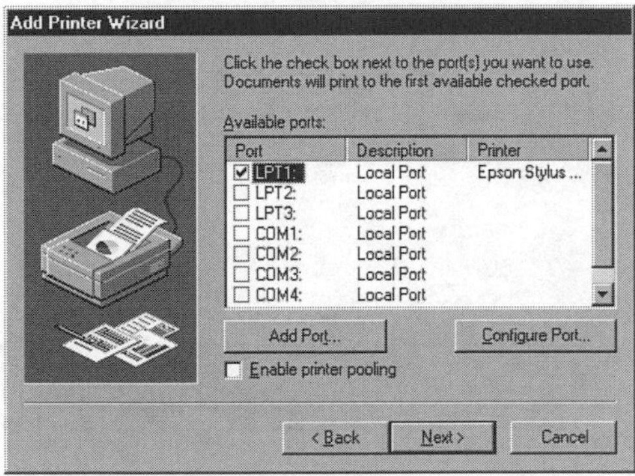

Figure 42.6. You select the port from the Available ports box. If the port is not listed, click the Add Port button.

For more information on adding an LPR/LPD port, see "Selecting the Port," later in this chapter.

If you want to enable printer pooling, click the check box shown in Figure 42.6 and select more than one port for the output. That's all there is to do to create a printer pool.

The Printer Wizard will then prompt you to select the type of printer so that it can load the correct driver. Figure 42.7 shows the dialog you use. First select the manufacturer from the left-hand box and then the correct printer from the selections presented in the right-hand box. If you do not see your printer listed, use the Have Disk button if you have obtained a driver from the manufacturer (or a driver that has been updated since the NT distribution CD-ROMs were created).

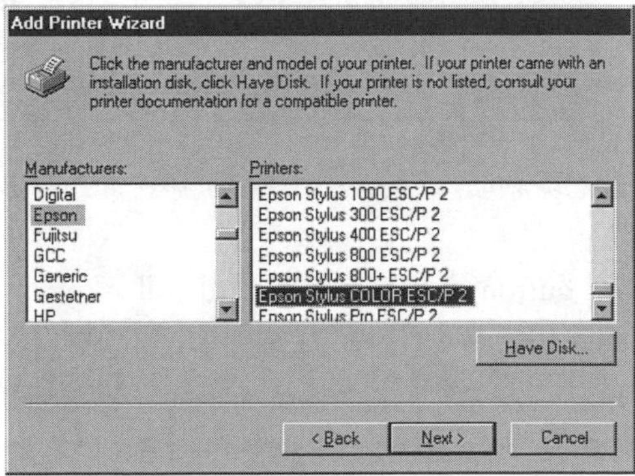

Figure 42.7. This dialog allows you to select the manufacturer and printer model so that a driver can be installed.

The wizard will then load the driver. If it is not already on the disk, it will prompt you for the location of the distribution files. If you selected the Have Disk button, it will prompt for the location of the disk or path to the necessary files.

Next, the Printer Wizard will ask you to name the printer and to designate whether or not you want to use this printer as the default when your applications print. (See Figure 42.8.)

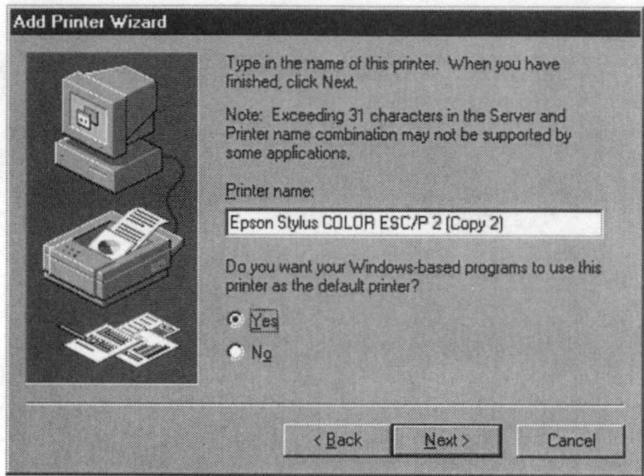

Figure 42.8. *Select a name for the printer you are adding and decide if it will be the default printer for your applications.*

Next, the wizard will prompt you to share the printer on the network (see Figure 42.9) and to load any additional printer drivers for clients that may connect to the printer.

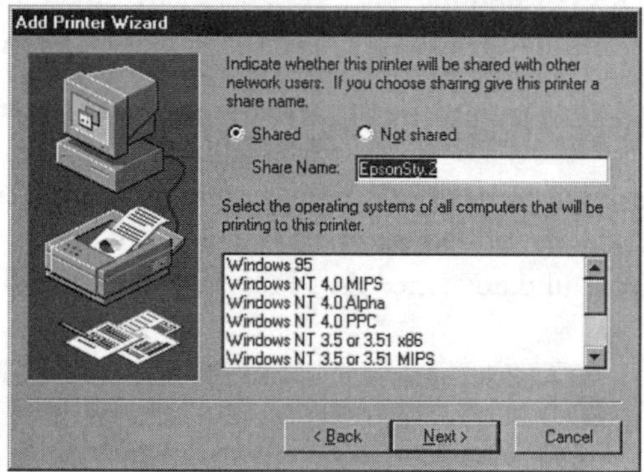

Figure 42.9. *If you decide to share the printer on the network with other clients, you should select additional drivers if clients use a different operating system.*

After you click the Next button, the Printer Wizard will ask you to print a test page. If it prints successfully, you can click the OK button to close the wizard. The new printer will now show up in the Printers folder, where you can view its properties and documents sent to it.

Using the Printer Wizard is the *only* way you can create a printer under Windows NT. However, if you want to connect to a printer on the network (or a print server), you can connect to it using the Printer Wizard or you can browse for the printer in your Network Neighborhood. (See Figure 42.10.) Some applications, especially those native to NT, allow you to browse for the printer under the File | Printer Setup menu selection.

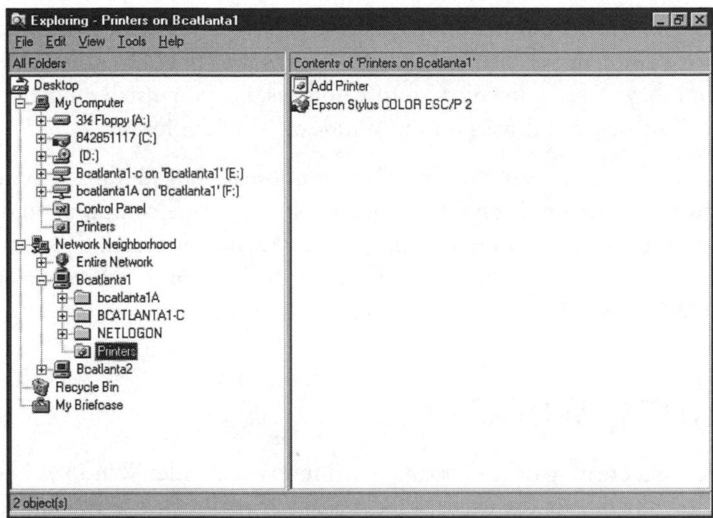

Figure 42.10. *You can browse to find a printer on the network you want to connect to.*

Connecting to a Printer

You can connect to a printer by browsing for it or by using the Printer Wizard. By far, the easiest method is to browse for the printer. In Figure 42.10, you can see the printer named Epson Stylus Color being offered on the network by the server BCATLANTA1. All you have to do to connect to the printer is double-click it, provided you have permission to do so.

Tip: You can also use the `NET USE` command at the command prompt to connect to a printer that you want to use for an MS-DOS type of program—for example,

```
> NET USE LPT1: \\server\printershare
```

works just like it did in a LAN Manager 2.*x* network.

When you create a printer, you have to tell the Printer Wizard where the correct driver for the client/printer combination is stored so that the driver can be installed on the computer. This is usually the CD-ROM that you used to install Windows NT. It can be a floppy disk or a directory where you have placed an updated driver from the manufacturer.

If you connect to a printer offered by an NT server from a client that is not using NT, you also have to install the driver locally.

However, if you are connecting from an NT computer to an NT computer that offers a printer, you will not have to install the printer locally. When you connect to the printer, the Windows NT computer will automatically download the correct printer driver from the server computer. When you update the driver on the print server, the new driver will be downloaded to client NT computers when they next access the printer.

You can do this with Windows 95 clients also—with an exception. Windows 95 clients will download the printer driver the first time they connect to the NT computer offering the printer as a share, but they will not download future updates that you install on the print server. You will have to install subsequent drivers on the Windows 95 client locally.

If your network consists only of Windows NT computers, your administrative tasks become much easier, because you need only apply an updated driver to one computer, and you don't have to worry about the clients. As discussed in the previous section on creating printers, you must be sure to install the Windows 95 driver on the Windows NT computer when you create the computer if you want Windows 95 clients to have the benefit of the first download.

How Printing Works

As you have seen, creating or connecting to print services under Windows NT is fairly easy. The automatic downloading of drivers to Windows NT clients makes setting up new workstations on your network much less complicated. The inner workings of the printing process, however, can be substantially more complex. Understanding the background might help when diagnosing printing problems.

Figure 42.11 shows a diagram of the printing process. A user on Computer A decides to print a document. The application makes calls to the GDI (Graphics Device Interface), which uses the printer driver to create a file (DDI journal file) containing Device Driver Interface (DDI) calls. This file is sent to the client side of the print spooler (`Winspool.drv`).

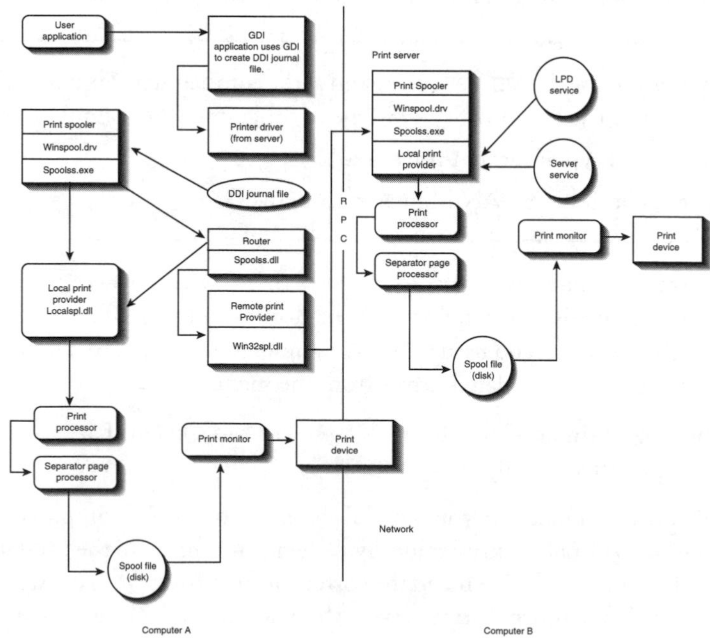

Figure 42.11. Overview of the internal printing process.

As you can see in Figure 42.11, the print spooler consists of more than one program. The `WINSPOOL.DRV` program makes calls to the `SPOOLSS.EXE` program, which performs the server side of the spooler's function. `SPOOLSS.EXE` makes API calls to the router program `SPOOLS.DLL`, which sends the job to the local print provider (`LOCALSPL.DLL`). Finally, the print job is spooled to a disk file.

The local print provider then polls any print processors on the system to determine which processor can accept the job. The print processor may modify the data in the print job, if needed, to make it print correctly. The separator page processor next adds a separator page, if it was requested by the user, and sends the spooled file to the print monitor.

Finally, the job is sent to the port monitor and then to the print device.

Note in Figure 42.11 that the router (`SPOOLSS.DLL`) can route the job to the local print provider if the printer is located on the same computer as the application that is trying to print. Otherwise, it establishes communications using remote procedure calls (RPCs) with the print spooler on the server system, which then continues to handle the print job.

Also note in the diagram that the Server service can also feed jobs to the print spooler. Clients that are not running Windows NT, such as MS-DOS or Windows 3.1 clients, send the print job to the server using the NetBIOS redirector. If the client computer is using LPR, the LPD service on the print server computer feeds the job to the print spooler.

Print Job Data Types

Depending on the type of client and the print device, the spooler can receive a print job in one of several data types. If the client is a Windows NT client, the job data type is called EMF, for enhanced metafile. The Raw data type is used for PostScript printers that interpret the text files they receive. The data types used in the Windows NT printing system are as follows:

- EMF

  The enhanced metafile format is used by clients running Windows NT 4.0. The print driver creates a print job based on the GDI calls. This information is used by a background thread process to recreate the print image that is sent to the print device.

- Raw

  The spooler does not modify a job with this data type, which comes in two flavors:

  - Raw [FF Appended]

    If a job consists of this data type, the spooler will add a form-feed character to the end of the print job to ensure it will be ejected from the printer at the end of the job.

  - Raw [FF Auto]

    The spooler will only add a form-feed character to the end of the print job if there is not one present.

- Text

  The spooler assumes a job of this data type to consist of ANSI text. Each character is represented by a numerical value from 0 to 255. Similar character sets are in existence that are basically the same as the ANSI character set for the values 0–27.

  This data type is used to send text files to printers that do not print text files on a one-to-one basis. For example, a PostScript printer will try to interpret the text as instructions on how to print the text.

  The spooler takes print jobs with this data type and reformats the print job into a series of commands the printer can understand. It uses the default font, form, and orientation of the print device to format the new print job. Those parameters, along with the print resolution, are taken from the Document Properties dialog.

- PSCRIPT1

  Macintosh clients usually send PostScript code to printers. On a printer located on a Windows NT computer, the client can print to non-PostScript printers. For jobs of this data type, the spooler will interpret the PostScript code and create an output file that the printer can understand.

If a print job is making it to the printer but is not producing the correct hardcopy output, you might try changing the document or printer's default data type. If you are printing from Windows NT applications, the default data type should be EMF.

Typical symptoms of using an incorrect data type for a print job include

- The final page does not print or an extra page prints for a client that uses Microsoft networking (LAN Manager 2.*x* or Windows NT networking, for example).
- PCL or Postscript code is reproduced on the output rather than the desired print image.
- Jobs sent from Macintosh clients do not print in color or they do not print.

Printer Driver Files

If you upgrade your Windows NT 3.51 systems to Version 4.0, you will have to reload your printer drivers. The changes surrounding the GDI require a new type of device driver and the older NT versions will most likely not work. If your printer is not on the Windows NT Hardware Compatibility List (HCL), you may need to check your manufacturer's Web page (or telephone service department) to get a new driver.

The printer graphics driver file takes the DDI commands and converts them to commands in the print device's language. The printer interface driver is used to allow the user to interact with the printer driver. When you select defaults or options, this is the program that you are interacting with. The characterization data file contains descriptive information about the capabilities of the printer and is used by the other two programs.

Managing Printers

When you double-click a printer in the Printers folder, you get a dialog that shows you the documents waiting to print. From this dialog you can also manage all of the properties of the printer and of each document that is waiting to print.

Figure 42.12 shows the dialog with the Printer menu open. As you can also see, there are a number of documents waiting to print. The Set As Default Printer option is checked, indicating that when you print from an application, this is the printer that will be the default in the Print dialog.

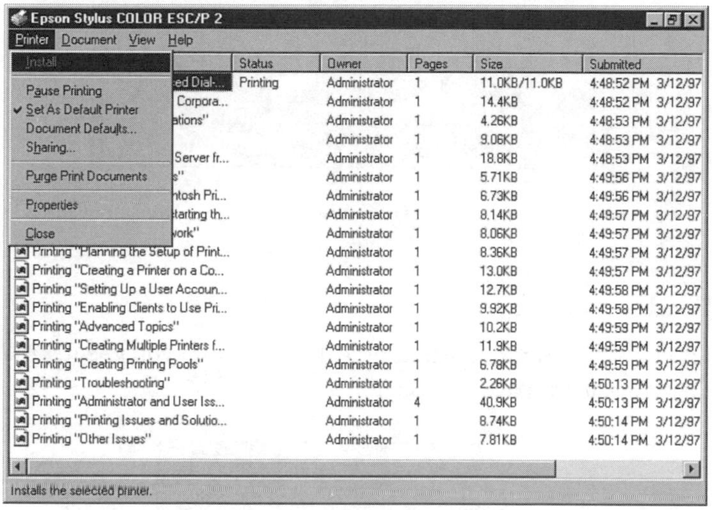

Figure 42.12. *The Printer dialog shows the documents waiting to print for the selected printer.*

Other selections in the menu enable you to pause the printer, set defaults for documents that come to the printer, purge documents that are waiting to print, and offer the printer as a shared printer to other computers. The Properties selection allows you to configure a wide range of options for the printer.

Figure 42.13 shows the first tab in the Printer dialog. These are general properties about the printer. As you can see, you can designate a separator page (if needed), install new drivers, set comments for users to see, select the print processor, and print a test page.

When troubleshooting client printing problems, use the Print Test Page button as a starting point to see if the printer can communicate with the print device at all. If this fails with a printer that has been working and if you have made no software changes, you probably have a hardware problem with the printer or other physical media (cables, serial or parallel port, and so on). If the test page will not print, the problem is not with the client.

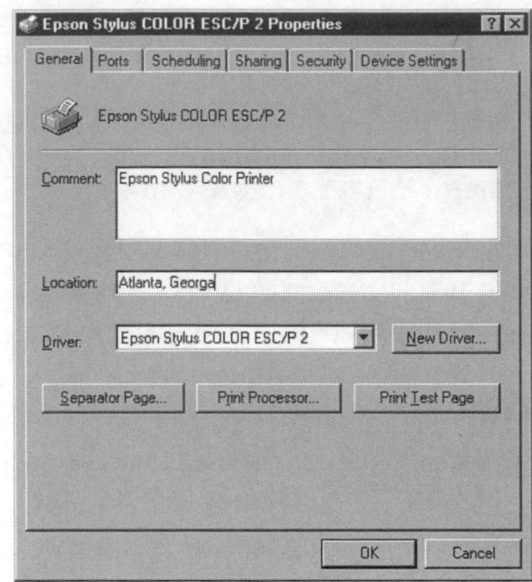

Figure 42.13. *The General tab on the printer's property sheet allows you to configure basic printer properties.*

Using Separator Pages

When you click the Separator Page button, NT will prompt you to enter the path to the file that will be used as a separator page. (See Figure 42.14.)

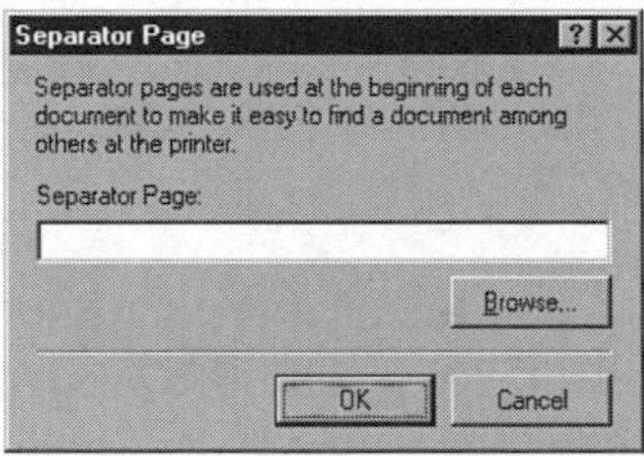

Figure 42.14. *Enter the path to the text file you want to use for a separator page.*

You can create a file yourself, using escape codes, or you can use the separator pages provided with the system, located under the directory `%SYSTEMROOT%\SYSTEM32`:

- `SYSPRINT.SEP`

  This separator page is compatible with printers that understand the PostScript language and prints a page before each document.

- `PCL.SEP`

  This page is compatible with HP printers that are dual-language printers. That is, they can switch between PCL and PostScript. This page sends the necessary codes to the printer to switch it to PCL mode.

- `PSCRIPT.SEP`

  This page is also used for HP-compatible printers that are dual-language, but this page will switch the printer back to PostScript mode.

You can copy one of these pages to use as a starting point to design your own page. You can print everything from your company's name to the user's name on the page by using the following codes in your text file:

- `\` This character should be used as the first character in the file. It tells the system that this is a separator page.
- `\N` This code prints the name of the user that submits the print job.
- `\I` This code prints the number of the print job.
- `\D` This code prints the time that the job was printed.
- `\L` This code is used to print text on the page. You follow the `L` character with the text. Any text following this code will print as is until another escape character is encountered.
- `\F` You follow the `F` character with a path/filename. The contents of the file you specify will print at the place that this code is placed in your separator page. If you are creating many different separator pages and want to put your company's name and address on the page, for example, you can put the text in a file and use this code to insert the text into the page.
- `\H` Characters following this code should be specified in hexadecimal, to represent printer-specific codes that you want to send to the printer. You can use this to set characteristics for the printer. Consult the printer manual for the correct codes.
- `\W` This code specifies the width of the separator page. The default is 80 characters, and you can specify up to 256 characters. Place the digits immediately after the `W` character.
- `\B\S` This causes any following text to be printed in single-width block characters, much like the big letters you used to see on line printer separator pages. The `\U` code will turn off this feature.
- `\B\M` This causes any following text to be printed in double-width block characters, again turned off by the `\U` code.
- `\U` This code turns off the two previous block-mode codes.
- `\n` Replace the *n* character with a number from 0–9. This will cause the interpreter to skip the number of lines indicated by *n*.

You can use any good text editor to edit and create separator pages. In an environment where a lot of users share printers, separator pages can help users easily locate their documents.

Configuring the Print Processor

Print providers (local and remote) are the processes that write the document out to a spool file. A print processor works with the print provider when the file is despooled and sent to the physical print device. Windows NT comes with two built-in print processors that are implemented as dynamic link libraries: `WINPRINT.DLL`, which is the Windows print processor, and `SFMPSPRT.DLL`, which is the print processor for Macintosh clients. Additionally, if needed, printer manufacturers can write their own custom print processors.

When you select the Print Processor button on the printer's property sheet, the Print Processor dialog appears. (See Figure 42.15.)

Note: The print processor for Macintosh clients will not show up in the Print Processor dialog unless you have installed the Services for Macintosh component.

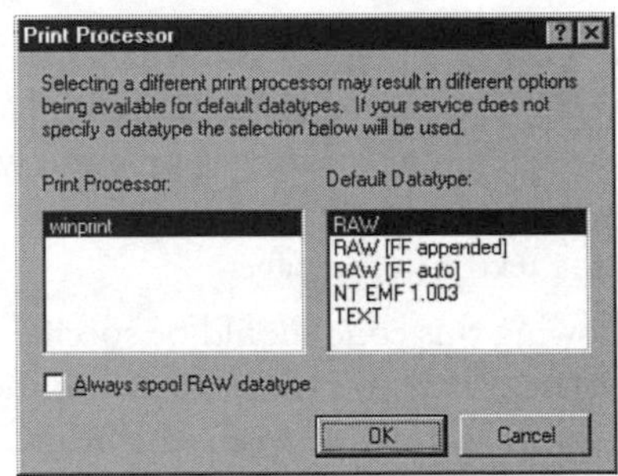

Figure 42.15. *Select the print processor in this dialog.*

If more than one processor is available, you can select the one you want to use in this dialog. You can also set the default data type for this print processor. (See "Print Job Data Types," earlier in this chapter.)

Selecting the Port

If you do not configure a printer to use the correct port, you will not get output on the print device. This should seem obvious, but, many times, users will not understand the different types of ports that are offered by Windows NT and simply will select LPT1:. If the printer is not connected locally to the printer port on the computer, this selection will not work.

The Ports tab on the printer's property sheet shows you which port(s) the logical printer is configured to send output to. (See Figure 42.16.) Note that you can select more than one port. This is how you create printer pools, which were discussed at the start of this chapter. You can also select to send the output to a file.

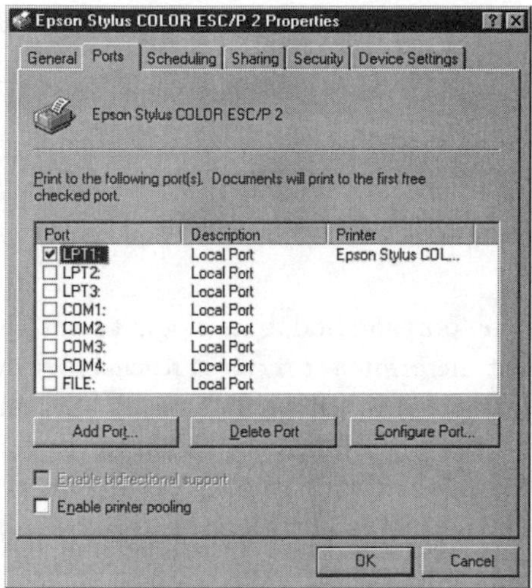

Figure 42.16. The Ports property sheet in the printer's property sheet shows the ports the printer will try to send output to.

In Figure 42.16, you can see three LPT*x*: ports, 4 COM: ports, and the FILE: port designation. If you want to use an LPR port to send jobs to a printer on the network using the TCP/IP protocol, you must create the port first. To do so, select the Add Port button. Figure 42.17 shows the Printer Ports dialog where you select the type of port to add.

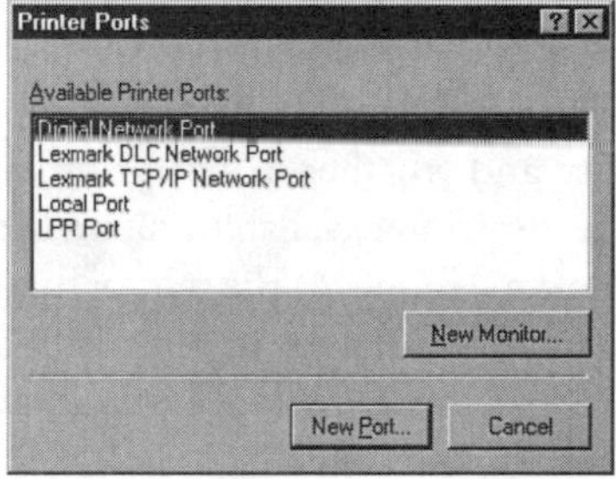

Figure 42.17. To add a port, select it in the Printer Ports dialog.

If you want to add a new type of port, such as one supplied by a manufacturer, use the New Port button on the Printer Ports dialog. You can also add a third-party print monitor using this dialog. Otherwise, select the port you want to add. For example, if you add any of the ports listed in Figure 42.17, you will be prompted to enter the location of the source files. Again, this is usually the CD-ROM you used to install Windows NT or a directory or network share where the files are stored.

If you select to add an LPR port, you will get a different type of dialog. Figure 42.18 shows the Add LPR compatible printer dialog box. You need only to enter the IP address (or host name) of the networked printer or the print server computer and then enter the name of the printer (if an NT printer) or the print queue (on a UNIX system, for example) to add the port.

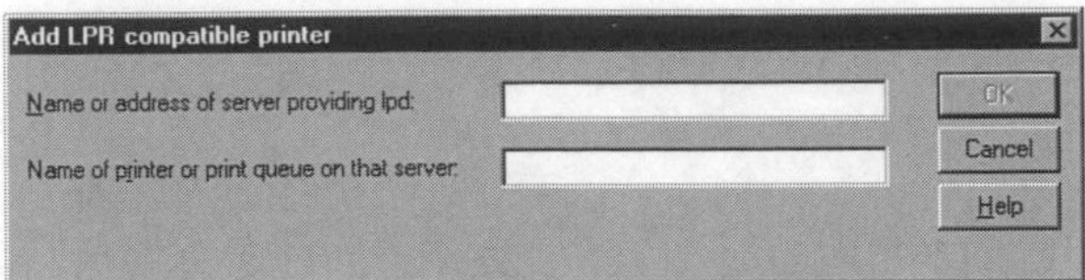

Figure 42.18. *The Add LPR compatible printer dialog box is where you specify the address and printer name when using TCP/IP to connect to a printer.*

If you create an LPR printer port and find that it doesn't print (using the Print Test Page button, for example), be sure that the printer or server is reachable from your computer. Use the `ping` command at the command prompt to determine this. If the printer or server is reachable, check to be sure you have entered the correct printer or queue name. If you are printing to an NT print server computer, the printer name you used when you created the printer should go here. If you are printing to an HP JetDirect card, you can usually get the name of the printer by printing out a test or configuration page from the test menu. If you are trying to connect to a printer on a UNIX computer, have the administrator check the `PRINTCAP` file to determine the name or alias of the printer.

Tip: If you have UNIX clients that cannot correctly print to a printer on an NT computer that is using the LPD protocol, reconfigure the UNIX client to send the lowercase `l` command.

The Scheduling Tab

The Scheduling tab (see Figure 42.19) in the printer's property sheet is where you specify things such as the printer's priority and whether or not print jobs should be spooled. The Available selection allows you to make the printer available around the clock or to restrict the printer so that it prints only within a certain time frame. At the start of this chapter, this was discussed as a means for using one print device to allow most users to print ordinary jobs during the day while allowing them to send less important jobs to a different printer (that uses the same print device) that will hold the jobs until after office hours.

If you want your users to continue working while print jobs are being processed, you should select to spool the printer. The user's job will be written to a disk file and stay there until the print device is ready to render it into hard copy. You can choose two modes for print spooling:

- Start printing after last page is spooled

  This mode will not send any output to the print device until the application has finished sending the entire document to the printer.

- Start printing immediately

  For long print jobs, you might want to have the spooler start despooling the print job as soon as it can, regardless of whether or not the application has finished sending the data to the printer. The document will still be spooled, but the printer will not wait for the entire print job before it starts to send output to the print device.

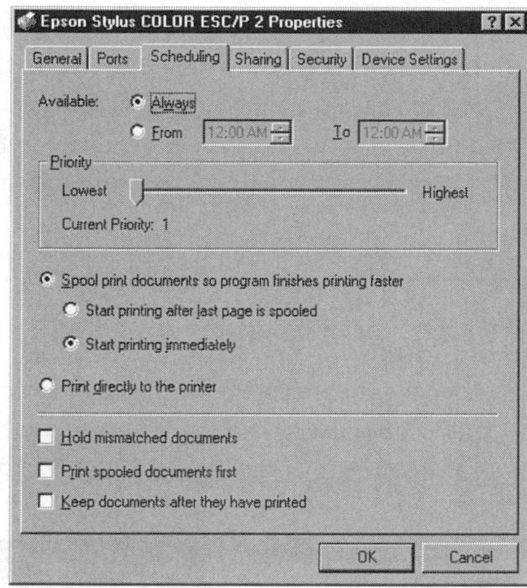

Figure 42.19. *You can set the printer priority, among other features, using the Scheduling tab.*

Sharing a Printer on the Network

Although you usually share a printer at the time you create it, you can use the Sharing tab in the printer's property sheet to share or unshare a printer. Figure 42.20 shows that you can also use this tab to select additional print drivers so that when NT clients connect to the printer, the appropriate print driver for the client will be downloaded to the client.

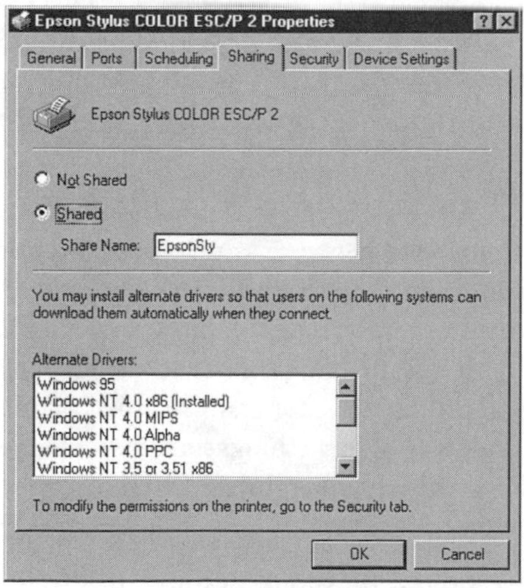

Figure 42.20. *The Sharing tab allows you to share or unshare a printer on the network and to select additional print drivers for clients of the shared printer.*

Keep in mind that the name you give to a printer share can be different than the name you give to the logical printer. When trying to connect to a printer using the LPR protocol, the name you use is the printer name, not the share name. When you connect to a printer using the `NET USE` command at the command prompt, you use the share name, not the printer name. However, it is quite possible that the printer name and the share name are the same.

Assigning Permissions to Printers

One of the best features of Windows NT is its security model. You can protect files as well as directories, and you can protect other resources such as printers. If you have a printer that is supposed to be used only by selected users, use the Security tab in the printer's property sheet to grant or deny users access to the printer. (See Figure 42.21.)

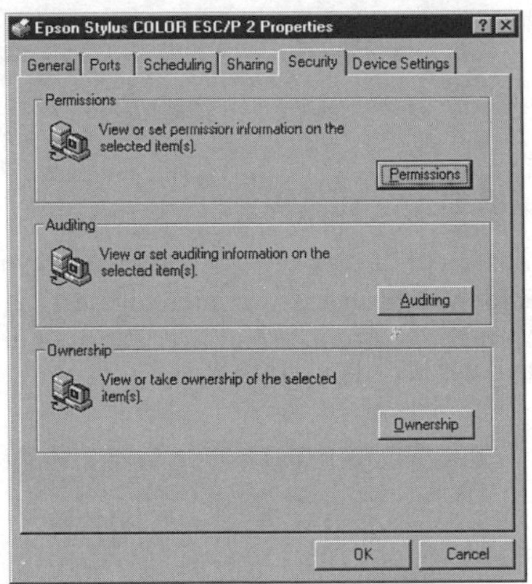

Figure 42.21. *The Security tab is where you apply permissions to printers.*

Again, this is a good place to look when a user cannot print to a printer. Make sure the user is logged on to the correct username and then check to see what kind of permissions (if any) have been granted to the user for the printer. Note again that a printer is not the physical print device. You can have several logical printers directing output to a single physical print device, and granting permission on one logical printer does not grant permission on any other printer that feeds jobs to the print device. This allows you to do things such as set up a general printer for most users, and then set up another printer with a higher priority, and restrict its use to those who need to get their documents done in a hurry.

To add permissions, select the Permissions button in the Security tab. The Printer Permissions dialog (see Figure 42.22) will appear, showing the users and groups that currently have access to the printer. You can expand the Type of Access field by using the down arrow to show different types of access and the users/groups that are granted that type of access.

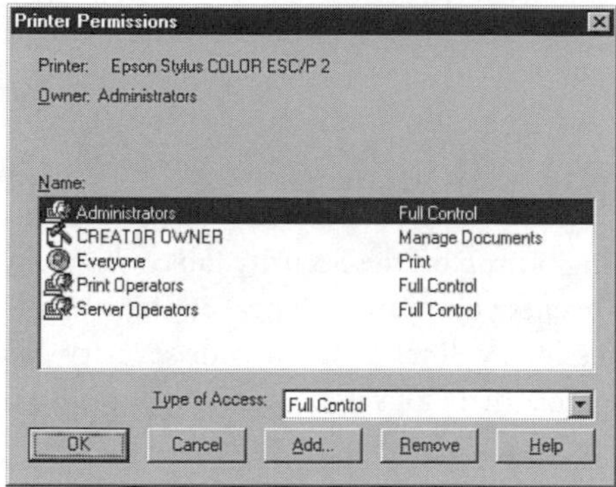

Figure 42.22. *The Printer Permissions dialog shows the current users and groups according to the type of access they have been granted.*

To remove users, select the type of access, highlight the user or group, and click the Remove button. To add new users, select the Add button and the Add Users and Groups dialog (see Figure 42.23) appears.

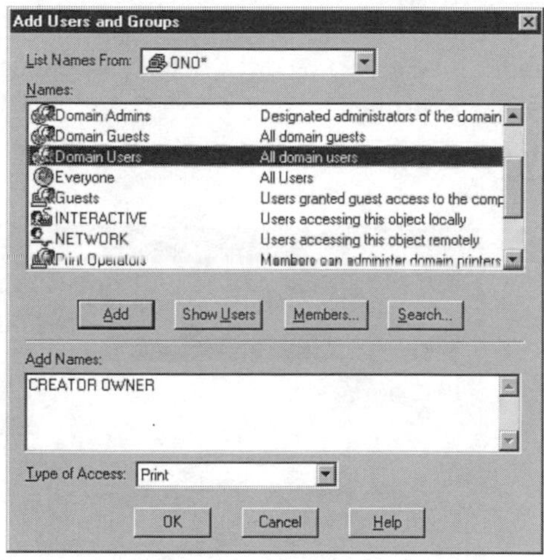

Figure 42.23. *Selecting the Add button causes the Add Users and Groups dialog to appear so you can add permissions for a printer.*

In the Add Users and Groups dialog, you first select the domain (the List Names From field) and then select the user or group you want to add from the Names box. Select the appropriate access from the Type of Access list box, and click the Add button to move that user or group name to the Add Names box.

If you select a group from the Names box, you can then click the Members button to show the individual users who are members of the group. If you select a different domain in the List Names From box, you can use the Show Users button to get a list of users in that domain instead of just the groups.

When you are finished selecting names, click OK to apply the permissions and return to the Printer Permissions dialog.

Auditing Printer-Related Events

If you select the Auditing button on the Security tab of the printer's property sheet, you can then choose which types of events you want to appear in the event log for this printer. Although you might think that permissions will take care of your security problems, you also need to keep an audit trail to protect against malicious users who might abuse the permissions you have granted them.

Figure 42.24 shows that you can audit the following types of events:

Print	Create a record in the event log when a user prints a document (or when a document fails to print).
Full Control	Create a record when a user changes job settings for a document, pauses, restarts, moves or deletes documents, shares a printer, or changes a printer's properties.
Delete	Create a record when a user deletes a printer.
Change Permissions	Create a record when a user changes the permissions for a printer.
Take Ownership	Create a record when a user takes ownership of a printer.

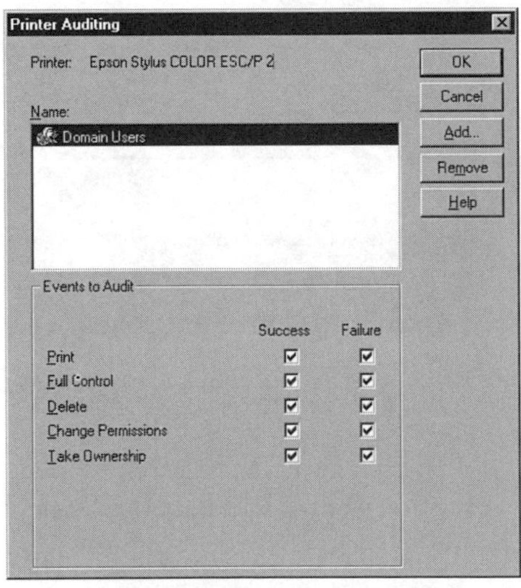

Figure 42.24. *You can select the type of printing events to audit using the Printer Auditing dialog.*

Auditing printing events can not only aid in security matters but can assist the administrator in other ways. If you want to set up a charge-back system, you can use a third-party utility (such as SomerSoft's DUMPEVT program, which will dump event logs to a file for processing with a spreadsheet or other program) to bill your clients. You can use it for troubleshooting purposes, also. If a user has inadvertently (or maliciously) changed printer properties, you can determine which property was changed and fix it and discipline the user if necessary.

When a print job fails to print, you are alerted to the fact that something may be wrong with the printer, provided the correct permissions for your users have been applied.

To remove permissions, you simply click the user or group name and click the Remove button. To add a user or group, use the Add button and add users in a similar manner that is described in the "Assigning Permissions to Printers" section, earlier in this chapter.

Use the Event Viewer found on the Administrative Tools menu to examine the records created by audited events. Figure 42.25 shows the main window of the Event Viewer with the System Log selected. (Use the Log menu to change to the Security, Application, or System Log files.)

Event Viewer - System Log on \\BCATLANTA1

Log View Options Help

Date	Time	Source	Category	Event	User	Computer
3/12/97	5:22:25 PM	Print	None	9	Administrator	BCATLA
3/12/97	5:21:03 PM	Print	None	10	Administrator	BCATLA
3/12/97	5:20:31 PM	Print	None	10	Administrator	BCATLA
3/12/97	5:20:06 PM	Print	None	9	Administrator	BCATLA
3/12/97	5:19:48 PM	Print	None	10	Administrator	BCATLA
3/12/97	5:19:28 PM	Print	None	10	Administrator	BCATLA
3/12/97	5:16:23 PM	Print	None	10	Administrator	BCATLA
3/12/97	5:16:22 PM	Print	None	10	Administrator	BCATLA
3/12/97	5:15:53 PM	Print	None	10	Administrator	BCATLA
3/12/97	5:15:17 PM	Print	None	10	Administrator	BCATLA
3/12/97	5:14:46 PM	Print	None	10	Administrator	BCATLA
3/12/97	5:14:10 PM	Print	None	10	Administrator	BCATLA
3/12/97	5:13:40 PM	Print	None	10	Administrator	BCATLA
3/12/97	5:13:21 PM	Print	None	10	Administrator	BCATLA
3/12/97	5:12:01 PM	Print	None	10	Administrator	BCATLA
3/12/97	5:11:38 PM	Print	None	10	Administrator	BCATLA
3/12/97	5:11:03 PM	Print	None	10	Administrator	BCATLA
3/12/97	5:10:50 PM	Print	None	10	Administrator	BCATLA
3/12/97	5:10:26 PM	Print	None	10	Administrator	BCATLA
3/12/97	5:09:29 PM	Print	None	10	Administrator	BCATLA
3/12/97	5:09:27 PM	Print	None	10	Administrator	BCATLA
3/12/97	5:08:53 PM	Print	None	10	Administrator	BCATLA
3/12/97	5:08:21 PM	Print	None	10	Administrator	BCATLA
3/12/97	5:07:51 PM	Print	None	10	Administrator	BCATLA

Figure 42.25. *The Event Viewer allows you to view the events logged by the audits you set up.*

To see the entire detailed event record, you need only double-click the event. Figure 42.26 shows a detailed event record for a successful print. As you can see, you can tell who printed what document, the number of pages, and the time that the document was printed.

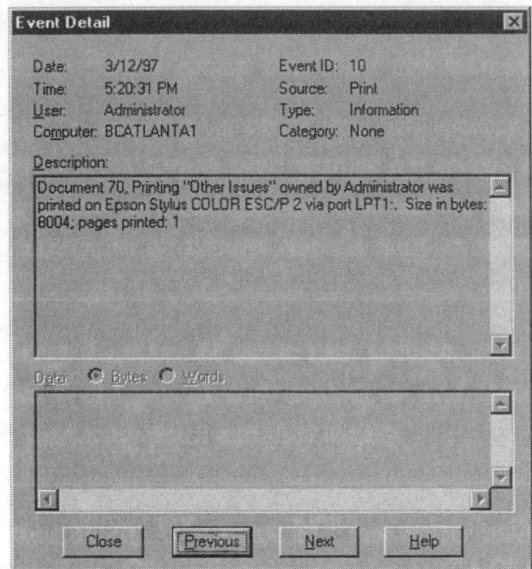

Figure 42.26. *A detailed Event Log record showing that a user has successfully printed a document.*

Configuring Device Settings

If your users encounter problems, such as the printer selects the wrong paper tray or the print quality comes out at a lower resolution than expected, you should check the Device Settings tab in the printer's property sheet. (See Figure 42.27.) Here you can set the paper tray and other options that are configurable for the selected printer.

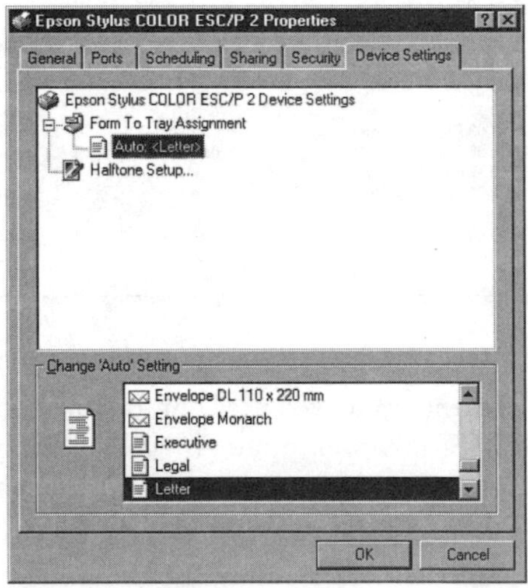

Figure 42.27. *You can select device-specific options to configure in the Device Settings tab of the printer's property sheet.*

Figure 42.28 shows the Device Color/Halftone Properties dialog for a printer. Again, the properties you see in this dialog are specific to a particular printer (in this case, an Epson Stylus COLOR printer), and your display will depend on the actual physical print device you are using.

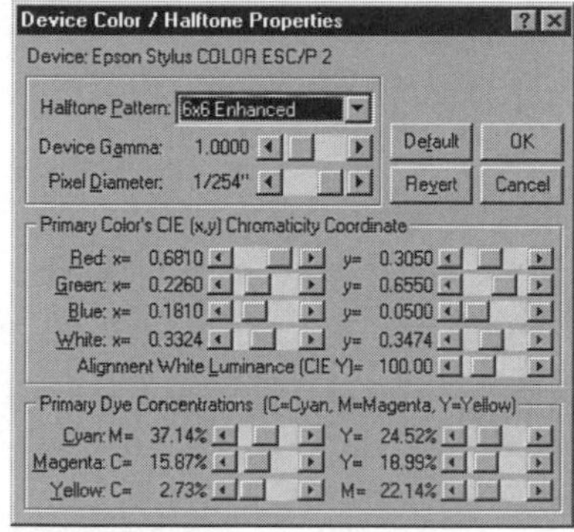

Figure 42.28. *You can configure color or B/W halftone options using this dialog. Your print device may have different attributes, however.*

Summary

Solving printer problems becomes easier if you can first determine where the problem lies. Using the Event Viewer, you can examine the system log files to look for problems due to security or failure of printing components. You should look first to the event logs because messages there can sometimes give you a hint if another problem, such as a hardware problem, exists.

In addition to providing print services for all types of clients, Windows NT also supports the TCP/IP-based LPR/LPD printing system. UNIX and NT clients can print using the LPR protocol to both UNIX and NT servers that are running the LPD service (daemon). Macintosh clients and NetWare clients can also make use of NT printer services and offer their printers to NT clients.

When troubleshooting printing problems, be sure to check the document and printer properties. The data type may be set incorrectly for the print device, or the client (as in an LPR situation) may be sending the wrong control codes.

When upgrading from Windows NT 3.*x* systems, remember that you must upgrade your printer drivers. If your printer is not on the Hardware Compatibility List, you should contact the manufacturer for an updated printer driver.

Identifying, Isolating, and Repairing Network Problems

by Brett Bonenberger

Everyone has had network problems. Whether it is on the client side or the server side, troubleshooting the problem can often be a headache. This chapter attempts to shed some light on troubleshooting your own network problems. It is not entirely NT-specific, but rather brings a general approach to network troubleshooting, presenting some troubleshooting tips that you can use with Ethernet networks, Token Ring networks, and TCP/IP as well as a couple of tools you can use for troubleshooting an NT network.

General Troubleshooting

To be able to troubleshoot network problems, you must first understand how the network communicates. A network is made up of a series of computers that communicate with one another through a standard protocol. Each node on the network transmits electronic packets of information through a network interface card (NIC). Each network packet or frame consists of a source address of the originating computer, a destination address of the computer receiving the data, the protocol header, and finally the data being transmitted. If there is something wrong with the network, it is because these packets of information are not reaching their destination. There are many possible causes, but the two most common are these:

- A break in the communication medium (a broken wire)
- Malfunction in the computer (node)

To pinpoint the cause of a network problem, take these steps:

1. Find out whether anyone else has reported a problem.
2. Always start with the client having the problem. Check physical connections (NIC, patch cable, wall jack, and so on).
3. Check client configuration.
4. Check network cable in wall from client workstation to hub.
5. Check concentrator connection for client workstation. Make sure the port is active and functioning properly.
6. Check server connections to concentrator. Make sure the port is active and functioning.
7. Check server configuration.

Determine Whether the Problem Is Common or Isolated

The first step is to find out whether anyone else is reporting the same or similar problems. If someone is, the location of the problem is narrowed down to the server, hub, router, or other major network component. You can then begin troubleshooting the problem from the system room and wiring closets.

Check the Client

If no one else reports similar problems, the next step is to check the client. This is for obvious reasons. How many times do you have a user who just likes to play around and see what things do? Although most will not admit doing something, it is still a possibility. Another reason to start with the client is there is not as much that can go wrong on the client side as on the communication medium or server side.

On the client side, first check the Network Interface Card to see if it is bad. Some NICs have a light indicating whether there is network activity. Check the light to see if it is on. If it is not on, that could mean two things: a bad NIC or a bad connection to the network. Before you start opening the computer to replace the NIC, be sure to check the physical connection from the computer to the network jack in the wall. Is the patch cable firmly seated at both ends? Could the patch cable be bad? Replace it and see whether the problem is corrected. If the problem is not corrected, you may want to look more closely at the NIC. Even before you do that, though, check the network configuration on the client.

The network configuration is the likely place where the user may have changed something and not known it. This is one of the reasons I like Windows NT Workstation. It is easy to restrict users from gaining access to Control Panel functions. Within the configuration, pay particularly close attention to the settings of IP addresses (if using TCP/IP) or to the IPX/SPX files (if using IPX/SPX). Check to make sure all files needed are present and that all network addresses are valid.

Check the Network Infrastructure

If all configuration settings are correct, then there must be a problem independent of the network client. If you are lucky enough to have and understand a network analyzer, you can begin to monitor the traffic from the client. Some of you may even have a cable scanner that you can plug into the wall jack and test the cable connection running through the wall. The cable scanner may be able to send a series of packets across the wire. A report is generated and a level of service is shown. If there is a good level of service, the wire is good. If it is poor, the wire is bad. Sometimes I have had a perfectly good connection with a client and then something went wrong somewhere in the wall and I had to rerun the wire.

Check the Concentrator and Patch Panel Connections

Your next step is to test the client connections to the concentrator. You should check in two places: the concentrator and the patch panel. Start with the patch panel. All of your network connections from throughout your office are brought into the patch panel. Each jack is labeled, and you should have your labeling scheme next to the patch panel and concentrator. Look for the client jack that is having problems and check the back connection on the patch panel. The back will look like a huge mess, unless it was done properly and tightly. If you have ever seen a wiring closet for a phone system, you have seen the punch down blocks where client connections are made to the phone system. This is similar to what you will see on the back side of a concentrator. A wire coming from the client is taken and the shroud removed to expose all of the smaller wires. A special tool called—you guessed it—a punch down tool is used to place the smaller individual wires into the punch down block. With a loud click, the connection is made.

At my place of employment we have a rack that is on hinges so that we can open the rack, similar to a door. Shortly after we installed the rack and cabling, we opened the "door" to label different ports (printers versus clients). Because of the wonderfully clean and tight wiring done, we managed to pull a few wires off of the punch down blocks. This resulted in lost clients. If your wiring is done nicely, you will need to be careful not to make the same mistake we did. By making sure there is not too much tension on your patch panel you will avoid this problem. From the patch panel to the concentrator is another patch cable. You need to check the connections of the patch cable on the panel and on the concentrator. You should also try a spare cable.

If you still have not corrected the problem, you should be testing the network port on the hub. This can be done easily by taking a client that is working, disconnecting it from the hub and plugging it into the port you suspect to be having problems. If that does not work, then chances are good that you have a bad port.

Check the Server Connections

Every server on your network will need to be connected to the concentrator some way. These connections are probably similar to the connections that each client uses. If this connection were bad, then all clients would be having similar problems. You only need to check this if all users are reporting problems. The methods of testing this connection are similar to those for checking the client, except the connection will most likely be directly to the concentrator. On our network, we have two UNIX servers and several NT servers. The UNIX machines are connected to the concentrator through a thin net connection. I don't recommend using thin net.

Our connections have failed us many times. We have lost communication because of a faulty coax connection on the concentrator, a bad T-connector, and a crimp that was pulled out. I don't know how a T-connector can go bad, or the coax connector, but it has happened. Unless you have the tools on site to correct the problem or maintain plenty of spare cabling, your servers could be down for an extended period of time. In fact, my advice is to have plenty of spare cabling available and learn to make the cables yourself.

Is the Server Configured Properly?

A bad configuration on the server is common, especially when the server is newly installed. Often the problem is a typo. When we added an application server to a network, the clients were unable to access the applications. Although we were able to log on to the domain from the application server, no one could access the applications. After looking for a few minutes, we realized our mistake—a typo in the share name. Other things to look at are the addresses the machine uses or needs, proper user rights, and correctly configured shares.

It is easy to miss something when setting up an additional server. As your network continues to grow, you need to remember more and more settings. This is especially true when you work in a multiple domain environment. Establishment of trust relationships, replication servers, and domain controllers can become very confusing. Make a map of what exists. Label each machine with its address, name, function, and location. When reaching this complexity, I don't think you can have too much documentation.

If you have gone through the preceding list and problems still exist, you may have missed something. Look at what you have done so far. Is there a step you could have missed or a configuration that you did not check. Go back through and look at the problem in greater detail. The preceding sections only briefly cover the steps for troubleshooting a network. Depending on the type of network operating system (NOS) that you have, there can be many other configuration items to look at. Because this is an NT book, we will look at troubleshooting TCP/IP networks.

Troubleshooting on a TCP/IP Network

TCP/IP seems to be the protocol to use. The Internet uses TCP/IP and because many LANs are being connected to the Internet, most are set up with TCP/IP. Consider this simple scenario. A workstation on the network appears to not be able to communicate with other workstations. The noncommunicating workstation has an IP address of `192.19.1.162`. The default gateway on the network is `192.19.1.30`. The default gateway is also your primary network server.

Note: Remember that if you are connecting your LAN to the Internet, you will need to have unique IP addresses assigned. This example involves a made-up IP address. To get more information about IP addresses, visit `rs.internic.net`.

The first thing you can do is use a utility that is common on all TCP/IP networks, `ping`. (By the way, `ping` stands for Packet InternetGroper.) This utility works much the same way that radar works. A signal is sent away and if something is present, a reply is sent back. The reply sent back is called an echo. From `192.19.1.162`, try to ping another workstation on the same segment. The following shows how to use the `ping` command.

```
Ping 192.19.1.30
```

If your ping is successful, you will receive an echo similar to the one shown in Figure 43.1.

```
C:\WINNT\System32\cmd.exe

C:\>ping 192.19.1.30

Pinging 192.19.1.30 with 32 bytes of data:

Reply from 192.19.1.30: bytes=32 time<10ms TTL=32
Reply from 192.19.1.30: bytes=32 time<10ms TTL=32
Reply from 192.19.1.30: bytes=32 time<10ms TTL=32
Reply from 192.19.1.30: bytes=32 time<10ms TTL=32

C:\>_
```

Figure 43.1. *Sample output of a successful ping to the IP address* `192.19.1.30`.

If you are unable to ping another workstation, you will get a response similar to Figure 43.2. If this happens, you need to verify whether the IP stack on your machine is functioning. Use the loopback address that is reserved for local use only. Every machine running TCP/IP has the same loopback address of `127.0.0.127`. Figure 43.3 shows a successful ping to the loopback address.

```
C:\WINNT\System32\cmd.exe
C:\>ping 192.19.1.201

Pinging 192.19.1.201 with 32 bytes of data:

Request timed out.
Request timed out.
Request timed out.
Request timed out.

C:\>_
```

Figure 43.2. *Sample output of an unsuccessful ping.*

```
C:\WINNT\System32\cmd.exe
C:\>ping 127.0.0.127

Pinging 127.0.0.127 with 32 bytes of data:

Reply from 127.0.0.127: bytes=32 time<10ms TTL=128
Reply from 127.0.0.127: bytes=32 time<10ms TTL=128
Reply from 127.0.0.127: bytes=32 time<10ms TTL=128
Reply from 127.0.0.127: bytes=32 time<10ms TTL=128

C:\>_
```

Figure 43.3. *A successful ping to the loopback address.*

If you are able to ping your loopback, the problem may extend to other workstations. Move to another workstation and try to ping another workstation or server. If you still can't hit another machine, the problem may exist in that segment. If you were unsuccessful in pinging your loopback address, the problem is in the workstation.

From here you need to check the IP configuration on the workstation. Some of the common things under NT to check are the domain name, default gateway, WINS server address, or DHCP server address. To help you with this, use `ipconfig` for Windows NT Workstation or use `winipcfg` for Windows 95 Workstations.

Windows NT Tools

Many network operating systems do not come bundled with any troubleshooting tools. This makes third-party software and hardware a very profitable business. Windows NT is the first to provide any type of network monitoring tools. One of these tools, Performance Monitor, is discussed in detail in Chapter 18, "Performance Monitor."

The other tool, Network Monitor, is mentioned briefly in Chapter 42, "Solving Printer Problems," but it is worth taking a more detailed look at it in this chapter because it deals with troubleshooting capacity and communication of a network. The robust version of Network Monitor discussed here is not included with NT Server but as part of a Microsoft BackOffice application called System Management Server (SMS). Starting with NT Server 4.0, a scaled-down version of Network Monitor was included. As you may recall from Chapter 42, it is only able to monitor two nodes on the network.

Network Monitor

A tool that I will talk about in a little greater detail is Network Monitor. Network Monitor is part of the System Management Server, a part of Microsoft BackOffice.

Note: Even though NT Server does not include this robust version, it is important to cover the capabilities of Network Monitor and some of the things that it can do. Most of the information discussed here still applies to the scaled-down version in NT 4.0.

Network Monitor is a very useful and powerful network diagnostic tool with many useful features. The Network Monitor Agent, which is now included as part of Windows NT 4.0, is used to set or change the capture password and to configure the network interface cards in the computer being used as the agent. With Network Monitor, you can capture and display network statistics to troubleshoot problems on your local area network.

If you are familiar with System Management Server (SMS), Server Network Monitor will be easy for you to use because it is very similar. The biggest difference is that SMS will capture frames sent to or from any computer on the network, but Server Network Monitor will only capture frames sent to or from the local computer. Still, Network Monitor has many features, including the capturing of network frames, displaying captured frames, and viewing network statistics.

How Does Network Monitor Work?

Each packet of data that is sent over the network contains a source address, destination address, protocol header, and data. All this information is captured by the Network Monitor software and displayed in an easy-to-read graphical interface, as shown in Figure 43.4. Network Monitor uses the Network Driver Interface Specification (NDIS) Version 4 to accomplish this. It captures the information and places it into a capture buffer.

The information that is captured is not written to disk but rather stored in memory, so the size of the capture buffer is dependent on the amount of memory you have in your computer. You do not need to capture a large amount of data to effectively analyze the network performance; a small amount of data often has enough information to analyze.

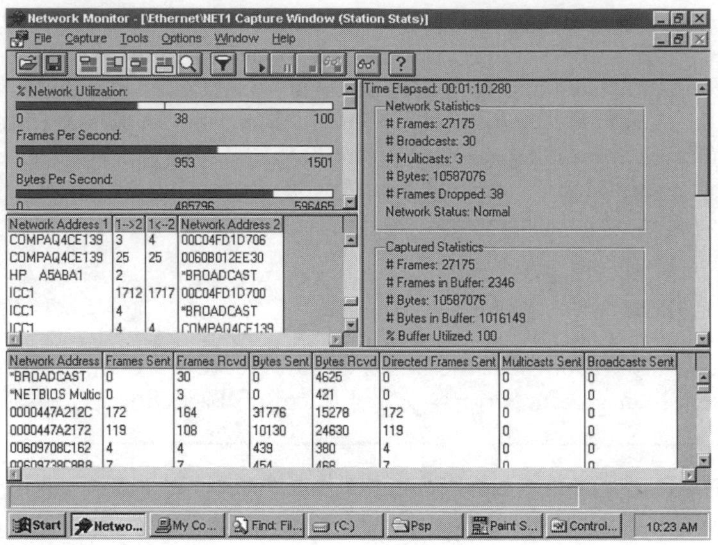

Figure 43.4. *Microsoft System Management Server Network Monitor.*

Installing Network Monitor

To install Network Monitor for the Windows NT Server 4.0, you need to use the Network applet under Control Panel. The installation steps are as follows:

1. Open Control Panel.
2. Double-click the Network Applet icon.
3. Under the Network applet, select the Services tab and click the Add button.
4. Select the Network Monitor Tools and Agent from the list of services and click OK.
5. You will be prompted for the location of the NT Distribution files. Use the default or type in the location of the files.
6. Setup will copy the needed files and review your bindings. After this is finished, click the Close button.
7. You will have to shut down and restart your computer for the changes to take effect.

The Network Monitor for NT Server 4.0 is located in the Administrative Tools folder and can be run from there or from a command line. The advantage of the command line is the custom configuration of switches that you can use. If you enjoy the UNIX and DOS environments, you will probably prefer to use the command line. Start the Network Monitor from the command line by using the following command:

```
START NETMON [options]
```

The following switches can be used with the NETMON command:

```
/REMOTE: remotename
/NET: #
/CAPTUREFILTER: path
/DISPLAYFILTER: path
/QUICKFILTER: type, Address
/AUTOSTART
/AUTOSTOP
/BUFFERSIZE: # bytes
```

Configuration of Network Monitoring Agent

The configuration of Network Monitor is simple; most of it is done within Network Monitor itself. The Monitoring Agent is configured through a Control Panel applet. (See Figure 43.5.)

Figure 43.5. *Open Control Panel with the Network Monitoring Agent applet highlighted.*

Figure 43.6 shows the open Configure Network Monitoring Agent dialog. There you can see the Change Password, Describe Net Cards, and Reset Defaults buttons.

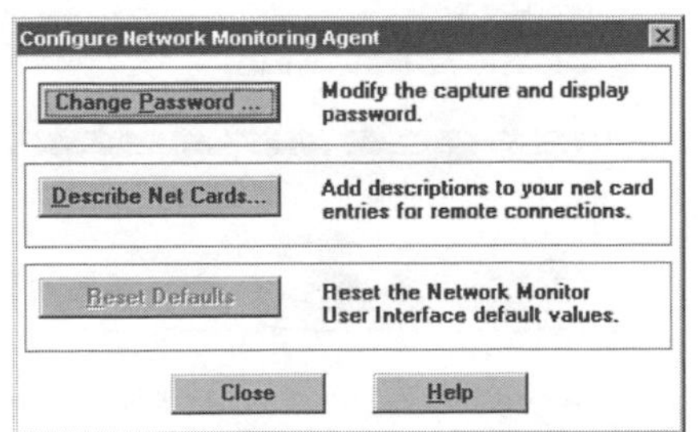

Figure 43.6. *The Configure Network Monitoring Agent dialog showing the Change Password, Describe Net Cards, and the Reset Defaults buttons.*

Changing Network Monitor Passwords

Click on the Change Password button to activate the Network Monitoring Password Change dialog shown in Figure 43.7. From this dialog, you can change the Display Password and Capture Password. The Display Password is used to grant permission to authorized users to view previously saved capture statistics. The Capture Password is to allow users to capture frames and to view capture files.

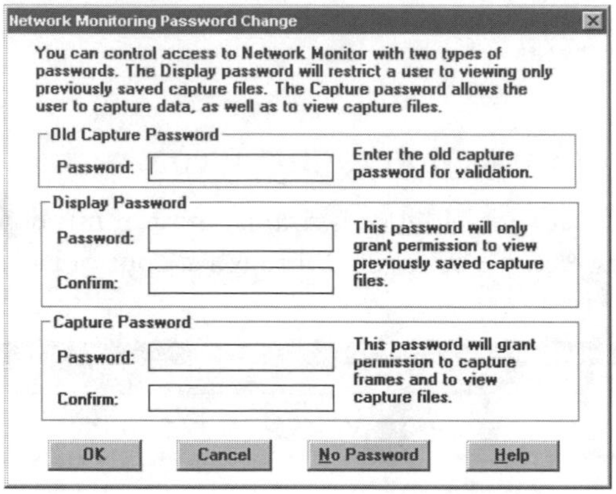

Figure 43.7. *Click the Change Password button to display this dialog box showing all the change password options.*

Describing Network Cards

The Describe Net Cards button enables you to describe the network cards in your computer. This can be a very helpful feature when you have multiple cards in your computer. You will be able to distinguish which computer and which card the captured frames are coming from. Figure 43.8 shows the Describe Net Cards dialog.

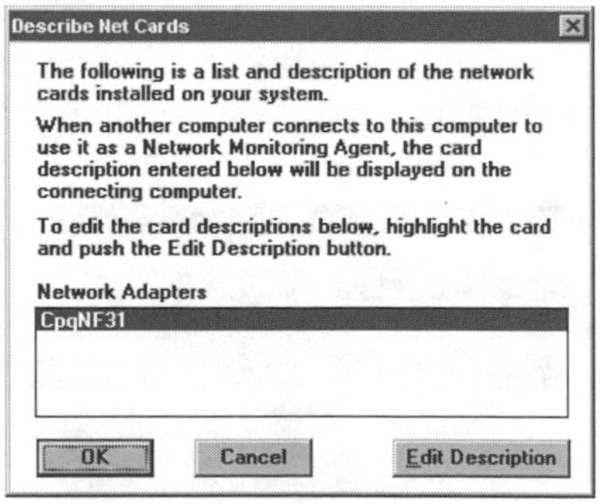

Figure 43.8. *The Describe Net Cards dialog allows you to set unique descriptions for each network card.*

Using Network Monitor

The process of network monitoring focuses on capturing information from the network. Capturing is the process of taking transmitted frames or packets of information from the network and using the information captured to analyze network communications. This is accomplished through the Network Monitor Capture window.

Network Monitor Capture Window

When the frames are captured, the statistics are displayed in the Capture window. Figure 43.9 shows the Network Monitor Capture window with some information displayed. As can also be seen in Figure 43.9, the Capture window is divided into four panes, each of which has a different function. The four panes are Graph, Session Stats, Station Stats, and Total Stats. The Graph pane is a horizontal bar graph showing current network activity. Session Stats show statistics on each individual session taking place on the network. Station Stats shows statistics about sessions being participated in by the computer that is running Network Monitor. Total Stats shows summary statistics about all network activity detected since the capture process was started. The Total Stats pane also shows the number of dropped frames.

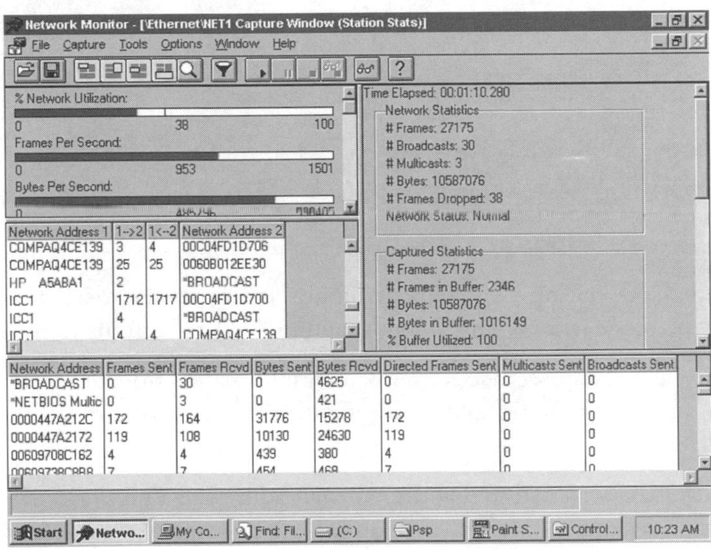

Figure 43.9. *The Network Monitor Capture window displaying information captured from a network.*

Capture Buffer

As mentioned earlier in this chapter, the size of the capture buffer is limited to the amount of memory that you have in your computer. Because of this, it is important to understand what factors will affect the size of your buffer. Those factors are the capture buffer size, frame size, capture filter, and the volume of the network traffic.

The default capture buffer size is 8MB less than the amount of RAM on your computer. Your buffer size should be large enough to catch enough information for analysis. If you exceed the configured amount, captured data will be written to virtual memory. The speed of virtual memory can cause frames to be dropped.

If the number of dropped frames is increasing, you need to reduce the capture buffer size. To do so, go to the Capture pull-down menu in Network Monitor and choose the Capture Buffer Settings option. Figure 43.10 shows the Capture Buffer Settings dialog.

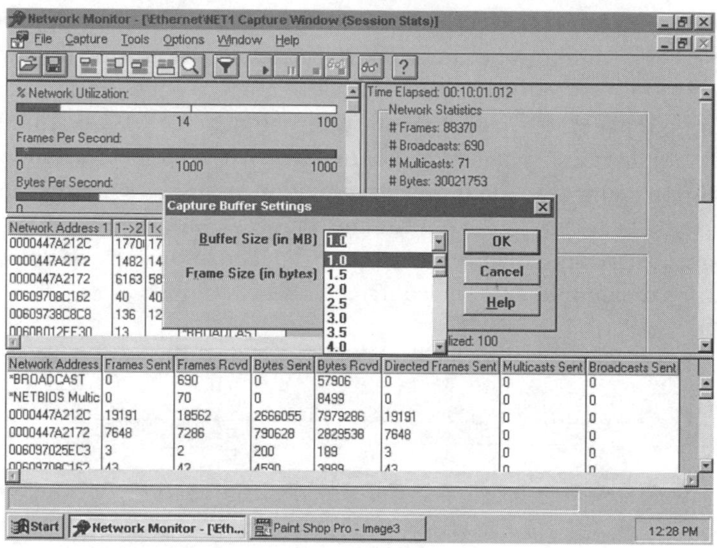

Figure 43.10. *Setting the capture buffer size in the Capture Buffer Settings dialog.*

Another method of reducing the amount of captured information is to set the Frame Size to match that of only the frame header. This will not capture the data but only frame information.

A capture filter allows the user to selectively sample information from the network traffic. By using a filter, you can select a certain subset of computers or protocols through the use of an address database.

An address database is created so that the hardware address of a network client can be associated to a more familiar name and then saved to a file for reuse—same concept as with a WINS server. You can then use the address file to monitor traffic from that subset of computers or from a single computer.

The capture filter is a series of decision-making statements similar to a query. You can use the Capture Filter dialog shown in Figure 43.11 to create filters.

You can also use the capture filter to capture protocols. To selectively capture protocols, you can use the Capture Filter SAPs and ETYPEs dialog shown in Figure 43.12.

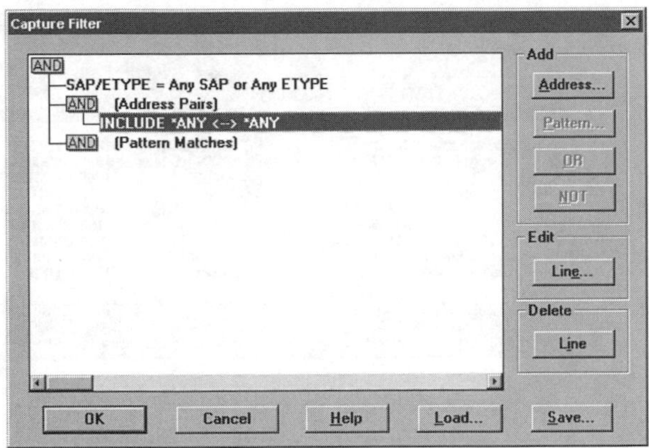

Figure 43.11. *The Capture Filter dialog allows for a graphical representation of capture filters.*

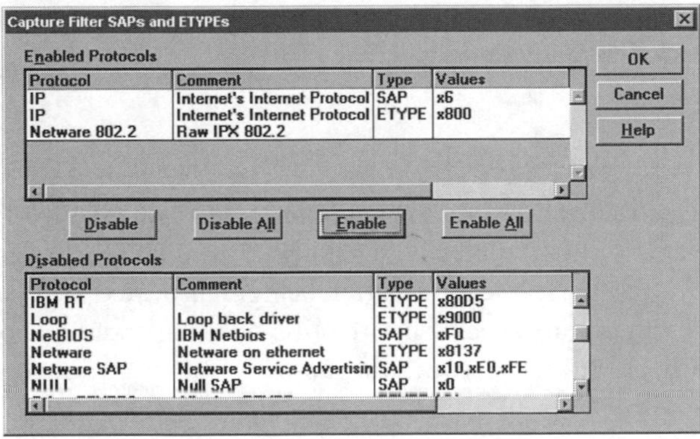

Figure 43.12. *The Capture Filter SAPs and ETYPEs dialog.*

By default, Network Monitor monitors all protocols that it supports. To specify a particular protocol, you need to disable all other protocols in the list. For example, on my network we use IPX/SPX for our accounting software but TCP/IP for all other network traffic. Because we only have a few people using IPX/SPX, the application generates a minimal amount of traffic. We are only interested in monitoring the TCP/IP traffic. To do this, we disable all protocols and then enable IP ETYPE 0x800 and IP SAP 0x6.

Address Filtering

Address filtering enables you to monitor the communications between two specific computers on the network. With the SMS Network Monitor, you can monitor traffic on up to four pairs of computers. Figure 43.13 shows the Address Expression dialog.

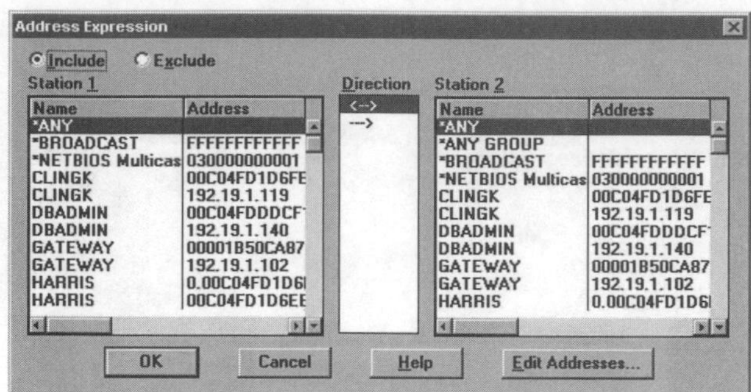

Figure 43.13. The Address Expression dialog, which is used to include and exclude frames and determine the direction of traffic you want to monitor.

The Include and Exclude radio buttons allow you to determine what you want Network Monitor to do with a frame of data that is being received. Exclude statements are always evaluated before any include statements. The arrows in the center of the dialog determine which traffic direction the include or exclude statement will look at.

Network Monitor Conclusion

The information presented here should help you to begin using Network Monitor. This is not an all-inclusive explanation of the tool; it is merely a brief introduction to a great tool. Using Network Monitor, you can view the frame information being transmitted over your network, save it, and view it later. You can capture specific information by using address or protocol filters. Network Monitor is a fairly easy-to-use network diagnostic tool that all network administrators should become familiar with.

Summary

This chapter has presented some simple troubleshooting steps that you can use to help troubleshoot your own network. The steps are as follows:

1. Find out whether anyone else has reported a problem.
2. Always start with the client having the problem.

   Check physical connections (NIC, patch cable, wall jack, and so on).
3. Check client configuration.
4. Check network cable in wall from client workstation to hub.
5. Check concentrator connection for client workstation. Make sure the port is active and functioning properly.

6. Check server connections to concentrator. Make sure the port is active and functioning.
7. Check server configuration.

The chapter also discussed monitoring performance on your NT network. One of the tools I mentioned was Performance Monitor, which is included with NT 4.0; the other, a scaled-down version of Network Monitor, is included with NT, but the more robust version is part of System Management Server. Both are great tools.

Network Monitor is a more advanced diagnostic tool that is part of the System Management Server. Only the basic uses of this tool were covered here. Because of the complexity of the tool, an entire chapter would be necessary for a thorough explanation.

Registry Recovery

by Robert Reinstein

The Windows NT Registry is the database that holds the system together. This is done by supplying the operating system with configuration settings that allow device drivers and services to be loaded at boot time. It also functions as a centralized application settings repository.

A corrupted or an improperly edited Registry can result in an unstable computer or a totally unbootable configuration.

Luckily, Microsoft has devised ways of backing up and restoring the Registry. This also involves the capability to save parts of the Registry from a remote computer onto other computers.

This chapter includes the following:

- Backing up the Registry
- Working with hives
- Remote Registry repair
- Backing Out after using the Last Known Good Configuration

Registry Hives

The Windows NT Registry was designed with a form of fault tolerance.

Hives are Registry subkeys that are kept in separate files located mainly in the `%SystemRoot%\SYSTEM32\CONFIG` directory. Other hives are in the `%SystemRoot%\PROFILES\username` directories.

The other parts of the Registry are not kept in hives, but rather are built dynamically whenever Windows NT is booted.

Transaction Logs

Each of the hives have an associated log file associated with it. These logs contain transaction data that shows changes made to these hives.

When a change is made to a Registry entry, which is actually a change to a hive, the first action to occur is an entry made to a log file. Then the hive is marked as ready to accept the change. Once the change is made, the hive is marked as changed.

Changes are only made to the hive if a flush has occurred. A flush is performed either by force from a programmed routine or after a few seconds, for instance, when making a manual change.

In all cases, changes to the Registry will either occur or not occur. If an unforeseen system shutdown occurs during a Registry change, the activity of the log file and the marking of the hive file will ensure that changes to the Registry will either not be made, or will be made, but in no way will there be a partial change, thus rendering the Registry corrupted.

The Registry subkeys, their associated hive files, logs, and backups are shown in Table 44.1.

Table 44.1. Registry subkeys and their hive files.

Registry Subkey	*Hive File*	*Log File*	*Backup*
HKEY_LOCAL_MACHINE\SAM	Sam	Sam.log	Sam.sav
HKEY_LOCAL_MACHINE\Security	Security	Security.log	Security.sav
HKEY_LOCAL_MACHINE\Software	Software	Software.log	Software.sav
HKEY_LOCAL_MACHINE\System	System	System.log	System.sav
System.alt			
HKEY_CURRENT_CONFIG	System	System.log	System.sav
System.alt			
HKEY_USERS\.DEFAULT	Default	Default.log	Default.sav
HKEY_CURRENT_USER	Ntuser.dat	Ntuser.dat.log	

Each of the hives has a backup file that has the file extension SAV. These SAV files actually contain a copy of the hives as they were after the text mode segment of the Windows NT installation program completed.

The System hive also creates a backup file, SYSTEM.ALT, which is a current backup of the SYSTEM hive.

When Windows NT boots, the dynamic parts of the Registry are built. Next, the hives are loaded. If there is any indication that the SYSTEM hive file may be corrupted, the `System.alt` file is used in its place.

Working with Hives

It is possible to load hives from one Windows NT computer into the Registry Editor (`REGEDT32.EXE`) running on another computer.

Note: Both `REGEDT32.EXE` and `REGEDIT.EXE` can be used for this purpose. They both use different file formats, however. Thus, you cannot save with one program and then restore with the other.

If the computer is on the network, the active Registry can be loaded into Registry Editor by choosing Select Computer from the Registry menu. Saving and loading hives is usually used for troubleshooting when a computer cannot communicate on the network.

Loading a hive from another Windows NT computer enables you to change certain configuration settings on another computer that requires changes. For instance, if another computer running Windows NT requires a service to be disabled or added, the hive file (both `SYSTEM` and `SYSTEM.LOG`) can be copied to a disk or placed out on the network for editing by another Windows NT computer.

Note: The SYSTEM hive cannot be copied while the computer is running Windows NT, so this file will have to exist on a FAT partition or another copy of Windows NT must be loaded to copy the SYSTEM hive for the Windows NT installation that is having problems.

Individual subkeys can also be saved using the method about to be described. The subkeys that are dynamically built at Windows NT boot time cannot be saved.

Troubleshooting a Computer That Is Not on the Network

For this scenario, a user in a different office is unable to connect to the network. The user has saved hives for sending to an administrator located in another location. These files are saved to a disk and then sent by another user to the administrator through e-mail.

Saving a hive is accomplished by highlighting the subkey you want to save as a file that can be sent to another user. The `HKEY_LOCAL_MACHINE\SOFTWARE` subkey has been highlighted, and Save Key has been chosen from the Registry menu. Next, a destination for the file needs to be chosen. Figure 44.1 shows the destination being a file called `SW` that will be put on the A: drive.

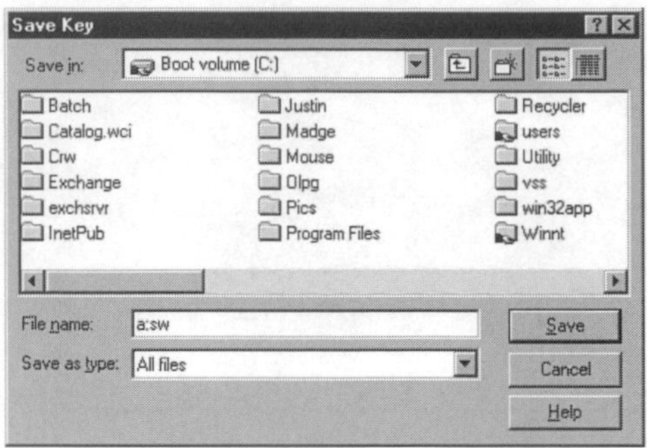

Figure 44.1. Saving a hive to a file.

Once saved, the file is then sent to the user who will load it into the Registry Editor for examination.

Editing a hive from another computer is achieved by choosing Load Hive from the Registry menu, as shown in Figure 44.2.

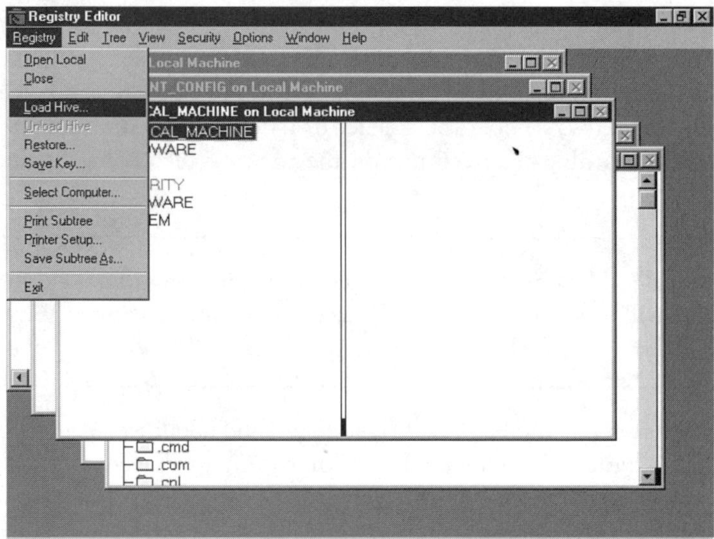

Figure 44.2. Loading a hive.

> **Note:** In order to have the Load Hive menu item enabled, the root key `HKEY_LOCAL_MACHINE` or `HKEY_USERS` must be selected. The person logged on must be a member of the Administrators group and have backup and restore rights.

The Load Hive dialog lets you choose the hive that will be added to the currently selected root key. Figure 44.3 shows the Load Hive dialog with a file named `sw`, which is the SOFTWARE hive saved from another computer.

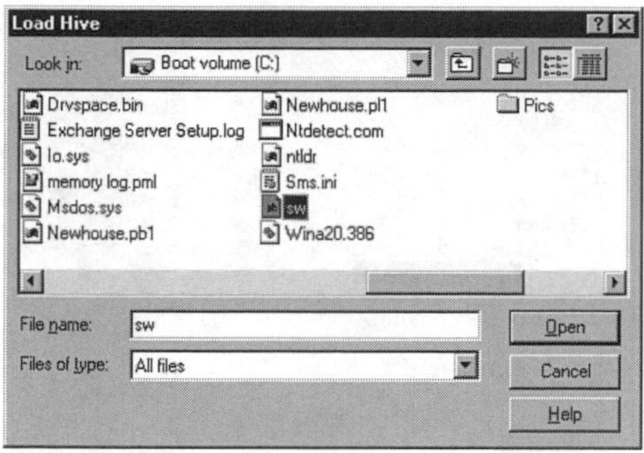

Figure 44.3. The Load Hive dialog.

After selecting the hive to load, a prompt for a key name is displayed, which is shown in Figure 44.4. You can name this key anything you want to easily identify it.

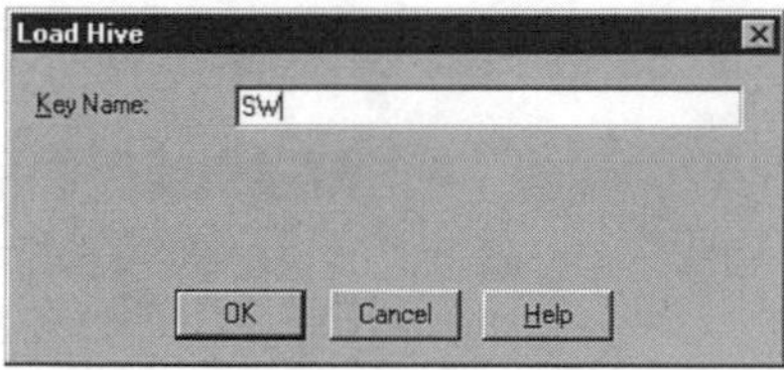

Figure 44.4. Naming the key for a loaded hive.

Click the OK button and the new hive will be added under the root key. Figure 44.5 shows the hive added to the `HKEY_LOCAL_MACHINE` root key.

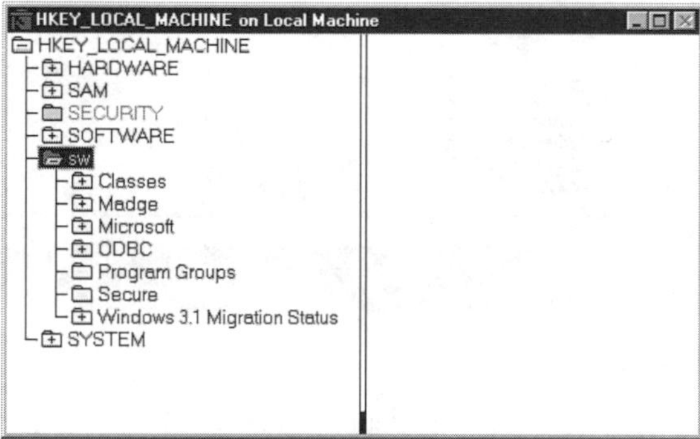

Figure 44.5. `HKEY_LOCAL_MACHINE` *with added hive.*

The administrator can then go through the `SW` subkey and check for version numbers. In this case, as shown in Figure 44.6, the network card driver is examined and determined to be an older version that requires updating.

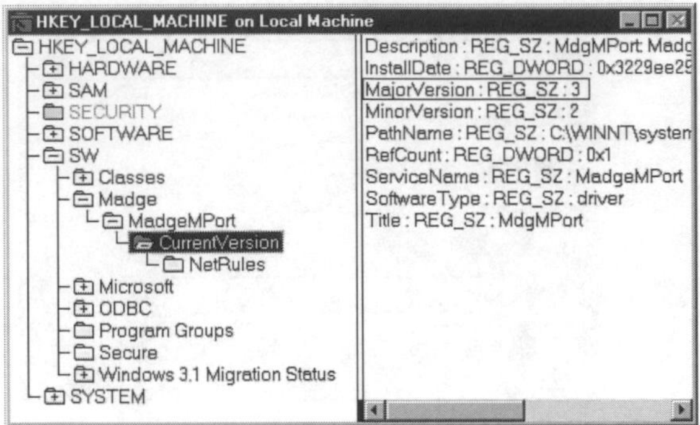

Figure 44.6. Checking for a network card version number.

Now, this subkey needs to be removed from the `HKEY_LOCAL_MACHINE` root key.

This is done by highlighting the hive to be removed and then choosing Unload Hive from the Registry menu, which is shown in Figure 44.7.

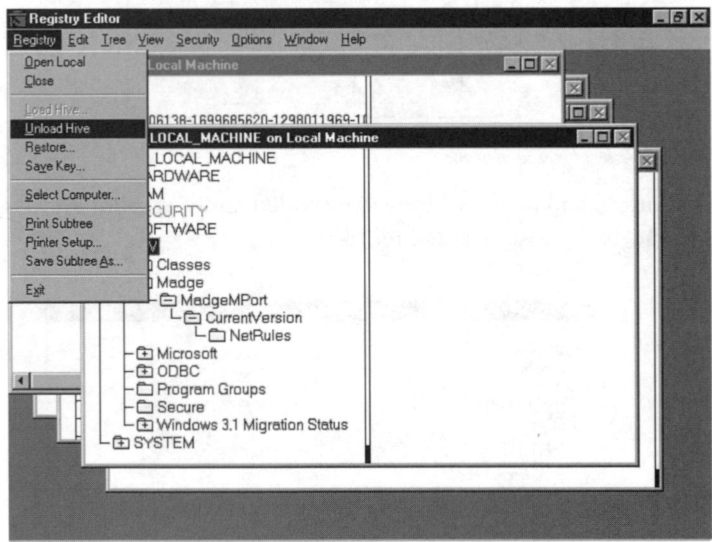

Figure 44.7. Unload Hive menu choice.

After making this selection, a warning dialog, shown in Figure 44.8, will confirm the choice to remove that subkey.

Click the Yes button and that subkey will be removed. The user can now be informed to update the driver and then see if connecting to the network is still a problem.

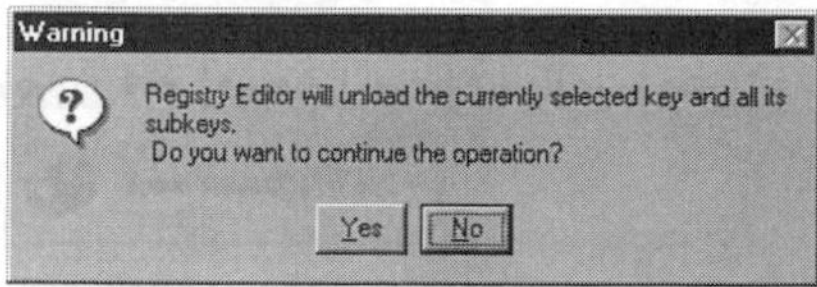

Figure 44.8. *Confirming removal of a subkey.*

Working with User Profiles Through the Registry

Another reason to work with hives from another computer is to access user profiles. When a user is logged on to a computer, his or her profile can easily be viewed from that computer. If, however, the user is not logged on, the only way to view or modify his or her profile is through the Registry.

For instance, to view the desktop settings for a user, you first need to find out the SID for that user account.

This is done by looking on the computer that the user logs on to or where the user profile is stored.

By looking at the subkey `HKEY_LOCAL_MACHINE\SOFTWARE\Microsoft\CurrentVersion\ProfileList`, you will see subkeys under there that are account SIDs. This is shown in Figure 44.9.

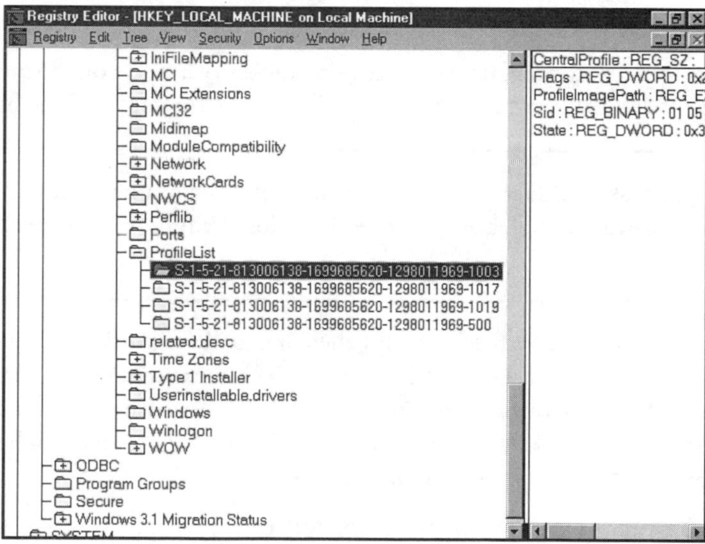

Figure 44.9. *List of user profiles in the Registry.*

Highlight a SID and check the value entry for `ProfileImagePath`. The name of the user profile will appear at the end of the path. Either you can read the value directly in the value entry list, or double-click to bring up the String Editor. The profile name, derived from the path shown in the String Editor (see Figure 44.10), is `robertr.000`.

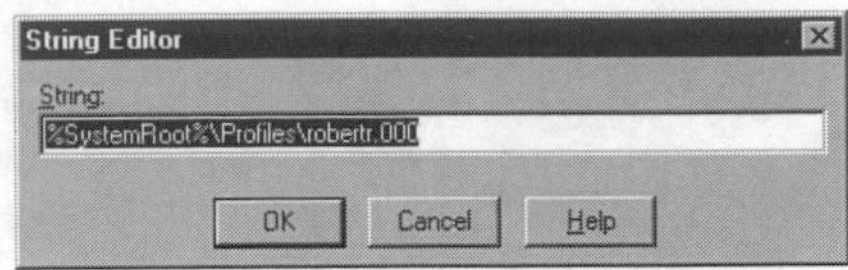

Figure 44.10. `ProfileImagePath` *value.*

Now, using this SID, the `HKEY_USERS` root key can be examined to find the same SID. Under that SID will be all the value entries for that user profile.

This profile can now be modified if a change is required, or simply viewed for troubleshooting or informational purposes.

Backing Up the Registry

There is always the chance of corruption in the directory where the hive files are stored.

This is why the Windows NT Backup utility has the option to create a full backup of the Windows NT Registry. When using the GUI mode Windows NT Backup, you will see a checkbox labeled "Backup Local Registry" that you can check in order to back up the Registry. In command-line mode, use the `/B` switch to back up the Registry. Many third-party backup utilities also have the capability to back up a Registry.

Without using a backup program, which requires the use of a tape, you can save copies of the hives by using the `RDISK.EXE` program. `RDISK.EXE` will copy recent copies of the hives to a disk.

Warning: `RDISK.EXE` does not copy all value entries. It can be used to make a computer bootable, but will not necessarily restore all the lost settings (such as the `SAM` and `SECURITY` hives).

Another way to back up hive files is to copy them manually to a disk or other drive location. This can only be done when Windows NT is not running on the computer. Either another installation of Windows NT must be running, or if the files have been stored on a FAT partition, the computer can be booted with MS-DOS and then the files may be copied. These files are in the `%SystemRoot%\SYSTEM32\CONFIG` directory.

Restoring these files is a different story. The `SAM` and `SECURITY` hives cannot be restored while Windows NT is active, so you might want to think about being prepared for such an operation.

By installing a second copy of Windows NT, you can always boot the other copy and then restore the Registry that belonged to the failed version. If a FAT partition had been used as the system partition, MS-DOS can be booted and a copy of `SECURITY` and `SAM` hives, from any type of backup, can be restored to the `%SystemRoot%\SYSTEM32\CONFIG` directory.

Modifying a Failed Configuration

The Last Known Good Configuration is a great method of recovering from having made changes to your Windows NT configuration, which then renders Windows NT unstable, or possibly not even startable.

The Registry stores multiple configurations. These are kept in the `HKEY_LOCAL_MACHINE\SYSTEM` subkey under the subkeys `CurrentControlSet`, `ControlSet001`, `ControlSet002`, and so forth.

The subkey `HKEY_LOCAL_MACHINE\SYSTEM\Select` contains value entries that identify these different configurations.

In Figure 44.11, the `Select` value entries identify the current configuration as `ControlSet001`.

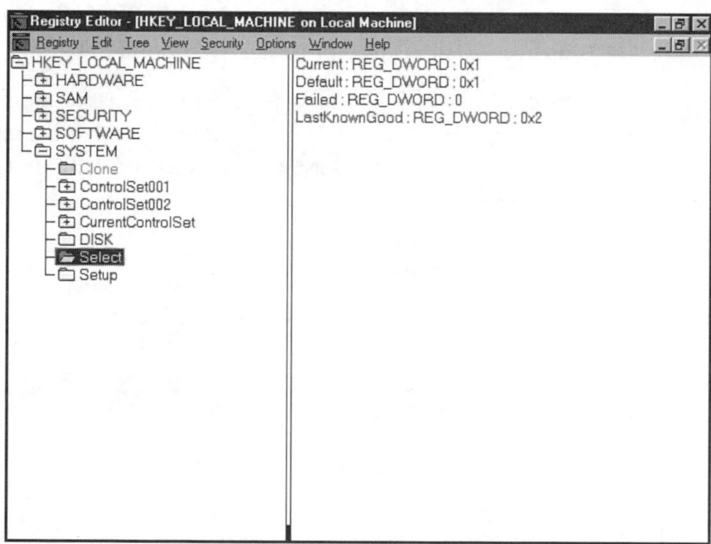

Figure 44.11. *Multiple configurations stored in the Registry.*

To understand how `ControlSet001` is flagged as the current configuration, see Table 44.2 for an explanation of the different value entries in `Select`.

Table 44.2. `HKEY_LOCAL_MACHINE\SYSTEM\Select` value entries.

Value Entry	*Explanation*
`Current`	The currently used configuration.
`Default`	The configuration that is used by Windows NT by default.
`Failed`	If the Last Known Good Configuration has been used, the configuration that was the default is identified here.
`LastKnownGood`	The configuration that will be used if the Last Known Good Configuration is chosen from the Last Known Good Configuration menu.

In the case of the `Current` value entry, the value is `1`, which refers to `ControlSet001`. This value is also used for `Default`. The value for `Failed` is `0`, which means that Last Known Good Configuration has not yet been used. The `LastKnownGood` value entry has a value of `2`, which means that `ControlSet002` will be copied into `CurrentControlSet` during Windows NT startup, and then the value of `Failed` will change to `1`.

Sometimes the configuration that is flagged as `LastKnownGood` does not contain all the settings—such as device configurations and hardware profiles—that you want to retain, even in the event of a failed Windows NT startup. This is because any changes made since the last successful boot will be lost and not part of the Last Known Good Configuration.

Using the Last Known Good Configuration can make your computer startable again, but then you may have a lot of configuring to do after finally starting the computer.

Using the settings in `Select` and modifying the configuration that is flagged as `Failed` is a good solution for backing out from a failed attempt to start Windows NT.

If the computer (the Registry of which is shown in Figure 44.11), has its configuration altered and Windows NT fails to start, the computer is restarted and the spacebar is pressed when Windows NT prompts to press the spacebar for the Last Known Good Configuration menu. The Last Known Configuration is then chosen and the computer restarts, with the configuration that was flagged as `LastKnownGood` now also flagged as `Default`.

After Windows NT restarts using the Last Known Good Configuration, the `HKEY_LOCAL_MACHINE\SYSTEM\Select` value entries will look like the ones shown in Figure 44.12.

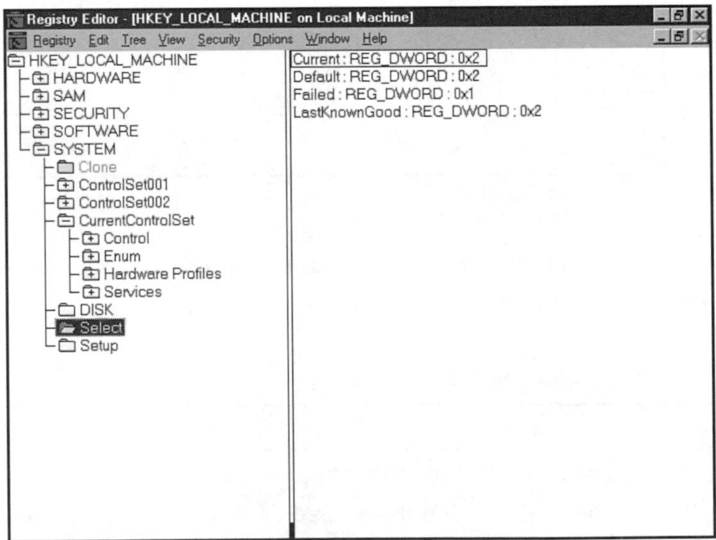

Figure 44.12. *The* `Select` *subkey after using the Last Known Good Configuration menu.*

As you can see, the `Current` and `Default` values have changed to `2`, the `Failed` value is now `1`, and `LastKnownGood` remains the same.

But the configuration in ControlSet002, which is now the CurrentControlSet, does not have all of the values that were in the previously used ControlSet001. Of course, the reason that ControlSet002 is now being used is because of one or more values in ControlSet001 that are making Windows NT unable to start properly.

By editing the Registry directly, you can alter the values for the Select subkey and make changes to the failed configuration to let it be used again as the default configuration.

Caution: When editing a configuration, use extreme caution in making sure you are editing the configuration you had intended to edit. It is very difficult to determine which configuration is which without closely examining each value entry.

The Services subkey, such as the one found in HKEY_LOCAL_MACHINE\SYSTEM\ControlSet001\Services, contains subkeys for each service and device available to a Windows NT computer. Each of these subkeys contains value entries that identify certain attributes for the named service or device.

A configuration that will no longer allow the system to start properly usually has just had a new service enabled that is critically affecting the system.

By identifying and properly altering that service, a value entry can be changed to manually disable that service or device.

First, let's examine the value entries for a service/device using the Modem device as an example, as shown in Figure 44.13.

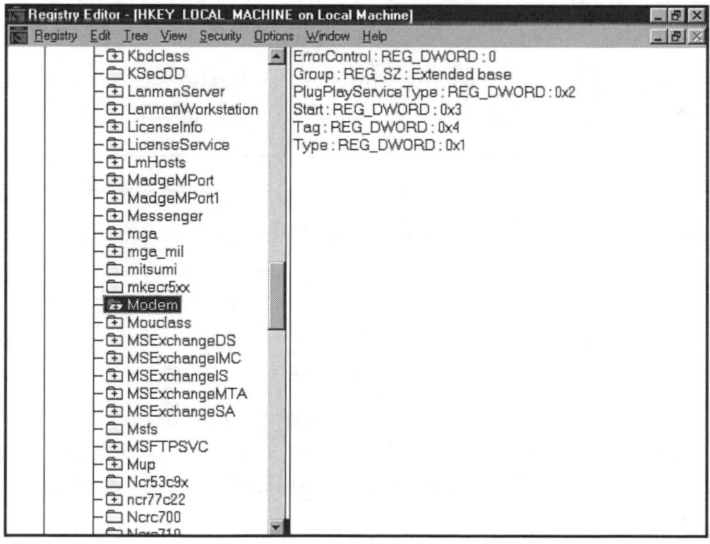

Figure 44.13. *The* Modem *device value entries.*

Each service/device in the Registry has a few value entries associated with them that contain information regarding dependencies, enabling or disabling, pathnames (where applicable), and an error level that determines how the system will react to a failed load of an enabled driver.

For the `Modem` device, the `ErrorControl` value entry has a value of `0`, which means that an error will be ignored.

An `ErrorControl` value of `3` signifies a Critical Error, `2` is a Severe Error, and `1` is a Normal Error.

Both Critical and Severe errors attempt to automatically use the Last Known Good Configuration. A Normal error will display an error message upon startup.

When an error occurs, the system responds accordingly based on the `ErrorControl` value. However, what cannot be determined is how the success of one service will interact with another service. If the `Modem` device interferes with another service or device that requires the COM port specified for an installed modem, it can result in a halted system. Many times I've seen services or devices interfere with network adapters or SCSI devices. In an extreme case, the boot process may result in a Windows NT blue dump screen.

If a service or device has just been installed, or enabled, that service/device needs to be disabled.

This is where the value entry `Start` applies. A `Start` value of `0` means that the service/device is started as a boot process. A value of `1` makes the service/device a system process. A value of `2` is an automatic startup. A `Start` value of `3` means Load on Demand. And the final value, `4`, disables the service/device.

The `Modem` example shows the `Start` value entry with a value of `3`. If this `Service` entry needs to be disabled, the value for `Start` can be changed to `4`, as shown in Figure 44.14.

Caution: Making manual modifications to the Registry can result in an unstable or nonbootable system. Use extreme caution when working with the Registry.

Note: The `Modem` device that is being used as an example is by no means a special device that should be investigated when troubleshooting a Windows NT computer. The service or device that applies in this example is any service or device that was added to the Windows NT system since the last successful Windows NT boot.

After this value has been changed, it is time to go back to the `Select` subkey and change the value entries that will determine which configuration will be used for the next boot and which configuration will become the Last Known Good Configuration choice.

This is done by setting the values back to the ones that are depicted in Figure 44.11.

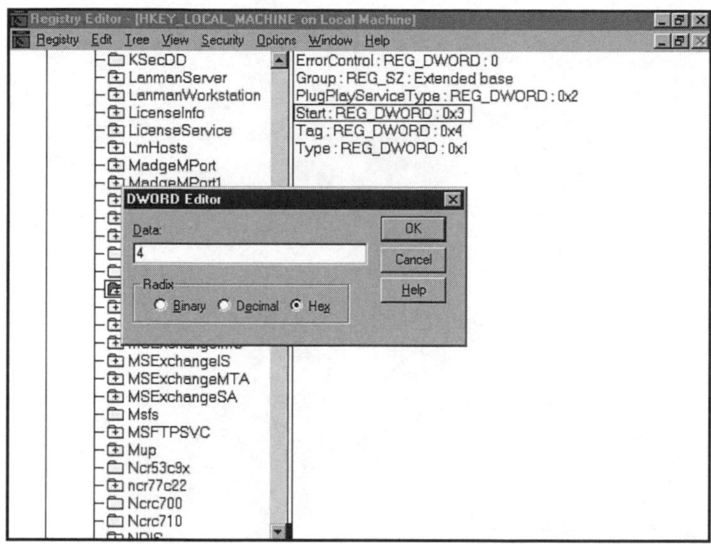

Figure 44.14. *Changing a* `Start` *value to* `4` *(disabled).*

Restart the system, and if the system fails again, use the Last Known Good Configuration again and try to determine what device or service may be causing the system to halt.

Summary

Mastering usage of the Registry puts a lot of power in your hands when you are trying to troubleshoot a computer—whether local or remote—or when just trying to get a better understanding of how a computer is configured.

Making manual modifications to the Registry can usually help make a computer stable again, but extreme caution should be used when making changes to the Registry. The standard Windows NT administrative tools should be used instead of directly modifying the Registry whenever possible.

Disaster Recovery

by Brett Bonenberger

This chapter is split into two different yet similar topics. The first section covers preventive maintenance and the second section covers disaster recovery planning. Both are important issues that are taken for granted or overlooked by many network administrators.

With the ever-increasing reliance on computer systems by businesses, good preventive maintenance and a disaster recovery plan are critical. Preventive maintenance includes using tape backups, uninterruptible power supplies, RAID technologies, clustering, and utilities built into NT 4.0. Disaster recovery plans are usually complex and expensive. Your plan can be simple or very complex depending on your needs; however, most plans should cover the entire business including computer systems, telephone systems, and media relations.

Preventive Maintenance

There are many topics that could be considered preventive maintenance. Some could be viewed as common sense, but some are things that people never think of. When I first started getting into computers, I had a now archaic desktop. I used it primarily to type papers and, of course, play games. I always thought that nothing would happen to my computer, that everything would always work fine. I believed this for several years, until the one time I was up late writing a final term paper for a graduate class. I lost power to my apartment. I figured that I could wait until the power came back on and continue. When the power did come back on, I found my paper had been corrupted. From what I could tell, the word processing program was in the middle of auto saving. It took a small disaster for me to realize the importance of having some preventive maintenance. This is a true story, and I ordered my first Uninterruptible Power Supply the next day! Even as I write this chapter, I frequently pause and save to a floppy disk for safekeeping.

Tape Backups

The simplest method to ensure that your data is kept safe is to implement a tape backup system. There are many backup software packages on the market to choose from offering a variety of features. Even Windows NT 4.0 comes with rather limited but effective backup software. Figure 45.1 shows the front end to NT Backup.

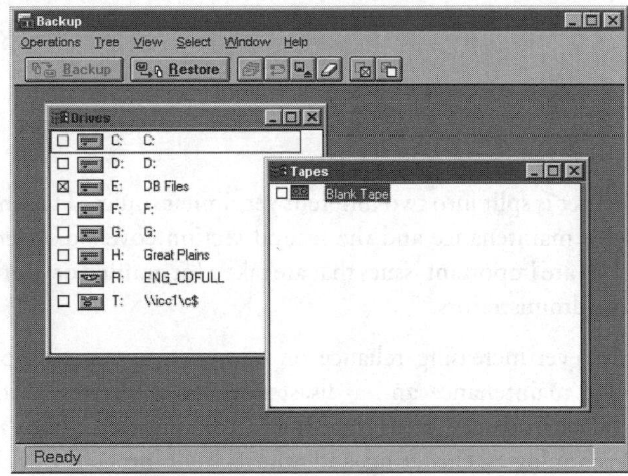

Figure 45.1. *The NT Backup main application screen.*

NT Backup

NT Backup is limited by the number of features it employs. Scheduling, for example, is done through a command-line syntax that you can place inside of a batch file. The command-line syntax follows:

```
ntbackup op path [/a] [/b] [/d "text"] [/e] [/hc:{off¦on}] [/] "filename"][/r]
➥[/t {opt}] [/tape:{n}] [/v]
```

All these options are explained in Table 45.1. There are two options that are not defined in the table or used in the preceding syntax. They are not included because they require user input. The `[/missingtape]` option specifies that a tape is missing from the backup set and that each tape should be treated as a separate entity, and `[/nopoll]` causes the tape to be erased.

Table 45.1. NT Backup command options.

Options	*Description*
`op`	Specifies the operation, backup, or eject
`path`	Specifies one or more paths to be backed up
`/a`	Causes backups to be appended after the last backup set on the tape
`/v`	Verifies the operation
`/r`	Restricts access
`/d "text"`	Specifies a description of the backup contents
`/b`	Specifies the local Registry to be backed up
`/hc:on¦off`	Specifies whether hardware compression is on or off
`/t {option}`	Specifies the backup type: normal, incremental, daily, copy, differential
`/l "filename"`	Specifies the filename for the backup log
`/e`	Specifies the backup log include exceptions only
`/tape:{n}`	Specifies the tape drive to use for the backup operation

You can then automate the backup by using the NT scheduler program, AT. The AT command-line syntax follows:

```
at [\\computername] time [/interactive] [/every:date[,...] ¦ /next:date[,...]] command
```

This will then allow you to schedule the backup that you created earlier. The command-line options are defined in Table 45.2. Table 45.2 was created by running at the command line

```
at /?
```

Table 45.2. The AT command options.

Options	*Description*
`\\computername`	Specifies a remote computer. Commands are scheduled on the local computer if this parameter is omitted.
`Id`	An identification number assigned to a scheduled command.
`/delete`	Cancels a scheduled command. If `Id` is omitted, all the scheduled commands on the computer are canceled.
`/yes`	Used with cancel all jobs command when no additional confirmation is desired.
`time`	Specifies the time when command is to run.
`/interactive`	Allows the job to interact with the desktop of the user who is logged on at the time the job runs.

continues

Table 45.2. continued

Options	*Description*
`/every:date[,...]`	Runs the command on each specified day(s) of the week or month. If date is omitted, the current day of the month is assumed.
`/next:date[,...]`	Runs the specified command on the next occurrence of the day (for example, next Thursday). If date is omitted, the current day of the month is assumed.
`"command"`	The Windows NT command or batch program to be run.

This might seem backward if you understand that NT was built based on the UNIX platform. All other backup software that I have used, uses a graphical scheduling system. Another limitation is report generation. NT Backup uses the Event Viewer to show when a successful backup occurs, but not when one fails or why it failed. Although Event Viewer is a wonderful tool, it lacks detailed reporting functions. Figure 45.2 shows a sample Event Viewer Detail screen showing a successful backup.

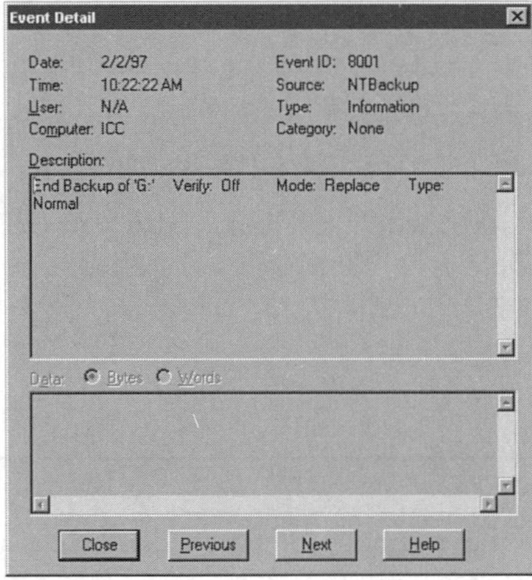

Figure 45.2. *Event Viewer Detail screen showing a successful NT Backup.*

Another limitation is the inability to configure and use media pools. A media pool allows you to maintain a group of tapes that have a common factor among them. Having a large amount of data to back up, a media pool will help you maintain your sanity by telling you what is on each tape of the pool. The largest problem with NT Backup is its reliability. Because of limited reporting, it is often difficult to determine why a backup may have failed. Most times the only way to know is to watch it run. For a small network administrator (10–15 users) this may not be difficult to do. The backup can usually be run manually at the end of the day without the need for scheduling. This way the backup process is known to start and, if there is not a lot of data, can be monitored to ensure its reliability.

On larger networks, backups often are run late at night so that the workaholics can complete what they need to. It is therefore impractical, in most cases, for a network administrator of a large network to watch the backup process. When I installed my first NT 3.51 network, I had many problems with NT Backup. The biggest and most frustrating problem is that NT Backup would occasionally decide not to run—not because of the scheduler but through the GUI application itself. The problem, as I soon discovered, was that the NT Backup process was still alive. To correct this problem I had to either reboot the server, which is almost impossible in the middle of a business day, or find the process and kill it manually. I am not aware if the same problem exists under NT Server 4.0, because I have since used only third-party products.

Types of Backups

There are several types of backups that you can perform worth mentioning. Choosing a type depends largely on the capacity of your tape drive.

- A normal backup will back up all files selected. This method should be performed at least once because it backs up all data and applications on the server. After it archives a file, the file is marked as being archived.
- An incremental backup will back up only those files that have changed or been added since the last normal backup. It will also mark files as being archived. Using a combination of normal and incremental backups, you will need to first restore the normal backup and then restore any incremental backups.
- A differential backup will also back up those files that have been changed or added since the last normal backup, but will not mark the file as such. To restore using this type of backup, you will need to first restore from the normal backup and then restore from the last differential backup.

In my experience, I have found it to be much easier to always perform a normal backup. It is a simple restoration process because you will need only the last normal backup tape. But if you do have a small capacity drive, using an incremental or differential backup will work great; it just involves a few extra steps.

Tape Rotation

Speaking of steps, tape rotation is another topic that you need to be aware of when planning your backup strategy. Because I always perform a normal backup, I have set up a simple tape rotation plan. I use five tapes, one for each day of the week (see Figure 45.3). At the end of each day, the previous day's backup tape is taken and stored offsite. Because each tape is written to once a week, I must follow the recommended life span the manufacturer has given the tape. A lot of wear on the tape can cause data to be lost.

Figure 45.3. *My tape rotation using a normal backup.*

If I were to use an incremental backup plan, the following tape rotation could be used. It involves two sets of five tapes. You can add more sets of five and become very elaborate with your backup plan, but for now this will help you understand the basic incremental process. Figure 45.4 shows the rotation plan. On Monday through Thursday an incremental backup is performed. On Friday a normal backup is performed. Each set of tapes is then stored offsite. After the normal backup is performed on the second week, the first week's tapes are returned and the second week's tapes are stored offsite. You can get as elaborate a tape rotation plan as you want. The important thing to remember is offsite storage.

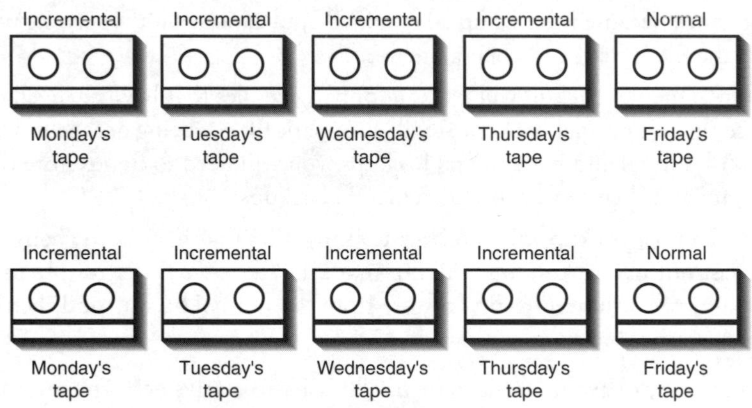

Figure 45.4. *A sample tape rotation for an incremental tape rotation.*

Other Backup Applications

There are many backup applications on the market. I do not know which is best and the purpose of this book is not to decide that. To determine what backup software will be the best for you, look at the size of your network, how much data you need to back up, and how much control you need over the backup process. Many magazines that are NT-specific offer a review of backup software about every six months. In those reviews they will rate the restoration process of the software. This is the most critical feature. No backup software can offer a 100 percent reliable restoration process, but some will perform better than others. Some backup software solutions are reviewed in Chapter 37, "Third-Party Utilities." Whichever backup software you choose, the first test that should be completed is restoring from the tape. If the server is live, create a directory and copy a large amount of data into it. After the first backup occurs, delete that directory and attempt to restore it from tape. If the server is not live on the network, attempt a full recover from tape. Although this is quite a bit of work, you will have at least gone through the process of restoring before you really need to restore because of a real failure.

Tips for Your Backup Plan

Now you have implemented your new backup routine and purchased your tape drive, backup software, and backup tapes. You have tested the backup and restoration processes and have been feeling good that you have made this step to secure critical data needed to run the company on backup tapes. After a few weeks of backing up the data, a small fire erupts and causes the automatic sprinklers to turn on making everything wet, including your backup tapes. Not only did the business lose money because of the fire, but also because all their customer information was lost. The moral here is be sure to store your backup tapes offsite, in a secure, water- and fire-proof environment. The most you will lose then is a day's worth of data. Another tip is to replace tapes periodically so that they do not become worn and lose their integrity. Some backup software will allow you to re-tension the tapes. This will help lengthen the life of the tape, but will not make the tape indestructible. Clean your tape drive after approximately 15 hours of use with an approved cleaning tape. Most manufacturers of drives will recommend a specific brand of cleaning tape to use—usually their own!

Uninterruptible Power Supplies

Uninterruptible Power Supplies (UPS) are another critical component to have in place to protect your computer system. A UPS helps to control damaging power surges, filter Electro-Magnetic Interference and Radio Frequency Interference (EMI/RFI) noise, and supply power to equipment when utility power is cut off.

A power surge is usually caused by lightning or motor load from air conditioners and elevators. EMI/RFI can be caused by radio transmissions and neon lights. Common causes of power failure include blackouts, brownouts, and sags. A blackout is defined as a total loss of power caused by an act of nature or accident. Brownouts are defined as temporary reductions in power that can be caused by huge power requirements from a nearby location or in extreme cases by the power company itself. Sags are defined as temporary reductions in the normal line Vac of 120 and are also caused by a huge requirement in power from a nearby location or equipment.

Before you go out and buy a UPS for your system, you need to determine what the power demands of your equipment are. To do this is actually a simple process. Every computer equipment manufacturer must provide a power rating for its equipment. This rating can usually be found on a sticker on the back of the equipment and will be given in either amps (A), watts (W), or volt-amperes (VA). Because of the different units of measurement you will need to convert each measurement to a common unit. For this example we will convert all measurements to an estimate of volt-amperes. If the unit of measurement is given in watts, multiply the value in watts by 1.4. If the load is given in amps, convert it by multiplying the value in amps by 120. See Table 45.3 for an example.

Table 45.3. Load calculation for a UPS.

Equipment Label	*Load*
`Server 1 VA = 120 X 4 A =`	480 VA
`Monitor 1 VA = 100 X 1.4 =`	140 VA
`Server 2 VA = 110 X 4 A =`	440 VA
`Monitor 2 VA = 100 X 1.4 =`	140 VA
	TOTAL = 1,200 VA

In this example, you would need to purchase a UPS that has a capacity of at least 1,200 VA.

Most major computer manufacturers will overrate the requirement for power. This is both bad and good. It is unfortunate when calculating requirements because the total power requirements will be higher than what you actually need. And the higher the power capacity of the UPS, the more expensive it is. On the other hand, it is fortunate that they overrate because you need not worry about the power requirements of expansion boards and drives.

However, just because the computer manufacturers overrate, does not mean you should buy a lower rated UPS. If you underestimate your requirements, you will defeat one of the purposes of the UPS, backup power. In the event of a power failure, the UPS will overload and will shut down abruptly.

A UPS should not be used only on your servers, but on all critical components of your network. Routers, concentrators, switches, or anything on the physical layer that requires power, should have a UPS.

Most UPSs will come with software that can be used to monitor power stability, fluctuations, and outages. Some of the software is also able to safely shut down the servers in case of a power failure. Once power is cut off, the software will usually begin shutting down the system after a short amount of time. This allows users to save any work they are doing and safely back out of their applications. I have only had the opportunity to work with such software on a Novell network, so I am not sure how well the software will work with an NT Server.

Redundant Array of Inexpensive Disks

Redundant Array of Inexpensive Disks, RAID, is a system configuration that uses multiple drives to write data across all drives. RAID typically will use four or five drives, but can be implemented on more or less. The array of drives is seen by the user as a single drive. Reading and writing data is determined by which level of RAID the system supports. These levels are designated with a number between 0 and 5. Each value then represents a different way of dealing with data. The most common RAID levels are Level 1 and Level 5.

RAID Levels

RAID Level 0 is called data striping or disk spanning. In data striping, the data is written block-by-block with each block being written once to one drive. With disk spanning, a block of data is written to the next available disk that is not full or busy. This level of RAID provides no fault tolerance and complete loss of data is possible. Many do not view this as a level of RAID, but I felt it should be discussed to help you understand the importance of fault tolerance.

RAID Level 1 is the simplest form of RAID. It involves using disk mirroring or duplexing to duplicate data over multiple disks. Figure 45.5 shows an example of mirroring where each block of data is written to two disks through the same channel. If one of the drives becomes damaged, the data is still accessible from the other drive. If the channel for writing fails, then the data is lost. This is when duplexing is a benefit. Figure 45.6 shows an example of duplexing where the data is written to two different drives but through separate channels. This protects the data even more, unless the worst happens, which is both drives fail or both channels.

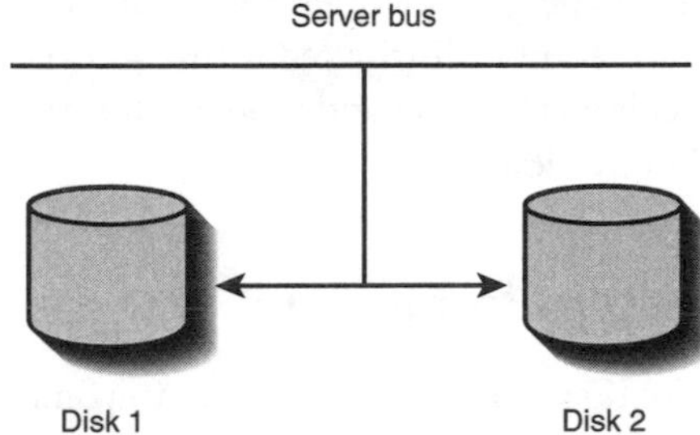

Figure 45.5. *This image shows how data travels through the use of disk mirroring. Notice the path for both drives is the same channel.*

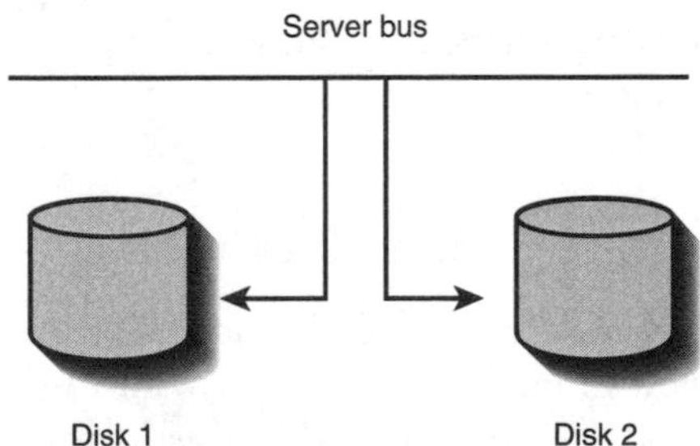

Figure 45.6. *This image shows how data travels to the disk drives through the use of duplexing.*

RAID Level 2 is called data striping, bit interleaving. Each bit is written to a different drive and uses a Hamming Code for Error Correction, which is used to reconstruct the data in the event of a disk failure. The Hamming Code information is nothing more than a checksum. The checksum information is written to a special checksum drive. RAID Level 2 is very slow and quite unreliable because any of the checksum drives can fail as well.

RAID Level 3 is similar to Level 2 except that it uses a single disk as a parity checker instead of using checksums and multiple checksum drives. The array of drives transfers data in parallel with one drive functioning as a parity check disk. Together, all drives function as one large virtual drive. In the event of a disk failure, data from the failed disk can be rebuilt by reading the remaining bits and calculate the missing bits using the parity data from the parity disk. RAID Level 3 offers high transfer rates that are suitable for graphics, imaging, and any application that requires fast or large data transfers.

RAID Level 4 is called disk striping, block interleaving, parity checking. This is almost identical to Level 3 except that an entire block is written to each hard disk each time. The chunks are read and written independently. The redundancy is obtained through the use of a parity disk. When a block is written to a disk, parity for that block is written to a corresponding block on the parity disk. The next time a block of data is written to a disk, the parity block must be checked to avoid overwriting the parity data. If you can imagine having to check the parity disk every time that a block of data is written, you will quickly realize that this can slow down drive access dramatically.

RAID Level 5 is called data striping, block interleaving, distributed parity. It is similar to Level 4 except that the parity information is distributed across all drives in the array rather than being written to special drives. This level is faster and more reliable than the others. For data to become lost, two drives must fail in this level.

Deciding Which Level to Implement

Before you implement a RAID solution for your systems, you must first know your applications and how they handle files. Database applications and engineering applications have many large files that are read and written sequentially. Transaction-processing applications such as reservation systems will typically perform a large number of concurrent requests. These concurrent requests will each make a small number of disk accesses. So, if your applications are dependent on disk transfer rates, RAID 3 would be your better solution. For high transaction rate applications, RAID 5 would be your better solution.

Hardware- and Software-Based Solutions

Now that you know the different levels of RAID and how to choose the right level to implement, you need to decide on how to implement. Do you want to use a hardware- or software-based solution? There are some advantages and disadvantages to each.

Hardware-based solutions offer the following advantages over a software-based solution:

- Hot swap and hot spare drives with almost instantaneous replacement of failed drives
- Improved disk performance through integrated disk caching
- A separate, dedicated processor
- Additional levels of RAID

The biggest disadvantage of a hardware RAID solution is the cost. They are expensive to implement although the cost is probably worth it. If you have a server that has to be up 24 hours a day, 7 days a week, having hot swappable drives is invaluable. Again, you have to look at what the downtime of the system will cost versus the cost of the solution.

Windows NT Server 4.0 has a built-in software RAID solution called Disk Administrator. Figure 45.7 shows the main application screen for Disk Administrator. Disk Administrator is limited to RAID Levels 0, 1, and 5. This is perfectly acceptable for most applications. The advantage of using Disk Administrator is that it is included with NT and doesn't require additional cost. The disadvantage of Disk Administrator is that you cannot implement a full RAID solution.

RAID is an expensive solution to implement and it is often argued as to whether it is worth the cost. The best alternative to using RAID is disk duplexing. The battle continues to rage on as to whether disk duplexing or RAID is the better choice. In my opinion, that is something that each network administrator must decide on his own.

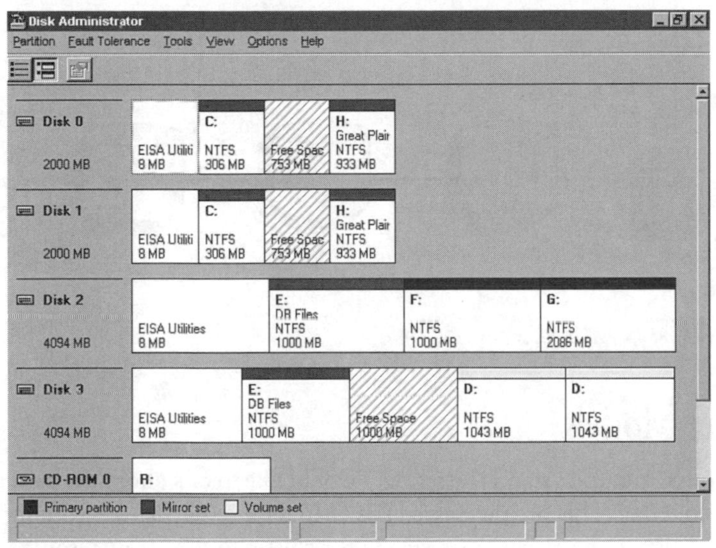

Figure 45.7. *Disk Administrator's main application screen.*

Server Clustering

Server clustering is the method of taking a group of independent systems that work together as a single system. Clients on a network will access the cluster as if it were a single system. Administrators will also view a cluster as if it were a single system. By using clustering, your network will have a greater level of availability and scalability. Figure 45.8 shows the normal operation of a two system cluster. Server 1 is handling all requests while server 2 sits in the chance server 1 fails. If a server in the cluster were to fail, the work from the downed server will then be dispersed over the remaining servers in the cluster. Figure 45.9 shows server 1 as failed and server 2 taking over the operation of the network. With scalability, you will avoid the cost of trying to maintain large systems that are capable of expanding memory, processors, or drives. With clustering, a smaller server can be added to support the needed processing requirements.

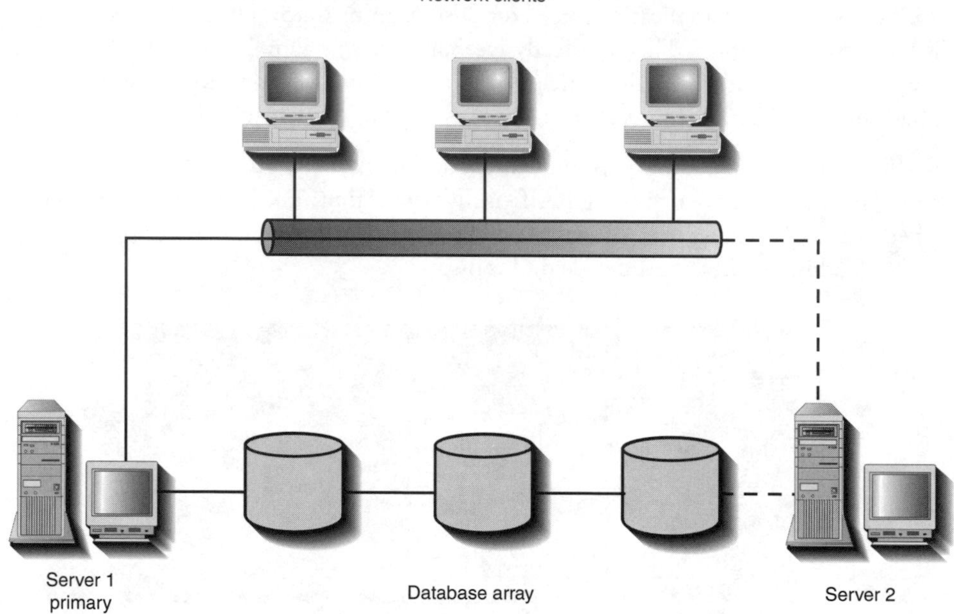

Figure 45.8. *Normal operations in a two server cluster.*

Clustering Models

To help you better understand clustering, I would like to talk about the primary software models that are used today. They are the Shared Disk Model and the Shared Nothing Model. The Shared Disk Model allows any system operating in the cluster to access any resource that is connected to another system in the cluster. If multiple systems need the same data, the data must be copied from one system to another or read twice from the resource.

In the Shared Nothing Model, each system in the cluster has exclusive ownership rights to any resource that it is accessing. If a request comes in from a client that needs data from a resource, the system hosting the request must use a sub-request to retrieve the data. The system holding ownership of the resource will send the requested data back to the host, and the host must assemble the final response to send back to the client.

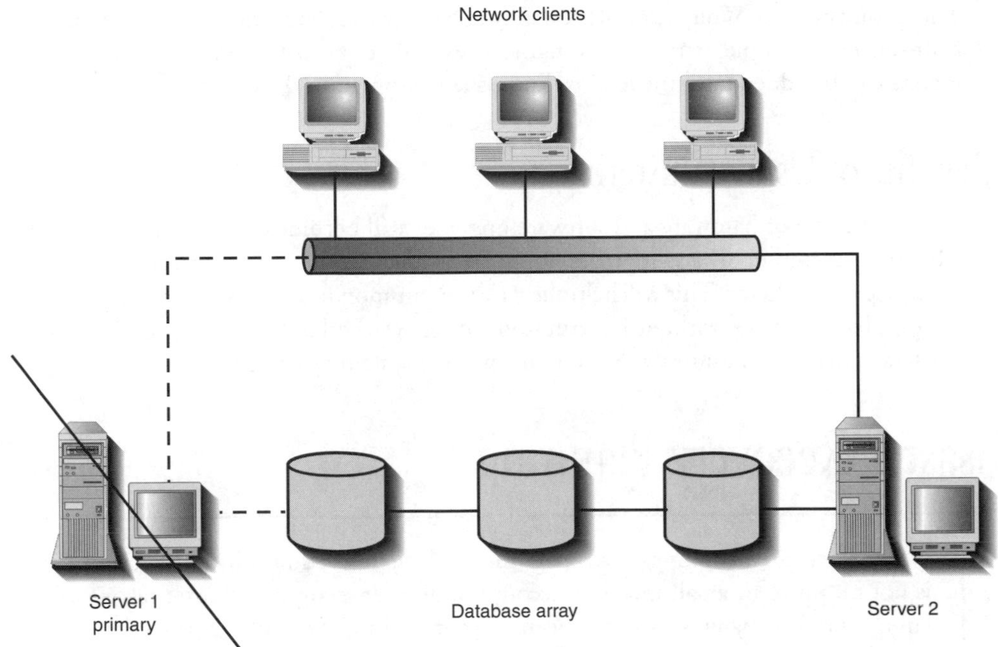

Figure 45.9. Server 1 failed, and now server 2 controls the operation of the network.

Why Clustering Is Important

Clustering is important when you are developing a strategic operating plan. System downtime costs businesses more than $4 billion per year. Clustering can help keep systems running by providing an architecture that is capable of withstanding a server failure. Clustering has been around for some time. Digital Equipment Corporation has had clustering on its VAX systems for more than 10 years and many UNIX-based clusters have emerged. Microsoft is now extending clustering to the NT environment. This strategy for clustering is called Wolfpack.

Microsoft's Answer to Clustering

Wolfpack is going to be released in two phases. The first phase is the failover solution and will address two-node clustering. Manufacturers are expected to begin releasing cluster-ready systems in the spring of 1997. In the failover implementation, the servers will be connected by a dedicated high speed link. This link will handle data replication between servers and verification of the other servers' "vital signs." Each server will be dependent on each other as failover partners. If one of the servers crashes, the other will automatically stand in and handle the lost resource until it can be replaced or repaired.

The second phase of Wolfpack will break through the two-node barrier and address load-balancing features. For example, when the overall load exceeds the capabilities of the cluster, additional servers can be added until the load is diminished throughout the cluster.

Benefits of Using Clustering

Administration of hardware and software upgrades will become easier with a Wolfpack cluster. The software and hardware upgrades can be performed on one system at a time without any loss of service to the clients. This will help alleviate the common headaches and late nights spent trying to complete upgrades without interruptions in service. Perhaps the greatest advantage to using clusters is that the end-users will not know when a system has failed.

Disaster Recovery Planning

Note: There are two things to keep in mind before proceeding with this section. First, this is not meant to be an all-inclusive account of disaster recovery. Disaster recovery is such a large issue that many books have been written about it. Secondly, this section is not NT-specific. Disaster recovery is such an important issue that it is presented in a broad general sense, but it pertains to an NT system just as much as a UNIX or VAX system. At the end of this chapter, I will discuss some NT-related disaster recovery tips.

If there is one thing in your lifetime that you can be sure will happen, it is a disaster. Each day as you look through the paper or watch the news a disaster has occurred somewhere. A disaster is not only an act of nature such as an earthquake or tornado, but also fire, water damage, and even malicious ex-employees. Chances are good that a disaster could affect you and your employer. After the excitement surrounding the disaster has died down, you will have to begin re-building the business and assessing damages. Some businesses will not survive the disaster.

What Is a Disaster Recovery Plan?

A disaster recovery plan is a detailed set of steps that are to be taken before, during, and after a disaster has occurred. These are steps that must be exercised on a regular basis to ensure the steps work and to keep employees knowledgeable of their roles in the plan.

Benefits of a Disaster Recovery Plan

The benefits of a disaster recovery plan are great in number. The following is a short list of the typical benefits for a business:

- Minimization of economic loss
- Calmer and more organized staff during a disaster
- Quicker recovery from a disaster
- Possible reduction in insurance premiums
- Shorter disruption time of normal business operations
- Less decision-making during a disaster
- Increased safety for employees
- Assurance that important items are not overlooked

Beginning Your Disaster Recovery Plan

Keep in mind that a disaster recovery plan is not something that can be developed overnight. It will take from several months up to a year to develop, depending on the size of the business and the number of other projects that may be going on. Although disaster recovery is important, it often gets pushed to the back burner.

The first step to developing your disaster recovery plan is to make a plan for development. Because this plan is critical to the operations of your business in the event of a disaster, time must be taken to analyze each step of development. First, determine who should be responsible for the plan. The ultimate responsibility does not lie with the Information Systems personnel, but with upper-management. They hold the purse strings and are the ones who need to have it proven to them that such a plan would be a benefit. Secondly, develop a team that will work through the creation and implementation of the plan. Team members should include department managers and anyone who would be responsible for emergency procedures within his area. The first responsibility of the team is to prove to management the value of the plan. This can sometimes be a difficult step. I know colleagues of mine who have been pushing for disaster planning within their companies for months and even years. Most of the time, management will not want to spend money on something that does not immediately provide any tangible benefits.

Note: To help you get management motivated, there are several videos that are available through the public library that will show what a disaster did to an actual company that had a plan and one that did not. Although most are humorous in their presentation, the message delivered should strike home. If you search for Disaster Recovery Planning, several books and videos should be shown.

After you have management approval to begin your plan, you need to start an in-depth analysis of the operations of your business and determine the impact a disaster would have. This is formally called a Business Impact Analysis. It is a broad look at the business and defines what the critical areas are, the financial impact, and how a disaster would affect your customers. A Business Impact Analysis will also help you to identify the role each employee would assume in the event of a disaster. If your focus is on development of a plan for your data center, a smaller than scale plan called a Data Center Risk Analysis should be performed. This plan is much smaller than the Business Impact Analysis, but answers the same questions: What are the critical areas? What is the financial impact? How would a disaster affect your users?

Recovery Strategies

The next step is to create a strategy for recovering from a disaster. Many different options exist, and each one has a different cost.

Hot Site

A local vendor that my company works with for our disaster recovery plan maintains a hot site within its facility. A hot site is a location, usually in the vendor's facility, that is equipped with computer hardware, phone equipment, and support personnel. In the event of a disaster, a company may relocate its critical operations to this location and function as if nothing has happened.

Note: If you recall from the last section on tape backups, I said to maintain offsite storage of your backup tapes. This is one instance where the offsite storage is absolutely necessary.

With today's advancements in technology, phone lines and leased lines can be transferred to a remote site in a matter of hours, thus minimizing the downtime from the disaster. Of course, the cost of having a hot site available is high, but the cost of not having one during a disaster could be even higher.

Cold Site

A cold site is similar to a hot site. It is an offsite facility, but it does not maintain equipment for its clients to use. Equipment will usually need to be ordered and could take several days to arrive. After the equipment is finally available, you will need to set it up, thus causing even greater delays. This solution is cheaper than a hot site but presents even greater downtime.

Internal Relocation

If you work for a large company that has offices in different locations, it is possible for you to plan on sharing the facilities. If the offices are connected via lease lines, the battle of bringing the computer systems online is half done, provided replication among the servers has occurred. It is also possible that the relocation office could temporarily provide the services the damaged office provided.

Selection of a Disaster Recovery Vendor

If you choose to work with a Disaster Recovery Vendor, you need to select a vendor that can meet your needs. This sounds like common sense, but not all vendors will be able to provide the equipment that you need. Some are focused on mainframes, while others are focused on midrange, and still others on LANs. I have not heard of any vendors in my area having support for all three. If you are looking at using a hot site in your plan, ask to see the facility, look to see if the floor layout is adequate for your space needs, examine the equipment they have available for you to use, and ask plenty of questions. The following are some good questions to ask whether planning a hot site or not:

- Ask to see the vendor's disaster recovery plan. This might sound like a stupid question, but you would be surprised to discover how many do not have a plan!
- Find out whether they have any business partnerships with your computer and telecommunication hardware manufacturers or who their business partners are. Although an exact match of equipment may be impossible, a close one can be a benefit.
- See, especially if you're looking at a hot site, what happens in a city-wide disaster. Who gets the facilities first?

Document

This step is probably the most tedious and most important step of the plan development. This is the step that outlines who does what, where, and why. Documentation must be maintained through periodic updates and testing. This can be developed in several ways. There are several companies that make Disaster Recovery Plan software that will help you create the documentation for your company. The simplest and cheapest form is to type it in any word processor. Both options are effective; one just has a larger price tag. I have not used any of the recovery plan software, but have heard that it is expensive and will take quite some time to catch on.

Training

After you have documented the plan, you will need to train others in their roles and responsibilities. You should take into careful consideration using and training backup personnel in case of someone being sick, on vacation, or having quit.

Simulation

Simulation is the most important step of your plan. This step must be performed routinely. A simulation will help your team to identify weaknesses in the plan, missed steps, and help to teach collaboration among those involved. After simulating a disaster, every member of the developing team needs to begin to critique his or her role identifying where things can be improved or are unnecessary. After the documentation for the plan has been created, making changes should be easy.

Summary

This chapter explained preventive maintenance and disaster recovery planning. You learned the importance of and how to implement various tape backup systems. You now understand why Uninterruptible Power Supplies are necessary when utility power is cut off. We also covered RAID and server clustering. In the next chapter, we discuss Microsoft Exchange and Microsoft Mail.

PART IX

The Components of BackOffice

Troubleshooting: Microsoft Exchange and Microsoft Mail

by Terry W. Ogletree

All Windows operating systems (with the exception of Windows 3.1) include the Microsoft Mail utility to enable users to communicate with each other using electronic mail. This electronic postoffice solution uses a centralized file-storage method for holding messages from users until the recipient can retrieve them. Although the stored messages can reside on a LAN server, the messages are manipulated by processes that run on the Mail client computers. The server only holds the necessary files that client computers can access by mapping a network drive.

This method works well in a small LAN environment where the volume of e-mail is not huge and there is little need to communicate outside the LAN by other means, such as WAN or Internet connections.

In larger network environments, the Microsoft Exchange Server BackOffice product is the choice for enterprise-wide messaging services. Microsoft Exchange gives you all the functionality of the Microsoft Mail utility and adds a multitude of features that can enhance your employees' productivity through groupware approaches to problems. In addition to providing e-mail capabilities, Exchange also provides Schedule+ to enable users to access shared appointment-schedule databases. The Outlook application that currently ships with Office 97 carries this concept one step further, and probably will be included in future Exchange releases.

A key difference between MS Mail and Exchange is that Exchange is a client/server-based application. Processes run on servers that take care of forwarding mail to other sites or foreign mail services. The administrator can perform functions by using the Exchange Administrator program to control and optimize features of Exchange. When administering MS Mail (adding a new user, for example), the administrator must map a network drive to the location of the postoffice just like Mail clients must. To administer more than one postoffice, each of which is located on a different server, the administrator must map a network drive to each of those servers. Exchange uses *remote procedure calls* (RPCs) instead, and mapping a network drive is not necessary.

By centralizing control over the administrative functions and by adhering to X.400/X.500 standards, Exchange can function in a much larger environment than would be possible for MS Mail.

Microsoft Exchange includes connectors that enable you to connect your Exchange sites to other mail systems that use standard messaging protocols. You will find site connectors you can use to connect to other Exchange sites, Internet connectors to connect to other mail services using SMTP, an X.400 connector for mail services that use that standard protocol, and so on.

Other differences between MS Mail and Exchange follow:

- The Exchange Information Store is divided into public and private sections, whereas MS Mail uses the *shared file system* (SFS) postoffice to hold messages. Users of MS Mail must connect to the file share that holds the message files. This is not necessary using Exchange.
- Exchange directory services adhere to the X.500 standard, so exchanges of Directory information with other compliant systems usually are possible. MS Mail uses a proprietary format for its Directory.

If it sounds like Microsoft Exchange is a complex product, that's because it is. But if you plan your implementation based on a careful review of your network and messaging needs, you will find that although Exchange is complex, it does not have to be difficult. If your organization is sufficiently large, you should consider dividing the implementation tasks among several employees so that each can devote the time necessary to ensure a smooth installation of Exchange. In addition to careful planning, be sure to document everything. Documentation can be a lifesaver when you have to troubleshoot later.

Using Microsoft Exchange

Microsoft Exchange was designed to be an enterprise messaging solution. Although Exchange is very well integrated into the Windows NT operating system and makes extensive use of the security features that NT provides, it does not use the domain concept for organizational purposes as NT does. The domain or local security Directory database is used for validating users when secure functions are performed using Exchange. For organizational purposes, though, you can think of Exchange as an organization containing sites that consist of a collection of servers, as illustrated in Figure 46.1. Directory replication services are offered by Exchange to provide a distributed messaging database, and connectors are used to logically join sites or other mail services to Exchange sites.

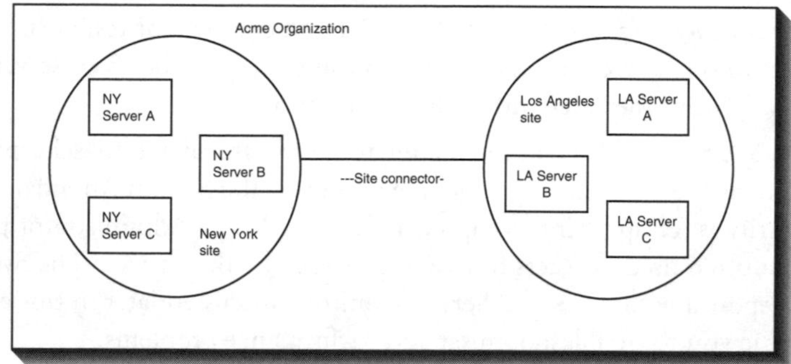

Figure 46.1. *Exchange divides administrative tasks among the organization, sites within the organization, and servers located at each site.*

Tip: The Microsoft BackOffice Resource Kit (Volumes 1 and 2) has recently been released. Both kits contain printed documentation on Microsoft Exchange and Microsoft Systems Management Server (SMS), along with utilities not included with Windows NT, Exchange, or SMS. Any administrator who will have Microsoft Exchange responsibilities as a primary part of his job should acquire these Resource Kits.

Core Components

The Exchange server consists of several services that run under Windows NT. Each service performs a different function related to the core components of Exchange:

- *The Directory:* This is the central Information Store that contains all the information about the organization's Exchange server configuration. Applications use the Directory to find information about any object used by Exchange. Each object in the database has properties that can be configured using the Exchange Administrator program to view or modify Properties dialogs. Objects include information on each connector and sites and servers within the organization. The directory also maintains addressing information for all users in the organization. The actual messages that users send or receive, however, are not stored here. Directory replication is used between servers in a site to ensure that all servers have a complete copy of the database, which is updated periodically. Bridgehead servers allow for directory replication among other sites in the organization. Bridgehead servers can be configured with the Exchange Administrator program. You use this utility to create the schedule that is used by bridgehead servers for replication. You can use one or more bridgehead servers in your site to connect to one or more other sites.

- *The Information Store:* This component is the database that contains the users' messages. Each server in a site maintains its own Information Store, which consists of public and private Information Stores. Private Information Stores contain user mailboxes. Public Information Stores contain folders that can be made accessible to one or more users in the organization. You can create both types of stores on a server, or you can dedicate a server to either a public or private Information Store to improve performance.
- *The Message Transfer Agent:* The MTA is the component responsible for routing messages to the correct destination. It can route messages between servers within a site and to MTAs at other sites within the organization.
- *The System Attendant:* This component performs general housekeeping duties for the Exchange server. Routing tables are rebuilt by the System Attendant, and advanced security is set up by this component. The Exchange Administrator program is the utility most often used to access functions provided by this service. The System Attendant also is responsible for Link and Server Monitors (discussed later in this chapter), which enable you to troubleshoot user and performance problems.

These four components perform separate, distinct functions, but they all work together to provide a complete messaging service. As with any service that runs under Windows NT Server, you can view the Exchange services and their configurations by double-clicking the Services icon in the Control Panel or by selecting the server using the Server Manager Administrative Tool to show the services. Figure 46.2 shows the Services Properties dialog with the Exchange services scrolled into view.

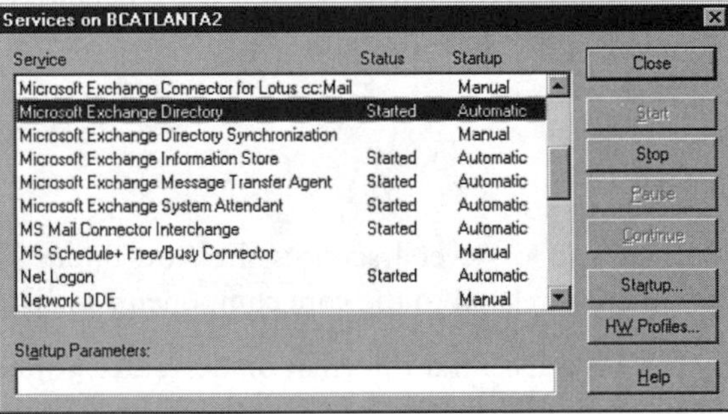

Figure 46.2. *You can configure all Windows NT services, including those that perform Exchange core functions.*

Optional Components

The core components discussed in the preceding section are all you need to give a small company an enterprise network solution for messaging. If you need to connect to remote sites (using the Internet or a dial-up connection), however, or if you need to connect to foreign mail services, you need to establish connections to those other sites or services.

In addition to the site connector, which you can use to join Exchange sites, you can use these three optional connectors:

- The Internet Mail connector
- The Microsoft Mail connector
- The X.400 connector

Another optional component you can install is the Key Management service, which you can use for security issues such as signing digital certificates and encrypting messages.

The Microsoft Mail connector enables you to exchange messages with clients that use a Microsoft Mail postoffice. At the same time, you can use the Internet Mail connector to exchange messages with a *Simple Mail Transport Protocol* (SMTP)–compliant messaging service and the X.400 connector to communicate with any mail service that uses the X.400 protocol standard.

In addition to these supplementary server components, you can install support for Schedule+ to maintain an enterprise scheduling system for your employees, and you can use the Forms Processor to create unique documents that can be used to facilitate company paperwork and processes.

Installing Exchange Server

When you install Exchange Server, you must be logged on to an account on the server that has at least the rights granted to the local Administrator account. You also have to designate a service account the Exchange Server will use for accessing system objects. The Install program will grant the Logon as a Service and Restore Files and Directories rights to the service account that you designate if the account does not yet have those rights.

You are prompted to create a new site or to join an existing site by the Install program. If you choose to create a new site, the names you give to the Setup program for the organization and site names will be added to the directory that is created. If you are installing Exchange on a server that is going to join an existing site, the process is a little different. The information you provide to the Setup program is used to add information to the directory of the site you are joining. Then, the directory database from the remote site is replicated back to the new server member.

Using Link and Server Monitors, Objects, and Counters

With a complex system of programs such as Microsoft Exchange, you should expect there to be an equally complex set of tools and utilities you can use to probe the system when user or performance problems arise. If you install the complete distribution from the Exchange CD-ROM, and if you have the Windows NT Server 4.0 Resource Kit and the BackOffice Resource

Kits on your system, you will find that you have more than enough resources to safely troubleshoot and explore your NT domain and the Exchange messaging system that provides support to your clients.

Because an organization in Exchange consists of a group of one or more sites, and because those sites are joined by connectors, it is natural that Exchange would include a monitor utility that could show you the status of a connection at any time. You will find this capability in the Exchange Administrator program.

You also can monitor the status of any server in a site by using a Server Monitor. You can configure this type of monitor by using the Administrator program. Both these types of monitors can be powerful troubleshooting tools. You can configure each type of monitor to record a log file and alert you (by mail, by an alert message, or by launching a program) when problems arise.

Creating a Server Monitor

You use the Exchange Administrator program to configure a Server Monitor. To invoke the Exchange Administrator program, choose Start | Microsoft Exchange | Microsoft Exchange Administrator.

If you want to set up a monitor to keep track of the status of one or more Exchange Server computers, choose File | New Other | Server Monitor. You then can fill in the required and optional information in the link's Properties dialog, as shown in Figure 46.3.

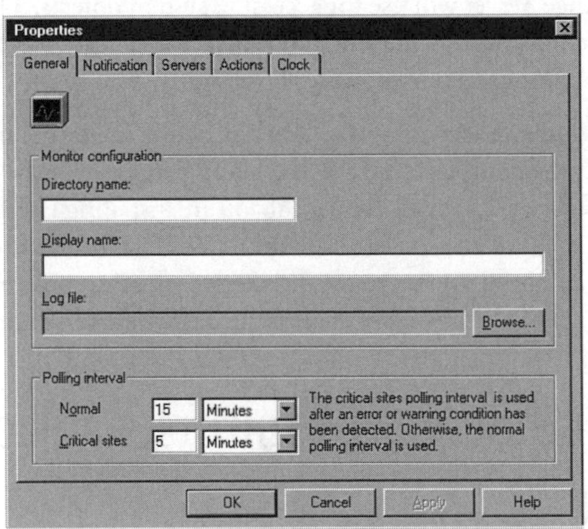

Figure 46.3. *You use the link's Properties dialog to name and configure a Server Monitor.*

The General Tab

The Properties dialog consists of five tabs that group information by function (refer to Figure 46.3). You select the General tab to specify a directory and display name for the monitor. A directory name (of up to 64 characters) is used for identification purposes by the system, and the display name (256 characters) is used for display purposes in the Administrator program's window.

You also can configure the monitor to create a log file. All communications performed by a Server Monitor are done by using RPCs. If you specify a path and filename for a log file, you will have a record of the results of all RPCs the monitor issues to the remote server(s). To add a filename, click the Browse button. Another dialog then appears that enables you to specify the path and filename to use for the log file.

The monitor will poll servers you specify using the time intervals you specify at the bottom of the General tab. You set the time in minutes, seconds, or hours that will elapse between each polling event.

The Notification Tab

Figure 46.4 shows the monitor's Properties dialog with the Notification tab selected. When you first use this tab, no notifications are listed in the When, How, and Who columns. You click the New button to add the information needed to produce a notification for the monitor.

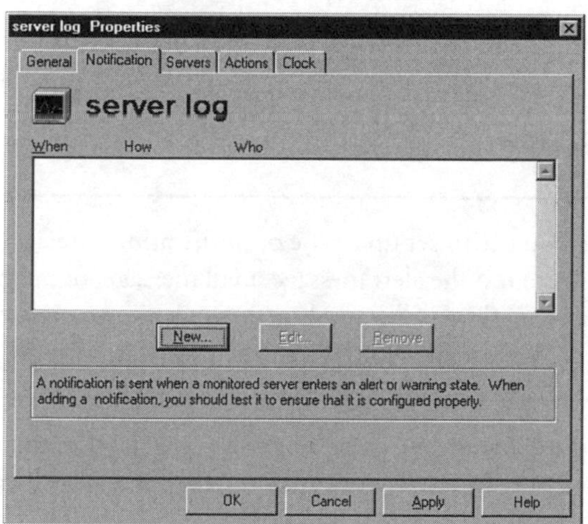

Figure 46.4. *The Notification tab of the Properties dialog.*

The first thing you need to specify for a notification is the type of notification. After you click the New button, the New Notification dialog appears, as shown in Figure 46.5. Here, you can choose to send an alert, send a mail message, or start a process (a batch file or executable program) to provide notification of a warning or alert.

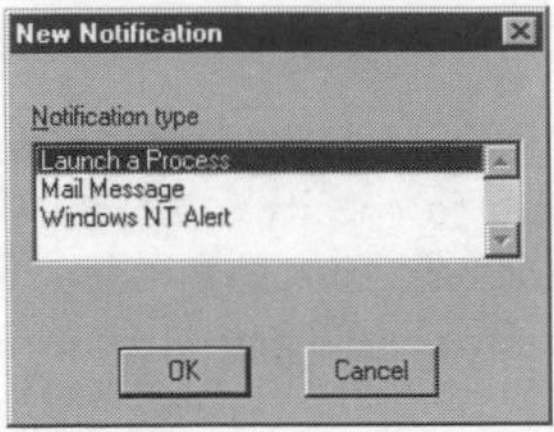

Figure 46.5. Using the New Notification dialog to select the type of notification used.

If you want to display an alert message when notification of an event is required, select Windows NT Alert from the New Notification dialog and click OK. The Escalation Editor (Windows NT Alert) dialog appears, as shown in Figure 46.6. Here, you enter the name of the computer on which you want the alert message to be displayed. If you use this type of notification, the target computer must be booted and a user must be logged on to that computer. Otherwise, the alert messages will not be displayed.

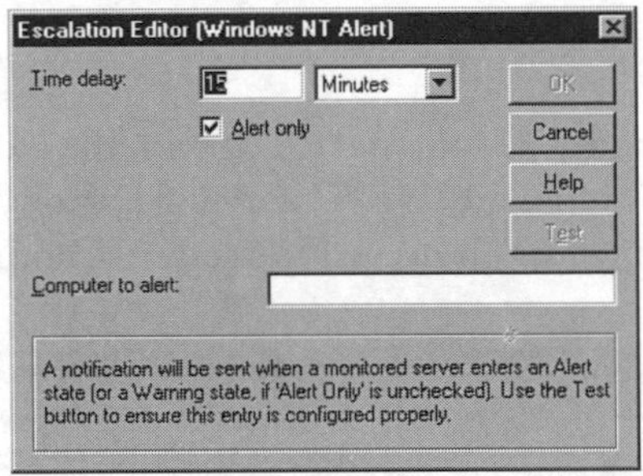

Figure 46.6. Entering the name of the computer that will be notified when an alert occurs.

> **Tip:** Each dialog you use to set up a type of notification offers a Test button. Use it! This button enables you to test the alert message, mail message, or program launch to make sure that the notification method will work. You do not have to wait until an event occurs to find out whether you have correctly configured the notification!

In the Escalation Editor dialog (and the dialogs discussed later in this section), you can enable the Alert only checkbox if you want to have only alerts sent via this notification method. If you disable this checkbox, both warnings and alerts will be sent. A *warning* usually indicates a small problem, such as when a target computer's clock has drifted from the correct time by a small amount. An *alert* is issued when a serious problem occurs, such as a service stopping or a system clock drifting a significant amount from the correct time.

If you decide that an alert message is not sufficient (remember that alerts don't work if the computer is down or no one is logged on to the target computer), you might want to use the mail-messaging capability of the monitor. Choose Mail Message from the New Notification dialog. The Escalation Editor (Mail Message) dialog, shown in Figure 46.7, appears.

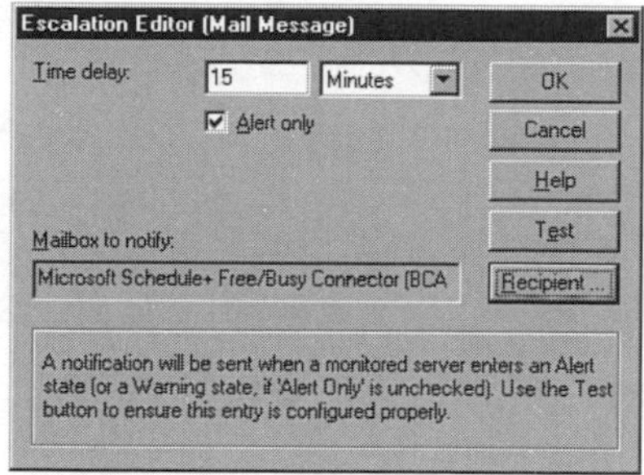

Figure 46.7. *Click Recipient to add usernames that will receive mail messages when an alert occurs.*

> **Tip:** Each type of notification (mail, application, and alert message) enables you to set a time interval to be used for that particular notification. You can use the Time delay field to issue more than one alert of the same kind for a particular event. This way, you can notify a primary user (or computer) when an event occurs and then create staggered notifications that, after a longer period of time elapses, notify the next person on your contact list, and so on; this chain of notification is called an *escalation path.*

If a user already has been selected to receive messages, the username appears in the Mailbox to notify field. If you want to add or change the user to be notified, click Recipient. The Recipient dialog appears, as shown in Figure 46.8. Here, you can select the mailbox to which you want the message to be sent. You can type the name of a valid Exchange user mailbox, or you can select one from the list. You also can click Properties to view more information about the mailbox that you select. Figure 46.9 shows the Properties dialog for the selected user; as you can see, Exchange enables you to store a large amount of information about a user.

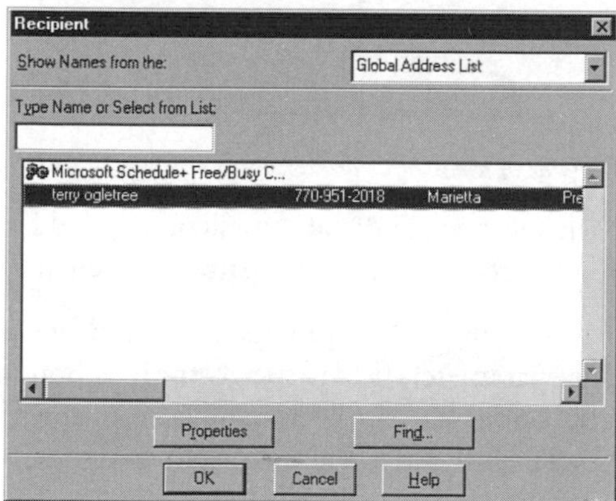

Figure 46.8. *Selecting the user's mailbox to be the target for any monitor messages.*

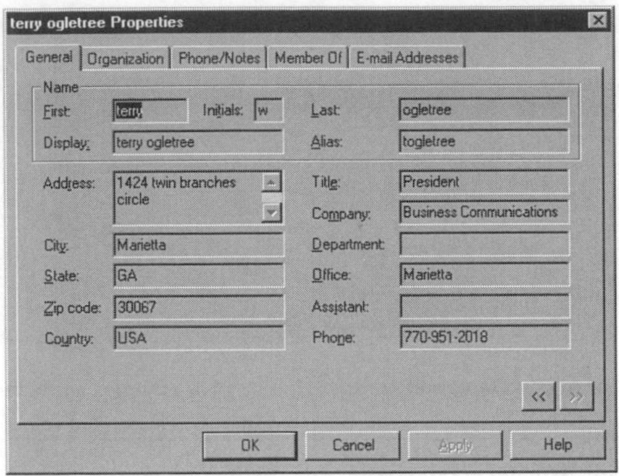

Figure 46.9. Viewing the properties of the selected user's mailbox.

Finally, you can choose to have a process started when an alert occurs by choosing the Launch a Process selection in the New Notification dialog. The Escalation Editor (Launch Process) dialog appears for you to enter the necessary information, as shown in Figure 46.10.

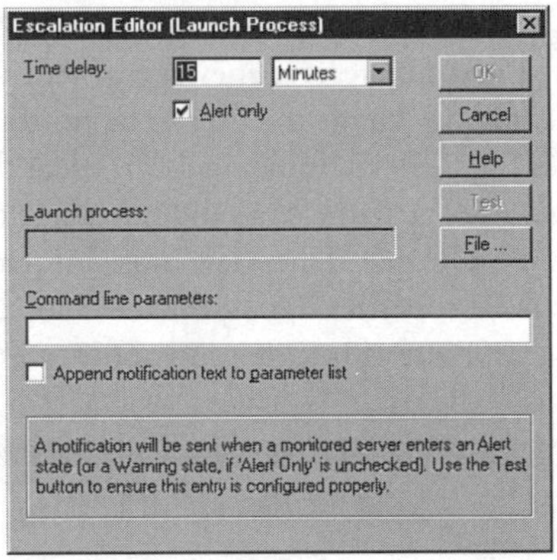

Figure 46.10. Configuring the name of a batch file or executable program to be launched when an alert occurs.

To specify a path and filename, click File (the Launch process field is a display-only field). A dialog appears that enables you to browse and select a path and filename.

In the Launch Process dialog, you also can provide command-line parameters to the process. You can use the Command line parameters field to specify the telephone number to be used by a paging program, for example. Also, if you enable the Append notification text to parameter list check box, any text generated by the alert is added to the text specified in the Command line parameters field. This might be useful if you use an executable program to update a data file to keep track of selected alerts, for example.

Of all the notification methods available, the Launch a Process method is the most flexible. You even could simulate the Mail Message and Windows NT Alert methods by using the Launch a Process method. You should analyze the impact a warning or alert will have on your network and decide on the best method (or methods) of notifying one or more users.

Tip: You don't have to choose just one of the three types of notification. Indeed, you can set up all three types of notification to be sure that someone gets the message!

The Servers Tab

The Servers tab of the monitor's Properties dialog enables you to select the servers to be monitored by this Server Monitor, as shown in Figure 46.11. The process of selecting servers is simple. On the right side of the Properties dialog, you see a list of monitored servers. To add a server, click any server listed on the left side of the display (in the Servers list) and then click Add. To remove a server from the Monitored servers list, select the server name and click Remove.

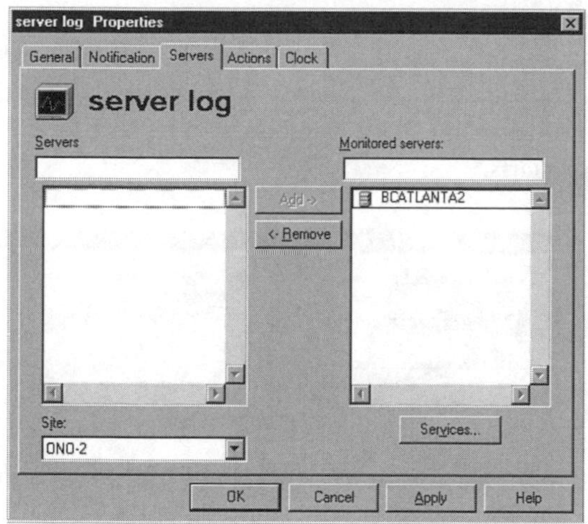

Figure 46.11. *Specifying the servers the monitor will watch.*

You also can choose to view servers from another site in the organization by using the Site drop-down listbox in the bottom-left corner of the Properties dialog.

After you select the server, you can click Services to access the Services dialog for the selected server. Here, you can add or remove services that are running on the target server from the Monitored services list. To choose a service, highlight it by clicking it in the Installed services list, and then click Add. To remove a service from monitoring, select the service in the Monitored services list and click Remove. When you are done adding or removing servers, click OK to return to the Servers tab.

Note: If you use the Servers tab to select a server and do not specify any services to be monitored, the services for the Directory Information Store and the MTA are monitored by default. You can use the Exchange Administrator's Link Monitor function, however, to monitor *any* service that runs under Windows NT Server—not just Exchange services.

By choosing which services you want to monitor on any server for which the Server Monitor is responsible, you can eliminate annoying messages about processes that are not essential to your network's operation and focus instead on just the critical processes.

The Actions Tab

The previous sections discuss how to set up a Server Monitor and how to select who will be notified about what kind of event. Because services running on an Exchange server are critical processes, the Server Monitor enables you to specify actions to be taken when a service is found to be stopped by the monitor. Note that you still have to use the Servers tab to select the servers and services to be monitored.

You use the Actions tab to specify what type of action to take when a service is stopped, as shown in Figure 46.12. You can specify that no action be taken if you have set up notification and are confident with that. Or, you can select to have the service restarted or the computer rebooted. You also can set the restart delay and specify a message to be sent to any logged-on users before the service or computer restarts.

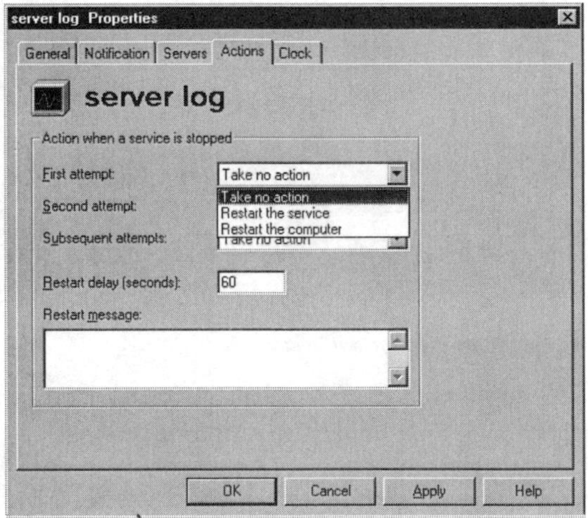

Figure 46.12. *Deciding which action will be taken when one of the servers/services enters the stopped state.*

The Clock Tab

The final tab on the Server Monitor's Properties dialog is the Clock tab, as shown in Figure 46.13. Here, you can specify the amount of seconds that a targeted server's system clock can be off from the correct time (or the system time of the polling server) before a warning or alert is issued.

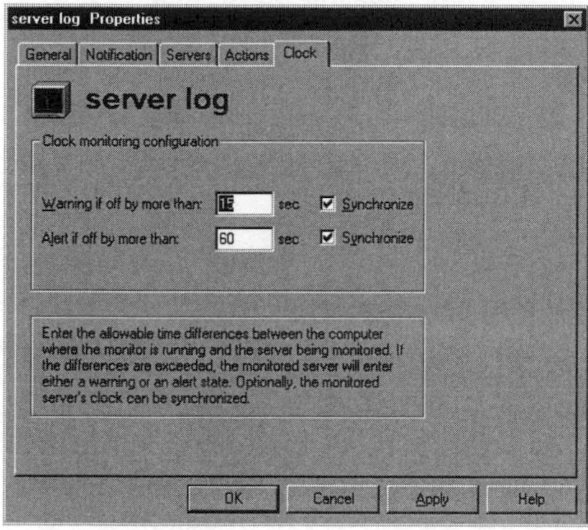

Figure 46.13. *Specifying the amount of time a target server's system clock can deviate from the polling server's clock.*

In addition to sending a notification, you can specify (using the Synchronize check box) that the polling server set the target server's time if it is incorrect by the time factor you specify.

Creating a Link Monitor

The monitors just discussed are for tracking events on servers in a site. Other important components in Exchange that need to be monitored are the various links you can create between sites. To set up a Link Monitor, choose File | New Other | Link Monitor. The Properties dialog displayed is similar to the Properties dialog used for the Server Monitor, with a few exceptions.

Note: The configuration information for a monitor is stored in the Exchange Directory component. The Directory is replicated at regular intervals to other servers in the site. For changes to take effect for a Link Monitor, you must stop and restart the monitor. Thus, if you want the Link Monitor to run on more than one server, and you want the changes you make to be reflected on all servers, you must wait until the Directory has been replicated and then stop and restart the specified Link Monitor.

The General tab of the Link Monitor Properties dialog is the same as the General tab of the Server Monitor Properties dialog. You only have to fill in the directory and display names to be used for the Link Monitor, the log file path (if any), and the polling intervals. In the case of a Link Monitor, the log file does not store RPC results, but instead stores changes to the status of the link and the notifications issued. This can be useful information in problem resolution. The Link Monitor does not poll remote systems for information. Instead, it sends test messages (called *ping messages*—not to be confused with the TCP/IP PING utility) to the servers you designate and monitors the round-trip time after a response is received.

The Notification and Servers tabs of the Link Monitor dialog are also the same as those of the Server Monitor. The Permissions tab does not appear by default—you use the Tools menu to make it visible:

1. Select Options from the Tools menu in the Microsoft Exchange Administrator.
2. Click the Permissions tab in the Options dialog box.
3. Select the checkbox titled Show Permissions page for all objects.

The Permissions tab will now appear in the Link Monitors Property dialog. When you no longer need to expose the Permissions tab, you can deselect the checkbox by using Tools | Options | Permissions. The Link Monitor dialog does not have a Clock tab, however, because time is a server function rather than a link function. There also is no Actions tab. The Link Monitor Properties dialog does offer two new tabs, though: Recipients and Bounce.

The Bounce Tab

You use the Bounce tab to set the amount of time the monitor waits for a response from a remote system before issuing a warning or alert. In Figure 46.14, you can see that the Bounce tab only requires you to enter these time values. You should test the amount of time it takes for a response from a remote system (by sending an undeliverable mail message and waiting for the non-delivery response) and adjust the warning and alert times according to your network's needs.

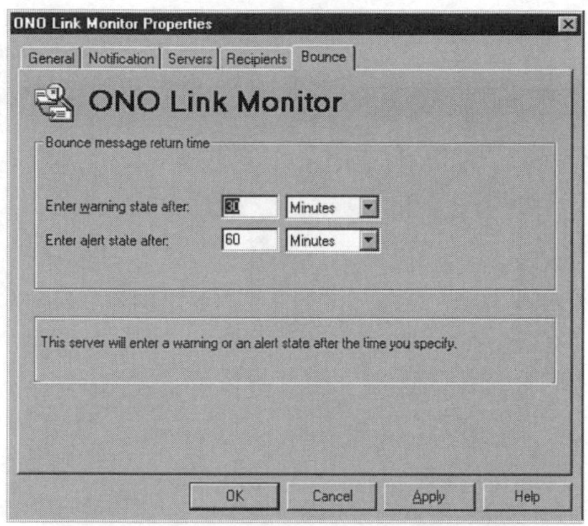

Figure 46.14. *Setting the warning and alert time intervals.*

The Recipients Tab

The Recipients tab is *not* used to indicate which users will receive notification of warnings or events from the Link Monitor. You perform that function by using the Notification tab, just like you do to configure a Server Monitor.

When the monitor needs to send a test message to a remote server, it sends a mail message to a user on that system. If the monitor is sending the message to another Exchange server, that server responds with an e-mail message that contains the same text in the Subject field that was in the Subject field of the original message.

You also can configure the Link Monitor to use the body of the message if necessary. This is useful when sending a message to a foreign system that does not respond with the original subject text in the Subject field. If you are dealing with many foreign systems, select a nonexistent username. An undeliverable mail message will be returned with the entire message (including the Subject field) contained in the body of the reply message.

Figure 46.15 shows the Recipients tab of the Link Monitor's Properties dialog; notice that you can use two distinct fields to add usernames. The list on the left (Message subject returned from) can be used with Microsoft Exchange servers, whereas the list on the right (Message subject or body returned from) can be used for systems that might return the Subject line in the Subject field or body of the mail message.

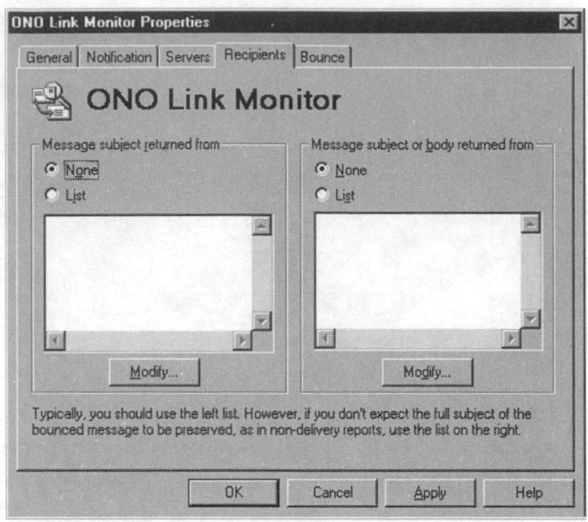

Figure 46.15. Specifying usernames to which test messages will be sent after the monitor verifies that a remote link is working.

To add usernames to either list, click the Modify button below the appropriate list. You then can browse for the usernames and select the ones you want to add.

Starting and Stopping Monitors

You can use the Exchange Administrator program to start and stop Link and Server Monitors. First, select a monitor from the Monitors directory entry in the main window of the Administrator program. Then choose Tools | Start Monitor. Figure 46.16 shows a display of a sample Server Monitor that has been started.

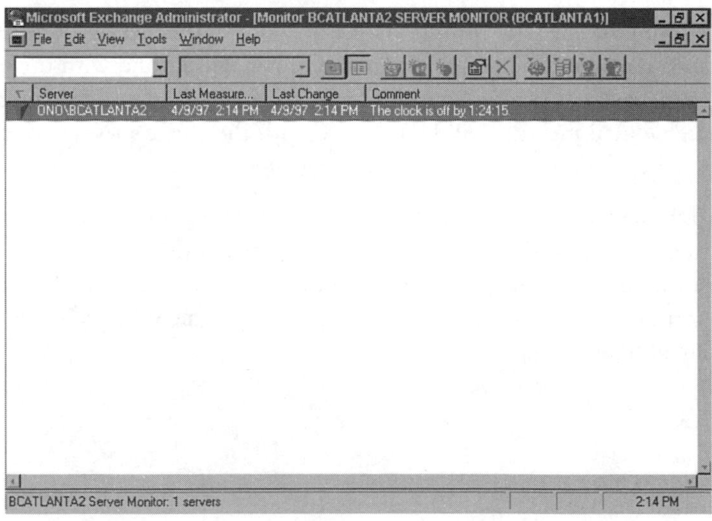

Figure 46.16. A Server Monitor that has been started.

In the far left column of the Server Monitor display, you quickly can evaluate the status of the server by the icon that appears. A question mark (?) indicates that the status of the server is unknown. Up and down arrows indicate that the server is up or down. If any component of the server being monitored is not functioning correctly, the server is considered to be down, and you should investigate further.

Other columns show the server that is being monitored, the last time the monitor polled the server, and the last time a change was made on the server (such as a time synchronization, if enabled).

Tip: If you double-click a monitor name, you can view the properties of that monitor. Figure 46.17 shows the properties for a Server Monitor. You can see the status of the Exchange services for the target server; you can even start, pause, or stop them. Other tabs on this Properties dialog enable you to view clock statistics, notifications, and other information.

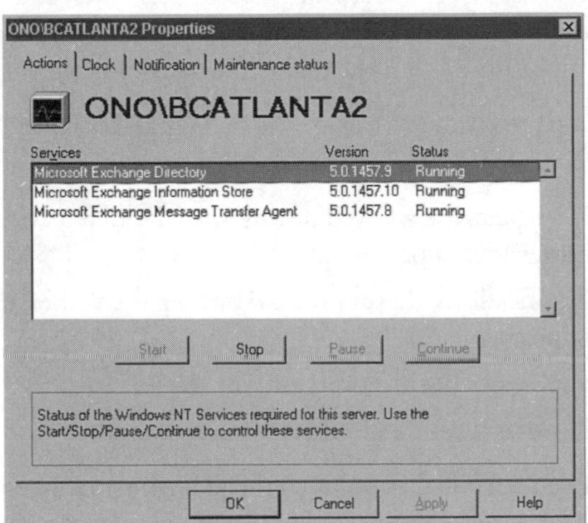

Figure 46.17. *The Properties dialog for a Server Monitor gives you a quick overview of the server and the configuration of the Server Monitor.*

Link Monitors show much the same information. The Server column shows the server to which ping messages are sent, the Last Measurement column shows the last time a ping message was sent, and the Last Change column shows the last time the status of the connection being monitored changed. The Last Time column shows the actual time it took for the last ping message to make the round trip. You can use this value to fine-tune the timing parameters you set for the link.

The Comment field for a Server Monitor can tell you several things:

- `Not measured yet`: A ping message has not yet been sent.
- `The link is operational`: All is OK, according to the measurement parameters you set. The ping message was returned from the target server in the allowable time.

- `Bounced mail took (time)`: Although the ping message was returned, it took longer than the threshold time you configured.
- `A message was due on (time)`: The last ping message sent has not been returned, and the time limit has expired.
- `Not monitored yet`: Ping messages have been sent but not yet returned. The time limit has not yet expired, however.

To stop a monitor, you do not use the Tools menu as you do to start a monitor. Instead, you simply close the monitor window. Remember that monitors run only when you are logged in and start the monitor.

The Command-Line Admin Program

If you are going to take a server down for maintenance or repair and do not want a Link or Server Monitor to generate warnings or alerts for that computer, you can use the command-line version of the Exchange Administrator program, Admin, to temporarily suspend notifications or repairs (such as fixing the clock time) until the maintenance is finished.

To execute the Admin program, you can use the following command-line options at the command line or in a batch file to specify the action the Admin program should take:

`-r`	No repairs are allowed during the Maintenance mode. Notifications, however, will be sent.
`-n`	Notifications are suppressed, but repairs will be carried out. (This is the opposite of `-r`.)
`-nr`	Suppresses notifications and repairs.
`-t`	Restores monitors to their normal operating mode.

Because computers that can poll the computer that is having maintenance performed on it can have different polling time periods set, you should be sure to issue the correct `Admin` command before the server is made unavailable. You then should wait until all polling servers have been able to poll the server undergoing maintenance. Otherwise, if the server is taken down and the polling servers have not been updated, warnings and alerts are issued for the nonresponding server.

Restarting Monitors Automatically After Reboot

If you want the monitors to start automatically after a system is rebooted, you can do it in several ways. The easiest way is to place the Admin program into the Startup group and provide command-line parameters that start the monitors you want to run. To place a program into the Startup group, follow these steps:

1. Click the Start button and choose Settings | Taskbar.
2. From the Taskbar Properties dialog, select the Start Menu Programs tab, as shown in Figure 46.18. Then click Add. The Create Shortcut dialog appears.

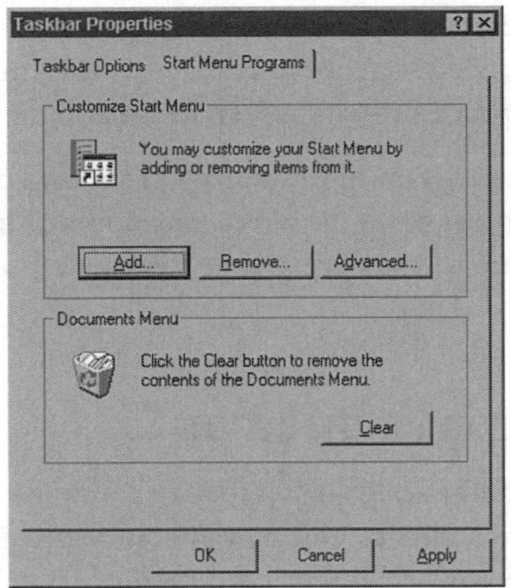

Figure 46.18. *Adding programs to the Startup group.*

3. You can enter the commands necessary to start the Admin program in the Command line field and then click Next, or you can click Browse to find the Admin program.

   If you click Browse, you quickly can locate the Admin program in Exchange's `\BIN` directory.
4. After clicking the Admin program, click Open.
5. The Create Shortcut dialog appears with the Admin program listed in the Command line field.

   You can add a few parameters to the command line to start a monitor. You use the `/m` parameter to designate a monitor name and the server on which it is to run. For example, you could enter the following command:

   ```
   c:\exchsrvr\bin\admin.exe /mAtlantaLink1\BCAServer1
   ```

   Be sure to use the directory name for the monitor instead of the display name. Click Next to continue.
6. The Select Program Folder dialog appears next. Scroll until you find the Startup folder. Select it and click Next.
7. The next dialog prompts you to enter a name for the shortcut. Provide a name that will be meaningful to you when you browse the Start menu. You might want the name to include a hint as to the monitors it is starting. Click Finish.
8. You return to the Start Menu Programs dialog. Click OK.

In these steps, the command-line option should be in exactly the same syntax you would use to run the program yourself from the command prompt. You also can place more than one `/m` parameter on the command line if you separate each instance with a space. If you use this method, you can use one command line to specify a number of monitors that should be started when the system reboots.

The only problem that remains to be solved before you can have monitors start automatically is that of a username. In order for a monitor to run, a user must be logged in to the computer. Monitors run as normal processes—not as services that hide in the background.

You can place the Admin program in the Startup group and configure the appropriate monitors to start. Then, after a user logs on to the server, the monitors begin their monitoring activity. Or, if you need your monitors to start every time a server reboots, you can enable the server for automatic logon.

Setting Automatic Logon for the Server

If you want a server to automatically log on to a user account after it reboots, you can specify the parameters needed for this action by editing values in the Registry, or you can use the Autologin utility included in the Windows NT Server 4.0 Resource Kit. The Resource Kit utility makes the same edits, but it is helpful because it prevents you from making any errors when you are editing the Registry.

To set up the server for automatic logon by editing the Registry, follow these steps:

1. Start the Registry Editor at the command prompt by typing the following and then pressing Enter:

   ```
   c:\> REGEDT32.EXE
   ```

   This command brings up the graphical interface to the Registry Editor, as shown in Figure 46.19.

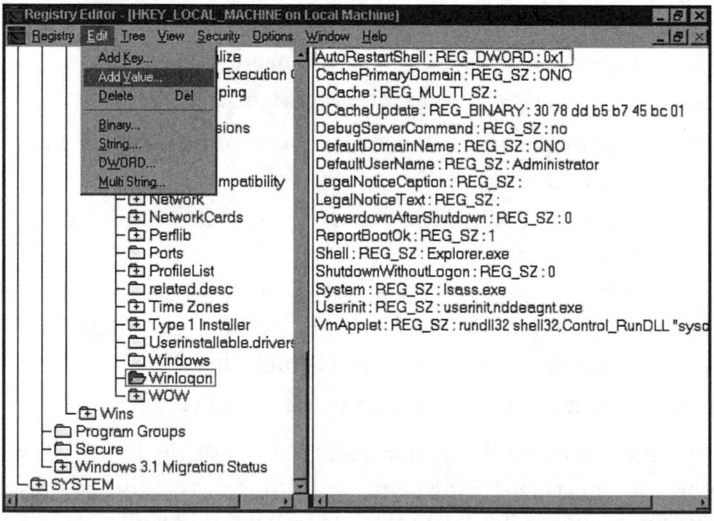

Figure 46.19. *Using the Registry Editor to locate specific entries in the Registry so that you can add or edit values.*

2. Select the HKEY_LOCAL_MACHINE window.
3. Locate the subkey `SOFTWARE\Microsoft\WindowsNT\CurrentVersion\Winlogon`.
4. If the entry `AutoAdminLogon` is available, double-click it to edit it. If `AutoAdminLogon` does not appear, choose Edit | Add Value.

   In the Add Value dialog, enter the name `AutoAdminLogon`, as shown in Figure 46.20. For the Data Type field, select REG_SZ from the drop-down list. Click OK.

   Whether you have just created the `AutoAdminLogon` value or you just double-clicked it, the String Editor dialog appears, as shown in Figure 46.21.
5. In the String Editor, enter the value `1` in the String field and click OK.

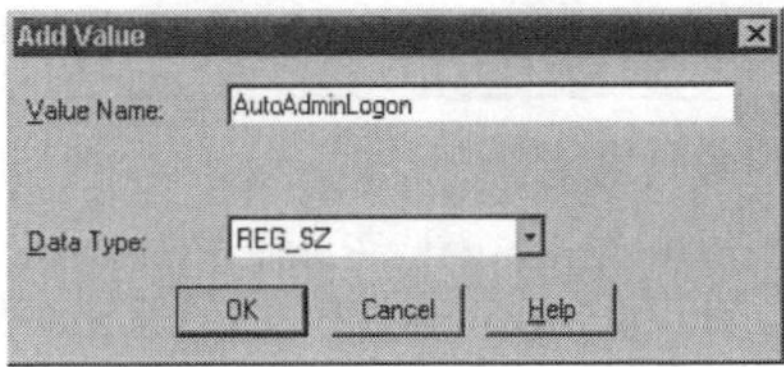

Figure 46.20. *Using the Add Value dialog to add values.*

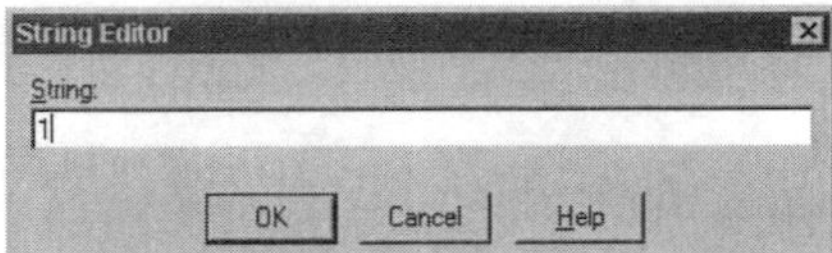

Figure 46.21. *Using the String Editor to set the* `AutoAdminLogon` *value to* `1`.

6. Next, select the value `DefaultUserName` by double-clicking it. This will once again bring up the String Editor, and the user account stored in this value should be present in the String Editor. To accept the current value, click the OK button. To change it, click the String field in the dialog box, enter a new user account, and then click OK.
7. To set the password to be used for the default user account, choose Edit | Add Value. Enter the name `DefaultPassword` in the Value Name box. Select REG_SZ as the datatype. When the String Editor appears, enter the password in the String field and click OK.
8. If any text has been entered for the following values, you must remove it before the automatic logon can occur:

   ```
   LegalNoticeCaption
   LegalNoticeText
   ```

   To remove the values for these entries, double-click each value and use the String Editor to erase it.
9. Exit the Registry Editor (exit from the Registry menu) and log off the system to test the automatic logon.

Caution: You should be extra-careful in how you set up security on the server that you configure for automatic logon. Any user who has permission to view the Registry keys used for automatic logon can see the default username and password by using the Registry.

Also, any user can log off the computer from the keyboard and log on as another user by pressing Shift as the computer boots (or when the user logs off). If a user bypasses the automatic logon in this manner, the username used for the logon is assigned to the `DefaultUserName` Registry parameter. Therefore, when the user finishes and logs off, the password stored in the Registry will not match the new `DefaultUserName`, and the automatic logon will fail.

In the case of a high-availability system, you should be sure that the computer enabled for automatic logon also is physically secured against the unknowing or unwitting user.

If you have the Windows NT 4.0 Resource Kit, you can use the Auto Logon utility to make the Registry entries for you. Because editing the Registry can be a dangerous thing to do (one wrong step and you can render the computer unbootable), using the Auto Logon utility seems to be a wise choice. To run the utility, choose Start | Programs | Resource Kit 4.0 | Configuration | Auto Logon. Figure 46.22 shows the dialog for the Auto Logon utility that appears.

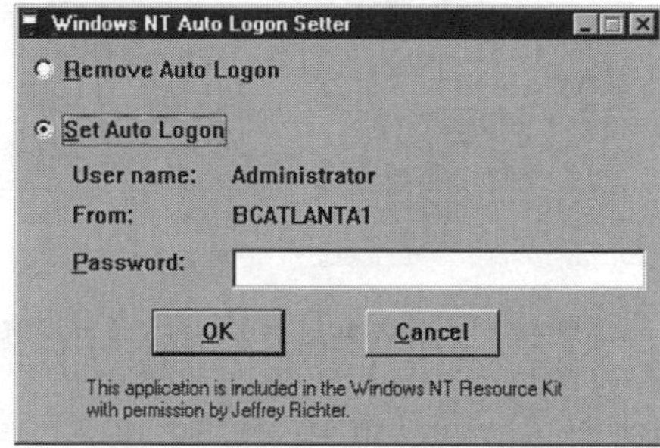

Figure 46.22. *The Auto Logon utility from the Resource Kit makes editing the Registry safer and simpler.*

All you have to do is select Set Auto Logon and fill in the password. Because this utility only allows you to enter the password for the user who is currently logged on, you must log on to the account before you run the utility.

You can select Remove Auto Logon to disable the Automatic Logon feature.

Using Exchange Objects and Counters for the Performance Monitor

Chapter 36, "Windows NT Troubleshooting Utilities," covers the problem-solving tools that are part of the Windows NT operating system. You can refer to that chapter for a complete overview of the Performance Monitor tool. This chapter discusses only the objects and counters that relate to performance optimization and troubleshooting for Exchange Server.

Objects and Counters

The Performance Monitor tracks and reports on selected aspects of discrete system components called *objects*. For the purpose of this discussion, an object can be a process, a section of shared memory, or an actual physical device. For each object, a set of *counters* is defined to track relevant aspects of the operation of the object.

You can use the Performance Monitor to examine data related to the operation of the Processor object, for example. More than 10 counters are associated with the Processor object. The Processor Time counter associated with the Processor object displays the percentage of time during which a processor is busy executing a non-idle thread. The Interrupts/Sec counter shows the number of device interrupts the processor is experiencing.

When you use the Event Viewer to examine System log files, you can review only records for events that you have chosen to audit. You can select to write audit records to the Security log file when users log on and off, for example. You first must set this up through User Manager for Domains (choose Audit | Policies). After you select events to be sent to the log file, you can use the Event Viewer to examine them.

When you use the Performance Monitor, you do not have to perform any setup tasks for the many counters that can be reviewed, with the exception of counters for disk-related objects. Instead, you simply open the Performance Monitor application, choose Edit | Add to Chart, and then select the objects/counters you want to view by pointing and clicking. The Add to Chart dialog appears, where you can select objects/counters to add to the chart, as shown in Figure 46.23.

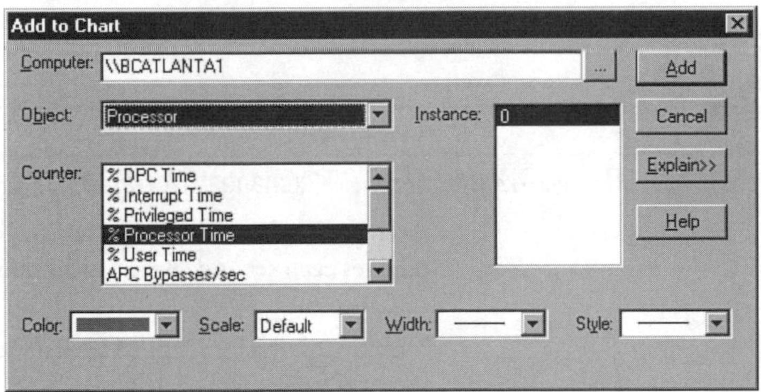

Figure 46.23. Selecting counters to be graphed on the chart.

Note: Activating counters for disk-related activities can place a small burden on the system. For this reason, disk-related counters are disabled by default. If you experience problems that you think might be related to disk performance, you can enable the disk counters by using the DISKPERF command:

```
DISKPERF [-Y[E] ¦ -N] [\\computername]
```

You can use the following command-line parameters to control the action of the `DISKPERF` command:

- `-Y` When the system is rebooted, normal disk counters are activated.
- `-E` When the system is rebooted, counters used for measuring the performance of physical disks used in striped disk sets are activated.
- `-N` When the system is rebooted, all disk counters are disabled.

After you activate the disk counters and reboot the system, you can use the Event Viewer to select disk-related objects and their associated counters.

If you are using the Chart view for the Performance Monitor, each counter you select is plotted on the chart using a different color. You can select the colors or let the Performance Monitor assign them for you. A legend is located at the bottom of the main display window of the Performance Monitor (Chart view) that shows each color and the counter it represents.

Exchange-Related Objects and Counters

In addition to the objects and counters automatically activated by the operating system and the disk counters, you will find that a host of new objects have been added on servers that are running Exchange Server. The easiest way to determine what each counter does is to click Explain in the Add to Chart dialog. Table 46.1 lists some of the most commonly used objects and counters with Exchange.

Table 46.1. Exchange-related objects and counters.

Counter	*Description*
Message Transfer Agent (`MSExchangeMTA` Object)	
Messages/Sec	Average number of messages the MTA sends and receives each second. A statistical sampling—not an actual count.
Queue Size	Number of objects in all MTA queues sent to and received from each connection.
Work Queue Length	Number of messages waiting in MTA queues to be processed by the MTA or delivered to other servers.

Counter	*Description*
Directory **(`MSExchangeDS` *Object)***	
Pending Replication Synchronization	Number of unanswered synchronization requests received by the directory.
Remaining Replication Updates	Number of outstanding updates for synchronization to be applied to this directory. If `0`, synchronization is complete.
Information Store **(`MSExchangeISPriv` *and* `MSExchangeISPub` *Objects)***	
Average Time for Delivery	An average of the time spent by the last 10 messages waiting in the Information Store before being delivered to the MTA.
Average Time for Local Delivery	An average of the time the last 10 local messages spent while waiting for delivery to a mailbox found in the same Information Store (local).
Logon Active Count	Number of users who have performed some kind of server activity within the last 10 minutes.
Logon Count	Number of clients currently logged on to the Information Store.
Messages Delivered/Min	Average of the number of messages delivered to the Information Store (both local and from the MTA).
Message Recipients Delivered/Min	Average of the number of messages sent divided by the number of recipients of those messages.
Messages Sent/Min	Average of the number of messages sent to the MTA from the Information Store for delivery to other systems.
MS MAIL CONNECTOR **(`MSExchange MSMI` *Object)***	
File Contentions/Hour	Number of times an Exchange component tries to write exclusively to a keyfile in use by another component.
LAN/WAN Messages Moved/Hour	Hourly number of messages moved by the MS Mail Connector (PC) MTA.
Messages Received	Number of messages received by Exchange.

continues

Table 46.1. continued

Counter	*Description*
***Internet Mail Connector* (`MSExchangeIMC` *Object*)**	
Inbound Messages Awaiting Conversion	Total count of messages from the Internet Mail connector waiting to be converted to the format used by Exchange.
Inbound Messages Awaiting Delivery	Number of messages received (from the Internet connector) and converted that are waiting in an Information Store queue for processing by the MTA.
Outbound Messages Awaiting Conversion	Number of messages from Exchange waiting to be converted to Internet format by the connector.
Outbound Messages Awaiting Delivery	Number of Exchange messages the Internet connector has received and converted, waiting for delivery to the Internet.
Total Internet Messages Delivered	Number of messages delivered to the Internet by the Internet connector since it was started.
Total Messages Transferred to Exchange	Total number of messages (since the Internet connector was started) that have been received, converted, and placed in the MTS-In queue in the Information Store awaiting processing by the MTA.

Using Exchange Built-In Performance Monitors

When you choose Programs | Microsoft Exchange, you can see that—in addition to the Admin program, crystal reports, Help files, and Migration Tool—many options are available. Each of these utilities brings up a version of the Performance Monitor that has been configured to chart selected object counters (which are related to the name of each utility). These preconfigured Performance Monitors can be excellent troubleshooting tools in themselves. You might find that using these utilities helps you understand the interaction between various objects and counters so that you can create your own charts using the full Performance Monitor tool.

Table 46.2 lists the Performance Monitor Server utilities and the counters they display.

Table 46.2. Microsoft Exchange Server Performance Monitor utilities and counters.

Utility	*Counter*
Health	% Processor Time (for the main Exchange services, including the total processor time used by all services, expressed as a percentage of the whole; see Figure 46.24)
History	User Count Work Queue Length (MTA) Pages/sec (memory)
IMS Queues	Queued Inbound (IMC) Queued MTS-IN (IMC) Queued MTS-Out (IMC) Queued Outbound (IMC)
IMS Statistics	Inbound Messages Total (IMC) Outbound Messages Total (IMC)
IMS Traffic	Messages Entering MTS-Inbound (IMC) Messages Entering MTS-Outbound (IMC) Messages Leaving MTS-Outbound (IMC) Connections Inbound (IMC)
Load	Message Recipients Delivered (Public) Message Submitted/Minute (Public) Adjacent MTA Associations (MTA) RPC Packets/sec AB Browses/sec AB Reads/sec ExDS Reads/sec Replication Updates/sec
Queues	Work Queue Length (for the MTA) Send Queue Size (Private) Send Queue Size (Public) Receive Queue Size (Private) Receive Queue Size (Public)
Users	User Count

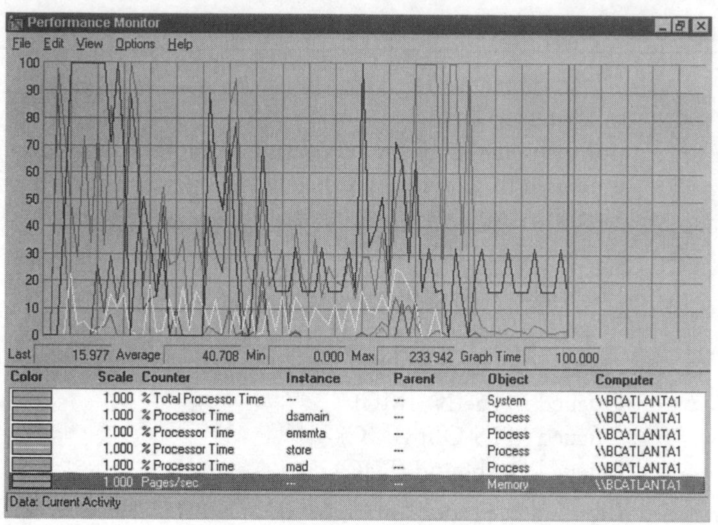

Figure 46.24. *Using the Health utility to chart the processor time of various Exchange components.*

Diagnosing Problems Using the Event Viewer

You can configure Exchange server to write records to the System Event logs based on a severity level that enables you to filter the types of events to be logged—specifically, Exchange write records in the Application Event log.

You can enable diagnostic event logging for each component by using the Diagnostics Logging Properties dialog for each component. Figure 46.25 shows the Diagnostics Logging tab for the MS Mail Connector Properties dialog.

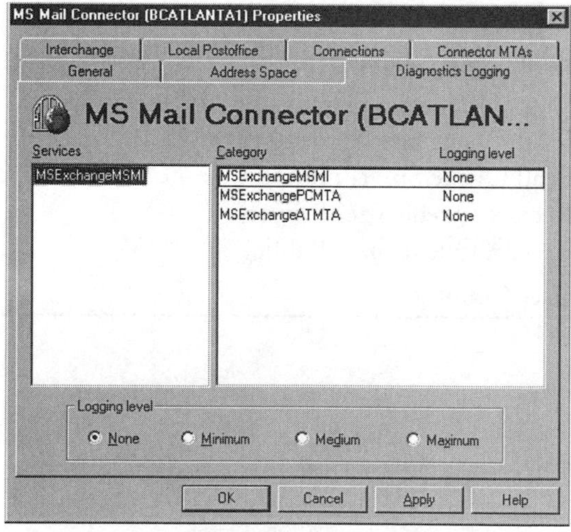

Figure 46.25. *Setting the level of diagnostic logging by using the Diagnostics Logging Properties dialog for each component.*

The Diagnostics Logging tab of a component's Properties dialog is similar for all components, with the exception of the Microsoft Schedule+ Free/Busy connector. The services that perform functions for the component are listed in the Services box. On the right, you will see a box that has two columns: Category and Logging Level. Each category consists of a group of functions that are related to each other. The Security category for a particular component, for example, logs any event considered a security function by the component if you set a logging level for the security component. You can decide which categories for any (or all) components you want to log event records for and set each category to the logging severity level that is sufficient to help you diagnose problems.

To change the logging level for a category, select the category and then choose from the buttons at the bottom of the dialog to set the logging level.

For some categories, you can set the logging level to cause the component to generate text log files in addition to the event records written to the Windows NT System log files. By setting the appropriate values for certain categories in the MTA component, for example, you can generate Interoperability and ADPU text log files. If you set the correct values for the SMTP category for the Internet Mail connector, you can create an SMTP log file.

You can view or modify the level of diagnostic logging for all components at the same time by using the Diagnostics Logging Properties dialog for the server itself, as shown in Figure 46.26.

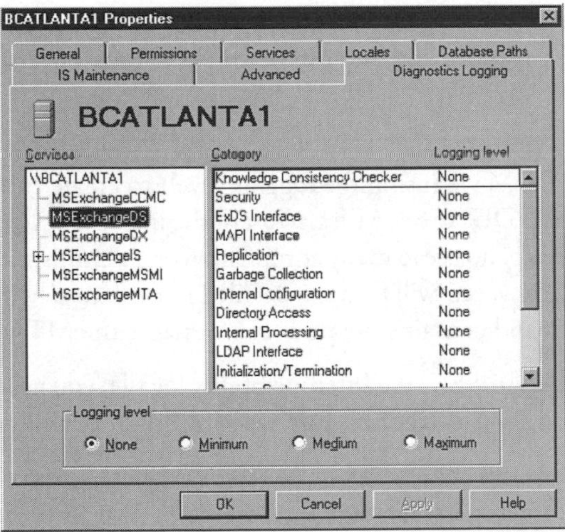

Figure 46.26. *Using the Diagnostics Logging Properties dialog for the server to set the logging level for all components.*

Because the amount of information that can be recorded in the Event logs can become quite voluminous, it is a good idea to set the logging level for all components to None (zero) when you first set up your Exchange Server. When set to zero, only critical events and error events are recorded in the Event logs. Table 46.3 lists the values you can use to set the logging level.

Table 46.3. Exchange Server logging severity levels.

Level	*Description*
None (0)	This is the default. Only critical events and error events are written to the file.
Minimum (1)	This selection should be used when first starting your troubleshooting effort. Instead of logging a lot of detailed records, only one or two records are logged for each major task that generates an error.
Medium (3)	This level causes more detailed events to be written to the log. Each of the basic steps performed by a service or task can generate a record.
Maximum (5)	You should rarely ever have to set diagnostic logging to this level. All possible event records that Exchange can generate are written to the log files as they occur. This level generally is used when conducting troubleshooting with the Microsoft Support team.

Because a level of 0 still catches all severe errors and writes the minimum number of records to the Event log files, it is the default level. When trying to narrow down a problem to a specific service or program, you first should consider increasing the diagnostic level to 1 and then possibly to 3 if further refinement is necessary.

Tip: Remember to reset the diagnostic level back to 0 when you finish. Depending on the activity on your server, the log files can become full rather quickly when you use values of 3 or 5.

You can configure the MTA (using the logging level) to create Interoperability and *Application Protocol Data Unit* (APDU) text log files. Most of the information logged to these files is of a very technical nature and is of no use to many administrators. Administrators who have experience with the X.400 protocol, however, will find the detailed information helpful, because the information is in a binary format and contains the protocol messages the MTA has transported.

To configure the MTA to create the Interoperability log file, you need to set the diagnostic logging level for two of the MTA's categories: Interface and Interoperability.

To log protocol messages sent between MTAs on different servers (and between MTAs and applications) to the Interoperability log, set the logging level of the Interoperability and Interface categories to Medium. If you want to add the messages passed between the MTAs and gateways to your log file, set both values to Maximum.

Note: Setting a value for the Interoperability category has no effect on messages logged to the System Application Event log. It only affects the creation of the text log files.

Interoperability logs are stored in the `MTADATA` directory. The naming convention for the files is `AP48.LOG`, where the current log is `AP0.LOG` and older logs have a non-zero digit.

To configure the MTA to create the APDU log file, you need to set the diagnostic logging level of the X.400 service and APDU categories.

If you set this level to Minimum, the following APDU events are logged to the text file:

- `Bad APDU transferred in from another MTA` (event 200)
- `Bad APDU submitted to this MTA` (event 220)
- `APDU delivery failed temporarily` (event 269)
- `APDU delivery failed permanently` (event 270)

If you set the value of the X.400 service and APDU categories to Maximum, two additional types of events are logged to the APDU log file:

- `APDU sent` (event 271)
- `APDU received` (event 271)

There is no difference between the Minimum and Maximum logging level for the APDU category, and setting a level for this category only affects logging to the APDU text log file. Setting a logging level for the X.400 Service category affects events that are written to the System Application Event log and the types of events recorded in the APDU text log file.

You can create SMTP log files by setting the logging level of the SMTP category for the Internet Mail connector. The type of records written to the text file depend on the logging level you set for the category, as listed in Table 46.4.

Table 46.4. Logging levels for the SMTP category.

Level	*Description*
None	The default for the category. No text log files are generated.
Minimum	Only connection information is logged to the text file.
Medium	SMTP commands and headers also are written to the text log file.
Maximum	Unformatted protocol packets are written in their entirety to the text log file.

The SMTP log files are written to the directory `\EXCHSRVR\IMCDATA\LOG`. Each concurrent connection produces a separate log file in this directory.

When troubleshooting problems with SMTP and the Internet connector, you also can set the logging level of the Message Archival category to Medium or Maximum to write a copy of each message (both inbound and outbound) to a text file. The messages are written to the directories `\IMCDATA\IN\ARCHIVE` and `\IMCDATA\OUT\ARCHIVE`.

The MS Mail connector differs from the other applications in that the logging level is set by subcomponent rather than category. The Schedule+ Free/Busy connector also differs from the other components in that it does not use categories; instead of four logging levels, it uses the six levels shown in Table 46.5.

Table 46.5. Schedule+ Free/Busy connector logging levels.

Level	*Description*
None (0)	Only critical events and error events are logged.
Minimal (1)	The same as None for the Free/Busy connector.
Basic (2)	The number of messages received and information messages created are added to the events that are logged.
Extensive (3)	The number of changes made and the names of users who receive messages from the Free/Busy connector are added to the events that are logged.
Verbose (4)	The same as Extensive for the Free/Busy connector.
Internal (5)	All events are written to the Event log. This includes configuration changes, unknown address notifications, and validations of accounts.

Tracking Down Lost Messages

If you have problems with mail not being delivered, you can use the message-tracking feature of the Exchange server to help locate which component is causing the error. You first have to enable message tracking for each component, which causes tracking information to be written to a log file that is re-created each day: `\EXCHSRVR\TRACKING.LOG`. When you decide to track message(s), the log files must be present for the days that you intend to search. In other words, if you want to track messages, you need to enable message tracking for each component you want to search later. Only components of Exchange used for mail handling can be used for message tracking:

- MTA
- Information Store
- MS Mail connector

Note: Message tracking is enabled by component, not by server. If you enable message tracking for any component at a site, message tracking is enabled for that component on all Exchange servers in the site.

You must restart each component after you enable tracking before it takes effect. This means that you have to restart the component on each server in the site before tracking begins. If you enable tracking for the MTA, for example, you must stop and restart all MTAs at the site.

Enabling Message Tracking for the Information Store

You must enable message tracking for each component responsible for handling mail messages. To do this for the Information Store, you use the Exchange Administrator utility. Follow these steps:

1. Double-click the Configuration entry in the main window of the Administrator program. On the right side of the screen, the Display Name window should now contain many configuration entries for this site.
2. Double-click the entry named Information Store Site Configuration.
3. Select the General tab on the Information Store dialog.
4. Click the Enable Message Tracking checkbox to select it.
5. Restart the Information Store on each server at the site; you must do this before tracking can start.

Enabling Message Tracking for the MS Mail Connector

Enabling message tracking for the MS Mail Connector is also a simple thing to do. Remember that you must enable tracking for each component in order to get a complete history of the route the message can take through your system. To enable message tracking for the MS Mail Connector, follow these steps:

1. Double-click Connections in the main window of the Administrator program. On the right side of the window, you will see connectors for your site listed in the Display Name window.
2. In the Display Name window, double-click the MS Mail connector.
3. Select the Interchange tab.
4. Click the check box labeled Enable Message Tracking to select it.
5. Restart the MS Mail connector component.

Tracking a Message

After you enable message tracking for one or more of the components, and daily log files are created, you can use the Track Message option to locate messages. Follow these steps:

1. Bring up the Admin utility (Start\Microsoft Exchange\Microsoft Exchange Administrator).
2. Choose Tools | Track Message. The Connect to Server dialog box appears. Enter the name of a server to connect to or use the Browse button to locate the server.

   The first thing you must do to track a message is to find an instance of it in the server's log file. After you identify the message, the tracking utility locates other instances of the message in log files for all other servers in the site.

3. The Select Message to Track dialog appears, as shown in Figure 46.27. Here, you can specify the originator and recipient(s) of the mail message.

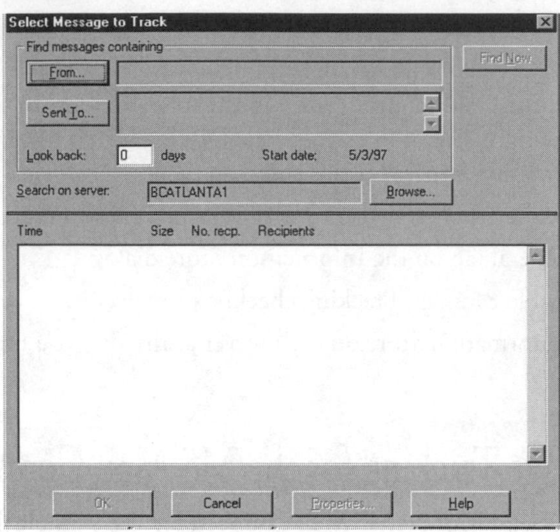

Figure 46.27. *Using the Select Message to Track dialog to specify the search criteria to find a message.*

4. Click From to specify the originator of the message. A dialog appears that you can use to browse the Global Address List to locate the originator, as shown in Figure 46.28.

   You can click Properties to view details about the user you select to be sure you are selecting the right username, and you can click Find to quickly locate a name.
5. Click Sent To. A dialog appears that enables you to select the recipients of the message, as shown in Figure 46.29.

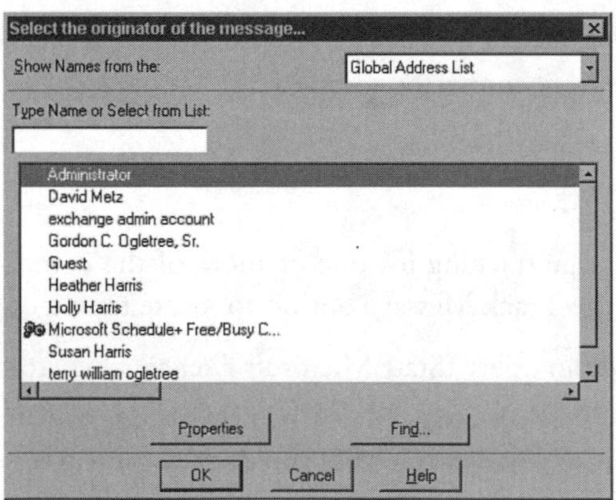

Figure 46.28. *Browsing the Global Address List to find the originator of the mail message to be tracked.*

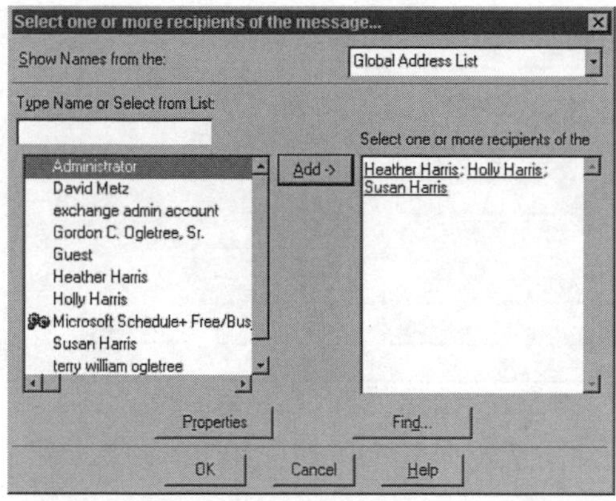

Figure 46.29. Selecting one or more recipients to which the message was directed.

6. Select the username from the left-hand box (Type Name or Select from List) and click Add to place the name into the right-hand box (Select one or more recipients of the ...). Then click OK.

   You are returned to the Select Message to Track dialog.

7. (Optional) In the Look Back field, enter the number of days previous to the current date that the utility will go back to search log files for the message.
8. To begin the search, click Find Now.
9. (Optional) Double-click an event that is listed in the Select Message to Track dialog to view details about the event (which functions were performed in reference to the message by the component that logged the information).
10. Select a message by double-clicking it; the Message Tracking Center dialog appears, as shown in Figure 46.30.

    Each line in the Tracking history box shows one segment of the path the message travels to get to its destination.

11. You can select any of the events in the Tracking history box and then click Properties to view more details.

When you track a message and find that it does not get to the recipient, you can check the message queues (of the MTA, Internet Mail Connector, and/or the MS Mail connector) to see whether the message still remains. To check the queues for these connectors, select Queues in the Properties dialog for the specific component.

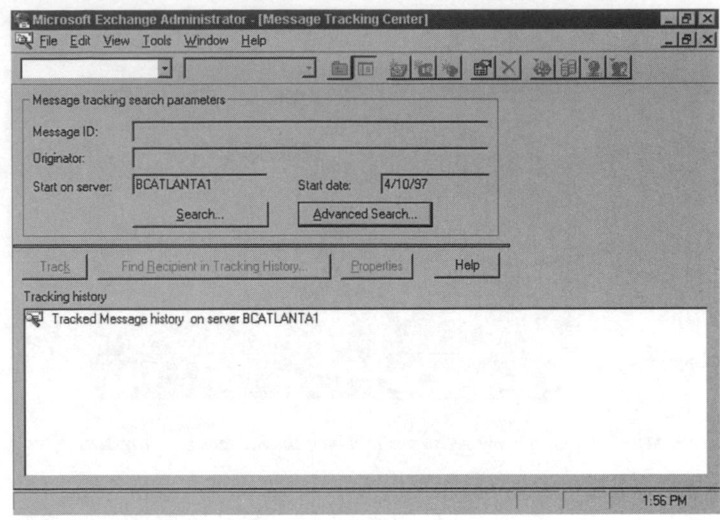

Figure 46.30. *Viewing the path of the mail message you are tracking.*

Summary

This chapter covered some of the basic utilities you can use to help solve problems you might encounter when using Microsoft Exchange. You can use the Windows NT utilities, such as the Event Viewer and the Performance Monitor, as well as Exchange-specific utilities, such as the Message Tracking utility.

To better prepare yourself for troubleshooting activities, it always is best to start out with an in-depth knowledge of the layout of your organization and network. Using this knowledge along with the tools described in this chapter can help you quickly locate problems.

Microsoft Exchange includes other utilities in the Exchange `\BIN` directory. For a description of these, see Chapter 17 of the *Microsoft Exchange Administrators Guide.*

SNA Server

by John West

Microsoft's SNA Server is the component of Microsoft BackOffice suite that gives network clients of Windows NT and other network operating systems easy access to legacy SNA systems such as IBM's AS/400 and mainframes. In this chapter, you will explore the following topics:

- SNA Server 2.11 and the features that make it one of the best gateway products on the market
- SNA gateways and the history of their development
- The benefits of using SNA Server
- The hardware you need to make SNA Server work for you
- The new features offered in SNA Server 3.0

Purpose

In the 1980s, users saw the rise and dominance of the mainframe and midrange computer. In the absence of network standards, IBM created the *Systems Network Architecture* (SNA) to allow communications between its mainframe and midrange systems. SNA uses the Data Link Communications (DLC) protocol for communications, and as long as you are communicating between midrange and mainframe systems, this works just fine.

In the mid-80s, the rise and growth of the *local area network* (LAN) began. Common protocols that were used on the LAN included TCP/IP, NetBEUI, and IPX/SPX. I did not mention DLC; that's because none of the more common *network operating systems* (NOSs) uses the DLC protocol to communicate file and application services across the network. DLC is used in a few cases to send data to printers but not for file and print services.

So, if DLC is not used by NOSs for most communications, what does this mean for people on LANs who want to have access to their company's AS/400 or mainframe? Well, to be able to get access to both the AS/400 and the LAN, the client has to install both a LAN protocol (TCP/IP, IPX/SPX, or NetBEUI) and the DLC protocol. The client then needs to bind these two protocols to the same network card. This method does not work very well; it usually leads to unpredictable freezing on the network client. Gateways were created to provide a more effective means of communicating with both the LAN and mainframe or midrange environments through the same network card.

Gateways enable network clients to run standard network protocols (TCP/IP, NetBEUI, and IPX/SPX) to communicate with the mainframe. The gateway acts as a translator between the LAN and the SNA network. Microsoft SNA Server is the component of Microsoft BackOffice that acts as a robust gateway application. This capability enables network clients to use Windows NT Server systems running SNA Server to communicate with a mainframe or midrange system using the common LAN protocols.

Features

SNA Server takes full advantage of the Windows NT operating system. It can work effectively as a stand-alone system or with the other components of the Microsoft BackOffice Suite. It can use the Windows NT 32-bit flat-memory model, integrate with a Windows NT security database, and take advantage of Windows NT multithreading and multiprocessing capabilities. Being tightly integrated with the Windows NT operating system also means that SNA Server has the same portable and scalable features of Windows NT. So, as the workload of your SNA Server increases, it can accommodate the growth by hardware upgrades and distributed network mechanisms.

SNA Server consists of two major components: the server and the client.

Server

The *server* component of Microsoft SNA is responsible for receiving all client and SNA requests and making sure that these requests are translated and forwarded to the proper recipient. When a Windows NT client makes a request to access resources on a mainframe, for example, the request is forwarded to SNA Server first. SNA Server translates the request into a language the mainframe can understand and sends the translated request to the mainframe. The same process occurs when the mainframe sends communications intended for clients.

SNA Server uses a number of features in the server component to provide consistent and reliable service:

- Load balancing
- Hot backup
- Multiprotocol support
- Flexible configuration models
- SNA Open Gateway Architecture
- Remote access support

These features are described in the following sections.

Load Balancing

Load balancing gives SNA an edge as a scalable application by enabling multiple SNA Servers to operate in the same domain to intelligently and transparently balance the number of client connections equally across all servers. As your network grows, you easily can add a new server to the network and watch it immediately take up an equal share of the client load.

Hot Backup

When accessing the mission-critical data that mainframes and midrange systems typically store, it is important that adequate fault tolerance is available to ensure that your system is available during critical times. SNA Server addresses this need by providing hot backup. *Hot backup* enables clients to dynamically switch servers in a failure situation. As shown in Figure 47.1, SNA Server accomplishes this task by creating a ghost connection to a backup server whenever a client connects to a server. If the server fails, the user at the client computer simply clicks the Connect button, and the client system instantly connects to the backup server.

Multiprotocol Support

To provide maximum support for clients of various platforms, SNA Server provides support for clients on most popular network protocols. As shown in Figure 47.2, this support is for clients using Windows NT, Windows 95, Windows for Workgroups, Windows 3.1, Mac OS, OS/2, and popular network protocols such as TCP/IP, IPX/SPX, NetBEUI, and AppleTalk. Because SNA Server uses Windows NT as its base platform, Microsoft enjoys the same capability of supporting multiple protocols simultaneously. IPX/SPX, TCP/IP, and NetBEUI clients therefore can access the system simultaneously.

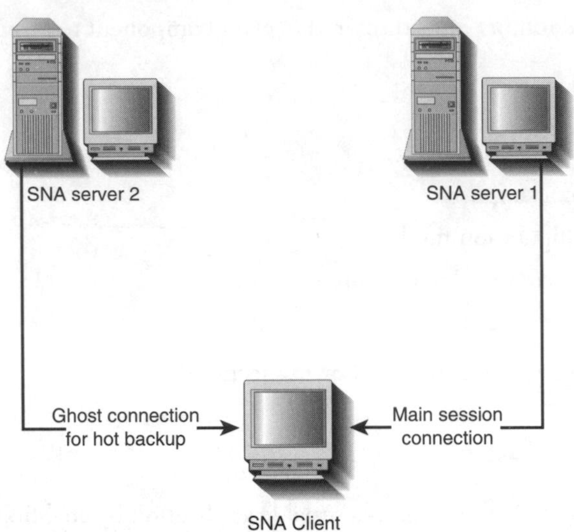

Figure 47.1. *SNA Server clients maintaining a hot backup connection.*

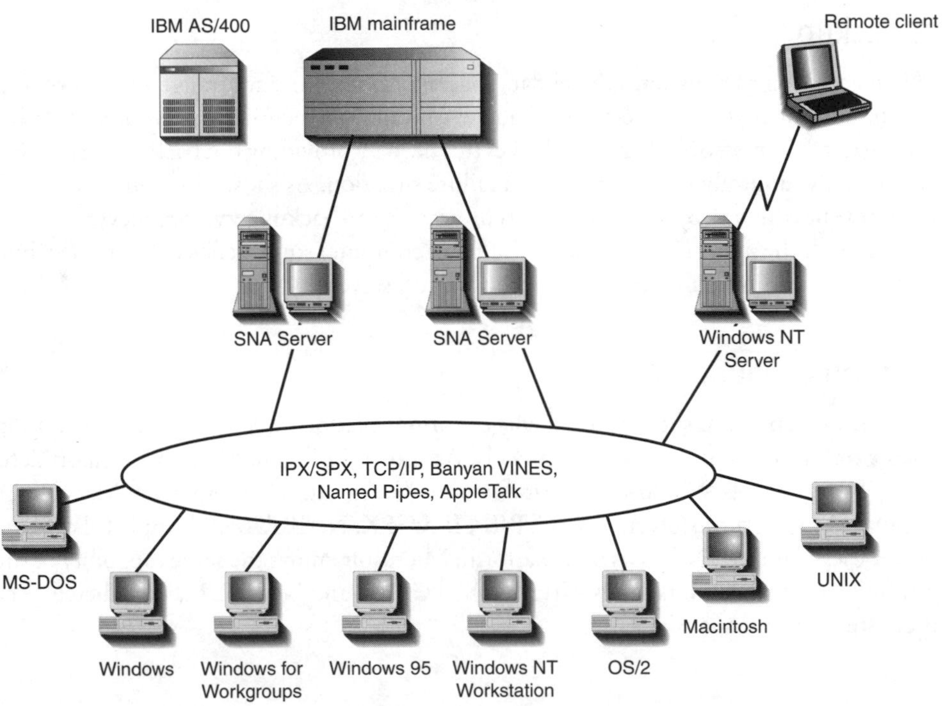

Figure 47.2. *The supported platforms of SNA Server.*

Flexible Configuration Models

Because of its flexible architecture and multiprotocol support, SNA Server offers a variety of configuration models. The models used most often by SNA Server consist of three basic configurations: the branch, centralized, and distributed models.

The Branch Model

The branch configuration, as shown in Figure 47.3, puts the SNA Server's physical location at the branch. This configuration can use SDLC lines or routers that support DLC switching. Each site server is capable of providing services other than SNA. File and print services and other application services can run on the same server with SNA Server.

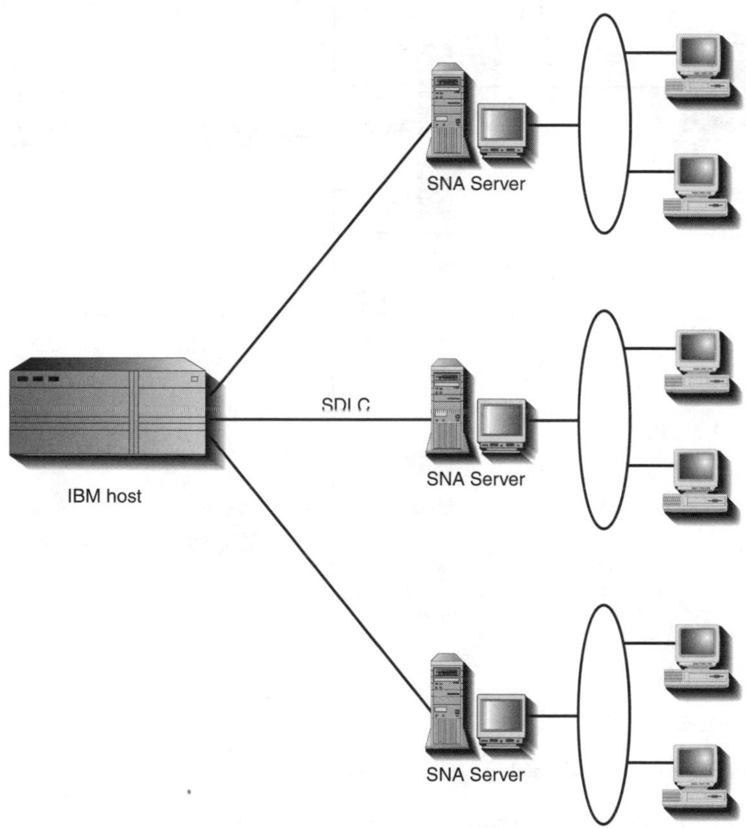

Figure 47.3. *The branch configuration.*

The branch model offers the following advantages:

- It reduces *wide area network* (WAN) traffic for services related to file or printing or other applications that otherwise might have been stored on a central site.
- It enables administration tasks to be performed at a remote site.

The branch model does have this drawback, though:

- ◆ It requires DLC switching to work over routers. This requirement generally inflates the cost of the routers.

The Centralized Model

Centralized configuration places all SNA Servers on the same physical network as the midrange or mainframe system. As shown in Figure 47.4, the remote sites run only a standard routable protocol across the WAN links. All client requests are sent across the WAN.

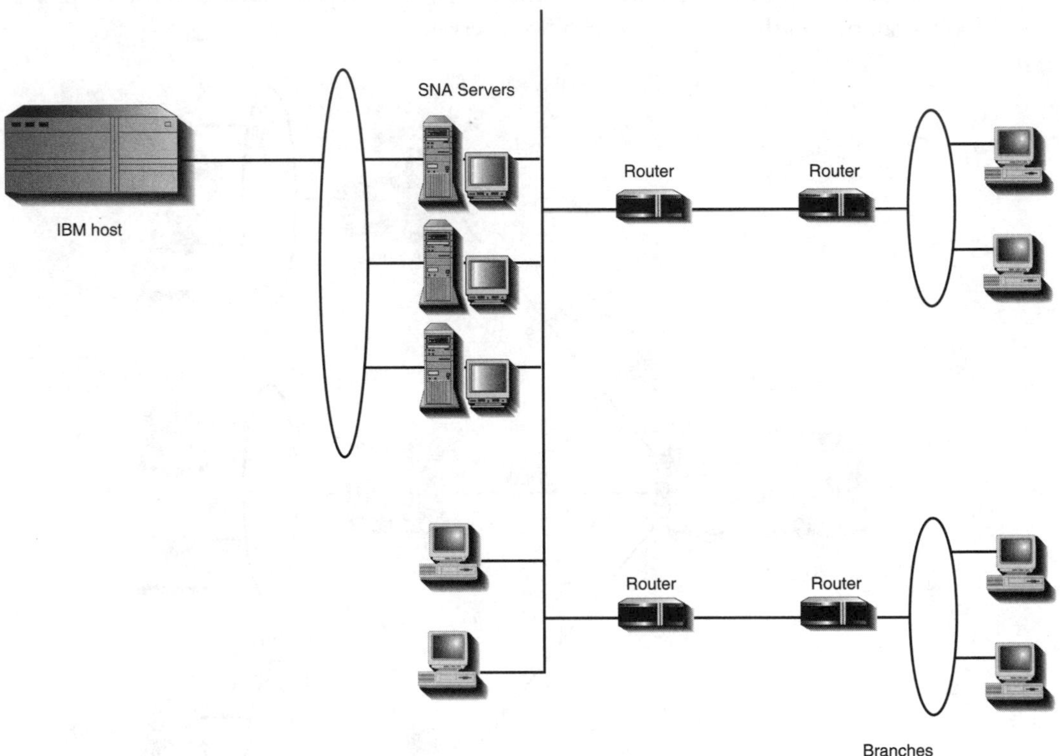

Figure 47.4. *The centralized model.*

The centralized model offers these advantages:

- ◆ It provides a central location from which to manage all servers.
- ◆ SNA Servers can take advantage of a high-speed channel attachment to the mainframe.

The centralized model does have this disadvantage, however:

- ◆ It increases data traffic across the WAN.

The Distributed Model

The distributed installation uses the recent *SNA Open Gateway Architecture* (SOGA is a standard that is covered in detail in the next section). The distributed model offers the best of both worlds: the branch model and the centralized model. Figure 47.5 shows an example of the distributed SNA Server installation concept. In a distributed installation, SNA Servers are located in the central locations and the branch offices. The branch offices use common LAN protocols such as TCP/IP to communicate with the SNA Servers at the central office. The SNA Servers at the central office then handle communications with the midrange or mainframe systems.

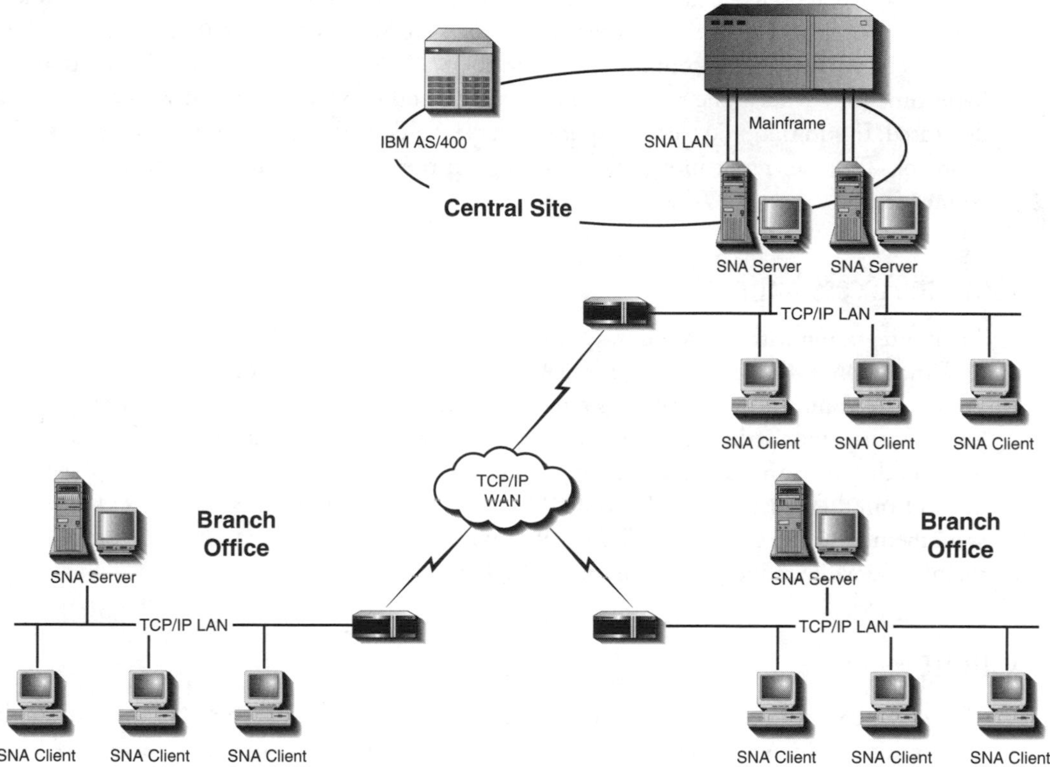

Figure 47.5. *The distributed model.*

The distributed model offers the following advantages:

- It isolates DLC traffic to the mainframe.
- It can use high-speed channel attachments to the mainframe.
- It reduces network traffic from file and print services, because the local server is capable of providing those services.
- It uses load balancing and hot backup.

The distributed model does have the following disadvantage, though: It is slightly more complicated to configure.

SOGA

SNA Open Gateway Architecture (SOGA) offers a unique advantage generally not provided by other vendors' gateways. SOGA enables you to set up SNA Server as a distributed model. The distributed model uses common network protocols across routers that enable SNA Servers to communicate with each other. As shown in Figure 47.5, the distributed model uses one or more servers located at the same site as the midrange or mainframe system. The model then uses at least one SNA Server at each of the remote sites. The remote SNA Servers use routable protocols such as TCP/IP or IPX/SPX to communicate with the SNA Servers at the central site. By doing this, login time for clients at the remote site is decreased and network traffic between the two sites is decreased. In addition, you are not required to have routers at the remote site that support the DLC protocol. This can result in significant savings in the cost of the routers and their associated connections.

Remote Access Support

Tight integration with the Windows NT operating system enables SNA Server to take advantage of Windows NT *Remote Access Server* (RAS). RAS enables clients to dial in to the network from a remote location and use network resources as though they were located on the network, including SNA Server. Suppose that you have field offices that are not large enough to qualify for a dedicated line, but they need to access the company's midrange or mainframe system. Your employees could dial in from their client system by using RAS and have access to the SNA services as though they were members of the network. This capability is very useful for providing access to the central mainframe while reducing costs on the dedicated circuits.

Client

The *client* component of SNA Server is responsible for encapsulating SNA calls from client applications and sending them via a common network protocol to the SNA Server. SNA Server accomplishes this task by using a client software component that must be installed on each SNA Server client. This client component receives all SNA configuration calls and ensures that they are converted to the proper protocol. The SNA client offers several features that make it a very successful component of SNA Server. These features include easy installation, support for a wide variety of client software, support for comprehensive application development, and troubleshooting tools.

Easy Installation

In general, the installation of the client component of SNA Server takes only a few minutes. The actual installation generally replaces a few key *dynamic link library* (DLL) files that most standard SNA programs use. SNA Server offers client software for MS-DOS, Windows, Windows 95, and Windows NT.

Support for Client Software

SNA Server has gained wide support from the client software industry. Client software generally takes the shape of emulation programs such as Wall Data's Rumba 5250 emulation package. Most of the recent emulation packages even include the SNA client as part of their installations.

Comprehensive Application Development Support

SNA Server offers a broad range of support for development *application programming interfaces* (APIs), including the following:

- APPC
- CPI-C
- LUA
- CSV
- EHLLAPI

These protocols are fully compliant with the *Windows Open Systems Architecture* SNA API standards. WOSA APIs give programmers a standard set of controls for creating applications. Following these standards produces applications that have a similar look and feel as other WOSA-based applications.

Troubleshooting Tools

Trace tools are provided in the client software to assist in any troubleshooting. The trace tools in SNA Server enable you to perform comprehensive traces on all components and communications between the SNA Server, SNA client, and SNA application. You can use these tools to quickly resolve problems in the software.

Features Summary

Now you have gotten a pretty good idea of what SNA Server is and what it has to offer. The following sections, provide a summary of the features offered in Microsoft SNA Server.

SNA PU and LU Protocols

The SNA environment describes systems as physical units (PUs) or logical units (LUs). This terminology is similar to the client/server terminology that describes devices on the LAN. *Physical units* describe server-like devices, such as a mainframe or a cluster controller. To a mainframe or AS/400, the server side of SNA Server appears as a physical unit.

Logical units describe client sessions; these can be printers or emulation sessions. With SNA Server, a client running a 5250 emulation server appears as an LU 6.2. This section summarizes the following PUs and LUs that SNA Server's client and server sides can appear as to the server:

PU 2.0
PU 2.1
APPN LEN node
DSPU
TN3270

LU 0
LU 1
LU 2
LU 3
LU 6.2

Data-Link Protocols

Data-link protocols are the languages SNA Server uses when communicating with mainframes or midrange systems through the various adapters that SNA Server supports. To communicate with an AS/400 via an Ethernet network, for example, SNA Server uses the 802.2 protocol. SNA Server can support a variety of adapter types. (A list of these adapter types appears later in this section.) The data-link protocols SNA Server supports follow:

802.2/LLC	Token Ring, Ethernet, or FDDI DLC connections
SDLC	Leased or switched telephone line connections
X.25/QLLC	Public or private packet-switched X.25 connections
DFT	Coaxial or twisted-pair connections via an IBM 3x74 cluster controller
Twinax	Twinaxial connections to an AS/400
Channel	Bus and tag or ESCON connections directly to a mainframe

LAN Protocols

As mentioned previously in this chapter, SNA Server offers support for a wide variety of LAN protocols. The supported protocols follow:

TCP/IP	Industry-standard LAN/WAN protocol
Named pipes/NetBEUI	Microsoft proprietary LAN protocol

IPX/SPX	Novell proprietary LAN/WAN protocol
Banyan VINES IP	Banyan proprietary LAN/WAN protocol
AppleTalk	Apple proprietary LAN protocol

Server Capacity

Windows NT's scalable and robust architecture enables SNA Server to support numerous clients and LU sessions. This flexibility gives SNA Server an edge on competitors products. SNA Server's capacities follow:

- Up to 2,000 clients per server
- Up to 10,000 LU sessions per server
- Up to 50 SNA Servers in a Windows NT Server domain configured for load balancing and hot backup
- Up to 250 connections per server, in any combination of upstream, peer-to-peer, and downstream
- Any combination of LU, PU, and data-link protocols concurrently

Distributed SNA APIs

For any platform to become successful, it must provide the tools that enable software makers to easily develop software for the platform. Microsoft provides access to every major SNA programming standard, including the following:

CPI-C, APPC	For peer-to-peer applications using LU 6.2 and EHNAPPC
CSV	For EBCDIC-to-ASCII conversion and communication with NetView
LUA	For direct access to LU 0, 1, 2, and 3 datastreams
EHLLAPI	For interfacing with 3270 or 5250 applications (offered by ISV emulators)

By providing these programming APIs, Microsoft provides the tools necessary to make SNA Server flexible enough to fit in just about any environment.

Administration

Easy setup, graphical support tools, and integration with Windows NT make Windows NT easy to support and administer. The features of the Microsoft Administration Set follow:

- Graphical setup, configuration, monitoring, and tracing tools
- Remote configuration across bridges and routers, via RAS, and from NetView

- Full dynamic tracing and self-diagnostics of APIs, SNA protocols, and connections
- Integration with Windows NT Event log, Performance Monitor, security, and service architecture

NetView

NetView is a system-monitoring and control console that runs on a mainframe or AS/400. SNA Server support for NetView enables SNA Server to send error messages to the NetView console. In addition, NetView operators can send commands through the console to be executed by SNA Server.

SNA NetView support includes the following features:

- API support for bi-directional communications
- Automatic data-link alerts for notification of communications problems
- A response-time monitor and user-defined alerts for ISV 3270 emulators
- Operator-configurable Windows NT Event log messages sent to NetView
- Any Windows NT Server command available from NetView console (`runcmd` support)

Reliability Features

As mentioned previously, SNA gateways are responsible for providing access to a company's mission-critical corporate data. Access to data this sensitive must be secure and reliable. SNA uses these features to provide the necessary security environment:

- Enhanced security through C2-level security integrated with Windows NT
- LU session load balancing and fault tolerance across SNA Servers and connections

RAS Support

SNA Server's capability to leverage Microsoft Windows NT RAS makes SNA Server a very flexible connection option. You also can use inexpensive modems or ISDN devices to act as SNA backbones. The RAS support includes the following:

- SNA over RAS, using Asynchronous, X.25, or ISDN
- RAS over SNA, using LU 6.2 protocol over SNA backbone

Included Utilities

To help you get started, Microsoft provides some basic emulation packages. These are single session packages that are really only meant to be used to test your connection to the mainframe or AS/400. In addition to the emulation packages, Microsoft includes an ODBC/DRDA driver.

This driver is necessary to provide access for client/server applications to the databases stored on the mainframe or AS/400. Microsoft also provides demo scripts that enable you to demonstrate connectivity. I have found this demo to be very useful when showing a client how easy it is to manage SNA Server. The utilities and tools that ship with SNA Server follow:

- 3270 applets for MS-DOS, Windows, Windows 95, and Windows NT clients
- 5250 applets for Windows, Windows 95, and Windows NT clients
- ODBC/DRDA driver for Windows, Windows 95, and Windows NT clients
- AFTP file transfer
- Demo host facility

Supported Emulators

Emulators act as miniature dumb terminals and operate in the framework of the client PC. 5250 emulation gives users access to systems such as IBM's AS/400. 3270 emulation is used to access most IBM mainframe systems. Emulator support is important for a gateway to be successful. SNA Server has support from most software vendors who create emulation packages, including the following:

5250	Andrew, Attachmate, DCA, Eicon Technology, IBM, Myrsis, NetSoft, Wall Data, WRQ
3270	Attachmate, DCA, Eicon Technology, Farabi, FutureSoft, IBM, Icot, NetSoft, Olivetti, Passport Communications, Siemens Nixdorf, Wall Data
TN3270	Any TN3270 emulator

Supported Adapters

By providing support for a variety of adapters, SNA Server easily can integrate into a number of environments. Supported adapters follow:

802.2/LLC	Any Token Ring, Ethernet, or FDDI adapter supported by Windows NT
DFT	Attachmate, DCA, IBM
Twinax	Andrew, IBM
Channel	Barr Systems, Bus-Tech
SDLC, X.25/QLLC	Atlantis, Attachmate, Barr Systems, Cirel, DCA, Eicon Technology, IBM, MicroGate, Passport Communications

SNA Server 2.11 Versus SAA 2.0

Microsoft's SNA Server has one major competitor: NetWare's SAA. SAA 2.0 provides many of the same features that SNA Server 2.11 offers. SAA is missing a couple of major components, however, including the following:

- No support for hot backup
- Licensing by session
- No graphical installation utility
- No built-in performance-monitoring tools

These drawbacks are discussed in the following sections.

No Support for Hot Backup

SAA does not provide support for hot backup for the AS/400 out of the box. In the event of a system failure, you might need to take the time to remove and add a new server before the system comes back online and operational. In a mission-critical environment, such a configuration can lead to catastrophic failures.

Licensing Is Available by Session Only

Microsoft offers very flexible client-licensing schemes. Users are given two choices for licensing: by seat or server.

For SAA, the only option is to purchase a group of sessions. Each session represents an emulation session for the printer or display. This means that each client might use as many as two sessions just to be fully operational, and that does not include any additional sessions that might be incurred from users opening additional emulation sessions. This drawback can be quite costly.

No Graphical Installation Utility

The installation of SAA is nongraphical and cumbersome. You must navigate your way through a series of text-based menus before the installation is complete. You also are responsible for making sure that you have DLC bound to your network card.

SNA Server uses a graphical user interface and provides many of the parameters necessary to get the system running. If SNA Server does not detect the DLC protocol, it gives you the option to install the protocol as part of the SNA Server installation process.

No Built-In Performance-Monitoring Tools

Because of its tight integration with Windows NT Server, SNA Server can use the Performance Monitor built in to Windows NT to monitor performance of the SNA Server. This capability enables network administrators to keep an eye on how the system is running. It also enables administrators to plan accurately for future upgrades. Novell NetWare does not offer these types of tools out of the box.

SNA Server 2.11 Versus SAA 2.0: A Summary

Table 47.1 lists the differences between SAA 2.0 and SNA Server 2.11.

Table 47.1. SAA 2.0 versus SNA Server 2.11.

	SAA 2.0	*SNA Server 2.11*
	Installation and configuration tools	
Setup	Character-based	Graphical. Context-sensitive help. Familiar Windows Help format.
Configuration	Not graphical for 5250. Graphical for 3270. Separate tools for configuration and monitoring.	Graphical SNA Admin. Single tool for configuration and monitoring.
Trace tools	Not dynamic—requires server stop and restart. Character-based.	Dynamic, graphical.
Local and remote administration	Character-based. CSSTATUS utility running under the MS-DOS operating system. Works with the IPX/SPX protocol but not TCP/IP. Separate tools for configuration and monitoring.	Graphical SNA Admin. Single tool for configuration and monitoring. Any Windows Windows NT computer. Any client-to-server LAN protocol.
Internal error diagnostics	No	Yes
Reconfiguration	Not dynamic. Requires an SAA server to stop and restart.	Dynamic changes without requiring a server restart. Includes adding or removing LUs, adding or removing groups, adding LUs to pools, and adding or removing user access rights.

continues

Table 47.1. continued

	SAA 2.0	*SNA Server 2.11*
	Desktop connection options	
IPX/SPX	Yes	Yes
Native TCP/IP	Yes. Requires emulator upgrade.	Yes
NetBEUI	No	Yes
802.2 DSPU	Yes	Yes
Banyan VINES IP	No	Yes
AppleTalk	Yes	Yes
Remote desktop	Yes	Yes
	Desktop API support	
MS-DOS	LU1, LU2, LU3, LU6.2, TN3720, DSPUAPPC, CPI-C	LU0, LU1, LU2, LU3, LU6.2, TN3720, TN3270E, DSPUAPPC, CPI-CLUA, RUI, LUA SLI
Windows	LU0, LU1, LU2, LU3, LU6.2, TN3270, DSPUAPPC, CPI-CLUA RUI	LU0, LU1, LU2, LU3, LU6.2, TN3720, TN3270E, DSPUAPPC, CPI-CLUA RUI, LUA SLIODBC/ DRDA
OS/2	LU1, LU2, LU3, LU6.2, TN3270, DSPUAPPC, CPI-C	LU0, LU1, LU2, LU3, LU6.2, TN3720, TN3270E, DSPUAPPC, CPI-C, LUA RUI, LUA SLI
NetWare	LU6.2, DSPU, APPC, CPI-C, LUA-RUI	DSPU
Macintosh	LU1, LU2, LU3, TN3270	LU1, LU2, LU3,TN3720, TN3270E
UNIX	TN3270	TN3270, TN3270E
Windows 95	LU1, LU2, LU3, TN3720, DSPU	LU0, LU1, LU2, LU3, LU6.2, TN3720, TN3270E, DSPUAPPC, CPI-CLUA RUI, LUA SLIODBC/ DRDA

	SAA 2.0	*SNA Server 2.11*
	Desktop API support	
Windows NT	LU1, LU2, LU3, TN3270DSPU	LU0, LU1, LU2, LU3, LU6.2, TN3720, TN3270E, DSPUAPPC, CPI-CLUA RUI, LUA SLIODBC/ DRDA
SDK included with product	Available separately	Yes. Open, published APIs. IBM SNA and WOSA.
Desktop API support	SAA 2.0	SNA Server 2.11
MS-DOS	APPC, CPI-C	APPC, CPI-C
Windows	APPC, CPI-C, EHNAPPC	APPC, CPI-C, ODBC/ DRDA, EHNAPPC
OS/2	APPC, CPI-C	APPC, CPI-C
NetWare	APPC, CPI-C	None
Windows 95	None	APPC, CPI-C, ODBC/ DRDA, AFTP
Windows NT	None	APPC, CPI-C, ODBC/ DRDA, AFTP
SDK included with product	Available separately	Yes. Open, published APIs. IBM SNA and WOSA.
	Integration with OS	
Command-line facility	Yes. NetWare command lines can be used to start, stop, and restart a NetWare for SAA NLM or host connection.	Yes. The Windows NT NET command line provides extensive capabilities to start, stop, and query status on SNA Server services.
User database and security	Yes. Requires bindery emulation to be turned on for all NetWare servers providing validation of access rights to SAA. Minimal integration with NetWare 4.1's NDS optional single logon to multiple SAA servers if deployed in a single tree.	Yes. The central Windows NT domain user database and users/groups security profiles provide validation of rights to access all SNA Server resources.

continues

Table 47.1. continued

	SAA 2.0	*SNA Server 2.11*
	Integration with OS	
Events	Separate character-based utility.	SNA Server is integrated with the graphical Windows NT Event Viewer.
Performance	Separate character-based utility.	SNA Server is integrated with the graphical Windows NT Performance Monitor.
	NetView support	
Alerts	Forwards predefined set of alerts to NetView. Forwarding additional alerts involves programming. Forwards gateway link alerts to NetView.	Forwards any Windows NT event to NetView as an alert simply by editing a familiar `INI` file. Forwards gateway link alerts to NetView. Displays RTM data in Performance Monitor.
`RunCmd`	Predefined set of commands supported.	Any Windows NT command-line statement can be executed remotely from a host NetView console as an `NVRunCmd`.
RTM	Forwards client and gateway RTM data to NetView.	Forwards client and gateway RTM data to NetView. SNA Server link alerts, RTM data, and 3270 applet RTM data are viewable on any Windows NT Workstation-based or Windows NT Server-based computer using the graphical Performance Monitor.
	Server capacity	
Max # host sessions per server	2,000 for mainframe 1,500 for AS/400	10,000
Max # users per server	2,000 (at 1 session per user)	2,000

	SAA 2.0	*SNA Server 2.11*
	Server capacity	
Max # PUs per server	32	250
Max # concurrent physical connections	10	250
Max # of servers grouped for load balancing	35	15
Max # of servers grouped for hot backup	2 (to avoid cost of additional licenses)	15
	Operating system	
Hardware	Intel	Intel, Alpha AXP, MIPS, PowerPC
Scalability on SMP systems	No	Yes
Preemptive multitasking	No	Yes
Server implementation	Set of NLMs	Set of Win32 apps
Internal messaging —async I/O	No	Yes
Multithreading	No	Yes
Virtual memory	No	Yes
	Fault tolerance	
Hot backup support	Mainframe but not AS/400. Requires a second dedicated server for favorable licensing.	Mainframe and AS/400. Works with load balancing.
Load balancing among servers	Yes. Requires NetWare for SAA 2.0 client emulator upgrades.	Yes. All shipping ISVs' products supported.
Load balancing of session types	3270 but not APPC.	All LU types supported.

continues

Table 47.1. continued

	SAA 2.0	*SNA Server 2.11*
	Host connections	
PUs per server	32	250
Active connections	10	250
Host types	IBM mainframe. IBM AS/400.	IBM mainframe. IBM AS/400. IBM Advanced 36IBM System/36IBM System/38.
	LAN adapter support	
Desktop-to-Server/Server-to-Host (802.2/LLC)	ODI 4.1-compatible and Novell Labs-tested Token Ring, Ethernet, and FDDI adapters.	200+ NDIS certified Token Ring, Ethernet, and FDDI adapters for ISA, EISA, Micro Channel, and PCI Local Bus.
	Host adapter support	
Channel attachment	Channel attachment solutions are not available directly from or supported by Novell.	Barr Systems Bus & Tag Channel Attachment. Bus-Tech Bus & Tag Channel Attachment. Enterprise Network Controller Bus & Tag Channel Attachment. IBM 3172-NT Bus & Tag Channel Attachment. Computer VMC SNA Server ESCON Channel Attachment. Dr. Materna GmbH SPOC-P.
Twinax	None	Andrew 3X Twin Adapter. Attachmate Twinax Adapter. IBM 5250 Emulation Adapter.
DFT	None	Attachmate 3270 Adapter. IRMA Adapter. IBM 3278/9 Emulation Adapter. 3278/9 Enhanced Emulation Adapter. 3270 Connection Mod A Adapter. 3270 Connection Mod B Adapter.

	SAA 2.0	*SNA Server 2.11*
	Deployment models	
Branch-based	Yes	Yes
Centralized	Yes	Yes
Distributed	No	Yes

Additional Benefits

In addition to the benefits of SNA Server listed in this chapter, using a gateway product such as SNA Server provides other benefits that are not obvious to the user:

- It acts as a terrific platform on which to migrate your network to TCP/IP.
- It reduces overall multiprotocol network traffic.
- It helps reduce the processor load on the AS/400.

This section takes a closer look at these benefits.

Terrific Platform for Migrating to TCP/IP

Midrange and mainframe system developers have recognized the need to provide support for LANs. To help meet this need, they have begun rolling in support for the TCP/IP protocol as part of their operating system's protocol support. The only downside to this trend is that most businesses are not yet using TCP/IP as their protocol. TCP/IP can be difficult to manage and is not something a network can migrate to overnight. SNA Server can assist in the migration because of its multiprotocol support and its tight integration with Windows NT. Windows NT has management tools such as DHCP, WINS, and DNS that help the network administrator manage the network more easily.

Reduces Overall Network Traffic

Working with SNA Server enables you to reduce the DLC network traffic on your LAN. You can reduce your traffic by setting up the mainframe and midrange systems on a separate network and using SNA Server to link the two networks together.

Reduces Processor Load on the AS/400

When a client system connects to the AS/400 via DLC, the AS/400 is forced to use a processor cycle to maintain the connection. With SNA Server, only the one physical connection created by the SNA Server exists. All other client connectivity appears as virtual connections and does not require a CPU cycle from the AS/400. This capability can reduce CPU loads by up to 30 percent!

Requirements

Now, to take advantage of all the neat features that Microsoft SNA Server offers, you need the right equipment. The following topics outline the requirements for the server to run Microsoft SNA Server.

Equipment Required for the Server

- A system using an Intel 386, 486, Pentium, MIPS R4xxx, Alpha AXP, or PowerPC processor
- Microsoft Windows NT Server 3.5 or later
- 16MB of memory
- 30MB available hard disk space
- A CD-ROM drive

Host Link Options (Any Combination)

The following lists the different ways you can connect SNA Server to your host system:

- 802.2 (Ethernet, Token Ring, or FDDI)
- SDLC
- X.25/QLLC
- DFT
- Twinax
- Channel

Networking Options (Any Combination)

The following list shows the networking environments that SNA Server can integrate into:

- Microsoft Windows NT Server
- Microsoft LAN Manager
- IBM LAN Server
- Novell NetWare
- TCP/IP-based networks
- Banyan VINES
- Apple AppleTalk

Licensing

SNA Server uses the same standard licensing policies as other products in the Microsoft BackOffice suite. A license is required for each SNA Server, and a license is required for each client. This license is in addition to any licenses you have for Windows NT or other BackOffice products. The licenses can come in one of two forms: per seat or per server.

Per Seat

Per seat licensing is generally the best choice for environments that have more than one server and have high usage. A *per seat* license allows a client to connect to as many servers as exist on the network. The client must have the same username and must log in from the same workstation as the name that appears on this license.

Per Server

The *per server* licensing model enables you to purchase a license for the total number of simultaneous users for each server. This licensing strategy is good for an environment that does not have high demand for mainframe use from the same set of users at all times.

SNA Server 3.0

Microsoft continues its tradition of providing the best gateway system on the market with the introduction of SNA Server 3.0. SNA Server 3.0 shows that the SNA Server team really listened to customer comments. Just about every comment that started with, "I wish SNA Server had…" has been included in this version. The new features of SNA Server 3.0 follow:

- A host print server
- Host security integration
- A TN5250 server
- A new SNA interface
- Data encryption between client and SNA Server
- An AS/400 shared folders gateway

This section includes details about these new services.

Host Print Server

The host print server enables SNA Server to give AS/400s and mainframes access to the network-based printers available to Windows NT. This capability provides a central point of management for all printing services that occur on the network.

Host Security Integration

Host security integration enables users in an SNA Server environment to automatically integrate their logon session between Windows NT and the mainframe. In SNA Server 2.11 and earlier, users have to log on twice. One logon is used to access SNA Server, and another logon is required to access the midrange or mainframe client.

A TN5250 Server

The TN5250 server was created to support a new feature that appears in most of the 5250 emulators now. This feature gives emulators the capability to have an emulation session across TCP/IP. The downside of this capability is that the AS/400 must be running TCP/IP in order to work. Running TCP/IP on all but the latest version of the AS/400 operating system (OS/400 V3R1 and later) can cause severe performance problems with the AS/400. The TN5250 feature of SNA Server takes care of this problem by enabling clients to use TCP/IP to the SNA Server and then converting the call to DLC. This feature enables the AS/400 to communicate with TN5250 clients without running the TCP/IP protocol.

A New SNA Interface

Figure 47.6 shows the new Explorer interface that ships with SNA Server 3.0. The Explorer interface enables you to easily and centrally manage multiple SNA Servers across your network. It falls right in line with the new Explorer interface provided in Windows NT 4.0. If you are using SNA Server 2.11 or earlier, you will have to make some adjustments, but they are definitely worth it.

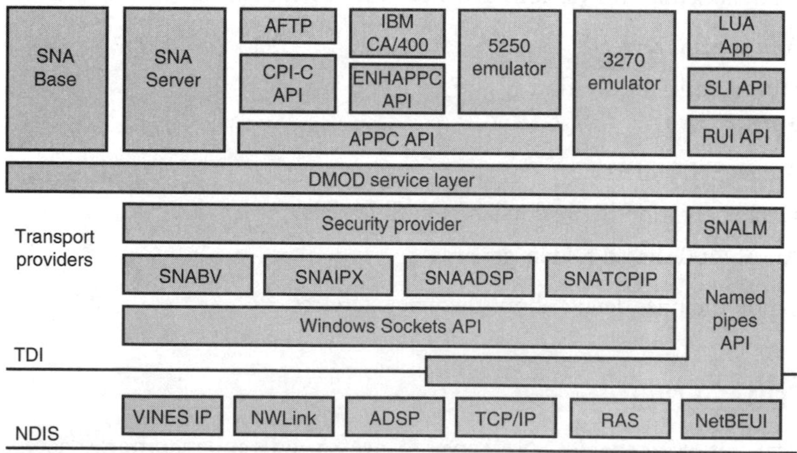

Figure 47.6. *The new Explorer interface of SNA Server 3.0.*

Data Encryption Between Client and SNA Servers

This feature comes in handy if you want to use the Internet as a possible network backbone. The new version of SNA Server will support data encryption in all communications between the client and SNA Server. The only requirement is that you must be operating in a distributed configuration.

An AS/400 Shared Folders Gateway

Accessing shared folders using SNA Server traditionally has been a less-than-straightforward process. SNA Server 3.0 solves this problem by offering a service similar to the gateway service for NetWare. The shared folders gateway enables the NT Server to connect to the shared folders service on the AS/400. The NT Server then can share the folders with the rest of the network's clients, including clients who are not even using the SNA Server client. This is a terrific way to help migrate AS/400 data from shared folders to network servers.

Summary

You now have been exposed to and should have a good understanding of SNA Server. In this chapter, you explored the purpose of SNA Server and looked at the features it offers. You took a look at the benefits you can experience by using SNA Server as your gateway solution. You now know what the necessary hardware for a minimum installation is, and you have had a chance to see what new features are going to be available in the next version of SNA Server.

SNA Server is just one of the robust components of the Microsoft BackOffice family that help provide integrated solutions for the Windows NT Server operating system. The following chapters will expose you to other components that make up the BackOffice family and help make Windows NT Server the robust platform it is today.

Systems Management Server

by Terry W. Ogletree

Microsoft Systems Management Server (SMS) is the BackOffice application that you use to perform administration tasks on client computers in a large network. Rather than having to physically go to each client computer to perform tasks (such as installing software or inventorying hardware and software), SMS enables the network administrator to accomplish this goal from one or more SMS servers.

Depending on who you ask, network client administration tasks can vary. However, the tasks performed by SMS include the following:

- Hardware and software inventorying
- Software installation and upgrades on client computers (including operating systems)
- Querying clients for hardware configuration information
- Establishing help desk functions that enable you to more directly access client computers to assist users in diagnosing problems

The computer on which you install the SMS server software must be a domain controller—either Primary (PDC) or Backup Domain Controller (BDC). Additionally, SMS uses the Microsoft SQL database to maintain its data. You must have at least one instance of the SQL product running in order to use SMS.

SMS uses the concept of a *site* for administrative purposes. A site represents a collection of one or more domains and computers. Only one domain, however, is required. Because SMS must be installed on a PDC, one domain remains the minimum requirement. You can't have SMS without at least one domain. Each site that you create must contain at least one domain. If you create more than one site, you must have more than one domain in your network.

You can distribute the many functions of SMS across many servers—you do not have to use a single server to perform all functions. The types of servers can have are the following:

- Primary Site Server

  A primary site server represents an SMS server that has *its own* SQL database. Sites can be organized into a hierarchical format in which a site can be a child or parent of another site. A primary site server can have both child and parent sites.

- Central Site Server

  This primary site server has no parent and is found at the top of the hierarchy. All other sites report up the chain of sites to this server. Because all child sites report their data back up the chain of child-parent servers, the central site server holds information about all sites in the hierarchy.

- Secondary Site Server

  This server type does not have its own SQL database. Consequently, it cannot have child sites because it cannot store their data. It must, however, have at least one parent server that it reports to.

You can also have Logon Servers that assist other servers in processing logon request, Helper Servers that can help to distribute the functions performed by other servers (running the Scheduler process, for example), a Distribution Server that holds the source files for a software package that SMS distributes, and a Database Server that can hold the SQL database. Thus, a primary site server does not actually have to run the SQL database software on the same machine; it simply has to be a server that can access an SQL server to store its data.

Senders make up the components of SMS that form communications links with other sites and servers. The LAN sender is the default. Two other types also exist:

- The SNA sender
- The Remote Access Service sender

Considering the many types of servers you can use in a large network for SMS purposes, you can see that having a good set of troubleshooting tools becomes a necessity.

Checking SMS Services and Processes

Most of the functions performed by SMS are performed by services run on Windows NT servers. You can view services installed on a Windows NT computer by using the Services applet found in the Control Panel, or you can use the Windows NT Service Manager utility (located under the

Administrative Tools group) to examine services running on any server that the utility can access. Figure 48.1 shows the Services dialog box with some of the SMS services scrolled into view.

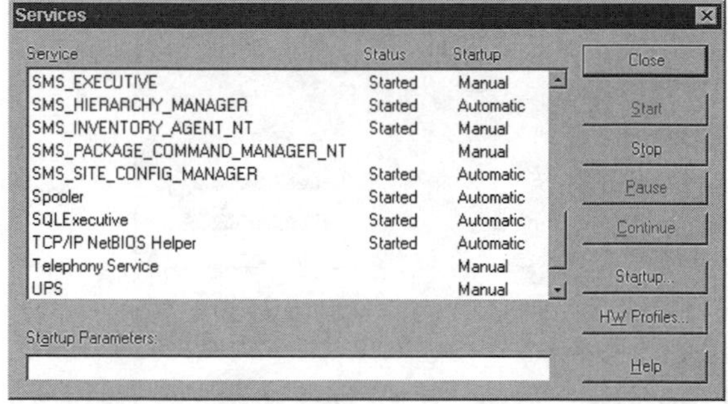

Figure 48.1. *The Services applet is where you can start, stop, or configure selected aspects of services running on a Windows NT Computer.*

The following list provides the services that SMS installs on a Site Server (and the service startup type):

- `SMS_HIERARCHY_MANAGER`—Automatic startup
- `SMS_SITE_CONFIG_MANAGER`—Automatic startup
- `SMS_INVENTORY_AGENT_NT`—Manual startup
- `SMS_PACKAGE_COMMAND_MANAGER`—Manual startup
- `SMS_EXECUTIVE`—Manual startup

The `SMS_SITE_CONFIG_MANAGER` service will start the services that are set to start up manually. If a particular SMS service does not start up correctly, you should first check the Services applet to make sure that it is correctly configured. Is the service set up to start automatically or manually?

Tip: You can also use the SMS Service Manager utility to examine services specific to SMS. However, the Windows NT Services applet found in the Control Panel will allow you to see all services running on the computer.

To view the startup type and the account under which a particular service appears, you can use the Startup button from the Services applet (refer to Figure 48.1). You first select the services from this dialog box and then click the Startup button. The Startup dialog box appears, as shown in Figure 48.2.

Using this dialog box, you can check to make sure the correct account gets used. You can also see if the account has accidentally been disabled. If everything looks correct, you can use the User Manager for Domains utility (found under the Administrative Tools menu) to verify that the account for the particular service has the correct setup. For example, does the account (or a group it is a member of) have the right to run as a service? Any account you use to start a service *must* have the "Logon as a service" right granted to it.

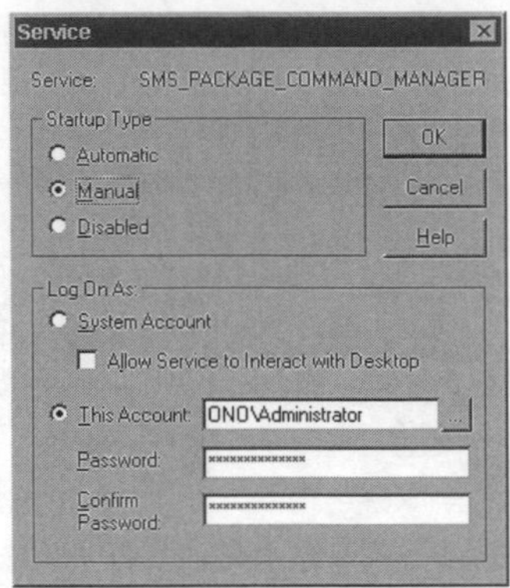

Figure 48.2. *The Service dialog box enables you to view or modify the startup method for a particular service (automatically or manually) and to specify the user account and password for the account under which the service will run.*

Also, think about whether the user account been disabled or the password changed. If you change the password for an account that is used by a service, you *must* also change it in the Service dialog box. You can use the User Manager for Domains to do this. If you use the default Local System Account to run SMS services, you should know that some features will not be available, including replication services and running scheduled tasks that relate to other servers.

You can also check the event log file, using the Event Viewer Administrative Tool, to see if errors are being logged either by SMS or by the operating system. For instance, some services have dependencies that require other services to be started before they can run. You can diagnose problems of this sort using the Windows NT Event log files (see the "Windows NT Troubleshooting Utilities" section later in this chapter).

In addition to installing these services on the NT Server, the `SMS_EXECUTIVE` service starts several processes on the server, including

- Maintenance Manager
- Inventory Processor
- Site Reporter
- Scheduler
- Despooler
- Inventory Data Loader
- Applications Manager
- Alerter
- LAN Sender

You can use the Windows NT Task Manager to make sure the required services are running and to get a quick overview of your system's performance. To bring up the Task Manager, right-click the Task Bar and select Task Manager from the menu. Figure 48.3 shows the Task Manager with the default Applications tab selected. You can see that the basic SQL and SMS applications are running.

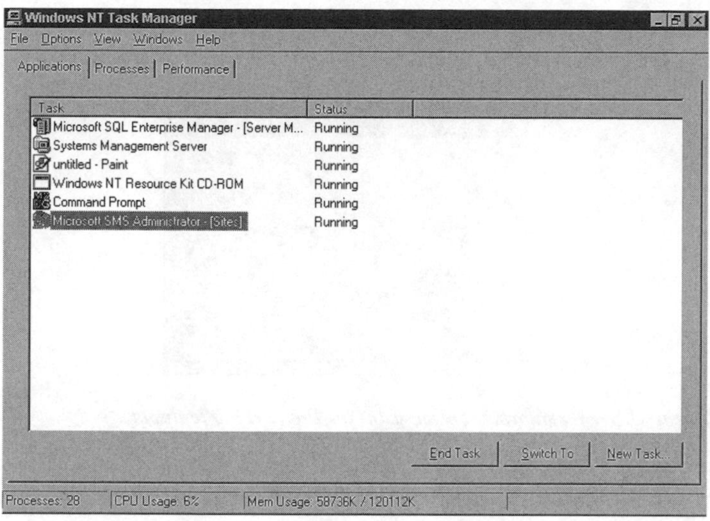

Figure 48.3. The Applications tab of the Windows NT Task Manager enables you to find out quickly whether the required applications are running.

This vastly improved Task Manager does much more than the Task Manager in previous versions of Windows NT. If you select the Processes tab, you can see the individual processes running on the system (see Figure 48.4). This tab can provide a great source of information for troubleshooting performance problems.

Windows NT Task Manager
File Options View Help
Applications Processes Performance

Image Name	PID	CPU	CPU Time	Mem Usage
SPOOLSS.EXE	70	00	0:00:10	1496 K
cmd.exe	71	00	0:00:00	32 K
SQLSERVR.EXE	87	00	0:00:22	8180 K
llssrv.exe	96	00	0:00:00	164 K
INVWIN32.EXE	104	00	0:00:01	44 K
LOCATOR.EXE	114	00	0:00:00	0 K
SQLEXEC.EXE	116	00	0:00:03	2364 K
nddeagnt.exe	118	00	0:00:00	88 K
SQLEW.EXE	120	00	0:00:17	676 K
explorer.exe	125	00	0:00:39	2924 K
rpcss.exe	131	00	0:00:01	496 K
PREINST.EXE	137	00	0:00:08	132 K
taskmgr.exe	143	04	0:01:16	940 K
TCPSVCS.EXE	151	00	0:00:02	692 K
SMSEXEC.EXE	158	00	0:01:38	4796 K
DNS.EXE	160	00	0:00:00	120 K
WINS.EXE	171	00	0:00:01	860 K
SITEINS.EXE	180	00	0:00:15	280 K
SMS.EXE	209	01	0:00:14	500 K
CDSETUP.EXE	265	00	0:00:00	92 K

End Process

Processes: 28 CPU Usage: 6% Mem Usage: 59492K / 120112K

Figure 48.4. The Processes tab shows each process running on the computer, along with information about the processes.

In the default configuration for this tab, you can see the Process Identifier (PID), the CPU Usage (CPU), the amount of CPU time the process has used (CPU Time), and the amount of memory the process is using (Mem Usage). You can, however, view other data. If you click the View menu selection and then choose Select Columns, you will get a dialog box that you can use to select the information you want to see (see Figure 48.5).

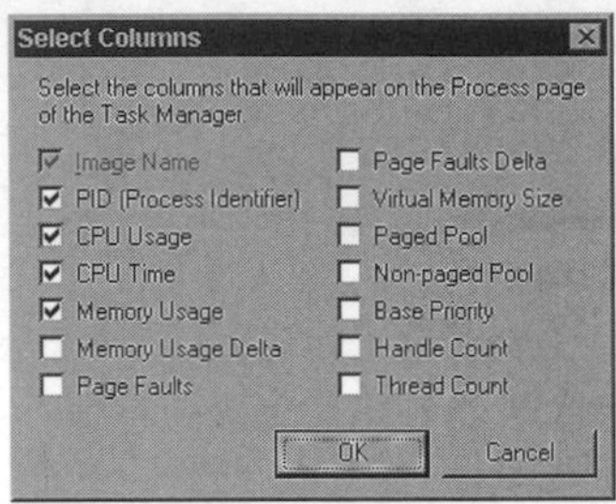

Figure 48.5. *You can choose the information you want the Processes tab to display.*

Unless you possess a great deal of experience in the internal workings of Windows 4 NT, many of the items you can choose from this dialog box will not have meaning. The Page Faults selection, however, is one you might want to consider if you have performance problems. When Windows NT needs more memory for a process than you have available in actual physical memory, it has to swap some pages of memory out to the page file—on disk. This process, known as page faulting, enables the system to appear to have much more memory than it actually has. When the number of processes demanding memory grows far beyond the amount of physical memory actually present, the system has to continually swap pages of memory in and out of the disk page file. Consequently, performance suffers because accessing data in memory happens much faster than retrieving it from a slow, mechanical disk.

Tip: When running Microsoft SQL Server and Microsoft Systems Management Server, the more memory you have, the better performance you will see. If you check the installation requirements for both products, you will see that you won't get much done at all if your machine has less than 64MB of physical memory. Even with that amount, you should plan to place your page file on a separate disk from the system disk—on a dedicated disk if you can spare it—to improve performance. If the system must place I/O requests in a queue to the same disk used for system processes or for data access, then the single disk becomes a bottleneck. Disks already run slow enough as it is!

Because you will probably use SMS as a business product, the cost of a single separate disk for a large page file becomes inconsequential compared to the performance improvement.

The last tab is the Performance tab (see Figure 48.6). When you first suspect a performance problem, you can use this tab to get a quick overview of the CPU and memory usage on the system. If you detect a problem (this figure shows the CPU usage at 100 percent, which represents a problem if it persists), then you can bring up the Performance Monitor tool found in the Administrative Tools menu to further refine your search for the cause of the overload.

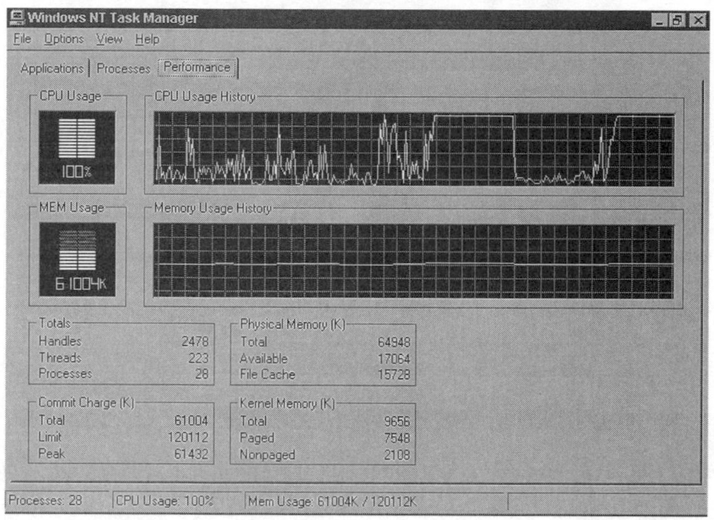

Figure 48.6. *The Performance tab gives you a quick look at how the system currently uses the CPU and memory resources.*

Using SMS Utilities to Diagnose Problems

You can use SMS applications, such as the Help Desk, to troubleshoot problems on clients in your network. Many built-in features exist that you can also use to troubleshoot the operation of the SMS services themselves.

Administering Services with the SMS Service Manager

The SMS Service Manager application enables you to administer services on the local computer or on other SMS servers in the site. You can start and stop (or pause) services, turn tracing on and off, provide parameters for a service's startup, and check on the status of a service.

To start the SMS Service Manager, click the Start button, and then select Programs, Systems Management Server; finally, choose SMS Service Manager (see Figure 48.7).

The local computer provides the default view when you start the utility. You use the Connect menu to connect to another server in the site, or to reconnect to the local server. To change the width of any column so that you can view long server names or service names, place your cursor on the vertical line that separates the column heads in the display, and then hold down the left mouse button and drag. Use the Startup Parameters box to enter parameters for a service to use when it is restarted.

To start or stop a service, double-click that item. You can also highlight a service and use the Start, Stop, Pause, and Continue buttons.

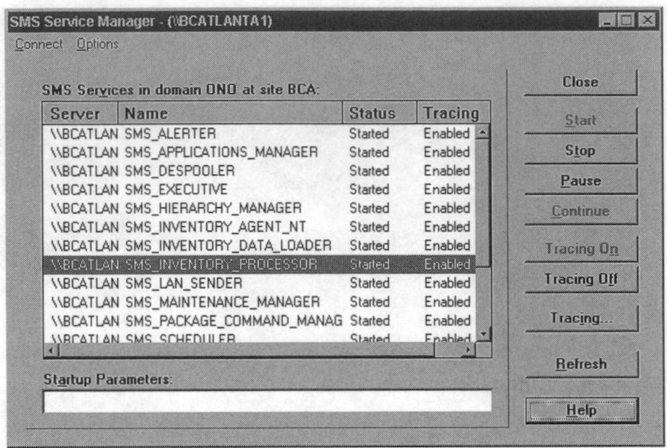

Figure 48.7. The SMS Service Manager utility enables you to start and stop services, and enables tracing for diagnostic purposes.

By enabling tracing, SMS services can be made to write to log files. Depending on the service you plan on examining, you can use these trace log files to troubleshoot many types of problems. Remember when enabling tracing that you have to keep in mind the amount of disk space you can allocate to these files. To set the maximum size for a log file, highlight the service, and click the Tracing button. The Tracing Properties dialog box (see Figure 48.8) enables you to both set the maximum size of the log file for the particular service and to modify the path or log filename if you choose.

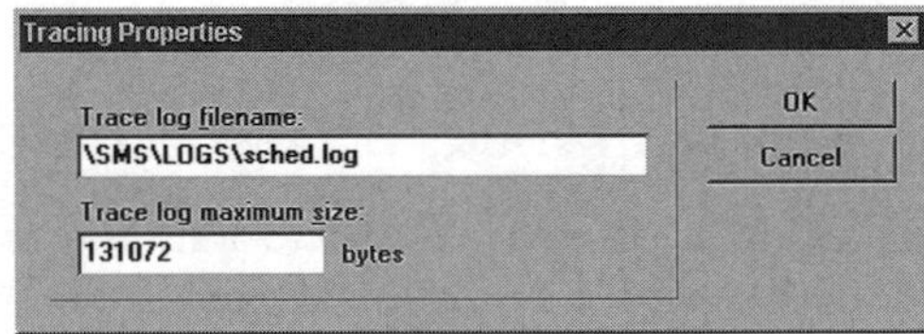

Figure 48.8. You can modify the name of the log file or the maximum size to which it can grow using the Tracing Properties dialog box.

Caution: When a log file reaches the maximum size you have specified, it is renamed and a new file is created. The renamed file will have the same name as the original file except that a trailing underscore gets added to the filename extension. Consequently, the log file data kept by *each* service that you enable can potentially use up twice the amount of disk space that you have specified. When a backup file already exists and the service needs to rename the current file, it overwrites the old backup file and you lose the data, unless you perform regular backups on your server and have the data saved offline.

The default location for the tracing log files is `\SMS\LOGS`. The default names for the log files for each service appear in Table 48.1:

Table 48.1. Default log filename for each service.

Service	*Log Filename*
Alerter	ALERTER.LOG
Applications Manager	APPMAN.LOG
Bootstrap	BOOT.LOG
Client Configuration *Manager*	CLICFG.LOG
Despooler	DESPOOL.LOG
Hierarchy Manager	HMAN.LOG
Inventory Agent	INVAGENT.LOG
Inventory Data Loader	DATALODR.LOG
Inventory Processor	INVPROC.LOG
LAN Sender	LANSEND.LOG
Maintenance Manager	MAINTMAN.LOG
Package Command Manager	PACMAN.LOG
RAS Sender *(Asynchronous)*	RASASYNC.LOG
RAS Sender (ISDN)	RASISDN.LOG
RAS Sender (X.25)	RASX25.LOG
Scheduler	SCHED.LOG
Site Configuration *Manager*	SCMAN.LOG
Site Reporter	SITEREPT.LOG
SMS Executive	SMSEXEC.LOG
SMS Administrator	UI.LOG
SNA Sender (BATCH)	SNABATCH.LOG
SNA Sender (INTER)	SNAINTER.LOG
SNA Receiver	SNARECV.LOG
SNMP Trap Receiver	TRAPFLTR.LOG

If the computer operates as a primary or secondary site, then tracing is turned on by default. You can turn tracing on or off for any of the SMS services, or any of the components of the SMS Executive service, by highlighting the service or component and then using the Tracing On or Tracing Off buttons. If tracing has already been turned on, the Tracing On button appears grayed out. The same goes for the Tracing Off button, if the service is not writing to a log file.

Note: You can also edit Registry parameters for these services to modify tracing attributes, but this action is not recommended. Any time you edit the Registry, a chance exists, even if only slight, that you will make a mistake, which can cause the system to behave unpredictably or fail to function at all.

Tip: Each service has its own log file, as previously described. If it becomes more convenient for your purposes, however, you can use the same log filename for one or more services, and they will write their data to the same log file sequentially.

You do not have to create the directory for the log file. If you specify a directory for a log file that does not exist, it will be created. Also, the path you use for the log file represents a relative path. The disk drive on which the particular service is located and running from will be prefixed to the path to determine the absolute location of the log file.

Furthermore, do not use a UNC path for a log file. If you do this, every copy of a service or component on other computers in the site will write to the same log file.

The log files contain one line for each action that the service or component logs. At the start of the line a description of the event appears, followed by two dollar signs ($$). After the dollar signs comes the component's name. The date and time of the event and the thread ID occur next, each enclosed by angle brackets(<>) to separate the data. The following short excerpt comes from the log file for the SMS Executive component.

```
~SMS_EXECUTIVE is starting...   $$<SMS_EXECUTIVE><Sun Apr 13 17:00:57
➥1997~><thread=EA>
Max working set size is now 6815744~   $$<SMS_EXECUTIVE><Sun Apr 13 17:00:57
➥1997~><thread=EA>
~Going through the thread list...   $$<SMS_EXECUTIVE><Sun Apr 13 17:01:07
➥1997~><thread=EA>
NewThread SMS_ALERTER~   $$<SMS_EXECUTIVE><Sun Apr 13 17:01:07
➥1997~><thread=EA>
Starting SMS_ALERTER~   $$<SMS_EXECUTIVE><Sun Apr 13 17:01:07 1997~>
➥<thread=EA>
NewThread SMS_APPLICATIONS_MANAGER~   $$<SMS_EXECUTIVE>
➥<Sun Apr 13 17:01:08 1997~><thread=EA>
Starting SMS_APPLICATIONS_MANAGER~   $$<SMS_EXECUTIVE>
➥<Sun Apr 13 17:01:08 1997~><thread=EA>
NewThread SMS_DESPOOLER~   $$<SMS_EXECUTIVE><Sun Apr 13 17:01:08
➥1997~><thread=EA>
```

```
Starting SMS_DESPOOLER~    $$<SMS_EXECUTIVE><Sun Apr 13 17:01:08
➥1997~><thread=EA>
NewThread SMS_INVENTORY_DATA_LOADER~    $$<SMS_EXECUTIVE><Sun Apr 13
➥17:01:08 1997~><thread=EA>
Starting SMS_INVENTORY_DATA_LOADER~    $$<SMS_EXECUTIVE><Sun Apr 13
➥17:01:08 1997~><thread=EA>
~Going through the thread list...    $$<SMS_EXECUTIVE><Sun Apr 13
➥17:11:13 1997~><thread=EA>
NewThread SMS_INVENTORY_PROCESSOR~    $$<SMS_EXECUTIVE><Sun Apr 13
➥17:11:13 1997~><thread=EA>
Starting SMS_INVENTORY_PROCESSOR~    $$<SMS_EXECUTIVE><Sun Apr 13
➥17:11:13 1997~><thread=EA>
```

From this example, you can see that after the Executive begins, it immediately starts up a host of other processes. If you began troubleshooting using the SMS Service Manager and saw that the `SMS_INVENTORY_DATA_LOADER` service was in a stopped state, you could check this log to see when it had been started (if at all) and when it had been stopped, either by error or intentionally by another administrator. The following excerpt from the SMS Executive's log file shows where services had been stopped and started:

```
Stopping SMS_INVENTORY_DATA_LOADER~    $$<SMS_EXECUTIVE>
➥<Mon Apr 14 00:09:19 1997~><thread=EA>
~Registry change notification triggered    $$<SMS_EXECUTIVE>
➥<Mon Apr 14 00:10:38 1997~><thread=EA>
~Going through the thread list...    $$<SMS_EXECUTIVE>
➥<Mon Apr 14 00:10:43 1997~><thread=EA>
Stopping SMS_SCHEDULER~    $$<SMS_EXECUTIVE>
➥<Mon Apr 14 00:10:43 1997~><thread=EA>
~Registry change notification triggered    $$<SMS_EXECUTIVE>
➥<Mon Apr 14 00:10:45 1997~><thread=EA>
~Going through the thread list...    $$<SMS_EXECUTIVE>
➥<Mon Apr 14 00:10:50 1997~><thread=EA>
Starting SMS_SCHEDULER~    $$<SMS_EXECUTIVE>
➥<Mon Apr 14 00:10:50 1997~><thread=EA>
```

In some record types, you will encounter `Job Types` and `Status` fields. This information appears numerically in Table 48.2.

Table 48.2. Log file `Job Types` and `Status` fields.

Value	*Job Type*	*Status*
1	Arrival	Pending
2	Workstation	Active
3	Server	Canceled
4	Completed	Complete
5	Reserved	Failed
6	Reserved	Retrying

Windows NT Troubleshooting Utilities

The Windows NT operating system includes several useful utilities that you can use to diagnose problems. SMS components, you will remember, run as services under Windows NT. Thus, you can use the same tools to administer these services as you do with any other Windows NT service.

Viewing the System Log Files

The Event Viewer offers perhaps the most useful tool, enabling you to display and print error (or event) messages written to the system log files. System Management Server services write records to the Application log file. Figure 48.9 presents a detailed record written by SMS showing that the service `SMS_INVENTORY_DATA_LOADER` failed to start.

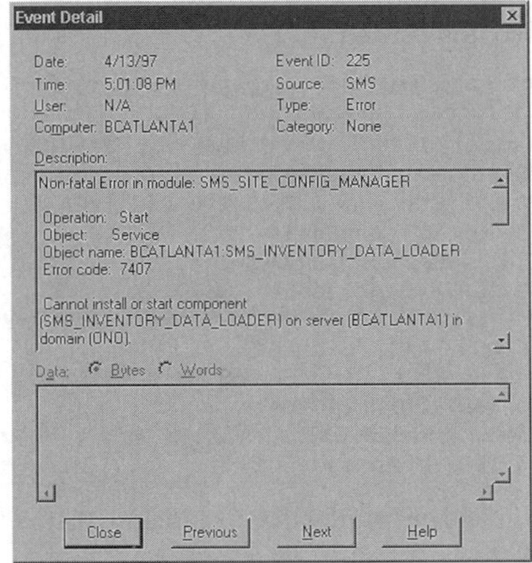

Figure 48.9. *The detailed event record showing that an SMS service did not start.*

If you use the scroll bar in the `Description` field of the Event Detail dialog box, you can bring further details into view that can be useful when you start to troubleshoot this problem. Figure 48.10 shows the same event detail information with additional text scrolled into view.

As you can see, several reasons can exist for the failure of this service to start. In this case, you could quickly check the logon account that the service uses by using the Control Panel\Services applet as described at the beginning of this chapter. You could then use the Event Viewer to look at records in the Security log file and see whether the logon account generated errors—login failures, for example. Did someone change the password? Using the User Manager for Domains to look at the properties for the account, you may find that it has expired or been disabled, or perhaps an important right (such as the necessary "Logon as a service" right) has been removed.

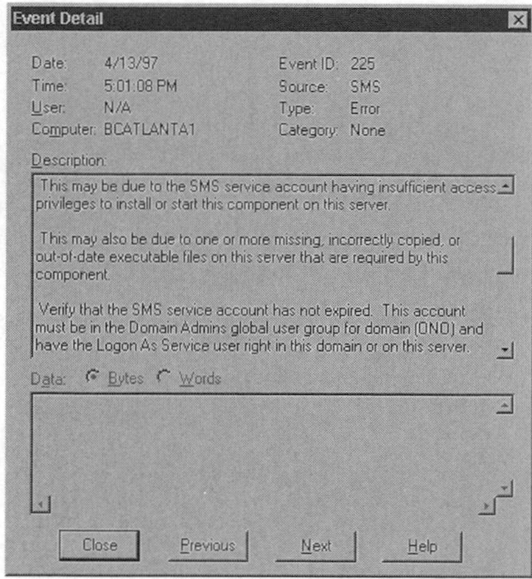

Figure 48.10. Some error messages can seem cryptic. This one actually suggests possible causes of the problem.

Scrolling down to reveal the remainder of the Description text, you can see the name of the computer on which the service could not get started, the site code of the SMS site that the service runs in, and the component (`SMS_SITE_CONFIG_MANAGER`) that tried to start the service (see Figure 48.11).

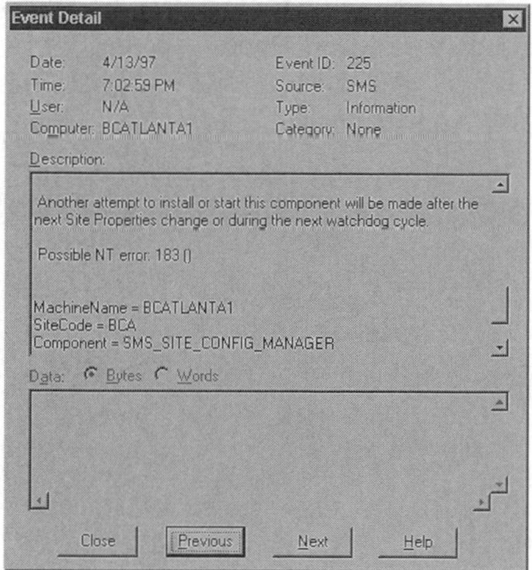

Figure 48.11. The remaining text in the event detail message shows you the computer site that the service was to start under and the name of the SMS component that tried to start the service.

Because a primary site server depends on an SQL database server as its data storage mechanism, you should also check to make sure that no problems exist with that application. If the Microsoft SQL Server fails to start, then the SMS components cannot access data necessary to perform their tasks. Figure 48.12 shows an event detail record indicating that the SQL server did successfully start.

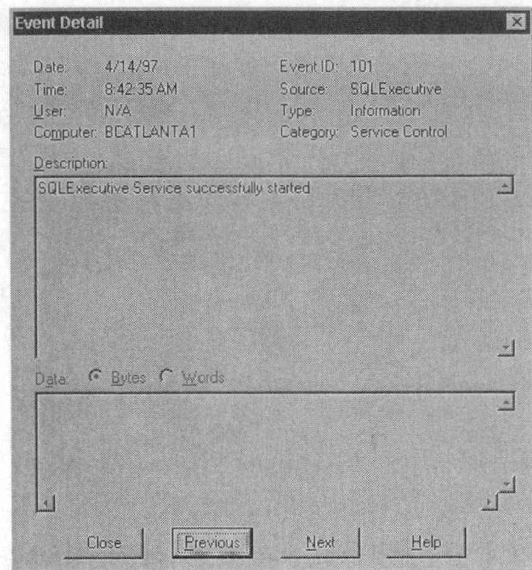

Figure 48.12. *The SQL server must be started on a primary site server for the SMS components to work properly.*

Performance Monitor Counter for SMS

The Performance Monitor utility can help gather information for tuning your Windows NT system and the applications that run on it. This utility can aid in detecting resource bottlenecks that slow services, or in come cases, cause them to fail. To start the Performance Monitor, choose that option from the Administrative Tools menu. The default view, called Chart view, enables you to see real-time data plotted on a graph as you add object counters to be tracked. To add a counter to the graph, you select the Add To Chart option from the Edit menu, as shown in Figure 48.13.

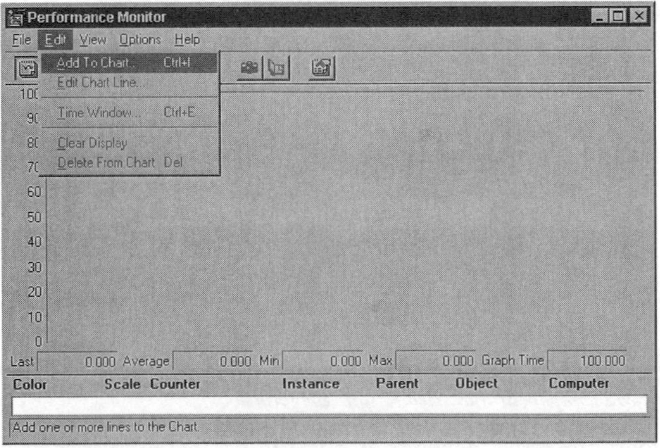

Figure 48.13. *The Add To Chart option enables you to add the Performance Monitor counters you want for tracking the graphical Chart view display.*

For a more complete explanation of objects and the counters associated with them that the Performance Monitor can track, see Chapter 36, "Windows NT Troubleshooting Utilities."

Windows NT operates as a multitasking/multiprocessing operating system that allows many processes to compete for available system resources as needed. The overall performance of any one process or application depends on not just its own internal workings, but also on the activities of all other processes running on the computer at the same time. In addition to requiring resources on the local computer, SMS applications can require network resources, as well as system resources on other SMS server computers and on the client computers. When using the Performance Monitor to evaluate performance problems, make sure to examine more than just one part of the problem.

The following list provides the objects that Microsoft recommends as most useful for diagnosing problems with SMS:

- Memory Object/Committed Bytes counter
- PhysicalDisk Object/%Disk Time counter
- Processor Object/%Processor Time
- Redirector Object/Current Commands counter
- SQL_Server Object/User Connections counter
- SQL_Server Object/Cache Hit Ratio counter

To add a counter to the chart, you use the Add to Chart dialog box as shown in Figure 48.14. In this figure, note that the Explain button appears grayed (it has been selected); consequently, you can see the `Counter Definition` field at the bottom of the dialog box. This field gives you a short explanation of what the counter represents.

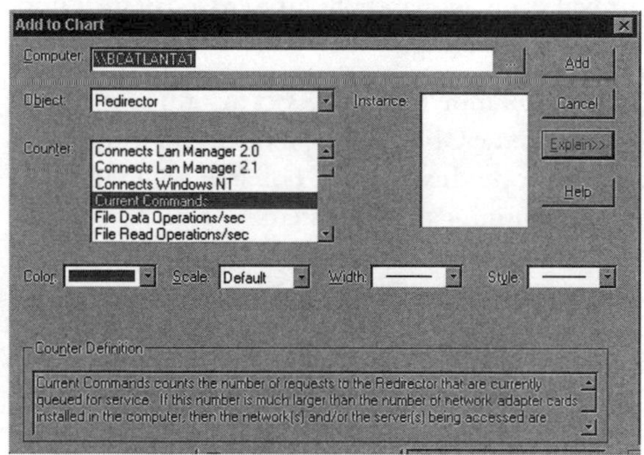

Figure 48.14. *The Add to Chart dialog box is used to select the object and then the counter that you want to chart.*

To switch to another object, simply use the Object pull-down menu. Once you have selected an object, the counters for that object appear in the scrollable Counter list box. After you select the counter, you can either use the default color shown in the Color pull-down menu, or you can select a specific color. Usually when you plot several counters, the color attribute offers enough differentiation on the chart display. If you want to further enhance the display, you can use the Width and Style list boxes to further customize the display you will see.

Figure 48.15 shows the Chart view with several counters added to it.

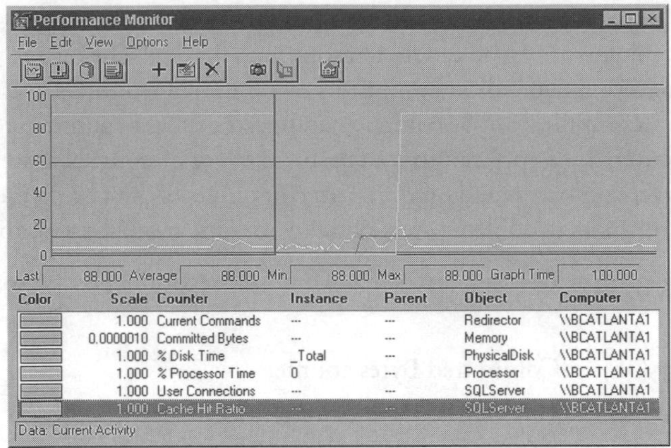

Figure 48.15. *The Chart view can show many different counters at the same time so that you can observe the interaction between different system resources.*

After you select an object and counter and any of the presentation attributes (color, width, and so on), click the Add button to add the counter to the chart. You can continue to select and add counters and press the Done button when you are finished (refer to Figure 48.14). You can always return to this dialog box to add more counters as you track down your problem.

In Figure 48.15, note that at the bottom of the chart display a legend displays each counter you have selected, the color used to graph it, and other useful information. The Alt+PrintScreen key combination will provide a quick snapshot of the chart. (Paste it into the Paint accessory or some other graphics program for printing.)

You can also view statistics for individual processes that run under NT. Use the Add to Chart dialog box and select Process from the Object list box; then, you will see the names of processes running on the system displayed in the Instance list box (see Figure 48.16). The Process object has an instance for each process running on the system.

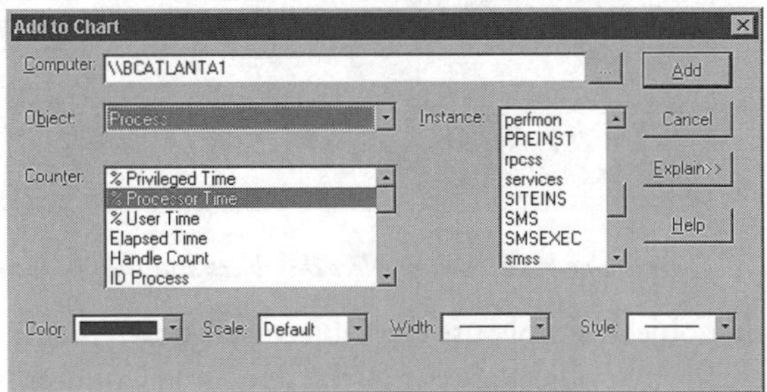

Figure 48.16. *You can select the process you want from the Instance list box and then display counters for just that process.*

Important processes you might want to monitor in your SMS environment include:

- PERFMON
- PREINST
- SITEINS
- SMS
- SMSEXEC
- SQL_SERVER (if using version 4.x of SQL Server)
- MSSQL_SERVER (if using version 6.x of SQL Server)

BackOffice Resource Kit Troubleshooting Utilities

The Microsoft BackOffice Resource Kit (parts 1 and 2) contains additional documentation for SMS, as well as new utilities that can help with troubleshooting. The following sections provide descriptions of some of the more helpful programs.

BUGDATA.EXE—The Bug Data Collector

SYNTAX:

```
BUGDATA /S:server /V filename
```

The BUGDATA.EXE program will collect data from several places including

- SMS Registry entries
- SMS log files
- The Site Control Image

Collected data gets placed into a compressed file. To view the data, you use the HDECOMP.EXE program. The syntax for running the BUGDATA program remains simple. Just enter the command at the command prompt. You can use the /S qualifier to specify a server, or else the one you logged into will get examined. The /V is the verbose mode qualifier, which causes the program to report more fully on its progress as it collects data. You can also specify a filename, after the command, that will be used to store the compressed data, or you can omit that step and the BUGDATA.SMS default will get used.

The following command line code shows the output of the program as it collects data from a primary site server using the verbose qualifier:

```
C:>\BORK\SMS BUGDATA /V

SMS Bug Data Collector v1.3
Microsoft Systems Management Server Utility
```

```
Creating working directory _bugdata.tmp...
Saving master site control file...
Saving trace files...
No tracing data in SMS site server registry for component
➥SMS_INVENTORY_AGENT_NT on server BCATLANTA2
No tracing data in SMS site server registry for component
➥SMS_PACKAGE_COMMAND_MANAGER_NT on server BCATLANTA2
    copying \\BCATLANTA1\SMS_SHRC\LOGS\alerter.log...
    copying \\BCATLANTA1\SMS_SHRC\LOGS\alerter.lo_...
    copying \\BCATLANTA1\SMS_SHRC\LOGS\appman.log...
    copying \\BCATLANTA1\SMS_SHRC\LOGS\appman.lo_...
    copying \\BCATLANTA1\SMS_SHRC\LOGS\despool.log...
    copying \\BCATLANTA1\SMS_SHRC\LOGS\despool.lo_...
    copying \\BCATLANTA1\SMS_SHRC\LOGS\smsexec.log...
    copying \\BCATLANTA1\SMS_SHRC\LOGS\smsexec.lo_...
    copying \\BCATLANTA1\SMS_SHRC\LOGS\hman.log...
    copying \\BCATLANTA1\SMS_SHRC\LOGS\hman.lo_...
    copying \\BCATLANTA1\SMS_SHRC\LOGS\invagent.log...
    copying \\BCATLANTA1\SMS_SHRC\LOGS\invagent.lo_...
    copying \\BCATLANTA1\SMS_SHRC\LOGS\datalodr.log...
    copying \\BCATLANTA1\SMS_SHRC\LOGS\datalodr.lo_...
    copying \\BCATLANTA1\SMS_SHRC\LOGS\invproc.log...
    copying \\BCATLANTA1\SMS_SHRC\LOGS\invproc.lo_...
    copying \\BCATLANTA1\SMS_SHRC\LOGS\lansend.log...
    copying \\BCATLANTA1\SMS_SHRC\LOGS\lansend.lo_...
    copying \\BCATLANTA1\SMS_SHRC\LOGS\maintman.log...
    copying \\BCATLANTA1\SMS_SHRC\LOGS\maintman.lo_...
    copying \\BCATLANTA1\SMS_SHRC\LOGS\pacman.log...
    copying \\BCATLANTA1\SMS_SHRC\LOGS\pacman.lo_...
    copying \\BCATLANTA1\SMS_SHRC\LOGS\sched.log...
    copying \\BCATLANTA1\SMS_SHRC\LOGS\sched.lo_...
    copying \\BCATLANTA1\C$\scman.log...
    copying \\BCATLANTA1\C$\scman.lo_...
    copying \\BCATLANTA1\SMS_SHRC\LOGS\siterept.log...
    copying \\BCATLANTA1\SMS_SHRC\LOGS\siterept.lo_...
    copying C:\SMSSETUP.LOG...
    copying C:\SMSSETUP.LO_...
Saving SMS.INI file...
Saving registry data...
Creating compressed output file bugdata.sms...
Removing working directory _bugdata.tmp...
Done!
```

As you can see, the utility collects data from a wide variety of sources, even from the service tracing logs discussed earlier in this chapter.

DUMPSEND.EXE—Display Send Request

SYNTAX:

`DUMPSEND /p` *`filename`*

You can use this utility to read the contents of a send request file. If you are running the utility in a command prompt window that will close after the command execution (running the program as a shortcut, for example), then you can use the `/p` (pause) switch to cause the display to stop after each page of data displays. Pressing any key enables the utility to continue.

Information that you can find in a send request file includes

- Send Request Data (destination, priority, job name, and so on)
- Cancel (used to cancel a send request)
- Action Code (Is this a deleted request or is the sender retrying this request?)
- Address (gateway and destination addresses)
- Package File (name of the package file being sent)
- Instruction File (name of instruction file for the package)
- Sender (information about the sender's actions on this request, such as the start time, number of times the sender took the request, and the size of the request)
- Access (information about file access)
- SSPS (remote site installation information)

ERROR32.EXE—Translate Error Code Number to Text Message

SYNTAX:

```
ERROR32 code [:code] [source ¦ message DLL]
          [insertion_string[…]]
```

Often, you will get an error code returned by a utility in the form of a decimal number. This utility translates that number into the text message that is associated with it so that you can actually understand the information from the system. In the preceding syntax statement, you substitute the number for the *code* variable. If you want to get the text for a range of messages, use the colon character and place the ending number of the range after the colon.

The `source` parameter can aid in specifying the name of the application that generated the code (take this from an Event Viewer record). Furthermore, you could use the `message_DLL` parameter to indicate a Windows NT message file (`NETMSG.DLL`, for example) that the utility can use to look up the error code. You cannot, however, use both `source` and `message_DLL` together; use one or the other.

The `insertion_string` parameter can be used to make the output more understandable by adding text (specified by `insertion_string`) to the output.

The following code shows the output from requesting the text for a range of error messages:

```
C:>\BORK\SMS ERROR32 16:19

Error code:  16  (0x10)
The directory cannot be removed.

Error code:  17  (0x11)
The system cannot move the file to a different disk drive.

Error code:  18  (0x12)
There are no more files.
```

```
Error code:  19  (0x13)
The media is write protected.
```

FILEPERF.BAT—Adding File Counter to the Performance Monitor

SYNTAX:

`FIPERF` *`sms_directory`*

In addition to the standard objects and counters that come with the Performance Monitor database, you can use this batch file to add counters to monitor directories and files used by SMS. You need to supply the only *`sms_directory`* parameter, which should be the root installation directory used for your SMS installation (`C:\SMS`, for example).

The following example displays the output generated when the counters are added to your database:

```
C:\BORK\SMS\FIPERF C:\SMS

This script will install the SMS_FILES Performance Monitor
(perfmon) counters so that you will be able to monitor certain
directories on your NT server using the  Windows NT Performance
Monitor utility.  See the smstools.hlp for details

Note, the regini.exe utility will be needed in the path.
Press any key to continue . . .
Creating the registry script...
Done.
Loading the registry...
Done.
Initializing counters...
Done.
Installing file(s)...
        1 file(s) copied.
        1 file(s) copied.
Done.
```

Note: You can remove these counters if you want by using the `UNLODCTR` (unload counter) command:

```
c:> UNLODCTR SMS_FILES
```

To see which directories are being monitored, use the Registry Editor (`REGEDT32.EXE`) to view the following Registry key:

```
\\HKEY_LOCAL_MACHINE\System\CurrentControlSet
    \Services\SMS_Files\Linkage
```

Figure 48.17 shows the default directories installed by this batch file. You can use the string editor to add or remove directories that suit your monitoring needs.

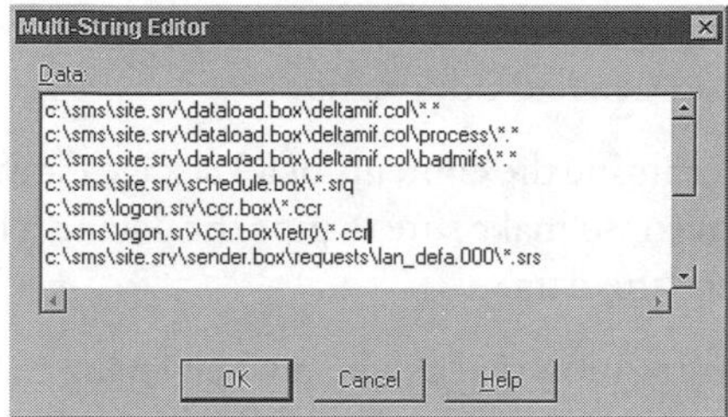

Figure 48.17. *The* `FIPERF.BAT` *file adds counters to monitor these SMS directories to the Performance Monitor.*

You can see the counters associated with the `SMS_Files` object by using the Add to Chart dialog box (see Figure 48.18). Notice that you should also choose which file to monitor by using the Instance list box.

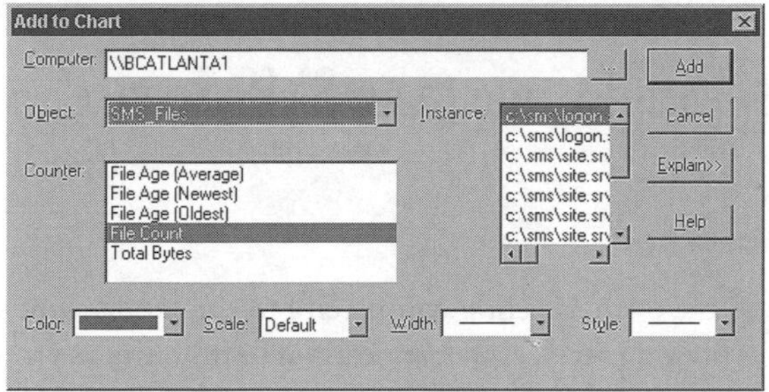

Figure 48.18. *The Add to Chart dialog box now enables you to add counters for the* `SMS_Files` *object.*

As always, when using the Performance Monitor, use the Explain button in the Add to Chart dialog box to get a brief explanation of each counter.

Note: In a similar manner, you can also use the `MIPERF.BAT` file to add counters for MIF files (the `SMS_Mifs` object) that are processed by SMS.

`PCMDUMP.EXE`—Package Command Manager Instruction File Dump Utility

SYNTAX:

```
PCMDUMP [optional switches] instruction_file
```

Optional switches include

/L	List the PCM Instruction box contents
/R	Dump the file from the instruction box
/P	Pause before exiting the command prompt window

/A	Dump all of the files in the instruction box
/D	Dump detailed information

This utility can help you examine the contents of a Package Command Manager instruction file. The output goes to the screen, so make sure to pipe the data to a file (using the `> pipe` command) if you want to save or print the data.

This utility will dump information that can help when trying to diagnose why a package did not get installed. For example, you can see the Install By date, which tells the date before which the package must be installed by the user. The Install Flag can be viewed, which tells whether or not a fast network connection is required to install the package.

If you are having problems getting a package to install on one or all of your client computers, use this command with the package instruction file to make sure the package contains the data you thought you had configured!

SENDCODE.EXE—Send Code to an SMS Service

SYNTAX:

`SENDCODE` *`service code`*

This utility will send the numeric code you specify to the service you want to test, which comes in handy for troubleshooting services that appear not to function as you expect. The codes you can send include

- 128—Starts memory allocation tracking.
- 129—Stops memory allocation tracking.
- 130—Dumps memory allocation data files to a file.

  The files are

  `C:\ALERTER.MEM`

  `C:\APPMGR.MEM`

  `C:\HMAN.MEM`

  `C:\SCMANMEM.LOG`

  `C:\SCHED.MEM`

  `C:\SMSEXEC.MEM`

- 131—The SQL cache for the `SMS_EXECUTIVE` service will be dumped to a file `C:\SQLCACHE.LOG.`
- 132—Toggles the `NET PAUSE` support if supported by an SMS service.
- 133—Causes the Registry to be read again and resets the SMS trace logging settings (locating and size).
- 192—Performs a watchdog cycle. That is, the current installation will be verified; stopped components will be restarted.

- 193—Performs a watchdog cycle and writes a status file with the .CT2 extension.
- 194—Performs a watchdog cycle as if an upgrade were being performed. You should first use the `SENDCODE` utility with a value of 234 to ensure a more effective execution of this code.
- 195—Performs a watchdog cycle and creates a user group MIF.
- 196—Performs a watchdog cycle; if Automatically Configure Logon Scripts and Use All Detected Servers are enabled, logon scripts may be modified.
- 234—On the site server, and on all logon and other helper servers, services (SMS) are first stopped, and then de-installed.
- 235—The site is de-installed. All components get removed and files and shares get removed (from the site server and helper and logon servers as well).

`SMSTRACE.EXE`—MS Log File Viewer

SYNTAX:

```
SMSTRACE
```

This utility has a graphical user interface that enables you to view the logs created by services when tracing is enabled. The `SMSADDIN` utility helps you to add this program to the SMS Administrator's Tools menu. The advantage to using this interface rather than a text editor to read the files is that a real-time update gets performed using `SMSTRACE` so that you can view data as it is added to the log file. With a text editor, you must exit and reload the file to view new data.

`TRACER.EXE`—Text File Viewer

SYNTAX:

```
TRACER logfilename
```

This utility will display, in real-time mode, changes made to a text file.

`RSERVICE.EXE`—Remote Control of Services

SYNTAX:

```
RSERVICE [options] initialization_file
```

Command-line options include

- `/INSTALL`

  Installs a service on the machines defined in the control file.
- `/START`

  Starts the service on the defined computers.

- `/STOP`

  Stops the service on the defined computers.
- `/DEINSTALL`

  Removes the service from the defined computers.
- `/QUERY`

  Sends a query to the service on the defined computers.
- `/PAUSE`

  Pauses the service on the defined computers.
- `/CONTINUE`

  Causes a paused service on the defined computers to resume.
- `/SENDCODE:`*`code`*

  Sends a control code to the defined computers.

  Numeric control codes exist in the range of 128–255. Some WIN32 services are written to interpret codes in this range.
- `/C`

  Causes the utility to make a connection to the computer using the service's account before any service commands are carried out.
- `/L:`*`logfile`*

  Gives a path and filename for a log file, to which output of the command is directed.
- `/M:`*`machine`*

  If you designate a specific computer with this qualifier, other computers listed in the initialization file are ignored.
- `/T:`*`thread-count`*

  Indicates the maximum number of threads that can be used, with the default being 10.
- `/V`

  Causes verbose output. The utility will more fully report its operations. Use this if you are just becoming familiar with the utility.

You can use this utility to exercise control over services on remote computers. First, you have to create an initialization file that contains data about the computers that will be accessed using the utility, and all of the computers must reside in the same domain. The utility has an extensive set of command qualifiers, however, that allow you to exercise a great deal of control over services on the designated computers; this characteristic helps make the utility one of the best included in the Resource Kit.

The initialization file represents a standard ASCII text file that is divided up into sections enclosed in square-brackets ([]). Within each section, entries define attributes related to the section. For a complete listing of the sections and values that you can define in the initialization file, see the help file that comes with the BackOffice Resource Kit.

SRVINFO.EXE—Server Information

SYNTAX:

```
SRVINFO server
```

This utility will return a summary of general information about the specified server (or the server on which the command is executed if no server is given) and about the services on the computer. The following code shows a sample output of this command:

```
C:\>SRVINFO

Server Name: BCATLANTA1
Security: Users
NT Type: WinNT Server
Version: 4.0, Build = 1381, CSD = Service Pack 1
Domain: ONO
PDC: \\BCATLANTA1
IP Address: 10.10.10.100
CPU[0]: x86 Family 5 Model 2 Stepping 6
Drive: [Filesys] [Size] [Used] [Free]
  C$     NTFS     1223   1018    205
Services:
   [Running]    Alerter
   [Running]    Computer Browser
   [Stopped]    ClipBook Server
   [Stopped]    DHCP Client
   [Running]    Microsoft DHCP Server
   [Running]    Microsoft DNS Server
   [Running]    EventLog
   [Running]    Server
   [Running]    Workstation
   [Running]    License Logging Service
   [Running]    TCP/IP NetBIOS Helper
   [Running]    Messenger
   [Stopped]    MSDTC
   [Running]    MSSQLServer
   [Stopped]    Network DDE
   [Stopped]    Network DDE DSDM
   [Running]    Net Logon
   [Running]    NT LM Security Support Provider
   [Running]    Plug and Play
   [Stopped]    Directory Replicator
   [Running]    Remote Procedure Call (RPC) Locator
   [Running]    Remote Procedure Call (RPC) Service
   [Stopped]    Schedule
   [Running]    SMS_EXECUTIVE
   [Running]    SMS_HIERARCHY_MANAGER
   [Running]    SMS_INVENTORY_AGENT_NT
   [Running]    SMS_PACKAGE_COMMAND_MANAGER_NT
   [Running]    SMS_SITE_CONFIG_MANAGER
   [Running]    Spooler
   [Running]    SQLExecutive
   [Stopped]    Telephony Service
   [Stopped]    UPS
   [Running]    Windows Internet Name Service
```

```
Network Card [0]: 3Com Etherlink16/Etherlink16 TP Adapter
Protocol[0]: [NET0] WINS Client(TCP/IP) 4.0
Protocol[1]: [NET1] NetBEUI Protocol 4.0
System Up Time: 0 Hr 33 Min  2 Sec
```

Summary

Microsoft Systems Management Server is the BackOffice component that enables you to effectively and efficiently manage computers throughout the network. Although you can use SMS to troubleshoot problems on client computers in your network, you can also troubleshoot problems with your implementation of SMS by using the regular Windows NT utilities, such as the Performance Monitor and the Event Viewer. Furthermore, SMS, and especially the BackOffice Resource Kit, comes with additional utilities that can be useful in trying to figure out problems with your SMS configuration.

PART X

Supporting the Internet with Windows NT

Internet Information Server

by John West

Microsoft's Internet Information Server (IIS) gives you everything you need to publish documents to the Internet. Internet Information Server is provided as part of the Windows NT Server package and includes support for WWW, FTP, and Gopher publishing services. This chapter will show you how to provide the information you need to effectively use these publishing services. It starts by taking a closer look at the services of IIS, and then shows you how to install and configure the Internet Information Server. Finally, the chapter gives a chart that summarizes the features of IIS. Let's get started.

Introduction to Internet Information Server (IIS)

The Internet Information Server shipping with Windows NT provides everything you need to begin publishing Web documents to your intranet or Internet. For those of you new to Web services, this section will give you an introduction to the concepts and differences between the Internet and an intranet. You will then be introduced to the services of IIS.

The Difference Between the Internet and an Intranet

You have probably heard a lot of talk about the Internet and about companies' intranets, but what do these terms mean? Well, an intranet is a Web server that serves a specific group and network, like a corporation or a small business. Only individuals in this group and network have access to Web pages on the intranet. A common use for an intranet is to publish HR information such as corporate phone lists and benefits and make them available to everyone in the company.

The Internet is a really big network that is basically available for anyone to log in to. Once you are on the Internet you can connect to any resource that is on the Net. If you have pages being published to the Internet, anyone with access to the Net can see the Web pages you are publishing.

To sum it up, an intranet serves a specific group of people, and the Internet is a huge network that virtually anyone can have access to.

The Services of IIS

During the evolution of the Internet, various methods for publishing and retrieving data across the Net were developed. To be useful, the methods had to be capable of working with any platform that was currently attached to the Internet. This could include UNIX, Windows NT, and others. To meet this goal, the methods were broken down into two components: a client and a server. The client component initiates the conversation with the server. The server component listens for the incoming requests from clients and processes their requests. IIS provides the server side of these components. The server services supported by IIS are WWW, FTP, and Gopher.

World Wide Web (WWW)

The World Wide Web is one of the most recent methods developed for publishing information across the Internet. Traditionally, information passed over the Net was in a text-only format. The WWW changed all this by allowing users to view graphics, sounds, and formatted text that had been passed to them across the Internet.

FTP

The File Transfer Protocol was developed to allow files to be easily transferred between different operating systems. FTP takes incoming requests for files from clients and fills the requests.

Gopher

Before the World Wide Web there was Gopher. Similar to the WWW, Gopher allows a user to drill down through menus to allow users to access the information they are looking for. Unlike the WWW's rich graphical interface, Gopher supports text-based menus, which can be kind of dull.

Installing Microsoft Internet Information Server

Installing Microsoft Internet Information Server is not difficult and is a fairly straightforward process. All that is required is the NT 4.0 CD. The following steps take you through the installation process.

1. Open the NT control panel and double-click the network icon. The Network dialog box shown in Figure 49.1 should now appear.

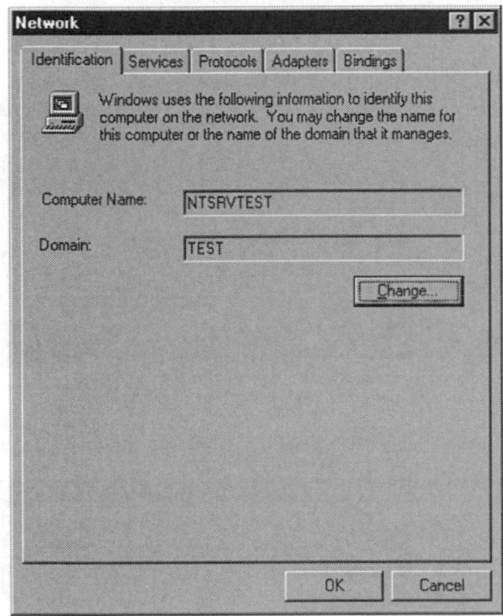

Figure 49.1. *The Network applet is used to install Microsoft Internet Information Server.*

2. In the Network dialog box, click the Services tab, bringing it to the foreground. The Networks dialog box should now appear as shown in Figure 49.2
3. In the Networks dialog box with the Services tab selected, click the Add button. This will bring up the Select Network Service dialog box shown in Figure 49.3.
4. In the Select Network Service dialog box find and double-click Microsoft Internet Information Server.
5. You will now be prompted for the path to the NT installation files. Insert the NT 4.0 CD in the CD-ROM drive, and type the drive letter and path that is appropriate for your installation of NT. For example, if you have NT installed on an Intel processor-based machine and the NT 4.0 CD is in the CD-ROM drive lettered D:, then the correct path would be D:\i386.
6. You will be presented with the Internet Information Server Setup dialog box as shown in Figure 49.4. From this box select the options you want to install and the directory where you will be installing IIS. Click the OK button to continue.

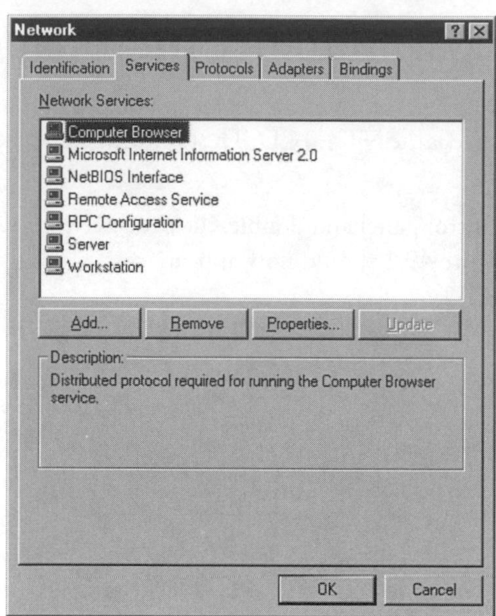

Figure 49.2. The Services tab.

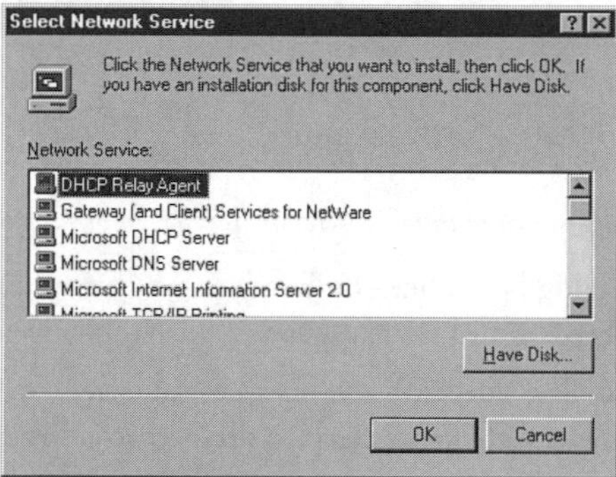

Figure 49.3. The Select Network Service dialog box.

7. Next, you will be prompted with the dialog box shown in Figure 49.5. This dialog box allows you to configure what the default root directory for each service will be. Select the desired directories and click OK. You may be prompted to confirm the creation of the directories if they did not already exist. If so, click OK.
8. NT will now begin copying the files necessary for IIS to your hard drive.
9. Once the files have been installed, you will be given the opportunity to install the SQL ODBC driver. This driver will allow the IIS services to access databases running on an SQL server. Install this driver if you plan to access any databases stored on SQL server.

10. After completing the IIS installation, click OK in the IIS Setup dialog box to close the dialog box.
11. Click Close in the Network Properties dialog box.
12. IIS is now installed and should now be running.

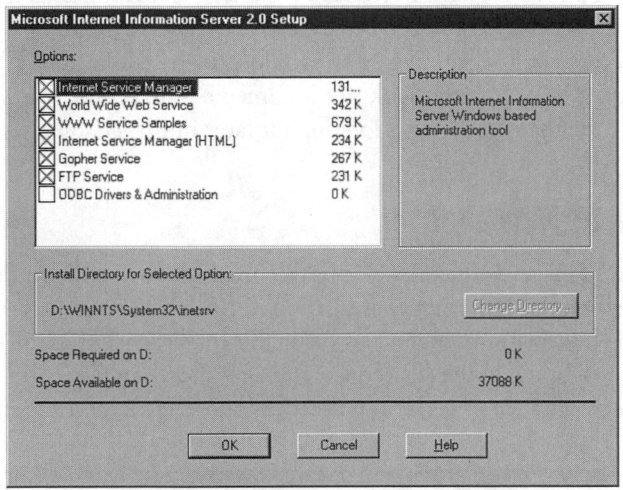

Figure 49.4. *The Internet Information Server dialog box.*

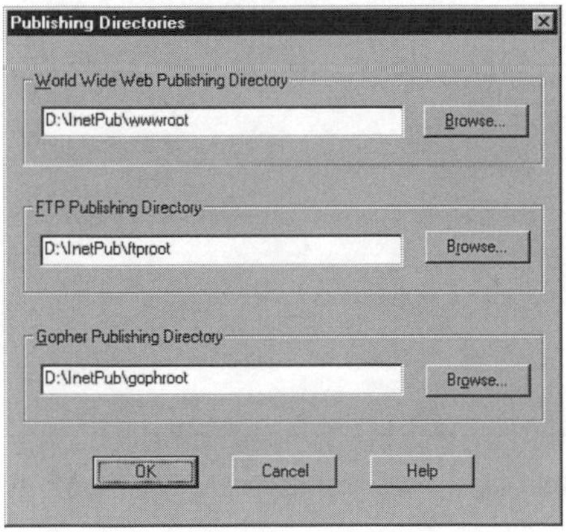

Figure 49.5. *The root directory dialog box.*

Configuring IIS

Now that you have IIS installed, you can optimize IIS for your environment. The following sections will show you what you can configure and how to configure it. Let's get started.

Overview of IIS Directory Structure

During the installation of IIS, you were prompted to enter the path for each of the services' directory. This directory acts as the root directory for each service. For information to be visible to the service, it must be put in the root directory or below. By default, the installation of IIS creates WWWROOT, FTPROOT, GOPHROOT, and scripts directories. These directories act as the root for all the services offered by IIS. For example, to have your initial Web index page come up when clients access your Web server, you would put the file in the WWWROOT folder. By default, the file the WWW server looks for is named `default.htm`. You will learn how to change the name of the file that the server is looking for later in this chapter.

The IIS Service Manager

The IIS Service Manager is the central interface used for the configuration and operation of all services provided by IIS. During the installation of IIS, a folder named Microsoft Internet Server was installed to your Programs menu bar. From this folder, click the icon labeled Internet Service Manager. This will bring up the IIS Service Manager shown in Figure 49.6. From the IIS Service Manager, you can see a list of servers and services running IIS and the status of the service.

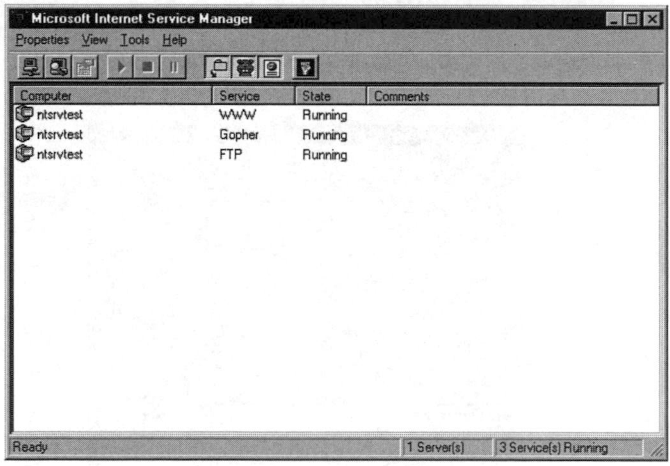

Figure 49.6. *The IIS Service Manager.*

Changing Views

The IIS Service Manager allows you to view services in many different views. Available views include

- By Server
- By Service State
- By Service

To change the way you are currently viewing services, simply click View from the menu bar of the IIS Manager and select the settings you desire.

The flexibility allows you to easily configure and manage multiple servers across your network.

Working with Multiple Servers

The flexible interface of the IIS Manager enables you to view the status of more than one server at a time. This is good for multi-server environments where a single administrator might be charged with the task of keeping up with multiple systems across the network.

To add another server to the IIS Manager, do the following:

1. From the IIS Manager menu bar, click Properties.
2. From the Server menu drop-down select Connect to Server to specify which server you want to connect to, or click Find All Servers if you want the IIS Manager to search for all IIS servers on the local subnet.
3. Once connected, the server and the status of its services will appear in the IIS Manager.

Security

IIS integrates with the security features built into Windows NT. Users can also be granted anonymous access, but then the user will only have the rights assigned to the Internet server account that is created during the IIS install. Some of the additional security features built into IIS include the following:

- Secure Socket Layer
- Packet filter on IP address
- Support for user authentication

Secure Socket Layer

The Secure Socket Layer is designed to allow the client and server components to share data of a secure line. This means that any information sent between the two systems will be readable by only those two systems, and not by other users on the Internet who may be looking around at data floating on the Net. To accomplish this, a key is created and registered with a key verification server. Then, when a client system connects to the secured server, it will receive the key necessary to decrypt the data from the server.

Packet Filter on IP Address

IIS gives you the ability to determine which workstations can access the server. IIS is able to do this by filtering data from specific IP addresses. Every machine that communicates on the Net has an IP address. If you configure IIS not to listen to that IP address, the machine will not be able to communicate with the server.

Support for User Authentication

Internet Information Server supports the ability to restrict access to only users listed in the NT user account database, requiring any client wishing to access services on the server to log in. IIS offers two forms of user authentication: basic or challenge and response.

Basic authentication provides no methods for securing the information that is passed between the client and the server. This means that the user ID and password of the user logging in to the IIS server has the potential of being intercepted by a network sniffer.

The challenge and response method of authentication uses the encrypted authentication methods supported by Windows NT. This prevents the user ID and password from being intercepted from the network. The downside is that not all network clients support the challenge and response method of user authentication.

WWW

You have already taken a look at some of the configuration options available with IIS. This section and the FTP and WWW sections are going to review in greater detail specific items available for configuring the services in IIS.

Each service in IIS has a properties sheet that lists configurable values. To access the properties sheet for the WWW service, open the IIS Manager and double-click the WWW service whose property sheet you want to view. You should see a dialog box similar to the one shown in Figure 49.7. Let's take a closer look.

Service

The Service tab shows the basic configuration parameters that provide the broadest effect. The parameters available here are as follows:

- TCP Port—This is the port number that the IIS WWW service listens for client requests to come in on.
- Connection Timeout—The time period that the server will maintain an inactive connection before disconnecting the client.
- Maximum Connections—The number of simultaneous connections the server allows.
- Anonymous Logon—This box shows what user account an anonymous user is assigned when logged in. The account shown here should have very limited access to the system.
- Password Authentication—The password authentication field is used to determine what types of authentication are allowed to the system. For more information on the security options listed here, check the section on security located earlier in this chapter.

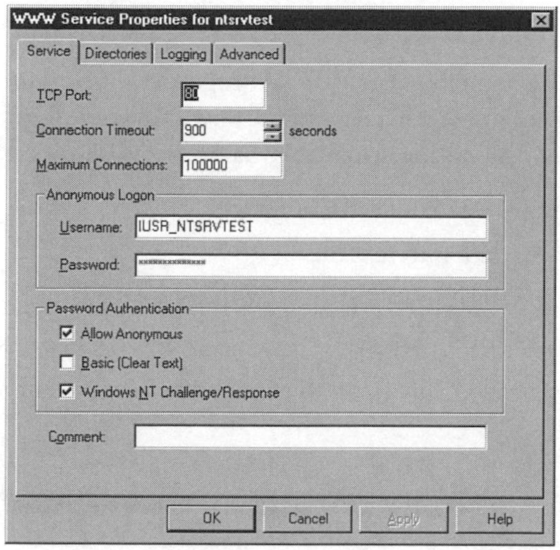

Figure 49.7. The WWW Service Properties sheet.

Directories

By clicking the Directories tab of the WWW Properties sheet, you will see a dialog box similar to the one shown in Figure 49.8. From here, you can set the location of the root directories for the WWW service. You can add, delete, or modify directories from this window.

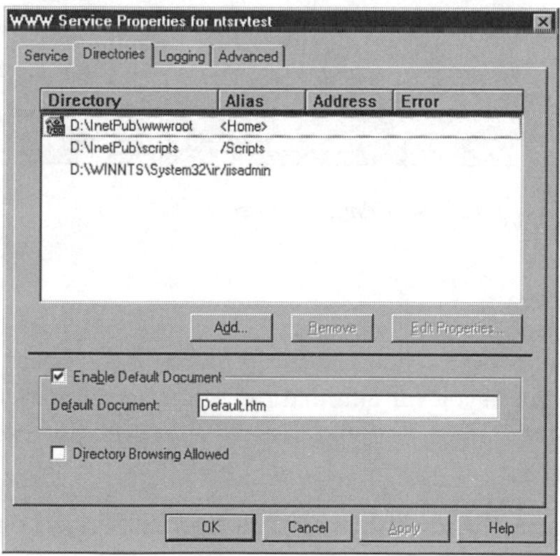

Figure 49.8. The Directories tab of the WWW Properties sheet.

Logging

You can click the Logging tab in the WWW Properties sheet to bring up the windows shown in Figure 49.9. This sheet allows you to configure how and where logs showing the use of the WWW server will be stored. The options from this dialog are as follows:

- ◆ Enable Logging—Enables or disables logging.
- ◆ Log to File—Stores log to text file.
- ◆ Log to SQL Server—Stores log to an SQL server database.
- ◆ Logging Format—Allows you to choose between NCSA or standard logging.
- ◆ Log File Directory—Allows you to specify where you want to store your logs when logging to file.

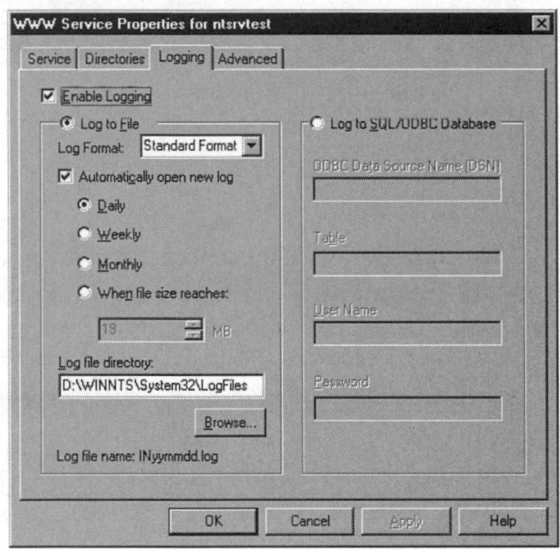

Figure 49.9. *The Logging tab of the WWW Properties sheet.*

Advanced

The Advanced tab provides two key features. The first is the Grant Access security feature. From here, you can determine if you will automatically grant access to everyone (the default setting) and filter out only a few machines, or if you wish to reject everyone except those users to whom you specifically grant access.

The other feature, Limit bandwidth used by all Internet Services on this computer, allows you to actually limit the amount of bandwidth the services of IIS can use. This is very important if you feel your pipe to the Internet is being wiped out by a constant inflow of hits to your Web page or other services.

Virtual Servers

The concept of virtual servers is very neat. Basically, it allows one IIS server to service requests to multiple domains. For example, if your domain name is `bitnet.net` and you want to service requests for `paranet.com`, you make the IIS server look like two different servers by creating a virtual server. The following steps outline how you make one:

1. First, you need another valid TCP/IP address.
2. Set up your DNS server so that any request for `bitnet.net` goes to IP address one and that all requests for `paranet.com` go to IP address two.
3. On the IIS server, click the Directories tab in the WWW Service Properties sheet.
4. Click the Add button. You should now see the Directory Properties dialog box shown in Figure 49.10.

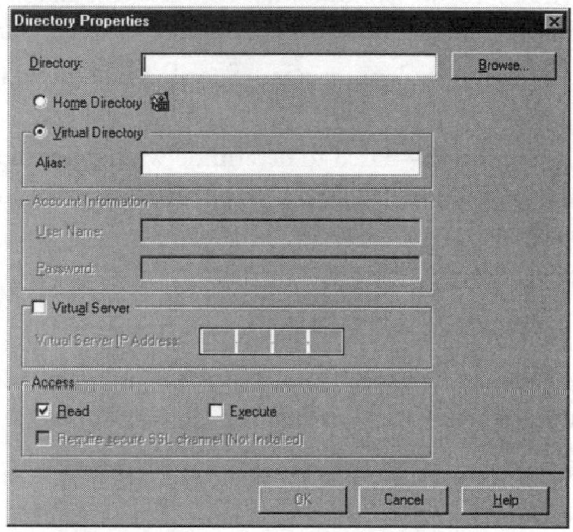

Figure 49.10. *The Directory Properties dialog box.*

5. From this dialog box you need to enter the following information.

   Directory—Specifies the path to the physical directory in which the files for the domain reside.

   Home Directory—Determines that the path in the directory statement is the home directory.

   Virtual Directory—Allows you to specify a name that represents the directory.

   Virtual Server—Indicates that the Virtual Server option be active. Once checked, enter the IP address that you have selected to be used by the virtual server.

   Access—Determines the type of access that clients have to the IIS server component.

   After completing this configuration, your IIS server will be able to service requests to the virtual domain.

FTP

The FTP service of IIS allows FTP clients to retrieve and place files on your NT server. The following sections describe the tabs of the properties sheet for the FTP service.

Services

The Services tab of the FTP service contains the following information:

- TCP Port—The port number that the IIS FTP service listens to for client requests.
- Connection Timeout—The time period that the server will maintain an inactive connection before disconnecting the client.
- Maximum Connections—The number of simultaneous connections the server allows.
- Allow Anonymous Logon—Shows what user account an anonymous user is assigned to when logged in. The account shown here should have very limited access to the system.
- Allow Only Anonymous Connections—Specifies whether any user other than anonymous can log in to the system.
- Password Authentication—Used to determine what types of authentication are allowed to the system. For more information on the security options listed here, check the section on security located earlier in this chapter.

Messages

The Messages tab enables you to specify messages that you want to appear to clients of the FTP server of IIS. Options include the following:

- Welcome Message
- Exit Message
- Maximum Connections Message

Directories

The Directories tab enables you to specify which directories are accessible to the FTP service. Options from this tab allow you to add, edit, or delete directory pointers. Keep in mind that you are only deleting or creating pointers, and not actual files. This box also allows you to specify the type of directory listing that the FTP service will use. You have a choice of UNIX, default, or MS-DOS.

Logging

Click the Logging tab in the FTP Properties sheet. This sheet allows you to configure how and where logs showing the use of the FTP server will be stored. The options from this dialog are as follows:

- Enable Logging—Enables or disables logging.
- Log to File—Stores log to text file.
- Log to SQL Server—Stores log to an SQL database server.
- Logging Format—Allows you to choose between NCSA or standard logging.
- Log File Directory—Allows you to specify where you want to store your logs when logging to file.

Advanced

The Advanced tab of the FTP Properties sheet is the same available in all IIS services property sheets. It provides two key features. The first is the Grant Access security feature. From here, you can determine if you will automatically grant access to everyone (the default setting) and filter out only a few machines, or if you want to reject everyone except those users to whom you specifically grant access.

The other feature, Limit bandwidth used by all Internet Services on this computer, allows you to actually limit the amount of bandwidth the services of IIS can use. This is very important if you feel your pipe to the Internet is being wiped out by a constant inflow of hits to your Web page or other IIS services.

Gopher

The following sections describe the properties sheets for the Gopher service of IIS.

Services

The Services sheet contains the following options:

- TCP Port—The port number that the IIS Gopher service listens to for client requests.
- Connection Timeout—The time period that the server will maintain an inactive connection before disconnecting the client.
- Maximum Connections—The number of simultaneous connections the server allows.
- Service Administrator—Used to specify the name and the e-mail address of the service administrator for the Gopher server.

- Anonymous Logon—Shows what user account an anonymous user is assigned to when logged in. The account shown here should have very limited access to the system.
- Comment—Allows you to specify any comments that you want to be seen from the IIS Manager.

Directories

This Directories dialog box allows you to specify which directories are available for use from the Gopher server. You have the option to add, delete, or modify the properties directories to be used.

Logging

Click the Logging tab in the Gopher Properties sheet to bring up the Logging Options dialog box. This sheet allows you to configure how logs showing the use of the Gopher server will be stored. The options from this dialog are as follows:

- Enable Logging—Enables or disables logging.
- Log to File—Stores log to text file.
- Log to SQL Server—Stores log to an SQL database server.
- Logging Format—Allows you to choose between NCSA or standard logging.
- Log File Directory—Allows you to specify where you want to store your logs when logging to file.

Advanced

The Advanced tab of the Gopher Properties sheet is the same available in all IIS services property sheets.

The Advanced tab provides two key features. The first is the Grant Access security feature. From here, you can determine if you will automatically grant access to everyone (the default setting) and filter out only a few machines, or if you wish to reject everyone except those users to whom you specifically grant access.

The other feature, Limit bandwidth used by all Internet Services on this computer, allows you to actually limit the amount of bandwidth the services of IIS can use. This is very important if you feel your pipe to the Internet is being wiped out by a constant inflow of hits to your Web page or other IIS services.

Upgrading to IIS 3.0

Microsoft has released an update to the version of IIS that ships with Windows NT 4.0. This version, 3.0, now supports active server pages. Active server pages provide features that make developing Web-based applications easier. The upgrade is available for free from Microsoft at `www.micorsoft.com/IIS`.

Troubleshooting

The IIS service is a simple service and usually runs trouble free. If you do encounter problems, the following are excellent resources for resolving issues:

- The Microsoft Technet CD—This CD is available via a yearly subscription and is updated monthly. It provides a wealth of knowledge on IIS and other Microsoft Products. For more information on Microsoft Technet, check the Microsoft Web site at `www.microsoft.com`.
- The Microsoft Web site—Microsoft's Web site provides some of the most current information on IIS and other NT products. It provides bulletins, patches, and updates that are downloadable to your system free of charge. You can find the Microsoft Web site at `www.microsoft.com`.

Summary of Features

IIS contains many features. This chapter has covered the details of these features. The following sections summarize the features that can be found in IIS.

Internet Services

The Internet services will probably be the most used services of IIS. The following outlines the features included in the Internet services of IIS:

- Includes high performance HTTP, FTP, and Gopher engines
- Compatible implementation of the current open Internet HTTP 1.0 standard for Web servers
- Fully integrated into the operating system
- Only Web server integrated into a network operating system
- Part of the Windows NT Server installation, which means that IIS is up and running with Windows NT Server
- Single user directory for all Web servers
- Uses the Windows NT Server user database
- Uses the same Windows NT Server access controls (ACLs) as all other Windows services
- Optimized performance through a lightweight single-process design with a multi-threaded architecture

- Scalable to high-performance, multi-processor–based systems ensuring your site can handle the heaviest traffic loads
- Instant access to the BackOffice Product Suite
- Easy remote administration
- Flexible monitoring and logging
- Server-side scripting

Summary

You should now have a pretty good idea of what IIS is and how it works with the NT operating system. In this chapter, you gained an overview of the Internet and intranets and how IIS can work in these environments. You became familiar with IIS installation and the configuration options, and learned how to effectively manage the services of IIS. For more information on this or other Microsoft products, check out the Microsoft home page at `www.microsoft.com`.

Microsoft Proxy Server

by John West

Accessing the Internet is quickly becoming a requirement to maintain competitiveness in the business environment. Connecting to the Internet, however, has traditionally been a time-consuming and complicated task. To enable companies to quickly and easily gain access to the resources of the Internet, the proxy server was created. A proxy server does the following:

- Enables you to connect your entire local area network to the Internet using a Windows NT dial-up connection
- Enables users to access TCP/IP application while running only the IPX/SPX protocols
- Saves money by auto connecting to your ISP when needed

This chapter's focus is on the proxy server being offered by Microsoft: Microsoft Proxy Server. In this chapter, you get to go through the components of a proxy server and see how it works. You will learn how to install and configure Microsoft's Proxy Server and take a look at administering and troubleshooting it. Let's get started.

What Is a Proxy Server?

A proxy server takes all Internet requests from network clients, and processes them on behalf of the client. For example, as shown in Figure 50.1, the local area client wants to view `www.microsoft.com`. The system first contacts the proxy server, which then packages the request with the proxy server's IP address and contacts `www.microsoft.com`. When the data is sent from `www.microsoft.com`, the data will first pass to the proxy server before going on to the local client. By acting on behalf of the client, the proxy server enables the client to access the Internet without requiring the client to have a legitimate IP address or run the TCP/IP protocol. In addition to allowing clients that run the IPX/SPX or TCP/IP protocols access to the Web, the proxy server acts as a terrific security barrier to your network. The only system visible to the Internet is the proxy server. All other systems are shielded from the Net by the proxy server.

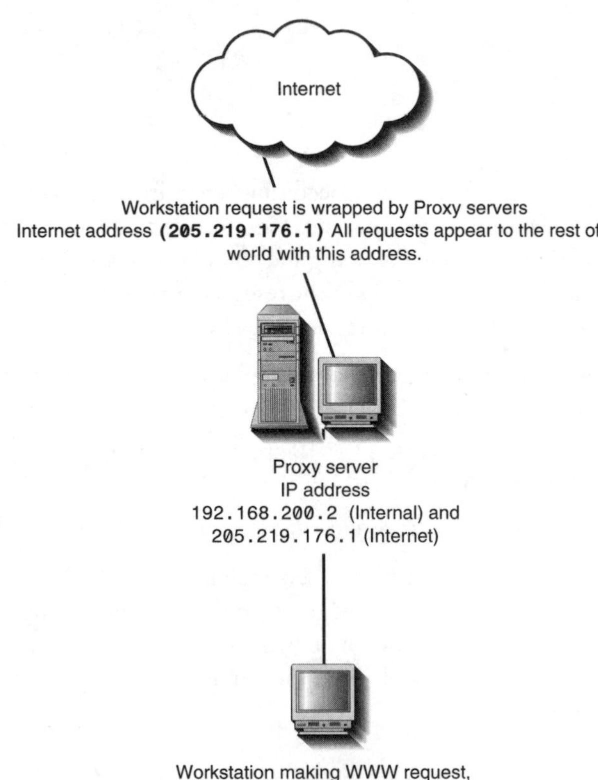

Figure 50.1. *The network client tries to contact the Internet through a proxy server.*

The Components of Microsoft's Proxy Server

Microsoft Proxy Server provides the capability to act as a proxy for most Internet applications. The capabilities that Microsoft Proxy Server offers are broken down into two services: the Web proxy service and the WinSock proxy service.

Web Proxy Service

The Web proxy service in Microsoft's Proxy Server handles all Web requests from clients of the proxy server. The http requests from proxy clients are sent to the Web proxy service, which generally runs on socket 80. This service then wraps the request with the proxy server IP address and forwards the request to the intended recipient.

WinSock Proxy Service

The WinSock proxy service provides the same services as the Web proxy except it does it for other TCP applications. You see, each TCP/IP application listens to a particular socket to receive information. The WinSock proxy service for NT can be configured to receive requests from many different WinSock applications—such as Real Time Audio or Internet Relay Chat—and forward those services to the appropriate socket. The WinSock proxy service also has the capability to receive and process multiple requests at the same time.

Features

Microsoft's Proxy Server includes many features to allow it to easily integrate with most network environments. The following outlines some of the features included in Microsoft's Proxy Server:

Integrates easily with existing networks

- Supports both TCP/IP and IPX/SPX protocols, so you can use it with your existing network without modification
- Requires no end-user training because it works with existing Web browsers, desktop operating systems, and hardware platforms
- Integrates tightly with the Windows NT Server networking, security, and administrative interface, so you can centrally administer Proxy Server using the same tools

Supports open standards for broad compatibility

- Complies fully with the CERN-proxy standard, which supports the HTTP, FTP, and Gopher protocols, providing access to the widest possible range of browsers and Internet applications
- Supports the Secure Sockets Layer (SSL) for secure data communication through data encryption and decryption

- Includes WinSock proxy, which supports Windows Sockets version 1.1-compatible applications running on a private network, including LDAP, IRC, SMTP, Microsoft SQL Server, RealAudio, and VDOLive, without any modification

Delivers high-performance access to the Internet and your intranet

- Improves response times and minimizes network traffic by caching a local copy of frequently requested Internet or intranet data on the proxy server
- Dynamically analyzes Internet and intranet use and automatically identifies the most frequently used data to be cached, ensuring that users can access the most popular information quickly
- Enables administrators to define a Time-to-Live for all objects in the cache, helping to keep the information fresh and ensure maximum efficiency

Provides secure, managed access

- Prevents unauthorized Internet users from connecting to your private network, keeping your sensitive data secure
- Integrates tightly with Windows NT Server user authentication, enabling the administrator to control who uses the Internet and which services they use
- Blocks access to restricted sites by IP address or domain so you can ensure that your users are using their Internet privileges appropriately

Installation

The installation of the Microsoft Proxy Server is quick and straightforward. In addition to the Proxy Server installation, you also have the option of installing just the admin tool for administering proxy servers from a system that does not have the proxy server installed. Another option is a client piece that enables programs that are not proxy aware the capability to make use of the proxy server. The purpose of this section is to show the steps involved in installing the Proxy Server and its components.

Server Installation

To install Microsoft's Proxy Server, you will need to obtain the proxy server software. Microsoft Proxy Server can be purchased directly from Microsoft or from a reseller of Microsoft products. You can also download a 120 day fully functional evaluation copy from Microsoft's World Wide Web site at `www.microsoft.com/proxy`. Before running the Microsoft Proxy Server installation, make sure to review the requirements section and make sure your system meets them.

Installation Requirements

Microsoft's Proxy Server is currently available for the Intel and RISC-based platforms. The installation requires very little in the way of hardware requirements. In the next section, you will find the hardware requirements for the specific platforms.

Hardware Requirements

Microsoft Proxy Server has the same hardware requirements as Microsoft Windows NT Server Version 4.0. The Windows NT Server Version 4.0 System Requirements are as follows:

Intel and compatible systems:

- 486/33 MHz or higher, or Pentium or Pentium PRO processor
- 15MB of available hard disk space minimum

RISC-based systems:

- RISC processor compatible with Windows NT Server Version 4.0
- 20MB of available hard disk space

All Systems:

- 16MB of memory (RAM)
- CD-ROM drive
- VGA, Super VGA, or video graphics adapter compatible with Windows NT Server 4.0

Software Requirements

Microsoft Proxy can be broken into two components, the server and the client. Each of these has its own specific set of operating system requirements. These requirements are outlined in the following sections.

Server

- Microsoft Windows NT Server Version 4.0
- Microsoft Internet Information Server Version 2.0 (included with Windows NT Server 4.0)
- The Windows NT Server 4.0 Service Pack 1 (provided on the Microsoft Proxy Server compact disc)

Client

The following is a list of operating systems supported by Microsoft Proxy Server:

- Windows 3.*x*
- Windows for Workgroups

- Windows 95
- Windows NT Workstation
- Apple Macintosh
- MS-DOS OS/2
- UNIX (Requires ODBC client software from Visigenic Software, San Mateo, California.)

Installing the Proxy Server Software

Installing the Microsoft Proxy Server is a simple and straightforward process. It should be noted that the Proxy Server setup will require that you stop all IIS services during the installation. The steps for installing the Microsoft Proxy Server follow:

1. Start the Microsoft Proxy installation by double-clicking the setup program on the CD-ROM.
2. You will be presented with a Welcome to Proxy Server setup dialog box. Click the Continue button.
3. Next, you will be prompted to enter your CD key. You can find this on the back of the CD-ROM case that the Microsoft Proxy Server CD-ROM came in.
4. You will be asked to confirm your settings and then will be prompted with a dialog box showing the location that setup plans to use to install files. When you are ready to continue, press the large button next to Installation Options.
5. You will now be prompted with the Installation Options dialog box. Choose the options you want to install. When ready, click the Continue button.
6. Next, you will be asked to set the drives and the amount of space the Proxy Server will use to cache the files downloaded by proxy clients. Cache files to the drive will allow proxy clients to experience faster access time and can reduce the amount of traffic sent over your Internet link. Choose the appropriate settings for your site and then click the OK button.
7. After you click OK, you will be presented with the Local Address Configuration dialog box. From this box, enter the beginning and ending IP address that your network will be using. Note that the address ranges that you will see entered are addresses that the InterNIC has set aside for the specific purpose of Internal networks.
8. The Client/Installation dialog box will now appear. From this dialog box, choose the settings you want to use when configuring your client software. When completed, click OK.
9. The Proxy Server setup program will now copy the Proxy Server files to your hard drive. Once the files are copied, the IIS services will be restarted and the Installation will be complete.

Removing the Proxy Server Software

It should be noted that WWW services will be shut down during the Uninstall process. Use the following steps to remove Microsoft Proxy Server:

1. Select Uninstall from the Start | Programs | Microsoft Proxy Server folder.
2. You will be prompted with a dialog box asking you to confirm that you want to uninstall Proxy Server. Click the Yes button.
3. The Proxy Server will stop the IIS services and remove the Proxy Server files.
4. When completed, the uninstall process will restart IIS services and present a dialog box stating that setup completed successfully.

Client Installation

In order to provide transparent access for Internet applications to the proxy server, Microsoft has created the proxy server Web client. This client intercepts and redirects client software requests to the proxy server. Installation of this client piece is not mandatory. It is possible to configure applications that are proxy aware to use the proxy server without the client piece. Examples of software packages that are proxy aware include Internet Explorer, Real Time Audio, and the Point Cast Network software. This section takes you through the installation and removal of the client software.

The Installation

Here are the steps to install the Microsoft Proxy Client:

1. The server that has the Microsoft Proxy Client service installed will automatically make the client software available in a share named `mspclnt`. From the client workstation you will choose to install the proxy client software and map a drive to the server running proxy server to the `mspclnt` share.
2. From the drive that is mapped to the `mspclnt` share, run `setup.exe`.
3. Setup will present you with a dialog similar to the one shown in Figure 50.2. From this dialog box, select the directory you want to install the proxy server client software into, and then click the Install Microsoft Proxy Client button.
4. The installation will begin copying files to the hard drive.
5. Microsoft Proxy Client setup will then present a dialog box stating the software was installed successfully. Click OK.
6. The installation is now complete.

You should now be able to use any TCP/IP apps to access the Net through the proxy server.

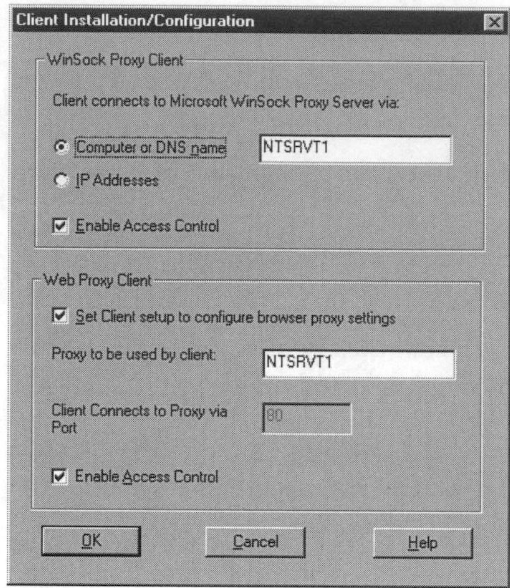

Figure 50.2. *The Proxy Client setup box.*

Removing Client Software

Removing the software is simple and straightforward. To remove the Microsoft Proxy Client software, perform the following steps:

1. Open the Microsoft Proxy Client folder and run Uninstall.
2. The Microsoft Proxy Uninstall program will prompt you to confirm the Uninstall. Click Yes.
3. The Uninstall program will now remove the files from your hard drive. Once completed, you will be prompted to reboot the system to complete the uninstall.
4. After the system finishes rebooting, the uninstall will be complete.

Configuration

Both the Web proxy server and the WinSock proxy server offer options that the administrator can and will need to configure in order to use these services. This section shows each of the options that these services offer and explains their meaning.

Web Proxy Server

The Web proxy component is responsible for processing Web-based requests made by proxy clients. This section covers the options that can be configured for the Web proxy server component of Microsoft Proxy Server.

Setting Up Proxy Users for the First Time

Microsoft Proxy Server is integrated into the Windows NT user account database. As the proxy administrator, you have the following security options for users of the Web proxy server:

- Determining whether the proxy server authenticates clients using Anonymous, Clear Text, or Windows NT Challenge/Response messages
- Limiting users' access to specific services such as HTTP, FTP, Gopher, and Secure Socket Services

Choosing Authentication Method

Microsoft Proxy Server works in cooperation with Microsoft Internet Information Server. There are instances where settings in the configuration of Microsoft's IIS Web server affects settings to Microsoft Proxy Server as well. The configuration of authentication methods is one of those instances. Perform the following to configure the authentication methods for Microsoft Proxy Server:

1. Start the Microsoft Internet Service Manager by going to the Microsoft Proxy folder and clicking it. You should now see the dialog box shown in Figure 50.3.

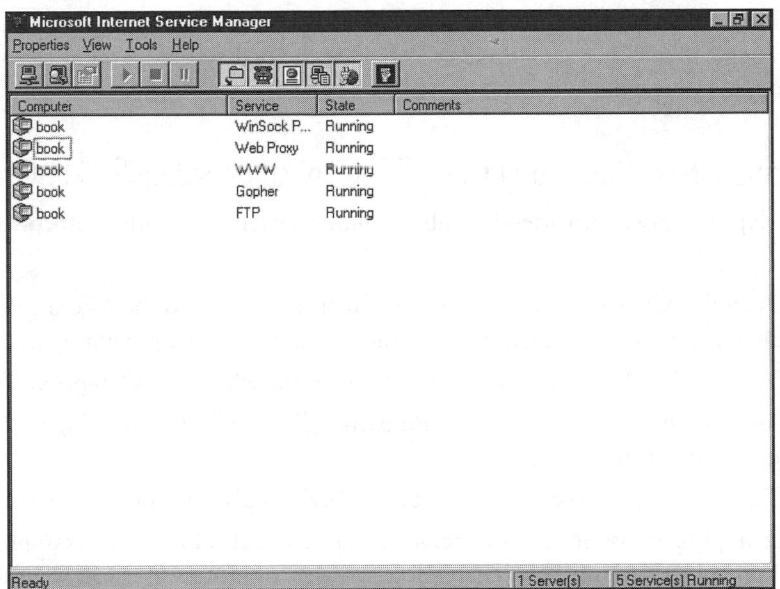

Figure 50.3. *The Internet Information Server Service Manager.*

2. Double-click the server name that appears next to the WWW service.
3. You should now see the WWW Services dialog box similar to the one shown in Figure 50.4. Notice the check boxes under password authentication.

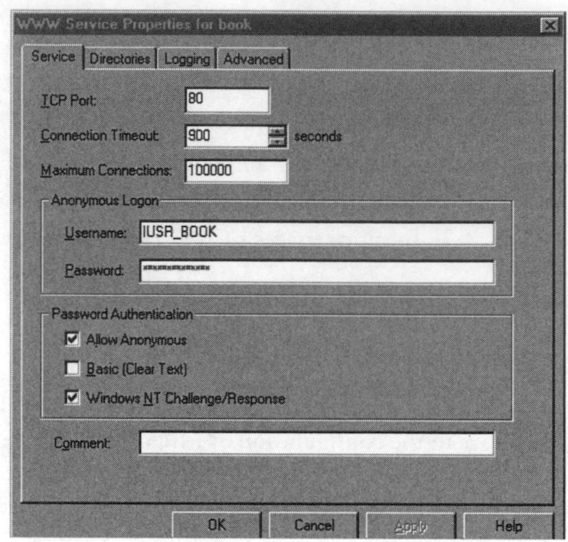

Figure 50.4. *The WWW Services dialog box.*

4. Choose the setting appropriate for your installation. Selecting Anonymous will allow any user to use the services. Clear Text creates the possibility that passwords can be captured from the network. Using NT Challenge/Response will guarantee the security of your system. If you choose all three, NT will use the best system authentication that the client logging in can do.

Configuring Users' Access to HTTP, FTP, Gopher, or Secure Socket Protocols

The Web proxy service provides the ability to limit users from specific protocols. Here is how you do it:

1. Open the Microsoft Internet Service Manager by going to the Microsoft Proxy folder and clicking it. You should now see the dialog box shown previously in Figure 50.3.
2. Double-click the server name that appears to the left of the Web proxy service.
3. You will now see the Web Proxy Properties dialog box shown in Figure 50.5. From here, select the Permissions tab.
4. Check the Enable Access Control box to begin applying protocol-specific permissions.
5. To apply permission to a service, select the protocol (HTTP, for example) from the Protocol drop-down box. Then select the users or groups that you want to permit to use this service.

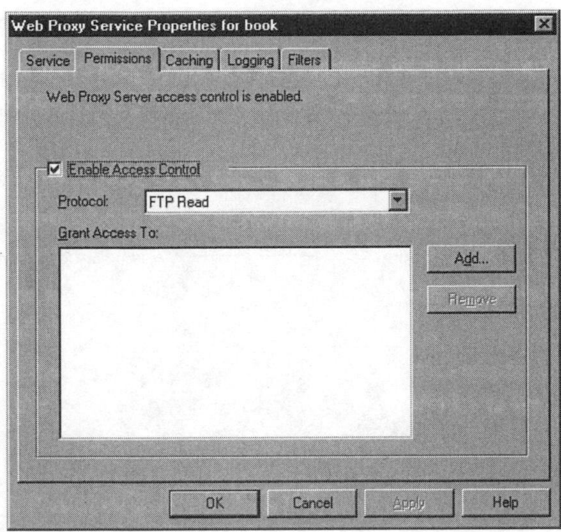

Figure 50.5. *The Web Proxy dialog box.*

Caching

Caching allows data retrieved from the Internet to be stored on the Proxy Server's local hard drive. This is useful for increasing response time to clients and reducing bandwidth usage on wide area network lines. The following describes how to configure caching on your Proxy Server:

1. Select the Caching tab from the Web Proxy Properties dialog box shown in Figure 50.5.
2. The Caching tab will appear as shown in Figure 50.6. To enable caching, check the Enable Caching check box. Adjust the caching option as appropriate for your installation. This setting varies depending on the amount of hard drive space you have available.

Local Address Table

The local address table (LAT) defines what address ranges make up your local area network. This basically lets the proxy server know from what addresses the server should service requests. An improperly set LAT can cause unauthorized access to the proxy server. The following describes the steps for configuring the LAT:

1. From the Web Proxy Properties dialog box shown in Figure 50.5, click the Edit Local Address Table button.
2. You will now see the Local Address Table Configuration dialog box shown in Figure 50.7. From this dialog box, click the Construct Table button.

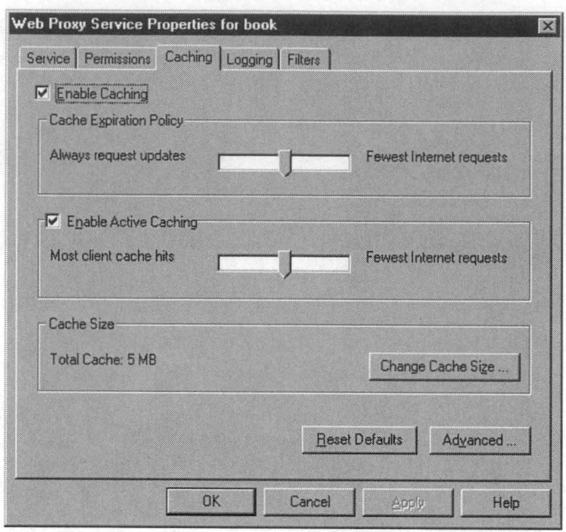

Figure 50.6. *The Caching tab.*

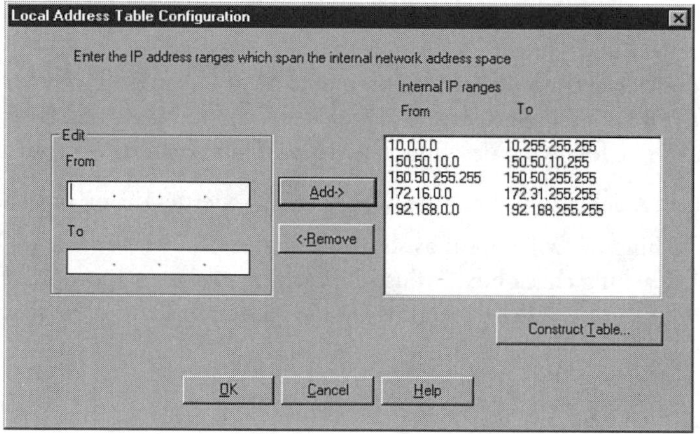

Figure 50.7. *The Local Address Table Configuration dialog box.*

3. This will add all IP addresses that are stored in the routing table. You now need to remove any addresses that represent external networks. This will allow these addresses access to the proxy server. If the addresses for your network are not entered here, they will not be able to access the rest of the network.
4. The system is now ready to receive requests from the Internet.

Dial-Up Support

Microsoft Proxy Server can use Remote Access connections to provide proxy services. In addition, this service can be provided on demand. This means that whenever a proxy client goes to access a Web page, the proxy server will automatically connect to your Internet service provider and then pass the request. This can be very helpful in keeping the costs of your Internet connectivity to a minimum. To configure automatic dial up, perform the following steps:

1. Open the Microsoft Proxy Server folder.
2. Click Auto Dial Configuration.
3. The Auto Dial Configuration dialog box will appear. From the Dialing Hours tab, check the Enable Dial on Demand check box.
4. Click the Credential tab.
5. On the Credential tab, select a remote access phone entry of your ISP. Enter your user ID and password for this connection.
6. Click the OK button at the bottom of the window.
7. Now you are ready to begin using Auto Dial.

Security

The security of Microsoft Proxy Server is integrated tightly with the security of the Windows NT operating system. This allows Microsoft Proxy Server to take full advantage of the C2 security feature of Windows NT. The following section describes some features of the security modes of the system.

Authentication Methods

Microsoft Proxy Server uses various forms of authentication methods. These methods can allow any user to access the proxy server or allow only select users access to the proxy server. This is useful when working in an environment where you may have limited bandwidth out to the Internet and only want certain users accessing this resource. The authentication methods used by Proxy Server follow:

- Anonymous

  The anonymous setting allows any users to use the proxy server. This setting provides the highest availability with the least security.

- Basic/Clear Text

  This setting requires that a user of the proxy system have a valid user ID and password. However, the user ID and password are not encrypted. This means that it is possible for people to detect and capture your user ID and password. This option provides some security.

- Windows NT Challenge/Response

  Windows NT Challenge/Response provides the highest security by encrypting passwords, but requires clients to be able to support Microsoft's encryption technology.

Logging

To give you an idea of who is coming and going on your system, the Microsoft Proxy Server offers the capabilities to log events as they occur on the system to either a local text file or to an SQL server database.

Logging Activity

By default, logging is configured to write to local text files for the system. Here are the steps for adjusting the options for logging:

1. Select the Logging tab from the Web Proxy Properties dialog box shown previously in Figure 50.5.
2. The Logging tab, shown in Figure 50.8, will appear. Select the options you want to enable.

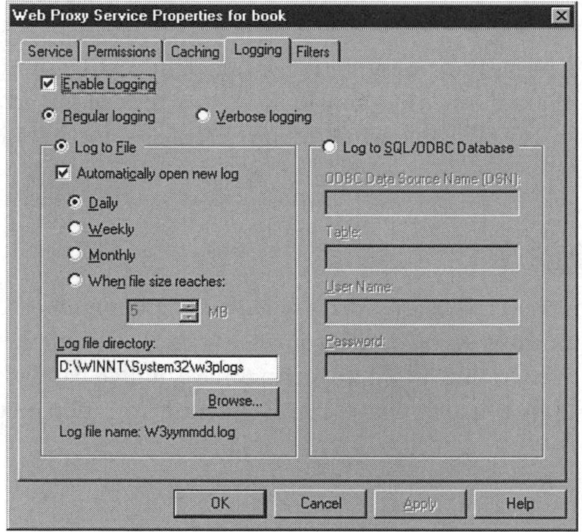

Figure 50.8. *The Logging tab.*

3. When finished, click the OK button. The dialog box will disappear and your log setting will now be active.

WinSock Proxy Server

The WinSock proxy server handles all proxy requests for client software that uses the WinSock 1.1 interface. An example of a WinSock application is Real Time Audio. Most popular applications are already configured in the proxy server. This section will show you how to add applications that are not already configured.

Setting Up Web Proxy Applications

To set up an application in the WinSock proxy service, you need two settings. First, the socket number used to initiate the call (a socket that the server part of the application listens to requests on), and second, the subsequent inbound and outbound sockets that the application will require. These details can usually be found in the Web server's documentation or by contacting the software manufacturer directly. With this information in hand, perform the following steps to add the application to the WinSock proxy server:

1. Start the Microsoft Internet Service Manager by selecting Start | Programs | Microsoft Proxy | Microsoft Internet Service Manager.
2. Double-click the server name that appears to the left of the WinSock proxy service.
3. You will now see the WinSock Proxy Properties dialog box shown in Figure 50.9. Select the Protocols tab.

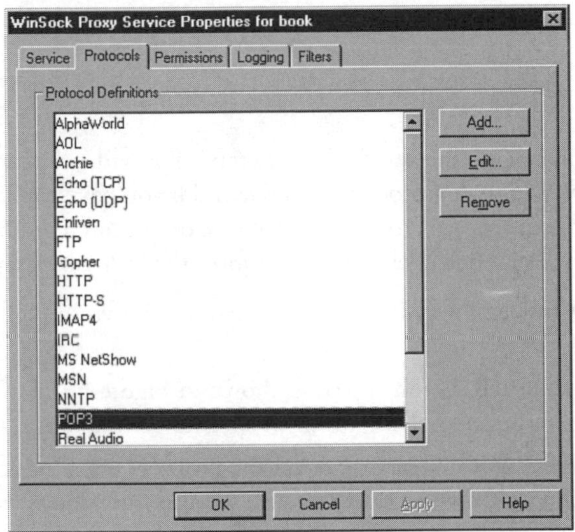

Figure 50.9. *The WinSock Proxy Properties dialog.*

4. In the Protocols tab shown in Figure 50.9, click the Add button.
5. You will now see the Protocol Definition dialog box, shown in Figure 50.10. Insert the name of the protocol and the protocol numbers that you collected earlier.
6. When finished, click OK to close the Protocol Definition dialog box, and then click OK again to close the WinSock Properties dialog.
7. Your new settings are now ready to be used.

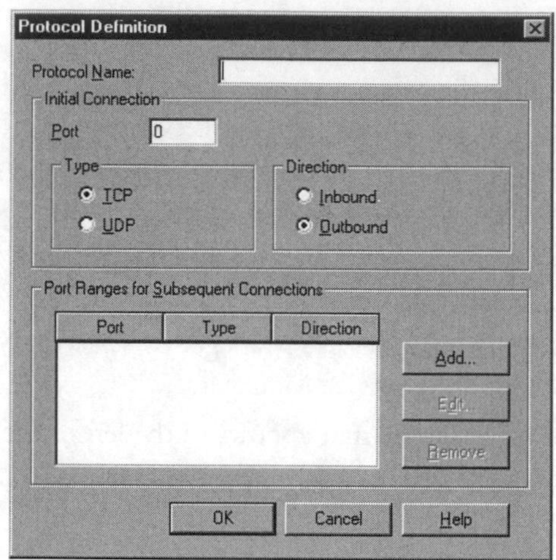

Figure 50.10. *The Protocol Definition dialog.*

Security

Like the Web proxy service, the WinSock proxy service provides the capability to allow user access to all or individual WinSock protocols. This is useful if you have applications that take up a great deal of bandwidth that you want to make available to only a certain number of users. To configure permissions for the WinSock Web Service, perform the following steps:

1. From the WinSock Proxy Properties dialog box, shown in Figure 50.9, select the Permissions tab.
2. The Permissions tab should appear as shown in Figure 50.11. Check the Enable Access Control box to begin applying protocol-specific permissions.
3. To apply permission to a service, select the protocol (`msnetmeeting`, for example), from the Protocol drop-down box. Then select the users or groups that you want to permit to use this service.

Logging

The WinSock Service provides the same logging options that are provided in the Web Proxy Service. To access the logging option for the WinSock Proxy Service, open the WinSock Proxy Service Properties dialog box and bring up the Logging tab. Set your options and then click OK.

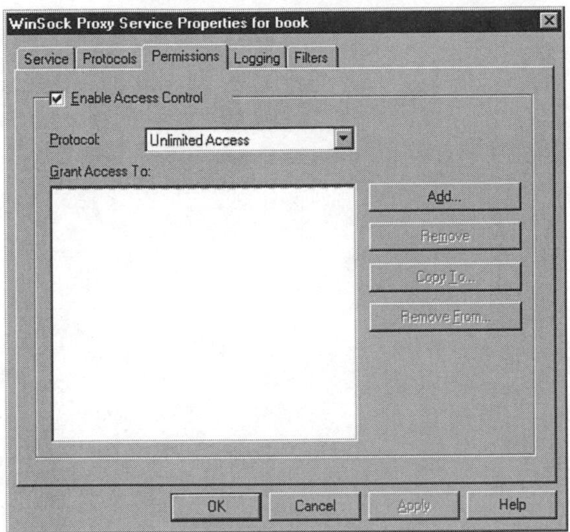

Figure 50.11. *The Permissions tab.*

Summary

You have gained a good look at Microsoft's Proxy Server and the options it offers. You should now have a good understanding of what a proxy server is and how it works. The proxy server system offers a terrific way to securely access the Internet with little configuration necessary by the client. For more information on this and other Microsoft products, check out the Microsoft home page at `www.microsoft.com`.

CHAPTER 51

Internet Explorer

by John West

On August 17, 1995 Microsoft entered the Internet browser market with the initial release of Internet Explorer. This chapter is designed to introduce users to Internet Explorer 3.0, otherwise known as IE 3.0.

This chapter provides the following:

- An overview of the purpose of a Web browser
- The features found in IE 3.0
- A walk-through of the installation process of IE 3.0
- The configuration of Internet Explorer and its optional components

Let's get started.

Overview of Internet Explorer

A Web browser acts as the window and the interpreter through which you can view the splendors of the Internet. When you use a Web browser to view a Web site, you are actually connecting to a computer that could be located anywhere in the world. When your Web client connects to that server, the server sends your client a series of text-based commands and images that make up the Web site. The text is relatively small in size and does not take too long to download. The pictures are much larger in size and take longer. The Web browser then processes the commands and produces the Web page in the viewing window, as shown in Figure 51.1.

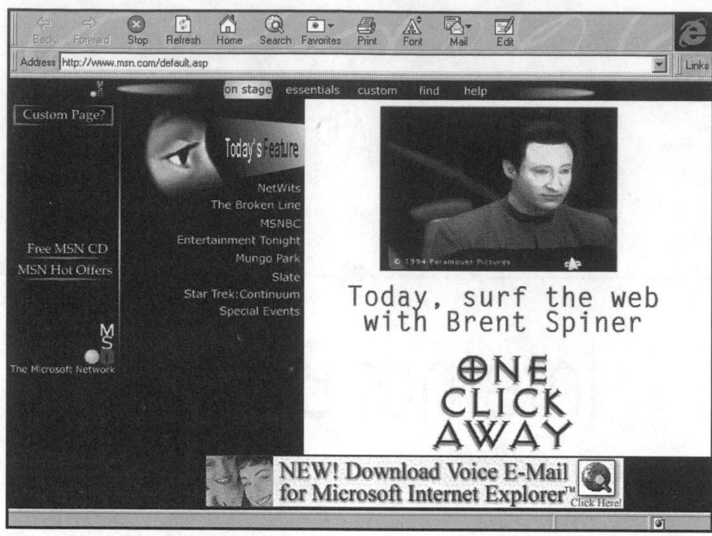

Figure 51.1. *Internet Explorer lets you view the splendor of the Internet.*

Internet Explorer is the Web browser created and distributed by Microsoft. The latest version of Internet Explorer, IE 3.0, supports many important features that allow it to understand the commands that the Internet servers are sending. IE 3.0's feature set includes the following:

- Support for all HTML standards including HTML 3.2

  HTML (Hypertext Markup Language) is the command language used by servers to send commands to the Web browser. By supporting these standards, IE 3.0 will be able to understand and perform the commands that the servers are sending.

- Support for ratings

  Ratings enable you to put password protection on supporting sites that would be inappropriate for children. This can help make the Web experience enjoyable for the whole family.

- Support for style sheets

  Style sheets enable Web creators to easily develop a consistent look and feel to their Web site.

- Support for ActiveX controls

  ActiveX controls are software components that have been designed to be small, lightweight, and fast on the Internet. They include the thousands of existing ActiveX controls, Java applets, and new ActiveX controls.

- Support for Java applets

  Java, which was originally developed by Sun Microsystems, has become a standard for developing more active Web sites. Java allows commands to be downloaded to your system and then executed. This is important for applications whose constant download of their command set would be too slow over traditional telephone links.

- Support for ActiveX Script

  With its support for VBScript and JScript, Microsoft Internet Explorer 3.0 provides the most comprehensive and language-independent script capabilities offered by a Web browser. You can plug any scripting language, such as VBScript or JScript, into your HTML code to create interactive pages that link ActiveX controls, Java applets, and other software components together.

- Includes ActiveMovie

  ActiveMovie provides playback of all popular video and audio formats on the Internet.

Optional Components

Optional components are add-on components that add more functionality separate from the Web browser. For example, Internet Mail and Internet News are considered optional components. This section covers the optional components available with the Internet Explorer install.

Internet Mail

Internet Mail is used to retrieve and send e-mail to and from e-mail servers. This product is compatible with any POP3 and SMTP e-mail server. POP3 and SMTP are common Internet-based e-mail standards.

Internet News

Internet News enables users to explore and view items posted to a Usenet server. Usenet is a collection of groups where users can find postings from other Internet users. Groups cover a very broad area of topics. At last count, there were more than 12,000 newsgroups available. Generally, your Internet service provider will provide connection information for your local news server.

Microsoft Netmeeting

Microsoft Netmeeting enables users to conduct conferences over the Internet or local intranet. Users of Netmeeting can collaborate on documents, carry on conversations, and even send files back and forth to each other across the network.

Support of these features and others allows Microsoft's Internet Explorer to interact with many different types of servers available on the Internet. In the following sections we will see how to install and configure I.E 3.0 on your system.

Installation

The installation of Internet Explorer is a simple, straightforward process that generally takes less than ten minutes.

1. First, you need to obtain a copy of Internet Explorer 3.0. The application can be found at `www.microsoft.com/ie` for download. Microsoft makes the following packages available for download:

   Full Install

   The full installation includes Internet Explorer and all the optional components. This download is quite large (10 Megabytes) and will take awhile to retrieve (approximately 2 hours at 28.8). This is the recommended download for enjoying all the features of the Internet.

   Typical Install

   The typical install includes Internet Explorer, Internet News, and Internet Mail. These components will give you most of the functionality needed on the Web. Use this option if you do not want to wait around for the full install download.

   Minimal Install

   The minimal install gives you just the basics, the Web browser. Use this for the fastest download time and if you just want to bum around the Web without any additional features.

2. Once you obtain IE 3.0, you can begin the installation by double-clicking the `.exe` file.

   The Microsoft licensing agreement appears, stating the usual Microsoft legal information as shown in Figure 51.2. You must agree to these terms before continuing the installation.

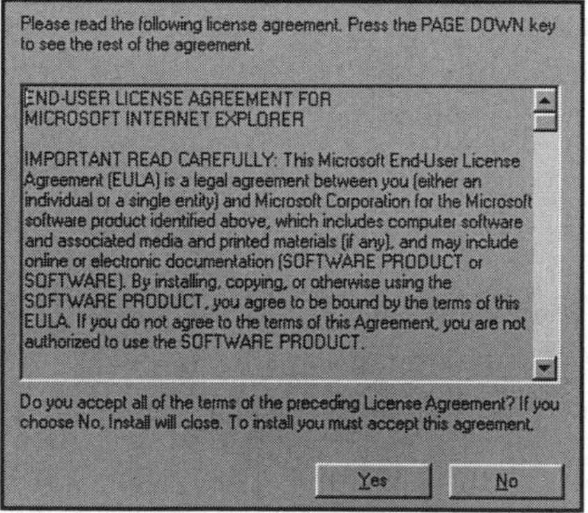

Figure 51.2. *The Microsoft licensing agreement.*

3. After agreeing to the licensing agreement, you will be presented with the dialog box that inquires whether you want to select which optional components are installed. The default setting of No installs all the optional components of Internet Explorer. If you have limited disk space or don't want some of the optional components installed, select Yes. You are then presented with a list of the optional components shown in Figure 51.3: Netmeeting, Internet Mail, Internet News, HTML Layout Control, and ActiveMovie. After selecting the components you want, click the OK button to continue the installation.

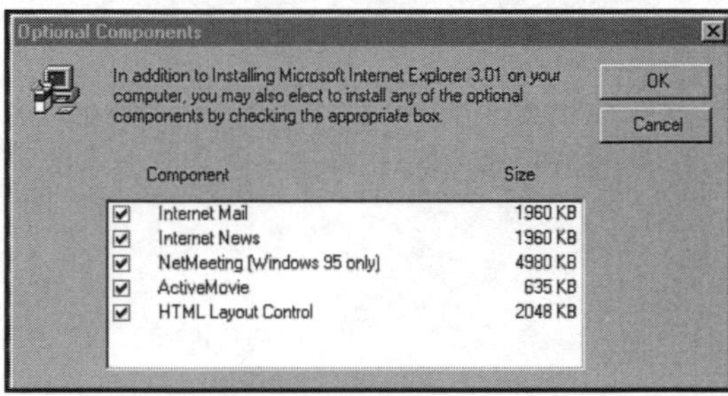

Figure 51.3. *Optional Components dialog box.*

4. The Installation Wizard will now install Internet Explorer and the optional components selected.
5. Once the file installation is complete, you will be prompted to restart the computer. You must restart the computer for the installation changes to take effect.

After Installation

After you have installed Internet Explorer, the next step is configuring the connection to the Internet. Under Windows NT, the Internet icon that appears on your desktop opens the Internet Connection Wizard as displayed in Figure 51.4. This wizard will appear if you don't already have an Internet connection in your dial-up network configuration, and allows for a fast, simple way of connecting to the Internet. If you already have an Internet connection, you can select it as your default. If you are connecting to the Internet through a permanent connection, select this option and finish the installation.

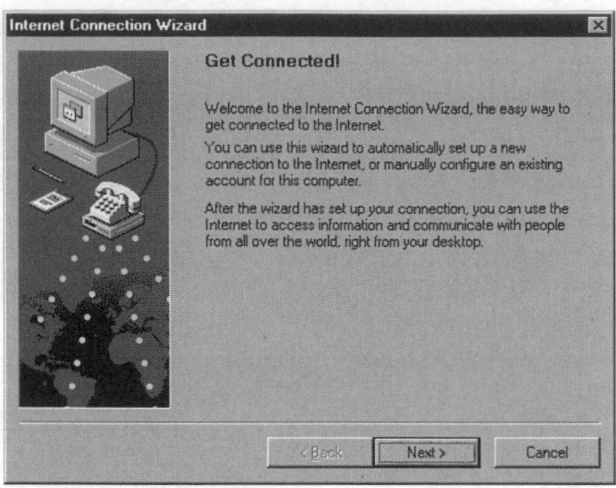

Figure 51.4. *Internet Connection Wizard.*

Configuration

The following sections cover the configuration of Internet Explorer and its optional components.

Internet Explorer 3.0

Internet Explorer has a number of options that can be configured. The following section outlines and covers the features available in Internet Explorer and how to configure them.

Accessing Internet Explorer

After the installation of IE 3.0 and the configuration of your client, you are ready to open your browser. There are several ways to open Internet Explorer. Two of the most common ways are the Internet icon on your desktop and the Internet Explorer shortcut located under Programs on the Start menu. The desktop icon will open your default Internet connection, allowing you to get connected.

Using Internet Explorer for the First Time

As shown in Figure 51.5, when you open Internet Explorer for the first time, you should be very familiar with the user interface if you have any experience with Microsoft products. I will assume no prior experience on your part, so a good amount of detail will be presented.

Across the top of the browser window you will see the words File, Edit, View, Favorites, and Help. This area is called the menu bar and allows for control of the browser and its features.

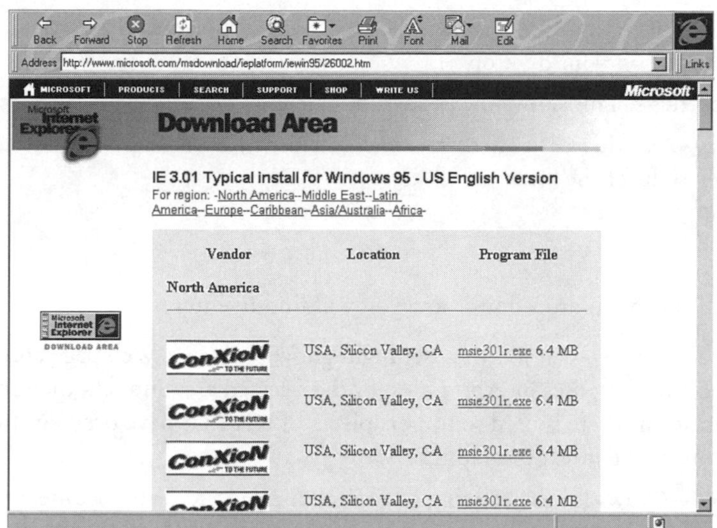

Figure 51.5. *The Internet Explorer interface.*

Overview of the Menus in IE 3.0

The following sections cover the menu items found in IE 3.0.

File

Under the File tab you will see the following:

- New Window—This opens another Internet Explorer window so you can explore multiple sites concurrently.
- Open—Use this to open a particular Web document or graphics file that is accessible from the open window.
- Save and Save As File—These two operations enable you to save whatever is in the screen of the browser, allowing you to keep Web documents.
- New Message—This tab is for the sending of Internet mail. When you select this item, your Internet Mail feature opens for easy access e-mail.
- Send To—Send To enables the user to send a file quickly to numerous locations such as your C drive or your Briefcase.
- Page Setup and Print—These two options allow for the printing of a page located in the browser window. Page Setup shows the page as it would look printed and enables the user to specify the different page properties, such as page format and size. The Print option allows the selection of such things as the default printer, number of copies to print, and so on.

- Create Shortcut—Use this feature if you want a shortcut to a particular Internet document on your desktop.
- Properties—This shows the properties of a Web document.
- Close—Use this as an alternative way to close Internet Explorer instead of the X on the upper-right of the browser.

Edit

Under the Edit menu drop-down box, you will find five items:

- Cut and Paste—Cut lets the user highlight an area in a Web page and remove it either for editing purposes or exportation of the selected area into another document or application. Paste is used to import pieces of text that have been cut from another document, be it text or graphics.
- Copy—Allows for the copying of a selected area in a Web document without removing it. Use this instead of Cut if you want to leave the original document intact.
- Select All—Select all allows for the selection of the entire Web page for editing purposes. For example, you can use the Select All feature to delete or copy an entire page.
- Find—The Find feature lets you locate a particular word located in a Web page.

View

The View tab allows for customization of the layout of the browser. There is also the Options feature located under View, which allows for some more sophisticated customization. Located under View, you will find the following:

- Toolbar and Status Bar—If you want to activate or disable either of these in the browser, you need to click the feature and either put a check mark by it (activated), or remove the check (disabled).
- Fonts—The Font option allows you to select the size of the text in the browser window.
- Stop and Refresh—Stop allows for the interruption of data flow from a Web site. Refresh lets a user reload a Web page. This feature is very useful due to the caching that IE 3.0 does. If you revisit a particular Web page, Internet Explorer will load a cached page to increase transfer speed, whether any new information is found on the page or not. Hitting Refresh will allow the new data to be downloaded.
- Source—Ever wonder how a particular Web page does all that cool, nifty stuff like frames or motion? The Source option will show you the HTML coding behind a Web page. When selected, the coding will be opened under your default text browser (Notepad under Windows 95).

- Options—The Options control is probably the most important control found in Internet Explorer. Accessing this option opens the Options dialog box, shown in Figure 51.6.

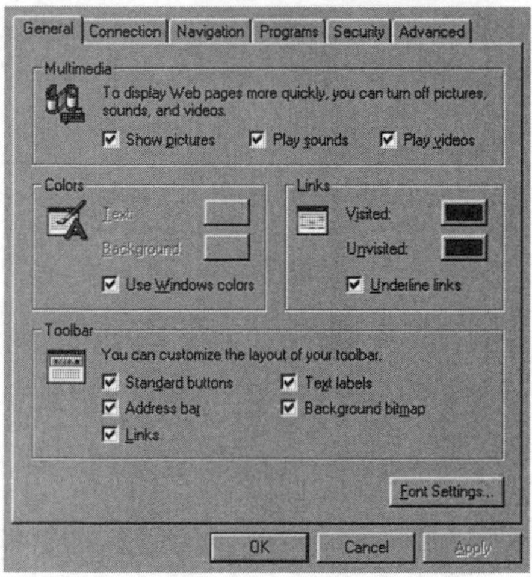

Figure 51.6. *The Options menu item.*

There are six configuration tabs located on the Options dialog box:

General—The General tab allows for several different customization features. Under multimedia, a user can specify whether pictures, sounds, and movies should be played. A colors box displays information on the different color characteristics of the text and background of the browser. Under the Links box you can determine what color the visited links should be. The Toolbar customization box gives a user the ability to change the layout of the toolbar to his specifications. Finally, the Font Settings button presents the ability to change the font style of the browser.

Connection—Under the Connection tab, shown in Figure 51.7, you will find specifications for your Internet connection. This is where you select which connection opens when you double-click on the Internet icon on your desktop. You can also configure the Dial-Up connection using the Properties button. At the bottom of the Connection box you will see the Proxy Server option, a very important feature that will hold great interest for any Windows NT network administrator. If you want to use a Proxy server connection to link to the Internet, you will need to configure the proxy settings shown here. To learn more about configuring IE to use a proxy server, see the section titled "Configuring IE to Use a Proxy Server."

Navigation—Under the Navigation tab, shown in Figure 51.8, a user can select which Web page Internet Explorer uses as a start page. There is also a history of Web pages viewed (a record of visited Web pages). You can select how many days you want the visited pages to be kept.

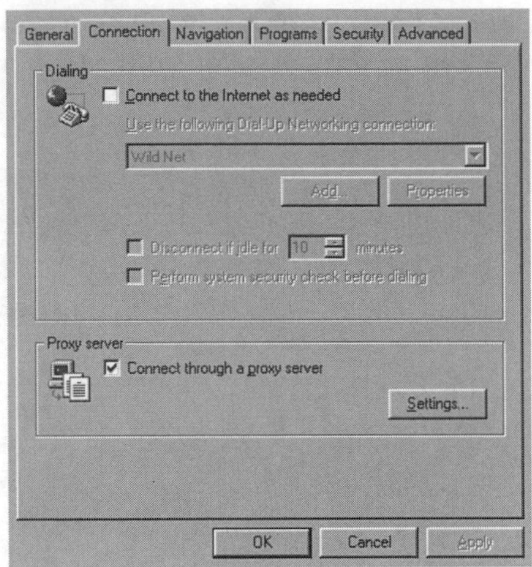

Figure 51.7. *The Connection tab.*

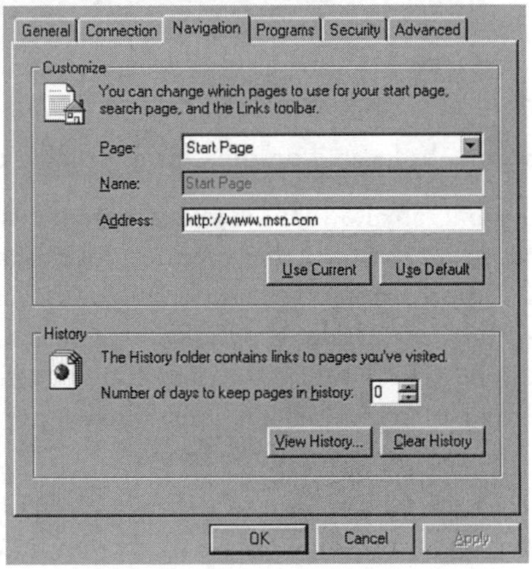

Figure 51.8. *The Navigation tab.*

Programs—Displayed on the Programs tab shown in Figure 51.9, are the options for which Mail and News browsers are used while on the Web. Whereas Internet Explorer comes with its own Mail and News readers, some users may already use applications to carry out these functions. Also found on the Programs tab is the Viewers box. Under this option you can determine what application to use to open a particular file. For example, say you run into a new type of audio file with the `.zzz` extension that has its own player, Zaudio. Under the File Types box you can associate the `.zzz` file with its player. (See Figure 51.10.)

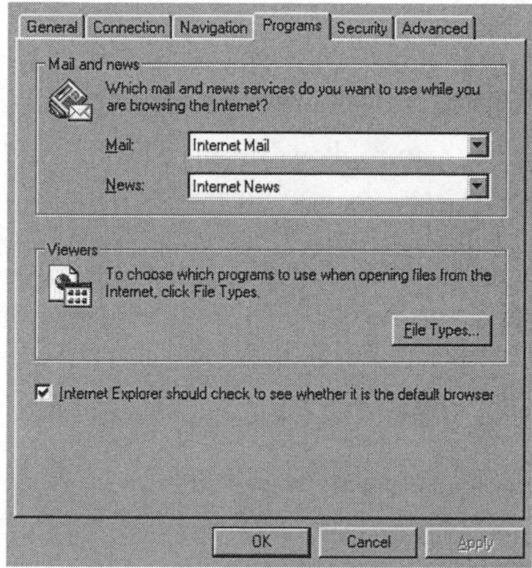

Figure 51.9. The Programs tab.

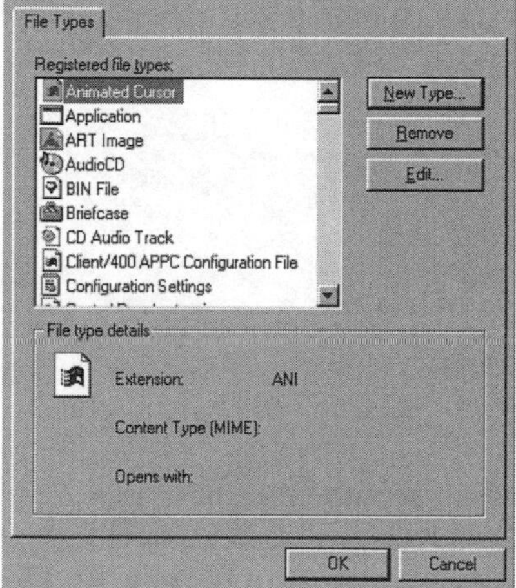

Figure 51.10. The File Types box enables you to determine what programs are used to display or run files.

Security—This tab, shown in Figure 51.11, allows users to specify options dealing with security. There are three main components that comprise the Security tab:

- The Content advisor enables a security supervisor to select what content can be viewed by users. The site ratings are maintained by the Recreational Advisory Council. To activate the Content advisor, click the Enable Ratings button. You will then be prompted for a Supervisor password. After supplying a password, the Content Advisor window opens, enabling you to set different levels of site censorship for language, nudity, sex, and violence. Clicking the General tab in the Content advisor opens the User Options box that controls the Password feature.

Also on the General tab is the Change Password box. The last tab under the Content advisor is Advanced. This tab lets the user specify another Ratings Provider.

- The Certificates feature allows for the use of identification certificates to verify the identity of Web sites, the publishers of Web sites, and your own identity to Web sites. This feature is extremely important for electronic commerce; you don't want to give your credit card number to just anyone. Personal identification certificates can be found at the VeriSign Web site (`www.verisign.com`).
- The Active content security option allows for the selection of the code that enables motion or interaction on a Web site, such as with Java applets.

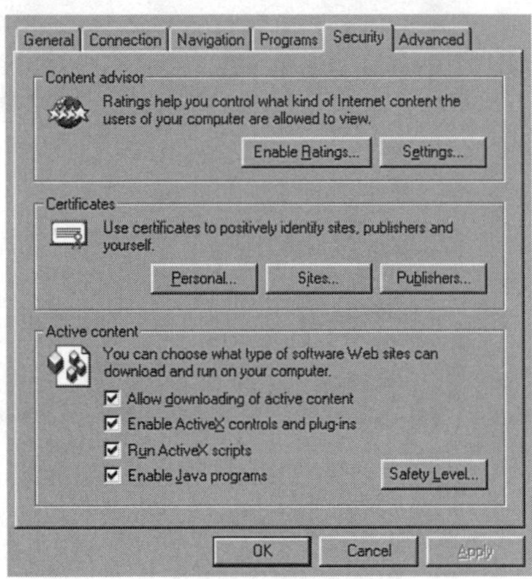

Figure 51.11. *The Security tab.*

Advanced—The last tab found under the Options feature is Advanced. On the Advanced tab you will find settings for Warnings, Temporary Internet files, and some varied settings for viewing as seen in Figure 51.12. The Warnings box specifies which warnings Internet Explorer displays during downloading of data off the Internet.

The next option found on the Advanced tab is the Temporary Internet files box. All images viewed during your Internet browsing are stored under the Temporary Internet files folder under the Windows directory. The Temporary Internet files option lets you specify the properties of your cache of images. Clicking the Settings button opens the Settings window for your temporary files. Here you can specify how much disk space the file can occupy and the location of the files. You can also clear the entire file from this menu.

At the bottom of the Advanced tab you will see the Cryptography Settings button, which lets a user decide what type of encryption protocols to use.

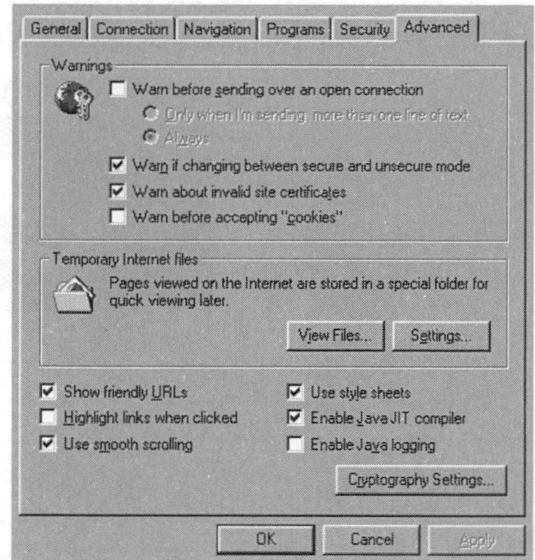

Figure 51.12. *The Advanced tab.*

Go

The Go menu item has the same browsing features that the toolbar has, such as Back, Forward, and so on. Also found under the Go tab is a listing of the sites visited during the current operation of Internet Explorer and a shortcut to the History folder.

Favorites

The Favorites menu item lets you add shortcuts to your favorite Web sites. Under Favorites you will see options to add and organize your list of favorites as displayed in Figure 51.13. All you have to do to make a Web site part of the Favorites links is click the Add to Favorites button while viewing the page to which you want the link to point. Internet Explorer will add the link to your favorites list. Another neat feature found on the Favorites tab is the Imported Bookmarks folder. When you upgrade from either an older version of Internet Explorer or switch from Netscape Navigator, all your previous bookmarks are imported and saved in this folder.

The Toolbar

Located beneath the menu bar is the Internet Explorer toolbar, shown in Figure 51.14. The toolbar is the main instrument for Internet navigation. From the toolbar you have quick access to many of Internet Explorer's functions. Printing, Internet Mail, and your favorites are all readily available. There are also shortcuts to Microsoft's Search page and the default Start page at `home.microsoft.com`.

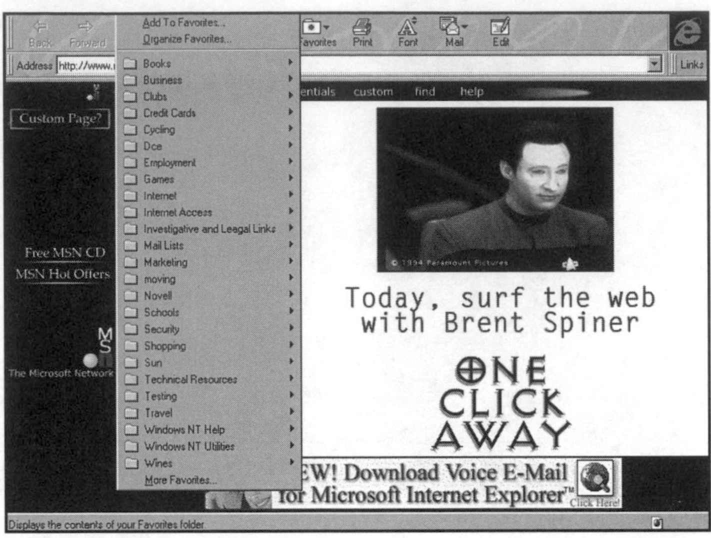

Figure 51.13 *The Favorites menu.*

Figure 51.14. *The Internet Explorer toolbar.*

Address

Below the toolbar is the address menu that shows the URL of the page you are currently viewing. You can also type in the Web address of the Web page that you want to visit. For example, if you want to travel to `www.nasa.gov`, just type it in at the address bar.

Links

To the right of the address bar you will see the Links menu bar. When you click the word Links, the menu bar replaces the address space with a series of buttons that provide shortcuts to the Internet links shown in Figure 51.15.

Configuring IE to Use a Proxy Server

Proxy servers act on behalf of client machines to provide them access to the Internet. When Internet Explorer is configured to use a proxy server, all requests are sent to proxy server first. The proxy server then processes the requests and sends the results back to the client. To configure Internet Explorer to use a proxy server, perform the following:

1. From the IE menu, click View | Options.
2. This will bring up the Options dialog box shown in Figure 51.16. From here select the Connection tab.

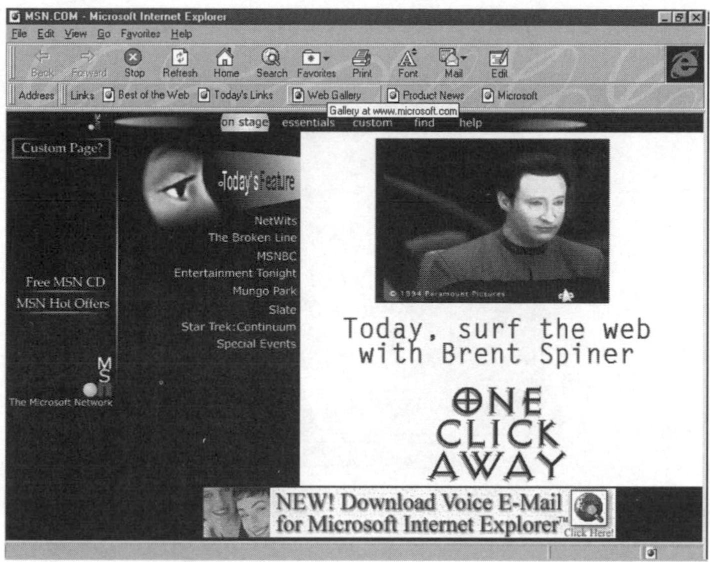

Figure 51.15. *The Links bar.*

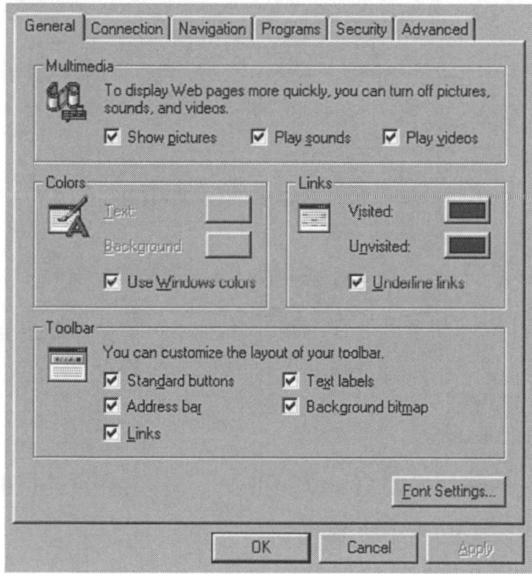

Figure 51.16. *The Options box.*

3. From the Connection tab, shown in Figure 51.17, check the *Connect through a proxy server* box and then click the Settings button.
4. You will now see the Proxy Server settings dialog shown in Figure 51.18. Enter the values that are appropriate for your network. If you are not sure what to put, contact your network administrator.

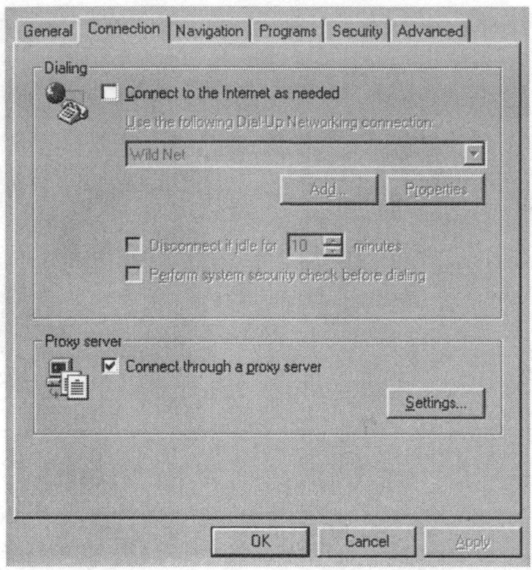

Figure 51.17. *The Connection tab.*

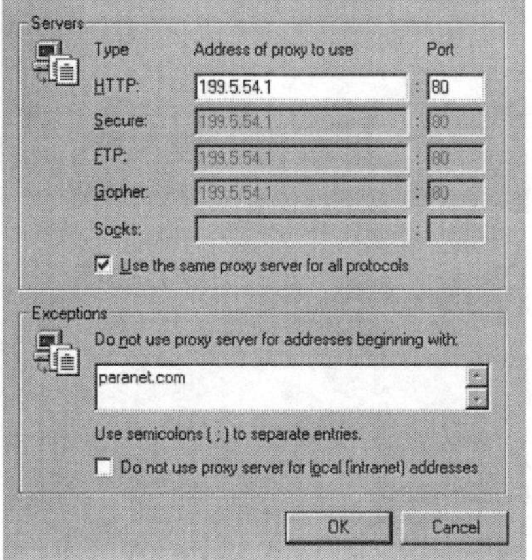

Figure 51.18. *The Proxy Server settings.*

5. Once completed, click OK to close the Proxy Connection Properties dialog. Then click OK to close the Options dialog.
6. You are now configured to use a Proxy Server.

Configuring Access to Web Sites Using Ratings

Ratings enable you to restrict the sites that can be viewed by Internet Explorer based on a content rating. A site must be configured to use ratings for Internet Explorer to know the ratings. If the site does not support ratings, you have the option of always or never letting the site be viewed. The ratings system is divided into four areas and four levels. The areas (violence, language, nudity, and sex) are broken down as follows:

- Violence
    1. Creatures killed; creatures injured; damage to realistic objects; fighting—no injuries
    2. Humans killed; humans injured; rewards injuring nonthreatening creatures
    3. Blood and gore; rewards injuring nonthreatening humans; rewards killing non-threatening creatures; accidental injury with blood and gore
    4. Wanton and gratuitous violence; rape
- Language
    1. Mild expletives
    2. Expletives, nonsexual anatomical references
    3. Strong, vulgar language; obscene gestures
    4. Crude or explicit sexual references
- Nudity
    1. Revealing attire
    2. Partial nudity
    3. Frontal nudity; nonsexual frontal nudity
    4. Provocative frontal nudity
- Sex
    1. Passionate kissing
    2. Clothed sexual touching
    3. Nonexplicit sexual activity; sexual touching
    4. Sex crimes; explicit sexual activity

Perform the following steps to configure Internet Explorer to use ratings:

1. From the IE menu, click View | Options.
2. This will bring up the Options dialog box shown in Figure 51.19. From here select the Security tab.
3. From the Security Properties tab under Content advisor, shown in Figure 51.20, click the Settings button.
4. You will be prompted to create a Supervisor password. Enter something that you can easily remember, but won't be easily guessed, and confirm it. You will need this password to be able to enable and disable the Ratings option.

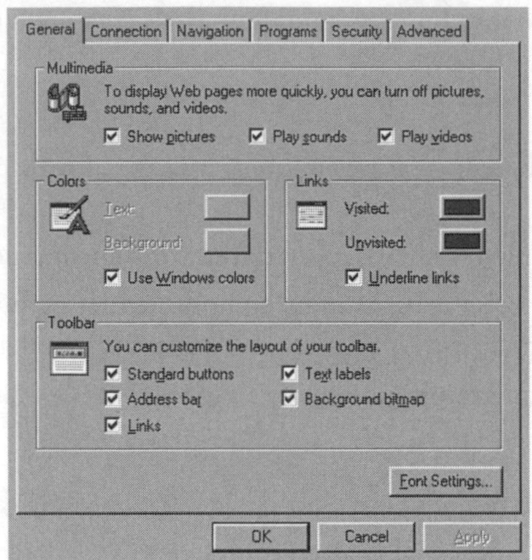

Figure 51.19. *The Options dialog box.*

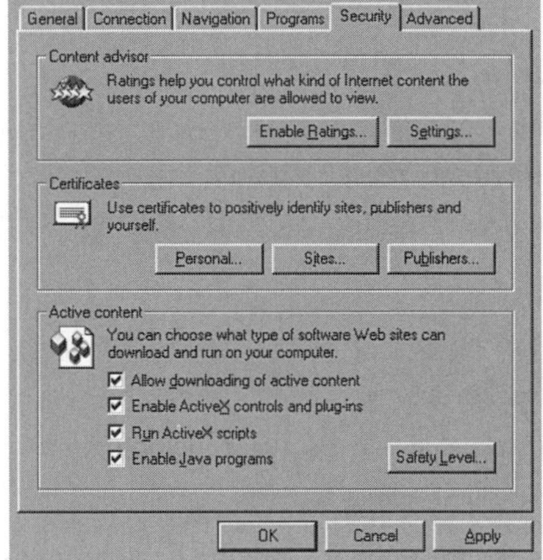

Figure 51.20. *The Security tab.*

5. You will now see the Ratings configuration dialog box shown in Figure 51.21. Configure the options to the desired level. Once complete, click the OK button to close the dialog.
6. Now click the Enable Ratings button. You will be prompted to enter the password you created earlier. Enter it now.
7. After the proper password has been entered, the Ratings option will be enabled.

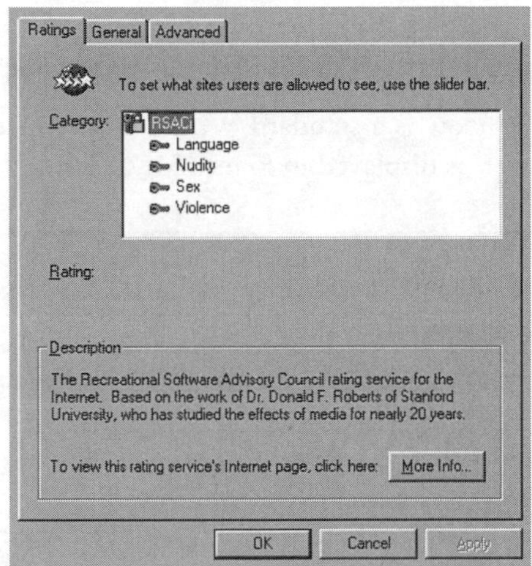

Figure 51.21. *Ratings configuration dialog box.*

Options

In addition to the Internet Explorer, Microsoft also includes options such as an e-mail program and a newsreader. This section covers the configuration of these options.

Mail

One of the most exciting things about the Internet is the ability it gives you to send electronic mail to people in places all over the world. The Internet Mail component that comes with Internet Explorer makes sending and receiving e-mail fairly simple.

Mail Setup

When you first access Internet Mail, a setup wizard begins to guide you through the setup procedure:

1. You will be prompted for your username and e-mail address.
2. Then you will need to enter the address for your POP3 server for incoming mail and your SMTP server address for outgoing mail.
3. Next, you will need to supply your e-mail account name where your POP3 stores messages. You must also supply the password for your POP3 server.
4. To finish, you must specify what type of connection you use to access your mail server. If you use a modem for mail access, you can specify to use a dial-up connection or configure a new one.

After the installation of Internet Mail, you will be able to send and receive e-mail over the Internet. You can open the Internet Mail window by either going through the Programs menu of the Start button or by accessing it through the toolbar in Internet Explorer.

The Internet Mail window is a standard Windows interface that enables easy point-and-click electronic mail control, as displayed in Figure 51.22.

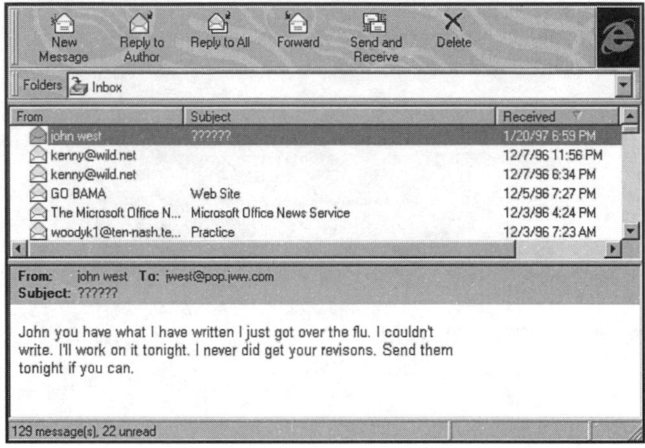

Figure 51.22. *The Internet Mail windows.*

Internet News

As mentioned earlier in this chapter, Internet News enables you to connect to Usenet news servers. These servers contain a wealth of information on almost any topic imaginable. Follow these directions to configure the Internet News Service:

1. Open Internet News by selecting it from the Start | Programs menu.
2. You will now see the Internet News program shown in Figure 51.23.
3. Bring up the Options dialog box shown in Figure 51.24 by clicking News from the menu bar and selecting Options from the drop-down box.
4. Select the Server tab.
5. From the Server tab shown in Figure 51.25, enter the appropriate information in the text boxes.
6. To add a news server, click the Add button at the bottom of the properties dialog box. Enter the server's information and click OK.
7. Once complete, click OK.
8. You are now ready to make use of your Internet News server.

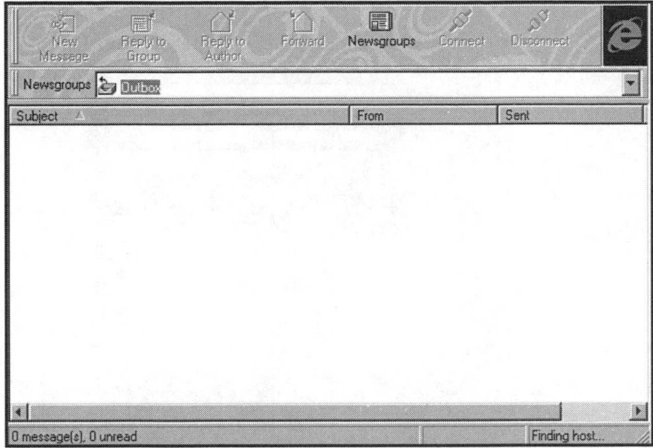

Figure 51.23. *Internet News window.*

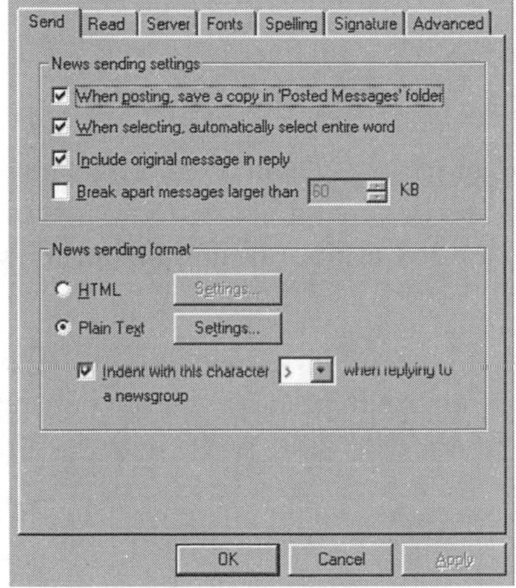

Figure 51.24. *The Internet News Options dialog box.*

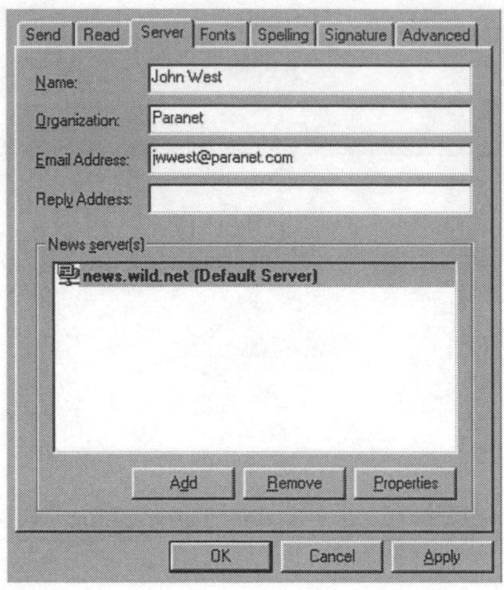

Figure 51.25. *The Server dialog box.*

Summary

You now have a great idea of what a Web browser is and how it works. In this chapter you have installed Internet Explorer and become familiar with all its features. You have also seen the optional components that come bundled in the full installation set of IE 3.0, their uses, and how to configure them.

The Internet provides a user access to incredible amounts of information. The Internet Explorer is the tool used by users to retrieve this data. For more information on Internet Explorer and its optional components, go to the Microsoft Web site at `www.microsoft.com`.

APPENDIX

Microsoft Training and Certification

The information in this appendix is from Microsoft's excellent Web site: www.microsoft.com.

The Microsoft Training and Certification Web pages are kept up-to-date; you should visit the site if you are considering pursuing a Microsoft certification. Also, since the time of this writing, I'm sure that many more courses and exams have been added—so be sure to get to the Web site to see up-to-date listings. The specific URL is www.microsoft.com/train_cert.

In 1992, I received my first certification as a Microsoft Certified Product Specialist for Microsoft Windows 3.1. To get this certification, I had to pass two exams, "Introduction to MS-DOS 5.0 and Microcomputer Hardware" and "Implementing and Supporting Microsoft Windows 3.1." The former exam no longer exists, and the latter is all that is now required to become a Microsoft Product Specialist for Windows 3.1.

The Microsoft Certified Professional courses and exams have changed a lot since then. The exams seem to get more challenging, and the number of authorized courses grow almost every month.

Also, in 1992, not too many people knew about the Microsoft Certified Professional program, but now, Microsoft Certified professionals are very much in demand. I can attest that these certifications have been very helpful in my career.

Pursuing the certification of a Microsoft Certified Systems Engineer, both on the Windows NT 3.51 and Windows NT 4.0 track, is a very rewarding experience. A lot of studying, education, and hands-on learning goes into understanding what is necessary to pass these exams. I highly recommend that anyone who is serious about Microsoft networking try taking these exams. Many people don't pass the exams the first time. You need an in-depth knowledge of the products—not only book knowledge, but real hands-on experience.

Step-by-Step Guide to Becoming a Microsoft Certified Professional

Before you pursue your Microsoft certification, it is important to create a plan. Since attaining a Microsoft certification can be a costly and time-consuming process, follow these steps to identify your goal.

1. Decide which certification you plan to pursue. Microsoft currently offers four certifications:
    - Microsoft Certified Systems Engineer

      Microsoft Certified Systems Engineers are qualified to effectively plan, implement, maintain, and support information systems with Microsoft Windows NT and the Microsoft BackOffice integrated family of server software.
    - Microsoft Certified Solution Developer

      For developers, Microsoft offers the Microsoft Certified Solution Developer (MCSD) credential. Microsoft Certified Solution Developers are qualified to design and develop custom business solutions with Microsoft development tools, technologies, and platforms, including Microsoft Office and Microsoft BackOffice.
    - Microsoft Certified Product Specialist

      For individuals who would like to demonstrate their expertise with a particular Microsoft product, Microsoft offers the Microsoft Certified Product Specialist (MCPS) credential. Microsoft Certified Product Specialists have demonstrated in-depth knowledge of at least one Microsoft operating system. Candidates may pass additional Microsoft certification exams to further qualify their skills with Microsoft BackOffice products, development tools, or desktop applications.
    - Microsoft Certified Trainer

      Microsoft Certified Trainers (MCTs) are instructionally and technically qualified to deliver Microsoft Official Curriculum through Microsoft authorized education sites.
2. When you are ready to prepare for a specific exam, read the exam preparation guide for that exam. The exam preparation guide contains information on resources that will help you prepare for the exam and a list of the topics on which you will be tested. Exam preparation guides are available on the Internet at `www.microsoft.com/train_cert`.

3. Determine the appropriate training you need to prepare for the exam. Microsoft offers a number of learning aides to help you prepare for the Microsoft Certified Professional exams. You might decide you need to use just one of these methods, or a combination. The training options include instructor-led, online, or self-paced. In addition, there are a variety of resource kits, product documentation, and other materials available.
4. Get hands-on experience with the product. This is a prerequisite for passing a Microsoft Certified Professional exam.
5. Take the appropriate assessment exam for practice. Assessment exams will give you a good idea of the types of questions that will be asked on the exams, as well as some experience using the test driver that delivers the exams electronically. You can download the assessment exams from `www.microsoft.com/train_cert`.

Note: Passing the assessment exam does not ensure a passing score on the certification exam.

6. When you feel prepared, register with Sylvan Prometric to take the exam at an Authorized Prometric Testing Center. In North America, call Sylvan at (800) 755-EXAM to register and find the location of an authorized Prometric testing center in your area. Outside the United States and Canada, contact your local Microsoft subsidiary.

The Microsoft Certified Professional Benefits

Each of the Microsoft certifications offers great benefits. Both MCSE and MCPS offer a look at Microsoft TechNet, which is an invaluable resource for professionals who deal with any of the Microsoft products, and my favorite resource for technical information. The following paragraphs take a look at these benefits, and should offer extra incentives for becoming a Microsoft Certified Professional.

MCSE Benefits

Why should you become a Microsoft Certified Systems Engineer? The reason is so that you can demonstrate to your customers and colleagues you have what it takes to plan, implement, and support business solutions with Microsoft Windows NT and Microsoft BackOffice. As a Microsoft Certified Systems Engineer, you receive the following benefits:

- Industry recognition of your knowledge and proficiency with Microsoft products and technologies.
- Access to technical information directly from Microsoft. Microsoft Certified Systems Engineers receive a complimentary one-year subscription to the Microsoft TechNet Technical Information Network, providing valuable information via monthly CDs. If you currently have a Microsoft TechNet subscription, an additional year will be added to your existing subscription, free of charge.

- One free priority comprehensive support ten-pack from Microsoft and a 25 percent discount on purchases of additional priority comprehensive support incident ten-packs. You gain access to support for any Microsoft product, 24 hours a day, 7 days a week. This provides the opportunity to resolve customer issues, with the help of Microsoft support engineers.
- A one-year subscription to the Microsoft Beta Evaluation program. This benefit provides you with up to 12 free monthly CDs containing beta software (English only) for many of Microsoft's newest software products, allowing you to become familiar with new versions of Microsoft products generally before they are available.
- A free annual subscription to *Microsoft Certified Professional Magazine,* a career and professional development magazine created especially for Microsoft Certified Professionals.
- Microsoft Certified Systems Engineer logos and other materials to let you identify your Microsoft Certified Systems Engineer status to colleagues or clients.
- Dedicated forums on MSN (The Microsoft Network) and on CompuServe, which allow Microsoft Certified Professionals to communicate directly with Microsoft and one another.
- Certification Update bimonthly newsletter from the Microsoft Certified Professional program, keeping you informed of changes and advances in the program and exams.
- Invitations to Microsoft conferences, technical training sessions, and special events.

MCPS Benefits

The reason to become a Microsoft Certified Product Specialist is to demonstrate to your customers and colleagues that you have the specialized knowledge required to use or support specific Microsoft products. As a Microsoft Certified Product Specialist, you receive the following benefits:

- Industry recognition of your knowledge and proficiency with Microsoft products and technologies.
- Access to technical information directly from Microsoft. Microsoft Certified Product Specialists receive a complimentary Microsoft TechNet CD, plus a 50 percent discount toward a one-year membership to the Microsoft TechNet Technical Information network, providing valuable information via monthly CDs.
- A free annual subscription to *Microsoft Certified Professional Magazine*, a career and professional development magazine created especially for Microsoft Certified Professionals.
- Microsoft Certified Product Specialist logos and other materials to enable you to identify your Microsoft Certified Product Specialist status to colleagues or clients.

- Dedicated forums on MSN and on CompuServe that allow Microsoft Certified Professionals to communicate directly with Microsoft and one another.
- Certification Update bimonthly newsletter from the Microsoft Certified Professional program, keeping you informed of changes and advances in the program and exams.
- Invitations to Microsoft conferences, technical training sessions, and special events.

The Microsoft Certified Professional Requirements

Each of the Microsoft certifications requires passing a certain number of specific exams. Here are the requirements for the two technical certifications—Microsoft Certified Systems Engineer (MCSE) and Microsoft Certified Product Specialist (MCPS).

MCSE Requirements

Microsoft Certified Systems Engineers are required to pass four operating system exams and two elective exams that require a valid and reliable measure of technical proficiency and expertise. These exams are developed with the input of professionals in the industry and reflect how Microsoft products are used in organizations throughout the world. The exams are administered by an independent organization, Sylvan Prometric, at more than 800 authorized Prometric testing centers around the world.

The Microsoft Certified Systems Engineer certification now has two tracks: the Windows NT 3.51 track and the Windows NT 4.0 track.

The operating system exams require candidates to prove their expertise with desktop, server, and networking components. The elective exams require proof of expertise with Microsoft BackOffice products.

To become an MCSE on the Windows NT 3.51 track you must pass both of these exams:

- Exam 70-43: Implementing and Supporting Microsoft Windows NT Server 3.51
- Exam 70-42: Implementing and Supporting Microsoft Windows NT Workstation 3.51

In addition to those two, you are required to pass one of these exams:

- Exam 70-30: Microsoft Windows 3.1
- Exam 70-48: Microsoft Windows for Workgroups 3.11-Desktop
- Exam 70-63: Implementing and Supporting Microsoft Windows 95

For your fourth core exam, you must pass one of these exams:

- Exam 70-46: Networking with Microsoft Windows for Workgroups 3.11
- Exam 70-47: Networking with Microsoft Windows 3.1
- Exam 70-58: Networking Essentials

In addition to the four core exams, you must also pass two elective exams, which are listed below the Windows 4.0 track core exams.

To become an MCSE on the Windows NT 4.0 track, you must pass both of these exams:

- Exam 70-67: Implementing and Supporting Microsoft Windows NT Server 4.0
- Exam 70-68: Implementing and Supporting Microsoft Windows NT Server 4.0 in the Enterprise

Note: If you are already an MCSE on the Windows NT 3.51 track, you are required to pass only the preceding two exams to also be an MCSE on the Windows NT 4.0 track.

For your third core exam, you must pass one of these exams:

- Exam 70-30: Microsoft Windows 3.1
- Exam 70-48: Microsoft Windows for Workgroups 3.11-Desktop
- Exam 70-63: Implementing and Supporting Microsoft Windows 95
- Exam 70-73: Implementing and Supporting Microsoft Windows NT Workstation 4.0

And for the fourth core exam, you must pass one of these exams:

- Exam 70-46: Networking with Microsoft Windows for Workgroups 3.11
- Exam 70-47: Networking with Microsoft Windows 3.1
- Exam 70-58: Networking Essentials

For either the Windows NT 3.51 track or the Windows NT 4.0 track, you must pass two of the following elective exams:

- Exam 70-12: Microsoft SNA Server
- Exam 70-14: Implementing and Supporting Microsoft Systems Management Server 1.0
- Exam 70-21: Microsoft SQL Server 4.2 Database Implementation
- Exam 70-22: Microsoft SQL Server 4.2 Database Administration for Microsoft Windows NT
- Exam 70-26: System Administration for Microsoft SQL Server 6
- Exam 70-27: Implementing a Database Design on Microsoft SQL Server 6
- Exam 70-37: Microsoft Mail for PC Networks 3.2-Enterprise
- Exam 70-53: Internetworking Microsoft TCP/IP on Microsoft Windows NT (3.5-3.51)
- Exam 70-75: Implementing and Supporting Microsoft Exchange Server 4.0

For SQL Server electives, candidates can pass the following:

- Exam 70-26: System Administration for Microsoft SQL Server 6 or Exam 70-22: Microsoft SQL Server 4.2 Database Administration for Microsoft Windows NT
- Exam 70-27: Implementing a Database Design on Microsoft SQL Server 6

MCPS Requirements

Microsoft Certified Product Specialists are required to pass one operating system exam, proving their expertise with a current Microsoft Windows desktop or server operating system.

To become a Product Specialist for Windows NT Workstation, you must pass one of these exams:

- Exam 70-73: Implementing and Supporting Microsoft Windows NT Workstation 4.0
- Exam 70-42: Implementing and Supporting Microsoft Windows NT Workstation 3.51

To become a Product Specialist for Windows NT Server, you must pass one of these exams:

- Exam 70-67: Implementing and Supporting Microsoft Windows NT Server 4.0
- Exam 70-43: Implementing and Supporting Microsoft Windows NT Server 3.51

Each of the following exams allows you to become a Product Specialist for the respective operating system:

- Exam 70-30: Microsoft Windows 3.1
- Exam 70-48: Microsoft Windows for Workgroups 3.11-Desktop
- Exam 70-63: Implementing and Supporting Microsoft Windows 95
- Exam 70-150: Microsoft Windows Operating Systems and Services Architecture I
- Exam 70-151: Microsoft Windows Operating Systems and Services Architecture II

Microsoft Training

Microsoft offers training in many ways. There are online courses at MOLI, Microsoft On-Line Institute, self-paced study materials, and instructor-led courses, held at Microsoft Authorized Training Education Centers (ATECs). All these courses help prepare you for Microsoft certification.

The following is a sample of the instructor-led courses that were available as of November 1996. For updates, check the Microsoft Training and Certification Web site at `www.microsoft.com/train_cert`.

Capacity Planning Windows NT Server Networks

Course No. 635 takes two days to complete, and enables network administrators and planners to analyze and optimize their Microsoft Windows NT Server–based network. The goal of this course is to provide the network planning and implementation skills needed to identify, analyze, and optimize the network traffic patterns associated with specific services of Microsoft Windows NT operating system and domain models.

At the end of the course, students will be able to describe the requirements of capacity-planning a Windows NT Server–based network, explain the process of analyzing network traffic, analyze client-to-server traffic, analyze server-to-server traffic, optimize network traffic, and predict network traffic.

This course helps you prepare for Microsoft Certified Professional exam 70-68, Implementing and Supporting Microsoft Windows NT Server 4.0 in the Enterprise.

Supporting Microsoft Windows NT 4.0 Core Technologies

Course No. 687 takes five days to complete and provides the core foundation for supporting Microsoft Windows NT operating system version 4.0. The goal of this course is to provide support for professionals with the skills necessary to install, configure, customize, optimize, network, integrate, and troubleshoot Windows NT 4.0.

Content primarily of interest in a complex environment—such as capacity planning on a server and a network, multiple domain management, and trust relationships—is covered in depth in a series of courses that make up the Microsoft Windows NT Enterprise series. Content specific to the administration of the Windows NT Server network operating system can be found in the Administering Microsoft Windows NT 4.0 course.

At the end of the course, students will be able to describe the system strategy for Windows NT 4.0; install Windows NT; configure the Windows NT environment; create and implement system policies; create and manage partitions, file systems, and fault-tolerant volumes; support running applications under Windows NT; identify network components and describe their functions on a Windows NT–based computer; install and configure network transport protocols; install and configure network services on Windows NT Server; implement remote access service (RAS); install and configure Microsoft Internet Information Server and Services for NetWare; install, configure, and support printers and printer resources; install client software; implement and troubleshoot directory replication and synchronization; recognize problems related to the boot process; and determine the appropriate action to take for common problems.

This course helps you prepare for the Microsoft Certified Professional exam 70-67, Implementing and Supporting Microsoft Windows NT Server 4.0.

Installing and Configuring Microsoft Windows NT Server 4.0

Course No. 685 takes one day to complete. The topics covered in Installing and Configuring Microsoft Windows NT Server 4.0 include Overview of Windows NT Server network operating system version 4.0, Installation, Administration, Configuration, Fault tolerance, NetWare integration and migration with Windows NT, and Microsoft Internet Information Server.

At the end of the course, students will be able to install Windows NT Server, assess and plan network needs for a given situation, configure server components, create accounts, manage system resources, migrate from NetWare, and use Internet Information Server.

This course teaches some of the skills required to successfully pass exam 70-67, Implementing and Supporting Microsoft Windows NT Server 4.0. Additional skills and knowledge required to pass exam 70-67 are taught in Course 803, Administering Microsoft Windows NT 4.0, and course 687, Supporting Microsoft Windows NT Core Technologies.

Supporting Microsoft Windows NT Server 4.0 Enterprise Technologies

Course No. 689 takes five days to complete and provides a training solution for support professionals working in a Microsoft Windows NT Server 4.0–based enterprise environment. It is assumed that students of this course have experience supporting a Windows NT Server–based network. The goal of Supporting Microsoft Window NT Server 4.0 Enterprise Technologies is for support professionals to be able to design, implement, and support the Windows NT Server network operating system in a multidomain enterprise environment.

The topics covered in this course are Windows NT Server 4.0 Directory Services and the enterprise challenge, Directory Services components and features, one-way and two-way trust relationships, managing groups and accounts across trusts, implementing trust relationships, determining the optimum number of domain controllers, determining effective server locations, implementing effective synchronization, implementing efficient pass-through authentication, considerations in implementing Directory Services, Windows NT Server–based approach to system analysis and planning, collecting system data, creating a measurement base, using the Performance Monitor, measurement bases in the server environment, establishing a database of measurement information, performance analysis, determining workload characterization, system bottlenecks, setting system usage expectations, analysis in the Windows NT Server–based environment, proposing solutions, resource allocation, and long-term record keeping.

This course helps you prepare for the Microsoft Certified Professional exam 70-68, Implementing and Supporting Microsoft Windows NT Server 4.0 in the Enterprise.

Implementing Directory Services Using Microsoft Windows NT Server 4.0

Course No. 690 takes one day to complete. This course is part of a group that comprises the Microsoft Windows NT Enterprise Series. It is assumed that students of this course have experience supporting a Windows NT Server–based network. The goal of Implementing Directory Services Using Microsoft Windows NT Server 4.0 is to enable support professionals to design, implement, and support Directory Services on a Windows NT Server–based network.

At the end of the course, students will be able to define Windows NT Server Directory Services, establish trust relationships, examine the effects that the different Directory Services structures have on a network implementation, and plan a Directory Services structure.

This course helps you prepare for Microsoft Certified Professional exam 70-68, Implementing and Supporting Microsoft Windows NT Server 4.0 in the Enterprise.

Microsoft Windows NT Server Expert Series

Course No. 729 takes five days to complete and provides a training solution for support professionals working in a Microsoft Windows NT Server–based enterprise environment. It is assumed that students of this course are experienced support professionals and have experience supporting a Windows NT Server–based network. The goal of the Microsoft Windows NT Server Expert series is to support professionals so that they can design, implement, and support enterprise technologies on a Windows NT Server–based network.

At the end of the course, students will be able to plan and implement Windows NT Server–based environments—defining capacity planning as it relates to the Windows NT Server network operating system, creating a measurement database, analyzing system performance, and implementing a capacity-planning strategy. Students will also be able to plan and implement a Windows NT–based network—describing the requirements of capacity planning, explaining the process of analyzing network traffic, analyzing client-to-server traffic and server-to-server traffic, optimizing network traffic, and predicting network traffic. Students will be able to diagnose and repair Windows NT–based systems in the context of the Windows NT architecture, the Registry, and the operating system file structure—identifying troubleshooting resources and tools, isolating problems to specific components in the architecture using Windows NT tools, tracing the system dependencies for devices and services using the Registry, identifying the files used in the Windows NT load sequence and repairing damaged files, interpreting blue screens, and using the kernel debugger. Finally, students will be skilled at integrating Windows NT Server version 3.51 with the Novell NetWare environment—integrating Windows NT Server with NetWare, migrating to Windows NT Server from a NetWare server, and implementing a single network logon in a mixed environment.

When combined with course 772, Microsoft Windows NT 4.0 Upgrade Training, this course helps you prepare for exam 70-68, Implementing and Supporting Microsoft Windows NT Server 4.0 in the Enterprise.

Administering Microsoft Windows NT 4.0

Course No. 803 takes three days to complete and provides students with the knowledge and skills necessary to perform post-installation and day-to-day administration tasks in a single-domain or multiple-domain Microsoft Windows NT–based network. It also provides students with the prerequisite knowledge and skills required for course 687, Supporting Microsoft Windows NT 4.0 Core Technologies.

At the end of the course, students will be able to create and administer user and group accounts by determining account policies, troubleshooting problems that prevent users from logging on to the network, managing network resources, setting up and administering permissions for files and folders, taking ownership of folders, and troubleshooting when users are unable to gain access to disk resources. Students will also be able to set up a printing environment, administer printers, and troubleshoot why a user cannot print; use auditing functions to generate and view security logs; monitor network resources to track usage and disk space; back up and restore files and folders using tapes; and administer the Windows NT Server and Windows NT Workstation operating systems in real-world situations.

This course helps you prepare for the following Microsoft Certified Professional exams:

- Administering Windows NT 4.0 self-administered assessment
- Exam 70-73: Implementing and Supporting Microsoft Windows NT Workstation 4.0
- Exam 70-67: Implementing and Supporting Microsoft Windows NT Server 4.0

Installing and Configuring Microsoft Windows 95

Course No. 546 takes two days and helps students gain the knowledge and skills needed to install and configure Microsoft Windows 95. These skills include installation, configuration, customization, optimization, network integration, administration, troubleshooting, messaging, and other support issues.

The topics covered in this course are installation and configuration; user interface; networking; printing; administration; transitioning, interoperability with Windows-based networks, Novell networks, and Transmission Control Protocol/Internet Protocol (TCP/IP) networks; dial-up Networking services; and troubleshooting.

At the end of the course, students will be able to install Windows 95; configure the system to meet the requirements of different users; identify and correct problems when running applications for Microsoft MS-DOS, 16-bit Windows, or 32-bit Windows; discuss the networking architecture; manage a remote workstation in a network; implement either share-level or user-level security as required; manage printing; implement message services; and diagnose and solve problems.

Because this course is an abbreviated version of the full, five-day Supporting Microsoft Windows 95 course, it does not include all information covered by the Microsoft Certified Professional exam for supporting Windows 95.

Supporting Microsoft SNA Server 2.11

Course No. 562 takes three days and provides a practical introduction to Microsoft SNA Server version 2.11. The background and theory presented in the modules is reinforced through hands-on labs that give students experience with all aspects of installing, configuring, managing, and troubleshooting SNA Server 2.11.

The topics covered in this course are Systems Network Architecture (SNA) and Microsoft SNA Server, the installation and configuration of SNA Server, the configuration of link services, 802.2, synchronous data link control (SDLC), X.25, distributed function terminal (DFT), the configuration of SNA Server for 5250 emulation in an AS/400 environment, security, debugging techniques, fault tolerance, NetView, event logging and alerts, the Performance Monitor, and SNATRACE. At the end of the course, students will be able to describe SNA Server using hierarchical and peer models, list components and protocols, install and configure in various environments, implement SNA Security at workgroup and domain levels, determine and implement appropriate SNA fault tolerance for a given site, configure NetView to monitor and receive alerts, enable event logging, and use the information to locate and resolve problems, monitor and maximize performance, troubleshoot problems that might occur during setup, and use the trace tool to identify and solve problems.

Core Technologies of Microsoft Exchange Server

Course No. 632 takes five days to complete and provides an introduction to the core technologies of Microsoft Exchange Server. It will prepare students to implement and administer Microsoft Exchange in a single-site environment.

At the end of the course, students will be able to describe Microsoft Exchange Server features and core technology components; explain the Microsoft Exchange hierarchy; plan and install the first and subsequent Microsoft Exchange Servers in a site; troubleshoot installation problems and address post-installation considerations; discuss the core technology architecture—including core and optional services and how a message flows through a single-site system; effectively manage all types of recipients; describe the client architecture; install, configure, and use a Microsoft Exchange client; explain how Microsoft Exchange interacts and communicates in a single-site environment; effectively administer the Microsoft Exchange configuration; manage public folders; install and configure Microsoft Schedule+; explain and set up advanced security; effectively monitor and maintain Microsoft Exchange Server–based computers; plan, configure, and manage Internet Mail Connector; design, create, install, and administer Microsoft Exchange forms; migrate from Microsoft Mail Server for PC networks; and integrate Microsoft Exchange clients in a NetWare environment.

Fundamentals of Microsoft Exchange Server

Course No. 730 takes three days and provides an overview of Microsoft Exchange Server. Students learn how to plan and install a Microsoft Exchange Server–based system.

At the end of the course, students will be able to discuss how a client/server mail system addresses the limitations of a shared-file mail system; list the five main functions of Microsoft Exchange Server; describe the hierarchy of Microsoft Exchange; describe Microsoft Exchange Server and client components; install Microsoft Exchange; create Microsoft Exchange recipients; configure each Microsoft Exchange core component by modifying its property page; install and configure Microsoft Exchange clients; create and configure a public folder; identify the 12 steps to implementing a Microsoft Exchange system; install a second Microsoft Exchange Server at a site; install and configure a site connector and an X.400 connector, and perform directory replication between sites; configure and perform public folder replication; configure a Microsoft Mail connector; configure and perform directory exchange across the Microsoft Mail connector; install and configure an Internet Mail connector; and create an interpersonal form, and post it to a public folder.

Supporting Microsoft Systems Management Server 1.2

Course No. 732 takes five days to complete and provides students with the knowledge and skills required to install, configure, administer, and troubleshoot Microsoft Systems Management Server version 1.2. Students will have an opportunity to implement multiple Systems Management Server sites, collecting hardware and software inventory, distributing software to client computers, managing shared applications, and using remote control functions to diagnose and solve common problems. The course is an updated and more in-depth version of course 646, Supporting Microsoft Systems Management Server 1.1. This course supports the Microsoft Certified Systems Engineer program.

At the end of the course, students will be able to describe how Systems Management Server features solve desktop management problems; describe the components that make up the Systems Management Server environment; install and configure primary and secondary sites; use the remote control functionality for Microsoft MS-DOS, Windows, and Windows NT clients; install, configure, and use the remote access server (RAS), local area network (LAN), and systems network architecture (SNA) senders to communicate between sites; install, configure, and administer the inventory process; retrieve specific information from a system management software database; manage the inventory within such a database; define a Systems Management Server package for both distributing software and sharing network applications; define a Systems Management Server job for both distributing software and sharing network applications; identify changes made to the client computer for a software package installation; and troubleshoot functions.

Planning a Microsoft Systems Management Server 1.2 Site

Course No. 733 takes two days to complete. In this course, students will gain the knowledge and skills necessary to plan for a successful Microsoft Systems Management Server deployment, integrate the product with existing software in the enterprise, and work with third-party network products. Students will practice the planning tasks required for a Systems Management Server rollout in different enterprise scenarios. These include determining the hierarchy, resource needs, and integration needs for each enterprise. Students also will configure and plan the maintenance of the Microsoft SQL Server database for the Systems Management Server site.

At the end of the course, students will be able to plan a Systems Management Server environment for a given situation, plan the maintenance of a Systems Management Server database including backup/restore and integrity checks, and integrate Systems Management Server with an existing network enterprise, including Macintosh and OS/2 clients, NetWare, and other management products such as Hewlett-Packard Openview.

Implementing a Database Design on Microsoft SQL Server 6.5

Course No. 750 takes five days to complete and provides students with the technical skills required to implement a database solution with the Microsoft SQL Server client/server database management system, based on a case-study design. Lab exercises allow hands-on implementation of the case-study design.

The topics covered in this course are roles and responsibilities of an SQL Server implementor, data-modeling components, storage for devices and databases, creating database objects (tables, indexes, views, defaults, and rules), stored procedures, triggers, data retrieval and data manipulation (`SELECT`, `UPDATE`, `INSERT`, and `DELETE`), constraints to enforce data referential integrity, performing row operations with cursors, implementing distributed data in a client/server environment, extending the capabilities of SQL Server through distributed management objects (DMOs), the messaging application programming interface (MAPI), and Open Data Services libraries (ODS).

At the end of the course, students will be able to create database devices, databases, user-defined data types, and tables; write Transact-SQL statements to query data, manipulate data, and program the server; identify issues to consider when creating indexes; create views, triggers, and stored procedures; enforce data integrity by creating and implementing constraints, defaults, and rules; describe how to use cursors to perform row operations; determine how to distribute data; and determine which external components to use. This course helps you prepare for exam 70-26, System Administration on Microsoft SQL Server 6.0.

System Administration for Microsoft SQL Server 6.5

Course No. 756 takes five days to complete and provides students with the knowledge and skills required to install, configure, administer, and troubleshoot Microsoft SQL Server client/server database management system version 6.5.

At the end of the course, students will be able to install and configure SQL Server 6.5; manage the storage requirements of a database; manage user accounts, login security, and database permissions; manage the import, export, and replication of data; and maintain the system and perform day-to-day operations including backing up and restoring a database, recovering from a system disaster, scheduling tasks, setting alerts, monitoring, and tuning.

This course helps you prepare for exam 70-26, System Administration on Microsoft SQL Server 6.5.

Supporting Microsoft Internet Information Server 2.0

Course No. 758 takes three days to complete and teaches students how to support the various features of Microsoft Internet Information Server. Students will gain understanding of the product by installing, configuring, and supporting Internet Information Server. (This course does not cover the publishing of Web page content.)

At the end of the course, students will be able to describe how hosts connect across the Internet; define the components of a uniform resource locator (URL); determine which Microsoft products would be needed to create a specific Internet site; install Internet Information Server; add support for file transfer protocol (FTP) and the World Wide Web; describe the architecture of Internet Information Server; describe the security architecture used by Internet Information Server; determine the best security for a specific setup; configure Internet Information Server to connect to a database; implement Microsoft Index Server; use Internet Service Manager to administer an Internet Information Server site; set up the domain name system (DNS); create and use virtual directories and virtual servers; plan a complete Internet site by determining necessary hardware, estimating bandwidth, and specifying appropriate connectivity methods; explain the role of Internet service providers; monitor and interpret performance data about an Internet Information Server site; indicate which Registry settings affect Internet Information Server; maintain a log for tuning purposes; troubleshoot problems that might occur; and identify the minimum hardware.

Installing Microsoft Internet Information Server 2.0

Course No. 769 takes one day to complete and teaches students how to install and configure Microsoft Internet Information Server. The cost and performance of various configurations are discussed. Students will learn about the factors involved in setting up external Internet information sites and publishing on the Internet.

At the end of the course, students will be able to explain the advantages of using Internet Information Server; describe the performance of various connectivity options on the basis of number of users, speed of data transmission, and cost; identify minimum hardware requirements; install Internet Information Server; configure Internet Information Server to use World Wide Web, Gopher, and file transfer protocol services; set up Internet Information Server to meet specific security requirements; and create a home page using Hypertext Markup Language (HTML) and Microsoft Internet Assistant for Word.

Installing and Configuring Microsoft Exchange Server 4.0

Course No. 781 takes one day to complete and provides students with the preliminary knowledge and skills required to install, configure, and use Microsoft Exchange Server version 4.0 in a small organization. Installing and Configuring Microsoft Exchange Server 4.0 uses lectures, labs, and demonstrations to deliver hands-on exposure to Microsoft Exchange Server essentials. The course concludes with an introduction to Microsoft Exchange Server version 4.5.

In-depth technical content, such as advanced security, server maintenance, coexistence, and migration, is not in the scope of this course. Topics such as these are the focus of the five-day course, Core Technologies of Microsoft Exchange Server.

At the end of the course, students will be able to describe the core components and features of Microsoft Exchange clients and servers; install Microsoft Exchange Server in a site; create and manage each recipient type in a Microsoft Exchange environment; install and configure Microsoft

Exchange clients; configure and manage Internet Mail Connector; and describe the impact of Microsoft Exchange Server 4.5 on Internet protocols, Microsoft Exchange clients, and electronic forms.

The Microsoft Certified Professional Exams

There are too many Microsoft Certified Professional exams to outline without dedicating an entire book to them. At the time of this writing, there were new exams in development, and I'm sure that by the time this book is published many more exams will be available.

The following pages outline a few of the exams that are required for the MCSE certification. To get the most current information about Microsoft Certified Professional exams, go to `www.microsoft.com/train_cert`.

Exam 70-67: Implementing and Supporting Microsoft Windows NT Server 4.0

The Implementing and Supporting Microsoft Windows NT Server 4.0 certification exam measures your ability to implement, administer, and troubleshoot information systems that incorporate Windows NT Server 4.0 in a simple computing environment. A simple computing environment is typically a homogeneous LAN. It might include one or more servers, a single domain, and a single location—and it might have file-sharing and print-sharing capabilities. This exam can be applied toward core credit for the Microsoft Certified Systems Engineer certification and for the Microsoft Certified Product Specialist certification.

This certification exam tests your ability to apply a comprehensive set of skills to the tasks necessary to administer, implement, and troubleshoot Windows NT Server 4.0.

The following list of exam objectives outlines the specific skills measured by the exam:

- Planning

  Plan the disk drive configuration for various requirements. Requirements include choosing a file system and choosing a fault-tolerance method.

  Choose a protocol for various situations. Protocols include TCP/IP, NWLink IPX/SPX Compatible Transport, and NetBEUI.

- Installation and Configuration

  Install Windows NT Server on Intel-based platforms.

  Install Windows NT Server to perform various server roles. Server roles include primary domain controller, backup domain controller, and member server.

  Install Windows NT Server by using various methods. Installation methods include CD-ROM, over-the-network, Network Client Administrator, and express versus custom.

Configure protocols and protocol bindings. Protocols include TCP/IP, NWLink IPX/SPX Compatible Transport, and NetBEUI.

Configure network adapters. Considerations include changing IRQ, IObase, memory addresses, and configuring multiple adapters.

Configure Windows NT Server core services. Services include Directory Replicator and License Manager.

Configure peripherals and devices. Peripherals and devices include communication devices, SCSI devices, tape device drivers, UPS devices and UPS service, mouse drivers, display drivers, and keyboard drivers.

Configure hard disks to meet various requirements. Requirements include allocating disk space capacity, providing redundancy, improving performance, providing security, and formatting.

Configure printers. Tasks include adding and configuring a printer, implementing a printer pool, and setting print priorities.

Configure a Windows NT Server computer for various types of client computers. Client computer types include Windows NT Workstation, Microsoft Windows 95, and Microsoft MS-DOS–based.

- Managing Resources

Manage user and group accounts. Considerations include managing Windows NT user accounts, managing Windows NT user rights, managing Windows NT groups, administering account policies, and auditing changes to the user account database.

Create and manage policies and profiles for various situations. Policies and profiles include local user profiles, roaming user profiles, and system policies.

Administer remote servers from various types of client computers. Client computer types include Windows 95 and Windows NT Workstation.

Manage disk resources. Tasks include copying and moving files between file systems, creating and sharing resources, implementing permissions and security, and establishing file auditing.

- Connectivity

Configure Windows NT Server for interoperability with NetWare servers by using various tools. Tools include Gateway Service for NetWare and Migration Tool for NetWare.

Install and configure Remote Access Service (RAS) configuration options including RAS communications, RAS protocols, and RAS security.

Configure Dial-Up Networking clients.

Monitoring and Optimization.

Monitor performance of various functions by using Performance Monitor. Functions include processor, memory, disk, and network.

Identify performance bottlenecks.

- Troubleshooting

  Choose the appropriate course of action to take to resolve installation failures.

  Choose the appropriate course of action to take to resolve boot failures.

  Choose the appropriate course of action to take to resolve configuration errors.

  Choose the appropriate course of action to take to resolve printer problems.

  Choose the appropriate course of action to take to resolve RAS problems.

  Choose the appropriate course of action to take to resolve connectivity problems.

  Choose the appropriate course of action to take to resolve resource access problems and permission problems.

  Choose the appropriate course of action to take to resolve fault-tolerance failures. Fault-tolerance methods include tape backup, mirroring, stripe set with parity, and disk duplexing.

Exam 70-68: Implementing and Supporting Microsoft Windows NT Server 4.0 in the Enterprise

The Implementing and Supporting Microsoft Windows NT Server 4.0 in the Enterprise certification exam measures your ability to implement, administer, and troubleshoot information systems that incorporate Windows NT Server 4.0 in an enterprise-computing environment. An enterprise-computing environment is typically a heterogeneous WAN. It might include multiple servers and multiple domains, and it might run sophisticated server applications. This exam can be applied toward core credit for the Microsoft Certified Systems Engineer certification.

This certification exam tests your ability to apply a comprehensive set of skills to the tasks necessary to administer, implement, and troubleshoot Windows NT Server 4.0 in an enterprise computing environment. Review the following tasks and then review the list of objectives that follows them. Before taking the exam, you should be able to accomplish these tasks by applying your in-depth knowledge of the skills covered in these objectives.

The following list of exam objectives outlines the specific skills measured by the exam:

- Planning

  Plan the implementation of a directory services architecture. Considerations include selecting the appropriate domain model, supporting a single logon account, and allowing users to access resources in different domains.

  Plan the disk-drive configuration for various requirements. Requirements include choosing a fault-tolerance method.

  Choose a protocol for various situations. Protocols include TCP/IP, TCP/IP with DHCP and WINS, NWLink IPX/SPX Compatible Transport Protocol, Data Link Control (DLC), and AppleTalk.

- Installation and Configuration

  Install Windows NT Server to perform various server roles. Server roles include primary domain controller, backup domain controller, and member server.

  Configure protocols and protocol bindings. Protocols include TCP/IP, TCP/IP with DHCP and WINS, NWLink IPX/SPX Compatible Transport Protocol, DLC, and AppleTalk.

- Configure Windows NT Server core services. Services include Directory Replicator and Computer Browser.
- Configure hard disks to meet various requirements. Requirements include providing redundancy and improving performance.
- Configure printers. Tasks include adding and configuring a printer, implementing a printer pool, and setting print priorities.
- Configure a Windows NT Server computer for various types of client computers. Client computer types include Windows NT Workstation, Windows 95, and Macintosh.
- Managing Resources

  Manage user and group accounts. Considerations include managing Windows NT user accounts, managing Windows NT user rights, managing Windows NT groups, administering account policies, and auditing changes to the user account database.

  Create and manage policies and profiles for various situations. Policies and profiles include local user profiles, roaming user profiles, and system policies.

  Administer remote servers from various types of client computers. Client computer types include Windows 95 and Windows NT Workstation.

  Manage disk resources. Tasks include creating and sharing resources, implementing permissions and security, and establishing file auditing.

- Connectivity

  Configure Windows NT Server for interoperability with NetWare servers by using various tools. Tools include Gateway Service for NetWare and Migration Tool for NetWare.

  Install and configure multiprotocol routing to serve various functions. Functions include Internet router, BOOTP/DHCP Relay Agent, and IPX router.

  Install and configure Internet Information Server.

  Install and configure Internet services. Services include World Wide Web, DNS, and intranet.

  Install and configure Remote Access Service (RAS). Configuration options include configuring RAS communications, RAS protocols, and RAS security.

- Monitoring and Optimization

  Establish a baseline for measuring system performance. Tasks include creating a database of measurement data.

Monitor performance of various functions by using Performance Monitor. Functions include processor, memory, disk, and network.

Monitor network traffic by using Network Monitor. Tasks include collecting data, presenting data, and filtering data.

Identify performance bottlenecks.

Optimize performance for various results. Results include controlling network traffic and server load.

- Troubleshooting

  Choose the appropriate course of action to take to resolve installation failures.

  Choose the appropriate course of action to take to resolve boot failures.

  Choose the appropriate course of action to take to resolve configuration errors. Tasks include backing up, restoring, and editing the Registry.

  Choose the appropriate course of action to take to resolve printer problems.

  Choose the appropriate course of action to take to resolve RAS problems.

  Choose the appropriate course of action to take to resolve connectivity problems.

  Choose the appropriate course of action to take to resolve resource access and permission problems.

  Choose the appropriate course of action to take to resolve fault-tolerance failures. Fault-tolerance methods include tape backup, mirroring, and stripe set with parity.

  Perform advanced problem resolution. Tasks include diagnosing and interpreting a blue screen, configuring a memory dump, and using the Event Log service.

Exam 70-14: Implementing and Supporting Microsoft Systems Management Server 1.0

The Implementing and Supporting Microsoft Systems Management Server 1.0 certification exam measures your ability to implement, administer, and troubleshoot information systems that incorporate Microsoft Systems Management Server version 1.0. This exam can be applied toward elective credit for the Microsoft Certified Systems Engineer certification.

The following list of exam objectives outlines the specific skills measured by the exam:

- Systems Management Server (SMS) Features

  Solve specified system management problems by using SMS.

  Describe how SMS can be integrated with third-party network management systems.

- Planning

  Plan an SMS environment for Microsoft Windows NT–based networks and NetWare-based networks.

  Install and configure an SMS site.

Install SMS on Microsoft Windows NT–based networks and NetWare-based networks.

Add NetWare and Windows NT Server domains to an SMS site.

Identify the changes to a site, helper, or logon server that occur when SMS is installed.

- Installing and Configuring an SMS Client Computer

  Identify changes made to a Microsoft MS-DOS computer after the Client Setup program is executed.

  Identify changes made to a Microsoft Windows computer after the Client Setup program is executed.

  Identify changes made to a Microsoft Windows NT Workstation computer after the Client Setup program is executed.

  Identify changes made to a Macintosh computer after the Installer program is executed.

  Choose the appropriate way to run the Inventory Agent service for a given situation.

  Configure the Windows NT Replicator service to replicate logon script information.

- Communicating Between Sites

  Identify the default senders and choose which should be used for a given situation.

  Explain how multiple senders can be used to provide fault tolerance.

  Install, configure, and use a RAS Sender to communicate between two SMS sites.

  Install, configure, and use an SNA Sender to communicate between two SMS sites.

  Install, configure, and use a LAN Sender to communicate between two SMS sites.

- Collecting Hardware and Software Inventory

  Identify the information inventoried for a given situation.

  Identify the changes made to the logon server after SMS has been installed.

  Configure the inventory collection process.

  Create packages to inventory software and to collect files.

  Add custom inventory to an SMS database.

  Querying the Inventory Database

  Retrieve specified information from a given inventory database by using the SMS user interface.

- Executing Activities on Remote Client Computers

  Create a package for a given situation.

  Create and configure the Run command on a workstation job for a given situation.

  Use the Package Command Manager to run jobs received by the client computer.

  Identify the tasks that can be performed with the runtime version of Microsoft Test.

  Establish and update client computer access to applications and data (packages) stored on the server.

  Create and configure a shared application package.

Create program groups and icons.

Identify the changes to the client computer that occur after the computer receives a Share Package On Server job.

- Disaster Recovery Planning

  Create and configure SMS alerts.

  Back up and restore the SMS database.

  Identify the computer types that support remote control.

  Identify the requirements for remotely monitoring and controlling client computers.

  Identify the types of functions that can be used remotely.

  Configure remote control.

- Troubleshooting

  Identify where the configuration process failed for a given troubleshooting situation.

  Identify where the communication process failed for a given troubleshooting situation.

  Identify where the Package Command Manager application failed for a given troubleshooting situation.

  Identify where the software distribution process failed for a given troubleshooting situation.

  Identify where the inventory collection process failed for a given troubleshooting situation.

  Identify where the shared application process failed for a given troubleshooting situation.

  Trace the operation of each SMS component.

  Track SMS errors.

  Collect a Network Monitor trace to send to Microsoft PSS.

  Identify troubleshooting utilities that come with SMS.

Exam 70-53: Internetworking Microsoft TCP/IP on Microsoft Windows NT (3.5–3.51)

The Internetworking Microsoft TCP/IP on Microsoft Windows NT (3.5–3.51) certification exam measures your ability to implement, administer, and troubleshoot information systems that incorporate Microsoft TCP/IP. This exam can be applied toward elective credit for the Microsoft Certified Systems Engineer certification.

The following list of exam objectives outlines the specific skills measured by the exam:

- Installation and Configuration

  Identify valid network configurations for devices on a TCP/IP network.

  Install Microsoft TCP/IP on a Windows NT Server computer.

Install Microsoft TCP/IP on a Windows NT Server computer to support multiple network adapters.

Configure a Windows NT Server computer to support TCP/IP printing.

Install a DHCP server.

Create and manage scopes by using DHCP Manager.

Install and configure a WINS server.

Configure multiple WINS servers to support replication.

Configure static mappings for clients that are not WINS-enabled.

- IP Addressing

  Describe how the individual IP address classes are configured to support different combinations of networks and hosts on an IP network.

  Configure a network by assigning appropriate IP addresses to devices on the network.

- Subnet Addressing

  Configure a network that comprises multiple subnets by using subnet masks.

- Implementing IP Routing

  Describe how packets are routed between networks by using IP routers.

  Compare and contrast static and dynamic IP routing.

  Configure routes within a static routing table.

  Configure a Windows NT Server computer to function as an IP router.

- IP Address Resolution

  Explain the purpose of the Address Resolution Protocol (ARP).

  Explain how ARP maps an IP address to a hardware address on a local network.

  Use the `arp` diagnostic command to add, modify, or delete entries in a translation table used by ARP.

- Host Name Resolution

  Explain how a host name is resolved to an IP address by using the Domain Name System (DNS).

  Configure a Windows NT Server computer to use DNS.

  Modify the `HOSTS` file so that host names are resolved correctly.

- NetBIOS Name Resolution

  Explain how NetBIOS names on a local area network are resolved by using broadcasts.

  Explain how NetBIOS names are resolved to IP addresses on remote networks by using the `LMHOSTS` file.

  Configure local and centralized `LMHOSTS` files.

  Configure an `LMHOST` file across domains.

  Explain how WINS can be used to resolve a NetBIOS name to an IP address.

- Connecting to Heterogeneous Environments

  Install and configure an FTP server on a Windows NT Server computer.

  Connect to and exchange files with a TCP/IP-based UNIX host by using the `ftp` command.

  Connect to a TCP/IP-based UNIX host by using the `telnet` command.

- Implementing the SNMP Service

  Configure the SNMP service to be monitored by an SNMP manager application.

  Configure SNMP security and agents.

- Performance, Tuning, and Optimization

  List and describe characteristics in a network environment that affect performance.

  Identify and explain the TCP/IP parameters that affect performance.

  Identify and explain the meaning of specific TCP performance counters.

- Troubleshooting

  Diagnose IP address resolution problems.

  Diagnose IP configuration problems by using Microsoft TCP/IP utilities.

  Diagnose problems that commonly occur with host name resolution.

  Diagnose address resolution problems by using Microsoft TCP/IP utilities.

  Diagnose name resolution problems by using Microsoft TCP/IP utilities.

  Diagnose problems that occur with a DHCP Server.

Exam 70-63: Implementing and Supporting Microsoft Windows 95

The Implementing and Supporting Microsoft Windows 95 certification exam measures your ability to implement, administer, and troubleshoot information systems and provide technical support for Windows 95 users. This exam can be applied toward core credit for the Microsoft Certified Systems Engineer certification and for the Microsoft Certified Product Specialist certification.

The following list of exam objectives outlines the specific skills measured by the exam:

- Planning and Installation

  Identify appropriate hardware requirements for Microsoft Windows 95 installation.

  Maintain program groups and user preferences when upgrading from Windows 3.1.

  Determine when to use Windows 95 and when to use Microsoft Windows NT Workstation.

  Configure a Windows 95 computer on a network using the appropriate protocol.

  Select the appropriate security to meet various needs.

  Determine the appropriate installation method for various situations.

Install the Windows 95 operating system.

Troubleshoot setup and system startup.

Set up files for network installation and for shared use.

Recognize files used in troubleshooting the installation process.

- Architecture and Memory

  Compare and contrast the memory usage of a Microsoft MS-DOS–based application, a 16-bit Windows-based application, and a 32-bit Windows-based application operating in Windows 95.

- Customizing and Configuring Windows 95

  Identify and explain the differences between the Windows 3.1 and the Windows 95 interfaces.

  Set up a dual-boot system for Windows 95.

  Install new hardware devices on various systems that support Plug and Play.

  Given a specific bus configuration, identify areas of limitation for full Plug and Play.

  Configure the taskbar.

  Configure shortcuts.

  Add items to the Start menu.

  Choose an appropriate method to accomplish a specified task, by using the user interface.

  Customize the desktop for a specified set of criteria.

  Use the Windows 95 interface to create, print, and store a file.

  Configure and use Windows Explorer.

  Access the network through Network Neighborhood.

  Configure the property sheet for an object.

  Define the purpose of the Registry.

  Classify types of information in the Registry.

  Determine where the Registry is stored.

  Identify situations in which it is appropriate to modify the Registry.

  Modify the contents of the Registry.

  Choose the appropriate course of action when OLE information in the Registry becomes corrupted.

- Editing User and System Profiles

  Modify a user workstation to meet specified criteria.

  Grant remote administration privileges on your computer.

  Modify user profiles.

Set up user profiles.

Set up computer policies.

Define the System Policy Editor and describe how it is used.

Create, share, and monitor a remote resource.

Administer a remote computer.

- Networking and Interoperability

  Configure a Windows 95 computer to access the Internet.

  Configure a Windows 95 computer to use NetWare user-level security.

  Configure a Windows 95 computer as a client or server in a NetWare network.

  Identify the limitations of a Windows 95 NetWare server.

  Configure a Windows 95 computer to use Windows NT Server user-level security.

  Configure a Windows 95 computer as a client in a Windows NT Server domain.

  Configure a Windows 95 computer as a client in a NetWare network.

  Recognize how the UNC is used.

  Configure Browse Master for Microsoft networks.

  Configure Browse Master for NetWare.

  Identify advantages and disadvantages of user-level and share-level security.

  Identify elements of the Windows 95 operating system network architecture.

  Install and configure TCP/IP for use with Windows 95.

- Managing Disk Resources and Utilities

  Manage long and short filenames in a mixed environment.

  Troubleshoot problems and perform disk compression.

  Select the appropriate disk-management tool for a given situation.

  Use Disk Defragmenter to optimize for speed.

  Use ScanDisk in appropriate situations.

  Use Backup in appropriate situations.

- Managing Printers

  Implement printers for Windows 95.

  Identify situations in which metafile spooling is appropriate.

  Set up point-and-print printing.

  Access a printer through a NetWare network.

  Create, reorder, and delete a Windows 95 print queue.

  Set up and remove printer drivers in Windows 95.

  Use Windows 95 to share a printer on the network.

- Running Applications

  Configure Windows 95 to run MS-DOS–based applications.

  Predict potential problems when configuring 16-bit Windows-based applications.

  Distinguish between MS-DOS mode and the standard method for running MS-DOS–based applications.

  Determine when an application should be run in MS-DOS mode.

  Resolve general protection faults.

- Determine the appropriate course of action when the application stops responding to the system.
- Mobile Services

  Implement the appropriate level of security for use with dial-up networking.

  Choose applications that would be appropriate to run over dial-up networking.

  Configure dial-up networking to be a client.

  Configure dial-up networking on a server.

  Configure a modem to meet a specific set of user requirements.

  Implement the various telephony options to meet a specific set of user requirements.

  Use a "briefcase" to transfer and synchronize data between two computers.

- Microsoft Exchange

  Share a fax.

  Configure a fax for both stand-alone and shared situations.

  Configure Microsoft Exchange to access the Internet.

  Configure a Windows 95 computer to send and receive mail.

  Configure a Windows 95 computer to access CompuServe mail.

- Plug and Play

  Explain how Windows 95 handles components that are not compatible with Plug and Play.

  Explain hot docking and the potential consequences of the dynamic device changes.

  Given a specific configuration, use Device Manager to manually reconfigure a Plug-and-Play device.

- Troubleshooting

  Resolve problems using appropriate resources.

  Select appropriate tools for troubleshooting.

  Monitor Windows 95 performance and resolve performance problems.

  Audit access to a Windows 95 local resource.

  Optimize the system to use the Windows 95 drivers.

Optimize a computer for desktop performance.

Optimize a computer for network performance.

Optimize printing.

Discriminate between preemptive and cooperative multitasking.

Explain Windows 95 multitasking of 16-bit, Windows-based and 32-bit, Windows-based applications.

Differentiate between a process and a thread.

Differentiate between resource usage in Windows 3.1, Windows 95, and Windows NT.

Explain how Windows 95 performs memory paging as compared to Windows 3.x.

Choose the appropriate course of action when the installation process fails.

Use the startup disk to repair a faulty network setup.

Choose the appropriate course of action when an application fails.

Choose the appropriate course of action when a print job fails.

Choose the appropriate course of action when the boot process fails.

Choose the appropriate course of action when file system problems occur.

Choose the appropriate course of action when dial-up networking problems occur.

Predict the consequences to the operating system when MS-DOS–based applications, 16-bit Windows-based applications, and 32-bit Windows-based applications fail to respond to the system while running under Windows 95.

Exam 70-58: Networking Essentials

The Networking Essentials certification exam measures the essential networking skills required to implement, administer, and troubleshoot information systems that incorporate Microsoft Windows 95 and any products in the Microsoft BackOffice family. The exam covers only the networking knowledge and skills common to both Windows 95 and BackOffice products.

This exam can be applied toward core credit for the Microsoft Certified Systems Engineer certification and toward elective credit for the Microsoft Certified Product Specialist certification.

The following list of exam objectives outlines the specific skills measured by the exam:

- Standards and Terminology

  Define common networking terms for LANs and WANs.

  Compare a file-and-print server with an application server.

  Compare user-level security with access permission assigned to a shared directory on a server.

  Compare a client/server network with a peer-to-peer network.

Compare the implications of using connection-oriented communications with connectionless communications.

Distinguish whether SLIP or PPP is used as the communications protocol for various situations.

Define the communication devices that communicate at each level of the OSI model.

Describe the characteristics and purpose of the media used in IEEE 802.3 and IEEE 802.5 standards.

Explain the purpose of NDIS and Novell ODI network standards.

- Planning

  Select the appropriate media for various situations. Media choices include twisted-pair cable, coaxial cable, fiber-optic cable, and wireless. Situational elements include cost, distance limitations, and number of nodes.

  Select the appropriate topology for various token-ring and Ethernet networks.

  Select the appropriate network and transport protocol or protocols for various token-ring and Ethernet networks. Protocol choices include DLC, AppleTalk, IPX, TCP/IP, NFS, and SMB.

  Select the appropriate connectivity devices for various token-ring and Ethernet networks. Connectivity devices include repeaters, bridges, routers, brouters, and gateways.

  List the characteristics, requirements, and appropriate situations for WAN connection services. WAN connection services include X.25, ISDN, frame relay, and ATM.

- Implementation

  Choose an administrative plan to meet specified needs, including performance management, account management, and security.

  Choose a disaster-recovery plan for various situations.

  Given the manufacturer's documentation for the network adapter, install, configure, and resolve hardware conflicts for multiple network adapters in a token-ring or Ethernet network.

  Implement a NetBIOS naming scheme for all computers on a given network.

  Select the appropriate hardware and software tools to monitor trends in the network.

- Troubleshooting

  Identify common errors associated with components required for communications.

  Diagnose and resolve common connectivity problems with cards, cables, and related hardware.

  Resolve broadcast storms.

  Identify and resolve network performance problems.

I

Index

C

D

E

F

G

H

J-K-L

N

O

Q-R

S

U

V

W

X-Y-Z

A VIACOM  SERVICE

The Information SuperLibrary™

CHECK OUT THE BOOKS IN THIS LIBRARY.

You'll find thousands of shareware files and over 1600 computer books designed for both technowizards and technophobes. You can browse through 700 sample chapters, get the latest news on the Net, and find just about anything using our massive search directories.

All Macmillan Computer Publishing books are available at your local bookstore.

We're open 24-hours a day, 365 days a year.

You don't need a card.

We don't charge fines.

And you can be as **LOUD** as you want.

The Information SuperLibrary

http://www.mcp.com/mcp/ ftp.mcp.com

Copyright © 1997, Macmillan Computer Publishing-USA, A Simon & Schuster Company

Technical Support:

If you need assistance with the information in this book or with a CD/Disk accompanying the book, please access the Knowledge Base on our Web site at **http://www.superlibrary.com/general/support**. Our most Frequently Asked Questions are answered there. If you do not find the answer to your questions on our Web site, you may contact Macmillan Technical Support **(317) 581-3833** or e-mail us at **support@mcp.com**.

Robert Cowart's Windows NT 4 Unleashed, Professional Reference Edition

Robert Cowart

The only reference Windows NT administrators need to learn how to configure their NT systems for maximum performance, security, and reliability. This comprehensive reference explains how to install, maintain, and configure an individual workstation as well as connect computers to peer-to-peer networking. Includes comprehensive advice for setting up and administering an NT server network, and focuses on the new and improved administration and connectivity features of version 4.0.

CD-ROM includes source code, utilities, and sample applications from the book. Covers Windows NT 4 Server and Workstation.

$59.99 USA/$84.95 CDN | *Intermediate—Expert* | *1,044 pp.*
0-672-31001-5 | *Operating Systems* | *3/1/97*

Programming Windows NT 4 Unleashed

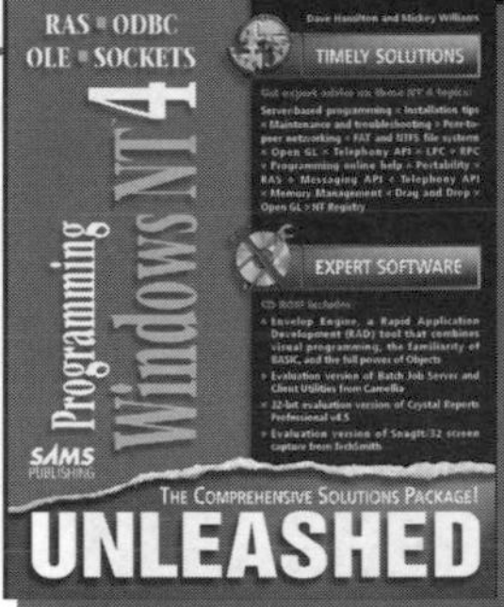

David Hamilton, Mickey Williams, & Griffith Kadnier

Readers get a clear understanding of the modes of operation and architecture for Windows NT. Everything—including execution models, processes, threads, DLLs, memory, controls, security, and more—is covered with precise detail.

CD-ROM contains source code and completed sample programs from the book.

Teaches OLE, DDE, drag and drop, OCX development, and the component gallery. Explores Microsoft BackOffice programming.

$59.99 USA/$84.95 CDN | *Accomplished—Expert* | *1,200 pp.*
0-672-30905-X | *Programming* | *7/1/96*

Peter Norton's Complete Guide to Windows NT 4 Workstation

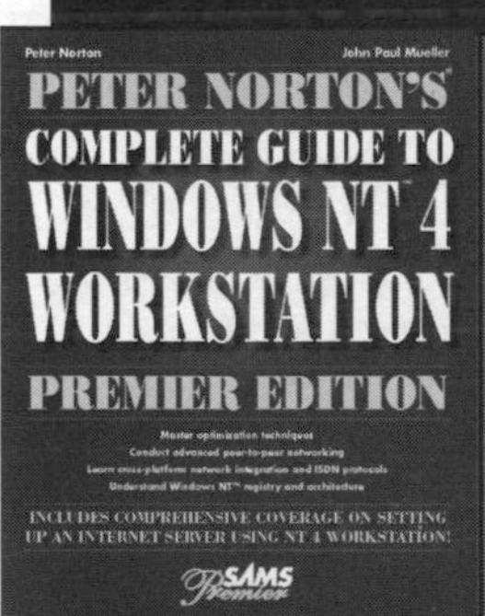

Peter Norton

Readers will explore everything from interface issues to advanced topics, such as client/server networking, building their own Internet server, and OLE.

Readers will master complex memory management techniques.

Teaches how to build an Internet server and explores peer-to-peer networking.

$39.99 USA/$56.95 CDN | *Casual—Accomplished* | *936 pp.*
0-672-30901-7 | *Operating Systems* | *7/1/96*

Peter Norton's Guide to Windows 95/NT 4 Programming with MFC

Peter Norton & Rob McGregor

Following in the wake of the best-selling *Peter Norton* series, this book gives the reader a "rapid tour guide" approach to programming Windows 95 applications. The reader will learn to use, change, and augment the functions of the MFC library.

Readers will use the Microsoft Foundation Class libraries to get the information they need to begin programming immediately. Covers the latest version of MFC for Windows 95 and Windows NT 4.

$49.99 USA/$70.95 CDN *New—Casual* *1,200 pp.*
0-672-30900-9 *Programming* *10/1/96*

Building an Intranet with Windows NT 4

Scott Zimmerman & Tim Evans

This hands-on guide teaches readers how to set up and maintain an efficient intranet with Windows NT. It comes complete with a selection of the best software for setting up a server, creating content, and developing intranet applications.

CD-ROM includes a complete Windows NT intranet toolkit with a full-featured Web server, Web content development tools, and ready-to-use intranet applications.

Includes complete specifications for several of the most popular intranet applications—group scheduling, discussions, database access, and more. Covers Windows NT 4.0.

$49.99 USA/$70.95 CDN *Casual—Accomplished* *608 pp.*
1-57521-137-8 *Internet—Intranets* *7/1/96*

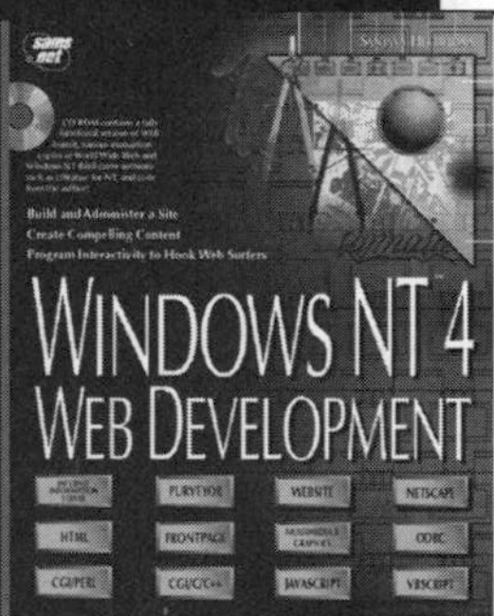

Windows NT 4 Web Development

Sanjaya Hettihewa

Windows NT and Microsoft's newly developed Internet Information Server is making it easier and more cost-effective to set up, manage, and administer a good Web site. Since the Windows NT environment is relatively new, there are few books on the market that adequately discuss its full potential. *Windows NT 4 Web Development* addresses that potential by providing information on all key aspects of server setup, maintenance, design, and implementation.

CD-ROM contains valuable source code and powerful utilities.

Teaches how to incorporate new technologies to your Web site.

Covers Java, JavaScript, Internet Studio, Visual Basic Script, and Windows NT.

$59.99 USA/$84.95 CDN *Accomplished—Expert* *744 pp.*
1-57521-089-4 *Internet—Programming* *8/1/96*

Microsoft Internet Information Server 3 Unleashed, Second Edition

Arthur Knowles

Following in the tradition of the best-selling *Unleashed* series, this all-in-one guide to Microsoft Internet Information Server covers everything users need to know—from installing and configuring the server and working with other BackOffice products to administration and security issues. This version was updated to cover Microsoft Index Information Server 1.1, Active Server Pages, Netshow Server, and FrontPage 97 IIS extensions.

Covers content development for Web sites, including Visual Basic Scripting and CGI programming. Shows how to use Internet Information Server to work with SQL Server databases.

CD-ROM is loaded with all the source code from the book as well as examples and third-party software. Covers Microsoft Internet Information Server 3.0.

$49.99 USA/$70.95 CAN	*Accomplished—Expert*	*972 pp.*
1-57521-271-4	*Internet—Networking/Servers*	*4/1/97*

Microsoft BackOffice 2 Administrator's Survival Guide, Second Edition

Arthur Knowles

This all-in-one reference describes how to make the components of BackOffice version 2 work best together and with other networks. BackOffice is Microsoft's complete reference for networking, database, and system management products.

Contains the fundamental concepts required for daily maintenance, troubleshooting, and problem solving.

CD-ROM includes product demos, commercial and shareware utilities, and technical notes from Microsoft's vendor technical support personnel.

Covers BackOffice version 2.

$59.99 USA/$84.95 CDN	*Accomplished*	*1,136 pp.*
0-672-30977-7	*Client/Server*	*11/1/96*

Add to Your Sams Library Today with the Best Books for Programming, Operating Systems, and New Technologies

The easiest way to order is to pick up the phone and call

1-800-428-5331

between 9:00 a.m. and 5:00 p.m. EST.

For fastest service please have your credit card available.

ISBN	Quantity	Description of Item	Unit Cost	Total Cost
0-672-31001-5		Robert Cowart's Windows NT 4 Unleashed, Professional Reference Edition (Book/CD-ROM)	$59.99	
0-672-30905-X		Programming Windows NT 4 Unleashed (Book/CD-ROM)	$59.99	
0-672-30901-7		Peter Norton's Complete Guide to Windows NT 4 Workstation (Book/CD-ROM)	$39.99	
0-672-30900-9		Peter Norton's Guide to Windows 95/NT 4 Programming with MFC (Book/CD-ROM)	$49.99	
1-57521-137-8		Building an Intranet with Windows NT 4 (Book/CD-ROM)	$49.99	
1-57521-089-4		Windows NT 4 Web Development (Book/CD-ROM)	$59.99	
1-57521-271-4		Microsoft Internet Information Server 3 Unleashed, Second Edition (Book/CD-ROM)	$49.99	
0-672-30977-7		Microsoft BackOffice 2 Administrator's Survival Guide, Second Edition (Book/CD-ROM)	$59.99	
		Shipping and handling: See information below.		
		TOTAL		

Shipping and handling: $4.00 for the first book and $1.75 for each additional book. If you need to have it immediately, we can ship your order to you in 24 hours for an additional charge of approximately $18.00, and you will receive your order overnight or in two days. Overseas shipping and handling costs an additional $2.00 per book. Prices subject to change. Call for availability and pricing information on latest editions.

201 W. 103rd Street, Indianapolis, Indiana 46290

1-800-428-5331 — Orders 1-800-835-3202 — FAX 1-800-858-7674 — Customer Service

Book ISBN 0-672-30941-6

What's on the Disc

The companion CD-ROM contains an assortment of third-party tools and product demos. The disc creates a new program group for this book and utilizes Windows Explorer. Using the icons in the program group and Windows Explorer, you can view information concerning products and companies, and install programs with just a few clicks of the mouse.

Some of the utilities and programs mentioned in this book are included on this CD-ROM. If they are not, a reference to a Web site or FTP location is usually provided in the body of the reference. If a reference is missing, up-to-date information can almost always be obtained from a comprehensive shareware site such as Beverly Hills Software (`www.bhs.com`), TUCOWS (`www.tucows.com`), or C|Net (`www.shareware.com`) for third-party Windows NT products.

To create the program group for this book, follow these steps:

Windows NT Installation Instructions

1. Insert the CD-ROM disc into your CD-ROM drive.
2. With Windows NT installed on your computer and the AutoPlay feature enabled, a Program Group for this book is automatically created whenever you insert the disc into your CD-ROM drive. Follow the directions provided in the installation program.
3. If AutoPlay is not enabled, using Windows Explorer, choose `Setup.exe` from the root level of the CD-ROM to create the Program Group for this book.

4. Double-click the “Browse the CD-ROM” icon in the newly created Program Group to access the installation programs of the software or reference material included on this CD-ROM.

   To review the latest information about this CD-ROM, double-click the icon “About this CD-ROM.”

Note: For best results, set your monitor to display between 256 and 64,000 colors. A screen resolution of 640×480 pixels is also recommended. If necessary, adjust your monitor settings before using the CD-ROM.

Technical Support

If you need assistance with the information in this book or with the CD-ROM accompanying this book, please access the Knowledge Base on our Web site at

`http://www.superlibrary.com/general/support`

Our most Frequently Asked Questions are answered there. If you do not find the answer to your questions on our Web site, you may contact Macmillan Technical Support at (317) 581-3833 or e-mail us at `support@mcp.com`.